COMPUTER LAW

Second Edition

Other books in the *Essentials of Canadian Law* Series

ESSENTIALS OF CANADIAN LAW

COMPUTER LAW

Second Edition

GEORGE S. TAKACH

Partner, McCarthy Tétrault

Adjunct Professor,
Osgoode Hall Law School,
York University

COMPUTER LAW, Second Edition

© George S. Takach, 2003

Published in 2003 by

Irwin Law Inc.
Suite 501
347 Bay Street
Toronto, Ontario
M5H 2R7
www.irwinlaw.com

ISBN: 1-55221-053-7

National Library of Canada Cataloguing in Publication Data

Takach, George S. (George Steven)
    Computer law / George S. Takach. — 2nd ed.

Includes index.

ISBN 1-55221-053-7

    1. Computers—Law and legislation—Canada. I. Title.

KE452.C6T35 2003   343.7109'99   C2003-902663-9
KF390.5.C6T34 2003

The publisher acknowledges the financial support of the Government of Canada through the Book Publishing Industry Development Program (BPIDP) for our publishing activities. The publisher also acknowledges the Government of Ontario through the Ontario Media Development Corporation's Ontario Book Initiative.

Printed and bound in Canada.

1 2 3 4 5   07 06 05 04 03

SUMMARY
TABLE OF CONTENTS

DETAILED
TABLE OF CONTENTS

CHAPTER 7:
INTERNET LIBEL AND JURISDICTION ISSUES   *620*

FOREWORD

to the First Edition

This book is a gem. It is essential for anyone — lawyer or non-lawyer — interested, intrigued, or impaled by the challenge modern information technology poses for the rule of law. It is Canadian in the sense that much of its data is Canadian-based. But it will be read with profit by anyone, in any jurisdiction, who must deal with the information revolution and the necessary adjustments in private and public law.

The book is a judicious, well-tempered balance of theory and practice. It gives enough technological background to understand the problem and challenge of the computer and communications transformation. It selects legal puzzles drawn from a kaleidoscope of fact patterns from a busy and rapidly changing law practice. It explains and expounds the law, its adaptability, its limits, and then advances reforms concisely and clearly. It will be valuable to specialized, as well as general, lawyers and law students and to non-lawyers interested in these technological changes and the law's response. It is organized elegantly and written eloquently — in short, a joy to read. Choice, selection, focus, and synthesis are precious gifts in crafting the knowledge society from the Information Age. The author displays these gifts splendidly.

The author has practised computer law for a dozen years and taught it for half that time at two eminent Canadian law schools. The book reflects the distilled wisdom of that experience. The author wrestles with practical, urgent, and endlessly novel problems by imaginatively conceptualizing them in an intellectual framework that takes one back to first principles. The book also demonstrates a scholar's love of history. The author skilfully compares the law's response to other related technologies from the printing press forward. And, in one especially intriguing analysis of the evolution of the "signature" for contractual authentication, he reaches back to the Old Testament book of *Ruth* to describe the giving over of one of a pair of sandals to a contracting party trader in a commercial transaction. The one sandal would be measured for equivalent wear against the other when the contract was to be executed. Thus, in the author's words we are now striving not for the electronic signature but the electronic "sandal," or perhaps its footprint. Reaching forward, he then anticipates new biomedical technologies for authentication by retinal scan or the reading of a fingerprint finely calibrated to ensure it is live and not severed from its owner.

The book comprehensively canvasses Canadian reported — and some unreported — law. But it also navigates confidently among leading and novel U.S. and U.K. precedents with occasional excursions into the European Community. It carefully distinguishes between situations that are genuinely new — a qualitative change — and those that simply represent modest enhancements on the technological scale as viewed through the law's eye. In making those distinctions it insists on a rigorous functional analysis of novelty and an avoidance of the dangerous and loosely applied metaphors that mask the change.

Canada is in an enviable position to lead the information technology revolution. One test of this leadership is whether we have the human resource and human science skills — law, finance, accounting, entrepreneurship — to undergird and enhance impressive scientific and technological accomplishment. This book is a telling testimony that we do in law.

David Johnston
Faculty of Law
McGill University
Chair, Canadian Information Highway Advisory Council
President, University of Waterloo

To the two women in my life —
Janis for your unending support and
Natalie for the daily wonder and joy

PREFACE
to the Second Edition

It has been only five years since the publication of the first edition of *Computer Law*, but in the world of technology that is a very long time. In terms of the Internet alone, one calendar year generally equals about four or five "Internet years." So, much has happened in the past half-decade. In this preface, I mention the highlights, organized along the lines of the book itself; for the details, see the corresponding chapter. Although many questions have been usefully answered by courts and legislatures, a number of open issues remain, and of course new ones will arise. The objective of this book is to explain succinctly the issues that have been settled, and to give sensible guidance as to the way ahead on the open and new matters.

Technology and Business Trends

The first dynamic of computer law — namely, the rapid pace of techno-logical change — is as alive and as well as ever. Moore's Law (which states that computer processing power doubles every eighteen months) is not going to be proven wrong anytime soon. IBM, for example, has announced a super computer capable of processing 12.3 trillion calcula-tions per second (which is about as powerful as 30,000 personal com-puters put together). And if you're wondering where all the data crunched by this behemoth will reside, IBM has also conveniently announced a data storage device that holds one terabite per square inch — in effect storing 25 million textbook pages on a surface the size of a postage stamp. It is these sorts of technical developments that lead some to argue that the computer revolution is only now starting to hit its stride.

In the past five years a number of new technology applications have come to the fore. E-mail continues to embed itself into the rou-tine of everyday life. Currently, about 10 billion — that's right, *billion* — e-mail messages are sent a day. This number is poised to rise as wireless devices become ubiquitous, such as the Blackberry (invented right here in Canada by Research In Motion). And now we also have instant messaging, "texting" on cell phones, and in another context, peer-to-peer file sharing (which is the technology underpinning Napster and subsequent music sharing services on the Internet). Yes, we've experienced a couple of difficult years for technology companies; no, this has not had an adverse impact on technology innovation.

Nowhere is the inexorable march of the Computer Revolution more pronounced than in respect of the Internet. We are up to about 600 million users of the Internet globally. Let me repeat the e-mail figure: 10 *billion* a day. Or, consider that the Web site for the 1996 Atlanta Olympics received 187 million visits, while the figure for the 2000 Sydney games was 7.2 *billion*. As for the new technology's impact, consider how the Internet facilitated vote swapping between Gore and Nader supporters during the 2000 U.S. presidential election — unprecedented, and impossible without the Internet. And beyond the Internet, I should mention, for example, the digitization of the military, as exemplified by the campaigns in Kosovo and Afghanistan in 1999 and 2000 respectively, and most recently in Iraq. Truly we live in the Information Age.

Of course, we've also had the dot-com boom (in 1998–99) and bust (in 2000–1), but this was nothing more than the usual shakeout that follows the early frenzy around each new transformative technology. We've seen the exact same cadence play itself out for the telegraph, railways, and canals (and any number of other technologies, including the automobile); in each case, after the crash comes the steady build-out of the technology and related business models by serious commercial enterprises. Witness the current positive fortunes of leading Internet companies such as Workopolis, TD Waterhouse, eBay, and Yahoo; they are transforming old industries, or creating entirely new ones, and in each case, profitably. And remember, it's still early days on the Internet: Yahoo is less than ten years old.

Intellectual Property Legal Issues

In the past five years, a number of computer-related intellectual property legal questions that were outstanding in the early and mid-1990s have now been completely or in substantial part answered. With the recent Ontario Court of Appeal decision in *Delrina* (leave to appeal to the Supreme Court refused), we now have a good sense of the scope of copyright protection for software. This was a difficult issue, but we now have sufficient judicial direction. Equally, the Supreme Court has rendered decisions recently on the question of whether the ink on a poster can be removed and transferred to another surface (a decision that has broad ramifications for copyright works in a digital environment), and whether higher life forms can be patented. In both cases, the respective close decision (one by 4–3, the other by 5–4) may not be the last word if a legislative response follows, but again, at least for now, we have useful judicial guidance.

The United States has also achieved some clarity as to whether software and Internet business methods can be patented. In both cases the answer from the patent office is affirmative, but courts are also not averse to finding some issued patents in need of pruning. Thus, it was held recently that the Internet's hyperlinks feature is not covered by a patent. At the same time, a patent has been issued for instant messaging. And the number of issued U.S. patents has exploded over the past five years, driven in large part by the information technology and biotechnology industries. In 1999, about 161,000 U.S. patents were issued, which is double the number ten years before; and in 2001, the number was 344,717. Clearly, the message has gotten through to owners and managers of tech businesses that patents are the new currency of the Information Age.

The United States has also witnessed leading cases that have given clear direction as to the protection under intellectual property legal regimes for electronic databases, the practice of reverse engineering software, and the transmission of traditional copyright content, such as music, over the Internet. We have less clarity on the legality of the new practices of Internet-based linking and framing. In relation to online music, we have also seen the introduction of technology-based digital rights management systems, and the passage of legislation in the United States that prohibits their disablement. These judicial decisions, technological developments, and law reform initiatives are aimed at addressing the second dynamic of computer law, namely, the elusive nature of information. Interestingly, while these legal and technological efforts have been successful in shutting down Napster and MP3.com, many of their successors continue to facilitate the sharing of illegally copied content.

In Canada we have also seen some of these issues debated in legal fora, but we do not yet have the same number of answers as in the United States. In the leading Canadian *Tariff 22* decision, a liability regime for third-party intermediaries is being crafted (we're awaiting the final appellate court review, particularly on the vastly important question whether Internet service providers (ISPs) can cache material). Equally, we're waiting for the Supreme Court to hear the *CCH/LSUC* case, in order to determine the appropriate scope of copyright protection for compilations. We have not yet, in Canada, passed anticircumvention legislation.

We do have clarity, however, on the legality of unauthorized direct-to-home satellite service decoders; the Supreme Court sided with the Canadian licensee, such that in Canada only dealers carrying the authorized Canadian services can lawfully sell receiving units — and only for the licensed Canadian services. As well, the Canadian federal government passed Bill C-11 to ensure that Internet retransmitters were not permitted to take advantage of the *Copyright Act's* compulsory licence regime for distant transmission of broadcast signals; the potential loophole for JumpTV- and iCraveTV-type services has been plugged.

In the area of Internet domain names, we have witnessed a gold-rush mentality, as companies and individuals feverishly staked out their claims in this new, virtual territory. The figures are staggering as to how many dot-com addresses were scooped up over the past five years:

    1998 — 1,745,000;
    1999 — 5,970,600;
    2000 — 17,472,000;
    2001 — 3,200,000; and
    2002 — minus 3,000,000.

Not surprisingly, many of these were registered by persons for the sole purpose of selling them to relevant trade-mark holders at a profit. The result has been literally thousands of cases brought under the dot-com domain name's mandatory dispute resolution process; more recently a similar regime has begun the same exercise for the dot-ca space. Trade-mark holders have generally been extremely successful under these arbitral rules; other battles have been won by them under traditional passing-off and trade-mark infringement rules (including under a fascinating "initial interest confusion" doctrine where the defendant uses the plaintiff trade-mark holder's brands in the meta-tags of the defendant's Web site), and under a new anticybersquatting law in the United States. But trade-mark holders are not always successful, such as when both dot-com arbitrators and courts have refused to turn domain name registrations over to plaintiffs when defendants were making legitimate use of them, including for cybercriticism.

Criminal Law

Computer crime continues to be a significant concern and an important preoccupation of law enforcement authorities. Over the past five years, virus attacks, ironically with innocent-sounding names like Melissa, Love Bug, and Anna, have caused billions of dollars in damage. And it's not just unsavoury, marginalized computer criminals perpetrating these virus attacks: in New York, a computer consultant intentionally placed a virus in a law firm's computer system so the consultant would have additional work detecting the virus and fixing its effects when it was triggered. Also, software piracy continues to rack up large losses for software companies. To these can be added fairly new forms of computer-based criminal behaviour, such as identity theft and debit card scams. At the same time, we should not overstate the problem: in 1999, for example, overall credit card fraud fell to a record low of .06 percent of purchases (i.e., .06¢ for every $100 of transactions).

Some online criminal behaviour, however, is truly out of control. It is estimated that there are 100,000 Web sites offering child pornography, many hosted by computers in locations outside of North America. Ready access to these sites illustrates well the third and fourth dynamics of computer law, namely, the blurring between private/public and national/international, and makes it easier for many more people to become criminals. In a couple of high-profile Ontario cases involving child pornography, for example, the convicted accused were a scientist with a doctorate in philosophy and an accountant. Hacking is also no longer the preserve of the subversive computer criminal: in a recent case the associate dean at an Ivy League university was caught gaining unauthorized access to the computers of other universities to learn their admissions data. Online hate speech is also proving difficult to combat, particularly where the computer serving up the illegal material is not in Canada, though some headway was made recently in the recent Zündel decision. The blurring of national/international, and the difficulty this fourth dynamic of computer law poses for the enforcement of criminal law, can also be seen in recent contempt of court proceedings, where publication bans in Canada are now routinely undermined by non-Canadian Web sites.

In the past five years we've witnessed a huge growth in spending in information-technology security, such as antivirus protection, firewalls, and encryption, to name three categories. We are also using technology in many other ways to combat criminal and quasi-criminal behaviour. For example, time-challenged university professors can now use Turnitin.com to scan student papers for plagiarism (the service compares them to many thousands of papers in its huge database to detect even slight similarities). Technology, however, is no "one-size fits all" silver bullet. Indeed, the new surveillance technologies, including miniature cameras and thermal image detectors, present their own legal challenges to civil liberties precisely because they are so powerful. Particularly in the wake of the 9/11 terrorist attacks, the legal system needs to work out the appropriate balance between assisting with necessary law enforcement, and the huge responsibility of preserving individual freedoms and privacy. In this regard, seemingly simple (yet upon reflection, fiendishly difficult) questions still remain, such as under what circumstances should an e-mail be considered private for the purposes of necessitating a judicially approved search warrant before it is accessed by law enforcement agencies?

Regulating Information, Technology, and E-Commerce

Much has happened in the past five years in the arena of government regulation of cyberspace and related matters. While some commentators in the early days of the Internet, such as John Perry Barlow, thought and hoped that the government's mandate to enact and enforce laws for the general good would not extend to this new communications medium, it is now beyond question that there is an important — indeed critical — role for government in making the Internet safe and efficient for education, commerce, and leisure. Frontiers tend not to be safe until they are tamed.

Nowhere is this more apparent than in the area of privacy, given the large volumes of personal information collected by Web sites or otherwise subject to transmission over the Internet. Thus, several years ago the federal government brought in general coverage privacy legislation for the private sector, which becomes effective in phases, with the non-federally–regulated private sector coming under the purview of this law on January 1, 2004. By then it is likely that provincial equivalents will be in place in British Columbia, Alberta, and (subject to the vicissitudes of electoral politics) Ontario; Quebec has had such a law since 1994.

Some argue such laws are not needed. The United States, for example, has opted for specific laws in certain sectors (such as children's privacy, health, and personal financial information), although at Europe's behest a "safe harbour" arrangement has also been negotiated between the European Union and the United States that mimics the most salient aspects of typical general coverage private sector privacy laws in Europe and Canada. Others contend that all these legislative efforts, however well intentioned, are too little, too late, and that these legislative measures simply cannot withstand the onslaught of privacy-eroding information and surveillance technology (in effect, they would argue that the four dynamics of computer law, namely, the rapid pace of technological change, the elusive nature of information, and the blurring of private/public and national/international, inexorably lead to a loss of privacy). Canada's current privacy commissioner, however, does not take such a defeatist attitude. In numerous decisions over the past few years he has made it clear that modern surveillance and business methods (including surveillance cameras operated by a security company, the practice of monitoring e-mail of employees, and a marketing plan to use personal information from a loyalty program on an opt-out basis) must respect the fair information practices in the new legislation.

Other areas of regulation germane to the technology industry have also undergone interesting development over the past few years. Canada's export control regime has witnessed a major revision over the past little while, with the result that fewer exports of dual-use technologies (such as powerful computers and encryption software) are controlled — recognition of the fact that top-tier computing power is now fairly ubiquitous around the world, and so it simply doesn't make sense for one country, or a handful, to try to regulate the flow when the digital dyke has burst. Equally, the Canadian government has decided that it will not regulate the domestic importation or use of encryption technologies or products. Looked at historically, this is a stunning development, given that until the advent of the Internet, encryption was the preserve of kings, governments, and the military. We have witnessed in this subarea nothing less than the fundamental democratization of a technology. John Perry Barlow would be proud.

Canada's broadcast regulator is also under fairly intense pressure courtesy of the Internet. While a couple of recent labour law decisions make it clear that the federal government has jurisdiction over activities such as Internet Web casting and an ISP generally, the CRTC has opted, in its *New Media* decision, to exempt Internet content retransmitters from regulation. At the same time, the government passed Bill C-11 to deny such entities the benefit of the compulsory licence regime under the *Copyright Act* (under which cable companies and satellite direct-to-home distributors carry off air television broadcast signals to distant subscribers in return for monthly licence fees calculated per subscriber). In short, the Internet will make the CRTC's life much more difficult.

In other online areas, however, governments are not at all considering giving up their traditional role of passing and enforcing laws that protect consumers. Recently, the Ontario government and certain other provinces have updated their consumer protection laws to require Internet agreements to contain certain base information. Governments are also busy pursuing entities that perpetrate false claims, fraud schemes, and other harmful online activity, such as "page-jacking" — Web sites that trap consumers at a certain site and do not let them leave. In the United States, some state governments have also taken steps to regulate spam; while Canada has not yet done so, Ottawa has indicated it is considering various options. In short, while the four dynamics of computer law make regulation much more difficult, governments are not abdicating their all-important regulatory role in the online world. Markets need rules to operate well: this is as true in cyberspace as it is in the traditional offline world. And "private law enforcement" has also come to the fore, as in the U.S. Web-crawling and spam cases where plaintiffs have been successful in arguing that the defendant's activities constitute a trespass against the plaintiff's chattels.

Commercial Law

Canada's competition law regulator has enforced in the online world its misleading advertising rules, and indeed has published guidelines on how not to run afoul of them when making representations on a Web site. Equally, the Competition Bureau in Ottawa, and its counterpart in Washington (the Federal Trade Commission [FTC]), have taken coordinated regulatory action against illegal multilevel marketing schemes implemented online. In the United States, the FTC has also investigated B2B exchanges to ensure they do not operate in a manner adverse to competition. And of course in the United States, the competition law authorities recently completed a gargantuan monopolization case against Microsoft, a proceeding that illustrates that the dynamism of the computer industry should inform how competition laws are applied to this sector of the economy.

In the licensing arena, we continue to see U.S. cases that uphold the "pay now, contract later" mass market software licence mechanic, whereby the consumer pays for the software at a retail outlet, but doesn't see the actual licence agreement until he or she loads the software at home, at which point an "I Agree" button must be clicked in order to be able to use the software. There is no equivalent case law yet in Canada; ideally, a Canadian court will find this U.S. jurisprudence compelling when answering the same question.

As for substantive licence rights, the traditional conundrum (attributable to the first dynamic of computer law) continues of determining whether licence grant language negotiated some time ago includes new technologies and business models. In a cluster of cases in both the United States and Canada, courts have held that newspapers do not have the right to use freelancers' work in their online database collection of articles; a different result likely would apply where the entire newspaper is replicated online, as is happening with some Internet-based journals. Similarly, in a recent case a U.S. court held that the licence grant in a book publishing contract did not extend to the electronic version of the work.

In the negligence area, makers and distributors of particularly violent video games have not been held responsible for copycat violence, including murders. On the other hand, the maker of a defective laptop computer settled a class action claim for $2.1 billion. To avoid such mass claims, a large Canadian cable company was recently successful in inserting an arbitration clause into its agreement with subscribers by posting the amendment on its Web site. Under Ontario's new consumer protection legislation, however, such contracting out of the class action regime is not permitted.

In the bankruptcy law area, we have had a recent decision in Canada that saw an insolvency proceeding disclaim an intellectual property licence. Whatever the merits of the reasoning that led to this conclusion, the fact that the case now exists makes it more urgent that the government pass a remedial provision, along the lines of the U.S. amendment to their bankruptcy statute in the 1980s, that makes it clear that a trustee in bankruptcy or similar official cannot upset previously granted technology and intellectual property licence rights.

In the tax area there continues to be fine-tuning of the retail sales tax regime insofar as the sale of software products and related products are concerned. As for tax issues related to the Internet, after numerous studies, governments are starting to issue useful guidance, such as can be found in a GST Information Bulletin that explains, through concrete examples, how the federal tax authority is approaching various GST issues in respect of online sales.

We have seen over the past five years quite a few insurance law cases on the question whether traditional insurance policies cover some of the new risks posed by computer-related activities, including whether software and data are covered by the "property" language of insurance policies. Much turns on the precise wording of the policy. Equally, courts have been giving guidance on the issue whether these same policies cover various forms of intellectual property claims, involving unauthorized software copying, or patent, copyright or trade-mark infringement, or trade secret misappropriation.

Contract Formation/Evidence Law

In the 1990s there were a number of nagging questions surrounding the legality of doing business online. Would e-mails and other electronic messages satisfy the writing requirement found in various *Statute of Frauds*-type provisions? How could signatures be given in the Internet environment? What constituted offer and acceptance for e-commerce purposes?

We now have answers to most of these questions. Some of the responses have been articulated by courts, where judges have distilled the policy rationale of the traditional rule, and found that the new electronic process, if designed and executed properly, more than satisfies the purpose of the law. Some other answers reside in the new electronic commerce statutes that have as their overriding objective putting electronic communications on the same plane as paper. Thus, whenever a law calls for something to be in writing, these statutes stipulate how that can be done in an electronic environment. We've also witnessed amendments to our corporations law, and securities law policies, to achieve much the same objective, in order that proxies and other shareholder material be able to be distributed to shareholders electronically.

Although these developments represent major, positive progress, we are not entirely out of the woods yet. Sometimes the legislature tells us that an electronic format will not suffice, such as in the preparation of a will. Or a judge reminds us that every now and then, as in some situations involving the telephone, a confirmatory writing still needs to be sent — even if just by e-mail — to the consumer. As well, great care must still be exercised in designing the user's online contract formation experience. The judicial decisions and legislation referred to above confirm that messages conveyed electronically will not be unenforceable merely because they are electronic. That doesn't mean, however, that all contracts purportedly concluded online are enforceable. Lawyers still have to design them in a way that has the user giving express or implied consent in a meaningful way, which is not a trivial exercise. Similarly, we are starting to witness a line of jurisprudence where judges find that the particular avalanche of e-mail exchanged between two parties actually does not result in a clear offer and acceptance. In short, the electronic commerce statutes, while very helpful, are not a panacea.

Equally, in the evidence law area, over the past number of years courts have been comfortable in admitting copies of data stored in computers because of the trustworthiness represented by the data entry and business processes surrounding these machines. To err on the side of certainty, we amended our evidence law statutes to confirm these cases statutorily. Subsequently, the case law has even held that where computer glitches come to light during the relevant time the data was being captured, this would not affect admissibility, but would go only to weight.

Again, however, while these developments are all welcomed by those utilizing computers to operate their businesses (and who isn't today?), and especially by those doing business online, thought still has to be given to certain related nuances. For example, text residing on a Web site has not been found to be trustworthy, and in a couple of cases has not been admitted into evidence. As well, while e-mail of the two litigants is invariably admitted, e-mails of non-litigant parties has been excluded. And then there is the very difficult question of how lawyers should respond when a client, for cost reasons driven by the expense of storage of spam and other unofficial e-mail, decides to implement a document retention/destruction policy.

Libel

In the 1990s, the Internet presented libel law with a series of novel questions. As in the contract formation area, we now have some helpful answers to many of these. An Ontario case recently made it clear that the province's *Libel and Slander Act* newspaper rules apply equally if the journal is put online. In another case it was determined that the single publication rule ought to apply to the Internet; thus, the relevant date for a libel on a Web site is the time at which the offending material is first posted on the site. Another decision holds that posting material to a Web site constitutes publishing (even though a relatively small number of visitors accessed the site) for the purposes of an insurance policy. We have also recently witnessed Canada's first online criminal libel case.

Successful actions against posters of the libellous material on the Internet are now fairly routine. In a recent Ontario case the court also awarded punitive damages. And in both Canada and the United States we now have jurisprudence detailing the test for when an ISP has to provide to a libel plaintiff the identity of an anonymous Internet poster. More intriguing is the possible liability of ISPs for libellous transmissions they carry or host, but do not originate. In a U.K. decision, an ISP was held liable for not taking down offending material sufficiently quickly after being notified of it. On the other hand, the United States has passed a fairly sophisticated limitation of liability regime for ISPs (and other Web site operators). This is one area where law reform lags sorely behind in Canada.

Jurisdiction

In the 1990s it was unclear what online behaviour would be sufficient before a court would take jurisdiction over a foreign Web site operator defendant solely on the basis of the Internet activity of the defendant. We now have many cases addressing this challenging point, particularly in the United States, but also in Canada. It is an extremely important question given that, technically, the World Wide Web is a supremely global medium, and all users of it, in fact, can access every Web site worldwide, thereby raising the spectre of courts potentially taking jurisdiction all the time over all Internet Web site operators.

In the criminal/regulatory area, something along these lines is indeed what is happening. Courts, governments, and law enforcement agencies are taking jurisdiction over criminal activity, including securities law matters and Internet gaming, on the basis that the impugned activity is occurring in Canada when Canadians access the problematic Web site hosted on a computer outside of Canada. Similarly, in a line of U.S. gaming decisions, courts have been consistent in finding that when a U.S. resident dials up a betting site hosted on a server in, say, Central America, the gaming is taking place in the United States (and not in Central America as argued by the Web site operator).

On the civil side a more nuanced approach is being taken. Where the foreign Web site operator is conducting full bore online e-commerce, including having the consumer order products online, courts are fairly consistently taking jurisdiction. On the other hand, depending on the particular type of substantive case that is at issue (i.e., a trade-mark claim can differ from a libel claim), the fact that persons in the subject forum can merely access a passive, informational Web site usually does not result in a real or substantial connection, and the courts regularly decline jurisdiction in such cases. And then there are many cases in between, where a detailed assessment of the quality and quantity of electronic contacts is assessed to determine whether jurisdiction is taken.

* * *

Although new legislation and case law have answered a number of nagging questions, they do not resolve every query that is outstanding. Moreover, they also raise a host of new issues. And so the avalanche of case law, government reports, and new legislative initiatives continues, both in Canada and within our major trading partners, especially the United States. Thus, while much recently enacted statute law, and a great number of recent judicial decisions, are reflected in this new manuscript, I have once again taken pains to advise of trends, overarching developments, skill sets, and other conceptual means of making sense of the continual tidal wave of information that crashes forth each day onto our desks and into our computers through e-mail.

This second edition attempts to state the law as at December 31, 2002.

George S. Takach
April 15, 2003

UPDATED PREFACE
to the First Edition

The computer was the defining technological device of the last quarter of the twentieth century. Encircling the globe with high-capacity computer networks, the Internet included, will be the major technological feat of the first quarter of the twenty-first century. These computer and communications developments have made information the critical asset of our time, surpassing in importance the traditional assets of land and physical goods. Such technological, economic, and social trends have brought into focus the importance of computer law. Therefore, after practising it for more than fifteen years at McCarthy Tétrault, Canada's pre-eminent law firm for technology law, and teaching it as an adjunct professor in Computer Law at Osgoode Hall Law School, York University, for more than a dozen years, it gives me great pleasure to discuss the principal features of computer law and to canvass its primary controversies and challenges. As part of the *Essentials of Canadian Law* series, this book does not purport to be comprehensive, but it does throw its light widely, illuminating the peaks and even some of the valleys of computer law.

The Theory and Practice of Computer Law

Although some readers may question whether computer law should be considered a separate jurisdiction on the legal map, I believe that well before reaching the final chapter, they will agree with me that there is indeed a discernible legal subdiscipline worthy of this title. This cannot be surprising given the enormous impact of the computer and information industries on the economy and on society at large. Law is a reflection of the human environment from which it emanates. Therefore, how could there not be a computer law, given that we are witnessing the computer revolution usher in the Information Age? Moreover, the diverse subtopics that constitute computer law are united by common dynamics and themes. This book, by proposing the four dynamics of computer law, makes a particularly strong case for the legal subdiscipline of computer law. Such an approach — a theory of computer law — has important ramifications both from an academic perspective as well as from the point of view of the day-to-day practice of law.

This book is accessible to the newcomer to computer law, as well as interesting to the expert, and useful to both. The time-starved practitioner will use it mostly as a quick reference guide, entering it by means of the index, or table of cases, or table of contents, in a non-linear manner, as if it were a Web site. And such use is to be welcomed; if the book helps a harried lawyer meet a deadline or assists an articling student find a case just on point, well, that is wonderful. I should, however, alert practitioners to the fact that there are many cross-references in the text, and I hope they will follow up on these when considering a particular issue. As a reference work, the usefulness of this book can be enhanced by a cover-to-cover read. Understanding the dynamics and themes that recur and animate the different areas of computer law can help the busy practitioner solve day-to-day problems. By the same token, legislators, academics, and regulators need to learn about the specific cases in order to make good law and policy. Macro and micro. Forest and trees. In this book I have tried to fuse theory with practice, as each illuminates, informs, and improves the other.

The importance of mastering and integrating theory and practice in the computer law field is a principle I teach my law students. Theory and practice, so often two solitudes in other subdisciplines of the law, simply must converge in the computer law area if the law hopes to remain relevant in this hugely important realm of human endeavour. Thus, when teaching computer law, law school must act as both a social science faculty and a professional school preparing students for the practice of law. And computer law is an ideal course for teaching substantive law and legal method. Most law school courses focus on an area of law, like contracts, and draw on examples from a range of industries, activities, and fact patterns. This is a valuable pedagogical approach, but so is one that focuses on an industry and then draws on the various subareas in the law that apply to the technologies and business practices within it. At the level of theory, this teaching method allows for comparative learning, as the nature and effect of different legal subfields are compared and contrasted. And with respect to legal practice, this method of education is indispensable because, of course, clients rarely prepackage their problems into neat, tidy, legal pigeonholes; instead, the file comes in the door as a mess of facts that cuts across a wide swath of potential legal (and extralegal) remedies. Former students of mine who never intended to practise computer law — they took the course because it sounded interesting in the law school syllabus – have commented that even though they now practise family law, general corporate-commercial law, or what have you, they very much appreciated the skill sets they acquired during the computer law course. In a similar vein, but at another level, before delving into an analysis of the law, this book begins with a first chapter that canvasses the key elements and societal implications of computer-based technologies, thus firmly grounding the theoretical law in the practical technology.

How did I choose the particular topics covered by this book? Partly, the selection is intended to reflect what computer lawyers do. This should please those of my partners at McCarthy Tétrault who still ask me from time to time what my law practice is all about. And my practice does touch on all the topics covered in this book, though some with more frequency than others.[1] Also, the book covers many of the topics that are included in the computer law courses I have taught over the past twelve years at Osgoode Hall Law School, York University, and the Faculty of Law, University of Toronto. In short, the topics covered by this book are the ones of most relevance and interest to my clients and students, and to me. It should be noted, however, that this book does not delve into any detail on the impact of computers on lawyers and their practice of law. This is an interesting and important area, but it is simply a different topic from the substantive legal issues that I consider to make up computer law, and thus is not treated at any length here.[2]

---

1   One aspect of my practice, however, that is not reflected here is the mergers, acquisitions, and financing legal work I do for technology companies and their investors. More precisely, the discussion does not extend to share and asset purchase agreements, or the shareholders and lending arrangements, but in other respects the material in this book is very relevant to high-tech M&A/financing legal work. For a useful book covering these and other business law topics related to technology companies, see George S. Takach, *The Software Business in Canada: Financing, Protecting and Marketing Software*, 2d ed. (Toronto: McGraw-Hill, 1997), and for a book focusing on the venture capital financing business from a U.S. perspective (venture capital and related financing being such an important driver of computer businesses), see Joseph W. Bartlett, *Venture Capital: Law, Business Strategies, and Investment Planning* (New York: John Wiley & Sons, 1988).

2   For a perceptive study of the profound impact that computers, and particularly computer networks, are having on the legal profession, their place in society, and on the nature of legal practice, see M. Ethan Katsh, *Law in a Digital World* (New York: Oxford University Press, 1995). For a discussion of the use of computers in the courtroom, see Deana Driver, "Software Developed in Swissair Crash Probe Used By Both Sides for Saskatchewan Murder Trial," *The Lawyers Weekly*, 30 August 2002. Lawyers are also using the Internet in many novel ways: Lisa

A word is perhaps in order about the title of this work. I have chosen *Computer Law*, notwithstanding that other works in the field are appearing under the titles of *Information Technology Law, Droit d'Informatique* (in France), *Internet Law, E-Commerce Law*, and a host of other names. Indeed, I added the word "Information" to my law school course title a few years ago, so that it now reads "Computers, Information, and the Law." And I was tempted to call this work *Computer and Internet Law* because the Internet features prominently in its pages. Although all these monikers are valuable, in the end I have settled on *Computer Law* because it is short, pithy, and, when all is said and done, the computer (in all its variegated permutations) is still the glue that connects the many facets of law discussed in the following pages.

Inevitable Obsolescence

All books about the law become dated rather quickly, as new statutes are passed, new court decisions are rendered, and new issues make their way onto the legal radar screen. This occupational hazard of the legal writer is perhaps most acute in the computer law field, given the breakneck pace of change within the technological and business spheres that underpin this area of law. Some would even question the utility of a book in such an environment. Obviously, I strongly disagree. Of course, there will be new technical and legal developments — in the computer law field, they are a daily occurrence. It is, however, precisely the daily avalanche of new legal precedents and conundrums that make it necessary to stand back and take stock from time to time. Canadian computer law practitioners can be forgiven for sometimes feeling overwhelmed at the daunting task of staying current with new developments. In addition to keeping abreast of Canadian happenings, the global nature of the computer business and of their clients' activities requires them to at least have a passing knowledge of developments in the United States, Europe, and increasingly in Asia as well. And while the Internet assists in this endeavour, it also compounds the

---

Girion, "Lawyers Compete for Evidence in eBay Auctions," *The Mercury News* (21 July 2002); and Dina Temple-Raston, "Class-Action Lawsuits Gain Strength on the Web," *The New York Times*, available at <nytimes.com/2002/07/28/business/yourmoney/2BCLAS.html> (28 July 2002). Also noteworthy is the rise of Internet-based dispute resolution services, such as <cybersettle.com>; see also Mark Thompson, "Settling Online: Litigation Without Lawyer Noise," available at <callaw.com/weekly/edge/edge419.html>, and Gerry Blackwell, "Online Dispute Resolution," *Canadian Lawyer*, July 2002.

challenge by bringing to the Canadian lawyer's desktop yet another stream of digital information to be reviewed and digested.

Thus, there is a need for a framework of analysis — a user interface — by which to manage this huge amount of legal information. While this book attempts to state the law as at December 2002, it equally strives to provide a conceptual architecture within which lawyers, judges, law students, computer business and technical people, legislators, regulators, and policy analysts can make sense of the vast mass of computer-related legal material that buffets them daily. What follows is an astrolabe for legally navigating the digital seas. As well, it provides skill sets that people involved in the computer and network industries can use to weather the next information-based storm. Of course, even these tools will need to be recalibrated from time to time; and the new cases and statutes will need to be chronicled, so there will be subsequent editions of this book. Accordingly, I would be obliged if you would send me your comments on the following discussion, including references to cases and developments you think are important that have been left out, and other matters (or unreported cases, etc.) you think should be mentioned in the next edition. A truly meaningful legal text is like a living tree: it needs nourishment from its readers. Or, drawing on a computer analogy, a subsequent edition of a book is like a successful new release of a software product — both require active input from their users. I look forward to hearing from you, and you can contact me at

George S. Takach
McCarthy Tétrault
Suite 4700, Toronto Dominion Bank Tower
Toronto-Dominion Centre
Toronto, Ontario
Canada
M5K 1E6

Phone: (416) 601-7662
Fax: (416) 601-8249
E-mail: gtakach@mccarthy.ca

Quality versus Quantity

A word is required about the depth of treatment of the subjects covered by this book. Some will wonder why a particular issue was not expanded upon, or why a subtopic was not worthy of an entire chapter, and so on. Clearly, this book could be twice as long (and still these same questions could be reasonably asked). In keeping with the mandate of the *Essentials of Canadian Law* series, however, I have endeavoured to focus on that which is essential, just as an artist might try to capture the "essence" of a bowl of fruit in a still life painting. In the law school course I teach, I purposely limit the student essays to a rather short length, and not because I have to read them all. When students first learn of the brief paper length they are elated. It is only later, as they get into the research and writing, that they learn the hard truth that it is easier (by far) to write a long paper than a short paper. And so it is, I think, with a book. The reason I limit the length of the papers is to force the students to think and, most importantly, to exercise judgment. In a seventy-page student paper even the least inspired author will eventually stumble across all the relevant points, but in the meantime may force the reader through forty-five pages of unnecessary chaff. To write a good paper that does not exceed twenty pages, now that is a skill.

I learned this lesson from two people. One was a university professor who had every student in his course write a five-page paper every week; I have never been as intellectually challenged, and I have never learned so much, before or since. In a legal context the point was brought home to me early in my career by John J. Robinette, perhaps the greatest legal advocate this country has ever known. I was just back from the bar admission course as a junior lawyer at McCarthy Tétrault (then still McCarthy & McCarthy) when I had to research and draft a legal opinion that was to be signed (and liberally revised) by Mr. Robinette. In my first draft of the opinion I cited three cases as authority for a particular point. I'll never forget Mr. Robinette looking up from the draft and asking, gently but firmly, "Which of these three decisions is the leading case?" I pointed to it. He then smiled, and in a manner that endeared him to his colleagues, he put a thin pencil line through the other two and said, "Then we won't be needing these." I tried to remember this advice as I wrote each paragraph of this book.

A sentiment similar to the one expressed by Mr. Robinette came frequently to mind as I read many of the older cases that I cite in this book. The cases that date from the late 1800s and the early part of 1900s are so much shorter than today's decisions, but without any appreciable diminution in quality. As a junior lawyer some years ago I asked a secretary at McCarthy's who was close to retirement how lawyers managed to prepare complex legal documents before the advent of computer-based word processing, when adding or subtracting something meant a lengthy manual retyping of the whole document. I asked the secretary this as I returned a draft for what must have been its sixth rewrite, and I added, "You must be delighted with this new technology that makes revisions so much simpler and faster." The secretary thought for a moment, smiled, and replied: "Not really. I actually work more on a document now because of all the changes the young lawyers make. You see, in the days of the manual typewriter, lawyers simply got it right the first time, and they managed to close deals with a lot less paper." Again, I have taken the advice to heart; I have tried to get it right, succinctly.

Foreign Judicial Decisions

The judicial decisions referred to in the following pages are, not surprisingly, primarily Canadian. There is, however, a liberal sprinkling of American, British, and even Australian case law in this book. Some will find this startling, but it really should not raise eyebrows. The simple truth is it is an extremely common practice for Canadian judges to cite judicial authorities from other countries.[3] In literally every subarea of the law covered by this book — from intellectual property, to criminal law/constitutional law, to privacy/data protection, to commercial law, to electronic commerce and Internet-related issues — courts in this country have made use of the thinking of members of the bench in other countries.[4] Bora Laskin, the former Chief Justice of the Supreme Court

---

3   The compliment is also repaid: see, for example, *Howley v. Whipple*, 48 N.H. 487 (1869), an early U.S. telegraph case that cites an even earlier Upper Canada telegraph case, *Kinghorne v. The Montreal Telegraph Co.* (1859), 18 U.C.Q.B.R. 60. The English also pay the same compliment to the Americans: consider the hundred-year-old U.K. copyright case, *Hollinrake v. Truswell*, [1894] 3 Ch. 420 (C.A.), that draws upon U.S. copyright jurisprudence. In a recent case from Texas, *Bradshaw v. Unity Marine Corporation, Inc.*, 2001 WL 739951 (S.D. Tex.), the judge notes that "the Court often gives heed to dicta from courts as far flung as those of Manitoba." The highest court in Australia recently cited a Canadian decision (*Libman v. The Queen*, [1985] 2 S.C.R. 178) for the proposition that "Judges have adopted the common law to new technology in the past": *Dow Jones & Company Inc. v. Gutnick*, [2002] HCA 56 (2002), at para. 123.

4   For example, the three leading cases in Canada (from courts in Quebec, Ontario, and British Columbia, respectively) on the scope of copyright protection for computer software all cite U.S. case law at length: *Matrox Electronic Systems Ltd. v. Gaudreau*, [1993] R.J.Q. 2449 (Que. Sup. Ct.); *Delrina Corp. v. Triolet Systems Inc.* (1993), 47 C.P.R. (3d) 1 (Ont. Gen. Div.), affirmed (2002), 17 C.P.R. (4th) 289 (Ont. C.A.); and *Prism Hospital Software Inc. v. Hospital Medical Records Institute* (1994), 57 C.P.R. (3d) 129 (B.C.S.C.). Similarly, in *BCAA et. al. v. Office and Professional Employees Int. Union et. al.*, 2001 BCSC 156 (B.C.S.C.), the court, in considering for the first time in Canada the novel situation of applying the passing-off rules to a union's commentary Web site, stated (at para. 69): "I am mindful that the American authorities are not binding but I think

of Canada, wrote about this phenomenon some thirty years ago while he was a justice of the Ontario Court of Appeal and concluded that "Canadian courts are hospitable to cases from other common law jurisdictions, and that, English cases apart, American decisions are the most frequently cited from such other jurisdictions."[5] Laskin also foresaw the day when the use of U.S. case law would exceed that from England.

Of course, great care must be exercised when utilizing foreign decisions to interpret Canadian statutes or in determining the next phase of development of the common law in a particular subarea of the law.[6] Thus, Canadian courts in a number of contexts have warned against an unthinking deference to foreign legal decisions.[7] This is particularly true in the intellectual property area where, although Canada shares a common legal heritage with, for example, the United Kingdom, the United States, and Australia, there now exist numerous important differences in the statutes in these respective jurisdictions. Recent international initiatives such as the *1996 WIPO Copyright Treaty*, however,

---

they are of some guidance to me in considering the elements of the tort of passing-off in the internet context." The court then went on to review extensively the U.S. jurisprudence.

5 Bora Laskin, *The British Tradition in Canadian Law* (London: Stevens & Sons, 1969), at 104–5 [*Tradition*].

6 In this regard, the degree of reliance by some Canadian courts on foreign jurisprudence can be quite disconcerting. Consider the following passage from *R. v. Crane and Walsh* (1985), 45 C.R. (3d) 368 at 373 (Nfld. Dist. Ct.), a decision that had to consider the privacy issues surrounding a traditional letter (and cited later in this book in the context of e-mail/Internet privacy issues) and where apparently access to U.S. legal sources was unavailable: "Neither counsel cited any case referring to search and seizure of personal mail. Further, by not having access to American case law I am left in a rather disadvantageous position when considering this novel legal point. When considering the application of s. 8 of the *Charter* it is helpful to consider the experience of the American courts in applying the Fourth Amendment to the American Constitution."

7 *Compo Company Limited v. Blue Crest Music Inc.*, [1980] 1 S.C.R. 357 [*Compo*]; *Cie Générale des Etablissements Michelin-Michelin & Cie v. C.A.W.-Canada* (1996), 71 C.P.R. (3d) 348 (F.C.T.D.). In the *Compo* case, however, after stating at 367 that U.S. copyright cases "must be scrutinized very carefully because of some fundamental differences in copyright concepts which have been adopted in the legislation of that country," the court goes on to cite liberally from a number of U.S. decisions. An English court has also warned against the unthinking use of American computer law decisions involving copyright matters: *Ibcos Computers Ltd. v. Barclays Mercantile Highland Finance Ltd.*, [1994] FSR 275 (H.Ct.); but see also *John Richardson Computers Limited v. Flanders*, [1993] FSR 497 (H.Ct.), a decision involving the first full hearing of a software copyright case in the United Kingdom that cited liberally American case law.

generally have the effect of increasingly harmonizing the intellectual property laws of different countries.[8] Where the underlying statutory or common law principle is similar in Canada to another jurisdiction, Canadian courts have not hesitated to at least consider the jurisprudence in that other jurisdiction when coming to a resolution on a novel or thorny problem. And this is to be encouraged, particularly with respect to the law related to an industry as global in its outlook as the computer industry. The litmus test, however, for determining whether to use a foreign case should not be the decision's jurisdiction or author, but rather the quality of the reasoning and its applicability to Canadian conditions.[9]

---

8   The *1996 WIPO Copyright Treaty* is available from the WIPO Web site: <wipo.org>.

9   Or, as Bora Laskin stated in *Tradition*, above note 5 at 105, "*Stare decisis* apart, it is the fitness of the solutions to legal issues offered by the cases and not their source that should be the moving consideration of their value." Seven years later, the same writer (then Chief Justice of the Supreme Court of Canada) expressed a similar view in *Morgentaler v. R.*, [1976] 1 S.C.R. 616 at 629, when he commented on the use by Canadian judges of U.S. constitutional law authorities when considering the then Canadian *Bill of Rights*: "This Court has found such decisions to be helpful in the past and remains receptive to their citation, but they do not carry any authority beyond persuasiveness according to their relevance in the light of context."

ACKNOWLEDGMENTS

Although the writing of a book is an intensely solitary experience, books like this one simply do not get written in a vacuum. I therefore wish to acknowledge, first and foremost, the primary debt I incurred while working on this project to my wife, Janis, and my daughter, Natalie, who continue to provide a constant source of encouragement and solace throughout my working, writing, and teaching endeavours. Family is so important. I also want to give a heartfelt thanks to my extended family at McCarthy Tétrault, the firm where I practise law. There is simply no doubt in my mind that I practise law at the finest law firm in the country; for the stimulating intellectual and professional environment created by my partners and our firm's associates I am truly grateful. A number of my partners will recognize elements of their intellectual handiwork in the following pages and to them I am particularly indebted. Yet another part of the McCarthy Tétrault family are the clients of the firm that I work with; thank you for the constant stream of interesting files. And as for Fonda Chau, my secretary, who tamed the ungainly manuscript with her cool professionalism and word processing magic, I simply could not have done it (and run a busy law practice at the same time) without her. Thank you very much.

I should also like to acknowledge my gratitude to the two great law schools in Toronto, Osgoode Hall Law School at York University and the Faculty of Law, University of Toronto, where I have taught computer law courses over the past dozen years. Teaching serves to sharpen my thinking about legal issues and allows me periodically to take stock and assess the big picture. It also pushes me to stay current with legal developments, lest I be embarrassed by a particularly bright student who stays up half the night surfing Internet legal sites in New Zealand for the latest Kiwi computer law case (this has happened). A great pleasure that I derive from my students is the symbiotic relationship we share: they tell me about the latest technology gizmos (and neat New Zealand legal Web sites) and I help them make sense of computer law. It's a wonderful arrangement. Finally, I would like to thank Irwin Law, and particularly William Kaplan, Jeffrey Miller, and Pamela Erlichman for allowing me to aggregate and focus my thinking into a single work that they have published with such professionalism.

George S. Takach
Toronto, May 2003

LAW IN THE INFORMATION AGE

Law is the set of rules created by governments to order social and economic behaviour and to mediate and resolve conflicts among people. Law (which includes publicly sanctioned force) may be contrasted with private force. There was a time, for example, when a person who felt aggrieved by another's malicious statements would resort to the sabre or pistol for a duel, and a bloody family feud might have erupted. Today, the maligned person would commence a lawsuit for libel. And lawsuits have multiplied because the fabric of society has become complex, with many more interests and entities and many more situations where interests collide than in the past. Thus, the areas of law have multiplied beyond the traditional subjects of property, contract, and criminal law, to include negligence (tort), commercial, corporate, family, securities, environmental, labour, and tax. Although some bemoan the number of laws, lawyers, and legislators in Canada, consider what our country would be like without the rule of law. It is not such a hard thing to imagine; one has only to look at the evening television news to see agonizing, bloodstained reports of communities that refuse to adopt, or for some unfathomable reason decide to jettison, the rule of law, and replace it with the arbitrary, capricious, and violent rule of private force.

Computer law is the body of legal rules related to the broad spectrum of activities and transactions involving computing technologies. Drawing upon the general concept of law noted above, computer law

1

strives to order relations among people who create and use computer and information-based assets, to manage the conflicts that invariably arise among them. If this conceptualization seems somewhat "authority-heavy," an equally valid view would be that computer law is the grease that makes the interconnected wheels and sprockets of the computer and information industries operate more efficiently. Under either approach, computer law encompasses a wide variety of subdisciplines of the law, including intellectual property, criminal law, regulatory regimes, and commercial law, as well as legal issues related to doing business electronically, including contract and evidence law, and libel and jurisdiction.

A. COMPUTER LAW: DYNAMICS, THEMES, AND SKILL SETS

As this book surveys a diverse landscape of subdisciplines in the law and examines how each area applies to computer and networking technologies, and software and information-based products, four principal dynamics — referred to in this book as the four dynamics of computer law — emerge. Most important is the rapid, almost torrid, pace of technological change, not only in terms of the development and release of new high-technology products, but also in terms of the new delivery systems of traditional content, such as the Internet. A second dynamic is the elusive nature of information and the fact that it derives its economic value from its context; as well, most information is never complete, but is in a continual state of becoming. A third dynamic is the melding of the two spheres that hitherto were distinctly private or public, as technological developments blur the line between them; the ultimate example is the Internet, which brings the world's largest communications network directly into a person's home through a personal computer or laptop. The final dynamic is the erosion of the borders between matters national and international. The computer industry is probably the most globally oriented business; the Internet has since confirmed high technology's contempt for geographic frontiers.

Each of these dynamics presents computer law and its practitioners with several fundamental challenges. In meeting these challenges, the legal system can consider four themes, the elements of which weave themselves through this book. First, there is the goal of consistency; that is, the legal rules related to the computer industry should be consistent with the best jurisprudence related to earlier technologies, and should also be consistent today around the world, as well as across the different subdisciplines of computer law. A second theme relates to control points and the roles played by geography, identity, and paper as regulatory control points; the corollary is that in an electronic world the traditional control points are under pressure, and new ones have to be devised. A third theme involves the liability regimes applicable to intermediaries. Entities that do not themselves initiate infringing, or criminal, or libellous conduct, but that propagate or facilitate it, pose some difficult questions for the law. And finally, one must consider the dangers of mischievous metaphors. Lawyers, judges, and legislators all tend to analyse current activities and persons or entities associated with them in terms of categories developed in the past. This is a useful approach but must be carried out carefully, as there is a serious danger of remaining trapped in outdated and ill-fitting legal paradigms.

Bolstered by the analytical tools offered by these dynamics and themes, the legal practitioner can approach any legal challenge posed by new technology and related business practices by employing one or more of the following skill sets. The common law entails assisting a judge to learn thoroughly the technological bases for a particular problem, and then bringing the tremendously flexible common law to bear by adapting and shaping it as required. Time and again, courts have shown a receptiveness to understand the new technology, a keen ability to tackle the various dynamics and themes of computer law, and a willingness to use their significant latitude to craft appropriate rules for a specific technologically driven problem. Where the common law falls short, contracts can be harnessed, in effect, to create private law between the contracting parties. Contracts can be particularly helpful in responding to the dynamics and themes of computer law. Similarly, technological skills can be employed to the same end; for example, technology can be used to prevent unauthorized use of intellectual properties. Technology drives the dynamics and themes of computer law, so it is not surprising that technology can also be used to address a number of the issues it raised in the first place. Contracts and technology, however, are not without their limitations, including concerns about uniformity of treatment (i.e., different contracting parties can be treated unequally), cost of access, lack of transparency (i.e., contracts can be kept confidential), and transaction costs. Hence, the fourth skill set, law reform, is important. Changing statute-based law often remedies a shortcoming in the previous state of statute- or judge-made law and is the desirable method for responding to a particular challenge posed by technology. To be efficient and effective, however, law reform in the computer law area must exhibit a sustained ability to stay abreast of technological developments and to effect statutory change in smaller but more regular increments than has traditionally been the case in Canada.

B. TECHNOLOGY TRENDS, SOCIETAL IMPACT, AND THE LAW

Before turning to a discussion of substantive questions of computer law, it is worth describing, however briefly, a few key aspects of the technology that underpins the computer revolution and that has brought us into the Information Age. Thus, it is important to understand what hardware, semiconductor chips, and software do, what data and databases are, how communications technologies and networks work, and what the primary features of the Internet are. More important, however, is to appreciate the dramatic and continuing drop in the price of computing power and telecommunications services and the enormous social and economic impact of this. The discussion of technology in this book centres not on technical questions such as how many bits or bytes can be — or even will be — compressed onto the head of a pin, but rather on the legal aspects of the technology and its trends and applications. And central to this is an understanding of the fantastic speed with which technological change occurs in this area. The first dynamic of computer law, namely, the rapid pace of technological change, figures prominently in the discussion in chapter 1.

With respect to technology applications, an understanding of the key principles of computer law, let alone its more subtle nuances, requires some familiarity with the powers that have been unleashed by the digitization, manipulation, mass storage, and communication of information. It is also important to appreciate the trend toward increasingly smaller and more intelligent computers. The collective result is an Information Age in which distance has been eliminated, mass customization has been enabled, and all businesses and organizations have become dependent on computers and networks. The discussion of these issues in chapter 1 serves as the technical, societal, and economic backdrop for a host of legal issues that are the subject of the book.

C. INTELLECTUAL PROPERTY LAWS

Intellectual property laws provide legal protection for products emanating from the minds of people. In order to understand intellectual

property laws, it is necessary to appreciate the economics of information, which differ radically from the economics for traditional property such as real estate and tangible goods. These traditional assets operate in a world of natural scarcity, but information does not, given the second dynamic of computer law, namely, the elusive nature of information. Information can be reproduced (and transmitted) at virtually no cost (particularly over the Internet), and is also capable of universal possession. Thus, the rationale for intellectual property law regimes is to bring various degrees of artificial scarcity to bear on information-based assets, thereby creating protection for the works of authors and inventors in order to encourage the production of these works and ultimately their dissemination for the benefit of all people. Accordingly, trade secrets/breach of confidence protects information that is not publicly known. Patents protect novel ideas that are not kept secret. Copyrights afford protection not for ideas but for the form of expression of ideas. Chip protection covers certain elements of the designs used to develop semiconductor chips. Trade-mark law prevents unfair competition by prohibiting competitors from using confusing marks and symbols to sell their goods or services. This book looks at intellectual property as its first substantive topic because the issues surrounding the economics of information will animate a number of other areas of the book.

With technological change advancing quickly, the intellectual property regimes face a number of challenges. Indeed, all four of the dynamics of computer law are being felt very acutely in the intellectual property area. Moreover, the intellectual property statutes emanate from the Industrial Revolution and will be hard-pressed to remain current in the Information Age. How, and indeed whether, patents should apply to software are burning questions in the computer industry. Similarly, copyright protection for software has yielded a number of judicial answers over the last few years. The application of traditional intellectual property laws to new information-based products, such as electronic databases, and to new technologies, such as multimedia works and the Internet (including the Internet domain name system, and Internet practices such as linking and framing), also raises a host of questions. Should there be other means of legal protection for information-based products? Besides these substantive issues, there are process-related questions regarding the way intellectual property issues are posed and resolved in our current legal system. Of particular interest in this regard are the new domain name dispute resolution procedures created for the domain name registries.

D. CRIMINAL LAW

Criminal law is another means that can be employed to protect information-based assets, but, of course, the criminal law does much more in its attempt to safeguard a number of other interests important to people, businesses, organizations, and governments. Unfortunately, a society dependent on computers, telecommunications, networks, and information is extremely vulnerable to computer crime. Indeed, computers and networks can figure in criminal activity in a multitude of ways. They can be the subject of crime, as when a computer is stolen or when one is accessed without authorization. As well, computers and networks can be the means by which other crimes are perpetrated. The exact amount of computer crime is difficult to measure because much harmful computer-related activity cannot be detected, and many organizations are reluctant to report themselves being victimized by computer criminals. Computer crime is a significant and growing problem, however, and it manifests itself in the following guises: unauthorized gain (including theft, software piracy, stealing computing or telecommunications resources, high-tech forgery, and unauthorized computer-based gambling including via the Internet); unauthorized destruction (including the deletion of data and the implantation in software, computers, and networks of "viruses," "worms," and other malicious software-based devices); unauthorized manipulation (including "hacking"); unauthorized intrusion (including wire-tapping and other means of scanning electronic-based communications, and surveillance with miniature cameras, microphones, and other intelligent but very small devices); illegal images (such as obscene pornography and child pornography); and illegal speech (such as racist and hateful messages, and libel).

The criminal law, prescribed in Canada primarily by the *Criminal Code*, delineates the behaviour that society, acting through Parliament, has deemed to be socially unacceptable. In combatting persons who engage in harmful computer-related activity, law enforcement authorities use mainly the following offences of the *Criminal Code*: theft, fraud, computer abuse, data abuse, obscenity and child pornography, hate propaganda, offences regarding gaming, and interception of communications. A number of other offences in the *Criminal Code* may also be relevant from time to time, particularly where a computer is used to facilitate a crime. As well, new surveillance-related laws involving computer networks have been proposed (and some passed) in the wake of the terrorist attacks in New York and Washington on Septem-

ber 11, 2001. The criminal law has been traditionally concerned with protecting the integrity of the individual and tangible property. Thus, the four dynamics of computer law — the rapid pace of technological change, the elusive nature of information, the blurring of private/public and of national/international — coupled with the general rule of criminal law interpretation that *Criminal Code* provisions be construed strictly and in favour of the accused in the event of doubt as to the applicability of the particular provision, have challenged the ability of the *Criminal Code* to stay current with the new mischiefs possible with the widespread use of computers and networks. The result has been the amendment of the *Criminal Code* to include several new computer-related provisions. The Internet and other computer-based technologies and business practices raise many questions under these and the older provisions of the *Criminal Code* and highlight the challenges of enforcing a national criminal law in an increasingly global computer crime environment.

E. REGULATING INFORMATION, TECHNOLOGY, AND E-COMMERCE

Governments regulate information in order to achieve a number of objectives. They institute and administer data protection laws in an effort to protect the privacy of individuals. Privacy has been expressed as the fourfold right to control intrusion into a person's seclusion; control the disclosure of private facts about a person; prevent a person being put into a false light in the public eye; and control the exploitation of a person's image and likeness. It is increasingly difficult for individuals to protect these rights in the Information Age. Computers, databases, and telecommunications networks, not to mention current developments in photography and other surveillance technologies, present significant threats to people's privacy. Most observers view this as an unfortunate byproduct of modern technology, and accordingly many look to the law to offer a bulwark against the various technologies and business practices that threaten privacy. The four dynamics of computer law, however, conspire to make the law's task in this regard a difficult one indeed. Whether employers should have the right to monitor employee e-mails is but one contentious subtopic in this area.

Information is power, particularly in the Information Age, so it is not surprising that many governments attempt to control the export of strategically important technologies and information that might, in the hands of a country's enemies, prove to be extremely detrimental to the country's security interests. Thus, the Canadian government regulates the export from Canada of powerful computers and related technologies (such as software) that could be used in military applications. Also subject to export control are encryption technologies that interfere with the ability of law enforcement and intelligence agencies to eavesdrop on the communications of our adversaries. Given the technology trends enumerated in chapter 1, particularly to increased miniaturization and to the development of the Internet for transmitting software as well as data, the enforcement of export controls in the area of high technology is becoming more problematic.

The federal government has for many decades regulated the telecommunications and broadcasting industries in Canada. The traditional rationale for doing so with respect to the former related to protecting the public interest in the context of an important utility and transportation-like service provided by monopolists and quasi-monopolists. Subsequently, protecting the indigenous Canadian participants in the telecommunications industry also became an important foundation for regulation. On the broadcasting side, scarcity on the radiowave spectrum was an initial driver for regulation. Today, with the 500-channel universe upon us, protection of Canadian sovereignty through cultural policies is much more important. These and other reasons have led to the development of an extensive regulatory regime for telecommunications and broadcasting overseen primarily by the Canadian Radio-television and Telecommunications Commission. The four dynamics of computer law — the rapid pace of technological change, the elusive nature of information, and the blurring of both private/public and national/international — make the tasks of the gatekeepers and conduits of the Information Age daunting. The Internet, in particular, raises questions about whether the government can regulate the information highway effectively, assuming it decides to do so for policy and political reasons.

Governments in Canada and around the world have implemented many regulations to protect the public from nefarious activities. In all these areas, the Internet and other new technologies pose a number of challenges. Accordingly, governments have found it necessary to bring rules to bear on Internet securities-related activities, electronic banking, corporate meetings, and consumer protection generally to ensure that e-commerce transactions are treated commensurately with their offline counterparts. On the other hand, the government has indicated that it will not regulate the domestic use or importation of encryption technology. In the middle is the spam issue, where for the longest time the government indicated no new laws were needed, though recently it may be reconsidering this hands-off approach.

F. COMMERCIAL LAW

The business of selling computers, software, and information-based products differs from other enterprises in a number of legally important ways. To understand these differences, it is first necessary to appreciate that the computer industry is driven by three interrelated phenomena. Perhaps the most fundamental and far-reaching of these is the incredibly short product cycles; that is, hardware, software, and information-based products and services are developed, marketed to customers, and then overtaken by new products, in ever-decreasing timespans. This trend is closely linked to the first dynamic of computer law, namely, the torrid pace of technological change.

Short product cycles also influence a unique aspect of software, namely, that it invariably has errors, or "bugs" in it. It is important to understand for legal purposes that software cannot be made to be perfect. Another result of short product cycles is the fact that distribution channels for much hardware, and most software and information-based products, are typically multitiered and variegated.

Short product cycles and complicated product distribution channels also have implications under competition law. Canada's Competition Act provides for a number of criminal offences and reviewable practices provisions that, although they apply to the economy generally, are particularly germane to the high-tech business, including possibly B2B exchanges.

Another commercial law issue relevant to the computer industry is the fact that information-based products in electronic form tend to be licensed, rather than sold, to end-users.

Copies of books are sold; copies of software are licensed. There are a number of historic reasons for licensing software, as well as certain contemporary rationales for the practice. A particularly common vehicle for licensing mass market software is the shrinkwrap licence, a form of agreement whose enforceability has been questioned by a number of courts, though recent cases suggest some countries seem to be more amenable to the vehicle. Another area of licensing controversy involves the particular scope of rights granted to licensees, and whether the rights granted are broad enough to cover new technical delivery mechanisms and media. These cases illustrate some of the difficulties inherent in the field of technology licensing given the first dynamic of computer law, namely, the rapid pace of technological change.

Computer products also present several questions under negligence law. Some relate to the creation of software, particularly in light of the fact that bug-free software is an unattainable goal. As well, computers can be used in a variety of ways that are negligent. Ironically, negligence can also arise when computers are not used. The applicability of sales legislation to computer products raises a series of questions. Is software a "good" in order to come under the auspices of sale of goods statutes? How are the implied warranties and conditions of merchantable quality and fitness for a particular purpose to be applied to computer-based products? Can suppliers of these products exclude these warranties and conditions, and limit other liabilities, through contract? Questions regarding the application of bankruptcy legislation are also germane. Upon the bankruptcy of the licensor of software, can the trustee in bankruptcy disclaim previously granted licence agreements? Conversely, what are the rights of the licensor of technology if its licensee goes bankrupt?

As in all areas of commercial endeavour, tax questions can pose intriguing problems for the suppliers and users of computers, software, and information-based products. Somewhat reminiscent of the discussion in the area of sales legislation, a threshold question for sales tax regimes is whether software is a good or a service. Similarly, Canada's withholding tax on software has experienced several bouts of uncertainty over the years. The Internet creates some intriguing international tax questions. The application of certain international trade rules to the high-tech sector is also noteworthy. Categorizing computer-based goods for tariff classification raises yet another challenge for public authorities, different in substance but similar in terms of process to those of sales and tax legislation. Government procurement rules have particular poignancy to the computer sector, since governments are major purchasers of high-tech products and their procurement practices in this area can be unfairly skewed against certain suppliers of computers, software products, and related services. Given the impact of technology on the workplace, whether in the office or on the factory floor, it is worth noting several kinds of labour and employment law ramifications related to information technology. Computer-related risks also pose interesting questions under insurance law, particularly from the perspective of asking whether software, data, and intellectual property infringement are covered under traditional insurance policies.

G. E-COMMERCE CONTRACT AND EVIDENCE LAW ISSUES

The sale of goods and services, and related activities such as the transport, insurance, and financing of goods, is accompanied by the generation and movement of information. For the past few hundred years, paper-based documents — contracts, purchase orders, invoices, bills of lading — have served as the predominant means to record and share commercial information. With the advent of the telegraph, commercial information began to be communicated electronically without paper. The telex and fax continued this trend, as did direct computer-to-computer communications, often referred to as electronic data interchange (EDI), an important means for transmitting commercial information in certain industries. Today, the Internet is poised to become the central means of doing business electronically, both for one-on-one transactions like those consummated by early electronic communication technologies, as well as for the new open environment of many-on-many ushered in by computer networks. As well, once data are received, they are also often stored electronically; increasingly, even paper-based documents are scanned and their contents stored electronically through imaging systems, both to save money and to improve accessibility to such information. This shift from a paper-based to an electronic-based commercial information environment raises numerous legal issues, particularly given the buffeting effect of the first two dynamics of computer law, namely, the rapid pace of technological change and the elusive nature of information.

Contract formation law has developed a number of principles and doctrines to promote certainty among business people in their commercial relations; these include the requirement that various contracts be in writing and be signed in order to be enforceable and other rules related to when and where a contract comes into existence. These rules are quite elaborate and well developed for contracts arising in a paper context, and their application to agreements concluded in an electronic environment has given rise to a number of judicial determinations. In virtually all these cases, courts have been adept at understanding the new technologies and business processes and at assisting business people in adopting them by recognizing their legal legitimacy. In a manner reminiscent of contract formation law, evidence law strives to ensure the predictable and fair ordering of relations among business entities, individuals, governments, and others by ensuring that only reliable evidence is permitted to be provided to judicial and other decision makers in legal, administrative, and related proceedings. Again, as with contract law, a number of evidence law rules were developed in a paper-based environment, such as those that make admissible records that were created in the normal course of business. The application of these common law and statutory rules, where express computer-related evidence law rules have not been enacted, in the past has raised some questions, but for the most part — again as with contract law — courts have endeavoured to understand the particular technology confronting them, and then have sensibly applied the relevant legal rule, almost invariably with the result that the computer-generated record has been admitted into evidence. Notwithstanding the positive track record, there have been some uncertainties in the law of evidence as it related to computer-generated records that probably warranted some law reform initiatives. Similarly, certain traditional records retention rules were too closely aligned with paper-based forms of recording and storage and required changes in statutory language to accommodate electronic formats. Equally, some organizations are revising their document retention policies to include all electronic materials, including e-mail.

To address a number of issues left open or uncertain by the courts, governments in Canada and around the world have adopted electronic commerce statutes and new evidence law statutes to deal with some of the challenges posed by the new technologies and the resulting business communications methods. While these statutes do not answer all the existing questions, they do go a long way to helping business people navigate the tides of the new e-commerce business models. It is important to note, however, that these new statutes do not, for example, provide that all agreements purportedly concluded online are enforceable. Rather, they provide that the electronic messages will not be unenforceable solely because they are in electronic form. Thus, it is still very much up to the parties to take care to design an online contract assent system that results in a binding offer and acceptance.

H. INTERNET LIBEL AND JURISDICTION ISSUES

In the history of computer law, the development and inexorable growth of the Internet has raised complex legal issues. This book, however, does not treat the Internet as a unique phenomenon. Rather, it views the Internet as another step in the steady evolution of computers and networks and integrates the analysis of Internet issues into the technologies and business processes of its predecessors, such as telegraphy, telephony, and broadcasting. Indeed, the four dynamics of computer law that have driven these industries are currently buffeting the Internet as well; moreover, the Internet may well be the phenomenon that best exemplifies the active and sustained operation of the rapid pace of technological change, the elusive nature of information, and the blurring of private/public and national/international. Accordingly, although there are some revolutionary characteristics of the Internet (such as framing, linking, and caching), for the most part the legal issues presented by it are best understood by carefully drawing on appropriate existing and historical analogies. Thus, intellectual property issues relating to the Internet are canvassed in the intellectual property chapter; its impact on criminal law is discussed in the criminal law chapter; regulation of it by the CRTC, together with Internet-related consumer protection issues, are addressed in the regulatory environment chapter; licensing and tax issues germane to it are covered in the commercial law chapter; and contract formation issues with respect to it are considered in the electronic commerce chapter. This is in addition to numerous other references to the Internet peppered throughout the book.

Two other Internet issues are particularly noteworthy. The Internet, as explained at the outset of the book, provides unprecedented opportunities for local, regional, national, and global communications of text and other content. Some of these messages will be defamatory. A pressing question is, What liability should be visited upon intermediary disseminators of libellous electronic messages? The same question is asked in the context of copyright and criminal law elsewhere in the book. In addressing these questions, courts must be wary of adopting mischievous metaphors and instead must thoroughly understand how much knowledge and control was exercised by the Internet participant regarding the alleged harm. Jurisdiction is also a fascinating Internet issue. The jurisdiction of a government to pass and enforce laws is generally limited in terms of the physical geography under the control of that government. The Internet, of course, allows users to cross borders (virtually) instantaneously. Thus, the fourth dynamic of computer law talks in terms of a blurring of national and international. Therefore, frequently courts must determine when to take jurisdiction over a person or legal entity physically resident outside the court's jurisdiction whose Internet-based activity is having some effect on people who are resident within the court's jurisdiction.

CHAPTER 1

TECHNOLOGY TRENDS, SOCIETAL IMPACT, AND THE LAW

An understanding of the key principles of computer law, let alone its more subtle nuances, requires some appreciation of the technology that underpins the computer revolution and that has brought us into the Information Age. Accordingly, there follows a brief exposition of some of the principal technical aspects of computers, software, data, and the networks (including the Internet) that are increasingly linking computers.[1]

---

1   There are numerous texts and journals where detailed information can be found regarding all the different aspects of computer and related technologies. For an engaging telling of the tale of computers since 1945, see Paul E. Ceruzzi, *A History of Modern Computing* (Cambridge, MA: MIT Press, 1998). A good, comprehensive and yet accessible volume for the non-technical reader is Anthony Ralston & Edwin D. Reilly, eds., *Encyclopedia of Computer Science*, 3d ed. (New York: Van Nostrand Reinhold, 1993) [*Encyclopedia of Computer Science*]; for a more recent work in the same vein, see Brian K. Williams, Stacey C. Sawyer & Sarah E. Hutchinson, *Using Information Technology* (Boston: Irwin/McGraw Hill, 2003). For an entry-level work with many helpful pictures consider Sherry Kinkoph, Jennifer Fulton, & Kelly Oliver, *Computers: A Visual Encyclopedia* (Indianapolis: Alpha Books, Macmillan, 1994) [*Visual Encyclopedia*]. For works that offer succinct descriptions of technical terms used in computing and networking, the following are recommended: George McDaniel, ed., *IBM Dictionary of Computing* (New York: McGraw-Hill, 1994); and Bryan Pfaffenberger, *Internet in Plain English* (New York: MIS Press, 1994) [*Plain English*]. Of course, the rapid pace of technological change dates books on computers and related technologies quickly, and so journals can be an invaluable source of information. *Scientific American* *and Communications of the ACM* have particularly strong and timely articles on various technical subjects related to computers and communications.

More importantly, several key technological trends and applications are also highlighted, namely digitization, manipulation, mass storage, communications, miniaturization, and expert systems. In this discussion the emphasis is not on technical questions. Rather, the focus is on the legal aspects of the technology. This chapter also discusses the impact the technology and the technological trends (specifically the elimination of distance, mass customization, our dependence on computers, and our development into an information-based society) are having on society. The law, with certain limited exceptions, is a reflection and outgrowth of the society in which it is rooted. To understand the main elements of computer law, therefore, it becomes important to grasp how these computer-based technologies and trends are shaping the world. The emphasis here will not be on the sociological, psychological, or political aspects of these transformations (though these are many and far-reaching), but on their legal significance.[2] This chapter will also begin to illuminate the contours of the four dynamics of computer law, namely, the rapid pace of technological change, the elusive nature of information, the blurring of public and private, and the blurring of national and international.[3]

Although an overview of computer technology and its trends and applications is useful — and so this chapter is particularly germane for those who are not technically proficient — the reader is cautioned that what follows is very general.[4] In fact, the technologies involved in com-

---

2   This is not to say the sociological, psychological, or political dimensions of the computer revolution are not important or fascinating, as they are certainly both. For example, for a penetrating study from a sociologist's perspective of computers and the Internet and their roles in redefining human identity and community through a culture of simulation and computer-based interaction, see Sherry Turkle, *Life on the Screen: Identity in the Age of the Internet* (New York: Simon & Schuster, 1995). For a description of the types of people transformed by the Internet — particularly youth — see Michael Lewis, *Next: The Future Just Happened* (New York: W.W. Norton & Company, 2002). As for the growing importance of the Internet to the world of politics, see "The Battle for the White House: America's Presidential Election Campaign is in Full Swing Not Least on the Internet," *The Economist*, 18 September 1999; "Political Campaigns Online: Beyond the Law's Reach," *The Economist*, 11 December 1999; and "Cyber Soapboxes," *The Economist*, 24 June 2000.

3   These dynamics are important, and are a unifying theme throughout this book. For a discussion of these dynamics, see chapter 8, section A, "Computer Law: Dynamics."

4   It should also be noted that the following discussion does not address in any technical detail various communications technologies that are also germane to parts of this book (especially chapter 6 on electronic commerce), such as telegraph, telex, teletype, EDI, and fax.

puters and networks can be exceedingly complex. Moreover, the rapid pace of change in the computer and related industries quickly outdates even a sophisticated, detailed explanation of the technologies currently underpinning the Information Age. These two factors — startling complexity and a breathtaking pace of change — have important ramifications for the legal process. They mean, for example, that lawyers must spend a significant amount of time and energy educating themselves, as well as judges and legislators, in technical matters and the new business processes engendered by groundbreaking technologies when they are involved in cases and law reform initiatives relating to computing and network technologies.[5] It also means the law is presented with a supremely difficult task when attempting to remain relevant and meaningful in the complicated and ever-changing world of computers and networks.

A. THE CORE TECHNOLOGIES

Computers can be described in a variety of ways. One approach is to break down the computer into several distinct components, namely the core technologies of hardware, software, and chips (semiconductor integrated circuits). It is also useful, however, to understand a computer purposefully, as in the following definition: "A digital computer is a machine that will accept data and information presented to it in its required form, carry out arithmetic and logical operations on this raw material, and then supply the required results in an acceptable form."[6] In short, computers process data and are used to communicate data as well. And most importantly for the purposes of the analysis in this book, computers are continually improving their ability to perform these functions, in terms of speed and ease of use, all the while dropping in price.[7] The performance–price ratio of computers is improving at a dizzying rate. The price of computer-processing power has declined by about 30 percent a year over the last twenty years; it is estimated that the cost of information processing is only 1/100 of 1 per-

---

5   For a discussion of the challenges posed to judicial decision making by sophisticated subject matter, including some startling admissions by certain judges, see chapter 2, section C.1, "Legal Dispute Resolution."

6   Ralston & Reilly, *Encyclopedia of Computer Science*, above note 1.

7   For a concise but extremely readable account of the history of the development of computers, see Maurice Estabrooks, *Electronic Technology, Corporate Strategy, and World Transformation* (Westport, CT: Quorum Books, 1995) [*Electronic Technology*].

cent of what it was in the early 1970s.[8] This trend will likely continue and therefore bring to the marketplace a host of new computer applications, as well as a wide array of new ways of performing the current functionality of computers. Thus, the first dynamic of computer law — the rapid pace of technological change — requires the reader to constantly update the discussion that follows.[9]

1) Hardware

As its name suggests, hardware is the collection of tangible components of the computer consisting of plastic, metal, glass, and other physical items. Each computer requires an input device in order for data to be entered into the computer. A common hardware device to accomplish this task is the keyboard, which permits a user to type data into the computer. Other hardware input devices include monitors that permit users to indicate choices by touching different parts of the screen, tablets that allow users to write data on them and then transform the handwriting into electronic equivalents, and most recently "digital pens" that convert the written word to digits that can be captured by a computer.[10] Another form of data entry device is a voice recognition system that can transform speech into electronically stored data.[11] However data are entered into the computer, they are processed in a central processing unit, which contains chips and other devices that perform the mathematical or other desired functions on the inputted data. Both before and after being processed, the data are stored on a memory device, another hardware component, that is able to maintain the data in electronic form. The data also have to be pre-

---

8   These figures are taken from "A Survey of the World Economy: The Hitchhiker's Guide to Cybernomics," *The Economist*, 28 September 1996 ["Cybernomics"]. This survey also notes that, compared to the declines in prices in other industrial inputs, the fall in prices of computing power has been dramatic indeed. For example, between 1890 and 1930, the price of electricity declined only 65 percent, roughly a 2 to 3 percent decrease a year.

9   For an overview of the devices and technologies that were being developed by the world's leading computer product laboratories in the late 1990s that will make much of the following discussion dated within the next few years, see Neil Gross, "Into the Wild Frontier," *Business Week*, 23 June 1997. See also Preston Gralla, "Five Live Ones," <darwinmag.com>, August 2001. This article chronicles five technologies that hold great promise: peer-to-peer networking; distributed computing; nanotechnology; Internet-on-a-chip; and wireless.

10   "Mightier Than the Pen," *The Economist*, 8 December 2001.

11   "Just Talk To Me," *The Economist*, 8 December, 2001; and Eric Hellweg, "Are You Talking To Me?" *Business 2.0*, February 1999.

sented to the human user by means of another hardware item, typically involving a terminal, by which a user can see representations of the data on a screen, and a printer that can transform the electronically stored data into printed words, figures, and images. There are then a myriad of hardware devices used to transmit data, such as modems, controllers, and routers. A number of companies are developing so-called network computers and other similar devices, which do little processing, because they are intended primarily for sending and receiving data over the Internet and other networks.[12]

Hardware devices, and computers generally, are categorized by the amount of data they can process and the speed with which they operate. At one end of the spectrum are very powerful mainframe computers that are used by large companies, governments, and other organizations to process vast amounts of data quickly.[13] At the other end of the spectrum is the personal computer that, as its name suggests, can be used by a single user, often in the home. Between the mainframe and the personal computer is the server-based network of personal computers, powerful enough to serve the data-processing needs of the mid-sized company. There are numerous other types of computers, as well as various configurations of computers. For example, super computers, as well as a large number of personal computers and more powerful workstations connected together, can provide huge amounts of computing power.[14] At the level of the personal computer,

---

12   See the articles contained in the "Annual Report on Information Technology: The Information Appliance," *Business Week*, 24 June 1996; and "The Network Computer: How Bill Became Larry," *The Economist*, 24 May 1997, "The Future of Computing: After the PC," *The Economist*, 12 September 1998, and "Microsoft: Winternet," *The Economist*, 1 July 2000. One view is that "network computers" will not do all that well because of the steep drop in the cost of the personal computer. Other, especially wireless, devices may well rise to prominence in their stead.

13   While mainframe computing seems to have been eclipsed by distributed computing (which uses groups of smaller machines linked together), one should not discount the importance of "big iron," as the mainframe computer is affectionately called: "Computing: Revenge of the Dinosaurs," *The Economist*, 21 July 2001.

14   IBM, for example, recently introduced a super computer capable of processing 12.3 trillion calculations per second, which is about 30,000 times more powerful than the average personal computer: Caroline Alphonso, "IBM Launches Fastest Computer," *The Globe and Mail*, 25 July 2000. Grid computing, where multiple supercomputers (or smaller computers) are closely integrated, offer even more collective computing power: see M. Mitchell Waldrop, "Grid Computing," *Technology Review*, May 2002; and Zack Medicoff, "Businesses Gird for Grid Computing Breakthroughs," *The Globe and Mail* (5 September 2002).

increasingly powerful and miniature semiconductor chips and other hardware components have spawned the lightweight and mobile laptop computer, as well as even smaller hand-held computers and some computerized personal organizers (personal digital assistants, as they are sometimes called) not much bigger than a pocket calculator. This is to say nothing of the tiny, special purpose computers that are increasingly imbedded in devices such as television sets, microwaves, and automobiles. As for the future, researchers are working at fusing computing technologies with materials science to produce intelligent construction materials, such as bridges that will be able to monitor a number of aspects of themselves.[15] Other researchers are working on computers that, because of the miracle of miniaturization, will be sewn into clothing.[16] Still others hope to make electronic devices out of single molecules, which would result in the as yet unimaginable hyperminiaturization of computers.[17] In short, hardware and computers generally are becoming smaller, better, and cheaper.

2) Chips

The critical hardware component is the semiconductor integrated circuit, or *chip*, as it is commonly called. Chips are very small pieces of semiconductor material, such as silicon, that contain miniaturized electronic circuits consisting of transistors, resistors, capacitors, and diodes, all electronically connected and packaged to form a fully operational circuit with a specific set of functions.[18] Chips are made by a painstaking and expensive process of placing photolithographic patterns — or masks — on a pure substrate, such as a silicon wafer, and then treating and etching the wafer with a conductive substance so that, at the conclusion of the process, extremely compact circuits are

---

15 Geoffrey Rowan, "Visionaries See Invisible Computing," *The Globe and Mail* (1 April 1997).

16 Mary Jo Dilonardo, "Wearable Tech Makes a Fashion Statement," *The Globe and Mail* (25 February 2001); Victoria Griffith, "Wearable Computers: Prêt à Portables," *Financial Times* (18 December 1996). See also Robert Everett-Green, "Joystick On Your Collar: Computers Get Ready-to-Wear," *The Globe and Mail* (28 February 1998). Computer garb is also being used to track a patient's medical condition by sewing different types of sensors into a short-sleeved shirt: "Medical Monitoring: Web Shirts," *The Economist*, 4 December 1999.

17 "Computing With Molecules," *The Economist*, 1 April 2000.

18 The latest chip technology involves reconfigurable integrated circuits, where the placement of elements can be rearranged to address multiple applications: "Programmable Chips," *Technology Review*, May 2002.

left on the wafer.[19] Transistors, invented just after the end of the Second World War, were the forerunner of the current chip and began to replace vacuum tubes in various electronic devices by the mid-1950s. The modern chip was invented in the early 1970s and came to prominence as a critical building block component of the first personal computer in the early 1980s. Ever since, chips have become smaller, cheaper, and more powerful at an astonishing rate. The processing power of chips generally has doubled every eighteen months to two years,[20] a trend likely to continue for the foreseeable future. It is not an overstatement that chip technology is the foundation of the computer revolution and a key driver of the Information Age.[21]

To fully appreciate the miracle of chip technology, and its other worldly rate of technical improvement, consider that in 1971 the Intel 4004 chip contained 2,300 transistors and was able to process at a speed of 0.06 MIPS (millions of instructions per second) (i.e., 60,000 instructions per second). By 1998 the Intel Pentium Pro chip contained 5.5 million transistors and operated at a speed of 400 MIPS (i.e., 400,000,000 instructions per second). By the year 2011, Intel believes chips will contain one billion transistors and operate at 100,000 MIPS.[22]

---

19   Newer chip development technologies also take advantage of software: "Hardware Goes Soft: Computer Chips That Can Rewire Themselves to Perform Different Functions Are Starting to Take the "Hard" Out of Hardware," *The Economist*, 22 May 1999. Another budding technology replaces the photo-lithographic process with a laser-assisted direct imprint: "Stamping on Tradition," *The Economist*, 22 June 2002.

20   This is often referred to as Moore's Law, after Gordon Moore, a founder and former chairman of Intel Corp. Moore said the power and complexity of the silicon chip would double every eighteen months: see Mary Gooderham, "Microchip at 25: More Power to It," *The Globe and Mail* (15 November 1996). See also Tim Jackson, *Inside Intel: Andy Grove and the Rise of the World's Most Powerful Chip Company* (New York: Dutton, 1997). New chip production technology should keep Moore's Law alive for the foreseeable future: "Extreme Measures," *The Economist*, 23 June 2001; this piece argues that the use of ultraviolet light lithography to print circuit patterns on slivers of silicon will allow still more transistors to be squeezed onto a single chip.

21   Bill Gates, one of the co-founders of Microsoft, pays appropriate homage to the chip in his extremely readable account of the rise to prominence of the personal computer industry and its inexorable extension through the Internet: Bill Gates, *The Road Ahead* (New York: Viking, 1995) [*Road Ahead*].

22   Otis Port, "The Silicon Age? It's Just Dawning," *Business Week*, 9 December 1996. See also Neil Gross, "How to Make Chips That Are Really Speedy," *Business Week*, 25 March 2002, which notes that a Dutch company thinks the billion-transistor chip should be achieved by 2005, and "Intel, AMD Unveil Fast Chips," *The Globe and Mail* (8 January 2002).

As for prices, if the automobile industry were able to produce the same performance-price improvements as the chip industry, a car today would cost under five dollars and would get 250,000 miles to a gallon of gasoline.[23] And we may be on the threshold of a breakthrough in chip processing power that will be as significant as the transition from vacuum tubes to electronically based devices in the 1950s, namely, the shift from chips based on electrical pulses to ones that use light to process and store information.[24] This photonic revolution is spawning a new set of acronyms, such as UDWDM (Ultra-Dense Wave-Division Multiplexing), and new performance metrics.[25]

3) Software

Software, or computer programs, are the statements and instructions that operate the computer and perform the various functions useful to the user of the computer.[26] Operating system software runs the computer by, among other things, coordinating the operation of the different hardware components of the computer. Application software, such as a word processing computer program, carries out the various functions on the data inputted into the computer by the user. Although resident on a diskette or a computer's hard drive memory device, or embedded right into a chip, the actual software instructions executed on a computer are intangible, having been converted from a high-level, almost written language (the source code of the program) into electronic bits (which are further described below).[27] Software is typically developed in a multistage process beginning with a high-level design of what the software is intended to do and what specific requirements of

---

23   "Cybernomics," above note 8.
24   Lawrence Surtees, "Scientists Harness Light to Speed Up Computers," *The Globe and Mail* (27 May 2000).
25   Moore's Law, based on a doubling of chip performance every eighteen months, looks anemic up against optically based networking technology, in which performance doubles every ten months: "Fiat Lux: In Telecommunications, the Long Day of the Electron has Reached its Twilight," *The Economist*, 5 February 2000; and "Communications: Laser-Guided," *The Economist*, 25 March 2000.
26   The term software was apparently coined in 1958, when it was used in an article to contrast it with hardware (which then consisted of tubes, transistors, wires, and tapes): "How Software Got Its Name," *The Economist*, 3 June 2000.
27   For a perceptive analysis of the different types of computer programming languages, and what their impact will be on the development of computers and the Internet, see "A Lingua Franca For The Internet," *The Economist*, 22 September 2001.

the user it will fulfil.[28] These functional specifications are then translated into a series of design specifications that plot and outline the various processes and procedures to be carried out by the software within the computer. The design includes the software's "user interface" (UI), which includes the "look and feel" of the program and how the user will interact with it.[29] Only after a great deal of time and effort has gone into the design of the program is the writing — or coding — of the specific computer-sensitive instructions and statements undertaken. Once the code is written, it is tested, and various errors are corrected, in a painstaking process of making the software stable enough for commercial use. This traditional process of software creation is being supplemented — and in some cases supplanted — by newer techniques where prewritten modules of code, sometimes called objects, are woven together to produce commercial quality software programs in much shorter time.[30]

However software is developed, it is a fact of life in the software world that software cannot be made perfect. The imperfections in software can take many forms. If the software is custom-developed for a particular user, the developer of the software may have failed to include all the functionality requested by the user. Or the user may have failed to adequately convey its requirements to the software developer. In either case, the software in such a circumstance will contain design deficiencies. Or, the software, including prewritten software, can have *bugs*, or errors, in it. These can be attributable to coding flaws, or to higher-level problems in the logic design or architecture of the computer program. In short, perfect software simply does not exist. As a result, most software developers offer ongoing support and mainte-

---

28   For a classic description of the software development process, first published in 1975, detailing the trials and tribulations involved from the software developer's perspective, see Frederick P. Brooks, Jr., *The Mythical Man-Month: Essays on Software Engineering, Anniversary Edition* (Reading, MA: Addison-Wesley, 1995).

29   The now ubiquitous design of the Microsoft Windows–oriented computer screen, with commands across the top and pop-up menu items, has influenced, for example, the redesign of the look and feel of the graphics on many news and sports-oriented television broadcasts. As well, a few years ago, Post Cereals redesigned, temporarily, its Alphabits breakfast cereal box to mimic a computer screen: see <alphapost.com> (thereby offering further evidence of the degree to which computers have insinuated themselves into our lives).

30   Peter M.D. Gray, Krishnarao G. Kulkarni & Norman W. Paton, *Object-Oriented Databases: A Semantic Data Model Approach* (Englewood Cliffs, NJ: Prentice-Hall, 1992).

nance programs for their products so that users can receive corrections to periodic problems.[31]

4) Data and Databases

Data are the elements of information put into, processed by, stored by, and then outputted and/or communicated by the computer. They might be the addresses on a mailing list, photographs from a gallery, excerpts of music from a digital jukebox, the words in a word processor, the figures on an electronic spreadsheet, or the prices of shares on a computerized stock ticker.[32] To be processed, stored, and transmitted electronically, data are digitized, or transformed in the computer into an electronic format, namely into 1s and 0s represented inside the computer by two electronic states: 1s are on (high-voltage electronic current), and 0s are off (low-voltage). Each binary value is one "bit," and eight bits make one byte, which in turn makes one character (such as a single letter or number). Data can also be stored optically, by means of little variegated bumps on a CD-ROM; these bumps can then be read by a laser in the CD-ROM machine; a CD-ROM is like a music CD and has read-only memory. Although such bit-based technology, whether in electronic or optical form, seems quite cumbersome, what makes it all work in a cost-effective manner is the lightning speed of the computer.

The predecessor of the computerized database is the paper-based directory, a book listing names, addresses, or other information about a specific group of persons or organizations. There are, of course, sev-

---

31   The legal implications of imperfect software are discussed in chapter 5, section D, "Negligence."

32   Although any material stored in a computer is generally referred to as data, it is sometimes useful for legal purposes to think of data as being one point along a longer continuum that includes symbols — the individual digits or letters; data — the aggregation of digits into numbers and letters into words; information — the aggregation of data into useful portions of meaning, such as sentences and paragraphs; knowledge — the distillation from information of ideas, concepts, and techniques; and wisdom — an advanced state of knowledge implying understanding. This typology is illustrated in Thomas A. Stewart, *Intellectual Capital: The New Wealth of Organizations* (New York: Doubleday, 1997) at 69 as follows: "*data*: The temperature is 77 degrees [Fahrenheit] ... *information*. ...That's hot for this time of year ... *knowledge*. ...We should postpone the ski trip ... *wisdom*: Everybody talks about the weather, but nobody does anything about it." See also the useful discussion of the difference between data, information, and knowledge in Thomas H. Davenport & Laurence Prusak, *Working Knowledge: How Organizations Manage What They Know* (Boston: Harvard Business School Press, 2000).

eral important differences between the computerized database and the paper-based directory, the most obvious being the space limitation inherent in the paper-based work; as discussed below, much more data can be stored electronically on, say, a CD-ROM disk than in even a thick paper-based directory. However, the paper-based directory, given its static medium, does not permit the user to select or edit the data; rather, the data are presented precisely how the compiler of the directory intended them to be presented. This can be as a listing of raw data, such as in a telephone White Pages, where all the people with phones in a given geographic area are included in alphabetical order. Or, in some cases, the compiler selects or edits the raw data for presentation in the way the editor feels will be the most useful to the reader; indeed, often space limitations of the paper-based medium force compilers to edit and present only a limited selection of the total data. The computerized database is a collection of data organized for storage in a computer and designed for easy retrieval of the data, or components thereof, by users of the computer.[33] In a computer-based, electronic environment, where storage capacity is increasingly less of an issue, vast quantities of data can be made available to the user. Moreover, if the data are contained in a relational database, the compiler of the data can empower the user to be the one who selects and edits the data in precisely the manner desired by the user. A relational database is a database management system that stores information in tables and conducts searches by using data in specified columns of one table to find additional data in another table. For example, consider the data in the human resources program of a large organization, which contains information regarding all employees. If data regarding these people were stored in a relational database, then one table might, for example, contain fields for employee name, employer department, and hire date. Another table might contain the person's name, salary, and age. Another table might contain the person's name and educational qualifications. By accessing such a database, a user could extract data in a number of different ways: for example, to determine how many persons earning over $80,000 are under the age of fifty, or how many have at least one graduate degree.[34] The relational database performs this

---

33   For a good introduction to database technology, see Fred R. McFadden & Jeffrey A. Hoffer, *Modern Database Management*, 4th ed. (Redwood City, CA: Benjamin/Cummings, 1994).

34   The privacy law implications of such a database are discussed in section A of chapter 4, while intellectual property protection for databases is addressed in section C.4 of chapter 2.

extremely useful, time-saving work by matching values in two or more tables to relate information in one to the others.

5) Networks

Computers do more than just process data; they also transmit them. The business of transmitting data, however, predates computers by about one hundred years, given that the telegraph first entered into widespread use in the 1850s.[35] The telegraph was a seminal technology; from the time that Gutenberg developed the movable type printing press in 1485 until the telegraph almost four hundred years later, information moved only as fast as goods and people, given that the mail was carried by horse-drawn carriage or sailing ship (or for expedited service in the American western frontier before the railroad, the pony express).[36] The telegraph was the first technology to disengage the transmission of

---

35   Samuel Finley Breese Morse transmitted the first telegraph message — "What hath God wrought" — over a line between Washington and Baltimore in 1844. For an insightful analysis of Morse's development and commercialization of the telegraph, as well as several other technological developments such as radio and the Internet, see Debora L. Spar, *Ruling the Waves: Cycles of Discovery, Chaos, and Wealth From the Compass to the Internet* (New York: Harcourt, 2001) [*Ruling the Waves*]. The more profound question than the one asked by Morse in his first transmission is "What hath Morse wrought?" the answer to which is, an incredible impact on the social and economic life of the world. The telegraph gave rise to modern markets, such as commodity exchanges, news wire services, futures trading, credit bureaus, and stock markets. It ushered in globalization, by expanding (to worldwide) the geographic area in which goods could meaningfully be sold. Considered like this, the telegraph is truly revolutionary, a complete break with precedent and genuinely "something new under the sun" when it was first unveiled, while the Internet, not to downplay its own breathtaking qualities, is in some senses merely an extension of numerous prior developments. The telegraph enabled a managerial revolution that (for good or ill) transformed the traditional agrarian economy of the early 1800s into the modern one based on manufacturing and services. It is not an overstatement that the modern firm sprang from the enabling technology of the telegraph. For a penetrating analysis of this phenomenon, see R.H. Coase, "The Nature of the Firm" (1937) 4 Economica N.S. 386.

36   In *Ruling the Waves*, above note 35 at 60–61, Debora L. Spar describes the pre-telegraph world of communications as follows: "Until the middle of the nineteenth century, information didn't move all that much faster than man. It moved the way it had nearly since biblical times, hastened only by sporadic improvements in transportation: stirrups for horses, for example, or sails for ships. In 1830, a message sent from London to New York or Bombay took almost as long to reach its destination as it had in the days of Vasco da Gama and Magellan. It still had to be written by hand, taken by coach to the nearest port, and then

information from general transportation, thereby commencing the collapse of geographic distance in human affairs.[37] The monumental importance of the telegraph cannot be overstated. The break it precipitated with the past, from a communications perspective, has no precedent, either before or since.[38] The telegraph was then followed by a succession of further technologies that continued the inexorable elimination of geographic distance. By the 1880s voice communication by telephone was beginning to challenge the telegraph's supremacy as the primary means of communications.[39] As for broadcasting, in the early

---

shipped across the globe. Along the way, just about anything could happen — either to the message itself or to the circumstances it was supposed to report. As a result, the world of 1830 was still very much a local one. People focused for the most part on the news of their town or village, and concentrated on business that could be conducted within several days' journey of home. To be sure, the ocean-going revolution of the late Middle Ages had opened vast new territories to Europeans' grasp, and the development of steam technologies presaged rapid gains in transportation by the end of the eighteenth century. But in communication terms, the world of 1830 differed only slightly from the world of 1380: it was unfathomably big, and it took seemingly forever to send information across it."

37   For a discussion of the development of the "information highway" (as the Internet was called in the mid-1990s), and its antecedents such as the telegraph, see W.T. Stanbury & Ilan B. Vertinsky, "Assessing the Impact of New Information Technologies on Interest Group Behaviour and Policymaking," in *Technology, Information and Public Policy*, ed. Thomas J. Courchene (Kingston, ON: John Deutsch Institute, Queen's University, 1995) [*Technology*]. For an entertaining study of the telegraph that draws a number of parallels between it and today's Internet, see Tom Standage, *The Victorian Internet: The Remarkable Story of the Telegraph and the Nineteenth Century's Online Pioneers* (Guernsey: Phoenix, 1998). By bifurcating communications from transportation, the telegraph, however, also spawned an unfortunate byproduct, the erroneous message, the legal implications of which are discussed in chapter 6.

38   Debora L. Spar, in *Ruling the Waves*, above note 35, at 61, describes the impact of the telegraph as follows: "All of this [the pre-telegraph communications world described in note 36] changed in the course of less than two decades. In 1838, Samuel Morse presented the U.S. Congress with a prototype of his electric telegraph — a machine, he claimed, that could instantly send messages across the nation and potentially around the world. Most members of Congress laughed. Yet by 1852, only fourteen years later, twenty-three thousand miles of telegraph wire had been laid across the United States and the industry was booming. By 1880, almost 100 thousand miles of subterranean cable stretched under the North Atlantic, across the Red Sea, and beneath the Caribbean. The same message from London to New York that had taken weeks or months in 1838 could now be transmitted in minutes. Suddenly, the world had become a great deal smaller."

39   For a fascinating study of the telephone, see Ithiel de Sola Pool, ed., *The Social Impact of the Telephone* (Cambridge, MA: MIT Press, 1977).

1900s radio technology came into use, twenty-five years later the first crude television was demonstrated, and in the mid-1960s cable television was beginning to rapidly penetrate the market in Canada. At the same time as cable television appeared in Canada, early efforts of data communications between computers were being perfected. By the beginning of the 1970s computers were being linked into local and wide area networks. In the early 1990s cellular radio telephone, as well as satellite transmission data services, were introduced. Today, the Internet, a network of networks, brings together many of the disparate elements of the computer and telecommunications revolutions.

Information can be transmitted by a number of different technologies, including traditional copper wire, still the basis for most telephone lines, and more recent vehicles such as fibre optics, coaxial cable (for cable television transmission), cellular radio telephone, and satellite.[40] Each of these technologies can transmit digital signals at different rates, thus making some technologies more or less appropriate for carrying various transmissions; for example, full motion video transmission needs significant transmission capacity or bandwidth, which currently fibre optics can satisfy, but which traditional copper wire traditionally has not been able to, although new digital data compression technologies (such as ADSL — Asymmetric Digital Subscriber Line) are being implemented that are able to pump more bits through copper wire. The foreseeable future will witness a great deal of competition between various service providers — the telephone companies, the cable companies, Internet service providers, satellite companies, cellular companies — in terms of technologies and in the regulatory arena.[41] Regardless of the short- and long-term outcomes of this competition, the trend, of course, is toward the implementation of better, faster, and smaller means of communication.[42] And again, massive price declines have already been precipitated by the latest communications technologies;

---

40 For a good discussion of the key technological and business aspects of each method, see Robert K. Heldman, *The Telecommunications Information Millennium: A Vision and Plan for the Global Information Society* (New York: McGraw-Hill, 1995).

41 Geoffrey Rowan, "Let the Internet Access Wars Begin" *The Globe and Mail* (14 May 1997).

42 Consider that a wire cable 3.25 inches in diameter contains 1300 pairs of copper wire, and each pair carries one telephone conversation; a 0.75 inch in diameter coaxial cable, used by the cable companies, carries 78 video channels, expandable to 500 with compression technologies; a fibre optic bundle .5 inch in diameter can carry 500,000 telephone calls or 5000 video channels over 32 hairlike strands. From Andrew Kupfer, "The Race to Rewire America," *Fortune*, 19 April 1993.

the increased competition will only continue the downward spiral in global telecommunications costs.[43]

6) The Internet

The Internet is an extremely important phenomenon, both for computer law and for society.[44] Begun in the early 1970s as a means of linking various U.S. military, industrial, and academic research partners by computers hooked up over telephone lines, in less than ten years[45] the Internet has expanded — indeed exploded — astonishingly to include millions of businesses and individual users.[46] For many people, a personal computer linked to the Internet is primarily a communications

---

43   In today's dollars, the cost of sending a single word in a transatlantic telegram in the 1860s would be US$60, and such high costs stunted the use of the telegram for many decades. By contrast, a three-minute telephone call in the fall of 1996 between New York and London was about US$2; in 1930 the same call would have cost more than US$200. By the year 2005 the cost of a transatlantic videophone call could drop to a few cents an hour. See "Cybernomics," above note 8.

44   A good history of the Internet can be found in Stephen Segaller, *Nerds 2.0.1: A Brief History of the Internet* (New York: TV Books, 1999). For an altruistic account of the development of the Internet, written by one of its architects, see Tim Berners-Lee, *Weaving the Web: The Original Design and Ultimate Destiny of the World Wide Web by Its Inventor* (San Francisco: Harper San Francisco, 1999). For an accessible account of the implications of the Internet for business, education, and home use, see Gates, *Road Ahead*, above note 21. See also Information Highway Advisory Council, *Preparing Canada for a Digital Future* (Final Report) (Ottawa: Industry Canada, 1997).

45   It is probably fair to mark the beginning of the commercialization of the Internet in 1993, the year the Mosaic browser began to be used widely; Yahoo and Netscape were founded in 1994.

46   No one really knows, at any one time, precisely how many users there are of the Internet. Its rapid growth, however, has been breathtaking. Vinton G. Cerf, one of the pioneers of the Internet, indicated in 1995 that the number of host computers (which is much smaller in number than the number of users) on the Internet increased from 200 to 5,000,000 between 1983 and 1995, a factor of 25,000: Vinton G. Cerf, *Computer Networking: Global Infrastructure for the 21st Century*, <cs.Washington.edu/homes/lazowska/cra/networks.html>. In 1995, an estimate, based on a survey, put the number of e-mail users on the Internet at 27.5 million: Federation of American Scientists, FAS Cyberstrategy Project, Cybersats, <fas.org/cp/netstats.htm>. A survey in the spring of 1997 put the estimate of the number of users of the Internet in the United States and Canada at 50.6 million, more than double the number shown in a similar survey done eighteen months before: "Internet Users Double," *The Globe and Mail* (1 April 1997). A major survey completed in March 2000 estimated the number of Internet users at over 300 million, up from 40 million in 1996: Angus Reid, "Face of

device, and only secondarily a data processor. With the advent of telephony on the Internet, the computer and communications industries will be merged, at least outwardly, to users.[47] As well, some argue that the Internet has moved beyond being a communications infrastructure to becoming a new software platform.[48] Most profound, however, is the Internet's role as a platform for the new "networked intelligence" that results from millions of people being able to communicate as never before with like-minded counterparts.[49] Given the importance of the Internet, it is worth describing, briefly, some of its services and features, as well as several of its principal participants.[50]

the Web Study Pegs Global Internet Population at More Than 300 Million," 21 March 2000, <internetangles.com>. To put this growth in other terms, the 1996 Olympics attracted 187 million hits to its official Web site, and the number for the 1998 Nagano winter games was 634 million, while for the 2000 Sydney games the figure was well over 7.2 billion: Robert MacLeod, "Wide World of Sport Big Hit on Web," *The Globe and Mail* (28 September 2000). Estimates in 2002 for the size of the worldwide Internet user base vary from 445 to 533 million: see statistics at <cyberatlas.com>. Canadians are particularly avid users of the Internet: Krista Foss, "Canadians at Forefront of Web Use in Schools," *The Globe and Mail* (11 September 2000); and Guy Dixon, "Canadian Internet Use Keeps Climbing," *The Globe and Mail* (17 November 2000). The latter piece cites a recent study that found 48 percent of Canadian homes have access to the Internet, compared with 43 percent in the United States.

47   Lawrence Surtees, "Internet Calls Go the Distance," *The Globe and Mail* (27 July 2000).

48   "The Age of the Cloud: A Survey of Software," *The Economist*, 14 April 2001; and "A World Gone Soft: A Survey of the Software Industry," *The Economist*, 25 May 1996. See also Amy Cortese, "The Software Revolution," *Business Week*, 4 December 1995, which discusses how small software programs called "applets" written in Java and other new object-oriented programming environments might be marketed and distributed over the Internet, thereby presenting an alternative to the current distribution model for software products.

49   See Derrick de Kerckhove, *Connected Intelligence: The Arrival of the Web Society* (Toronto: Somerville House, 1997) [*Connected Intelligence*]. De Kerckhove, the director of the McLuhan Program in Culture and Technology at the University of Toronto, highlights the importance of interactivity and hypertextuality in the context of the Internet. There can, however, be too much of a good thing. For studies on "Internet addiction," see the materials published by the Center for On-Line Addiction at <netaddiction.com>.

50   For a perceptive analysis of the Internet by a court, including how it differs from earlier communications technologies such as books, newspapers, radio, and television, see generally *American Civil Liberties Union v. Reno*, 929 F. Supp. 824 (E.D. Pa. 1996) [*ACLU*]; in this decision, at 844, the court labelled the Internet a "unique and wholly new medium of worldwide human communication." This decision was essentially confirmed by the U.S. Supreme Court: see *Reno v. American Civil Liberties Union*, 117 S. Ct. 2329 (1997). See also *Brookfield Communi-*

The Internet is a fascinating exercise in symbiotic anarchy. Technically, it is a network of computer networks.[51] Thousands of host computers serve as electronic repositories for huge volumes of data, stored according to an address system that gives each site, and "mailboxes" within sites, a residency within cyberspace. Untold and growing numbers of router computers serve as relay stations for the information travelling between host computers. The Internet is an intricate web of computers and networking infrastructure, able to operate by means of a series of non-proprietary standards — called data transfer protocols — for the naming of sites and for the sending of data.[52] While no single entity owns or controls the Internet, the Internet Society provides technical leadership in terms of planning its long-term architecture and engineer-

---

cations, Inc. v. *West Coast Entertainment Corp.*, 174 F. 3d 1036 (9th Cir. 1999) for a description of the Internet that includes developments that followed the *ACLU* decision.

51   In the *ACLU* decision, *ibid.*, at 830, the court stated that "[t]he Internet is not a physical or tangible entity, but rather a giant network which interconnects innumerable smaller groups of linked computer networks. It is thus a network of networks." For a good overview of various technological and other aspects of the Internet, see Pfaffenberger, *Plain English*, above note 1.

52   "The Internet is a distribution system that is capable of handling a wide variety of data (text, pictures, and sound) in any number of formats. In order to move through the Internet, however, data and requests for data made by users must adhere to sets of rules called 'protocols.' The Internet is a distributed, interoperable, packet-switched network that predominantly uses the TCP/IP protocol. A distributed network has no one central repository of information or control, but is made up of an interconnected web of 'host' computers, each of which can be accessed from virtually any point on the network. An Internet user can obtain information from a host computer in another province or another country just as easily as obtaining information from across the street and often with little knowledge of the location of its source. An interoperable network uses "open protocols" so that many different types of networks and facilities can be transparently linked together, and allows multiple services to be provided to different users over the same network. The Internet can run over virtually any type of facility that can transmit data, including copper and fibre optic circuits of telephone companies, coaxial cable of cable companies, and various types of wireless connections." From the Glossary of New Media Terms, *New Media*, Broadcasting Public Notice CRTC 1999-84/Telecom Public Notice CRTC 99-14, 17 May 1999 [*New Media*].

53   In the *ACLU* decision, above note 50 at 832, the court stated that "[t]here is no centralized storage location, control point, or communication channel for the Internet, and it would not be technically feasible for a single entity to control all of the information conveyed on the Internet." For a discussion of various controversies surrounding the governance of the Internet, and in particular the domain name registration system, see Jonathan E. Moskin, "Canada and the

ing.[53] Other groups are responsible for handing out network registrations so that an Internet address, such as <gtakach@mccarthy.ca>, continues to mean only a single place on the Internet.

There is a wide and varied range of services on the Internet. At one end of the spectrum is electronic mail, or e-mail, whereby electronic messages can be sent to specific electronic mailboxes registered to individuals. E-mail is a store and forward system, and it can take a few minutes for a message to pass through the various computers on its possibly roundabout way to its destination. E-mail can also be routed to multiple recipients.[54] A very different group-based feature is the Usenet, or usegroup, a discussion forum where participants can post messages and commentary about certain subjects or current interest topics. Sites that agree to carry a usegroup will then be sent all new postings, thus creating a propagation system whereby one posting is replicated thousands of times as it is sent to computers around the world. Some of these discussion forums operate in real time, such as MUDS (Multi-User Dungeons) and MUSES (Multi-User Simulation Environments). Perhaps the fastest growing dimension of the Internet is the World Wide Web, which allows organizations to create Web sites of information at a specific address — such as <www.mccarthy.ca> for the McCarthy Tétrault law firm — which can then be accessed by users from any point along the Internet. An incredibly powerful aspect of the "Web," as it is colloquially called, is the ability to link between different pages on a site — or to link between different sites half a world away — simply by clicking on highlighted words. This hypertext feature has allowed the Internet to become an invaluable resource of discovery for a whole population of only semi-computer-literate users. The Web has also given birth to Internet-based e-commerce, whereby goods and services are bought and sold through a number of new business models.[55]

Future of Internet Governance" (1998) 15 C.I.P.R. 247; Industry Canada, "Domain Name System Reform and Related Internet Governance Issues: A Consultation Paper," September 1998 and Industry Canada, "Consultation on ICANN Reform," 10 August 2002, both at <strategis.ic.gc.ca>; "Regulating the Internet: The Consensus Machine," *The Economist*, 10 June 2000; and Committee on ICANN Evolution and Reform, "ICANN: A Blueprint for Reform," 20 June 2002, at <icann.org>.

54   A form of e-mail that permits essentially real-time communication is ICQ and its variants: see "Instant Messaging Joins the Firm," *The Economist*, 22 June 2002; and Kevin Marron, "Instant Messaging Goes to Work," *The Globe and Mail* (9 November 2000).

55   More on this later in the chapter under section C.3, "Mass Customization."

There are a number of participants on the Internet who facilitate access to it. Online full-service providers, such as AOL (America Online), offer through their own computers a number of in-house services to their subscribers only, in addition to offering access to the Internet.[56] These companies will typically aggregate various types of content, services, and features for a variety of pricing schemes, depending on what the user finds most attractive. A much scaled-down variation on the online service provider is the bulletin board system (BBS) operator, who might even be an individual, who runs a computer with some group messaging software that allows the BBS operator to serve as a discussion moderator. At the other end of the spectrum is the Internet service provider, or ISP, that, in most cases, simply offers access to the Internet for a flat monthly fee, regardless of the amount of use.[57] In between these two are the services springing up from telephone and cable companies that offer greater or fewer customer services and the all-important Internet access. A variation on all of these facilitators is the "freenet," typically a community-based organization that provides access to the Internet as well as to some of its own services. And then, of course, there are the multitude of content providers, ranging from the entities noted above to libraries, universities, corporations, media companies,[58] governments, and individuals who, for a

---

56   See Anick Jesdanun, "AOL's 'Net on Training Wheels' Leads ISP Race: Simplified Interface Helps World's Largest Internet Provider Surpass 25 Million Users," *The Globe and Mail* (7 December 2000).

57   Internet Service Provider: a company or other organization that provides access to the Internet to its customers via one or a combination of dial-up lines (similar to telephone service), coaxial cable ISDN, xDSL, or other dedicated lines. The most typical example is to a home-user who pays a fee to connect to the ISP's server. The connection is made by a "modem" that makes the electronic data from the home-user's computer transmittable over a telephone line. The data then passes through the telephone company's facilities in the same way as a normal telephone call. The "call" is received by the ISP, which "routes" the user's requests for information to the server that is "hosting" the desired data. *Note*: The computer of an ISP customer is ordinarily never actually "online," it simply sends requests and receives information via the ISP's servers and routers (from the Glossary of New Media Terms, *New Media*, above note 52). For a detailed description of the operation of an ISP, including how a computer user in Prince Edward Island actually connects to the Internet through an ISP, see *Island Telecom Inc. et al.* [2000] CIRB no. 59.

58   For a discussion of how a Canadian media enterprise coordinates its traditional television broadcasting business with new online opportunities, and vice versa, see: *CITY-TV, CHUM City Productions Limited, MuchMusic Network and BRAVO!, Division of CHUM Limited* [1999] CIRB no. 22.

small investment, can create their own presence on the Internet through a custom home page. All these persons and entities are users of the Internet as well, given that the Internet blurs the distinction between listeners and speakers, namely, the consumers and producers of information.[59]

B. TECHNOLOGY TRENDS AND THE LAW

Now that some of the basics of computer and networking technologies, have been discussed it is worth describing, briefly, how these technologies are being put to use today, and how some of the current technological trends and applications might unfold over the coming years.[60] Since people often overestimate the short-term impact of technology — just as they underestimate its long-term impact! — it is fiendishly difficult to make specific accurate predictions in the technology world, given the first dynamic of computer law coupled with the inherent unpredictability of people.[61] When the telephone first appeared, it was widely believed that although it might be useful for calls of a personal nature, surely nobody would do business over the telephone.[62] Those who think

---

59   The legal implications of the complex and variegated pastiche of Internet business models and different service providers are discussed throughout the balance of this book.

60   There are a number of useful paper-based and online resources that track technological developments in this area, but more importantly the actual business and other applications being built on or utilizing these technologies, including the following magazines and their related Web sites: *The Economist* <economist.com>; *Business Week* <businessweek.com>; *Wired* <wired.com>; and *The Wall Street Journal* <wsj.com>.

61   For example, see "The Year That Wasn't: A Catalogue of Misguided Musings, Fallacious Forecasts and Erroneous Estimates from Technology Pundits in 1998," *The Globe and Mail* (31 December 1998).

62   Indeed, the operator of the U.S. telegraph system at the time, Western Union, did not think people would want to talk to one another over great distances, so they declined an offer to buy the telephone patents for $100,000, a decision they later came to regret; see Estabrooks, *Electronic Technology*, above note 7 at 23. For more modern near-misses, consider that Andrew Grove, one of the leaders of Intel over the past thirty years, initially did not see the potential of the microprocessor in 1971 (he was too busy producing memory chips) (recounted in the introduction to John Heilemann's interview with Andrew Grove in *Wired*, June 2001); and Bill Gates was a relative latecomer to understanding the paradigm-shifting importance of the Internet (see Paul Andrews, *How The Web Was Won* (New York: Broadway Books, 1999).

the Internet is a lot of hype[63] are, in the short term, partly right, but in the long run they will be woefully wrong, and they fail to understand the enormous impact that it will have on the development of computer law. This is not to say that the Internet will soon replace all forms of human communications, particularly because it is quite rare for a new communications medium to obliterate a predecessor entirely — witness how well radio and the cinema have held up against television and the videocassette player (but, by the same token, there are not many telegraphs in use today!).[64] The Internet is, however, steadily becoming embedded in the social and economic fabric of the world, an impressive development given that this new commercial communication medium is still less than ten years old.[65] Nonetheless, specific predictions made about this new communications infrastructure even a few years ago are proving incorrect, as certain anticipated uses for the Internet have not materialized — while unforeseen uses grow exponentially.[66] Indeed, with respect to this last point, consider "Takach's Law of Unintended Uses for Technology," namely, that a technology's most compelling uses

---

63   For example, Charles Jonscher, in *The Evolution of Wired Life* (New York: John Wiley, 1999), argues that the importance of the Internet has been overstated, particularly when contrasted to the technological developments of the first sixty years of the twenty-first century, such as the telephone system, jet aircraft, nuclear weapons, the modern automobile, and the national electricity grid.

64   For example, box office receipts of cinemas in the United States were up 8 percent in 1996, reversing a decline in the previous years: see *The Economist*, 4 January 1997. On the other hand, television-based storytelling has virtually wiped out radio dramas: "Radio's Golden Age: The World According to Lux," *The Economist*, 22 December 2001.

65   For a highly personal anecdote, consider that when the author and his fifteen-year-old daughter were planning a canoe trip in Ontario's Algonquin Park in June 2002, they found a wilderness outfitter that, by its Web site, seemed to have everything they would need, from a canoe to high-tech dehydrated meals. When the author called the 1-800 number to make reservations, he was directed back to the Web site as it had a detailed point-and-click system for selecting entries off the outfitter's menu. In short, a prospective customer of this wilderness outfitter would be hard pressed to get good service if he or she did not have Internet access.

66   See the insightful "A Survey of Electronic Commerce: In Search of the Perfect Market," *The Economist*, 10 May 1997, which points out that, for example, consumer sales on the Internet are still in an embryonic stage, but that business-to-business Internet commerce is booming, as witnessed by General Electric currently buying one billion dollars' worth of goods from suppliers online annually, and Cisco Systems (the leading supplier of internetworking technology) selling a similar dollar amount of products from its Web site.

are not anticipated.[67] In any event, the point is not to peer into a crystal ball simply for the sake of it, but rather to highlight the legal aspects of some of the key trends and applications of computing and network technologies.

1) Digitization

A fundamental application for computing technologies is digitization, which entails reducing all forms of representations of information into numeric-based electronic signals that can then be recorded electronically or on an optical medium.[68] Of course, with new documents it will not be a case of transforming them into a digital format, but of keeping them as such because they were created inside computers as digital word processing documents or some other files. Thus, scanning technologies, which allow for easy transformation of paper-based doc-

---

67   Take, for instance, the Internet and politics. It is no surprise that political parties and politicians are using the Internet for a variety of predictable purposes, like e-mail–based fundraising: see notes 2 above and 131 below. Pretty powerful, but still quite humdrum. Nothing in this particular application to invoke Takach's Law. On the other hand, consider the vote-swapping phenomenon in the 2000 U.S. presidential election. Democratic supporters of Al Gore, in a state where he was a shoo-in, could go to a Web site (like <votetrader.org>) and connect with supporters of Ralph Nader's Green Party in other states where Gore was in a tight race, and make the following deal. If the Green Party supporter agreed to vote for Gore, the Gore supporter would vote for Nader. This would help Gore in tight races (obviously it did not help enough), but would also help Nader try to attract 5 percent of the total vote so he could get federal matching grants for campaign funds (this didn't work out either, as Nader only garnered 3 percent of the vote). Notwithstanding that vote swapping wasn't entirely successful for Nader and Gore (and in fact may have hurt Gore in Florida: some of his supporters there may have swapped, not realizing how close the race in Florida would ultimately be), and may be illegal according to certain state government authorities, it is a fascinating application for the Internet. It essentially arbitrages the U.S. electoral college system, and institutes, through technology, a solution not unlike some of the proportional representation reforms floated as a result of the Bush–Gore election. It also collapses geography, and implements a strategic voting system that simply would not work, for all practical purposes, without the Internet. It is a classic example of Takach's Law of Unintended Uses for Technology. And another good example of why we can use the term *revolutionary* when referring to the Internet.

68   Bill Gates, in "Tech in a Time of Trouble," in *The World in 2002*, a year-in-review publication of *The Economist*, predicts the first ten years of the twenty-first century will be the digital decade, as products such as software, photographs, videos, and books become commonly distributed over the Internet in digital form.

uments into electronic, digital form, will be used to input only the previous generation of books, images, and other paper-based materials.[69]
The ability to store all information, including text, images (moving and
still), and sound, in a digital format is as revolutionary a development
as the invention of the Gutenberg printing press. The first CDs that
fused all the types of content — text, graphics, photos, music, narra-
tion, videos, animation, etc. — present as clear a core step in history as
the first books.[70] And this is perhaps more so, because with digitization
people have freed themselves from the shackles of the printed medium,
the primary platform for the preservation and presentation of information over the last five hundred years. Once digitized, information is in
its most fluid form. Reduced to electronic bits and bytes, information
can be stored, changed, adapted, transmitted, reproduced, all with
impunity, and at extremely low cost. Elusive, ephemeral, amorphous
digital information veritably dances. Digitization, therefore, highlights
the second dynamic of computer law — namely, the elusive nature of
information — and will have an enormous impact on the law. Previously, the fixation of information in a physical medium like paper dictated a number of key rules in areas as diverse as intellectual property
law, and especially copyright, to contract/commercial law, where legal

---

69   This is done ingeniously by the scanner changing light reflected from an image
into an electrical current, then using a chip that changes the electrical current
into a digital signal by using a series of mathematical formulas: see Kinkoph,
Fulton, & Oliver, *Visual Encyclopedia*, above note 1 at 297.

70   As to the impact of Gutenberg's revolutionary invention, see Marshall McLuhan,
The Gutenberg Galaxy: The Making of Typographic Man (Toronto: University of
Toronto Press, 1962). Although McLuhan was critical of much that was wrought
by Gutenberg, he was much more hopeful for the electronic age; see Marshall
McLuhan & Bruce R. Powers, *The Global Village: Transformations in World Life
and Media in the 21st Century* (New York: Oxford University Press, 1989). From
a legal perspective, Gutenberg's printing press kicked off the long development
of copyright law, which continues to this day: see Benjamin Kaplan, *An Unhur-
ried View of Copyright* (New York: Columbia University Press, 1967); Simon
Nowell-Smith, *International Copyright Law and the Publisher in the Reign of Queen
Victoria* (Oxford: Clarendon Press, 1968); and George A. Gipe, *Nearer to the
Dust: Copyright and the Machine* (Baltimore: Williams & Wilkins, 1967). For an
exploration of the impact of various media, from print to electronic, on the
development of law, see M. Ethan Katsh, *The Electronic Media and the Transformation of Law* (New York: Oxford University Press, 1989). Ethan Katsh, in this
book at 11, also gives due recognition to another great Canadian scholar, Harold
Innis who, more than a decade before McLuhan became popular, stressed that
the "materials on which words were written down have often counted for more
than the words themselves," which is a more accurate statement than McLuhan's
famous dictum that "the medium is the message."

rules have for several hundred years been devised with a paper-based business information environment in mind. As society travels the information highway from "papersville" to "electronicsville," a number of legal potholes will have to be attended to if the ride is to be a smooth and successful one.[71]

Digitization, of course, does not mean the end of books or other paper-based documents.[72] Much electronic mail is printed out so that a paper-based copy can be maintained as a record.[73] And bookstores continue to do a brisk business selling books.[74] Nonetheless, huge amounts of data never appear on paper, and over time this trend will continue. Or, the paper and electronic channels of distribution are being pursued

---

71 See George S. Takach, "Preventing Ambulance-Chasing on the Info Highway," *The Globe and Mail* (11 February 1994). Several of the shortcomings of Ontario's laws noted in this article have since been remedied by, among other measures, the repeal of the previous s. 5 of the *Sale of Goods Act* (Ontario), and the passage of the *Electronic Commerce Act, 2000*, as discussed in chapter 6, sections A.1(f), "Law Reform Approaches," and A.1(g), "Electronic Commerce Statutes."

72 Sales of printing and writing paper are up, but e-books are just now starting to come into their own: see "Bad News for Trees," *The Economist*, 19 December 1998; Marina Strauss, "The E-book Finds Its Mark," *The Globe and Mail* (2 March 2000); and "Electronic Books: Uncertain Prize," *The Economist*, 21 October 2000. Trying to predict, however, the likely future of e-books and other forms of electronic publishing is very difficult, as can be gleaned from the following headlines and titles: Andre Meyer, "Electronic Books Appear Stalled at the Technology Gate," *The Globe and Mail* (19 September 2002); Ian Simpson, "E-Books Remain Tough Sell," *The Globe and Mail* (15 February 2001); "Online Publishing: Offline?" *The Economist*, 9 December 2000; and "Steal This Ebook," *Wired*, December 2001, which lists the most pirated authors on the Internet and their works. See also Jason Epstein, *Book Business: Publishing Past, Present and Future* (New York: W.W. Norton, 2001), which has an upbeat vision of the digital future of books. And then there is the "e-paper" invention, essentially a soft plastic computer display that looks and acts like paper, but can be reprogrammed rather than recycled: "Display Technology: The Age of the Electronic Page," *The Economist*, 28 April 2001; "Digital Ink Meets Electronic Paper," *The Economist*, 9 December 2000; and Simon Tuck, "Plastic Pages Seen Altering Publishing" *The Globe and Mail* (6 September 2000).

73 From a legal perspective, this may not be as silly a practice as it first seems: see the discussion on e-mail retention/destruction policies in chapter 6, section B.3(b), "E-Mail Policies."

74 Including online, as, ironically perhaps, books are the biggest selling consumer item on the Internet; and while the online divisions of Indigo and Chapters (and Amazon.com, and now Amazon.ca) are most widely known, the Internet allows even a tiny CanLit specialist to turn a small profit: Charles Mandel, "Books E-tailer Charts Independent Course," *The Globe and Mail* (14 September 2000).

in a complementary manner.[75] In any event, the powers unleashed by digitization are compelling. For example, text that is in digital form can be searched and linked by keywords.[76] Thus, an encyclopedia on a CD-ROM allows the user to navigate various articles all related to the user's principal topic simply by clicking from one article to another connected by common keywords. While the traditional index in a paper-based encyclopedia serves a similar function, the ease with which the exercise is performed in an electronic environment makes the CD-ROM version of the work a revolutionary improvement.[77] Such keyword-based searching of digital-based content, through the use of HTML hypertext linking technology, is driving the explosive growth of the World Wide Web portion of the Internet.[78] Such linking technology also raises many legal issues. Consider a securities prospectus that has been put online and is available to potential investors instead of the traditional paper-based one. The use of hypertext links in such a document might mean that investors never see important warning sentences in the prospectus as they link from key passages describing the business to the financial

---

75 Canadian magazine Web sites, for example, tend to supplement, rather than supplant, the paper-based version: Kevin Marron, "Magazine Readers Stick to Print," *The Globe and Mail* (1 May 2002). For a different sort of fusion of electronic and paper, see Natalie Southworth, "Print on Demand's New Day," *The Globe and Mail* (17 May 2001), which describes a business process whereby newspapers are transmitted digitally over the Internet, but then printed out locally, perhaps with the content tailored to the specific reader. Or, the reader can have the whole newspaper delivered electronically in the paper-based format: Gayle MacDonald, "Globe Readers Can Subscribe on New Digital Newstand," *The Globe and Mail* (24 October 2001). A variation on "print on demand" is "books-on-demand," where the traditional book retailer downloads the content by computer, but then prints and binds the pages to form a traditional, paper-based book: see Marina Strauss, "E-books a New Chapter in Publishing," *The Globe and Mail* (5 April 2002).

76 See Cristina Brandao, "Rewiring the Ivory Tower," *Canadian Business Technology* (Winter 1996). This piece observes that an increasing number of academic journals are going online, and incorporating hyperlink features when they do. For articles on how the Internet is shaking up the world of academic journals, see "E-Conomic Publishing," *The Economist*, 5 August 2000; and "Publishing, Perishing and Peer Review," *The Economist*, 24 January 1998.

77 The paper-based book, however, remains an excellent format for presenting a linear story, such as a novel, where the reader proceeds page by page from the beginning, to the middle, and finally to the end of a story. For non-linear searching of fact-intensive sources, such as databases, the electronic environment is clearly superior to its paper-based predecessor. See, for example, the online edition of the *Encyclopedia Brittanica*, at <brittanica.com>.

78 See de Kerckhove, *Connected Intelligence*, above note 49, for an insightful discussion of the societal ramifications of hypertext linking technology.

statements later on. Or what if the prospectus has within it links to other documents, or even to other Web sites that might contain explanatory or supplemental material? Does that other document now become part of the prospectus? Or is a hypertext link to another Web site an endorsement of that other site, which might give rise to liability in a legal sense?[79]

2) Manipulation

Once digitized, the electronically stored information, be it a picture, music, video, drawing, text, or what have you, can be easily altered. Black-and-white movies can be coloured.[80] Music can be sampled and manipulated.[81] Text can be edited.[82] Photos can be digitally retouched to remove or add subjects.[83] The adage "a photo never lies" is no longer true.[84] Digital cameras take digital pictures so that the photos do not

---

79 For answers to these questions, see chapter 4, section E.1 "Securities Law."
80 Or, current movies can be edited by a video rental chain to remove passages of the work they consider to be sexually explicit or otherwise offensive, without the consent of, and to the dismay of, the producers and distributors of the films: Gayle MacDonald, "For a Few Bucks, We'll Launder Your Movie for You," *The Globe and Mail* (31 October 2002).
81 See, for example, Robert Everett-Green, "Guitar, Drums, Bass ... Laptop," *The Globe and Mail* (21 March 2002), which describes how music software can, among other things, make composers out of persons with no formal musical training.
82 To understand the impact of the digital revolution on the presentation and communication of the written word, see Roger E. Levien, "The Civilizing Currency: Documents and Their Revolutionary Technologies," in *Technology 2001: The Future of Computing and Communications*, ed. Derek Leebaert (Cambridge, MA: MIT Press, 1991).
83 See Kenneth Kidd, "Frontlines: Snap Judgments," *The Globe and Mail, Report on Business Magazine*, February 1995, about the business in Vancouver that specializes in digitally altering photographs to remove, for example, former spouses from vacation pictures. For a less innocent application of digital manipulation of photos, see note 143 in chapter 3 in the context of child pornography, together with the *Pecciarich* decision referred to in note 142 of chapter 3.
84 For an arresting example, see the two pictures of Pope John Paul II in *Computerworld*, 16 October 1995. On the left is the standard papal image, with the Pope wearing white robes, a gold cross, and a tall white-and-gold mitre on his head. On the right is a digitally retouched derivative of this image to make the Pope look like a leader of the Jewish faith, and has him dressed in black, with a Star of David, a black yarmulka, and a moustache and beard. A visitor from Mars would not be able to tell which is the "real" picture. For a lawsuit prompted by such digital gymnastics, see *Dustin Hoffman v. Capital Cities/ABC, Inc.*, 225 F.3d 1180 (9th Cir. 2001), where a magazine published a computer-altered "Tootsie" photo comprising Hoffman's head but another person's body.

even have to be scanned into the computer; rather, the "digital film" is played back on the computer, and then pictures can be printed out in hard copy or sent out over the Internet — after they are modified as required by the photographer.[85] The ability to manipulate digitized content without any degradation of quality is without precedent. As a result, in the digital world, artists and creators are challenging the old rules that dictated what is creative, what is original, and what is derivative. Advertisers are struggling to determine how much digital modification of a photo for use in an advertisement constitutes a misleading change in the representation of information.

Not surprisingly, digitization and manipulation of data, which underpin the second computer law dynamic — the elusive nature of information — have triggered a host of moral, ethical, and legal issues. The ease with which electronic data can be manipulated raises a wide array of legal challenges. In regard to intellectual property, numerous questions pertain to a creator's "moral rights" in a work and in its digitally produced and metamorphosed progeny. The criminal law relating to forgery and counterfeiting (and from a different perspective, child pornography) will be put to the test. In the areas of contract law and evidence law, there will be questions surrounding proof and authentication; for example, in an environment where digital-based material is manipulated regularly, what, if anything, constitutes the legal "original," and how is the existence of it proven in court? Given that copyright exists only in original works, manipulation of digital-based materials will also raise issues surrounding the ownership of copyright in such works. Further, the legal rules pertaining to misleading advertising will also need to be reassessed given that photographs can now be digitally altered without any degradation in the quality of the images.

3) Mass Storage

Once digitized, information is stored electronically or on an optical disk. Data storage is not a new human activity — the library at ancient Alexandria some three thousand years ago was said to store thousands of volumes of manuscripts. What has changed is the scale on which data storage can be effected. All the paper-based white pages telephone direc-

---

85   See Peter Burrows, "HP Pictures the Future," *Business Week*, 7 July 1997, which chronicles the strategy of Hewlett-Packard, a computer manufacturer, to compete in the photography market against companies such as Kodak; both companies have a range of digital photography products. See also "Digital Photography: Prints and the Revolution," *The Economist*, 8 June 2002.

tories for all the cities in Canada take up half a dozen long bookshelves; such a display can still be seen at some local reference libraries. The same amount of data can be stored digitally on a few CDs. All the information in Alexandria's library could be stored on a few more CDs. Computers allow us to record, store, and retrieve information in ways simply not possible in a paper-based environment.[86] Therefore, not surprisingly, huge databases have been developed, and more are being created each day. For example, the technological trend of mass storage permits retailers to record and store in "data warehouses" every individual's purchasing history — recorded down to the last intimate item bought at a pharmacy. And while the terms *storage* and *warehouse* have passive connotations in the world of physical objects, the data in electronic databases are anything but quiescent. They can be sorted and filtered, and merged with other databases, to provide "profiles" of data subjects, or to strategically link seemingly unrelated raw data into a meaningful whole.

The legal issues engendered by mass storage, and related activities and capabilities, are legion and novel. The ability to store vast quantities of personal information raises a host of privacy law issues. These concerns are heightened when the data are transmitted and stored outside of a data subject's domestic jurisdiction, possibly denying any effective legal recourse to the affected person. As such, mass storage brings sharply into focus the third and fourth dynamics of computer law, namely the blurring of both private/public and that of national/international. Criminal law concerns will also come to the fore as electronic mischief makers — as well as hard-core felons — gain remote access to these huge repositories of information. There are also new legal uncertainties that touch on the second dynamic of computer law: Who owns these mountains of data? Can data be bought and sold like traditional, tangible assets?[87]

4) Communications

Computers have always been used to store and manipulate information; indeed, they have traditionally been called "data processing" devices. An enormously important current technology trend is the

---

86   IBM recently announced a new data storage technology that can hold one terabit per square inch, effectively storing 25 million textbook pages on a surface the size of a postage stamp (which is about twenty times better than previous technology): *The Globe and Mail* (11 June 2002).

87   Again, while these questions are seemingly enumerated solely for pedagogical reasons, answers to them are to be found in the balance of this book.

development of the computer into a communications device as well — computation, processing, and now communication. In the first phase of computing, roughly from 1960 to 1980, mainframe computers automated large batch-based data calculating activities, as in running a payroll or keeping track of financial information. In the 1980s, the second phase of computing saw personal computers appear on desks and on factory floors, but still primarily oriented to processing data on a stand-alone basis. Since the early 1990s, we have witnessed the rise of the third phase of computing, namely, networking, whereby the personal computers on desks have been exchanging e-mail[88] and sharing documents through various groupware applications. Hence there follows the rise of ubiquitous computer networks, where the previously stand-alone personal computer now becomes a gateway to access a vast array of other computers belonging to individuals, corporations, and organizations, all of them also hooked up to the network, including the mother of all networks, the vast Internet. And the next important phase in the development of the computer into a networked communications device is being implemented currently with the new wireless world being constructed by telecommunications companies and a host of other businesses.[89] Mobile phones and other compact Internet access devices will have more and more intelligence stuffed into them, and they will become as important for conveying data as voice.[90] The result will be a raft of new Internet and other services that will permit people to access any information, any time from anywhere at a reasonable cost.[91] The

---

88   E-mail is, so far, the "killer" application of the Internet, with over 9.7 billion e-mails sent daily in 2000: IDC (International Data Corporation), cited in Stacy Lawrence, "The Agony and the Ecstasy," *The Industry Standard*, 25 December 2000. The volume and nature of e-mails, however, results in its own set of new legal challenges: see chapter 6, section B.3(b), "E-Mail Policies."

89   For a solid overview of the wireless present and likely future, see "Telecommunications: The World in Your Pocket," *The Economist*, 9 October 1999. Even kids are getting into the act: Mariam Mesbah, "Teenie Beepers: Parents Are Using Wireless Gadgets to Track Down Teens and Tweens," *The Globe and Mail* (11 September 1998).

90   It is useful to think of the coming world of data over wireless as the last of four important stages in telecommunications, preceded by voice over a fixed wire, data over wire, voice over wireless and, now, data over wireless: see Richard E. Talbot, *Portable Telecom Directory: Telecom Tsunami*, 30 March 2000, at 10 (a research report from RBC Dominion Securities).

91   Edward Trapunski, "Next Big Wave: Mobile Commerce," *The Globe and Mail* (28 January 2000); "America Rides the Wireless Wave," *The Economist*, 29 April 2000; and Gail El Baroudi, "Banks Roll Out Services to Catch the Wireless Wave," *The Globe and Mail* (5 October 2000).

wireless revolution will have a huge impact on consumers, as well as businesses.[92]

Of course, networks are not entirely new. The telephone system is a network, as is cable television. To date, however, these two types of networks have been very different from computer networks. The telephone has been essentially single point to single point interactive communication, while cable television (and its predecessor off-air broadcast) has been single point to multipoint non-interactive communication. Computer networks facilitate single point to multipoint, and increasingly multipoint to multipoint, interactive communications.[93] This particular dynamic has never been seen before, and its impact will be profound, with huge ramifications for our educational, retail, financial, and political systems, to mention but a few areas that will be impacted importantly by the Internet.[94] Elizabeth Eisenstein has chronicled the far-reaching social changes precipitated in Europe around 1500 as a result of the shift from scribe processes (monks and other persons copying manuscripts) to Gutenberg's print technology, including the fundamental and irreversible impact on education, language, religion, science, and on social trends such as the growth in censorship, intellectual property, and national cultures.[95] The shifts and accelerations

---

92   "The Internet, Untethered: A Survey of the Mobile Internet," *The Economist*, 13 October 2001. Of course there will be setbacks and specific business failures along the way: Karen Howlett, "BMO Pulls Plug on Retail Wireless Banking," *The Globe and Mail* (22 June 2002). Interestingly, a week after this announcement, the *Globe and Mail* reported that its readers selected Mike Lazaridis, a co-founder of Research in Motion, the Waterloo, Ontario, developer of the Blackberry "always on" e-mail device, as Canada's Nation Builder of the Year: Erin Anderssen, "'Why Not Be Branded the Wisest Nation in the World,'" *The Globe and Mail* (29 June 2002). For a discussion of the wireless e-mail product category invented by Research in Motion, see "Sending a Message," *The Economist*, 11 May 2002.

93   De Kerckhove, *Connected Intelligence*, above note 49, gives a penetrating analysis of how the interactivity of the Internet makes it a radical departure from any other communications medium.

94   See, for example, Patrick Butler *et al.*, "A Revolution in Interaction" (1997) 1 The McKinsey Quarterly 4, which argues that the new networking technologies, including the Internet, are decreasing transaction costs related to searching and contracting with partners, and that this will have widespread beneficial effects for the global economy.

95   Elizabeth L. Eisenstein, *The Printing Revolution in Early Modern Europe* (Cambridge, UK: Cambridge University Press, 1983).

resulting from the displacement of print by electronic media centred on the Internet will be as basic and far-reaching in their own right.[96] Not surprisingly, the Internet also presents the legal system with fundamental challenges. From a narrow, regulatory perspective, how and where — or even whether — to slot the Internet into the current framework of telecommunications and broadcasting regulation raises some real conundrums. The growth in international telecommunications will eliminate distance as a legal fact, thereby illustrating the fourth computer law dynamic, namely the blurring of the national and the international. However, laws are stubbornly national in scope, with nationalism being understood primarily as a geographic concept. Thus, core jurisdictional questions will need to be revisited in all legal areas — including contract, criminal, intellectual property, commercial, and tort. Over the past few years, answers to many of these questions have been hammered out, both through judge-made decisions and legislative law reform, as is chronicled in the balance of this book.

5) Miniaturization

If all of the above is not already reason enough to gape in awe at the computer revolution and the Information Age that it has spawned, consider that the computer on today's desk (and everywhere else) and its software is a "Model T" compared to what is coming over the next decade. This is largely because of the continued miniaturization of the computer, which in turn has been made possible by stunning advances in the design and fabrication of the semiconductor chip, the fundamental building block of computers and the foundation technology of the Information Age.[97] As computers, and chips, get smaller and more powerful, they will insinuate themselves into every last nook and cranny of society. For good or ill, no part of human endeavour will be free from the effects of the computer. Already, it is the rare corporation or government entity that has not automated its financial/accounting systems with computers. In most computing environments, however, this

---

96   For a touching example, see Jerry Nolfi, "How We Saved Smarties," *The Globe and Mail* (21 May 2001), where the author, the father of a son with severe allergies to nuts, organizes a successful Internet-based lobbying campaign to convince a chocolate manufacturer to keep a particular factory nut-free.

97   It has been a remarkable story so far, considering that the world's first business computer occupied 5000 square feet of floorspace: "Computer History: It All Started with Pies," *The Economist*, 17 November 2001. The reference to pies is to the fact that the machine was built by a catering company, which used it initially to evaluate weekly the costs, prices and margins on its bread, cakes, and pies.

is only the beginning. Computers have spread to the factory floor, and onto every desktop, and lately lap, in the organization. Consider any business, government department, school, university or other place of learning, any store, place of amusement, hospital or other medical facility, any hotel, airplane, or army unit — all have become increasingly dependent on the compact computer.

A key legal outcome of the ubiquitous computer will likely be a rise in lawsuits dealing with a wide array of liability issues as computers — as small as the size of a wristwatch — infiltrate every crevice of human endeavour. Notwithstanding their incontestable success as a base technology — clearly the defining technological device of the last quarter of the twentieth century and the first decade of the current century — computers are nevertheless risky devices. Custom software projects often fail because of the limits of the current technology. Even computer systems that can be built usually arrive over budget and well after the initially scheduled completion date. And computers and networks have a nasty habit of performing poorly from time to time. When they do, chaos follows. An important question is whether our liability regimes, both contract- and tort-based, are up to the challenge posed by computers. The widespread adoption of computing technology will also have an impact on the rate of computer crime, as the number of potential victims increases exponentially. And the pervasive spread of computers and networks will mean overall that many more cases involving the other legal issues discussed in this book will arise as the number of computer law incidents multiplies exponentially. One has difficulty envisaging unemployed practitioners of computer law.

6) Intelligent Computers

Computers will also become smarter, meaning easier to use and more efficient. Already we are witnessing the growing use of *expert systems and artificial intelligence*, software that has the capacity to learn over time based on the data fed into it.[98] A decade ago, a thoughtful report prepared by Canada's National Research Council included a précis of a

---

98   For an overview of expert systems, see Frank Puppe, *Systematic Introduction to Expert Systems: Knowledge Representations and Problem Solving Methods* (Berlin: Springer-Verlag, 1993); and Amar Gupta & Bandreddi E. Prasad, eds., *Principles of Expert Systems* (New York: The Institute of Electrical and Electronics Engineers, 1988). See also Frederick Hayes-Roth & Neil Jacobstein, "The State of Knowledge-Based Systems" (March 1994) 37(3) *Communications of the ACM* 27, and "AI By Another Name," *The Economist*, 16 March 2002.

number of artificial intelligence/expert systems being worked on by computer scientists around the world at that time.[99] The titles of articles of some of these initiatives are revealing, and one can only imagine what has transpired in this field in the interim: "REGWASTE: An Expert System for Regulating Hazardous Wastes"; "Air Traffic Control Using AI [Artificial Intelligence] Techniques"; "Potential Defence Applications of Expert Systems"; and "Expert Systems for University Admissions." There is even talk of intelligent legal software.[100] Robotics is another area that makes heavy use of artificial intelligence systems.[101] Yet a further development worth noting is *neural network* technology that apparently mimics the stimulus and response action of the human brain, resulting in computers that are able to analyse extremely complex situations in a matter of minutes rather than days, as is the case with conventional computing technology.[102] And to deal with information overload, the fact that there is too much information available on the Internet, there is intelligent agent software that learns, over time, what interests the user, and then goes out on the Internet

99 National Research Council Canada, Associate Committee on Artificial Intelligence, *The Social Context of Artificial Intelligence: Guideline and Discussion Paper* (Ottawa: the Committee, 1989). For a more current example, dealing with the self-running automobile, see "When Crashing Is Not an Option: The Blending of Car and Computer Technologies Promises Much — So Long As a Few Teething Problems Can Be Overcome," *The Economist*, 28 November 1998. Or see "The Needle in the Haystack," *The Economist*, 14 December 2002, which mentions how banks are using artificial intelligence software to detect money laundering. And then there is the computer that can beat the world's human chess champion: see Simon Houpt, "Can Unorthodox Moves Confound a Computer," *The Globe and Mail* (4 February 2003).

100 Adam Szweras, "Expert Computer Systems Could Give Legal Opinions, Make Administrative Decisions, Law Prof. Predicts," *The Lawyers Weekly*, 14 January 1994. As for how legally oriented software programs and the Internet will impact the delivery of legal services, see Brad Daisley, "Legal-Advice Websites Seen as Threat to Lawyers," *The Lawyers Weekly*, 30 June 2000.

101 For several articles on the state of the industry researching and commercializing robots, see "Briefing — Robotics: Machines Push the Boundaries of Science and Engineering" (and accompanying articles), *Red Herring*, December 2001.

102 Geoffrey Rowan, "'Unique' Software Thinks like a Human," *The Globe and Mail* (31 December 1996). For discussion of an example of a neural network application, namely a household-control system, see: "The Learning Home," *The Economist*, 22 May 1999. On the other hand, for a critical assessment of the state of development of artificial intelligence, see Geoffrey James, "Out of Their Minds," *Red Herring*, August 2002.

and retrieves information of particular relevance to the user, while the user enjoys an energetic game of tennis.[103]

Such agent software devices, and artificial intelligence/expert systems/neural network technology in general, raise some fundamental ethical questions. Immanuel Kant, the brilliant eighteenth-century German philosopher, believed that the quality that set humans apart from all other species was our ability to make moral, autonomous judgments throughout our lives; in a sense, our ability to decide makes us humans.[104] One wonders, if Kant were alive today, whether he would be distressed by the development of thinking machines that, in many areas of human endeavour, displace the need for human judgment and decision making.[105] In effect, prior to the advent of the computer, humans possessed a monopoly on information-processing tasks. Now that is no longer the case. Perhaps Kantian philosophy would be willing to draw a distinction between those computing and networking technologies that are tools to assist humans make better decisions, and those that represent a wholesale abdication of what is essential to the human condition.[106] As for the legal issues surrounding these systems, again liability will be a major focus. Consider a medical expert system that misdiagnoses a patient. Who is responsible? The doctor using it? The software company that created it? The eminent doctors who contributed to the knowledge base within the product? Or some combination of all three? And what should be the negligence standard by which such products are judged?[107]

---

103 For a discussion of intelligent agents, and one possible scenario for the unfolding of the computer revolution over the coming years, see Nicholas Negroponte, Being Digital (New York: Vintage Books, 1995). See also Communications of the ACM 37(7) (July 1994), an issue devoted to intelligent agents.

104 Immanuel Kant, Groundwork of the Metaphysic of Morals, trans. H.J. Paton (New York: Harper & Row, 1964).

105 For a modern-day critique of artificial intelligence, see Robert J. Sawyer, "Get Ready for the Killer Robots," The Globe and Mail (16 March 2000).

106 In a somewhat similar vein, some commentators have begun to question whether various features of the computerized/networked world are not dysfunctional, if not downright dangerous for the human soul. For example, Alan Lightman, an MIT professor, in an essay entitled "Prisoners of the Wired World," published in The Globe and Mail (16 March 2002), finds some of the negative attributes of the Wired World to include: "1. An obsession with speed and an accompanying impatience for all that does not move faster and faster … 2. A sense of overload with information and other stimulation … 3. A mounting obsession with consumption and material wealth … 4. Accommodation to the virtual world … 5. Loss of silence … 6. Loss of privacy."

107 For a discussion of such liability issues, see chapter 5, section D, "Negligence."

C. SOCIETAL IMPACT AND LEGAL ISSUES

Now that several key technologies and technological trends and applications have been briefly considered, it is worth asking what their impact has been, and will continue to be, on society at large. In a word, immense.[108] The computer revolution, by which is meant the widespread, sustained, and irreversible use of the computer in every area of economic and social activity, ushered in the Information Age. Understanding several of the key dynamics of this information era is critical to a discussion of computer law. Accordingly, the remainder of this chapter reviews the phenomena of elimination of distance and mass customization, both brought about by the computer-network technological developments discussed above. To understand these aspects of the Information Age, it is useful to consider the underpinnings of two earlier eras in history, the agrarian and the industrial. And again, the interplay of the four dynamics of computer law — rapid pace of technological development, the elusive nature of information, and the blurring of private/public and national/international — can be identified throughout the remaining pages of this chapter.

1) The Information Age

A comparative, analytical approach clarifies the defining indicia of the Information Age. During the Agricultural Revolution, land was the prime asset in the economy, the source of most wealth, and the vehicle that determined many social and power relationships. The defining assets of the Industrial Revolution were the physical goods first produced in mass production factories in England and other industrialized countries in the mid-1800s. In 1860, agriculture accounted for about 45 percent of Canada's gross domestic product.[109] By 1920, this figure was at about 15 percent, and manufacturing, the product of industrialization, was at its peak as a percentage of GDP, at about 25 percent.[110]

---

108 For an overview of the pervasive and fundamental societal changes wrought by the information highway (as the Internet was called in the mid-1990s) and related technological developments, see Gilles Paquet, "Institutional Evolution in an Information Age," in Courchene, *Technology*, above note 37. For a management guru's perspective on the profound changes occurring in our computer-networked world, see Don Tapscott, *The Digital Economy: Promise and Peril in the Age of Networked Intelligence* (New York: McGraw-Hill, 1996).

109 These and the following GDP statistics on Canada have been compiled by Statistics Canada and John Kettle: see *The Globe and Mail* (2 August 1996).

110 By 2020, factory jobs should make up just 10 percent of the Canadian workforce: John Kettle, "Manufacturing Gearing Down as Employer," *The Globe and Mail* (16 September 1999).

The Information Age should not be viewed as displacing the two previous eras. Land is still an important component of the economy — people still need to live and work in buildings and to eat food, for which land is also necessary — and the economy still produces and uses vast amounts of factory-produced goods; put another way, while processing information/symbols (the defining economic activity of the Information Age) is the key activity today, processing natural resources (the hallmark exercise during the Industrial Revolution) and harvesting natural resources (the primary activity of the agrarian age) are still important. Thus, information must be seen as an additional layer, important itself, but also incredibly strategic in the agriculture,[111] manufacturing,[112] and service[113] sectors. Today, the information services sector of the Canadi-

---

111 See Alanna Mitchell, "Cattle Left Home on the Range in Satellite Auction," *The Globe and Mail* (3 October 1996), which describes the use of video, satellite, and Internet technologies to replace face-to-face cattle auctions, with the positive results of saving costs and increasing prices due to the ability to reach a larger number of buyers. See also Alexander Wooley, "Harvesting High Tech," *The Globe and Mail* (15 March 1997), which discusses how farmers are using satellite-based global positioning systems and computers on board combines to obtain valuable data on soil moisture and past chemical use patterns in order to optimize crop yields.

112 For a discussion of how various advanced computer-based information technologies, because of their cheap processing power, large storage capacities, and efficient networking capabilities, have infiltrated and changed key aspects of the Canadian manufacturing sector, see John Baldwin, Brent Diverty & David Sabourin, "Technology Use and Industrial Transformation: Empirical Perspectives," in Courchene, *Technology*, above note 37. See also Gene Bylinsky, "The Digital Factory," *Fortune*, 14 November 1994, which analyses the role of software and computer networks in profoundly transforming the factory floor, with superb economic results. For a more recent example involving that pillar of the manufacturing sector, the auto industry, see "Ford To Expand On-Line Buying," *The Globe and Mail* (7 September 2001). See also "How About Now: A Survey of the Real-Time Economy," *The Economist*, 2 February 2002, an analysis that concludes that information technology's ability to eliminate the delays in doing business will bring about a real-time economy, with many beneficial results. As for the use of high-tech gadgetry in the construction industry, see Gordon Pitts, "Ellis-Don Focussed on Construction Innovation," *The Globe and Mail* (22 July 2002).

113 See Jon. E. Hilsenrath, "Services Help Spur Economy," *The Globe and Mail* (22 April 2002), for discussion of a research paper that emphasizes the importance of information technology investment in increasing productivity in thirty-five service industries. For a specific example, consider the chip-based "smart label" technology that will likely replace bar-codes in the retail sector in a few years: "The Best Thing Since the Bar-Code," *The Economist*, 8 February 2003. These intelligent labels will be able to communicate automatically with the check-out till, and perform other amazing feats; they also raise intriguing privacy issues if they are kept turned on after they leave the store and begin to beam back to the supplier information about the consumer. On a more human note, consider also

an economy — comprising publishing, television, communications, advertising, banking, research, education, government, etc. — accounts for about 30 percent of GDP. This includes those entities whose final product comes in the form of information. If entities that make information machines, such as computers and telephones, are included, as well as service organizations where information is the lifeblood but not the primary product, the percentage of the economy based on information can comfortably be put at 60 percent; agriculture, industry, and general services make up the remainder.[114]

For over twenty years social scientists have chronicled the growing importance of the information sector in the economy, by measuring either GDP statistics or the percentage of people engaged in the generation and transmission of information.[115] In a seminal work in the mid-1970s, Daniel Bell concluded that the United States was undergoing a profound shift to a "post-industrial" stage of development.[116] More recently, another scholar in this field concluded that the production, processing, and distribution of information accounts for 40 percent of

---

that online personals are a fast-growing segment of the e-commerce market: Showwei Chu, "On-line Dating Firms Heat Up Cyberspace," *The Globe and Mail* (13 February 2003).

114 A recent OECD study, working with a somewhat different definition of "knowledge economy," found that knowledge-based industries accounted for 51 percent of all business output (up from 45 percent in 1985): "Knowledge Gap," *The Economist*, 16 October 1999. Another way of assessing the importance of high-tech knowledge industries is by jobs: for example, a recent American study estimated that in the U.S., the Internet economy alone directly supported 2,476,000 workers: Center for Research in Electronic Commerce, University of Texas, "June 2000 Internet Economy Indicators," <internetindicators.com>. Reasonable people, however, can disagree on these various statistics (though not on the general conclusions they point to): see "E-xaggeration: The Digital Economy is Much Smaller Than You Think," *The Economist*, 30 October 1999.

115 For a review of how economists have handled the information economy, see D. McL. Lamberton, "The Information Economy Revisited," and Robert E. Babe, "The Place of Information in Economics," both in *Information and Communication in Economics*, ed. Robert E. Babe (Boston: Kluwer, 1994).

116 Daniel Bell, *The Coming of Post-Industrial Society: A Venture in Social Forecasting* (New York: Basic Books, 1973; 1976). This is truly one of the great works of the twentieth century. Bell did more than predict the ascendancy of the services sector, and its eclipsing of agriculture and manufacturing. He understood the importance of knowledge and technology, and the huge impact they would have not merely on the economy, but on society at large. He then went on to analyse the role of the corporation, and universities, in such an environment. Almost three decades after its first publication, *The Coming of Post-Industrial Society* is still a fine road map to our complex, technology-centric world.

the world's industrial production.[117] Although criticism has been levelled at the methodology used in some of these studies,[118] it is difficult to dispute that information has attained a pre-eminent role in the economy and society, thereby justly earning for the current era the label Information Age.[119] In fact, some economists, led by Paul Romer at Stanford University, have recognized in what is called New Growth Theory that knowledge, ideas, and information are as important — if not more so — as labour, capital, and natural resources, in fuelling economic growth.[120] Other recent research highlights the importance of innovation as a key to corporate success.[121] Put another way, while physical, tangible elements of the economy are still important, the key wealth creators and drivers today are intangibles, like software, knowledge[122] and information,[123] and of course, the people who create them.[124]

---

117 Herbert S. Dordick, *The Information Society: A Retrospective View* (Newbury Park, CA: Sage, 1993).

118 For a critical analysis of the key Information Age theorists, see Frank Webster, *Theories of the Information Society* (London: Routledge, 1995).

119 For an excellent overview of the economic, technological, and sociological implications of the Information Age, see Jorge Reina Schement & Terry Curtis, *Tendencies and Tensions of the Information Age: The Production and Distribution of Information in the United States* (New Brunswick, NJ: Transaction, 1995).

120 See Paul M. Romer, "Endogenous Technological Change" (1990) 98 Journal of Political Economy S71. Romer believes that technological change, namely the improvement in the instructions for mixing together raw materials, lies at the heart of economic growth and at S72 states that "One hundred years ago, all we could do to get visual stimulation from iron oxide was to use it as a pigment. Now we put it on plastic tape and use it to make videocassette recordings." For a similar perspective, but focusing on the critical role of information and knowledge at the level of the individual firm, see Stewart, *Intellectual Capital*, above note 32.

121 David Landes, *The Wealth and Poverty of Nations* (New York: W.W. Norton: Little, Brown, 1998). See also Ronald Jonash & Tom Sommerlatte, *The Innovation Premium* (Cambridge, MA: Perseus, 1999), and "Fear of the Unknown," *The Economist*, 4 December 1999.

122 In a recent trenchant analysis, Peter Drucker, the eminence grise of management gurus, argues that we are well along the way to becoming a knowledge-based world: "The Next Society: A Survey of the Near Future," *The Economist*, 3 November 2001. This important piece expounds on the profound implications for economics, politics, and society more generally of the rise to paramountcy of the knowledge worker. And especially the youthful knowledge worker that is the first generation to have grown up on the Internet: Chris Anderson, "Bright Young Things: A Survey of the Young," *The Economist*, 23 December 2000.

123 Chris Meyer, "What's the Matter?" *Business 2.0*, April 1999; and Bill Birchard, "Intangible Assets Plus Hard Numbers Equal Soft Finance," *Fast Company*, October 1999. See also Bruce Little, "IT Helps Spur Productivity," *The Globe and Mail* (17 December 2002), which reports that Statistics Canada has concluded

For a number of observers, the "new economy" of ideas, computers and networks has definitely come into its own in the last decade of the twentieth century.[125] These commentators highlight how, for example, while the economy grew by between 2.5 and 4.5 percent annually during much of the 1990s, new economy industries (such as manufacturers of computers and communications systems, communications carriers and suppliers of computer services) expanded at a phenomenal annual rate of 17.9 percent. Employment in these industries grew by 13 percent a year, compared with 2.5 percent for the rest of the private economy; indeed for much of this period there have been shortages of skilled workers in the new economy.[126] And even the slowdown

---

that productivity growth in Canada accelerated significantly in the late 1990s as a result of additional investment in information technology, especially in sectors such as retail and banking (through technologies such as bar code scanning in the former and Internet and telephone banking in the latter).

124 Don Tapscott, "Mind Over Matter," *Business 2.0*, March 2000. One of the features, however, of the new economy is that fewer people are required to produce wealth: see John Kettle, "Internet Surge is More Than Hype," *The Globe and Mail* (30 September 1999), which includes an analysis that points out that America Online recently had sales per employee for a recent quarter of $86,000, while the similar figure for General Motors was $57,000. For an excellent analysis of the "new economy," including the labour pains caused by it among some workers, see Pam Woodall, "Untangling E-conomics: A Survey of the New Economy," *The Economist*, 23 September 2000. This article explains the massive repercussions caused by an information technology revolution that has resulted in, for example, a Ford Taurus car today containing the same computing power as the mainframe computer used in the Apollo space program.

125 For macro reports, see Bruce Little, "Don't Dismiss New Economy Hype As Hot Air," *The Globe and Mail* (18 September 2000); and "The New Economy: Work in Progress," *The Economist*, 24 July 1999. For micro reports, see Bruce Little & Wendy Stueck, "New Economy Going on Buying Spree to Load Up on Technology," *The Globe and Mail* (20 July 2000); and Bruce Little, "GDP Rises Sharply in August as New Economy Fuels Growth," *The Globe and Mail* (1 November 2000). And even reports of a slowdown in technology spending means companies will spend only 12 percent more on computers, communications and software, and not the 25 percent annual increases of previous years: Gary McWilliams, "Companies Trim Tech Budgets," *The Globe and Mail* (28 December 2000). See also Bruce Little, "Nobel-winning Economist Hails Internet's Potential," *The Globe and Mail* (30 October 2002).

126 Mark Evans, "High-Tech Sector Expected to Add 30,000 Jobs in Two Years," *The Globe and Mail* (10 February, 1999); Lawrence Surtees, "Lack of E-workers May Hurt Profit: Survey," *The Globe and Mail* (9 March 2000). Even the unemployed have begun to make use of the Internet: Showwei Chu, "Panhandlers Stake Out Cyberspace," *The Globe and Mail* (4 November 2002).

in the technology sector in the 2000 to 2002 period[127] cannot dampen the generally positive outlook for the new economy sector over the next fifteen to twenty years.[128] It is no wonder, therefore, that every government, Canada's included, is being encouraged by numerous commentators[129] to create local conditions within its boundaries that foster replicas of California's Silicon Valley.[130]

127 "The Great Telecoms Crash" and "Too Many Debts: Too Few Calls," *The Economist*, 20 July 2002;"That Falling Feeling," *The Economist*, 17 March 2001; and "Telecoms in Trouble: When Big Is No Longer Beautiful," *The Economist*, 16 December 2001. It should be noted, however, that while 2001, for example, was a very tough year for Canadian companies that make telephone apparatus (down 62 percent), semiconductors (down 57 percent) and computers (down 32 percent), the high-tech services sector actually did quite well: telecommunications services (up 12 percent), software (up 14 percent) and data processing service companies (up 15 percent): Bruce Little, "New Economy Showing Signs of Its Old Self," *The Globe and Mail* (12 August 2002). And even some of the players caught in the dot-com meltdown are making a comeback: David Alain, "Startup Wizards Make 2nd Debut," *The Globe and Mail* (11 November 2002).

128 "The New Economy: What's Left," *The Economist*, 12 May 2001; Bruce Little, "Canada's New Economy Sectors Down But Far From Out," *The Globe and Mail* (15 May 2001); and "The Same – Only More So," *The Economist*, 8 December 2001. In a very perceptive analysis of Statistics Canada data on Canada's information and communications technology sector, Bruce Little notes that in the 2000–1 period, while makers of "telephone apparatus" (such as Nortel Networks) saw their production drop precipitously, software and services providers saw gains of 8.5 percent and 17 percent, respectively, during the first eleven months of 2001, leading this analyst to conclude that the information revolution is far from over: Bruce Little, "High-tech Horror Stories Clouding Brighter Spots," *The Globe and Mail* (4 February 2002). See also W. Brian Arthur, "Is the Information Revolution Dead?" *Business 2.0*, March 2002. The author concludes that if history is any guide, it is not. This essay observes, with the inspiration of the renowned economist Joseph Schumpeter, that canal mania (around 1790) and railway mania (around 1845) each lead to spectacular share crashes, but that both of these technological marvels only came into their own after these investment shake-outs. The piece posits that we are in a similar situation today with computational and Internet technologies; now that the dot-com frenzy and crash are behind us, we can get on with the true building ,out of the wired, digital world. Incidentally, in the late 1840s and 1850s, the telegraph industry underwent the same boom, bust and then mature growth cadence.

129 For example, the Canadian e-Business Initiative has lobbied the federal government for regulatory and tax reform, and is now helping to facilitate small and medium-sized businesses to implement e-commerce strategies: Charles Mandel, "Embrace E-biz or Lose Edge, Stodgy SMEs Told," *The Globe and Mail*, *Report on E-Business* (28 June 2002). See also David Pecaut, "The Budget Must Look to the E-Future," *The Globe and Mail* (7 December 2001) and "B+ for the E-budget," *The Globe and Mail* (29 February 2000); Guy Dixon, "Canada Needs Dot-com Future: Economist," *The Globe and Mail* (22 February 2000); Heather Scofield, "Ottawa to Spend $1-billion on Internet Initiative," *The Globe and Mail* (17 October 2000). See also *Fast Forward*

The Information Age title, however, is deserved not merely as a result of economic theory or statistics related to GDP and employment. As relevant is the fact that computers are embedded in every activity undertaken in the economy and society. Today, businesses could not operate, banks could not bank, schools could not educate, the media could not inform, hospitals could not heal, professionals and other service providers could not provide services, governments could not govern, political parties could not fight elections,[131] and the military could not fight wars,[132] if they did not have computers and the

---

3.0: Maintaining the Momentum, a report from the Canadian E-Business Roundtable, March 2002, available at <ebusinessroundtable.ca>. One commentator points out that corporate Canada's investment in information technology infrastructure lags well behind that of the United States, and probably accounts for the superior productivity and growth rates achieved south of the border: Bruce Little, "Canada's Frugal IT Investment Imperils Growth," *The Globe and Mail* (11 June 2001).

130 The following is a guide to the various "Silicon" monikers around the world: Silicon Alley — New York City; Silicon Valley North — Canada; Silicon Alps — Carinthia, Austria; Silicon Bog — Ireland; Silicon Fen — Cambridge, England; Silicorn Valley — Fairfield, Iowa; Silicon Polder — The Netherlands; Silicon Vallais — Switzerland; Silicon Forest — Byron Bay, Eastern Australia; Silicon Glen — Edinburgh to Glasgow, Scotland; and Silicon Wadi — Israel. Source: "Silicon Wannabes," *Business 2.0*, October 1999. And although it does not have a silicon prefix, the Indian State of Karnataka, which includes Bangalore, should not be left off any such list: see <bangaloreit.com>. Governments can give tech companies a wide range of assistance, including a hospitable regulatory environment for raising investment: see Peter Kennedy, "B.C. Considers Regulatory Aid For Tech Firms," *The Globe and Mail* (14 January 2003).

131 For an example of a Canadian political party's use of the Internet, see *Reform Party of Canada* v. *Western Union Insurance Co.* (1999), 3 C.P.R. (4th) 289 (B.C.S.C.) rev'd (2001), 12 C.P.R. (4th) 475 (B.C.C.A.). For a survey of the American experience, see Michael Totty, "Get Out the Vote," *The Wall Street Journal* (15 April 2002). To understand how "digital democracy" and "e-politics," both fuelled by the Internet and wireless text messaging, have transformed the landscape of political campaigning in South Korea, see Geoffrey York, "In South Korea, It's the Mouse That Roars," *The Globe and Mail* (30 December 2002).

132 For a compelling analysis of the computerization and digitization of the military, both during and since the 1991 Gulf War, the 1999 war in Kosovo, and most recently the conflict in Afghanistan in 2002, see "Defence Technology: The Information Advantage," *The Economist*, 10 June 1995, "The Future of Warfare: Select Enemy, Delete," *The Economist*, 8 March 1997; "'Twas a Famous Victory, But ...," *The Economist*, 18 December 1999; "Look, No Pilot," *The Economist*, 11 November 2000; "Satellites and Horsemen," *The Economist*, 9 March 2002; Paul Koring, "High-Tech, High Cost, High Hopes," *The Globe and Mail* (6 September 2002); and "Clipping the Enemy's Wings," *The Economist*, 8 March 2003. Apparently the Pentagon also has plans to develop high-tech weapons to attack the domestic computer systems of its adversaries: see Gary H. Anthes, "Info Warfare Risk Growing," *Computerworld*, 22 May 1995; and for the obverse, see "The New Ter-

huge volumes of information stored, processed, and disseminated by computers. A negative view of this dependency would highlight the risks posed to these activities if the computers on which they depend malfunctioned, as often happens. By contrast, a positive view is that businesses,[133] banks,[134] schools,[135] the media,[136] professionals,[137] the

---

rorism: Coming Soon to a City Near You," *The Economist*, 15 August 1998, and Steve Mertl, "Cyberspace Experts Await Full-Scale Attack," *The Globe and Mail* (27 December 2002). See also: Joseph Nye, "The New Rome Meets the New Barbarians," *The Economist*, 23 March 2002, in which the argument is advanced that even the United States, clearly the number one military power in the world by far, cannot dictate the course of international relations unilaterally because of the global information revolution and the democratisation of technology.

133 Even the businesses related to funerals and organized religion are embracing computing technologies: Margaret Stafford, "Death has a Future in Cyberspace: Funeral Industry Finds a New Internet Niche," *The Globe and Mail* (4 November 1999) (people can also memorialize a loved one at <obituariestoday.com>; and Guy Dixon, "Ecclesiastics Embrace E-business: Canada's Evangelical Lutheran Church Uses Web to Streamline Searches for Pastors, Link Far-flung Congregations," *The Globe and Mail* (26 October 2000). To understand how a core pillar of the economy, namely the world of finance, will adopt (and adapt to) the Internet, see Simon Long, "The Virtual Threat: A Survey of Online Finance," *The Economist*, 20 May 2000.

134 "Online Foreign Exchange: At Last, FX Online," *The Economist*, 19 August 2000. In Oliver Bertin, "Amex in No Rush to Move into Canada," *The Globe and Mail* (13 February 2003), the CEO of American Express is quoted as stating that servicing a credit card customer online is 90 percent less expensive than through a telephone representative.

135 Many universities, for example, are offering courses over the Internet, including traditional top-tier schools as well as new entrants created just for online learning: Karen W. Arenson, "A Different Transition: The Move to the Wired World," *The Globe and Mail* (9 November 1998); Kathleen Morris, "Wiring the Ivory Tower," *Business Week*, 9 August 1999; Keith McArthur, "Internet MBA Program Shakes Ivory Towers," *The Globe and Mail* (14 January 2000), and Charles Forelle, "Elite Colleges Finally Embrace Online Degree Courses," *The Wall Street Journal* (15 January 2003). Even younger students can benefit from the use of computers in the classroom: David Atkin, "It Computes: Laptops Equal Learning," *The Globe and Mail* (2 November 2002).

136 Susan Bourette & Jack Kapica, "Election Night Internet Surge Put News Web Sites to the Test," *The Globe and Mail* (30 November 2000).

137 An accounting firm has recently introduced a novel service whereby for a fixed, annual fee, it will answer questions sent in via e-mail by subscribers to the service: see Ernst & Young's Online Tax Advisor, at <ey.com>. A Canadian public relations firm is pioneering providing its services over the Internet to smaller clients: Wendy Stueck, "Vancouver PR Firm Sets Up On-line Service," *The Globe and Mail* (13 November 2000). Even law firms are beginning to use the Internet to deliver legal information: see, for example, the online products of a leading Australian law firm, Mallesons Stephen Jaques at <mallesons.com> and the online services of Clifford Chance in the United Kingdom at <cliffordchance.com>.

military,[138] health-care professionals,[139] life sciences researchers,[140] and governments[141] can now achieve ambitious new goals in the Informa-

---

138 For an analysis of the importance of the computer in training for and fighting a war, and the use of the Internet in waging the propaganda war surrounding the physical fighting, see, respectively, "The 21st Century Army: A New But Risky Sort of War," *The Economist*, 2 January 1999; and "War on the Web: A Guide to Following the War in Yugoslavia on the Internet," *The Economist*, 15 May 1999. As for the most recent war fought by Americans, see John Lloyd, "As Ye Sow, So Shall Ye Reap," *The Globe and Mail* (7 January 2002), for a discussion of the effectiveness of the high tech, unmanned and aptly named Predator drone that could hover silently for twenty-four hours, send back high-resolution images to its command centre, and then use its own missiles when it saw a promising target. As an ad for Northrop Grumman states: "In tomorrow's conflicts, information will be a resource, a target and a weapon, all at the same time"; in *The Economist*, 8 June 2002. A former vice-chairman of the U.S. Joint Chiefs of Staff, Admiral Williams Owens (ret.), believes there is a lot more the U.S. military could do to implement comprehensive computer and networking systems: William Owens, *Lifting the Fog of War* (New York: Farrar, Straus & Giroux, 2000); see also Mark Williams and Andrew P. Madden, "Military Revolution," *Red Herring*, 1 August 2001.

139 Todd Woody, "How the Net Could Save Your Life," The Industry Standard, 13 September 1999. See also Krista Fuss, "Consult Your MD on the Net, For a Price," *The Globe and Mail* (14 August 2000); "An Un-killer App: A Combination of 'Biochips' and Databases Could Lead To More Effective Diagnosis and Treatment for a Wide Range of Diseases," *The Economist*, 23 October 1999; and Kevin Marron, "Electronic Records Offer Instant Access," *The Globe and Mail* (30 July 1999).

140 Biotech and pharmaceutical companies rely extremely heavily on powerful computing systems to extract information from genes and proteins, then to store and manipulate the resulting data, the amount of which is (amazingly) doubling every six months, all of which gives rise to the new discipline of bioinformatics: Kevin Marron, "Health Sector Seen Giving Booster Shot to Tech Firms," *The Globe and Mail* (13 June 2002).

141 A recent report indicates that Canada has the highest proportion of citizens among industrialized countries using the Internet to access and use government services: "E-government: No Thanks, We Prefer Shopping," *The Economist*, 4 January 2003. See also Marissa Nelson, "Renewal Of Licence From Home Not Far Off, Minister Pledges," *The Globe and Mail* (5 September 2001), which highlights the Ontario government's ambitious plans for offering services over the Internet. See also Simon Tuck, "Dawn of the E-State," *The Globe and Mail* (22 March 2001), and Jennifer Lewington, "City Looks at Ways to Put Services On-line," *The Globe and Mail* (2 September 2002). For a wide-ranging analysis of the impact that the Internet is having, and likely will have, on the delivery of government services, see "Government and the Internet: The Next Revolution," *The Economist*, 24 June 2000, and Gassan Al-Kibsi, Kitode Boer, Mona Mourshed & Nigel P. Rea, "Putting Citizens On-Line, Not In Line," *The Mckinsey Quarterly, Special Edition, On-Line Tactics*, 2001. See also Charles Bedford, "Winnipeg MP Finds IT, Internet Help Serve Constituents," *The Globe and Mail* (1

tion Age because of computers and computer networks.[142] Regardless of one's assessment of the prospects for a society where information is the defining asset, it simply cannot be denied that this is the Information Age. This has even been recognized in a recent judicial decision, where the court stated: "Information is the currency of modern life. This has been properly called the information age."[143]

Law is a reflection of the economy and the society from which it emanates. Thus, it is not surprising that land-related laws first developed with the ascendancy of the role of land as the principal asset in the agrarian era. It is for this reason that mortgage legal principles, and related documents, still contain a healthy dose of "olde English," given that the legal rules for mortgages date from several hundred years ago. Similarly, the enactment of the first *Sale of Goods Act* in England in 1894 is the quintessential legal development in the industrial era, which was so concerned with the production and distribution of physical goods. Therefore it is appropriate to ask, living as we are in the Information Age, if our laws have stayed current with the rise to prominence of

---

August 2002). As for the importance of computer technology to the government's intelligence gathering agencies, see Justin Hibbard, "Mission Possible: The CIA Is Increasingly Dependent On Its Fledgling Venture Capital Arm," *Red Herring*, December 2001. And on a cautionary note, the use by the government of the Internet to promote adoptions has caused some controversy: Arthur Schafer, "Beware e-Adoptions," *The Globe and Mail* (14 February 2003).

142 It should also not be forgotten what a significant impact computer-based devices have had on the entertainment industry, including the development of diversionary technology for the home: Jack Kapica, "Fun and Games Drive Computer Innovations," *The Globe and Mail* (18 July 1998); Kevin Marron, "New Technology Alters Business Model for TV," *The Globe and Mail* (23 January 2002); and Erin Anderssen, "Children Abandon Remote, Grab Mouse: Lured By Computer Games, Internet Canadian Children Watching Less TV," *The Globe and Mail* (3 December 2002). Or, consider that computer games are today a US$20 billion industry: "Counter-Culture," *The Economist*, 6 January 2001; in the United States in 2001, sales of video-game equipment and software, at US$9.4 billion, exceeded American movie box-office receipts of US$8.35 billion: *The Globe and Mail* (7 February 2002). Many of these are now of the multiplayer variety involving contests with participants all over the Internet connected in real-time virtual combat: see "Console Wars," *The Economist*, 22 June 2002. For a discussion of the uneven impact the digital revolution has had on the entertainment industry to date, see "Thrills and Spills: A Survey of E-entertainment," *The Economist*, 7 October 2000. And even more traditional games, such as bridge, are being played over the Internet: Ingrid Pentz, "Gates Tries His Hand at Bridge," *The Globe and Mail* (16 August 2002).

143 *Vancouver Regional FreeNet Assn. v. M.N.R.* (1996), 137 D.L.R. (4th) 206 at 213 (F.C.A.).

information as the pre-eminent asset. Put another way, do we need to develop new laws and legal principles for the new era, or can we make do relying, for the most part, on laws intended for a previous era? These questions form a constant theme throughout this book. And thus it is not surprising that a statute such as Ontario's *Electronic Commerce Act, 2000* was passed in the first year of the new millennium.[144]

The comparative analytic approach of understanding law (at least partially) as a product of the underlying economics and defining assets of respective eras can also help explain "legal regulatory infrastructure" issues. For instance, we can ask what was the primary means of transporting to market an era's defining asset. Thus, in the agrarian age, ships competed with roads to deliver foodstuffs. More interestingly, at the height of the Industrial Age, canal companies, railroads, and later trucking firms competed vigorously to see which would win the battle of taking industrial goods to market.[145] Therefore, it is not surprising that today telephone companies (such as Bell Canada) and cable companies (such as Rogers) are in an epic battle to bring the Internet (and thereby the informational assets of our age) to the consumer.[146]

2) Elimination of Distance

Almost by definition, geography played an important role in the agrarian era. In the industrial era, geographic space was still important because it was (and still is) expensive to send physical goods to distant customers. In contrast, a central feature of the Information Age is how computers linked to electronic networks eliminate physical distance.[147]

---

144 S.O. 2000, c. 17. For a discussion of this new statute, and its counterparts passed by other jurisdictions in Canada, see chapter 6, section A.1(g), "Electronic Commerce Statutes."

145 The analogy between railroads and high-speed Internet access is made in Gordon Pitts, "Axia Claiming Middle of Net Road," *The Globe and Mail* (1 July 2002). This article focuses on the Supernet initiative, intended to bring broadband Internet service to rural Alberta.

146 Keith Damsell, "Internet Providers Slug it Out in Ads: Sympatico, Rogers Battle for Lucrative High-Speed Service Market," *The Globe and Mail* (6 September 2000). Similarly, the battle between Telus's phone-based ADSL dial-up service, and Shaw's "always on" high-speed Internet over cable service, is being fought mainly through marketing campaigns, but has also seen a skirmish in an Alberta courtroom: see Brent Jang, "Shaw-Telus Wrangling Over Internet Speed Gets Nasty," *The Globe and Mail* (11 December 2001).

147 See Frances Cairncross, *The Death of Distance* (Boston: Harvard Business School Press, 1997). Cairncross believes one of the wonderful benefits of the telecommunications revolution will be a global diffusion of knowledge that will be a boon

Current telephony, broadcast, and cable systems have already caused the world to shrink. Full electronic networks that can transmit all forms of digital information and content will eliminate geographic distance as a factor in a number of areas of human endeavour, including education, medicine, engineering, most business services, finance, and entertainment. Consider the growing area of telemedicine. Arthroscopic surgery involves inserting compact medical instruments into a patient and having a doctor perform the operative procedure by viewing a monitor that displays the images conveyed by the instruments and by manipulating dials on a computer that in turn control the instruments in the patient.[148] With this sort of procedure it no longer matters whether the doctor is in the same room as the patient or half a continent away. Indeed, access to medical expertise may increase dramatically as specialists are able to ply their trade around the world over networks. This is not science fiction; there are currently numerous telemedicine facilities up and running.[149] Activities capitalizing on the same technological dynamics that are driving telemedicine include the rapidly growing phenomena of Internet banking and distance education by universities that offer courses through a combination of satellite, broadcast, and Internet facilities.

The legal impact of the elimination of distance will be enormous. Computer networks are a prime exponent of the fourth dynamic of computer law, namely, the blurring of the national with the international. Hence, novel legal questions abound when a person or organization

---

not just to developed countries, but to poorer ones as well. Other observers are not so sanguine. For example, Harvard professor Jeffrey Sachs worries about a yawning technology gap between the world's haves and have-nots: "Sachs on Globalisation: A New Map of the World," *The Economist*, 24 June 2000.

148 Jerry Zeidenberg, "Cut the Cuts: The Trend to Minimally Invasive Surgery," *The Globe and Mail* (30 July 1999).

149 David Orenstein, "Remote Surgery," *Business 2.0*, December 2001. This piece describes an operation in which two surgeons in New York performed a gall bladder removal on a patient lying in a hospital in Strasbourg, France, using remote surgery techniques involving endoscopic cameras and secure fibre-optic communications lines. See also Joanne Sommers, "Nortel, Bell Linking Doctors, Patients in Different Cities," *The Globe and Mail, Report on Telecommunications* (6 May 1997). Physicians are also starting to make sustained use of e-mail in order to communicate with patients: Joanne Sommers, "Doctors Bring Back the House Call, Virtually," *The Globe and Mail, Report on E-Business* (28 June 2002). See also Josh Fischman, "Bringing Doctors to Day Care," *U.S. News & World Report*, 27 May 2002, which describes a project whereby a child-care centre is linked to a hospital by the Internet in order to permit physicians to make diagnoses on the children remotely.

is able to convey a presence in another jurisdiction electronically, or when someone in one jurisdiction accesses a Web site located on a computer resident in another jurisdiction. When is a company legally carrying on business in another jurisdiction, such that it is subject to that other jurisdiction's laws, simply because people in that other jurisdiction can access its Web site?[150] Or, in the telemedicine example, is a doctor who is physically present in Toronto, operating remotely on her patient resident in a hospital in Denver, Colorado (the patient broke his leg skiing), required to be licensed in Colorado to practise medicine in Colorado? Is the doctor in fact practising medicine in Colorado? Does the Canadian doctor's malpractice insurance cover the doctor for procedures effected on patients who are physically outside of Canada at the time? These questions will multiply exponentially as new and intriguing applications are found to help eliminate the concept of geography as a factor in human endeavours.[151]

3) Mass Customization

With information exchange becoming such an important activity in our society, and with data capture, storage, and manipulation becoming less and less expensive, businesses, public sector agencies, and governments are getting to know individuals as never before. In one sense, this is not an entirely new phenomenon. In the agrarian era, the local butcher, for example, knew intimately what each of his hundred customers in the village preferred by way of types and cuts of meat, and the appropriate item would be waiting on the relevant day of the week because the butcher knew each customer personally. The quality and selection may not have been very exciting, and products were quite expensive because economies of scale were hard to come by in such an environment. In other words, the benefits of mass production could not be realized, but at least the customer received what the customer desired, and when the customer wanted it, from the limited selection. In the industrial era the production of goods — and services — moved into factories. Economies of scale were realized in factories that produced goods, as well as services such as education (i.e., the "factory" is the school), cul-

---

150 A number of parts of this book address these questions, including chapter 7, section B, "Jurisdiction."

151 For a discussion of some legal and non-legal obstacles confronting telemedicine in certain jurisdictions, such as the unwillingness of medical insurance companies to pay for non–face-to-face consultations, see Mitch Betts, "Network Medicine Offers Its Share of Headaches," *Computerworld*, 26 September 1994.

ture (opera house, concert hall, cinema), medicine (hospital), information (library), and government (Parliament, city hall). These factories
were marvels of efficiency, and they caused costs to drop dramatically,
thereby ushering in the era of mass consumption. Knowledge of the
individual customer, however, and of that customer's preferences — the
dual hallmarks of the earlier era — were lost. More consumers were
able to buy a car, but all Model Ts were black. The defining benefit of
mass production — a dramatic decrease in prices — was able to be realized, but the benefits of customization became elusive.

The technology trends noted above today permit *mass customization*, the result obtained from fusing the intimacy of the customized
agrarian era with the mass production efficiency of the industrial era.[152]
Networked computers running huge databases can now recreate the
detailed knowledge that the butcher had of each of his customers; today
each retailer, or government, or school can know each customer or citizen or constituent.[153] The fundamental difference, of course, is that
while the medieval butcher's geographic term of reference was the village, the modern database creator's field of activity is literally the world,
thereby permitting large economies of scale to result in lower unit
prices.[154] This is both an exhilarating prospect (for the retailer), and
possibly an uncomfortable one too (for the data subject)! Contributing
to the phenomenon of mass customization is the ability of computers
and networks to divide a product or service into its information and
physical delivery components. Currently, a patient goes to a hospital
both for information and the delivery of the requisite service. Similarly,
a consumer goes to a retail store for information (i.e., to find out price,
quality, availability, colour, etc.) and to take physical delivery of the

---

152 Two authors recently explained this phenomenon in the following way: historically, the delivery of information presented a trade-off between richness (the quality
and depth of the information) and reach (how distant the information could be
effectively communicated). Today, over the Internet, information can be both rich
and have worldwide reach, a unique combination relative to past experience, and
one that presents enormous opportunities (and challenges) for businesses: Philip
Evans & Thomas S. Wurster, *Blown To Bits: How The New Economics of Information Transforms Strategy* (Boston: Harvard Business School Press, 2000).

153 See "Mass Customisation: A Long March," *The Economist*, 14 July 2001. For a
treatment of mass customization from the perspective of the management guru,
see Don Peppers & Martha Rogers, *The One to One Future: Building Relationships
One Customer at a Time* (New York: Doubleday, 1993).

154 See, for example, the service offerings of Net Perceptions, an e-commerce personalization company that utilizes several technologies to place appropriate products, ads, and content before prospective online customers: <netperceptions.com>.

product. Increasingly, these two functions are being separated, and performance of the former will no longer require physical attendance at the site of delivery of the latter. Instead, information will be provided in advance to the prospective user of the service or product.

This is already occurring in a number of areas, for example, in the low-tech environments of direct-mail catalogues or ordering pizzas by telephone. With full digitization of content, where product catalogues or medical information or customer information is online, the bifurcation process will be complete. Moreover, the information delivery component will be by far the more valuable of the two parts of the system. It is the primary value-added activity, while shipping product will become a commodity-like function with relatively low margins. Airlines, for example, make more profit from moving information over their computer-based reservation networks than from moving people in their planes.[155] And as the consumer learns about a particular product or service in an online or networked environment, the provider of this information will be learning about the consumer, adding yet more personal information to the already burgeoning database.

Mass customization is driving the development of a range of new business models over the Internet,[156] giving rise to a new nomenclature.[157] In assessing the long-term impact of these new commercial paradigms, it is important not to focus too much on the day-to-day announcements concerning online consumer sales,[158] the amount of

---

155 A number of airlines have realized there is probably more money in moving information than people: Keith McArthur, "Air Canada To Launch On-Line Travel Agency," *The Globe and Mail* (7 September 2001).

156 Don Tapscott, a leading thinker about the new world of e-commerce, conceptualizes a number of new business models as follows: the Agora, Aggregation, Alliance, Value Chain, and Distributive Network: Don Tapscott, David Ticoll & Alex Lowy, "The Rise of the Business Web," *Business 2.0*, November 1999; and Don Tapscott, "Internet Firms Change Model of Traditional Business," *The Globe and Mail* (17 July 1998).

157 For example, B2B (business to business); B2C (business to consumer); and C2C (consumer to consumer), each denoting a specific focus for an online business. For a description of a "B2B exchange," in this case operating in the hospital procurement area, see Grant Buckler, "On-Line Exchanges Yield Healthy Hospital Savings," *The Globe and Mail* (21 March 2002). For a discussion of the fortunes (and misfortunes) of various B2B exchange models (such as a horizontal one versus a consortium-based vertical marketplace), see the various articles in *The Mckinsey Quarterly, Special Edition, On-Line Tactics*, 2001.

158 The reports can be bewildering. For a positive spin, see Marina Strauss, "E-Shoppers Spend $2 – Billion in Half; *The Globe and Mail* (9 October 2002); Marina Strauss, "Canadian Tire, Future Shop Sales Beat Expectations," *The Globe and Mail* (10 January 2002) (which notes that Canadian Tire's online sales during Decem-

electronic commerce,[159] or on the gyrations of the valuation of dot-com companies on the stock markets,[160] but rather to consider how in less than a decade, certain industries have already been fundamentally transformed by online business dynamics,[161] and how others will be impacted

---

ber, 2001 increased 252 percent, and its Web site traffic grew 70 percent from the previous year); "On-Line Purchases Surged in 2000: Statscan," *The Globe and Mail*, 24 October 2001; Steven Chase, "Growth Seen in Net Purchases," *The Globe and Mail* (3 November 2000); and Natalie Southworth, "$20-billion Expected in On-Line Shopping: Report Forecasts Big Holiday Sales," *The Globe and Mail* (6 September 2000); and for a contrary view see: Marina Strauss, "The E-tailing Retreat," *The Globe and Mail* (28 September 2000); Bob Tedeschi, "Plenty of Retailers Pass on E-commerce," *The Globe and Mail* (4 November 1999); and Marina Strauss, "Forzani E-Commerce Site Gets Axe as Customers Fail to Log On," *The Globe and Mail* (1 October 2002). Moreover, in the strange world of the Internet, when actual online consumer sales grow by only 60 to 100 percent, that is not good enough: Keith McArthur, "Internet Sales A Disappointment for Retailers," *The Globe and Mail* (30 December 2000). And in some industries it may simply be too early to tell; thus, while online food retailing has not caught on in the United States, it has in the United Kingdom: see "Tesco and Safeway Online: Surfing USA," *The Economist*, 30 June 2001. On the other hand, Internet-based new product marketing is successful in the United States: John Gaffney, "How Do You Feel About a $44 Tooth Bleaching Kit?: Procter & Gamble Discovers What The Web is Really Good For – Test Marketing," *Business 2.0*, October 2001.

159 For an even-handed assessment of the amount and nature of electronic commerce in Canada at the beginning of the new millenium, see Statistics Canada, "Electronic Commerce and Technology," *The Daily*, April 3, 2001, available at <www.statcan.ca>. This is an annual report on e-commerce and technology; for the 2002 edition, see "Survey of Electronic Commerce and Technology," 14 August 2002.

160 What goes up can come down, particularly after the "correction" in tech stocks in the spring of 2000: Peter Kuitenbrouwer, "Millionaire Ranks Thinning: Sliding Market Taking its Toll of Dot.com Rich," *The Financial Post* (14 April 2000); "E-Commerce: Too Few Pennies from Heaven," *The Economist*, 1 July 2000; "Shades of Hype," *The Economist*, 17 June 2000; and a sober analysis of the bursting of the dot-com bubble: John Cassidy, "*dot.con: The Greatest Story Ever Sold*" (New York: HarperCollins, 2002). The result has been a shake-out in a number of Internet industries: "Dot.com Death Count Accelerating: Study," *The Globe and Mail* (23 November 2000).

161 For example, online businesses have captured, or will by 2005, 60 percent of retail stock trading; 33 percent of adult entertainment, 20 percent of the sales of books and videotapes and the gaming market (source: OECD, as reported in *Fast Company*, March 2000): not too shabby for a technology infrastructure that is less than a decade old. Also consider the success of Internet-based job search sites, auction sites, and certain B2B exchanges: "Workopolis.com Revenue Hits $1 million in October," *The Globe and Mail* (9 November 2000); Tyler Hamilton, "Net Auctions Catch On," *The Globe and Mail* (27 April 2000); "The Heyday of the Auction," *The Economist*, 24 July 1999; "Going, Going, Gone: Online Haggling is the Hottest Thing Happening in E-Commerce," *Business Week* (12 April 1999); Simon Tuck,

to a greater or lesser extent.[162] In short, while business over the Internet will not replace traditional commerce, it will impact every player in the economy to some extent,[163] and those that ignore it do so at their peril.[164]

"Canada's Hottest Dot-Coms," *The Globe and Mail* (22 June 2000); Nick Wingfield, "Profit Triples at eBay," *The Globe and Mail* (17 January 2003); and Mylene Mangalindan, "Yahoo Breaks Dot-Com Mold, Sees a Rebound," *The Wall Street Journal* (15 January 2003). Particularly intriguing, and revolutionary, is Priceline.com, which operates a "name your own price" Internet ticket service: David Carpenter, "More Big Airlines Sign Up With Priceline," *The Globe and Mail* (18 November 1999). In a similar vein, the Internet is helping to disintermediate the travel agent: Keith McArthur, "Travel Agents Gird for Turbulence," *The Globe and Mail* (30 March 2002), although those agents that specialize in sophisticated travel services are doing all right: Laszlo Buhasz, "Survival of the Travel Agent," *The Globe and Mail* (16 April 2003). For an analysis of three of the leading "pure play" Internet companies, namely Yahoo!, eBay, and Amazon, see "Internet Pioneers: We Have Lift-Off," *The Economist*, 3 February 2001. At the end of 2001, for example, eBay, the world's largest online trading community, had 42.4 million users worldwide, and in the previous three months listed 126.5 million items: "Internet Firms: Party Like It's 1999?" *The Economist*, 23 February 2002. Not bad for a Web site started in 1995 to sell Pez candy dispensers; although some products, such as fine art, seemingly do not sell well over the Internet, as they require more "high touch" than "high tech": "Just the Two of Us," *The Economist*, 1 March 2003. It is not, however, just new dot-com companies that are riding the Internet wave. For example, some offline retailers are doing very well by their online presence: Rob Lever, "Bricks and Clicks Beat out Pure Plays," *The Globe and Mail* (28 December 2000). See also Wendy Stueck, "Ritchie Bros. Takes Reserved Approach to Net," *The Globe and Mail* (14 June 2002), for an example of how an established company (in the industrial auction market) has carefully integrated the Internet into its general business model.

162 The auto industry, for example, stands poised to transform both the selling of cars and their production courtesy of the Internet: Greg Keenan, "Auto Firms Set to Expand Net Sales," *The Globe and Mail* (22 November 2000); "Riding the Storm," *The Economist*, 6 November 1999; and "Internet Economics: A Thinker's Guide," *The Economist*, 1 April 2000. The latter piece cites a study that reckons that auto company procurement portals on the Internet could reduce the cost of making a car by 14 percent.

163 To understand how General Electric is instituting a culture of "e-buy," "e-sell," and "e-make," see "While Welch Waited: E-Strategy Brief: GE," *The Economist*, 19 May 2001. In June 2001, *The Economist* ran three more such analyses, focusing on very different companies, but in each case illustrating how the Internet is in the process of significantly impacting each of them: "Electronic Glue: E-Strategy Brief: Siemens," *The Economist*, 2 June 2001; "A Reluctant Success: E-Strategy Brief: Merrill Lynch," *The Economist*, 9 June 2001; "The Cemex Way: E-Strategy Brief: Cemex," *The Economist*, 16 June 2001; and "E-Management: Older, Wiser, Webbier," *The Economist*, 30 June 2001.

164 Peter Kennedy, "Forestry Firms Neglect Net: Study – Says Sector Must Embrace E-commerce Technology to Stem Poor Profitability," *The Globe and Mail* (9

This is why few companies are avoiding the Internet,[165] even if some cannot yet show a positive return on their investment.[166] The collection, aggregation, and especially dissemination to third parties of personal information and corporate data over the Internet, of course, brings to light a set of legal issues involving privacy, data protection, and a host of commercial issues. It is not surprising that such a fundamental shift in the way that much of business will be done will result in an important re-evaluation of a number of the legal principles in effect today, all with a view to bringing into the Information Age those laws that are currently completely out of date or in need of partial upgrading. It will be important to be able to conclude enforceable contracts online.[167] The third dynamic of computer law — involving the blurring of the private and public spheres — will also bring to the fore a number of legal questions. Data protection and surveillance laws will have to be updated (where they exist) or enacted (where none exists). For example, so-called cookies can be embedded in the software that users employ to access the various Web sites of the Internet. This cookie software can tell its creator what Web sites were visited by the user, and eventually will be able to convey information on the actual purchases made, money spent, etc. All this can be done without the user having any knowledge of the cookie. The law of privacy will likely be called upon to address this type of technology.[168]

November 2000). For a more general call to arms, see Shikar Ghosh, "Making Business Sense of the Internet," *Harvard Business Review*, March–April 1998. See also Don Tapscott, Convocation Speech, University of Alberta, 4 June 2001, available at <dontapscott.com>.

165 John Partridge, "Bell to Target B2B E-commerce," *The Globe and Mail* (23 November 2000); and Marina Strauss, "Canadian Tire Launches New E-biz Site," *The Globe and Mail* (21 November 2000). And it is not just big-name companies that stand to gain from e-commerce; in 2001, Vesey Seeds of Prince Edward Island, Canada's largest pre-Internet mail-order gardening supplies company, saw its Internet sales account for 25 percent of its total business: Charles Mandel, "Embrace E-biz or Lose Edge, Stodgy SMEs Told," *The Globe and Mail, Report on E-Business* (28 June 2002).

166 Keith Damsell, "The Fight to Rule Toronto On-line: Plenty of Web Sites Focus on the City But None Make Money," *The Globe and Mail* (30 October 2000). On a very different plane, it is interesting to note that Enron's Internet-based energy trading business may be one of the few divisions of this failed behemoth that had residual value: "Enron's Ghost: Recharging," *The Economist*, 20 April 2002.

167 This topic is analysed in chapter 6, section A.3(c), "Express and Implied Click-Consent Agreements."

168 For a discussion of privacy law, see chapter 4, section A, "Privacy and Data Protection."

4) Dependency on Computers

As computers become pervasive, our dependency on them grows.[169] The ability to store all the key financial and operating data of a business on a single CD, permitting an executive to access it on a laptop computer while she is at her summer cottage, illustrates the power and benefits of the new technology.[170] Powerful and beneficial indeed, until it is stolen from the executive's car.[171] Then an ugly Achilles' heel of the Information Age is revealed. Some thieves may only think about fencing the laptop for a few hundred dollars; more sophisticated felons, however, are beginning to realize that the data in the laptop are far more valuable.

---

169 Though at least one court has determined that a household is not as dependent on the computer as it is on the television. In *Re Larsen*, 203 B.R. 176 (Bankr. W.D. Okl. 1996), an American bankruptcy court concluded that the personal computer in 1996 is where the television was in the mid-1950s, an intriguing and entertaining device, but not yet critical enough to be excluded from a secured party's lien as a necessary household item in a personal bankruptcy, though the judge conceded that one day it may well attain such an important status. The court noted that the television has gone from an expensive curiosity to a necessity as a family's relatively inexpensive primary source of information and entertainment, but that the personal computer is not yet at this stage. Persons exhibiting symptoms of Internet addiction may disagree with this court's assessment: see Ed Susman, "Studies Identify Internet Addiction," *The Globe and Mail* (16 August 1997). These symptoms include: having an inability to control Internet use; lying to family members or friends to conceal the extent of involvement with the Internet; and going through withdrawal when not online. See also *Re Ratliff*, Guide to Computer Law (CCH) ¶47,745 at 70,529 (Bankr. E.D. Okla. 1997), where a bankruptcy court did find that in view of the computer's role as a key resource for gathering information, the debtors' use of the computer for school purposes, and the importance of learning computer skills, the personal computer was exempt from a lien as being protected household goods. See also the discussion in chapter 3, section B.5(d), "Sentencing and Computers," where at least one court in Canada has concluded that Internet access is today too important for employment and other purposes so as to completely deny an accused access to use of the Internet.

170 Unless one takes the view that laptops have no place in a cottage. On the other hand, busy people would use the cottage a lot less if they could not remain connected to the rest of the world while there.

171 For example, American nuclear weapons secrets appear to have been compromised recently when two computer hard-drives went missing, and British spies have gotten in trouble for leaving laptops on trams and in pubs: "Nuclear Security: Cuckoo NEST," *The Economist*, 17 June 2000. More recently, the Canadian government (presumably inadvertently) made available on the Internet security details related to the G8 gathering of world leaders in Kananaskis, Alberta, in June 2002: Graeme Smith, "Summit Blueprint Turns Up on Web," *The Globe and Mail* (2 April 2002).

They can be used for extortion through a slow sale of individual files back to the executive or for industrial espionage through a quick sale to the executive's competitor. Obviously, these risks to security must be addressed by all users of the new technology.[172] A further problem is the inadvertent disclosure of information, particularly through unintentional e-mail distribution.[173] Another risk presented by dependency involves malfunction or breakdown of the computer infrastructure of the organization.[174] Soon all businesses and organizations will be unable to function if their computers are not operating properly.

As well, huge costs in financial and operational terms can occur if a proposed new system was simply too complicated and could not be built.[175] An insatiable appetite has been created for ever more powerful computers, software, and networks to perform more Herculean tasks: a computer-based expert system to run part of Canada's air traffic control regime; a gargantuan automated baggage handling system at Denver's new international airport; a revolutionary computerized stock trading system for the Toronto Stock Exchange, just to name a few examples.

---

172 A further unfortunate side effect of computers is the stress they can cause to users: see Steven Chase, "Computers Take Beating As 'IT Rage' Grips Offices," *The Globe and Mail* (24 January 2001); and Virginia Galt, "Workers Say E-Mail Can Get Stressful," *The Globe and Mail* (18 July 2001).

173 See Paul Wilde, "Canadian Firms on Global Crossing List," *The Globe and Mail* (11 April 2002), which chronicles the mistaken disclosure of a confidential list of bidders by a New York–based law firm.

174 For a discussion of a number of risks posed by computers, particularly in the health sector, see Jacques Berleur, Colin Beardon & Romain Laufer, eds., *Facing the Challenge of Risk and Vulnerability in an Information Society* (Amsterdam: North-Holland, 1993).

175 For a discussion of a number of famous, as well as lesser-known computer meltdowns, see Lauren Ruth Wiener, *Digital Woes* (Reading, MA: Addison-Wesley, 1993). A 1994 study of large, computer software development projects reported that only 9 percent are concluded on time and on budget, and fully one-third are abandoned prior to completion: see Barrie McKenna, "Cancelled Contracts Cost Ottawa Millions," *The Globe and Mail* (4 September 1996). A U.S. study in 2000 found that about 25 percent of all software projects are cancelled, with a cost to the firms involved of some $67 billion: Charles C. Mann, "Why Software Is So Bad," *Technology Review*, July/August 2002. For some wise yet practical advice on how to avoid disappointments in the implementation of information technology projects, see Alistair Davidson, Harvey Gellman & Mary Chung, *Riding the Tiger* (Toronto: HarperCollins, 1997). Of course other sophisticated technologies are also susceptible to birthing pains: see Mira Oberman, "Two Bombardier Trains Stopped by Amtrak," *The Globe and Mail* (16 August 2002), for a discussion of problems with the yaw damper bracket part of a hydraulic tilting system on a train.

Incidentally, these three (and many other large software development projects) all experienced huge technical problems, commensurate delays in completion, and mountainous cost overruns.[176] Other examples of high-profile high-tech heartburn include the one-day outage experienced by America Online, a leading Internet service provider, similar outages by MCI WorldCom and AT&T, IBM's trials and tribulations with its computer systems at the 1996 Atlanta Olympic Games, the crashing of the Toronto Stock Exchange's computerized trading system on various occasions, and the cost overruns and delays associated with the Ontario government's Integrated Justice Project, reportedly the world's largest justice technology implementation exercise.[177] The causes of such problems can vary widely, from design flaws in computer chips,[178] to interference with network connections,[179] to soft-

---

176 High-profile failures caused by errors in software are also not new: in 1962, a single character error in the control software for the Mariner I Venus probe sent the rocket booster off course, leading mission control to destroy it, and in 1990 the AT&T long distance network was knocked out for nine hours due to a problem with the routing software: see *Encyclopedia of Computer Science*, above note 1. Closer to home, a news report attributed to software glitches several deaths and injuries related to overdoses of radiation therapy: see Barbara Wade Rose, "Fatal Dose," *Saturday Night*, June 1994. For more recent government-related computer messes, see: "Gun-Registry System Had to be Rebuilt, McLellan Says," *The Globe and Mail* (17 December 2002); and "The Health Service's IT Problem," *The Economist* (19 December 2002).

177 Mitch Wagner, "AOL Unplugged," *Computerworld*, 12 August 1996; Jason K. Krause, "A Tale of Two Network Outages," *The Industry Standard*, 13 September 1999; Mindy Blodgett, "IBM Misses Chance for the Gold," *Computerworld*, 29 July 1996; Janet McFarland, "Latest TSE Computer Crash Angers Investors, Members" *The Globe and Mail* (2 April 1997); Richard Blackwell, "Technical Problems Hit TSE Again," *The Globe and Mail* (22 February 2000); David Gambrill, "Waiting for IJP," Canadian Lawyer (April 2002); John Jaffey, "Ontario's Integrated Justice Project Heading Back to the Drawing Board," *The Lawyers Weekly*, 1 November 2002; and David Gambrill, "Integrated Justice Project in Tailspin," Law Times, 21 October 2002. See also the brief story in *The Economist*, 8 June 1996, regarding the destruction of $500-million worth of uninsured spacecraft and scientific satellite when apparently a software failure made the launch rocket go off course just after lift-off.

178 For an article on a defective chip leading to a multibillion dollar settlement of a class action claim, see David P. Hamilton & Robert A. Guth, "Why Did Toshiba Bite the $2 –billion Bullet," *The Globe and Mail* (4 January 2000). See also Showwei Chu, "Glitches Force Intel to Recall Superfast Chip," *The Globe and Mail* (29 August 2000).

179 Showwei Chu, "Train Derailment Interrupts Internet," *The Globe and Mail* (26 April 2002). See also Roma Luciw, "Internet, TV Service Cut as Rail Crew Slices Cable," *The Globe and Mail* (20 July 2000).

ware snafus.[180] The results can be harm to reputation,[181] lost business,[182] and, more positively, a more sober and level-headed approach to information technology.[183]

A dispassionate observer of these trends could be forgiven for having the uneasy feeling that our mastery of the technology has not kept pace with our stratospheric expectations.[184] Many computer programmers are working well outside their comfort zone, a situation with profound legal implications. Of course, many software development projects can fail because of problems caused by the customer as well. In any event, the dependency that society has developed on computers brings to the forefront questions about legal liability. How should neg-

---

180 "Sydney Baggage Glitch," *International Herald Tribune* (5 July 2000) and "Computer Glitch Blamed for Incorrect Price Readings," *The Globe and Mail* (7 September 2002).

181 Andrew Willis, "Stone-age TSE Loses Credibility by the Day: Computer Troubles Again Prove that Canada's Top Stock Exchange Isn't Ready for the 21st Century," *The Globe and Mail* (8 March 2000). This piece comments on how the TSE's technology woes will drive stock trading to the United States in the 220 stocks of Canadian companies that are listed on the TSE and U.S. exchanges. If it is any consolation, the TSE is not the only stock exchange in Canada to be hit by technology problems: see "Software Glitch Halts CDNX," *The Globe and Mail* (29 January 2000). And U.S. exchanges are not immune from technology bugs either: Richard Blackwell, "Computer Snag Hits NYSE But TSE Declines to Gloat," *The Globe and Mail* (9 June 2001) and "Worker's Error Downs Nasdaq," *The Globe and Mail* (30 June 2001).

182 See Guy Dixon, "Investors Cite On-Line Delays for Losses," *The Globe and Mail* (24 August 2000), which chronicles the losses that can accrue to investors who use online brokerages that experience trading delays due to computer problems; "Heathrow Airport Recovers After Computer Chaos," *The Globe and Mail* (19 June 2000), which cites cancelled flights as one of the fallouts from an airport's computer breakdown; Oliver Bertin, "Software Cited in Vistajet Shutdown," *The Globe and Mail* (16 September 1997), which blames malfunctioning customer reservations software as partly to blame for the demise of a discount airline; and Andrew Tarisz, "Crashes Can Be Fatal with Rivals a Click Away," *The Globe and Mail* (28 January 2000), which reported that online auction sites can lose as much as $5.3 million in revenue during a one-day system outage.

183 Bernard Wysocki, Jr., "High Tech's Value Can Be Elusive: Ill-Fated Projects in the Information Revolution Spawn a Backlash Among Computer-Savvy Executives," *The Globe and Mail* (30 April 1998).

184 On the other hand, there are also situations where computers do a better job than humans, as in the case of a recent midair collision between two jets where, apparently, the catastrophe could have been avoided had one of the pilots followed the computer's instructions, instead of those of the human air controllers: Paul Koring, "Air Crash Stirs Man-or-Machine Debate: Automatic Systems May Provide More Safety than Humans Who Create Them," *The Globe and Mail* (13 July 2002).

ligence be assessed with respect to software programmers, given the lack of software programming standards? Should society contemplate some form of licensing regime to help ensure the competence of persons working in the software field? A university degree in engineering and an engineer's licence is required of someone designing a bridge for our concrete highways, yet no such accreditation or licensure is required of the persons constructing our information superhighways. Is insurance available to either the developer or the user to cover computer-related risks? Can contracts be used to allocate risks, and in some cases completely limit one party's liability? In short, how well have our legal liability regimes, both in contract and tort/negligence, kept pace with developments driven by the first dynamic of computer law, the torrid pace of technological change?[185]

5) Legal Implications

The societal trends discussed above have important legal ramifications, and a number of these have already been alluded to in the previous paragraphs. Other questions can be contemplated. With an increasing proportion of society's wealth linked to the generation and dissemination of computer and information-based assets, are traditional intellectual property laws appropriate to ensure optimum levels of production of information? With ubiquitous networks presenting criminals with untold new opportunities to cause harm, is the criminal law adequate to ensure public safety? Should the government regulate the content flowing over these networks, and if they do so, how can they do so effectively? Should laws regulate the massive databases that collect copious amounts of personal data? A government's jurisdiction to regulate has traditionally been geographically oriented (for example, the government of British Columbia can only make laws in the province of British Columbia); how will governments exercise jurisdiction over a network like the Internet that ignores geographic boundaries? How should traditional principles of contract, evidence, and tort law be customized to deal with the challenges posed by the computer revolution? It is to these and a host of similar questions that we turn in the remainder of this book.[186]

---

185 These questions are discussed in chapter 5, section D, "Negligence."
186 In March, 1998, a justice of the Supreme Court of Canada asked very similar questions about cyberlaw:

> Searching for the right metaphors which relate cyberspace to conventional law is a huge challenge precisely because there are no precise analogies to cyberspace in the real world. Moreover, many questions are implicated by

When approaching these questions, it is worth being mindful of how uncontrolled and unruly it all is. Primarily contributing to this sense of anarchy is the speed with which all these developments are unfolding. It was 350 years before the first major improvement was

---

the nature of cyberspace which have never been previously raised and which pose insoluble problems for legal doctrine as currently constituted. Questions such as: [w]hen users are in different countries, where is a contract made over the Internet for jurisdictional purposes? When a defamatory statement is made on the Internet, does every state where the statement is accessible have jurisdiction over that tort? Are criminal sanctions against, for example, hate speech, gambling, or pornography subject to the authority of any jurisdiction in which that speech is accessible? What type of communication on the Internet should be considered private and what should be considered public? Is a "chat-room" public or private? How private does the "chat-room" have to be before it is considered analogous to the privacy of one's home? Does, for example, the delicate balancing required under the *Charter* apply with equal force to all forms of speech on the Internet, even though that speech and the opportunity for response, rebuttal, control, and tuning-out are greater than in any other "public" forum?

The Internet raises a host of other issues which I have not canvassed here, particularly in the realm of intellectual property law. In fact, it is hardly an exaggeration to say that cyberspace is sufficiently distinct from any other model of communication and human interaction that almost every important issue in civil law, and many in the criminal context, may need to be reviewed according to the particular circumstances of this new technology. Moreover, courts will need to be aware as in no other domain of developments in other jurisdictions and the dictates of inter-jurisdictional comity. But this will be an elusive task for a medium where a message posted onto the Internet can simultaneously be available in every country in the world. The borders of cyberspace do not map onto the borders of real space, which poses a fundamental problem for courts whose jurisdiction is based on geography. New tools and new doctrines will need to be developed, and perhaps certain doctrines that have been developed heretofore, particularly in the realm of conflict of laws, will need to be revisited. While this challenge may not require the acceptance of a new normative order, as in the case of aboriginal or international law, it does present a whole area of such rapid technological change that it will be a challenge for legal models to adapt quickly and yet remain coherent and comprehensible over time. And depending on the response of other jurisdictions and users of cyberspace, what amounts to an independent normative code could develop and demand deference from Canadian courts.

The Honourable Michel Bastarache, "The Challenge of the Law in the New Millennium" (1998) 25 *Manitoba Law Journal* 411. In a subsequent communication with the media, the current Chief Justice of Canada indicated she also thought technology would have a profound impact on the legal system: see note 9 in chapter 3.

made to Gutenberg's original printing press — replacing human power with steam. In contrast, the commercial use of the Internet is barely a decade old, but rarely a month passes without the announcement of some new Internet technology! Technological advances occur at break-neck speed, but law reform moves at a much slower pace. Contributing to the difficulties surrounding the development of sensible legal rules for computer and network technologies is the fiendishly elusive nature of information itself — it is a hard asset to pin down. Adding to the feeling of anarchy is the profoundly democratic nature of much of the new technology; for example, a personal computer and a handheld scanner can make a computer user a budding publisher on the Internet. In other words, even if the legal system could craft the rules necessary for the Information Age, how will they be implemented and enforced locally and in each home? And how will all this be done in foreign jurisdictions, given the global nature of the computer revolution, but the parochial domestic reach of national laws? These factors — what this book refers to as the four dynamics of computer law — and how lawyers, judges, and legislators come to understand and master them, will have an important effect on how the legal questions raised in this book are ultimately answered.

CHAPTER 2

INTELLECTUAL PROPERTY LAWS

Intellectual property laws provide legal protection for products emanating from the minds of people and, accordingly, cover a variety of computer and information-based technologies and products. The rationale for intellectual property laws lies in the peculiar economics associated with intellectual properties. This chapter begins by discussing several important economic differences between intellectual properties, on the one hand, and real property and tangible physical, movable property (goods), on the other hand. Understanding these differences will bring into focus the core principles and more subtle nuances of the various intellectual property law regimes. The chapter then discusses how the core intellectual property law regimes of trade secrets/breach of confidence, patents, copyrights, semiconductor chip protection, and trade-marks apply to information-based products. Of course, not all questions regarding intellectual property laws and their application to information-based products are settled. The four dynamics of computer law, namely, the rapid pace of technological change, the elusive nature of information, and the blurring of private/public and national/international,[1] conspire to ensure that the application of intel-

---

1   These dynamics are important, and are a unifying theme throughout this book. For a discussion of these dynamics, see chapter 8, section A, "Computer Law: Dynamics." In section C.8 of this chapter, "Other Measures of Protection," the concept of the four skill sets is introduced — the common law; law reform; contract; and technology — that can be deployed to address the challenges posed by

lectual property laws to software and other information-based assets is in a constant state of flux. Accordingly, the last part of the chapter discusses how these laws apply (or may not apply) to software, multimedia content, databases, and to activities on the Internet. Finally, in addition to covering the substantive aspects of intellectual property law regimes, the material in this chapter explores the process-related question of how well, or poorly, the current civil procedure system is wrestling with these complicated matters. Of particular interest in this regard are the new domain name dispute resolution procedures created for various domain name registries.

A. THE ECONOMICS OF INFORMATION

In the previous chapter, a number of differences between the agrarian and industrial eras, on the one hand, and the Information Age, on the other hand, were highlighted.[2] Similarly, economic differences exist among the principal assets of these three epochs. Illustrative of the second dynamic of computer law — the elusive nature of information — information-based assets differ radically from those of tangible assets, such as land and goods. Understanding these differences is vital to an appreciation of the rationale and role of intellectual property laws, as well as the specific substantive provisions of these legal regimes. Although the following discussion is not comprehensive, a brief overview of the key concepts will assist the reader to become comfortable with the discussion of legal issues that follows.

1) Tangible Assets — WHAT - ETAMPLES

The central economic fact governing the traditional assets of land (including buildings) and goods (such as tables, chairs, and automobiles) is natural scarcity. There is a finite amount of land in the world. Similarly, notwithstanding recycling efforts, natural resources such as minerals are inherently scarce commodities. Equally, the energy sources required to transform natural resources into finished goods are also, for the most part, non-renewable. In a world characterized by finite physical assets, economics can be understood as the study of the

---

the four dynamics of computer law. These skill sets are further elaborated on in chapter 8, section C, "Computer Law: Skill Sets."

2   See chapter 1, section C.1, "The Information Age."

allocation within society of scarce resources. As for the legal system, an economy based on land and goods that recognizes private property need only have a criminal law prohibiting trespass (for land) and theft (for goods). Once the law provides that non-owners cannot occupy the land and cannot take goods of others, the economic rules of supply and demand will operate to determine how much of a particular asset is sold and purchased, and at what price.[3] Moreover, it is easy to determine if a non-owner is squatting on someone else's land or is occupying someone else's premises. It is also easy to ascertain whether a car owner has been deprived of that good; if she wakes up in the morning, and the car is not in the driveway, it has been stolen.[4] In essence, tangible, physical goods lend themselves to simple property ownership regimes. Further, they are not subject to the four dynamics of computer law. They are not nearly as susceptible to technological change, they are not elusive, and their delimitation both within the private/public and national/international spheres is simple and constant. Tangible goods are static, and hence the legal system for their protection can be quite straightforward.

Of course, ownership of even the traditional assets of land and goods has become more complicated over time. Real property rights are now hemmed in and overlaid by a host of public and quasi-public rights, such as easements in favour of utilities, and zoning restrictions in favour of the common good.[5] Through condominium law, for example, we have created ownership rights in a type of real property that, in a sense, is disassociated from the underlying earth; for units on the second and subsequent floors, these real property rights literally hang in midair.[6] Laws governing relationships also permit security interests and other contingent ownership rights to be granted in movable goods, such as automobiles. Nonetheless, we have in our real property and

---

3   For a seminal elaboration of these concepts by one of the pioneers of the law-and-economics school of thought, see Richard A. Posner, *Economic Analysis of Law*, 4th ed. (Boston: Little, Brown, 1992).

4   Or repossessed by the finance company: see the discussion in chapter 5, section D.2(a), "Malfunctioning Computers"of *Ford Motor Credit Company* v. *Swarens*, 447 S.W. 2d 53 (Ky. App. 1969), where the finance company was held liable when it repossessed a car due to the failure of its computer to record instalment payments that had actually been made.

5   For analysis of property as a cluster of rights, and not as a thing, see C.B. Macpherson, ed., *Property: Mainstream and Critical Positions* (Toronto: University of Toronto Press, 1978); and Arnold S. Weinrib, "Information and Property" (1988) 38 U.T.L.J. 117.

6   See, for example, Ontario's *Condominium Act, 1998*, S.O. 1998, c.19.

LAND → KNOW
HOW
MUCH

personal property security registration systems relatively simple and efficient mechanisms by which these various interests can be ordered and recorded. Thus, when a person buys a house (or a condominium), a lawyer can give a very meaningful opinion as to who owns title to the property and what third party interests affect such title. In contrast, a lawyer's title opinion to a purchaser of the intellectual property in a computer program generally would be so full of qualifications as to be meaningless. The four dynamics of computer law raise all sorts of questions as to the ownership of the intellectual property in the software. Who, exactly, contributed what to the software, so as to have had an ownership interest in it? Were aspects of it created by persons at their homes, and does this mean they might own parts of it personally even if they were employees at the time? Were there international contributors to the software, perhaps collaborating over the Internet? Which intellectual property laws apply to them? The lack of an effective ownership registration system compounds these questions. Tangible assets raise few of these questions.

2) Information-Based Assets

Information-based assets differ radically from land and goods. The fundamental difference is that today information can be reproduced at virtually no cost.[7] This was not always true. Prior to the printing press, copying a book by hand in monasteries in Europe in the Middle Ages was as laborious a task as writing the original copy. Gutenberg changed all this with his invention of the movable type printing press, which dramatically reduced the time, effort, and cost involved in producing copies. More recently, the photocopier has driven the marginal cost of reproduction even lower.[8] The printing press and the photocopier did not, however, reduce the still significant cost of transporting books, newspapers, and other paper-based media on which information has traditionally resided. Today, digital-based content can be reproduced by computers *and* transmitted around the world by telecommunication networks at no cost and with no degradation in the quality of the work.

---

7   For a perceptive analysis of the legal ramifications of this fact and other related indicia of information, see R. Grant Hammond, "Quantum Physics, Econometric Models and Property Rights to Information" (1982) 27 McGill L.J. 47. See also R.J. Roberts, "Is Information Property?" (1987) 3 I.P.J. 209.

8   An early discussion of the legal impact of the photocopier is provided in George A. Gipe, *Nearer to the Dust: Copyright and the Machine* (Baltimore: Williams & Wilkins, 1967).

In many respects, it is no longer appropriate to talk about scarcity of information in the current technological environment. To illustrate this point, several commentators make reference to the story in The Gospel According to Matthew of the fishes and loaves, where the disciples fed the crowds from a few baskets that miraculously replenished themselves with fish and bread; apparently after everyone ate, twelve baskets were still filled with food.[9] This is a rare situation in which physical, tangible goods behaved like information. What was truly a miracle in the corporeal world, however, is an everyday occurrence in the incorporeal sphere of information-based assets. Just like the adage says, in the physical world cake cannot be held after it is eaten. By contrast, in the world of information, you can eat your cake and still have it, too.

The fact that information can be copied and transmitted at no incremental cost leads to the second fundamental aspect of information, that it is capable of universal possession. A touchstone of traditional, physical assets is that at any one time only one person is capable of possessing a particular table, chair, or automobile. Indeed, exclusive possession and the ability to exclude others from the asset are the hallmarks of ownership for traditional assets like land and goods. An ownership regime based on exclusion gave rise to the old legal adage that "possession is nine-tenths of the law," which is a pithy way of saying that with traditional assets ownership and possession are usually synonymous, because possession of tangible assets tends to be exclusive. This turn of phrase clearly predates the Information Age. Given the second dynamic of computer law, exclusive possession becomes fiendishly difficult with information-based assets, where multiple, simultaneous or near-simultaneous possession is the norm. Put another way, because we can physically see and experience fences, doors, and locks, it is easy to forget that ownership of real and tangible property is about relationships. Perhaps it is also important that all real estate has been claimed and is owned by someone. An exception is the land under the oceans, and this fact, along with the fluid nature of water and the migratory habits of fish, actually brings to mind other fish examples that somewhat approximate the information world: the salmon, cod, and other fish disputes that break out between Canada, the United States, and (on the east coast) other countries. Another example is air, also generally not owned, and migratory, and the cause of cross-border disputes because of airborne pollution. Intellectual property constantly has to be carved out of the ether, or like nomadic fish,

---

9   *The Bible*, Matthew 14:17–20.

pulled from the ocean. Information is diffusive, it leaks, it spreads, it ebbs and flows. Historically, we used a physical net, namely paper,[10] to catch it, but after the invention of the printing press and the photo-copier this net began to tear. And once information is stored, aggregat-ed, processed, and disseminated electronically, leaving all physical carriers behind, the analogy with water and air is complete. The evanescent nature of information — essentially, the second dynamic of computer law —combined with the ability to reproduce and transmit it at extremely low cost seriously affects the legal ownership regimes applicable to information-based assets.

3) The Rationale for Intellectual Property Laws

Given the ease with which information can be reproduced and trans-mitted, how should society implement a private property ownership regime for elusive information-based assets? This question assumes, of course, that a system of private property protection is both desirable and required in order that sufficient amounts of information be creat-ed. If cars were not protected by the criminal offence of theft, they would not be produced because they would be stolen from factories, thus denying the manufacturer a return on effort; for markets to oper-ate efficiently, a private property regime is required in order that pro-ducers be able to recoup economic rewards for their work.[11] Put another way, laws impose barriers to free consumption so that manu-facturers and distributors can earn a return for their efforts. It is no dif-ferent for information and intellectual property.[12] If there were no

---

10   Even paper can be made to be a transitory medium of fixation. In *Théberge* v. *Galerie d'Art du Petit Champlain, Inc.*, [2002] SCC 34 (Sup. Ct. Can, 2002) [*Théberge*], a well-known Quebec painter objected to a gallery transferring his images from a paper-based poster, by means of a sophisticated ink removal process, to a canvas backing (thus making the new "poster" look more like a real painting). For the denouement of this conflict, see below at note 100.

11   See for example, "World Hunger: Stop Blaming the Weather," *The Economist*, 15 June 2002, which includes the passage: "In eastern Congo, nobody wants to raise cattle, because marauding soldiers steal them." At the same time, however, certain less developed countries may need to modify somewhat first world intel-lectual property laws when adopting them, at least for some period of time: "Imitation v. Inspiration: How Poor Countries Can Avoid the Wrongs of Intellec-tual Property Rights," *The Economist*, 14 September 2002.

12   This view has had proponents in the economic literature since the time of Adam Smith, who wrote that while monopoly was hurtful to society, a temporary monopoly granted to an inventor was a good way of rewarding risk and expense: Adam Smith, *An Inquiry into the Nature and Causes of the Wealth of*

means of capturing some economic returns for investing in the human and other capital required to create, say, software, a great deal less software would be produced.[13] This point is particularly salient for creators of information-based assets, like software or movies, because these assets typically are extremely expensive to produce but, once created, are incredibly inexpensive to reproduce (illustrating another dimension of the second dynamic of computer law). There are, of course, other economic models that might result in sufficient production of intellectual properties. For example, several hundred years ago, rich patrons, rather than copyright, were responsible for underwriting the creation of most artistic works, and more recently the state has been an important patron of the arts. These alternatives to the market system,

---

Nations, book V, chapter I, part III (London: W. Strahan and T. Cadell, 1776, [New York: A.M. Kelley, 1966]). For a study that canvasses the views of pro-patent and antipatent economists, see Fritz Machlup, *An Economic Review of the Patent System* (Washington: U.S. Government Printing Office, 1958). For a more recent analysis of the economics literature on the rationale for patents — and whether the theory behind patents is actually borne out by the evidence, see "Patently Absurd," *The Economist*, 23 June 2001. One of the studies referred to in this article concluded that the most patent-conscious business of all — the semiconductor industry — did not become more innovative as the patenting activity increased. On the other hand, see Debora L. Spar, *Ruling the Waves: Cycles of Discovery, Chaos and Wealth* (New York: Harcourt, Inc., 2001) [*Ruling the Waves*], for an analysis of the very important role played by patent protection in the early development of a number of technological breakthroughs that animated society from the late nineteenth century to today.

13 In a recent case involving patent infringement, *Polansky Electronics Ltd.* v. *AGT Limited*, [1999] A.J. No. 1230 (Alta. Q.B.) [*Polansky Electronics*], the court, in discussing the basics of patent law, put it simply at para. 35: "Without patents, ideas have little protection." This trial decision was subsequently set aside, and a new trial ordered: *Polansky Electronics Ltd.* v. *AGT Ltd.*, [2001] A.J. No. 153 (Alta. C.A.). In a recent brochure for a conference titled "WIPO Summit on Intellectual Property and the Knowledge Economy," to be held in Beijing in April, 2003, WIPO put the case for intellectual property legal regimes more positively as follows (the e-version of the brochure is available at <wipo.org>):

> Today, a state does not have to be "lucky" — in terms of its possession of land, labor and capital — to succeed. Creativity and innovation are the new drivers of the world economy and national well-being increasingly depends on the strategy a country develops to harness its intellectual capital. An effective intellectual property system is the foundation of such a strategy. Within knowledge-based, innovation-driven economies, the intellectual property system is a dynamic tool for wealth creation — providing an incentive for enterprises and individuals to create and innovate; a fertile setting for the development of, and trade in, intellectual assets; and a stable environment for domestic and foreign investment.

however, are not without their own disadvantages, as the many angst-filled relationships between composer and patron, and between cash-strapped government and state-subsidized artist, can attest.[14]

One option for protecting information in a free market system is simply to draw on the legal regime associated with tangible goods, and make the theft of information a criminal offence. The problem with this approach, however, is that the criminal law is too blunt an instrument to apply to information.[15] Consider the theft of a book. If someone physically removes a book from a store without paying for it, that person has stolen the book, the physical medium on which the information resides, and the person would be guilty of the offence of theft but only of the paper-based good that is the book. Thus, the criminal law works well enough for the physical containers into which information is poured, the units of tangible media on which information is imprinted (i.e., paper) or electronically (i.e., a computer disk) stored. Matters become more complicated, however, when that which is taken is not the physical medium. For example, what if the thief reads the book, with the intention of writing her own book on a similar subject? If the thief copies each sentence, word for word, so that her book is the same as the author's book, and the thief sells multiple copies of "her" resulting book, one may still envisage a role for the criminal law. What should happen, however, if the thief merely copies a few sentences from the existing book into her own manuscript? Or what if she merely writes, in her own work, about ideas also articulated in the first book? And what if the thief had not stolen the first book, but bought it from

---

14   For a modern equivalent of the "rich patron," see Sarah Hampson, "He Calls the Tunes," *The Globe and Mail* (12 December 2002), which depicts the largesse of the world's most generous donor to the arts, and the control he exercises over the donations. Another model is the one that gave rise to Linux and other "open source" software that is distributed for free over the Internet. The creation of this software is undertaken by thousands of computer programmers around the world collaborating on a part-time basis via the Internet. These people can spend part of their time working on open source software because they have regular paying jobs at universities, companies or governments, and the Internet allows their individual, intermittent efforts to bear collective fruit. For yet another model, consider the arrangements established by typeface designers in the late 1960s through the International Typeface Corporation to promote protection for their font designs: the interface between this industry and companies such as Adobe and Microsoft is described in *Monotype Corporation PLC* v. *International Typeface Corporation*, 43 F. 3d 443 (9th Cir. 1994).

15   For an answer to the question whether one can "steal" confidential information under the criminal law in Canada, see the discussion of *R*. v. *Stewart* (1988), 41 C.C.C. (3d) 481 (S.C.C.) in chapter 3, section B.1, "Theft."

a retailer who in turn acquired it from the authorized publisher of the work? These questions are more problematic from a legal perspective, and they raise a host of additional issues. Is it clear the author of the previous book was the first to describe a particular idea, or even use the particular words he used to describe it? Many ideas and information-based works and the form of expression found in them are, to a greater or lesser degree, derivative in their form and/or content.[16] The great scientific thinker, Sir Isaac Newton, articulated this concept well when, in paying homage to the authors of the great scientific works that preceded him and their influence upon his own thinking, exclaimed: "If I have seen further it is by standing on ye sholders of Giants."[17] Could there have been a Mozart without a Haydn to precede him, or a Brahms, Bruckner, or Mahler without a Beethoven? The stylistic similarities among the paintings of the Group of Seven Canadian landscape artists (and Tom Thomson) are uncanny. Of course, each bona fide painter, author, composer, or other creator adds new and different elements, but what exactly is old and what is new is often difficult to separate.[18] The criminal law is not well suited to this enquiry with information-based assets because the parameters of criminal offences should be very well delineated, given the serious consequences that flow from a conviction. The certainty of the physical parameters of tangible goods permits the criminal law to determine the ownership of such assets; the ephemeral nature of information — in essence, the second dynamic of computer law — requires the legal system to look beyond the criminal law for a regime to perform the same function.

Given the shortcomings of applying the criminal law of theft to information the way it is applied to physical assets, but cognizant of the need to protect at least certain aspects of information-based assets, the legal system has devised several specific regimes in order to afford protection to the creators and owners of intellectual properties, assets

---

16 For a short, but incisive, discussion of this point, see Rick Salutin, "Intelligent Theft Is a Pillar of Artistic Creation," *The Globe and Mail* (29 November 1996). See also James Adams, "What a Great Idea: I Think I'll Steal It," *The Globe and Mail* (19 February 2003).

17 This passage is cited in *Lotus Development Corporation* v. *Paperback Software International*, 740 F.Supp. 37 at 77 (D. Mass. 1990) [*Paperback*], where the court, rightfully, points out that in a copyright law context the tricky exercise is to determine just how broad these shoulders are and just how much a subsequent creator can step on them.

18 And the task of determining originality and degree of derivation becomes fiendishly complex when digitization tools are used in the production of works: see the discussion in chapter 1, section B.2, "Manipulation."

that emanate from the mind. The major regimes are: trade secrecy/ breach of confidence — to protect secret information; patents — to protect certain non-secret ideas that are implemented in inventions; and copyrights — to protect the expression of ideas. Each of these regimes, in its own particular manner, affords creators the right to limit the copying, use, and economic exploitation of specific aspects of information created by them. In economic terms, these intellectual property legal regimes exist to maintain artificial scarcity in information assets, thereby compensating for the lack of natural scarcity in information. To counteract the second dynamic of computer law — the elusive nature of information — intellectual property regimes have been crafted to give legal substance and form to certain aspects of information; that is, they cut down certain trees from the forest of ideas and with these trees build legal fences around certain creative content and inventions. The exercise is more daunting, though, because the better analogy is trying to carve chunks of air out of the atmosphere. Once this difficult task is accomplished — once the forest of ideas is subdued — the regimes that relate to publicly available information, namely patent and copyright, also recognize that the legal scarcity they establish should not continue indefinitely because society has a long-term interest in the wide dissemination and use of information. Therefore, these regimes protect for periods of time that are considered sufficient to provide adequate economic returns to creators, after which the protection ceases. In some cases, there are even limited exceptions to the exclusivity during the term of protection, as in the case of fair dealing with a copyright work for private study or research; to return to the forest metaphor, having cleared the land and given most of it over to private ownership, some parks and other public spaces are created for the betterment of all people.[19] In short, ensuring that adequate amounts of information are created, and guaranteeing the appropriate allocation of information resources within the economy and society at large, given their critical importance to the economy and society, require the establishment of sophisticated intellectual property legal regimes that carefully regulate the exploitation and disclosure of information so as to balance the needs of creators and users

---

19   Or, as the Federal Court of Appeal put it in a recent case, *CCH Canadian Ltd.* v. *Law Society of Upper Canada*, [2002] F.C.J. No. 690 (F.C.A.) [*CCH Canadian*] at para. 23: "The person who sows must be allowed to reap what is sown, but the harvest must ensure that society is not denied some benefit from the crops." The Supreme Court of Canada, in *Théberge*, above note 10, also stressed the importance of achieving a balance in copyright law between creators and users of copyright works.

of these important assets.[20] This involves a delicate balancing act among diverse and competing interests, an exercise the criminal law simply is incapable of fulfilling, and that the intellectual property law regimes strive to achieve.

B. THE ESSENTIALS OF INTELLECTUAL PROPERTY LAW REGIMES

Now that the rationale for intellectual property laws has been briefly discussed, this section describes, concisely, the key parameters of the principal intellectual property law regimes — trade secrecy, patents, copyright, semiconductor chip protection, and trade-marks. There are additional regimes, but they are of lesser importance, such as industri-

---

20 Nonetheless, there are cases that state that the sole purpose of copyright is the protection of authors: see for example, *Canadian Assn. of Broadcasters v. Society of Composers, Authors and Music Publishers of Canada* (1994), 58 C.P.R. (3d) 190 (F.C.A.). But see also *Apple Computer Inc. v. MacKintosh Computers Ltd.* (1986), 10 C.P.R. (3d) 1 (F.C.T.D.) [*Apple Computer*], where one of the purposes of the *Copyright Act* was said to be to encourage disclosure of works for the advancement of learning. Indeed, very early on in English copyright law the requirement for a balance between private and public interests was recognized: see *Sayre v. Moore* (1785) 1 East's Reports 361 at 362 (K.B.), in which the court, in deciding the scope of copyright protection in a map, stated: "The rule of decision in this case is a matter of great consequence to the country. In deciding it we must take care to guard against two extremes equally prejudicial; the one, that men of ability, who have employed their time for the service of the community, may not be deprived of their just merits, and the reward of their ingenuity and labour; the other, that the world may not be deprived of improvements, nor the progress of the arts be retarded."
    A contemporary articulation of this dual role of copyright law can be seen in the following two recitals in the Preamble of the *1996 World Intellectual Property Organization (WIPO) Copyright Treaty*:

    The Contracting Parties,
    ...
    Emphasizing the outstanding significance of copyright protection as an incentive for literary and artistic creation,
    Recognizing the need to maintain a balance between the rights of authors and the larger public interest, particularly education, research and access to information, as reflected in the Berne Convention,
    Have agreed as follows:
    ...

    This treaty is available from the WIPO Web site: <wipo.org/>.

al design registration and plant breeders' rights.[21] Some would also view the personality rights conferred by tort law as a species of intellectual property law, or at least affording intellectual property-type protection, but in this work they are dealt with in the context of privacy rights.[22] As for the regimes that are covered, the intent is to give a useful overview that focuses on the computer industry. Trade secrets/breach of confidence protects information that is not publicly known. Patents protect novel and inventive ideas that are not kept secret. Copyrights afford protection not for ideas but for the form of expression of ideas. Chip protection covers certain elements of the designs used to develop semiconductor chips. Trade-mark law prevents unfair competition by prohibiting competitors from using confusing marks and symbols to sell their goods or services. After discussing the core parameters of these intellectual property regimes, this section also explains a number of ownership issues and the principal remedial measures (such as injunctions and damages) common to them. The section ends with an overview of several of the international aspects of intellectual property law systems. The following section deals with particularly contentious issues in the intellectual property area.

1) Trade Secrets/Breach of Confidence

The law of trade secrets and breach of confidence affords important protection for a wide range of information-based assets that are not publicly known, by prohibiting someone from using or disclosing, or otherwise misappropriating, another person's trade secret or confidential information. Based on judge-made common law in Canada,[23] trade secrets/breach of confidence protection is particularly attractive to many creators of information because no administrative formalities are

---

21 See *Industrial Design Act*, R.S.C. 1985, C. I-9; and *Plant Breeders' Rights Act*, S.C. 1990, c. 20. For a discussion of the history and rationale of the latter, see *Harvard College* v. *Canada (Commissioner of Patents)* (2002) SCC 76 [*Harvard College*].

22 See chapter 4, section A.1, "Privacy Laws."

23 As compared with the United States, where most states have adopted a trade secrets statue: see Roger M. Milgrim, *Milgrim on Trade Secrets* (New York: Matthew Bender, 1986) (looseleaf, updated) [*Milgrim on Trade Secrets*]. Thus, in Canada, trade secrecy law is not governed by a federal statute, the way patents, copyrights and registered trade-marks are. It should be noted the United States also has a federal criminal law that covers theft of trade secrets: *Economic Espionage Act*, 18 U.S.C. §§1831–39.

required to obtain a trade secret and the protection extends indefinite-ly for so long as the information remains confidential.[24] The leading Canadian breach of confidence case, the decision of the Supreme Court of Canada in *LAC Minerals*,[25] articulates a three-part test for a breach of confidence to be actionable: first, the information must have the nec-essary quality of confidence; second, the information must be impart-ed in circumstances giving rise to an obligation of confidence; and third, there must be a misuse or unauthorized use of that information.[26] Prior to this decision, the doctrinal basis for trade secrets/breach of confidence protection in Canada was unclear, in some cases being based on property rights, in others on contract, and in yet others on

---

24   While persons in the computer industry often agree contractually that they can disclose each other's trade secrets after a certain period of time, such a limitation on the term of trade secrets is not required by law; indeed, for example, the *North American Free Trade Agreement*, in Article 1711(3), confirms that trade secret protection is to extend indefinitely (so long as the information maintains its confidential quality).

25   *LAC Minerals Ltd.* v. *International Corona Resources Ltd.* (1989), 26 C.P.R. (3d) 97 (S.C.C.) [*LAC Minerals*]. See also *Cadbury Schweppes Inc.* v. *FBI Foods Ltd.* (1999), 83 C.P.R. (3d) 289 (S.C.C.) [*Cadbury Schweppes*].

26   In some U.S. cases there has not yet been a disclosure or misuse, but the court grants relief because it finds it will be "inevitable" that trade secrets will be dis-closed. For an early example of this, involving the potential disclosure of a secret film manufacturing process of Kodak, see *Eastman Kodak Co.* v. *Powers Film Products*, 179 N.Y.S. 325 (4th Dep't 1919). See also *Pepsico, Inc.* v. *Redmond*, 54 F. 3d 1262 (7th Cir. 1995) [*Redmond*]. In Canada, the "inevitable disclosure" doctrine is receiving a lukewarm reception: see *ATI Technologies Inc.* v. *Henry*, [2000] O.J. No. 4596 (Ont. Sup. Ct.); and *Future Shop Ltd.* v. *Northwest–Atlantic (B.C.) Broker Inc.*, [2000] B.C.J. No. 2659 (B.C. Sup. Ct.). And even in the Unit-ed States not every form of trade secret disclosure warrants an injunction. For example, in *Ford Motor Company* v. *Robert Lane*, 67 F.Supp. 2d 745 (E.D. Mich. 1999), the court, on the strength of First Amendment rights, refused to enjoin disclosure of Ford's trade secrets on an Internet site, concluding: "The last cen-tury has seen substantial advances in communications, of which the Internet is only the most recent development. Each new medium, as it was introduced, changed the balance of power in the constitutional equation involving the First Amendment. Every advance in mass communication has enhanced the immedi-ate and widespread dissemination of information, often resulting in great poten-tial for immediate and irreparable harm. With the Internet, significant leverage is gained by the gadfly, who has no editor looking over his shoulder and no pro-fessional ethics to constrain him. Technology blurs the traditional identities of David and Goliath. Notwithstanding such technological changes, however, the Courts have steadfastly held that the First Amendment does not permit the prior restraint of speech by way of injunction, even in circumstances where the disclo-sure threatens vital economic interests."

equitable principles, including unjust enrichment.[27] The court in *LAC Minerals* concluded the right of action is *sui generis*, and is essentially a reflection of the policy that disclosures made in confidence between business people should be protected.[28] Essentially the same rationale has underpinned the law of breach of confidence in a non-commercial setting as well, as can be seen in the English "privacy" cases.[29]

A broad spectrum of information and information-based assets in the computer industry can come within the ambit of trade secrets/confidential information, including software, as well as the designs and specifications for software.[30] To appreciate the breadth of coverage of this branch of intellectual property protection, consider the following definition of a trade secret found in the Alberta law reform commission report on trade secrets: "information including but not limited to a formula, pattern, compilation, programme, method, technique, or process, or information contained or embodied in a product, device or mechanism which (i) is, or may be used in a trade or business, (ii) is not generally known in that trade or business, (iii) has economic value from not being generally known, and (iv) is the subject of efforts that are rea-

---

27   For a good discussion of the doctrinal underpinnings of trade law secret law prior to the decision in *LAC Minerals*, above note 25, see Institute of Law Research and Reform (Edmonton, Alberta) and A Federal Provincial Working Party, *Trade Secrets* (Report No. 46, July 1986) [*Trade Secrets*]. See also *Cadbury Schweppes*, above note 25. For a similar discussion from a Quebec perspective, see *Tri-Tex Co. v. Ghaly* (1999), 1 C.P.R. (4th) 160 (Que. C.A.) [*Tri-Tex*], where it was held that confidential information does not constitute "moveable property" under section 734(1) of the Quebec *Code of Civil Procedure*.

28   This same sentiment has animated U.S. trade secret law: see *Burten v. Milton Bradley Company*, 763 F.2d 461 at 467 (1st Cir. 1985), where the court expounded a dual rationale for trade secret law; first, to encourage the formulation and promulgation of ideas by ensuring that creators benefit from their creations; second, the "public has a manifest interest ... in the maintenance of standards of commercial ethics."

29   See chapter 4, section A.1(c), "Breaches of Confidence." See also *Interbrew SA v. Financial Times Ltd.*, [2001] EWHC B216 (H.C. Ch.), where the court reasoned that a duty of confidence attached to a third party merely by the fact of receiving a confidential document.

30   *Software Solutions Associates Inc. v. Depow* (1989), 25 C.P.R. (3d) 129 (N.B.Q.B.); *Matrox Electronic Systems Ltd. v. Gaudreau*, [1993] R.J.Q. 2449 (Que. Sup. Ct.) [*Matrox*]; and *Ticketnet Corp. v. Air* Canada (1987), 21 C.P.C. (2d) 38 (Ont. H.C.J.) [*Ticketnet*]. In a U.S. case, the architecture, organization, and structure of a computer program were protected as trade secrets: *Fabkom, Inc. v. R.W. Smith & Associates, Inc.*, 1997 Copyright Law Decisions (CCH) ¶27,590 at 29,476 (C.D. Cal. 1996) [*Fabkom*].

sonable under the circumstances to maintain its secrecy."[31] A trade secret, therefore, could include a plan for a new information-based product or service, before it was disclosed to the marketplace.[32] Even an amalgam of several publicly available elements of information is susceptible of protection where the final collection results in a unique composite of information.[33] The key is that the information not be available generally and that the discloser take reasonable steps to keep the information confidential.[34] One case found that the following protective measures taken by a software company were adequate to establish a trade secret: confidentiality issues were discussed with employees; employees signed confidentiality agreements; confidential documents were kept in locked filing cabinets; employees used passwords and confidential "log in" numbers to ensure computer security; employees and visitors wore identification badges; the premises were secured by an alarm system and patrolled by a security guard twenty-four hours a

.

---

31 *Trade Secrets*, above note 27 at 256. The idea, however, must be original and have some concreteness: see *Promotivate International Inc.* v. *Toronto Star Newspapers Ltd.* (1986), 8 C.P.R. (3d) 546 (Ont. S.C.). See also *Lueddeke* v. *Chevrolet Motor Co.*, 70 F. 2d 345 (8th Cir. 1934) where the court concluded that the act of pointing out a defect in the design of an automobile does not warrant proprietary rights protection. On the other hand, for an example of a finding of breach of confidentiality in the biotech/pharmaceutical field, see *Apotex Fermentation Inc.* v. *Novopharm Ltd.* (1998), 80 C.P.R. (3d) 449 (Man. C.A.) [*Apotex*].

32 For a discussion as to whether "strategic content planning" for an Internet content company can be a trade secret, see *EarthWeb, Inc.* v. *Mark Schlack*, 71 F. Supp. 2d 299 (S.D.N.Y. 1999) [*EarthWeb*].

33 In *ICAM Technologies Corp.* v. *EBCO Industries Ltd.* (1991), 36 C.P.R. (3d) 504 (B.C.S.C.) [*ICAM*], a business plan for a new venture involving several high-technology elements and government procurement opportunities, none of which was secret in itself, was held to be confidential when considered as a whole. See also *Telex Corporation* v. *International Business Machines Corporation*, 367 F.Supp. 258 (N.D. Okla. 1973) in which a combination of material that was not new, novel, secretive, or innovative was protected as a trade secret because together they formed a valuable "design composite."

34 Milgrim, *Milgrim on Trade Secrets*, above note 23, cites a U.S. case, *Management Science America, Inc.* v. *Cyborg Systems, Inc.*, 1977-1 Trade Cases (CCH) ¶61,472 (N.D. Ill. 1977), in which a software program was still considered to be a trade secret after 600 copies of it were distributed because each was accompanied by a restrictive software licence. See also *Data General Corporation* v. *Digital Computer Controls, Inc.*, 188 U.S.P.Q. 276 (Del. Cir. Ct. 1975), where the court upheld the secrecy of multiple copies of documentation distributed with computers because of, among other reasons, the proprietary rights notice contained on them.

day; and access to every section of the premises was regulated by a "Cardkey" reader.[35]

Just as a wide variety of information is capable of being protected under the doctrine of trade secrets/breach of confidence, so there are numerous circumstances in which a duty of confidence can arise. Probably the most common problematic confidee — if the volume of litigation is any indicator — is the employee of the knowledge-based business.[36] Many judicial decisions have found former employees liable under trade secret law for disclosing the former employer's trade secrets to the new employer, an entity often owned by the departing employees.[37] In these employee-related cases, courts have the fiendishly difficult task of distinguishing between the general skill and knowledge of the employee, which the employee is able to exercise after leaving the employer, as compared with the proprietary information of the former employer, which may not be so used by the former employee. Information, however, is an elusive asset (as noted by the second dynamic of computer law), and drawing the line between that which is owned by an employer and that which is owned by the employer's former employee can be an almost Sisyphean exercise.[38] In one case, for

---

35 *Matrox*, above note 30. Similar measures were held to support the finding of trade secrets in the American software-related case in *Vermont Microsystems, Inc. v. Autodesk, Inc.*, 5 Computer Cases (CCH) ¶47,210 at 67,224 (D. Vt. 1994) [*Vermont Microsystems*].

36 The amount of litigation should be judged not simply by decided cases, but by the number of claims begun that ultimately settle before a decision, such as the following: Lawrence Surtees, "Nortel Loses Bid to Stop Rival From Raiding Work Force: But Judge Bans 10 Employees From Divulging Trade Secrets," *The Globe and Mail* (4 November 1999); and Wendy Stueck, "Burntsand Denies It Conspired to Obtain Trade Secrets," *The Globe and Mail* (25 November 1999).

37 For example, see *Matrox*, above note 30. And in *Equus Computer Systems, Inc. v. Northern Computer Systems, Inc.*, Civ. No. 01-657 (DWF/AJB; D.C. Minn. 22 July 2002), detailed customer information that was not publicly available was held to be a trade secret deserving of protection. For a recent low-tech example of this kind of holding, see *Clayburn Industries Ltd. v. Piper*, [1998] B.C.J. No. 2831 (B.C.S.C.).

38 In *Matrox*, above note 30, the court at 2461–62 stated: "Unfortunately, this artificial classification of human knowledge is simply unworkable and unrealistic in today's information economy. As most of the personnel employed in the computer and electronic industries today are highly specialized, the old classifications, generalized v. specialized, and subjective v. objective (which were always difficult to apply in any event) have been rendered almost meaningless. In passing, the Court suggests that there is no such thing as objective knowledge that was not previously somebody's subjective knowledge!" See also the passage from the *Teleride Sage* case at note 42 below. If it is any consolation, while this dilemma of separating general skill and knowledge from proprietary information is particularly acute in

example, portions of a plaintiff's statement of claim were struck out for not describing with sufficient particularity the specific confidential information that was allegedly taken by the former employees.[39] Given the difficulty of differentiating between the two, and the difficulties caused by the second dynamic of computer law generally, employers often address the issue in a contract with the employee, sometimes adding a non-competition provision to help ensure, prophylactically, the protection of the employer's trade secrets. Such agreements must be drafted with great care, as the restrictions in them must be reasonable from the perspective of the term of the restriction, the actual activity being restricted, and the geographic scope of the restriction.[40] Many courts generally disfavour post-employment non-competition restrictions, and will not enforce them if, for example, the protection can be secured through a customer non-solicitation provision in the same agreement, unless the company has a special proprietary interest to protect, which will often be the case in the technology industry.[41] In

---

technology-related situations, this conundrum predates the computer age: see *Amber Size and Chemical Company, Limited* v. *Menzel*, [1913] 2 Ch. 239.

39   *SLM Software Inc.* v. *Dimitri* (1996), 65 C.P.R. (3d) 330 (Ont. Gen. Div.). For a similar result in the United States, see *ECT International, Inc.* v. *John Zwerlein*, 8 CCH Computer Cases ¶47,973 at 71,870 (Wis. Ct. App. 1999). Particularly where the former employee was employed in a sales capacity, it can be difficult to prevent subsequent competition by means of a breach of confidential information claim, even where the employee was a fiduciary: see *Edac Inc.* v. *Joseph Tullo*, [1999] O.J. No. 4837 (Ont. Sup. Ct. 1999) [*Edac*].

40   Non-compete agreements can be used in a number of other scenarios where one party is concerned that, upon the disclosure of sensitive information, the recipient of the information will use the information to compete against the discloser. For example, in *Ben Israel* v. *Vitacare Medical Products Inc.*, [1999] O.J. No. 2272, 122 O.A.C. 57 (C.A.), a contract manufacturer was held liable in damages for breaching an oral non-competition arrangement with a commercial customer when the manufacturer began selling therapeutic pillows that were very similar to the ones made by the manufacturer. The importance of the non-compete in this case was heightened because it was questionable whether the type of information disclosed to the contract manufacturer would be sufficiently confidential to come within the *LAC Minerals* test.

41   See, for example, *Lyons* v. *Multari* (2000), 50 O.R. (3d) 526 (C.A.). However, even in this decision the court acknowledged that non-compete restrictions are warranted where the discloser had a "proprietary interest worthy of protection." And courts are particularly willing to assist former employers where the departing executive can be characterized as a fiduciary: see *McCormick Delisle & Thompson Inc.* v. *Ballantyne*, [2001] O.J. No. 1783 (Ont. C.A.). In the context of the difficult competing interests at play in these agreements (see Caroline Alphonso, "Corporate Confidentiality's Balancing Act," *The Globe and Mail* (26

one case, a six-month non-competition period for a software programmer that covered North America and the United Kingdom was upheld,
the court concluding that such non-competition covenants are "about
the only efficacious means that an employer has to gain some measure
of protection [over its trade secrets]."[42] In the United States, when
there are overt thefts of trade secrets, a court may, in rare circumstances, enjoin an employee from working for a competitor, typically
for up to six months, even in the absence of an express non-compete
agreement.[43] On the other hand, in one American case, a twelve-month
non-compete restriction for an employee in an Internet content business was considered too long, and hence unenforceable, given the
dynamic nature of the online content industry.[44] In short, technology

---

April 2002)), it is interesting to note that Canada's largest technology company
uses a post-employment incentive vehicle whereby if the former employee
makes any profit on stock options from the company, these must be given up to
the company if the individual joins a competitor to the company within a specified time after leaving the company. In *Nortel Networks Inc. v. Jervis*, [2002] O.J.
No. 12 (Sup. Ct.), this mechanism was found enforceable, and the employee was
required to transfer $626,857.74 (for which he was reimbursed by his new
employer, Newbridge Networks, due to a separate agreement he made with
them).

42   *Teleride Sage Ltd. v. Ventures West Management Inc.* (1996), 67 C.P.R. (3d) 361 at
362 (Ont. Gen. Div.) [*Teleride Sage*]. In this case the court stated at 361–62: "It
is obvious in an industry based on innovation, inspiration, rapid obsolescence,
shared information and group dynamics that it will always be exceedingly difficult to determine what skills and information fall within the definition of confidential information, that it will be difficult for the most honest employee to
know what skills and knowledge he can share with his new employer and that it
will be exceedingly difficult for the former employer to determine what the former employee is, in fact, sharing with the new employer. What is not sophisticated, difficult of interpretation, or difficult to police is the non-competition
clause of reasonable length and geographical scope." For a good text covering
restrictive covenants, including those found in an employment context, see
Michael J. Trebilcock, *The Common Law of Restraint of Trade: A Legal and Economic Analysis* (Toronto: Carswell, 1986).

43   In *DoubleClick, Inc. v. Henderson*, 1997 N.Y. Misc. LEXIS 577 (Sup. Ct. N.Y. Co.
1997), two senior executives of the Internet advertising company were enjoined
from launching their own company or joining a competitor for six months, after
having been caught taking trade secrets as they surreptitiously plotted to form
their own company to compete directly with *DoubleClick*. See also *Redmond*,
above note 26.

44   *EarthWeb*, above note 32. It also did not help the former employer's case that the
non-compete had no geographic limit. Importantly, though, the court in *Earth-
Web* did acknowledge that non-compete clauses are enforceable in appropriate
circumstances, just not those in the specific case before it.

companies must give careful consideration to the crafting of non-competition provisions to try to ensure that they are not overly broad and that they protect truly proprietary interests, and ideally these agreements should be negotiated and not merely imposed.

The flip side of the claims that employers bring against former employees is what responsibility the new employer has when hiring the former employee of another company. While intellectual property claims are, of course, about intellectual property, in trade secret/confidential information claims they are invariably about people as well. That is, it is virtually always the case that an individual who is "contagious" with a previous employer's information "contaminates" the new employer. Sometimes the employee is specifically hired to work in an area directly competitive with the former employer.[45] In one case, however, the employee was not initially hired to work on a competitive product, but rather over time he insinuated himself into the new employer's competitive product.[46] And even where the new employer consciously requests the employee not to infringe the former employer's proprietary information, this admonition will be ignored by the court and a finding of vicarious liability entered, particularly where the court finds evidence that the new employer was wilfully blind as to the risk of contamination posed by the new employee.[47] Thus, the lesson to be drawn from all these cases (given the elusive nature of information, as posited by the second dynamic of computer law) is that employers must be extremely vigilant when hiring or otherwise retaining staff who worked on potentially competitive projects previously. It is also prudent to continually review the activities and practices of employees, so that any industrial espionage will be discovered and enjoined promptly.[48]

Beyond employees, courts have been prepared to impress a duty of confidence on a number of recipients of trade secrets. For example, in one case an interim injunction was granted against an entity that had been previously negotiating a potential joint venture arrangement in the high-technology industry when this company apparently threatened to launch a competing business on its own, thereby possibly mis-

---

45   *Computer Associates International, Inc.* v. *Altai, Inc.*, 3 Computer Cases (CCH) ¶46,505 at 63,357 (E.D.N.Y. 1991), aff'd 982 F.2d 693 (2d Cir. 1992).
46   *Vermont Microsystems*, above note 35.
47   *Apotex*, above note 31.
48   See "Procter & Gamble, Unilever Settle Espionage Suit," *The Globe and Mail* (7 September 2001), for an example of how rogue employees can get a company in trouble in this area.

appropriating trade secrets of the plaintiff.[49] In another case, a partner in a high-technology initiative was stopped from having business discussions with another potential partner, as this could cause a leak of information.[50] As well, a supplier of computer services has been prohibited from possibly disclosing one customer's information to another client,[51] and a purchaser of high-technology equipment has been held liable for disclosing one supplier's trade secrets to another supplier.[52] In an American case, a user was held to have violated a software supplier's trade secrets when the user conveyed to a third party specifications for a bond trading system, the court finding that the user's list of specifications was influenced by the plaintiff's software that the user had been operating for years.[53] This case, as well as others, illustrates with poignancy the second dynamic of computer law, the elusive nature of information, and should teach recipients of trade secrets/confidential information to be extremely circumspect in respect of what

---

49   *Alphanet Telecom Inc.* v. *Delrina Corp.* (1994), 53 C.P.R. (3d) 156 (Ont. Gen. Div.) [*Alphanet*]. In the United States, there are a number of "submission of idea" cases, where, for example, a (plaintiff) inventor with an idea for a new product or service approaches a (defendant) potential business partner, with a view to jointly developing and exploiting the idea. For a good review of the American case law, which is extremely fact-specific, that results when the defendant confidee decides to take the idea forward without the plaintiff inventor, see *Nadel* v. *Play-by-Play Toys & Novelties, Inc.*, 208 F.3d 368 (2d Cir. 2000). For a recent Canadian case in the same genre, see *Enterprise Excellence Corp.* v. *Royal Bank of Canada*, [2002] O.J. No. 3086 (Ont. Sup. Ct.), where the plaintiffs argued that the defendant bank misappropriated their concept for a certain marketing program idea targeted at small and medium sized businesses. The court concluded the bank did not take the idea for the program, as it was independently working on its own equivalent program. However, the court did find the bank took the plaintiffs' name for the program, "Today's Entrepreneur," and awarded damages of $520,000, based on the interesting finding that by taking the name, the bank precluded the plaintiffs from proceeding with their entire program. One wonders why the plaintiffs could not have simply changed the name of their program.

50   *Ticketnet*, above note 30. For a low-tech trade secret case involving one potential business partner bringing a claim against the other, see *Sweet Factory Inc.* v. *Hudson's Bay Co.* (1995), 85 C.P.R. (3d) 417 (Ont. Gen. Div.).

51   *Computer Workshops Ltd.* v. *Banner Capital Market Brokers Ltd.* (1990), 74 D.L.R. (4th) 767 (Ont. C.A.).

52   *Wil-Can Electronics Can. Ltd.* v. *Ontario (Ministry of the Solicitor General)*, [1992] O.J. No. 2537 (Gen. Div.) [*Wil-Can Electronics*].

53   *Fabkom*, above note 30. For a recent British case where the court found the defendant's bond-trading system to infringe the proprietary rights in the plaintiff's software, see *Cantor Fitzgerald International* v. *Tradition (U.K.) Ltd.*, The Times, 19 May 1999 [*Cantor Fitzgerald*].

they have access to in order to avoid contaminating themselves.[54] Given that the parameters of confidential information are difficult to determine in advance — judges often have difficulty even in hindsight — parties should through contract, technology, and by minimizing exposure attempt to reduce the likelihood of a breach of trade secrets/confidence claim. As noted above in respective of the "contagious" employee, all organizations should manage their use of trade secrets/confidential information in a pro-active manner: an ounce of prevention is worth a pound of painful cure.[55]

2) Patents

The *Patent Act*[56] grants the holder of a patent the exclusive right within Canada to make, use, or sell the invention covered by the patent for a period of twenty years from the date the application for the patent was filed.[57] Inventions that can be patented comprise processes, machines, manufactures, and composition of matter; by contrast, scientific formulae cannot be patented. Trade secrets, then, are secret ideas; patents cover applied ideas. As a result, patents have been issued for a wide range of devices associated with computers and their predecessors, including the telegraph, the telephone, the radio,[58] many components of the computer, the semiconductor chip, and encryption technologies.[59]

---

54 In *TDS Healthcare Systems Corporation* v. *Humana Hospital Illinois, Inc.*, 880 F.Supp. 1572 (N.D. Ga. 1995), the defendant acquired a hospital that used the plaintiff's software. When an affiliate of the defendant that developed software competitive with the plaintiff's software obtained access to the plaintiff's software, the defendant was found liable for, among other reasons, not using best efforts to prevent the unauthorized disclosure of the plaintiff's software, as required by the relevant software licence agreement.

55 The expense of the cure is not merely in damages awarded, or the competition-stunting injunction, nor even the (usually not insubstantial) legal fees attendant on litigating such cases, but is also partly (and perhaps most importantly) in the huge amount of senior management time that needs to be invested in such matters once they become litigious.

56 R.S.C. 1985, c. P-4. The *Patent Act* is federal legislation, as the subject matter of "Patents of Invention and Discovery" is a federal power under the *Constitution Act, 1867* (U.K.), 30 & 31 Vict., c. 3, s. 91(22). The *Constitution Act, 1867* can be found in R.S.C. 1985, Appendix II, No. 5.

57 For patents granted with respect to applications filed in Canada and the United States prior to 1 October 1989 and 8 June 1995, respectively, the term of protection is seventeen years from the date of issuance of the patent.

58 For an analysis that recounts the importance of patents in the development of the radio, and other early communications technologies such as the telegraph, see Spar, *Ruling the Waves*, above note 12.

Today, patents cover a variety of devices, such as the writing heads in computer hard drives, a device for allowing cellular phones to send faxes,[60] and more controversially, numerous software programs and specific features in computer programs, as well as Internet-based and other business methods.[61] For example, it is not surprising that IBM applied for the largest number of patents at the U.S. Patent Office in 1999,[62] and indeed in each of the nine years prior to 2001.[63] IBM and other like-minded companies find patents attractive because, notwithstanding that their duration is quite short relative to copyright protection, a patent is the most powerful form of intellectual property protection.[64] A patent is effective against everyone, not just a copier or someone who misappropriates, as is the case with copyrights and trade secrets; in other words, independent creation, which is a defence to a copyright or trade secret claim, is not a defence to a patent infringement claim. Given this high level of protection, several important tests must be met before a patent is issued, and indeed, even after a patent is issued a third party can

59   For the patent on the first public key encryption system, see U.S. Patent No. 4,405,829, issued September 20, 1983. Many have been issued since. For a discussion of the regulation of encryption technology, see chapter 4, sections B.3, "Regulating the Export of Encryption Technologies," and C, "Regulating the Domestic Use of Encryption Technologies."

60   *Polansky Electronics*, above note 13. See also Brad Daisley, "Alberta Digital Fax Inventor Wins Patent Infringement Lawsuit," *The Lawyers Weekly* (17 December 1999).

61   See section C.2, "Patent Protection for Software and Business Methods."

62   Tom Foremski, "IBM Breaks Record for US Patents," *Financial Times* (12 January 2000). This article notes that while IBM's patent portfolio covers a wide range of technologies, including semiconductors, data storage systems and network equipment, recently its patents have been focusing on e-business applications: in 1999, 900 of its 2756 patents related to these activities, including many for software and business processes. This article also states that IBM earned more than $1 billion in annual revenues from its patent licensing program.

63   Erika Jonietz, "Economic Bust, Patent Boom," *Technology Review*, May 2002 ["Patent Boom"]. This article points out that by 2001, IBM's patent licence revenue had increased to $1.5 billion.

64   The U.S. Patent and Trademark Office issued 161,000 patents in 1999, double the number ten years before: "Who Owns the Knowledge Economy," *The Economist*, 8 April 2000 ["Who Owns the Knowledge Economy"]. Erika Jonietz, in "Patent Boom," above note 63, notes that while the technology sector was in a downturn in 2001, the U.S. Patent Office received a record number of patent applications that year, 344,717. Canadian companies are also coming to understand the value of patents: Lily Nguyen, "Wi-Lan Names Radiata in Suit: Alleges Patent Infringement," *The Globe and Mail* (25 November 2000). This article states that Wi-Lan, based in Calgary, is claiming more than $780-million in this patent infringement litigation.

attack the patent on the grounds that one of these tests was not in fact met at the time the application was filed, notwithstanding that the patent office was of a different view when it issued the patent. The first requirement is that the invention be "useful," that is, that it work and have utility in an industrial sense. Most computer and software-related inventions have little difficulty meeting this test. Also, the invention must be novel, meaning that it cannot have been known or disclosed more than twelve months prior to the filing of the application for the patent. Given Canada's "first to file system," where the first person to lodge the patent application with the Patent Office has priority even if someone else may have invented it earlier, prudence dictates filing the application before any public disclosure is made of the invention. This practice of early, pre-disclosure filing is reinforced by the fact that some countries consider any disclosure prior to filing to invalidate the patent. Thus, in the fast-paced computer business one must be extremely vigilant not to disclose the invention prematurely, perhaps at a trade show or user group meeting or some other venue, where a description of the invention before a filing of a patent application can be fatal to the hopes for the patent. Equally, in a university environment, where the doctrine of "publish or perish" often leads professors to disclose patentable material before a patent filing, professors and administrators involved with software (and other) patentable technologies and research must realize that early publication may cause the patent to perish. Notwithstanding the importance of the novelty requirement, perhaps the most difficult test that an invention must meet in order to be patented is that it not be obvious; in other words, courts have long required the invention to exhibit a certain degree of inventiveness beyond that which would be considered average in the industry.[65] A leading case summarizes this test as whether an unimaginative technician (and not a competent expert) skilled in the art would have come upon the solution taught by the patent; if so, then the invention is not deserving of a patent.[66] Put another way, the invention

---

65   Traditionally, the requirement for inventiveness was judicially inferred from the term invention; since the enactment of s. 283 in 1993, the *Patent Act* has contained a specific provision requiring an invention to be non-obvious.

66   See *Beloit Canada Ltd.* v. *Valmet Oy* (1986), 8 C.P.R. (3d) 289 at 294 (F.C.A.), in which the court stated: "The test for obviousness is not to ask what competent inventors did or would have done to solve the problem. Inventors are by definition inventive. The classical touchstone for obviousness is the technician skilled in the art but having no scintilla of inventiveness or imagination; a paragon of deduction and dexterity, wholly devoid of intuition; a triumph of the left hemisphere over the right. The question to be asked is whether this mythical creature

or the improvement, to be patentable, must go beyond what was common knowledge at the time of the filing of the application.

The patent application, and, if it issues, the patent itself, contains a rather detailed description of the invention and its proposed application, including a disclosure of prior art related to the invention as well as the best mode of working the patent. This detailed disclosure represents a key public policy rationale for patents, namely, that in return for what is often an extremely strong monopoly position, albeit for a limited time, the patent holder must disclose the invention to the public.[67] This disclosure then allows others to learn the workings of the patent, and to prepare to work it after the patent expires, as well as possibly to work around it during its term. Following the detailed description will be the specific claims, which set out the particular parameters of the monopoly by describing the precise features that the patent holder claims are new and inventive and for which the monopoly is granted. It is these claims that are examined to determine if the impugned device infringes upon the patent, either because the infringer's product clearly comes within the purview of the patent claims, or because the invention has been taken in terms of its substance, or "pith and marrow," as some judges refer to the essence of the patented invention.[68] In a recent Supreme

---

(the man in the Clapham omnibus of patent law) would, in the light of the state of the art and of common general knowledge as at the claimed date of invention, have come directly and without difficulty to the solution taught by the patent. It is a very difficult test to satisfy." See also *Xerox of Canada Ltd. v. IBM Canada Ltd.* (1977), 33 C.P.R. (2d) 24 (F.C.T.D.), in which the court reviewed a number of English cases that have considered the obviousness test.

67   As Binnie J. put it in *Whirlpool Corp. v. Camco Inc.*, [2000] 2 S.C.R. 1067 (Sup. Ct. Can.) [*Whirlpool*] at para. 42: "The disclosure is the quid provided by the inventor in exchange for the quo of a 17-year [now 20-year] monopoly on the exploitation of the invention." Similarly, in *Free World Trust v. Électro Santé Inc.*, [2000] 2 S.C.R. 1024 (Sup. Ct. Can.) [*Free World*], Binnie J. states: "Patent protection rests on the concept of a bargain between the inventor and the public. In return for disclosure of the invention to the public, the inventor acquires for a limited time the exclusive right to exploit it. It was ever thus." Binnie J. expresses the same sentiment in his minority decision in *Harvard College*, above note 21.

68   *AT&T Technologies v. Mitel*, [1989] F.C.J. No. 604 (F.C.T.D.). In this case Madam Justice Reed, at 9, also confirmed another key principle of patent interpretation, namely, that "in construing a patent one must adopt a purposive construction and not engage in an overclose parsing of the words." In *Whirlpool*, above note 67, the Supreme Court of Canada confirmed the importance of purposive construction as a key mechanic of patent interpretation. In this case, Binnie J. also took the view, at para. 53, that a broader interpretative approach to patent claim construction is to be preferred to a strictly literal, "dictionary" approach: "A second difficulty with the appellants' dictionary approach is that it urges the Court

Court of Canada decision,[69] Binnie J. sets out a process for undertaking claims analysis that is intended to achieve predictability and fairness.[70] Nevertheless, patent interpretation and claims analysis will always be difficult and controversial because, while the claims of the patent serve as the inventor's fence around the relevant invention, this fence is not a physical one, but (given the second dynamic of computer law, namely, the elusive nature of information) rather it is one built with words, and therefore always subject to ambiguity and uncertainty, especially after withering cross-examination by an expert patent litigator. Thus, it takes significant skill to draft patent claims well, particularly in the area of software patents, and in Canada expert patent agents perform this task. Patent agents, who alone can prosecute a patent application to issuance before the Patent Office other than the inventor, are also able to perform searches of existing patents at various patent offices to obtain a preliminary sense of whether a proposed patent will be permitted.

---

to look at the words through the eyes of a grammarian or etymologist rather than through the eyes and with the common knowledge of a worker of ordinary skill in the field to which the patent relates. An etymologist or grammarian might agree with the appellants that a vane of any type is still a vane. However, the patent specification is not addressed to grammarians, etymologists or to the public generally, but to skilled individuals sufficiently versed in the art to which the patent relates to enable them on a technical level to appreciate the nature and description of the invention." At the same time, however, Binnie J., in *Free World*, above note 67, warns against using such vague interpretative notions as the "spirit of the invention," when conducting claims analysis.

69   *Free World*, above note 67.
70   *Ibid.*, at para. 43: "Predictability is achieved by tying the patentee to its claims; fairness is achieved by interpreting those claims in an informed and purposive way." A debate about the proper scope of a patent monopoly has also been resolved in the United States through a re-examination and narrowing of the "doctrine of equivalents" (which traditionally had provided a fairly broad protection beyond the literal terms of the patent): see *Festo Corporation v. Shoketsu Kinzoku Kogyo Kabushiki Co., Ltd.*, 234 F.3d 558 (Fed. Cir. 2000); affirmed 535 U.S. 722 (Sup. Ct. 2002) [*Festo*]. It is interesting to note that in *Free World*, above note 67, no infringement is ultimately found because the patent-in-issue's essential element was a circuit-based system, while the allegedly infringing (but judicially determined non-infringing) product utilized a microcontroller, such as a personal computer. This led Binnie J., at para. 32, to another colourful analogy, especially for men who are follicly challenged: "Based on the foregoing principles, I conclude that the appellant's arguments must be rejected. As stated, the ingenuity of the patent lies not in the identification of a desirable result but in teaching one particular means to achieve it. The claims cannot be stretched to allow the patentee to monopolize anything that achieves the desirable result. It is not legitimate, for example, to obtain a patent for a particular method that grows hair on bald men and thereafter claim that anything that grows hair on bald men infringes."

Companies in the computer industry are well advised to consult with a patent agent in order to gauge the opportunities for achieving competitive advantage through filing for patents. Equally important is reviewing the patent filings of competitors to ensure, from a defensive perspective, that all necessary precautions in terms of product design are being taken to avoid infringing the rights of others. At a minimum this would involve searching for patents and patent applications filed under the name of competitors. More extensive searches would include infringement searches, and even prior art searches in some situations, to gauge the state of patents and patentability generally vis-à-vis an inventor's handiwork. In short, patents should be thought of both offensively and defensively. It should be noted, however, that currently a patent search cannot reveal all filings submitted to the Patent Office because patent applications are kept confidential for eighteen months after they are filed. Therefore, it can happen that a patent search result comes up clear, and a person relies on this result to start marketing her particular product, only to be confronted subsequently by a patent the filing date of which predates the commencement of the person's marketing, and hence is enforceable against the person. While this problem exists in any sector of the economy where patents are a factor, this is a particularly dangerous problem in the hyperkinetic computer industry (given the first dynamic of computer law, namely the rapid pace of technological change).

3) Copyright

Where trade secrets protect ideas (that are kept secret) and patents protect applied ideas implemented in an invention, copyright protects only the form of expression of ideas.[71] The *Copyright Act*[72] grants this pro-

---

71   See *Matrox*, above note 30 at 2455: "It is fundamental that copyright can protect the form of expression of computer programs, but not the ideas embodied therein." See also *Delrina Corp. v. Triolet Systems Inc.* (1993), 47 C.P.R. (3d) 1 (Ont. Gen. Div.); affirmed (2002) 17 C.P.R. (4th) 289 (Ont. C.A.) [*Delrina*]. Note as well Article 2 of the *WIPO Copyright Treaty*, available from the WIPO Web site <wipo.org> that provides "Scope of Copyright Protection: Copyright protection extends to expressions and not to ideas, procedures, methods of operation or mathematical concepts as such." The case of *Cuisenaire v. South West Imports Ltd.*, [1969] S.C.R. 208, gives a good low-tech example of this principle, as it held that the copyright in a book describing a method of teaching mathematics through "teaching rods" cannot protect, or preserve for the author any protection in, the method of teaching itself or the "teaching rods." See also *Tri-Tex*, above note 27, where it was held that chemical formulae are ideas and therefore not subject to copyright.

72   R.S.C. 1985, c. C-42. The *Copyright Act*, like the *Patent Act*, is federal legislation as copyrights are a federal power under the *Constitution Act, 1867* (U.K.), 30 &

tection for expression by reserving to the copyright owner the exclusive right to reproduce the copyright work or any substantial part of it, and to exercise certain other rights including publication and translation of the copyright work, the right to perform the work in public, and the right to communicate the work to the public by telecommunication, as well as the right to authorize any of the foregoing. The *Copyright Act* also prohibits the rental, for a motive of gain, of computer software and sound recordings that are capable of being reproduced. Relatively recent amendments to the *Copyright Act* also give performers (such as actors, singers, and musicians), the makers of sound recordings, and broadcasters copyright in the reproduction of their respective performances, sound recordings, and communication signals, as well as the right of sound recording performers and makers to receive royalties for public and broadcasting performances of such works (previously only composers and lyricists were entitled to such royalties). Other fairly recent amendments to the *Copyright Act*[73] also established a compensation regime whereby performers, producers, and composers are to be paid the proceeds of a new tax levied on blank audio recording media, such as cassettes, in return for private copying of musical works no longer being an infringement of copyright.[74] These new provisions

---

31 Vict., c. 3, subs. 91(23), found in R.S.C. 1985, Appendix II, No. 5. Canada's original *Copyright Act* came into force in 1924. Copyright is a creature of the *Copyright Act*; there is no more a common law copyright; for example, see *Apple Computer Inc.* v. *Mackintosh Computers Ltd.* (1986), 10 C.P.R. (3d) 1 (F.C.T.D.).

73   The most recent large-scale amendments to the *Copyright Act*, contained in Bill C-32, *An Act to Amend the Copyright Act*, S.C. 1997, c. 24, amending R.S.C. 1985, c. C-24, amending R.S.C. 1985, c. C-42, were passed by Parliament in April 1997 (and are referred to herein as the "Bill C-32 amendments" or "Bill C-32"). Most recently, Bill C-11 (formerly Bill C-48) received Royal Assent on December 13, 2002. This latest narrow amendment of the *Copyright Act* is discussed in note 303 below.

74   Retailers, of course, do not like the levy: Keith Damsell, "Groups at Odds Over Hidden Copyright Fees," *The Globe and Mail* (11 December 2002). More interestingly, the software industry, which buys a lot of CDs for distributing its software and not for copying music, does not like this new system, as it requires them to "pay for the sins of others": Caroline Alphonso, "Software Firms Fume Over Proposed CD Levy," *The Globe and Mail* (18 July 2000). See also David Paterson, "Recordable Media Levy Handicaps High-Tech Sector," *The Globe and Mail* (4 January 2000); and David Akin, "Plan Could Boost CD Prices," *The Globe and Mail* (12 March 2002). Mr. Paterson, the head of the Canadian Advanced Technology Alliance, bemoans the fact that "The industry uses millions of CD-Rs to distribute low-volume software for operating manuals and data storage. None of these uses has anything to do with the private copying of music."

recognize the third dynamic of computer law, namely, that the boundary between the private and public realms is blurring, and that enforcement of the law against copying for private use is very difficult but of increasing concern because of the improved quality of copies made with digital technologies; thus, this radically different approach to compensation for creators of copyright materials.[75] The *Copyright Act* also prohibits what may be termed *secondary infringement*, namely, where a person sells, leases, distributes, exhibits, or imports into Canada any work that to the person's knowledge is infringing copyright or would infringe copyright if it had been made in Canada. Mention should also be made of the fact that in addition to giving copyright owners the right to control the copying and the other protected uses of their copyright works, the *Copyright Act* also gives to creators so-called moral rights, which permit the creator to protect the integrity of the work, namely, to prevent it from being distorted or mutilated, and to have the author's name remain associated with the work.[76] Moral rights, which prohibit anyone other than the creator from modifying or altering the work in a manner that would dishonour the creator's reputation, are particularly germane in respect of multimedia works where images, among other elements, can be easily manipulated and modified once they are in digital form (once again providing evidence of the second dynamic of computer law, namely, the elusive nature of information, particularly after it is freed from the constraints of paper and allowed to "dance around" in electronic form). While moral rights cannot be assigned or transferred, they can be waived, and it is fairly common practice in the computer and online industries to have creative staff waive their moral rights in the works they create.

---

75 A government background document to Bill C-32 cites a report of the Task Force on the Future of the Canadian Music Industry that notes that nearly 44 million blank tapes were sold in Canada in 1995, of which it is estimated 39 million were used by consumers to copy sound recordings: "Legislative Highlights" available at <pch.gc.ca/main/c32/back.htm>. Nonetheless, as noted in note 74 above, criticism has been levelled at the new private copying exemption/blank tape levy on the basis that it is a blunt instrument and legitimizes a free copying mentality that may well spill over to other works. It is interesting to speculate if the blank tape levy will, over time, be the model for compensation regimes in other areas such as home movies and computer software.

76 For a case involving a claim of violation of moral rights in a computer game's graphic display, and the underlying software, see *Nintendo of America Inc.* v. *Camerica Corp.* (1991), 36 C.P.R. (3d) 352 (F.C.A.) [*Camerica*]. See also *Snow* v. *The Eaton Centre Ltd.* (1982), 70 C.P.R. (2d) 105 (Ont. H.C.J.). For a case that makes a clear distinction between, on the one hand, the economic, and on the other hand, the moral, rights of copyright, see *Théberge*, above note 10.

Creators of software, multimedia products and other information-based assets find copyright protection attractive because of its relatively long term; in Canada, the copyright in a work generally subsists for the lifetime of the author of the work plus 50 years, though certain rights, such as the rights of performers and sound recording makers, are only 50 years in duration; in some countries, notably recently the United States, the term of copyright has been extended to the lifetime of the author plus 70 years. In the case of works of joint authorship, which would include most software and other information-based assets, the 50-year period begins to run from the death of the last joint author to die, and therefore protection for software is afforded for between 80 and 100 years, given the relative youthfulness of many software programmers. A further attraction is the lack of formalities involved in obtaining copyright protection, as copyright arises automatically upon creation of the work, unlike the case with patents, which must be registered.[77] There is a registry of copyrights maintained in Ottawa, but registration is voluntary, though particularly with the statutory damages provision added to the *Copyright Act* by Bill C-32, copyright owners should be registering their copyrights even if they did not do so previously. Although it is easier to obtain a copyright than a patent, the protection afforded by copyright is weaker than by patent. While a patent holder's rights are effective against all others in the jurisdiction, even persons who have had no previous contact with the patent holder or the patented invention, truly independent creation is a defence to a copyright claim. To attract copyright, a work must be an "original" literary, dramatic, musical, or artistic work fixed in some material form.[78] Originality in a copyright context is not at all similar

---

77 *Fletcher v. Polka Dot Fabrics Ltd.* (1993), 51 C.P.R. (3d) 241 (Ont. Gen. Div.) [*Fletcher*]. While not mandatory, it is advisable to place on the work the "c" in a circle copyright symbol "©" and the word "copyright," as these give notice to potential infringers and hence more favourable remedies to the copyright owner. The *Copyright Act* limits a copyright owner's remedies to an injunction if the defendant can prove it was unaware and had no reasonable ground for suspecting that copyright subsisted in the work; it should also be noted that this provision does not apply if the copyright is registered. As well, it is extremely useful to register early on in respect of a work that may be the subject of criminal copyright remedies given that a certificate of copyright ownership obtained after the alleged offence occurred will not be acceptable to show that someone other than the accused owned the copyright: see *R. v. Laurier Office Mart Inc.* (1995), 63 C.P.R. (3d) 229 (Ont. Gen. Div.).

78 See *Canadian Admiral Corporation Ltd. v. Rediffusion, Inc.* (1954), 20 C.P.R. 75 (Ex. Ct.) [*Canadian Admiral*] where the fixation requirement is referred to. In the context of software, there is American authority for the proposition that

to the patent standards of novelty or inventiveness; rather, an original copyright work is merely one that is not copied from another source.[79]

A wide range of information-based assets can come within the scope of original literary works, including books, reports, and other written material. Multimedia products on, for example, a CD-ROM, will often contain literary, artistic, and musical works, thus touching three of the four protected categories.[80] For the most part, the *Copyright Act* is relatively technology-neutral, concentrating on acts (such as reproduction) and types of works (such as a literary work) rather than on particular technology-based content delivery mechanisms. Periodically, however (given that the second dynamic of computer has analogues with prior technologies as well), the statute is usefully updated to remove doubt in respect of new technologies. For example, the 1909 U.S. copyright statute was updated expressly to accommodate perforated rolls in player pianos (sometimes called pianola rolls) after the U.S. Supreme Court held that these were not protected by the predecessor statute.[81] In a similar vein, the Canadian *Copyright Act* was amended to cover a live telecast of a sporting or similar event if it is simultaneously taped. This was a result of an earlier case that held that televised live sporting events do not qualify for copyright protection given that they did not come within the then existing categories of photography or films.[82] As well, prior to 1988 the *Copyright Act* did not expressly mention computer software, and thus there was uncertainty as to whether copyright protection extended to computer programs.[83] This uncertainty was resolved in the

---

even transitory fixation in RAM-type memory suffices: *MAI Systems Corporation v. Peak Computer, Inc.*, 991 F.2d 511 (9th Cir. 1993). This issue has not been definitely determined yet in Canada, although see *International Business Machines Corporation v. Ordinateurs Spirales Inc./Spirales Computers Inc.* (1984), 80 C.P.R. (2d) 187 (F.C.T.D.) [*Spirales*].

79   *Fletcher*, above note 77.

80   See, for example, the U.S. case of *Playboy Enterprises, Inc. v. Starware Publishing Corp.*, 900 F. Supp. 433 (S.D. Fla. 1995), where the defendant was found to have infringed *Playboy*'s copyright in photographs by reproducing digitized versions of them on 10,000 CD-ROM disks.

81   *White-Smith Music Publishing Company v. Apollo Company*, 209 U.S. 1 (2d Cir. 1908). Two years later, the English (and by implication the Canadian) *Copyright Act* was similarly revised to cover pianola rolls, to counteract the decision on *Boosey v. Wright*, [1900] 1 Ch. 122 (C.A.).

82   *Canadian Admiral*, above note 78.

83   See, for example, the decision in *Apple Computer, Inc. v. MacKintosh Computers Ltd.* (1987), 18 C.P.R. (3d) 129 (F.C.A.), aff'g *Apple Computer*, above note 20, where judges disagreed as to whether software embedded on a chip was protected as a "translation" or "reproduction" of the original software.

1988 amendments to the *Copyright Act* by expanding the definition of literary work to cover "computer programs," and providing a definition for computer programs.[84] However, the scope of protection of software under copyright law, beyond the literal statements of source code, has generated vigorous debate (providing evidence yet again of the first and second dynamics of computer law).[85]

The *Copyright Act* prohibits anyone from copying or exercising the other rights granted under the statute without the permission of the copyright owner. A person or entity infringes the rights of the copyright owner by doing something only the owner has the right to do under the *Copyright Act*. With respect to infringement by copying, a qualitative as well as quantitative analysis is undertaken, with the result that the reproduction of relatively small, but qualitatively important, parts of a copyright work can lead to a finding of infringement.[86] For larger scale unauthorized commercial copying, the *Copyright Act* contains criminal sanctions against piracy, which can range from a fine of $25,000 and/or imprisonment of up to six months for a summary offence conviction, to a fine of $1 million and/or imprisonment of up to five years, for an indictable offence conviction, as well as destruction or other disposition of the copies and plates used to make the infringing copies.[87] This provision may be relevant when, as in the *Rexcan Cir-*

---

84 The *Copyright Act*, above note 72, s. 2, defines *computer program* as a set of instructions or statements expressed, fixed, embodied, or stored in any manner that is to be used directly or indirectly in a computer in order to bring about a specific result.

85 For a further discussion of the scope of protection of software under copyright law, see section C.3 of this chapter, "Copyright Protection for Software."

86 *Prism Hospital Software Inc.* v. *Hospital Medical Records Institute* (1994), 57 C.P.R. (3d) 129 (B.C.S.C.) [*Prism*]. See also *University of London Press, Limited* v. *University Tutorial Press, Limited*, [1916] 2 Ch. 601 [*University of London Press*], where the court at 610 put forward the arguably questionable proposition that "what is worth copying is prima facie worth protecting," though the court did note this was a "rough practical test." For a low-tech American example, see *Castle Rock Entertainment, Inc.* v. *Carol Publishing Group, Inc.*, 150, F.3d 132 (2nd Cir. 1998), where a trivia book based on the *Seinfeld* television series was found infringing because the excerpts of dialogue in the questions were copied from the show. As for a recent case that is critical of the "test" articulated in *University of London Press*, see *Cantor Fitzgerald*, above note 53.

87 The term *plate* is broadly defined in the Canadian *Copyright Act*. In *R.* v. *Ghnaim* (1988), 28 C.P.R. (3d) 463 (Alta. Prov. Ct.) [*Ghnaim*], the court concluded that the term *plate* was broad enough to cover videocassette recorders used to make unauthorized videotapes, such that thirty-three of them were ordered forfeited to the Crown. Arguably, a similar result would follow where computers are used to make illegal copies of software.

cuits case, an organization acquires some software legally but then makes unauthorized copies of it.[88] Such activity, euphemistically dubbed "corporate overuse" of software, or more pointedly "non-commercial piracy," continues to be a serious concern to software developers, as many users of software continue to refuse to acknowledge the illegality of making unauthorized copies of software.[89] The criminal provisions of the *Copyright Act* have been used to convict illegal copiers of videotapes and sound recordings,[90] and more recently the operator of a bulletin board that made illegal copies of software available from it.[91] It should be noted that while the *Copyright Act* contains a limitation period of three years for civil remedies, summary conviction proceedings (but not indictable offence ones) must be brought within six months.[92]

The *Copyright Act* also includes, however, several specific fair dealing exceptions to infringement by providing that certain acts do not constitute unlawful copying.[93] An important defence is the right of fair

---

88   *R. v. Rexcan Circuits Inc.*, [1993] O.J. No. 1896 (Prov. Ct.) (QL). In this case a company was fined $50,000 for making unauthorized copies of software for its use within the company.

89   See Mitch Betts, "Dirty Rotten Scoundrels?" *Computerworld*, 22 May 1995, which reports the results of an ethics survey conducted among information systems professionals and found, among other things, that 47 percent of respondents admitted to making unauthorized copies of software, even though 78 percent of respondents agreed this should not be done. See *Adobe Systems Inc. v. KLJ Computer Solutions Inc.* (1999), 1 C.P.R. (4th) 177 (F.C.T.D.) [*KLJ Computer Solutions Inc.*] for a civil case involving "corporate overuse" of software or, as the plaintiffs referred to it, "softlifting." For examples of U.S. software piracy cases, see note 13 in chapter 3.

90   *Re Adelphi Book Store Ltd. and The Queen* (1972), 7 C.P.R. (2d) 166 (Sask. C.A.); *Ghnaim*, above note 87; *Photo Centre Inc. v. R.* (1986), 9 C.P.R. (3d) 425 (Que. Sup. Ct.); and *R. v. Miles of Music Ltd.* (1989), 24 C.P.R. (3d) 301 (Ont. C.A.).

91   *R. v. M. (J.P.)* (1996), 107 C.C.C. (3d) 380 (N.S.C.A.) [*M. (J.P.)*]. The accused in this case was a young offender (age seventeen); he was sentenced to eighteen months' probation and 150 hours of community service.

92   *R. v. Shimming* (1991), 35 C.P.R. (3d) 397 (Sask. Prov. Ct.); *Ghnaim*, above note 87.

93   The Federal Court of Appeal, in *CCH Canadian*, above note 19, in para. 150 enumerated these factors to be considered when applying the fair dealing defence: (1) the purpose of the dealing; (2) the nature of the dealing; (3) the amount of the dealing; (4) alternatives to the dealing; (5) the nature of the work in question; and (6) the effect of the dealing on that work. In the U.S., an operator of an Internet search engine was entitled to rely on the American fair use defence when importing small, lower resolution images owned by the plaintiff, but linking to the full-sized version of the images was not covered by the same defence: *Kelly v. Arriba Soft Corporation*, 280 F. 3d 934 (9th Cir. 2002).

dealing with any work for private study or research.[94] The fair dealing provisions may be an important element of any defence related to a claim of reverse engineering, though the legalities of reverse engineering software and related products have not yet been addressed by a Canadian court;[95] in several U.S. decisions,[96] the American "fair use" defence was found to be important by both courts, though it should be noted that American fair use is somewhat broader than its Canadian fair dealing counterpart.[97] The Bill C-32 amendments added several limited exceptions relevant to educational institutions, such as the use of copy-

---

94   Also important is the defence of fair dealing for the purpose of criticism, review, or newspaper summary: see *Allen* v. *Toronto Star Newspaper Ltd.* (1995), 26 O.R. (3d) 308 (Gen. Div.), rev'd (1997), 36 O.R. (3d) 201 (Div. Ct.) [*Allen*]. In some jurisdictions certain public entities may also be able to sidestep an infringement claim on the grounds of sovereign immunity. For example, there is a line of cases in the United States holding that state public bodies, such as universities, are not subject to federal copyright law: *Chavez* v. *Arte Publico Press*, 204 F.3d 601 (5th Cir. 2000).

95   For an analysis supporting the proposition that the fair dealing exception under the Canadian *Copyright Act* would allow the reverse engineering of software, see M.F. Morgan, "*Trash Talking: The Protection of Intellectual Property Rights in Computer Software*" (1994) 26 Ottawa L. Rev. 425.

96   *Sega Enterprises Ltd.* v. *Accolade, Inc.*, 977 F.2d 1510 (9th Cir. 1992); and *Atari Games Corp.* v. *Nintendo of America Inc.*, 975 F.2d 832 (Fed. Cir. 1992). In *Sony Computer Entertainment Inc.* v. *Connectix Corp.*, 203 F.3d 596 (9th Cir. 2000) [*Connectix*], for example, the court concluded that the "intermediate copying" of the Sony basic input-output system as part of the reverse engineering by Connectix of the Sony PlayStation was permitted under the U.S. fair use doctrine. This allowed Connectix to make its own, non-infringing Virtual Game Station emulation software, which allowed Sony PlayStation games on CD-ROMs to be played on a regular computer. See also *Sony Computer Entertainment America, Inc.* v. *Bleem*, LLC 214 F. 3d 1022 (9th Cir. 2000), where the court, also under the fair use doctrine, allowed another developer of emulator software that competed with Sony's Play Station to use screen shots from Sony's game disks in comparative advertising — provided it shows what the games look like on a television screen (the output device for the Sony Play Station) relative to a computer monitor (the emulator's output device). For a British perspective with a different result than in *Connectix*, see *Mars U.K. Ltd.* v. *Teknowledge Ltd.*, The Times (23 June 1999).

97   See, for example, *Cie Générale des Établissements Michelin-Michelin & Cie* v. *C.A.W.-Canada* (1996), 71 C.P.R. (3d) 348 (F.C.T.D.), where the court concluded that use of a copyright for purposes of "parody" is not fair dealing under Canada's *Copyright Act* the way it is a fair use under American copyright legislation. As well, even in the United States it may be possible to prohibit reverse engineering contractually, if the relevant licence agreement expressly bans the practice: *DVD Copy Control Association, Inc.* v. *McLaughlin*, 2000 WL 48512 (Santa Clara Sup. Ct. 2000).

right materials for testing purposes, and by libraries and archives in order, for example, to maintain their permanent collections. Bill C-32 also added the exception for the private copying of sound recordings, the trade-off for the levy on blank audio recording tapes mentioned earlier. Two specific defences in the *Copyright Act* that date from 1988, the year computer software was expressly added to the statute, permit owners of a copy of a computer program to make back-up copies of the program, and to make modifications to the program necessary for the interoperability of the program with other programs, but both of these defences are of little practical use because the vast majority of software is licensed and not sold,[98] and hence it is the rare user of a computer program who owns the copy of the software being used.[99] It should also be noted that, under what is sometimes called "the first sale doctrine," once a copy of a copyright work is sold with the permission of the copyright owner, the copyright owner cannot control any further resale of such copy (so long as no further copies are made) because the right to distribute or resell a work is not included in the bundle of rights afforded the holder of a copyright under the current version of the Canadian *Copyright Act*. Similarly, the Supreme Court of Canada has recently confirmed that once an artist sells a paper-based poster, he cannot prevent its transfer to a canvas backing where no additional copy of the image is made,[100] this decision may have interesting repercussions for works in digital form, given the second dynamic of computer law, namely, the elusive nature of information.

---

98 See chapter 5, section C.1, "Why Software and Content Are Licensed."

99 By contrast, for example, the similar defences under the U.K. copyright law apply to "lawful users" of a computer program: see *Copyright, Designs and Patents Act*, 1988 (U.K.), 1988, c. 48, ss. 50A, 50B, & 50C.

100 *Théberge*, above note 10. In coming to this conclusion, Binnie J., speaking for a 4–3 majority, stated, at pars. 31 and 65 respectively, "Once an authorized copy of a work is sold to a member of the public, it is generally for the purchaser, not the author, to determine what happens to it. ... Generally, the copyright holder does not by virtue of his or her *economic* rights retain any control over the subsequent uses made of authorized copies of his work by third party purchasers." This decision has prompted an artists group to call for a change in the law: James Adams, "New Copyright Protections Urged in Wake of Ruling," *The Globe and Mail* (6 April 2002).

4) Semiconductor Chip Protection

The *Integrated Circuit Topography Act*[101] protects registered chip topographies, which are the stencil-like designs that lay out the various interconnections for the electronic elements embedded on a semiconductor chip. While the *ICT Act* has a much narrower application than the three other intellectual property regimes reviewed above, there are a number of chip manufacturers in Canada (and abroad) who stand to benefit from it. It should be noted, however, that there have been relatively few registrations under the *ICT Act*, and apparently no proceedings brought to date under it (and only one case under the equivalent U.S. statute[102]), probably because of the constant avalanche of new developments in the technologies used to design chips (that is, ironically, the first dynamic of computer law — the rapid pace of technological change — may have obviated the need for the *ICT Act*) and the basic economic fact that the immensely expensive, intricate process technologies used to fabricate chips may afford sufficient practical protection to this industry. Nevertheless, it is still worth considering the *ICT Act*, even if only briefly, because it might represent an example of the type of *sui generis* solution that could be applied to software (and possibly other technologies or information-based assets), given that a number of commentators are uncomfortable with software being protected by both copyright and patent.[103] In essence, the *ICT Act* is a unique amalgamation of copyright and patent concepts, following largely the U.S. semiconductor chip protection statute to respond to the seeming inappropriateness of trying to protect chip topographies under either patent or copyright; topographies were considered too machine-like to come within the copyright regime, and yet were too much like writing to come within the patent system; put another way, topographies are too functional for copyright and not inventive enough for patent. Therefore, in this area the first two dynamics of computer law (namely the rapid pace of technological change and the elusive nature of information) were addressed (perhaps unnecessarily, as noted above) by a statutory solution rather than piecemeal development of existing intellectual property laws applied to a new technology.

---

101 S.C. 1990, c. 37, referred to herein as the *ICT Act*. Like the *Patent Act* and the *Copyright Act*, the *ICT Act* is federal legislation. The *ICT Act* is quite recent legislation, having come into force only in May 1993.

102 *Brooktree Corporation* v. *Advanced Micro Devices, Inc.*, 757 F.Supp. 1088 (S.D. Cal. 1990), aff'd 977 F.2d 1555 (Fed. Cir. 1992).

103 See section C.3 of this chapter, "Copyright Protection for Software."

Nonetheless, the *ICT Act* should not be viewed as a panacea, because it contains several concepts that are by no means self-defining, and these raise a number of new questions.

The *ICT Act* gives the owner of a registered topography the exclusive right to reproduce, make, import, or commercially exploit the topography or any substantial part thereof. The *ICT Act* shows its hybrid nature by providing that only "original" topographies may be registered and then by defining as an original topography one that has not been copied from another topography and is not "commonplace" within the chip industry. Thus, the standard of originality lies somewhere above the copyright test, but arguably below the patent test of absolute novelty. There is no decided case yet as to what commonplace means, and this will be one area of uncertainty regarding the *ICT Act* that will require judicial determination before an accurate assessment of the test can be made. Other hybrid elements of the *ICT Act* include a term of protection for registered topographies that is quite short, at least by copyright standards, being ten years from the earlier of the filing date in Canada or first use in Canada or anywhere else in the world (the latter global element illustrating nicely the fourth dynamic of computer law, namely the blurring of domestic and international). In order to be protected, the topography must be registered. While these aspects of the *ICT Act* are patent-like, the *ICT Act's* relatively broad "fair dealing" provisions for the purpose of analysis, education, research, or teaching, coupled with a reverse engineering exception that permits third parties to strip away and study the various layers of the topography so long as they do not use any copies in their subsequent product, are conceptually derived from the fair dealing provisions of the *Copyright Act*, though are arguably broader in scope. The *ICT Act* also provides, in a copyright-like manner, that no infringement of a registered topography can occur where the second topography is "independently created." The provision of the *ICT Act* that states that no rights are granted under it for "any idea, concept, process, system, technique or information that may be embodied in a topography" is also derivative of the black letter copyright law principle that copyright does not protect ideas and concepts, and specifically is reminiscent of section 102(b) of the U.S. copyright law that articulates this copyright principle expressly by providing that copyright does not extend to any "idea, procedure, process, system, method of operation, concept, principle, or discovery."[104] While the Canadian *Copyright Act* does not currently

---

104 *Copyright Act of 1976*, as amended and codified, 17 U.S.C. §102(b).

contain such a statutory provision, there are cases under the *Copyright Act* that articulate the same principles.[105]

5) Trade-marks

A trade-mark is a word, slogan, or symbol that is used to distinguish the products or services of one supplier from those of another. Trade-marks are widely used in the computer and information industries to permit suppliers to differentiate themselves in an increasingly crowded and international marketplace. Trade-mark law is as much about consumer protection as it is about intellectual property, given that trade-marks do not protect information itself or its expression, but rather serve to prevent fraud and confusion by giving purchasers guarantees of quality regarding the many different goods and services in the marketplace. As an indication of this purpose, it is worth noting that the *Criminal Code* contains several provisions making it a criminal offence to forge or deface a trade-mark or to take a number of other steps regarding trade-marks or passing off goods that have the effect of misleading the purchasers of such goods.[106] These criminal provisions are not utilized very often, and instead owners of trade-marks tend to rely on the civil law to protect their interests.[107] Under the common law tort doctrine of passing-off, the owner of an unregistered trade-mark can stop another supplier from using a confusingly similar trade-mark to pass off its goods or services as those of the original trade-mark owner.[108] The essence of the tort of passing-off is to prevent unfair com-

---

105 See, for example, *Moreau* v. *St. Vincent*, [1950] Ex. C.R. 198 at 204 [*Moreau*], wherein the court concluded that copyright does not extend to a "system or scheme or method for doing a particular thing"; and *Hollinrake* v. *Truswell*, [1894] 3 Ch. 420 at 427 (C.A.) [*Hollinrake*], where the court held that copyright does not extend to "ideas, or schemes, or systems, or methods." See also Article 2 of the *1996 WIPO Copyright Treaty*, above note 71, which has been adopted by Canada, and, therefore, will require Canada to adopt a similar statutory provision.
106 See ss. 406 to 412 of the *Criminal Code*, R.S.C. 1985, c. C-46, as amended.
107 See, however, *R.* v. *Locquet* (1985), 5 C.P.R. (3d) 173 (Que. Sess. Ct.), where an accused was convicted under the *Criminal Code's* trade-mark provisions for falsifying a trade-mark on a computer program.
108 In *Ciba Geigy Canada Ltd.* v. *Apotex Inc.*, [1992] 3 S.C.R. 120 (S.C.C.), the Supreme Court of Canada set out a three-part test for passing off: the existence of reputation or goodwill in the mark in favour of the plaintiff; deception of the public by the defendant by a misrepresentation that leads the public to believe the defendant is associated with the plaintiff; and damage suffered by the plaintiff. But see also *Consumers Distributing Company Limited* v. *Seiko Time Canada Ltd.*, [1984] 1 S.C.R. 583 [*Seiko*], where adequate notice posted to buyers at the

petition by which one supplier sells his goods or services as being those of another supplier. In order to make out a passing-off claim, however, the plaintiff must show actual confusion in the relevant geographic marketplace, which in turn requires that the supplier bringing the action prove that it has built up a sufficient reputation in its trade-mark in the relevant marketplace. Given these difficulties with unregistered trade-marks, suppliers of computer and information-based goods and services are well advised to register their trade-marks under the *Trade-Marks Act*,[109] particularly given that registration under this statute affords nationwide protection, even if the product or service has not been sold from coast to coast. A registered trade-mark gives its owner the exclusive right to its use throughout Canada in respect of the wares and services for which it is registered.[110] Thus a third party infringes the registered owner's exclusive rights in the trade-mark if the third party uses the trade-mark, or a confusingly similar mark, in association with similar products and services. The *Trade-Marks Act* also prohibits the use by a third party of a registered trade-mark in a manner that depreciates the goodwill in the trade-mark. Once products bearing registered trade-marks are sold with the consent of the owner of the registered trade-mark, however, the owner cannot restrict or control further sales of the goods bearing the mark.

A further limitation to the protection afforded by registered trade-marks is that not all use of a trade-mark attracts liability under the *Trade-Marks Act*. Rather, in respect of goods, a trade-mark is only deemed to be used if, at the time title to the goods, or possession of them, is transferred, the trade-mark is affixed to the goods or related packaging. In respect of services a trade-mark is used if it is displayed

---

point of sale regarding the differences in services offered with a product precluded a finding of passing-off; and George S. Takach, "Passing Off, Trade Mark Protection and Parallel Imports After *Consumers Distributing* v. *Seiko*" (1985) 63 Can. Bar Rev. 645. The *Seiko* case may be of important precedential value to certain suppliers in the computer industry.

109 R.S.C. 1985 c. T-13; like the other intellectual property statutes, the *Trade-Marks Act* is federal legislation. In addition to registering under this statute, consideration should be given to securing the relevant domain name(s), as discussed further in section C.7, "Trade-marks, Domain Names, and the Internet."

110 In *Canada Post Corp.* v. *IBAX Inc.* (2001), 12 C.P.R. (4th) 562 (T.M. Opp. Bd.) [*IBAX*], the Trade-marks Opposition Board concluded that wares described as "computer software" were too broad and generic, and that it was necessary to provide specifics as to the type of software or the purpose for which it was designed, such as to assist in targeted mailings (which was the purpose of the applicant's software).

or used in conjunction with the advertising of those services. In other words, persons other than the registered owner of the trade-mark may make use of the mark where it is not being used in a trade-mark manner, subject to such use not constituting dilution of the value of the registered trade-mark. A variation on this point can be seen in an American case where the defendant created a small computer to calculate golfing handicaps based on a formula of the plaintiff, the United States Golf Association (USGA).[111] When the defendant publicly referred to the fact that its device used the USGA handicapping algorithm, the plaintiff argued that it had protection in the handicapping system on a trade-mark–related basis, but the court did not agree, concluding that the formula was functional. The court also found that there was no misappropriation by the defendant under the *INS* doctrine (for a discussion of the *INS* doctrine, see section C.8, "Other Measures of Protection") because the plaintiff and the defendant did not compete directly with one another.

In order to be registered under the *Trade-Marks Act*, the trade-mark must meet several tests, the two principal ones being that it must be distinctive of a single supplier or source of products and that it not be clearly descriptive. Distinctiveness is important given that the very purpose of a trade-mark is to distinguish one supplier's products or services from those of all other suppliers. Accordingly, a trade-mark that is not distinctive will not be registrable, though it is possible for a trade-mark to acquire a secondary meaning in Canada over time, and thus become distinctive and registrable; but a trade-mark will not be registrable if it is confusing with an existing registered trade-mark.[112] Also, a trade-mark

---

111 *United States Golf Association v. St. Andrews Systems, Data-Max, Inc.*, 749 F.2d 1028 (3d Cir. 1984).

112 For example, in *Cognos Inc. v. Cognisys Consultants Inc.* (1994), 53 C.P.R. (3d) 552 (T.M. Opp. Bd.) [*Cognos*], the applicant's proposed trade-mark "Cognisys" was refused registration on the ground of being confusing with the opponent's trade-mark "Cognos," particularly in light of the aural and visual resemblance between the trade-marks. See also *Motorola Inc. v. Fonorola Inc.* (1996), 66 C.P.R. (3d) 537 (T.M. Opp. Bd.), where the applicant's proposed trade-mark registration for "Fonorola" was refused in light of the opponent's trade-mark "Motorola"; *Ready Systems Corp. v. Financial Models Co.* (1993), 52 C.P.R. (3d) 125 (T.M. Opp. Bd.), where the applicant's proposed trade-mark registration "Vertex" for software was refused in light of the opponent's trade-mark "VRTX"; and *Dialog Information Services, Inc. v. PMS Communications Ltd.* (1995) , 62 C.P.R. (3d) 406 (T.M. Opp. Bd.), where the applicant's proposed trade-mark registration for "Dialnet" for software and data communication services was refused in light of the opponent's registered trade-mark "Dialog."

must not be clearly descriptive. This test often poses a challenge to suppliers of computer and information-based products because of their tendency to choose product names that do indicate something essential about the nature of the product. Thus, IBM was refused registration of "Business Solution Centre" for use in association with services for providing pre-installation planning, user education, technical support, and installation assistance,[113] "Money Machine" was found to be too descriptive for automated teller machines,[114] and "The Complete Networking Solution" was found to be too descriptive for computer, hardware, and local area network hardware.[115] In the United States, the term "CD Creator" was held to be too descriptive of a product used to develop CD-ROM titles.[116] In contrast, the federal court, on appeal from the Registrar of Trade-marks, permitted the registration of "AuditComputer" for use in association with the services of examining and testing bookkeeping records by computer and related consulting services.[117] Relatively innocent distinctiveness and descriptiveness problems can also arise in the computer industry because of the habit of using contractions for trade-names and trade-marks, as in the *Cognos* case[118] and as in *Digicom, Inc.*

---

113 *Computer Innovations Distribution Inc.* v. *International Business Machines Corp.* (1988), 23 C.P.R. (3d) 530 (T.M. Opp. Bd.). In the United States the mark "iMarketing" was found generic and not protectable: *Courtenay Communications Corp.* v. *Hall*, 2001 U.S. Dist. LEXIS 7717 (S.D.N.Y. 2001). Also, the phrase "You Have Mail" has been held not to be protectable: *America Online, Inc.* v. *AT&T Corp.*, 243 F. 3d 812 (4th Cir. 2001).

114 *Canada Trustco Mortgage Co.* v. *Guaranty Trust Co. of Canada* (1987), 15 C.P.R. (3d) 86 (T.M. Opp. Bd.).

115 *IBM Canada Ltd.* v. *Cabletron Systems, Inc.* (1995), 66 C.P.R. (3d) 343 (T.M. Opp. Bd.). See also *Mitel Corporation* v. *Registrar of Trade Marks* (1984), 79 C.P.R. (2d) 202 (F.C.T.D.), where Mitel was refused registration for the trade-mark "Superset" for telephone instruments as the term was laudatory and descriptive.

116 *Lewis Management Company, Inc.* v. *Corel Corporation*, 6 Computer Cases (CCH) ¶47,472 at 68,863 (S.D. Cal. 1995). See also *Interstate Net Bank* v. *NetB@nk, Inc.*, 221 F.Supp. 2d 513 (D.N.J. 16 Sept. 2002), where "Netbank" was held to be too generic to be able to stop the use of "Net Bank"; moreover, the mark originally was registered for "electronic payment services featuring a system of electronic money coupons that are exchanged by means of an online computer service," and therefore the court was unwilling to extend it to all of online banking.

117 See *Clarkson Gordon* v. *Registrar of Trade Marks* (1985), 5 C.P.R. (3d) 252 (F.C.T.D.), where the court at 255 allowed this application because in order to get from the trade-mark to its meaning, "one has to separate the two words of which it is formed, reverse them and add a verb between."

118 *Cognos*, above note 112. In *IBAX*, above note 110, the applicant was refused a registration for "Compumail" for, among other reasons, the word *mail* being associated with Canada Post.

v. *Digicon, Inc.*,[119] where the plaintiff's name was a contraction of "digital communications" and the defendant's was a contraction of "digital consultants." The court found the two names confusing, as the parties operated in the same industry, and found for the company that had adopted its name first in time. This case illustrates well that the best trade-marks and trade-names are those that are not descriptive, but rather are completely new and coined words, or words that may have a common meaning but are not related to the business of the entity.

The registration process involves submitting an application that includes the trade-mark and a description of the specific wares or services in respect of which the trade-mark is being or proposed to be used. The Trade-marks Office reviews the application as to form and substance, and if the registrar finds the trade-mark registrable and not confusing with other prior applications or registrations, the application is advertised in the *Trade-marks Journal* to allow third parties to object to the proposed registration. If the application is unopposed, or if the opposition is unsuccessful, a certificate of registration will issue upon payment of the registration fee. The registration is effective for fifteen years, and may be renewed indefinitely. The indefinite term is defensible because a trade-mark does not really protect information *per se*, the way a patent or even a copyright does; rather, a trade-mark serves a consumer protection function by designating a single source for a particular good or service. If at some point the trade-mark ceases to be used, or is otherwise challenged for non-registrability or lack of distinctiveness, a party may bring expungement proceedings to remove the trade-mark from the register. Once it is registered, the trade-mark must be used in association with the wares or services for which it is registered, unless the application was based on proposed use, in which case the applicant must also file a declaration of use indicating that the applicant has actually begun to use the trade-mark in Canada. This typically means being attached to the good, as in the case of hardware, or used in marketing literature in the case of services, but in the case of software it may also be shown in the screens of the computer program.[120] The trade-mark must also be used in the form it is registered

119 328 F.Supp. 631 (S.D. Texas 1991).

120 *BMB Compuscience Canada Ltd.* v. *Bramalea Ltd.* (1988), 20 C.I.P.R. 310 (F.C.T.D.). In a similar vein, in *Riches, McKenzie & Herbert* v. *Source Telecomputing Corp.* (1992), 46 C.P.R. (3d) 563 (T.M. Opp. Bd.), a trade-mark registration for an online information service was permitted on the basis of showing the trade-mark on the screens accessed by subscribers to the service.

in; in one case the registered trade-mark "Bull" was stricken from the register because the owner never used it as such, but rather only as part of the composite mark "CII Honeywell Bull," the name of a French computer company.[121]

6) Ownership Issues

Given the elusive nature of information-based assets, and the fact that most information is the product of some form of collaboration, it is not surprising that a number of complicated issues arise in respect of the ownership of these assets. Generally, the creator of the intellectual property is the first owner of it, subject to an important exception where the creator is an employee and creates the intellectual property in the course of employment, in which case the employer usually is the first owner of the work.[122] An author, for copyright purposes, is the individual(s) who actually writes the work — it is not enough merely to contribute ideas to the project to become an author (or co-author) of the work — and similarly, someone does not obtain a copyright interest in a work merely because she participated in a conversation.[123] Moreover, under the Canadian *Copyright Act* the author has to be a human being, thus raising interesting questions in respect of the ownership of computer-generated output — such as written, musical, or artistic material — where the bulk of "creativity" was generated by the

---

121 *Registrar of Trade Marks* v. *Compagnie internationale pour l'informatique CII Honeywell Bull, Société Anonyme* (1985), 4 C.P.R. (3d) 523 (F.C.A.).

122 For operation of this rule in the context of patents, see *Spiroll Corp. Ltd.* v. *Putti* (1975), 64 D.L.R. (3d) 280 (B.C.S.C.); and *Seanix Technology Inc.* v. *Ircha*, [1998] B.C.J. No. 179 (S.C.). In *Medforms, Inc.* v. *Healthcare Management Solutions, Inc.*, 290 F.3d 98 (2d Cir. 2002), a non-employee programmer was held not to own the resultant software as he was under the close and constant direction of a supervisor (who was an employee).

123 *Hanis* v. *Teevan*, [1995] O.J. 981 (Gen. Div.); aff'd (1998), 162 D.L.R. (4th) 414 [*Hanis*]; *Gould Estate* v. *Stoddart Publishing Co.* (1996), 30 O.R. (3d) 520 (Ont. Gen. Div.); aff'd on the copyright ownership question, namely that the photographer owned the negatives of pictures taken of Glenn Gould, but circumspect on the trial judge's reliance on the misappropriation of personality claim by the Gould Estate: *Gould Estate* v. *Stoddart Publishing Co.* (1998), 39 O.R. (3d) 545 (Ont. C.A.). See also *Visitor Industries Publications, Inc.* v. *NOPG, L.L.C.*, 91 F.Supp. 2d 910 (E.D. La. 2000), where, in respect of a CD-ROM product, the court held that mere assistance is insufficient to become a joint author; rather, each party's contribution must be a separate copyrightable work for joint ownership to be able to arise.

advanced computer rather than any human.[124] It is also worth noting that the Crown can own copyright in information-based materials produced by or for it, and it is not contrary to the constitutional freedom of expression to limit exploitation of the Crown's copyright.[125]

The *Copyright Act* provides that the author of the copyright work is the first owner of the copyright, and that any transfer of copyright must be in writing. These two rules, however, are subject to the important exception, noted above, that where an author is an employee who creates copyright works in the course of his or her employment, the employee is deemed to transfer his or her copyright to the employer unless there is a written agreement between the employee and the employer to the contrary.[126] Taken together, these rules can often frustrate the intention of a party commissioning the creation of a knowledge-based asset, as was the case in the *Mainville* case where an independent contractor, hired to do some programming work, ended up owning the software he wrote because he did not assign in writing his intellectual property rights to the company.[127] As software and other

---

124 In the United Kingdom's 1988 copyright law amendments, and in several government reports in Europe and Canada, this question is being answered on the basis that the computer/software is merely a tool, and the copyright rests with the person manipulating the tool to actually produce the output: *Copyright, Designs and Patents Act, 1988* (U.K.), 1988, c. 48, subs. 9(3).

125 *R. v. James Lorimer & Co. Ltd.* (1984), 77 C.P.R. (2d) 262 (F.C.A.). In other jurisdictions, however, different results may arise. For example, under the law of New York State, the ability to copy and distribute public records (in this case maps) under freedom of information legislation overrides the government's copyright: *County of Suffolk, New York v. Experian Information Solutions, Inc.*, 2000 WL 1010262 (S.D.N.Y. 2000).

126 In the *Hanis* case, above note 123, it was held that the "agreement to the contrary" must be between the employees and their employer, and thus a professor was unsuccessful in arguing that the software written by employees of the university was owned by the professor as a result of an agreement between the employees and the professor. See also *Canavest House Ltd. v. Lett* (1984), 2 C.P.R. (3d) 386 (Ont. H.C.J.), where the court gave ownership of copyright in certain software to an employer in the absence of a written agreement to the contrary. Similarly in the patent context, the employer is generally held to be the owner of a device invented by an employee (on the basis of an implied term in the employment contract), or at least the employer has a licence to work the invention: see *W.J. Gage Ltd. v. Sugden*, [1967] 2 O.R. 151 (H.C.J.).

127 *Amusements Wiltron Inc. v. Mainville* (1991), 40 C.P.R. (3d) 521 (Que. Sup. Ct.). For an opposite conclusion, see *Massine v. de Basil*, [1936-45] M.C.C. 223 (cited in *John Richardson Computers Limited v. Flanders*, [1993] FSR 497 at 499 (H. Ct.)), where the court concluded that it was an implied term of a retainer arrangement for an independent contractor that the copyright in the work

knowledge-based companies increasingly allow employees to work at home and connect to the office and co-workers electronically, another example of the blurring of private/public (the third dynamic of computer law), ownership disputes are also arising where employees claim to have developed a particular information-based item at home and not on company time.[128] Another factor that can muddy the analysis is the use by the employee of his or her own computer, such as a personal laptop, partly for business purposes.[129] In order to avoid doubt, and lengthy and costly disputes, it is prudent for organizations in any way involved in the development of software and other information-based works to clarify and confirm in writing with their staff, meaning employees and literally anyone else who works on the particular project, which of them will own the work product emanating from the relationship.[130] Failure to do so results in cases such as *Allen v. Toronto Star Newspapers Ltd.*, where a freelance photographer was held to be the owner of a photograph taken for a magazine cover, given the custom in the relevant industry and the absence of an agreement to the contrary.[131] It should also be noted that while moral rights cannot be assigned, they can be waived by the author. In short, it is advisable to

---

developed by the independent contractor, which was one component of a larger work, would rest with the commissioning party. In a recent U.S. case, where the Web site developer and his customer failed to execute a written agreement, the developer ended up with ownership of the relevant software, but the court found an implied, non-exclusive, irrevocable licence in favour of the user (though the court also noted that without consideration, an implied license may be revoked by the licensor): *Holtzbrinck Publishing Holdings L.P. v. Vyne Communications, Inc.* 2000 WL 502860 (S.D. N.Y. 2000).

128 See the U.S. case *Avtec Systems, Inc. v. Jeffrey G. Peiffer*, 1995 Copyright Law Decisions (CCH) ¶27,432, at 28,477 (4th Cir. 1995), where the copyright in a software program written by an employee software developer was held to be owned by the employee personally, rather than the employer company. Notwithstanding his employee status, the court concluded he developed the software at home and not in the course of his employment.

129 For an example of an employee using his own laptop for business use, see the *Edac* case, note 39 above, though in this case no adverse inference was drawn against the employee as the evidence showed the employee used his own computer because the company's was malfunctioning.

130 In some jurisdictions, family law or community property marital law rules may also provide spouses with certain rights related to the subject intellectual property. In *Rodrique v. Rodrique*, 218 F.3d 432 (5th Cir. 2000), the court concluded the husband was the sole owner of the copyright in his paintings, but the wife had an undivided one-half interest in the economic benefit flowing from these works.

131 *Allen*, above note 94.

counteract the four dynamics of computer law by addressing through a written agreement who will own the resulting intellectual property rights regardless of what new technologies may be worked on, regardless of how evanescent these work products emanating from these technologies may be, and whether they are developed in a private or international setting.

Joint creators of information-based assets will often agree to be co-owners of the intellectual property in the work or invention. Such an ownership arrangement means that, in the absence of an agreement to the contrary, neither co-owner can exploit the work without the consent of the other, and where there is such exploitation each co-owner must remit to the other, one-half of the profit generated by such exploitation.[132] For many joint venturers this is not a desired state of affairs, and the parties would be better off to have ownership vest in a single entity with the other obtaining adequate licence rights to it. In any event, to achieve maximum certainty co-owners are also usually well advised to agree contractually as to the scope of use and exploitation that each of them can make of the particular intellectual property. Another area of uncertainty relates to the granting of enforceable security interests in patents, copyrights, and trade-marks. As the statutes governing these properties do not expressly provide for the registration of security interests, there is some question as to how to perfect a security interest in these assets. It is a common practice to record in the relevant registry the applicable security agreement, though it is not clear what the legal effect of doing so is. As a result, some secured lenders insist on obtaining a written assignment of the intellectual property, which assignment is then registered in the relevant intellectual property office. This assignment is coupled with a grant back to the borrower of exclusive distribution rights, which grant includes collateral security language indicating that the secured lender cannot exercise any effective rights with or over the intellectual property until the borrower is in default. Such a security arrangement may cause problems under trade-marks and even copyrights, and therefore in some cases lenders merely require the initial delivery of unsigned and undated assignments, which only become effective upon the borrower's default. The risk with this sort of arrangement is that such an assignment, when ultimately completed, may not be good against a previously registered assignment

---

132 For application of the consent requirement in a patent context, see *Forget* v. *Specialty Tools of Canada Inc.* (1995), 62 C.P.R. (3d) 537 (B.C.C.A.). For a recent case involving a copyright work of joint authorship, see *Editions Chouette (1987) Inc.* v. *Desputeaux*, 2003 SCC 17 [*Editions Chouette*].

if the borrower takes the unscrupulous step of assigning the same intellectual property interest twice to two different people.[133]

7) Remedies for Infringement

The copyright, patent, chip protection, and trade-marks statutes, and the common law of trade secrecy and breach of confidence, together with the rules of civil procedure of Canada's various courts, provide a wide range of remedies where the creator of an information-based asset believes its intellectual property rights have been infringed. These remedies are extremely important because protecting information-based assets can be particularly difficult, given their intangible, elusive nature (echoing again the second dynamic of computer law). If the creator has a strong *prima facie* case that infringement has occurred, and where serious damage is occurring or about to occur to the creator as a result, and where there is clear and compelling evidence that the infringer has incriminating material in its possession or control that the infringer would destroy if he or she were served with a regular infringement claim, the creator may apply *ex parte* to a court for an "Anton Piller order."[134] Such an order serves essentially as a civil search warrant, permitting the creator to attend unannounced at the premises of the alleged infringer to protect vital evidence from being destroyed, and thus responds to the second dynamic of computer law.[135] The Anton Piller order is particularly useful for combatting the "fly-by-

---

133 See, for example, the discussion in Michel Racicot & George S. Takach, "Agaguk — Un Nouveau Conflit Fédéral-Provincial" (1992) 4 Les Cahiers de Propriété Intellectuelle 401. As for a U.S. discussion of perfecting a security interest in software/copyright, see *Re Avalon Software, Inc.*, 209 B.R. 517 (Bankr. D. Ariz. 1997).

134 *KLJ Computer Solutions Inc.*, above note 89. See also *Capitanescu* v. *Universal Weld Overlays Inc.* (1996), 71 C.P.R. (3d) 37 (Alta. Q.B.). This remedial measure takes its name from *Anton Piller K.G.* v. *Manufacturing Processes Ltd.*, [1976] 1 All E.R. 779 (C.A.), the English case that first granted this powerful order.

135 The rationale for the Anton Piller order was well expressed by the English House of Lords as follows in *Rank Film Distributors Ltd.* v. *Video Information Centre*, [1982] A.C. 380 at 439 [*Rank Film*]: "They are designed to deal with situations created by infringements of patents, trade marks and copyright or more correctly with acts of piracy which have become a large and profitable business in recent years. They are intended to provide a quick and efficient means of recovering infringing articles and of discovering the sources 'from which these articles have been supplied and the persons to whom they are distributed before those concerned have had time to destroy or conceal them. Their essence is surprise. ... They are an illustration of the adaptability of equitable remedies to new situations."

"night" counterfeiting operation.[136] Given the draconian effect such an order can have on an unsuspecting defendant, the plaintiff must make full and complete disclosure of all relevant information in the application for the order.[137] Moreover, the court invariably requires the plaintiff to give several undertakings, including that the plaintiff will compensate the defendant for any damages as a result of the order, and the order must be carried out in good faith and in strict compliance with all undertakings.[138] Notwithstanding the requirement to give these safeguards, the Anton Piller order is an important procedural remedy to creators of information-based assets, given the unfortunate side effect of the second dynamic of computer law, namely the ease and speed with which digitally stored information on computer disks and computers containing the incriminating evidence can be wiped clean.

Another strong remedy for software developers, manufacturers of computer products, and content creators is the interlocutory injunction (as well as the related interim injunction), which prohibits the defendant from continuing any alleged acts of infringement from the time the injunction is granted until trial.[139] Three conditions generally

---

136 *Nintendo of America, Inc.* v. *Coinex Video Games Inc.* (1983), 69 C.P.R. (2d) 122
(F.C.A.).

137 In *Pulse Microsystems Ltd.* v. *SafeSoft Systems Inc.* (1996), 67 C.P.R. (3d) 202 (Man.
C.A.), an Anton Pillar order was set aside because the plaintiffs failed to provide the
court with full and fair disclosure of all material facts. See also *Top Star Distribution
Group Inc.* v. *Sigma* (2000), 4 C.P.R. (4th) 168 (F.C.T.D.), where, in addition to
failing to provide full and frank disclosure of all material facts, the plaintiffs
failed to convince the court that the defendants would destroy the evidence.

138 In *Rank Film*, above note 135 at 439, the court stated: "Because they operate
drastically and because they are made, necessarily, ex parte, i.e., before the persons affected have been heard, they are closely controlled by the court. ... They
are only granted upon clear and compelling evidence, and a number of safeguards in the interest of preserving essential rights are introduced."

139 *Omega Digital Data Inc.* v. *Airos Technology Inc.* (1996), 32 O.R. (3d) 21 (Gen.
Div.) [*Omega*]; and *Kamengo Systems Inc.* v. *Seabulk Systems Inc.* (1996), 26
B.L.R. (2d) 43 (B.C.S.C.) [*Kamengo*]. But see also *Digital Equipment Corporation*
v. *C. Itoh & Co. (Canada) Ltd.* (1985), 6 C.P.R. (3d) 511 at 512 (F.C.T.D.),
where, in refusing an interlocutory injunction because the plaintiff could not
demonstrate that it would suffer irreparable harm, the court noted that an
injunction is an "extraordinary remedy" and "ought not to be lightly granted."
Equally, an application for an interlocutory injunction must be brought promptly or the plaintiff will lose the ability to enjoin conduct that has been ongoing
for some time: see *Amdahl Canada Ltd.* v. *Circle Computer Services Inc.* (4
December 1994), 92CQ-30531 (Ont. H.C.J.); and *Magnet Communications, LLC*
v. *Magnetcommunications, Inc.*, 2001 U.S. Dist. LEXIS 14460 (S.D. Fla. 2001) (in
the latter case a twelve-day delay precluded a finding of irreparable harm).

need to be met before a court will grant an interlocutory (or interim) injunction. First, the plaintiff must show that there is a "serious question" or a "fair question" to be tried,[140] and therefore the court, on an interlocutory injunction application will generally not enquire as to whether the defendant has in fact copied or misappropriated the relevant intellectual property. An exception to this rule may come into play where the granting of the order will effectively bring the matter to an end because the defendant will be unable to survive until trial, or where the interlocutory injunction would impact on the employment plans of individuals, in which case the court is entitled to pay closer attention to the likely outcome of the merits of the case.[141] Second, the plaintiff must show that it will suffer irreparable harm not compensable in damages if the injunction is not granted.[142] Third, the balance of convenience must favour the plaintiff. As an example of this latter factor, courts will sometimes seek to preserve the status quo, for example, by granting the plaintiff's motion for an interlocutory injunction if the defendant has not entered the market with the allegedly infringing product, while often refusing the motion if the defendant has entered the market, particularly if the defendant will be able to satisfy any damages ultimately awarded at trial.[143] It should be noted that there is a line of case law in Canada supporting the proposition that once a clear violation of intellectual property rights has been established, the balance of convenience need not be considered, with the result that an injunc-

---

140 *Omega*, above note 139 ("serious question"); and *Kamengo*, above note 139 ("fair question").

141 *Omega*, above note 139; and see also *RJR-MacDonald Inc. v. Canada (A.G.)* (1994), 54 C.P.R. (3d) 114 (S.C.C.).

142 See *ITV Technologies, Inc. v. WIC Television Ltd.*, [1997] F.C.J. No. 1645 (T.D.) (interim injunction granted); and *ITV Technologies, Inc. v. WIC Television Ltd.*, [1997] F.C.J. No. 1803 (T.D.) (interlocutory injunction denied) [*ITV*]. In *Amazon.com Inc. v. BarnesandNoble.com, Inc.*, 73 F. Supp. 2d 1228 (W.D. Wash.), an injunction was granted on December 1, 1997, enjoining Barnes and Noble from using a patented one-click Web site ordering method because, the court concluded, Amazon would suffer irreparable harm, given that the important Christmas online shopping season was approaching, Amazon's 1-Click system meaningfully differentiated Amazon from its archival Barnes and Noble, and it would be impossible to gauge damages in terms of customer loyalty if Barnes and Noble were allowed to use its single-action ordering system. On appeal, this injunction was ultimately lifted (in a decision that did not address the substantive merits of the case): *Amazon.com, Inc. v. BarnesandNoble.com, Inc.*, 239 F.3d 1343 (Fed. Cir. C.A. 2001). See also note 199 below.

143 *Camerica*, above note 76.

tion is granted,[144] though where the validity of the claim of the copyright or trade-mark is put into question this approach is not followed.[145] In one case, a court granted a temporary injunction, mindful of the fact that the actual trial was to be brought on extremely quickly.[146] On the other hand, a court can refuse to grant an injunction if the plaintiff failed to bring its action promptly against the defendant as soon as the plaintiff first learned of the misappropriation or infringement.[147]

If infringement or misappropriation of an intellectual property right is proven at trial, the owner of the relevant copyright, patent, trade secret, chip topography, or trade-mark will be entitled to enjoin any further infringing activity by the defendant through a permanent injunction. The term of the injunction if issued in respect of a trade secret may extend beyond the time that the information becomes generally known, in order that the misappropriator not be entitled to use the information as a "springboard," even after honest competitors have access to the information.[148] In some cases the injunctive order is cast in extremely broad terms. In one case the defendants were ordered to cease using the plaintiff's product, which is understandable, as well as *any* other software product that performed a similar function, which constitutes an incredibly broad prohibition.[149] The order granting the permanent injunction may even provide for the return to the plaintiff of copies of the infringing work that have been provided to third parties.[150] The

144 *Jeffrey Rogers Knitwear Productions Ltd.* v. *R.D. International Style Collections Ltd.* (1985), 6 C.P.R. (3d) 409 (F.C.T.D.). See also *Spirales*, above note 78, where reference is made to the principle that courts are more willing to grant interlocutory injunctions in copyright infringement actions when the copying by the defendant is very clear.

145 *Upjohn Co.* v. *Apotex Inc.* (1993), 51 C.P.R. (3d) 292 (F.C.T.D.); *ITV*, above note 142.

146 *Alphanet*, above note 49.

147 See *Cadbury Schweppes*, above note 25.

148 *Kamengo*, above note 139; and *Matrox*, above note 30. The duration of protection provided by the springboard injunction can be extended if the defendant's conduct is found to be particularly egregious: see *Apotex*, above note 31, and *Apotex Fermentation Inc.* v. *Novopharm Ltd.* (2000), 4 C.P.R. (4th) 148 (Man. Q.B.).

149 *Gemologists International Inc.* v. *Gem Scan International Inc.* (1986), 7 C.I.P.R. 225 (Ont. H.C.J.) [*Gemologists*].

150 *Prism*, above note 86. On the other hand, while a court will order a licensee to remove a licensor's trade-marks if the former is in breach of a trade-mark licence agreement, the court will not grant an order permitting the licensor to disable the licensee's Web site, as this was considered to be too draconian a remedy: *Florists' Transworld Delivery Inc.* v. *Originals Florist & Gifts Inc.*, 57 U.S.P.Q. 2d 1079 (N.D. Ill. 2000).

Copyright Act provides that in a copyright case, a permanent injunction may be all the plaintiff is entitled to if the defendant did not have knowledge that copyright subsisted in the work. An injunction granted at trial in a patent infringement case, however, may be stayed pending the result of an appeal provided the defendant has an arguable appeal, it will suffer irreparable harm if the judgment is enforced, and the balance of convenience favours a stay.[151]

Damages based on a wide variety of measures can be awarded when infringement of an intellectual property right is proven. With respect to a violation of trade secrets or the misappropriation of confidential information, compensation has been based on the lost profits of the plaintiff,[152] as well as the development costs of the information.[153] Compensating the plaintiff for foreseeable damages is a common copyright measure of damages.[154] Yet another approach is to determine fair compensation for the right to use the information.[155] The *Copyright Act* also permits a plaintiff to recover conversion damages if the defendant destroys the infringing copies without the copyright owner's permission.[156] This remedy is linked to another provision of the *Copyright Act*, which deems the holder of the copyright to be the owner of the infringing copies as well, and requires the defendant to deliver up the infringing copies to the copyright holder. A court may award damages for copyright infringement even where the infringer made no profits.[157] The *Copyright Act* also contains a statutory damages provision that permits a court to award monetary damages between $500 and $20,000.[158] Punitive or exemplary damages for copyright infringement or trade

151 *Polansky Electronics Ltd. v. AGT Limited*, [2000] A.J. No. 146 (Alberta C.A.). The technology that was at issue in this case was an interface device that enabled the transmission of facsimiles by computers and fax machines over mobile radios.
152 *McCormick Delisle & Thompson Inc. v. Ballantyne et al.*, [2001] O.J. No. 1783 (C.A.); *Kamengo*, above note 139; *Wil-Can Electronics*, above note 52; and *Cadbury Schweppes*, above note 25.
153 *ICAM*, above note 33.
154 *Prism*, above note 86. This case illustrates well the practice of granting multiple damage claims in appropriate circumstances.
155 *Pharand Ski Corp. v. Alberta* (1991), 37 C.P.R. (3d) 288 (Alta Q.B.).
156 *91439 Canada Ltée v. Editions JCL Inc.* (1994), 58 C.P.R. (3d) 38 (F.C.A.).
157 *Fletcher*, above note 77.
158 In a recent U.S. case, the court concluded that when a music CD is infringed, statutory damages should be determined on a per-CD basis, and not on a per-song basis: *UMG Recordings, Inc. v. MP3, Inc.*, 109 F.Supp. 2d 223 (S.D.N.Y. 2000). In a subsequent decision in this case, the court determined the appropriate measure of damages per CD was $25,000: *UMG Recordings, Inc. v. MP3.com, Inc.*, 2000 WL 1262568 (S.D.N.Y. 2000).

secret misappropriation can also be awarded where the defendant's conduct is egregious and shows virtual contempt for the intellectual property rights of the plaintiff.[159] An infringer of another person's patent is liable for all damages sustained by the patent holder, and such damages may be expressed as a payment of reasonable or generous royalties in such a manner as is considered to be fair in all of the circumstances of the case.[160] A court may also award punitive damages in a patent infringement suit.[161] A patent holder may choose to order an accounting of the infringer's profits in lieu of damages in appropriate circumstances.[162] It should also be noted that in certain situations, such as where an individual established a corporate vehicle predominantly for the purpose of undertaking the infringing activity, or where the individual was the controlling mind and the driving force behind the company's infringement, the court will be able to hold the individual liable together with the company.[163] These remedies are all in addition to the criminal offence of piracy provided in the *Copyright Act*.[164] Finally, with copyright works fixed in paper and other traditional intellectual properties, an owner could often press the Canadian customs authority to stop the offending goods at the border.[165] Such a useful "control point" is more problematic in the Internet era given the third

---

159 See *Wil-Can Electronics*, above note 52; and *Prism*, above note 86, where an employee of the defendant (in addition to the corporate defendant) was also found personally jointly liable (together with his corporate employer) for copyright infringement. For a recent discussion of when it is appropriate to award punitive damages, see *Whiten* v. *Pilot Insurance Co. et al.* (2002), 209 D.L.R. (4th) 257 (S.C.C.).

160 *Unilever PLC* v. *Procter & Gamble Inc.* (1995), 61 C.P.R. (3d) 499 (F.C.A.).

161 *Lubrizol Corp.* v. *Imperial Oil Ltd.* (1996), 67 C.P.R. (3d) 1 (F.C.A.). See also *Polansky Electronics*, above note 13.

162 In a case that an appellate court (in *Beloit Canada Ltée* v. *Valmet Oy* (1995), 61 C.P.R. (3d) 271 at 274 (F.C.A.)) termed "almost Dickensian in its length and complexity," a judge commented on the "pitfalls of granting the remedy of an accounting of profits other than in in exceptional and appropriate circumstances and after due deliberation by the court": *Beloit Canada Ltée* v. *Valmet Oy* (1994), 55 C.P.R. (3d) 433 at 435 (F.C.T.D.).

163 For copyright, see *Ital-Press Ltd.* v. *Sicoli* (1999), 86 C.P.R. (3d) 129 (F.C.T.D.) and *Prism*, above note 86; for patent, see *Mentmore Manufacturing Co.* v. *National Merchandise Manufacturing Co.* (1978), 40 C.P.R. (2d) 164 (F.C.A.); and for trade secret/confidential information, see *Apotex*, above note 31.

164 See section B.3 of this chapter, "Copyright."

165 See, for example, *Dennison Manufacturing Co.* v. *M.N.R.* (1987), 15 C.P.R. (3d) 67 (F.C.T.D.), where a copyright owner tried to compel the minister responsible for customs to stop allegedly infringing materials at the border.

and fourth dynamics of computer law, where copyright material is being copied and uploaded and downloaded by personal computers around the world.

8) International Aspects

The computer and information industries are extremely global in nature. This fact, highlighting the fourth dynamic of computer law (the blurring of national/international), was true even before the advent of the Internet. With Canadian suppliers of computer and information-based products exploiting their wares around the world, it is important that they be able to obtain intellectual property protection in foreign countries. This is done through a variety of international treaties and conventions. In the copyright field, Canada is a signatory to the *Berne Convention*[166] and the *Universal Copyright Convention*.[167] Most recently, Canada has become a party to the *Rome Convention*,[168] with many of the amendments to the Canadian *Copyright Act* effected through Bill C-32 aimed at implementing Canada's obligations under this convention. These treaties grant the nationals of signatory countries reciprocal protection based on the principle of national treatment, as well as establishing certain minimum substantive requirements, such as the term of copyright not being shorter than the life of the author plus fifty years. Thus, a copyright work by a Canadian is automatically granted the same protection in, for example, the United States (another signatory to the *Berne Convention*) as a work by an American, which protection may be different than that afforded the work in Canada. With respect to patents and trade-marks, Canadians must file applications in foreign jurisdictions in order to obtain protection there and vice versa.[169] This is assisted somewhat by the *Paris Convention*, to which Canada and (at

---

166   *Berne Convention for the Protection of Literary and Artistic Works*, 9 September 1886, as revised, CTS 1948/22. The general current version of this convention, and the one to which Canada has adhered, is the one done in Paris in July 1971. For a list of signatory countries to this convention, see the WIPO Web site <wipo.org>.

167   The *Universal Copyright Convention*, 6 September 1952, as revised, UNTS 216/132, T.I.A.S. 3324, was adopted by UNESCO in 1952.

168   *International Convention for the Protection of Performers, Producers of Phonograms and Broadcasting Organisations* (1961), done in Rome on 26 October 1961, UNTS 496/43.

169   See *Vanity Fair Mills, Inc. v. T. Eaton Co. Limited*, 234 F.2d 633 (2d Cir. 1956) [*Vanity Fair*].

October 15, 2002) 163 other countries are parties.[170] The *Paris Convention* provides that if a filing is made in one *Paris Convention* country, the filing date in any other *Paris Convention* country is the earliest filing date in a *Paris Convention* country so long as the subsequent filing is effected within six and twelve months in the case of trade-marks and patents, respectively. For example, if a Canadian files in Canada for a trade-mark on January 1 and files for a U.S. trade-mark registration any time before June 30 of the same year, the filing date in the United States will be deemed to be January 1. Canada and more than one hundred other countries are also parties to the *Patent Cooperation Treaty*, which allows patent applications filed in one treaty country to be deemed applications in other treaty countries, thereby greatly assisting the international patent filing process.[171]

There is no international treaty covering chip protection. Rather, the *ICT Act* provides for bilateral reciprocity by allowing Canada to extend protection to those nationals whose countries provide similar protection to Canadians. Currently, Canada has such reciprocal arrangements with the United States and most countries in Europe.[172] The World Intellectual Property Organization (WIPO) is advocating an international treaty for chip protection, but to date this effort has not been successful.[173] WIPO is particularly active in encouraging a number of countries to improve the level of intellectual property protection provided by their domestic laws, especially in developing countries. This process has also become a part of multilateral trade agreements. The *North American Free Trade Agreement* contains a chapter on intellectual property that sets out minimum requirements for copyright,

---

170 *Paris Convention for the Protection of Industrial Property*, 20 March 1883, as revised, CTS 1928/3. For a list of signatory countries, see the WIPO Web site <wipo.org>. See also the *Madrid Agreement Concerning the International Registration of Marks*, another international intellectual property treaty that allows a trade-mark filing in one country to be effective in other signatory countries, of which there are currently 70. Canada is currently considering becoming a party to the Madrid Agreement.

171 *Patent Cooperation Treaty* (1970), done in Washington on 19 June 1970, as amended, CTS 1990/22.

172 See SOR/93-282, 28 May 1993, for the United States, Australia, and Japan, and SOR/94-677, 1 November 1994, for most European countries.

173 WIPO is a Geneva-based specialized agency of the United Nations. Canada is one of the currently 179 countries that are members of WIPO. WIPO undertakes numerous efforts to promote the protection of the intellectual property around the globe, including by administering various international treaties related to intellectual property.

patent, trade-mark, and trade secrecy protection that must be adopted by each signatory country.[174] The World Trade Organization, the successor to the GATT, also has an agreement on intellectual property that, as with the earlier NAFTA, requires a number of countries to update their intellectual property laws.[175] Most recently, WIPO was instrumental in effecting the conclusion in December 1996 of two "Internet treaties," the *WIPO Copyright Treaty* and the *WIPO Performances and Phonograms Treaty*, which became effective when thirty countries adopted them; but like other international intellectual property conventions, they are only binding on the signatory countries.[176] Of course, having laws in the statute books that provide, in writing, adequate substantive protection for intellectual property are not worth much if these laws cannot be practically enforced through the country's judicial system. In this regard, a number of organizations, such as the Business Software Alliance (BSA) and the Software Publishers Association (SPA), groups of largely American-based producers of mass market software products, expend significant financial and human resources in tracking down pirates of intellectual property and trying to convince local authorities to bring legal action against them.[177]

---

174 The NAFTA, to which Canada, the United States, and Mexico are parties, was implemented in Canada by the *North American Free Trade Agreement Implementation Act*, S.C. 1993, c. 44. Chapter 17 of the NAFTA is devoted to intellectual property issues.

175 The WTO's new regime on intellectual property is contained in the *Agreement on Trade-Related Aspects of Intellectual Property Rights, Including Trade in Counterfeit Goods*, one of the subsidiary agreements to result from the Uruguay Round of international trade negotiations. The text of this Agreement can be found at <itl.irv.uit.no/trade_law/documents/freetrade/wta-94/art/iialc.html>. Canada made a number of WTO-related amendments to its intellectual property statutes through the *World Trade Organization Agreement Implementation Act*, S.C. 1994, c. 47, including the adoption of performers' rights. For a good overview of the WTO's new intellectual property agreement, see Klaus Stegemann, "Uruguay Round Results for New Issues," in Technology, Information and Public Policy, ed. Thomas J. Courchene (Kingston, ON: John Deutsch Institute, Queen's University, 1995).

176 As of 6 December 2002, 39 countries, not including Canada, have signed the *WIPO Copyright Treaty* and 39, not including Canada, have signed the *WIPO Performances and Phonograms Treaty*; the WIPO Web site <wipo.org> can be used to review up-to-date lists of signatories. These treaties cover a number of topics, including a range of digital rights management issues, such as prohibiting anti-circumvention measures, and establishing a new right of "making available" a work to the public.

177 These groups have their work cut out for them. In 1996 the BSA compared the number of personal computers sold to the number of software packages sold, and using a ratio of 1:3 (every PC uses roughly three software programs), the

These international efforts of adopting stronger intellectual property laws around the world are particularly welcome in the age of the Internet. Indeed, the territorial basis of patent, copyright, and other intellectual property laws will probably have to be modified to adequately cope with a number of challenges posed by the Internet's ability to facilitate sustained cross-border remote access activities. In effect, the fourth dynamic of computer law is sorely testing the current global intellectual property legal regime that is still stubbornly nationalist in orientation. There are, however, some signs of progress. For example, in a recent case in the U.K., a defendant who operated a server/ computer that infringed a U.K. patent was found to be subject to the U.K. court's jurisdiction, and to have infringed the U.K. patent, even though the server was operated out of Antigua.[178] The patent was for a computerized gaming system, and bettors who were resident in the United Kingdom accessed the Antiguan-based server over the Internet. In a manner reminiscent of the criminal gaming cases referred to in chapter 3, section B.7, "Gaming and Betting," and the jurisdiction cases referred to in chapter 7, section B.2(a), "Regulatory/Criminal Jurisdiction," the court concluded that the U.K. resident "used" the infringing computer in the United Kingdom, even though the computer was physically located offshore.

BSA estimated that half the software programs in use are pirated, illegal copies: "Intellectual Property: The Property of the Mind," *The Economist*, 27 July 1996. In 1995 the SPA estimated that in 1994 the software industry lost $8 billion in revenues to piracy: Stuart J. Johnston, "Microsoft Pilot Helps Firms Pinpoint Piracy," *Computerworld*, 12 June 1995. More recently, the Internet has helped fuel the increase in software piracy: Rebecca Buckman, "Microsoft Makes War On Pirates," *The Globe and Mail* (2 August 2000); and "Sega Crusades Against Piracy," *The Globe and Mail* (27 July 2000). At the same time, the Internet allows Microsoft to use a new search engine to ferret out illegally copied software, "Microsoft Finds Pirate Software Sites," *The Globe and Mail* (3 August 2000). Retailers, in some cases large, multistore, reputable ones, can also contribute to the problem of software piracy: Terry Weber, "Microsoft Settles Piracy Case," *The Globe and Mail* (13 November 2000). In any event, the piracy rate (by the figures of the industry), continue to remain stubbornly in the 40-percent range: "Ontario Takes Biggest Hit on Software Piracy Losses," *The Globe and Mail* (2 November 2000); and Showwei Chu, "Software Piracy Rises in 2001: Study," *The Globe and Mail* (11 June 2002).

178 *Menashe Business Mercantile Limited* v. *William Hill Organization Limited* [2002] EWCA Civ. 1702. But see also *Freedom Wireless, Inc.* v. *Boston Communications Group, Inc.* Civ. No. 00-12234-EFH (D.C. Mass, April 16, 2002), where Rogers, a Toronto-based wireless phone operator, was held not to infringe a U.S. patent on a database resident in Boston when Rogers merely used the Boston-based service on an ancillary basis; that is, it was used only in analysing billing information for a prepaid wireless billing service, and was not a control point.

C. CONTENTIOUS ISSUES

With technological changes advancing at a fast pace, the intellectual property legal regimes face a number of challenges. Indeed, all four of the dynamics of computer law are being felt acutely in the intellectual property area. Moreover, for the most part the intellectual property statutes emanate from the Industrial Age, and therefore are hard-pressed to remain current in the Information Age. How, and indeed whether, patents should apply to software and Internet-based business methods are burning questions in the computer industry. Similarly, copyright protection for software has yielded a number of judicial answers over the past decade. The application of traditional intellectual property laws to new information-based products, such as electronic databases, and to new technologies, such as multimedia works and the Internet, also raises a host of questions. Are there other means of legal protection available for information-based products? Besides these substantive issues, there are process-related questions regarding the way intellectual property questions are posed and resolved in our current legal system.

1) Legal Dispute Resolution

Before turning to the substantive topics, it is worth looking at the difficulties inherent in legal decision making in the high-technology intellectual property arena. First, there is the need for the legal system, including lawyers, judges, and legislators, to be able to understand the new technologies. This is not a trivial exercise, as noted by an American judge in an early computer law case:

> [I]n the computer age, lawyers and courts need no longer feel ashamed or even sensitive about the charge, often made, that they confuse the issue by resort to legal "jargon", law Latin or Norman French. By comparison, the misnomers and industrial shorthand of the computer world make the most esoteric legal writing seem as clear and lucid as the Ten Commandments or the Gettysburg Address; and to add to this Babel, the experts in the computer field, while using exactly the same words, uniformly disagree as to precisely what they mean.[179]

---

179 *Honeywell, Inc. v. Lithonia Lighting, Inc.*, 317 F.Supp. 406 at 408 (N.D. Ga. 1970).

This language barrier between technologists and the legal community means that legislators must be extremely careful to draft laws in this area without using jargon, and in as technology-neutral a fashion as possible. In the contractual area, lawyers should also strive to describe technological concepts in functional, objective terms, rather than in techno-speak (or as some would argue, techno-babble) shorthand.

The complexity of the subject matter, coupled with the first dynamic of computer law, might be taxing the traditional adversarial system of civil litigation to the limit. Consider the following passage from the decision of an American judge presiding over a lengthy, complicated patent lawsuit involving semiconductor chip technologies developed by Hitachi and Motorola, the parties to the litigation:

> For reasons stated above, the Court is constrained to find damages both for infringements by Hitachi and by Motorola. It is both in making the initial infringement determination and in fashioning the remedy that this Court is made acutely aware of the travesty of justice cases such as this pose upon courts. The subject matter of this suit is extremely complex and delicate; not the sort of thing the lay person should be put in a position of judging. The intricacies of the patents and devices involved is [sic] clear only to the engineer. The far-reaching effects of infringement is [sic] known only to the business persons and marketing specialists involved with Motorola and Hitachi. What is more perplexing to this Court is these two parties have dealt personally with each other for years. They have negotiated their differences with the skill and expertise only they can possess. Yet suddenly they left behind their prior relationship and expected this Court to ferret out the wrongdoings of which each is accused. Even worse, they hired lawyers to compound and exponentially increase their disputes and damages. This court has seen more than ninety motions filed in this case, replete with bickering and petty insults. The parties would have saved time, money, feelings, and relations had they curbed their emotions and sat down to settle their difference out of court. In short, this suit is not the sort of thing Federal Courts should spend time and energy upon. The parties present this Court not with legal questions, but with questions related to engineering and electronic technology more suitably determined by those intimately familiar with the art.
>
> With that, the Court shall begin its bewildering foray into the issue of damages.[180]

---

180 *Motorola, Inc.* v. *Hitachi, Ltd.*, 2 Computer Cases (CCH) ¶46,280 at 62,103, quote at 62,118-19 (W.D. Texas 1990).

A similar admission was made by a judge in a Canadian case involving technical subject matter:

> The matter of a serious question to be tried is doubtful. The plaintiff avers that the defendant's device infringes the plaintiff's patent, because as it seems, the defendant's device is capable of the basic functions claimed for the plaintiff's patented device. The defendant's counsel says it is clear and obvious that his client's device, because of its functions, does not infringe. Quite simply, the parties' respective technologies and the comparison between them are unintelligible to this judge, as presented by the parties' respective counsel. This judge is just unable to form an opinion on the basis of the parties' respective submissions, involving as they do, functions of electromagnetic formulae.
>
> One often hears complaints by members of the so-called "patent bar" or "intellectual property bar" that Federal Court judges lack the scientific and technical formations for easy understanding of patent cases involving electrical and chemical and other scientific inventions. That complaint is probably true, and this judge openly admits it. On the other hand, it is said that members of those bars from which the complaint arises, will never accept an appointment to this bench, because they already earn from their generally affluent clients, incomes which significantly surpass judicial salaries. Present-day Canadian society does not seem to be imbued with the ideal of sacrifice in order to give service to the country and its institutions and the truth of that observation may well lie at the root of the lack of judges of a scientific or technical background, such as this judge.[181]

Finally, consider the following passage from a recent Canadian case involving a technical subject matter, in this case chemical compounds; the court had to determine whether a particular fabric softener infringed the patents that protected another brand of fabric softener:

> The trial of these actions on the claim and counterclaim was not ordinary in its duration. The public litigation extended over 35 long (early until late) days, from October 16, 1990, until February 8, 1991, in both Toronto and Ottawa. No doubt because of the high incidence of unfilled vacancies, and some illness among the judges of the Trial Division, no sufficient duration of uninterrupted reflexion and writing time could be accorded to this judge until October 1992. Given the mind-boggling volume of documentary evidence, conflicting scientific and other testimony, and written and oral argument, it

---

181 *Geonics Ltd. v. Geoprobe Ltd.* (1991), 37 C.P.R. (3d) 346 at 348 (F.C.T.D.).

is admittedly difficult for this judge now to sort out the evidence, especially the chemistry which was all new to the judge upon reading over the file prior to the opening of the trial in Toronto. Expert witnesses — called because, one supposes, of their eminence in the chemical science in which they proudly purport to be expert — are a large hindrance rather than much help because, of course, they are paid to contradict the eminent scientists on the opposite side. They remind one of another ancient profession (law, or soldiery) rather than learned experts of technical precision seeking to find and to explain scientific verities.

When one considers the apparent silliness of trial by a judge who is utterly unschooled in the scientific substance of a patent, hearing conflicting testimony of so-called experts to speak the antithesis of scientific verity, and lawyers who have been engaged in the particular case for years before the trial, one knows that this field cries out for reform. It wastes the scarce resources of the court, which is not configured for getting at the truth of arcane scientific contradictions. A judge unschooled in the arcane subject is at difficulty to know which of the disparate, solemnly mouthed and hotly contended "scientific verities" is, or are, plausible. Is the eminent scientific expert with the shifty eyes and poor demeanour the one whose "scientific verities" are not credible? Cross-examination is said to be the great engine for getting at the truth, but when the unschooled judge cannot perceive the truth, if he or she ever hears it, among all the chemical or other scientific baffle-gab, is it not a solemn exercise in silliness? Reform is much needed in the field of non-mechanical patents' litigation.[182]

On the other hand, many courts do not seem to have a problem wading into the technical details of intellectual property cases, immersing themselves in the scientific minutiae (a particularly relevant exercise in patent matters), and dispensing informed justice. For a good example, consider the decision of Madam Justice Reed in *AT&T Technologies, Inc. v. Mitel Corp.*[183] that dealt with the validity of a patent related to complex technology surrounding the fabrication of transistors in the 1960s. Specifically, the patent claims at issue read as follows:

---

182 *Unilever PLC v. Procter & Gamble Inc.* (1993), 47 C.P.R. (3d) 479 at 488-89 (F.C.T.D.) [*Unilever*]. One of the counsel in this case, now a justice of the Supreme Court of Canada, has called upon lawyers and judges to consider carefully how science may be better understood in the courtroom: Richard Furness, "Lawyers, Judges Must Become More Science-Friendly, Binnie Tells Toronto Audience," *The Lawyer's Weekly*, 7 March 2003.

183 (1989), 26 C.P.R. (3d) 238 (F.C.T.D.) [*AT&T*].

1. In the method for making a semiconductor structure in which a diffused region of one conductivity type is formed in a semiconductor substrate having the opposite conductivity type and which requires an insulating layer and an overlying conductive layer having a critical spatial relationship with respect to the diffused region the improvement which comprises forming the insulating layer on the semiconductor substrate, forming a silicon layer over selected portions of the insulating layer, using the silicon layer as a mask, diffusing impurities into the semiconductor substrate to form the diffusion layer using the silicon layer as a diffusion mask and simultaneously or separately diffusing impurities into the silicon layer to render it conductive.

9. In an insulated-gate silicon field effect transistor, the improvement which comprises a gate electrode which is of polycrystalline silicon.

10. The transistor of claim 9 in which the gate insulator comprises silicon dioxide.[184]

In this complicated case, Reed J. seemed to have no trouble figuring out the science and applying the relevant law. Indeed, at the end of the judgment she even noted why she had not referred to some of the diagramatic evidence: because, as far as she was concerned, it contained errors.

Notwithstanding Reed J.'s decision in the *AT&T* case, the judicial pronouncements noted earlier in this section are disturbing. They raise a number of questions about the capacity of the traditional civil litigation system to deal with highly technical subject matter. In essence, is the first dynamic of computer law — namely, the rapid pace of technological change — presenting a material obstacle to effective judicial dispute resolution? Several remedial measures are possible. One remedy is to remove intellectual property disputes from the standard judicial system and submit these cases to alternative dispute resolution processes such as mediation and, in particular, arbitration. Arbitration is a legal dispute process where the parties to the dispute choose their own decision maker. For a case involving a software-related patent or a software copyright issue, arbitration permits the parties to choose an arbitrator who has experience in the software field, or who has technology/business or technology/legal experience. Or if the case merits the additional expense, a panel of three arbitrators could be chosen, with each member having a technical, business, or legal background. This was

---

184 *Ibid.*, at 249.

done in the arbitration between IBM and Fujitsu in the mid-1980s.[185] In addition to allowing parties to choose their own expert "judge," arbitration has the further advantage of permitting the parties to keep confidential their dispute; of course, in some cases a party to a dispute does not want to keep matters quiet, and indeed wants the glare of publicity to pressure the other party into a settlement. In regular court proceedings there are means by which certain sensitive evidence can be ordered sealed by the court in files that the public does not have access to. This can be very important in an intellectual property case where disclosure of the trade secret or other information would defeat the very relief sought by the plaintiff. Nonetheless, the existence of the litigation in court will be a matter of public record, as will certain papers filed with the court. By contrast, at least in theory, an arbitration and all documents related to it can be kept private, though depending on the parties and the facts of the case, rumours may begin to circulate regarding the arbitration. Indeed, in the case of a major arbitration where the parties have agreed contractually to keep the matter confidential, an invidious situation can arise where inaccurate and highly speculative stories surface in the trade press regarding the arbitration, and the underlying positions and claims made by the two parties, but these cannot be rectified or even rebutted because of the non-disclosure rules, thereby potentially causing damage to at least one of the parties' relationships with third parties.

A further advantage often touted for arbitration is the greater speed with which the matter can be brought to a determination in an arbitral setting. In many Canadian cities the courts are so clogged that it can take months, if not years in some cases, before the substantive merits of the case can be heard, as opposed to motions for interim or interlocutory relief that can generally be heard within a matter of weeks, or days if required; the ability to obtain interim relief in a rather timely fashion, and usually in less time than it takes to appoint the arbitrator, argues for the practice of reserving the right to resort to the regular judicial system for such relief even if the substantive merits of the case are subject to arbitration. And in the computer industry, with its short and ever-shrinking product cycles (a further manifestation of the first

---

185 The "clean room procedure" established by this arbitration for the creation of non-infringing software is referred to in Richard A. Brait, "The Unauthorized Use of Confidential Information" (1991) 18 C.B.L.J. 323. For a discussion of Michigan's foray into creating a hospitable regime for arbitration of high-tech disputes, see Daryl-Lynn Carlson, "States Initiate Cyber Courts to Specialize in Technology," *Law Times*, 9 July 2001.

dynamic of computer law), justice delayed is truly justice denied. Moreover, prompt decisions can also result in cost savings. Full-blown court-based litigation can be extremely expensive, primarily because of the protracted nature of the pre-trial skirmishing. Therefore, a short arbitration, even with the parties paying the fees and expenses of the arbitrator, can be cheaper than litigation. Of course, sometimes parties to an arbitration get what they pay for, particularly given the preference of a number of arbitrators who are business people to achieve "justice" by merely splitting the difference between the two protagonists. High-quality dispute resolution determination, which often entails finding completely in favour of one of the parties, is an art honed through long experience, precisely the expertise that seasoned judges bring to any dispute. This is why retired judges are in such demand as arbitrators.

Parties not resident in the same jurisdiction and affected by the fourth dynamic of computer law — the blurring of national and international — will often resort to arbitration in a neutral third country as a means of not giving the appearance of advantage to one party by using its legal system for disputes. Again, this is an example of resorting to a contractual solution to address one of the four dynamics of computer law. One further benefit to arbitration is the ability of parties to an arbitration to craft the procedural rules that will apply to their dispute resolution process.[186] For example, the parties may wish to provide for intensive education of the arbitrator(s) in the relevant technical subject matter, perhaps even by having a neutral instructor provide at least certain background material. Of course, a critical objective for every advocate in an intellectual property case is to educate the judge by distilling the essence of the technologies or science involved and then imparting this in a manner that is both intellectually honest and easily understandable — no mean feat! Arbitration can arguably assist this process by allowing a greater panoply of teaching and demonstra-

---

186 To the extent the parties are silent on a procedural point, the relevant provincial arbitration statute will apply; for example, in Ontario the *Arbitration Act*, 1991, S.O. 1991, c. 17, for arbitrations among Ontario entities, and the *International Commercial Arbitration Act*, R.S.O. 1990, c. I.9, for arbitrations with a party that is outside of Ontario. Another benefit of arbitration, particularly to an entity providing products or services to multiple customers, is the ability to preclude class action claims: see the discussion of the *Kanitz* case in chapter 6, section A.3(c), "Express and Implied Click-Consent Agreements," though it should be noted that some jurisdictions prohibit parties from contracting out of the class action regime. Notwithstanding such legislation, the trend is clearly for courts to support arbitration: see *Editions Chouette*, above note 132, where the Supreme Court of Canada held that copyright ownerships disputes can be resolved by arbitration.

tive aids, given the generally more relaxed approach to the rules of evidence in an arbitration setting than those found in the courtroom.

In this regard it should be noted that judges will sometimes attempt to bridge the technology knowledge gap by appointing a technical expert (nominally) to assist the judge. As noted above in the passage from the *Unilever* case,[187] typically in each intellectual property case the plaintiff and defendant each retain a subject matter expert to explain why the position of the party retaining the expert is firmly buttressed by the technical evidence. Given, however, that these experts invariably vehemently disagree, a judge will on occasion recruit an "independent" expert to assist the judge in sorting through the technical evidence and the respective experts' reports of the parties. For example, such an expert was appointed by the trial judge in the *Altai* software copyright infringement case.[188] Indeed, in this decision the influence of the court-appointed expert was so great as to raise the question whether the judge at trial overly deferred to the views of the expert. For instance, the expert developed a mechanistic formula for weighing certain aspects of the two software programs in issue in the litigation (i.e., source code counted for 1000 points, organization of the program counted for 100 points, etc.) that would result in a finding of copyright infringement only if there was copying by the defendant of the source code of the plaintiff's program. Interestingly, while the trial decision, concluding that there was no copyright infringement by the defendant, was upheld on appeal, the appeal court made no mention of this formula and instead devised a very different legal test for copyright infringement, which is discussed below. There is, then, the danger that a judicial decision maker overly defers to a court-appointed expert. Interestingly, this concern is not evident in an arbitration setting, where the technical expert is the decision maker because the parties can engage in a dialogue directly with the expert, a key concern with the court-appointed expert being that the parties neither appoint the expert nor have any direct interaction with him or her. Nonetheless, there may well be a place for court-appointed technical experts in intellectual property cases provided suitable respect for due process principles can be guaranteed the parties. In short, the regular judicial system continually needs to take advantage of new means by which the distance between the technical and legal worlds can be abridged.

---

187 *Unilever*, above note 182.
188 *Computer Associates International, Inc. v. Altai, Inc.*, 3 Computer Cases (CCH) ¶46,505 at 63,357 (E.D.N.Y. 1991), aff'd 982 F.2d 693 (2d Cir. 1992).

2) Patent Protection for Software and Business Methods

Whether computer software should be able to be patented has engendered significant debate in Canada, the United States, and other countries, notably in Europe and Japan. The *Patent Act* provides that mere scientific principles or abstract theorems are not patentable subject matter. In the *Schlumberger* decision, it was held that the particular computer program before the court was not patentable because the program merely performed a series of mathematical calculations in order to extract useful information.[189] Accordingly, in the mid-1980s, the Canadian Patent Office issued guidelines (which have since been superseded) on the patentability of computer-related subject matter that included the statement that computer programs *per se* are not patentable. The *Schlumberger* case, however, did not preclude a computer program or a data processing system from being proper patentable subject matter. Indeed, the Canadian[190] and, especially, the U.S.[191] Patent Offices have been allowing patent applications that consist largely of, and in many cases entirely of, computer software, particularly where they are artfully and skilfully drafted to include some hardware elements in the claims and so long as they do not focus overly on stand-alone algorithms but rather refer to systems, processes, or methods to achieve a concrete solution to a specific problem. As a result, the current guidelines for the patentability of computer-related subject matter issued by the Canadian Patent Office no longer contain

---

189 *Schlumberger Canada Ltd.* v. *Commissioner of Patents* (1981), 56 C.P.R. (2d) 204 (F.C.A.). For a discussion of the general requirements for patentability (i.e., utility, novelty, and inventiveness), see the discussion above in section B.2 of this chapter, "Patents."

190 See *In Re Motorola Inc. Patent Application No. 2085228* (1998), 86 C.P.R. (3d) 71 (Pat. Appeal Bd.); *Re Honeywell Information Systems Inc.* (1986), 11 C.I.P.R. 81 (Pat. Appeal Bd.); and *Re Application of Fujitsu Ltd.* (1985), 9 C.P.R. (3d) 475 (Pat. Appeal Bd.). See also *Re Application of Vapor Canada Ltd.* (1985), 9 C.P.R. (3d) 524 (Pat. Appeal Bd.), where, in allowing some claims, the decision denied other claims that were directed only to the extraction of information from recorded data or that describe a computer performing the kinds of steps for which computers were invented. Or consider *Re Application for Patent of General Electric Co.* (1984), 6 C.P.R. (3d) 191 (Pat. Appeal Bd.), where a software program was held patentable as part of a large engine control system.

191 See *AT&T Corp.* v. *Excel Communications, Inc.*, 172 F. 3d 1352 (Fed. Cir. 1999), cert. denied, 120 S. St. 368 (1999) [AT&T Corp.]; *State Street Bank & Trust Co.* v. *Signature Financial Group*, 149 F.3d 1368 (Fed. Cir. 1998), cert. denied, 119 S.Ct. 851 (1999) [*State Street Bank*]; *Re Alappat*, 33 F.3d 1526 (Fed. Cir. 1994); and *Arrhythmia Research Technology Inc.* v. *Corazonix Corporation*, 958 F.2d 1053 (Fed. Cir. 1992) [*Arrhythmia*].

the statement that computer programs *per se* are unpatentable.[192] Similarly, the lengthier U.S. guidelines regarding computer-related inventions are also quite amenable to appropriately drafted software-related patents.[193]

The U.S. guidelines give a useful discussion of the criteria for patent protection for software-related inventions.[194] Processes will be found to be non-patentable if, for example, they consist solely of mathematical operations or simply manipulate abstract ideas without some practical application. Thus, the guidelines indicate that patent claims that define a "data structure" *per se* will be considered to relate to information rather than a computer-implemented process, and hence will not be patentable. By contrast, algorithms implemented by a computerized process that actually manipulate data to achieve a specific result are patentable. In this regard, the U.S. guidelines cite the American *Arrhythmia* case, where the patent, based on complex algorithms, was allowed as it was found directed to the analysis of electrocardiographic signals in order to determine certain characteristics of heart function.[195] That is, the output from the patented system was not an abstract number but signals related to a patient's heart activity.

The decision in *Arrhythmia* (which involved a computer program) was followed by what many commentators consider to be the landmark decision in *State Street Bank* (which involved a novel business method implemented through software). In this latter American case, Signature Financial's patent[196] covered a data processing system, identified by its proprietary name "Hub and Spoke," that facilitated a financial investment structure whereby mutual funds (Spokes) pool their assets in an investment portfolio (Hub) organized as a partnership. This configuration provides the mutual fund administrator with the advantage of

---

192 Canadian Intellectual Property Office, The Patent Office Record, "Notice 16," Vol. 123, No. 8, 21 February 1995.

193 United States Department of Commerce, Patent and Trademark Office, "Examination Guidelines for Computer-Related Inventions" 61 Fed. Reg. 7478, 29 March 1996 (also reproduced in Guide to Computer Law (CCH) ¶60,530 at 82,103).

194 The U.S. guidelines, and the U.S. case law on the patentability of software and Internet business method patents, are of more than academic interest to Canadians, given that virtually all Canadian technology companies are active in the huge American market, and thus Canadians are effectively very much affected by U.S. patent law.

195 *Arrhythmia*, above note 191.

196 U.S. Patent No. 5,193,056, "Data Processing System for Hub and Spoke Financial Services Configuration."

combining economics of scale in administering investments, together with the tax advantages of a partnership. State Street Bank wished to license this patented data processing system, but when the parties' negotiations failed, State Street Bank brought an action to declare the patent invalid. The court, however, upheld the patent, concluding that:

> Today, we hold that the transformation of data, representing discrete dollar amounts, by a machine through a series of mathematical calculations into a final share price, constitutes a practical application of a mathematical algorithm, formula, or calculation, because it produces "a useful, concrete and tangible result" — a final share price momentarily fixed for recording and reporting purposes and even accepted and relied upon by regulatory authorities and in subsequent trades.[197]

The decision in *State Street Bank* made it clear beyond all doubt that a business method implemented through software can be patented in the United States if it is limited to a practical application of the abstract idea or mathematical algorithm. Moreover, the decision in *AT&T Corp.* completed the "dephysicalization" of these business process patents by concluding that they were not limited to patents involving "machine" claims. These decisions have caused a flurry of patent applications aimed at software and Internet-based business methods. Coupled with the continuing deluge of software patent applications, the U.S. Patent Office is issuing a significant number of these new patents. Many relate to various features involved in e-commerce. Amazon used its "one-click" patent[198] to enjoin Barnes and Noble from using a similar online ordering feature just before the 1999 Christmas shopping season.[199]

---

197 *State Street Bank*, above note 191 at 1373.

198 U.S. Patent No. 5,960,411, "A Method and System for Placing a Purchase Order Via a Communications Network." Amazon's "1-Click" ordering system allows pre-registered consumers to buy an item from the Amazon Web site with a single click, as the system involves pre-set parameters for payment, shipping, and address that are stored with Amazon. Amazon invented this feature to combat the problem of 50 to 65 percent of shopping carts being abandoned by online consumers, many because of the complexity of ordering products over the Internet.

199 *Amazon.com, Inc. v. BarnesandNoble.com, Inc.*, 73 F.Supp. 2d 1228 (W.D. Wash. 1999). Interestingly, Barnes and Noble's response to the injunction, namely adding a second, "confirming" screen to the ordering process that had users confirm the order they were about to submit, has advantages under certain of the recently enacted electronic commerce statutes from the perspective of denying buyers the ability to rescind transactions: see the discussion in chapter 6, section A.4(b), "Law Reform." Subsequently, in *Amazon.com Inc. v. BarnesandNoble.com, Inc.*, 239 F.3d 1343 (Fed. Cir. C.A. 2001), the injunction was lifted, without a determination of the merits of the case. Ultimately, the parties settled this matter before it went to trial.

Priceline.com has received a patent on its "name your-own-price" travel reservation business model,[200] upon which it has based a claim against Microsoft's Expedia travel subsidiary when the latter began to offer a competing service.[201] Literally hundreds of other software, Internet and business process patents have been issued in the United States.[202]

While the Canadian Patent Office has not been as enthusiastic about issuing these sorts of patents, Canadian companies have pursued them in the United States.[203] Moreover, a number of practitioners

---

200 U.S. Patent No. 5,794,207. Jay Walker, the principal behind Priceline.com, through Walker Digital Corp., has reportedly filed some two hundred patents, with a dozen related to electronic commerce: N. Wingfield, "Former President of First USA Joins Internet Firm Walker Digital as CEO," *Wall Street Journal* (16 September 1999). See also Thomas E. Weber and Andrea Petersen, "Entrepreneur Finally Strikes Billion Dollar Idea," *The Globe and Mail* (2 April 1999).

201 *Priceline.com Inc. v. Microsoft Corp. and Expedia, Inc.*, Civil No. 99-CV-01991 (D. Conn., filed 13 October 1999).

202 British Telecom, for example, claims that it has a sixteen-year-old patent covering hyperlinks: Thorold Barker, "BT Holds US Hyperlink 'Patent'," *FT.com/Financial Times* (19 June 2000); and Jeri Clausing, "Patent Claims Pop Up All Over the Internet," Cyber Law Journal (23 June 2000) <nytimes.com/library/tech/00/06/cyber/cyberlaw/23law.html>. In *British Telecommunications, Plc v. Prodigy Communications Corporation*, 189 F.Supp. 2d 101 (S.D.N.Y. 2002), the claims of the BT patent (U.S. Patent No. 4,873,662) were construed in a so-called Markman hearing, and subsequently, in *British Telecommunications PLC v. Prodigy Communications Corporation*, 217 F.Supp. 2d 399 (S.D.N.Y. 2002) [*British Telecommunications*], a court rejected BT's infringement argument, concluding that the Internet does not drive off a central computer or use blocks of information, as claimed in the patent in question (BT claimed that every Web server is a "central computer," and that HTML files constituted "blocks of information"). More recently, AOL was granted two U.S. patents for instant messaging software: David Akin, "Instant Messaging Battle Pending: Patents Could Give AOL the Upper Hand," *The Globe and Mail* (20 December 2002). See notes 62–64 above for figures on the overall volume of patents being issued in the United States in the technology sector, a good number of which relate to software, Internet, and business methods.

203 See, for example, U.S. Patent 5,890,138, issued to Bid.com International Inc., of Mississauga, Canada (now known as ADB Systems International). The patent covers an Internet-based auction system, and the patent shows as the two inventors "Paul B. Godin and Jeffrey Lymburner, Etobicoke, both of Canada." See also *Zi Corporation of Canada Inc. v. Tegic Communications Inc.*, 2000 U.S. App. Lexis 26659 (Fed. Cir. 2000). Canadian companies are both bringing patent suits (Showwei Chu, "RIM Launches Lawsuits, Claims Patent Infringed," *The Globe and Mail* (15 October 2002)), and settling them (Showwei Chu, "RIM Drops Handspring Patent Suit: Negotiates Licensing Deal with Rival," *The Globe and Mail* (6 November 2002); and "Nortel Settles Patent Lawsuit with Extreme," *The Globe and Mail* (1 October 2002)).

believe that the Federal Court of Appeal in Canada would uphold a business method patent if one came before it.[204] A recent decision of this court in the *"Harvard Mouse* case,"[205] gives support to this position. In this case, the Federal Court of Appeal concluded, contrary to the views of the Commissioner of Patents and the Federal Court, Trial Division, that genetically altered non-human mammals can be patented.[206] In coming to this conclusion, the court found useful guidance in the related U.S. decision that also held the Harvard mouse patentable, because the definition of "invention" in the Canadian patent statute was derived virtually word-for-word from the American patent statute.[207] Therefore, if there is increasing convergence in Canadian and U.S. patent law in the biotechnology area, one could expect a similar consistency in the software and Internet business methods patents area.[208] It should be noted, however, that by a narrow margin (5 to 4), the Supreme Court overturned the Federal Court of Appeal's decision in *Harvard Mouse*, concluding that higher life forms cannot be patented under Canada's

---

204 Mark Bourrie, "Widening the Scope of Patent Protection," *Law Times*, 14 January 2002.

205 *Harvard College* v. *Canada (Commissioner of Patents)* (2000), 7 C.P.R. (4th) 1 (F.C.A.) [*Harvard Mouse*]. But note that the Supreme Court has overturned this decision: see note 209 below.

206 Prior to this decision, biotech patents were restricted to lower life forms consisting of uni-cellular organisms: see *Re Application of Abitibi Co.* (1982), 62 C.P.R. (2d) 81 (Com'r. Pat.) where microorganisms such as yeast were found to be patentable. It should be noted, however, that the Federal Court of Appeal, in *Harvard Mouse*, above note 205, at para. 127, did make it clear that human beings cannot be patented (at least at the non-genetic level): "Patenting is a form of ownership of property. Ownership concepts cannot be extended to human beings. There are undoubtedly other bases for so concluding, but one is surely section 7 of the *Canadian Charter of Rights and Freedoms*, which protects liberty. There is, therefore, no concern by including non-human mammals under the definition of 'invention' in the *Patent Act*, that there is any implication that a human being would be patentable in the way that the oncomouse is."

207 While all patent law derives generically from the common law of England and the British royal prerogative to grant monopolies for new inventions (see H.G. Fox, *The Canadian Law and Practice Relating to Letters Patent for Invention*, 4th ed. (Toronto: Carswell, 1969), the court in *Harvard Mouse* noted that Canada's first patent law [*Patent Act* of 1869, S.C. 1869, c.11] was modelled on the American statute of 1836.

208 Such increased commonality would be welcomed by counsel practising in the information technology area: see Sheldon Gordon, "A Patent Revolution," <cba.org>, December 2001. However, this increased commonality on both sides of the Canada-U.S. border in biotech patent matters is not welcomed by all commentators: see Richard Gold, "Building A Better Patent Law," *The Globe and Mail* (17 May 2002).

current *Patent Act*; the court invited Parliament to amend the statute if it wished to provide for the patenting of transgenic animals.[209]

A number of commentators have criticized the issuance by the U.S. Patent Office of software-, Internet- and business method-oriented patents. The criticism stems from several arguments, including in respect of software: software is too mathematical and scientific; software is not embodied in a physical device; changes to software programs are effected too incrementally to be inventive; the difficulties of searching the Patent Office for software patents, particularly given that the search will not reveal current applications, are particularly onerous for individual software developers and smaller companies; the Patent Office has issued a number of patents that would not have been issued had the relevant state of prior art been brought to the Patent Office's attention; the Patent Office's staff are inexpert in matters related to software; and for many years the software industry got along fine relying solely on copyright and trade secrets.[210] A Canadian law professor specializing in Internet and electronic commerce law has commented on the "absurdity of such patents and the danger they pose to e-commerce growth."[211] A number of journalists have bemoaned these new types of patents.[212] One of the leading thinkers about the Internet, Canada's

---

209 *Harvard College*, above note 21. This decision, and the issue of patenting higher life forms, has generated a great deal of commentary, on both sides of the issue: Jonathan Kimmelman, "Free the Harvard Mouse," *The Globe and Mail* (4 December 2002); and Carolyn Abraham, "Mouse Ruling May Stall Research," *The Globe and Mail* (6 December 2002).

210 For a canvassing of these and other criticisms of software patents, see Richard Stallman, "Against Software Patents: The League for Programming Freedom" (1992) 14 Hastings Comm. & Ent. L.J. 295; and Pamela Samuelson, "*Benson* Revisited: The Case Against Patent Protection for Algorithms and Other Computer-Related Inventions" (1990) 39 Emory L.J. 1025.

211 Michael Geist, "A Patently Obvious Threat to E-Commerce," *The Globe and Mail*, (27 January 2000). Professor Geist also argues that "Sadly, the costly and complex process of patent applications may well exclude many smaller e-commerce companies who lack the funding and expertise to file such applications." An article in a recent European trade journal, Philip Jolly, "Software Patent Stalemate," *infoconomy Business Briefings 2001*, counts among the most vocal opponents of software patents the leader of the French Linux community, who is quoted as saying that widespread patenting will "stifle" innovation, with "potentially catastrophic consequences." The same article quotes the French secretary of state for industry as warning that software patents "would kill innovation and promote judicial terrorism."

212 For example, J. McHugh, "Barbed Wire on the Internet," *Forbes*, 17 May 1999, in which the danger of the "slippery-slope" question is asked: "What's to stop someone from patenting the idea of franchising a restaurant chain? Or offering

Don Tapscott, who generally favours patents, thinks these may have gone "too far."[213]

The contrary view is that applications for software, Internet, and business methods patents should be treated no differently than other patent applications.[214] Thus, if the patent application reveals only a scientific formula, or if it is not novel or inventive, the patent should not be issued. In this regard, it should be noted that the U.S. and Canadian Patent Offices have upgraded their skills in the software and Internet areas so that they are better able to analyse the prior art and inventiveness questions. In addition, the U.S. Patent Office is willing on occasion to "recall" an issued patent, as it did when it recognized that the controversial patent it had issued for a multimedia interface device was issued in error, and revoked it.[215] Moreover, these patents, just like those in other areas of technology, can be and will be challenged, and a

---

cents-off coupons? Or paying interest on credit balances?" See also Scott Rosenberg, "Amazon to World: We Control How Many Times You Must Click," *Salon Technology* <salon.com/tech/log/1999/12/21/bezos/index.html>. In "Who Owns the Knowledge Economy," above note 64, the editorial board of the *Economist* levels the following thoughtful criticism at the patent system: "The trouble with the law is that it does not differentiate between the incentives needed to invest in different kinds of technologies. It accords as much protection to an idea thought up in the bath as to a drug that may have taken many years and hundreds of millions of dollars to move from conception to marketplace."

213 Don Tapscott, "Patenting of Ideas Becomes a Serious Issue for Business," *National Post* (29 March 1999).

214 See David Bender, "The Case for Software Patents" (1989) 6(5) The Computer Lawyer 2. And in many cases the defendant's activity simply is not found to be infringing: see *Fantasy Sports Properties, Inc. v. Sportsline.com, Inc.*, 287 F. 3d 1108 (Fed. Cir. 2002), where Yahoo's online fantasy football game (where visitors pick teams and direct strategy virtually) was held not to infringe a patent covering such games; and *Charles E. Hill & Associates, Inc. v. Compuserve, Inc.*, 33 Fed. Appx. 527 (Fed. Cir. 2002), where Compuserve's online shopping service was held not to infringe defendant's patent claiming an electronic catalog shopping system.

215 The U.S. Patent Office took this step after much criticism had been levelled at the broad scope of the patent: see Michael D. Bednarek, "Comptons New Media's Patent Saga: Lesson for the Software Industry and Others in Emerging Technologies" (1995) 69 Patent World 29. And the U.S. Patent and Trademark Office is simply being tougher recently on business method patents: see Declan McCullagh, "Are Patent Methods Patently Absurd?" *CNET News.com* (15 October 2002), which quotes the head of the office as saying that while previously the office allowed 65 or 70 percent of these, now they are rejecting the same percentage. That is not to say, of course, that some patents will not continue to raise eyebrows: see William M. Bulkeley, "Controversial Patent Granted," *The Globe and Mail* (3 October 2002), which describes the issuance of a U.S. patent on any computerized process for automating international-commerce paperwork.

good number of them will be held invalid (just as in other areas of technology).[216] Indeed, in this regard, as is often the case, a (supposed) problem caused by the Internet is to a degree being solved by the Internet, in that various online means are being used to help ferret out prior art that can be used against patents that are overly broad.[217] As well, to the extent these patents are upheld, they will not signal the end of innovation or competition. We have seen all this before. Patents have played an incredibly important role in the discovery, development, and commercialization of every communications technology since the telegraph.[218] In the early 1980s, when Merrill Lynch obtained a patent on its cash management account system, many commentators predicted gloom and doom for the financial services sector.[219] Instead, many companies paid a fee to use the Merrill Lynch system, and then they promptly turned around, innovated, and obtained their own patents,

---

216 For example, in *Mossman* v. *Broderbund Software Inc.*, 51 USPQ 2d 1752 (E.D. Mich. 1999), the plaintiff argued that its patent, which involved a method of teaching children in which words or syllables are displayed on a video screen, covered the "Living Books" CD-ROM products of the defendant. The defendant responded that the plaintiff's patent was not inventive because it was anticipated by the prior art, namely several segments on the children's television program "The Electric Company." The court agreed and held the patent invalid. Note also the adverse result to the patent holder in the *British Telecommunications* case, above note 202. To illustrate the see-saw nature of some of these cases, consider that most of the scope of the famous (or infamous) "Freeny patent" was rejected in *Interactive Gift Express, Inc.* v. *Compuserve Inc.*, 231 F.3d 859 (Fed. Cir. 2000), but on appeal the U.S. Federal Circuit allowed several of the claims (231 F. 3d 859 (Fed. Cir. 2000)), and then subsequently in *Interactive Gift Express, Inc.* v. *Compuserve Incorporated*, 256 F.3d 1323 (Fed. Cir. C.A. 2001) the matter was remanded for further proceedings. The Freeny patent (U.S. Pat. No. 4,528,643, 9 July 1985), currently owned by E-Data Corp., describes a method of doing business whereby users select a digitally distributed product from an online catalogue and then have it transmitted electronically to a point of sale location, which could include a house. For a sense of the controversy in the computer and network industries surrounding this patent, see Neil Gross, "E-Commerce: Who Owns the Rights," *Business Week*, 29 July 1996.

217 See, for example, the BountyQuest service, an online network of engineers, scientists, and patent law experts that offers rewards for submitting prior art for given patents: Ashby Jones, "Searching For Silver Bullets: BountyQuest Uses the Tricks of the Wild West to Help Kill Bad Patents," *American Lawyer*, May 2001.

218 See Spar, *Ruling the Waves*, above note 12, which chronicles, among other things, the pivotal role played by patents in the development of the telegraph, telephone, radio, and various other technologies.

219 D.B. Moskowitz, "Using Patents to Protect Innovative Financial Products," *The Washington Post* (20 August 1990).

which Merrill Lynch then had to contend with.[220] And to the criticism that these patents favour large companies over small, consider the successful software patent infringement claim brought by Stac Electronics in 1994 against Microsoft in respect of the unauthorized use of certain data compression technologies for which the former owned several patents.[221] More recently, a survey of the patents issued to technology companies in 2001 noted that while industry behemoths like IBM, Lucent, NEC, and Microsoft received most of the patents, many small companies also did very well, particularly in the bio-tech area.[222] In effect, software, Internet and business-method patents seem firmly embedded in the intellectual property landscape of the United States. Even in Europe, where the *European Patent Convention*[223] expressly states that computer software is not patentable material, the European Patent Office and some national courts have been willing to grant patent protection for certain software-related inventions.[224]

In principle, software, Internet, and business-method patents should not cause alarm. Of course there will be a period of uncertainty, and even angst in some circles, as the patent offices, and the courts, work out the parameters for these patents. This, however, is nothing new. Each wave of innovation, not surprisingly, brings its attendant

---

220 *Paine, Webber, Jackson & Curtis, Inc.* v. *Merrill Lynch, Pierce, Fenner & Smith, Inc.*, 564 F Supp. 1358 (D. Del. 1983).

221 The suit resulted in a jury awarding Stac $120 million for patent infringement, though the parties ultimately settled on the basis of Microsoft paying Stac $40 million in royalties and $40 million for an equity investment. The importance of this litigation in highlighting the strategic value of patents in the computer industry prompted a number of stories about it in the general press: see Anthony Aarons, "Software Giant Dealt Big Loss in Patent Fight," *Los Angeles Daily Journal* (24 February 1994); Lawrence M. Fisher, "Judge Rules Microsoft Must Recall DOS Software," *New York Times* (11 June 1994); and Lawrence M. Fisher, "Microsoft in Accord on Patent: Agrees to Pay Stac in Data Storage Case," *New York Times* (22 June 1994).

222 "Patent Boom," above note 63. Patent lawsuits can also involve the clients of a defendant, thus triggering the intellectual property indemnity in the relevant agreement: see Don Clark, "Microsoft Facing Lucent Claims," *The Globe and Mail* (11 April 2003).

223 The *EPC Convention on the Grant of European Patents* (European Patent Convention) of 5 October 1973, as amended, is available at <epo.co.at/epo.co.at/epo/>.

224 See Laurence Tellier-Loniewski and Alain Bensoussan, "Europe Extends Patent Protection to Software," *The National Law Journal*, (September/October 1996) available at <ljx.com/practice/computer/p6europe.html>. In this piece the authors note Japan is also actively issuing software patents, given that in 1994 the Japan Patent Office received 335,000 patent applications, of which 24,000 (7 percent) were software-related.

flood of patent activity. It was thus with chemicals, transportation devices, certain pharmaceuticals, and a range of other classes of industrial products and technologies over the past hundred years (given that the first dynamic of computer law has analogues with other technologies as well).[225] Indeed, it would be surprising if we did not experience a similar degree of patenting activity in respect of today's critical assets. In short, these new patents will not cause the sky to fall. Accordingly, participants in the Canadian technology community should approach patents proactively, both defensively and offensively. The former involves keeping a close eye on the patents of others, to try to avoid infringing upon them; the latter requires developing a patent strategy, so as to obtain optimum competitive advantage from this important form of intellectual property.

3) Copyright Protection for Software

The *Copyright Act* has always been an uncomfortable home for software. Affording copyright protection to computer programs by calling them literary works has been an effective and efficient way of combatting wholesale piracy, the practice of reproducing all or almost all of a computer program and selling the illegal copy on a bootleg basis. By amending the definition of literary work in the *Copyright Act* to cover computer programs in 1988, software developers were given quick protection in Canada and abroad through Canada's participation in the *Berne Convention*. The alternative of crafting a separate legal regime for software, as has been done with chip topography technology, would have resulted in a much slower pace of protection both domestically and globally. It is, nonetheless, something of a fiction to call software a "literary work." Novels, plays, art, and music, the traditional core copyright works, are communicative vehicles intended to express artistic or aesthetic values. The real genius in these types of works is their expressive flair. Of course Shakespeare crafted intriguing plots and created notorious or endearing characters, but his really profound contribution to English literature is his dialogue, the actual words he chose to express and give life to his eternal themes. There is no "correct" or best way to write about a love between two young people whose families

---

225 First-rate inventors have always been attracted to patents. Thomas Alva Edison (1847-1931), of light bulb fame, still holds the record for most patents, at 1,093: "Who Owns the Knowledge Economy," above note 64. For a book that Edison would enjoy were he able to read it today on why and how to use patents for strategic purposes, see Stephen C. Glazier, *Patent Strategies for Business*, Third Edition (Law & Business Institute: Washington, 2000).

stand in the way. Shakespeare expressed it one way in *Romeo and Juliet*, but Leonard Bernstein expressed it another way in *West Side Story*. Monet and Cézanne both painted the French countryside, but with very different styles — each with his own expressive imprint; the same can be said of Emily Carr and Tom Thomson with respect to Canadian landscape painting.

In contrast, a computer program that runs a company's payroll is a utilitarian device that controls a machine to perform certain predetermined functions.[226] Other software processes document, sort data, perform calculations; these are very different activities than the purpose of a book, which is simply to convey information. Even maps and charts, which have long been covered by copyright, merely convey information — they do not operate machines. Thus, in a case more than one hundred years ago,[227] a British court refused to recognize copyright in

---

226 Some would argue computer program statements do not even look very literary; consider the following sampling of source code, in a mixture of English and French computer commands, reproduced in an early Canadian software infringement case, *Dynabec Ltée* v. *La Sociéte d'Informatique R.D.G. Inc.* (1985), 6 C.P.R. (3d) 322 at 327 (Que. C.A.):

```
Ok
LIST
10   LPRINT<La Compagnie d'Informatique ABC>:
     LPRINT:LPRINT:LPRINT:LPRINT
20   LPRINT TAB (31) <MON CLIENT LTEE>
30   LPRINT:LPRINT:LPRINT
40   LPRINT TAB (29) <LISTE DU SALAIRE BRUT>:
     LPRINT:LPRINT:LPRINT
50   LPRINT TAB (10) <NOM DE L'EMPLOYE>,
     TAB (30) <TAUX>, TAB (45) <HEURES>, TAB (60)
     <BRUT>
60   LPRINT:LPRINT:LPRINT
70   CLS LPRINT<La Compagnie d'Informatique
     ABC>:LOCATE 10,25
80   INPUT>Entrez le nom de l'employé>;
     NOM:LOCATE 12,25
90   INPUT<Entrez son taux horaire>;
     TAUX:LOCATE 14,25
100  INPUT<Entrez le nombre d'heures>;
     HEURES
     ...
```

The second dynamic of computer law — the elusive nature of information — is heavily at work here; for example, does written information protected by copyright have to be comprehensible to humans generally? This is only one of the finicky questions posed by the question of the copyrightability of software.

227 *Hollinrake*, above note 105.

a cardboard pattern with writing and scales on it that was used for making sleeves for clothes. The court concluded that the item did not convey information or pleasure but rather was for practical use, and therefore its protection should be sought in the bailiwick of patent; the court was particularly concerned about giving the long term of copyright protection to such an industrial device.[228] A similar unease and ambivalence towards software can be seen in three reports that addressed intellectual property protection for software prior to the 1988 addition to the *Copyright Act* of computer programs. In 1971 the Economic Council of Canada argued against extending copyright protection to software, lest it grant protection to ideas.[229] In 1984, a government white paper responded to the same concern by proposing that software be divided into two categories, that which is human-readable and that which is executed on a computer, and that the former should have the same term of protection as other copyright works, but protection for the latter be limited to five years.[230] This highly controversial and much criticized proposal was not adopted by a subsequent Parlia-mentary report, which nonetheless had its own strange suggestion, namely, that using part of one program as a non-substantial part of another program be a permitted exception to copyright protection as a form of fair dealing.[231] The government rejected all these concerns and proposals when it amended the *Copyright Act* in 1988 to provide express protection for computer programs as literary works, much in

---

228 In coming to its conclusion, the court in *Hollinrake*, above note 105, stated at 428: "[A] literary work is intended to afford either information and instruction, or pleasure, in the form of literary enjoyment. The sleeve chart before us gives no information or instruction. It does not add to the stock of human knowledge or give, and is not designed to give, any instruction by way of description or otherwise; and it certainly is not calculated to afford literary enjoyment or pleasure. It is a representation of the shape of a lady's arm, or more probably of a sleeve designed for a lady's arm, with certain scales for measurement upon it. It is intended, not for the purpose of giving information or pleasure, but for practical use in the art of dressmaking. It is, in fact, a mechanical contrivance, appliance or tool." For a discussion of copyright more generally, including the difference between it and patent, see section B.3, "Copyright," earlier in this chapter.

229 Economic Council of Canada, *Report on Intellectual and Industrial Property* (Ottawa: Information Canada, 1971).

230 Consumer and Corporate Affairs Canada, Department of Communications, *From Gutenberg to Telidon, A White Paper on Copyright: Proposals for the Revision of the Canadian Copyright Act* (Ottawa: Supply and Services Canada, 1984).

231 House of Commons, Standing Committee on Communications and Culture, *Report of the Sub-Committee on the Revision of Copyright: A Charter of Rights for Creators* (Ottawa: Supply and Services Canada, 1985).

keeping with the trend of other industrialized countries.[232] Nevertheless, given the differences between software and traditional copyright works, a number of respected commentators have called for software to be protected under its own statute, a *sui generis* solution that is capable of responding to the unique attributes of software.[233] One common theme in these proposals is to reduce the term of protection for software. Given the relative youthfulness of many software programmers, the copyright term of protection of life of the author plus 50 years effectively gives software 80 to 100 years of copyright protection, a term that many consider too lengthy in light of the first dynamic of computer law (namely, the rapid pace of technological change in the industry) and the related short, and ever-shortening, life cycles for technology-related products. In effect, the spirit of concern that animated the court in the *Hollinrake* case[234] continues to find expression in these proposals.

In light of the foregoing discussion, it is not surprising that determining the appropriate scope of protection for software within the parameters of the *Copyright Act* — except when presented with the case of wholesale copying — has proven to be an extremely difficult and controversial exercise, indicative of the first two dynamics of computer law, namely, the rapid pace of technological change and the elusive nature of information. Put another way, separating non-protectable idea from protectable expression in software presents courts with a daunting task. In the *Whelan* case, the leading U.S. case of the 1980s, the court determined that the purpose or function of a computer program would be its idea, and that everything not necessary to that purpose would be protectable expression.[235] Therefore, in that case, copyright protected not just the actual computer statements and instructions that made up the program, but extended as well to the "sequence, structure, and organization" of the program, thus providing the initial creator of the program with a very strong level of protection for the software through copyright. In Canada the *Gemologists* case

---

232 For example, the *1996 WIPO Copyright Treaty*, available from the WIPO Web site <wipo.org>, provides in Article 4 that computer programs are to be given copyright protection as literary works.

233 See, for example, Pamela Samuelson *et al.*, "A Manifesto Concerning the Legal Protection of Computer Programs" (1994) 94 Colum. L. Rev. 2308; and Robert A. Arena, "A Proposal for the International Intellectual Property Protection of Computer Software" (1993) 14 U. of Pa. J. Int'l Bus. L. 213.

234 *Hollinrake*, above note 105.

235 *Whelan Associates, Inc. v. Jaslow Dental Laboratory, Inc.*, 797 F.2d 1222 (3d Cir. 1986) [*Whelan*].

exhibited a similarly broad scope of protection by finding that the defendants had copied the "overall logical structure" and "sequence of menus" of the plaintiff.[236]

Partly in response to a torrent of scholarly and industry criticism levelled at the decision in Whelan, a new standard emerged for separating idea from expression in software copyright cases. Expressed in the Altai decision at the appellate level,[237] the current American leading case, as the "abstraction-filtration-comparison test," a key element of the new approach is to recognize that computer programs, rather than having a single overriding idea or purpose, comprise numerous sub-ideas, and thus the initial step in the test requires a dissection of the software into these constituent ideas. Then, in the all-important filtration stage, a number of elements of the software are identified that are not afforded copyright protection, such as those portions of software code that are in the public domain or those aspects of the software that are dictated by the external computing environment[238] or simply by efficiency, as is the case where there is only one way, or a very limited number of ways, in which to program a particular idea. In this latter situation it is sometimes said that there is a "merger" of idea and expression; low-tech examples of this are the silhouettes of a man and a woman on the respective washroom doors, as these symbols are classic examples of the merger of idea with expression. After applying the two steps of abstraction and filtration, the court is left with a smaller number of kernels of protectable software, which are then compared with the defendant's product to see if they have been copied.[239] This

---

236 Gemologists, above note 149.

237 Computer Associates International, Inc. v. Altai, Inc., 982 F.2d 693 (2d Cir. 1992) [Altai].

238 See, for example, Computer Management Assistance Company v. Robert F. De Castro, 220 F.3d 396 (5th Cir. 2000) where no finding of infringement was found because, among other things, the similarities between the two computer programs was driven by particular external business factors. In pre-software cases of copyright infringement, this is often called the "scènes à faire" doctrine, translated from the French to be a "stock scene." For example, in a movie about Pierre Elliott Trudeau, a producer could not copyright the "scene" where the prime minister, after invoking the War Measures Act at the height of the FLQ crisis, in response to a reporter's question as to "how far he would go," replies "Just watch me." No Trudeau biography could be complete without this passage, and so no producer could claim a monopoly on it.

239 Since the decision in Altai, above note 237, some nuances have been added to the test by various U.S. circuit appellate courts. For example, in Gates Rubber Company v. Bando Chemical Industries, Limited, 9 F.3d 823 at 834 (10th Cir. 1993), the court, in a footnote, indicated that in some cases the order in which

abstraction-filtration-comparison standard results in a lower level of copyright protection for software than resulted from the test articulated in the *Whelan* case.[240] The concept of filtering out unprotectable elements of a software program as part of the infringement analysis has been adopted in the important *Delrina* case in Canada.[241] After a lengthy review of the *Altai* case, the trial decision concluded that whether or not the U.S. "abstraction-filtration-comparison" method should be followed by a Canadian judge, some filtering process should be undertaken under the Canadian *Copyright Act* as well, when separating protectable expression from unprotectable idea in a software case; this approach was not disturbed by the Ontario Court of Appeal in *Delrina*. In *Delrina*, as in the *Altai* case, there was no finding of infringement, the court having concluded that the significant similarities in the two programs were attributable largely to the fact that both programs had to correspond to the same external programming constraints given that they were both used to monitor the performance of a particular computer system.[242] In contrast, in the Canadian *Prism* case, while the *Altai* standard of infringement is preferred over that articulated in *Whelan*, infringement was found because the court con-

---

the components of the test are applied may be different; for example, it might be in a certain case that the comparison step should come before filtration as even unprotectable elements are useful to consider in carrying out the evidentiary analysis as to whether there has been copying.

240 Copyright infringement, however, will still be found in the United States under even the *Altai* standard, above note 237, if the two programs' similarities are not dictated by external constraints or the use of common programming techniques, but rather are attributable only to copying, as was the case in *CMAX/Cleveland, Inc. v. UCR, Inc.*, 804 F.Supp. 337 (M.D. Ga. 1992).

241 *Delrina*, above note 71. See also *Matrox*, above note 30, where the court reviews the *Whelan*, above note 235, and *Altai*, above note 237, decisions and decides to adopt the approach found in the latter case.

242 See also *Systèmes informatisés Solartronix v. Cégep de Jonquière* (1990), 38 C.P.R. (3d) 143 (Que. Sup. Ct.), where the defendant's program that automated the operation of a cement plant was found not to copy or plagiarize the plaintiff's program that performed the same function because the design and methodology of the two programs were based on factors common to cement plants, and therefore the court found it not surprising that the two programs were very similar. Equally, in *Hunter Group, Inc. v. Smith, Deloitte & Touche, LLP, et al*, 8 CCH Computer Cases ¶47,903 at 71,442 (4th Cir. 1998), the plaintiff was an implementer of PeopleSoft software, and its claim for trade secret misappropriation of its training materials by departing employees was refused because the court found that most of the relevant information originated from PeopleSoft, not the plaintiff.

cluded that the similarities in the two programs were not driven by external constraints, but were simply the product of copying.[243]

It should be noted that the British standard for determining copyright infringement in software cases is articulated differently from the U.S. "abstraction-filtration-comparison" test. In the U.K. approach, the court asks the following series of questions: What is the work in which copyright is claimed? Is this work original? Was there copying from this work? and perhaps most importantly, If there was copying, has a substantial part of the work been reproduced?[244] With respect to this last question, in one of these cases[245] the court specifically notes that it would be a mistake to adopt the often-quoted proposition "what is worth copying is worth protecting,"[246] because in a utilitarian work like a computer program, each line of code may well be necessary for the software to operate. Thus, a qualitative analysis is preferred to a purely quantitative one, with the focus not being on viewing each copied element in isolation, but rather by considering the collection of copied elements as a whole and then weighing them against the relevant skill and labour in design and coding. It will be interesting to see in the coming years whether this test is adopted by courts in Canada.

The reduction of the scope of protection for software represented by the *Altai, Delrina,* and *Matrox* cases has a counterpart in the degree of protection afforded by copyright to a program's "user interface," which are the various aspects of the program's screen layout, including the use of particular words in menu commands. In the area of user interfaces, the high-water mark for U.S. copyright protection came in the *Softklone* case, in which the court determined that the particular words, such as "speed" and "data," used in a status screen were protected such that the defendant had to select alternative words in its functionally equivalent product.[247] A similar result was arrived at in the trial decisions in various cases brought by Lotus against other developers of spreadsheet programs who imitated the menu commands in the Lotus 1-2-3 product.[248]

---

243 *Prism*, above note 86.
244 *Cantor Fitzgerald*, above note 53; and *Ibcos Computers Ltd. v. Barclays Mercantile Highland Finance Ltd.*, [1994] FSR 275 (H.Ct.).
245 *Cantor Fitzgerald*, above note 53.
246 The questionable quote appears in *University of London Press*, above note 86.
247 *Digital Communications Associates, Inc. v. Softklone Distributing Corporation*, 659 F. Supp. 449 (N.D. Ga. 1987).
248 *Paperback*, above note 17; and *Lotus Development Corporation v. Borland International, Inc.*, 799 F.Supp. 203 (D. Mass. 1992), 831 F.Supp. 223 (D. Mass. 1993). These cases, together with those referred to below in note 249, are collectively referred to as the *Lotus* cases.

In the *Lotus* cases, the defendants felt it important to recreate the same "look and feel" of the plaintiff's products given the leading position in the marketplace of the Lotus products, and the need to be able to sell the defendants' products without having to retrain users. In an important reversal, the appeal court in a *Lotus* case denied protection for the user interface, concluding that the series of commands were a method of operation, and hence expressly precluded copyright protection under subsection 102(b) of the U.S. copyright law.[249] The First Circuit appeals court in this decision analogized the Lotus software's user interface to the symbols and words on the display panel of a videocassette recorder machine, another method of operation and system the court found to be incapable of protection under copyright law. Although the Canadian *Copyright Act* does not contain a provision equivalent to subsection 102(b) of the U.S. statute, the Canadian decision in *Moreau*[250] states that copyright does not extend to a "system or scheme or method for doing a particular thing," and thus the door is open for a Canadian court to adopt the First Circuit appeals court's reasoning in *Lotus* in an appropriate Canadian case involving user interfaces.

4) Copyright Protection for Electronic Databases

Computers are able to collect, aggregate, process, store, and transmit huge volumes of data.[251] These technological and business trends have resulted in many compilers of facts, who traditionally made available the fruits of their effort in a paper-based directory (i.e., a telephone book or a business directory), now providing customers with two computer disks: one containing the raw data and one containing search software to access the data.[252] It is clear from the discussion in the previous section that under copyright law the compiler has protection for

---

249 *Lotus Development Corporation v. Borland International, Inc.*, 49 F.3d 807 (1st Cir. 1995), aff'd 116 S.Ct. 804 (1996). The decision of the U.S. Court of Appeals for the First Circuit was affirmed by the U.S. Supreme Court on 16 January 1996 by a 4–4 deadlock vote; one Supreme Court justice had earlier recused himself, and upon such a tie, the lower court decision is affirmed. See also *Ilog, Inc. v. Bell Logic, LLC* No. 01-10648-WGY (D.C. Mass, 2002), where certain non-literal elements of a computer program were held not to be copyrightable.

250 *Moreau*, above note 105. See also *Hollinrake*, above note 105 at 427, which held that copyright does not protect "ideas, or schemes, or systems, or methods."

251 See chapter 1, section A.4, "Data and Databases."

252 Or both the search software and the data are made available on a single CD-ROM, or via an Internet service: see *ProCD, Incorporated v. Zeidenberg*, 86 F.3d 1447 (7th Cir. 1996).

the software contained on the latter disk. More problematic is the scope of protection for the data residing on the former disk; in other words, could the compiler use copyright to prevent someone from making unauthorized copies of the data? This question is emblematic of the second dynamic of computer law, namely, the elusive nature of information. In order to be protected under the *Copyright Act*, an electronic database would have to come within the Act's definition of a *compilation*.[253] Interestingly, prior to 1994 the *Copyright Act* did not contain a definition of compilation, and it was left up to courts to determine what scope of protection would be provided for compilations of data and other works.[254] In the pre-1994 compilation cases, Canadian courts applied a "sweat of the brow" approach and afforded copyright protection to compilers that expended either (a) intellectual effort, in the sense of selecting or arranging the material comprising the compilation, or (b) labour or menial effort in compiling the material. Unfortunately, the pre-1994 cases do not take pains to distinguish between these two types of effort, and regularly intersperse words such as *selection, skill, taste, judgment, thought*, and *arrangement*, which connote the intellectual activity of selection or arrangement, with words such as *work, industry*, and *labour*, which denote the task of physically compiling material. This distinction is important because since 1994

---

253 Subsection 5(1) of the *Copyright Act* provides protection to "every original literary, dramatic, musical and artistic work," and the definition of literary work in s. 2 includes "tables ... and *compilations* of literary works" (italics added).

254 The following are the primary pre-1994 compilation cases, together with a description of the particular type of compilation that was protected: *Stevenson v. Crook*, [1938] 4 D.L.R. 294 (Ex. Ct.) — bridge tallies; *Deeks v. Wells*, [1931] 4 D.L.R. 533 (Ont. C.A.); *Underwriters Survey Bureau Ltd. v. American Home Fire Ass'ce Co.*, [1939] 4 D.L.R. 89 (Ex. Ct.) — instruction manual; *National Film Board v. Bier* (1970), 63 C.P.R. 164 (Ex. Ct.) — glossary of terms; *British Columbia Jockey Club v. Standen* (1985), 8 C.P.R. (3d) 283 (B.C.C.A.) — horse racing form; *Horn Abbot Ltd. v. W.B. Coulter Sales Ltd.* (1984), 77 C.P.R. (2d) 145 (F.C.T.D.) — game of questions and answers; *Slumber-Magic Adjustable Bed Co. Ltd. v. Sleep-King Adjustable Bed Co. Ltd.* (1984), 3 C.P.R. (3d) 81 (B.C.S.C.) — advertising brochure; *École de conduite tecnic Aube Inc. v. 15098858 Québec Inc.* (1986), 12 C.I.P.R. 284 (Que. Sup. Ct.) — driver training manual; *L'Index téléphonique (N.L.) de notrel localité v. Imprimerie Garceau Ltée* (1987), 18 C.I.P.R. 133 (Que. Sup. Ct.) — telephone directory; *Euclid Industries Can. Ltd. v. Reg Holloway Sales Inc.* (1989), 25 C.I.P.R. 290 (F.C.T.D.) — catalogues; *Éditions Hurtubise HMH Ltée v. Cégep André-Laurendeau* (1989), 24 C.I.P.R. 248 (Que. Sup. Ct.); *Caron v. Assoc. des Pompiers de Montréal Inc.* (1992), 42 C.P.R. (3d) 292 (F.C.T.D.) — charts in a calendar; *Pool v. Pawar* (1993), 50 C.P.R. (3d) 396 (B.C.S.C.) — foreclosure listings; *U & R Tax Services Ltd. v. H&R Block Canada Inc.* (1995), 62 C.P.R. (3d) 257 (F.C.T.D.) — an income tax form.

the *Copyright Act* has included the following definition of compilation: "'compilation' means (a) a work resulting from the selection or arrangement of literary, dramatic, musical, or artistic works or of parts thereof; or (b) a work resulting from the selection or arrangement of data."[255] Part (b) of this definition, which would apply to the raw data contained in electronic databases, is noteworthy because of its emphasis on "selection or arrangement" of data. Does this mean that since 1994 Parliament intended to no longer extend protection to compilers who expend effort in compiling data but who present it in a straightforward, unoriginal manner?

This is precisely the state of the law in the United States as a result of the *Feist* case, in which the U.S. Supreme Court held that copyright does not protect a White Pages telephone directory because it consisted of facts presented in a completely ordinary, uncreative way.[256] Moreover, the court in *Feist*, clearly repudiating a line of case law based on the "sweat of the brow" approach that had developed in the United States, concluded that facts and raw data are not copyrightable in any event, even where they are arranged or selected in an original manner. Thus, in the United States copyright protection for factual compilations is quite thin, given that the second compiler can copy facts from even a compilation whose selection and arrangement is protected by copyright so long as the facts, as presented by the second comer, are selected or arranged differently.[257] The *Feist* decision makes extremely problematic the protection of certain electronic databases through copyright.[258]

---

255 *Copyright Act*, above note 72, s. 2.
256 *Feist Publications, Inc.* v. *Rural Telephone Service Co., Inc.*, 499 U.S. 340 (1991) [*Feist*].
257 There have been, however, a number of U.S. cases decided after *Feist* where paper-based directories have been protected under copyright because of the selection and arrangement of facts within them. See, for example, *CCC Information Services, Inc.* v. *Maclean Hunter Market Reports, Inc.*, 44 F.3d 61 (2d Cir. 1994). In this case the infringing work was resident in electronic form. In *American Massage Therapy Association* v. *Maxwell Petersen Associates*, 209 F. Supp. 2d 241 (N.D. Ill. 2002), the court held that the copying of 17,617 names from an association's membership directory did not constitute copyright infringement as the listings were unprotected facts.
258 See John F. Hayden, "Copyright Protection of Computer Databases after *Feist*" (1991) 5 Harv. J.L. & Tech. 215. For a recent decision that illustrates how difficult it is to protect facts in the U.S. in the post-*Feist* world, see *EPM Communications, Inc.* v. *Notara, Inc.*, 2000 U.S. Dist. Lexis 11533 (S.D.N.Y. 2000). In this case, the operator of a Web-based directory service took around one-quarter of its listings from the plaintiff's paper-based directory, but this was insufficient for the court to grant a preliminary injunction.

In one Canadian case that addresses the scope of protection for fact-intensive works, the trial court, after clearly being briefed on the point by both sides, declined to decide on the express question of whether to follow the reasoning in *Feist*.[259] Nonetheless, the decision, involving the scope of protection for headings and other materials in a Yellow Pages business directory, in many important respects resembles a Feistian analysis by not extending copyright to cover such elements of a Yellow Pages directory. Moreover, it should also be noted that in a leading Canadian copyright case involving software, *Feist* was cited for the proposition that an author's original literary work does not cover underlying facts.[260] As well, the CRTC has also taken a rather Feistian approach to the protection — or rather lack of protection — afforded basic telephone directory listing information.[261] Finally, it should also be pointed out that only two of the pre-1994 Canadian compilation cases involved fact-intensive works of the "data" variety; for the most part these cases would be ones that would fall into subsection 2(a) of the current compilation definition. Thus, Canadian courts have simply not had a great deal of experience with fact-intensive, let alone data-related, compilations in the pre-1994 *Copyright Act* era, and this should make courts less inclined to maintain a sweat of the brow approach to protecting electronic databases in the face of a clear alternative in the *Feist* case.

Thus it came as no surprise that the Federal Court of Appeal in the *Tele-Direct* case, in upholding the trial decision, went beyond the trial decision to expressly approve of the U.S. *Feist* approach to protecting compilations and to unequivocally jettison in Canada the sweat of the

---

259 *Tele-Direct (Publications) Inc.* v. *American Business Information Inc.* (1996), 27 B.L.R. (2d) 1 (F.C.T.D.). This decision was upheld by the Federal Court of Appeal, which latter court did expressly consider the *Feist* case: see above note 256.

260 *Prism*, above note 86.

261 Telecom Decision CRTC 92-1, *Bell Canada-Directory File Service* (3 March 1992). In this decision the CRTC concluded at 8 that: "In the Commission's view, copyright could attach to a compilation of basic non-confidential listing information as a result of the sorting, arrangement or classification of that information. However, in the Commission's opinion, basic non-confidential listing information cannot attract a claim of copyright in and of itself. Thus, while it may be possible to claim copyright for a directory, either in hard copy or in electronic form, the raw listing information contained in the directory is not subject to being copyrighted." In a subsequent decision the CRTC seemed more ambivalent about the scope of copyright protection for such information: see Telecom Decision CRTC 95-3, *Provision of Directory Database Information and Real-Time Access to Directory Assistance Databases* (8 March 1995).

brow theory of copyright protection for databases and other fact-intensive works.[262] The Federal Court of Appeal confirmed that some amount of creativity must exist for a creator to obtain copyright protection in a fact-intensive work, and that the in-column listings of a Yellow Pages directory were too obvious and commonplace to satisfy this test. The court specifically put its mind to the question of whether Parliament intended, by the 1994 amendment to the *Copyright Act*, to support the "creativity" school of thought on compilations, or the "industrious collection" school; the court concluded in favour of the former. Echoing the sentiments of the *Feist* case and its U.S. progeny, the court therefore concluded that certain compilations of routine data are so mechanical as to be denied copyright protection.[263]

More recently, however, the Federal Court of Appeal seems to have pulled back from this endorsement of *Feist*. In a case involving the scope of protection for legal materials produced by law publishers, and particularly the "headnotes" that accompany judicial decisions, the Federal Court Trial Division followed the approach in *Tele-Direct* on the "creativity" versus "industrious collection" issue, concluding that headnotes were insufficiently creative to attract copyright protection.[264] On appeal, however, the Federal Court of Appeal[265] concluded that the trial judge was mistaken in adopting a U.S.-like originality test that included the requirements of "creative spark" or "imagination."[266] In this decision, the court stated that the test for originality should be as follows (which the court takes from the *Tele-Direct* case):

---

262 *Tele-Direct (Publications) Inc. v. American Business Information, Inc.* (1997), 76 C.P.R. (3d) 296 (F.C.A.) [*Tele-Direct*].

263 *Ibid.*, at para. 32.

264 *CCH Canadian Ltd. v. Law Society of Upper Canada* (1999), 179 D.L.R. (4th) 609 (F.C.T.D.). See also *Ital-Press Ltd. v. Sicoli* (1999), 86 C.P.R. (3d) 129 (F.C.T.D.), a telephone directory case, where the court agreed that a *Feist*-oriented interpretation ought to be made of Canada's *Copyright Act* compilation provision (but nevertheless found infringement because the White Pages listings at issue involved selection requiring skill and judgment). For an American decision along the lines of the above-noted trial decision in the *CCH Canadian Ltd. v. LSUC* case, holding that the factual portions of the material added to judicial judgments were not sufficiently creative to warrant copyright protection, see *Matthew Bender v. West Publishing Co.*, 158 F.3d 674 (2d Cir. 1998). For the view from Australia, see *Desktop Marketing Systems Pty Ltd. v. Telstra Corporation Limited*, [2002] FCAFC 112 (Fed. C.A., Australia, 2002), which refused to follow the approach in *Feist*, and reaffirms "sweat of the brow" as the law down under.

265 *CCH Canadian Ltd. v. Law Society of Upper Canada*, [2002] F.C.J. No. 690 (Fed. C.A.).

266 *Ibid.*, at para. 48.

[F]or a compilation of data to be original, it must be a work that was independently created by the author and which displays at least a minimal degree of skill, judgment and labour in its overall selection or arrangement.[267]

Thus, until the Supreme Court of Canada clears up this question, it appears the Canadian standard for copyright originality in respect of fact-intensive works rests somewhere between the Anglo and American poles. In effect, the Supreme Court will have to wrestle with the second dynamic of computer law — the elusive nature of information — and determine which of the "creativity" or "industrious collection" approaches should be followed when determining the proper scope of copyright for fact-intensive works.

Regardless of whether our Supreme Court ultimately adopts a Feistian view of the protection of databases, it should be noted that some have argued that the *Feist* approach affords too little protection to compilers of fact-intensive works, particularly where the products are provided to users in an electronic form. In this regard, it is interesting to note that the European Union has adopted a directive, which member states are required to implement into national law, that offers specialized protection to databases.[268] The directive provides that copyright laws only protect databases where there is originality in the selection or arrangement of their contents. This approach follows *Feist*. On the other hand, the directive would establish a new form of right that protects the factual contents of the database. This *sui generis* right will prevent the unauthorized extraction of all or a substantial part of the contents of a database, and prevent such contents from being made available to the public. The new right would be shorter in duration than copyright — only fifteen years — though a new term would begin to run whenever the database is significantly changed. In light of the appellate decision in the *Tele-Direct* case, the adoption in Canada of a right of data extraction similar to the new right created by the European Union's database directive should be strongly considered, though it would be preferable if such a new right were adopted in the United States at the same time it was made law in Canada. In this regard it should be noted that a bill was introduced in the 104th U.S. Congress

---

267 *Ibid.*, at para. 44.
268 *Directive 96/9/EC of the European Parliament and of the Council of 11 March 1996 on the Legal Protection of Databases.* This directive was required to be implemented into national law by the members of the European Union by 1 January 1998 and can be found in the *Official Journal of the European Communities* of 27/3/96 No. L77 at page 20 or at <2.echo.lu/legal/en/ipr/database/database.html>.

in 1996 that would have given protection to databases along the lines of the European directive, albeit the new right of extraction would have been for a period of twenty-five years (rather than fifteen years as under the European directive), but primarily because of intense opposition from a number of users and disseminators of online services, this bill was not enacted into law.[269] Similarly, in December 1996, WIPO had proposed the adoption of an international treaty regarding the protection of databases together with two other proposed treaties (one dealing with copyright and the other with performers' rights), but again, due to vociferous opposition in the U.S., only the latter two treaties were adopted and the database treaty was dropped.[270] Of course, it can be expected that database protection initiatives will appear again on the U.S. and WIPO agendas, and in Ottawa as well when the next round of amendments to the *Copyright Act* are contemplated. In the meantime, in the absence of intellectual property protection for the facts in a database, it may be possible, in appropriate circumstances, for creators and distributors of databases to protect their fact-intensive, information-based products by contract.[271]

5) Multimedia Works

The ability to digitize all the different traditional forms of copyright content and to fuse the resulting material into digital compilations presents copyright law with a number of challenges. Until recently, most copyright content was made available in a single format. A book was sold to the public on paper. Music was supplied on a vinyl record, or more recently on a cassette tape. In effect, content was presented to the public as one of the four categories of works recognized by the *Copyright Act*, namely, artistic, musical, dramatic, or literary works. There was some co-mingling of the categories — as when a movie contained

---

269 *Database Investment and Intellectual Property Antipiracy Act of 1996*, H.R. 3531. See Julius J. Marke, "Database Protection Acts and the 105th Congress," The New York Law Journal (18 March 1997); also found on the Web at <ljx.com/copyright/0318dbase.html>.

270 See Pamela Samuelson, "Confab Clips Copyright Cartel: Big Media Beaten Back," *Wired*, March 1997, and John Browning, "Confab Clips Copyright Cartel: Africa 1, Hollywood 0," *Wired*, March 1997. Ostensibly another reason why the database treaty did not pass is the conflicting views of the Europeans and the Americans that the data extraction right should last fifteen and twenty-five years, respectively.

271 See section C.8, "Other Measures of Protection," in this chapter, and chapter 5, section C.1, "Why Software and Content Are Licensed."

a musical soundtrack — but not much. In the digital era, all this has changed rapidly. A current good example is the CD-ROM (and more recently DVD) multimedia product that contains, on a single disk, full-motion video, text, photographs, music, animation, and video clips. Moreover, these different content elements can be altered and melded, so that the result is a seamless, single product rather than discreet portions of pre-existing content. These CD-ROM/DVD products exemplify the second dynamic of computer law, namely the elusive nature of information. One legal question that arises from such a CD-ROM/DVD product is how to categorize it under the *Copyright Act*'s four categories of works. Is it a literary, dramatic, artistic, or musical work? This can be an important question because, while many of the *Copyright Act*'s rules apply to all these works in the same way, there are some differences in treatment depending on the nature of the work. To help resolve this problem, the *Copyright Act* includes a definition of compilation, the first part of which provides that a compilation means a work resulting from the selection or arrangement of literary, dramatic, musical, or artistic work or of parts thereof.[272] Equally important, the statute provides that where a work contains two or more of these elements, the work will be considered of the type whichever of which there is the most. Although this is helpful, it is not a self-defining concept in all cases. There are many CD-ROM/DVD products where it will not be a simple task to determine what type of copyright work they are. Accordingly, it can usefully be asked whether the distinctions in the *Copyright Act* between the treatment afforded different works is still sensible. Perhaps it is time to recognize that the artificial differences perpetuated in the *Copyright Act* are anachronistic and should be abolished. For example, why the compulsory licensing regime only applies to books and mechanical sound recordings is puzzling, when these have become intermingled in the marketplace with so many other types of media.

Another legal challenge posed by CD-ROM/DVD and other multimedia works is how difficult and time-consuming it is for a creator or distributor of such a work to obtain the permission from the holders of the copyright and other proprietary rights to use their components of content in the collective work. For example, the publisher of the paper-based version of a book may not have the electronic rights to the book, in which case the creator of a CD-ROM/DVD product wishing to use all or part of the book would have to deal directly with the author or his or her estate. Similarly, whoever holds the copyright in a film — perhaps

---

272 See section C.4 of this chapter, "Copyright Protection for Electronic Databases."

the film studio, director, or producer — may not have the electronic rights in the underlying book where the film is based on a story from a book. As well, the copyright in the soundtrack may be held by another entity. Or the actors may not have signed releases covering multimedia rights. In a similar vein, the publisher of a magazine that contains a photo often does not have the copyright, let alone electronic rights, in the photo. And again, if there are people in the photo, releases should be obtained from them. Music rights are also complicated. First, there is the need for a synchronization licence if the music is to be used in conjunction with video or other images. Then, if the music is to be put on a separate, stand-alone soundtrack release, either on CD or cassette, a mechanical licence would also be required. And if use of a particular recording is required, then a further recording licence is required. Finally, if the resulting multimedia product were to be shown in public, then a performance licence would also be required. No wonder clearing the various rights for use of a work in a CD-ROM or other product, perhaps on the Internet, can be a fiendishly difficult exercise.

To assist in this process there are various collectives and rights administration groups that have been sanctioned and facilitated by the *Copyright Act*. Perhaps the best known is SOCAN (Society of Composers, Authors and Music Publishers, in Canada), which tracks the number of times certain songs are played, and then obtains payment from the radio stations and other broadcasters and distributes this money to the composers and performers.[273] Given that music can be transmitted over the Internet, SOCAN has proposed a tariff for musical works accessed over this medium.[274] As for synchronization rights, these can be cleared in Canada through the CMRRA (Canadian Musical

---

273 For an explanation of how SOCAN's rates are set by the Copyright Board under the *Copyright Act*, see SOCAN (Re) (1991), 37 C.P.R. (3d) 385 (Copyright Board). For an article that includes, in one handy annex, a list of all Canadian copyright collectives (together with their Internet addresses), see Daniel J. Gervais, "Collective Management of Copyright and Neighbouring Rights in Canada: An International Perspective," 1 C.J.L.T. 21 (July 2002).

274 See proposed tariff No. 22 in *Transmission of Musical Works to Subscribers Via a Telecommunications Service Not Covered Under Tariff Nos. 16 or 17*, Canada Gazette, Supplement, Part I, 19 October 1996. This tariff is being opposed by Internet service providers who argue that the Internet is not a broadcast medium and therefore does not require a "per subscriber-type tariff"; rather, the Internet allows people to contract for the right to use intellectual property rights: see Canadian Association of Internet Providers, *Report on Political and Regulatory Activities for 1996-1997*, 23 April 1997, available at the CAIP Web site <caip.ca/>. For the initial results of this skirmish before the Copyright Board and the Federal Court, see below notes 311 and 318.

Reproduction Rights Agency). Yet another copyright collective is Access Copyright (formerly called CANCOPY), which administers the rights to photocopy pages of literary works. Access Copyright facilitates large users of photocopy materials, such as universities and governments, in reproducing such materials with the permission of the relevant authors/publishers. One current shortcoming of Access Copyright is that it has not yet obtained the electronic rights for all of the works it represents, and thus for these rights users must continue to go to individual authors or publishers, which is an extremely laborious process.

With these various copyright collectives as the precedential backdrop, several commentators have called upon the establishment of a similar rights clearance organization for multimedia works purposes. These proposed schemes would still require, however, voluntary participation by the copyright holder; that is, they do not include a proposal for compulsory licensing of copyright works for use by others, as there currently exists for books after a period of time and for mechanical musical recordings at all times. Of course, a compulsory licence regime for multimedia works would raise numerous questions about the protection afforded the integrity of the copyright work through the exercise of moral rights, and much resistance to such a scheme could be expected from artists and their representative organizations. In effect, the most efficient manner in which to address the second dynamic of computer law, namely, the elusive nature of information, may not be the one that is most respectful of the artistic rights (versus economic rights) of creators.

6) Copyright and the Internet

a) The Challenges of Digital Transmission
Copyright owners view the Internet and the other networks encircling the globe with great hope and, at the same time, immense trepidation given the four dynamics of computer law, namely, the rapid pace of technological change, the elusive nature of information, and the blurring of private/public and national/international. The former sentiment derives from the Internet representing a new and extremely cost-efficient mechanism for distributing copyright content to vast numbers of users. Ironically, it is these same features, and the four dynamics of computer law, that make the Internet the ultimate copyright infringement technology. Not only can the computers on the Internet reproduce copyright content at extremely low cost and without a degradation of quality, but also these unauthorized copies can be transmitted over the myriad of

telecommunications networks that comprise the Internet — all in a matter of seconds. The Internet can be used in a number of other ways to reproduce and disseminate copyright works. There is, for instance, the phenomenon of fans of movies, television shows, rock bands, and other elements of modern culture who create Web sites using copyright material in the form of images, photos, and music without permission of the copyright owners.[275] In the late 1990s, a series of more challenging threats emerged to content providers courtesy of technological breakthroughs in digital compression and transmission. MPEG-3,[276] abbreviated to "MP3," was fine-tuned to compress digital audio files and then send them quickly as e-mail attachments or some other file transfer protocol.[277] MP3.com took this technology to a new level by replaying for users converted sound files purportedly already purchased by the users, to allow them to listen to music over the Internet any time and anywhere. In November 1999, Napster.com added a search and transmission functionality that allowed users to swap MP3 files over the Internet. In the same month iCraveTV.com was launched in Toronto as a site for retransmitting television signals over the Internet; subsequently, another Canadian entity, JumpTV, announced a somewhat similar business model. None of these sites sought or obtained permission from the relevant content owners. They were also hugely successful, measured by the number of discrete user visits.[278]

---

275 See Constance Sommer, "Hollywood Readies for Fight over Internet Ownership" *The Globe and Mail* (11 January 1997).

276 MPEG-3 (for Motion Picture Experts Group) is a standard file format for the storage of audio recordings. For a detailed discussion of the technology, see *Recording Industry Ass'n of America v. Diamond Multimedia Systems Inc.*, 180 F.3d 1072 (9th Cir. 1999) [*Diamond*].

277 Music, however, is not the only type of content challenged by the new compression and transmission technologies. Other cultural industries buffeted by the same storm include: film ("Movies and the Internet: Napster All Over Again," *The Economist*, 23 March 2002; Patrick Brethour, "On-Line Movies Worry Makers," *The Globe and Mail* (7 February 2002); Simon Tuck, "Hollywood Tackles On-Line Monster," *The Globe and Mail* (3 August 2000); Steven Chase and John Heinzl, "Pirate Films Are Big Again: But This Time, The Plunderers Are Teens Who Grab First-Run Movies Off the Internet," *The Globe and Mail* (8 February 2001); literature (Spider Robinson, "Literary Piracy: Napster On Steroids," *The Globe and Mail* (9 January 2001); computer games (Daniel McItardie, "Sega Moves to Shut Hundreds of Pirate Sites," *The Globe and Mail* (5 August 2000); and images (Josipa Petrunic, "Napster Is Dead, Long Live Morpheus," *The Globe and Mail* (3 September 2001).

278 In the first half of 2000, the Napster song-swap software was the fastest-growing computer program ever tracked by Media Metrix, a firm that measures Internet usage: "Napster Software Use Quadruples: Study," *The Globe and Mail* (14 Sep-

The above-noted technologies and business models have prompted some commentators to conclude that the Internet has sounded the death knell of copyright. For example, John Perry Barlow has argued that the copyright law system, which he believes is intrinsically connected to paper-based media, simply no longer works in a digital, networked environment.[279] Barlow does not believe incremental change in copyright law will do the trick; he advocates a wholesale jettisoning of the copyright system.[280] In effect, Barlow would argue that the four dynamics of computer law make an anachronism of copyright law. However, the rejoinder to Barlow, drawing on a highway analogy, would be that it is precisely because automobiles can reach speeds of 200 kilometres an hour that we need speed limits. It is because the Internet permits copying and transmission capabilities never before witnessed that copyright law must rise to the new challenge. And it is not just music company executives and their lawyers who support respect for copyright in the context of the Internet. For example, Lars Ulrich, a member of the rock band Metallica, testified before the U.S. Senate in opposition to Napster.[281] Other musical groups responded to Napster and inserted a voice-over in early versions of some songs that

---

tember 2000). And Canadians, particularly young Canadians, courtesy of the most inexpensive high-speed Internet access in the world, became world leaders in using Napster: Simon Tuck, "Canadian Youth Download Music the Most: Poll," *The Globe and Mail* (9 December 2000). Due to Internet-based file sharing piracy, it is estimated sales of recorded music fell by almost 10 percent in 2002: "In a Spin," *The Economist*, 1 March 2003.

279 John Perry Barlow, "The Economy of Ideas: A Framework for Rethinking Patents and Copyrights in the Digital Age (Everything You Know about Intellectual Property Is Wrong)," *Wired*, March 1994. See also John Perry Barlow, "The Next Economy of Ideas," *Wired*, October 2000. In an earlier incarnation, Mr. Barlow was a member of the rock group the Grateful Dead.

280 Many teenagers echo Barlow's way of thinking: Thalia Kapica, "Bummer! No more Napster," *The Globe and Mail* (28 July 2000); this op-ed piece indicates that Ms. Kapica is a Grade 10 student.

281 Lars Ulrich, "Nobody Else Works For Free. Why Should Musicians?" *The Globe and Mail* (17 July 2000). This piece, which is excerpted from Mr. Ulrich's testimony before the U.S. Senate, includes the following telling statement: "We have many issues with Napster. First and foremost: Napster hijacked our music without asking. They never sought our permission — our catalogue of music simply became available as free downloads on the Napster system." In closing his address, Mr. Ulrich, noting that the terms of use on Napster's Web site make it very clear that Napster claims full ownership of its Napster software, concludes: "Napster itself wants — and surely deserves — copyright and trademark protection. Metallica and other creators of music and intellectual property want, deserve and have a right to that same protection."

they knew would be transmitted over the Internet that encouraged listeners to buy a legitimate copy of the CD.[282] It is not surprising that people who earn their livelihood in cultural industries would support intellectual property rights, given it is what they sell for a living.

In essence, Barlow's exhortation that the Internet heralds the demise of copyright law is too extreme. Copyright law is flexible and resilient and very much able to adapt to technological challenges, just as it has over the last hundred years when confronted with new reproduction and transmission technologies — photographs, pianola rolls, sound recordings, broadcasting, cable transmissions, cassette recordings, and photocopies. Put another way, over the years the pioneers of each new communications technology initially confront and threaten the existing legal regime; but then commercial interests take over the development and mass roll-out of the particular technology, and these companies do an about-face on the utility of the legal system by inviting — usually demanding — the law to protect their new business models.[283] Nonetheless, there are aspects of the Internet that will require careful thought and creative law reform from a copyright law perspective. For example, one issue related to the mechanics of Internet transmission is that sending content in a digital format requires the making of at least one additional copy at the user's computer terminal, but often at an intermediate server and other computers as well. This presents an interesting dilemma. If someone in Vancouver buys an authorized copy of a book, this person may send this book to a friend in Halifax by courier or regular (as opposed to electronic) mail. If the person has an electronic version

---

282 Simon Houpt, "Artsists Use Trojans to Defeat MP3s," *The Globe and Mail* (9 September 2000).

283 This view of the relationship between technology and the law/government regulation is the subject of a fine book: *Ruling the Waves*, above note 12, by Debora L. Spar. Spar surveys a half-dozen communications technologies, including the telegraph, radio, and direct-to-home satellite television, and chronicles how each was invented by "pioneers and pirates," who sparked innovation in the absence of applicable laws. She concludes, however, that in each case full-scale commercialization required property rights, standards, and regulation. Her thesis, applied to cyberspace, will see the Internet increasingly subject to the rule of law as commercial dynamics come to replace the initial anarchic tendencies exemplified by John Perry Barlow. In essence, what Barlow does not get is that markets need rules in order to work properly; markets cannot prosper without the rule of law. In this regard, see Douglass C. North, "Institutions," *Journal of Economic Perspectives* 5, No. 1 (Winter 1991), where the Nobel Prize-winning economist concludes: "Undergirding … markets are secure property rights, which entail a policy and judicial system to permit low cost contracting." See also Douglass C. North and Robert Thomas, *The Rise of the Western World: A New Economic History* (Cambridge, UK: Cambridge University Press, 1973).

of the text of the book, the electronic version cannot be sent over the Internet without making a copy of it. Similarly, a person can today go into a bookstore or a library and browse through the books before deciding to buy or borrow one (and the principle noted above permits the library to lend out the book assuming the library bought an authorized copy of it in the first place). Such browsing in the case of a physical work like a book does not require a copy of the work to be made; but, in an electronic, online environment, it would entail making one or more copies of the digital-based work.

b) Government Studies

Issues such as these have prompted the American, and subsequently, the Canadian governments to appoint experts to consider whether the copyright laws of their respective countries need modification in light of the Internet.[284] The resulting study in the United States, the *Lehman Report*, advocated a number of changes to copyright law to bolster protection on the Internet, including making clear that digital transmissions fall within the U.S. distribution right; abolishing the "first sale" rule for digital transmissions; eliminating "fair-use rights" where digital copies could be licensed; and promoting digital licensing and "metering" technologies by making it illegal to circumvent technological means used to prevent unauthorized copying.[285] The Canadian report echoed many of the positions in its American counterpart, deriving its basic outlook from the premise that any access of copyright content on the Internet requires the making of one or more additional copies on intermediate computers or on an end-user's terminal, and that any such copying, to be legal, must

---

284 Governments outside of North America have also commissioned studies of the intellectual property and other questions related to the Internet. These studies include: Commission of the European Communities, *Copyright and Related Rights in the Information Society* (Luxembourg: Office for Official Publications of the European Communities, July 1995); Ministère de la Culture et de la Francophonie, *Industries Culturelles et Nouvelles Techniques* (Paris: 1994); Australia, Report of the Copyright Convergence Group, *Highways to Change: Copyright in the New Communications Environment* (August 1994). These studies are referred to in the study commissioned by the Canadian government of the state of the law in Canada regarding the liability of participants in the Internet content distribution chain for liability under copyright, trade-mark, criminal, privacy, and civil laws: see Michel Racicot *et al.*, *The Cyberspace Is Not a "No Law Land": A Study of the Issues of Liability for Content Circulating on the Internet* (Ottawa: Industry Canada, 1997).

285 United States, Information Infrastructure Task Force, *Intellectual Property and the National Information Infrastructure: The Report of the Working Group on Intellectual Property Rights*, Bruce A. Lehman, Chairman (September 1995).

be done with the permission of the copyright owner.[286] Therefore, the Canadian report concludes that online browsing would constitute an infringement unless expressly authorized.[287] With respect to the liability of online service providers, the Canadian report recommends that BBS operators be liable for infringement and not be treated as common carriers, but that this rule should be subject to a defence if they did not have actual or constructive knowledge of the offending material and they acted reasonably to limit potential abuses.

The *Lehman Report* has been criticized for being overly concerned with the rights of copyright owners, while ignoring the legitimate requirements of users, including individuals and libraries.[288] For example, critics of the *Lehman Report* suggest that consideration should be given to creating a first sale provision in the digital environment that would allow someone to transmit to someone else a digital work provided that upon completion of the transmission the originator deleted its copy of the work.[289] There is also a concern that content tracking and metering devices will apply to all available copyright content, thereby effectively eliminating the fair use provisions of the *Copyright Act* in the digital Internet environment, a result that will cause serious hardship to innumerable users and destroy an important aspect of the copyright law regime.[290]

---

286 Canada, Information Highway Advisory Council (IHAC), Copyright Subcommittee, *Copyright and the Information Highway: Final Report of the Copyright Subcommittee* (Ottawa: The Council, March 1995) available at <xinfo.ic.gc.ca/info-highway/reports/copyright/copy_e.txt>. The final phase 1 IHAC report, *Connection, Community, Content: The Challenge of the Information Highway: Final Report of the Information Highway Advisory Council* (Ottawa: the Council, 1995) incorporated most of the copyright subcommittee recommendtions: <strategis.ic.gc.ca/IHAC> and also at <xinfo.ic.gc.ca/info-highway/final.report/eng/>.

287 The report of the Copyright Subcommittee referred to above in note 286 points out that the Canadian *Copyright Act* does not require the addition of an electronic transmission right because the statute already includes the right in para. 3(1)(f) "to transmit the work by telecommunication." Similarly, Canada does not require the "first sale" doctrine, as is the case in the United States, because the Canadian *Copyright Act* does not control distribution of copyright works, and hence a Canadian copyright owner ceases to be able to control distribution of the work once it is published with authorization, in effect giving rise to the same results as the first sale doctrine.

288 Pamela Samuelson, "The Copyright Grab," *Wired*, January 1996 ["Copyright Grab"]. For a more balanced approach to online copyright issues than that provided in the *Lehman Report*, see: Committee on Intellectual Property Rights and the Emerging Information Infrastructure, National Research Council, *The Digital Dilemma: Intellectual Property in the Information Age*, 1999, available at <nas.edu>.

289 See James V. McMahon, "A Commentary on Proposals for Copyright Protection on the National Information Infrastructure" (1996) 22 Rutgers Computer and Technology Law Journal 233.

These and other critical views are based on the premise that copyright law represents a delicate balance between the creators and users of copyright works, and that as each new reproduction and transmission technology comes to the fore this balance has to be carefully recalibrated to ensure that the fundamental objectives of the statute continue to be achieved. Those critical of the *Lehman Report* argue that by ignoring the needs of the first sale doctrine, browsing, and fair use/fair dealing, the prospect for a digital environment that is overly weighted to creators looms as a real threat to the preferred balance in copyright matters.

c) Law Reform

The United States was the first country to implement WIPO's so-called Internet treaties by enacting the *Digital Millennium Copyright Act* (DMCA) in October 1998.[291] One of the key objectives of the DMCA was to implement the anticircumvention provisions in the WIPO Internet treaties. These provisions respond to the fact that in order to combat unauthorized copying over the Internet, content developers and distributors, together with technology companies, are creating various mechanisms, known as digital rights managements (DRM) systems, to track the use of copyright works and to prevent their illegal reproduction.[292] Of course, as soon as any encryption or similar technology is created by

290 Pamela Samuelson talks ominously about the transformation of the "information superhighway into a publisher-dominated toll road": Samuelson, "Copyright Grab," above note 288.

291 Pub. L. No. 105-304, 112 Stat. (1998) (adding §§ 512 and 1201-05 to the U.S. *Copyright Act* of 1976). The *1996 WIPO Copyright Treaty* and the *1996 WIPO Performances and Phonograms Treaty* are discussed in section B.8 of this chapter, "International Aspects."

292 Some DRM systems work through encryption technology (for a discussion of encryption technologies see chapter 4, sections B.3, "Regulating the Export of Encryption Technologies," and C, "Regulating the Domestic Use of Encryption Technologies" and chapter 6, section A.2(c), "Law Reform"); others implement "digital watermarks." Essentially, through a DRM system a content publisher can set certain parameters of use for a particular digital file sent to a user, and the user's computer, typically running some other software from the content owner, will not allow a further use to be made of the item; this software would also effect payment, in some ambitious systems, even tailored to the particular user (i.e., the user gets a discount if she purchased a pair of tickets to see the band live). For a description of various such schemes, see Dr. Ian Kerr, Alana Mavrushat, and Christian S. Tacit, "Technical Protection Measures: Part 1 — Trends in Technical Protection Measures and Circumvention Technologies," 10 March 2003, available at <pch.gc.ca/progs/ac-ca/progs/pda-cpb/pubs/protection/index-e.cfm>; Guy Dixon, "Music Companies Test Ways to Combat Copying of CDs," *The Globe and Mail* (30 January 2003); "Digital Rights and Wrongs," *The Economist*, 17 July 1999; and "Digital Copyright: Going Straight," *The Economist*, 7 April 2001.

the business community, the code breakers come along to hack it, as happened in November 1999 when a sixteen-year-old Norwegian cracked the Content Scrambling System that encrypts digital video discs. Thus, the DMCA makes it an offence, among other things, to circumvent a technological measure that effectively controls access to a work protected under the U.S. *Copyright Act*, and to manufacture, import, or sell devices that are designed to effect such circumvention.[293] The DMCA also protects the integrity of copyright management information (CMI) by prohibiting the distribution of false CMI in order to enable or conceal infringement, and by making it illegal to remove or alter CMI.[294]

Concerns have been expressed that DRM systems and technologies might shift the delicate balance in copyright law between creators and users inexorably in favour of the former at the expense of the latter.[295] Accordingly, as a result of heavy lobbying when the DMCA was making its way through Congress, a number of exceptions were added to the non-circumvention provisions, including allowing an override or dismantling of the relevant device by non-profit libraries for certain purposes; law enforcement agencies; a person who has a lawful copy of the software for reverse engineering to achieve interoperability of an independently created program with other programs;[296] a person undertaking encryption research; and a person to discover and disable an undisclosed information-gathering feature, such as a cookie.[297] For some commentators, these exceptions still did not go far enough.[298]

The other major objective of the DMCA was to create four significant new limitations on the liability for copyright infringement by online service providers.[299] Perhaps the most important is that a service

---

293 *DMCA*, Section 1201. The *DMCA* was held to be constitutional in *U.S. v. Elcom Ltd.*, 203 F.Supp. 2d 1111 (N.D. Cal. 2002), a case involving technology intending to compromise the copyright protection device in Adobe's e-book format.

294 *DMCA*, Section 1202. Another way to protect DRM systems is through trade secret protection: see *DVD Copy Control Association, Inc. v. McLaughlin* 2000 WL 48512 (Santa Clara Sup. Ct. 2000).

295 See "Copyright Grab," above note 288. See also David Ticoll, "Building a Wall of Cyber Trust," *The Globe and Mail* (8 November 2002), which describes briefly the ramifications (including the privatization of public goods) of the Trusted Computing Platform Alliance that aims to build into a chip the software necessary to prevent digital piracy.

296 Fascinatingly, the language for this exception comes verbatim from the *European Union Software Directive*, which may be a first in U.S. copyright law.

297 For a discussion of "cookies" and related privacy concerns, see chapter 4, section A, "Privacy and Data Protection."

298 See Pamela Samuelson, "*Intellectual Property and the Digital Economy: Why the Anti-circumvention Regulations Need to Be Revisited*" (1999) 14 Berkeley Tech. L.J. 519.

299 These are contained in section 512 of the *DMCA*.

provider will not be liable for infringement for transmitting content if it was acting merely as a data conduit at someone else's request.[300] The other major limitation removes responsibility for infringing material on Web sites hosted by the service provider, provided it did not have knowledge of the infringing activity, and upon receiving proper notification of the claimed infringement, the service provider expeditiously removes the material. There are similar limitations for system caching. To be eligible for these limitations, the service provider must adopt and implement a policy of terminating the accounts of repeat offenders. The DMCA implements all this through a fairly elaborate "notice and take down" process whereby the complainant must identify the infringing material and certify it can act for the copyright owner. Then the service provider must notify the poster that the material will be removed unless he speaks up; and if he does, this notice is sent to the complainant, and the material is kept up on the site unless the complainant indicates it has commenced a lawsuit. In effect, this is a sensible process that recognizes that the service provider is caught in the middle, and allows it to deal reasonably with a difficult situation. In Canada, the amendments to the *Copyright Act* effected by Bill C-32[301] did not include Internet-related provisions similar to those in the DMCA, whether proposed by the Canadian Information Highway Advisory Council (IHAC) report or otherwise. There likely will be, at some point in the future, such amendments, but Canada has not yet implemented into domestic legislation the *1996 WIPO Copyright Treaty*. In the summer of 2001, the Canadian government began a consultation process on the question of whether Canada's *Copyright Act* should be amended to reflect the WIPO Internet treaties, as well as whether to implement a limitation of liability regime for Internet service providers similar to that found in the DMCA.[302] One of the proposals put forward

---

300 To be eligible for this limitation, among other things the transmission must be initiated by a person other than the service provider, must be carried out by an automatic process, and must not modify the content.

301 See above note 73.

302 See Copyright Policy Branch, Canadian Heritage and Intellectual Property Policy Directorate, Industry Canada, *Consultation Paper on Digital Copyright Issues*, June 22, 2001, available at <strategis.ic.gc.ca/ssg/rp01099e.html>; and *Consultation Paper on the Application of the Copyright Act's Compulsory Retransmission License To The Internet*, June 22, 2001, available at <strategis.ic.gc.ca/ssg/1/rp00008e.html>. More recently (October 2002), the Canadian government released *Supporting Culture and Innovation: Report on the Provisions and Operation of the Copyright Act*, available at <strategis.ic.gc.ca/pics/rp/section92eng.pdf>. This report sets out a fairly detailed law reform agenda, both in terms of timing and the particular copyright reform issues the government would like to tackle in the coming years.

by the government would be a complaints-driven "notice and take down" regime where the intermediary is hosting or caching, coupled with a limit of liability regime for copyright infringement.

The *iCraveTV* and *JumpTV* matters also prompted the Canadian government to recently enact Bill C-11,[303] which is a partial response to the Internet retransmission issue. Essentially, under the *Copyright Act* certain cable companies and other distributors (such as DTH satellite signal delivery operators) could retransmit a television broadcaster's signals in markets in Canada outside of the reach of the television broadcaster's regular over-the-air territory by paying a royalty set by the Copyright Board. This system worked because the retransmitters had a closed system of subscribers. The issue arose, however, whether persons operating Internet television streaming services (who were exempt from CRTC licensing requirements courtesy of the CRTC's *New Media* decision discussed in chapter 4, section D.3(c), "The *New Media* Decision") could take advantage of this distant signal retransmission compulsory licence regime. Bill C-11 answers this in the negative, as it makes it clear that the *Copyright Act's* retransmission regime can only be utilized by entities that are not exempt transmitters under the *New Media* decision. The government, however, has indicated that it will now await the report of the CRTC as to what the CRTC wishes to do with the regulatory environment surrounding Internet retransmission. Presumably, if there were a way, ostensibly through technological means, to counteract the effect of the fourth dynamic of computer law, such that Internet-based transmissions could be made more secure and certain in terms of their destination, then there might be an argument for expanding the retransmission right to include some Internet-based players.

d) Litigation and Case Law

Until law reform is fully effected in Canada, it is useful to consider what activities on the Internet conducted by which parties might constitute an infringement of copyright under the current *Copyright Act*. In undertaking such an analysis, each fact situation must be considered on its own merits. There are so many different participants on the Internet, and they each engage in a multitude of activities. Fact-specif-

---

303   Bill C-11, *An Act to Amend the Copyright Act*; now S.C. 2002, c. 26. The bill received Royal Assent on 12 December 2002. For a helpful discussion of a predecessor of this law, see Monique Hébert, "Bill C-48: An Act to Amend the Copyright Act," *Parliamentary Research Branch, Library of Parliament* (22 January 2002).

ic, function-oriented determinations must be made, and generalized phrases — such as *common carrier* or *bulletin board service provider* or *Internet service provider* — must be avoided, given that with the wide range of "push" and "pull" technologies available today, various types of end-users and service providers can participate in a plethora of posting, transmission, and receipt activities. For example, in terms of intermediary liability, the phrase *common carrier*, particularly in the context of a "common carrier defence for copyright infringement," is no longer useful. With respect to some of their activities the telephone companies (the traditional common carriers) do have knowledge (real and constructive based on negligence) and the ability to control passage of the content, while some non-telephone company entities should be counted among common carriers for activities where they serve as passive conduits of transmission. The same point is made in this book in the discussions regarding intermediary liability under criminal law[304] and libel law.[305] It must be determined what knowledge the Internet participant had of the infringing or harmful activity, in terms of both actual knowledge and "constructive knowledge" through either negligence or related criminal law concepts. As well, it must be made clear what control the Internet participant could exercise over the offensive activity, involving either directly or indirectly its ongoing storage or electronic distribution.

The three rights in the *Copyright Act* most relevant to the Internet are the rights of reproduction, transmission to the public by telecommunication, and the secondary distribution rights. An end-user that posts or initiates the transmission of content by sending an e-mail or putting content on a Web site will likely violate the reproduction right, and often the transmission and distribution rights as well. Thus, bulletin board operators on the Internet will be liable for copyright infringement when they make copies of software available to third parties via the bulletin board service.[306] Entities that make other copyright content available by means of Web sites and bulletin boards will also

---

304 See chapter 3, section B.5(b), "Intermediary Liability."
305 See chapter 7, section A.2(c), "Internet Intermediaries."
306 See M. (J.P.), above note 91. See also "Computer Bulletin Board Raided as Companies Allege Software Piracy," *The Lawyers Weekly* (30 August 1996); and a press release of CAAST (the Canadian Alliance Against Software Theft), "Vancouver-based Bulletin Board Faces Charges for Software Theft," dated 20 June 1994, announcing a raid by the RCMP against a Vancouver-based bulletin board operator that resulted in charges involving sixteen counts of copyright infringement for unauthorized software copying.

be liable.[307] If, however, the end-user is small and relatively judgment-proof, as many are on the Internet, then a key question is when might larger, more solvent service providers also be liable for transmitting content that they did not initiate? This question has been asked by courts in a number of copyright contexts involving a range of pre-Internet environments. The fact patterns are usually the same: the infringer is an individual of modest financial means who carries out or sets in motion the infringement and then disappears (or if caught is not worth suing). And so courts have been asked by plaintiffs to turn their attention to others involved, directly or indirectly, in the infringing activity. Thus, in an American case involving bootleg musical recordings, the "bad guy" made the master bootleg recordings without paying relevant royalties, then effected distribution and marketing through a fulfilment house (which made, packaged, and mailed the records) and through radio stations and an advertising agency.[308] In this decision, the court dismissed the threshold defence claims of the three latter entities that they could not be liable; the court concluded that the excessively low sales price of the records was so suspiciously below the usual market price that they either deliberately closed their eyes or were recklessly indifferent to it. Going even further back in a number of U.S. cases, proprietors of dance halls were held to be liable for copyright infringements committed by the musical bands they hired, even where the musicians were independent contractors who selected the actual compositions played by them without any input from the dance hall owner.[309] A landlord, however, was held not to be liable for copyright infringement committed by a tenant where the landlord had no

---

307 See *Playboy Enterprises Inc. v. Webbworld Inc.* (N.D. Texas, 27 June 1997), mentioned in *Computer & Online Industry Litigation Reporter*, 15 July 1997, at 24,433, where a judge found a Web site operator liable for illegally copying Playboy's adult photographs and assessed $310,000 in damages ($5000 for each of the sixty-two photos). In an earlier case, *Playboy* brought suit against Event Horizons, a bulletin board operator that also scanned Playboy pictures, and settled for $500,000: see *Computer Industry Litigation Reporter*, 15 October 1992 at 15,710. Interestingly, this report of this case and settlement indicated that *Playboy* has also decided to sponsor its own electronic bulletin board system; thus, in 1992, one could ask whether Event Horizons did not in fact provide *Playboy* with valuable market testing services!

308 *Screen Gems-Columbia Music, Inc. v. Mark-FI Records, Inc.*, 256 F.Supp. 399 (S.D.N.Y. 1966).

309 *Irving Berlin, Inc. v. Daigle*, 26 F.2d 149 (E.D. La. 1928). For a similar result in Canada, see *Canadian Performing Right Society Ltd. v. Canadian National Exhibition Assn.*, [1938] 2 D.L.R. 621 (Ont. S.C.).

power or control over the tenant and did not benefit financially beyond receipt of the usual rent.[310]

These issues all came to a head, and were extensively analysed, in an important decision of the Canadian Copyright Board (Board) released in October 1999, called the *Tariff 22* decision.[311] The case has this name, as it involved the proposed Tariff 22, a tariff submitted to the Copyright Board by SOCAN, a collective under the *Copyright Act* that collects royalties on behalf of authors and songwriters.[312] The tariff was introduced to deal with the increasing presence of music on the Internet. Through other tariffs, SOCAN collects revenues from commercial radio stations and television broadcasters. SOCAN proposed that Internet service providers (ISPs) in Canada pay SOCAN a percentage of their revenues, amounting to roughly 25 cents per customer per month. SOCAN was keen to have ISPs responsible for paying for music transmitted over the Internet, because the alternative, collecting royalties from individual Web site operators, including many in the United States, posed an administrative nightmare for SOCAN. Therefore, a lot was riding on this decision, and the Board responded with a detailed analysis of how the *Copyright Act* should be applied to the phenomenon of music over the Internet.[313] In a methodical decision, the Board, drawing on previous decisions regarding television broadcasting and cable transmissions under the *Copyright Act*, came to the following conclusions:

- A musical work is not communicated when it is made available on a server.[314] However, the Board also found that by making a work available, a person authorizes its communication, such authorization being a right reserved to the copyright owner.
- Internet transmissions of musical works are communications by telecommunication, thereby bringing such transmissions within the

---

310 *Deutsch* v. *Arnold*, 98 F.2d 686 (2d Cir. 1938). Similarly, in Canada in *de Tervagne* v. *Beloeil (Town)* (1993), 50 C.P.R. (3d) 419 (F.C.T.D.) [*de Tervagne*], a municipality and a cultural centre were not liable when they merely rented a hall to the infringer.

311 *Re SOCAN Statement of Royalties, Public Performance of Musical Works 1996, 1997, 1998 (Tariff 22, Internet)*, (1999) 1 C.P.R. (4th) 417 (Cop. Bd.).

312 See section C.5 of this chapter, "Multimedia Works," for a brief discussion of copyright collectives.

313 Another reason *Tariff 22* is important is because its principles will be applicable to other content categories. Not surprisingly, SOCAN appealed the decision of the Board; see note 318 below.

314 This will be otherwise if and when Canada adopts the *1996 WIPO Copyright Treaty*, which expressly provides that making available a work for transmission is a right of the copyright owner.

Copyright Act. Therefore, it does not matter that the musical digital files being transmitted are compressed, or broken into packets for transmission, so long as at the receiving end they are reassembled to allow the recipient to recognize the work.

- Internet communications are to the public even when transmitted to a small segment of the public. Thus, services restricted to a small group of subscribers, or to a particular usegroup will still be caught; however, an e-mail communication from one individual to another would not be.[315]

- To be captured by the *Copyright Act,* the transmission need not be instantaneous or simultaneous; thus, communications may be made at different times, as determined by the sender (for example, with fax transmissions) or the recipient (as happens with Internet transmissions).[316]

- The person who actually posts the work to a Web site or server (for example, a content provider) is the one who makes the communication.

- Thus, and this is the key part of the decision, ISPs can take advantage of section 2.4(1)(b) of the *Copyright Act*[317] provided they act merely as a "conduit" for the communication.

This final conclusion is important and has far-reaching ramifications beyond music transmissions to other types of content. The Board concluded that the liability of a participant is assessed by its function, and not its function generally, but in respect of each particular transmission. Thus, where an ISP limits its role to passive intermediary, it will avoid liability. However, if the ISP posts content, creates embedded links or moderates newsgroups, then, the Board concluded, they are no longer acting as intermediaries, and they will not be entitled to the defence afforded by section 2.4(1)(b) of the *Copyright Act.*[318]

---

315 For a similar analysis, see the *New Media* decision of the CRTC, discussed in chapter 4, section D.3(c), "The *New Media* Decision."

316 Again, the parallels with the CRTC's *New Media* decision are worth noting.

317 Section 2.4(1)(b) of the *Copyright Act* provides that "a person whose only act in respect of the communication of a work ... to the public consists of providing the means of telecommunication necessary for another person to so communicate the work ... does not communicate the work ... to the public." This section was the key battlefield in the *Tariff 22* proceeding. See also the decision in the *Electric Despatch Company* case, referred to in note 186 in chapter 3.

318 The Board's decision was largely upheld upon appeal to the Federal Court of Appeal: *Society of Composers, Authors and Music Publishers of Canada v. Canadian Association of Internet Providers,* 2001 FCA 166 (Fed. C.A.), though the FCA did modify the Board's decision in two important respects. First, the FCA concluded that transmission from a cache is not protected by Section 2.4(1)(b) of the

In the United States, a number of cases have addressed the issue of copyright infringement liability by third parties in an Internet context. In a simple case, a defendant copies the plaintiff's material for use on the defendant's Web site, and the court has no difficulty entering a finding of copyright infringement, and often that the infringement was wilful.[319] Where the defendant is an intermediary, the issues are not as simple. Nevertheless, in *Sega Enterprises Ltd. v. MAPHIA*, a BBS operator was held liable for soliciting users to upload video games for use by other subscribers of the service.[320] In this case, and others like it, the third party is not merely a passive conduit, but rather actively encourages subscribers to disseminate bootleg copies. In the subsequent *Netcom* case, however, it was held that where an online service provider's computer merely copies content as part of the automatic and natural functioning of the Internet, the service provider will not be directly liable for infringement.[321] The *Netcom* court, however, concluded that the service provider may be liable under a theory of contributory infringement once the service provider is put on notice of the existence of the infringing material on the service provider's computer. More recently, the music industry has been successful in shutting down

---

Copyright Act; this could have important ramifications on various Internet-related services. Second, the FCA reversed the Board's finding that a communication by telecommunication occurs in Canada only if it originates from a host server in Canada. Rather, the FCA reasoned, the Board should undertake an analysis using the "real and substantial connection test" (described in chapter 7, section B.1(a), "Canadian Civil Matters") in each instance; this could have important ramifications for ISPs located outside of Canada, particularly in light of the fourth dynamic of computer law (namely, the blurring of the domestic and the international).

319 See *Perfect 10, Inc. v. Talisman Communications Inc.* 2000 U.S. Dist. Lexis 4564 (C.D. Cal. 2000), where the defendant's <supersex.com> Web site reproduced three of the plaintiff's photographs without authorization, as a result of which the court awarded $300,000 in statutory damages.

320 857 F.Supp. 679 (N.D. Cal. 1994). See also *Playboy Enterprises, Inc. v. Frena*, 839 F.Supp. 1552 (M.D. Fla. 1993) [*Frena*], where a BBS operator was found responsible for facilitating the distribution of unauthorized copies of content over the BBS. In a similar vein, in *Los Angeles Times v. Free Republic*, 2000 U.S. Dist. Lexis 5669 (C.D. Cal. 2000), a Web-based bulletin board forum, where registered users posted complete articles from the *Los Angeles Times* and *The Washington Post* (who both had fee-based online archive services for the same articles), was unable to justify its Web-based service on grounds of fair use, as it reproduced the entirety of the articles, among other reasons.

321 *Religious Technology Center v. Netcom On-Line Communication Services, Inc.*, 907 F.Supp. 1361 (N.D. Cal. 1995).

MP3.com[322] and Napster.com.[323] In the latter case, for example, Napster argued the fair use, the "time-shift,"[324] and other defences, but to no avail. The court concluded that Napster's active participation in facilitating the uploading and downloading of MP3 music files made it a contributory infringer. As a result, MP3.com and Napster.com have decided that, rather than go it alone, they will work with the music industry to bring music over the Internet in a manner that respects copyright law.[325] Content owners and suppliers of digital rights man-

322 UMG Recordings, Inc. v. MP3.Com, Inc., 92 F.Supp. 2d 349 (S.D.N.Y. 2000) [MP3]. The court in this case found clear infringement, and refused to accept MP3.com's fair use defence on the grounds, among other reasons, that its use of the plaintiffs' works was not transformative; that is, it merely repackages those works for transmission over the Internet, thereby taking a market away from the plaintiffs. These types of proceedings are not limited to the music industry. In Video Pipeline, Inc. v. Buena Vista Home Entertainment, Inc., 192 F. Supp. 2d 321 (D.N.J. 2002), the same reasoning as in the MP3.com case was brought to bear to preclude the unauthorized creation and Internet distribution of movie trailers.

323 A&M Records, Inc. v. Napster, Inc., 239 F.3d 1004 (9th Cir. 2001) [Napster]. Even before this victory in court, more than two hundred U.S. universities had banned Napster on campus, partly in response to a lawsuit brought by the rock band Metallica and two record companies against one university: see Spar, Ruling the Waves, above note 12 at 362; and Nicole St. Pierre, "Why More Schools Are Expelling Napster," Business Week, 9 October 2000.

324 In Diamond, above note 276, the so-called time-shift defence was successful in respect of the Rio portable MP3 player, because it merely made copies already in a hard drive in order to render them portable. This defence also fell on deaf ears in In Re Aimster Copyright Litigation, 2002 WL 31006142 (N.D. Ill. 2002), where a music file-sharing service was held to be a contributory and vicarious copyright infringer.

325 See Anna Wilde Wathews & Colleen DeBaise, "MP3.com and Seagram Singing the Same Song," The Globe and Mail (15 November 2000). For its part, Napster tried to make a go of it with Bertelsman ("Bertelsman Buys Napster More Time," The Globe and Mail (18 May 2002)), but ultimately this failed to stave off bankruptcy (Jonathan Stempel, "Napster Files for Bankruptcy," The Globe and Mail (4 June 2002)), and Napster's assets were sold for $5 million: a short, titleless piece in The Globe and Mail (28 November 2002) announces this grim demise. Of course successors to Napster have appeared, including Grokster, which is apparently appreciative of the publicity surrounding its own litigation with the music companies, which it says increases its traffic: Bernhard Warner, "Internet File Sharer Glad of Lawsuits," The Globe and Mail (5 March 2003). For their part, the music companies have started online music services: Nick Wingfield, "Music Retailers Go On-Line," The Globe and Mail (27 January 2003); Patrick Brethour, "Tech Giants Vie to Bring Web, Video, Music Hubs to Your Den," The Globe and Mail (9 January 2002); Patrick Brethour, "On-Line Music Service Coming," The Globe and Mail (15 February 2002); Showwei Chu, "Bell Launches Web-based Music Service," The Globe and Mail (26 September 2002); and Rob Lever, "Vivendi to Offer Music On-Line for Fee," The Globe and Mail (21 November 2002), and have paid $1.2 million for an ad campaign in Canada to convince

agement systems have also been successful in pressing into service the DMCA in order to enjoin various types of defendants.[326]

Canada has not yet seen cases precisely like the *MP3* and *Napster* ones. A claim was brought by a number of content owners against iCraveTV when it first appeared, and an injunction was obtained in the United States, but the parties settled in Canada, so we do not have guidance emanating from this case.[327] Similarly, JumpTV contemplated Webcasting television signals, but then withdrew before any jurisprudence could be made.[328] So it is still open to speculation how Canadian courts will handle these issues, though the *Tariff 22* decision gives some guidance. In any event, it can be stated that not all the elements of the *MP3* and *Napster* decisions would be directly applicable in Canada. For example, Canadian copyright law does not have a doctrine of contributory infringement. In pre-Internet cases, the question has arisen whether the supplier of equipment, services, or facilities can infringe the right to authorize the exercise of the reproduction and other substantive rights in the *Copyright Act*.[329] In these cases, suppliers of equipment and related items have not been found liable in situations where they do not exercise effective ongoing control of the equipment in a manner sufficient to influence the use to which the equipment is put by its immediate user (i.e., the principal infringer). Moreover, if the

---

consumers to pay for music: John Heinzl, "Anti-Piracy Ads to Stress Buying Music is Better," *The Globe and Mail* (8 November 2002).

326 *CSC Holdings, Inc. v. Greenleaf Electronics, Inc.*, 2000 WL 715601 (N.D. Ill. 2000): preliminary injunction against suppliers of pirate decoders; *Universal City Studio, Inc.v. Reimerdes*, 82 F.Supp. 2d 211 (S.D.N.Y. 2000) (preliminary injunction), 111 F.Supp.2d 294 (S.D.N.Y. 2000) (decision on liability): Internet service providers enjoined from supplying DeCSS circumvention technology, being unable to rely on various exemptions in the DMCA or on fair use defence; *RealNetworks, Inc. v. Streambox, Inc.*, 2000 WL 127311 (W.D. Wash. 2000): injunction against supplier of the Streambox VCR technology that circumvents Realnetwork's security technologies; and *A&M Records, Inc. v. Napster, Inc.*, 2000 WL 573136 (N.D. Cal. 2000): Napster cannot take advantage of the safe harbour protections of the DMCA.

327 *Twentieth Century Fox Film Corporation v. iCraveTV,* (2000) U.S. Dist. LEXIS 1091 (W.D. Penn. 2000). See also *Infinity Broadcasting Corporation v. Wayne Kirkwood*, 8 CCH Computer Cases ¶47,999 at 72,039, where a company that streamed radio over the Internet was found to be unable to rely on the "passive carrier defence" under the U.S. copyright law.

328 Simon Tuck, "JumpTV Considers Webcasting," *The Globe and Mail* (21 September 2000); Bertrand Marotte, "JumpTV.com Withdraws From Copyright Hearings," *The Globe and Mail* (12 October 2000).

329 See, for example, *de Tervagne*, above note 310; and *Vigneux v. Canadian Performing Right Society Ltd.* (1945), 4 C.P.R. 65 (P.C.). See also *CBS Songs Ltd. v. Amstrad Consumer Electronics plc.*, [1988] 2 All E.R. 484 (H.L.).

equipment supplier were to have such control, and the commensurate knowledge, then in Canada the basis for liability would not likely be the authorization right, but rather by finding the equipment supplier a co-infringer in its own right. Other grounds of liability may be relevant as well, such as "aiding and abetting," as well as the concept of "acting in concert" that was discussed in the *Tariff 22* decision.

In some situations, the service provider may be able to argue certain defences available under the *Copyright Act* or otherwise. In the case of the transmission right, the question can arise as to who is the "public" in the context of the Internet because the transmission right applies only to "transmissions by telecommunication to the public." This issue raises squarely the third dynamic of computer law, namely, the blurring of private/public. In this regard, one Canadian decision took the position that radio or television broadcasts are not performances in public when received in private homes.[330] A more recent decision expresses the better view that a broadcasting signal beamed into private homes either off air or over cable transmission is to the public, given that it is much more in keeping with the plain and usual meaning of the words "in public," namely, "openly, without concealment and to the knowledge of all."[331] Moreover, there is authority in the United Kingdom for the proposition that even a part of the public, such as a group or club, can constitute the public.[332] Under such an approach the concept of "private" is essentially limited to activities that take place wholly within the confines of a private dwelling house for the occupants of such house and their relatives and close friends. A not dissimilar concept of public can be derived from the criminal cases referred to in chapter 3, section B.6, "Illegal Speech," with perhaps the added nuance that a domestic unit can retain its quality of privateness even if it undertakes an activity outside of the home (e.g., there can be a private showing of a movie in a community hall normally open to the public where only members of a family and their private invitees have access to the hall). Following this line of reasoning, it may be possible to have circumstances on the Internet where the concept of "private" is recreated in an electronic, networked environment, such as through the transmission of material to a small e-mail list of family members who otherwise meet the necessary criteria of the term as it is under-

---

330 *Canadian Admiral*, above note 78.
331 *Canadian Cable Television Assn. v. Canada (Copyright Board)* (1993), 46 C.P.R. (3d) 359 at 370 (F.C.A.).
332 *Jennings v. Stephens*, [1936] 1 All E.R. 409 (C.A.). See also *R. v. Continental Cablevision Inc.* (1974), 5 O.R. (2d) 523 (Prov. Ct.), and more recently the CRTC's *New Media* decision, discussed at length in section D.3(c), "The *New Media* Decision," of chapter 4.

stood in a physical, pre-Internet context. In other words, the law should countenance a degree of privateness on the Internet where the functional rationales for such a state are duplicated in an Internet environment (i.e., the transmission is by a non-commercial entity to a reasonable number of relatives or acquaintances without charge such that it does not take away sales of copies of the relevant work by the copyright holder, etc.).[333] Support for this position can be found in a case that held that the transmissions of programs from a television network head office to its affiliates did not constitute a communication to the public.[334] Nevertheless, given the third dynamic of computer law, it is becoming more difficult to carve out a private space in our computerized, networked world.

7) Trade-marks, Domain Names, and the Internet

a) Domain Names and Meta-Tags

The Internet's domain name system, and the Internet-based practice of meta-tagging, present the intellectual property system and especially trade-mark law with some interesting challenges. To understand the nature of these challenges, it is important to briefly review the functions of the domain name system and meta-tags that result from Internet communications. As described in two recent cases, each host computer on the Internet is assigned its own Internet Protocol (IP) number or address, which specifies the "location" of the computer on the Internet.[335] For example, the IP number for the court that rendered the *Umbro* decision is 208.210.219.101; however, because people can remember names rather than long numbers, Internet registration authorities provide a service to give each IP address a word name (a domain name), which is mapped onto the numerical IP address.[336] Thus, the previously

---

333 See chapter 3, section B.6, "Illegal Speech."

334 *CTV Television Network Ltd. v. Canada (Copyright Board)* (1993), 99 D.L.R. (4th) 216 (F.C.A.).

335 *BCAA et al. v. Office and Professional Employees' Int. Union et al.*, 2001 BCSC 156 (B.C.S.C.) [*BCAA*]; and *Network Solutions, Inc. v. Umbro International, Inc.*, 529 S.E.2d 80 (Vir. Sup. Ct. 2000) [*Umbro*].

336 In this sense, domain names serve a purpose not unlike the mnemonics of telephone numbers (where the numbers are proxies for various electrical connections). However, as pointed out in one of the first cases dealing with an ownership dispute over a domain name, *MTV Networks v. Curry*, 867 F.Supp. 202 (S.D.N.Y. 1994), Internet domain names are more important than telephone numbers because there is no single, comprehensive Internet equivalent to a telephone company directory (though Internet search engines come close, but not without their own challenges, legal and otherwise) and users will often try to guess a domain name.

mentioned court's domain name is <courts.state.va.us> with "us" being the top-level domain; in this case "us" is a country code indicating that it is registered in the United States. American authorities administer the "open" or "generic" top-level domains, including dot-com,[337] whereas associations in other countries administer the country-specific ones. For example, in Canada, the Canadian Internet Registration Authority (CIRA) manages the dot-ca top-level domain database.[338]

Several problems bedevil the domain name registration process. One is a function of the fact that there can be only one registration for, say, Stellar.com, even though Stellar Books and Stellar Financial, to use fictitious examples, and possibly a number of other companies using Stellar as a trade-mark, use the trade-mark for their respective goods or services. That is, there can be, and often are, multiple registrations of trade-marks in the same country so long as they relate to uses in different, non-overlapping channels of business. In this sense, the Internet domain naming system is not as robust as the trade-mark system because the domain name, in addition to serving as a marketing vehicle like a trade-mark, also plays the key function of being an address. In other words, the Internet domain naming system has created, in its present guise, too much scarcity, to put the issue in terms of the analysis set out in section A, "The Economics of Information," in this chapter.[339] The domain name authorities have recently created several new top-level domain registers, such as dot-biz to help alleviate this problem.[340] Although only one Stellar can exist on the dot-com registry, another Stellar can be registered under the Canadian registry of dot-ca,

---

337 The other generic top-level domains administered by NSI are dot-net and dot-org.

338 CIRA was established in 1999. Prior to that date, the dot-ca system was organized by the University of British Columbia. Before CIRA took over the dot-ca registration process, it was fairly difficult to obtain a dot-ca registration; a registrant typically had to be a federally incorporated company and have offices in multiple provinces, and a registrant was limited to a single domain name. Not surprisingly, by the year 2000, the number of dot-ca registrations paled in number (about 100,000) against its dot-com counterpart (20 million registrants, about 600,000 by Canadians): see John Partridge, "The Dot-ca Revolution," *The Globe and Mail* (26 October 2000). Usefully, the new Canadian presence requirements under the CIRA regime are more flexible, and even permit non-residents who own trade-marks to register for the equivalent dot-ca domain name. Information on these rules, and CIRA generally, can be found at <cira.ca>.

339 See "Can You?: The Internet is Running Out of Addresses," *The Economist*, 4 March 2000.

340 Ted Bridis, "Seven New Web Suffixes Picked," *The Globe and Mail* (17 November 2000); and Showwei Chu, "New Web Names May Spur Cybersquatters," *The Globe and Mail* (23 November 2000).

and similarly in other national registries around the world, even for the same types of goods and services. In this sense, given the fourth dynamic of computer law (and the fact that all domain names may be accessed by all computers hooked up to the Internet), the international domain naming system does not create enough scarcity.

The Internet trade-mark and domain name problems, particularly in the context of national trade-mark registration regimes, have precursors in the pre-Internet era. For example, in the *Vanity Fair* case, a U.S. court had to wrestle with a Canadian retailer and a U.S. clothing manufacturer, each owning trade-mark registrations for their respective countries and coming into conflict when they made cross-border sales and distributions of catalogues.[341] In other words, the increase in international trade in goods over the decades has pointed out the shortcomings of national-based trade-mark registration regimes. But, given the fourth dynamic of computer law — namely, the blurring of national/ international — what was a periodic inconvenience in the physical world has become a major design flaw in the Internet system, where success depends on the ability to connect users across borders. Accordingly, numerous initiatives have been undertaken to study and alleviate the problems associated with the international Internet domain name system. For example, a WIPO group has studied the problem,[342] and an international *ad hoc* group appointed by a number of international organizations has produced a report and agreement addressing a few aspects of the problem.[343] The various solutions proposed include expanding the number of top-level domains (which has happened to a limited extent), expanding domain names themselves to accommodate trade-mark and country references, creation of single global databases and directories to assist in the screening and selection of domain names and trade-marks, and even a proposal for a *sui generis* system of intellectual property protection for domain names. Whichever of these solutions, or combinations of them, come to be widely accepted by the Internet community, it is clear that (given the fourth dynamic of computer law) only through a coordinated, fully

---

341 *Vanity Fair*, above note 169.

342 See the memorandum prepared by WIPO entitled *Issues Relating to Trademarks and Internet Domain Names* prepared for the consultative meetings on trademarks and Internet domain names held in May 1997 at <wipo.org>.

343 See the *Final Report of the International Ad Hoc Committee: Recommendations for Administration and Management of gTLDs*, 4 February 1997, and the related Establishment of a Memorandum of Understanding on the Generic Top Level Domain Name Space of the Internet Domain Name System, 28 February 1997, both available at <iahc.org>.

international response will the pressing Internet-related trade-mark issues be settled.

One of the primary factors that cause conflict between the registered trade-mark system and domain names is that registries such as NSI and CIRA have generally accepted domain name registrations on a "first come, first served" basis, without an initial, independent review of whether the name being registered is another party's registered trade-mark.[344] At the same time, a domain name in some respects is more powerful than a trade-mark, as there can only be one company name registered for each top-level domain.[345] In this sense, domain names are like telephone numbers or the addresses for physical street locations in that, although they are now used as valuable marketing devices, their underlying purpose remains an IP address.[346]

Websites are coded in a computer language known as HTML, and a computer's browser can read and interact with this HTML informa-

---

344   This was particularly true in the early days of the commercial Internet. Currently, both the NSI and CIRA rules ask the registrant to certify that it has the right to use the domain name and that such use does not interfere with the rights of any other party, but this is still a very weak screening mechanism.

345   On the other hand, prefixes and suffixes can be added to register for close equivalents, a practice that has also led to much litigation: see below note 378.

346   For example, an American court in *Umbro*, above note 335, has held that there exist no property rights in domain names, in the traditional sense, rather it is merely a "contractual right" between the registrant and the operator of the domain name directory; though it did concede that the right to use a domain name is a form of intangible personal property. In the *Umbro* case Umbro International, the well-known sportswear and equipment supplier, obtained a default judgment against a Canadian corporation that registered the <umbro.com> domain name in order to sell it to Umbro for, apparently, a payment of $50,000 and a lifetime supply of Umbro equipment and apparel. Umbro then attempted to execute on this judgment by seizing the domain name through garnishment, effectively demanding NSI to turn over to Umbro a number of domain names related to Umbro and registered in the defendant's name. Although the court refused to characterize a domain name as property that is capable of being subject to garnishment, it was willing to admit that appellate courts have concluded differently in respect of telephone numbers: see *Georgia Power Co. v. Security Inv. Properties, Inc.*, 559 F.2d 1321 (5th Cir. 1977), though there are also courts going the other way on telephone numbers as well: *Slenderella Sys. of Berkeley, Inc. v. Pacific Tel. & Telegraph Co.*, 286 F.2d 488 (2nd Cir. 1961). In another U.S. decision, *Dorer v. Arel*, 60 FSupp. 2d 558 (E.D. Va. 1999), the court gingerly sidestepped concluding on the issue of whether a domain name is property, by noting that NSI has a policy of turning over the registration to a new owner if so ordered by a court, thus effecting the same result. In Canada, a court has intimated that a domain name may be able to be characterized as intangible property: *Easthaven, Ltd. v. Nutrisystem.com Inc.* (2001), 55 O.R. (3d) 334 (Sup. Ct.).

tion.[347] When a user does not know a Web site's precise domain name, an Internet search engine that compiles massive indices containing information on most sites is useful. The search engine tracks a Web site's meta-tags, key descriptive information about the site done in HTML. Meta-tags created by a Web site owner specify keywords that will be matched to keywords entered by a user conducting an Internet search.[348]

b) Cybersquatting

Given the steadily increasing value of domain names, and the ease with which they can be registered, it is not surprising that the practice has arisen where a person registers a domain name with the intention of selling it, at a profit, to someone else who owns a registered trade-mark for the same word(s).[349] Nevertheless, where someone registers a domain name that comprises or includes a registered trade-mark of a third party with a view to selling the domain name to the trade-mark owner at a profit, the trade-mark owner will generally be able to have the domain name transferred from the "cybersquatter," as such registrants have come to be called.[350] There are a number of different means by which this can be done. In Canada, some trade-mark owners have successfully used the doctrine of passing off,[351] while in other cases

---

347 HTML stands for Hypertext Markup Language. HTML, among other things, permits the practice of embedding links in Web pages.
348 *BCAA*, above note 335, paragraph 33. See also the description of meta-tags in *Brookfield Communications Inc.* v. *West Coast Entertainment Corp.*, 174 F.3d 1036 (9th Cir. 1999) [*Brookfield*].
349 See Patrick Brethour, "Firms Cash in on Web Addresses," *The Globe and Mail* (4 December 1996). In effect, wherever markets create get-rich-quick opportunities, it is to be expected that legal friction will follow: Elizabeth Raymer, "Battles over Domain Names on the Rise," *The Lawyers Weekly* (21 February 1997). See also Paul M. Eng, "Get Your Hands Off My .COM," *Business Week*, 28 July 1997. Some sales, however, do not reflect a speculative animus, but merely involve one legitimate user transferring to another: for example, apparently the Professional Golfers Association (whose acronym is pga) paid $25,000 to the Potato Growers Association of Alberta (whose acronym is also pga) for the domain name <pga.com>.
350 "Cybersquatting involves the registration as domain names of well-known trademarks by non-trademark holders who then try to sell the names back to the trademark owners": *Sporty's Farm L.L.C.* v. *Sportsman's Market, Inc.*, 8 CCH Computer Cases ¶48,031, at 72,319 (2d Cir. 2000) [*Sporty's*].
351 In *Law Society of British Columbia* v. *Canada Domain Name Exchange Corp.*, [2002] B.C.J. No. 1909 (B.C.S.C.) [*Law Society of British Columbia*], the Law Society of BC was successful in obtaining an interlocutory injunction against an entity that registered <lawsocietyofbc.ca> for an adult entertainment site. Interestingly, the court found the plaintiff did not have to show irreparable harm. In *Saskatoon Star Phoenix Group Inc.* v. *Noton*, [2001] S.J. No. 275 (Sask. Q.B.), the

have simply argued trade-mark infringement under the *Trade-Marks Act*.[352] In Canada, it might also be possible to argue "depreciation of goodwill" under Section 22 of the *Trade-Marks Act*,[353] as well as misappropriation of personality rights.[354] In a U.K. decision[355] involving the registration of well-known marks such as "Marks and Spencer" by a pair of dealers in Internet domain names (that is, they registered them merely to sell them), the court went so far as to characterize some of the domain names as "instruments of fraud":

> I also believe that the names registered by the appellants were instruments of fraud and that injunctive relief was appropriate upon this basis as well. The trade names were well-known "household names"

publisher of *The Star Phoenix* newspaper, who also operated the related Web site at <thestarphoenix.com>, was successful against the defendant, who offered to sell the plaintiff <thestarpheonix.com> and <starpheonix.com>. In a subsequent case, *Itravel2000.com Inc. v. Fagan* (2001), 11 C.P.R. (4th) 164 (Ont. Sup. Ct.), the owner of a business carried on under the name Itravel, who also operated a Web site at <itravel2000.com>, was successful in its claim against the defendant, who offered for sale the domain name <itravel.ca>. In a similar vein, interim orders not to sell domain names were entered in *Weight Watchers International, Inc. v. Value Printing Ltd.*, [2000] F.C.J. No. 777 (F.C.T.D.) and *Innersense International Inc. v. Manegre*, [2000] A.J. No. 613 (Alta. Q.B.).

352 In *Bell Actimedia Inc. v. Puzo (Communications Globe Tête)*, [1999] F.C.J. No. 683 (F.C.T.D.), the owner of the Canadian trade-marks "Yellow Pages" and "Pages Jaunes" obtained an interlocutory injunction against the operators in Montreal of the <lespagesjaunes.com> Web site. Interestingly, the defendants argued that they should have been able to use the site in respect of their business outside of Canada (where the plaintiff had no registered trade-marks), but the court (perhaps unconsciously reacting to the fourth dynamic of computer law) did not address this jurisdictional issue. See also Tyler Hamilton, "Bell Winning Battle to Protect Yellow Pages Brand Name On Web," *The Globe and Mail* (7 July 1999).

353 The goodwill depreciation argument failed in *BCAA*, above note 335, but this was not a cybersquatting case, but rather a cybercriticism case (see note 358 below). More relevantly, in the United States successful claims against cybersquatters have been brought under the American doctrine of trade-mark dilution. See, for example, *Panavision International, L.P. v. Dennis Toeppen*, 141 F.3d 1316 (9th Cir. 1998). The U.S. Federal *Trademark Dilution Act*, 15 U.S.C. §1125(c) states, in part: "The owner of a famous mark shall be entitled … to an injunction against another person's commercial use in commerce of a mark or trade name, if such use begins after the mark has become famous and causes dilution of the distinctive quality of the mark …"

354 For an offline analogy, see *Baron Philippe de Rothschild, S.A. v. La Casa de Habana Inc.* (1987), 19 C.P.R. (3d) 114 (Ont. H.C.), where the court granted an order prohibiting the defendant from using the plaintiff's well-known name on the defendant's storefront sign.

355 *British Telecommunications plc v. One In A Million*, [1998] 4 All E.R. 476 (C.A.) [*One in a Million*].

denoting in ordinary usage the respective respondent. The appellants registered them without any distinguishing word because of the goodwill attaching to those names. It was the value of that goodwill, not the fact that they could perhaps be used in some way by a third party without deception, which caused them to register the names. The motive of the appellants was to use that goodwill and threaten to sell it to another who might use it for passing-off to obtain money from the respondents. The value of the names lay in the threat that they would be used in a fraudulent way. The registrations were made with the purpose of appropriating the respondents' property, their goodwill, and with an intention of threatening dishonest use by them or another. The registrations were instruments of fraud and injunctive relief was appropriate just as much as it was in those cases where persons registered company names for a similar purpose.[356]

Not all use by a defendant of a plaintiff's trade-mark in the defendant's domain name will be actionable, given that courts have recognized a number of legitimate uses in these circumstances.[357] So-called cybercriticism will not result in infringement, so long as the defendant's Web site is non-commercial.[358] Again, if the defendant does not make use of the plaintiff's mark in a "trade-mark sense" but merely

356 *Ibid.*, at p. 498. For a Canadian decision that cites and follows the decision in *One in a Million, ibid.*, see *Law Society of British Columbia*, above note 351.
357 In some cases, defendants have been let off the hook not because of substantive trade-mark law reasons, but because the plaintiff could not make out the three-part test for an interim or interlocutory injunction: see the *ITV* case, above note 142, and *Toronto.com v. Sinclair* (2000), 6 C.P.R. (4th) 487 (F.C.T.D.), where the plaintiff, operating <toronto.com>, could not obtain an interlocutory injunction against the operator of <toronto2.com> due to a failure of establishing irreparable harm. In other cases the court ostensibly is responding to extenuating local circumstances: there is really no other way to explain the decision in *PEINET Inc. v. O'Brien* (1995), 61 C.P.R. (3d) 334 (PEI Sup. Ct.), where the court concluded that the defendant's use of lower case <pei.net> would not be confusing with the plaintiff's use of PEINET trade-mark [and domain name].
358 See *BCAA*, above note 335, where a union was permitted to keep up the site <bcaaonstrike.com>, notwithstanding the plaintiff's site <bcaa.com> and "baa" trade-mark. See also *Bell Expressvu Limited Partnership v. Tedmonds & Co. Inc.*, [2001] O.J. 1558 (Ont. Sup. Ct.), where the defendant's <expressvu.org> survived a challenge from the plaintiff owner of the Expressvu trade-mark and <expressvu.com> domain name, partly because the defendant's site was aimed at commentary and not commerce. In the United States, see also *Bally Total Fitness Holding Corp. v. Faber*, 29 F.Supp. (2d) 1161 (C.D. Cal. 1998), where the term "Ballysucks" survived challenge, because its purpose was consumer commentary. As well, in *Lucent Technologies, Inc. v. Lucentsucks.com*, 2000 U.S. Dist. Lexis 6159 (E.D. Va. 2000) [*Lucentsucks*], the court observed that if <lucentsucks.com> were a

uses the word on its site in a passive manner, it may be able to sidestep liability.[359] And of course there will not be a finding for the plaintiff where the defendant uses the conflicting domain name for a legitimate business purpose that does not conflict with the plaintiff trade-mark owner's reputation.[360] It may also be possible, in appropriate cases, to avoid a finding of infringement or passing off through use of a written disclaimer that clearly indicates to the Internet surfer that the defendant is not affiliated with the plaintiff.[361] In this regard, it is interesting to note that some defendants argue that disclaimers should be a complete answer to a plaintiff's concern with the defendant using the plaintiff's marks in the context of meta-tagging; that is, there will not be any confusion as to source once the user lands on the defendant's Web site, as he will see it is different from the plaintiff's. In response, courts have concluded that while meta-tagging does not generate "source confusion," it does lead to "initial interest confusion," and therefore is actionable if it is done with commercial motive.[362]

---

parody or criticism Web site, it would be difficult for the plaintiff to successfully bring a trade-mark infringement or dilution action. On the other hand, the initial registrant of <walmartcanadasucks.com> lost this registration to Wal-Mart under the UDRP policy noted below given that the registrant's goal in registering this domain name was not to foster consumer commentary, but rather to generate a sale of the domain name to Wal-Mart: *Wal-Mart Stores, Inc. v. Walsucks and Walmarket Puerto Rico*, WIPO D2000-0477; in a subsequent decision, however, the same respondent was able to keep virtually the same domain name <wallmartcanadasucks.com> (i.e., it has an extra "l") before a different arbitrator, who held that using it for criticism was a legitimate use: see John Partridge, "Wal-Mart Loses Dispute," *The Globe and Mail* (7 December 2000). See also the support given to counteradvertising by the Supreme Court of Canada in *R. v. Guignard* (2002), 209 D.L.R. (4th) 549 (S.C.C.): the court stated that posting messages on the Internet is an important means of communication for discontented customers.

359 *Pro-C Ltd. v. Computer City Inc.* (2001), 55 O.R. (3d) 577 (Ont. C.A.).
360 For example, in *Hasbro, Inc. v. Clue Computing, Inc.*, 232 F.3d 1 (1st Cir. 2000), a company called Clue Computing was entitled to go on owning <clue.com> in conjunction with its computer business, notwithstanding the plaintiff's famous "Clue" board game. Indeed, in some cases it is the complainant that abuses the process by participating in reverse domain name hijacking, namely by bringing a claim in bad faith: *Prom Software, Inc. v. Reflex Publishing, Inc.*, WIPO-D2001-1154.
361 A disclaimer played a role in the refusal to grant an interlocutory injunction in *ITV*, above note 142, and in *Playboy Enterprises, Inc. v. Welles*, 7 F.Supp. (2d) 1098 (S.D. Cal. 1998).
362 Initial interest confusion occurs when the meta-tags cause a consumer initially interested in, and searching for, the plaintiff's Web site, to ultimately use the defendant's Web site. In *Brookfield*, above note 348, the court gave a useful offline hypothetical example of initial interest confusion caused by meta-tagging someone else's trade-marks for commercial gain: "Using another's trademark in one's

Cybersquatting has also elicited a specific statutory response in the United States, in the form of the *Anticybersquatting Consumer Protection Act (ACPA)*.[363] The *ACPA* amended the U.S. *Trademark Act* of 1946 by creating a specific federal remedy where a person has a bad faith intent to profit from another's mark and registers it as a domain name. The *ACPA* goes on to list nine non-exhaustive factors to assist courts in determining when a defendant has acted with a bad faith intent to profit from the use of a mark.[364] In

---

metatags is much like posting a sign with another's trademark in front of one's store. Suppose West Coast's competitor (let's call it "Blockbuster") puts up a billboard on a highway reading — "West Coast Video: 2 kilometres ahead at Exit 7" — where West Coast is really located at Exit 8 but Blockbuster is located at Exit 7. Customers looking for West Coast's store will pull off at Exit 7 and drive around looking for it. Unable to locate West Coast, but seeing the Blockbuster store right by the highway entrance, they may simply rent there. Even consumers who prefer West Coast may find it not worth the trouble to continue searching for West Coast since there is a Blockbuster right there. Customers are not confused in the narrow sense: they are fully aware that they are purchasing from Blockbuster and they have no reason to believe that Blockbuster is related to, or in any way sponsored by, West Coast. Nevertheless, the fact that there is only initial consumer confusion does not alter the fact that Blockbuster would be misappropriating West Coast's acquired goodwill." For an example of initial interest confusion from a Canadian perspective, see Val Ross, "Chapters Apologizes for Internet 'Confusion,'" *The Globe and Mail* (27 March 1999), wherein the practice is described of getting people looking for <Indigo.com> to end up at <chapters.com> (during the time the two retail chains were competitors). There will not, however, be initial interest confusion where a cybercriticism site does not stand to gain financially from its site: *Northland Insurance Companies* v. *Blaylock,* 115 F.Supp. 2d 1108 (D. Minn. 2000); or where there is "legitimate" and "non deceptive" use of another party's trade-mark in a Web site's meta-tags: *Promatek Industries Ltd.* v. *Equitrac Corp.,* No. 00-4276 (7th Cir. 2002).

363 Pub. L. No. 106-113 (1999).

364 These factors are
- the trademark or other intellectual property rights of the person, if any, in the domain name;
- the extent to which the domain name consists of the legal name of the person or a name that is otherwise commonly used to identify that person;
- the person's prior use, if any, of the domain name in connection with the *bona fide* offering of any goods or services;
- the person's *bona fide* non-commercial or fair use of the mark in a site accessible under the domain name;
- the person's intent to divert consumers from the mark owner's online location to a site accessible under the domain name that could harm the goodwill represented by the mark, either for commercial gain or with the intent to tarnish or disparage the mark, by creating a likelihood of confusion as to the source, sponsorship, affiliation, or endorsement of the site;
- the person's offer to transfer, sell, or otherwise assign the domain name to the mark owner or any third party for financial gain without having used,

the first case[365] determined under this new legislation, the court granted injunctive relief to the trade-mark owner when the defendant registered as a domain name the plaintiff's well-known mark, and then
produced a lame story (that the court found more "amusing than credible") as to how it made legitimate use of it; rather, the court concluded, the defendant merely intended to block the plaintiff's use of the
domain name.[366] Interestingly, the ACPA permits plaintiffs to bring an
in rem action, in order to deal with the situation where the cybersquatter is anonymous, or if known, refuses to respond to the plaintiff's

---

or having an intent to use, the domain name in the *bona fide* offering of any
goods or services, or the person's prior conduct indicating a pattern of such
conduct;

- the person's provision of material and misleading false contact information
  when applying for the registration of the domain name, the person's intentional failure to maintain accurate contact information, or the person's prior
  conduct indicating a pattern of such conduct;

- the person's registration or acquisition of multiple domain names which the
  person knows are identical or confusingly similar to marks of others that
  are distinctive at the time of registration of such domain names, or dilutive
  of famous marks of others that are famous at the time of registration of
  such domain names, without regard to the goods or services of the parties;
  and

- the extent to which the mark incorporated in the person's domain name
  registration is or is not distinctive and famous within the meaning of subsection (c)(1) of section 43.

365 *Sporty's*, above note 350. See also *Shields v. Zuccarini*, 89 F.Supp. 2d 634 (E.D.
Pa. 2000), where the creator of the Joe Cartoon business (which included at the
time a Web site <joecartoon.com> that received 700,000 hits per month) was
able, courtesy of the ACPA, to enjoin the defendant who had registered <joescar-
toon.com> and other variations on the plaintiff's registration. In *Wright v.
Domain Source, Inc.*, 2002 WL 1998287 (N.D. Ill. 2002), the defendant was in
breach of ACPA by registering a person's name as a domain name, and then
offering to sell it to them for $1,855. In *Coca-Cola Co. v. Purdy*, 2002 WL
1634277 (D. Minn. 2002), the ACPA was used to shut down sites that incorporated famous brands (like Coke and Pepsi) in domain names for antiabortion
sites, which in turn linked to antiabortion fundraising sites.

366 Other decisions in favour of trade-mark owners under the ACPA include: *Virtual
Works, Inc. v. Network Solutions, Inc.*, 238 F.3d 264 (4th Cir. 2001): <vw.net>
transferred to Volkswagen; *Northern Light Technology, Inc. v. Northern Lights
Club*, 236 F.3d 236 (1st Cir. 2001): <northernlights.com> transferred to owner of
"Northern Light" trade-mark; *Advance Magazine Publishers, Inc. v. Vogue International*, 123 F.Supp. 2d 790 (D.N.J. 2000): <teenvogue.com> transferred to publisher Vogue; and *People for the Ethical Treatment of Animals, Inc. v. Doughney*,
2000 U.S. Dist. Lexis 9474 (E.D. Va. 2000): <PETA.ORG> transferred to the
owner of the famous PETA trade-mark (court also refused parody defence based
on registrant's Web site titled "People Eating Tasty Animals").

claim.[367] The ACPA even applies retroactively in cases where the impugned domain name was registered before the ACPA came into force.[368] The ACPA has also been used by a U.S. law firm to obtain the transfer of various domain names related to its firm name from a cyber-squatter.[369]

In a manner akin to the ACPA, in December 1999 the Internet Corporation for Assigned Names and Numbers (ICANN, which is the successor to NSI), established the Uniform Dispute Resolution Policy (UDRP).[370] The objective of the UDRP is to give rightful trade-mark owners the ability to have domain names that comprise or include their trade-marks to be transferred to them from cybersquatters who registered them in bad faith. The UDRP is a fascinating form of quick arbitration, facilitated by one of several dispute resolution service providers, including eResolution in Montreal. They appoint a panel of one or three arbitrators who collect the relevant facts and argument by e-mail and then deliver a decision within sixty days, all for a cost of about $1000, which compares extremely favourably with the much longer time and, especially, greater cost of a traditional court proceeding. There are, however, some important differences between the ACPA and the UDRP; the former, for example, permits plaintiffs to recover damages, while the latter does not. In short, it is fair to ask how these two similar but distinct systems will coexist over time.

To make a successful case under the UDRP, the complainant has to prove three elements: first, that it owns a trade-mark and that the respondent's domain name is identical or confusingly similar to this

---

367 Another benefit of an *in rem* action is that it allows a claimant to proceed against a foreign registrant that might not otherwise be subject to personal jurisdiction: see Michael Geist, "New Net Laws Reach Beyond Borders," *The Globe and Mail* (27 June 2002). For example, in *Heathmount A.E. Corp.* v. *Technodome.com*, 106 F.Supp. 2d 860 (E.D. Va. 2000), the U.S. court asserted jurisdiction over two Canadian parties as the domain names were registered in the United States. In *Lucentsucks*, above note 358, however, Lucent was not permitted to proceed on an *in rem* basis against the domain name <Lucentsucks.com>, as the court determined it could have pursued the domain name registrant on an *in personam* basis.

368 *Porsche Cars North America, Inc.* v. *AllPorsche.com*, 55 U.S.P.Q. 2d 1158 (4th Cir. 2000); and *Mattel, Inc.* v. *Internet Dimensions, Inc.*, 2000 U.S. Dist. Lexis 9747 (S.D.N.Y. 2000).

369 In *Morrison & Foerster LLP* v. *Wick*, 94 F.Supp. 2d 1125 (D. Colo. 2000), the defendant registered domain names for over 90 law firms, and in the case of the ones involved in this case, linked them to various racist and offensive sites. For a non-ACPA case resulting in an injunction against a trafficker in law firm domain names, see *Debevoise & Plimpton* v. *Moore*, 2000 U.S. Dist. Lexis 6126 (D.D.C. 2000).

370 The rules of the UDRP are available at <icann.org>.

mark; second, that the respondent has no rights or legitimate interests in the domain name; and third, the respondent has registered and is using the domain name in bad faith.[371] Up to December 31, 2002, complainants have brought about 7000 claims under the UDRP, involving a total of 11,000 domain names, and complainants have been successful in about 80 percent of cases.[372] Indeed, some arbitrators have taken very expansive interpretations of the principal elements of the UDRP. For example, celebrities have been held to have sufficient common law trade-mark rights in their well-known names that they are not required to have registered their names as trade-marks or service marks.[373] As for the "confusingly similar" test, minor grammatical differences between the registered trade-mark and the domain name, such as misspelled words,[374] use of lowercase words,[375] absence of spaces,[376] and

---

371 UDRP, section 4(a).

372 The league tables of the four dispute resolution services can be tracked at <icann.org/udrp/proceedings-stat.htm>. Numerous Canadian owners of dot-com domain names have taken advantage of the UDRP; for example, the Government of Quebec achieved a transfer of <gouvernementduquebec.com> in *Gouvernement du Quebec contre Peter McCann*, WIPO-D2002-1010.

373 Thus, Julia Roberts, the actor, was able to have <juliaroberts.com> turned over to her: *Julia Fiona Roberts v. Russell Boyd*, WIPO D2000-0210; and Madonna achieved a similar result: *Madonna Ciccone, p/k/a Madonna v. Parisi and "Madonna.com,"* WIPO-D2000-0847. But see also *Gordon Sumner, p/k/a Sting v. Michael Urran*, WIPO No. D2000-0596, where the rock star Sting was unsuccessful, as "sting" is a common word, the respondent made some legitimate use of the "sting" word, and the respondent did not register the domain name in bad faith; it was Sting who offered $25,000 to buy it. On the other hand, in *Peter Frampton v. Frampton Enterprises, Inc.*, D2002-0141, the famous rock star Peter Frampton was able to achieve a transfer of the domain name, notwithstanding that the registrant was called Lyle Peter Frampton, given that the registrant made no legitimate use of the domain name, but rather used it to sell merchandise in competition with the rock star.

374 For example, Microsoft was successful in obtaining <Microesoft.com> [emphasis added] (*Microsoft Corporation v. Audrey Tumakov*, WIPO-D2002-1039); and American Express was successful in obtaining <Americaexpress.com> [i.e.- the "n" is missing] (*American Express Company v. Americaexpress.com*, NAF-FA-0210000-128700). See also *Bama Rags, Inc. v. John Zuccarini*, NAF-FA-94380. Zuccarini has also been sued successfully under the ACPA: in *Electronics Boutique Holdings Corp. v. Zuccarini*, 2000 WL 1622760 (E.D. Pa. 2000), the plaintiff was awarded damages of $500,000 as a result of the defendant's practice of using typosquatting Web sites that "mousetrap" a user and do not let them leave until they have clicked on a number of advertisements. The court concluded that the defendant's business model is based entirely on deceiving Internet users, which redounds to the detriment of the plaintiff whose business is built on user-friendliness and trust.

375 In *Educational Testing Service v. TOEFL*, WIPO D2000-0044, the well-known "TOEFL" trade-mark in upper case letters [TOEFL stands for Test of English as a Foreign Language] trumped the lower case <toefl.com> domain name, while in

use of hyphens,[377] and even the addition[378] or deletion[379] of words (or prefixes or suffixes), has not deterred a finding in favour of the holder of the registered trade-mark. As for whether the respondent has a "legitimate interest" in the domain name,[380] interestingly, a number of

---

Pharmacia & Upjohn Company v. *Moreonline*, WIPO-D2000-0134, the "ROGAINE" upper case trade-mark prevailed over the lower case <rogaine.net> domain name.

376 In *National Football League Properties, Inc. and Chargers Football Company* v. *One Sex Entertainment Co.*, WIPO-D2000-0118, the respondent's <chargergirls.com> domain was found confusing with the "Charger Girls" trade-mark.

377 In *Creo Products Inc. & anor* v. *Web site in Development*, WIPO-D2000-0160, the <creo-scitex.com> domain name was found confusing with the "creoscitex" business name (though the domain name was not ordered transferred as it was not used in bad faith).

378 Adding "888" before "celebrex," as in <888celebrex.com>, still produces a domain name confusing with the "Celebrex" trade-mark: *G.D. Searle & Co.* v. *Sean a/k/a Sean Kim*, NAF-FA-0211000-129128 (December 27, 2002). Similarly, in *Nokia Corporation* v. *Nokiagirls.com*, WIPO-D2000-0102, the addition of "girls" in <nokiagirls.com> did not distinguish this domain name from the well-known "Nokia" trade-mark. Equally, adding "greatings" to "icq" (to form <icq-greatings.com>) did not save John Zuccarini (again), in light of AOL's trade-mark in "icq": *America Online Inc.* v. *John Zuccarini*, WIPO-D2000-1495. And in *Dr. Ing. h.c.f. Porsche AG* v. *Takeda, Jim*, WIPO-D2002-0994, the respondent's <porschefinance.com> was found confusing with the complainant's well-known auto-related trade-mark, given that Porsche also provides financing. Closer to home, Canadian Tire was successful against <ecanadiantire.com> (*Canadian Tire Corporation, Limited* v. *849075 Alberta Ltd. carrying on business as Par5Systems*, WIPO-D2000-0985); but interestingly, was not against the registrant of <crappytire.com>, as this domain name was not found to conflict with "Canadian Tire" (*Canadian Tire Corporation, Limited* v. *Mick McFadden*, WIPO-D2001-0383).

379 In *Royal Bank of Canada* v. *D3M Domain Sales*, DeC AF-0147, dropping "Group" from the trade-mark "Royal Bank Financial Group," to come up with <royalbank-financial.com>, did not save the latter from being found confusing with the trade-mark. Another Canadian bank also used the UDRP to get the domain names <cibconline.net> and <cibconline.com> from the same respondent: John Partridge, "CIBC Wins Internet Domains," *The Globe and Mail* (6 October 2000).

380 The UDRP, in Section 4(c), sets out guidelines as to how the respondent can show a legitimate interest in the domain name: "Any of the following circumstances, in particular but without limitation, if found by the Panel to be proved based on its evaluation of all evidence presented, shall demonstrate your rights or legitimate interests to the domain name for purposes of Paragraph 4(a)(ii): (i) before any notice to you of the dispute, your use of, or demonstrable preparations to use, the domain name or a name corresponding to the domain name in connection with a bona fide offering of goods or services; or (ii) you (as an individual, business, or other organization) have been commonly known by the domain name, even if you have acquired no trademark or service mark rights; or (iii) you are making a legitimate noncommercial or fair use of the domain name, without intent for commercial gain to misleadingly divert consumers or to tarnish the trademark or service mark at issue."

decisions have held that the marketing of domain names is such a legitimate interest,[381] while others have found the opposite, in particular in respect of domain name "speculators."[382] And as to the "bad faith" test, a key determinant, of course, is whether the respondent registered the name with a view to flipping it to the trade-mark owner for cash;[383] for a classic example of this behaviour, consider the case where the respondent registered the name <vivendiuniversal.com> and various other derivatives the same day he heard about the merger between Vivendi and Universal, and immediately offered to sell these to the merged firm at a tidy profit.[384] Another type of case involving bad faith sees the respondent registering multiple domain names to prevent the owner of the registered trade-mark from using its trade-marks on the Internet.[385] And where a respondent registers a domain name primarily for the pur-

---

381 These cases have typically involved generic, non-source identifying domain names, such as <allocation.com> (*Allocation Network GmbH* v. *Steve Gregory*, WIPO-D2000-0016; this decision mentions that the respondent had registered some four hundred short phrases or common words, but not with the specific intent to cybersquat against anyone in particular.

382 *J. Crew International, Inc.* v. *crew.com*, WIPO-D2000-0054.

383 The UDRP, in section 4(b), also has guidelines as to what constitutes "bad faith": "*Evidence of Registration and Use in Bad Faith*. For the purposes of Paragraph 4(a)(iii), the following circumstances, in particular but without limitation, if found by the Panel to be present, shall be evidence of the registration and use of a domain name in bad faith: (i) circumstances indicating that you have registered or you have acquired the domain name primarily for the purpose of selling, renting, or otherwise transferring the domain name registration to the complainant who is the owner of the trademark or service mark or to a competitor of that complainant, for valuable consideration in excess of your documented out-of-pocket costs directly related to the domain name; or (ii) you have registered the domain name in order to prevent the owner of the trademark or service mark from reflecting the mark in a corresponding domain name, provided that you have engaged in a pattern of such conduct; or (iii) you have registered the domain name primarily for the purpose of disrupting the business of a competitor; or (iv) by using the domain name, you have intentionally attempted to attract, for commercial gain, Internet users to your web site or other on-line location, by creating a likelihood of confusion with the complainant's mark as to the source, sponsorship, affiliation, or endorsement of your web site or location or of a product or service on your web site or location."

384 *Vivendi S.A. et al.* v. *CPIC Net*, WIPO D2000-0685.

385 *Sanrio Company, Ltd. and Sanrio, Inc.* v. *Neric Lau*, WIPO-D2000-0172. See also *Volkswagen of America Inc.* v. *Ian Carson*, NAF-FA94394, where the respondent's <driverswanted.com> was found to have prevented Volkswagen from using its trade-mark "Drivers Wanted" in a domain name; in this case, the respondent was also found to have committed the other tell-tale indicia of cybersquatting, namely trying to pass off his site as an authorized Volkswagen site, and offering to sell the domain name for $20,000.

pose of disrupting business of a competitor, again the UDRP will provide the trade-mark owner with relief.[386]

Not all cases brought by complainants under the UDRP are successful in having the domain name transferred. In many cases brought under the UDRP, the trade-mark owner is unsuccessful in obtaining a transfer of the registrant's domain name because the registrant is making *bona fide* use of the domain name.[387] A similar good faith defence exists under the ACPA.[388] It is interesting to note, however, that even where a registrant makes legitimate use of a domain name, a court can require the registrant to use a prominent notice on the site to avoid confusion with the trade-mark owner.[389]

The CIRA Domain Name Dispute Resolution Policy (CDRP), which governs domain names in the dot-ca space, came into effect on

---

386 *Microsoft Corporation* v. *Amit Mehrotra*, WIPO-D2000-0053.

387 For example, in *H-D Michigan, Inc.* v. *Gary Skaggs*, NAF-FA-0211000-132449 (December 24, 2002), the complainant was the well-known Harley-Davidson motorcycle manufacturer that owned many "Harley-Davidson"-related trade-marks and some 600 domain names, 154 of which used some version of "Harley" or "Harley-Davidson." Nonetheless, the respondent was entitled to keep his domain name <usedharleys.com> because he legitimately used it to sell used Harley-Davidson motorcycles, a line of business the complainant was not in (they sold only new bikes). See also *GA Modafine S.A.* v. *Mani.com*, WIPO-D2001-0388, where the respondent was permitted to keep the <mani.com> domain name, as it was the respondent's surname and he used it for a *bona fide* purpose, notwithstanding that the complainant was a well-known fashion house selling goods internationally under the "Mani" brand. Or consider *FUNDUS Hotelentwicklungs-und Verwaltungsgesellschaft mbH* v. *Adlon Hotel*, WIPO-D2001-0339, where the respondent was entitled to keep using the <Adlon.com> domain name, notwithstanding that the complainant owned the German trade-mark for "Adlon" in respect of hotel services, because the respondent operated the "Adlon Hotel" in San José, California. In all these cases, it should be noted, the complainant might consider bringing a regular trade-mark claim, notwithstanding that it was unsuccessful under the UDRP. The opposite is also true: in *Black* v. *Molson Canada*, [2002] O.J. No. 2820 (Sup. Ct.), an Ontario court reversed a UDRP ruling, concluding that the Molson beer company was not entitled to have transferred the <Canadian.biz> domain name.

388 *Greenpoint Financial Co.* v. *The Sperry & Hutchinson Company*, 116 F.Supp.2d 405 (S.D.N.Y. 2000). See also *Chatam International, Inc.* v. *Bodum, Inc.*, 157 F.Supp. 2d 549 (E.D. Pa. 2001). In *Newport Elects., Inc.* v. *Newport Corp.*, 157 F.Supp. 2d 202 (D. Conn. 2001), the court held that both parties were entitled to keep using "Newport" in their respective domains, namely <newportus.com> and <newport.com>.

389 *Nissan Motor Co., Ltd.* v. *Nissan Computer Corp.*, 2000 U.S. App. Lexis 33937 (9th Cir. 2000). In this case, the court also ordered the registrant to cease displaying automotive-related advertisements and links so as not to exploit consumer confusion.

June 27, 2002.[390] While the CDRP is modelled generally after the
UDRP, as the CDRP was developed later than its dot-com counterpart,
CIRA made some revisions to its rules aimed at ameliorating some
shortcomings that CIRA and some other Canadian commentators
detected in the UDRP. For example, the CDRP gives more guidance as
to the bad faith and legitimate interest tests, and expressly permits use
in respect of good faith criticism, an activity that has resulted in diver-
gent decisions under the UDRP. Perhaps most importantly, the CDRP
generally requires a three-member arbitration panel because the predominantly single arbitrator process favoured by the UDRP was seen in
some quarters as overly favouring trade-mark owners.[391] Moreover,
CIRA believes its process of having panel members appointed random-
ly from lists submitted by the parties will prove superior to the UDRP
system. Another difference is that the CDRP permits a panel to award
costs of up to $5000 against a complainant found guilty of reverse
domain name hijacking. As well, the CDRP reflects some of the ele-

390 The CDRP is available at <cira.ca>. Two dispute resolution services provide the
     decision-making infrastructure under the CDRP: the British Columbia Commer-
     cial Arbitration Centre (<bcicac.ca>), based in Vancouver; and Resolution Cana-
     da Inc. (<resolutioncanada.ca>), based in Toronto.
391 See, for example, Dr. Milton Mueller, *Rough Justice: An Analysis of ICANN's Dis-
     pute Resolution Policy*, 9 November 2000, available at
     <dcc.syr.edu/roughjustice.htm>, which argues that some dispute resolution serv-
     ices are more complainant friendly than others due to a difference in approach-
     ing the policy, and the report prepared by Michael Geist, "*Fair.com?: An
     Examination of the Allegations of Systemic Unfairness in the ICANN UDRP*" (2001)
     University of Ottawa, <aix1.uottawa.ca/~geist/geistudrp.pdf>. However, under
     the CDRP, if the holder of the domain name refuses to participate in the pro-
     ceedings, the complainant may choose to have a single person adjudicate the
     case. Thus, in the first two cases under the CDRP, single arbitrators ordered
     transfers of the relevant .ca domain names when the registrants failed to respond
     to the complainants' allegations: *Browne & Co. Ltd. v. Bluebird Industries*, ECO-
     020822-001005 (<browneco.ca> found confusing with the "Browne & Co."
     business name; decision available at <resolution-canada.ca>); and *Red Robin
     International, Inc. v. Greg Tieu* (<redrobin.ca> transferred to owner of "Red
     Robin" trade-mark; decision available at <bcicac.ca>). Interestingly, under the
     UDRP system, known cybersquatters default between 70 and 100 percent of the
     time: see Dr. Milton Mueller, *Success by Default: A New Profile of Domain Name
     Trademark Disputes Under ICANN's UDRP*, 24 June 2002, available at
     <dcc.syr.edu/markle/mhome.htm>. This report also concludes that the gold rush
     mentality vis-à-vis domain names may be subsiding, as the number of new regis-
     tration levels off; the report cites the following figures for new registrations in
     the .com, .net, and .org spaces: 1997 — 1,464,000; 1998 — 1,745,000; 1999 —
     5,970,600; 2000 — 17,472,000; 2001 — 3,200,000; and 2002 — minus
     3,000,000. Thus, there likely will be fewer domain name disputes in the future.

ments of the underlying CIRA domain name registration system, such as the requirement that complainants either be owners of the registered Canadian trade-mark or qualify under CIRA's Canadian presence rules. Notwithstanding these purported improvements, some litigators remain critical of certain aspects of the CDRP (and the UDRP).[392]

8) Other Measures of Protection

A creator or owner of information-based assets can look to three means to protect them: intellectual property legal regimes (both judge-made and statutory); contract, whereby a user of the asset agrees not to make certain use of the asset; and technology, by which the owner of the asset, through technical means, restricts what users can do with the asset. These different vehicles correspond with the four approaches referred to in chapter 8, section C, "Computer Law: Skill Sets," that can be utilized by lawyers and others in meeting the challenges posed by the four dynamics of computer law. Thus, on the legal front, the common law can be used by relying on judge-made decisions to address new legal issues, or law reform can be pursued through the legislature. A third skill set centres on contract law, namely, the ability of entities, when confronted with new or uncertain situations, to craft their own laws (as it were) for use as between the private parties. And finally, technology can also be employed to fill gaps and fissures in the law by channelling behaviour through the use of specific technological devices contained within computers, networks, and software programs.

It should be noted that within the intellectual property area new rights can be created from time to time, typically by the legislative branch, as when the European directive on databases created the right of data extraction for a fifteen-year term (discussed earlier in this chapter in section C.4, "Copyright Protection for Electronic Databases"). Such a new right, however, can also be created by judges exercising their prerogative under the common law, as exemplified in the famous *INS* case in the United States.[393] In this decision, the court created a

---

392 For example, in "CIRA Adopts Domain Name Dispute Resolution Policy," *The Lawyers Weekly* (9 August 2002), Bradley J. Freedman argues that the following constitute deficiencies of both systems: the lack of an oral hearing mechanism by which panels could determine credibility or motive; the limited right to make reply submissions; the lack of an appellate body to provide interpretive guidance; and failure of the policy to indicate the intended interaction between it and court proceedings.

393 *International News Service v. Associated Press*, 248 U.S. 215 (2d Cir. 1918) [*INS*].

"quasi-property" right in "hot news" when it prevented the defendant news wire service from transmitting to its subscribers news stories that it learned of by reading the newspapers that used the plaintiff's news wire service. The majority of the court concluded there is no copyright in news, but felt it necessary to give a remedy to the plaintiff, given that the defendant

> admits that it is taking material that has been acquired by complainant as the result of organization and the expenditure of labor, skill, and money, and which is salable by complainant for money, and that defendant in appropriating it and selling it as its own is endeavoring to reap where it has not sown, and by disposing of it to newspapers that are competitors of complainant's members is appropriating to itself the harvest of those who have sown. Stripped of all disguises, the process amounts to an unauthorized interference with the normal operation of complainant's legitimate business precisely at the point where the profit is to be reaped, in order to divert a material portion of the profit from those who have earned it to those who have not; with special advantage to defendant in the competition because of the fact that it is not burdened with any part of the expense of gathering the news. The transaction speaks for itself, and a court of equity ought not to hesitate long in characterizing it as unfair competition in business.[394]

A recent decision in the United States stated that the "hot news" misappropriation doctrine can be invoked when the plaintiff expends resources generating or collecting information; the value of the information is time-sensitive; the defendant's use of the information constitutes free riding on the plaintiff's costly efforts; the defendant's use is in direct competition with the product offered by the plaintiff; and this ability to free ride reduces the incentive to produce the product or service such that its continued existence may be threatened.[395] Thus, in the INS case, the court concluded that if the plaintiff collector of news was not protected, it would cease to collect news, to the detriment of the news-reading public.

Justice Brandeis registered a strong dissent in the *INS* case, largely on the basis of a review of the previous British cases that, Brandeis concluded, did not afford protection for a quasi-property right in informa-

---

394 *Ibid.*, at 239–40.
395 *National Basketball Association v. Motorola, Inc.*, 105 F.3d 841 (2d Cir. 1997) [*Basketball*].

tion outside of the known parameters of copyright and the other intellectual property regimes.[396] Brandeis was of the view that

> The general rule of law is, that the noblest of human productions —
> knowledge, truths ascertained, conceptions, and ideas — become, after
> voluntary communication to others, free as the air to common use.[397]

Brandeis was not blind to the free-rider problem encountered by the plaintiff; he simply thought that a common law creation of a property right in news was a dangerous remedy that did not take into account all the relevant factors. Thus, Brandeis thought the legislature was the appropriate place to consider such issues as the following: If a property right is extended to the plaintiff, what happens to the newspapers dependent on the defendant? Is the plaintiff required to give them access to the news wire service at a reasonable price? Should the property right sound in damages alone, or should injunctive relief be available? Brandeis believed it was dangerous for the court to venture into these areas:

> The injustice of [the defendant's] action is obvious. But to give relief
> against it would involve more than the application of existing rules of
> law to new facts. It would require the making of a new rule in analo-
> gy to existing ones. The unwritten law possesses capacity for growth;
> and has often satisfied new demands for justice by invoking analogies
> or by expanding a rule or principle. This process has been in the main
> wisely applied and should not be discontinued. Where the problem is
> relatively simple, as it is apt to be when private interests only are
> involved, it generally proves adequate. But with the increasing com-
> plexity of society, the public interest tends to become omnipresent;
> and the problems presented by new demands for justice cease to be
> simple. Then the creation or recognition by courts of a new private
> right may work serious injury to the general public, unless the
> boundaries of the right are definitely established and wisely guarded.
> In order to reconcile the new private right with the public interest, it
> may be necessary to prescribe limitations and rules for its enjoyment;

396 For example, in *INS*, above note 393, Justice Brandeis at 255 cited *Sports and General Press Agency, Limited v. "Our Dogs" Publishing Company, Limited*, [1916] 2 K.B. 880, where the court held that the "official photographer" of a dog show could not prohibit others from making and publishing photos of the show where there was no condition to entry to the show not to take photographs. The court added that even if there were such a condition on entry, it would not restrict someone who, from a high roof, could take photos without buying a ticket to the show; that is, the plaintiff would have had to have built a high wall if it wanted to keep out unwanted photographers.
397 *INS*, above note 393 at 250.

and also to provide administrative machinery for enforcing the rules. It is largely for this reason that, in the effort to meet the many new demands for justice incident to a rapidly changing civilization, resort to legislation has latterly been had with increasing frequency.[398]

The admonition of the majority judgment in *INS* that it was wrong, and constituted "unfair competition" for the defendant to "reap where it had not sown," has become a very difficult test to operationalize in subsequent cases because it just begs the questions: what was sown, what was reaped, and on what basis should the decision be made to protect any particular element of what was sown? Thus, while in the United States a number of cases have found protection for a plaintiff on the basis of *INS*, others have declined. For example, in one case, the court granted protection to a person who recorded and sold copies of a tape of animal sounds used by hunters and photographers to attract animals when the defendant copied these sounds for a competing product.[399] By contrast, in a recent case the National Basketball Association was unsuccessful in using the *INS* doctrine against the defendants who operated a pager service that provided subscribers with simultaneous key data about NBA basketball games by utilizing modern information processing and communications.[400] The defendants' staff watched telecasts of the games and transmitted the facts of the game to subscribers by means of the pagers. As in the *INS* and other related cases, there was no violation of copyright because only facts were being disseminated, and there is no copyright in the underlying facts. The appellate court in the *Basketball* case, however, concluded that the *INS* doctrine did not apply because at the time the NBA did not have a service competitive with that of the defendants. Even if the NBA did, the court stated, it would still not apply the *INS* case so long as the defendants continued to collect the facts as they had done previously and did not derive them from the NBA pager service.

The American *INS* doctrine of "hot news quasi-property" has not been welcomed into Commonwealth jurisdictions. Juxtaposed against

---

398 *Ibid.*, at 262.

399 *United States Sporting Products, Inc.* v. *Johnny Stewart Game Calls, Inc.*, 865 S.W.2d 214 (Tex. App. 1993).

400 *Basketball*, above note 395. See also *Morris Communications Corp.* v. *PGA Tour, Inc.*, 117 F.Supp. 2d 1322 (M.D. Fla. 2000), where a court held that the PGA, under antitrust law, did not have to give the plaintiff access to real-time golf scores, as the plaintiff's service would have competed with the PGA's existing golf scores distribution business. Accordingly, the PGA was entitled to continue using its rules that prohibited unauthorized use of wireless communications devices on golf courses during PGA events.

the *INS* case, for example, is the *Victoria Park Raceway* decision of Australia's highest court.[401] In this case, the operator of a horse-racing track wanted to prevent a radio station from broadcasting coverage of the horse races. A platform had been built by the radio station adjacent to the horse track for just such a purpose. The court considered the *INS* decision, but refused to adopt the approach of the majority, opting instead for reasoning that approximated closely the Brandeis dissent, which the court stated represented the *"English view."*[402] The approach in *Victoria Park Raceway* was reconfirmed in Australia in a decision almost fifty years later, in which the High Court of Australia unequivocally stated that the doctrine of misappropriation of information in which someone has a quasi-property right is simply not a part of Australian law.[403] It should be noted, however, that the court in *Victoria Park Raceway* stated that if the plaintiff did not want the defendant seeing what went on on its land, it should build a higher fence. Similarly, the court also noted that had the broadcasts originated from within the race track from patrons who were granted entry to it, it would have been open for the plaintiff to impose a condition on the entry of such persons that they not communicate to anyone outside the race track the knowledge they obtained inside it, and such a covenant could be enforced against both the patron as well as any person who induces the patron to breach this contract. In support of this proposition the court cited one of the *Exchange Telegraph* cases.[404]

The latter points raised by the court in *Victoria Park Raceway* illustrate the ability of creators and owners of information-based assets to protect them through contractual means in certain circumstances. An

---

401 *Victoria Park Racing and Recreation Grounds Company Limited* v. *Taylor* (1937), 58 C.L.R. 479 (Austl. H.C.) [*Victoria Park Raceway*].

402 In refusing to accede to the argument that the races should be protected as quasi-property given the enterprise and labour of the plaintiffs in establishing the race course and conducting the races, the court in *Victoria Park Raceway, ibid.*, stated at 509: "[C]ourts of equity have not in British jurisdictions thrown the protection of an injunction around all the intangible elements of value, that is, value in exchange, which may flow from the exercise by an individual of his powers or resources whether in the organization of a business or undertaking or the use of ingenuity, knowledge, skill or labour. This is sufficiently evidenced by the history of the law of copyright and by the fact that the exclusive right to the invention, trade marks, designs, trade name and reputation are dealt with in English law as special heads of protected interests and not under a wide generalization."

403 *Moorgate Tobacco Co. Ltd.* v. *Philip Morris Ltd.* (1984), 56 A.L.R. 193 (Austl. H.C.).

404 *Exchange Telegraph Company Limited* v. *Central News, Limited*, [1897] 2 ch. 48. See also *Exchange Telegraph Company Limited* v. *Giulianotti*, [1959] Scots Law Times 293 (O.H.).

Exchange Telegraph case a year before the one cited by the Australian court gives a good example.[405] In this case the London Stock Exchange had given to the plaintiff the exclusive right to disseminate the stock ticker and other time-sensitive information related to the activities of the stock exchange, subject to the condition that it not be provided to certain brokers. The plaintiff, therefore, in turn made the financial information available to subscribers only on the basis of a written contract that prohibited the subscriber from conveying the information to any third party. The defendant induced a subscriber to breach this restriction so that it could obtain the information, and the court upheld an injunction issued against the defendant prohibiting such conduct. In the subsequent *Exchange Telegraph* case (cited in *Victoria Park Raceway*) involving the same plaintiff's horse racing information, a similar result was achieved even in circumstances where the race results transmitted to subscribers had already become relatively widely available through other means.

These *Exchange Telegraph* cases stand for the proposition that disseminators of information can utilize contractual means to limit the use and further distribution or disclosure of that information.[406] These cases, therefore, would be useful for creators or distributors of databases, particularly where the underlying information in the database was given thin or no legal protection under copyright law. The usefulness of these cases may also be enhanced in a mass market environment if Canadian courts adopt the reasoning of the leading U.S. case in upholding so-called shrinkwrap licences.[407] In the *Exchange Telegraph* cases, the courts imply that in addition to the plaintiff protecting its information-based assets through contract, it could also protect them under a common law property right prior to their publication, after which they would be protected by copyright. Although the courts in these cases did not use the now familiar terms of *trade secret* or *confidential information*, in all likelihood these are the kinds of information-based legal rights they were defining, rather than the broader property

---

405 *Exchange Telegraph Company* v. *Gregory & Co.*, [1896] 1 Q.B. 147.
406 A similar result was obtained in a U.S. Supreme Court case, *Board of Trade of the City of Chicago* v. *Christie Grain and Stock Company*, 198 U.S. 236 (1905), where the distribution of commodity price quotes was protected by contract.
407 *ProCD, Incorporated* v. *Zeidenberg*, 86 F.3d 1447 (7th Cir. 1996); incidentally, this case dealt with the distribution of a White Pages directory listing in an electronic format. For a discussion of this case and shrinkwrap licences, see chapter 5, section C.2, "Shrinkwrap Licences." As for the enforceability of contracts concluded in an online environment, see chapter 6, section A.3(c), "Express and Implied Click-Consent Agreements."

right referred to in the majority in *INS*. Confirmation of this view can be seen in the references in the *Stewart*[408] decisions at both the Ontario Court of Appeal and the Supreme Court of Canada to the *Exchange Telegraph* cases as authority for a property-based trade secret right.

Where the owner of an information-based asset is unable to bring the item under one or another intellectual property law regime, or where use of a contract is awkward or impractical, or where an intellectual property or contract is available but the owner is concerned about the practical ability to enforce either, the owner may turn to one of several technical devices to thwart the unauthorized use or copying of the asset. For some time, copy protect technology has been available for use on diskettes in order to prohibit the making of extra copies of mass marketed software, but the inconvenience of these devices largely stunted their acceptance and widespread use by software suppliers. With respect to the transmission of information in the broadcasting environment, encoding techniques are used to scramble signals so that only paying subscribers can access the broadcast. And for shipping digital assets over the Internet, various technological mechanisms are being considered and tested to code and tag specific digital documents or files with so-called rights management information (information that identifies the work, the owner, and author of it and information about the terms and conditions of its use) so that use of the work can be limited in accordance with the respective payment made by the user.[409] The law supports these technical efforts in several ways. For example, the *Radiocommunication Act*[410] makes it an offence for anyone but an authorized subscriber to decode encrypted subscription programming signals or to retransmit such illegally obtained signals.[411] In

---

408 *R. v. Stewart* (1983), 5 C.C.C. (3d) 481 (Ont. C.A.), rev'd (1988), 41 C.C.C. (3d) 481 (S.C.C.). This property-based approach has been superseded by understanding trade secrecy/breach of confidence protection in Canada as being a *sui generis* form of protection, as noted in the *LAC Minerals* case discussed in section B.1 of this chapter, "Trade Secrets/Breach of Confidence."

409 See, for example, Art Kramer, "Web Becoming World's Biggest Juke Box," *The Globe and Mail* (2 August 1997).

410 R.S.C. 1985, ch. R-2, as amended.

411 This and related provisions in the *Radiocommunication Act* have been used in several cases against entities importing into Canada devices for descrambling U.S. direct-to-home (DTH) satellite television services: *Expressvu Inc. v. NII Norsat International Inc.*, [1997] F.C.J. No. 1004 (T.D.) (QL), aff'd [1997] F.C.J. No. 1563 (C.A.); *R. v. Knibb* (1997), 198 A.R. 161 (Prov. Ct.); but see also *R. v. Ereiser* (1997), 156 Sask. R. 71 (Q.B.), for a contrary view. This dichotomy has now been resolved in favour of the authorized program provider. In *Bell ExpressVu Limited Partnership v. Rex*, 2002 SCC 42 [*Bell ExpressVu*], the Supreme Court of

a similar vein, the U.S. *Lehman Report* on the Internet recommended the establishment of civil and criminal penalties for removing copyright management information contained in digital files, and this has now been implemented in U.S. law in the DMCA, as discussed above.

9) Internet Linking and Framing

To end this survey of contentious intellectual property issues, it is fitting to discuss two practices that have developed on the Internet, namely, linking and framing, as these have given rise to several legal proceedings that may have an impact on further development of the Internet. As discussed in chapter 1, section A.6, "The Internet," linking is a core feature of the Internet, perhaps its single most important dimension in terms of attracting millions upon millions of non-technical users to the medium. A link (sometimes called a hyperlink or hypertext link) is an area on a computer screen that, when activated, transports the user to another Web site. Links are often in bold blue lettering; by clicking on the blue letters, the user can travel around the world, seamlessly and effortlessly, from site to site (thus serving as a

---

Canada has made it clear that the *Radiocommunication Act* should be read in conjunction with the *Broadcasting Act*, with the combined effect that only distributors of DTH satellite services licensed by the CRTC, and their authorized dealers, can offer a DTH service in Canada and sell the related decoding equipment. As well, the "computer abuse" offence of the *Criminal Code* (see chapter 3, section B.3, "Computer Abuse") might also be pressed into action against persons who break computer-based encryption codes in an unauthorized manner. Based on the decision in *Bell ExpressVu*, private suits have been launched against the grey-market dealers (see Keith Damsell, "Bell Suing Satellite TV Dealers," *The Globe and Mail* (22 October 2002)), but others in the Canadian broadcasting community argue still more needs to be done, including greater enforcement by the RCMP: Bertrand Marotte, "Coalition Targets Illegal TV Signals," *The Globe and Mail* (23 November 2002). Cable companies, however, argue that the licensed Canadian DTH companies are not doing enough about the grey-market problem: Bertrand Marotte, "CRTC Called to Act on Signal Piracy: Cable Firms Want Satellite — TV Hearing," *The Globe and Mail* (22 November 2002); and Bertrand Marotte, "Quebecor Complains of Satellite Piracy," *The Globe and Mail* (28 November 2002). For its part, one of the two Canadian satellite DTH providers argues that cable companies are not doing enough to stem piracy of their own cable-originating signals: Keith Damsell, "Cable Piracy Pegged at $400-million," *The Globe and Mail* (17 December 2002). Leaving aside the competitive rationales that may account for these accusations between the cable companies and the DTH provider, what is clear is that the four dynamics of computer law are conspiring to make it quite a challenge to keep unauthorized grey marketers out of the market.

bold testament to the fourth dynamic of computer law, namely the blurring of national and international). It is one of the features of the Web that is truly magic. Most links simply connect a user to the first page of another Web site. Some entities, however, have devised rather clever uses for linking.

In one case, an online news service in Scotland linked to the stories of the Scottish *Shetland Times* newspaper's Web site; that is, the link did not deposit the user at the electronic doorstep of the online newspaper, but took the user well inside, by-passing advertising and other content the online newspaper wanted its users to see.[412] In another case, a Microsoft Internet city guide Web site linked to a site operated by Ticketmaster for online ordering of tickets to live events; again, the Microsoft link allegedly took the user beyond the screens that Ticketmaster would have liked users to visit.[413] This practice of linking to an interior page of linked party's website, instead of linking to its home page, is known as "deep linking." Another example of deep linking involved a second *Ticketmaster* situation, in this case when Tickets.com deep-linked to event pages in the Ticketmaster Web site, again bypassing the latter's home page.[414] A clever variation on deep linking is framing, which was the subject of a lawsuit commenced by The Washington Post, CNN, and a number of other media companies with news Web sites, against a defendant that linked to these sites, but in a novel manner.[415] When a user from the defendant's Web site clicked on the link space, say of CNN, rather than being a regular link

---

412 *Shetland Times Co. Ltd.* v. *Wills*, [1997] FSR 604 (Scotland Court of Session) [*Shetland Times*], reported in *Computer & Online Industry Litigation Reporter*, 21 January 1997 at 23,534. See <shetland-times.co.uk/> for materials from the plaintiff's perspective.

413 *Ticketmaster Corporation* v. *Microsoft Corporation*, No. CV97-3055 RAP (C.D. Ca.), reported in *Computer & Online Industry Litigation Reporter*, 6 May 1997 at 24,087 and complaint reproduced at 24,144 [*Ticketmaster*]. For a copy of the complaint, see "Web Suit," *The National Law Journal* (12 May 1997) and also available at Web Suit at <ljx.com/internet/tktmaster.html>. See also Larry Armstrong, "Ticketmaster vs. Microsoft," *Business Week*, 12 May 1997.

414 *Ticketmaster Corp.* v. *Tickets.com, Inc.*, 54 USPQ 2d 1344 (C.D. Cal. 2000) [*Tickets.com*]. Each event page would list the basic facts relevant to the event, such as date, place, price, ticket availability, and instructions for ordering tickets. Tickets.com was able to deep link to a Ticketmaster event page because each such page had its own URL.

415 *Washington Post Co.* v. *Total News Inc.*, No. 97 Civ. 1190 (S.D.N.Y., complaint filed 20 February 1997) [*Washington Post*], reported in *Computer & Online Industry Litigation Reporter*, 6 May 1997, at 24,091 and complaint reproduced at 24,148ff.

the CNN site was displayed in a *window frame* that contained the defendant's logo and advertising. A similar phenomenon is often seen on television when, at the end of a program, the screen splits and additional information or content (perhaps about the next show) is broadcast on one side of the screen as the credits from the previous program are scrolling in another window.

In all of these situations the company whose site was linked took exception to the practice and commenced legal proceedings claiming a wide array of infringements. Interestingly, the prime motivator in these cases is not the direct loss of revenue due to unauthorized copying of the linked party's material, if indeed any such copying even goes on. Instead, what rankles is that the deep linking causes the user to bypass one or more screens on which advertising is placed, and the linked party charges fees to advertisers based on the number of users who see this advertising; in essence, the greater the amount of deep linking, the less money is generated from Web site traffic. Similarly, framing cuts down on advertising revenue because, again, the linked party's ads are not seen by users. In the *Shetland Times* case, the plaintiff argued copyright infringement and was successful in securing an injunction.[416] In the *Ticketmaster* case, Ticketmaster claimed trade-mark dilution, misleading representation, and unfair competition, among other heads of liability. In the *Washington Post* case, the plaintiffs argued misappropriation along the lines of the *INS* case,[417] trade-mark dilution, trade-mark infringement, copyright infringement, false advertising, and unfair competition; most of these claims were also alleged in the *Tickets.com* case, but in addition Ticketmaster argued breach of contract (the Ticketmaster Web site term and conditions), trespass, passing off and reverse passing off. The tenor of all these claims is similar to that which animated the majority in the *INS* case, namely, that persons linking and framing in these particular ways are trying to reap where they did not sow. Thus, Ticketmaster claimed that Microsoft was "feathering its own nest at Ticketmaster's expense."[418] The Washington Post labelled the defendant's Web site "parasitic."[419] The defendants were accused of "pirating" copyrighted materials.[420] Of course, moral outrage (real or feigned) does not a recognized legal claim make. The *Shetland Times*

---

416 *Shetland Times*, above note 412.
417 *INS*, above note 393.
418 See "Web Suit," above note 413 at 3.
419 *Washington Post*, above note 415 at 24,148.
420 *Ibid.*, at 24,150.

injunction case is not very helpful, given that its main finding was centred on the copyright that the court concluded the plaintiff had in the titles to its news stories (and which appeared on the defendant's site for purposes of effecting the link).[421] The *Washington Post* case settled rather quickly, and therefore there will not be a judgment forthcoming from that proceeding. Microsoft initially contested the Ticketmaster claim, arguing fair use and news reporting as defences, and that being linked is simply part of the operation of the Internet; therefore, Ticketmaster should not be able to complain about Microsoft's links.[422] This case, however, also settled, so again it is not of jurisprudential value.

The *Tickets.com* case did proceed to a judicial decision upon Tickets.com's motion to dismiss the claim brought by Ticketmaster. The court held in favour of Tickets.com, concluding that there was no copyright infringement;[423] the Ticketmaster Web site terms, which prohibited deep linking, were not enforceable because users were not given adequate notice of them and thus could not impliedly consent to

---

421 The parties have since settled this case, on the following terms: *The Shetland News* is permitted to link to *The Shetland Times* stories using the latter's headlines, provided there is an acknowledgment for each link along with the appearance of the latter's masthead or logo on a button beside the link, and this button and *The Shetland Times* button must link to the online headlines page on the latter's site. Details of the settlement are on the parties' respective Web sites: <shetland-times.co.uk> and <shetland-news.co.uk>.

422 "Microsoft Answers Ticketmaster's Charges of Electronic Piracy," *Computer & Online Industry Litigation Reporter*, 1 July 1997, at 24,421.

423 "Further, hyperlinking does not itself involve a violation of the *Copyright Act* (whatever it may do for other claims) since no copying is involved, the customer is automatically transferred to the particular genuine web page of the original author. There is no deception in what is happening. This is analogous to using a library's card index to get reference to particular items, albeit faster and more efficiently": *Tickets.com*, above note 414, at 1346. In a subsequent decision involving this same case, *Ticketmaster Corp. v. Tickets.com, Inc.*, 2000 U.S. Dist. Lexis 12987 (C.D. Cal 2000 (August)), the court found that it is also not copyright infringement for Tickets.com to copy the Ticketmaster event information, extract the facts therefrom, and then reformat them on Tickets.com's Web site. In coming to this conclusion, the court relied on *Connectix*, above note 96, where it was held that it is fair use for a defendant to copy a plaintiff's copyrighted work to distill non-copyrightable material (in this case, event facts). Interestingly, a different result might follow in Europe, where a Dutch court has held that an Internet news aggregator's practice of deep linking to commercial newspaper sites violated the provisions of the Danish *Copyright Act* that implemented the European Union's Database Directive (see above note 268): *Danish Newspaper Publishers' Association v. Newsbooster.com ApS* (Copenhagen Bailiff's Court, 5 July 2002, Denmark).

them;[424] and deep linking does not necessarily involve unfair competition. By contrast, in a more recent decision a Canadian court granted a temporary injunction against a Web site operator that had facilitated an indirect framing of a competitor's logo, advertising and trade-mark.[425] While these are rather cursory decisions, and the other cases noted above ultimately settled, several observations can already be made at this point about these sorts of cases. First, they illustrate clearly the first dynamic of computer law. As well, they show the multifaceted legal response that accompanies new perceived mischiefs; that is, although the discussion in this chapter has segmented the analysis of intellectual property into its constituent categories, fact patterns often involve two or more of the intellectual property regimes at the same time. Indeed, in the *Washington Post* and *Ticketmaster* cases, there were also technical responses offered by the plaintiffs as they tried to neutralize the linking by programming countermeasures to the links, which of course were met by further linking measures. In terms of the law, the *Washington Post* case raised some particularly interesting issues; whereas a straight link to a Web site's first page should not be problematic under copyright law, as concluded by the court in the *Tickets.com* decision, since the link does not copy any material and serves only as an address to another location, in Canada questions such as moral rights may be raised in addition to those listed in the plaintiffs' claims noted above. As well, given that linking is such an essential feature of the World Wide Web, it may be possible to argue implied licence in defence of these claims; on the other hand, such a licence may be subject to revocation, if not through Web site terms and conditions (assuming they are designed and presented in a manner to make them enforceable), then through express notice to the unwanted linker or framer.[426] Also, in some framing cases in the United States the concept of derivative work may also arise; that is, in the United States the right to make derivative works rests with the copyright holder of the original material. This concept, for example, was used in a U.S. case to enjoin someone from taking the pages of an art book that contained pictures on each page and remounting the pages/pictures on tiles, and selling the

---

424 For a fuller discussion of this issue, see chapter 6, section A.3(c), "Express and Implied Click-Consent Agreements."

425 *Imax Corp. v. Showmax Inc.*, [2000] F.C.J. No. 69 (F.C.T.D.).

426 For an interesting variation on the linking case, see *Putnam Pit, Inc. v. City of Cookesville*, 2000 U.S. App. Lexis 17305 (6th Cir 2000), where a plaintiff argued that a city's refusal to provide a link to the plaintiff's site violates the plaintiff's freedom of speech rights.

tile product.[427] Although no copy was made of the page from the art book, the court held that an unauthorized derivative work was made, and found for the owner of the copyright in the book. Interestingly, a diametrically different result was obtained in a Canadian case where the defendant was permitted to transfer pictures from a magazine and mount and resell them in a different medium where no copies were made of them.[428] These sorts of analogies may play a role in sorting out the controversies surrounding linking and framing.[429]

---

427 *Mirage Editions, Inc.* v. *Albuquerque A.R.T. Co.*, 856 F.2d 1341 (9th Cir. 1988) [*Mirage Editions*].

428 *Fetherling* v. *Boughner* (1978), 40 C.P.R. (2d) 253 (Ont. H.C.J.). See also *Lee* v. *A.R.T. Company*, 125 F.3d 580 (7th Cir. 1997), where the appellate court disagreed with the approach in the *Mirage Editions* case, above note 427, and found that mounting art on tiles did not infringe the artist's copyright. This dichotomy has now been resolved in Canada courtesy of the Supreme Court decision in *Théberge*, above note 10, where it was held that once an artist sells a paper-based poster, he cannot prevent its transfer (in this case through a sophisticated ink transfer process) to a canvas backing where no additional copy of the image is made.

429 Though in a decision involving a form of Internet framing, the court discussed and refused to follow the analysis in *Mirage Editions*, above note 427, arguing that the facts in the two cases are clearly distinguishable: *Futuredontics, Inc.* v. *Applied Aragramics, Inc.*, 45 U.S.P.Q. 2d 2005 (C.D. Cal. 1998).

CHAPTER 3

CRIMINAL LAW

A society dependent on computers, telecommunications, networks, and information is extremely vulnerable to computer crime. Computers can be the subject of crime, as when they are stolen or accessed without authorization. As well, computers and networks can be the means by which other crimes are perpetrated. Computer crime involves some form of unauthorized gain, destruction, manipulation, or intrusion, or some form of illegal image or speech. In combatting computer crime, authorities are squarely faced with the four dynamics of computer law, namely, the rapid pace of technological change, the elusive nature of information, and the blurring of private/public and national/international.[1] These dynamics, together with the general interpretative principle that criminal laws must be construed narrowly, have resulted in the courts in Canada having an uneven track record of convicting persons charged with computer and information-related activities that cause wilful harm and damage to third parties. Nevertheless, and to a large degree because of certain of these cases that resulted in acquittals, the Canadian government has revised the *Criminal Code* on several occasions to give law enforcement agencies addi-

---

1   These dynamics are important, and are a unifying theme throughout this book. For a discussion of these dynamics, see chapter 8, section A, "Computer Law: Dynamics."

tional assistance in fighting computer crime.[2] Today the *Criminal Code* contains a number of different provisions that can be pressed into service against persons who perpetrate computer-related crime. In other cases, the applicability of the *Criminal Code* to certain harmful behaviour remains in question, requiring Parliament to be vigilant as to the adequacy of the criminal law to deal with new computer-related threats and risks, and to protect people, property, and governments in the Information Age.

A. A TYPOLOGY OF HARMFUL CONDUCT

The actual nature and amount of computer crime are not precise. Computer crime has been defined as "any illegal, unethical, or unauthorized behaviour involving automatic data processing and/or transmission of data."[3] Canada's Royal Canadian Mounted Police (RCMP) has used the following working definition of computer crime: "any criminal activity involving the copying of, use of, removal of, interference with, access to or manipulation of computer systems, computer functions, data or computer programs."[4] These definitions cast the net of computer crime broadly indeed. As for the quantum of computer crime, exact and reliable statistics are hard to come by because much malicious computer-related activity is difficult to detect. Moreover, many organizations do not report themselves as victims of computer crime since this could

---

2   R.S.C. 1985, c. C-46. The *Criminal Code* is federal legislation, as the *Constitution Act, 1867* (U.K.), 30 & 31 Vict., c. 3, s. 91(27), gives the federal government power over criminal law. The Constitution Act, 1867 can be found in R.S.C. 1985, Appendix II, No. 5.

3   Ulrich Sieber, *The International Emergence of Criminal Information Law* (Koln: Heymanns, 1992) at 5 [*Criminal Information Law*].

4   RCMP, Operational Policy 1992, cited in Donald K. Piragoff, "Computer Crimes and Other Crimes against Information Technology in Canada," in *Information Technology Crime: National Legislations and International Initiatives*, ed. Ulrich Sieber (Koln: Heymanns, 1994) at 86 [*Information Technology Crime*]. Ten years later, the Mounties' definition of computer crime is "any illegal act which involves a computer system whether the computer is the object of a crime, an instrument used to commit a crime or a repository of evidence related to a crime": Royal Canadian Mounted Police, "What is Computer and Telecommunication Crime," last updated 2001-07-25, available at <rcmp.ca>.

result in a loss of confidence among customers and investors.[5] At the
same time, some observers question whether the actual incidence of
computer crime is as great as is popularly thought. For example, a survey conducted by the Ontario Provincial Police in the early 1980s
reported that only 4 percent of respondents had been victimized by
computer crime.[6] Today, however, computer crime is a significant and
growing problem.[7] The statistics from a recent survey of 538 computer
security practitioners in the United States are indeed sobering: 85 percent of respondents detected computer security breaches; 64 percent
acknowledged financial losses due to computer breaches; 35 percent
were willing and/or able to quantify financial losses, reporting
$377,828,700 in financial losses; 70 percent cited their Internet con-
nection as a frequent point of attack; 38 percent detected denial of service attacks; and 94 percent detected computer viruses.[8] The Internet
raises particular problems from a computer crime perspective: the very
features that make it such a powerful, positive communication medium (ease of use, ubiquity, relatively low cost), make it a prime theatre
on which criminals can act out a range of traditional and more novel
nefarious behaviours. It came as no surprise when Madam Justice Bev-
erley McLachlin predicted, upon her being sworn in as Chief Justice of
the Supreme Court of Canada, that Canada's highest court will increasingly be faced with technology-oriented issues, including computer

---

5   See Patrick Brethour, "Newbridge Mum on Fraud Charge," *The Globe and Mail*
    (10 December 1996); and Joe Chidley, "Cracking the Net," *Maclean's*, 22 May
    1995. The *Criminal Code* does not require a victim of computer crime to report
    it. Thus, someone hit by a software "virus" can stay mute; compare this to cer-
    tain types of public health legislation, such as Ontario's *Health Protection and
    Promotion Act*, R.S.O. 1990, c. H.7, which requires physicians and certain other
    persons to report certain "virulent" diseases.

6   See Ulrich Sieber, *The International Handbook on Computer Crime* (New York:
    Wiley & Sons, 1986) at 33. Interestingly, 46 percent of respondents to the OPP
    survey thought computer crime to be an important concern, thereby leading
    some to conclude that the general level of concern expressed vis-à-vis computer
    crime is not borne out by real crime statistics. For a discussion of survey results
    reporting much higher rates of computer crime, see council of Europe, *Comput-
    er-Related Crime* (Strasbourg: Council of Europe, 1990).

7   For example, it is estimated that in 1995 losses in the United States from com-
    puter viruses alone amounted to $1 billion: Gary H. Anthes, "Old, New Viruses
    Swarm PC Users," *Computerworld*, 6 May 1996 ["Old, New Viruses"].

8   Computer Security Institute, "Financial Losses Due to Internet Intrusions, Trade
    Secret Theft and Other Cyber Crimes Soar," *Press Release* (12 March 2001). This
    press release gives highlights of the CSI's sixth annual "Computer Crime and
    Security Survey," and is available at <gocsi.com>.

crime.[9] Computer crime manifests itself in a wide variety of guises,[10] most of which fall within one or more of the following broad categories: unauthorized gain, destruction, manipulation and intrusion, and illegal images and speech. These categories are in addition to the many types of situations in which a computer is used to facilitate one of the "traditional" offences set out in the *Criminal Code*. The four dynamics of computer law (the rapid pace of technological change, the elusive nature of information, and the blurring of private/public and national/international), as explained in part B of this chapter, make it more difficult for the *Criminal Code* to deal with each type of these harmful activities. But first, in the balance of part A, there is provided a discussion of the problem.

1) Unauthorized Gain

In this category of damaging conduct falls a broad range of theft and theft-like activities. Stealing computer equipment,[11] and recently, valuable components like chips, is an age-old form of illicit conduct involving new devices.[12] Commercial piracy of software — making multiple copies of a computer program and selling them, including more recently over the Internet — is a modern means by which an owner of prop-

---

9 Brian Laghi, "Top Judge Predicts Jump in Internet Crime: New Supreme Court Chief Justice McLachlin Foresees Era of High-Tech Challenges," *The Globe and Mail* (12 January 2000). In an interview, the new Chief Justice was quoted as saying that: "Technology, in a variety of ways, is going to produce new issues that will one way or the other find their way before the courts. The Internet is having a big impact on society and it's going to make its impression felt profoundly."

10 For example, in 1991 German police registered 5004 cases of "computer crime" consisting of 3963 cases of cash dispenser manipulations, 787 cases of computer fraud, 82 cases of forgery of computer data, 95 cases of alteration of data and computer sabotage, and 77 cases of illegally obtaining computer data (especially hacking): Sieber, *Criminal Information Law*, above note 3 at 6–7.

11 For an article that describes an elaborate operation by six thieves that resulted in the theft of 81 laptops in a five-block area of office buildings, see Kim S. Nash, "Rising Laptop Theft Tacks on $150 a Box," *Computerworld* (3 August 1998).

12 A novel crime involving chips has the criminals acquiring genuine chips of a certain strength, then re-marking them as higher strength, therefore victimizing both disappointed buyers as well as the manufacturers, who lose sales of their higher-strength chips: see U.S. Department of Justice, "New York Electronic Crimes Task Force Arrests Two Individuals on Charges of Trafficking in Counterfeit Computer Chips and Software," *Press Release*, 22 June 2000 <cybercrime.gov/ptatinum.htm>.

erty can be deprived of the benefits accruing from the property.[13] Benefiting economically from others without paying compensation, and
thus "stealing their resources," would include the theft of computer,
telecommunications, and cable/satellite services.[14] The Internet is also
becoming a popular venue for various scams to bilk unsuspecting and
gullible users, such as taking a customer's money but not delivering the
agreed-upon goods.[15] Another use for computers in this area is to access
payroll, banking, and other records stored on computers to divert monetary amounts to the perpetrator's account.[16] New technologies, includ-

13   See the following U.S. Department of Justice News and Press Releases: "U.S.
Indicts 17 In Alleged International Software Piracy Conspiracy," 4 May 2000 (a
scheme masterminded by an international group known as "Pirates with Attitudes," which included several Intel employees who supplied hardware, illegally
copied software worth over US$1 million which was made available over the
Internet from a computer located at the University of Sherbrooke in Quebec);
"Two Defendants Sentenced for Distribution and Sales of Counterfeit Copyrighted Computer Software," 7 August 2001 (penalty included forfeiture of the Web
site, including the domain name <software-inc.com>, used to help sell $900,000
worth of software); "U.S. Customs Seizes $100 Million in Pirated Computer
Software, Biggest Case in U.S. History," 16 November 2001 (authorities found
over 47,000 copies of counterfeit Microsoft and Symantec software in a single
shipping container); "Federal Law Enforcement Targets International Internet
Piracy Syndicates: Multiple Enforcement Actions Worldwide Snare Top 'Warez'
Leadership," 11 December 2001 (over one hundred search warrants executed
worldwide), all available at <cybercrime.gov>. The latter arrests led to a forty-
six-month prison term, the longest imposed to that date for organized Internet
software piracy: see *The Globe and Mail* (20 May 2002).

14   For a good discussion of the types and amount of telecommunications fraud, see
chapter 2 of Robert W.K. Davis & Scott C. Hutchison, *Computer Crime in Canada: An Introduction to Technological Crime and Related Legal Issues* (Toronto: Carswell, 1997) [*Computer Crime*].

15   Some of these types of unauthorized gain are discussed in chapter 5, section
B.1(d), "Misleading Advertising," and chapter 4, section E.4(b), "False Claims."
Online purchasers have generated a large amount of complaints, as the Internet
presents criminals with several fraud promotion business models, including a
fraudulent seller simply not making good on the delivery of goods. For a good
example of a massive Internet Ponzi scheme, in which 13,000 investors were
bilked of US$58 million, see Wendy Stueck & Lily Nguyen, "Alleged Con Man's
Internet Game Nears Its End," *The Globe and Mail* (4 June 2002).

16   Ulrich Sieber, in *Information Technology Crime*, above note 4 at 9, gives an example of "salary-doubling," a common crime implemented by computer whereby a
person, typically an existing employee, enters fictitious employee/salary information into the company's computers in order to have such funds transferred to
the perpetrator at a later date. For recent American examples, see the following
U.S. Department of Justice Press Releases: "Former Chase Financial Corp.
Employee Pleads Guilty to Unlawful Access to Chase Manhattan Bank to
Defraud Chase Financial Corp. and Chase Manhattan Bank," 9 October 2001

ing pinhole cameras, altered cash dispensing machines, and doctored punch pads that facilitate "debit card skimming," have given rise to new forms of credit card fraud.[17] With the phenomenal growth in online auctions, it is no surprise that "auction fraud" is also a byproduct of this new form of e-commerce.[18] High-tech devices can also facilitate "identity theft," allowing thieves to impersonate the victim and ring up large credit card balances in their name.[19] High-tech forgery,[20]

(employee obtained credit card numbers which she provided to others to fraudulently purchase goods); "Former Cisco Systems, Inc. Accountants Sentenced for Unauthorized Access to Computer Systems to Illegally Issue Almost $8 Million in Cisco Stock to Themselves," 26 November 2001 (accountants accessed stock option disbursement software program to issue themselves stock), both available at <cybercrime.gov>.

17　See Alison Dunfield, "E-Bandits Target Credit Cards," *The Globe and Mail* (21 May 2002); Caroline Alphonso & Renée Huang, "Debit Data Swiped, Four Held in Scam," *The Globe and Mail* (2 June 2000); and Rob Carrick, "Police, Bankers Rush to Reassure Card Holders," *The Globe and Mail* (11 December 1999). On the other hand, in 1999 VISA reported that overall card fraud losses had reached a record low of only 0.06 percent of total purchases, essentially 6¢ for every $100 of transactions: *The Globe and Mail* (22 February 2000).

18　Auction fraud can take many forms, from failing to deliver purchased merchandise, to placing "shill" bids intended to artificially inflate prices: David Diamond, "The Web's Most Wanted," *Business 2.0*, August 1999. See also the following U.S. Department of Justice Press Releases: "Man Indicted for Auctioning Pirated Software on Ebay," 28 November 2001 (charged with both criminal copyright infringement and fraud for failing to disclose to purchasers that the software was not legitimate); "Man Pleads Guilty in eBay Fraud Case," 13 December 2001 (accused defrauded 30 victims of $50,000 by obtaining payment through money orders and PayPal, but then never delivering merchandise); "Man Indicted for Selling Fake Derek Jeter and Nomar Garciaparra Baseball Bats on eBay, Harassing E-Mails," 18 December 2001 (accused ordered the bats from the Original Maple Bat Company in Ottawa); and "Man Pleads Guilty to eBay Auction Fraud," 20 December 2001 (buyers sent money, accused did not send baseball cards), all available at <cybercrime.gov>.

19　Sandra Martin, "Is Little Brother Watching You?" *Report on Business Magazine*, September 2000; and Tom Clark, "Ontario Laws Toughened To Combat Identity Theft," *The Globe and Mail* (9 February 2002).

20　In a recent report by the Criminal Intelligence Service Canada (an umbrella group for the RCMP, the Ontario and Quebec provincial police, and 120 municipal and regional police agencies), the huge increase in counterfeit currency and credit card fraud is attributed to sophisticated scanning and desktop publishing equipment: Brian Laghi, "Canadian Police Confounded by Information-Highway Robbery," *The Globe and Mail* (22 August 1998). At the same time, advanced technology — but not involving computers — is being pressed into action against criminals in order to make it more difficult to counterfeit banknotes. Among these neat new technologies to hamper counterfeiting is the thin film patch that changes colour as the note is tilted, caused by the optical properties of the patch: "Counterfeit Prevention: The Colour of Money," *The Economist*, 29 April 2000.

manipulation of automated teller machines, and accessing a competitor's industrial secrets resident on computer systems, are three more examples of damage engendered through unauthorized gain. Another activity is gaming. Many Internet sites offer games of chance, ranging from blackjack to roulette to slot machines, all provided in a computerized environment and resident on a computer outside of Canada and the United States in an attempt to remove themselves from the federal, provincial, and state laws that prohibit or regulate gambling.[21]

Traditional and modern rationales for theft converge in the unauthorized taking of laptop computers. One report indicates that in 1996 the number of laptops stolen in the United States was 265,000, an increase of 27 percent over 1995.[22] The epidemic proportions of this problem indicate that laptop computers are stolen not only for the value of the machines, but also for the value of the data stored on them. Apparently one laptop stolen from a credit card company contained 314,000 credit card numbers. The trends of mass storage and miniaturization highlighted in chapter 1, sections B.3, "Mass Storage," and B.5, "Miniaturization," and implemented in laptop computers have produced a computing environment that is extremely vulnerable to computer crime. Indeed, all the trends detailed in chapter 1, such as the rise of ubiquitous communication networks, the explosive growth of the Internet, the ability to digitize and manipulate data and other content, and society's increasing dependence on the computer and networks, along with the four dynamics of computer law, contribute to a world where the computer criminal can operate more effectively, more internationally, more easily, more surreptitiously, and more dangerously than ever before. Computer crime is an unfortunate Achilles' heel of the Information Age.

2) Unauthorized Destruction

This category includes criminals who access computer systems remotely in order to destroy data. As well, many malicious computer-related

---

21   It is difficult to know with any certainty just how big an activity Internet-based gaming really is, but one estimate put it in the $2.5 billion range in 2001, predicting a rise to $5.0 billion by 2003: Tatiana Boncompagni, "Doubling Down," *The American Lawyer*, October 2001. This article notes that the number of Internet gambling sites stood at 1200 in 2001, compared with 25 in the mid-1990s.
22   Mindy Blodgett, "Laptop Thefts Escalate: Data Loss, Not Cost of Hardware, Top Concern," *Computerworld*, 31 March 1997; see also Beppi Crosariol, "Lap-jacked!" *The Globe and Mail, Report on Business Magazine*, October 1996.

activities are committed by disgruntled company employees.[23] This category also includes "viruses," "worms," and other software-based booby traps that are intended to infiltrate computer systems and cause damage.[24] The most drastic virus deletes data and/or causes a computer program to become completely inoperable. More subtle ones, however, can also take their toll, such as viruses that only change certain letters throughout data resident on a computer. Indeed, often these more circumspect perpetrators can inflict greater harm because they can go undetected for so long. Moreover, even viruses that are seemingly benign — some simply display a greeting — take up much time and effort on the part of computer users once they are detected.[25] Viruses are particularly dangerous due to their ability to replicate and transmit themselves over networks, as in the case of the famous one let loose by Robert Morris, which swept across the Internet to infect a large number of computers.[26]

The Internet has increased the virus problem dramatically. In a 1995 survey, 75 percent of respondents indicated that the viruses that attacked them came from diskettes, and 9 percent said the viruses came from e-mail attachments.[27] This latter form of dissemination did not exist the year before. In another survey, 76 percent of respondents at larger companies indicated they had been hit by a computer virus.[28] In a more recent survey, 80 percent of all virus infections were reported to

---

23 One survey recorded that 42 percent of larger company respondents indicated offensive computer-related behaviour by "company insiders": Bob Violino, "The Security Facade," *Information Week*, 21 October 1996 ["Security"]. In one case of employee computer sabotage, a terminated employee activated a time bomb that permanently deleted all of the employer's sophisticated manufacturing programs: U.S. Department of Justice, "Former Computer Network Administrator Guilty of Unleashing $10 Million Programming "Timebomb," *Press Release*, 9 May 2000.

24 For a historical overview of viruses, see David Ferbrache, *A Pathology of Computer Viruses* (London: Springer-Verlag, 1992). For a recent version, see John Saunders, "Computer Virus Infects Networks Around the World," *The Globe and Mail* (27 January 2003).

25 For a description of the good, the bad, and the ugly of viruses, see Alan Solomon, *PC Viruses: Detection, Analysis and Cure* (London: Springer-Verlag, 1992). It is open to question whether there can ever be a "good" virus: "Computer Viruses: The Good, the Bad and the Ugly," *The Economist*, 16 June 2001.

26 See *United States* v. *Morris*, 928 F.2d 504 (2nd Cir. 1991).

27 The National Computer Security Association, "1996 Computer Virus Prevalence Survey," reported in Anthes, "Old, New Viruses," above note 7. A recent survey puts the global costs attributable to viruses in 2001 at around US$13 billion: "Securing the Cloud," *The Economist*, 26 October 2002.

28 Violino, "Security," above note 23. See also Geoffrey Rowan, "Computer Viruses Cost Firms: Study," *The Globe and Mail* (17 December 1996).

have been transmitted over the Internet.[29] In the last few years, some of the most dangerous viruses have been given innocuous sounding names, which can mislead as to the damage wreaked by them: "Melissa,"[30] "Love Bug,"[31] and "Anna."[32] More appropriate are names such as "Goner,"[33] "Worm.ExploreZip,"[34] and "Code Red."[35] Wireless devices are not immune from viruses either,[36] nor are the products of the computer industry's leading suppliers.[37] Indicative of the extent of the virus

29 Barb Cole-Gomolski, "Hackers Hitch Ride on E-Mail: Lack of Security Opens Door," *Computerworld*, 28 April 1997.

30 The Melissa virus was the worst of 1999, in terms of the $1.2 billion financial damage caused by it: "Code Red Cost Hits Billions: Firm," *The Globe and Mail* (4 September 2001) ["Code Red"]. This virus proliferated exponentially; each infected computer sent out fifty messages to other computers, which in turn each distributed fifty more messages, etc: U.S. Department of Justice, "Creator of "Melissa" Computer Virus Pleads Guilty to State and Federal Charges," *Press Release* (9 December 1999).

31 The Love Bug, which apparently has hit 40 million computers since May 2000, has been estimated to be the most expensive ($8.7 billion) virus to-date: "Code Red," above note 30.

32 Susanne Craig & Jack Kapica, "'Anna' Computer Virus Served Worldwide, But It Was No Ace," *The Globe and Mail* (13 February 2001); and Anthony Deutsch, "Dutch Hacker Admits to Kournikova Virus," *The Globe and Mail* (15 February 2001). For an interesting inside view of the world of Dutch Internet hackers, see Michael Specter, "The Doomsday Click: How Easily Could a Hacker Bring the World to a Standstill?" *The New Yorker*, 28 May 2001.

33 The Goner virus, which, among other damage, caused the city of Calgary to shut down its entire e-mail system, was particularly malicious because it deleted virus-protection and Internet security software on a computer, and then sent out a flood of e-mails to new victims: Patrick Brethour, "E-mail Virus Hits Internet's 'Immune System,'" *The Globe and Mail* (5 December 2001).

34 The Worm.ExploreZip virus apparently wiped out 25,000 documents at the Deposit Insurance Corp. of Ontario, and hit other Canadian companies such as Rogers, Bell Canada, & Nortel: Simon Tuck, Natalie Southworth, & Ann Gibbon, "Companies Scramble to Fight E-mail Virus That Erases Files," *The Globe and Mail* (11 June 1999); and Simon Tuck & Natalie Southworth, "As the Worm Turns: A Viral Nightmare," *The Globe and Mail* (12 June 1999).

35 The worldwide cost of the Code Red computer worm is estimated to be in the $2.6 billion range: "Code Red," above note 30.

36 Steven Chase, "Handheld Headache: Virus Creator Strives to Fix Mistake," *The Globe and Mail* (6 September 2000); and Kevin Marron, "Cybercrime Takes to the Airwaves," *The Globe and Mail* (28 June 2001).

37 Steven Chase, "Hackers Attack Microsoft Secrets: Source Code Access Seen as Wake-up Call," *The Globe and Mail* (28 October 2000). Some software developers do not help themselves by allowing staff to program "easter eggs" into software products, which are extraneous files inserted mainly for humour: "Messages From the Hall of Tortured Souls," *The Economist*, 18 December 1999.

problem is the phenomenon of the spread, again over Internet e-mail, of virus hoaxes, namely, messages that carry warnings about non-existent viruses. These hoax messages, however, cause massive inconvenience and consume scarce information system personnel resources, and therefore are a scourge in themselves.[38] Of course, a number of public agencies and private companies combat viruses by detecting them and supplying the marketplace with antivirus scanning software.[39] Canada, for example, has established an Office of Critical Infrastructure Protection and Emergency Preparedness, in large measure to combat against potential attacks against this country's computer networks.[40] These efforts and products aimed at countering computer crime, however, are invariably reactive in nature, and therefore determined perpetrators of viruses can invariably stay one step ahead of these antidote measures; hence, the need to criminalize this antisocial, harmful behaviour (although the four dynamics of computer law make this a difficult task).

3) Unauthorized Manipulation

Just as *virus* has entered the modern lexicon, so too has *hacker*, though originally this term was used to denote a computer virtuoso. Hacker has acquired a darker connotation of late, being used to label individuals who spend inordinate amounts of time attempting, often successfully, to gain access to other computers connected to one or more networks.[41] The motivations of hackers vary, once they are inside the victim computer, from an intention to commit fraud, theft, or industrial espionage

---

38 Sharon Machlis, "Virus Hoax Make IS Sick: Warnings, Carried by E-Mail, Spread Hysteria and Waste Resources," *Computerworld*, 28 April 1997.

39 See "A Thousand Ills Require A Thousand Cures: Researchers are Borrowing from Immunology to Improve the Security of Computer Networks," *The Economist*, 8 January 2000; "Whodunnit: Forensic Computing Studies the Anatomy of Computer Crime," *The Economist*, 31 March 2001; and Dean Takahashi & Dean Starkman, "How the Melissa Case Was Cracked," *The Globe and Mail* (6 April 1999).

40 Jeff Sallot, "Guarding Canada's e-Frontier: New Federal Agency Aims to Protect Crucial Electronic Infrastructure from Hack Attacks," *The Globe and Mail* (20 February 2001).

41 In *United States* v. *Riggs*, 739 F.Supp. 414 (N.D. Ill. 1990), a "Legion of Doom" member objected to being referred to as a hacker on the grounds that it was prejudicial, but the court found that it was an appropriate term given his harmful activities. In coming to this conclusion, the court noted the dual use of the term hacker, namely to designate those who obtain unauthorized access to computers, as well as those who are computer hobbyists with an intense interest in exploring the capabilities of computers and communications.

to mere adventurism and egotistical gratification at being able to penetrate a security system implemented for just the purpose of trying to
keep hackers out.[42] In a profile on a notorious hacker, he is quoted as
explaining his rationale for breaking into computers as "it's neat ... it's a
challenge ... I love the game."[43] Even where there is no theft or destruction or damage, the very presence of the hacker in a third party's computer causes the third party to expend resources and incur costs. These
can sometimes be substantial, as when a Toronto-based hacker gained
unauthorized access into fifty university sites around North America.[44]
And the hacking mentality has engendered new forms of harmful
manipulation of computer resources and information-based assets, as
when hackers broke into Web sites at the U.S. Department of Justice
and the Central Intelligence Agency in order to add inflammatory text
and messages to these sites.[45] Yet another form of offensive behaviour is
the so-called denial of service, illustrated by the bombardment of an
Internet access company in September 1996 with electronic requests for
services that disabled the service provider for days.[46] The most notori-

---

42   For a "psychological profile" of various hackers, see Warwick Ford, *Computer
Communications Security: Principles, Standard Protocols and Techniques* (Englewood Cliffs, NJ: Prentice-Hall, 1994). For an in-depth chronicling of a young
(sixteen years old) computer hacker who for two years kept the FBI and computer security specialists busy with his hacking into systems around the world
in order to, among other things, collect thousands of passwords and credit card
numbers, see David H. Freedman & Charles C. Mann, *@Large: The Strange Case
of the World's Biggest Internet Invasion* (New York: Touchstone, 1998).
43   Jonathan Littman, "In the Mind of 'Most Wanted' Hacker, Kevin Mitnick," *Computerworld*, 15 January 1996. Upon his release from prison, Mitnick held fast to
his original defence that his hacking was driven by "curiosity," involved merely
finding out how networks and computer security worked, and were at most
crimes of trespass but not of fraud: see his statement dated 21 January 2000 at
<freekevin.com>.
44   Katrina Onstad & Barbara Wade Rose, "Is This Any Way to Run Cyberspace?:
Why the Hacker Ethos Is Bad for the Net," *Canadian Business Technology*, Summer 1996. See also Joe Chidley, "Cracking the Net," *Maclean's*, 22 May 1995. It
is not just troublemaking teens who hack into university computer networks.
Recently, the associate dean of an Ivy League university was reported to be gaining unauthorized access to another university's computers to learn important
admissions data: Miro Cernetig, "Princeton Dean Suspended Over Academic
Espionage: Confidential Data from Applicants' Files Used to Hack into Computers at Rival Yale," *The Globe and Mail* (27 July 2002).
45   Violino, "Security," above note 23. See also Jeff Sallot, "Hackers Altered Its Web
Page, CSIS Reports," *The Globe and Mail* (18 August 1999); and "'Loan Gunmen'
Crack Into Nasdaq," *The Globe and Mail* (16 September 1999).
46   Violino, "Security," above note 23.

ous spate of denial of service attacks occurred in February 2000, when the Web sites of such leading Internet companies as eBay, Yahoo, Amazon, eTrade and CNN were paralysed,[47] with the last site being attacked by software unleashed by a fifteen-year-old Montreal-area boy.[48] The ability to create harm and mischief over the Internet is limited only by the imagination of computer-savvy perpetrators. Companies have responded by instituting, or improving, previous security measures, but unfortunately it seems that in a manner reminiscent of Newton's famous law of physics, every security action prompts an opposite and equal criminal reaction.[49] The four dynamics of computer law — namely the rapid pace of technological change, the elusive nature of information, and the blurring of private/public and national/international — also exacerbate the achievement of effective solutions.

Society's use of the same term *hacker* to denote both computer criminal and computer expert illustrates a schizophrenic dimension of the modern computer-Internet age that links closely with the third dynamic of computer law, namely, the blurring of private/public.[50] The private activity of sitting in front of one's computer terminal and programming computer codes into the wee hours of the morning, or searching the Internet for neat information by uncovering and navigating within cool sites is, in a physical sense, no different from the manipulation required to hack into a secure site in order to perpetrate a criminal offence. The distinction is almost purely in the mental element (*mens rea*) of the hacker at the time of the two different activities. There are few crimes outside of the computer/Internet realm where the *actus reus* of the offence so closely approximates a common, legitimate

---

47 Ira Sagar, "Cyber Crime: First Yahoo! Then eBay. The Net's Vulnerability Threatens e-Commerce — and You," *Business Week*, 21 February 2000; "Internet Security: Anatomy of an Attack," *The Economist*, 19 February 2000; and "Denial of e-Commerce," *The Economist*, 12 February 2000. A Toronto-based music retailer's site was also hit: Chris Nuttall-Smith, "HMV Music Net Site Blocked by Hackers," *The Toronto Star* (12 February 2000).

48 A few months later, a second fifteen-year-old Montreal teenager pleaded guilty to illegally hacking into the computers of NASA, Harvard and MIT: Tu Thanh Ha, "15 On-Line Hours a Day Made Teen Hacker," *The Globe and Mail* (17 May 2000).

49 See Tyler Hamilton, "The Cyber-Terrorism Fight," *The Globe and Mail* (10 February 2000).

50 Adding to the confusion is the fact that many legitimate companies hire former hackers to help them test their systems from a security perspective: Theresa Ebden, "Ethical Hackers Spar Over What to Wear," *The Globe and Mail* (13 July 2000).

activity. For example, while driving a car may be said to be very similar to stealing a car, in fact the analogy is inapposite because a person very rarely drives another person's car (the correct analogy), while on the Internet a computer user is always in someone else's site when utilizing the Web. On another plane, withdrawing money from a bank teller is different from robbing the bank teller because one does the former so infrequently. On the other hand, deciphering the various features of a bank's complicated Web site, and its interface to various merchant sites, does not seem dissimilar to accessing an off-limits portion of the same bank computer. It also matters that in the tangible world, to commit a crime one has to physically remove oneself from one's home and enter a new and clearly marked physical space where it is invariably perfectly clear that a crime is being committed; there is no doubt the bank robber who enters a bank branch with a gun in hand and a ski mask on his face shouting "This is a hold-up" knows he is committing a crime. The fellow who accesses the bank's main "electronic vault" by a computer terminal in the privacy of his own home — the computer he just used to visit the same bank's Web site — may not feel the same physical indicia of blameworthiness. This is not offered as an excuse for the criminal activity of unauthorized access to a computer, but it is worth noting because it illustrates the extent of the difficulty in combatting it.

4) Unauthorized Intrusion

Modern technology affords a number of means by which persons can intrude into the private communications of others. Wire-tapping and related technologies were once the sole domain of law enforcement officers. Today, with the proliferation in communication technologies, it is not surprising that some of them lend themselves to intrusion quite readily. In particular, it is notoriously easy to scan and record conversations undertaken by analog cellular telephones. The equivalent of the previous era's wire-tapping equipment can be purchased in many electronics stores for eavesdropping on cellular telephone conversations. Efforts to make mobile phone transmissions more secure are, of course, being undertaken; but in one of the immutable laws of computer technology, for every security-related development "cause" there is the "effect" of the security-breaking counterdevelopment designed, manufactured, and on the market usually within a matter of weeks. For example, at one time digital wireless phones were heralded as the solution to the scanning-based intrusion problem. Digital phones include a chip that encrypts conversations into complex binary computer code. No sooner, however, did this technology appear then a new breed of digital scanners was developed that, in addition to monitoring digital cellular phone calls, could capture faxes and paging messages sent digitally over wireless networks.[51] Prudence, and security, continue to dictate that confidential conversations be reserved for wire-based phones.

Intrusive activities, particularly those practised by governments, pre-date the era of the cellular telephone. In 1591 Queen Elizabeth I effected censorship over international mail by requiring all letters sent out of England to be carried by messengers approved by the Crown; this decree had the effect of shutting down private mail services set up in London by foreign merchants.[52] James I extended the same prohibition to domestic mail in 1609, and Oliver Cromwell emphasized the importance of a centralized post office in 1657 in order to uncover the "many dangerous and wicked designs which have been and are daily contrived against the peace and welfare of this Commonwealth, the intelligence whereof cannot well be communicated but by letter of escript."[53] Subsequently, in England the post office was given a monopoly on the conveyance of telegraphic messages, which monopoly, in the last third of the nineteenth century, was held to cover the fledgling telephone as well.[54] Although one rationale for these actions was to bolster the revenue flowing to the public purse, the ability to eavesdrop on private communications was another. In the twentieth century, for example, postal censorship was not restricted to the two World Wars. In the United States, one infamous case in the late 1970s resulted from the massive mail search activities undertaken by the Central Intelligence Agency, wherein between 1953 and 1973 some 215,000 pieces of mail were opened, and 1.5 million names from these letters were entered into government computers.[55] One can only imagine the possibilities for intrusion and recordation in an environment of e-mail messaging, global voice messaging, and huge computer storage capacity.

Another kind of intrusion practised today involves private persons sending to others unsolicited and unwelcome e-mail messages that are harassing or even threatening in tone. Again, there is nothing new in

---

51   John J. Keller, "Wireless Security Still Way Down the Line," *The Globe and Mail* (21 March 1997).
52   See *Encyclopaedia Britannica*, 1965 ed., s.v. "postal services."
53   *Ibid.*, at 306.
54   *A.G.* v. *The Edison Telephone Company of London (Limited)* (1880), 6 Q.B. 244 (Ex. D.).
55   *Birnbaum* v. *United States*, 436 F.Supp. 967 (E.D.N.Y. 1977).

using the mails to send similar missives, or in using the telephone in an offensive manner, particularly given the archaic technology of the telephone that has it ring loudly until it is answered.[56] While not necessarily as audible as the telephone, e-mail can be particularly offensive and threatening because of its immediacy and its ability to be shared with third parties. In a recent Canadian case, a university student was warned that his computer privileges would be curtailed if he continued to send offensive e-mail to another student.[57] In a disturbing American case, a university student sent to an Internet acquaintance in Canada chilling e-mail messages regarding abduction, bondage, torture, humiliation, rape, sodomy, murder, and necrophilia including references to the Paul Bernardo murders.[58] When one of these diatribes, consisting of a gruesome story in which the victim had the name of a classmate, was shared with this classmate, the authorities charged the student with transmitting threats to kidnap or injure a person through interstate or foreign commerce. One of three appellate judges was prepared to convict, but the two in the majority acquitted the accused on the ground of there being an insufficient threat; rather, they concluded the communications were an attempt to foster a friendship based on shared sexual fantasies.

5) Illegal Images

Pornography is a huge business on the Internet.[59] The ability of computers to scan, and of networks to transmit, sexually explicit images, has caused sex to become an important commercial Internet activity. The keyword *sex*, entered into an Internet search engine in August 1997, produced a response indicating that there are 425,449 sites with the word *sex* in them; the equivalent figures for the terms *museum*, *art gallery*, and *symphony* were 388,110; 71,125; and 59,893, respectively. It should be noted that the following terms found more sites than *sex*: *university* — 7,801,043; *education* — 2,051,768; *pet health* — 1,354,091, and *god* — 554,599.[60] In 1997, *Playboy* estimated it received 5 million

---

56 *Motherwell v. Motherwell* (1976), 73 D.L.R. (3d) 62 (Alta. C.A.).

57 *Blaber v. University of Victoria* (1995), 123 D.L.R. (4th) 255 (B.C.S.C.).

58 *United States v. Alkhabaz*, 104 F.3d 1492 (6th Cir. 1997).

59 As with Internet-based gaming, it is impossible to know with certainty the size of the online pornography business, but one estimate puts it at $1 billion annually: David Diamond, "The Sleaze Squeeze," *Business 2.0*, February 1999.

60 Interestingly, the same search terms, run through Google, in January, 2002, produced the following responses: *sex* — 53,700,000; *museum* — 10,500,000; *art gallery* — 2,780,000; *symphony* — 1,780,000; *university* — 59,300,000; *education* — 52,500,000; *pet health* — 1,140,000; and *god* — 29,300,000. Alas, where-

hits a day at its Web site.[61] Much of the pornography on the Internet, or distributed on CD-ROM, is relatively non-controversial, and not illegal, at least in Canada. Where it involves the undue exploitation of sex, however, it risks being obscene under Canada's *Criminal Code*, and therefore illegal. It is apparently for this reason that a major Internet service provider in Canada decided to cease carrying certain news-groups.[62] Similarly, universities in Canada from time to time ban usegroups with sexual content they consider obscene,[63] generally flagged by adjectival monikers such as "alt.sex.bestiality," "alt.sex.sto-ries," and "alt.sex.bondage," though the effectiveness of such bans is often questionable given the ability of users to access these sources through multiple means. Child pornography, which is also illegal under the *Criminal Code*, has seen a resurgence in the last few years as a result of computer and network technologies. A decade ago, police forces had virtually won the battle against the domestic production and importa-tion into Canada of child pornography. Today, high quality child pornog-raphy can be created using relatively inexpensive camcorders.[64] The Internet has breathed new life into this form of pornography, with digi-tal images crossing national frontiers with impunity (illustrating graph-ically the fourth dynamic of computer law).[65] And with a computer on

---

as in 1997 the last four terms exceeded *sex*, only *education* does currently, with *sex* hits almost doubling up on *god*. And of course the growth in the number of *sex* entries is also astounding.

61 "Cybersex: An Adult Affair," *The Economist*, 4 January 1997 ["Cybersex"].

62 See the advertisement by i.star Internet Inc. in *The Globe and Mail* (13 July 1996), which reads, in part, "With Leadership Comes Responsibility ... Our recent decision to no longer offer access to Internet newsgroups that blatantly contravene the laws of Canada ..."

63 Joe Chidley, "Red-Light District: From S&M to Bestiality, Porn Flourishes on the Internet," *Maclean's*, 22 May 1995.

64 In *R. v. Jewell and Gramlick* (1995), 100 C.C.C. (3d) 270 (Ont. C.A.), Finlayson J. A. stated at p. 277: "The court must be responsive to emerging concerns that pornography, particularly child pornography, has become an area of criminality that increasingly menaces our young people and threatens our values as a socie-ty. Because pornography now can be so easily prepared and disseminated through relatively inexpensive means, such as the hand-held video used in the case under appeal, it has emerged as a very real problem in our society."

65 "Buried by a Pile of Porn: The Hunt for Consumers of Child Pornography is Overwhelming Police," *The Economist*, 18 January 2003. Jeff Sallot, "Internet Eases Sexual Exploitation," *The Globe and Mail* (27 August 1996). See also Peter Kuitenbrouwer, "A Mountain of Smut: Police Make an Arrest in Child Porn Ring on the Internet," *Maclean's*, 18 November 1996, which details the seizure by police of 30,000 files containing child pornography belonging to a young man in Kirkland Lake, Ontario, who allegedly participated in an international child

virtually every desk, no organization is immune from the phenomenon of one of its employees downloading such material at the office, as apparently happened recently with a Department of National Defence civilian employee in Ottawa, who was arrested for downloading and storing on his computer a large quantity of child pornography (this time illustrating compellingly the third dynamic of computer law).[66] In a subsequent case, the commander of Canada's naval forces on the West Coast was charged under the *National Defence Act* (under which there was a standing order that Department of Defence computers cannot be used to view pornography, even if the images are legal) and fined $200 for visiting adult entertainment sites on the Internet using his DND laptop.[67]

The Internet is not the first technology platform to be used so extensively by the sex trade. In a revealing survey, *The Economist* points out that sex-related applications have been in the vanguard of the development of videoconferencing, the cinema, the videocassette, the compact disk, pay-per-view television, and direct-to-home digital satellite technol-

---

pornography swap arrangement. The U.S. Customs Service estimates there are more than 100,000 Web sites offering child pornography: Robert Grove & Blaise Zerega, "The Lolita Problem: Illegal Child Pornography Is Booming, Thanks to the Internet — And the Unwitting Support of Corporate America," *Red Herring*, January 2002. See also Kim Lunman, "Child-Porn Probe Nets 2 Canadians," *The Globe and Mail* (21 March 2002). The Supreme Court of Canada, in *Little Sisters Book and Art Emporium* v. *Canada (Minister of Justice)*, [2000] 2 S.C.R. 1120, has recognized, at para. 17, the "exponential growth of pornographic sites on the Internet," and the fact that this might reduce the amount of pornographic goods coming across the border physically. At the same time, however, the court also recognized that to the extent the goods consisted of high-density materials like CD-ROMs, they too would put an intense strain on customs officials hoping to review all content coming across the border on physical media.

66 Scott Feschuk & Henry Hess, "Internet Porn Results in Arrest: Ottawa Scientist Faces Charges," *The Globe and Mail* (10 December 1996). For the sentencing decision (eight months in jail, no access to Internet chat rooms upon release during a three-year probation period), see *R. v. Evans*, [1999] O.J. No. 1831 (Ont. Ct. Justice) [*Evans*]. Interestingly, the accused in this case held a doctorate in philosophy, and was employed as an accomplished scientist. Police in Toronto have indicated that they could charge the employer if, after being notified that illegal material was resident on an employee's computer, the employer did not remove it: Gay Abbate, "Workplace Porn Could Mean Charges to Firms," *The Globe and Mail* (14 September 2002). This article mentions that Toronto police charged people with pornography-related offences in the first eight months of 2002, and seized 1.5 million pornographic images during the same period.

67 Robert Matas, "Web-Surfing Commodore Fined $200," *The Globe and Mail* (17 August 2001). Of course the real punishment in a case like this is the vast amount of publicity afforded the proceeding in the media, including prominent coverage in newspapers complete with photos of the accused.

ogy.[68] This survey points out that "adult entertainment" business activities often lead the way for the embryonic development of technology, including new online payment mechanisms. Development then continues to serve medicine, education, and a range of mainstream commercial and industrial applications. Similarly, the activities of watching and recording sexually explicit material at home gave impetus to the development of the video camera as well as the video rental store.[69] One can go even farther back in history, however, for example to the American Civil War, when one of the first widespread uses of the then latest photographic devices was to take pornographic pictures that were sent by mail to the soldiers on the front lines; and, perhaps not surprisingly, the U.S. postal service was pressed into action as a censor to try to stop this flow of pornographic images. Of course stopping it then was, and now will prove to be, extremely difficult given the volume of material. A recent survey estimates that about 10,000 adult entertainment sites generate $1 billion a year in revenues.[70] Perhaps most telling is another survey estimate that more than one-quarter of households that own computers visit adult sites each month (illustrating again the third dynamic of computer law).[71] And a particular problem with online "adult entertainment" is that children can access much of it, too.[72] Then there are the adult customers of these sites who become addicted to online pornography, a phenomenon causing its own adverse social implications.[73]

6) Illegal Speech

The Internet is an ideal technology for those people who wish to disseminate messages that are racist or hateful. The same features that make computers and networks attractive to corporations, governments, and others who wish to disseminate their messages make these technologies indispensable to bigots and hatemongers. The Internet is global, provides instant communication, is relatively inexpensive, permits

---

68 "Cybersex," above note 61.
69 Sara Silver, "Virtual Sex Drives On-Line Technology," *The Globe and Mail* (21 June 1997).
70 *Ibid.*
71 *Ibid.*
72 Danylo Hawaleshka and Robert Scott, "Beware the Internet Underground," *Maclean's*, 8 November 1999.
73 Peter Cheney, "A Solitary Obsession That Can Ruin a Life," *The Globe and Mail* (5 December 2000). This lengthy investigative report cites an estimated figure of 6 million Internet pornography addicts globally. It also chronicles a number of employees terminated from their jobs for watching pornography at work.

the transmission of text, video, audio, music, and pictures, and allows for feedback by readers. If the pen is mightier than the sword, the Internet is more powerful still. Again, the various features of the Internet, such as its ability to collapse geography, make this communication medium extremely attractive to persons who would spread perverse and problematic propaganda.[74] It is also worth recalling the assessment of the District Court in the *ACLU* case, namely, that there is no single point through which the vast amount of information flowing over the Internet can be controlled.[75] In the Supreme Court decision in the *ACLU* case, the court stated that on the Internet, "Through the use of chat rooms, any person with a phone line can become a town crier with a voice that resonates farther than it could from any soapbox. Through the use of web pages, mail exploders, and newsgroups, the same individual can become a pamphleteer."[76] It is almost as if an unrepentant racist or malicious hate propagator had designed the Internet; of course that is not the case, rather in combatting online hate material, governments are faced with the challenges posed by the four dynamics of computer law.

Just as not all pornography is criminally obscene, in Canada not all sharp or critical communication is illegal, only that which incites hatred or which wilfully promotes hatred. Assuming one is dealing with the latter, the Internet reveals yet another unfortunate strength, the ability of the hate propagator to attempt to evade arrest by establishing her server in a jurisdiction with laws more lax than Canada's (again illustrating the fourth dynamic of computer law). The United States, for example, takes a more lenient approach to hate speech than Canada, given the former's strong tradition of upholding freedom of speech through its constitution.[77] Thus, Canada has seen some of its undesirable elements relocate south of the border to establish Web sites.[78] Of

---

74   See chapter 1, section A.6, "The Internet."
75   *American Civil Liberties Union v. Reno*, 929 F.Supp. 824 (E.D. Pa. 1996) aff'd (*sub nom. Reno v. American Civil Liberties Union*) 117 S.Ct. 2329 (1997) [*ACLU*]. The supreme Court decision is available on the web at <ciec.org/SC_appeal/opinion.shtml>.
76   *Ibid.*, at 2344.
77   While many Americans are concerned about Web sites that preach hate, their typical response is to launch an Internet campaign of their own in rebuttal: "The Internet: Downloading Hate," *The Economist*, 13 November 1999.
78   See Donn Downey, "Rights Panel's Jurisdiction over 'Zundelsite' Disputed," *The Globe and Mail* (27 May 1997). The point is made in "Center Sees a Rise on Web in Hatred Made in Canada," *The Globe and Mail* (22 May 2002), that the number of hate sites in Canada has grown to about thirty from a handful a few years ago, and that there has been "tremendous growth" in the practice of operating these on servers located in the United States.

course, prosecuting these persons for their Internet activities poses the same risk as it does for paper-based activities: such prosecutions bring them significant notoriety and many more readers than if they had been left to peddle their drivel in some Internet cul-de-sac.[79] Nevertheless, even when successful prosecutions are brought against such persons resident outside of Canada, practical questions arise as to what steps can be taken to block their messages from reaching Canadian computer screens, given the anarchic nature of the Internet; more on this in the discussion of the *Zündel* decision of the Canadian Human Rights Commission, in section B.6(a), "The *Canadian Human Rights Act*."

B. *CRIMINAL CODE* OFFENCES

The criminal law, prescribed in Canada primarily by the *Criminal Code*, delineates the behaviour that society, acting through Parliament, has deemed to be socially unacceptable.[80] In combatting persons who seek to achieve in a computer context unauthorized gain, destruction, manipulation, or intrusion, or who seek to participate in the dissemination of socially unacceptable images or speech, law enforcement authorities turn mainly to the following provisions of the *Criminal Code*: theft, fraud, computer abuse, data abuse, obscenity and child pornography, hate propaganda, and interception of communications. A number of other offences in the *Criminal Code* may also be relevant from time to time, particularly where a computer is used to facilitate a crime. The criminal law, traditionally, has been largely concerned with protecting the integrity of the individual and tangible property. Thus, the four dynamics of computer law — the rapid pace of technological change, the elusive nature of information, and the blurring of private/public and national/international — along with the general rule of criminal law interpretation that *Criminal Code* provisions be construed strictly and in favour of the accused in the event of doubt or uncertainty as to the applicability of the particular provision, have challenged the

---

79   See Anthony Keller, "Patrolling the Internet," *The Globe and Mail* (2 December 1996), pointing out that one of the better-known hate peddlers was given a decade's worth of courtroom platforms in Canada, while in the United States he has become an anonymous crank since he is left alone by the authorities.

80   See Kent Roach, *Criminal Law* (Toronto, ON: Irwin Law, 1996), at 2: "Criminal laws are primarily designed to denounce and to punish inherently wrongful behaviour, and to deter people from committing crimes or engaging in behaviour that presents a serious risk of harm."

ability of the *Criminal Code* to stay current with the new mischiefs possible with the widespread use of computers and networks. The result has been the amendment of the *Criminal Code* to include several new computer-related provisions. The Internet and other computer-based technologies and business practices raise a number of novel questions under these and the older provisions of the *Criminal Code*, and highlight as well the challenges of enforcing a national criminal law in an increasingly global technology environment.

While the remainder of this chapter focuses on the *Criminal Code* and the legal means available in Canada to combat computer crime, it should be noted that technological solutions are also being pressed into action in this campaign.[81] In 2000, for example, about $5.1 billion was spent on Internet-security software, broken down by categories as follows: 27 percent on antivirus applications; 14 percent on firewall software; 55 percent on authentication and authorization applications; and 4 percent on encryption software.[82] Technology is also being deployed that, through the use of small tracking devices and cellular or GPS communication systems, can detect and locate stolen property such as an automobile.[83] While this does not prevent the theft, it makes it easier to nab the criminals, and eventually should act as a useful deterrent. And finally, it should also be noted that the new networked technology can also help catch criminals.[84] This Newtonian cat and mouse cadence in computer technology, namely that for every technical development there is an opposing reaction, can be seen, for example, in the market

---

81   This is a recurring theme in this book; namely that technology is a useful vehicle for responding to some of the legal issues precipitated by technology: see chapter 8, section C.3, "Technical Solutions."

82   "Out, Out, Damned Hacker," *Red Herring*, January 2000. Of course, while spending money on technology is important in order to properly counteract computer crime, one analysis suggests focusing on management processes and staff awareness is even more central: "Securing the Cloud," *The Economist*, 26 October 2002.

83   See Grant Buckler, "Homing Systems Thwart Theft," *The Globe and Mail* (11 April 2002). These systems, which include chips implanted in the human today, can also be used to make sure people on parole and probation stay where they are supposed to: "Surveillance: Something to Watch Over You," *The Economist*, 17 August 2002.

84   In Colin Freeze, "Parents Held in Swoop on Internet Pedophile Ring," *The Globe and Mail* (10 August 2002), the point is made that while the Internet facilitated the exchange of exploitative images — in this case horribly involving parents with their own children — e-mails passed along from an Internet hotline helped crack the case.

for plagiarized university term papers.[85] Students can buy papers online with ease,[86] and in response a U.K. company, Turnitin.com, has created an online service for professors that scans student papers and detects plagiarism against a database of hundreds of thousands of sources.[87] An Internet-created problem, an Internet-created solution.

1) Theft

Given Canada's market-based economy anchored in the institution of private property, it is no surprise that the offence of theft — stealing someone else's property — is a cornerstone of the *Criminal Code*. Thus, if an item of hardware or computer chips are wrongfully taken, the *Criminal Code*'s theft provision in subsection 322(1) could be used to prosecute the thief.[88] The question, however, whether the theft offence should apply to confidential information (a query directly following

---

85   "Cheat-Detection Software. Plagiarize. Let No One Else's Work Evade Your Eyes," *The Economist*, 16 March, 2002 ["Plagiarize"]. Students should not take comfort from the fact that plagiarism is also a problem in the entertainment industry: Simon Houpt, "Don't Stop Me If You've Heard This Before," *The Globe and Mail* (10 September 2002).

86   From Web sites such as <gradesaver.com>.

87   <turnitin.com>. "Plagiarize," above note 85, estimates that 30 percent of submitted papers are less than original. See Vernon Clement, "Cheating Carleton Students Punished," *The Globe and Mail* (4 July 2002), which notes that 29 engineering students received a zero in the same paper course, after lifting text directly from the Internet. Interestingly, similar technology now also exists to assist with detecting musical sources: "Music Recognition Software: Om Tiddly Om Pom," *The Economist*, 19 October 2002.

88   The theft offence currently reads as follows:

> 322.(1) Every one commits theft who fraudulently and without colour of right takes, or fraudulently and without colour of right converts to his use or to the use of another person, anything whether animate or inanimate, with intent,
>
> (a) to deprive, temporarily or absolutely, the owner of it, or a person who has a special property or interest in it, of the thing or of his property or interest in it;
> (b) to pledge it or deposit it as security;
> (c) to part with it under a condition with respect to its return that the person who parts with it may be unable to perform; or
> (d) to deal with it in such a manner that it cannot be restored in the condition in which it was at the time it was taken or converted.
>
> (2) A person commits theft when, with intent to steal anything, he moves it or causes it to move to be moved, or beings to cause it to become movable.
> . . .

from the second dynamic of computer law) has confronted a number of courts in Canada and abroad, and in particular was considered in two cases in the mid-1980s by well-respected appellate courts in this country. In *R. v. Stewart*,[89] the Ontario Court of Appeal concluded that information, in this case confidential information regarding employees of a hotel that a labour union wished to obtain for purposes of an organizing drive, could be "property," and therefore the accused was found guilty of counselling theft when he attempted to induce a hotel employee to provide him with the employee information.[90] By contrast, in *R. v. Offley*, the Alberta Court of Appeal held that information could not be property for purposes of the *Criminal Code*'s theft provision.[91] This divergence was resolved by the Supreme Court of Canada when it held in the *Stewart* case that information, for policy reasons, should not fall within the purview of "property" for purposes of the theft or fraud offences under the *Criminal Code*.[92] The court concluded that the offence required there to be a permanent "taking," and that when information is disclosed it is still available to the victim. The Supreme Court took a very physically oriented view of both property and deprivation, finding that, except in rare circumstances, someone cannot be deprived of information; the court found, by contrast, that someone can be deprived of confidentiality, but it in turn cannot be taken, as one enjoys it but cannot really own it. From a practical perspective, the court was also concerned about the difficulties of defining with adequate precision

89   (1983), 5 C.C.C. (3d) 481 (Ont. C.A.).

90   In a similar vein, in *R. v. Scallen* (1974), 15 C.C.C. (2d) 441 (B.C.C.A.), the British Columbia Court of Appeal concluded that a person's credit in a bank account could be subject to the theft offence, noting that the word *anything* in the relevant *Criminal Code* provision is very broad and does not require the subject matter to be tangible or in a material form.

91   (1986), 28 C.C.C. (3d) 1 (Alta. C.A.) [*Offley*]. In an earlier decision, *R. v. Falconi* (1976), 31 C.C.C. (2d) 144 at 148 (Ont. Co. Ct.) [*Falconi*], the court held that a pharmacy prescription cannot be property for purposes of the theft offence, but only after struggling valiantly with the tough questions presented by the case: "One may have little difficulty in conceptualizing a piece of land or a wrist watch, which are characterized by the classical common law terms of real property and personal property respectively. However, when one attempts to similarly characterize the written or spoken words of a person the task, couched as it is in metaphysics, becomes rather more difficult." This is a good illustration of the second dynamic of computer law — the elusive nature of information — busy at work.

92   *R. v. Stewart* (1988), 41 C.C.C. (3d) 481 (S.C.C.) [*Stewart*].

what constitutes confidential information.[93] The court noted, for example, that a finding contrary to its own would have a severe impact on the mobility of labour, such that the court did not want to criminalize the environment in which employees switched employers. The court recognized that the civil law of trade secrecy and copyright were available in appropriate cases to deal with misappropriation of information,[94] and that the court would not criminalize such behaviour unless Parliament clearly amended the *Criminal Code* to capture such conduct.[95]

The Supreme Court in the *Stewart* case was reacting to the second dynamic of computer law — the elusive nature of information — and, utilizing a narrow, strict interpretation approach to criminal law,[96] con-

---

93   The unease of the Supreme Court is captured in the following passage in *ibid.*, at 492: "Moreover, because of the inherent nature of information, treating confidential information as property *simpliciter* for the purposes of the law of theft would create a host of practical problems. For instance, what is the precise definition of 'confidential information'? Is confidentiality based on the alleged owner's intent or on some objective criteria? At what point does information cease to be confidential and would it therefore fall outside the scope of the criminal law? Should only confidential information be protected under the criminal law, or any type of information deemed to be of some commercial value?"

94   Interestingly, in one such civil case the court refers to a defendant having "stolen" a trade secret, which, strictly speaking, is not an appropriate term given the decision in *Stewart*, above note 92, and assuming that "steal" refers to "theft" under the *Criminal Code*: see *Apotex Fermentation Inc.* v. *Novopharm Ltd.* (1998), 80 C.P.R. (3d) 449 (Man. C.A.), at para. 75.

95   This has been done, for example, in the United States, where the *Economic Espionage Act*, 18 U.S.C. §§1831-1839, imposes criminal liability, which can include fines and prison terms, for theft of trade secrets. For a case brought under this statute, see *United States* v. *Martin*, 228 F.3d 1 (1st Cir. 2000). In *The People* v. *Alejandro Farell*, 48 P.3d 1155 (S.C. Cal. 2002), the court determined that theft of trade secrets (in this case design specifications for a computer chip) warranted time in jail. Those that consider this a harsh result should remember that in Renaissance Italy artisans who fled the famous Murano glassworks in Venice to work elsewhere, if caught, were imprisoned and faced the prospect of being put to death for revealing the secret glassmaking techniques of Murano (this enabled the wondrous style of Murano glass to remain a Venetian monopoly for centuries): "Venetian Glass: Red Hot," *The Economist*, 27 July 2002.

96   The principle that penal statutes are subject to rules of strict and narrow interpretation was articulated by Laskin, C.J.C. in *R.* v. *McLaughlin*, [1980] 2 S.C.R. 331 [*McLaughlin*] at 335, as follows: "the general rule [is] that in construing criminal statutes they should, where there is uncertainty or ambiguity of meaning, be construed in favour of rather than against an accused. In short, he must be brought fully within the statute and cannot be held guilty of a violation if it is only acceptable in part." A few years before the *McLaughlin* case, the Supreme Court of Canada expressed the doctrine of strict interpretation as follows: "It is unnecessary to emphasize the importance of clarity and certainty when freedom

cluded that the *Criminal Code*'s theft provision, as currently drafted, was inappropriate to handle the evanescent, ephemeral nature of information. The various decisions in the *Stewart* and *Offley* cases were the subject of some commentary.[97] And almost anticipating the Supreme Court's invitation to law reform, Alberta's Institute of Law Research and Reform produced an excellent report on trade secrets that included a proposed model law for both civil and criminal misappropriation of confidential information.[98] To date, however, the federal government has not adopted the recommendations from this report, and thus the theft provision of Canada's *Criminal Code* currently does not extend to the unauthorized disclosure of confidential information. Accordingly, creators and owners of trade secrets and confidential information must find protection for these information-based assets either under the *Criminal Code*'s fraud provision,[99] or under the civil intellectual property protection regimes.[100]

If Parliament at some point does decide to update the theft provision to cover confidential information, it should consider the statutory history, and jurisprudential treatment, of the current section 326 of the *Criminal Code* (a story that resonates with the first dynamic of computer law).[101] This provision was initially restricted to electricity when it

---

is at stake ... if real ambiguities are found, or doubts of substance arise, in the construction and application of a statute affecting the liberty of a subject, then that statute should be applied in such a manner as to favour the person against whom it is sought to be enforced. If one is to be incarcerated, one should at least know that some Act of Parliament requires it in express terms, and not, at most, by implication": *Marcotte* v. *Canada (Deputy A.G.)* (1975), 19 C.C.C. (2d) 257 at 262 (S.C.C.) [*Marcotte*]. For a more recent case that cites *Marcotte* for this proposition, see *R.* v. *McIntosh* (1995), 95 C.C.C. (3d) 481 (S.C.C.).

97   For an article in favour of the Supreme Court's position, see R. Grant Hammond, "Theft of Information" (1984) 100 L.Q. Rev. 252; for a contrary position, see Arnold S. Weinrib, "Information and Property" (1988) 38 U.T.L.J. 117.

98   Institute of Law Research and Reform (Edmonton, Alberta) and A Federal Provincial Working Party, *Trade Secrets* (Report No. 46, July 1986).

99   See section B.2 of this chapter, "Fraud."

100 See chapter 2, sections B.1, "Trade Secrets/Breach of Confidence" and B.3, "Copyright."

101 326. (1) Every one commits theft who fraudulently, maliciously, or without colour of right,

    (a)   abstracts, consumes or uses electricity or gas or causes it to be wasted or diverted; or

    (b)   uses any telecommunication facility or obtains any telecommunication service.

(2) In this section and section 327, "telecommunication" means any transmission, emission or reception of signs, signals, writing, images or sounds or intelligence of any nature by wire, radio, visual, or other electro-magnetic system.

first came to Canada from England and was implemented through *The Electric Light Inspection Act*, 1894 (Canada), chapter 39, section 10. The provision was brought into the *Criminal Code* in 1906, and in 1934 was extended to include "telephone or telegraph line" and "obtains a telephone or telegraph service" (the current phrase is "telecommunication facility or service"). In 1954 gas was added to the provision, and in 1960 "telephone or telegraph line" was changed to "telecommunication wire or cable" in order to capture cable television service. This brief history illustrates that as new utilities and technology-based services come to the marketplace, and as unscrupulous persons abuse them, the provision has been amended to protect such new product offerings and technologies.[102] Given the first dynamic of computer law, however, such amendments can have a difficult time staying current with both new technologies and unanticipated technology-related activities. Thus, in *Maltais v. R.*[103] the Supreme Court had to decide whether the 1960 version of the provision, which covered a "telecommunication wire or cable," was broad enough to capture an accused who had broadcast propaganda over the radio waves when a radio station was overtaken in the course of a labour dispute. The court answered in the negative, and acquitted, on the basis that the phraseology of "wire or cable," while broader than telephone and telegraph line, was not broad enough to cover transmission by Hertzian waves sent through the air.

Subsequent to the charge being laid in the *Maltais* case, the theft of a telecommunications service provision was updated yet again so that "wire or cable" was replaced by "facility." While this change made it clear that the provision covers radio and television broadcasting, in yet a further decision the current wording was held not to extend to the unauthorized manipulation of a computer.[104] As well, in a case a few years after the *Maltais* decision, a husband and wife were accused of stealing a pay television service when the husband, who had expertise in electronic communications, hooked up a device to his television set to improve regular cable television reception but which also, apparently inadvertently, descrambled the pay-tv signal, with the result that until their arrest, the couple enjoyed a pay-tv service for free.[105] The

---

102 It should also be noted that the *Radiocommunication Act*, R.S.C. 1985, c. R-2 as amended, contains provisions prohibiting the decoding or use of encrypted broadcasting signals.

103 (1977), 33 C.C.C. (2d) 465 (S.C.C.) [*Maltais*].

104 See the discussion of *McLaughlin*, above note 96, in section B.3 of this chapter, "Computer Abuse."

105 *R v. Miller and Miller* (1984), 12 C.C.C. (3d) 466 (Alta. C.A.).

court believed the accused's statement that the device was not intended to receive pay-tv signals, and therefore concluded that the couple merely enjoyed a windfall in respect of which they should not be held responsible. The Alberta Court of Appeal concluded that ensuring adequate scrambling was up to the pay-tv company, as viewers who receive unscrambled signals through no connivance of their own do not offend paragraph 326(1)(b). Indeed, the court speculated whether "electronic technology has again outpaced the legislation passed for its own protection."[106] In effect, the history of the current section 326 of the *Criminal Code* illustrates how difficult it is for the law to stay current with rampaging technology.

Courts in countries other than Canada have also been confronted with the challenge of applying existing criminal law provisions to new technologies. In many such cases property and theft have been restricted to tangible, physical assets, with acquittals being entered as in the *Stewart* case. For example, in the English case *R. v. Gold*, the accused, who accessed data in a computer by using another person's access code and password, was acquitted under an antiforgery and counterfeiting statute, which required the making of a false "instrument," because the court concluded that electronic messages do not constitute an instrument.[107] In some cases, however, courts are willing to take a broader view of the criminal law. In one recent American case, the court had to determine whether a CD-ROM disk, containing obscene images, could come within the definition of "obscene material," which was defined as any "photographic product" in the form of still photographs, undeveloped film, videotape, or a purely photographic product or a reproduction of such product in any book, pamphlet, magazine, or other publication.[108] The court acknowledged that a computer's monitor screen is not a photosensitive surface such as the silver halide surfaces of traditional photographic film. Nonetheless, the court decided the CD-ROM was a photographic product because "the video capture board and scanner used to record the obscene images produced by these discs reproduced the images — aided by appropriate computer hardware and software — with the exactness of a photograph."[109] In

---

106 *Ibid.*, at 470.
107 [1988] 2 All. E.R. 186 (H.L.).
108 *Anthony Aloysius Davis v. State of Oklahoma*, 7 Computer Cases (CCH) ¶47, 533 at 69,232 (Okla. Crim. App. 1996) [*Davis*].
109 *Ibid.*, at 69,236.

RE-DEFINED photograph!

another U.S. case,[110] an accused argued that a criminal statute prohibiting the transmission of obscene material by "computer or mails" did not cover the downloading of images over the Internet. The court disagreed and concluded:

> The use of the words "by computer" are sufficient to cover this conduct. Congress was no more required to explain in intricate detail the technology of sending pictures over the Internet than it was to explain the chemical process of developing film into photographs. This court will not indulge in metaphysical hair-splitting to rule that "by computer" does not give constitutionally adequate notice that defendant's alleged activity in this case is prohibited.[111]

In these two U.S. cases a much more purposive approach was taken to the criminal law, with seemingly little heed being paid to the principle of narrow interpretation of criminal law statutes.[112]

2) Fraud

Harmful activity that may not be subject to the theft offence as a result of the *Stewart* decision may nevertheless come within the *Criminal Code*'s fraud provision.[113] For example, in R. v. *Marine Resource Analysts Limited*,[114] a former employee of the federal government continued using the government's computer facilities for his consulting business, without paying for such use, after he left the employment of the government. The cost of such usage came to $27.30. Ostensibly because of the principle involved, the Crown charged the accused with theft of a telecommunications service and with fraud. For reasons similar to

---

110 *United States of America* v. *Michael Lamb*, 7 Computer Cases (CCH) ¶47,622 at 69,719 (N.D.N.Y. 1996) [*Lamb*].

111 *Ibid.*, at 69,726.

112 See also *United States* v. *Coviello*, 225 F.3d 54 (1st Cir. 2000), where software on a CD-ROM was held to come under the *U.S. National Stolen Property Act*, 18 U.S.C. §2314, notwithstanding that the real value in the property is attributable to an intangible component, namely the software.

113 The *Criminal Code*'s fraud provision reads as follows:

> 380 (1) Every one who, by deceit, falsehood or other fraudulent means, whether or not it is a false pretence within the meaning of this Act, defrauds the public or any person, whether ascertained or not, of any property, money or valuable security, [is guilty of an offence] …

114 (1980), 41 N.S.R. (2d) 631 (Co. Ct.), leave to appeal refused (1980), 43 N.S.R. (2d) 1 (C.A.).

those given in the *McLaughlin* case,[115] the court acquitted on the former charge (i.e., a computer is not a telecommunications facility), but the court did convict on the fraud charge, finding that the accused defrauded the government of $27.30; that is, in order to make out a fraud case there must be a dishonest deprivation. Where an intangible like information is at issue, however, the deprivation is not in the "taking" of the information because, as with the theft offence, information will not constitute property for purpose of the fraud offence. The deprivation, rather, comes from the accused denying the owner of the information or intellectual property a revenue stream that would otherwise be generated from the information. Thus, in the *Stewart* case no finding of fraud was made both because the information was not property and also because the hotel was not in the business of selling its employee information and hence would lose no revenue from a disclosure of this information. Similarly, there was no finding of fraud in the *Falconi* case because the court found there is no property in a pharmacy prescription, and pharmacists do not earn revenue from the mere fact of making out prescriptions.[116]

By contrast, in *R. v. Leahy* the court found that the accused's making of unauthorized copies of software under the guise of a software rental business warranted a finding of fraud because of the economic deprivation this activity visited upon the owners of the intellectual property in the software.[117] In support of this finding, the court stated:

> On this inquiry, a number of highly-placed executive officers of the computer companies alleged to have been victimized testified. All these witnesses spoke of the extremely high cost of producing and marketing computer programs, which they stated involved programmers, writers and other personnel, many man-hours of work over an extended period of years, and an investment in the production of millions of dollars before any returns could be realized at all and thereafter, a similar investment in advertising and marketing the product, including support services. It is clear that these manufacturers have a substantial economic interest in their product to protect. They claim that the unauthorized making and distribution of copies of their software is highly damaging to their own enterprises through loss of sales, increased costs of providing support services and loss of reputation.[118]

---

115 *McLaughlin*, above note 96.
116 *Falconi*, above note 91.
117 (1988), 21 C.P.R. (3d) 422 (Ont. Prov. Ct.).
118 *Ibid.*, at 430–31.

In a similar vein, in *R. v. Kirkwood* an accused was convicted of fraud for making, selling, and renting videotapes because the accused was thereby depriving the rightful owner of the videos of revenues that the rightful owner would have earned but for the accused's activities.[119] Thus, in appropriate circumstances, creators and owners of intellectual property can find the *Criminal Code's* fraud provision helpful in combatting bootleggers, counterfeiters, and others who would unfairly misappropriate the fruits of intellectual labour.

3) Computer Abuse

Hackers, as noted above, compromise the integrity of computers by gaining access remotely, and then typically manipulating data and computer files. Even if they do not take the next step of destroying data, or committing a further act such as stealing money or copying sensitive information, hackers cause great anxiety by merely roaming unwelcome through a computer. A stranger breaking into a house and wandering around in the rooms is quite disconcerting, even if she leaves the VCR as she departs. So it is not surprising that the *Criminal Code* has been used to fight hackers for some time, though the initial skirmish did not end in a conviction for many of the same reasons that led to acquittals in the *Stewart* and *Maltais* cases. In *McLaughlin*, a student at the University of Alberta hacked his way into the university's computers.[120] The hacker was charged with theft of a telecommunications service because at the time (mid-1970s) that was the closest provision to hacking available in the *Criminal Code*. The Supreme Court of Canada, however, decided it was not close enough. The court concluded that a computer is not a telecommunications facility, holding that the function of a computer is not to channel or transmit information to outside recipients so as to be susceptible to unauthorized use; rather, a computer is a data processing device. The court also noted that the definition of *telecommunications* in the *Criminal Code* is the same as that found in Canada's broadcasting legislation, and that broadcasting legislation does not cover computers. Again, in the face of the first dynamic of computer law, the court took a very restrained, circumspect approach to a technology-oriented section of the *Criminal Code* and declined to give an expansive interpretation of the relevant provision, calling on Parliament to undertake this task if the country's legislators

---

119 (1983), 35 C.R. (3d) 97 (Ont. C.A.).
120 *McLaughlin*, above note 96.

so wished. It is interesting to speculate whether the court, if it were to render its decision today, would come to a different conclusion given that now computers are used as much to transmit data as to process it, particularly in light of the development of the Internet. In an ironic sense, the technology may have "caught up" to the law in this instance.

Whereas Parliament declined to change the law in response to the Supreme Court's invitation in the *Stewart* case, in 1985 Canada's law-makers responded to the call to action in the *McLaughlin* case by adding to the *Criminal Code* section 342.1 that, with subsequent amendment, today reads as follows:

(1) Every one who, fraudulently and without colour of right,

(a) obtains, directly or indirectly, any computer service,

(b) by means of an electromagnetic, acoustic, mechanical or other device, intercepts or causes to be intercepted, directly or indirectly, any function of a computer system,

(c) uses or causes to be used, directly or indirectly, a computer system with intent to commit an offence under paragraph (a) or (b) or an offence under section 430 in relation to data or a computer system, or

(d) uses, possesses, traffics in or permits another person to have access to a computer password that would enable a person to commit an offence under paragraph (a), (b) or (c)

is guilty of an indictable offence and liable to imprisonment for a term not exceeding ten years, or is guilty of an offence punishable on summary conviction.

(2) In this section,

"computer password" means any data by which a computer service or computer system is capable of being obtained or used;

"computer program" means data representing instructions or statements that, when executed in a computer system, causes the computer system to perform a function;

"computer service" includes data processing and the storage or retrieval of data;

"computer system" means a device that, or a group of interconnected or related devices one or more of which,

(a) contains computer programs or other data, and

(b) pursuant to computer programs,

(i) performs logic and control, and

(ii) may perform any other function;

"data" means representations of information or of concepts that are being prepared or have been prepared in a form suitable for use in a computer system;

"electro-magnetic, acoustic, mechanical or other device" means any device or apparatus that is used or is capable of being used to intercept any function of a computer system, but does not include a hearing aid used to correct subnormal hearing of the user to not better than normal hearing;

"function" includes logic, control, arithmetic, deletion, storage and retrieval and communication or telecommunication to, from or within a computer system;

"intercept" includes listen to or record a function of a computer system, or acquire the substance, meaning or purport thereof;

"traffic" means, in respect of a computer password, to sell, export from or import into Canada, distribute or deal with in any other way.[121]

This provision, often referred to as the "computer abuse" offence, is aimed at several potential harms: paragraph 342.1(1)(a) protects against the theft of computer services, paragraph 342.1(1)(b) is intended to protect privacy, and the more recently added paragraph 342.1(1)(d) is aimed at persons who trade in computer passwords (such as personal identification numbers and similar codes) or who crack encryption systems. Paragraph 342.1(1)(b) is required because the wiretap provision in section 184 arguably is limited to person-to-person communications and therefore may not be adequate to cover computer-to-computer communications.[122] Thus, this provision is continuing the concern of the *Criminal Code* with the preservation of privacy and secrecy, just as the *Criminal Code* has provisions making it illegal to open a person's correspondence, the low-tech equivalent to computer-related communications.[123] With respect to paragraph 342.1(1)(d), it should be

---

121 While the bulk of s. 342.1 dates from 1985, para. 342.1(1)(d), and the corresponding definitions of *computer password* and *traffic* in subs. 342.1, were enacted in April 1997 by *An Act to Amend the Criminal Code and Certain Other Acts*, S.C. 1997, c. 18 (Bill C-17).

122 For a discussion of s. 184, see section B.10 of this chapter, "Interception of Communications."

123 *Criminal Code*, s. 345: "Everyone who stops a mail conveyance with intent to rob or search it is guilty of an indictable offence and liable to imprisonment for life."

noted that section 342.2 makes it an offence to make, possess, or distribute any instrument or device primarily used for committing an offence under section 342.1. This new provision is similar to subsections 191(1), 327(1), and 351 of the *Criminal Code*, which make it an offence to possess a scanning device and instruments used to tap into telecommunications transmissions or break and enter into a house.

The potentially wide breadth of the computer abuse provision can be seen in, among other things, paragraph 342.1(1)(c), which makes it an offence merely to use a computer to *intend* to commit either of the two above offences or to commit mischief in relation to data.[124] The rationale for paragraph 342.1(1)(c) is that the law enforcement authorities, and potential victims, should not be required to wait until actual harm is inflicted before the computer abuse behaviour is considered criminal. In effect, paragraph 342.1(1)(c) creates the equivalent of the offence of trespass for real property, where it is also the case that one does not have to wait for the "real" harm to occur. Several other aspects of this provision make it extremely broad. The definition of *computer system* is quite expansive, covering every device that contains some software-related functionality. With the pervasive diffusion of computers today, a personal organizer, pocket calculator, and even a car or television (which both contain software-based features) can come within the ambit of the section. The definition of *data* is also wide-ranging, including data "in a form suitable for use in a computer system," which would include data in the process of being transmitted, or in offline storage, in addition to data inside a computer. The key limitation on the expansive scope of the abuse of computer section is provided by the *mens rea* required by the provision, namely that the perpetrator effect one of the activities enumerated in paragraphs 342.1(1)(a), (b), (c), or (d) "fraudulently and without colour of right." Interestingly, these words are also found in the definition of *theft* in section 322 of the *Criminal Code. Fraudulently* essentially means dishonestly and unscrupulously, and with an intent to cause deprivation to another person.[125] The phrase without colour of right means without an honest belief that one had the right to carry out the particular action. To establish a colour of right, one would have to have an honest belief in a state of facts that, if they existed, would be a legal justification or excuse. Thus, the computer abuse provision should not apply where a person accidentally did one of the enumerated acts, or mistakenly believed she

---

124 See section B.4 of this chapter, "Abuse of Data," for a discussion of the provisions of the *Criminal Code* relating to mischief in respect of data.

125 *R. v. Zlatic* (1993), 79 C.C.C. (3d) 466 (S.C.C.).

was authorized to do so (and given the third dynamic of computer law, and the discussion in section A.3, "Unauthorized Manipulation," such accidental or mistaken activity may not be all that far fetched in the Internet environment as the line between legitimate and problematic online behaviour can be blurry in some cases).

There have been a number of prosecutions under section 342.1 that have resulted in convictions.[126] Courts are also attuned to the seriousness of computer abuse in their sentencing.[127] In one case, however, an accused was held not to come within paragraph 342.1(1)(a) because he was considered too far removed from the actual activity of accessing the particular computer at issue.[128] In *Forsythe* there was a chain of three accused, one (Curtis) who accessed the Canadian Police Information Computer, a second accused (Wagner) who previously worked for the Edmonton police department and arranged for Curtis to do the accessing, and the third (Forsythe) who dealt only with Wagner and employed him in Forsythe's firm of private detectives. The court concluded that Curtis and Wagner came comfortably within the "directly

---

126 In the United States, similar convictions have been obtained against hackers under the American *Computer Fraud and Abuse Act*, 18 U.S.C. §1030: see, for example, *United States* v. *Middleton*, 231 F.3d 1207 (9th Cir. 2000), as well as the following U.S. Department of Justice Press Releases: "Computer Security Expert Sentenced to 27 Months' Imprisonment for Computer Hacking and Electronic Eavesdropping," 13 June 2001 (a computer security specialist with a failed dot-com company hacked into the computers of his former venture capital investor firm); and "Brian K. West, Employee of Oklahoma ISP, Pleads Guilty to Unauthorized Access Charge Under 18 U.S.C. §1030 (a)(2)(c)," 24 September 2001 (the accused penetrated a security hole and downloaded computer files of value), both of which are available at <cybercrime.gov>. In the United States, some of the criminal computer abuse statutes are broad enough to support a conviction where the accused used an e-commerce Web site to receive orders and payments for goods, but then never delivered products: *Commonwealth of Pennsylvania* v. *Murgalis*, 2000 Pa. Super Lexis 748 (Pa. Sup. Ct. 2000).

127 In *R.* v. *Mewhinney*, [2000] O.J. No. 2095 (Ont. Sup. Ct.), the court, in sentencing the twenty-three-year-old accused to six months in a reformatory, stated: "Much has been made in the film media about computer hacking to the point where it is almost glorified. The little computer operator pitted against the best minds available in this computer security community. However, this should be viewed at no higher a level than a safe cracker attempting to steal from a bank. This type of crime should be viewed more seriously than simple fraud and mischief because of the possible consequences. The disruption that can be caused to commerce and the possible security of a nation dictates that these crimes must be dealt with swiftly and sternly so that others will be deterred from similar conduct."

128 *R.* v. *Forsythe* (1992), 137 A.R. 321 (Prov. Ct.) [*Forsythe*].

or indirectly" language of paragraph 342.1(1)(a) (and Wagner had pleaded guilty previously), but that Forsythe was too remote to come within the provision. This is perhaps an overly conservative reading of section 342.1, given that the court found that Forsythe knew exactly what Wagner was doing, Forsythe had copies of the computer information in printout form, and Forsythe billed his clients for the information derived from the computer. Nonetheless, the court's approach again exemplifies the judicial restraint that will be shown when, as in the *McLaughlin* and *Maltais* cases, a judge believes an accused does not come squarely within an offence.

4) Abuse of Data

The computer abuse offence created by section 342.1 of the *Criminal Code*, which protects the integrity of computers and computer-related communications, does not address data *per se*. This was left to a companion addition to the *Criminal Code* in 1985, namely the provisions relating to mischief with respect to data that read as follows:

> 430(1.1) Every one commits mischief who wilfully
> (a) destroys or alters data;
> (b) renders data meaningless, useless or ineffective;
> (c) obstructs, interrupts or interferes with the lawful use of data; or
> (d) obstructs, interrupts or interferes with any person in the lawful use of data or denies access to data to any person who is entitled to access thereto.
>
> ...
>
> (5) Everyone who commits mischief in relation to data
> (a) is guilty of an indictable offence and liable to imprisonment for a term not exceeding ten years; or
> (b) is guilty of an offence punishable on summary conviction.
>
> (5.1) Everyone who wilfully does an act or wilfully omits to do an act that it is his duty to do, if that act or omission is likely to constitute mischief causing actual danger to life, or to constitute mischief in relation to property or data,
> (a) is guilty of an indictable offence and liable to imprisonment for a term not exceeding five years; or
> (b) is guilty of an offence punishable on summary conviction.

As with the abuse of computer provisions discussed above, the abuse of data offences are drawn in broad terms. Note that the definition of data is found in subsection 342.1(2) and is expansively defined to capture, in addition to information, specific representations of information; that is, in addition to covering information, this definition would also apply to individual binary digits as well as letters or numbers that, at a higher level of aggregation, comprise information. This wording attempts to address the second dynamic of computer law, namely, the elusive nature of information. As with section 342.1, the limitation in the scope of section 430(1.1) comes from the *mens rea* requirement, namely, that the accused, to be convicted, must have acted "wilfully." In this regard, it is necessary to note that section 429 of the *Criminal Code* provides (in part):

(1) Every one who causes the occurrence of an event by doing an act or by omitting to do an act that it is his duty to do, knowing that the act or omission will probably cause the occurrence of the event and being reckless whether the event occurs or not, shall be deemed ..."wilfully" to have caused the occurrence of the event.

(2) No person shall be convicted of an offence ... where he proves that he acted with legal justification or excuse and with colour of right.

The abuse of data provision in section 430(1.1) is broad enough to encompass most every kind of virus imaginable, particularly where the virus destroys data in some manner.[129] It should be noted, however, that section 430(1.1) requires the accused to have actually interfered with data; thus, mere possession of a virus computer program just before it is disseminated over a network or more generally released into the stream of commerce is not sufficient for a conviction under this section. This may be contrasted with section 342.2 implemented in April 1997 by Bill C 17,[130] and subsections 191(1) and 327(1) of the

---

129 For similar results in the United States, see U.S. Department of Justice, Press Release, "Jury Convicts Herbert Pierre-Louis of Sending Computer Virus to Destroy Purity Wholesale Grocers Inc.'s Computer Systems," 2 September 2001 (virus brought down company's computer for several days and cost them $75,000); and Jeffrey Gold, "Melissa Virus Creator Gets 20 Months in Jail," *The Globe and Mail* (2 May 2002). For an early prosecution against (and conviction of) an implementer of a widespread virus, see *United States* v. *Morris*, 928 F.2d 504 (2d Cir. 1991); in this case, the court refused the defence of the accused (who was a university student) that he was merely trying to point out, by releasing the virus, how vulnerable computers were to such attacks, thereby performing a useful public service. Also in the United States, a computer consultant has been sued civilly for compensatory and punitive damages for intentionally placing a virus in a law firm's computer system (the consultant wanted to make extra work for himself): *Werner, Zaroff, Slotnick, Stern & Askenazy* v. *Lewis*, 558 N.Y.S. 2d 960 (N.Y. Cir. Ct. 1992).

130 See section B.3 of this chapter, "Computer Abuse," and above note 121.

Criminal Code, the companion sections to the provisions that prohibit the interception of private communications and the theft of telecommunications services, that make it, respectively, an offence to possess or deal in any scanning device or any device that can be used to tap into telecommunications transmissions;[131] similarly, section 351 makes it an offence to possess instruments that may be used to break and enter into a house. It should also be noted that section 430(1.1) is aimed at more than just activity that destroys data. Actions that obstruct the use of data are also covered, as was the case in *Re Turner and the Queen*, where the accused, by modifying software operated on the computer of a service bureau, caused a customer of the service bureau to be unable to access its data resident on the service bureau's computer.[132] Considered under subsection 430(1), the general mischief in relation to property section because the data abuse provision had not then been enacted, the court held that the accused's defence that no data were destroyed was immaterial given that obstructing the use of the physical media on which the data were resident was sufficient to constitute the offence. In a more recent case, an accused was convicted under subsection 430(5) for deleting what he argued was his own data from a computer owned by someone for whom the accused worked.[133] This case illustrates the second dynamic of computer law; the elusive nature of information led the accused to believe he could deal with "his data" as he pleased, but the company he worked for also believed it had rights in such data. As noted generally in the context of trade secrets in chapter 2, section B.1, "Trade Secrets/Breach of Confidence," this case also argues for the utility of written agreements between persons to confirm their respective rights in the information that each discloses to the other and that they develop together.

---

131 In *R. v. Duck* (1985), 21 C.C.C. (3d) 529 (Ont. Dist. Ct.) it was held that the "Telefreak" computer program, when operated on a Commodore computer, allowed the user to make long distance calls so that they didn't appear in the telephone company's records. *Phreaking* is hacker lingo for stealing a telecommunications service.

132 (1984), 13 C.C.C. (3d) 430 (Ont. H.C.J.). For a recent similar American case, see U.S. Department of Justice, Press Release, "Chardon, Ohio Woman Sentenced for Computer Fraud via Unauthorized Access of Employee's Computer System," 4 December 2001 (accused logged into computer remotely and changed CIO's password of her employer so he could not access the computer system); available at <cybercrime.gov>.

133 *R. v. Downs*, [1996] S.J. No. 703 (Prov. Ct.).

5) Obscenity and Child Pornography

Most criminal law concerns itself with the owner's rights in particular information, and not that much attention is paid in the *Criminal Code* to the content itself of the information; content concerns are much more the purview of the privacy and export control discussions that follow in chapter 4. Nevertheless, there are several *Criminal Code* provisions that contain restrictions on the content of communications, including sedition (section 61), obscene material (section 163), child pornography (section 163.1), criminal harassment (section 264), uttering threats (section 264.1), criminal libel (sections 296–301), hate propaganda (sections 318 and 319), and false messages (section 372). Of these sections, perhaps the most actively enforced by prosecutors are the following provisions that prohibit the creation and distribution of obscene materials:

163. (1) Every one commits an offence who
(a) makes, prints, publishes, distributes, circulates, or has in his possession for the purpose of publication, distribution or circulation any obscene written matter, picture, model, phonograph record or other thing whatever; or

. . .

(2) Every one commits an offence who knowingly, without lawful justification or excuse,
(a) sells, exposes to public view or has in his possession for such a purpose any obscene written matter, picture, model, phonograph record or other thing whatever;
(b) publicly exhibits a disgusting object or an indecent show; . . .

Also important are the following provisions related to child pornography:

163.1(1) In this section, "Child Pornography" means
(a) a photographic, film, video or other visual representation, whether or not it was made by electronic or mechanical means,
(i) [depicting a person under 18 years in sexual activity], or
(ii) [having its dominant characteristic the depiction of a minor's sexual organs or anal region]; or
(b) any written material or visual representation that advocates or counsels sexual activity [with a minor, which would be an offence under the *Criminal Code*].

(2) Every person who makes, prints, publishes or possesses for the purpose of publication any child pornography [is guilty of an offence].

(3) Every person who transmits, makes available, distributes, sells, imports, exports or possesses for the purpose of transmission, making available, distribution, sale or exportation any child pornography [is guilty of an offence].

(4) Every person who possesses any child pornography [is guilty of an offence].

(4.1) Every person who accesses any child pornography [is guilty of an offence]. [Subsection 4.2 provides that "access" means knowingly causing child pornography to be viewed or transmitted to himself or herself.][134]

The constitutionality of section 163.1(4) was upheld recently, subject to certain exceptions for material created by and for the accused alone.[135] It should be noted that section 163 is subject to the defence that the material was distributed for the public good, and section 163.1 is subject to the defences that the material had artistic merit, or an educational, scientific, or medical purpose. In terms of remedies, section 164.1 gives the court wide powers to order the custodian of a computer system, such as an Internet service provider, to deliver up to the court child pornography stored on and made available through a computer system defined under section 342.1(2).

It is useful to note the differences in the kinds of material to which these provisions are directed. The types of media through which child pornography may be depicted are arguably narrower than obscene material under section 163, given that the former would not include sound-based materials or written materials (other than those that advocated or counselled sexual offences under the *Criminal Code*). By contrast, written descriptions involving the undue exploitation of sex could violate section 163. Any visual representation of a minor in a sexual situation would qualify as child pornography, whereas sexually explicit material will be found to violate section 163 of the *Criminal Code* if it involves the undue exploitation of sex, either because of the images involving explicit sex with violence or explicit sex that is

---

134 Section 163(4.1) was added to the *Criminal Code* in 2002 by the *Criminal Law Amendment Act, 2001*, S.C. 2002, c. 13 [*2002 Criminal Code Amendments*]. The *2002 Criminal Code Amendments* included a number of measures to protect children from sexual exploitation, including sexual exploitation involving use of the Internet, as well as a provision that permits a judge to order a Web site operator to remove child pornography from a Web site. See Rheal Seguin, "Web Site Lured Girls, Officials Say," *The Globe and Mail* (20 December 2002).

135 *R. v. Sharpe*, [2001] S.C.J. No. 3 (S.C.C.).

degrading or dehumanizing, or other explicit sex where children are used in the production.[136] The determination of whether there is an "undue exploitation of sex" is based on community standards of tolerance; a key question in an obscenity case is whether the Canadian community as a whole would tolerate the impugned materials.

a) Community Standards

Given the vast amount of pornographic material available on the Internet, it is not surprising that this new distribution medium raises some interesting questions in respect of the *Criminal Code*'s obscenity and child pornography provisions. One such question is how the "community standard" under section 163 in respect of obscene material ought to be discerned in an Internet environment. Should the traditional approach continue, or should a narrower community standard evolve that focuses on the Internet and, for example, the specific subscribers to a particular Internet service or newsgroup? These questions bring into play the third and fourth dynamics of computer law, namely the blurring between private/public and national/international. While not yet explored in any Canadian proceeding in respect of the Internet, such an argument was offered in the *Thomas* obscenity case in the United States.[137] In this matter the San Francisco-based operators of an Internet "bulletin board service" that disseminated child pornography were charged with obscenity in Tennessee, where the authorities downloaded material from the computer server located in California. The law enforcement authorities consciously sought out a conservative community in which to bring the case in order to improve their chances of success in convicting the service's owners. The co-accused argued that the court should fashion an Internet-based standard for considering the appropriate scope of the community standard by which to judge their material. The court refused to take this approach, and simply followed the long-standing obscenity rule in the United States that prosecutions may be brought either where the material is produced or where it is obtained.

In pre-Internet obscenity cases Canadian courts have also expressed the view that they will not carve out narrow communities, such as a

---

136 R. v. *Butler* (1992), 89 D.L.R. (4th) 449 (S.C.C.); and R. v. *Jorgensen*, [1995] 4 S.C.R. 55 [*Jorgensen*]. See Kirk Makin, "Man Fined for Obscenity over 'Snuff Film' Web Site," *The Globe and Mail* (3 December 2002). The government is also considering beefing up its child pornography laws: Sue Bailey, "New Child-Porn Bill Unveiled," *The Globe and Mail* (6 December 2002).

137 *United States* v. *Thomas*, 74 F.3d 701 (6th Cir. 1996).

university film-viewing audience, for purposes of determining the applicability of section 163.[138] At the same time, however, Canadian courts have recognized that the manner and circumstances of distribution are relevant in determining whether or not a publication is obscene; that is, as one court put it, while distribution of certain magazines to a neighbourhood store accessible to all ages would not be tolerable, distribution to an "adult" bookstore to which children of a certain age are not admitted might not be objectionable, and packaging and pricing of material may be relevant as well.[139] For example, in R. v. O'Reilly, a sexually explicit performance was held not to be obscene when performed in a small theatre with admittance restricted to persons above eighteen years of age, with an admission fee charged and a notice posted near the box office indicating the nature of the performance.[140] In the context of the Internet, it is useful to consider several findings in the ACLU case, namely, that currently no effective technology exists to prevent minors from accessing a particular Web site but that this may change in the not too distant future;[141] at the same time, however, Internet communications are much less intrusive than broadcasts, in the sense that a user must take active steps to access a particular Web site, and so users of the Internet cannot be "surprised" the way viewers might be watching television or listening to radio (though certain advertising, such as pop-up ads discussed in chapter 4, section E.4(d), "Other Harmful Online Activity," is indeed intrusive and can appear on a computer screen without warning or request). See also the sentencing decision in Pecciarich, referred to in note 142 below.

b) Intermediary Liability

An important question in respect of both sections 163 and 163.1 is who is liable under these provisions, given that in the computer industry, and particularly over the Internet, multiple participants can be involved in or facilitate the distribution of material to end users. In the context of the Internet, for example, there are Internet service

---

138　R. v. Goldberg and Reitman (1971), 4 C.C.C. (2d) 187 (Ont. C.A.).

139　This is a summary of a lengthier passage in R. v. Sudbury News Service Limited (1978), 39 C.C.C. (2d) 1 (Ont. C.A.); this passage was cited and adopted by Dickson J. in Towne Cinema Theatres Ltd. v. R. (1985), 18 C.C.C. (3d) 193 (S.C.C.). For a similar concept considered in the context of the Internet, see the discussion of the ACLU case, above note 75, in section B.5(e) of this chapter, "Legislative Responses."

140　(1970), 1 C.C.C. (2d) 24 (Ont. Co. Ct.).

141　ACLU, above note 75.

providers, information suppliers, telecommunications carriers, Web site operators, newsgroup moderators, e-mail list distributors, and other distributors of content, as well as governments, corporations, and other users (including individuals) who both access as well as disseminate material. Mindful of the four dynamics of computer law, and the ever-changing landscape of the Internet, an analysis of each fact situation must always be undertaken based on its own merits, and on the basis of the particular technology and activities specifically involved in the case. Great care must be taken, as well, in attempting to apply metaphors of the real world to the various actors and activities on the Internet. In some cases, it may be appropriate to think about an Internet service provider that merely provides technical Internet access as a telecommunications carrier, or the moderator of a usegroup as a newspaper publisher, or a Web site operator that offers access to third party databases such as a bookstore or library. In other cases, however, these analogies may not be helpful, and one must always be vigilant not to fall into the trap of using the easy but ultimately incorrect metaphor in place of independent fact gathering and analysis. Moreover, in some respects the Internet will defy analysis by analogy. Nevertheless, where an individual is responsible for the creation of the obscene material or the child pornography, there is little doubt the person will come within subsections 163(1) and 163.1(2), as was the case in R. v. Pecciarich, where the accused was charged under both provisions.[142] In terms of the creation of the offensive materials, this case illustrates all too graphically the blurring of private/public (the third dynamic of computer law), in that prior to the ascendance of computer and network technology, an individual would be hard-pressed to create and disseminate on a large scale high-quality pornography; that is, the resources and funding of a larger organization would typically be required both for production and distribution purposes. By contrast, the accused in the Pecciarich case single-handedly scanned pictures of children's bodies from retail store catalogues and then manipulated the images into

---

142 (1995), 22 O.R. (3d) 748 (Prov. Ct.) [Pecciarich]; see R. v. Pecciarich, [1995] O.J. No. 2238 (Prov. Ct.) for the sentencing decision, which resulted in the first-time offender being sentenced to two years' probation and 150 hours of community service. Interestingly, the court did not ban the accused from using a computer modem, as requested by the Crown, as this would affect the accused's learning and employment opportunities; the judge did order him not to upload or download any computer material that is erotic, obscene, or pornographic in nature.

pornographic contexts using a standard personal computer.[143] The accused then distributed the child pornography over the Internet. The case illustrates how in today's technology environment (courtesy of the four dynamics of computer law) everyone can become a publisher, distributor, retailer, marketer, and seller, with a global reach, of sexually explicit material.

Turning from the creation of pornographic material to its dissemination, it was well established under section 163 that to be found to be a distributor under paragraph 163(1)(a), or to be found to be a seller under paragraph 163(2)(a), the accused had to have knowledge of the obscene nature of the contents of the materials. While subsection 163(1) is a strict liability offence, (i.e., there is no "knowingly" requirement as in subsection 163(2)), an honest and reasonable belief in a state of facts which, if true, would render conduct innocent constitutes a defence.[144] It should be noted, however, that such a mistake cannot be a "mistake of law," as where an accused, knowing of the sexually explicit materials, believes them not to be obscene, for if a court ultimately concludes that the materials are obscene, the accused will be liable even if he had an honest and reasonable belief to the contrary. With respect to a retailer under subsection 163(2), the pre-Internet cases are clear that the person who sells to the ultimate consumer must have knowledge of the obscene material, and thus in a paper-based environment an accused news seller was acquitted because it did not know it had materials that were obscene.[145] Indeed, for the Supreme Court of Canada in the *Jorgensen* case, which dealt with a retailer of pornographic videos charged under section 163, the distinction between producer/distributor and retailer is an important one:

In my view there are sound reasons for such a distinction. Producers and distributors can be presumed to be familiar with the content of the material that they create or distribute. Furthermore, if the law

143 In Paul Knox, "Child Porn Flood Swells: High-Tech Era Catches Nightmare," *The Globe and Mail* (27 August 1996), there is mention of technology soon being able to create computer-generated images of lifelike child pornography without using real children. The definition of *child pornography* in s. 163.1 is seemingly broad enough to capture such material, though arguably in one sense such technology is to be welcomed because it avoids one harm to which s. 163 is aimed, namely, the exploitation of minors in the creation of child pornography; see, for example, the *Ashcroft* case at note 171 below.
144 R. v. *Metro News Ltd.* (1986), 32 D.L.R. (4th) 321 (Ont. C.A.); and *Jorgensen*, above note 136.
145 R. v. *Dorosz* (1971), 4 C.C.C. (2d) 203 (Ont. C.A.) [*Dorosz*].

casts upon them the obligation of being familiar with the material they make or distribute, that can easily be discharged. On the other hand, a seller of pornographic material may include among her merchandise magazines, books and a myriad of other products. Until the materials arrive at the seller's shop, he or she has had nothing to do with the material. It might be suggested that the seller can ask the distributor or producer about content when the material is ordered. This is not likely to produce a helpful response. Anyone in the business of producing or distributing pornographic material for profit is not likely inclined to scare off buyers by telling them his or her product can potentially subject the potential purchaser to criminal liability. It would, therefore, be perfectly reasonable for Parliament to have assumed that the seller would ordinarily not be aware of the specific nature of the contents of the material sold, in which circumstance imposing criminal liability would result in the conviction of many persons who did not possess a blameworthy mind state.

Conversely, the producer or distributor will generally be aware of the contents of the material which may result in its being found to be obscene. The imposition of criminal liability in the absence of knowledge of the contents will be less likely to result in the conviction of those that are mentally blameless. In addition, a producer or distributor who knows that absence of knowledge in default of a reasonable inquiry cannot be relied on can easily find out what the material contains. On the other hand, it would be unreasonable to expect the seller to read every book or magazine and view every video or film to ferret out the portions that may run afoul of the obscenity provisions.[146]

The *Jorgensen* decision also makes it clear that the quality of knowledge on the part of the retailer must be more specific than just knowing of the nature of the material, i.e., that it is generally pornographic. Thus, the operator of a video retail outlet must be aware of the relevant facts that made the material obscene, i.e., the specific parts of a videotape that go beyond legal pornography to illegal obscenity, such as the scene where there are images of explicit sex with violence. This knowledge may be directly acquired, as when the operator views the videotape, and indeed in one case a retail outlet that made copies of videos for sale or rental was assumed to have such knowledge.[147] The requisite knowledge for subsection 163(2), however, may also be acquired indirectly, as

---

146 *Jorgensen*, above note 136 at 96–97.
147 *R. v. Harris and Lighthouse Video Centres Limited* (1987), 35 C.C.C. (3d) 1 (Ont. C.A.).

when the proprietor receives warnings from authorities, or statements from others; and wilful blindness will also suffice if the accused suspects the materials may be obscene but does not review them because he knows that looking would fix him with knowledge. This standard of liability is not unlike the one for disseminators of material under civil libel.[148] Section 163.1 regarding child pornography does not include a "knowledge" requirement on the part of sellers, though we do not yet have a case indicating the precise *mens rea* required under this provision and what, if any, defences might be available.

c) Internet Distribution

The state of affairs for pre-Internet intermediary liability for distribution of obscene material now having been discussed briefly, the analysis now turns to the Internet-based scenario. The liability of Internet-based bulletin board system (BBS) operators under section 163 has been considered in several Canadian cases. Where the BBS operator creates the obscene materials, as in the *Pecciarich* case,[149] the court has little difficulty in finding the accused guilty of distribution as well by uploading files containing the obscene material onto bulletin boards, which the public was then able to access through an application process. In the *Hurtubise* case, however, the BBS operator did not create the obscene material, and argued it should be considered a seller (and not a distributor), and that it did not have knowledge of the specific files being uploaded by it and subscribers on its BBS, and therefore did not have the requisite knowledge for a seller under subsection 163(2).[150] The court disagreed, finding the accused to be a distributor, based on a number of factors, including the large number of people that could access the BBS, and the ability of the obscene material, in digital form, to be further distributed, in electronic or hard copy form if printed out, once made available electronically on the BBS. The court, after citing from the *Jorgensen* and *Dorosz* cases, concluded that the distinction between retailer and wholesaler (distributor) drawn in the latter case "makes sense with print material" but "is not one which is necessarily applicable to computer technology."[151] This could be a very important decision. It determines the dichotomy between distributor and retailer not on the basis of whom a party sells to, but rather whether the purchaser can in turn further disseminate copies of the material. Under

---

148 See chapter 7, section A, "Cyber Libel."
149 *Pecciarich*, above note 142.
150 *R. v. Hurtubise*, [1997] B.C.J. No. 40 (S.C.) [*Hurtubise*].
151 *Ibid.*, at para. 11.

such an approach, the transmission of digital-based products in electronic form may effectively negate the concept of retailer, thus making a distributor of all participants, including end users, because they in turn can retransmit the obscene materials. In essence, the third dynamic of computer law, namely, the blurring of private/public, appears to have obliterated the previously important distinction between subsections 163(1) and 163(2) of the *Criminal Code* drawn by the Supreme Court of Canada in the *Jorgensen* case.

In addition to distributing and selling obscene material and child pornography, an accused can be convicted under sections 163 and 163.1 for publishing or exposing to public view these materials. These elements raise the beguiling question of how the concept of "public" should be determined in the context of the Internet. In a pre-Internet case, *R. v. Rioux*,[152] a private showing of obscene films in the accused's home was not found to constitute "circulation" for purposes of paragraph 163(1)(a). Further along the private–public continuum, in *R. v. Harrison*[153] it was held that an obscene film was not exposed to public view under paragraph 163(2)(a) where it was shown only to relatives and friends of the groom at a stag party in a community hall that, while generally open to the public, was being used for a private gathering; there was a notice posted on the wall outside the hall indicating that this was a private party and warning even the invited guests that stag films were going to be shown. In concluding that the persons in this case constituted a private group, and that the situation was tantamount to showing a film in one's home, the court relied, in part, on the definition of *private* in the Oxford dictionary, which includes the phrases: "kept or removed from public view … not within the cognizance of people generally … not open to the public; intended only for the use of particular and privileged persons," and which were contrasted to the following definitions of *public*: "done or made by or on behalf of the community as a whole … generally accessible or available" and *public place*: "A place to which the general public has a right to resort. … Any place so situated that what passes there can be seen by any considerable number of persons, if they happen to look."[154] By contrast, in *R. v. Vigue*[155] a film was held to be exposed to public view because it was shown to invited guests as well as to two people who paid an admission charge. In coming to this conclusion, however, the court was

152 (1969), 10 D.L.R. (3d) 196 (S.C.C.).
153 (1973), 12 C.C.C. (2d) 26 (Alta. Dist. Ct.).
154 *Ibid.*, at 28–29.
155 (1973), 13 C.C.C. (2d) 381 (B.C. Prov. Ct.) [*Vigue*].

clearly troubled by the fact that the two paying viewers were not invited by the person organizing the screening; they were simply allowed in the room by the person who was helping to run the film projector (who was not the organizer of the viewing).[156] In the course of the judgment the court struggled with the concept of public and private in the following terms:

> I have been troubled as to what is the test of privacy. Does the invitation have to be extended by the accused or may he delegate one or more people to invite guests? May invited persons invite others? Would it still be a private occasion if the accused stands on the street and invites everybody who comes past? Is a personal invitation the only criterion of privacy? Or is acquaintance with the invited person part of the test?
>
> In addition does the payment of money affect the question of privacy and to what extent? In this case the accused says that he received money which he did not ask for and he used it simply to replace the bulb in the projector.[157]

These sorts of considerations and factors animate the third dynamic of computer law and will likely loom large in analyses of the public/private determinations involving Internet situations.

The *Hurtubise* case addressed both the publication and exposing to public view issues under section 163. In respect of the former, the court held that there was possession of the obscene material for the purpose of publication given the ability of the computer to show material to a number of people and to produce material easily and inexpensively, as discussed above. In respect of the offence of "exposing to public view," the counsel for the accused argued that his clients should have been charged under this provision (for which counsel argued his clients did not have the requisite *mens rea*), and in this regard it is interesting to note that the bulletin board service in *Hurtubise* took active steps to limit access to specific subscribers who were adults; that is, this case is consistent with the trend in other cases involving the

---

156 The Court's willingness to convict in the *Vigue* case, above note 155, may also have been coloured by the nature of the films in issue, and the court's reaction to them at 382: "The films I saw were of poor quality and would, I think, be quite loathsome to many people because of their subject-matter. To have shown them to a pre-wedding party as accused testified he had, would be in execrable taste and destructive, if young people are to commence married life with any respect for their relationship."

157 *Vigue*, above note 155 at 383.

"private/public" differentiation, such as in the case of copyright infringement[158] and regulation of broadcasting,[159] namely, that it is increasingly difficult to retain a concept of private in the world of modern communications, at least in respect of those applications where people generally are able to participate in or subscribe to the particular activity. In the case of the Internet, this is arguably exacerbated by the fact that solicitation and subscription is far easier in a networked environment than was previously the case. Nonetheless, the application of the provisions in sections 163 and 163.1 to Internet services such as e-mail or usegroups will have to be determined on a case-by-case basis, and may turn on the particular nature of the service involved; for example, a limited and closed e-mail list should be treated differently than a large, open-ended usegroup. Obviously, any material posted to a generally accessible Web site will be considered to reside in a public place. With certain present and future technologies such as passwords based on biometric features[160] and encryption, however, it should be possible to carve out private enclaves within the broader Internet and to recreate, in a virtual environment, the privacy that courts have accorded a person's own physical house (that is, to use personalization, authentication, and security technologies to counteract the effects of the third dynamic of computer law).

Subsection 163.1(4) makes it an offence to "possess" child pornography. Computers, and particularly networks (and especially the Internet), raise some new questions as to the concept of possession. Under subsection 4(3) of the *Criminal Code*, a person possesses something when (a) it is in that person's personal possession; (b) the person knowingly has it in the actual possession of another person; or (c) the person knowingly has the item in a place for use or benefit of himself or another person. Pre-computer/Internet cases have held that the key ingredients of possession are knowledge and control, each of which must occur simultaneously. Thus, where a subscriber to a BBS consciously downloads some child pornography to his computer, there is likely a strong case that he had both the requisite knowledge and control. But what if the end user merely accesses a Web site that has the

---

158 See the last paragraph of chapter 2, section C.6(d), "Litigation and Case Law." See also the discussion relating to a "public place" in section B.6, "Illegal Speech," later in this chapter.

159 See chapter 4, section D.3, "Regulating Broadcasting over the Internet," as well as the discussion of "public" in the *Tariff 22* decision (referred to in note 311 of chapter 2).

160 See chapter 6, section A.2(b), "The Authentication Function."

offending material? Does it matter if the user has an account there? Interestingly, the new e-commerce statutes require more than mere Web site access in certain circumstances to effect adequate "delivery" of certain electronic documents; see the discussion in chapter 6, section A.1(g), "Electronic Commerce Statutes." As for a third party intermediary on the Internet, they may be exonerated in respect of the particular activity involving the child pornography if they lacked the knowledge of its presence. More problematic is the control issue. Does this factor require, for example, an Internet service provider to request a BBS to delete some child pornography of which it has knowledge? Or does it require the wholesale disconnection of the BBS's connection to the Internet, given that the Internet service provider does not exercise editorial control over the particular pornography? These questions regarding possession of pornography in an electronic environment remain to be answered in Canada.

d) Sentencing and Computers

The question often arises what use an accused convicted of a child pornography offence can make of the Internet during any period of incarceration, conditional sentence, or subsequent probation. In *Evans*,[161] the Crown asked that the accused not be allowed access to the Internet, as this would increase the likelihood of recidivism. The court, however, concluded that Internet access is today too important for legitimate employment and other purposes to make such an order; rather, the accused was ordered not to possess or use software that allows access to Internet relay chat channels. In another case, the court ordered that the offender's use of computers be limited as follows:

---

161 See above note 66. It is interesting to note that the offender in this case was a scientist with a doctorate in philosophy. In the United States, some appellate courts have upheld a restriction on the total prohibition of the Internet as a release condition, while others have not. For the former, see *United States* v. *Crandon*, 173 F.3d 122 (3d Cir. 1999); and *United States* v. *Paul*, 274 F.3d 155 (5th Cir. 2001). For the latter, see *United States* v. *Sofsky*, [No. 01-1097] (2d Cir. 2002) [*Sofsky*]; and *United States* v. *Peterson*, 248 F.3d 79 (2d Cir. 2001). In this last case the court noted, at 83, that "computers and the Internet have become virtually indispensable in the modern world of communications and information gathering," and therefore cannot be completely denied to people on parole or serving conditional sentences. In the *Sofsky* case the court argued that this would be tantamount to denying someone who committed fraud by means of a telephone the right to subsequently use the telephone. On a somewhat related point, see *State* v. *Davis*, 1998 WL 809632 (W. Va. November 20, 1998), which held that inmates do not have a constitutional right to have a personal computer in their prison cell.

- for employment purposes only;
- the offender shall not have access to or hold a personal (non-employment) account or have access to an Internet service provider;
- the offender shall not engage directly or indirectly in the use of electronic media for the purpose of communicating with Internet web-sites, commonly known as bulletin boards, whether interactive or static in nature;
- the offender will maintain "Net Nanny" or equivalent program on his work computer(s), and, if called upon to do so, will forthwith provide satisfactory evidence that this has been done.[162]

In this case, given that the court imposed upon the offender a conditional sentence of ninety days of house arrest (as opposed to incarceration in a jail), the court also discussed the practice of electronic monitoring, whereby the offender wears a transmitting bracelet around the ankle that immediately pages a supervisor if the offender moves more than the permitted distance from a monitoring device.

e) Legislative Responses

The foregoing discussion of sections 163 and 163.1 of the *Criminal Code* illustrates that there are a number of uncertainties associated with these provisions when considered in the context of computers and networks, particularly for intermediaries such as Internet service providers. As a result, some ISPs have ceased to carry a number of pornographic usegroups, both on their own volition or at the suggestion of public authorities. Similarly, a number of Canadian universities have taken steps to restrict access to "alt.sex" newsgroups.[163] Given the amorphous nature of the Internet, such activities may not limit access to people determined to reach these sites, since they can usually find another electronic route.[164] Not surprisingly, some elements within government wish to go further and legislate certain measures to fight child pornography in particular. For example, Bill C-396, a private member's bill entitled *An Act to Restrict the Use of the Internet to Distribute Pornographic Material Involving Children*, was introduced into Canada's House

---

162 *R. v. Patterson*, [2000] O.J. No. 736 (Ont. Ct. Justice). It is interesting to note that the offender in this case was a senior chartered accountant. See also the sentencing decision in *Pecciarich*, referred to in note 142 above.

163 See Richard S. Rosenberg, "Free Speech, Pornography, Sexual Harassment, and Electronic Networks: An Update and an Extension," in *The Electronic Superhighway: The Shape of Technology and Law To Come*, ed. Ejan Mackaay, Daniel Poulin & Pierre Trudel (The Hague: Kluwer, 1995).

164 See Warren Caragata, "Crime in Cybercity," *Maclean's*, 22 May 1995.

of Commons on 8 April 1997. This bill, which died on the order paper when the 1997 federal election was called, would have required the licensing of all persons who facilitate access to the Internet, with such licences being refused (or cancelled if previously issued) to anyone who has been convicted under section 163.1 of the *Criminal Code*. The bill would also have made it an offence to knowingly permit the use of its service for the placing of child pornography on the Internet or the viewing, reading, copying, or recovery of child pornography from the Internet. The bill would also have required Internet service providers to check whether subscribers had been convicted under section 163.1, and to refuse service to such persons, and to block access by its subscribers to any material that the government determines to be child pornography. The bill would also have made directors of corporations liable if they were aware of the circumstances giving rise to the offence.

Elements of the broad parameters of Bill C-396 can also be seen in the U.S. *Communications Decency Act of 1996* (CDA), which criminalizes the transmission to minors of obscene or indecent messages and the use of interactive computer services to display to minors sexually explicit material that is patently offensive by contemporary community standards.[165] This legislation is relevant to Canadians for a number of reasons (mostly animated by the fourth dynamic of computer law), including the fact that Canadian users acquire much content from U.S. information providers, the statute may have an impact on Canadians providing services to Americans, and the statute may contain elements that one day might be adopted in Canada. Important provisions in this statute are several affirmative defences on behalf of Internet service providers, including where they take effective technologically feasible actions to prevent minors accessing knowledge of the offending material, or where they restrict access to the sexual material by requiring use of a credit card, debit account, adult access code, or adult personal identification number. In a ruling by the United States Supreme Court in the *ACLU* case, two of the core provisions of the CDA were held to be unconstitutional for being overly broad.[166] While upholding the provision of the CDA aimed at prohibiting the transmissions of obscene messages, the majority of the court found that the provisions regarding "indecent" and "patently offensive" messages were too vague to pass muster under the First Amendment of the U.S. Constitution (which

---

165 This legislation is Title V of the *Telecommunications Act of 1996*, Pub.L. 104-104, 110 Stat. 56.
166 *ACLU*, above note 75.

protects freedom of speech). Drawing upon the extensive findings regarding the Internet made by the lower court,[167] the majority also concluded that the affirmative defences provided by the CDA were not technologically or economically feasible for most content providers on the Internet. In an ironic variation of the first dynamic of computer law, where it is usually the law that cannot keep pace with technology, the *ACLU* case illustrates the problem of a law being ahead of the then available technology! In a perceptive partial minority opinion, Justice Sandra O'Connor noted that in the past the U.S. Supreme Court would uphold a law that regulates pornography by creating an "adult zone" in the physical world because in such an environment geography and identity can enable the owner of an adult establishment to prevent the entry of children. Justice O'Connor noted that effecting the same protection of children through zoning on the Internet in 1997 is not possible because speakers and listeners can mask their identities; she added, however, that content "tagging," screening, and other technologies are being developed that, if they come into widespread use, may permit effective zoning on the Internet in the future.[168] In effect, the *ACLU* case is required reading for all legislators who wish to regulate the Internet because the case makes it clear how difficult it will be to tame the Internet tiger, given the four dynamics of computer law.

In response to the striking down of parts of the CDA, the U.S. Congress enacted the *Child Online Protection Act* (COPA), which required that Web site operators take positive steps to avoid liability, such as undertaking credit card checks or utilizing adult access codes and personal identification numbers; however this law too was struck down on First Amendment grounds as being too burdensome on protected speech.[169] Subsequently, however, the *Child Pornography Protection Act*

---

167 *Ibid.* As noted in chapter 1, section A.6, "The Internet," this decision gives a very thorough description and analysis of the structure, operations, uses, and nuances of the Internet. Another lower court decision also found the CDA unconstitutional: *Shea* v. *Reno*, 930 F.Supp. 916 (S.D.N.Y. 1996). This latter decision gives a good discussion of "tagging" and various other measures being developed to permit the private screening of content over the Internet.
168 Private tagging and content categorization schemes have their own critics, particularly as they raise the spectre of censorship by persons not accountable to the public at large: see Lawrence Lessig, "Tyranny in the Infrastructure," *Wired*, July 1997.
169 *American Civil Liberties Union* v. *Janet Reno*, 8 CCH Computer Cases 71,643 (E.D. Pa 1999). Subsequently, though, the U.S. Supreme Court partially upheld this law: *Ashcroft* v. *American Civil Liberties Union*, 535 U.S. 564 (U.S. Sup. Ct. 2002).

of 1996 (CPPA) fared better than the CDA and COPA.[170] In a number of cases convictions have been registered under the CPPA where the accused used the Internet to download, and a computer to store, child pornography. However, the United States Supreme Court has struck down the provision within the CPPA that criminalized "virtual" child pornography, that is, material that does not depict an actual child.[171] In one recent case, the court refused to accept as a defence that child pornography can be received unintentionally by spam.[172] In another case, in addition to the conviction for possession of pornographic material, the accused was convicted for attempting to seduce a minor who was first contacted by the accused in an online chat room.[173] In regard to this latter American decision, it is important to note that the *2002 Criminal Code Amendments*, above note 134, introduced the new offence of using a computer to communicate with a child for the purpose of facilitating certain other offences.[174] It is not a defence under this new provision that the accused believed the person was above the relevant fourteen-, sixteen-, or eighteen-year age limit, "unless the

---

170 Four appellate courts have upheld it: *United States* v. *Hilton*, 257 F.3d 50 (1st Cir. 2001); *United States* v. *Mento*, 231 F.3d 912 (4th Cir. 2000); *United States* v. *Fox*, 248 F3d 394 (5th Cir. 2001); and *United States* v. *Acheson*, 195 F.3d 645 (11th Cir. 1999).

171 *Ashcroft* v. *The Free Speech Coalition*, 535 U.S. 234 (U.S. Sup. Ct. April 16, 2002) [*Ashcroft*]. The court concluded that these computer-generated images do not harm children in the production process, and refused to accept the government's argument that to destroy the market for pornography that uses real children in its production it is necessary to ban all virtual pornography as well, as the two types of pictures are indistinguishable.

172 *United States* v. *Hay*, 231 F.3d 630 (9th Cir. 2000); also see the decision in *Daniels*, at note 294 below, where the court concluded that subscribing to a child pornography Web site did not necessarily mean that any offending material was downloaded. See also *United States* v. *Simons*, 206 F.3d 392 (4th Cir. 2000), where the court concluded that the accused's Fourth Amendment rights (against unreasonable search and seizure) were not violated when the accused's employer searched the accused's e-mail messages (and found over fifty files of child pornography), because the employer's Internet use policy clearly stated that the employer would monitor the employee's use of the Internet.

173 *Hatch* v. *The Superior Court of San Diego County*, 80 Cal. App. 4th 170 (Cal. Ct. App. 2000).

174 The luring a child provision is contained in the new s. 172.1(1) of the *Criminal Code*, implemented by s. 8 of the *2002 Criminal Code Amendments*, above note 134. Unfortunately, some teenagers (so-called camgirls) seem to invite trouble by operating sexually provocative Web sites in return for gifts: Erin Anderssen, "Camgirls: Empowerment or Predator Enticement," *The Globe and Mail* (19 October 2002).

accused took reasonable steps to ascertain the age of the person."[175] This begs the question how the jurisprudence will determine how one may come to determine someone else's age over the Internet.[176]

6) Illegal Speech

The *Criminal Code* makes certain types of speech illegal. Subsection 319(1), for example, provides that "[e]very one who, by communicating statements in any public place, incites hatred against any identifiable group where such incitement is likely to lead to a breach of the peace" is guilty of an offence. As well, subsection 319(2) provides that "[e]very one who, by communicating statements other than in private conversation, wilfully promotes hatred against any identifiable group" is guilty of an offence.[177] Significant definitions related to these "hate speech" provisions are contained in subsection 319(7), namely that *communicating* includes communicating by telephone, broadcasting, or other audible or visible means; *public place* includes any place to which the public have access as of right or by invitation, express or implied; and *statements* includes words spoken or written or recorded electronically or electromagnetically or otherwise, and gestures, signs, or other visible representations. These provisions raise a number of particularly interesting and difficult issues in terms of their application in an electronic environment like the Internet. The intention here, therefore, is not to examine the various elements of these offences, such as the meaning of *promote* and other keywords or defences, but rather to review the application of these offences in the context of computer and network technologies.[178]

---

175 *Criminal Code*, s. 172(4).
176 Apparently the first case of "Internet luring" under this provision has now been commenced: see Estanislao Oziewicz & Jane Gadd, "Province Gives Police $2-million to Fight Web Exploitation of Kids," *The Globe and Mail* (16 October 2002).
177 Other provisions of the *Criminal Code* include s. 318, which makes it an offence to advocate or promote genocide, and s. 320, which authorizes the seizure of copies of hate propaganda. Regulations under the *Broadcasting Act* also prohibit licensees from distributing programming that exposes individuals to hatred or contempt on the basis of discrimination: see *Pay Television Regulations, 1990*, SOR/90-105, para. 3(2)(b), 25 January 1990; *Specialty Services Regulations, 1990*, SOR/90-106, subs. 3(b), 25 January 1990; *Television Broadcasting Regulations, 1987*, SOR/87-49, para. 5(1)(b), 9 January 1987; and *Radio Regulations, 1986*, SOR/86-982, subs. 3(b), 18 September 1986.
178 For a discussion of the hate speech offences generally, see *R. v. Keegstra* (1990), 61 C.C.C. (3d) 1 (S.C.C.).

With respect to subsection 319(1), a key question is whether a networked computer environment, and particularly the Internet, can be considered to be a "public place." A threshold point in this regard is whether the concept of public place, as used in this provision, is limited to physical places, which then begs the question whether the Internet is a physical place. When Canadian novelist William Gibson coined the term *cyberspace* in the early 1980s, it was intended to describe a space without physical or even temporal dimensions.[179] In many areas, however, the Internet has become a virtual version or alter ego for physical counterparts. Justice Sopinka of the Supreme Court of Canada suggested outside the courtroom that the message-posting capability of the Internet approximates the ability to hang posters from physical telephone poles; considered in this light, cyberspace is a place for purposes of subsection 319(1).[180] Justice Sopinka made this analogy in the context of a Supreme Court of Canada decision that struck down as unconstitutional a municipal bylaw that prohibited posters on public property; the law was held to be an unjustifiable infringement on the freedom of expression, preventing the communication of political, cultural, and artistic messages.[181] In this context, Justice Sopinka stated:

> In many ways, it may be said that electronic media such as Internet are the posters of the late twentieth century providing an invaluable means of expression to a wide audience. Like posters, the cost is relatively inexpensive and therefore it is available to people of modest economic means. In some cities, electronic mail services are entirely free. Just as with posters, we must be cognizant of the tremendous value of electronic mail.[182]

At the same time, however, Justice Sopinka discussed the less positive aspects of the electronic media, and in particular its potential to be used for obscene and hateful expression. In this regard, he noted:

---

179 William Gibson, *Neuromancer* (New York: Ace Books, 1984).

180 Hon. John Sopinka, "Freedom of Speech and Privacy in the Information Age" (Address to the University of Waterloo Symposium on Free Speech and Privacy in the Information Age, 26 November 1994) [*Freedom of Speech*]. See also an updated version of this address delivered at the Faculty of Law, Queen's University, on 21 November 1996. Both versions are available at <canniff.com/tdenton/sopinka.html>.

181 *Peterborough (City) v. Ramsden* (1993), 106 D.L.R. (4th) 233 (S.C.C.).

182 Sopinka, *Freedom of Speech*, above note 180 at 5.

The freedom of speech over computer networks is no more absolute than for any other means of expression. ... The ability of computer networks to provide a new and expansive forum for sexual and racial harassment, obscenity and violent messages may in fact demand government attention.[183]

Assuming the Internet is a place for purposes of subsection 319(1) of the *Criminal Code*, is it a *public one*? The third dynamic of computer law makes the answer to this question quite difficult. Consider that the Internet comprises a multitude of services, features, and participants, and the facts of each scenario would have to be analysed carefully in order to apply subsection 319(1) sensibly. For example, an open bulletin board or discussion forum on a so-called freenet, where no fees are charged to participate and all users have access to all messages posted by all other users, is a good candidate to be considered a public place. By contrast, private e-mail, particularly if encrypted and resident on a personal computer in a private home, may not be a message resident in a public place. There are pre-Internet indecent exposure or prostitution solicitation cases, however, that hold that a person, although physically on private property, can be deemed to be in a public place if the person is in view of the public. Thus, in *Hutt* v. *R.*, an automobile was held not to be a public place because the particular offence occurred wholly within the vehicle.[184] In contrast, in other cases the subject automobile lost its private character because while the indecent or other impugned act was performed in the automobile it was able to be viewed from the public street.[185] After the *Hutt* decision the term *public place* in section 195 of the *Criminal Code* was amended to include *any motor vehicle in a public place and any place open to public view*. These cases have some consequences for the Internet. First, by analogy to them it may be possible to argue that someone comfortably ensconced in the seemingly private environs of her own home nevertheless is deemed to be in a public place, depending on the quality and nature of the person's connections with public portions of the Internet. Second, at some point

---

183 *Ibid.*, at 6.
184 (1978), 38 C.C.C. (2d) 418 (S.C.C.) [*Hutt*].
185 *R.* v. *Wise* (1982), 67 C.C.C. (2d) 231 (B.C. Co. Ct.); and *R.* v. *Figliuzzi* (1981), 59 C.C.C. (2d) 144 (Alta. Q.B.). See also *R.* v. *Buhay* (1986), 30 C.C.C. (3d) 30 (Man. C.A.), where it was held that a public place includes a doorway in a private house if the accused performs the indecent act in such a way as to be exposed to public view; in essence, the private dwelling takes on a public presence for the narrow purpose of the commission of the offence. See also the discussion of "public" in section B.5(c), "Internet Distribution," earlier in this chapter.

Parliament may take up the challenge and legislate the meaning of public and private on the Internet in an attempt to clarify these blurring definitions in the computer environment, particularly given the challenges posed by the third dynamic of computer law.

With respect to the potential liability of Internet intermediaries under section 319, much will turn on the approach taken by courts to the word communicating in both provisions. The dictionary meaning of this word is broad enough to encompass mere carriage or transmission of messages initiated by someone else. Nonetheless, it will be interesting to see if courts adopt reasoning analogous to that in *The Electric Despatch Company of Toronto* v. *The Bell Telephone Company of Canada*, which held that a person who transmits a message is the sender of it, and that a telecommunications carrier should not be considered to have transmitted the message where it did not have knowledge of it.[186] Great care, however, must be taken when assessing the jurisprudential value of this century-old case, as it involved two litigants disputing a non-competition covenant in a purchase and sale agreement; moreover, a reading of the trial decision in this case shows that the key concern of the plaintiff was not the transmission of messages but the act of permitting a certain competitor of the plaintiff to connect to the defendant's telephone system. In any event, again a detailed analysis will have to be undertaken of each case, including understanding what the specific role of the intermediary was in the particular circumstances. Different considerations will apply to a passive provider of a telecom service than to a moderator of a discussion group that posts inflammatory messages.

a) The *Canadian Human Rights Act*

Although the term *public place* in section 319 of the *Criminal Code* raises questions with respect to the Internet, the definitions of *communicating and statements* in subsection 319(7) likely capture every form of message, regardless of its medium. As with the definitions of *data* in section 342.1 discussed earlier, these definitions in subsection 319(7) are technology-neutral and apply regardless of the particular mode of transmission utilized. The same may not necessarily be said of another federal statute that is aimed at prohibiting hate messages. Under subsection 13(1) of the *Canadian Human Rights Act* (CHRA), it is a discriminatory practice to repeatedly communicate telephonically, or cause to be so communicated by means of the facilities of a telecommunications

---

186 (1891), 20 S.C.R. 83 [*Electric Despatch Company*]. See also the decision in the *Tariff 22* case, referred to in note 311 in chapter 2.

undertaking, any matter that exposes a person to hatred based on prohibited grounds of discrimination.[187] It is clear this provision applies to telephone answering machines, as determined in the *Taylor* case, where the subsection also withstood constitutional scrutiny.[188] Prior to the recent decision involving Ernst Zündel, it was not clear how the provision would be interpreted in relation to the Internet. One argument could focus on the concept of *telephonically* within the provision and draw on the case law that stands for the proposition that "telephone" relates to the transmission of sounds or voice, thereby not extending the provision to text-based Internet messages.[189] Several arguments, however, may be mustered against this approach, including the fact that modems (the devices still used by many people to connect to the Internet) transmit sound-based tones in the process of transmitting text and digital content over telephone lines. A somewhat broader approach is that *telephonically* should cover all communications over the Internet, since many people use telephone lines to connect to the Internet, and computing and telephony technologies converge in respect of the Internet. Essentially this approach was articulated by a U.S. court in a case involving the issue of a person's reasonable expectations of privacy in e-mail transmissions.[190] Such an approach would be consistent with the principle that human rights legislation should be given a liberal and purposive interpretation, and that any doubts are to be resolved in a manner that promotes the goals of the legislation.[191] Support for this approach can be gleaned from the Taylor decision, where Justice Dickson pointed out that human rights legislation operates differently from the *Criminal Code*. Therefore, the principle of narrow construction of

---

187 R.S.C. 1985, c. H-6.

188 *Canada (Canadian Human Rights Commission)* v. *Taylor* (1990), 75 D.L.R. (4th) 577 (S.C.C.) [*Taylor*].

189 See, for example, *IBM Canada Ltd.* v. *Deputy M.N.R., Customs and Excise*, [1992] 1 F.C. 663 (C.A.) [*IBM*], though it should be noted that this is a customs case and hence its applicability in a human rights context is questionable.

190 *United States* v. *Maxwell*, 45 M.J. 406 (U.S. Ct. App. Armed Forces 1996) (Westlaw). In this case the court stated, at paras. 416–17: "In answering these questions, we have examined the relationship between appellant and AOL [America Online] from four different perspectives. First, the technology used to communicate via e-mail is extraordinarily analogous to a telephone conversation. Indeed, e-mail is transmitted from one computer to another via telephone communication, either hard line or satellite. We have recognized that '[t]elepone conversations are protected by the Fourth Amendment if there is a reasonable expectation of privacy.'"

191 See Ruth Sullivan, *Driedger on the Construction of Statutes*, 3d ed. (Toronto: Butterworths, 1994).

criminal statutory provisions, as articulated in the *Maltais*[192] and *McLaughlin*[193] cases, should not come into play in respect of subsection 13(1) of the CHRA, and indeed the more purposive approach taken in the U.S. *Davis*[194] and *Lamb*[195] cases should be adopted.

These very arguments were indeed aired when a Canadian Human Rights Tribunal had to determine whether hate material posted on a Web site was communicated telephonically for purposes of section 13(1) of the CHRA. Both the Tribunal[196] and the Federal Court of Canada in an earlier judicial review decision[197] concluded that the provision should be given a broad, purposive construction, one that can take into account advances in technology, and thus the section was held to apply to the Internet.[198] Both the Tribunal and the court also found Zündel to have caused the communication, given his intimate control of the material on the Web site, notwithstanding that another person actually operated the relevant computer on a day-to-day basis.[199] And finally, both the Tribunal and the court refused Zündel's argument that individual visitors to the site actually caused the communication of materials when they clicked with their browser.[200] Thus

---

192 *Maltais*, above note 103.

193 *McLaughlin*, above note 96.

194 *Davis*, above note 108.

195 *Lamb*, above note 110.

196 *Sabrina Citron, Toronto Mayor's Committee on Community and Race Relations, and Canadian Human Rights Commission v. Ernst Zündel*, Canadian Human Rights Tribunal, 18 January 2002.

197 *Zündel v. Canada (Attorney General)*, [1999] F.C.J. No. 964 (F.C.T.D.) [*Zündel*].

198 The Tribunal concluded that the word telephonically relates to the general means of communication by a telephone network, rather than being limited to one type of device that operates in respect of voice communications. See also *Mark Schnell, Canadian Human Rights Commission, Machiavelli and Associates Emprize Inc., John Micka, Canadian Association For Free Expression Inc.*, Canadian Human Rights Tribunal, 20 August 2002, for a similarly broad interpretation of "telephonically" in relation to an antigay Web site. For another example of a court (in an area unrelated to human rights) willing to go beyond the narrow language of a statute when confronted with new technological developments, see *SONG Corp., Re* 31 C.B.R. (4th) 97 (Ont. Sup. Ct. 2002), where the court held that the phrase *put into type*, which clearly referred to books, in a bankruptcy statute should not be an obstacle to concluding that the specific statutory regime at issue applied to all copyright works (including musical works), having regard to changes in technology.

199 For a similar result involving an answering machine that was moved to the U.S., see *Canada v. Canadian Liberty Net*, [1998] 1 S.C.R. 626.

200 The Tribunal drew an analogy with a telephone answering machine, possibly in light of the comfort provided by the *Taylor* case, above note 188, and concluded

the Tribunal found Zündel in violation of section 13.1 of the CHRA, and ordered him to cease disseminating hate material over the site.[201] Subsection 13(3) of the CHRA provides an exemption from the prohibition in subsection 13(1) for an owner or operator of a telecommunications undertaking that is used by others. This provision is similar to the general principle, seen often in this book, that innocent disseminators of third party messages should not be liable for the content of those messages, but only so long as the disseminator does not have actual knowledge of the offending nature of the third party's message or fails to have knowledge due to negligence or wilful blindness; the same general principle is articulated by the law in respect of copyright,[202] libel,[203] obscene material under the *Criminal Code*,[204] criminal libel,[205] and broadcasting.[206] The knowledge elements, however, are lacking in subsection 13(3) of the CHRA, ostensibly because it dates from a time when only telephone companies carried telephonic messages, and did so as true common carriers in a manner that saw them fulfil this role without having any occasion to monitor a customer's conversations. Today, however, over the Internet an owner or, especially, an operator of a network may well have reason to monitor messages. In effect, just as the provision in subsection 13(1) could be drafted more broadly,[207] the

---

that it would be equally disingenuous to argue that the telephone answering machine is not communicating because it has to be activated by the specific caller. The Federal Court was even more dismissive of this argument, and responded it to it thus, at para. 68: "This is the merest sophistry and provides no basis for the Court to intervene in the proceedings now before the Tribunal. It would follow from counsel's submission that the person who opens the morning's newspaper causes its content to be communicated to her, rather than the journalists who wrote the items that are published and printed in the newspaper."

201 The Tribunal was mindful of the fact that, with mirror sites carrying Zündel material (exemplars of the fourth dynamic of computer law), it might be more of a symbolic than practical measure to order Zündel to cease Internet operations. Indeed, Zündel appears to have moved to the U.S. himself, presumably to be out from under the CHRA's jurisdiction, and to continue his campaign in a more hospitable American First Amendment environment: Kirk Makin, "Rights Group Orders Zündel to Kill Hate Site," *The Globe and Mail* (19 January 2002).

202 See chapter 2, section C.6, "Copyright and the Internet."

203 See chapter 7, section A, "Cyber Libel."

204 See section B.5 of this chapter, "Obscenity and Child Pornography."

205 See section B.7 of this chapter, "Criminal Libel."

206 See chapter 4, section D.3, "Regulating Broadcasting over the Internet."

207 For example, the equivalent provision in s. 14.(1) in Saskatchewan's legislation uses the phrase *or by any other medium*, which casts a much broader net: *The Saskatchewan Human Rights Code*, ss. 1979, c. 5–24.1.

exemption in subsection 13(3) is too broad, because it is based on "status" rather than an assessment of function. The real question should be whether the owner or operator of the telecommunications undertaking had knowledge of (actually or through negligence or wilful blindness) and control over the offending message.

7) Criminal Libel

Another form of illegal speech is criminal libel. Under section 301 of the *Criminal Code*, someone convicted of publishing a criminal libel is liable to imprisonment for two years; the sentence can be increased under section 300 to five years if the publisher of the libel knows it to be false. A defamatory libel is defined as a "matter published, without lawful justification or excuse, that is likely to injure the reputation of any person by exposing him to hatred, contempt or ridicule, or that is designed to insult the person of or concerning whom it is published."[208] Perhaps the most interesting provisions relating to criminal libel are the sections addressing the liability of persons who publish newspapers and sell other works. The former, contained in section 303, provides as follows:

> 303.(1) The proprietor of a newspaper shall be deemed to publish defamatory matter that is inserted and published therein, unless he proves that the defamatory matter was inserted in the newspaper without his knowledge and without negligence on his part.
>
> (2) Where the proprietor of a newspaper gives to a person general authority to manage or conduct the newspaper as editor or otherwise,

---

208 *Criminal Code*, subs. 298(1). For a discussion of the criminal libel rules and their historic rationale and development, see *R. v. Stevens* (1995), 96 C.C.C. (3d) 238 (Man. C.A.). These criminal libel provisions withstood a constitutional challenge in *R. v. Lucas*, [1998] 1 S.C.R. 439. Canada's first Internet-related criminal libel charge was brought against the disgruntled purchaser of two dogs who had posted on a Web site material critical about the breeder of the animals. When the breeder complained to the poster's ISP, the ISP took down the site, but the poster then moved his site to a server hosted in El Salvador: Eric Atkins, "Internet Dogfight in Criminal Court," *Law Times* (1 May 2000). In *R. v. Barrett*, [2000] O.J. No. 2055 (Ont. Sup. Ct.), an early skirmish in this case, the court, at para. 5, noted: "The accused's conduct since 1995 has been, if the allegations are proven, bizarre, rude, insensitive and quite possibly criminal. His weapon of choice is the computer and through the computer, the World Wide Web. When he chose this weapon, the complainant was unarmed. Since arming herself, she has, if the documents produced are proven, demonstrated that she "gives as good as she gets."

the insertion by that person of defamatory matter in the newspaper shall, for the purposes of subsection (1), be deemed not to be negligence on the part of the proprietor unless it is proved that

(a) he intended the general authority to include authority to insert defamatory matter in the newspaper; or

(b) he continued to confer general authority after he knew that it had been exercised by the insertion of defamatory matter in the newspaper.

(3) No person shall be deemed to publish a defamatory libel by reason only that he sells a number or part of a newspaper that contains a defamatory libel, unless he knows that the number or part contains defamatory matter or that defamatory matter is habitually contained in the newspaper.

The definition of newspaper is in section 297, and reads as follows:

any paper, magazine or periodical containing public news, intelligence or reports of events, or any remarks or observations thereon, printed for sale and published periodically or in parts or numbers, at intervals not exceeding thirty one days between the publication of any two such papers, parts or numbers, and any paper, magazine or periodical printed in order to be dispersed and made public, weekly or more often, or at intervals not exceeding thirty one days, that contains advertisements, exclusively or principally.

As a threshold matter, it may be asked whether section 303 applies to publications circulated in an electronic environment, given that the definition of newspaper speaks in terms of being "printed." The traditional method of printing is to imprint ink onto paper by mechanical means. A more purposive approach, however, would focus on simply the process of making multiple copies of a document. Thus, in one case unrelated to the *Criminal Code*, there is a suggestion that photocopies should be considered printed.[209] In this regard, the cases in chapter 7, section A, "Cyber Libel," in the civil libel discussion, that address

---

209 *Xerox of Canada Ltd.* v. *IBM Canada Ltd.* (1977), 33 C.P.R. (2d) 24 (F.C.T.D.). In this case, one party had to prove, in respect of a patent infringement action, that a particular document had been "printed" given the *Patent Act's* then requirement for a "printed publication" for this particular purpose. After reviewing the sketchy evidence before it, the court approached the "printed" question by being sensitive to "the state of printing and reproducing methods," and concluded at 85: "Without deciding, I would suggest that today a run of so-called 'photostatic copies,' might well be held to be 'printed.'"

whether a newspaper or a periodical is only paper-based or could also exist in an Internet context, are indirectly relevant and should be referred to on this point. To avoid doubt, Parliament, in light of the first dynamic of computer law, might consider amending the definition of newspaper to make it more technology-neutral. The next noteworthy point about subsection 303(1) is that a proprietor of a newspaper may not avoid responsibility simply because he did not have knowledge of the defamatory material; in addition, he cannot have been negligent in respect of its insertion in the newspaper. This mirrors the standard of liability for "innocent disseminators" under civil libel.[210] Subsection 303(2) addresses the situation where the proprietor has appointed someone else, such as an editor, to manage the editorial content of the newspaper and who serves to relieve the proprietor of responsibility, unless she gave a general permission to the editor to insert libellous material or she does not revoke the editor's responsibility after the proprietor learns of the editor's insertion of libellous material in the newspaper. This particular provision has interesting counterparts in the Internet world, where it is not uncommon for an online service provider to contract out to a third party responsibility for overseeing the editorial aspect of a particular electronic information-based service, as was the case in *Cubby, Inc.* v. *CompuServe Inc.*[211]

With respect to persons who sell newspapers that happen to contain libellous material, such vendors are only liable, as a result of subsection 303(3), if they have knowledge of the defamatory material or if they know that the particular newspaper habitually carries such libellous matter. Interestingly, the second prong of this knowledge test is arguably narrower than the equivalent test for civil libel with respect to newsvendors and other innocent disseminators;[212] that is, there are likely circumstances where one could attract liability as a distributor under the civil standard of negligence but not come within subsection 303(3). Similarly, persons who sell books, magazines, or other things (other than newspapers) under subsection 304(1)[213] must have knowledge of the defamatory material, and again this seems narrower than

210 See chapter 7, section A, "Cyber Libel."
211 776 F. Supp. 135 (S.D.N.Y. 1991). This case is discussed in chapter 7, section A, "Cyber Libel."
212 See chapter 7, section A, "Cyber Libel."
213 "304(1) No person shall be deemed to publish a defamatory libel by reason only that he sells a book, magazine, pamphlet or other thing, other than a newspaper that contains a defamatory matter if, at the time of the sale, he does not know that it contains the defamatory matter."

the equivalent civil libel standard, which would also include negligence, unless knowledge is interpreted rather broadly as including wilful blindness along the lines articulated in the *Jorgensen* case.[214] Equally, under subsection 304(2),[215] where an employee sells such material, the employer's liability requires actual knowledge or knowledge that defamatory material was habitually contained in the subject material, again establishing a standard arguably narrower than the civil libel one. Moreover, the distinction in these provisions between newspapers and other publications appears to be unjustifiable in an electronic environment, where CD-ROMs and online databases blur the definitions.

a) Contempt and the Internet

Although not directly related to the criminal libel provisions, it is worth speculating how another control on the media — the law of contempt of court in the guise of bans on the publications of trial proceedings — will be applied in a computer and networked environment. It was traditionally the law that a newspaper or broadcaster had absolute liability if it published or broadcast any material that was subject to a court-ordered ban.[216] More recently, however, this strict rule in respect of so-called contemptuous publications has been loosened in those circumstances where, for example, a reporter is ignorant of the ban, in which case a due diligence defence might be raised provided the parties involved acted with all reasonable care and had no intention of interfering with the court process.[217] Of course, regardless of the prospects for liability or immunity of an Internet participant in respect of publication bans, the practical question should also be asked to what extent they can be made to work in an Internet environment (particularly in light of the fourth dynamic of computer law, namely the blurring of national/international). Consider the experience with the notorious court-imposed ban on information related to the 1993 legal proceedings involving Karla Homolka, who at the time was alleged to have assisted Paul Bernardo in carrying out the grisly murders of three young

---

214 *Jorgensen*, above note 136.
215 "304(2) Where a servant, in the course of his employment, sells a book, magazine, pamphlet or other thing, other than a newspaper, the employer shall be deemed not to publish any defamatory matter contained therein unless it is proved that the employer authorized the sale knowing that
    (a) defamatory matter was contained therein; or
    (b) defamatory matter was habitually contained therein, in the case of a periodical."
216 *R. v. Odham's Press, Ltd.*, [1956] 3 All E.R. 494 (Q.B.).
217 *R. v. Edge*, [1988] 4 W.W.R. 163 (B.C.C.A.).

women in St. Catharines, Ontario. Soon after the court-imposed ban, some Internet newsgroups began carrying material from the trial. A number of these were deleted from university access by university administrators, but as an Internet expert stated at the time, "As soon as one news group is closed down, the story shows up somewhere else."[218] In short, although bringing legal action against particular Internet participants is possible, regulating the whole of the Internet is a close to impossible task. It would appear that the judiciary is cognizant of these dynamics of the Internet. In the recent *Dagenais* case, the Supreme Court of Canada, in overturning a publication ban, stated:

> It should also be noted that recent technological advances have brought with them considerable difficulties for those who seek to enforce bans. The efficacy of bans has been reduced by the growth of interprovincial and international television and radio broadcasts available through cable television, satellite dishes and shortwave radios. It has also been reduced by the advent of information exchanges available through computer networks. In this global electronic age, meaningfully restricting the flow of information is becoming increasingly difficult.[219]

Justice Sopinka, in a speech that resonated with the four dynamics of computer law, commented on the *Dagenais* case as follows:

> Those opposing bans express concern about the efficacy of some publication bans. They note that recent technological advances such as satellite dishes and computer networking have created substantial difficulty in enforcing such bans. The fact that it is becoming much more difficult to meaningfully restrict the flow of information must

---

218 See Mark Nichols, "Wired World," *Maclean's*, 17 January 1994. In another case, a Web site carried explicit information about the case against two suspects notwithstanding a publication ban imposed by a BC court: Robert Matas, "Forbidden Air-India Details Posted on Internet," *The Globe and Mail* (13 February 2001). More recently, defence counsel argued that a Canadian publication ban was violated by U.S. media outlets posting information on their Web sites: Rod Mickleburgh, "Publicity Problems Suspend Pickton Testimony," *The Globe and Mail* (15 January 2003). In this proceeding, one of the counsel suggested that Canadian media might also be violating the ban merely by mentioning the U.S. Web sites. In a somewhat similar vein, Canada's election law that prohibits dissemination of voting results until all polls have closed across Canada has come under intense pressure from Web sites that consciously, or inadvertently, violate this law through Internet postings: see Mary McGuire & Janice Neil, "Give Up: Voters Will Find Out," *The Globe and Mail* (13 February 2003).
219 *Dagenais v. Canadian Broadcasting Corp.*, [1994] 3 S.C.R. 835 at 886.

be weighed into the balancing equation. If the efficacy of a ban is minimal due to technology, then it becomes harder to justify its existence. Once again, we see that the courts will have to consider the impact of the information age on the balancing of rights and freedoms under the Charter.[220]

Both passages noted above reflect a heightened awareness of the difficulty in regulating, let alone prohibiting, the dissemination of information in our computerized, globally networked Information Age.

8) Gaming and Betting

The proliferation of computers and networks, particularly the Internet, raise a number of novel issues under the *Criminal Code*'s provisions related to gaming and betting.[221] The legal regime for gaming in Canada created by sections 201 to 207 of the *Criminal Code* operates on the basis that sections 201 to 206 prohibit gaming and numerous other betting activities (including lotteries, sports betting, and the like) unless they are regulated by a province. As well, paragraph 207(4)(c) effectively requires that any lottery scheme using a computer or video device be operated by a provincial government (which can include a provincial Crown corporation). As a result, Canadian companies involved in the online gaming business generally are careful to restrict their activities to developing the software used by foreign operators of Internet casinos,[222] or operate their online gaming systems from computers located in non-Canadian jurisdictions where Internet gaming is legal, such as Antigua (assisted in this endeavour by the fourth dynamic of computer law).[223] However, one such company was investigated by the police, charged with possessing a device that facilitated gaming, and pleaded guilty.[224] Given the regulatory regime in Canada for gaming, a provincial government (or more likely one of the provincial

---

220 Sopinka, *Freedom of Speech*, above note 180 at 7.
221 Even the traditional activity of wagering on horse races is witnessing the application of Internet-related technologies: see Neil A. Campbell, "Tracks Decry Lack of Help With 'Illegal' Betting," *The Globe and Mail* (16 January 1997).
222 Tyler Hamilton, "CryptoLogic Stock Jumps On Listing Plans," *The Globe and Mail* (28 August 1999).
223 John Partridge, "Entrepreneur Seeks Web Gambling Jackpot," *The Globe and Mail* (28 August 2000); Peter Kennedy, "Starnet Seen As Test of On-Line Gambling," *The Globe and Mail* (7 September 1999); and Peter Kennedy, "Starnet Communications Moving Office to Antigua," *The Globe and Mail* (3 September 1999).
224 Peter Kennedy, "Vancouver Police Raid Starnet Offices," *The Globe and Mail* (21 August 1999).

Crown corporations that operates one of Canada's offline casinos) could create an Internet-based gaming site, subject to a number of considerations discussed below. One challenge would be to recreate in an online, virtual environment the various regulatory protections that are provided in provincial law with respect to the current offline casinos. For example, these casinos generally restrict admittance to persons above a certain age, and they prohibit the use of devices such as calculators. These same issues will be difficult to address in an Internet environment,[225] but with the ongoing development of various biometric authentication devices, technology will likely appear in the marketplace to solve these problems.[226]

An interesting constitutional/jurisdiction issue posed by Internet-based casinos is whether such a licensed site offered by one province could accept customers from another province. The *Criminal Code*'s gaming provisions do not expressly contemplate the Internet era where a person physically resident in one province could access the casino Web site operated by another province.[227] In this regard, it should be noted that a province cannot legislate activities outside its physical boundaries. However, a province whose residents access another province's Internet casino likely could take jurisdiction of the activity within its province, in light of the discussion on Internet jurisdiction in chapter 7, section B.2(a), "Regulatory/Criminal Jurisdiction," though it is open to question how one province could bring enforcement action against another province, as they each enjoy immunity from one another. Equally, in light of the fourth dynamic of computer law, namely, the blurring between national/international, a provincially sanctioned gaming Internet site in Canada may well run afoul of the laws of another jurisdiction outside of Canada, such as the United States[228] if the site

---

225 For a discussion of recreating in an Internet environment the same security as provided by geography and identity in a physical environment, see Justice O'Connor's decision in the Supreme Court decision in *ACLU*, above note 75.
226 See chapter 6, section A.2(b), "The Authentication Function."
227 Other provisions in the *Criminal Code*'s gaming rules also illustrate their pre-Internet nature. For example, subs. 201(1) makes it an offence to keep a "common gaming house" or "common betting house." Does "house" include an Internet site? What if the server for the Web site is situated in a house?
228 Notwithstanding that some states in the United States have indicated they would like to decriminalize Internet gaming (e.g., in 2001 the Nevada Senate passed Bill AB466, which enabled casinos to operate Internet gaming sites), most American judicial and legislative sentiment is still heavily against it in that country. For example, the state of Missouri obtained an injunction against a Pennsylvania corporation that offered gaming over the Internet: see *State of Missouri v. Interac-*

accepted patrons from that jurisdiction, and in this context the Canadian province might not enjoy immunity if its activities were characterized as "commercial" rather than governmental in nature. Similarly, a provincial government could take action against non-Canadian operators of gaming Web sites, just as the attorneys general of certain U.S. states have done against out-of-state operators, as illustrated by the *Granite Gate*[229] and other cases discussed in chapter 7, section B.2(a), "Regulatory/Criminal Jurisdiction." In this regard, it is interesting to note that in the United States, Internet gaming is generally illegal, with gaming Web site operators being prosecuted under the *Wire Act*, which makes it an offence to be engaged in the business of betting or wagering by means of a wire communication in interstate or foreign commerce.[230] On the other hand, some forty other countries, including Australia, have legalized Internet gaming.[231]

Two recent cases, one in Ontario and the other in Prince Edward Island, have started to shed light on how licensed gaming entities will fare on the Internet distribution question, at least under the current Canadian regulatory regime in Canada. In *Ontario Jockey Club v. Canada*,[232] the licensed operator of a horse-racing track applied to extend its permit to include the ability of bettors to place their wagers over the Internet. When the regulator refused, the applicant brought this application for judicial review, arguing that when an online system is used the bets are made on the racecourse where the races are held. Unfortunately for the applicant, section 204(1)(2) of the *Criminal Code* provides that for purposes of the racecourse betting provision in section 204(1)(c), bets made by telephone calls to the racecourse are deemed

tive Gaming & Communications Corp., No. 197CF0014(1) (Mo. Cir. Ct., 23 May 1997), reported in *Computer & Online Industry Litigation Reporter*, 15 July 1997 at 24,441, and in *United States of America v. Jay Cohen* (Docket No. 00-1574, 2nd Circuit 2001), it was held that an Antigua-based sports betting business that took bets from Americans over the phone and the Internet violated the U.S. Federal *Wire Act*, which criminalizes the transmission of sports bets over interstate phone lines. In Canada, it will be interesting to see how regulators respond to computerized gaming in aircraft: see Ralph Schoenstein "The Odds Favour In-Flight Gambling," *The Globe and Mail* (23 August 1997).

229 *State of Minnesota v. Granite Gate Resorts, Inc.*, 1996 WL 767431 (D. Minn.) (Westlaw) [*Granite Gate*].

230 *Wire Act*, 18 U.S.C. §1084. In 1998 alone, the U.S. Department of Justice brought charges under this statute against 22 American citizens involved in managing Internet gaming sites outside of the United States. See also the cases mentioned in note 228 above.

231 "Betting Against the House," *The Economist*, 4 September 1999.

232 [1998] F.C.J. No. 154.

to be made on the racecourse, and the court concluded that as this deeming provision did not include online bets, the statutory interpretation inference would be that online bets are not made at the racecourse.[233] In a decision with a similar outcome, *Earth Future Lottery, Re.*, a charity based in Prince Edward Island wished to operate an Internet-based lottery, such that residents from across Canada could participate online through the lottery operator's Web site.[234] The lottery operator was very careful to structure the ticket-purchasing process to ensure that the transaction took place in PEI. Thus, their Web site made it clear that the Web site merely constituted advertising and an invitation to treat, that purchasers submitted an offer when they wished to purchase a ticket, but that the offer was subject to acceptance, and that the contract was made only when the lottery operator accepted the offer in PEI. In short, the lottery operator attempted to do all that it could for contract law purposes, including providing for PEI governing law, to make the purchases of tickets "occur" in PEI, and thus permitted under the lottery operator's licence. The court, at the behest of lottery operators in other Canadian provinces, concluded, at 325, that regardless of contract law rules,[235] from a criminal law perspective a trans-border transaction would be taking place every time an offer is made over the Internet to sell a ticket to a consumer located outside Prince Edward Island and every time he or she buys one.[236] In this regard, the court also found that the language of section 207(1)(b) of the *Criminal Code* requires the lottery to stay within the physical boundaries of the province; it reads conducted and managed "in" the province, and not just "from" the province. Both of these Canadian decisions are consistent with U.S. Internet gaming cases where courts have also taken jurisdiction in the place where the bettors are located.[237] In effect, to-date

---

233 The court also relied on the provision in section 204(1)(C)(ii) of the *Criminal Code* that required all relevant rules to be complied with, in light of an Ontario regulation that provided that no racecourse accept bets by "telephone, telegram or any other means of communication that originates from outside the racecourse at which the race is taking place": *Pari-Mutuel Betting Supervision Regulations*, SOR/91-365, s. 53.

234 (2002) 633 A.P.R. 311 (PEI C.A.).

235 For a discussion of offer and acceptance in the online world, see chapter 6, sections A.3(b) "Online Offers, Acceptances, and Auctions" and A.3(c), "Express and Implied Click-Consent Agreements."

236 The court also hung its hat on section 207(4)(c) of the *Criminal Code*, which prohibits anyone other than a provincial government from using a computer in a lottery scheme.

237 See the *Granite Gate and World Interactive Gaming* cases discussed in chapter 7, section B.2(a), "Regulatory/Criminal Jurisdiction."

courts in North America have taken very restrictive views of the regulatory regimes and prohibitions on Internet gaming.

9) Other Offences

The foregoing discussion has focused on those provisions of the *Criminal Code* most relevant to computer crime. Other offences, however, may also be germane in certain circumstances. There are, for example, a number of provisions that can come into play where a computer or a network facility is used as a means to facilitate an otherwise traditional offence, or where information stored on a computer is the subject of the criminal behaviour. Into these categories of offences fall forgery (section 366), uttering a forged document (section 368), drawing or using a document without authority (section 374), falsification of books and documents (section 397), falsification of employment records (section 398), and the making, circulating, or publishing of a false prospectus (section 400). With respect to those offences that refer to documents, the 1985 amendments to the *Criminal Code* that enacted the computer abuse and abuse of data provisions also implemented a revised definition of *document* in order to cover computer-based materials:

> "document" means any paper, parchment or other material on which is recorded or marked anything that is capable of being read or understood by a person, computer system or other device, and includes a credit card, but does not include trademarks on articles of commerce or inscriptions on stone or metal or other like material.[238]

This was a useful amendment since today so much information is stored electronically and the copying, scanning, and other technologies allow non-technical people to engage in counterfeiting and forgery activities.[239] It is also worth noting that sections 406 to 409 contain offences regarding the forging of trade-marks, and in one case these provisions were used to convict an unauthorized distributor of software who had reproduced a third party's trade-mark on the software product to deceive purchasers of the product.[240]

---

238 *Criminal Code*, s. 321.
239 See *R. v. Sebo* (1988), 42 C.C.C. (3d) 536 (Alta. C.A.), where a photocopier was used to create a forged document.
240 *R. v. Locquet* (1985), 5 C.P.R. (3d) 173 (Que. Sess. Ct.).

Computers and networks can be used in other *Criminal Code* offences, such as criminal harassment (section 264),[241] uttering threats (section 264), extortion (section 346), obtaining a benefit through false pretences (section 362), fraudulent fortune-telling for consideration (section 365), making false messages (sections 371 and 372), and making anything resembling a banknote (section 457). Some of these provisions, such as those relating to uttering threats, extortion, and fortune telling, are drafted without a specific reference to a particular communications medium and therefore should apply without difficulty in a computer and networked environment. Others, however, use phrases that may be problematic, such as the appearance of "writing" in the false pretences offence, which raises the question whether electronic messages (such as e-mail over the Internet) constitute writings; for a discussion of this issue see chapter 6, section A(1), "The Writing Requirement." Some provisions are also tied to certain communication vehicles, such as the telegram, cablegram, and radio message in section 371 or the telephone call in subsections 372(2) and (3). Again, the question arises whether either of these provisions would capture text-based messages transmitted over the Internet; in the case of subsections 372(2) and (3) because of the *IBM* case referred to in note 189 above, but see also the discussion of the *Zündel* case (and its broad interpretation of "telephonically") in section B.6(a), "The *Canadian Human Rights Act*." It should also be noted that the various offences related to the "mails," such as sections 345 (stopping a mail conveyance with intent to rob or search), 356 (theft from mail), and 381 (using mails to defraud) only apply to "mailable matter" conveyed by Canada Post Corporation, and thus would only apply to e-mails transmitted by or through this corporation.[242] In effect, in order to ensure that the *Crimi-*

,241 In the United States, in *New York v. Kochanowski*, 2000 N.Y. Misc. Lexis 535 (N.Y. Sup. Ct. 2000), an accused was convicted of aggravated harassment for creating an anonymous Web site that cast the accused's former girlfriend in an unfavourable light by stating, among other things, that she had an infatuation with sex.

242 The *Canada Post Corporation Act*, R.S.C. 1985, c. C-10, subs. 2(1), contains the following definitions:

"mail" means mailable matter from the time it is posted to the time it is delivered to the addressee thereof;

"mail conveyance" means any physical, electronic, optical, or other means used to transmit mail;

"mailable matter" means any message, information, funds, or goods that may be transmitted by post;

nal Code is always and consistently relevant to the needs of the computer and network dynamics coursing through the economy and society at large, the statute needs to be constantly reviewed and updated.

It is worth noting that criminal or quasi-criminal provisions are also dealt with in other parts of this book: section B.3, "Copyright," in chapter 2 includes a discussion of the criminal piracy provisions of the *Copyright Act*; section B.1, "Criminal Offences," in chapter 5 discusses the criminal offences under the *Competition Act*; and section E.4(a), "Online Contests," in chapter 4, dealing with regulation, makes mention of the *Criminal Code*'s provisions relating to contests and promotions. Another provision in the *Criminal Code* worthy of brief mention is section 21, the aiding and abetting section, which provides that everyone is a party to an offence who does or omits to do anything for the purpose of aiding any other person to commit the offence. It might be asked, for example, whether certain participants on the Internet might come within the purview of section 21 depending on their activities in disseminating content or facilitating an activity that is otherwise problematic under one of the other provisions discussed in this chapter. In this regard, it should be noted that to be a party to an offence, the aider or abetter must have knowledge that the principal was intending to commit the relevant offence and the aider/abetter must have acted with the intention of assisting in the commission of the offence; that is, the person accused of aiding and abetting must know the circumstances necessary to constitute the offence the person is accused of aiding, although in certain situations recklessness or wilful blindness may suffice as well.[243] In the context of the Internet, this test appears to be quite close to that set out for intermediary liability for libel on the Internet.[244]

"post" means to leave in a post office or with a person authorized by the Corporation to receive mailable matter;

"post office" includes any place, receptacle, device, or mail conveyance authorized by the Corporation for the posting, receipt, sorting, handling, transmission, or delivery of mail;

"transmit" means to send or convey from one place to another place by any physical, electronic, optical, or other means;

"transmit by post" means to transmit through or by means of the Corporation.

243 See, for example, *R. v. Roan* (1985), 17 C.C.C. (3d) 534 (Alta. C.A.); *Dunlop and Sylvester v. R.* (1979), 47 C.C.C. (2d) 93 (S.C.C.); and *Director of Public Prosecutions for Northern Ireland v. Maxwell*, [1978] 3 All E.R. 1140 (H.L.).

244 See chapter 7, section A, "Cyber Libel."

10) Interception of Communications

Since the passage in 1974 of the *Protection of Privacy Act*, Canada's criminal law has concerned itself with countering unauthorized telephone wire-tapping and electronic surveillance.[245] Initially aimed only at police authorities, the *Criminal Code's* interception of communications provisions has a much wider application as the technological devices that permit electronic eavesdropping have become widely available; thus, the heightened importance of the following:

> 184 (1) Every one who, by means of any electro-magnetic, acoustic, mechanical or other device, wilfully intercepts a private communication is guilty of an indictable offence and liable to imprisonment for a term not exceeding five years.
>
> (2) Subsection (1) does not apply to
> (a) a person who has the consent to intercept, express or implied, of the originator of the private communication or of the person intended by the originator thereof to receive it;
> (b) a person who intercepts a private communication in accordance with an authorization or pursuant to section 184.4 or any person who in good faith aids in any way another person who the aiding person believes on reasonable grounds is acting with an authorization or pursuant to section 184.4;
> (c) a person engaged in providing a telephone, telegraph or other communication service to the public who intercepts a private communication,
> (i) if the interception is necessary for the purpose of providing the service,
> (ii) in the course of service observing or random monitoring necessary for the purpose of mechanical or service quality control checks, or
> (iii) if the interception is necessary to protect the person's rights or property directly related to providing such service; or
> (d) an officer or servant of Her Majesty in right of Canada who engages in radio frequency spectrum management, in respect of a private communication intercepted by that officer or servant for the purpose of identifying, isolating or preventing an unauthorized or interfering use of a frequency or of a transmission.

---

245 S.C. 1973-74, c. 50.

Important definitions related to this prohibition are contained in section 183 and are as follows:

"electromagnetic, acoustic, mechanical or other device" means any device or apparatus that is used or is capable of being used to intercept a private communication, but does not include a hearing aid used to correct subnormal hearing of the user to not better than normal hearing;

"intercept" includes listen to, record or acquire a communication or acquire the substance, meaning or purport thereof;

"private communication" means any oral communication, or any telecommunication, that is made by an originator in Canada or is intended by the originator to be received by a person who is in Canada and that is made under circumstances in which it is reasonable for the originator to expect that it will not be intercepted by any person other than the person intended by the originator to receive it, and includes any radio-based telephone communication that is treated electronically or otherwise for the purpose of preventing intelligible reception by any person other than the person intended by the originator to receive it;

To complete the picture under the *Criminal Code*, it should be noted that *telecommunications* is defined in the *Interpretation Act* as "any transmission, emission, or reception of signs, signals, writing, images, sounds, or intelligence of any nature by wire, radio, visual, or other electromagnetic system."[246] As well, section 193 of the *Criminal Code* makes it an offence to unlawfully use or disclose an intercepted private communication, and section 193.1 makes it illegal to use or disclose a radio-based telephone communication. Other statutes also have provisions aimed at preserving the confidentiality of communications. Subsection 9 (1.1) of the *Radiocommunication Act*, for example, makes it an offence to intercept and make use of, or intercept and divulge, any radiocommunication, which essentially covers any transmission of signals lower than 3,000 Ghz.[247] Certain provincial privacy statutes also contain provisions making it a tort to, among other things, listen to or record a person's conversation, or to listen to or record messages travelling to or coming from that person by telecommunications. This can

---

246 R.S.C., c. I-21, subs. 35(1). This is similar to the definition in the *Telecommunications Act*, discussed in chapter 4, section D.1, "Regulating Telecommunications."

247 R.S.C. 1985, c. R-2.

serve as an important supplement to section 184 of the *Criminal Code*. For example, in *R. v. Dunn*[248] the court held that a policeman listening to a telephone conversation on an extension was not in violation of section 184 because one of the parties to the conversation consented to the policeman's eavesdropping; essentially the same activity, however, was held to be actionable under Manitoba's *Privacy Act* in the *McBee* case.[249] Finally, it should also be noted that, as discussed in the next part of this chapter, with the enactment of the *Canadian Charter of Rights and Freedoms* (*Charter*) in 1982,[250] eavesdropping, surveillance, and related activities carried out by government also come under scrutiny of the *Charter's* various provisions, and specifically section 8 of the *Charter,* which provides that "[e]veryone has the right to be secure against unreasonable search or seizure."

a) What Information Is Protected

Various technologies and business processes have raised questions under section 184 of the *Criminal Code* and section 8 of the *Charter*, largely because of the second dynamic of computer law — the elusive nature of information. For example, a number of cases in Canada have considered whether the signals obtained by a dial number recorder (DNR) (in the United States referred to as a "pen register") constitute a telecommunication for purposes of section 184. A DNR is a device that is used by a telephone company to track the numbers called by a telephone subscriber and the length of those calls, but it does not record the content of the calls. In the *Samson* case,[251] the Newfoundland Court of Appeal concluded that DNR-type information is not covered by section 184, as that provision is aimed at protecting only conversations. In several later cases, the holding in the *Samson* case was not followed, and the courts in these subsequent cases decided that DNR information related to at least local calls should be protected as these calls are not normally monitored by DNR technology, as opposed to long-distance calls which are so monitored for billing pur-

---

248 (1975), 28 C.C.C. (2d) 538 (N.S. Co. Ct.).

249 *Ferguson v. McBee Technographics Inc.* (1989), 24 C.P.R. (3d) 240 (Man. Q.B.). The various provincial privacy statutes are discussed in chapter 4, section A.1(a), "Tort-Oriented Privacy Statutes."

250 The *Charter* is Part I of the *Constitution Act, 1982*, being Schedule B to the *Canada Act 1982* (U.K.), 1982, c. 11. The *Canada Act 1982* can be found in R.S.C. 1985, Appendix II, No. 44.

251 *R. v. Samson* (1983), 45 Nfld. and P.E.I.R. 32 (Nfld. C.A.) [*Samson*].

poses.[252] More recently, however, the Ontario Court of Appeal in the *Fegan* case followed *Samson*, without any mention of the decisions finding to the contrary.[253] In contrast, the Manitoba Court of Appeal in a decision rendered around the time of the *Fegan* case indicated it believed the police required judicial authorization to obtain information about an individual's utility records.[254] In any event, the *Criminal Code* now contains, in section 492.2, a provision for obtaining a warrant for a number recorder. Interestingly, outside of Canada, courts have been equally divided about DNR information. In a U.S. Supreme Court decision,[255] the majority concluded that such information should not be protected by the U.S. Fourth Amendment (which protects against unreasonable search and seizure). The eloquent dissent in this case, however, was subsequently followed in a decision regarding Colorado's state constitution.[256] In the *Malone* case originating in the United Kingdom, the European Court of Human Rights concluded that providing the police with the telephone numbers and duration of calls made by the accused, but without the contents, was an invasion of the accused's right of privacy and contrary to section 8 of the *European Convention of Human Rights*, which guarantees against unreasonable search and seizure.[257]

---

252 *R. v. Griffith* (1988), 44 C.C.C. (3d) 63 (Ont. Dist. Ct.) [*Griffith*]; *R. v. Mikituk et al.* (1992), 101 Sask. R. 286 (Q.B.); and *R. v. Kutsak (T.L.)* (1993), 108 Sask. R. 241 (Q.B.).

253 *R. v. Fegan* (1993), 80 C.C.C. (3d) 356 (Ont. C.A.) [*Fegan*].

254 *R. v. Makwaychuk* (1993), 81 C.C.C. (3d) 186 (Man. C.A.).

255 *Smith v. Maryland*, 442 U.S. 735 (1979).

256 *People v. Sporleder*, 666 P.2d 135 (Colo. 1983). This case notes and cites the two lines of authority that have developed over this question in the United States. In coming to the conclusion that DNR information should be protected, the court, reminiscent of the decision of Justice McLachlin in the *Plant* case, below note 258, stated at 142: "Knowledge of these facts can often yield inferential knowledge of the content of the conversation itself. In addition, a pen register record holds out the prospect of an even greater intrusion in privacy when the record itself is acquired by the government, which has a technological capacity to convert basic data into a virtual mosaic of a person's life." The reasoning in the *Sporleder* court would also go further than that exhibited by the Canadian decisions in note 252, and hold long distance call data protected as well; just because these data are recorded by the telephone company as an incidence of the service it provides does not make it fair game for police scrutiny, to paraphrase the conclusion of the court.

257 The *Malone* case is discussed in James Michael, *Privacy and Human Rights: An International and Comparative Study, with Special Reference to Developments in Information Technology* (Aldershot, U.K.: Dartmouth, 1994).

A debate similar to the one in the DNR cases arose in the Supreme Court of Canada decision in *R. v. Plant*.[258] In this case the police, without a warrant, were given access to a suspect's electricity consumption records, which showed roughly quadruple the level of usage compared to neighbours, and which indicated the probable growing of marijuana in a hydroponic environment, a suspicion originally conveyed to the police by an anonymous tip. The majority of the court stated that such electricity consumption records should not be protected under section 8 of the *Charter*, having regard to, among other factors, the type of information (the majority felt they did not reveal personal information about the accused, i.e., the court was only willing to provide protection for a "biographical core of personal data"), the nature of the relationship between the original data collector and the accused (the utility collected this information in the normal course of business), the place where the information was obtained (not in the accused's home or any other place ordinarily considered private), and the manner in which it was obtained (the police had computerized access to the utility's computers, albeit on a password basis, and the majority was under the impression the utility records were made available to the general public upon request). In a spirited separate opinion, Justice McLachlin disagreed with many of these conclusions, stating that the police should have to obtain a warrant to access utility records for a number of reasons, including the following: the records were not public, and there was no evidence that the general public could access them; and the records are capable of telling much about one's personal lifestyle, and this is precisely why the police wanted access to them. Justice McLachlin also disagreed with the majority on the issue of where the information was found and (echoing the issues raised by the third dynamic of computer law) stated:

> Computers may and should be private places, where the information they contain is subject to the legal protection arising from a reasonable expectation of privacy. Computers may contain a wealth of personal information. Depending on its character, that information may be as private as any found in a dwelling house or hotel room.[259]

The DNR and *Plant* cases illustrate in dramatic fashion the second dynamic of computer law, but with an interesting twist. In these cases it is not the content of the communications that is elusive, but rather the inferences that can be drawn from them. Put another way, what is

---

258 [1993] 3 S.C.R. 281 (S.C.C.) [*Plant*].
259 *Ibid.*, at 303–4.

valuable is not the content of the message, but its context. In the recent *Kyllo* decision,[260] the U.S. Supreme Court understood this point when it had to consider whether the use of a thermal-imaging device[261] used by police to detect different amounts of heat coming from various rooms within a home constitutes a search under the U.S. Fourth Amendment.[262] As in *Plant*, the police suspected the growing of indoor marijuana, which usually required high-intensity lamps, that would then register on the infrared search. The government argued, among other things, that the thermal imaging search was constitutional because it did not "detect private activities occurring in private areas," and hence did not reveal "intimate details." The majority of the U.S. Supreme Court, however, held otherwise, concluding that:

> In the home, our cases show, all details are intimate details because the entire area is held safe from prying government eyes.[263]

Thus the court, in a 5–4 decision, concluded that obtaining, by sense-enhancing technology that is not generally available to the public, any information regarding the interior of the home that could not other-wise have been obtained without physical intrusion constitutes a search under the U.S. Fourth Amendment for which a warrant is required. This decision implicates two of the dynamics of computer law in a very interesting manner. On the one hand, it responds to the third dynamic — the blurring of private/public — by attempting to protect prophylactically all that goes on within the home. On the other hand, by restricting the protection only to invasive threats posed by

---

260 *Kyllo v. United States*, 533 U.S. 27 (2001) [*Kyllo*].
261 The Agema Thermovision 210 thermal imager detects infrated radiation, and then converts different degrees of heat into colour images (i.e., white is hot, black is cool). The court in *Kyllo, ibid.*, at 1, analogized the system to a video camera that shows heat images.
262 The U.S. Fourth Amendment provides that "[t]he right of the people to be secure in their persons, houses, papers, and effects, against unreasonable search-es and seizures, shall not be violated." In confronting the question of the scope of the Fourth Amendment in the modern age, the court noted that "The ques-tion we confront today is what limits there are upon this power of technology to shrink the realm of guaranteed privacy."
263 *Kyllo*, above note 260 at 10. For a recent Ontario decision that discusses both *Kyllo* and *Plant*, above note 258, and follows the former and distinguishes the lat-ter (on the grounds that the utility records were generated and stored by a third party, the hydro company), see *Her Majesty The Queen v. Walter Tessling*, [2003] O.J. No. 186 (Ont. C.A.) [*Tessling*], where the Ontario Court of Appeal held that an infrared aerial camera that detected heat rays emanating from a private home cannot be used as a surveillance technique without obtaining a search warrant.

non-readily available technologies, the court is seemingly blind to the first dynamic, which predicts that in fairly short order those surveillance technologies that were previously the exclusive preserve of law enforcement agencies will become available to the general public. Thus, *Kyello* probably affords in the longer term much less protection than would at first glance appear to be the case, given that the rapid pace of technological change invariably means the ongoing democratization of a technology through price decreases and marketing diffusion. For a stunning example of this phenomenon, see the discussion of encryption technologies in chapter 4, section C, "Regulating the Domestic Use of Encryption Technologies."

b) Expectation of Privacy

Both section 184 of the *Criminal Code* and section 8 of the *Charter* will only afford protection to communications that are made in circumstances where the originator of the communication had a reasonable expectation that the communication would not be intercepted. Numerous cases, therefore, have had to wrestle with the difficult question of which technologies may be said to afford their users a reasonable expectation of privacy. Again, the elusive nature of information has resulted in judicial divergence. For example, courts have disagreed as to whether a sealed letter sent through the mail is a private communication. In *R. v. Newell*, the court concluded that the sender of a letter should not have a reasonable expectation of privacy because, among other things, the recipient of the letter might voluntarily show the letter to others, or it might be misplaced and come into the hands of a third party:

> Letters and mailed tapes are different from a normal telephone call or private discussion. An average person is entitled to expect no one will listen to a telephone call or record a private discussion by a body pack. Unlike a letter, a telephone call or private discussion is not given to others for the purpose of transmission nor is it intended by the originator that the words be preserved for later reference.[264]

In contrast, in *R. v. Crane and Walsh*,[265] the court held that the privacy of the mails is an important and highly confidential element of society, and should be protected just as telephone calls are. Thus, the court concluded that the section 8 *Charter* protection against unreasonable search and seizure applied to mail.

---

264 (1982), 69 C.C.C. (2d) 284 at 286 (B.C.S.C.) [*Newell*].
265 (1985), 45 C.R. (3d) 368 (Nfld. Dist. Ct.).

Similar disagreement has accompanied cellular phone technology. In *R. v. Solomon*, a conversation over a cellular phone was held not to be confidential because the radio waves used to transmit cellular messages could be scanned by third parties.[266] By contrast, in *R. v. Cheung* cellular phone messages were held to be confidential because although cellular phone messages could be scanned, the state of scanner technology before the court did not easily permit the use of a scanner to intercept the cellular calls of any particular person.[267] Thus, the police in the *Cheung* case intercepted the cellular calls of the suspect at the switchboard of the phone company rather than by use of a general scanner device because they would have "little to no chance to intercept communications of the target individuals by using scanners."[268] In coming to this conclusion, the court in *Cheung* was very conscious of having to discern the intricacies of the specific technology before it in order to make a sensible determination, thereby heeding the first dynamic of computer law: "As technological advance and counteradvance leapfrog over each other, I am sure that ease and difficulty of interception will shift from time to time. The state of technology at the time of any disputed interception will be important, because it will bear upon the reasonable expectations of the caller."[269] It should be noted that the definition of *private communications* was amended to include any radio-based communication that is encrypted, and in addition subsection 193(1) has been added to the *Criminal Code* to make it an offence to use or disclose any private communication that has been intercepted.

Another problematic technology that has been considered in the context of section 184 is pager devices. In *R. v. Nin*, the court concluded that a pager communication is not private because the paging unit that receives the message plays the message audibly such that anyone in the vicinity of the recipient would hear the message.[270] The same pager technology was similarly treated in *R. v. Lubovac*.[271] As well, in this case a further ground for not finding privacy was the fact that the

---

266 (1992), 77 C.C.C. (3d) 264 (Que. Mun. Ct.). It should be noted, however, that in a subsequent decision ((1993), 85 C.C.C. (3d) 496 (Que. Mun. Ct.)), the court in *Solomon* reversed its earlier ruling by holding that under the *Charter* a person nevertheless expects that the police will not intercept and record his or her conversations made over a cellular phone.

267 (1995), 100 C.C.C. (3d) 441 (B.C.S.C.) [*Cheung*].

268 *Ibid.*, at 447.

269 *Ibid.*, at 443.

270 (1985), 34 C.C.C. (3d) 89 (Que. Sess. Ct.) [*Nin*].

271 (1989), 52 C.C.C. (3d) 551 (Alta. C.A.).

person leaving the pager message dictated it on the pager company's tape-recording device, and that this consensual recording broke the chain of confidentiality. In a subsequent American case, it was also held that a pager message was not private because the pager device might be in the possession of someone other than the intended recipient of the message.[272] Interestingly, this specific rationale was considered and not approved in the *Nin* case. Again, one is struck by the diversity of judicial response to a particular technology. In any event, these cases are extremely dependent on the specific types of devices being considered. Thus, a court might come to a different conclusion if presented with a more modern paging technological process where the caller's message is merely forwarded to the recipient's pager (without being recorded by the paging company), and the pager only displays the message on a small readout screen after being called up by a password.

A number of questions arise when section 184 of the *Criminal Code* and section 8 of the *Charter* are considered in the context of the Internet. Based on the holding in the *Fegan* and *Plant* cases that only the content of conversations is protected, would this imply that Internet service providers or network operators could monitor which Web sites a user visited, so long as the Internet service provider did not pry into the actual information retrieved? For instance, is cookie technology, comprising software that a third party can attach to an Internet browser in order to monitor the Web sites visited by another person without her knowledge (described in more detail in chapter 4, section A.1, "Privacy and Data Protection") outside the purview of subsection 184(1) so long as it does not relay the content of messages? And if subsection 184(1) does not apply to cookies, is paragraph 342.1(1)(b) applicable? (This provision is discussed in section B.3, "Computer Abuse.")

Given that the originator of the communication must have a reasonable expectation of privacy in her message for section 184 to apply, how will courts treat e-mail? Some would argue that most users are aware that system and network operators are always able to view e-mail, such that the proper analogy to e-mail is not the sealed envelope but the open-faced postcard (and hence senders of postcards, like e-mail, are more circumspect in what they say in their respective messages). The trial court in the *ACLU* decision observed that unlike mail in the postal system, e-mail sent over the Internet is not sealed or secure and can be accessed or viewed by intermediary computers between sender and recipient unless it is encrypted.[273] As well, e-mail

272 *United States v. Meriwether*, 917 F.2d 955 (6th Cir. 1990).
273 *ACLU*, above note 75.

can be easily, and is often, forwarded electronically by the recipient to other users; indeed, this is a prime feature of e-mail and makes it a very powerful and functional service. These attributes, consistent with the *Newell* case, would argue for the proposition that most e-mail over the Internet would not come within the definition of a private communication under subsection 184(1), and neither would messages posted to Web sites, bulletin boards, newsgroups, discussion forums, and the like. In support of this view is the American case law that holds that employees do not have a reasonable expectation of privacy in their e-mail generated at work.[274] In another American case, however, an appellate military court concluded that an e-mail user did have a reasonable expectation of privacy in those messages stored on computers of an online service which he alone could retrieve by use of a password and which had not yet been forwarded by the user to others.[275] In this case the court usefully differentiated between e-mail sent over the Internet and e-mail transmitted within the much more secure America Online system. Even within the latter, however, the court concluded there was a range of privacy expectations, with no right of privacy, for example, attaching to e-mails once they are forwarded from subscriber to subscriber. In effect, the court carefully dissected the different technologies and message-passing techniques to sensibly arrive at a result appropriate to the circumstances. This case illustrates that it is important to look at e-mail not as a single mode of communication, but rather to consider its various permutations, with the result that some, but not others, of it might meet the test for private communication under subsection 184(1). In such an analysis, for example, it would be important whether the particular type of e-mail is encrypted.

Put another way, one can envisage a continuum of electronic communications on the Internet from the perspective of determining which ones should reasonably attract an expectation of privacy. Clearly, messages posted to Web sites are "public" and should not be protected. At the other end, e-mail that is encrypted generally should be considered private, particularly where only one, or a small group of, recipient(s) is

---

274 See *Smyth* v. *Pillsbury Company*, 914 F.Supp. 97 (E.D. Pa. 1996), and *Bill McLaren, Jr.* v. *Microsoft Corp.*, 8 Computer Cases (CCH) ¶47,970 at 71,857 (Tex. Ct. App. 1999). These cases are discussed in chapter 4, section A.1(d), "Monitoring Employee E-mails."

275 *United States* v. *Maxwell*, 42 M.J. 568 (U.S. Air Force Ct. of Crim. App. 1995) [*Maxwell*]. For a case coming to essentially the same conclusion, and intimating that the user of a commercial ISP e-mail service may well be entitled to a reasonable expectation of privacy, see *R.* v. *Weir* (2001), 156 C.C.C. (3d) 188 (Alta. C.A.).

able to retrieve the message. But also in the private category, deserving of the protection of section 184, is the regular, unencrypted e-mail message that is intended for a single recipient, or a small group of recipients, where it is not reasonably foreseeable that the message would be further transmitted by the recipient without the permission of the sender. Such messages are not unlike regular mail or telephone conversations. They can be intercepted by network or system operators, but this monitoring is done to promote the technical and operational maintenance of the e-mail system, and not in order to hack into personal messages. It is similar to the phone company incidentally listening in on telephone calls as part of supporting the communications network. Thus lawyers, for example, should not have to encrypt their e-mails to clients to be able to maintain attorney-client privilege, as it would be an offence under section 184 to intercept these e-mails.[276]

11)   Search, Seizure, and Surveillance

In the previous section the issues related to section 184 of the *Criminal Code* were discussed and mention was made of section 8 of the *Charter*, which provides that "[e]veryone has the right to be secure against unreasonable search or seizure." A key question in light of this *Charter* section and the inexorable development of more and more sophisticated electronic and optical devices by which to monitor, track, and probe various aspects of individuals is, When should the police require prior judicial authorization, through the means of search warrants, before they can employ these high-tech products and mechanisms? In this regard it is important to note that the Supreme Court of Canada in the *Dyment*[277] case concluded that section 8 of the *Charter* should be interpreted in a broad and liberal manner so as to secure the citizen's right to a reasonable expectation of privacy against governmental encroachments. In this case the court adopted the views of a leading American proponent of privacy rights by stipulating that "society has come to realize that privacy is at the heart of liberty in a modern state. ... [G]rounded in man's physical and moral autonomy,

---

276 A number of U.S. state bar associations have rendered opinions to this effect: see Illinois State Bar Association, *Electronic Communications: Confidentiality of Client Information, Advertising and Solicitation*, Op. No. 96-10, 1997 WL 317367 (16 May 1997).

277 *R. v. Dyment*, [1988] 2 S.C.R. 417. In this case a police officer's receipt of a blood sample of the accused taken by a doctor who was administering medical treatment before any charges were laid was held to constitute an unreasonable search and seizure under s. 8 of the *Charter*.

privacy is essential for the well being of the individual."[278] The court then adopted the reasoning in a task force report of the Canadian government titled *Privacy and Computers* that privacy, in addition to protecting a person's home and person, also should arise in an information context. The court stated:

> Finally, there is privacy in relation to information. This too is based on the notion of the dignity and integrity of the individual. As the Task Force put it (13): "This notion of privacy derives from the assumption that all information about a person is in a fundamental way his own, for him to communicate or retain for himself as he sees fit." In modern society, especially, retention of information about oneself is extremely important. We may, for one reason or another, wish or be compelled to reveal such information, but situations abound where the reasonable expectations of the individual that the information shall remain confidential to the persons to whom, and restricted to the purposes for which it is divulged, must be protected. Governments at all levels have in recent years recognized this and have devised rules and regulations to restrict the uses of information collected by them to those for which it was obtained; see, for example, the *Privacy Act*.[279]

Notwithstanding these sentiments, the Supreme Court's approach to informational privacy in the context of search and seizure does not extend to records related to electricity consumption, given the decision in the *Plant* case.[280]

In a trio of important cases, the Supreme Court of Canada has held that three forms of high-tech surveillance offended section 8 of the *Charter*; though in all of them the evidence obtained was admitted because the court held doing so would not bring the administration of justice into disrepute.[281] In *R. v. Wise*, the court concluded that the

---

278 *Ibid.*, at 427.

279 *Ibid.*, at 429–30.

280 *Plant*, above note 258. But see also the discussion in *Kyllo*, above note 260.

281 Subsection 24(2) of the *Charter* provides that if evidence was obtained in a manner that infringes the freedoms of the *Charter*, the evidence is excluded if its admission would bring the administration of justice into disrepute; thus, evidence can be admitted even if it was obtained in a manner that violates s. 8 of the *Charter* if the court believes its admission will not bring the administration of justice into disrepute. But see also the decision of the Ontario Court of Appeal in *Tessling*, above note 263, where yet a fourth form of new technology, namely an infrared aerial camera that detects heat rays emanating from a house, was held to offend section 8 of the *Charter*, and the resulting evidence was excluded.

police could not use an electronic tracking device that attached to an automobile without first obtaining a search warrant.[282] In R. v. Wong the court also believed that judicial oversight was required for the use of tiny hidden cameras and microphones in a hotel room setting.[283] In concluding that the Charter protects against surreptitious video surveillance conducted by agents of the state, the court noted that "modern methods of electronic surveillance have the potential, if uncontrolled, to annihilate privacy."[284] Finally, in R. v. Duarte the court concluded that concealed audio surveillance through a small microphone violated section 8 of the Charter.[285] These are noteworthy cases for the Information Age, though their impact is somewhat dulled by the fact that the illegally obtained evidence was admitted in any event.

Notwithstanding this trio of Supreme Court cases, police are able to utilize high-tech equipment to conduct warrantless surveillance where the subject matter was in an open space. Thus, in R. v. Elzein, videotaping and photography by the police were found to be acceptable because the suspect was in a public place.[286] In a similar vein, in a recent case a court held that there was no violation when police conducted surveillance of a computer bulletin board operation by using a false identity to obtain online access to it, and when they kept a verbatim record of communications they had with the operation; again, an important element of the court's reasoning centred on the public nature of this particular bulletin board service.[287] The implications of these rulings could become disturbing given that, in respect of the Elzein case, more and more high-powered miniature cameras are being used to monitor more and more public areas, such as in some cities in England where whole sections of the downtown are blanketed with cameras.[288] When connected by powerful computer networks and visual image and data processing links, these cameras can produce an envi-

---

282 (1992), 70 C.C.C. (3d) 193 (S.C.C.) [Wise].
283 (1990), 60 C.C.C. (3d) 460 (S.C.C.) [Wong].
284 Ibid., at 479.
285 (1990), 53 C.C.C. (3d) 1 (S.C.C.) [Duarte].
286 (1993), 82 C.C.C. (3d) 455 (Que. C.A.) [Elzein].
287 R. v. Morin, [1996] R.J.Q. 1758 (Crim. Ct.). The court in this case summarized its view at 1764 as follows: "En somme, l'accusé a lancé des invitations générales de communiquer avec lui, et ce, à plusieurs reprises. Il est impossible de conclure qu'une personne raisonnable, dans la situation de l'accusé, pouvait s'attendre au respect de sa vie privée en de telles circonstances. Une personne raisonnable saurait que, lorsque de telles invitations sont lancées au public en général, elle ne peut pas s'attendre à ce qu'il n'y ait pas d'étrangers, y compris des policiers, qui communiquent avec elle."
288 See David Brin, "The Transparent Society," Wired, December 1996.

ronment where there is a conceptual shift from seemingly monitoring a physical place (for example, a specific lobby of a particular building), to tracking individuals. Similarly, it seems unreasonable that police should be able to conduct electronic surveillance on a bulletin board system operator in a sustained and detailed manner for as long as they please without some judicial oversight in the form of a warrant. Even if not problematic from a criminal search and seizure perspective, such camera-based environments and Internet-related activities raise serious privacy concerns of a more general nature, such as those discussed in chapter 4, section A, "Privacy and Data Protection."

In response to the *Wise*, *Wong*, and *Duarte* cases, the search warrant provisions of the *Criminal Code* have been recently augmented. The traditional provision, section 487, is virtually unchanged since the first Canadian *Criminal Code* in 1892, and permits a justice of the peace to issue a warrant for searching a "building, receptacle or place" where there are reasonable grounds to believe that an offence was committed therein and that there is anything that will afford evidence thereof. This provision is arguably limited to physical places, though it is open to question whether the word *place* might not be able to apply to a non-physical place, such as a site on the Internet.[289] As well, the evidence referred to in this provision again seems to contemplate physical items, as one court has concluded that it cannot be used to search for incorporeal items.[290] In the context of data, software, and other intangibles, therefore, this usually meant the police would take the whole computer and the tangible media on which the software resided. To remedy this deficiency, Bill C-17, enacted in April 1997, extended the coverage of section 487 to computers, so that police are now expressly permitted to search a computer system.[291] These new provisions are similar to

---

289 One commentator takes this view; see Davis & Hutchison, *Computer Crime*, above note 14.

290 See *Re Banque Royale du Canada and The Queen* (1985), 18 C.C.C. (3d) 98 (Que. C.A.), where a s. 487 warrant was held not to cover monies in a bank account.

291 The new additions to s. 487 read as follows:

(2.1) A person authorized under this section to search a computer system in a building or place for data may

(a) use or cause to be used any computer system at a building or place to search any data contained in or available to the computer system;

(b) reproduce or cause to be reproduced any data in the form of a print-out or other intelligible output;

(c) seize the print-out or other output for examination or copying; and

(d) use or cause to be used any copying equipment at the place to make copies of the data.

section 16 of the *Competition Act*, which since 1986 has permitted the investigating authorities to use the computers on the premises being searched to search any data available to the computer system.[292] This recognizes that in today's networked world an organization's data are often not physically located on its premises, or even in the computer located on its premises, but rather may reside in computers at distant locations. These are good examples of legislation striving to stay current with the new and ever-changing data processing and communications environment. In a recent case a court even upheld the ability of the investigating authorities under the *Competition Act* to bring their own software onto the premises to help facilitate a computer search.[293]

In 1993, several other search warrant provisions were added in light of the decisions in the *Wise, Wong,* and *Duarte* cases. Section 492.1 authorizes the issuances of warrants for electronic tracking devices, while section 492.2 does the same for telephone number recorders, the type of device discussed in the previous part in the *Griffith* and *Fegan* cases. In both of these new provisions the standard for issuing the warrant is a reasonable suspicion that an offence has occurred or will occur, which is lower than the reasonable belief standard in the traditional section 487. It should also be noted that the 1993 amendments included the new section 487.01, which permits the issuance of a warrant (on the reasonable belief standard) where no other provision in the *Criminal Code* or other statute authorizes the search. This latter provision is extremely broad and could conceivably be used to authorize any type of computer or network search imaginable. Section 487.1, also a new provision, establishes a procedure for applying for, and issuing, warrants by telephone, fax, and other telecommunications technologies.

Notwithstanding these new provisions, computer crime often presents investigators with thorny evidentiary problems. For example,

---

(2.2) Every person who is in possession or control of any building or place in respect of which a search is carried out under this section shall, on presentation of the warrant, permit the person carrying out the search

(a) to use or cause to be used any computer system at the building or place in order to search any data contained in or available to the computer system for data that the person is authorized by this section to search for;

(b) to obtain a hard copy of the data and to seize it; and

(c) to use or cause to be used any copying equipment at the place to make copies of the data.

292 R.S.C. 1985, c. C-34, as amended.
293 *Re United States Pipe and Founding Co.* (1994), 58 C.P.R. (3d) 463 (Ont. Gen. Div.).

given the elusiveness of information, it is common for the computer and Internet-based criminal to deny he had anything to do with the offensive conduct. Thus, in the *Pecciarich* case (above note 142), the defence counsel (echoing the second dynamic of computer law) argued that the accused should not be convicted because it was possible for someone other than the accused to have uploaded the pornographic material; that is, the defence contended that the connection between the accused and the impugned activity could not be conclusively proved in a computer-based environment. The court did not accept this argument, and held that the accused was responsible for the creation and distribution of the offending materials as a result of circumstantial evidence linking him to the materials. In another case, however, a court of appeal concluded that a bulletin board subscriber's payment for child pornography does not necessarily mean that the subscriber completed the download of the impugned material.[294] From time to time, accused also challenge the admissibility of computer-generated evidence, but, as explained in chapter 6, section B, "Evidence Law," these arguments usually fall on deaf ears given that most courts have been favourably disposed to admitting computer-generated evidence in criminal cases either under the *Canada Evidence Act* or the relevant common law rules. Counsel for accused can also propose some novel and intriguing arguments in respect of computer-related evidence. In one instance, the accused in an American first-degree murder case argued that he attempted to destroy completely the electronic version of a ransom note, but that it was retrieved from the computer's hard drive by authorities with the assistance of a software program.[295] The accused did not contest that the search warrant obtained by the police was improper with respect to the seizure of the computer, but argued it was inadequate to obtain the data from the computer that the accused mistakenly believed he had destroyed, and that a subsequent search warrant was required for this material. The court disagreed, and concluded:

> An attempt to destroy evidence is not equivalent to a legally protected expectation of privacy. Appellant's unsuccessful attempt to delete documents or files from his computer did not create a legally protected expectation of privacy which would have required a second warrant before the prosecution applied technology to elicit the content of files buried in the memory of the computer. At best, appellant had the

---

294 *R. v. Daniels* (1999), 177 D.L.R. (4th) 599 (Nfld. C.A.) [*Daniels*].
295 *Commonwealth v. Copenhefer*, 587 A.2d 1353 (Pa. 1991).

hope of achieving secrecy, but his hope did not prohibit the state from subjecting validly seized physical evidence from any scientific analysis possible within current technology.[296]

a) Post-9/11 Law Reform

It is trite to say that the terrorist attacks in New York and Washington on September 11, 2001, (referred to as "9/11") have changed dramatically the U.S. government's approach to security. Other governments, including those in Canada and the United Kingdom, have also responded to the increased threat to national security. This has resulted in a situation where the tension between security and freedom is palpable, problematic, and profound in the post-9/11 world along the information technology frontier. On the one hand, certain software, database, networking, and optical surveillance technologies greatly enhance the ability of law enforcement agencies to track, detect, and deter criminal and terrorist activity. On the other hand, these technologies of intrusion threaten informational and other freedoms. The result is one of the classic conundrums posed by information technology throughout this book: How do we balance its ability to promote both positive and negative conduct?

In terms of a legislative response, the United States has passed several statutes that enhance the government's electronic investigatory powers, including the *Patriot Act*[297] and the *Homeland Security Act*.[298] Collectively, these laws, among other things, expand the government's powers of wire-tapping and electronic surveillance, augmented the situations under which devices such as pen registers and trap and trace devices might be used during emergencies, and increase the penalties for various computer-related crimes. As well, they facilitate greater sharing of intelligence with foreign governments. They have also put a greater onus on intermediaries, such as Internet service providers, to disclose certain confidential information in various circumstances.

The Canadian government also responded to the new security environment of post-9/11. In a series of legislative initiatives,[299] Ottawa has

---

296 *Ibid.*, at 1356.
297 18 USC 2517. For a discussion of this legislation, see "A Question of Freedom," *The Economist*, 8 March 2003.
298 H.R. 5005. This statute includes the *2002 Cyber Security Enhancement Act*.
299 See the *Anti-Terrorism Act, 2001*, S.C. 2001, c.41 (Bill C-36); Bill C-44, an *Act to Amend the Aeronautics Act*, R.S. c.A-2; and Bill 55, the *Public Safety Act, 2002*. For an overview of the U.K.'s analogous laws, see "Freedom and Anti-Terrorism: Coming Quietly," *The Economist*, 1 March 2003.

increased its search and seizure and electronic investigatory powers. Several government departments also released, in August 2002, a discussion paper on the various options being considered by the government in the area of electronic surveillance and investigatory techniques.[300] The paper begins with express recognition of the problems posed to law enforcement agencies of the first and fourth dynamics of computer law, namely the rapid pace of technological change and the blurring of national/international. On the technology front, the paper is particularly conscious of the technical challenges posed by wireless communications, the Internet and e-mail. An overriding theme is that entities that operate transmission facilities, such as ISPs, should be required to ensure that their systems have the technical capability to provide government agencies with lawful access. This would be mandated in general terms, and then regulations would flesh out the specific technical details that each operator would have to implement. The paper also addresses the cost implications of this regime, which presumably would not be trivial. The paper also speaks to several initiatives to implement new production, assistance, and data-preservation orders in an electronic environment. In this area the paper calls for harmonization with the new *Convention on Cybercrime*.[301] And finally, the paper suggests greater clarity on the legal status of e-mail, given that it raises multiple questions (such as whether it is a "private communication").[302]

While the consultation paper on lawful access has been criticized, invariably many of its proposals will be implemented, given the heightened concern for security in the post-9/11 era.[303] Indeed, as Internet usage becomes ubiquitous, and as still more new and intrusive surveillance and electronic investigatory technologies come to market, many more issues involving the tension between electronic security and digital freedom will need to be resolved. May we have the collective sense and insight, fostered through deep and sustained dialogue between the government and interested citizens and organizations, to resolve them in a way that enhances our security to the fullest while preserving our personal privacy and other rights to the maximum.

---

300 Department of Justice, Industry Canada and Solicitor General Canada, *Lawful Access — Consultation Document*, 25 August, 2002, available at <Canada.justice.gc.ca/en/cons/la_al/.>.

301 See below, at note 310.

302 This question is discussed in various parts of this book, including at the end of section B.10(b), "Expectation of Privacy," earlier in this chapter.

303 Michael Geist, "Federal Proposal Tells Only Part of Cybercrime Story," *The Globe and Mail* (3 October 2002).

12)   International Issues

The global nature of the computer business and the transnational reach of computer networks highlight the fourth dynamic of computer law, the blurring of the national and international realms. The ability of computer criminals to access computer facilities easily in other countries through international telecommunications hubs, and the extremely mobile nature of data and information, raise a number of international legal issues in a criminal law context. Given Canada's federal structure, questions of jurisdiction between courts of different provinces are addressed in several provisions of the *Criminal Code*. For example, under paragraph 476(e), an offence committed through the mails can be prosecuted either where the letter was posted, or where it was received, or in any place in between where the letter passed. In the international sphere, notwithstanding subsection 6(2) of the *Criminal Code*, which provides that no one can be convicted in Canada of an offence committed outside the country, courts in Canada, the United States, and elsewhere (including in the United Kingdom) have routinely exercised criminal jurisdiction if the facts underlying the activity have a real and substantial connection to the host country or have an effect upon it.[304]

In addition to the jurisdiction question, transnational computer crime has brought into focus the need for international cooperation in the computer crime field. There is, for example, a need to harmonize computer crime laws because mutual assistance or joint efforts in bringing to justice felons using the Internet, through extradition and other forms of mutual assistance, are only possible if the underlying laws of the two relevant countries are more or less equivalent.[305] The alternative is the development of computer crime havens, countries from which computer felons operate with impunity. For example, law enforcement agencies were stymied initially in their attempts to bring to justice the Philippine-based perpetrator of the Love Bug virus because that country did not have adequate computer crime laws.[306] An example of this can already be seen with gaming on the Internet, as dis-

---

304 For a discussion of these and other jurisdiction-related cases see chapter 7, section B.2(a), "Regulatory/Criminal Jurisdiction."

305 For example, obtaining evidence in foreign jurisdictions for use in Canadian courtrooms is governed by the *Mutual Legal Assistance in Criminal Matters Act*, R.S.C. 1985, c. 30 (4th Supp.).

306 "Hacked Off in the Philippines," *The Economist*, 13 May 2000; and Daniel McHardie, "Cyber-crime Havens Seen Emerging," *The Globe and Mail* (10 May 2000).

cussed in section B.8, "Gaming and Betting." Canada regulates gaming, as does the United States. As a result, the bulk of the operators of Internet gaming sites operate from Central American or Caribbean countries in an effort to elude North American law enforcement efforts. Nevertheless, courts in the United States have taken the position that the government has jurisdiction to prosecute the provider of such a service in the state in which customers of the service access it.[307] One enforcement option if the prosecution is successful is to order all Internet service providers in the jurisdiction to cease to carry access to the offending Web site. This, of course, will be difficult, because the site likely will reappear again, under a different domain name. Given the fourth dynamic of computer law, truly effective action against international computer crime will require harmonization of computer crime laws. To this end, the members of the OECD, the Council of Europe, and the United Nations have all undertaken activities to create guidelines for, and to coordinate the implementation of, computer crime legislation. Canada has been extremely active in these efforts,[308] but more needs to be done including the crafting of an international convention that would specifically address the prosecution of computer crime with an international dimension.[309]

In light of the foregoing, it is interesting to note that the Council of Europe (which is a treaty-making body not formally associated with the European Union) has adopted the first international treaty dealing with computer crime issues, namely the *Convention on Cybercrime*.[310] The Convention strives to achieve several purposes. First, it attempts to harmonize substantive criminal law by setting out minimum standards for offences such as computer abuse, viruses, e-mail interception and copyright infringement.[311] Second, the treaty hopes to standardize

---

307 *Granite Gate*, above note 229; this case, and other similar ones, are discussed under the Internet jurisdiction in chapter 7, section B.2(a), "Regulatory/Criminal Jurisdiction." The state of Missouri takes a similar view: see above note 228.

308 For example, Canada's Donald Piragoff of the Federal Department of Justice was the primary author of the UN's computer crime handbook.

309 One positive development is that Interpol has turned its attention to fighting Internet crime: "Interpol to Target Web Crime," *The Globe and Mail* (6 November 2000).

310 The *Convention* was signed on 23 November 2001 by twenty-six Council of Europe member states and four non-member states that assisted with the drafting, including Canada.

311 Nine offences are slotted into four categories: offences against confidentiality, integrity, and availability of computer data and systems (covers illegal interception, access, data, and computer interference and misuse of computers); computer-related offences (includes forgery using a computer, and computer fraud);

the criminal law procedures related to computer and digital evidence and other matters related to the prosecution of computer crime.[312] And finally it hopes to facilitate more efficient and deeper processes for international cooperation on computer crime matters. As with all such efforts, the convention is not without its critics.[313] On balance, however, given the fourth dynamic of computer law, it is a welcome addition to the tool kit of law enforcement agencies that have the difficult task of combating computer crime in the context of a globally hyperactive Internet.

---

content-related offences (includes criminalizing child pornography); and copyright offences (makes wilful infringement of a copyright by means of a computer an offence).

312 Procedural powers contemplated by the Convention include search and seizure of computer data; interception of content-related data; collection of traffic data in real-time; and preservation of traffic and stored data.

313 See "Group Blasts Web Crime Treaty," *The Globe and Mail* (21 December 2000). This piece notes that The Global Internet Liberty Campaign, which includes the Canadian Journalists for Free Expression and the American Civil Liberties Union, contend that the Convention "would undermine network security, reduce government accountability and improperly lengthen the reach of law enforcement."

CHAPTER 4

REGULATING INFORMATION, TECHNOLOGY, AND E-COMMERCE

Governments regulate information in order to achieve a number of objectives. They institute and administer data protection laws in an effort to protect the privacy of individuals. Governments control the export of certain high-tech information in order to protect a nation's security interests. In the area of telecommunications and broadcasting, the Canadian government exercises the regulatory power to preserve and enhance Canadian culture, sovereignty, and a host of other objectives. Governments also pass laws to protect the interests of consumers, as there are many nefarious fraudsters who would perpetrate scams over the Internet. In each of these areas two important questions can be asked. The initial, threshold-level inquiry is whether governments should regulate these areas of endeavour at all. The answer to this question will be based on an amalgam of policy and political considerations. If the decision is made to introduce government regulation, then the analysis shifts to determining the optimum manner in which such regulation may be effected. In this regard it is important to understand that the four dynamics of computer law — the torrid pace of technological change, the elusive nature of information, and the blurring of private/public and national/international — are making it more difficult for governments to regulate computers, networks, data, and e-commerce activities effectively.[1]

---

1   These dynamics are important and are a unifying theme throughout this book. For a
    discussion of these dynamics, see chapter 8, section A, "Computer Law: Dynamics."

A. PRIVACY AND DATA PROTECTION

Privacy has been expressed as the fourfold right to control intrusion into a person's seclusion or solitude; control the disclosure of embarrassing private facts about the person; prevent being put into a false light in the public eye; and control the exploitation of a person's image and likeness.[2] It is increasingly difficult for individuals to protect these rights in the Information Age; indeed some commentators conclude that privacy does not stand a chance.[3] And if the prospects for privacy were bleak before the terrorist attacks of September 11, 2001, they are positively depressing after this date given the additional sacrifices privacy will have to make in the name of security.[4] Computers, databases,

---

2   William L. Prosser, "Privacy" (1960) 48 Calif. L.R. 383 ["Privacy"]. Each of these rights, which David H. Flaherty, in "Some Reflections on Privacy and Technology" (1999) 26 Man. L. J. 219 ["Privacy and Technology"] refers to as solitude, intimacy, anonymity, and reserve, is the subject of discussion in this book. Controlling intrusion is the subject of chapter 3, sections B.3, "Computer Abuse," B.10, "Interception of Communications," and B.11, "Search, Seizure, and Surveillance," as well as some discussion in the next section below; the regulation of personal information is dealt with in the bulk of section A, "Privacy and Data Protection"; the right to avoid being put in a false light is the subject of the libel discussion in chapter 7, section A, "Cyber Libel"; and the exploitation of image and likeness is touched upon briefly in section A.1 of this chapter, "Privacy Laws."

3   See "The End of Privacy" and "The Surveillance Society," *The Economist*, 1 May 1999. These articles take a decidedly gloomy view of the prospects for privacy: given the privacy-eroding impact of technology, in the not-to-distant future there will simply be no privacy left, and there is little that technology or legal solutions can do about this inexorable development. The authors' prescription? "Get used to it." Recent books that echo the sentiment about privacy losing the battle to technology include Simson Garfinkel, *Database Nation: The Death of Privacy in the 21st Century* (Cambridge: O'Reilly, 2000); Jeffrey Rosen, *The Unwanted Gaze: The Destruction of Privacy in America* (New York: Random House, 2000); and Reg Whitaker, *The End of Privacy: How Total Surveillance Is Becoming a Reality* (New York: New Press, 1999). Some commentary has also noted that many people are willing to give up some degree of privacy to private sector service suppliers in return for security or convenience: "Go On, Watch Me," *The Economist*, 17 August 2002.

4   "Liberty v. Security," *The Economist*, 29 September 2001. See also Miro Cernetig, "Uncle Sam and Big Brother," *The Globe and Mail* (25 November 2002), which describes a proposal to create a supercomputer that would search a massive database that would bring together, at the U.S. border, a traveller's credit card purchases, travel patterns, health and bank records and previous telephone conversations (see also "New U.S. Rules to Require More Data from Canadian Travellers," *The Globe and Mail* (4 January 2003)). A similar concept in Canada has Canadian privacy advocates up in arms: Kim Lunman, "Air-Travel Database Plan Alarms Rights Advocates," *The Globe and Mail* (28 September 2002). Canada's privacy commis-

and telecommunications networks, not to mention current developments in photography and other surveillance technologies,[5] present significant threats to people's privacy.[6] In particular, the Internet, and the computer and networking technologies that underpin it, allows for hitherto unknown degrees of data collection techniques, by express collection of data from consumers through sign-up activities and the like,[7]

---

sioner is fairly comfortable with new measures taken to combat terrorism, but is extremely concerned that these new measures not be utilized for governmental purposes completely unrelated to terrorism suppression, such as routine income tax investigations: Campbell Clark, "Canadian Privacy Rights at Risk, Radwanski Says," *The Globe and Mail* (30 January 2003). In Japan, a proposed new national database is also encountering serious opposition, in part because of the fear that data will leak from the system: "There's Always Someone Looking at You — And the People Don't Like It," *The Economist*, 10 August 2002.

5   For example, by hiding small cameras in the ceilings of stores, retailers can create "consumer observation laboratories" in order to track shoppers' behaviour: John Heinzl, "Some Retailers Watching Your Every Move," *The Globe and Mail* (3 May 2002). Employee surveillance is another application for video cameras. In a recent American survey, over 30 percent of companies acknowledged watching staff through them for security reasons; Marjo Johne, "Is Someone Watching You," *The Globe and Mail* (10 January 2003).

6   For a good survey of the various threats to privacy that have surfaced over the past decade, see *Privacy Commissioner of Canada, Annual Report, 1999–2000* (Ottawa: the Privacy Commissioner of Canada, 2000 [*2000 Privacy Commissioner Annual Report*]. The privacy commissioner who penned this report was Bruce Phillips, a former journalist. There is a large literature, authored principally by journalists, that focuses on the erosion of privacy in the face of new and ever-menacing technology; the other genre of privacy writing is the academic defence of privacy rights, as exemplified in Prosser's "Privacy," at note 2 above, and West-in's *Privacy and Freedom*, at note 55 below. For an example of the former, journalist variety, see David Brin, "The Transparent Society," *Wired*, December 1996, which gives a revealing description of new surveillance techniques engendered by miniature cameras. In a recent book, *The Transparent Society* (New York: Addison-Wesley, 1999), David Brin also argues that privacy is doomed. His prescription? Transparency: let everyone see everything on everyone else, with the result, he hopes, that this would result in less data being collected in the first place.

7   Including through online registration screens, survey forms, user profile requests, order fulfilment processes, mailing lists, etc. The Internet also is a very powerful tool for information dissemination, so much so that various Canadian provincial governments have decided to stop making certain family law court decisions available over the Internet due to the disclosure of personal information, even though the public can otherwise get copies of these decisions: Kim Bolan, "B.C. to Close Court Web Site Offering Lurid Case Details," *The Globe and Mail* (12 July 2002). Digital rights management systems, which will become ubiquitous for selling digital content rights over the Internet, also present some finicky privacy issues: see Information and Privacy Commissioner of Ontario, *Privacy and Digital Rights Management: An Oxymoron*, October 2002, available at <ipc.on.ca>.

but also by less visible means such as "cookies" and software that tracks online browsing and other activity and e-mail, fax, and other communications.[8] Each of the four dynamics of computer law presents significant obstacles to the preservation of privacy.[9] Most observers view this as an unfortunate byproduct of modern technology, given that privacy is necessary for people's emotional and psychological well-being.[10] Accordingly, many look to the law to offer a bulwark against the various technologies and business practices that threaten privacy, though it should also be stated that technology itself can assist in protecting privacy, as noted by a former justice minister of Canada in a speech on privacy and data protection.[11] For example, there are a number of services

---

8   For an exposition of some of these privacy-eroding technologies and techniques, see Paul M Schwartz, "Privacy and Democracy in Cyberspace" (1999) 52 Vand. L. Rev. 1609 ["Privacy and Democracy"]. Cookies pose a real conundrum. On the one hand, by storing information such as passwords, preferences, profiles, registration information, and personal buying history, they help make the Web experience more efficient and rewarding, as they help the user navigate through a huge ocean of choices and data by, for example, customizing advertisements to an individual's previous purchasing history. On the other hand, it is precisely these powerful positive aspects of cookies that, when misused, create such concerns from a privacy perspective. As for allegations of e-mail monitoring, see Terry Pedwell, "Canada's Eavesdropping on Citizens, Ex-Spy Says," *The Globe and Mail* (19 June 1999), which discusses Echelon, a computer system that allegedly monitors e-mail, fax and phone messages.

9   The third dynamic, the blurring of private and public, is particularly pronounced. When a user surfs the Internet, visiting, for example, political, religious or adult entertainment Web sites, it seems like a very private exercise: the user is in the privacy of her own home, and no one else is around (or so it seems). But in fact, the techniques and technologies described in Schwartz, "Privacy and Democracy," above note 8, cause the seemingly private activity of Web surfing to become public.

10 See Arthur R. Miller, *The Assault on Privacy: Computers, Data Banks, and Dossiers* (Ann Arbor: University of Michigan Press, 1971). Note, however, that not all commentators place such a high value on privacy: see Richard A. Posner, "The Right of Privacy" (1978) 12 Ga. Law Rev. 393, in which the author, an exponent of the law and economics school, concludes at 419 that keeping personal data private in certain circumstances is economically inefficient: "If what is revealed is something the individual has concealed for purposes of misrepresenting himself to others, the fact that disclosure is offensive to him ... is no better reason for protecting his privacy than if a seller advanced such arguments for being allowed to continue to engage in false advertising of his goods."

11 Hon. Allan Rock, Minister of Justice and Attorney General of Canada, "Notes for an Address to the Eighteenth International Conference on Privacy and Data Protection," 18 September 1996 [Notes]. These notes are available at: <infoweb@magi.com/~privcan/conf96/se_rock.html>. See also Flaherty, "Privacy

available on the Internet that, through the use of pseudonyms, encryption, and network technologies, can make a user's Internet presence anonymous.[12] There have also been a number of business responses to the call for greater privacy-enhancing practices.[13] Nevertheless, these will likely never obviate the need for some form of legislated regime for privacy protection. The legal subfield of data protection relates to the various statutory and other legal measures that have been implemented, or that are advocated, to control the collection, use, and dissemination of personal data. Before turning to this important area, however, it is worth highlighting several aspects of privacy law.

---

and Technology," above note 2, which discusses "privacy-enhancing technologies," such as biometrics, smart cards, active badges, passwords, and audit trails, and recounts how the transition, years ago, from the multiuser "party" telephone line, that permitted eavesdropping on neighbours' telephone calls, to the private line, was another good example of technology improving privacy. See also *2000 Privacy Commissioner Annual Report*, above note 6 at 17, regarding the "double-edged sword" dimension of new technology: it has potential for both good and harm, from a privacy perspective. For a court's recognition of the privacy-enhancing properties of technology, see *Bernstein v. U.S. Department of Justice*, 974 FSupp. 1288; on appeal 192 F.3d 1308 (9th Cir. 1999) rehearing ordered, opinion withdrawn. In this case, the court began by recognizing the privacy-eroding effects of technology, proving that it is not just journalists who tilt at this windmill: "Whether we are surveilled by our government, by criminals, or by our neighbours, it is fair to say that never has our ability to shield our affairs from prying eyes been at such a low ebb." Then the court offered the technology sinecure: "The availability and use of secure encryption may offer an opportunity to reclaim some portion of the privacy we have lost."

12   See, for example, <anonymizer.com>, <proxymate.com>, <onion-router.net/> and <zeroknowledge.com>. See also Steven Chase, "Users Flock to PrivacyX's No Questions E-mail Service," *The Globe and Mail* (12 September 2000). It should be noted, however, that with respect to some areas of the law, such as libel, operating under an alias can raise additional issues: see chapter 7, section A.3, "Anonymity and the Internet."

13   For example, see American Express' Private Payments system, which essentially creates a one-time use charge card by generating a new card number for every online purchase. Also, a company called Disappearing has created an e-mail technology that generates messages that wipe themselves from recipient computers after a period of time. For a book that encourages business to take the high ground in the technology versus privacy battle, by treating privacy enhancements as an important commercial opportunity, see Ann Cavoukian and Don Tapscott, *Who knows: Safeguarding Privacy in a Networked World* (New York: McGraw-Hill, 1997).

1) Privacy Laws

Canadian law,[14] like that of the United Kingdom,[15] does not recognize a general "right of privacy";[16] there is in Canada, for example, no general tort of invasion of privacy.[17] Contrast this to the American tradition of a much stronger support for a right of privacy, dating from at least the famous essay by Samuel Warren and Louis Brandeis,[18] in which these later-to-be famous judges articulated privacy as the "right to be let alone." They were reacting, obviously, not to the computer, but to their own era's new technology-based privacy usurper, namely photography, coupled with mass distributed, inexpensive newspapers (essentially, the tabloid press). One can only imagine what Warren and Brandeis would think about privacy rights in today's networked world. The American

---

14   For an overview of Canadian privacy law, see Barbara McIsaac, Rick Shields & Kris Klein, *The Law of Privacy in Canada* (Scarborough, ON: Carswell, 2000).

15   *Kaye* v. *Robertson*, [1991] FSR 62 (C.A.). For an excellent discussion of U.K. privacy law, see Raymond Wacks, *Personal Information: Privacy and the Law* (Oxford: Clarendon Press, 1989) [*Personal Information*]. For a more recent (and pessimistic) analysis by the same author, see Raymond Wacks, "Privacy in Cyberspace: Personal Information, Free Speech, and the Internet," in Peter Birks, ed. *Privacy and Loyalty* (Oxford: Clarendon Press, 1997). However, in a recent case, *Douglas* v. *Hello! Ltd.* [2001] F.S.R. 40 (C.A.) [*Hello!*], at least one judge was prepared to equate a breach of confidence to a right of privacy. In this decision, Sedley L.J. stated at pars. 110, 111 and 126: "Nevertheless, we have reached a point at which it can be said with confidence that the law recognizes and will appropriately protect a right of personal privacy. The reasons are twofold. First, equity and the common law are today in a position to respond to an increasingly invasive social environment by affirming that everybody has a right to some private space. What a concept of privacy does, however, is accord recognition to the fact that the law has to protect not only those people whose trust has been abused but those who simply find themselves subjected to an unwanted intrusion into their personal lives. The law no longer needs to construct an artificial relationship of confidentiality between intruder and victim: it can recognize privacy itself as a legal principle drawn from the fundamental value of personal autonomy."

16   At least one Canadian privacy rights advocate has called for the *Charter of Rights and Freedoms* to be explicitly amended to include the right to privacy: see Flaherty, "Privacy and Technology," above note 2, at 221.

17   While this has been the traditional view in Canada, there are some more recent cases that are coming very close to recognizing a common law right of privacy. For example, in *Dyne Holdings Ltd.* v. *Royal Insurance Co. of Canada* (1996), 138 Nfld. & P.E.I.R. 318 (PEI Sup. Ct.) the court, after a lengthy review of the authorities, concluded, at para. 63: "It would seem to me the courts in Canada are not far from recognizing a common law right of privacy if they have not already done so."

18   "The Right to Privacy" (1890) 4 Harv. L. Rev. 193. But see below, note 145.

constitution does not include an express right of privacy and that not all American courts have assiduously followed the noble sentiments expressed by Warren and Brandeis in their renowned essay. For example, in *Olmstead* v. *United States*,[19] the U.S. Supreme Court held that there was no privacy right against police wire-tapping because there was no physical intrusion; the articulate dissent by Brandeis in *Olmstead* does not carry the day until *Katz* v. *United States*,[20] which held that wire-tapping a public phone booth was unconstitutional under the U.S. Fourth Amendment (which protects against unreasonable search and seizure). Even today, however, the U.S. judiciary's support of informational privacy is not unanimous: see the *Dwyer* decision referred to in note 68. On the other hand, the United States does recognize four distinct torts, each of which constitutes an invasion of privacy:

1) intrusion upon the plaintiff's seclusion or solitude or into his private affairs;
2) public disclosure of embarrassing private facts about the plaintiff;
3) publicity which places the plaintiff in a false light in the public eye;
4) appropriation, for the defendant's advantage, of the plaintiff's name or likeness.[21]

a)   Tort-Oriented Privacy Statutes

Although Canada does not recognize a general right of privacy, there are a number of statutes and judicial principles that have been used by courts in Canada to support various privacy rights. In the constitutional setting, section B.10, "Interception of Communications," and section B.11, "Search, Seizure, and Surveillance," in chapter 3 discussed how the Supreme Court of Canada in several cases has concluded that section 8 of the *Charter*, which provides protection against unreasonable search and seizure, should be interpreted in a broad and liberal manner so as to secure the citizen's right to a reasonable expectation of privacy against governmental encroachments, including in the context of informational privacy.[22] As well, in four provinces there

---

19   277 U.S. 438 (1928) [*Olmstead*].
20   389 U.S. 347 (1967).
21   *Bill McLaren, Jr.* v. *Microsoft Corp.*, 8 Computer Cases (CCH) ¶47,970 at 71,857 (Tex. Ct. App. 1999) [*Bill McLaren*]. These four torts comprise the fourfold right to privacy referred to by Prosser in "Privacy," above note 2.
22   *Canadian Charter of Rights and Freedoms*, Part I of the *Constitution Act, 1982*, R.S.C. 1985, Appendix II, No. 44, being Schedule B to the *Canada Act 1982* (U.K.), 1982, c. 11. See also chapter 3, section B.11, "Search, Seizure, and Surveillance," for a discussion of privacy of messages sent over telecommunications networks under the criminal law.

are privacy statutes that establish a tort, actionable without proof of damages, where someone knowingly and unreasonably violates the privacy of another person.[23] These statutes do not define *privacy*, but generally set out the following as acts that constitute a violation of privacy: audio or visual surveillance of a person or the person's home by any means, including eavesdropping or spying on the person; except for British Columbia, listening to or recording a person's conversation or listening to or recording messages travelling to or coming from that person by telecommunications;[24] except for British Columbia, use of a person's letters, diaries, or other personal documents without the person's consent; and use of a person's likeness (or in British Columbia, "portrait"), name, or voice for advertising, sales promotion, or other commercial use without the person's consent. These rights are not absolute. Except for Manitoba's statute, these laws provide that the nature and degree of protection of privacy to which a person has a right is that which is reasonable under the circumstances, taking into account the interests of third parties. All statutes provide several

---

23   In Newfoundland — *An Act Respecting the Protection of Personal Privacy*, R.S.N. 1990, c. P-22; in Manitoba — *The Privacy Act*, R.S.M. 1987, c. P-125; in Saskatchewan — *An Act Respecting the Protection of Privacy*, R.S.S. 1978, c. P-24; and in British Columbia — *Privacy Act*, R.S.B.C. 1979, c. 336. It should be noted that while these statutes are generally animated by the same principles, there are a number of differences between them, and in particular the British Columbia statute differs in several important respects from the other three. Recently, a class action suit was commenced against a number of organizations, and the computer services company that managed their data on an outsourced basis, when a hard drive containing customer information went missing: Peter Kennedy, "Investors Group Warns Client Information Stolen," *The Globe and Mail* (3 February 2003); and Paul Waldie & Jacquie McNish, "Missing Computer Disk Spurs Suit," *The Globe and Mail* (4 February 2003). In the Statement of Claim (*Alex Taylor et al. v. Her Majesty The Queen in Right of Saskatchewan et al.*, Q.B. No. 243 of 2003, filed 3 February 2003), the plaintiffs frame their causes of action as breach of fiduciary duty, negligence, breach of confidence, breach of contract and confidentiality, violation of privacy, and statutory liability. The damages claimed include emotional trauma, as a result of the plaintiffs being exposed to the possible theft of their identities. With the hard drive being recovered shortly after it went missing, it will be interesting to see if this action is ultimately pursued by the plaintiffs.

24   See, for example, *Ferguson v. McBee Technologies Inc.* (1989), 24 C.P.R. (3d) 240 (Man. Q.B.), also discussed in chapter 3, section B.10, "Interception of Communications," where the prohibition against interception of communications in Manitoba's *Privacy Act* was held to be broader than the interception of private communications provisions in s. 184 of the *Criminal Code*.

defences, including explicit or implicit consent of the targeted individual, investigations by public authorities, news gathering activities, and publications that are in the public interest or constitute fair comment or that are privileged under the rules of the defamation law. Assuming these defences do not apply, the statutes provide for various remedies, including damages, injunctions, an accounting of profits, and delivery of documents that have resulted from the wrongful act.

These four privacy statutes raise several questions in the context of modern computer and network technologies. For example, how would the audio and visual surveillance provisions apply to the Internet? "Cookie" technology, for instance, comprises a software device that can be attached to a user's Internet browser when the user visits the cookie implanter's Web site.[25] The cookie can then tell the implanter what pages of the Web site were visited by the user, and in certain circumstances there is also the capability to have the cookie relay back to the implanter what other Web sites the user visits, and what the user buys there, etc. This information, which effectively tracks someone's "clickstream," could then be made available by the cookie implanter to third parties, such as merchants looking for high-quality data on the purchasing preferences of individuals, particularly if the cookie-derived data, which is generally anonymous in the sense it alone does not reveal the identity of the Web surfer, is combined with personally identified data.[26] It is unclear if the antisurveillance provisions of the above-noted privacy statutes cover cookie and cookielike technologies. As well, in terms of the unauthorized recording of messages provisions, the Newfoundland and Saskatchewan statutes afford protection for messages sent by telecommunications, whereas Manitoba's equivalent

---

25 For a brief overview of cookie technology, see Stephen H. Wildstrom, "They're Watching You Online," *Business Week*, 11 November 1996, and Stephen H. Wildstrom, "Privacy and the 'Cookie' Monster," *Business Week*, 16 December 1996. For more information on cookies, see <illuminatus.com/cookie.fcgi>.

26 This is what DoubleClick planned to do a few years ago when it bought Abacus. DoubleClick had amassed a vast amount of anonymous cookie-based data as a result of its "ad-serving" business; Abacus had a huge pool of personally identifiable consumer data from catalogue lists. DoubleClick planned to merge all this data, until an investigation by the Federal Trade Commission, several lawsuits by state attorneys general, a number of class action suits, and a significant backlash in the media and from privacy advocates precipitated a significant drop in DoubleClick's share price, and prompted an abandonment of this idea: see "DoubleClick Backtracks," *The Globe and Mail* (9 March 2000); and "The Internet's Chastened Child," *The Economist*, 11 November 2000.

provision refers to messages sent over the telephone. This latter formulation is arguably narrower, and may not be broad enough to capture certain Internet-related transmissions if, as in a 1992 decision, matters pertaining to the "telephone" are held to relate to the transmission of sounds and voice only.[27]

b) Quebec and Personality Rights

With respect to the other provinces, articles 3, 35, and 36 of Quebec's Civil Code expressly provide for the right of privacy, and specifically the interception of communications, surveillance, use of personal documents, and appropriation of image are enumerated as constituting invasions of the privacy of a person.[28] In a recent case, the Supreme Court of Canada affirmed the decision of the Quebec Court of Appeal that prohibited a literary magazine from using the picture of a woman seated in a public place on the grounds that it violated her right to privacy under the Quebec *Civil Code* and specifically her right to remain anonymous.[29] As for the right of publicity in the common law provinces beyond the aforementioned privacy statutes, judges in Canada have found there to be a tort of appropriation of personality where the likeness of a person has been used for commercial gain for purposes of commercial endorsement.[30] In a recent decision the court stressed that this right of publici-

---

27   *IBM Canada Ltd.* v. *Deputy M.N.R., Customs and Excise*, [1992] 1 F.C. 663 (C.A.). See, however, the discussion of this case in chapter 3, section B.6, "Illegal Speech," given that its precedential value in the context of a law such as a privacy statute may be questionable, and in particular note the *Zündel* decision in that section, which finds, under a human rights statute, that "telephonically" does capture Internet-related transmissions.

28   *Code Civil du Quebec*, R.S.Q. 1991, c. 64. Article 35 provides for "un droit a la vie privée." See *Houle* v. *Mascouche (Ville)* (1999), 179 D.L.R. (4th) 90 (Q.C.A.), where these provisions were relied on to prevent a municipality from using recordings made of an employee's wireless telephone conversations.

29   *Aubry* v. *Editions Vice-Versa Inc.*, [1998] 1 S.C.R. 591 [*Vice Versa*], affirming *Aubry* v. *Duclos* (1996), 141 D.L.R. (4th) 683 (Que. C.A.). The Quebec Court of Appeal decision contains a discussion of a number of earlier Quebec cases involving personality rights, which include, in appropriate circumstances, the right to privacy and anonymity. The court in *Hello!*, above note 15, talks at length about the *Vice Versa* case, and comments favourably on its rights-based genesis.

30   See *Athans* v. *Canadian Adventure Camps Ltd.* (1977), 17 O.R. (2d) 425 (H.C.J.); and *Krouse* v. *Chrysler Canada Ltd.* (1973), 40 D.L.R. (3d) 15 (Ont. C.A.) [*Krouse*]. For an American case, see *KNB Enterprises* v. *Matthews*, 92 Cal. Rptr. 2d 713 (Cal. Ct. App., 2d Dist. 2000), where a personality right, separate and distinct from the copyright in a photograph, was held to exist in a photograph of a model posted on a Web site.

ty is quite different from a right of privacy; for example, the latter, as provided in the abovementioned privacy statutes, ends upon the death of the subject individual, while the right of publicity, which the court characterized as "a form of intangible property akin to copyright or patent," can be inherited by heirs.[31]

c) Breaches of Confidence

From time to time, the law of nuisance has also been pressed into service in the interests of preserving privacy. In one case, the plaintiffs were granted an injunction and damages against the defendant public authority for following, watching, and besetting the plaintiffs' boat in Toronto harbour.[32] In another case, a plaintiff brought a case against relatives for continual harassment through telephone calls and letters.[33] In this latter decision the court recognized a claim in nuisance by invasion of privacy through the abuse of the telephone system, because of the annoying ringing of the telephone's bell and the fact that the plaintiff had to answer the phone to make it stop ringing. The court did not extend the same legal principle to the letters sent by the defendant, as the court held that the mail is not as intrusive a communications medium as the telephone.[34] As well, in appropriate circumstances, courts will also enjoin the disclosure of personal information, or award damages to the plaintiff after the disclosure, where the information was imparted in confidence and the subsequent disclosure betrays such confidence. For example, in several British cases newspapers have been prohibited from publishing personal information on this basis.[35] The

---

31 *Gould Estate* v. *Stoddart Publishing Co.* (1996), 30 O.R. (3d) 520 (Gen. Div.). In this case the court stated at 528 that "[r]eputation and fame can be a capital asset that one nurtures and may choose to exploit and it may have a value much greater than any tangible property. There is no reason why such an asset should not be devisable to heirs."

32 *Poole and Poole* v. *Ragen and The Toronto Harbour Commissioners*, [1958] O.W.N. 77 (H.C.J.).

33 *Motherwell* v. *Motherwell* (1976), 73 D.L.R. (3d) 62 (Alta. C.A.) [*Motherwell*].

34 See, however, *Mather* v. *Columbia House* (1992), 12 L.W.1226-004 (Ont. Sm. Claims), where unsolicited mailings that continued despite repeated requests to stop, were held to be a form of trespass.

35 *Duchess of Argyll* v. *Duke of Argyll*, [1967] 1 Ch. 302; *X.* v. *Y.*, [1988] 2 All E.R. 648 (Q.B.); *Stephens* v. *Avery*, [1988] 2 W.L.R. 1280 (Ch. D.) [*Stephens*]; *Fraser* v. *Evans*, [1969] 1 All E.R. 8 (C.A.) [*Fraser*]. More recently, a U.K. court, applying principles from a 1998 human rights law and the European Convention on Human Rights, enjoined the publication of sexually explicit photographs, but at the same time permitted the public narrative description of the events in a newspaper: *Theakston* v. *MGN Ltd.*, [2002] EWHC 137 (Q.B.).

jurisprudential basis for these decisions is not unlike that seen in section B.1, "Trade Secrets/Breach of Confidence," in chapter 2 in the discussion of the protection of trade secrets and confidential information. As Lord Denning stated in the *Fraser* case:

> [T]he court will, in a proper case, restrain the publication of confidential information. The jurisdiction is based, not so much on property or on contract, but rather on the duty to be of good faith. No person is permitted to divulge to the world information which he has received in confidence, unless he has just cause or excuse for doing so. Even if he comes by it innocently, nevertheless, once he gets to know that it was originally given in confidence, he can be restrained from breaking that confidence.[36]

Where, however, the information sought to be protected relates to persons who generally seek publicity, courts are reluctant to enjoin the publishing of confidential information.[37]

---

36 *Fraser*, above note 35 at 11. Emphasizing that pre-existing relationships are not critical to this form of protection, the court in *Stephens*, above note 35 at 1286, expressed the legal obligation as follows: "[the defendant] submits that in the absence of either a legally enforceable contract or a pre-existing relationship — such as that of employer and employee, doctor and patient, or priest and penitent — it is not possible to impose a legal duty of confidence on the recipient of the information merely by saying that the information is given in confidence. In my judgment that is wrong in law. The basis of equitable intervention to protect confidentiality is that it is unconscionable for a person who has received information on the basis that it is confidential subsequently to reveal that information. Although the relationship between the parties is often important in cases where it is said there is an implied as opposed to express obligation of confidence, the relationship between the parties is not the determining factor. It is the acceptance of the information on the basis that it will be kept secret that affects the conscience of the recipient of the information."

37 In *Woodward v. Hutchins*, [1977] 1 W.L.R. 760 (C.A.), pop singers including Tom Jones wanted the court to prohibit a former employee of the company that ran the singers' tours from divulging stories that occurred on various singing tours. The court refused, and Lord Denning stated at 763–64: "No doubt in some employments there is an obligation of confidence. In a proper case the court will be prepared to restrain a servant from disclosing confidential information which he has received in the course of his employment. But this case is quite out of the ordinary. There is no doubt whatever that this pop group sought publicity. They wanted to have themselves presented to the public in a favourable light so that audiences would come to hear them and support them. Mr. Hutchins was engaged so as to produce, or help to produce, this favourable image, not only of their public lives but of their private lives also. If a group of this kind seek publicity which is to their advantage, it seems to me that they cannot complain if a servant or employee of theirs afterwards discloses the truth about them. If the

In a manner akin to the above-noted British breach of confidence cases, in Quebec, the Canadian Broadcasting Corporation was found, on the basis of the *Civil Code*, to have caused damage to a viewer critical of a certain show by causing an invasion of that viewer's privacy by the host of the show reading the viewer's critical letter on the air, and in so doing identifying the viewer and encouraging other viewers to contact him, which subsequently resulted in the viewer receiving offensive phone calls and letters.[38] In Ontario, a court awarded damages to a plaintiff when the defendant, without authorization of the plaintiff, played in public a tape of a telephone conversation with the plaintiff; the court called this action an "invasion of privacy," and partly relied on the *Krouse* case for precedent.[39] It should also be noted that

---

image which they fostered was not a true image, it is in the public interest that it should be corrected. In these cases of confidential information it is a question of balancing the public interest in maintaining the confidence against the public interest in knowing the truth. ... In this case the balance comes down in favour of the truth being told, even if it should involve some breach of confidential information. As there should be "truth in advertising," so there should be truth in publicity. The public should not be misled. So it seems to me that the breach of confidential information is not a ground for granting an injunction."

Similarly, in *Lennon* v. *NewsGroup Newspapers Ltd. and Twist*, [1978] FSR 573 (C.A.), ex-Beatle John Lennon urged the court to block a newspaper from publishing revelations about Lennon provided to the paper by Lennon's first wife. Again the court refused, concluding at 574–75: "It seems to me as plain as can be that the relationship of these parties has ceased to be their own private affair. They themselves have put it into the public domain. They made it public to all the world themselves, and I do not think that one or other of them can obtain an injunction to stop it being published. One only has to read these articles all the way through to show that each of them is making money by publishing the most intimate details about one another and accusing one another of this, that and the other, and so forth. It is all in the public domain. I do not regard this as a breach of confidence at all. If there is any action it is for libel and, as she says it is true, there is no ground for an injunction."

But for a different result, based partly on the strength of a non-disclosure agreement, see *Campbell* v. *Frisbee*, [2002] EWHC 328 (H.C.Ch.).

38   *Robbins* v. *Canadian Broadcasting Corp.* (1957), 12 D.L.R. (2d) 35 (Que. Sup. Ct.). The particular provision of the Quebec *Civil Code* relied on by the court at 39 reads as follows: "1053. Every person capable of discerning right from wrong is responsible for the damage caused by his fault to another, whether by positive act, imprudence, neglect or want of skill."

39   *Saccone* v. *Orr* (1981), 34 O.R. (2d) 317 at 321 (Co. Ct.). See also the recent American decision, *Lake* v. *Wal-Mart Stores, Inc.*, 582 N.W. 2d 231 (Miss. S.C. 1998). In this case the plaintiff had brought some rolls of film to a Wal-Mart for developing, and a Wal-Mart employee had printed and circulated in the community a copy of a photograph that showed the plaintiff and a friend naked in a shower, even though the employee, following store policy, would not print the

a number of statutes also prohibit the interception of electronic communications.[40] At the same time, however, it is worth remembering that no right, however important, is absolute, and thus privacy rights will always have to compete against — and often yield to — other rights.[41]

d)   Monitoring Employee E-mails

A particularly contentious question in the privacy area is whether employees should have the right to preclude their employers from monitoring employee-related e-mail and other similar electronic communications. As is pointed out in a very perceptive article, this simple question invites complex answers depending on a wide range of facts, such as whether the employee is in the public or private sector, whether the employee is in a union or non-union environment, and what circumstances gave rise to the employer monitoring.[42] Adding to the complexity is the third dynamic of computer law, the blurring of private and public. Consider how it denotes the employee's and employer's interests and is compounded by the fact that the workplace is becoming more like home (for many telecommuters, the workplace is in the home), and home is becoming more like the workplace. On the one hand, many

---

photograph for the plaintiff because of its "nature." In response to the plaintiff's privacy claim against Wal-Mart for circulation of copies of the photograph, argued as a common law tort, the court concluded at 235: "One's naked body is a very private part of one's person and generally known to others only by choice. This is a type of privacy interest worthy of protection. Therefore, without consideration of the merits of Lake and Weber's claims, we recognize the torts of intrusion upon seclusion, appropriation, and publication of private facts."

40   See chapter 3, section B.10, "Interception of Communications."

41   For example, in the context of a search and seizure case, the Supreme Court has noted that: "It thus becomes necessary to strike a reasonable balance between the right of individuals to be left alone and the right of the state to intrude on privacy in furtherance of its responsibilities for law enforcement": R. v. Duarte (1990), 53 C.C.C. (3d) 1 at 11–12. Other rights and interests that compete with privacy include effective and efficient law enforcement; freedom of the press, including investigative journalism; and various commercial interests that may be hindered or thwarted altogether if individuals are afforded the possibility of full informational autonomy. Privacy also competes with national security, as discussed in chapter 3, section B.11(a), "Post-9/11 Law Reform."

42   Charles Morgan, "Employer Monitoring of Employee Electronic Mail and Internet Use" (1999) 44 McGill L.J. 849 ["Employer Monitoring"]. Morgan gives an exhaustive review of the Canadian and U.S. cases, and provides useful wisdom on how to reconcile the competing claims of employers and employees in this difficult area.

legitimate reasons exist for employer monitoring of e-mail, including concerns about transmission or reception by employees (consciously or not) of trade secrets or confidential information,[43] offensive or illegal content,[44] computer viruses,[45] or unauthorized copies of software or other copyright material,[46] libellous content,[47] to name but a few high-

---

43 For example, in the early 1990s Borland International Inc. brought a claim against Symantec Corp. for misappropriation of trade secrets via the e-mails of a former Borland employee (who reportedly sent Symantec the e-mails while still employed at Borland); this case has since settled — see News Release announcing settlement at <symantec.com/press>. See also *Shurgard Storage Centers, Inc.* v. *Safeguard Self Storage, Inc.*, 119 F.Supp. 2d 1121 (W.D. Wash. 2000), where the employee of the plaintiff sent the defendant e-mails full of the plaintiff's trade secrets; and *United States* v. *Martin*, 228 F.3d 1 (1st Cir. 2000), where the employee's impugned activity came to light when she sent a fellow employee an e-mail regarding the scam. See also the following U.S. Department of Justice Press Releases: "Former Lucent Employees and Co-Conspirator Indicted in Theft of Lucent Trade Secrets," 31 May 2001 (the defendants allegedly used e-mail and a password-protected Web site to steal and transfer source code, software, and the design of a new product); "New York City Law Firm Paralegal Pleads Guilty to Stealing Trial Plan," 4 October 2001 (paralegal working on a huge tobacco litigation file obtained an electronic copy of the Trial Plan, prepared at a cost of several million dollars, and transmitted parts of it by e-mail to counsel on the opposing side, offering to send the rest for $2 million); "Santa Clara Man Sentenced for Theft of Trade Secrets," 4 December 2001 (accused appropriated customer and order information databases related to employer's sales); "Silicon Valley Man Sentenced to Economic Espionage Act Violation Relating to Intel Trade Secrets," 11 December 2001 (partly using home computer, converted computer files containing Intel new product information with a view to using it at his new employer, Sun Microsystems), all of which are available at <cybercrime.gov>.

44 See the discussion in chapter 3, sections B.5, "Obscenity and Child Pornography," and B.6, "Illegal Speech," regarding obscenity, child pornography, and hate speech, and chapter 6, section B.3(b), "E-Mail Policies," for cases involving sexual harassment where e-mails played a part in the allegations. For examples of companies disciplining staff for inappropriate e-mail, see "Civil Servants Suspended Over E-mail," *The Globe and Mail* (30 July 1999); Ann Carns, "Staff Sacked Over Bawdy E-mails," *The Globe and Mail* (11 February 2000); and "Dow Fires, Suspends Staff For Pornographic E-mail," *The Globe and Mail* (29 July 2000).

45 See the discussion in chapter 3 regarding viruses, which includes the fact that the vast majority of viruses are today transmitted as attachments to e-mails.

46 See the discussion in chapter 2, section B.3, "Copyright," as to the illegal activity of "corporate overuse of software."

47 See chapter 7, section A, "Cyber Libel," for a description of the Internet as the ultimate libel machine.

risk e-mail activities.[48] It is true that these risks predate the e-mail era, but for reasons articulated elsewhere in this book,[49] e-mail heightens the risk profile greatly for employers (and employees) given the unique dynamics of this communication medium. On the other hand, is it reasonable to assume that employees should expect some degree of privacy to attach to their e-mail communications? This indeed is the key legal question, one that has not yet attracted judicial scrutiny in Canada.[50]

---

48   A recent survey in the United States of 538 computer security practitioners found that 91 percent detected employee abuse of Internet access privileges, including downloading of pornography or pirated software or inappropriate use of e-mail systems: Computer Security Institute, "Financial Losses Due to Internet Intrusions, Trade Secret Theft and Other Cyber Crimes Soar," *Press Release* (12 March 2001). This press release gives highlights of the CSI's sixth annual "Computer Crime and Security Survey," and is available at <gocsi.com>. There is also the problem of the inadvertent disclosure of information by e-mail (Sandra Martin, "Errant E-mail Leaks Prize List of Top Authors," *The Globe and Mail* (11 November 2000)), and the propensity of some employees to forward internal corporate e-mail to external publishers ("Web Site Discloses Corporate Memos," *The Globe and Mail* (31 July 2002)). Some employers also argue they need to monitor employee e-mail use because of the time that some employees might spend on personal matters through the medium: Showwei Chu, "Workers Waste 800 Million Hours on Web: Poll Finds Employees Surf for Personal Reasons, Unrestricted by Policies," *The Globe and Mail* (6 July 2000); Natalie Southworth, "Employers Crack Down On Free Web E-mail," *The Globe and Mail* (2 November 2000); and Kevin Marron, "Attack of the Cyberslackers," *The Globe and Mail* (20 January 2000).

49   Section B.3(b), "E-mail Policies," in chapter 6 makes the point that e-mail is very dangerous "truth serum." Thus, it is not surprising that many employers are actively monitoring computer use in the workplace in a number of different ways, tracking both e-mail but also other computer-based activities: Michael J. McCarthy, "Keystroke Cops Keep Tabs on Employees' Moves," *The Globe and Mail* (8 March 2000); and Liz Stevens, "Big Brother Invading Workplace," *The Globe and Mail* (29 September 1999). And all of this activity is made more problematic by the third dynamic of computer law (namely, the blurring of private and public), given that many employees are also working from home, either full- or part-time: "Firms Wiser About Personal E-mail Use," *The Globe and Mail* (8 December 2001).

50   In *R. v. Weir*, [1998] 8 W.W.R. 228 (Alta. Q.B.), affirmed (2001) 156 C.C.C. (3d) 188 (Alta. C.A.) the court held, in the context of an Internet service provider accessing a customer's e-mail files, that the customer should have a reasonable expectation that such files would not be accessed by third parties. It is open to question whether the court would have reached a similar conclusion had an employee's email been at issue, given the significant differences between the two situations in terms of ownership of the communications infrastructure, the personal versus corporate purpose of the general access rights, etc. For a review of the labour arbitration jurisprudence on the question of electronic surveillance of employees in the unionized workplace, see *Lenworth Metal Products Ltd.* v. *U.S.W.A., Local 3950*, [1999] L.V.I. 3062-5 (Ont. Arb. Board).

In the United States, though, there have been a number of decisions that considered whether employees have a reasonable expectation of privacy in e-mail. In *Smyth v. Pillsbury Company*,[51] the court, considering the privacy rights in an e-mail message sent from one employee to another in a company, concluded that once the employee sent the message over the e-mail system the employee lost any reasonable expectation of privacy. Similarly, in a recent decision in Texas,[52] a Microsoft employee argued that his employer should not have been able to access the personal electronic folders on his computer that contained his e-mails. In particular, the employee argued that Microsoft allowed him to keep this folder under a private password, and therefore the folder was like the locker that an employer gives an employee to store personal effects during work hours, and in respect of which a previous Texas court concluded an employee would have a reasonable expectation of privacy. The court in the *Bill McLaren* case (after wrestling with the third dynamic of computer law) disagreed, concluding that the computer-based folder can be distinguished from the physical locker on several grounds: namely, the locker stored personal belongings, whereas the computer was intended to store work items; the e-mail messages were not intended to be personal items, but were part of the employee's work environment; and in any event (and echoing the reasoning in *Smythe*), a reasonable person would not consider the employer's interception of these messages to be a highly offensive invasion.

---

51 914 F.Supp. 97 (E.D. Pa. 1996) [*Smyth*]. In this case the court also concluded, at 101, that even if it could be said the employee had a reasonable expectation of privacy in the contents of e-mail messages, the court would not find the interception of e-mail communications to be a substantial or offensive invasion of privacy: "Again, we note that by intercepting such communications, the company is not, as in the case of urinalysis or personal property searches, requiring the employee to disclose any personal information about himself or invading the employee's person or personal effects. Moreover, the company's interest in preventing inappropriate and unprofessional comments or even illegal activity over its e-mail system outweighs any privacy interest the employee may have in those comments." Charles Morgan, in "Employer Monitoring," above note 42, argues that *Smyth* must be read very carefully, and its applicability to Canada may be somewhat limited.

52 *Bill McLaren*, above note 21. Reinforcing the principle that the e-mail system belongs to the employer is the American case of *Pichelmann v. Madsen*, 2002 Wash. App. LEXIS 727 (7th Cir. 2002), which held that an employer could force an employee to remove a customized signature (in this case: "The truth shall set you free, but first it will piss you off! Gloria Steinem") given that the e-mail system was not a public forum for First Amendment purposes as it was not indiscriminately open for use by the general public (illustrating again the challenges posed by the third dynamic of computer law).

These American cases, and the Canadian *Weir* decision, lead to the conclusion that is useful, both from the perspective of the employer and the employee, for the employer to institute an e-mail usage policy that covers e-mails and Internet usage in the workplace.[53] The policy would allow for monitoring of e-mail and other electronic communications, and employees would consent to this. By the same token, either in the policy, or merely in its administration, the employer should consider restricting its monitoring to that which is reasonably required to protect its legitimate interests. A key benefit to the employer of such a policy is that it removes doubt as to whether the employee had a reasonable expectation of privacy in his or her use of the e-mail system. For example, in *United States of America* v. *Mark L. Simmons*,[54] an employee of the CIA argued that his employer violated his Fourth Amendment rights (protecting against unreasonable search and seizure) when they performed a warrantless search on his computer. The court noted that the Fourth Amendment requires the complainant to show he had a reasonable expectation of privacy in the place searched, and that because of the Internet policy that he was subject to (that clearly stated the employer would audit, inspect, or monitor employees' use of the Internet and all e-mail messages) he lacked such an expectation. Under Canada's new private sector privacy law (discussed later), the Canadian privacy commissioner has taken the view that all employer monitoring of employee e-mail usage should be reasonable, even if employee consent has been obtained.

---

53   For an example of a guide to creating such a policy, see Treasury Board of Canada Secretariat, *Policy on the Use of Electronic Networks*, 12 February 1998. In addition to addressing the privacy issue, such policies are useful in assisting an employer to revoke an employee's e-mail privileges when the employee uses the e-mail system for unauthorized purposes: see *Benson* v. *Cuevas*, 741 N.Y.S. 2d 310 (Sup. Ct. N.Y. App. Div. 2002). In this case, the court held that a government department was justified in cancelling the e-mail privileges of an employee (who was also a union representative) when, contrary to the employer's e-mail policy that required the e-mail network to be used only for official government business, the employee used the e-mail system to disseminate various union messages.

54   206 F.3d 392 (4th Cir. 2000). See also *Kelleher* v. *City of Reading*, Cir. No. 01-3386 (E.D. Pa. 2002), which held that an employee did not have a reasonable expectation of privacy in workplace e-mail as a result of an e-mail policy that read, in part, as follows: "Messages that are created, sent, or received using the City's e-mail system are the property of the City of Reading. The City reserves the right to access and disclose the contents of all messages created, sent, or received using the e-mail system. The E-mail system is strictly for official City of Reading messaging."

2) Data Protection

In terms of information privacy, a leading definition of privacy conceives of it as the "claim of individuals, groups, or institutions to determine for themselves when, how, and to what extent information about them is communicated to others."[55] Many commentators and the public at large worry that computers and networks (and particularly the Internet) are eroding the ability of individuals to make these determinations in respect of their personal information.[56] Although records have been kept about people for hundreds of years, the shift in the storage medium from paper to electronic files has raised multiple new concerns. Computers can gather and store much more information. The means for collection are automated, as when a point-of-sale system in a store automatically records every purchase made by a consumer. Computers also permit data to be readily combined from various sources.[57] And then the data can be reproduced at no cost. These and other factors have resulted in the creation of huge databases within governments and countless private sector companies.[58] In addition to collecting,

---

55 Alan F. Westin, *Privacy and Freedom* (New York: Atheneum, 1967), at 7 [*Privacy and Freedom*].

56 "Virtual Privacy," *The Economist*, 10 February 1996. Nor are handheld personal digital assistants safe: Almar Latour, "Wireless Devices Threaten to Be Achilles' Heel of Data Security," *The Globe and Mail* (28 December 2000).

57 The Privacy Working Group of the U.S. government's Information Policy Committee, Information Infrastructure Task Force, illustrated the phenomenon of computer-based data aggregation in the following manner. In the days before computers, in order to build a profile of an individual who had lived in various states, one would have to travel from state to state and search public records for information about the individual. This process would have required filling out forms, paying fees, and waiting in line for record searches at local, state, and federal agencies, such as the departments of motor vehicles, deed record offices, electoral commissions, and county record offices. Although one could manually compile a personal profile in this manner, it would be a time-consuming and costly exercise, one that would not be undertaken unless the offsetting rewards were considerable. In sharp contrast, today, as more and more personal information appears online, such a profile can be built in a manner of minutes, at minimal cost. See "Privacy and the National Information Infrastructure: Principles for Providing and Using Personal Information," 6 June 1995, at 1–2. This report is available at <iitf.nist.gov/ipc/ipc/ipc-pubs/niiprivprin_final.html>.

58 The data can then be used to send voluminous amounts of "spam," essentially junk e-mail. In order to fight back, many online consumers do not give accurate information about themselves, if they can avoid it: Showei Chu, "On-line Lies Cast Doubt On E-biz Databases," *The Globe and Mail* (10 August 2000). Or, they are opting for prepaid cards and other payment mechanisms that do not leave a data trail: Natalie Southworth, "Data Checks," *The Globe and Mail* (21 September 2000).

combining, and storing data, computers and telecommunication networks permit remote access to information in a manner not permitted previously.[59] The paper-based file, kept in a locked filing cabinet in a room with a locked door in a building that limits entry to authorized persons, is a rather secure mechanism for storing sensitive personal information. Polls indicate that the same information, when resident on a computer system to which many users have access, is perceived to be insecure, and indeed these concerns lead many people to view the loss of personal privacy as the chief threat of the Information Age.[60]

People have a broad range of concerns with the practices of collecting, aggregating, and disseminating information.[61] There is the frightening, and real, prospect of unsavoury and dangerous people, such as pedophiles and convicts gaining access to such information.[62] A "blagger" can take someone's publicly available data and easily trick companies into disclosing confidential information over the telephone.[63]

---

59   Consider the practice of data or account aggregation, where a single online service provider, perhaps a bank, keeps track of all of a consumer's online accounts: Rob Carrick, "On-Line Aggregate Accounts Ideal for Web Warriors," *The Globe and Mail* (7 February 2002). As with most new e-commerce applications, it provides the consumer with a very powerful and convenience-enhancing service, but at the same time presents privacy issues that need to be managed.

60   See, for example, the results of an attitudinal survey of a group of U.K. respondents that attempted to measure which of thirteen examples of invasion of privacy would most upset them, and whether they thought it should be prohibited. The "central computer" that would have data available to anyone who asks for it elicited the strongest reaction; 87 percent said it would constitute an invasion of privacy; 71 percent said they would be annoyed; 85 percent said it should be prohibited by law. Similar figures for private detectives were 39 percent, 19 percent, and 30 percent, respectively: reported in Wacks, *Personal Information*, above note 15. See also Ekos Research Associates Inc., *Privacy Revealed: The Canadian Privacy Survey* (Ottawa: Communications Canada, 1993), which, based on a survey of three thousand Canadian households, reported that 81 percent of respondents believed that computers are reducing the level of privacy in Canada.

61   For example, in a recent survey, almost 87 percent of U.S. respondents, all of whom were experienced Internet users, said they were very or somewhat concerned about threats to their privacy online: Lorrie F. Cranor, "Beyond Concern: Understanding Net Users' Attitudes About Online Privacy" <research.att.com/projects/privacystudy>. In a recent Canadian survey, 84 percent of respondents said they were concerned to some extent about providing their personal information to a Web site: Tyler Hamilton, "Web Sales Stunted By Security Fears: Survey," *The Globe and Mail* (27 April 2000). In another survey, the figure was 80 percent: "Poll Identifies On-line Concerns," *The Globe and Mail* (15 December 1999).

62   "Inside Information," *The Economist*, 29 June 1996.

63   "Living in the Global Goldfish Bowl," *The Economist*, 18 December 1999.

Miniature cameras, microphones without wires, computers that can sense images through walls, high-powered optical devices that can give full vision at night, to name but a few breakthroughs in surveillance technology, also generate concern, especially when these technologies are coupled with high-powered databases that can effect real-time monitoring.[64] The components of information technology are also being outfitted with more sophisticated data-tracking capability.[65] Then there is the problem that commercial Web sites that collect reams of data are not immune to technology or human errors, which can cause inadvertent disclosure of data.[66]

The net result of all these developments is that consumers, among other things, are intensely uncomfortable regarding the use of consumption-related data and mailing lists by credit card companies, retailers, and others.[67] And the common law has not responded to these issues very effectively. For example, in the case of *Dwyer* v. *American Express Company*, a credit card company ranked cardholders in different categories based on their spending habits, and then rented out its mailing lists of cardholders to merchants who would then target these individuals with marketing and sales programs.[68] The plaintiff cardholder argued that these practices amounted to an intrusion into the cardholders' seclusion, the disclosure of private financial information, and an appropriation of personality rights by trading on the personal spending habits of cardholders, and thereby caused damage to the cardholders. The court disagreed, concluding that the compilation by the card company of mailing data in its own records does not constitute an invasion of privacy, noting that the right to privacy does not

---

64 Dawn Walton, "Police Plan to Install Street-Watch Cameras," *The Globe and Mail* (22 June 2001); "Security Technology: Watching You," *The Economist*, 22 September 2001; and Adam L. Penenberg, "The Surveillance Society," *Wired*, December 2001.

65 Eric Reguly, "Big Brother Chip Defies Privacy Laws," *The Globe and Mail* (2 February 1999). This article discusses the plans Intel had to outfit each Pentium III chip with an electronic tracking device that would allow Web sites to more effectively monitor a user's clickstream than by cookie technology.

66 "Barclays On-Line Banking Shut By Security Breach," *The Globe and Mail* (1 August 2000); and Ted Bridis, "Windows XP Has Major Flaws," *The Globe and Mail* (21 December 2001).

67 Tyler Hamilton, "Getting To Know All About You," *The Globe and Mail* (29 October 1998); and Theresa Ebden, "Canadian Businesses Enticed By E-Billing: But Consumers' Privacy May Suffer: Critics," *The Globe and Mail* (23 June 2000).

68 652 N.E.2d 1351 (Ill. App. 1995) [*Dwyer*].

extend to the mailbox. As well, the court stated that including names on mailing lists does not disclose financial information about cardholders, particularly given that, as the court put it, "a single random cardholder's name has little or no intrinsic value to defendants (or a merchant)";[69] rather, the credit card company creates value by categorizing and aggregating the names, and therefore, the court concluded, the appropriation claim also failed. In effect, the court said, the only damages the plaintiffs could have suffered was an excess of unwanted mail, and thus the court dismissed the claim.[70] This case illustrates well the second dynamic of computer law, namely, the highly ephemeral nature of information and the fact that information, malleable and plastic asset that it is, often takes its value from its context. It also makes clear why governments have for some time been concerned with data protection matters. The Canadian government first focused on these issues when it appointed a Task Force on Privacy and Computers in the early 1970s, which resulted in an important report and a series of related studies.[71] Governmental concern continues to this day, as illustrated by the fact that privacy issues were treated by the national Information Highway Advisory Council as an important research topic.[72] This governmental concern has translated into a number of statutes in Canada, which are discussed later. As these laws draw their inspiration from recommendations issued by the Organization for Economic Cooperation and Development (OECD), developed in the 1970s, it is worth considering these guidelines first.

3) The OECD Data Protection Guidelines

The OECD, the Paris-based organization dedicated to promoting economic cooperation and growth among its members,[73] promulgated its *Guidelines Governing the Protection of Privacy and Transborder Flows of Personal Data (OECD Guidelines)* in 1980 in response to the rapid

---

69   *Ibid.*, at 1356.
70   Note that the jurisprudential value of this case in the U.S. may be adversely affected given the subsequent enactment of the *Gramm-Leach-Bliley Act*, Pub. L. 106-102 (1999), which contains privacy provisions that apply to the non-public personal information of clients of U.S. financial institutions.
71   *Privacy and Computers* (Ottawa: Information Canada, 1972).
72   *Privacy and the Canadian Information Highway* (Ottawa: Industry Canada, 1994).
73   OECD membership currently consists of the former "Western" European countries, Austria, Iceland, Norway, Finland, Denmark, Sweden, Greece, Turkey, Mexico, the Czech Republic, Hungary, Poland, Korea, the United States, Japan, Canada, Australia, and New Zealand: see <oecd.org>.

growth of the use of computer and telecommunications technologies in the OECD countries.[74] The *OECD Guidelines* essentially strive to reconcile the sometimes inconsistent objectives of personal information privacy with the free flow of information. With respect to data protection, the *OECD Guidelines* set out eight basic principles:[75]

1. **Collection Limitation.** There should be limits to the collection of personal data and any such data should be obtained by lawful and fair means and, where appropriate, with the knowledge or consent of the data subject.

2. **Data Quality.** Personal data should be relevant to the purposes for which they are to be used, and, to the extent necessary for those purposes, should be accurate, complete and kept up-to-date.

3. **Purpose Specification.** The purposes for which personal data are collected should be specified not later than at the time of data collection and the subsequent use limited to the fulfilment of those purposes or such others as are not incompatible with those purposes and as are specified on each occasion of change of purpose.

4. **Use Limitation.** Personal data should not be disclosed, made available or otherwise used for purposes other than those specified in accordance with paragraph 3 except: (a) with the consent of the data subject; or (b) by the authority of law.

5. **Security Safeguards.** Personal data should be protected by reasonable security safeguards against such risks as loss or unauthorized access, destruction, use, modification or disclosure of data.

6. **Openness.** There should be a general policy of openness about developments, practices and policies with respect to personal data. Means should be readily available of establishing the existence and nature of personal data, and the main purposes of their use, as well as the identity and usual residence of the data controller.

7. **Individual Participation.** An individual should have the right: (a) to obtain from a data controller, or otherwise, confirmation of whether or not the data controller has data relating to him; (b) to have communicated to him, data relating to him (i) within a reasonable time; (ii) at a charge, if any, that is not excessive; (iii) in a reasonable manner; and (iv) in a form that is readily intelligible to him; (c) to be given reasons if a request made under subparagraphs (a) and (b) is denied, and to be able to challenge such denial; and (d) to challenge data relating to him and, if the chal-

---

74   The *OECD Guidelines* are available at <oecd.org/dsti/sti/it/secur/index.htm>.
75   *OECD Guidelines*, ss. 7 to 14.

lenge is successful, to have the data erased, rectified, completed or amended.

8. **Accountability.** A data controller should be accountable for complying with measures that give effect to the principles stated above.

The *OECD Guidelines* also define *personal data* as "any information relating to an identified or identifiable individual (data subject)."[76]

The *OECD Guidelines* do not have the force of law and are a set of principles that each member country of the OECD is urged to implement in its national law. Nonetheless, the OECD "fair information practices" principles, as they are sometimes called, are important because they have formed the basis for many national data protection legal regimes, as well as numerous voluntary codes of conduct dealing with personal information.[77] With respect to the latter, the Canadian Standards Association has adopted a *Model Code for the Protection of Personal Information (CSA Code).*[78] The *CSA Code*, in its introduction, expressly states that the *OECD Guidelines* were used as the basis for the development of the *CSA Code*, which consists of ten interrelated principles. The *CSA Code* also includes commentary on each principle that elaborates on specific procedures that might be used by an organization to implement the principle. The *CSA Code* represents a marked improvement over other voluntary codes of conduct for data protection, and several financial institutions, for example, have indicated that they will be adopting it. Similarly, many e-tailers and other online Web-based merchants have adopted privacy policies, some of which are vetted and approved by companies operating "seal" programs; that is, the Web merchant can display the organization's seal if its privacy policy meets the organization's criteria.[79] The non-binding nature of the *CSA*

---

76   *OECD Guidelines*, subs. 1(b).

77   In 1998 the OECD issued "Implementing the OECD 'Privacy Guidelines' in the Electronic Environment," a report that analyses how well, on balance, the *OECD Guidelines* apply to the various practices becoming commonplace on the Internet. See also OECD, *Group of Experts on Information Security and Privacy, Practices to Implement the OECD Privacy Guidelines on Global Networks* (23 December 1998) <appli1.oecd.org/olis/1998doc.nsf/linto/dsti-iccp-reg (98)6-final>.

78   CAN/CSA — Q830-96. The CSA Code is available at <csa.ca>. The *CSA Code* was adopted as a national standard courtesy of the *Standards Council of Canada Act*, R.S.C. 1970 (1st Supp.), c. 41 [as am. by s. 4(2)(e)].

79   See, for example, seal programs operated by the Better Business Bureau (BBBOn-line <bbbonline.org>) and Trust-e (<truste.org>). See also <enonymous.com>, a service which reviews privacy policies for various sites, assesses them, and then qualitatively ranks them in accordance with a four-star system.

Code, however, coupled with the corresponding lack of an effective sanction mechanism, has led the federal privacy commissioner to conclude that the *CSA Code* is inadequate and that data protection legislation covering the private sector is required.[80]

4) Data Protection Legislation

a) Public Sector Coverage

The fair information practices contained in the *OECD Guidelines* have been enshrined in a number of federal and provincial statutes. Federally, the *Privacy Act* has regulated the collection and use of personal information by the federal government and a number of federal public agencies since 1982.[81] This statute applies to personal information recorded in any form and not merely that which is computer-based. The *Privacy Act* contains the principles of the *OECD Guidelines*, with some interesting nuances. Usefully, the statute sets out the only grounds on which personal information can be disclosed[82] though this provision also permits the government to disclose personal information where public interest in the disclosure clearly outweighs any invasion of privacy that could result from the disclosure.[83] The *Privacy Act* establishes the office of the privacy commissioner to receive and investigate complaints. The privacy commissioner acts as an information ombudsman, conducts audits on the government's information-handling practices, and prepares an annual report that serves as a report card on the government's progress in implementing responsible information-handling techniques. The role of the privacy commissioner is essentially advisory, however, given that legal appeals from decisions of the government as to matters pertaining to the statute are to the Federal Court and not to the privacy commissioner.[84]

The *Privacy Act* is coupled and coordinated with the *Access to Information Act*, a statute that gives Canadians the right to access informa-

---

80   *Privacy Commissioner of Canada*, Annual Report, 1996–97 (Ottawa: the Privacy Commissioner of Canada, 1997) at 30–31.

81   R.S.C. 1985, c. P-21.

82   *Ibid.*, subs. 8(2).

83   *Ibid.*, para. 8(2)(m).

84   For a discussion of the "privacy watchdog mandate" of the privacy commissioner, and the provincial counterpart of information commissioner, and their role in promoting systemic solutions for informational privacy issues, including conducting "privacy impact assessments," see Flaherty, "Privacy and Technology," above note 2 at 222–24, 228.

tion in records under the control of the federal government.[85] The term record is defined very broadly and in a technology-neutral manner, and includes correspondence, photographs, sound recordings, and computer-based material regardless of physical form.[86] The statute does, however, contain a number of exemptions from the right of access, an important one being that the government is not to disclose a record containing trade secrets of a third party; confidential financial, commercial, scientific, or technical information supplied by a third party that is treated consistently in a confidential manner by the third party; or information the disclosure of which could reasonably be expected to result in material financial loss.[87] The Federal Court, which decides appeals under the *Access to Information Act*, has construed these exemptions narrowly, only rarely finding against disclosure. For example, the court has set a very high onus on an applicant to show the probability of financial loss from disclosure.[88] In another case, the court has held that while aircraft maintenance records supplied by an airline to a government inspector come within the confidential information exemption, notes taken by the government inspector based on these records do not, as these would not have been "supplied" by the airline.[89] This latter case illustrates very well the elusive nature of information (being the second dynamic of computer law). In one of the few cases holding in favour of non-disclosure, the court decided that disclosing information regarding a quota to import cheese would satisfy the economic harm test provided in section 20 of the *Access to Information Act*.[90]

---

85   R.S.C. 1985, c. A-1. In the United States, such legislation is referred to as Freedom of Information (FOI) laws. FOI regimes can have wide-ranging effects. In *County of Suffolk, New York* v. *Experian Information Solutions, Inc.*, 2000 WL 1010262 (S.D.N.Y. 2000), a government's copyright in tax maps was overridden by the public's right to copy and distribute public records under the relevant FOI law.

86   *Access to Information Act*, s. 3. It is interesting to note that an American case has held that personal e-mails of government employees are not public records susceptible to access by third parties: *Times Publishing Co.* v. *City of Clearwater*, No. 2D01-3055 (Fla. Dist. Ct. App., 2002).

87   *Access to Information Act*, s. 20.

88   See *Canada Packers Inc.* v. *Canada (Minister of Agriculture)* (1988), 53 D.L.R. (4th) 246 (F.C.A.).

89   *Air Atonabee Ltd.* v. *Canada (Minister of Transport)* (1989), 27 C.P.R. (3d) 180 (F.C.T.D.).

90   *Canada (Information Commissioner)* v. *Canada (Minister of External Affairs)* (1990), 72 D.L.R. (4th) 113 (F.C.T.D.).

Privacy and access to information statutes covering information held by provincial governments have been enacted in all provinces (except Prince Edward Island).[91] All share the same general structure on the privacy front of implementing the principles found in the OECD Guidelines, coupled with an enforcement mechanism. One procedural difference between some of the statutes is in the role of the relevant information/privacy commissioner. For example, Ontario's statute provides for a right of appeal to the Ontario information and privacy commissioner, rather than to a judge.

b) Private Sector Coverage

As noted above, a number of commentators have called for data protection legislation for the private sector. Quebec was the first jurisdiction in Canada to heed this call, with the enactment in 1994 of the *Act Respecting the Protection of Personal Information in the Private Sector*[92] and amendments to the *Civil Code*. In April 2000, the federal government enacted its long-awaited data protection when Bill C-6 became law (PIPEDA).[93] PIPEDA applies to "personal information"[94] processed

---

91   For example, in Ontario, see the *Freedom of Information and Protection of Privacy Act*, R.S.O. 1990, c. F.31. This statute covers the ministries and agencies of the Ontario government; the *Municipal Freedom of Information and Protection of Privacy Act*, R.S.O. 1990, c. M.56, extends essentially the same legislative regime to Ontario municipalities and subsidiary bodies, such as municipal hydro-electric commissions.

92   S.Q. 1993, c.17 [*Quebec Privacy Act*].

93   An Act to support and promote electronic commerce by protecting personal information that is collected, used, or disclosed in certain circumstances, by providing for the use of electronic means to communicate or record information or transactions and by amending the *Canada Evidence Act*, the *Statutory Instruments Act*, and the *Statute Revision Act*, S.C. 2000, c. 5 [PIPEDA]. The privacy law is in Part 1 of PIPEDA; Part 2 contains the new federal rules on electronic documents, discussed in chapter 6, section A.1(f), "Law Reform Approaches." For a chronology of the milestones that led up to PIPEDA, from the adherence of the federal government to the *OECD Guidelines* in 1984, to the adoption of the *CSA Code* in 1996, to the passage of PIPEDA, see *2000 Privacy Commissioner Annual Report*, above note 6.

94   PIPEDA defines "personal information" as "information about an identifiable individual, but does not include the name, title or business address or telephone number of an employee of an organization." Personal information should be able to be anonymized if the data elements that identify the specific person are removed. Support for this position can be found in a recent decision of the British Court of Appeal, in *R. v. Department of Health*, [2000] W.L.R. 940 (C.A.).

as part of a commercial activity.[95] PIPEDA becomes effective in three phases. From January 1, 2001, it applied to organizations that use, collect, or disclose personal information in connection with the operation of a company under federal jurisdiction[96] or outside the province for consideration.[97] On January 1, 2002, the reach of PIPEDA extended to organizations in respect of personal health information. And finally, on January 1, 2004, PIPEDA will apply to all private sector entities that collect, use, or disclose personal information in the course of commercial activities, except in those provinces where provincial legislation similar to PIPEDA has been enacted.

95   Therefore, PIPEDA will not apply to any non-commercial activities; charities, universities, schools or hospitals; the professions except where these organizations are engaged in commercial activities; employee records in the provincially regulated private sector; agents of the Crown in right of the province; or municipalities. The "commercial" activity qualification was presumably added to help the federal government bring PIPEDA within the federal commerce power if a constitutional challenge is made against the legislation: see Daniel McHardie, "Internet Privacy Law Now On-Line," *The Globe and Mail* (2 January 2001), where a legal adviser to the federal privacy commissioner is quoted as anticipating a constitutional challenge from the provinces on the grounds that PIPEDA invades provincial jurisdiction in relation to property and civil rights (of course this adviser believes PIPEDA comes within federal powers).

96   Federally regulated entities include shipping companies, railways, airlines, banks, telecommunications companies, radio stations and, in light of the *Chum*, below note 256, and *Island Telecom*, below note 260, decisions referred to in section D.3(a) of this chapter, entities that carry on Web-casting activities. In respect of these organizations, PIPEDA also applies to employee information. Consider the measures a group like the Bell Companies has taken in light of PIPEDA: revised Bell Code of Fair Information Practices and implemented a Bell Privacy Policy; developed a privacy team with representatives from various business units (human resources, legal, regulatory, marketing, information technology); developed an opt-out mechanism from information sharing; obtained the Web Trust Seal from Ernst & Young for the <bell.ca site>; continued Bell Privacy Ombudsman to oversee compliance; appointed privacy coordinators in Ontario and Quebec for employees; implemented communications strategies regarding privacy with customers and employees; implemented employee training and annual sign-off; and added privacy audit processes to existing internal audits: David Elder (assistant general counsel, regulatory law, Bell Canada), *Compliance With PIPED Act by the Bell Companies*, presentation to the LL.M. in E-Business Law Program, Osgoode Hall Law School, 22 May 2001.

97   For example, credit reporting services. In *Thomas v. Robinson*, [2001] O.J. No. 4373 (Ont. Sup. Ct.), the court concluded that PIPEDA applied to a database that comprised personal information of insurance agents from across Canada. There are, however, a few curious aspects to this decision. For example, the deal at issue in this case involved a sale of shares, thus PIPEDA should not have come into play as there was no transfer of data; in sale of business situations, PIPEDA should only apply when there is a sale of assets.

PIPEDA requires every organization that is subject to its jurisdiction to comply with the fair information handling practices set out in its Schedule 1, which are essentially the CSA Code (discussed earlier in this chapter) with a few additional nuances. These practices can be summarized as follows:

Accountability. An organization is responsible for personal information under its control. The organization shall designate an individual or individuals who are accountable for the organization's compliance with the following principles.[98]

Identifying Purposes. The purposes for which personal information is collected shall be identified by the organization at or before the time the information is collected.

Consent. The knowledge and consent of the individual are required for the collection, use, or disclosure of personal information, except when inappropriate.

Limiting Collection. The collection of personal information shall be limited to that which is necessary for the purposes identified by the organization. Information shall be collected by fair and lawful means.

Limiting Use, Disclosure, and Retention. Personal information shall not be used or disclosed for purposes other than those for which it was collected, except with the consent of the individual or as required by the law. Personal information shall be retained only as long as necessary for fulfilment of those purposes.

Accuracy. Personal information shall be as accurate, complete, and up-to-date as is necessary for the purposes for which it is to be used.

Safeguards. Personal information shall be protected by security safeguards appropriate to the sensitivity of the information.

Openness. An organization shall make readily available to individuals specific information about its policies and practices relating to the management of personal information.

Individual Access. Upon request, an individual shall be informed of the existence, use, and disclosure of his or her personal information and shall be given access to that information. An individual shall be

---

98   Chief privacy officers are being appointed in Canada and the United States: "Corporate Privacy Officers Increasingly Important," *The Globe and Mail* (23 February 2001); and John Schwartz, "Chief Privacy Officers Forge Evolving Corporate Roles," *The New York Times* (12 February 2001).

able to challenge the accuracy and completeness of the information and have it amended as appropriate.

Challenging Compliance. An individual shall be able to address a challenge concerning compliance with the above principles to the designated individual or individuals for the organization's compliance.

Individuals who feel an entity has not complied with the provisions of PIPEDA may make a complaint to the federal privacy commissioner. Unresolved disputes may also be escalated to the Federal Court, which may exercise broad remedial powers, including awarding damages for humiliation and punitive damages not to exceed $20,000. The privacy commissioner may also act on his or her own initiative and conduct investigations, as well as audit the information-handling practices of any organization that he or she believes is violating the statute.[99] Fines up to $100,000 may be levied for failing to cooperate with an investigation or audit of the privacy commissioner.

Apart from Quebec, as at December 31, 2002, no other province has enacted comprehensive data protection legislation covering the private sector. Ontario has announced that it intends to do so, and that its legislation will have even broader coverage than PIPEDA in that it will cover personal information included in non-commercial transactions.[100] Given the inexorable rise of the Internet, and the enactment of PIPEDA, it is likely that all other Canadian provinces will follow suit and bring forward their own data protection legal regimes. Given the fourth dynamic of computer law (the blurring of national/international, or in the Canadian context, the blurring of provincial/national), one hopes this will be done in a manner whereby all the enactments will be harmonized as much as possible. Early in 2002, the Ontario government released a draft privacy law that was intended to cover both health information and other personal information.[101] Presumably, Ontario will want its privacy legislation in place by January 1, 2004, in order to avoid the purported application of PIPEDA to the provincial

---

99 PIPEDA, ss. 18 and 19.

100 A consultation draft of the proposed *Privacy of Personal Information Act* was released for comment in early 2002. Press Release available at <gov.on.ca>. British Columbia issued a consultation paper titled *Privacy Protection in the Private Sector* in May 2002 (available at <mser.gov.bc.ca>).

101 For commentary on this draft bill, see Information and Privacy Commissioner/ Ontario, "Submission to the Ministry of Consumer and Business Services: Consultation Draft of the *Privacy of Personal Information Act*, 2002," 27 February 2002, available at <ipc.on.ca/english/pubpres/reports/cbs-0202.pdf>.

private sector.[102] Some commentators predict a dandy constitutional fight if a province neither passes its own private sector privacy law nor accepts PIPEDA.[103]

Given its recent enactment, it is too early to gauge the impact of PIPEDA. Nevertheless, a few observations are in order. A threshold one is that a number of commentators have questioned the wisdom of building a legally enforceable privacy regime on top of the *CSA Code*, which was essentially a very general, voluntary, consensus document that was to be fine-tuned by different industries or companies for actual use.[104] It is also not helpful that the *CSA Code* is attached as a schedule to PIPEDA, but the body of Part 1 of the statute contains a number of provisions that amplify or override part of the *CSA Code* schedule. For example, retrofitted onto the entire *CSA Code* is the further generic obligation that an organization may collect, use, or disclose personal information only for purposes that a reasonable person would consider are appropriate in the circumstances.[105] The result is a cumbersome, some might say unwieldy, legislative regime that is not at all user friendly.[106] Thus, a number of questions arise when companies begin to try to apply PIPEDA to their specific situations, but particularly in an online context, given that the *CSA Code*'s pronouncements

---

102 See Barrie White, "Made-in-Ontario Privacy Legislation Coming," *Law Times* (11 March 2002).

103 Simon Chester, "Privacy Set To Become Constitutional Battleground," *The Lawyers Weekly* (28 June 2002).

104 For one such commentary, see Teresa Scassa, "Text and Context: Making Sense of Canada's New Personal Information Protection Legislation" (2000–1) 32 Ottawa Law Review 1 ["Text and Context"]. In hindsight, and for consistency's sake, it may have been wiser for the federal government to have used more of the Quebec privacy law as its own template. On the other hand, politics, especially privacy politics, is the art of the possible, and PIPEDA was heavily lobbied at its inception, so the government might have concluded that it is better to have half a loaf than no bread at all: Eric Reguly, "Privacy Act Is One Complicated Beast," *The Globe and Mail* (13 March 1999); Heather Scoffield, "Senate Delays Passing of Privacy Bill," *The Globe and Mail* (8 December 1999); and Shawn McCarthy, "Privacy Bill Splits Health Care, Commerce," *The Globe and Mail* (8 December 1999).

105 PIPEDA, s. 5(3). This clause will likely generate copious amounts of negotiation with the privacy commissioner, and litigation, until its parameters are defined.

106 And in any event, why did the federal government not put the privacy law regime into a statute of its own, instead of including it in an omnibus law that also addresses evidence law and contract formation issues? Privacy will be one of the defining rights of the twenty-first century; surely an area this important warranted its own statutory framework.

on matters of notice and consent contemplated a paper-based environment. For example, how should consent for disclosure to a third party be garnered from the user of a Web site? Does consent have to be express, or is implied consent permitted?[107]

The general nature of many of the paragraphs in the *CSA Code*, and thus the inherent ambiguity of PIPEDA on a number of points, gives scope for the privacy commissioner to fill this vacuum if he or she so wishes.[108] The current commissioner, George Radwanski, is doing just this. In his initial actions under PIPEDA during the course of 2001 and 2002, the first two years of operation of the statute, Mr. Radwanski has taken a very activist approach to the new law. In his inaugural decision, the privacy commissioner ruled that the use of a surveillance camera by a private store to monitor a public street in Yellowknife constituted the gathering of personal information and therefore was unlawful.[109] In a potentially far-reaching action, the privacy commissioner has criticized Air Canada's use of an opt-out system for securing the consent of Aeroplan members to the sharing of their personal data for marketing pur-

---

107 The *CSA Code*, in para. 4.3.2, contemplates that the data collector will use "reasonable effort" to advise the data subject of the use to be made of the personal information. Accordingly, it would appear that the discussion in chapter 6, section A.3(c), regarding "express and implied click-consent agreements," is relevant here. The same principles would apply: in the online world, consent for data protection purposes may be secured by either an "express click-consent agreement," where the user clicks an "I Agree" button at the end of a specific agreement, or by an "implied click-consent agreement" where, to reiterate the standard articulated in more detail in chapter 6, there is a direct link from the home page (or the page where the personal information is collected) to the privacy policy or the general terms that contain the consent language, there is on the home page or information collection page a prominent notice requiring data subjects to read and assent to the consent and stressing the importance of the consent, and the home page or information collection page should have a button that has the data subject confirm that he or she has read the consent and agrees to be bound by it, thereby manifesting assent to it.

108 To give an idea of how busy the privacy commissioner might be under PIPEDA, consider that in the first five years of Quebec's privacy law, 900 investigations were commenced as a result of a total of 2,000 inquiries: statistics cited in footnote 2 of Scassa, "Text and Context," above note 104.

109 Privacy Commissioner of Canada <privcom.gc.ca/media/an/nt_010620_e.asp>. In this decision, Mr. Radwanski held that both live and recorded video pictures qualify as personal information, and therefore cannot be collected or used without consent of the person being taped. In other early decisions, the commissioner has found that a credit score and Web site information is personal information, but physician's prescriptions are not. In another case the commissioner ruled that using a subscriber's email address to send spam was not a violation as the customer had consented in the subscription agreement.

poses.[110] Mr. Radwanski and privacy advocates do not like opt-out systems, where a data subject has to expressly indicate his or her refusal to prevent the data collector from doing something; they prefer opt-in systems, whereby the data collector cannot do something unless expressly approved by the data subject. The weakness, however, in this latter position is that PIPEDA clearly permits the use of the opt-out mechanism.[111] Presumably, if Mr. Radwanski and privacy advocates do not like opt-out systems, their displeasure should be directed at Parliament, not at the organizations that use them. Put another way, there is a tendency in some circles to view privacy law as the great battleground between those (typically commercial interests) who view data protection law as a means of facilitating the collection, use, and transfer of information, and those who approach this subject solely to carefully preserve personal privacy. Rather than side institutionally with the latter, a better role for the privacy commissioner would be to champion those who occupy the middle ground in this debate, namely, organizations that wish to use personal information of data subjects in a manner that is sensitive to the reasonable concerns of data subjects. Therefore, instead of fighting opt-out mechanisms on principle, the way a privacy interest group might, the privacy commissioner should spend his time working to improve the notification aspects of opt-out systems.[112]

---

110 Privacy commissioner, letter to Air Canada, July 18, 2001; see also Shawn McCarthy, "Federal Privacy Watchdog Criticizes Air Canada: Plan To Share Data From Aeroplan Cited," *The Globe and Mail* (19 July 2001). The final decision of the privacy commissioner in the Air Canada matter, dated April 4, 2002, summaries of which are available (as are summaries of the other decisions of the privacy commissioner) at <privcom.gc.ca>, received press coverage: see Janet McFarland, "Business Face Crackdown On Sharing Customer Secrets," *The Globe and Mail* (21 March 2002). This Air Canada decision is one of the most significant of the privacy commissioner's early decisions. Among other findings, the commissioner concluded that Air Canada breached Principle 4.1.3 of PIPEDA when it failed to have its third-party mailing house agree to contractually impose privacy restraints.

111 See PIPEDA, schedule 1, para. 4.3.7(b), which reads as follows: "a checkoff box may be used to allow individuals to request that their names and addresses not be given to other organizations. Individuals who do not check the box are assumed to consent to the transfer of this information to third parties."

112 As well, the privacy commissioner might usefully engage in helping to craft sectoral codes that would fine-tune the *CSA Code* for particular situations, such as activities that collect personal data in an online environment. In this regard, it is interesting to note that the U.K.'s *Data Protection Act 1998* (U.K.), 1998 c. 29, in s. 51 permits the data protection commissioner to approve codes of practice brought forward by trade associations. These codes are advisory and are not legally binding, but under s. 53 of New Zealand's *Privacy Act 1993* they are.

5) Other Legislation

While Quebec has been the only province to date to enact a general data protection statute covering the private sector, there are in the various common law provinces a number of other statutes and/or regulations that address data protection issues. It is quite common, for example, to institute fair information practices in the credit reporting industry.[113] Generally, these statutes require consumer credit reporting agencies to be registered with the government, and to adhere to the sound data-handling practices enumerated in the statutes and in related regulations. Given the use to which credit reports are put by financial institutions and others, these statutes also contain provisions regarding the type of information that may be collected on individuals and included in a credit report. For example, Ontario's statute provides that information in a consumer report regarding bankruptcy, court judgments, tax arrears, criminal convictions, and other negative information cannot be more than seven years old.[114]

Statutes regulating or relating to various other industries or sectors of the economy will often have provisions enumerating standards for dealing with personal information. For example, in the financial services field, federal and provincial statutes governing banks, insurance companies, and other entities have been amended over the past few years to give regulators the authority to make regulations in the data protection area.[115] To date, however, specific regulations have not been passed in this area.[116] One area where the necessity to protect personal information is particularly acute is the health care field. The Supreme Court of Canada, in the *Dyment* case, recognized this when it spoke of a patient's need to reveal information "of a most intimate character" in

---

113 For example, see the *Consumer Reporting Act*, R.S.O. 1990, c. C.33; *Consumer Reporting Act*, R.S.N.S. c. 93; and *Credit Reporting Act*, R.S.B.C. 1996, c. 81.

114 See also Alberta's *Financial Consumers Act*, R.S.A. 1990, c. F-95, which regulates how consumer information collected by financial institutions may be used; it requires, in s. 18(1), the consumers' consent to the use of their information for a purpose other than the purpose for which it was originally given.

115 For example, see the *Bank Act*, R.S.C. 1985, c. B-1, s. 459. Banks and other financial institutions are also subject to a common law duty of confidentiality that requires banks to hold their customers' data in confidence subject to several exceptions: see *Tournier v. National Provincial and Union Bank of England*, [1924] 1 K.B. 461 (C.A.).

116 It is interesting to note that banks were the first organizations to institute privacy codes based on the *CSA Code* back in 1996; now they come under PIPEDA as federally regulated entities.

order to obtain medical care.[117] Thus, it is not surprising that statutes governing hospitals, such as a regulation under Ontario's *Public Hospitals Act*, stipulate that a hospital may not disclose patient data to a third party except under the circumstances enumerated in the regulation.[118] Similarly, many statutes governing the various health care providers make it professional misconduct to divulge patient data without approval from the patient.[119] Courts in Canada have also held that doctors and other health care providers have a common law duty to keep patient information confidential, notwithstanding that the physician or dentist owns the patient record.[120] These statutory provisions and common law rules are useful, but there is concern that as the practice of medicine moves from the individual doctor–patient relationship in the doctor's office to a medical team-based approach in an institutional setting, with computer-based technologies storing and communicating personal health data among physicians and health care providers, new and broader protections are required.[121] Accordingly, Alberta,[122] Mani-

---

117 *R. v. Dyment*, [1988] 2 S.C.R. 417 at 433. This case is discussed in chapter 3, section B.11, "Search, Seizure, and Surveillance." In Lisa Priest, "Privacy Commissioner Called To Assess Medical Records Leak," *The Globe and Mail* (28 May 2002), the Ontario privacy commissioner is quoted as stating that health information is the most sensitive kind of information; her request to audit the health records of a large hospital were prompted by reports that celebrities' records had been accessed in an unauthorized manner. As for the particular challenges involved in keeping health information confidential, see "Medical Records: Whose File Is It Anyway," *The Economist*, 1 June 2002.

118 Hospital Management, R.R.O. 1990, Reg. 965, as amended.

119 See, for example, in Ontario, subs. 36(1) of the *Regulated Health Professions Act*, 1991, S.O. 1991, c. 18; and s. 1 of Regulation 856/93 under the *Medicine Act*, 1991, S.O. 1991, c. 30.

120 *Wells (Litigation Guardian of) v. Paramsothy* (1996), 32 O.R. (3d) 452 (Div. Ct.); *Axelrod (Re)* (1994), 20 O.R. (3d) 133 (C.A.); and *McInerney v. MacDonald*, [1992] 2 S.C.R. 138.

121 See, for example, Tom Onyshko, "Common-Law Protection for Doctor-Patient Confidentiality Needs Reform, U.S. Expert Says," *The Lawyers Weekly* (24 February 1995).

122 *Health Information Act*, R.S.A. 2000, c. H.5. Some have argued, however, that this law is not so much privacy legislation "as it is an information act that provides for disclosure under controlled conditions": statement of Alberta's *Information and Privacy Commissioner*, cited in *Privacy Commissioner of Canada Annual Report, 1999–2000* at 43. It is interesting to note that an earlier version of the law discussed in 1997 contained the word protection in the title: Health Information Protection Act, but this word has been dropped from the current law. Under this legislation, the Alberta privacy commissioner recently held that health service provider information cannot be provided to IMS without the provider's consent: Office of the Information and Privacy Commissioner, Alberta, Order H2002-003, Alberta Pharmacists and Pharmacies, 19 March 2003.

toba,[123] and Saskatchewan[124] have recently introduced comprehensive data protection legislation for the health care sector, and Ontario at one time contemplated doing the same.[125] While the health information privacy statutes resulting from these initiatives likely will resemble one another in terms of general principles, it is unfortunate that they are not based on a standard, model law. With telemedicine across provincial boundaries soon to be a reality, and given the impact of the fourth dynamic of computer law generally, differing regulatory treatment of health information will cause serious compliance problems for health care administrators.

6) International Developments

a) Europe

There have been plenty of international conventions and related efforts regarding the codification of rules related to data protection and privacy, including those at the international level[126] and the regional level, especially in Europe.[127] Many countries, particularly those in Europe, have enacted data protection laws, commencing with the Scandinavian countries in the 1970s.[128] More recently, to try to ensure a harmoniza-

---

123 The *Personal Health Information Act*, S.M. c. 51 (assented to June 28, 1997). Apparently part of the rationale for passage of this legislation was to bolster public confidence in light of the creation of a proposed computer network linking Manitoba's entire health care system, the SmartHealth computer project; see David Roberts, "Manitoba Bill Still Flawed, Critics Say," *The Globe and Mail* (25 June 1997).

124 *Health Information Protection Act*, S.S. 1999, c. H.O.012; Royal Assent, May 6, 1999, not yet proclaimed in force.

125 In December 2000, the Ontario government introduced Bill 159, *Personal Health Information Privacy Act, 2000*, but, after much criticism, this was withdrawn and as of December 31, 2002, it has not been reintroduced. It is now likely that Ontario's much-awaited private sector privacy statute will cover the health and non-health sectors in a single law.

126 United Nations: *Universal Declaration of Human Rights*, 1948 — Article 12; *Guidelines Concerning Computerized Personal Data Files*, 1990.

127 European Union — *European Convention for the Protection of Human Rights and Fundamental Freedoms*, 1950; Council of Europe — *Convention for the Protection of Individuals with Regard to Automatic Processing of Personal Data*, 1985.

128 The Swedes, in particular, have been strong supporters of data protection since 1776, the date of their first *Access to Public Records Act*, which mandated that publicly held information only be used for sanctioned purposes. This rich tradition in Europe of data privacy can also extend to the treatment of e-mail monitoring by employers: see "German Law May Keep E-mail Secret," *The Globe and Mail* (19 October 2000).

tion of various national laws dealing with the protection of personal data (and clearly with one eye firmly fixed on the fourth dynamic of computer law), the European Union has adopted a *Directive on Data Protection (Directive)*.[129] The *Directive* implements two objectives, one to protect the rights of individuals in respect of their personal information, the other to ensure that this data can move freely within the single European market; the first objective is a prerequisite for the latter one. The directive and the various existing national laws generally implement the fair information practices found in the *OECD Guidelines*, but sometimes with important nuances. For example, the *U.K. Data Protection Act 1984* required data users and computer services companies who process personal data for others to register under the statute.[130] Importantly, this statute and its successor also provide data subjects with civil remedies, including compensation for damages arising from inaccurate data or the unauthorized disclosure of personal data. Particularly noteworthy for Canadians is the provision in many of these European laws and the *Directive* that the export of personal data can be prohibited where the country of the transferee does not provide adequate data protection laws. These "export" rules ostensibly played an important part in first Quebec, and then the federal Government, deciding to implement data protection laws to cover the private sector. Late in 2001, the European Union released a decision indicating that the level of protection granted personal data under PIPEDA was adequate for the purposes of European law.[131]

b) The United States

The American response to the European *Directive* has been somewhat different from those of the Canadian and Quebec governments.

---

129 *Directive 95/46/EC of the European Parliament and of the Council of 24 October 1995 on the protection of individuals with regard to the processing of personal data and on the free movement of such data*. The Directive can be found in the *Official Journal of the European Communities* of 23 November 1995, No. L281 at page 31 or at <europa.eu.int/eurlex/en/lif/dat/1995/en_395L0046.html>. The Directive came into effect in October 1998, and is being implemented into the national law of the member states of the EU: for the status of these efforts, see <europa.eu.int/comm/internal_market/en/media/dataprot/law/impl.htm>.

130 *Data Protection Act 1984* (U.K.), 1984, c. 35, subs. 4(1). This statute has now been superseded by the *Data Protection Act 1998* (U.K.), 1998, c. 29, which continues this registration requirement.

131 The Commission of the European Communities, Commission Decision of 20 December 2001 pursuant to Directive 95/46/EC of the European Parliament and of the Council on the adequate protection of personal data provided by the *Canadian Personal Information Protection and Electronic Documents Act*.

Although the United States has had a fairly comprehensive data-handling law covering the federal public sector since the mid-1970s, its general approach in the private sector, to date at least, has been to implement sectoral legislation aimed at specific monitoring technologies and businesses, rather than a broad general regime.[132] Thus, the United States has the *Federal Wiretap Act* of 1968,[133] the privacy subscriber provisions in the *Cable Act* of 1984,[134] a *Fair Credit Reporting Act*,[135] the *Video Privacy Protection Act*,[136] an *Electronic Communications Privacy Act*,[137] the *Polygraph Protection Act*,[138] the *Telephone Consumer Protection Act* of 1991,[139] the *Children's Online Privacy Protection Act* of 1998,[140] The

---

132 *The Privacy Act of 1974*, 5 USC §552a (1974). The Canadian *Privacy Act*, R.S.C. 1985, c. P-21, passed eight years later, has the same general intent, to regulate how the government can collect, store, and use personal information of citizens. Other U.S. federal privacy law also exists vis-à-vis the public sector. See the *Driver's Privacy Protection Act of 1994*, 18 U.S.C. 2721, which the U.S. Supreme Court, in *Reno v. Condon* 528 U.S. 141 (2000), recently confirmed gives the U.S. Congress the right to regulate the marketing by state agencies of drivers' record information collected by them.

133 18 USC §2510-2520. Elements of this statute have an analogue in s. 184 of the Canadian *Criminal Code* (see chapter 3, section B.10, "Interception of Communications"), in that both address standards for the conduct of electronic surveillance by law enforcement authorities.

134 *Cable Communications Policy Act* of 1984. This prohibits the collection, storage, or disclosure to third parties of personal data of subscribers without their consent. The equivalent of this in Canada are the privacy protections afforded by the *Radiocommunication Act*, R.S.C. 1985, c. R-2, s. 9(1)(b) and the *Telecommunications Act*, S.C. 1993, c. 38, ss. 7(i), 41. Section 7(i) of the latter statute makes it one of the objectives of Canada's telecommunications policy "to contribute to the protection of privacy of persons."

135 15 USC §1681-81t (1988). Like its Canadian counterparts, the various provincial credit reporting agency laws (discussed in section A.5 of this chapter, "Other Legislation"), this statute does not control the collection, storage, or use of personal information except for credit-related data, and applies only to credit reporting agencies.

136 18 USC §2710. This statute prohibits the disclosure of customer data, or viewing habit data, relative to the rental of videotapes. It was prompted in large part by the disclosure of the viewing habits of Judge Robert Bork during his (unsuccessful) nomination hearing for the U.S. Supreme Court.

137 18 USC §2510-2522, 2701-2711 (1994). This statute amended the *Federal Wiretap Act* by extending it to cover most electronic communications, including e-mail.

138 This statute prohibits the disclosure of polygraph test results.

139 This regime controls the uses of telephone auto-diallers and the distribution of junk faxes.

140 Pub. L. 105-277; otherwise known by its acronym, COPPA. A key requirement of this legislation is that parental consent be obtained before a child's personal information is disclosed to third parties. One means of obtaining "verifiable" consent is to have the parent print out the consent form, sign it and fax it back

Gramm-Leach-Bliley Act,[141] privacy regulations under the *Health Insurance Portability, Accountability Act*,[142] the *Driver's Privacy Protection Act*,[143] and *Regulation S-P* of the U.S. Securities and Exchange Commissioner.[144] Although this legislative record amounts to a fairly extensive aggregation of regulation,[145] traditionally the United States has resisted

---

to the Web site operator. One of the author's clients recalls receiving faxes of this form, just as envisaged by COPPA, but with the parent's purported signature written in a very childlike cursive script.

141 Pub. L. 106-102 (1999). This legislation deals with a broad range of issues; in terms of privacy, it contains requirements for the financial institution with respect to the protection of non-public personal information. This law has prompted U.S. financial institutions to send millions of mailings to clients that include various opt-out options. Many of the mailings are vague and confusing, or often too detailed: John Schwartz, "Privacy Policy Notices Are Called Too Common and Too Confusing," *The New York Times* (7 May 2001). One bank has even adopted two privacy policies, the regular detailed one, and a short one in plain English. This is all fodder for future litigation if the institutions fail to abide by these policies and notices: see the FTC proceeding against GeoCities for failure of this entity to comply with the terms of its own privacy policy, which would constitute a deceptive practice for purposes of the FTC's enabling legislation: *Federal Trade Commission Act*, 15 U.S.C. §§41-58.

142 Federal Register, November 3, 1999. These extensive HIPAA rules, which are over 350 pages in length, implement a comprehensive regime of privacy fair information practices in respect of personally identifiable health-related information collected, stored, used, or transmitted by health plans, certain health care providers, and others. This rule came into effect in April 2001, with compliance required by April 14, 2003.

143 This statute promulgates rules for the disclosure and commercial exploitation of personal information stored in the databases of state motor vehicle registration departments. In *Reno* v. *Condon*, 120 S. Ct. 666 (U.S. Sup. Ct. 2000), this law was held to be constitutionally valid.

144 17 C.F.R. Part 248. This regulation requires financial institutions to notify consumers about the institution's privacy policies, and provide them with an "opt-out" method of refusing to allow sharing of this information with non-affiliated third parties.

145 This list is limited to federal initiatives. In addition, there is a fairly extensive state-based privacy-related statutory regime. For example, New York State enacted the *New York Right of Privacy Act*, N.Y. Civ. Rts. §§50–51, in 1903 in response to that state's highest court concluding, in *Robertson* v. *Rochester Folding Box Co.*, 64 N.E. 442 (N.Y. 1902), there was no common law right of privacy. More recently, the State of California enacted legislation that attempts to regulate the phenomenon of photographers and press hounding celebrities, and was prompted by the death of Princess Diana as a result of her being chased through the streets of Paris by the European paparazzi. Of course it remains to be seen whether this law will withstand a challenge under the First Amendment of the U.S. Constitution, which, in its support of free speech, has typically precluded such legislation.

adopting an overarching legislative privacy regime for the private sector, opting instead to rely on self-regulation and the common tort of privacy discussed earlier in this chapter. Indeed, some of the legislation noted above has been successfully attacked as infringing the First Amendment right of "commercial and corporate free speech," illustrating again the point that privacy is not an absolute right and often yields to other rights.[146] Therefore, rather than prompt the U.S. government to enact a general privacy law regime for the private sector, the European *Directive* resulted in the European Commission and the U.S. government concluding the "safe harbor" arrangement, under which U.S. companies that agree to adhere to the seven fair information practices of the arrangement will be deemed to provide adequate privacy protection for purposes of the European *Directive*, will thus be considered in a "safe harbor" in respect of the European *Directive*, and therefore can be transferred data from European companies.[147] The seven information-handling practices under the safe harbor arrangements are not dissimilar to those of the *OECD Guidelines*, and involve: Notice (indicating to data subjects the purpose for the data collection); Choice[148] (individuals must be permitted to opt out of third party disclosure or any other use not originally contemplated; disclosure of sensitive information requires explicit choice, or an opt-in approach); Onward Transfer (the data collector may only transfer data to an entity that agrees to adhere to the safe harbor arrangement); Security (data collectors must implement reasonable security safeguards); Data Integrity (data collectors should ensure the data they collect is reliable for its intended purpose); Access (data subjects must be given access to their information); and Enforcement (data collectors must provide meaningful, independent recourse mechanisms to ensure compliance). Companies that subscribe to the safe harbor arrangement must self-certify each year.[149]

---

146 In *U.S. West, Inc. v. FCC*, 182 F.3d 1224 (1999) the court annulled the rules of the Federal Communications Commission that required telephone companies to procure the express consent (opt-in) of customers before using their related network information for marketing purposes.

147 U.S. Department of Commerce, Safe Harbor Privacy Principles, July 2000, available at <ita.doc.gov/td/ecom/shprinciplesfinal.html>. Although this is a Canadian book, it will nonetheless defer to the American spelling of *harbor*, as this is the title of a legal treaty.

148 While Canadians and Europeans use the word *consent* to denote manifestation of assent in privacy matters, the Americans use the term *choice*.

149 For a list of companies that participate in the safe harbor arrangement, see <export.gov/safeharbor/index.html>. As of October 31, 2002, there were 291 companies registered in the program.

Another example of U.S. self-regulation can be seen in the private sector certification programs that have come into operation in respect of the privacy policies that a Web site could adopt regarding the use the operator of the site can make of personal information collected from users of the site. The certification program operated by TRUSTe[150] is perhaps the best known and most widely used. Essentially, to be certified by TRUSTe, and thereby to be entitled to display the TRUSTe trustmark,[151] a Web site operator must prepare a Web site privacy policy in accordance with the TRUSTe guidelines, comply with this policy, and subject itself to periodic review by TRUSTe. Interestingly, the TRUSTe privacy principles are not dissimilar to the fair information practices found under PIPEDA or the *OECD Guidelines,* and indeed they have the advantage of being more finely tuned to Internet practices and procedures. For example, the definition of "personally identifiable information" is sensitive to Internet-based data collection practices.[152] As well, the TRUSTe guidelines specifically address cookies, and require disclosure about their use and what will be done with the information collected by them. With respect to the all-important issue of consent, or "choice" as the Americans refer to it, TRUSTe recognizes the use of the "opt-out" mechanism, but at the same time requires that the privacy

---

150 See <truste.org>. Another well-known program, BBBOnline, is operated by the Better Business Bureau: <bbbonline.org>.

151 The TRUSTe logo is also known as a "seal," as in "seal of approval," and hence these Web site privacy certification programs are also known as "seal programs." For a discussion of these seal programs, and how they compare to PIPEDA, see John MacDonnell, "Exporting Trust: Does E-Commerce Need A Canadian Privacy Seal of Approval?" (2001) 39 Alberta Law Review 346.

152 The TRUSTe guide provides: "'Personally Identifiable Information' refers to any information that identifies or can be used to identify, contact, or locate the person to whom such information pertains. This includes information that is used in a way that is personally identifiable, including linking it with identifiable information from other sources, or from which other personally identifiable information can easily be derived, including, but not limited to, name, address, phone number, fax number, e-mail address, financial profiles, social security number, and credit card information. To the extent unique information (which by itself is not Personally Identifiable Information) such as a personal profile, unique identifier, biometric information, and IP address is associated with Personally Identifiable Information, then such unique information will also be considered Personally Identifiable Information. Personally Identifiable Information does not include information that is collected anonymously (i.e., without identification of the individual user) or demographic information not connected to an identified individual."

policy be a single click away from the home page.[153] The TRUSTe guidelines also address how the personal data should be dealt with upon a merger or acquisition of the business of the Web site operator.[154] Yet another variation on American self-regulation is the Platform for Privacy Preferences Project (generally known by its acronym P3P).[155] In short, P3P is a design standard for Web browsers that involves businesses crafting privacy policies for their Web sites in accordance with the template provided by P3P. Users' browsers, provided by P3P, would be equipped with related technology that would enable each user to pre-select his or her own privacy preferences. Then, whenever such a user visited such a Web site, the user's browser would immediately indicate how the Web site's policies compared to the user's privacy preferences. In his recent influential book, Lawrence Lessig is supportive of the P3P initiative and sees it as an important example of the American

---

153   The BBBOnline approach is somewhat more demanding, requiring the notice to be on the home page as well as at every point in the Web site where personal information is requested: BBBOnline, Sample Privacy Notice, available at <bbbonline.org/privacy/sample-privacy.asp>.

154   In this regard, it is interesting to note that in 2000 the U.S. Federal Trade Commission brought a proceeding against Toysmart.com when it threatened to transfer personal information upon its bankruptcy, as this would have violated the provision in the Toysmart privacy policy that stipulated the Internet toy e-tailer would "never" share this data with a third party. The FTC gets involved in these matters courtesy of its enabling legislation, which gives the FTC the power to pursue injunctive and other relief where it finds unfair and deceptive practices in or affecting commerce: *The Federal Trade Commission Act*, 15 U.S.C. §§41: *FTC v. Toysmart.com, LLC et al.* — Complaint, available at <ftc.gov/os/2000/07/toysmartcmp.htm>; Barrie McKenna, "E-Tailer Shakeout Punctures Privacy: Toysmart's Move to Sell Confidential Customer Information Sparks Renewed Debate Over the Need For Tougher Laws To Protect Consumers," *The Globe and Mail* (20 July 2000). The parties ultimately settled on the basis that the data could be transferred, but only to an entity that purchased the Toysmart business, and on condition that the purchaser would have to continue to abide by the Toysmart privacy policy; use the personal data only to fulfil customer orders; not disclose, sell, or transfer the data to a third party; and give prior notice to the data subjects of any change in the privacy policy, with any change related to the previously collected data requiring the affirmative consent ("opt-in") of the data subject. See also *In Re Toysmart.com LLC*, No. 00-13995-CJK (U.S. Bkr. Ct. 2000) available at <ftc.gov/os/2000/07/toysmarttbankruptcy.1.htm>, wherein the court overrode the *FTC-Toysmart* consent decree, and held that Toysmart could sell its customer database to a third party.

155   See <w3.org>. P3P is backed by the World Wide Web Consortium, which includes companies such as Microsoft, IBM, AOL, and TRUSTe.

preference for self-regulation of the Internet.[156] Others, however, are critical of P3P (and of Lessig's support for it!).[157] And the self-regulators may be losing ground, notwithstanding the safe harbor arrangement, given that the U.S. Federal Trade Commission, which traditionally was a staunch supporter of the self-regulation model,[158] has more recently come out strongly in favour of the enactment of a general privacy law regime to cover the private sector;[159] the FTC has concluded that self-

---

156 *Code and Other Laws of Cyberspace* (New York: Basic Books, 1999). Lessig's important thesis is that the overall technical architecture of the Internet, as well as the design of specific technologies and products, has an enormous impact on the rules governing this new communication medium: hence, from Lessig's perspective, software "code" is also, for all intents and purposes, "legal code" or law.

157 For a scathing attack on Lessig, see Marc Rotenberg, *"Fair Information Practices and the Architecture of Privacy (What Larry Doesn't Get)"* (2001) 1 Stan. Tech. L. Rev. Rotenberg, who is the executive director of the Electronic Privacy Information Center in Washington, D.C., would like to see the United States enact a general privacy law, and argues that to do so would be in keeping with the fairly extensive sectoral privacy regulation developed over the years (and enumerated briefly above).

158 The Federal Trade Commission (FTC) has undergone a fascinating evolution (and turnaround) in thinking on the question of self-regulation versus statutory regime. In its first pronouncements on the Internet, it was clearly pro–self-regulation. In June 1998, after conducting a survey of 1400 Web sites, which showed that only 14 percent of them provided notice of their information collection practices and only 2 percent had a comprehensive privacy policy, the FTC concluded more had to be done regarding privacy online, but it was still advocating this be done through self-regulation, except in respect of children, where it recommended legislation (and which spurred Congress to pass COPPA, which is noted above). Martha K. Landesberg *et al.*, FTC, Report to Congress on Privacy Online (4 June 1998). See also *Prepared Statement of the FTC on "Internet Privacy" Before the Subcommittee on Courts and Intellectual Property of the House Committee on the Judiciary, U.S. House of Representatives,* 26 March 1998. Incidentally, a survey of privacy policies on Canadian Web sites conducted two years later also resulted in a failing grade: Michael Geist, "A Troubling Snapshot of E-Privacy in Canada," *The Globe and Mail* (7 December 2000).

159 Federal Trade Commission, *Privacy Online: Fair Information Practices in the Electronic Marketplace,* May 2000 <ftc.gov/reports/privacy3/index.htm>. See also Tyler Hamilton, "FTC Joins in Push for Privacy: Stronger Internet Regulation Would Bring U.S. More in Line with Canada and Europe," *The Globe and Mail* (24 May 2000). In the meantime, however, regulators in the United States have also brought proceedings against online businesses in respect of alleged noncompliance with their own privacy policies: a short piece in "What's New," *The Globe and Mail* (27 August 2002); indicates that DoubleClick Inc. has settled an investigation with ten U.S. states regarding its ad serving practices, and in March 2002 paid $1.8 million to settle lawsuits alleging violations of privacy laws.

regulation is simply incapable of affording adequate privacy safeguards for Internet users, and recommends legislation that would enshrine fair information practices, as well as create an agency that would oversee the enforcement of the new legislation.

c)   Transborder Data Flow

The other major international dimension to data protection relates to the various measures that have been taken by international organizations, and in international treaties and agreements, to reduce national legal and regulatory obstacles to transborder data flows. For example, the *OECD Guidelines*, together with a subsequent OECD declaration,[160] exhort member countries to refrain from creating unjustified barriers to the international exchange of data and information. This sentiment found expression in the *Canada–U.S. Free Trade Agreement*, and now in the *North American Free Trade Agreement* (NAFTA), which includes Mexico.[161] Article 1302 of the NAFTA provides that governments cannot erect barriers to the free flow of information across their borders, subject to the ability to implement *bona fide* security or privacy rules. The free trade approach to transborder data flow, enshrined in the NAFTA, can be seen, for example, in the data processing provisions of the *Bank Act* and other federal financial institutions legislation. For example, while section 245 of the *Bank Act* requires a bank to maintain and process its data in Canada, the same provision, coupled with *Guideline No. E3*,[162] allows the Canadian subsidiaries of foreign banks to quite easily obtain an exemption to process their data outside of Canada so long as the Office of the Superintendent of Financial Institutions has adequate access to such records in a timely manner, and the business operations of the Canadian entity are not adversely affected.

B.   EXPORT CONTROL OF TECHNOLOGY

Since information is power — and in the Information Age it surely is — it is not surprising that many governments around the world attempt to control the export of strategically important technologies and information that might, in the hands of a country's actual or poten-

---

160   OECD, *Declaration on Transborder Data Flow*, adopted April 11, 1985.

161   *North American Free Trade Agreement Implementation Act*, S.C. 1993, c. 44.

162   Office of the Superintendent of Financial Institutions Canada, Processing Information Outside Canada, May 1992, found in *Consolidated Bank Act and Regulations 1998*, 10th ed. (Toronto: Carswell, 1997) at 636.

tial enemies, including terrorists, prove to be extremely detrimental to the country's security interests. Accordingly, the Canadian government enforces a pair of laws that can be used to curtail the export from Canada of relatively powerful computers and related technologies (such as certain software) that could be useful in military applications. Also subject to export control are encryption technologies that interfere with the ability of law enforcement and intelligence agencies from eavesdropping on the communications of our actual and potential adversaries. Given a number of the technology trends enumerated in chapter 1, particularly increased miniaturization and the development of the Internet as a means to transmit software as well as all sorts of data, the enforcement of export controls in the area of high technology is arguably becoming more problematic. The four dynamics of computer law — the rapid pace of technological change, the elusive nature of information, and the blurring of private/public and national/international — present significant challenges to those government regulators who wish to control the export of certain computer and related products and technologies.

1) The Law of Export Control

The Canadian government controls the export of computers, technology, and other products by means of two different statutes, the *Export and Import Permits Act (EIPA)*,[163] and the *United Nations Act*.[164] Under the latter statute, Canada can restrict the export of goods, as well as the movement of people and money, and the provision of services, to any country against which the United Nations has imposed economic sanctions. It was under the *United Nations Act* that Canada implemented economic sanctions against Iraq when it invaded Kuwait in 1991,[165] and against the various former territories of Yugoslavia.[166] As of December 31, 2002, the countries subject to embargo by Canada under the *United Nations Act* are Afghanistan, Angola, Libya, Rwanda, and Sierra Leone.[167] The *EIPA* is narrower in scope in that it only applies to the

---

163 R.S.C. 1985, c. E-19, as amended.
164 R.S.C. 1985, c. U-2, as amended.
165 United Nations Iraq Regulations, SOR/90-531, 7 August 1990, as amended.
166 United Nations Federal Republic of Yugoslavia (Serbia and Montenegro) Regulations, SOR/92-342, 2 June 1992, as amended; United Nations Republic of Bosnia and Hercogovina Regulations, SOR/95-145, 14 March 1995, repealed by SOR/96-222, 23 April 1996.
167 Readers are reminded to always check this and other lists like this because they change regularly.

export of goods, including software and technical data. Like the *United Nations Act*, however, under the *EIPA* the export of goods can be controlled on the basis of destination by placing a country on the Area Control List (ACL) kept under the *EIPA*.[168] Under the *EIPA* the export of munitions and certain strategic technologies are also controlled by placing such goods on an Export Control List (ECL).[169] An exporter shipping out of Canada any good on the ECL (regardless of its destination, except for most goods shipped to the United States), or shipping any good to an ACL country (regardless of the type of good), requires an export permit from the Canadian government. Since its enactment in 1947 until the fall of the Iron Curtain in the early 1990s, the primary rationale for the *EIPA*, and similar legislation in the United States and in Canada's other NATO allies and other like-minded democracies such as Japan and Australia, was to prevent the then Soviet Union and other Communist states from acquiring military goods, and strategic computer, software, and other dual-use technologies that could be used against the West in a military confrontation. The term *dual-use* illustrates another aspect of the elusive nature of information, seemingly cognizant of the second dynamic of computer law, namely, that it often assumes its value — in this case strategic and military value — from the context of its use.[170] When the countries of the former East Bloc came out from under Communism, there was a relaxation of certain aspects of export control, such as the disbanding of COCOM, the Paris-

---

168 Area Control List, SOR/81-543, 3 July 1981, as amended. The countries on the ACL as of December 31, 2002, were Angola and Myanmar: SOR/2001-42, s. 1.

169 Export Control List, SOR 89-202, 31 December 2001, as amended. The official current (as at 31 December 2002) ECL (the 1997 ECL) is at SOR/97-131, 4 March 1997, and is contained in *A Guide to Canada's Export Controls*, published in September 1996 by Canada's Department of Foreign Affairs and International Trade (FAIT). FAIT has published another ECL dated April 2002 (the 2002 ECL) that reflects the 1998 and 2000 Wassenaar agreements (see note 171 below), but as of 31 December 2002, the 2002 ECL has not been officially implemented through legislation. Nevertheless, FAIT is responding to export permit requests in light of the 2002 ECL, and therefore its key provisions are highlighted below.

170 For an example of a dual-use technology configuration, consider the "land warrior individual soldier weapon system," which includes a wearable computer/radio, complete with gun-mounted mouse and wrist-mounted keyboard; heads-up display (which projects maps onto a small screen connected to the soldier's helmet); microphone/speaker (which permits hands-free communication); and video sight (which relays images to heads-up display, permitting soldier to peer around corners): Mark Williams & Andrew P. Madden, "Military Revolution," *Red Herring*, 1 August 2001.

based committee that coordinated the implementation of the West's various export control regimes; the COCOM system, since July 1996, has been superseded by the Wassenaar Arrangement.[171] Nonetheless, the *EIPA* and its two lists remain, albeit the ACL, whose list of countries varies over time, has been much shorter since the removal of the countries formerly comprising the East Bloc. By the same token, particularly in response to Iraq's use of missiles in the 1991 Gulf War, the provisions in the ECL related to missiles have been augmented. Thus, it remains an offence under the *EIPA* to export a good from Canada without an export permit where one is required either by the ECL or the ACL. Under the *EIPA* a company may be fined and its employees may be fined or imprisoned or both if they violate the *EIPA*.

The *EIPA*, pursuant to the *Export Permit Regulations*,[172] provides for two types of export permits: the General Export Permit (GEP) and the Individual Export Permit (IEP). Under the former, an exporter is permitted to ship specific goods to certain countries without having to submit to the government an individual export permit application. If the particular export of an ECL item is not covered by a GEP, then the exporter may apply for an IEP by completing the requisite form, which includes a detailed description of the product or technology being exported together with its intended destination. The treatment of U.S. origin goods is also worth noting given the large amount of technology exports from the U.S. to Canada. Item 5400 of the ECL provides that all U.S. origin goods intended to be exported from Canada to a third country require a permit, which in most cases will be automatic under Gen-

---

171 *The Wassenaar Arrangement on Export Controls for Conventional Arms and Dual-Use Goods and Technologies* was established at meetings of thirty-three states in Vienna, Austria, on 11–12 July 1996. The arrangement is named after the small town in Holland where the negotiations took place that led to the arrangement. See <wassenaar.org>. The thirty-three participating states of the Wassenaar Arrangement are Argentina, Australia, Austria, Belgium, Bulgaria, Canada, the Czech Republic, Denmark, Finland, France, Germany, Greece, Hungary, Ireland, Italy, Japan, Luxembourg, the Netherlands, New Zealand, Norway, Poland, Portugal, the Republic of Korea, Romania, the Russian Federation, Slovakia, Spain, Sweden, Switzerland, Turkey, Ukraine, United Kingdom, and the United States. In light of the terrorist attack on the World Trade Center in New York City in September 2001, a recital was added to the Initial Elements document that serves as the enabling document for the Wassenaar Arrangement, to the effect that participating countries will continue to prevent the acquisition of conventional arms and dual-use goods and technologies by terrorist groups as well as individual terrorists.

172 Consolidated Regulations of Canada, 1978, c. 602; SOR/97-204, 15 April 1997, as amended.

eral Export Permit No. Ex.12 — United States Origin Goods,[173] as this allows the re-export from Canada of otherwise non–ECL-controlled goods of U.S. origin, except where the intended destination is an ACL country or one of the following: Cuba, North Korea, Iran, or Libya. In essence, there is an unfettered Canada–U.S. border from the perspective of export controls. Thus, a Canadian exporter can ship most goods in the ECL to the United States without a permit. Conversely, in order to allow the free flow of goods up to Canada from the United States, the Canadian government has agreed to honour U.S. trading restrictions on certain countries, but only insofar as U.S. origin goods are concerned. For example, goods made in Canada may be exported to Cuba and do not require a Canadian export permit. Indeed, Canada requires, by force of law, that Canadian-based companies do not comply with foreign directives in respect of the U.S. trade embargo of Cuba,[174] but this Canadian law does not apply in the case of U.S. origin goods re-exported from Canada. Particular problems can arise in the definition of *U.S. origin*. The Canadian government takes the position that once a U.S. input component undergoes significant transformation, such that it is shipped out of Canada pursuant to a different tariff classification than upon its importation, it is no longer a U.S. origin product. For its part, the U.S. government takes the view, generally, that any Canadian product that still contains at least 20 percent U.S. content is American for purposes of U.S. export controls, and in some cases, as with encryption products, the U.S. government takes the view that these products are always subject to U.S. rules regardless of how they may be integrated into other items. In these cases, the respective export control laws of Canada and the United States can be in direct conflict, with the unfortunate Canadian exporter caught in the crossfire.

2) Regulating High-Technology Exports

It is through the *EIPA*'s ECL that the government controls the export of certain computers, software, and other technologies. The ECL contains

---

173 SOR/97-107, 29 January 1997, amended by SOR/99-203, 30 April 1999. The Americans take their export control laws seriously: a short article in *The Globe and Mail* (6 January 2003) noted that Silicon Graphics Inc. was fined $1,182,000 in respect of sales of certain computers to a Russian government laboratory without an export permit.

174 See Foreign Extraterritorial Measures (United States) Order, 1992, SOR/92-584, 9 October 1992, as amended, enacted under the *Foreign Extraterritorial Measures Act*, R.S.C. 1985, c. F-29.

eight groups of goods.[175] Certain high-technology products could fall under Group 2, the military list, but most technology items are considered dual-use (i.e., they have both a civilian use and a military use) and thus are included in Group 1, the industrial list of goods. As noted above, a good listed in the ECL requires a permit in order to be exported from Canada, either a GEP or an IEP. Computers are a good example of a dual-use technology found on the ECL. The 1991 Gulf War, and the air wars in Kosovo and Afghanistan more recently, illustrated just how central sophisticated computers and software programs have become to the military, both for logistics purposes, as well as command, control, and communications, and integrated into smart bomb and missile technologies. The waging of war has become an increasingly high-tech exercise.[176] Recognizing, however, that personal computers and laptops are everywhere, the ECL does not attempt to control the export of every single computer. Rather, it controls only those digital computers that have a processing power of greater than 28,000 Mtops, an Mtop being roughly equivalent to one Megahertz (MHz) of a pentium processor;[177] that is, only relatively high-end computers are captured by the permit requirements of the ECL. In terms of structure, format, and approach, the method of regulation found in the ECL for computers is quite reasonable. The ECL is not product-specific; rather, it contains a set of technical specifications that are technology-neutral for the most part and that are functional in their description. Of course, given the first dynamic of computer law, the government must be vigilant in updating these specifications as individual computers become more powerful. As well, exporters of high-tech goods must be aware that multiple personal computers with co-processors, or one computer having more than one processor operating in parallel, could easily exceed the ECL's threshold for computers. It should also be noted that under a GEP a computer that exceeds the 260 Mtop threshold but is below 500 Mtops can be exported, provided the destination is not one of a few countries,

---

175 The groups are: Group 1 — Dual Use; Group 2 — Munitions; Group 3 — Nuclear Non-Proliferation; Group 4 — Nuclear-Related Dual Use; Group 5 — Miscellaneous Goods; Group 6 — Missile Technology Control Regime; Group 7 — Chemical and Biological Weapons Non-Proliferation; and Group 8 — Chemicals for the Production of Illicit Drugs.

176 See chapter 1, section C.1, "The Information Age," including footnotes 132 and 138 in that chapter.

177 See item 1041.3 of the ECL for a description of controlled digital computers. The 1997 ECL set this figure at 260 Mtops, but the 2002 ECL sets it at 28,000.

including currently Iran, Iraq, and North Korea.[178] As well, under another GEP, a computer not exceeding 1500 Mtops can be exported without an IEP if the destination is Hong Kong, Japan, Australia, New Zealand, Turkey, or one of seventeen countries in Europe.[179] Also, seemingly cognizant of the fourth dynamic of computer law, another GEP authorizes travellers to take personal computers and associated software out of Canada to any destination except a country on the ACL for a maximum of three months, provided that no transfer of technology takes place as a result of the exportation and that the computer is used only by the exporter and only for business or education purposes.[180] In short, as computers become more powerful and widespread, and in deference to the first dynamic of computer law, these thresholds will be constantly raised and the coverage within them revised; so it is always important to check the most current ECLs and GEPs to understand the current export control rules applying to computers.

As for software and technology, each controlled item on the ECL includes an entry for related software and the technology that is used to develop, produce, or use the controlled item. Thus, if an item is on the ECL, it is almost certain that the software and technology designed for its development, production, or use is also covered by the ECL. For example, item 1081 of the ECL controls, among other things, manned, untethered submersible vehicles designed to operate at depths exceeding 1000 metres, while item 1084 controls software specially designed or modified for the development, production, or use of, among other things, equipment controlled by item 1081, and item 1085 controls technology related to these submersible vehicles. With respect to separate, stand-alone software products, item 1044.3 of the ECL covers such products as the source code of operating system software and certain development tools and compilers specially designed for multidata stream processing equipment, and certain expert system software. As discussed in more detail below, Category 1150 of the ECL also covers

---

178 General Export Permit No. Ex. 29 — Eligible Industrial Goods, SOR/94-735, 24 November 1994 (GEP 29). With the 2002 ECL, this GEP 29 is somewhat moot on this point as the 2002 ECL sets the new controlled Mtop limit at 28,000.

179 General Export Permit No. Ex. 30 — Certain Industrial Goods to Eligible Countries and Territories, SOR/94-734, 24 November 1994 (GEP 30). With the 2002 ECL, this GEP 29 is somewhat moot on this point as the 2002 ECL sets the new controlled Mtop limit at 28,000.

180 General Export Permit No. Ex. 18 — Portable Personal Computers and Associated Software, SI/89-121, 10 May 1989, as amended.

certain encryption software.[181] All of the software items in the 2002 ECL, however, are subject to the General Software Note that appears at the beginning of Group 1 of the ECL and that provides that the ECL's control rules do not apply to software that is either:

1. Generally available to the public by being:
    a. Sold from stock at retail selling points, without restriction, by means of:
        1. Over-the-counter transactions;
        2. Mail order transactions;
        3. Electronic transactions; or
        4. Telephone call transactions; and
    b. Designed for installation by the user without further substantial support by the supplier; or
2. In the public domain.[182]

The intent of the General Software Note is to exclude from the coverage of the ECL, and hence to permit the export without a permit of, "off-the-shelf" mass market software and software "in the public domain," unless the software is destined for a country on the ACL, or U.S. origin software in which case the considerations noted above apply. While the General Software Note therefore serves a useful purpose, and again is a reflection of the general recognition that personal computer-based software is now ubiquitous in the world and therefore its export from Canada need not be controlled, the particular provisions of the General Software Note contain a problem, specifically the use of the phrase *without restriction* in subsection 1(a) of the General Software Note to qualify the manner in which the software must be sold from stock at retail selling points. In short, what does *without restriction* mean? As discussed in chapter 5, section C.1, "Why Software and Content are Licensed," software invariably is licensed subject to an agreement that does in fact contain restrictions on its use, disclosure, and further dissemination or transfer, though the licence restrictions pertaining to certain "shrink-wrapped" software often contain fewer of these restrictions. In effect, it is not clear how the *without restriction* language in the General Software Note is to be applied to

---

181 These are only two of the software items contained in the ECL. Essentially, before an exporter ships, or transmits, software from Canada, she should check to see if the particular product or program is covered by the ECL, and if the destination is on the ACL.

182 The General Software Note is at the beginning of the list of Group 1 items in the ECL.

software licences. It should also be noted that the "mass market" exception of the General Software Note does not apply to Category 1150, which is instead subject to a slightly different exception.

A further problem centres on the phrase *public domain* in section 2 of the General Software Note. Use of this wording is confusing. In copyright parlance, a copyright work enters the public domain when it is no longer protected by copyright, typically because the copyright term has expired.[183] Accordingly, the use of the term *public domain* in the General Software Note is unfortunate because the definition of *in the public domain* in the ECL means software (or technology) that has been made available without restrictions upon its further dissemination, and this definition expressly provides that copyright restrictions do not disentitle software (or technology) from being in the public domain. Moreover, given that most software is licensed subject to restrictions on its further dissemination (i.e., as discussed in chapter 5 most software licences restrict the ability to transfer the software to a third party), it is arguably only a relatively small number of commercial software programs that would qualify as being in the public domain under the General Software Note. Perhaps by *in the public domain* the government really means *freeware*, software in which copyright subsists but which is given away without restriction. There is, however, not much of this kind of software in commercial use. In any event, the term *in the public domain* could be more precise to better reflect the policy rationale behind the provision.

The General Technology Note that appears at the beginning of Group 1 of the ECL refers to *technology* as being specific information necessary for the development, production, or use of a product, such information taking the form of *technical assistance* (which includes instruction, training, and consulting services) and *technical data*. In turn, technical data is stated to be able to take many forms such as blueprints, plans, diagrams, models, formulae, tables, engineering designs and specifications, manuals, and instructions written or recorded on other media or devices such as disk, tape, or read-only memories. This broad definition of technical data would cover most information in electronic form, and therefore would encompass the

---

183 In the United States, before that country adhered to the *Berne Convention*, a work could also cease to be protected by copyright, and hence fall into the public domain, if it failed to comply with certain formalities, such as the marking of each copy of the work with the "©" copyright symbol. As Canadian copyright law never required such formalities, works in Canada could not enter the public domain for failure to mark the work in a particular manner.

transmission of controlled technology over the Internet. In today's networked environment, where researchers even within the same company may collaborate with colleagues in other countries via a high-speed, broad bandwidth intranet, organizations must be extremely careful not to violate the export control rules by inadvertently transmitting controlled technical data over the intranet, either directly, or simply by permitting someone outside of Canada to pull down the problematic material from the Canadian site.

3) Regulating the Export of Encryption Technologies

Encryption is a critical feature of computers and networks in the Information Age. Maintaining the security of computers and confidentiality of transmissions over networks is seen as a fundamental weakness of the computer-enabled environment. Many users, for example, are uncomfortable sending personal or otherwise sensitive data over the Internet, or conducting commerce by means of it, because of concerns about security and privacy. Encryption is seen by many as the chief means of allaying these fears. There are many cryptography systems now commercially available. Most are based on a system of scrambling messages by means of a mathematical algorithm, transmission of the sensitive message in the scrambled form, and then descrambling the message by means of a second algorithm or device made available only to the authorized recipient.[184] Password-based cryptography systems are also used to secure limited access to computers, including highly mobile (and highly prone to theft) laptop computers. Not surprisingly, encryption systems of all varieties are finding their way into software, computer, and Internet products and services around the world at a very rapid rate. As a result, Category 1150 of the ECL is assuming greater importance.

Category 1150 of the 2002 ECL covers encryption technologies and provides as follows:

---

184 For an overview of encryption systems, see Lorijean G. Oei, "Primer on Cryptography" in *Online Law: The SPA's Guide to Doing Business on the Internet*, ed. Thomas J. Smedinghoff (Reading, MA: Addison-Wesley, 1996) [*Online Law*]. See also Deborah Kerr, "Public Key Mystery," *Computerworld*, 9 September 1996; and Industry Canada, Task Force on Electronic Commerce, *A Cryptography Policy Framework for Electronic Commerce: Building Canada's Information Economy and Society* (February 1998) [*Cryptography Policy*] available at <strategis.ic.gc.ca/SSG/cy00005e.html>. See also the discussion of encryption in the next section, "Regulating the Domestic Use of Encryption Technologies," and in chapter 6, section A.2(c), "Law Reform."

1150 Information Security

Note 1:
The control status of "information security" equipment, "software," systems, application specific "electronic assemblies," modules, integrated circuits, components, or functions is determined in this Category even if they are components or "electronic assemblies" of other equipment.

Note 2:
Category 1150 does not control products when accompanying their user for the user's personal use.

Note 3:
Cryptography Note:
1151 and 1154 do not control items that meet all of the following:
a.   Generally available to the public by being sold, without restriction, from stock at retail selling points by means of any of the following:
    1.   over-the-counter transactions;
    2.   mail-order transactions;
    3.   electronic transactions; or
    4.   telephone call transactions;
b.   The cryptographic functionality cannot easily be changed by the user;
c.   Designed for installation by the user without further substantial support by the supplier; and
d.   When necessary, details of the items are accessible and will be provided, upon request, to the appropriate authority in the exporter's country in order to ascertain compliance with conditions described in paragraphs a) to c) above.

Note: The "appropriate authority" means an officer of the Export Controls Division of the Department of Foreign Affairs and International Trade.

Technical Note:
In Category 1150, parity bits are not included in the key length.

1151 Systems, Equipment and Components
1.   Systems, equipment, application specific "electronic assemblies", modules or integrated circuits for "information security", as follows, and other specially designed components therefore:

Note: For the control of global navigation satellite systems receiving equipment containing or employing decryption (i.e., GPS or GLONASS), see 1071.5.

a. Designed or modified to use "cryptography" employing digital techniques performing any cryptographic function other than authentication or digital signature having any of the following:

Technical Note:
1. Authentication and digital signature functions include their associated key management function.
2. Authentication includes all aspects of access control where there is no encryption of files or text except as directly related to the protection of passwords, Personal Identification Numbers (PINs) or similar data to prevent unauthorized access.
3. "Cryptography" does not include "fixed" data compression or coding techniques.

Note: 1151.1.a. includes equipment designed or modified to use "cryptography" employing analogue principles when implemented with digital techniques.

1. A "symmetric algorithm" employing a key length in excess of 56 bits; or
2. An "asymmetric algorithm" where the security of the algorithm is based on any of the following:
    a. Factorization of integers in excess of 512 bits (e.g., RSA);
    b. Computation of discrete logarithms in a multiplicative group of a finite field of size greater than 512 bits (e.g., Diffie-Hellman over Z/pZ); or
    c. Discrete logarithms in a group other than mentioned in 1151.1.a.2.b. in excess of 112 bits (e.g., Diffie-Hellman over an elliptic curve);
    d. Designed or modified to perform cryptanalytic functions;
    e. Deleted;
    f. Specially designed or modified to reduce the compromising emanations of information-bearing signals beyond what is necessary for health, safety or electromagnetic interference standards;
    g. Designed or modified to use cryptographic techniques to generate the spreading code for "spread spectrum" systems, including the hopping code for "frequency hopping" systems;

h. Designed or modified to use cryptographic techniques to generate channelizing or scrambling codes for "time-modulated ultra-wideband" systems;

i. Designed or modified to provide certified or certifiable "multilevel security" or user isolation at a level exceeding Class B2 of the Trusted Computer System Evaluation Criteria (TCSEC) or equivalent;

j. Communications cable systems designed or modified using mechanical, electrical or electronic means to detect surreptitious intrusion.

Note: 1151 does not control:

a. "Personalized smart cards" where the cryptographic capability is restricted for use in equipment or systems excluded from control under entries b. to f. of this Note. If a "personalized smart card" has multiple functions, the control status of each function is assessed individually.

b. Receiving equipment for radio broadcast, pay television or similar restricted audience broadcast of the consumer type, without digital encryption except that exclusively used for sending the billing or program-related information back to the broadcast providers;

c. Equipment where the cryptographic capability is not user-accessible and which is specially designed and limited to allow any of the following:
    1. Execution of copy-protected software;
    2. Access to any of the following:
        a. Copy-protected contents stored on read-only media; or
        b. Information stored in encrypted form on media (e.g., in connection with the protection of intellectual property rights) when the media is offered for sale in identical sets to the public;

    or
    3. One-time copying of copyright protected audio/video data.

d. Cryptographic equipment specially designed and limited for banking use or money transactions:

Technical Note:
"Money transactions" in 1151 Note d includes the collection and settlement of fares or credit functions.

e. Portable or mobile radiotelephones for civil use (e.g., for use with commercial civil cellular radiocommunications systems) that are not capable of end-to-end encryption;

f.   Cordless telephone equipment not capable of end-to-end encryption where the maximum effective range of unboosted cordless operations (i.e., a single, unrelayed hop between terminal and homebase station) is less than 400 metres according to the manufacturer's specifications.

1152 Test, Inspection and Production Equipment

1.   Equipment specially designed for:
   a.   The "development" of equipment or functions controlled by Category 1150 including measuring or test equipment;
   b.   The "production" of equipment or functions controlled by Category 1150 including measuring, test, repair or production equipment.
2.   Measuring equipment specially designed to evaluate and validate the "information security" functions controlled by 1151 or 1154.

1153 Materials
None.

1154 Software

1.   "Software" specially designed or modified for the "development," "production" or "use" of equipment or "software" controlled by Category 1150.
2.   "Software" specially designed or modified to support "technology" controlled by 1155.
3.   Specific "software" as follows:
   a.   "Software" having the characteristics, or performing or simulating the functions of the equipment controlled by 1151 or 1152;
   b.   "Software" to certify "software" controlled by 1154.3.a.

Note: 1154 does not control:
   a.   "Software" required for the "use" of equipment excluded from control under the Note to 1151;
   b.   "Software" providing any of the functions of equipment excluded from control under the Note to 1151.

1155 Technology

1.   "Technology" according to the General Technology Note for the "development," "production" or "use" of equipment or "software" controlled by Category 1150.

It should be noted that words in quotations are defined in the "Definitions for Terms in Groups 1 and 2" section in the ECL. In particular, the following terms are defined in the ECL as follows:

"Cryptography": The discipline which embodies principles, means and methods for the transformation of data in order to hide its information content, prevent its undetected modification or prevent its unauthorized use. "Cryptography" is limited to the transformation of information using one or more secret parameters (e.g., crypto variables) or associated key management. Note: "Secret parameter": a constant or key kept from the knowledge of others or shared only within a group.

"Information security": All the means and functions ensuring the accessibility, confidentiality or integrity of information or communications, excluding the means and functions intended to safeguard against malfunctions. This includes "cryptography," cryptanalysis, protection against compromising emanations and computer security. Note: "Cryptanalysis": the analysis of a cryptographic system or its inputs and outputs to derive confidential variables or sensitive data, including clear text (ISO 7498-2-1988 (E), paragraph 3.3.18).

"Microprogram": A sequence of elementary instructions maintained in a special storage, the execution of which is initiated by the introduction of its reference instruction register.

"Program": A sequence of instructions to carry out a process in, or convertible into, a form executable by an electronic computer.

"Software": A collection of one or more "programs" or "microprograms" fixed in any tangible medium of expression.

Category 1150 of the ECL is drafted in very broad terms and covers a wide variety of software and hardware products that implement cryptographic functionality. For example, it covers not only items that perform cryptography functionality, but also items "designed or modified to use cryptography," thus capturing software that includes, for example, an interface for a specific encryption device but does not yet contain it. However, Category 1150 tries to strike a reasonable balance by providing for numerous exceptions. This form of lengthy, but detailed, regulation is to be preferred, so long as the contents of the provision are regularly reviewed and amended to ensure that it stays current with the reality of the global marketplace. It should also be noted that, interestingly, the rationale for the control of encryption technologies is somewhat different than for other high-technology products, given that the concern is not so much that these cryptography products will be "used against the West" in the manner that other dual-use technologies might be turned against us. Rather, the concern is that if foreign governments and other entities are provided with encryption features, they will be able to keep their messages free from eavesdropping by Western intelligence services. Nonetheless, subsection 1(z.4) of the Schedule to GEP 29, and GEP 30, subsection 5(1)[185] contain important exceptions to item 1151, stipulating that, subject to the other provisions of such general export permits, the following may be exported:

(i)   access control equipment, including automatic teller machines, self-service statement printers and point-of-sale terminals, that protects password or personal identification numbers (PIN) or similar data to prevent unauthorized access to facilities, but that does not allow for encryption of files or text, except as directly related to the protection of the password or PIN;

(ii) data authentication equipment that calculates a Message Authentication Code (MAC) or similar result to ensure that no alteration of text has taken place or to authenticate users, but that does not allow for encryption of data, text or other media other than that needed for the authentication; and

(iii) cryptographic equipment specially designed, developed or modified for use in machines for banking or money transactions, such as automatic teller machines, self-service statement printers and point of sale terminals.

These exceptions are forerunners of the exemptions contained in Note d to Item 1151 of the 2002 ECL. These provisions are useful, for example, for banks and other financial institutions in Canada that are increasingly providing non-Canadian clients with access to computer systems in Canada, and that wish to implement as much security as possible around these access mechanisms. These exemptions, however, relate essentially to encryption devices that authenticate the identity of users of a particular system, but do not cover technologies that encrypt the underlying data itself, though the exemption in Note d to Item 1151 of the 2002 ECL appears to be broader. As well, and importantly, GEP 39 permits Canadians to export "mass market cryptographic software" that does not exceed 128 bits to all countries on the

---

185 See above notes 178 and 179, respectively. As noted above, with the 2002 ECL, these GEPs will be somewhat moot on these exceptions given that note 1151(d) decontrols "Cryptographic equipment specially designed and limited for banking use or money transactions."

ACL and three more listed in GEP 39 (totalling seven in all).[186] GEP 39 defines "mass market cryptographic software" as software described in item 1154 of the ECL and that meets all of the following conditions:

(a) generally available to the public by being sold, without restriction, from stock at retail selling points by any of the following means:
   (i) over the counter transactions;
   (ii) mail order transactions;
   (iii) electronic transactions; or
   (iv) telephone transactions;

(b) the cryptographic functionality cannot easily be changed by the user;

(c) designed for installation by the user without further substantial support by the supplier; and

(d) does not contain a symmetric algorithm employing a key length exceeding 128 bits.

A company making available its software for download from its Web site would want to implement reasonable controls to help ensure that the software does not find its way to countries to which Canada's export control laws prohibit the export of the relevant software. The techniques for doing so might include IP address filtering, reverse DNS look up, and independent address verification, as well as including appropriate provisions in the applicable software licence to be entered into by the user, such as representations and warranties as to the country in which the software will ultimately be used.[187]

Category 1150 is subject to the General Software Note discussed above as well as GEP 39 (as well as the mass market cryptography product exception set forth in Note 3 to Category 1150 of the 2002 ECL), and therefore encryption devices implemented on most off-the-shelf software do not require Canadian export permits, unless they are of U.S. origin. Moreover, the United States government views encryption devices as military goods, and the United States has traditionally

---

186 General Export Permit No. Ex. 39 — Mass Market Cryptographic Software, SOR/99-238, 1 June 1999 (GEP 39). The seven controlled countries are: Afghanistan, Angola, Federal Republic of Yugoslavia, Myanmar, North Korea, Iran, and Iraq. Again, this part of GEP 39 will be superseded by the 2002 ECL given that the latter, in Note 3 to item 1150, decontrols mass market cryptography products.

187 As for how to create enforceable "click-consent agreements" online for this purpose, see chapter 6, section A.3(c), "Express and Implied Click-Consent Agreements."

imposed a virtual ban on the export (outside of North America) of all products containing cryptography features, even if found in off-the-shelf commercially available products.[188] This is why it has been common for a U.S. software company to have a North American version of a product and a non–North American version, the latter having a lower level of encryption protection built into it because of the U.S. export controls on cryptography technologies. Over the past few years, however, in recognition of the fourth dynamic of computer law, Washington has on more than one occasion loosened its approach to the regulation of encryption technologies.[189] Late in 1998, the U.S. government decided to allow the export of 56-bit encryption to all but a handful of countries, and even 128-bit strength crypto can be exported from the United States provided a key recovery system is implemented.[190]

C. REGULATING THE DOMESTIC USE OF ENCRYPTION TECHNOLOGIES

Encryption technologies and products present some very finicky regulatory challenges for governments. Cryptographic mechanisms, typically embedded in software, allow users of the Internet and other communications networks to exchange messages and data securely, in order both to preserve their confidentiality and to authenticate the rel-

---

188 For a discussion of the U.S. controls on the exports of encryption technologies, see Thomas J. Smedinghoff, "Export Controls and Transnational Data Flow," in Smedinghoff, *Online Law*, above note 184.

189 See Wendy R. Leibowitz, "Encryption Takes Centre Stage: Is Government a Trusty Neighbour?" (7 July 1997) The National Law Journal; and see more recently, U.S. Department of Commerce, Bureau of Export Administration, Office of Strategic Trade and Foreign Policy Controls, Information Technology Controls Division, *Commercial Encryption Export Controls: Encryption Fact Sheet* (19 October 2000). See also *Bernstein v. U.S. Department of Justice*, 176 F.3d 1132 (9th Cir. 1999), upholding *Bernstein v. United States Department of State*, 945 F. Supp. 1279 (N.D. Cal. 1996), in which it was held that the U.S. government's licensing scheme of cryptographic software was unconstitutional (under the U.S. "free speech" First Amendment) as a prior restraint on speech because it failed to meet certain constitutional procedural safeguards; but note that the 9th Circuit granted an *en banc* rehearing: see *Bernstein v. United States DOJ*, 192 F.3d 1308 (9th Cir. 1999). See also *Junger v. Daley*, 209 F.3d 481 (6th Cir. 2000).

190 Debora L. Spar, *Ruling the Waves: Cycles of Discovery, Chaos, and Wealth From the Compass to the Internet* (New York: Harcourt, 2001) [*Ruling the Waves*], at 278–79.

evant parties.[191] It is not surprising, therefore, that cryptography has become an important enabler of electronic commerce and other activities on the Internet. At the same time, the very features that make cryptography so attractive to law-abiding users of the Internet make it an equally compelling technology for criminals, terrorists, money-launderers and others who would use it to cover their illegal tracks on the Internet.[192] This conflict prompted the Canadian government to review its cryptography policy several years ago.[193] In an initial discussion paper issued in February 1998,[194] the government described cryptography and its current applications, various considerations that would underpin any policy in this area in an effort to address various human

191 For a discussion of the technologies and processes buttressing cryptography, see chapter 6, section A.2(c), "Law Reform." For a review of the history of cryptography, and the current debate about the regulation of cryptanalysis in the context of Internet messaging, see chapter 5 of Spar, *Ruling the Waves*, above note 190.

192 One author describes the concern of governments with encryption as follows: "When the Internet went mainstream, it thus thrust the national security and law enforcement agencies into an awkward dilemma. On the one hand, they, like the rest of the U.S. government, saw the inherent potential of the Net and were reluctant to impede its growth. On the other hand, they were terrified by what the Net could do to their own world of law enforcement and national defense. For just as cyberspace opened up vast new spaces for social and commercial contact, so too did it expand the possibilities for criminal exchange. On the Internet, terrorists could easily exchange information about bomb-making or chemical weapons. Hate groups could recruit new members; gangsters could launder money. New-age pirates would be able to manipulate the ever-growing flows of money and information, and hostile governments could extend their reach in subtle and undetected ways. While none of these threats was completely novel — there had always been hostile governments, and money launderers and terrorists — they all loomed larger in cyberspace, where contact was more immediate, communication more expansive, and activity of any sort more difficult to detect. In this context, secure encryption was seen, paradoxically perhaps, as a threat. If everyone could protect their communication, the agencies feared, then law enforcement would be thrust into an unprecedented vacuum and national security would suffer. In a world of perfect information and total privacy, governments would lose out." *Ruling the Waves*, above note 190 at 267–68.

193 The Canadian government is not alone in looking at the public policy ramifications of encryption technologies and products: the OECD, for example, has issued *Cryptography Policy Guidelines* and a report on the background and issues of cryptography policy, in March 1997, available at <oecd.org/dsti/sti/it/secur/prod/e-crypto.htm>.

194 Government of Canada, Task Force on Electronic Commerce, Industry Canada, *A Cryptography Policy Framework for Electronic Commerce: Building Canada's Information Economy and Society* (Ottawa: Industry Canada, 1998), available at <strategis.ic.gc.ca/crypto>.

rights, commercial, civil liberties, law enforcement and national security requirements,[195] and then various policy options.[196] Interestingly, each of the four dynamics of computer law can be seen animating various aspects of each option.

The most controversial potential policy option related to mandatory key access by law enforcement agencies; in short, that governments should be given the means of deciphering all encrypted messages, albeit only on receipt of court authorization. Several years before the Canadian review of its cryptography policy, a controversy erupted in the United States surrounding the proposed "Clipper chip," a device the U.S. government proposed building into each telephone, switching device, and computer that would serve the "mandatory access" function.[197] The Clipper chip would encrypt all communications, and would thereby make secure all messages and transmissions, with one fundamental exception, namely, the government and its agencies and law enforcement officials (the police) would be able to access each device once appropriate judicial wire-tapping authority was obtained. The U.S. government proposed this regime because it is rather difficult to tap into fibre optics transmission capacity, and the government wanted to maintain its surveillance capacity in the new networked environment. This is a legitimate concern for the United States and

---

195 The considerations included those pertaining to electronic commerce (cryptography increases competitiveness of business and creates jobs and industrial growth; government policies should avoid slowing down innovation and creating obstacles to commerce); lawful state access (cryptography can create significant obstacles to the detection and investigation of criminal activities and security threats); human rights and civil liberties (mechanisms that facilitate lawful state access could compromise human rights and civil liberties); technical security (the technical mechanisms that facilitate lawful state access could be used by illicit interests); and international considerations (whatever policy Canada adopts must be sensitive to its key trading partners).

196 The general options were classified in three areas, each with increasingly stronger intervention alternatives: encryption of stored data (do nothing — rely on the market; regulate minimum standards for back-up of encryption keys; or regulate mandatory access by government by prohibiting the use of encryption products without key recovery capabilities); encryption of real-time communications (rely on status quo search warrants; impose requirements on all carriers to be able to decrypt messages for law enforcement purposes upon receipt of court order; similar to mandatory access, prohibit use of any product for which the government does not have a key by which it can obtain access upon receipt of a court order); export controls (relax controls; maintain existing policy; extend controls).

197 For a discussion of the Clipper chip debate, see Lance J. Hoffman, ed., *Building in Big Brother: The Cryptographic Policy Debate* (New York: Springer-Verlag, 1995).

other governments as evidence obtained through wiretapping has been instrumental in prosecuting, for example, drug dealers. However, because of privacy concerns, the Clipper chip proposal engendered a great deal of criticism,[198] and the controversial proposal has since been superseded by a less intrusive, but still controversial alternative proposal whereby private parties can use various encryption technologies so long as a copy of the digital key necessary to decipher the technology is lodged with the U.S. government.[199] This escrow arrangement proposal, argues the government, is necessary to give the government the ability to track criminals in the modern era of telecommunications. Many U.S. civil libertarians remain sceptical and concerned.

Partly as a result of the Clipper chip controversy, the Canadian government received a large number of responses to its cryptography policy options paper. These were analysed on behalf of Industry Canada in a report[200] released in June 1998 that made the following general conclusions: perhaps not surprisingly, only law enforcement groups advocated more domestic controls on cryptography, and in particular only law enforcement respondents approved of any type of mandatory access regime for encryption of stored or real-time data. The non-law enforcement submissions were opposed to any mandatory key recovery system, largely because they think it would not work and would be too expensive.[201] Interestingly, several of the police agencies were also will-

---

198 For a summary of the arguments ranged against — and for — the Clipper chip proposal, see chapter 5 of Spar, *Ruling the Waves*, above note 190.
199 See John P. Barlow, "Save the Bill of Rights?: Jackboots on the Infobahn," *Wired*, April 1994. Barlow stated that trusting the government with privacy under the Clipper chip proposal was like having a peeping Tom install window blinds. For a more measured response, see Philip Elmer-Dewitt, "Who Should Keep the Keys?" *Time*, 14 March 1994. For the perspective of U.S. law enforcement agencies, see the transcript of testimony of the director of the FBI, Louis J. Freeh, before the U.S. Senate Judiciary Committee on 4 June 1997, at <epic.org/crypto/legilsation/freeh_6_4_97.html>. See also Todd Lappin, "Clinton's New Clothes: A New Report Lays Bare the Encryption Policy Scam," *Wired*, August 1996.
200 AEPOS Technologies Corporation, *Cryptography Policy Discussion Paper: Analysis of Submissions* (Ottawa: Industry Canada, 1998), available at <strategis.ic.gc.ca/crypto>.
201 The specific concerns with mandatory access policies included the following: any kind of key recovery for law enforcement would create points of vulnerability and weaken the value of the encryption; key recovery systems are less secure, cost more and are more difficult to use; key recovery requirements can be evaded; double encryption can be used to circumvent key escrow objectives; non-standard algorithms can be used; any mandatory key recovery infrastructure will be limited in its application; the cost of establishing and operating a key recovery infrastructure would be high and negatively affect industry's competitive-

ing to "recognize the technical difficulty, impracticality and cost implications of trying to apply mandatory access controls for stored data or mandatory access requirements on the carriers."[202] The report went on to make the following observation, which resonates from the perspective of the first dynamic of computer law:

> Implicit in a small number of the law enforcement submissions is a recognition that the problem faced by law enforcement is not one of cryptography alone, but of the rapid pace of technological change and development of technical capabilities that can be abused. Comments that law enforcement agencies are not equipped to deal with current technology appeared in several contributions including a number from the law enforcement agencies themselves. It was suggested that additional tools, technical information, technical support, more resources to monitor and detect breaches, plus a national strategy are needed to keep abreast of the technology and to help technology fulfil the promise of aiding, rather than hindering, law enforcement.[203]

Having considered the submissions made in response to its February 1998 discussion paper, the government released its cryptography policy in October 1998.[204] The policy indicated that although the government would encourage industry to establish responsible practices such as key recovery techniques, including through government procurement practices, it would not legislate mandatory key recovery requirements. Equally, there would be no regulation of the import into Canada, or the use or production within Canada, of encryption technologies or products. The government, however, would continue to implement export controls on cryptography consistent with its obligations under the Wassenaar Arrangement, but in a manner that would ensure that Canadian exporters would not be at a competitive disadvantage relative to their foreign counterparts.[205] Finally, the government

---

ness; key recovery is not possible for the type of strong encryption used with smart cards, *ibid.*, at 11.

202 *Ibid.*, at 15.

203 *Ibid.*, at 15.

204 The policy is contained in the notes of the Hon. John Manley, [the then] Minister of Industry, in his presentation to the National Press Club on Canada's Cryptography Policy, October 1, 1998, available at <e-com.ic.gc.ca/english/speeches/42d3.html>.

205 See section B.1 earlier in this chapter, "The Law of Export Control," regarding export controls on technology generally, and section B.3, "Regulating the Export of Encryption Technologies," for a discussion of export controls on encryption technology specifically. In particular, General Export Permit No. Ex. 39, Mass Market Cryptographic Software, SOR/99-238, 1 June 1999, facilitates the export of certain types of cryptographic products of up to 128 bits in length.

indicated it would make legislative amendments to protect consumers' privacy, by making it an offence to wrongfully disclose private encryption key information; at the same time, however, there would also be changes to the *Criminal Code* making it an offence to use cryptography to commit or hide evidence of a crime, and to clarify that search warrants and assistance orders apply in situations where encryption is encountered, so as to allow the law enforcement agency to obtain the decrypted material or decryption keys.[206]

That computer-based cryptography is not regulated domestically in either the United States or Canada is a rather stunning state of affairs, when considered historically. Traditionally, the ability to communicate in secret codes was the preserve of the state — initially Roman emperors, then kings and queens, and later governments.[207] Today, with encryption products used widely over the Internet by individuals and commercial users, we have witnessed a fascinating democratization of cryptographic technologies. It illustrates superbly the four dynamics of computer law, as well as the difficulty of regulating in the Internet age.[208]

---

206 See, for example, the addition of para. 342.1(1)(d) to the *Criminal Code*, in order to bolster the general computer abuse offence to cover persons who crack encryption systems: this is discussed in chapter 3, section B.3, "Computer Abuse."

207 As Debora L. Spar argues in *Ruling the Waves*, above note 190 at 248: "[T]he battle over encryption was one of the first and most significant contests of the Information Age. For by embracing encryption as a private good, the cypherpunks and their supporters had taken something — security — that used to belong to governments and thrust it into private hands. They had used technology — specifically, the combination of encryption and the Internet — to attack politics, arguing that technological advance had fundamentally changed the rules of the game. And when the politicians struck back, the cypherpunks used this same technology to circumvent the state's now-rusty laws and proclaim a new order."

208 Spar's following trenchant observation, at 283 of Spar, *Ruling the Waves*, above note 190, is worth noting at length: "[D]espite encryption's ancient bonds to wars and spies and governments, the Internet has categorically changed the rules that govern encryption. It has taken what was once a restricted technology and tool of the state and thrust it into private hands. It has created a market where one didn't exist and has denied states the power they once had to control the flow of secrets. Why has this change been so dramatic? According to the prophets and cypherpunks, it is because the Internet itself is so radical — because it inherently shifts power and erodes the basis of state control. It is because, as one author wrote in a 1993 *Harvard Business Review* article [Sam Piroda, "Development, Democracy and the Village Telephone," *Harvard Business Review*, November– December 1993, at 66], 'information technology is the great-

D. REGULATING COMMUNICATIONS INFRASTRUCTURES

The federal government has for many decades regulated the companies that operated the telecommunications and broadcasting infrastructures of Canada. The rationale for doing so with respect to the former related to protecting the public interest in the context of an important utility and transportationlike service provided by monopolists and quasi-monopolists. After 1987, Canadian ownership and control regulation was established, matching similar provisions that had long been in place in the United States and elsewhere. Recently, this form of regulation has come under increasing pressure, as the World Trade Organization and other international organizations press for the removal of barriers to international trade in telecommunications. Broadcasting regulation was initially aimed at creating and promoting the presence of an indigenous Canadian voice to provide to Canadians an alternative to U.S.-based radio (and subsequently television, and more recently satellite) programming. These and other reasons have led to the development of an extensive regulatory regime for telecommunications and broadcasting overseen primarily by the Canadian Radio-television and Telecommunications Commission (CRTC), although Industry Canada regulates radio spectrum allocation and use, as well as some other areas. The four dynamics of computer law — the rapid pace of technological change, the elusive nature of information, and the blurring of private/public and national/international — make the regulation of the gatekeepers and conduits of the Information Age, especially the Internet, a daunting task.

1) Regulating Telecommunications

The federal *Telecommunications Act*[209] regulates "telecommunications common carriers" operating in Canada, which are entities that own or operate transmission facilities used by the entities or others to provide

---

est democratizer the world has ever seen'; because 'high technology can put unequal human beings on equal footing.' Perhaps. But encryption also seems to have some special qualities, characteristics that make it particularly susceptible to this kind of a power shift and particularly immune to governmental involvement."

209 S.C. 1993, c. 38, as amended.

telecommunications services to the public for compensation.[210] The *Telecommunications Act* sets out the following telecommunications policy objectives for Canada:

> **Objectives.** – It is hereby affirmed that telecommunication performs an essential role in the maintenance of Canada's identity and sovereignty and that the Canadian telecommunications policy has as its objectives
>
> (a) to facilitate the orderly development throughout Canada of a telecommunications system that serves to safeguard, enrich and strengthen the social and economic fabric of Canada and its regions;
>
> (b) to render reliable and affordable telecommunications services of high quality accessible to Canadians in both urban and rural areas in all regions of Canada;
>
> (c) to enhance the efficiency and competitiveness, at the national and international levels, of Canadian telecommunications;
>
> (d) to promote the ownership and control of Canadian carriers by Canadians;
>
> (e) to promote the use of Canadian transmission facilities for telecommunications within Canada and between Canada and points outside Canada;
>
> (f) to foster increased reliance on market forces for the provision of telecommunications services and to ensure that regulation, where required, is efficient and effective;

---

210 *Ibid.*, s. 2. *Related definitions are:*

"exempt transmission" apparatus means any apparatus whose functions are limited to one or more of the following:

(a) the switching of telecommunications,

(b) the input, capture, storage, organization, modification, retrieval, output or other processing of intelligence, or

(c) control the speed, code, protocol, content, format, routing, or similar aspects of the transmission of intelligence;

"intelligence" means signs, writings, images, sounds, or intelligence of any nature;

"telecommunications" means the emission, transmission or reception of intelligence by any wire, cable, radio, optical or other electromagnetic system, or by any similar technical system; and

"transmission facility" means any wire, cable, radio, optical, or other electromagnetic system for the transmission of intelligence between network termination points, but does not include any exempt transmission apparatus.

(g) to stimulate research and development in Canada in the field of telecommunications services;

(h) to respond to the economic and social requirements of users of telecommunications services; and

(i) to contribute to the protection of the privacy of persons.[211]

Making sense of this policy in the real world is a challenge indeed. Like a multiheaded Hydra, the internal conflicts between the subparts of the policy soon become apparent. For example, it is not a trivial exercise to reconcile the promotion of Canadian ownership (subsection d) with fostering greater reliance on market forces (subsection f), which often involves non-Canadian interests. Indeed, in the fall of 2002 a significant debate commenced in political, regulatory, and industry circles about the merits of liberalizing the Canadian ownership control rules. Responsibility for implementing this Sisyphean telecommunications policy rests with the CRTC,[212] and with the federal government, which issues directives that are binding on the CRTC.[213] The CRTC is the present-day successor to a number of other bodies that have regulated telecommunications in Canada since 1906.

The *Telecommunications Act* sets out a number of rules that apply to telecommunications common carriers. As a threshold matter, in order to operate as a telecommunications common carrier, the carrier must be at least 80 percent Canadian owned and controlled in fact by Canadians.[214] As well, the regulated rates charged by a carrier must be just and reasonable, and in some cases are subject to prior approval by

---

211 *Ibid.*, s. 7.

212 The CRTC is established under the *Canadian Radio-television and Telecommunications Commission Act*, R.S.C. 1985, c. C-22, as amended.

213 The federal government currently exercises its responsibility for telecommunications through the Minister of Industry.

214 *Telecommunications Act*, subss. 161(1) and (3). This restriction, however, is affected by the provisions of the *Canadian Telecommunications Common Carrier Ownership and Control Regulations*, SOR/94-667, 25 October 1994, which permit, among other things, the indirect foreign ownership of up to 33-1/3 percent of the voting shares of a holding company that controls a Canadian carrier, and an even higher percentage of non-voting shares, provided there is no control-in-fact by a non-Canadian. These Canadian ownership restrictions may be dropped in the future if the ongoing negotiations on international telecommunications liberalization at the World Trade Organization bear fruit. In early 2003, the Canadian government conducted various hearings as to the advisability of continuing the Canadian ownership rules in the telecommunications sector: Dave Ebner, "Telecom Review Set to Begin: Foreign Ownership Limits to be Examined," *The Globe and Mail* (27 January 2003).

the CRTC.[215] In practice, fewer and fewer rates are subject to CRTC approval, as the CRTC "forbears" from regulating the increasingly competitive telecommunications markets under section 34 of the *Telecommunications Act*. More broadly, most aspects of the services provided by the carrier are subject to conditions imposed by the CRTC, contained in *"Conditions of Service."*[216] It is an offence to contravene any provision of the *Telecommunications Act* or any regulation or decision made under it.[217] The *Telecommunications Act* also provides that no carrier shall unjustly discriminate in respect of the services it provides or the rates it charges, nor shall it give any unreasonable preference to any person, including itself, nor subject anyone to an undue or unreasonable advantage.[218] Since the early 1980s, the duty on carriers to supply services to everyone at reasonable rates and without unjust discrimination has led to a number of CRTC decisions that have fostered increasing competition in the market for telecommunications services and ancillary products. For example, currently there is competition in the attachment and sale of terminal apparatus,[219] the provision of enhanced services (computer-based services provided on top of the core basic telephone service),[220] publication of directory listing information,[221] and long-distance and local telephony.[222] In a decision in early 1997, the CRTC determined that the provision by Bell Canada and its Stentor partner companies across Canada of the Sympatico Internet connection service did not constitute an unreasonable advantage or undue preference, as was argued by a number of independent Internet service

---

215 *Telecommunications Act*, subss. 25(1) and 27(1). Once approved, such rates are called "tariffs."
216 See *ibid.*, s. 24; however, the CRTC may also forbear from regulating the conditions of services, and has done so in the case of many competitive services.
217 *Ibid.*, s. 73.
218 *Ibid.*, s. 27. Again, the CRTC may forbear from regulation under this section.
219 Telecom Decision CRTC 82-14, *Attachment of Subscriber-Provided Terminal Equipment*, 8 C.R.T. 848 (23 November 1982).
220 Telecom Decision CRTC 84-018, *Enhanced Services*, 10 C.R.T. 486 (12 July 1984).
221 Telecom Decision CRTC 95-3, *Provision of Directory Database Information and Real-Time Access to Directory Assistance Databases* (8 March 1995).
222 For long distance, see Telecom Decision CRTC 92-12, *Competition in the Provision of Public Long Distance Voice Telephone Services and Related Resale and Sharing Issues* (12 June 1992). For local telephony, see Telecom Decision CRTC 97-8, *Local Competition* (1 May 1997) and Telecom Decision CRTC 98-8, *Local Pay Phone Telephone Competition* (30 June 1998).

providers.[223] The CRTC has also ordered cable operators to make available to independent ISPs their broadband service for resale.[224] As noted above, the CRTC has also decided to implement a policy of local telephony competition.[225] When the CRTC established the basic framework for opening local telephony to competition in 1997, it also announced that telephone companies could apply for broadcasting licences.[226] The ultimate goal was meaningful convergence, whereby the telephone and broadcast industries would be free to offer all services to all consumers in a single competitive environment. Shortly after these decisions, the CRTC gave two telephone companies permission to conduct market trials for broadcasting services, including the delivery of pay-per-view movies.[227] Another example of the impact of convergence is telephony over the Internet, a phenomenon that likely will come before the CRTC for greater scrutiny once the technology improves to the point of it becoming a viable alternative to long-distance calling; to date the CRTC has indicated that Internet service providers facilitating voice telephony over the Internet will be treated as telephone service resellers and will have to make contribution charges to the established telephone companies.[228]

---

223 Telecom Decision CRTC 97-1, *Bell Canada and Bell Sygma Inc. — Joint Marketing of Sympatico Internet Services* (13 January 1997). With respect to the regulation of incumbent affiliates, see CRTC Decision 2002-76 (12 December 2002).

224 Telecom Decision CRTC 99-11, *Application Concerning Access By Internet Service Providers to Incumbent Cable Carriers' Telecommunications Facilities* (14 September 1999).

225 Telecom Decision CRTC 94-19, *Review of Regulatory Framework* (16 September 1994).

226 Telecom Decision CRTC 97-8, *Local Competition* (1 May 1997), and Telecom Decision CRTC 97-9, Price Cap Regulation and Related Issues (1 May 1997).

227 Telecom Decision CRTC 97-11 and 97-12, *Applications Under the Broadcasting Act and the Telecommunications Act for Authority to Conduct Technical and Market Trials* (8 May 1997). Subsequently, broadcasting licences were awarded to the following telephone companies: NBTel — Decision CRTC 98-14 (23 June 1998); MT&T — Decision CRTC 2000-332 (16 April 2000); SaskTel — Decision CRTC 2001-171 (12 March 2001); and MTS — Decision CRTC 2001-235 (14 August 2002). The achievement of true convergence still remains a somewhat elusive goal. For example, the Bell Canada licence was revoked, at Bell's request, in Decision CRTC 98-449 (19 November 1998).

228 Telecom Order CRTC 97-590 (1 May 1997). But note that ISPs do not have to pay contribution charges where they offer only contribution — exempt ISP services: Telecom Order CRTC 98-929 (17 September 1998).

2) Regulating Broadcasting

The federal *Broadcasting Act*[229] regulates broadcasting in Canada. This statute in subsection 2.(1) defines broadcasting as:

> any transmission of programs, whether or not encrypted, by radio waves or other means of telecommunication for reception by the public by means of broadcasting receiving apparatus, but does not include any such transmission of programs that is made solely for performance or display in a public place.

Integral to this definition of broadcasting is the definition of *program*, which is as follows:

> sounds or visual images, or a combination of sounds and visual images, that are intended to inform, enlighten or entertain, but does not include visual images, whether or not combined with sounds, that consist predominantly of alphanumeric text.

Subsection 4(2) of the *Broadcasting Act* provides that it applies "in respect of broadcasting undertakings carried on in whole or in part within Canada." The *Broadcasting Act* further provides that a *broadcasting undertaking* includes a *distribution undertaking, a programming undertaking*, and a *network*, and these are defined as follows:

> "distribution undertaking" means any undertaking for the reception of broadcasting and the retransmission thereof by radio waves or other means of telecommunication to more than one permanent or temporary residence or dwelling unit or to another such undertaking;

> "programming undertaking" means an undertaking for the transmission of programs, either directly by radio waves or other means of telecommunication or indirectly through a distribution undertaking, for reception by the public by means of broadcasting receiving apparatus;

> "network" includes any operation where control over all or any part of the programs or program schedules of one or more broadcasting undertakings is delegated to another undertaking or person.[230]

It should also be noted that the term *other means of telecommunication* in these definitions is in turn defined to mean "any wire, cable, radio, optical or other electromagnetic system, or any similar technical system."[231]

---

229 S.C. 1991, c. 11.
230 *Ibid.*, subs. 2(1).
231 *Ibid.*, subs. 2(2).

The *Broadcasting Act* sets out a broadcasting policy for Canada. This policy is longer than the policy contained in the *Telecommunications Act*, but it is worth setting out in its entirety because the multitude of often competing demands placed on the Canadian broadcasting system are only evident upon a review of the complete policy, which provides as follows:

3.(1) **Declaration.** – It is hereby declared as the broadcasting policy for Canada that

(a) the Canadian broadcasting system shall be effectively owned and controlled by Canadians;

(b) the Canadian broadcasting system, operating primarily in the English and French languages and comprising public, private and community elements, makes use of radio frequencies that are public property and provides, through its programming, a public service essential to the maintenance and enhancement of national identity and cultural sovereignty;

(c) English and French language broadcasting, while sharing common aspects, operate under different conditions and may have different requirements;

(d) the Canadian broadcasting system should

(i) serve to safeguard, enrich and strengthen the cultural, political, social and economic fabric of Canada;

(ii) encourage the development of Canadian expression by providing a wide range of programming that reflects Canadian attitudes, opinions, ideas, values and artistic creativity, by displaying Canadian talent in entertainment programming and by offering information and analysis concerning Canada and other countries from a Canadian point of view;

(iii) through its programming and the employment opportunities arising out of its operations, serve the needs and interests, and reflect the circumstances and aspirations, of Canadian men, women and children, including equal rights, the linguistic duality and multicultural and multiracial nature of Canadian society and the special place of aboriginal peoples within that society, and be readily adaptable to scientific and technological change;

(e) each element of the Canadian broadcasting system shall contribute in an appropriate manner to the creation and presentation of Canadian programming;

(f) each broadcasting undertaking shall make maximum use, and in no case less than predominant use, of Canadian creative and other resources in the creation and presentation of programming, unless the nature of the service provided by the undertaking, such as specialized content or format or the use of languages other than French and English, renders that use impracticable, in which case the undertaking shall make the greatest practicable use of those resources;

(g) the programming originated by broadcasting undertakings should be of high standard;

(h) all persons who are licensed to carry on broadcasting undertakings have a responsibility for the programs they broadcast;

(i) the programming provided by the Canadian broadcasting system should

   (i) be varied and comprehensive, providing a balance of information, enlightenment and entertainment for men, women and children of all ages, interests and tastes,

   (ii) be drawn from local, regional, national and international sources,

   (iii) include educational programs and community programs,

   (iv) provide a reasonable opportunity for the public to be exposed to the expression of differing views on matters of public concern, and

   (v) include a significant contribution from the Canadian independent production sector;

(j) educational programming, particularly where provided through the facilities of an independent education authority, is an integral part of the Canadian broadcasting system;

(k) a range of broadcasting services in English and in French shall be extended to all Canadians as resources become available;

(l) the Canadian Broadcasting Corporation, as the national public broadcaster, should provide radio and television services incorporating a wide range of programming that informs, enlightens and entertains;

(m) the programming provided by the Corporation should

   (i) be predominantly and distinctively Canadian,

   (ii) reflect Canada and its regions to national and regional audiences, while serving the special needs of those regions,

   (iii) actively contribute to the flow and exchange of cultural expression,

   (iv) be in English and in French, reflecting the different needs and circumstances of each official language community, including the particular needs and circumstances of English and French linguistic minorities,

(v) strive to be of equivalent quality in English and in French,

(vi) contribute to shared national consciousness and identity,

(vii) be made available throughout Canada by the most appropriate and efficient means and as resources become available for the purpose, and

(viii) reflect the multicultural and multiracial nature of Canada;

(n) where any conflict arises between the objectives of the Corporation set out in paragraphs (l) and (m) and the interests of any other broadcasting undertaking of the Canadian broadcasting system, it shall be resolved in the public interest, and where the public interest would be equally served by resolving the conflict in favour of either, it shall be resolved in favour of the objectives set out in paragraphs (l) and (m);

(o) programming that reflects the aboriginal cultures of Canada should be provided within the Canadian broadcasting system as resources become available for the purpose;

(p) programming accessible by disabled persons should be provided within the Canadian broadcasting system as resources become available for the purpose;

(q) without limiting any obligation of a broadcasting undertaking to provide the programming contemplated by paragraph (i), alternative television programming services in English and in French should be provided where necessary to ensure that the full range of programming contemplated by that paragraph is made available through the Canadian broadcasting system;

(r) the programming provided by alternative television programming services should

(i) be innovative and be complementary to the programming provided for mass audiences,

(ii) cater to tastes and interests not adequately provided for by the programming provided for mass audiences, and include programming devoted to culture and the arts,

(iii) reflect Canada's regions and multicultural nature,

(iv) as far as possible, be acquired rather than produced by those services, and

(v) be made available throughout Canada by the most cost efficient means;

(s) private networks and programming undertakings should, to an extent consistent with the financial and other resources available to them,

(i) contribute significantly to the creation and presentation of Canadian programming, and

       (ii) be responsive to the evolving demands of the public; and

(t) distribution undertakings

       (i) should give priority to the carriage of Canadian program-
ming services and, in particular, to the carriage of local
Canadian stations,

       (ii) should provide efficient delivery of programming at afford-
able rates, using the most effective technologies available at
reasonable cost,

      (iii) should, where programming services are supplied to them
by broadcasting undertakings pursuant to contractual
arrangements, provide reasonable terms for the carriage,
packaging and retailing of those programming services, and

      (iv) may, where the Commission considers it appropriate, origi-
nate programming, including local programming, on such
terms as are conducive to the achievement of the objectives
of the broadcasting policy set out in this subsection, and in
particular provide access for underserved linguistic and cultural minority communities.[232]

As with the telecommunications policy noted above, this broadcasting
policy seemingly contains a number of objectives that could easily conflict with each other. Nonetheless, what is clear is that Parliament has
declared as Canada's broadcasting policy a series of objectives that go
well beyond merely parcelling out space along the finite radio spectrum.

The *Broadcasting Act* mandates the CRTC to "regulate and supervise all aspects of the Canadian broadcasting system with a view to
implementing the broadcasting policy."[233] Indeed the *Broadcasting Act*
provides in a further declaration that the Canadian broadcasting system constitutes a single system and that the objectives of the broadcasting policy can best be achieved by providing for a single,
independent, public regulator — the CRTC.[234] The power of the CRTC
in broadcasting matters is subject only to directions of the government,
which can be general[235] and specific,[236] but in both cases are binding on
the CRTC.[237] The CRTC carries out its functions under the *Broadcasting Act* primarily through imposing licence conditions on broadcasting

232 *Ibid.*, subs. 3(1).
233 *Ibid.*, subs. 5(1).
234 *Ibid.*, subs. 3(2).
235 *Ibid.*, subs. 7(1).
236 *Ibid.*, subss. 26(1) and 27(1).
237 *Ibid.*, subss. 7(3) and 27(2).

undertakings and passing regulations that are binding on them.[238] The CRTC's enforcement powers are bolstered by sections 32 and 33 of the *Broadcasting Act*, which make it a criminal offence to carry on a broadcasting undertaking without a licence or to contravene or fail to comply with the terms of a licence or a regulation made by the CRTC.

The CRTC and the federal government, acting largely through the Department of Heritage, have implemented the broadcasting policy in a myriad of regulations, policies, and licence conditions.[239] To illustrate the breadth of policy tools available to the CRTC and the government, consider the following mechanisms that have been deployed over the past number of years to foster Canadian content in television, which is a prime rationale for CRTC regulation of broadcasting today:

- *Government support for the CBC:* The *Broadcasting Act* proclaims the Canadian Broadcasting Corporation to be "the national public broadcaster,"[240] and notwithstanding recent budget cuts, hundreds of millions of public dollars continue to be contributed to the CBC.
- *Other government subsidies:* Other public monies are used to support Telefilm Canada, and provincial funding agencies, which fund productions that meet Canadian content rules.
- *Canadian content quotas:* Since 1961, television stations and networks have had to show a minimum amount of Canadian content, currently generally 60 percent during the eighteen-hour broadcast day and 50 percent during prime time. Specific spending quotas are also being imposed to support Canadian drama production. Certain stations are also being required to expend specific amounts on Canadian drama. Canadian-owned pay television and specialty program services on cable television have their own Canadian content rules, as do Canadian-owned pay-per-view undertakings that, for example,

---

238 The licensing and regulation-making powers are contained in subss. 9(1) and 10(1), respectively, of the *Broadcasting Act*.

239 For a useful collection of various CRTC policies, together with an annotated version of the *Broadcasting Act*, see McCarthy Tétrault (Peter S. Grant & Anthony H. A. Keenleyside), 2002 *Canadian Broadcasting Regulatory Handbook* (Toronto: McCarthy Tétrault, 2002). For a comprehensive work on the powers and procedures of the CRTC, together with its experience in regulating telecommunications, see Michael H. Ryan, *Canadian Telecommunications Law and Regulation* (Toronto: Carswell, 1993) (looseleaf, updated).

240 *Broadcasting Act*, para. 3(1)(l). The CBC has played a central role in fostering a Canadian presence on Canada's airwaves since its creation in 1935 when the prime minister of the day, R.B. Bennett, apparently quipped, "better the state than the States."

must ensure that at least one in twenty of their first-run film titles is Canadian.

- *Restrictions on distribution of U.S. television signals:* The number of U.S. off-air television signals that may be carried by cable companies is generally limited to the four U.S. commercial networks and PBS.[241] Also, the "simultaneous substitution rule" permits Canadian broadcasters to prevent U.S. off-air television signals from being delivered to Canadian cable homes when the Canadian station is showing the same program at the same time.[242] Indirect support for Canadian services is provided under section 19.1 of the *Income Tax Act*, which denies Canadian advertisers from claiming advertising on U.S. border stations as an allowable business expense. The number of U.S. satellite services carried by cable television and direct-to-home satellite companies is also limited.[243]

- *Levies on private sector participants:* Cable television companies and other distributors of broadcast programming provide direct financial support for Canadian production through a series of independently administered funds.[244] As well, 5 percent of gross revenues from pay-per-view undertakings such as direct-to-home satellite must be spent on funding the development of Canadian programming.[245]

---

241 See *Approval of Cable Distribution of Fox Network Affiliates*, Public Notice CRTC 1994-107, 29 August 1994.

242 See *Cable Television Regulations*, 1986, SOR/86-831, s. 20, 1 August 1986.

243 Public Notices CRTC 2001-90 and 2001-89, respectively, 3 August 2001, as amended by the Eligible Satellite Services list issued periodically by the CRTC.

244 The original fund, now called the Canadian Production Fund, is administered by the Department of Canadian Heritage. The CRTC maintains exclusive jurisdiction over the funding mechanism, which is set out in sections 29 and 44 of the *Broadcasting Distribution Regulations*, Public Notice 1997-150 (22 December 1997). Other funds are permitted by the CRTC, provided they qualify as "independent production funds," as defined in section 1 of the *Broadcasting Distribution Regulations*. Detailed related policies on production funds are set out in a number of CRTC Public Notices, notably 1994-10 (10 February 1994); 1997-98 (22 July 1997); 1999-29 (16 February 1999); 2001-30 (23 February 2001); and 2002-61 (10 October 2002), and in CRTC Circular Number 426 (22 September 1997).

245 *Licensing of New Direct-to-Home (DTH) Satellite Distribution Undertakings, and New DTH Pay-Per-View (PPV) Television Programming Undertakings*, Public Notice CRTC 1995-217, 20 December 1995. Some argue even these various regimes to promote Canadian participation in our consumption of cultural products are not sufficient. For an argument that our Canadian content rules should be extended to movies watched in theatres, see Jacques Bensimon, "Battle of the Big Screen," *The Globe and Mail* (22 June 2002).

It should be noted with respect to "Canadian content" that the CRTC does not define Canadian content by "content," *per se*, but by the origin of the content. The CRTC has adopted the point system developed by the Canadian Audio-Visual Certification Office, the federal agency that determines whether film productions qualify as Canadian for purposes of obtaining the benefits of a tax credit regime in the *Income Tax Act*. Under this system, each creative function is given a certain number of points (e.g., director, two points; writer, two points; leading performer, one point, etc.), and a production must earn a minimum of six points (or eight points under the new cable fund) to be considered Canadian, and at least one of the director or writer and one of the two leading performers must be Canadian.[246] In short, to be considered Canadian the program need not be about hockey, or any other Canadian story, but must have a critical mass of Canadians involved in the production.

3) Regulating Broadcasting over the Internet

The Internet poses a number of challenges to the regulatory regimes for telecommunications and broadcasting outlined above. Each of the four dynamics of computer law, namely, the rapid pace of technological change, the elusive nature of information, and the blurring of private/public and national/international, exacerbates these challenges. Consider an Internet environment of much greater bandwidth than today, where, in addition to text, a Web site could carry and would permit the truly efficient downloading of images, music, and full-motion video. One service that would arise would be sophisticated video-on-demand (VOD), where customers could rent movies over the Internet instead of trudging to the video rental store.[247] Of course the "full"

---

246 See *Certification for Canadian Programs — A Revised Approach*, Public Notice CRTC 2000-42 (17 March 2000); for the application of the point system to the cable fund, see 2(c) of *The Production Fund*, Public Notice CRTC 1994-10, 10 February 1994.

247 For an American initiative in this area, see James Lardner, "The Instant Gratification Project," *Business 2.0* (December 2001). This piece gives an even-handed account of the current state of play for VOD, including its great promise, but also its very significant technological challenges. Another service is streaming video, whereby television signals are delivered and accessed over the Internet. Given the compulsory licence regime for retransmission of television signals by cable and direct-to-home satellite operators, Parliament recently amended the *Copyright Act* (S.C. 2002, c. 26) to deny an entity relying on the CRTC's *New Media* exemption order (discussed below) from also benefiting from this compulsory licence regime. See the discussion of this issue in chapter 2, section C.6(d), "Litigation and Case Law."

Internet will offer much more than VOD. Just focusing on videos for a moment, newspapers delivered online will include video clips, rather than just text and fixed images. A company in the travel business will not only provide videos of prospective destinations, but may also provide travel videos supplied by satisfied clients. A hockey league may provide instructional videos, as well as Don Cherry's popular hockey video series. Universities and others will provide courses by distance education over the Internet; in cinema studies, this might entail downloading entire movies. Or book and magazine retailers might add video products to their Web sites. In a technical environment (which will not be attained for a number of years) comprising digitization and broadband networks, the content will be transmitted from all to all at modest cost, the sources of content will proliferate, and what people see on their information appliance (a computer or an interactive television set) will be determined by them rather than a broadcaster. The technical and business model for the full Internet will be the bookstore, magazine stand, and video rental store — with greater choice and with a great deal of "pull" technology, where the user dictates what she sees, rather than "push" technology, where the broadcaster determines what the viewer sees.[248] But even the pre-Internet examples of bookstore, magazine stand, and video rental store do not really capture the potential of the Internet. One important service for the baseball-crazed business person will enable her to pull down from the Internet highlights of her favourite team's latest game. Depending on how much time the harried viewer has, she can choose the two-, five-, or ten-minute versions, and she can watch these at any time. Moreover, this content might be available from any number of sources on the Internet. And this model can be multiplied by an almost infinite amount of content delivery operations over the Internet, just as the number of Web sites proliferate inexorably.

a) Constitutional Jurisdiction

Several questions regarding the *Broadcasting Act* arise from such an Internet environment. The first is whether the federal government has the legislative power to regulate the Internet. Paragraph 92(10)(a) of

---

248 That is not to say that a traditional broadcast model will not also arise on the Internet, though it will be more "narrow-cast" focused by being able to serve smaller, more specific types of demographics, but worldwide: see Stephanie Nolen, "CRTC Conundrum: Reality TV Moves On to Internet," *The Globe and Mail* (29 August 2000). See also David Akin, "Big Leagues Show First Game on Web," *The Globe and Mail* (27 August 2002).

the *Constitution Act, 1867* gives jurisdiction to the federal government over interprovincial "telegraphs," among other interprovincial works or undertakings.[249] In a consistent line of constitutional decisions, the federal government's jurisdiction over telegraphs has been extended to include telephones,[250] wireless radio communications and broadcasting,[251] and cable television facilities.[252] More recently, telephone companies operating in a single province have been held to come under federal jurisdiction because they invariably participated in the national telecommunications system.[253] In all these cases, however, the company over which federal jurisdiction was extended was a *work* or an *undertaking*, given the articulation of these terms in the *Radio Reference* case, namely, that a work is a physical thing and an undertaking,

---

249 *The Constitution Act, 1867* (U.K.), 30 & 31 Vict., c. 3, found in R.S.C. 1985, Appendix II, No. 5, is the old *British North America Act*, renamed by means of the *Canada Act, 1982* (U.K.), 1982, c. 11.

250 *Alberta Government Telephones v. Canada (C.R.T.C.)*, [1989] 2 S.C.R. 225 [*AGT*]. See also *Corporation of the City of Toronto v. Bell Telephone Company of Canada*, [1905] A.C. 52 (P.C.). In *Commission du Salaire Minimum v. The Bell Telephone Company of Canada*, [1966] S.C.R. 767, the federal jurisdiction over the telephone company was held to apply to all matters that are an important part of the operation of the interprovincial business, in this case minimum wage rules. See also Decision CRTC 2001-23 (25 January 2001), upheld by the Federal Court of Appeal in *Federation of Canadian Municipalities v. AT&T Corp.*, [2002] FCA 500, which confirmed CRTC jurisdiction over access to municipal streets by telephone and cable companies; but note *Barrie Public Utilities v. CCTA* (2001), 202 D.L.R. (4th) 272 (F.C.A.), denying jurisdiction over poles of provincially regulated power utilities (though leave granted to the Supreme Court of Canada as at December 31, 2002).

251 *Re Regulation and Control of Radio Communication in Canada*, [1932] A.C. 304 (P.C.) [*Radio Reference*]; and *R. v. Gignac*, [1934] O.R. 195 (H.C.J.) [*Gignac*]. See also *Re C.F.R.B. and Canada (A.G.)*, [1973] 3 O.R. 819 (C.A.), where the jurisdiction of the federal government was held to cover the whole of broadcasting, including matters pertaining to technology as well as intellectual content: the court thereby upheld a provision of the *Broadcasting Act* that prohibits political advertising on the day before an election; but see also *Quebec (A.G.) v. Kellogg's Company of Canada*, [1978] 2 S.C.R. 211, which upheld a Quebec law that regulated cartoons aimed at children, including those on television.

252 *Capital Cities Communications Inc. v. C.R.T.C.*, [1978] 2 S.C.R. 141. In this case the Supreme Court found in favour of the federal government's continuity of regulation from off-air broadcasting to cable transmission. See also *Public Service Board v. Dionne*, [1978] 2 S.C.R. 191 in which it was held that a provincial agency may not exercise regulatory authority over a cable company as this field of activity is reserved exclusively to the federal government.

253 *AGT*, above note 250; *Téléphone Guèvrement Inc. v. Québec (Régie des Télécommunications)*, [1994] 1 S.C.R. 878.

although not a physical thing, is an arrangement under which physical things are used. In other constitutional cases undertaking has been equated to organization or enterprise.[254]

Regarding the Internet, there is little doubt that the traditional carriers with respect to their traditional services, be it the telephone companies or the cable companies, come under federal jurisdiction. By contrast, what about the thousands of new content providers that have appeared on the Internet, as well as those that will be participating in the future, such as the schools, retailers, and travel agencies noted above? Are they interprovincial works or undertakings? And it is not clear that one can consider the Internet itself as an undertaking, given its anarchical, decentralized nature, as outlined in chapter 1, section A.6, "The Internet." Nevertheless, if the federal government assumed jurisdiction over every Web site in Canada, is the CRTC capable of regulating thousands of new "broadcasters"? This question raises the further question whether the current definitions of *broadcasting* and *program* in the *Broadcasting Act* are inclusive enough to capture all aspects of Web-based activity. The definition of program is very broad, covering sounds or visual images and excluding only visual images that consist predominantly of alphanumeric text. Thus, in its definition only text-based services, such as a stock market data feed or the cable wire news service that shows as text, are excluded from being a program. Moreover, the requirement that broadcasting involve transmission of programs "for reception by the public" is likely not an obstacle if they are made available to users of the Internet, and even if they are more targeted in their dissemination where the quality of the "audience" did not comprise only pre-existing friends or acquaintances.[255] And in any event, even if the definitions of broadcasting or programs were too narrow to capture all aspects of broadcasting on the Internet, Parliament could amend them to be more expansive.

Recent decisions have shed light on these various questions. With respect to how the Commission will approach its jurisdiction vis-à-vis the Internet, see the discussion of the *New Media* decision in section D.3(c), "The *New Media* Decision." As for the constitutional law question, two recent decisions of the Canadian Industrial Relations Board

---

254 *Canadian Pacific Railway v. British Columbia (A.G.)*, [1950] A.C. 122 (P.C.); *A.G. for Ontario v. Israel Winner*, [1954] A.C. 541 (P.C.); *Reference re Validity of the Industrial Relations and Disputes Investigation Act*, [1955] S.C.R. 529.

255 See the discussion of "public" in chapter 2, section C.6(d), "Litigation and Case Law," and chapter 3, section B.5(c), "Internet Distribution." See also *R. v. Continental Cablevision Inc.* (1974), 5 O.R. (2d) 523 (Prov. Ct.).

(CIRB) have held that Internet Web casting and Internet service provider activity both are federal undertakings, extending the constitutional jurisprudence in the telecommunications and broadcasting areas noted above to Internet activities. In the first case,[256] the union that represented the bargaining unit at the City-TV television station wanted to include in the bargaining unit the City Interactive staff who were employed by the same company and who worked in the same building as the television station (the famous City-TV building on Queen Street in Toronto). The company opposed the application, arguing that the CityInteractive unit, as a developer of Web sites (albeit for the company's broadcasting businesses) and a provider of various services over the Internet, should not be considered a federal undertaking. The CIRB agreed with the union for two reasons. First, it concluded that CityInteractive was an integral component of the broadcasting company in that it shared premises and senior management, and most importantly, its work was dedicated primarily to supporting the various broadcasting properties of the employer in the online environment.[257] The CIRB, however, went on to find that even if the CityInteractive business were a separate operation, in and of itself it would come under federal jurisdiction given that its Web casting services amounted to a form of broadcasting, and its other interactive services are interprovincial in nature.[258] Thus, while the board found that the design and marketing of Web sites and the posting of information on the Web constitute CityInteractive's primary activity, and these are not federally regulated, CityInteractive's extraprovincial activities are integral to its operations and are regular and continuous. In effect, concluded the CIRB,

> CityInteractive is not a mere publisher on the Web. It carries on activities that in effect take television on-line and the Internet to the air. The scope and complexity of the Internet as "a network of computer networks interconnected by means of telecommunications facilities using common protocols and standards that allow for the exchange of information between each connected computer" ... and the instantaneous, ubiquitous, and borderless nature that characterizes digital communications, lead to the natural conclusion that these activities, viewed functionally and realistically, bear a clear interprovincial communication stamp.

---

256 *CITY-TV, CHUM City Productions Limited, MuchMusic Network and BRAVO!, Division of CHUM Limited,* [1999] CIRB no. 22; 53 CLRBR (2d) 161 [*Chum*].
257 *Ibid.,* paras. 123, 130, 131, and 147.
258 *Ibid.,* paras. 164–66.

In the context of webcasting, CityInteractive is an essential link in the broadcasting chain. CHUM's television operation turns to CityInteractive to carry its signal to the world over the Internet. The reverse is also true in the context of on-line chat. In that case, CityInteractive is an essential link in the broadcasting chain by providing the digital signal to the television operation and making the necessary connections to ensure its on air transmission. The fact that CityInteractive's signal is carried on the Internet through an ISP does not change the nature of its day-to-day operations for constitutional purposes.[259]

In the second decision,[260] a telephone company clearly under federal jurisdiction rolled its Internet service provider business (ITAS) into a separate business. When the union wanted to extend its jurisdiction to the employees of ITAS, the employer argued that ITAS was not operating a federal work, undertaking, or business. The board again sided with the union, concluding, after an extensive review of its operations, that "ITAS is an integral part of the transmission of digital bits from one province to another, and from one country to another, via telephone lines, for interconnected computers."[261] By serving as a "gatekeeper" to the Internet, ITAS provides access to telecommunications, even though it only operates at the "application domain" stage and not the "transport domain" stage. Thus, the board found ITAS to be a federal communications business on its own account. In addition, however, as in the *Chum* decision, the board also found ITAS to be part of Island Tel, the telephone company that employed all of ITAS's employees, and provided it with senior management, thus resulting in ITAS and Island Tel being operated in common. In both this and the *Chum* decisions, the fourth dynamic of computer law can be seen at play, albeit the blurring of national/international in the domestic Canadian context becomes the blurring of provincial/national.

In the end, however, it is not statutory language that most brings into question the ability of the CRTC to regulate the Internet; rather, it is the unruly technology of the Internet as discussed in chapter 1, section A.6, "The Internet." For example, the Internet is extremely global. In light of the fourth dynamic of computer law, a user in Canada can access Web sites around the world. Consider a user of a broadband Internet in the near future accessing a Web site resident on a computer in Florida to pull down American movies. The CRTC may be able to

---

259 *Ibid.*, paras. 165 and 166.
260 *Island Telecom Inc. et al.*, [2000] CIRB no. 59 [*Island Tel*].
261 *Ibid.*, para. 52.

argue that the American Web site operator is carrying on a broadcasting undertaking in part in Canada, thus giving the CRTC jurisdiction under subsection 4(2) of the *Broadcasting Act*, but even if it could, to what end would this argument be made if the Florida Web site operator did not have assets in Canada? There is the technical option of requiring the Internet service provider in Canada, or the Canadian regulated carrier, to block access to the Web site, but again the practical difficulties of this sort of action become daunting when the example of this single Florida-based Web site is multiplied a thousand times over by the vast number of Web sites around the world.[262] It is almost like trying to regulate telephone conversations among individuals. In short, the Canadian government does not regulate the material carried in bookstores, music stores, and video rental stores in order to implement Canadian content rules because, quite frankly, it is an impossible task. Of course, the urge and impetus for the CRTC to regulate the Internet will be great, just as it was when all individual users of radios needed a licence from the government. Ottawa eventually gave up this practice, and the CRTC will also have to be realistic about its ability to tame the unruly Internet tiger.[263]

In order to regulate, governments need effective and efficient control points that permit regulation. To date, in the broadcasting field, tel-

---

262 See the example of the court order banning publication of the Homolka trial proceedings referred to in chapter 3, section B.7(a), "Contempt and the Internet," for a real-life case study of how difficult it is to regulate content on the Internet.

263 See *Gignac*, above note 251; and *Nolan v. McAssey*, [1930] 2 D.L.R. 323 (P.E.I.S.C.). Interestingly, the Canadian government's book retailer ownership policy, which requires bookstores in Canada to be owned by Canadians, came under e-commerce-induced scrutiny in the summer of 2002 when Amazon.com Inc., the leading U.S. Internet retailer, unveiled *Amazon.ca* aimed at the Canadian market (the service priced in Canadian dollars with all Canadian taxes included): Elizabeth Church, "Amazon.ca Set To Go Today," *The Globe and Mail* (25 June 2002); Elizabeth Church, "Ottawa Probes Amazon.com's Canadian Debut," *The Globe and Mail* (26 June 2002); and Tom Hawthorn, "Retailers Lament Amazon.ca," *The Globe and Mail* (12 July 2002). Amazon argued the ownership rules did not come into play as it did not have an office or a single employee in Canada, and its fulfillment in Canada was done by Canada Post, a Crown corporation. Canadian booksellers, large (such as Indigo Books and Music Inc.) and small (such as Misty River Books in Terrace, B.C.) were up in arms. Canadian book publishers (such as Porcupine's Quill Inc. in Erin, Ontario) were more ambivalent, particularly if Amazon.ca presented them with a new distribution channel in Canada and abroad. This controversy is perhaps the quintessential example of the fourth dynamic of computer law — the blurring of national with international — in this entire book.

evision and radio stations and cable companies have been extremely convenient control points. Telecommunications carriers, and even larger new entrants into the Internet content business with assets in Canada, will serve as manageable regulatory control points. The Internet, however, simply has many fewer effective control points relative to the thousands and thousands of its users. And if these unregulated entities take material market share away from the traditional broadcasters, the latter will clamour for a general deregulation. This is not to say that the future of the CRTC is doomed, because there will continue to be a traditional broadcast industry. Even elements of it on the Internet will be able to be regulated by the CRTC. Nevertheless, the huge fragmentation and democratization that will occur with so much content on the Internet will simply be beyond the practical regulatory purview of the CRTC. For an "early warning" indicator, one simply has to recall the problems encountered during the 1997 federal election by Elections Canada in enforcing the rules that public opinion polls must not be published in the forty-eight-hour period prior to election day and that election results may not be released in a region until the polls have closed there.[264] Of course this prediction may prove to be somewhat off the mark or it may not come to pass for some time. Given the phenomenon of information overload, there will always be a demand for services that aggregate, edit, and present information and content in manageable portions, and arguably these types of entities are reasonably convenient regulatory control points, particularly if broadcast regulators around the world band together in some coordinated fashion to impose their collective wills. In any event, there is no question that the four dynamics of computer law will make the broadcasting regulator's task much more difficult in the new computerized, Internet environment.

b)   The Convergence Report

The Canadian government and the CRTC are mindful that the Internet presents novel questions. In October 1994 the government requested

---

264 See Mary Gooderham, "Officials Rushing to Plug Cyberspace Loophole," *The Globe and Mail* (27 March 1997); and Mary McGuire and Janice Neil, "Give Up: Voters Will Find Out," *The Globe and Mail* (13 February 2003). See also "Chaos Theory in Action" in the "Briefly Noted" section of *The Globe and Mail* (23 May 1997), which describes election Canada's problem in enforcing another election law on the Internet. When an Ottawa-based Web site operator removed his material at the behest of Elections Canada, copies of it sprang up in six countries, including several sites in Canada. Regulating the Internet is like putting small fingers into huge cracks in the dyke. See also Drew Fagan, "Canada's Cultural Protections Are Bound to Come Tumbling Down," *The Globe and Mail* (30 April 2002).

the CRTC to conduct hearings and prepare a report on the regulatory issues of the Information Highway (as the Internet was then called). The resulting *CRTC Convergence Report*,[265] released in May 1995, as well as the 1995 report of the government's Information Highway Advisory Council (IHAC),[266] published a few months later, and the government's official *Convergence Policy Statement*,[267] issued in August 1996, contain a number of interesting observations and policies. With respect to carriage of telecommunications and broadcasting signals, the primary policy objective was articulated to be to allow for complete convergence between the telephone companies and the cable companies; that is, telephone companies will be permitted to provide broadcasting services, and cable companies and other broadcasting undertakings will be permitted to provide telecommunications services including local telephone service. As well, third-party service providers will be entitled to use the facilities of both to provide broadcasting and telecommunications services. Such convergence, and the access by third parties, will be subject to a host of rules related to interconnection, rate restructuring, and the prevention of cross-subsidies and other anticompetitive practices. In short, the liberalization process that has resulted in increased competition in the telecommunications sector will continue and will include the broadcasting sector; this policy objective is being implemented by the CRTC's decisions referred to in footnotes 226 and 227.

With respect to content issues and the ability of the *Broadcasting Act* to face the challenges posed by the Information Highway, the government's policy and the CRTC and IHAC reports are unanimous in observing that reinforcing Canadian sovereignty and cultural identity through the *Broadcasting Act* remains a paramount objective. The CRTC *Competition and Culture* Convergence Report is almost defiant in its tone when responding to the question whether it has sufficient regulatory tools to respond to a networked, digital world, as seen in the following excerpts from the report:

---

265 CRTC, *Competition and Culture on Canada's Information Highway: Managing the Realities of Transition*, 19 May 1995 [*Competition and Culture*].

266 Canada, Information Highway Advisory Council, *Connection, Community, Content: The Challenge of the Information Highway, Final Report of the Information Highway Advisory Council* (Ottawa: the Council, 1995), available at <strategis.ic.gc.ca/IHAC> and also at <xinfo.ic.gc.ca/info-highway/final.report/eng/>.

267 Industry Canada, *Convergence Policy Statement*, 10 July 1996. This document is available at <strategis.ic.gc.ca>.

Section 3 of the *Broadcasting Act* sets out detailed objectives for a distinctively Canadian broadcasting system. The Act is not a dusty and dated piece of legislation passed in the days of crystal sets and Victrolas. It is an expression of the will of Parliament studied, debated and passed just over four years ago. This legislation anticipated both the extraordinary pace of technological change and an explosion of broadcasting services in a competitive environment. Nevertheless, the framers of that legislation held to the primary importance of maintaining a Canadian system that offers Canadians programming of high standard and one that, in its totality, reinforces the sovereignty of their country and their own cultural identity.

The 1991 *Broadcasting Act* is the latest in a consistent set of responses to the two central questions that have preoccupied Canadians since before the 1919 sign-on of Canada's first radio station, XWA (now CIQC) in Montréal. How can Canada create and maintain a distinctive Canadian broadcasting system, and how can that system ensure the availability of high quality and diverse Canadian programming, particularly in the face of the attractive, low-cost, popular culture spilling over our southern border? Both of these goals have rested on the conviction that "Keeping Canada on its own airwaves" could never be guaranteed by U.S.-dominated market forces, but must rely on reasonable forms of Canadian public intervention. Like Canada itself, our national broadcasting system is not an accident of the market; it is an act of will.

The challenges facing Canadians today, as we adapt to a new era of information technology, do not differ in principle from the challenges posed by radio in the 1920s and 1930s; television in the 1940s and 1950s; cable in the 1960s and 1970s; and, communications satellites in the 1970s and 1980s. In each case, attractive new services were first available from U.S. sources. With Canadians rightly demanding access to these services, government policy had to ensure that attractive and viable domestic services were also available within the system.

The Canadian broadcasting system, as it exists today, is the product of more than five decades of cooperation between public and private elements; compromise between idealism and pragmatism; balance between national identity and continentalist market forces; and concentration on the principles in section 3 of the *Broadcasting Act*.

Canadians can be justifiably proud of their broadcasting system. It is studied and emulated by nations around the world. We live beside the world's most prolific exporter of popular culture and mass media, one whose products reach us in particular abundance, and in one of our own official languages. Despite this, and in a vast and thin-ly-populated land, Canadians have accomplished the following:

- established publicly-funded radio and television services, educational services and community services, in both official languages;
- extended public broadcasting services to over 97% of the population;
- established private conventional radio and television services that provide Canadians with a range of choices in virtually every community;
- established multilingual radio, television and specialty services directed to Canada's multicultural population, as well as services controlled by and dedicated to the aboriginal peoples of Canada;
- developed an advanced cable distribution system that is available to 94% of Canadian homes; and
- created over 30 specialty and pay television services available to cable subscribers.[268]

The CRTC and the government perceive the current regulatory model going forward to cover new culture-delivery technologies and distribution systems in the future. Thus, both documents stipulate that new licensed distribution undertakings will be required to make financial contributions to the production of Canadian programming, as currently is the case. Similarly, these entities will be required to provide an affordable and attractive base package of services that include predominant Canadian choice. For example, licensed VOD services will be required to offer a meaningful amount of Canadian titles, and they must make use of navigational systems that give priority to Canadian programs. The CRTC considers that the tools in the *Broadcasting Act* and the *Telecommunications Act* are sufficient to ensure cultural policy

---

268 *Competition and Culture*, above note 265 at 27–28. Since the date of this report, the number of analog and digital specialty, pay, pay-per-view, video-on-demand, and direct-to-home television services has increased to 130 (from the thirty mentioned in the report). With respect to the CRTC's approach to licensing digital-only pay, pay-per-view, VOD, and specialty services, see the following CRTC public notices and decisions: Public Notice 2000-6 (13 January 2000); Public Notice 2000-171 (14 December 2000); Public Notice 2000-172 (14 December 2000); Decisions 2000-449 to 469; Decisions 2000-470 to 731; Decisions 97-285 to 97-287; Decisions 2000-733 to 2000-736; and Decisions 2000-737 to 2000-738. These can be found in McCarthy Tétrault (Peter S. Grant, Grant Buchanan & Monique Lafontaine), *Regulatory Guide to Canadian Television Programming Services* (Toronto: McCarthy Tétrault, 2002).

objectives because it does not perceive this digital world to be a great deal different from the existing broadcasting environment. For example, the CRTC believes that VOD services will require significant financial resources to launch and market, will involve the acquisition of program rights, and generally will resemble the structure of licensed broadcasters today. This will be an accurate view for some time since currently the prime drivers behind large-scale VOD services will be telephone and cable companies that are already regulated. There is, however, the possibility that a new content distribution model will develop on the Internet involving very different entities. The CRTC, in its report, is willing to consider amending the definition of program in the *Broadcasting Act* to exclude, in addition to alphanumeric text-based services, other services that "while they likely fall within the definition of broadcasting, will not foreseeably contribute materially to the achievement of the *Broadcasting Act*'s objectives";[269] the *Competition and Culture* Convergence Report then provides a non-exhaustive list of such services as including interactive courses offered by accredited instructional organizations or used by medical institutions, online commercial multimedia services, and educational multimedia materials directed to schools. The CRTC also stated that it might be reasonable to simply issue exemption orders in respect of such activities, as it has already done in respect of home shopping.[270] Interestingly, the IHAC report and the government policy statement are not convinced that additional exemptions should be added to the definition of programs, and are willing only to concede that more study should be devoted to this issue. One is left with the impression after reading these reports and policy statements that the CRTC, the IHAC, and the government are not fully cognizant of the digital world that will be unfolding, or of the difficulty the CRTC and the government will have regulating it to achieve cultural sovereignty objectives as a result of the four dynamics of computer law.

c)   The *New Media* Decision
Given that Internet use increased dramatically in the years immediately following the CRTC's *Competition and Culture* Convergence Report, the Commission decided it would make sense to hear from the Canadian community, including broadcasters, telecommunications companies, and the multimedia/Internet companies, regarding the Internet's impact on

---

269 *Competition and Culture*, above note 265 at 30.
270 *Exemption Order Respecting Teleshopping Programming Service Undertakings*, Public Notice CRTC 1995-14, 26 January 1995.

the objectives of the *Broadcasting and Telecommunications* Acts. In July 1998 the CRTC initiated a proceeding calling for submissions on "new media" with a view to answering three questions:

a) In what ways, and to what extent, do new media affect, or are they likely to affect, the broadcasting and telecommunications undertakings now regulated by the Commission?

b) In what ways, and to what extent, are some or any of the new media either broadcasting or telecommunications services?

c) To the extent that any of the new media are broadcasting or telecommunications, to what extent should the Commission regulate and supervise them pursuant to the *Broadcasting Act* and the *Telecommunications Act*?[271]

The CRTC's call for comments prompted an unprecedented volume and range of responses: more than a thousand contributions were made in writing; hundreds more were submitted as e-mails to an online forum hosted for the CRTC by the McLuhan Program E-lab unit; and nearly a hundred parties made oral presentations to the Commission during eleven days of hearings.

The resulting *New Media* decision,[272] released in May 1999, begins by defining the term *new media* as, essentially, any and all services delivered over the Internet.[273] Then, in an effort to clarify whether new media services constituted "broadcasting" under the *Broadcasting Act* (in other words, did the CRTC have jurisdiction over new media), the Commission concluded that most of the content on the Internet, to the extent it consisted of alphanumeric text, would be excluded from the definition of *program* under the statute, and therefore would fall outside the purview of the CRTC.[274] As well, non-alphanumeric content that was customizable by the user, by allowing the end-user to create unique content in a one-on-one experience, would also fall outside the

---

271 Broadcasting Public Notice CRTC 1998-82, Telecom Public Notice CRTC 98-20, 31 July 1998.

272 *New Media*, Broadcasting Public Notice CRTC 1999-84/Telecom Public Notice CRTC 99-14, 17 May 1999 [*New Media*].

273 The Commission observed that "new media" includes a wide range of products, including video games, CD-ROMs, e-mail, online paging services, faxing, electronic commerce, IP telephony, and services delivered over the World Wide Web and the Internet, and that such products/services combine elements such as text, graphics, data, fixed images, audio, full motion video, and animation: *ibid.*, paras. 12 and 14.

274 *Ibid.*, para. 35.

definition of *broadcasting*.[275] All other content, however, would come within the Commission's jurisdiction, including transmissions where users could select camera angles,[276] and on-demand transmissions, even to a single individual.[277] Having asserted jurisdiction over everything on the Internet, other than alphanumeric text or personally customized content, the CRTC went on to propose exempting all this material from regulation for the following reasons: there is a substantial Canadian presence in the new media;[278] there is no evidence that the Internet has had an adverse impact on the advertising revenues of regulated broadcasters;[279] government initiatives help support Canadian content on the Internet;[280] and perhaps most importantly, rather than competing with traditional media, new media would be complementary to it.[281] The related actual exemption order was issued in December 1999.[282] As for the call by some participants in the *New Media* proceeding that the CRTC get involved in regulating illegal and offensive content, the Commission replied that generally applicable laws, such as the *Criminal Code*, together with industry self-regulation and content filtering software would be adequate to deal with this concern.[283] On the other hand, with respect to carriage, the Commission reiterated its concern with ensuring that Internet service providers be given meaningful access to the facilities of telephone and cable compa-

---

275 *Ibid.*, para. 45.
276 *Ibid.*, para. 46. This has important ramifications for digital television-type services.
277 *Ibid.*, paras. 43–44. The Commission does not believe that broadcasting requires a scheduled or simultaneous transmission of programs; therefore, self-selecting content on demand still involves "reception by the public," whereas "customizing" or interacting with the content itself to suit the user's needs would not.
278 *Ibid.*, para. 74. In a related information sheet released together with the *New Media* decision, the Commission noted that the record collected for the *New Media* proceeding indicated that 5 percent of content on the Internet is Canadian, and 5 percent is French.
279 *Ibid.*, para. 109.
280 *Ibid.*, paras. 77–78.
281 *Ibid.*, paras. 23, 91, and 96. Indeed, the Commission wondered whether the Internet would ever be able to create mass audiences in a manner similar to conventional television: para. 87, and that any hope of doing so would have to await new technological developments: para. 92.
282 Public Notice CRTC 1999-197, *Exemption Order for New Media Broadcasting Undertakings* (17 December 1999).
283 *New Media*, above note 272, paras. 117–23. It is interesting to note that the U.S. Supreme Court, in *Reno v. American Civil Liberties Union*, 117 S. Ct. 2329 (1997) made a similar point about the importance of self-help tools, such as filtering software that parents can install on the family personal computer in order to block their children from viewing certain questionable content.

nies, particularly for broadband services, so that there would be healthy competition in the Internet access market.[284]

The CRTC stated in the *New Media* decision that it anticipated that it would be a good ten years before the Commission, in light of new technology developments, would have to turn its mind to Internet regulation. This may well prove to be too cautious a time line. Since the *New Media* decision, large-scale mergers have taken place, in Canada and the United States, between traditional broadcasting entities and online service providers. In the United States, the merger of AOL with Time Warner in January 2000 exemplifies this activity, whereas in Canada, BCE's acquisition of CTV and the *Globe and Mail* represents convergence. As for technical developments, video and audio content streaming over the Internet is developing at a quick pace, for example, by Canadian companies such as Iceberg Media and iMagicTV, and by the new business models floated by iCraveTV and JumpTV.[285] Thus, when the Commission reviews its *New Media* exemption order in 2004,[286] it may not be able to postpone the really tough questions confronting it vis-à-vis the Internet (driven inexorably by the four dynamics of computer law): Are Internet service providers broadcasting undertakings?[287] How will the CRTC approach the regulation of foreign broadcasters streaming into Canada over the Internet? and How can the CRTC regulate the potentially thousands of non-traditional purveyors of broadcasting content?

---

284 *New Media*, above note 272, paras. 53–55. In this regard, the Commission pointed out that it already addressed this issue in *Telecom* Decision CRTC 98-9, Regulation Under the Telecommunications Act of Certain Telecommunications Services Offered by "Broadcast Carriers," 9 July 1998; as well, in 1999, the Commission mandated "open access," whereby telecommunications and cable companies were mandated to carry Internet service provider traffic over their facilities for a reasonable contribution charge.

285 For discussions of the *iCraveTV* and *JumpTV* cases, and the recent amendment of the *Copyright Act* to deny, at least currently, Internet re-transmitters access to the compulsory licensing regime in the statute, see chapter 2, section C.6, "Copyright and the Internet."

286 Exemption orders are automatically reviewed every five years, and the Commission recently indicated the *New Media* one will be reviewed on this same schedule: David Colville & Andree Wylie, *Notes for an Address to the Standing Committee on Canadian Heritage: Review of the Canadian Broadcasting System* (22 November 2001). Messrs. Colville and Wylie are chair and vice-chair, broadcasting, of the CRTC.

287 For a discussion of a somewhat related issue in the copyright law area, see the discussion in chapter 2, section C.6(d), "Litigation and Case Law," of the *Tariff 22* decision.

E. REGULATING E-COMMERCE

Governments in Canada and around the world have implemented many regulations to protect the public from nefarious activities. Unfortunately, as discussed in chapter 3 in the context of the criminal law, the Internet affords fraud artists and other unsavoury types many new and powerful opportunities to perpetrate wrongdoing. Other parts of this book discuss misleading advertising and criminal law[288] in the context of computers and the Internet. Other laws with similar objectives involve securities regulation and consumer protection statutes. In all these areas the Internet and other new technologies pose a number of challenges (all made more problematic by the four dynamics of computer law, namely, the rapid pace of technological change, the elusive nature of information, and the blurring of private/public and national/international). Of course the phenomenon of responding to new, technologically driven issues and activities is nothing new in this area of the law. Fraudsters have long used the mails and telephone to bilk unsuspecting members of the public from a distance.[289] The Internet is just another stage in the evolution of technology and business environments where the rules of consumer protection and industry regulation need to be applied; but is the existing legal regime adequate to deal with some of its novel aspects?

To illustrate the difficulties of regulating e-commerce activities (prompted in no small measure by the four dynamics of computer law), consider the case of Internet-based pharmacies. There are estimated to be some 15,000 online pharmacies worldwide, many selling counterfeit, illegal, or non-effective products (i.e., containing no active ingredient). But there are legitimate pharmacies that sell only to persons requiring refills, in order to comply with Canadian law that requires an in-person visit for a physician to prescribe medication.[290] The cross-border trade in pharmaceuticals between Canada and the United States is particularly robust given the ability of the Internet to

---

288   See chapter 5, section B.1(d), "Misleading Advertising," and chapter 3, "Criminal Law."

289   For example, in *Libman v. R.* (1985), 21 D.L.R. (4th) 174 (S.C.C.), the telephone was used by persons resident in Canada to perpetrate securities fraud on victims outside of Canada.

290   Andre Picard, "Bypassing Their MDs, Canadians Go On-Line For Drugs," *The Globe and Mail* (2 March 2002). See, for example, <onlinemed/23.com>. As for legitimate operators, see Linda A. Johnson, "Internet Medicine Firm Gets Drugs Up To 85% Cheaper From Canada," *The Globe and Mail* (7 October 2002).

efficiently arbitrage the differences in currency values, drug prices, and medical/patent law systems (and highlighting graphically the fourth dynamic of computer law).[291] It is extremely difficult to regulate in such an environment.[292] In a similar vein, in the United States the Internet is making it very difficult for state governments to prohibit direct shipments of out-of-state wine and cigarettes.[293] On the other hand, where the entity to be regulated is not the individual consumer (as in the case of sales of wine and cigarettes) but rather, for example, a large corporation or car dealers with physical places of business within the

---

291 Krista Foss, "A Borderline Case: Selling Cheap Canadian Drugs to U.S. Customers Is A Grey Area — But It's Putting Internet Pharmacies in the Black," *Report on Business Magazine*, May 2002.

292 But not impossible: see chapter 7, section B.2(a), "Regulatory/Criminal Jurisdiction," for examples of government agencies rising to the task. With respect to pharmacies, the Ontario College of Pharmacists has taken action against their members involved in Internet sales of drugs (Allison Lawlor, "Internet Pharmacy Faces Charges Over Drug Sales," *The Globe and Mail* (15 May 2002)), and pharmaceutical companies are also taking steps to cut off the flow of product to the Internet pharmacies (Leonard Zehr, "Glaxo Moves to Curb Net Sales," *The Globe and Mail* (11 January 2003); and Leonard Zehr, "Glaxo to Stop U.S.-bound Drugs: Medicines Won't Be Sold to Canadian Firms Selling them Over the Internet," *The Globe and Mail* (22 January 2003), though Internet pharmacies may push back: Leonard Zehr, "Manitoba Net Pharmacies May Sue if Glaxo Halts Sales," *The Globe and Mail* (14 January 2003)). As well, note the successful arbitration decision brought by a large U.S. chain pharmacy's franchisees when the chain began selling directly into the franchisees' territories by means of a Web site: Stuart Gittleman, "Franchisees Win Landmark Internet Arbitration Ruling," *Law.com* (12 September 2000), available at <law.com>. In this case, which presumably arose because the franchise agreements pre-dated the Internet, the franchisor was undercutting sales by franchisees by selling at much lower prices than the franchisees. To stop such disintermediation, or "Internet encroachment," the arbitration panel ordered the franchisor not to sell to any customer within the physical territory of a franchisee and to place a notice on its Web site that products cannot be shipped to such customers.

293 For a review of the various legislative efforts by state governments in the United States to stem the flow of out-of-state wine facilitated by unlicensed mail-order and Internet operations, see *Swedenburg* v. *Kelly*, 232 F.Supp. 2d 135 (S.D.N.Y. 2002), and 2000 WL 1264285 (S.D.N.Y.). As for cigarettes, again involving a growing volume of Internet sales, see *Santa Fe Natural Tobacco Co. Inc.* v. *Spitzer*, 2001 WL 636441 (S.D.N.Y.) [*Sante Fe*], and 2000 WL 1094307 (S.D.N.Y.). See also *American Libraries Association* v. *Pataki*, 969 F.Supp. 160 (S.D.N.Y. 1997), where the court stated at 168: "The borderless world of the Internet raises profound questions concerning the relationship among the several states and the relationship of the federal government to each state, questions that go to the heart of 'our federalism.'"

state, the government's ability to counteract the fourth dynamic of computer law becomes much easier.[294]

Another factor that makes regulating e-commerce — and the Internet generally — difficult is the culture of certain Internet constituencies. There are a number of proponents of the view that traditional laws and regulation, and government generally, have no place in Internet affairs. Consider the following promulgation of this view from the first three paragraphs of a longer "Declaration of Independence of Cyberspace" by John Perry Barlow:

> Governments of the Industrial World, you weary giants of flesh and steel, I come from Cyberspace, the new home of Mind. On behalf of the future, I ask you of the past to leave us alone. You are not welcome among us. You have no sovereignty where we gather.
>
> We have no elected government, nor are we likely to have one, so I address you with no greater authority than that with which liberty itself always speaks. I declare the global social space we are building to be naturally independent of the tyrannies you seek to impose on us. You have no moral right to rule us nor do you possess any methods of enforcement we have true reason to fear.

---

294 In *Ford Motor Company v. Texas Department of Transportation*, 106 F.Supp. 2d 905 (W.D. Texas); affirmed, 264 F.3d 493 (5th Cir. 2001), Ford challenged a Texas law prohibiting automobile manufacturers from acting as dealers, given that Ford wished to sell pre-owned cars in Texas through a Ford Web site. The trial judge, in finding against Ford, concluded at 913:

> The plaintiff's entire argument is an attempt to avoid the Texas Motor Vehicle Commission Code. The plaintiff has mounted a substantive attack on Texas' decision to prohibit manufacturers from selling vehicles to consumers and attempted to cloak that attack in a constitutional challenge. It is a legitimate exercise of the state's police power for Texas to regulate who is qualified to sell motor vehicles in Texas and under what conditions...
>
> The fact that the plaintiff is attempting to use the internet to disseminate this information is not constitutionally significant under these circumstances. If the Court were to accept the plaintiff's arguments about the interplay between the internet and the Commerce Clause, all states' regulatory schemes would be nullified. This is an absurdity that the Court declines to accept. The Court emphasizes that Ford is mounting a challenge to a regulatory scheme of general applicability, not one that attempts to regulate directly and primarily transactions that take place on the internet ...
>
> The plaintiff has identified various reasons why it is in the interest of the manufacturer, the dealer, and the public to permit the plaintiff to advertise fixed price vehicles on an internet site. These arguments are more appropriately addressed to the Texas Legislature than a federal district court.

Governments derive their just powers from the consent of the governed. You have neither solicited nor received ours. We did not invite you. You do not know us, nor do you know our world. Cyberspace does not lie within your borders. Do not think that you can build it, as though it were a public construction project. You cannot. It is an act of nature and it grows itself through our collective actions.[295]

Set against this sentiment, however, is a determination by governments not to abdicate responsibility for bringing sound regulation to the Internet, and this book chronicles such government activity across a broad spectrum of e-commerce and Internet activities.[296] And this effort is to be lauded and encouraged. It is extremely easy to disseminate misinformation over the Internet either consciously (in order to perpetrate a fraud) or by mistake (though often the mistaken poster of incorrect information was at least negligent). Regardless of the motive, disinformation and misinformation can harm consumers and other participants on the Web, and in many cases the third and fourth dynamics of computer law make it extremely inconvenient or impossible for someone so harmed to pursue a private damages claim against the wrongdoer. Thus, it is imperative that governments not abdicate their

---

295 This declaration is available on the site of the Electronic Frontier Foundation at <eff.org>. For a discussion of Barlow's (similar) views on intellectual property protection and the Internet, see chapter 2, section C.6(a), "The Challenges of Digital Transmission." A more recent press report, however, describes Mr. Barlow as now admitting that he was wrong in predicting that the Internet would evolve as a new society free of the laws and constraints of the real world: Doug Saunders, "Mr. Wrong — John Perry Barlow, Mr. Internet Utopia: What He Was Wrong About: That the Internet Would Be A Lawless Shangri-La," *The Globe and Mail* (10 August 2002). Notwithstanding that John Perry Barlow seems to have seen the error of his earlier ways, others still continue to express equally naive "Barlowian" sentiments publicly: see Ken Wiwa, "My Big Fat Geek Web Is Being Taken Over," *The Globe and Mail* (4 January 2003); and Ronald Deibert, "The Internet: Collateral Damage," *The Globe and Mail* (1 January 2003).

296 See, for example, chapter 7, section B.2(a), "Regulatory/Criminal Jurisdiction." As well, sometimes the Internet business model and its specific online purchase practices can help regulators. For example, in the *Santa Fe* case, above note 293, an expert testified that minors tend not to purchase cigarettes over the Internet for various reasons, including the requirement of most e-tailers to effect payment through credit card (which minors do not have), the minimum purchase requirement of one carton (which is more than most teenagers can afford at one time; and purchasing a carton, as opposed to a pack, greatly increases the risk of detection), and the difficulty of arranging delivery without interception by an adult.

responsibility, through prophylactic, *ex ante* regulation, to help make cyberspace a safe place in which to do business, obtain information, exchange messages, and do the myriad of other activities that the Internet facilitates so wonderfully.

1) Securities Law

In the area of securities regulation, the investment community, long a leading user of computers and networks, has discovered the many advantages of the Internet.[297] Indeed, it is fair to say that the Internet has caused a revolution in the capital markets when one considers the cumulative impact of the veritable explosion in online and day trading; the use of electronic roadshows and electronic delivery of disclosure information; the avalanche of financial and investment information available on the Internet, including from financial services and information portals; and the proliferation of finance-related Internet chat rooms.[298] For example, securities law administrators in Canada have implemented an automated system for the receipt, processing, and distribution of disclosure documents, known as SEDAR (System for Electronic Document Analysis and Retrieval).[299] SEDAR reduces the time, effort, and cost involved in filing disclosure documents required of public companies, and it should also enhance the efficiency of the securities market by allowing for a more rapid distribution of information in electronic form. Interestingly, although all documents are to be filed electronically under the SEDAR system, those that call for signatures require handwritten ones on certificates of authentication to be filed in a paper-based format soon after the electronic version is submitted. With the ongoing improvement and diffusion into the business world

---

297 A decade ago, for example, the decision in *Daniel v. Dow Jones & Company, Inc.*, 520 N.Y.S. 2d 334 (N.Y. City Cir. Ct. 1987) resulted from an investor utilizing an online financial information service.

298 In the United States, to help the Securities and Exchange Commission (SEC) grapple with all these developments, in 1999 the then SEC Chairman (Arthur Levitt) created the SEC's Advisory Committee on Technology: 31 BNA Sec. Reg. & L. Rep. 18 (7 May 1999). In a similar vein, the current chairman, Harvey Pitt, has appointed a chief technology officer.

299 The SEDAR system was established by *National Instrument 13-101, System For Electronic Document Analysis and Retrieval (SEDAR)* of the Canadian Securities Administrators. See <sedar.com>. A similar system, known as EDGAR, is used in the United States. See <edgar.com>.

of biometric and related authentication devices,[300] it may be that at some point adequate systems can be developed to replace this last vestige of paper in the SEDAR process.

As well as communicating with regulators, computers and networks are increasingly being used to assist companies, investment dealers, and others in the investment community to correspond with investors and members of the public. This has prompted securities law regulators to review their rules. How well do they apply in an electronic environment? Is there any new functionality that may be problematic and that was not addressed in the former rules? To take one example, rules related to the delivery of a prospectus looked at putting paper-based versions of the document in the mail.[301] When a prospectus is put on a Web site, many of these rules no longer work and must be updated to reflect the new technology. Securities commissions in Canada,[302] the United States,[303] and elsewhere,[304] together with stock

---

300 See chapter 6, section A.2(b), "The Authentication Function."

301 Prospectuses do matter. In one recent American case, *Steinberg* v. *PRT Group, Inc.*, 88 F.Supp. 2d 294 (S.D.N.Y. 2000), claims of fraudulent statements and omissions in the prospectus were successfully countered by a close reading of the document itself, based upon which the court found the company not to have misrepresented statements in the important document.

302 See National Policy 11-201 of the Canadian Securities Administrators, which became effective January 1, 2000 ["National Policy 11-201"]. The purpose of this policy is articulated as follows: "Developments in information technology provide market participants with the opportunity to disseminate documents to securityholders and investors in a more timely, cost-efficient, user-friendly and widespread manner than by use of paper-based methods. The securities regulatory authorities recognize that information technology is an important and useful tool in improving communications to securityholders and investors, and wish to ensure that the provisions of securities legislation that impose delivery requirements are applied in a manner that recognizes and accommodates technological developments without undermining investor protection."

303 The U.S. Securities and Exchange Commission has issued three cumulative releases dealing with electronic delivery and related issues: *Use of Electronic Media for Delivery Purposes*, Release No. 33-7233 (6 October 1995); *Use of Electronic Media by Broker-Dealers, Transfer Agents, and Investment Advisers for Delivery of Information, Additional Examples Under the Securities Act of 1933, Securities Exchange Act of 1934, and Investment Company Act of 1940*, Release No. 33-7288 (9 May 1996); and *Use of Electronic Media, Exchange Act* Release No. 34-42728, *Securities Act Investment* Release No. 33-7586, *Company Act of 1940* Release No. 10.24426 (28 April 2000).

304 The International Organization of Securities Commissions (IOSCO) has also published guidelines regarding Internet-based investor communications: see <iosco.com>.

exchanges,[305] have provided guidance as to how delivery, presentation, notice, access, and retention requirements may be implemented in an electronic environment. As discussed for electronic commerce statutes in chapter 6,[306] these securities law directives require that investors receive electronically the same type of delivery of disclosure information as if they were to receive the paper-based equivalents. Merely posting a prospectus to a Web site is generally insufficient; rather, the investor must also be sent an e-mail giving notice that the material has been posted electronically, unless the investor consents otherwise in advance. These rules also address matters such as hyperlinks, and generally provide that material hyperlinked from a prospectus will be deemed to be included in the prospectus for regulatory purposes.[307] A core recommendation of the Canadian National Policy 11-201 is that the deliverer obtain the consent of the shareholder to receive materials electronically, again echoing an important theme found in the general electronic commerce statutes; indeed, this policy contains fairly detailed provisions regarding consent and even includes a form of consent that deliverers should utilize. On the other hand, contrary to the consent requirement in general electronic commerce statutes, Canadian National Policy 11-201 states that a deliverer may effect electronic delivery without the benefit of a consent (in which case the deliverer bears a more difficult burden of proving that the intended recipient had notice of and access to the document, and that the intended recipient actually received it, than if a consent had been obtained).

With the Internet's ability to transmit a large volume of material to a great number of people at low cost, companies are exploring it as a vehicle for attracting investment capital. An early effort was the raising of approximately U.S. $1.6 million by Spring Street Brewing, a U.S. compa-

---

305 For the guidance of the Toronto Stock Exchange on these matters, see *Electronic Communications Disclosure Guidelines*, March 1999. These *Guidelines* discuss the disclosure rules applicable to distribution of information via a Web site, e-mail, or otherwise over the Internet, including the duty to correct and update information and ensuring that electronic communication complies with securities laws. The *Guidelines* also address what information should be on an issuer's Web site; employee misuse of electronic communications; the posting of analyst reports on a Web site; links to third-party Web sites; and how to deal with rumours on the Internet. Interestingly, notwithstanding the wide adoption of the Internet, these *Guidelines* require, among other things, that press releases be disseminated by a wire service before being posted on a Web site.

306 See specifically chapter 6, section A.1(g), "Electronic Commerce Statutes."

307 This is sometimes referred to as the "envelope" theory, because the hyperlinked pages are associated with each other as a virtual single electronic document, much like mailing two paper-based documents in the same envelope.

ny, in early 1996 by use of an online prospectus.[308] Indeed, software is now available that assists in compiling a prospectus, again helping the smaller firm raise money over the Internet.[309] "Roadshows," in which companies raising money by a prospectus give presentations to prospective investors, can now be done by video transmissions.[310] Retail investors have for some time used the Internet to buy and sell stocks — as early as 1996 it was estimated that in the United States about 800,000 individual investors use Internet discount brokers — but the move by larger companies and their financial advisers into underwriting and distribution is new.[311] Securities regulators will have to update rules promulgated for a different environment. For example, the ability of a company to offer shares to the public in British Columbia using only the Internet (a phenomenon driven by the fourth dynamic of computer law) is restricted by the requirement in that province that a person cannot trade in a security unless the person is registered as a securities dealer.[312]

---

308 After issuing these shares, Spring Street Brewing then established an "off-the-grid" securities trading system using its Web site: see Richard Raysman & Peter Brown, "Securities Offerings Over the Internet" (10 June 1997), The New York Law Journal ["Securities"]. By March 2001 there had been more than two hundred direct public offerings similar to that undertaken by Spring Street Brewery. In the United States, the primary guidance on such Internet-based offerings can be found in a no-action letter from the SEC to Wit Capital Corporation that outlines, among other things, a fairly elaborate process of online offer and acceptance by would-be investors implemented by an exchange of e-mails: see *Wit Capital Corporation*, 1999 SEC No-Act LEXIS 620 (14 July 1999).

309 "On-line Capitalism," *The Economist*, 23 November 1996.

310 Raysman & Brown,"Securities," above note 308. In Canada, guidance on the use of roadshows held over the Internet is provided by Canadian National Policy 47-201, *Trading Securities Using the Internet and Other Electronic Means*, 1 January 2000 [*Trading Securities*]. In the United States, the SEC has issued a series of no-action letters that provide guidance on the use of electronic roadshows, including addressing issues such as any access restrictions (by passwords or other similar means) by viewers; making available the related prospectus in electronic form (including by hyperlink); preventing further distribution of the electronic transmission; and, in the case of Regulation 5, making sure U.S. investors do not view the offshore roadshow: Net Roadshow, 1998 SEC No-Act LEXIS 107 (30 Jan. 1998); Charles Schwab, Inc., 2000 SEC No-Act LEXIS 194 (9 Feb. 2000).

311 Linda Himelstein & Leah Nathans Spiro, "The Net Hits the Big Game," *Business Week*, 28 October 1996. This article describes the marketing of a $500 million bond issue by General Motors Acceptance Corporation through a brokerage that uses a Web site from which the prospectus can be downloaded. In 1999, the SEC estimated that 25 percent of all retail stock trades were done from online brokerage accounts: "Plain Talk About Online Investing," speech by SEC Chairman Arthur Levitt to the National Press Club (4 May 1999), available at <sec.gov/news/speeches>.

312 See the British Columbia *Securities Act*, R.S.B.C. 1996, c. 418, s. 34.

Thus, a company considering using the Internet to raise investment capital must carefully consider what rules apply to it in its home jurisdiction, as well as in any other jurisdiction where the company intends to have investors.

The need to carefully scrutinize the securities law ramifications of Internet-based investment activities is illustrated by the first enforcement action by the Ontario Securities Commission (OSC) against a Web site that occurred when it contacted the operator of the Federal Bureau of Investments site to cease operation.[313] This site, by giving detailed advice about stocks, led the OSC to conclude that it ran afoul of the requirement that the operator of it be a registered adviser under Ontario securities law, which he was not. Apparently, the operator of the site did not know that the site's activities required him to be registered. This highlights a dimension of the Internet that has been referred to in previous chapters — the technology and communication infrastructure is so accessible to persons of even modest means that regulators will see more contravention of, for example, the unregistered investment adviser. There is also a strong element of the third dynamic of computer law at play here, namely, the blurring of private/public by means of Internet technology; for example, a "hobby" investment club among a few close friends can turn into a serious regulatory concern if the club's activities are posted on an Internet home page.[314]

Of course, the Web is crawling with more nefarious characters that view the Internet as an ideal communications vehicle for "pump and dump" schemes where they heavily promote a thinly traded stock so that the price of it rises, and then they sell their positions, often causing the price to collapse.[315] One press report on this phenomenon quotes a representative of a U.S. self-regulatory organization in the bro-

---

313 Janet McFarland, "OSC Shuts Investment Web Site," *The Globe and Mail* (21 June 1997). See also Richard Blackwell & Jacquie McNish, "OSC Orders Four Internet Firms Shut Down," *The Globe and Mail* (14 December 2000); and Richard Blackwell, "Small OSC Team Has Big Job Policing Net," *The Globe and Mail* (28 December 2000).

314 In a similar vein, the SEC is concerned that unregistered financial portals may become broker-dealers (who need to be registered and are subject to regulation): see the remarks of then SEC Acting Chairman Laura S. Unger at the SEC Portals Roundtable (23 May 2001); Web cast available at <sec.gov/news/headlines/portalsroundtable2.htm>.

315 Peter Morton, "Net Scams Leave Investors Burned: Old Fashioned Stock Fraud Thrives on High-Tech Internet," *The Financial Post* (15 June 1996); Bertrand Marotte, "QSC Probes Brokers Misusing the Internet," *The Globe and Mail* (3 October 2000); and Wendy Stueck, "B.C. Securities Agency Finds Internet Scam," *The Globe and Mail* (22 June 2002).

kerage industry as commenting: "I think the Internet is a wonderful tool because it's inexpensive, because it's easily accessed, because it provides massive amounts of information to people at virtually no cost. ... And for those very same reasons, it is a wonderful vehicle to perpetrate a fraud."[316] However, if the activity is illegal in the physical world, it is invariably illegal in cyberspace as well; thus, by early 1997 the Securities and Exchange Commission (SEC) in the United States had brought nine enforcement actions against persons selling unregistered securities over the Internet, and it had also halted trading in a number of stocks that were the subject of pump and dump schemes.[317] Over the past number of years the SEC has greatly expanded its Internet enforcement team,[318] established a Web-based complaint intake vehicle,[319] and conducted a number of major Internet fraud "sweeps."[320]

One issue that complicates enforcement in respect of the Internet is the fact that the perpetrators of the illegal act may be resident outside the geographic confines of a regulator's jurisdiction (echoing the fourth dynamic of computer law). As noted in chapter 7, section B.2(a), "Regulatory/Criminal Jurisdiction," however, public authorities will not be deterred from asserting regulatory oversight simply because the offender is not physically present in its jurisdiction, so long as the links between the perpetrator and the victim are meaningful. And this is not a new regulatory approach. In *R. v. McKenzie Securities Ltd.*,[321] two persons resident in Toronto were charged in Manitoba for selling securities without being registered when they sold stocks to a resident

---

316 Janet McFarland & Paul Waldie, "Hype Artists Spin Stocks on the Web," *The Globe and Mail* (9 August 1997).

317 Christopher Wolf & Scott Shorr, "Cybercops Are Cracking Down on Internet Fraud" (13 January 1997) The National Law Journal; also available at <ljx.com/internet/0113cops.html> ["Cybercops"].

318 In 1999, the size of the Internet surveillance team, called Cyberforce, was doubled from 125 to 250 staff: "Electronic Commerce: Levitt Announces Increased Inspections, Enforcement for Internet Brokerage Firms" (7 May 1999) 31 BNA Sec. Reg. L. Rep. 18.

319 The SEC's Enforcement Complaint Center, located on its Web site since 1996, receives about 250 e-mail messages a day, thus representing a valuable source of leads and, in effect, self-policing.

320 These sweeps generally focus on persons participating in illegal touting of stocks, and other forms of stock manipulation. When preparing for these enforcement actions, the SEC must be open about its presence in fora such as chat rooms, and not otherwise conduct undercover operations: Joseph J. Cella III & John Reed Stark, "SEC Enforcement on the Internet: Meeting the Challenge of the Next Millennium," *The Business Lawyer*, Vol. 2, May 1997.

321 (1966), 56 D.L.R. (2d) 56 (Man. C.A.).

of Manitoba pursuant to contacts made by mail and by telephone. The accused were registered in Ontario, but the court found this did not cure their unregistered status in Manitoba. In response to the argument that the accused did not trade in securities in Manitoba because they were never personally in that province, the court concluded:

> The sole point to be determined is whether the accused Dubros and the accused West, both of whom were unlicensed here, traded in securities in Manitoba. That they did not physically enter the borders of the Province is not conclusive of the matter. A person may, from outside the borders of a Province, do certain acts within the Province so as to make himself liable to the provisions of this statute. ... Although offences are local, the nature of some offences is such that they can properly be described as occurring in more than one place. This is peculiarly the case where a transaction is carried on by mail from one territorial jurisdiction to another, or indeed by telephone from one such jurisdiction to another. This has been recognized by the common law for centuries. Thus, where a threatening letter was written and posted in London, and delivered in Middlesex, it was held by the Court that the writer could properly be tried in Middlesex.[322]

By the same token, today if the operator of a Web site solicits purchasers of securities from foreign jurisdictions it should be prepared to comply with the laws of those countries. Where this is impractical or uneconomic, the operator should attempt to limit the geographic range of its customers by stating clearly at the beginning of the site those jurisdictions from which it will not accept customers; or it should list only those jurisdictions from which it will accept customers. For example, the British Columbia Securities Commission has indicated that such notices, which have the effect of keeping B.C. residents from using a particular Web site subject to certain conditions, would be sufficient to remove the communication from the registration and prospectus requirements of the B.C. securities law.[323]

---

322 *Ibid.*, at 63. See also *Gregory & Co. Inc.* v. *Quebec Securities Commission*, [1961] S.C.R. 584, where Canada's highest court concluded that Quebec's securities law regulator had jurisdiction over a promoter based in Quebec who offered securities for sale by correspondence to persons outside of Quebec.

323 Douglas M. Hyndman, chair, B.C. Securities Commission, "Notice: Trading Securities and Providing Advice Respecting Securities on the Internet," NIN 97/9, 3 March 1997. The U.S. Securities and Exchange Commission has also indicated that the use of disclaimers and various means to determine that a purchaser's residence is not in the United States, for example by obtaining their mailing address or phone number, could allow an offshore Internet offeror to

2) Corporate Meetings

Somewhat related to the previous topic of securities law, on a number of occasions courts have been asked to approve the use of various (then) new communications mechanisms that are intended to provide notice of a corporate meeting or to gather proxies to be used at the resulting meeting. Typically, these cases arise because the relevant corporations or partnership law statute is silent, or ambiguous, on the point of using the new vehicle. Thus, one or both parties may want the comfort of a court order sanctioning the new mechanism, and therefore apply for it prior to the meeting. Or, the case arises because the losing party wants to disqualify the other side's votes that were transmitted courtesy of the new technology. For example, in *Re English, Scottish and Australian Chartered Bank*,[324] a lower court judge was called upon, under the then current U.K. companies statute, to supervise a vote of creditors/shareholders regarding the proposed winding-up of a bank. The shareholders of the bank were in England, where the meeting was to be held, while the creditors were in Australia. The meeting was called on very short notice, and there was insufficient time to send to England through the postal service the Australian proxies; they would have arrived late, and the wishes of the Australians, which were diametrically opposed by the English shareholders, would have been ignored. Therefore, the judge ordered that the results of the proxies could be telegrammed to England, and acted upon at the meeting, which resulted in the Australian creditors prevailing over the English shareholders. The English shareholders appealed this order.

The Court of Appeal concluded that although the order was novel, it was not prohibited by the company's statute, which did not call for any particular method for giving notice of a meeting called to consider the wind-up of a company. Therefore, the judge had wide latitude, and the Court of Appeal found it was exercised to effect justice. One judge

---

stay clear of compliance with U.S. law: SEC, Statement of the Commission Regarding Use of Internet Web Sites to Offer Securities, Solicit Securities Transactions, or Advertise Investment Services Offshore, Release No. 33-7516 (23 March 1998), available at <sec.gov/rules/concept/33-7516.html>. Canada's securities regulators have taken essentially a similar approach, stating that they consider the posting of a document on the Internet that offers or solicits trades of securities not to be trade or distribution in a local jurisdiction if the document contains an appropriate disclaimer that identifies the jurisdictions in which the offering is qualified to be made (and excludes the local jurisdiction), and reasonable precautions are taken not to sell to anyone resident in the local jurisdiction: *Trading Securities*, above note 310, section 2.2(2).

324 [1891-4] All E.R. Rep. 775 (Eng. C.A.) [*Australian Chartered Bank*].

at the Court of Appeal held that "it [the order] is adapted to the necessities of the occasion. It is ingeniously using the improved methods of communication by telegraph which it would be folly to shut out and not to use if it can be done."[325] Another judge framed the question in the context of "[w]hether or not the electric telegraph can be brought into play to carry out what was eminently needed, and indeed was absolutely necessary to carry out, justice in this case."[326] This judge answered the question in the affirmative by focusing on the provision in the company's act that allowed the court, in winding-up matters, to have regard to the wishes of creditors "as proved to it by any sufficient evidence." The Court of Appeal noted that while the judge presiding at the meeting would not have the best evidence of the proxies before him, the judge was able to consider the telegrammed information as sufficient evidence, particularly given the time constraints and the fact that there was no reason to doubt the truthfulness of the telegrammed information.[327]

Decisions similar to the one in *Australian Chartered Bank* can be found in a pair of Canadian cases involving fax technology[328] and more recently in a case where a company wished to allow several thousand option holders to exercise voting rights by means of a secure Web site.[329] In all these cases, courts have considered the trustworthiness of the underlying technology and found that the new technology did not present a risk to the integrity of the meeting process; indeed, in the *Newbridge Networks* case, the court expressly points out that the high-tech system proposed to be used is inherently more secure than, and to be preferred to, the old paper-based system. Usefully, the rationale behind these cases has now been engraved in legislation, with the federal *Business Corporations Act*[330] being amended recently to expressly permit CBCA corpora-

---

325 *Ibid.*, at 779.

326 *Ibid.*, at 783.

327 See chapter 6, section B.1, "Admissibility of Business Records," for a discussion of the best evidence rule and its general relaxation in the face of computer-generated evidence.

328 *Beatty v. First Explor. Fund 1987 & Co.* (1988), 25 B.C.L.R. (2d) 377 (S.C.); and *Rolling v. Willan Investments Ltd.* (1989), 70 O.R. (2d) 578 (C.A.). Both of these cases are discussed in chapter 6, section A.1(c), "Fax Cases."

329 *Newbridge Networks Corp. (Re)* (2000), 48 O.R. (3d) 47 (Ont. Sup. Ct.) [*Newbridge Networks*]. This case is discussed in chapter 6, section A.1(d), "Electronic Messages."

330 R.S.C. 1985, c. C-44, as amended. Other jurisdictions in Canada have done more or less the same: see, for example, the following sections in Ontario's *Business Corporations Act*, R.S.O. 1990, c. B.16, as amended: s. 94(2) — shareholders' meetings may be held by telephonic or electronic means; and s. 110(4.2) — proxies may be sent to shareholders in electronic form.

tions to communicate with their shareholders electronically[331] and to hold meetings of shareholders electronically.[332] With these common law and legislative developments, and the steady improvement in the technology for group electronic communication,[333] corporate Canada will witness a rise in this type of shareholder communication and meeting.

3) Banking

Internet sites and other forms of network technology are also being used by banks and financial institutions to conduct banking and to provide financial services. As well, computers and chip technologies are finding their way into electronic payment systems, from well-established, large-volume clearing systems to debit card systems to stored value-card systems ("smart cards") that are still in their infancy.[334] Statutes that regulate banks and financial services companies are dealing with new issues, such as privacy (discussed in section A, "Privacy and Data Protection") and encryption technologies (discussed in sec-

---

331 Sections 252.4 and 252.5 of the CBCA permit a company to send various materials to shareholders electronically so long as, among other things, they are accessible so as to be usable for subsequent reference. This is similar to the provision in the electronic commerce statutes discussed in chapter 6, section A.1(g), "Electronic Commerce Statutes," contemplated for electronic delivery of information that statutorily must be in writing; a similar amendment was made to "National Policy 11-201," above note 302, on 13 February 2003. Section 132.5 of the CBCA permits meetings to be held electronically. In all cases, the corporation's bylaws must not be an impediment to doing such activities electronically.

332 Sections 141(3) and 141(4) of the CBCA permit voting at a shareholders' meeting to be conducted entirely by means of a telephonic, electronic, or other communication facility, so long as the mechanism is secure and permits the votes to be tallied to be presented to the corporation in a manner that does not identify to the corporation how each shareholder voted. The 2002 amendments to the *Criminal Code*, effected by the *Criminal Law Amendment Act*, 2001, S.C. 2002, c. 13, ss. 61 and 67, implement very similar provisions for technological appearances and the "virtual presence" of witnesses and counsel, so long as everyone involved can communicate simultaneously.

333 For example, in David Koenig, "Virtual Meetings Get Real," *The Globe and Mail* (3 January 2002), the benefits of video conferencing are extolled, particularly in a corporate environment that is concerned with the inefficiency, cost, and insecurity of air travel. See also Mark Evans, "Baystreetdirect Holds First On-Line Vote at Meeting," *The Globe and Mail* (31 May 2000).

334 Smart cards are essentially credit card-like devices fitted with a chip that can store "value" electronically, as well as intelligence, with the value being drawn down as purchases are made: see Shameela Chinoy, "Electronic Money in Electronic Purses and Wallets" (1996–97) 12 B.F.L.R. 15.

tion C, "Regulating the Domestic Use of Encryption Technologies"). Another is the legal nature of "electronic money," and the regulatory and consumer protection issues raised by electronic money, none of which seem to be insurmountable currently in Canada.[335] In the long run, it may be that paper and metal-based currency will be replaced completely by a digital system of exchanging credits and debits over computer networks in real-time.[336] To date, however, several "e-cash" systems have failed to catch on.[337] As well, consumers are very concerned about the security of using their credit card numbers in online transactions.[338] So-called peer-to-peer payment systems have had more success, however; in particular PayPal, whose online payment scheme, which is the payment mechanism of choice for users of eBay's auction site, attracts about 24,000 new users a day.[339] Interestingly, PayPal is not regulated as a financial institution, and therefore can dictate its terms of use with consumers in a lengthy contract concluded online.[340]

One banking issue that raises computer law considerations is *money laundering* — the term used to describe the criminal practice, especially of drug traffickers, to "cleanse" the proceeds from their criminal acts by running them through a series of financial institutions so they cannot be traced to the illegal source.[341] The primary law against money laundering in Canada is subsection 462.31(1) of the *Criminal Code*.[342] To assist in the enforcement of this law, in 1991 the govern-

---

335 See Bradley Crawford, "Is Electronic Money Really Money?" (1996–97) 12 B.F.L.R. 399.

336 Elizabeth Church, "Get Ready to Part With Your Last Loonie, OECD Says," *The Globe and Mail* (20 June 2002). See also Evan I. Schwartz, "How You'll Pay," *Technology Review*, December 2002–January 2003.

337 Services such as "Cybercash" and "Digi-cash" have gone bankrupt: Reuters, "Network 1 To Buy Cybercash Assets" (2001) (online: ZDNet, at <zdnet.com>). See also "Keep the Change," *The Economist*, 21 November 1998.

338 In response to fears about online security actually increasing, Visa is testing a system that will let cardholders use a password that will not be seen by merchants, while a Canadian bank is offering an encrypted signature for its e-banking clients: Grant Buckler, "The Drive To Curb Risky E-Business," *The Globe and Mail* (27 December 2001).

339 "Internet Firms: Party Like It's 1999?" *The Economist*, 23 February 2002. For a Canadian-based equivalent of PayPal, check out CertaPay at <certapay.com>.

340 For a discussion of the enforceability of these sorts of online agreements, including one involving PayPal, see chapter 6, section A.3(c), "Express and Implied Click-Consent Agreements."

341 It is estimated that between $300 billion and $500 billion of such funds are cycled through the United States each year: Steven Solomon, "Know Your Customer — Or Else," *Business Week*, 21 July 1997.

342 *Criminal Code*, R.S.C. 1985, c. C-46, subs. 462.31(1).

ment enacted the *Proceeds of Crime (Money Laundering) Act*,[343] which requires banks and other financial institutions to keep certain records to facilitate investigations under subsection 462.31(1) of the *Criminal Code* and several other money laundering provisions in federal statutes. The record-keeping requirements are set out in a regulation and require the financial institution to verify the identity of individuals who open accounts and to keep track of cash transactions of $10,000 or more.[344] Specifically, the regulation requires banks and other deposit-taking institutions to have persons complete a signature card when they open an account and to ascertain the identity of the person who signs this card by reference to the person's "birth certificate, driver's licence or passport, or to any similar document."[345] These requirements present interesting challenges in the age of the Internet and high-tech smart cards. For example, the identification regime assumes a face-to-face encounter between a representative of the financial institution and the new customer, and therefore poses a problem for some aspects of Internet banking. New technologies, however, such as biometric devices (retina scans, fingerprints)[346] and videoconferencing, may permit the identification process to occur in a remote, online mode. Similarly, if the cardholder is anonymous, it may become difficult to keep records of money exchanges done through smart cards. But technologies that feature less anonymity would increase privacy concerns, although they would assist money laundering enforcement. Clearly, these new technologies will require some creative thinking by regulators, business people, and technologists to integrate them into existing regulatory regimes.

4) Consumer Protection

Ontario's *Business Practices Act*, which prohibited certain forms of false representations and other unfair business practices, was drafted in a relatively technology-neutral manner such that its application to the Internet presented little difficulty.[347] In contrast, Ontario's *Consumer*

---

343 S.C. 1991, c. 26.
344 *Proceeds of Crime (Money Laundering) Regulations*, SOR/93-75, 11 February 1993. Financial Institutions are using sophisticated software to compy with many aspects of the new regime: see Kevin Marron, "Banks Investing in Systems to Bring Terrorists to Account," *The Globe and Mail* (27 March 2003).
345 *Ibid.*, subs. 11(2).
346 See chapter 6, section A.2(b), "The Authentication Function," for a discussion of biometric devices and their use to facilitate secure online transactions.
347 R.S.O. 1990, c. B.18; now superseded by the *Consumer Protection Act, 2002* (see below note 349).

Protection Act required that certain consumer "executory contracts" be "in writing," raising the question whether agreements concluded electronically over the Internet met this requirement.[348] As well, this statute allowed a consumer to rescind such a contract within two days if it is negotiated, solicited, or signed by the buyer at a place other than the seller's permanent place of business. Although this provision was primarily intended to capture itinerant salespeople (e.g., the door-to-door seller), would a Web site constitute a company's permanent place of business? These sorts of questions needed attention by regulators, legislators, and business people, not only in Ontario, but also in other jurisdictions where consumer protection statutes had not yet been updated in light of the Internet. In Ontario the response has been the enactment of the *Consumer Protection Act, 2002*.[349]

Given the dramatic rise in Internet-based consumer sales over the past decade, and the scope for misunderstanding (and worse) to creep into these transactions, during the past few years governments have indeed studied what sorts of changes should be instituted in consumer protection legal regimes courtesy of the new phenomenon of online sales involving the public. The OECD has proposed a set of guidelines,[350] the WTO has produced a useful study,[351] as has the Australian government,[352] the European Union has adopted several directives,[353] and the

---

348 R.S.O. 1990, c. C.31, subs. 19(1); now superseded by the *Consumer Protection Act, 2002* (see below note 349). Though, see the discussion in chapter 6, section A.1(d), "Electronic Messages," which concludes that electronic messages satisfy general writing requirements.

349 Bill 180 2002, *An Act to Enact, Amend or Revise Various Acts Related to Consumer Protection*, supersedes the *Business Practices Act* and the *Consumer Protection Act* (among others); however, these earlier laws continue to apply to agreements and matters that predate the enactment of the new law.

350 *Guidelines for Consumer Protection in the Context of Electronic Commerce*, available at <oecd.org>.

351 *Electronic Commerce and the Role of the WTO*, referred to in a press release available at <wto.org/english/news_e/pres98_e/pr96_e.htm>.

352 *A Policy Framework for Consumer Protection in Electronic Commerce*, available at <treasury.gov.au/publications/ConsumerProtectionInElectronicCommerce/index. as>.

353 *European Parliament and Council Directive on Certain Legal Aspects of Electronic Commerce in the Internal Market*, COM (1998) 586-98/03125 (COD) (13 December 1999); *Protection on Consumers in Respect of Distance Contracts*, Directive 97/7 EC of the European Parliament and of the Council (20 May 1997); and *Directive of the European Parliament and of the Council Concerning the Distance Marketing of Consumer Financial Services*, COM (1999) 468 Final — 98/0245 (COD) ([submitted] 19 November 1998).

American Federal Trade Commission has produced several publications that explains how the FTC will apply its general consumer protection laws to Internet-related activities.[354] Closer to home, the Canadian federal government proposed voluntary guidelines in 1999,[355] and a year later the Ontario government published a discussion paper.[356] Several other studies have also been performed.[357] Subsequently, various federal and provincial ministers adopted the Internet Sales Contract Template discussed in section E.4(c) "Internet Sales Contract Template."

a) Online Contests

Some consumer protection laws (both in Ontario and the other provinces), while arguably not requiring fundamental amendment as a result of the Internet, do require review. For example, promotional contests must not require contestants to pay any consideration (or must be based on an element of skill) in order not to be considered an illegal lottery under section 206 of the *Criminal Code*.[358] In this regard,

---

354 *Dot Com Disclosures*; *Guide to Online Payments*; *Advertising and Marketing on the Internet*, all available at <ftc.gov>.

355 *Principles of Consumer Protection for Electronic Commerce: A Canadian Framework*, available at <strategis.ioc.gc.ca/sfg/ca01028e.html>.

356 *Consumer Protection for the 21st Century*, available at <ccr.gov.on.ca/mccr/277a_ba2.htm>.

357 For example, in *Consumer Protection and Licensing Regimes Review: The Implications of Electronic Commerce* <aix1.uottawa.ca/~geist/mccrgeist.pdf>, Professor Michael Geist proposed that the government grant an official seal of approval to Web sites as a means of giving comfort to consumers. He also notes that many licensing regimes, such as that pertaining to travel agents, contemplates that the seller will have a physical presence in the jurisdiction. Thus, Geist calls for regulatory reform, together with aggressive enforcement against out-of-province sellers who fail to comply with the applicable regulatory regime. For an American example of such action, see *Ford Motor Company v. Texas Department of Transportation*, 106 F.Supp. 2d 905 (W.D. Tex. 2000) (Ford's Web site for selling used cars was found to violate a Texas law that prohibits an auto manufacturer from also operating a auto sales dealership); but see also *Santa Fe National Tobacco Co., Inc. v. Spitzer*, 2000 WL 1694307 (S.D.N.Y. 2000) (based on constitutional grounds relating to the commerce clause, the court refused to enforce a New York State health law that banned Internet, telephone, and mail-order sales of cigarettes by out of state retailers); and *Swedenburg v. Kelly*, 2000 WL 1264285 (S.D.N.Y. 2000) (the court denied the New York Liquor Authority's motion to dismiss a challenge brought by consumers against N.Y. State's ban on advertising and direct shipments by out-of-state wineries).

358 R.S.C. 1985, c. C-46; see chapter 3, section B.8, "Gaming and Betting," for a brief discussion of gaming issues as they apply to the Internet. Note that s. 59 of the *Competition Act*, R.S.C. 1985, c. C-34, also contains requirements for a legal promotional contest.

certain online requirements of a vendor's Web site (e.g., that the contestant fill out a survey, etc.), if made part of the contest, could be considered to constitute consideration. In other respects, however, the online contest might be made more regulatory-friendly if contestants signify their agreement to the rules by typing and transmitting an acknowledgment in conjunction with the screen that displays the rules.[359] And where the operator of the contest does not wish to comply with the requirements of any particular jurisdiction, it should be made clear at the beginning of the site that the contest is open to players from certain jurisdictions only or, conversely, that it is not open to persons from certain jurisdictions.

b) False Claims

Many consumer protection laws in Canada and in other countries will require little or no modification to apply to the Internet, so U.S. authorities, for example, have already been quite active in applying their core consumer protection laws to Internet-related mischiefs. By January 1997, the U.S. Federal Trade Commission had brought at least eight enforcement actions against companies in respect of their false claims in Internet communications.[360] The activities of Canada's Competition Bureau to combat Internet-related misleading advertising are discussed in chapter 5, section B.1(d), "Misleading Advertising."[361] In a recent case, the attorney general of New York State was held to be able to proceed against an online business that used false testimonials from fictitious consumers to promote a magazine subscription service; attempts to trace the authors of these testimonials were unsuccessful

---

359 For a discussion of this sort of online agreement, see chapter 6, section A.3(c), "Express and Implied Click-Consent Agreements."

360 Wolf & Shorr, "Cybercops," above note 317. The FTC has continued its efforts to crack down on illegal Internet marketing scams in annual "Surf Days," where the regulator sweeps the Web to find fraudulent Web site operators: "Internet Fraud Tackled," *The Globe and Mail* (22 December 1999).

361 See also note 385 below, regarding the Competition Bureau's actions against deceptive spam. The Competition Bureau, and the FTC, together with similar agencies in Europe and elsewhere, are increasingly sharing information about untoward Internet activities in order to more effectively counter the international scope of the perpetrators: see Adam Bisby, "Canada, 12 Others Share Net Fraud Data," *The Globe and Mail* (3 May 2001), which mentions one case where the U.S. FTC uncovered a credit-card scam perpetrated against Americans in the Caribbean by people operating out of Portugal; this is yet another stellar (though unfortunate) example of the fourth dynamic of computer law. For a recent example of joint Canadian-American co-operation to shut down a fraudulent Internet scheme, see Karen Howlett, "Promoters Settle Case with FTC," *The Globe and Mail* (25 March 2003).

because they did not exist.[362] Interestingly, in an attempt to reduce such frauds, the state of Georgia enacted a statute that prohibits the use of false names when communicating over the Internet.[363] Soon after its enactment, this statute attracted a constitutional challenge from a number of parties who argued that communicating anonymously and pseudonymously over the Internet served many legitimate functions and that banning all such activity is an overreaction to the problem.[364] The court agreed and, in a judgment reminiscent of the U.S. Supreme Court's opinion in the *ACLU* case,[365] found the statute vague and constitutionally overbroad.[366] This case illustrates, once again, the unruly nature of the Internet and the difficulties in controlling it.[367]

c) Internet Sales Contract Template

In order to address consumer protection for sales on the Internet, in May 2001, federal, provincial, and territorial ministers responsible for consumer affairs adopted a template for consumer protection legislation in Canada governing Internet sales and service contracts.[368] The template covers contract formation, cancellation rights, credit card charge-backs and information disclosures to consumers entering into Internet sales contracts. The *Internet Template* applies to any *Internet sales contract*. That term is defined to mean "a consumer transaction

---

362 *People* v. *Lipsitz*, 663 N.Y.S.2d 468 (Sup. Ct. 1997).

363 Act No. 1029, Ga. Laws 1996, codified at O.C.G.A. §16-9-93.1, which amends the *Georgia Computer Systems Protection Act*, Article 6, Chapter 9, Title 16 of the Official Code of Georgia. For a disturbing example of the mischief at which this statute is aimed, see *Zeran* v. *America Online, Inc.*, 958 F.Supp 1124 (E.D. Va. 1997), where a subscriber of America Online received multiple harassing and threatening calls, including death threats, after a third party anonymously affixed the plaintiff's name and telephone number to an America Online bulletin board advertising T-shirts and other items with slogans glorifying the Oklahoma City bombing in which 168 people died.

364 For a copy of the complaint in this case, *American Civil Liberties Union of Georgia* v. *Miller*, 977 F.Supp. 1228 (N.D. Ga. 1977) [*Miller*], see <aclu.org/issues/cyber/censor/GACOMPLT.html>.

365 *American Civil Liberties Union* v. *Reno*, 929 F.Supp. 824 (E.D. Pa. 1996), (*sub. nom. Reno* v. *American Civil Liberties Union*) 117 S. Ct. 2329 (1997). This case is discussed at the end of section B.5(e), "Legislative Responses," in chapter 3.

366 *Miller*, above note 364.

367 In this regard, the discussion of the *ACLU* case in chapter 3, section B.5(e), "Legislative Responses," and the discussion of the CRTC's prospects for regulating the Internet in this chapter, section D.3, "Regulating Broadcasting over the Internet," are relevant.

368 A copy of the *Internet Sales Contract Template* [*Internet Template*] is available at <strategis.ic.gc.ca/pics/ca/sales_template.pdf>.

formed by text-based Internet communications." The term *consumer transaction* means "the supply of goods or services by a supplier to a consumer as a result of a purchase, lease or other arrangement." The term *services* is defined broadly to mean "any services offered or provided primarily for personal, family or household purposes." Section 3(1)(b) of the *Internet Template* requires that a supplier must disclose and prominently display, before a consumer enters into an Internet sales contract, the following information in a clear, comprehensible, and accessible manner that ensures that the consumer has accessed the information and is able to retain and print the information:

- the supplier's name and, if different, then the name under which the supplier carries on business;
- the supplier's place of business and, if different, the supplier's mailing address;
- the supplier's telephone number, if available[369] and the supplier's e-mail address and facsimile number;
- a fair and accurate description of the goods or services being sold to the consumer, including any relevant technical or system specifications;
- an itemized list of the price of the goods or services being sold to the consumer and any associated costs payable by the consumer, including taxes and shipping charges;
- a description of any additional charges that may apply to the contract, such as custom duties and brokerage fees, whose amounts cannot reasonably be determined by the supplier;
- the total amount of the contract or, where the goods or services are being purchased over an indefinite period, the amount of the periodic payments under the contract;
- the currency in which amounts owing under the contract are payable;
- the terms, conditions and method of payment;
- the date when the goods are to be delivered or the services are to begin;
- the supplier's delivery arrangements, including the identity of a shipper, the mode of transportation and the place of delivery;
- the supplier's cancellation, return, exchange or refund policies, if any; and
- any other restrictions, limitations or conditions of purchase that may apply.

---

369   A recent survey of the Web presences of Fortune 50 businesses indicated that only 33 percent contained a telephone number, and only 50 percent included a physical address: Susan Stellin, "For Many Online Companies, Customer Service Is Hardly a Priority: Just Try to Find a Phone Number," *The New York Times*, (19 February 2001).

Under the *Internet Template*, a supplier must also provide a consumer who enters into an Internet sales contract with a copy of the contract in electronic form within fifteen days after the contract is entered into. A supplier is considered to have provided the consumer with a copy of the Internet sales contract if the copy is

(a) sent by e-mail to the e-mail address provided by the consumer to the supplier for the provision of information related to the contract;

(b) sent by facsimile to the facsimile number provided by the consumer to the supplier for the provision of information related to the contract;

(c) mailed or delivered to an address provided by the consumer to the supplier for the provision of information related to the contract;

(d) actively transmitted to the consumer in a manner that ensures that the consumer is able to retain the copy; or

(e) provided to the consumer in any other manner by which the supplier can prove that the consumer has received the copy.

In addition to the various measures noted above, several provinces have also enacted specific legislation or regulations addressing Internet-related consumer protection. Manitoba's *Electronic Commerce and Information Act*,[370] in addition to covering the usual "writing," "signature," and related issues (which are dealt with in chapter 6, section A.1(g), "Electronic Commerce Statutes"), also contains a number of sections that address cooling-off periods, disclosure, and credit card rules in respect of Internet transactions.[371] In a similar vein, Alberta has enacted the *Internet Sales Contract Regulation*[372] under its *Fair Trading Act*.[373] Most recently, Ontario passed the *Consumer Protection Act, 2002*, which, among other things, prescribes certain rules for "Internet Agreements," such as giving the consumer certain information, supplying the consumer with an opportunity to accept or decline the agreement and correct errors immediately before entering into it, and delivering to the consumer a copy of the agreement in a manner that allows the consumer to be able to retain the relevant information.[374]

---

370 S.M. 2000, c. E55.

371 See ss. 127–135 of the Manitoba *ECIA*, above note 370.

372 Alta. Reg. 81/2001. Interestingly, this regulation is subject to a sunset provision; it expires on September 30, 2006, unless it is renewed before then.

373 S.A. 1998, c. F-1.05. Section 42 of this law permits the government to make regulations regarding the marketing of goods and services through forms of electronic media.

374 *Consumer Protection Act, 2002*, S.O. 2002, c. 30, Sched. A. These provisions are not unlike certain of those relating to the delivery of information and the con-

d) Other Harmful Online Activity

There is other Internet-related activity that users complain about to government consumer protection agencies, such as ministries of consumer relations in Canadian provinces, or the Federal Trade Commission in the United States. For example, "page jacking" involves substituting one Web page for another, thereby sending the consumer to the wrong page. Similarly, "mousetrapping" involves keeping the consumer stuck in the substituted pages so that he or she cannot exit them without restarting the computer.[375] In another somewhat similar development, various well-known newspapers in the United States (including the *New York Times* and the *Wall Street Journal*) have obtained a preliminary injunction against Gator Corporation, the distributor of software that triggers pop-up ads.[376] These types of ads "pop up" on a user's screen, and require the user to click on them in order to make them disappear. Gator sells software that creates forms for use on the Internet, but when it installs this software, it also includes an additional application that tracks the user's Internet usage patterns and causes the display of certain pop-up ads when the user visits certain sites. In this litigation the media companies argued that users will associate these ads with them, and in some cases they can also cover other ads placed on the Web site by other advertisers. Although the court granted a preliminary injunction, it will likely require a full trial to sort out the competing claims raised by this new technology and business model. Interestingly, the adverse reaction of the public to pop-up ads has already caused some large online companies to cease to use them.[377] No doubt over the next few years governments, public regulators, agencies, and private parties will be faced with new forms of harmful online activity, given the inexorable march of the first dynamic of computer law.

---

clusion of online agreements found in the *Electronic Commerce Act, 2000* (and discussed in chapter 6, section A.1(g), "Electronic Commerce Statutes").

375 For example, in *Federal Trade Commission v. Zuccarini*, 2002 WL 1378421 (E.D. Pa. 2002), an operator of a Web site was ordered, pursuant to section 5 of the *FTC Act* (which prohibits unfair and deceptive practices), to cease the deceptive practice of using copycat addresses to draw users to his site, only to hold them captive as he ran multiple ads for pornography sites. Once "mousetrapped" in this site, a visitor could not close his or her browser and return to the previous page, but rather a back click merely unleashed another wave of new pages. In this case, the FTC also ordered the defendant to pay a fine of $1,097,166.

376 *Washingtonpost.Newsweek Interactive Co. v. Gator Corp.*, No. 02-909-A (E.D. Va., 2002).

377 Verne Kopytoff, "Consumer Backlash Helps Push Out Internet Pop-Ups," *The Globe and Mail* (8 November 2002), and "AOL Targets Pop-up Ads, but Rival Shoots Back," *The Globe and Mail* (13 March 2003).

5) Spam and Web Crawlers

a) Spam

Spam is the term used for bulk, unsolicited commercial e-mails sent over the Internet, usually in vast volumes.[378] Many e-mail marketers send spam, to the point where a market research firm predicts the average person will soon receive fifty such unsolicited messages a day.[379] Spam is also being distributed to cellphone users, courtesy of the phone's text messaging feature.[380] The extremely low cost of spam, as little as $500 to send 10 million messages, makes it an extremely attractive communications medium, at least for e-marketers.[381] Many consumers who receive this barrage of unsolicited messages, and the Internet service providers who have to transmit it, have a different, less positive view.[382] In effect, the same feature that makes the Internet an incredibly powerful tool for legitimate purposes becomes an Achilles'

---

378 The term *spam* to denote junk e-mail apparently comes from a silly sketch done by the British comedy group, Monty Python, which has a chorus of Vikings in a restaurant singing the word spam, the name of the well-known canned luncheon meat, over and over until they drown out all other conversation at the restaurant. Those who oppose electronic spam think it will choke off legitimate Internet communications: Steven Chase, "Spam Under Attack," *The Globe and Mail* (5 April 2001). Spam was invented by two American lawyers, who first used it to advertise their law practice, and later started a business built around it: see K.K. Campbell, "A Net Conspiracy So Immense…," 1 October 1994, at <eff.org/Legal/Cases/Canter_Siegal/c-and-s_summary.article>, and *Cybersell, Inc.* v. *Cybersell, Inc.*, 130 F.3d 414 (9th Cir. 1997).

379 Steven Chase, "'Spam' Gets Harder to Swallow," *The Globe and Mail* (8 August 2001). ["Harder to Swallow"]. There is also the problem, however, of employees becoming overwhelmed, and productivity being adversely affected, by "friendly" spam and the sheer volume of authorized e-mail: Jon Chavez, "E-mail Blamed for Wasted Work Time," *The Globe and Mail* (21 June 2001); Zack Medicoff, "Bitten by In-Box Overload at Work? Call a Spam-Buster," *The Globe and Mail* (20 June 2002); and Virginia Galt, "E-mail Doesn't Save Time: It Wastes It, Study Says," *The Globe and Mail* (26 June 2002).

380 Showwei Chu, "Spam Invades Cellphones As E-mail Goes Wireless," *The Globe and Mail* (8 July 2000). Of course e-mail sent in large volume can also be used as a legitimate communication vehicle: Zack Medicoff, "E-mail Seen Sending New Message As Publishing Tool," *The Globe and Mail* (31 July 2002).

381 Chase, "Harder to Swallow," above note 379. In contrast to traditional paper-based junk mail, where the marketing firm has material printing and postage costs, the originator of e-mail has virtually no distribution costs.

382 D. Ian Hopper, "Hotmail Users Get Burned with Spam," *The Globe and Mail* (6 March 2001); and Kevin Marron, "The Spam Arms Race," *The Globe and Mail* (13 December 2002).

heel in the hands of unscrupulous mass e-mail disseminators. Indeed, spam is quickly becoming a material burden for unhappy Internet users, as their in-boxes are becoming clogged with it; clearing it can take valuable time away from more productive pursuits. And Internet service providers are becoming fairly concerned because the volume of their e-mail messages, estimated to soon be almost 30 billion a day, is 50 percent unwanted spam, though because it receives revenue based on traffic volume, the ISP might not look unfavourably on spam until customers complain.

The Canadian federal government's response to spam has been that, for the time being, it will not enact new legislation or regulations to address it. In a report released in August 1999,[383] the government concluded that Internet-based promotional and product information should be treated commensurately with similar material in print, essentially in an unregulated manner. The report noted that the Canadian Marketing Association has a code and guideline for spam, which provides that consumers must be given the chance to "opt out" of any further communication with the marketer.[384] Most importantly, the report seems to place great emphasis on the ability of ISPs to take steps to curtail the practice of sending spam, by refusing to carry it on behalf of e-marketers. And of course if the communication conveyed by the mass e-mail contained deceptive or otherwise illegal messages or statements, then the law of misleading advertising, or the general criminal law, would apply.[385] In early 2002, the federal government still seemed

---

383 Industry Canada, *Internet and Bulk Unsolicited Electronic Mail (SPAM)*, available at <e-com.ic.gc.ca/using/en/201.html>.

384 For a discussion of opt-out v. opt-in consumer consent regimes, see section A.4(b), "Private Sector Coverage," earlier in this chapter.

385 See Steven Chase, "Canadians Peddling Web Scams Get Warning," *The Globe and Mail* (3 April 2002), which discusses how Canada's federal Competition Bureau sent warnings to fifty Canadians involved in Internet chain letter schemes. Similarly, mass e-mails implying further fees were required from domain name registrants have attracted charges under the misleading representation provisions of the Competition Act (discussed in chapter 5): see David Akin, "Internet Bills Called Deceptive," *The Globe and Mail* (29 October 2002). Also, the U.S. Federal Trade Commission has brought many proceedings against spammers who have distributed deceptive messages: see Federal Trade Commission, "Federal, State, and Local Law Enforcers Tackle Deceptive Spam and Internet Scams" (2002), online: Federal Trade Commission <ftc.gov/opa/2002/11/netforce.htm>. Note, however, in respect of the criminal law, that in *R. v. Hamilton*, [2002] 8 W.W.R. 334 (Alta. Ct. Queen's Bench), a spammer who sent mass e-mails that advertised homemade bomb-making instructions was acquitted under s. 464 of the *Criminal Code* (which makes it

to be of the view that legislative intervention on the spam issue was unnecessary,[386] but some commentators have called for legislation in this area,[387] and by early 2003 it appeared that the Canadian government was starting to consider some form of action in this area.[388]

The mechanism by which the ISP can prohibit spam is the agreement that contains the terms and conditions under which the ISP makes available its service. For example, in *I.D. Internet Direct Ltd. (c.o.b. Internet Direct)* v. *Altelaar*,[389] in a very short decision the court found that the respondent's delivery of bulk unsolicited commercial e-mail through the applicant's system breached the terms of e-mail use agreed to by the respondent with the applicant upon the opening of the e-mail account. In another case,[390] the relevant agreement did not expressly prohibit spam, but it did require the user to "follow generally accepted 'Netiquette' when sending e-mail messages." The court found that:

> The unrestricted use of unsolicited bulk commercial e-mail appears to undermine the integrity and utility of the Internet system. Network systems become blocked. The user expends time and expense reviewing or deleting unwanted messages. Of fundamental importance is the distortion of the essentially personal nature of an e-mail address.[391]

Given these findings, and after reviewing the American case law dealing with "trespass to chattels" (discussed below), the court in *Nexx Online* concluded that spam is "contrary to the emerging principles of 'Netiquette,'" and hence the ISP could terminate the user's access to the ISP's system.

---

illegal to counsel an offence such as making a bomb with the intent to cause an explosion) as the court concluded the spammer had insufficient knowledge of the messages he was disseminating.

386 See Estanislao Oziewicz, "Junk E-mail Scourge of Cyberspace," *The Globe and Mail* (23 February 2002), quoting the official who co-authored the Canadian government's 1999 spam policy as indicating he had received only a dozen or so calls complaining about spam since the release of the policy.

387 Michael Geist, "Time to Hit Delete Key On Weak Spam Policy," *The Globe and Mail* (30 May 2002).

388 Jonathan Fowlie, "Ottawa Looking for Way to Can the Spam," *The Globe and Mail* (24 January 2003).

389 [1999], O.J. No. 1804 (Ont. Sup. Ct.). Apparently the respondent in this case sent 600,000 e-mails over the applicant's system in a two-month period: Mark Evan, "Tough Law Needed to Bite Into Spam," *The Globe and Mail* (25 March 1999).

390 *1267623 Ontario Inc.* v. *Nexx Online Inc.* (1999), 46 B.L.R. (2d) 317 (Ont. Sup. Ct.).

391 *Ibid.*, at 324.

In the United States, there are many views as to how to approach the spam issue.[392] Legislation has been passed in a number of states prohibiting the sending of spam.[393] Others advocate "social action," effectively encouraging Internet users to boycott — or sometimes take stronger action — against sites, or ISPs, that transmit spam. For example, the Mail Abuse Prevention System's Realtime Blackhole List acts as a kind of virtual vigilante group that helps shut down ISPs that either generate or retransmit spam.[394] More conservative private action involves the use of filtering software that can detect spam and keep it out of a person's e-mail box.[395] Others, in particular ISPs, pursue spam-

---

392   See Eric Hellwig, "Debate: What Price Spam?" *Business 2.0*, April 1999.

393   For a list of U.S. state legislative activity in respect of anti-spam legislation, see <ncsl.org/programs/lis/legislation/spamleg02.htm>. For example, California's *Business and Professions Code*, §§17538.4, 17538.45, requires transmitters of business mass e-mail to indicate a reply address so the recipient can send a message cancelling further communications, and mass e-mailers must use an identifying three-character subject line, namely ADV for advertisement and ADV:ADLT for sexually explicit material. In *State of Washington v. Jason Heckel*, 2001 U.S. LEXIS 10036 (Sup. Ct. Wash.), Washington State's antispam law, which (among other things) prohibits e-mail solicitors from using misleading information in the subject line, was held to be constitutional. The effectiveness of this sort of law may be thought to be augmented by the fact that circumvention for telemarketers and junk faxers is an expensive proposition as telecommunications charges are generally higher outside of the United States; however, as the cost of sending spam over the Internet is exceedingly cheap anywhere in the world, circumventing U.S. law for spam by moving offshore is a realistic option (illustrating once again the fourth dynamic of computer law). But where the spam disseminator has stayed in the United States, these antispam statutes can be effective indeed, as illustrated by a recent case: "AOL Awarded Almost $7 Million in Spam Case," *The Mercury News* (16 December 2002).

394   See the MAPS Realtime Blackhole List at <mail-abuse.org/rbl>.

395   For a discussion of filtering software, see Gerry Miller, Gerri Sinclair, David Sutherland, and Julie Zilber, *Regulation of the Internet: A Technological Perspective*, March 1999, available at <strategis.ic.gc.ca/ssg/ito5082e.html>. But filtering technology is not perfect, as it has a tendency to screen some non-spam messages as well, thereby creating angst for the user; this has prompted the development of an intriguing business model whereby responsible mass e-mailers are bonded, and they lose their financial security if they abuse the rules of the new system: "E-mail Spam: Filter It Out," *The Economist*, 19 October 2002. Newer spam-blocking technologies may help, just as products are now on the market to block computer-generated telemarketing phone calls, which are in one sense more intrusive than e-mail spam: Shawna Richer, "Say Goodbye to Nuisance Calls," *The Globe and Mail* (27 April 2002). As for a decision that acknowledges the invasive nature of telephone calls due to the phone's ringing (at least e-mail is quiet), see the *Motherwell* case, at note 33 above.

mers in the courts, arguing (usually successfully), that bulk e-mailing constitutes trespass against chattels.[396]

b) Web Crawling and Trespass against Chattels

Another Internet-based technology that has raised novel legal questions is the automated querying software, sometimes referred to as a "bot" (short for "robot") or "spider" that allows its user to search another person's Web site and glean information from it in a very short period of time. This practice, often referred to as "Web crawling," allows, for example, an online merchant to quickly ascertain what prices another merchant is charging for goods sold through the latter's Web site.[397] One early adopter of Web-crawling technology was the online auction aggregator,[398] who would present what was available at multiple Internet auction sites, thereby making it very convenient for a user to follow several auctions for the same type of item. Bidder's Edge (BE), for example, was an online auction aggregator that was searching about one hundred other Internet auction Web sites in the late 1990s. However, as eBay was already then the leading online auction brand, BE was accessing eBay's site about 100,000 times a day, and approximately 70 percent of the items on the BE site were from auctions hosted by eBay.

eBay took umbrage at the activities of the online auction aggregators and in 2000 obtained an action for a preliminary injunction against BE.[399] In this high-profile proceeding,[400] BE argued that Web

---

396 See *America Online, Inc.* v. *IMS*, 24 F.Supp. 2d 548 (E.D. Va., 1998); *Hotmail Corporation* v. *Van Money Pie Inc.*, 47 U.S. P.Q. 2d (N.D. Cal 1998) (in this case the court also concluded that the spammer breached the ISP's terms and conditions); and *America Online, Inc.* v. *National Health Care Discount, Inc.*, 121 F.Supp. 2d 1255 (N.D. Iowa, 2000). In the latter case the court surmised that spam may also violate Virginia's computer crimes law.

397 This technology, for example, has allowed "shopping bots" such as <mysimon.com> to provide a price comparison service, whereby the consumer searches for a particular product, and *mysimon* presents a search result that shows at what price the item is offered at various Web sites: see also Natalie Southworth, "Bots Beaten in War with Portals," *The Globe and Mail* (28 September 2000).

398 An early pioneer was BiddersEdge (BE). At its peak, the BE Web site contained listings for 5 million items being auctioned on over one hundred auction sites. BE is no longer in operation. But see <Bidxs.com> for a current example of the online auction aggregator.

399 *eBay, Inc.* v. *Bidder's Edge, Inc.*, 100 F.Supp. 2d 1058 (N.D.Cal 2000) [*Bidder's Edge*].

400 See "Deep Blocking," *The Economist*, 16 October 1999.

crawling was permitted given that eBay's Web site was open to the public. The court disagreed and concluded that eBay's computers were private property, to which eBay granted the public conditional access, subject to terms and conditions that prohibited the kind of use made of the site by BE.[401] Moreover, eBay led evidence that BE's Web crawlers accounted for about 1.5 percent of the load on eBay's servers, which represented considerable expense to eBay. Accordingly, the court found that BE's use of the eBay computers constituted trespass against chattels, as EB intentionally and without authorization interfered with eBay's possessory interest in its computers, and this resulted in damage to eBay. As a result, the court ordered BE to stop using any form of automated query program to access eBay's computers until trial.[402]

---

401 It is interesting to consider what precisely is the appropriate offline analogy to an e-commerce Web site that displays merchandise and prices. Is it the interior of a store? If so, it is worth noting *A&B Sound Ltd.* v. *Future Shop Ltd.*, 2 C.P.C. (4th) 37 (B.C.S.C.), where it was held that a competitor's presence in a physical retail outlet to review prices constituted trespass. Or is it the storefront that faces the street, where presumably there would not be a cause of action for trespass if a consumer merely stopped to "window shop" and observed prices set out in the display (i.e., the consumer did not have to enter the store to see the prices)? Or, is it an enclosed mall, where even the "common areas" where consumers walk to get from one store to another is private property? Interestingly, the court in *Bidder's Edge*, above note 399, observed that if eBay were a bricks-and-mortar auction house, it could refuse access to those individuals who had no intention of bidding.

402 See also *Register.com* v. *Verio.Inc.*, 126 F.Supp. 2d 238 (S.D.N.Y. 2000), where a similar finding was made even though the host site's terms and conditions did not expressly prohibit the type of use made by the defendant, although the defendant had been given actual notice subsequently that its use of a Web crawler on the WHO IS database was not authorized. But see also *Ticketmaster Corp.* v. *Tickets.com, Inc.*, 2000 Lexis 12987 (C.D. Cal. 2000), where there was no finding of trespass against chattels as the use of the query software was quite limited, and there was no evidence that this use adversely affected Ticketmaster's site; thus there was no finding of irreparable harm, a requirement for the granting of an injunction. Both of these decisions are also discussed in chapter 6, section A.3(c), "Express and Implied Click-Consent Agreements," in the context of the enforceability of online agreements.

CHAPTER 5

COMMERCIAL LAW

The business of selling computers, software, and information-based products differs from other enterprises in a number of legally important ways. The computer industry is driven by three interrelated phenomena. Perhaps the most fundamental and far reaching, and a function of the first dynamic of computer law,[1] is the short product cycle in the computer business. Short product cycles also result in a unique aspect of software — it invariably has errors or bugs in it. Another result of short product cycles is that the distribution channels for much hardware, and most software and information-based products, are multitiered and complex. These three characteristics of the computer industry raise a number of legal issues. Short product cycles and complicated product distribution channels have implications under competition law. Information-based products also tend to be licensed, rather than sold, thereby differentiating them from most other goods. Licensing products in an environment of rapid technological change can be legally challenging. Computer products also present questions under negligence law and raise issues regarding the applicability to them of sale of goods legislation. As software is critical to a company's well-being, it is not surprising that bankruptcy issues are of concern to a supplier and user of

---

1   The four dynamics of computer law, namely, the rapid pace of technological change, the elusive nature of information, and the blurring of private/public and national/international, are an important, unifying theme of this book. For a discussion of these dynamics, see chapter 8, section A, "Computer Law: Dynamics."

technology-oriented products. And, as in all areas of commercial endeavour, tax questions can pose intriguing problems for the suppliers and users of computer, software, and information-based products. Two other subjects are also worth mentioning: international trade law because of the global nature of the computer industry and its strategic role in the world economy; and labour law because of the profound impact that technology has had on the workplace. This chapter concludes with a review of how well (or poorly) traditional insurance policies provide coverage against computer-related risks, and in particular whether software, data, and intellectual property are covered under these policies. In most of these subareas of the law there are few statutes, or even provisions within statutes, devoted to computer and information products.[2] Rather, the analysis often involves reviewing a general commercial law rule and assessing how well (or poorly) it applies to a high technology issue. In conducting this analysis, the dynamics of computer law should be kept in mind. As noted above, particularly relevant to this chapter are the rapid pace of technological change and, depending on the issue area (such as sales legislation and tax), the elusive nature of information and the blurring of the national and international realms.

A. MARKETING COMPUTER AND INFORMATION-BASED PRODUCTS

1) Short Product Cycles

The incredible rate of technology development, the first dynamic of computer law, translates into a commercial environment characterized by short, and ever-shortening, product cycles. In virtually all submarkets of the computer business, innovation is measured in weeks or months rather than years. Most computer software and information-based products have short shelf lives, at least for any particular version of the product. One report in the United States noted that the "extraordinarily rapid pace of technological change in information technology (IT) hardware and software ... creates the equivalent of three to five [automotive] model changes each year."[3] Moreover, every segment of the computer

---

2   An interesting exception is Quebec's *Charter of the French Language*, R.S.Q. 1977, c. C-11, which requires that a supplier's French-language version of software (if one exists) be made available in Quebec at the same time as the English-language version.

3   Cited in Margaret E. McConnell, "The Process of Procuring Information Technology" (Winter 1996) 25:2 Public Contract Law Journal 385.

market is characterized by intense competition. New entrants are continually bringing to market new products. Marketing people in the computer business talk in terms of narrow temporal windows of opportunity to get a new product or version out into the marketplace before it invariably collides with a competitor's subsequent version.

The business and legal impact of short product cycles is significant. It leads, for example, to the formation of numerous alliances within the industry among different companies and organizations. These arrangements vary in terms of degree and intensity from product distribution agreements, to joint R&D agreements, to full-blown mergers. In each case, however, there is the common thread of understanding that in today's technology business it is very difficult for one firm to possess in house all the required core competencies. Some large technology firms, such as Microsoft, Intel, and Cisco, are acquiring minority positions in smaller companies to bolster the market for products that will increase demand for these companies' core products, as well as to use these investment targets as surrogate R&D test beds.[4] All these different types of arrangements raise competition law issues. From another perspective, the short product cycles raise, often to unreasonable levels, expectations within the user community. This can result in liability claims, sounding both in contract and in negligence, if ultimately the products or services do not measure up to these expectations.

2) Imperfect Software

The creation of software normally involves several distinct phases, from the initial high-level design, through coding the instructions and statements, and finally to an exercise of testing to find and fix as many problems as possible before it is shipped to customers.[5] Although most software products undergo a significant amount of testing, it is a central fact of software development that it is virtually impossible to detect and eradicate all the bugs in advance. Bug-free software, if such a state were even attainable, would be so expensive and time-consuming as to make it impractical in a commercial setting, at least given how that environment is structured currently. Thus, suppliers of software offer support programs to users of their products, a major element of which is the correction of bugs that come to light once the customer has commenced to use the software product. Another component of the typical software support program is the provision of future versions and

---

4   "Silicon Valley's New Sugar Daddies," *The Economist*, 12 July 1997.
5   See chapter 1, section A.3, "Software."

upgrades of the software. A prime rationale for such follow-on versions is to provide the user with new or enhanced features, but upgrades are also used to distribute to users new copies of the previous software with a number of the bugs corrected. Software and other information-based products, such as CDs based on software, are unique in the world of commerce in that they involve an ongoing relationship between the supplier and the user not seen with other products.

3) Multiple Marketing Channels

Most industries have a rather well-defined set of procedures and mechanisms for getting products and services into the hands of the ultimate customer. Not so the computer industry. There are a myriad of ways in which computer products are distributed, and new channels are constantly being explored. Again, as with so much of the computer business, change is the only constant. Thus, in some cases, an end-user can buy a computer product directly from a hardware manufacturer or software developer. However, there may be several intermediate layers of distribution and other players between the developer and the end-user. There may be the general distributor, who buys from the software developer or hardware manufacturer and resells to dealers, who may resell to retailers or to companies that integrate the diverse products into particular solutions for ultimate sale to end-users. Third parties, some authorized by the product's creator and some not, may also offer to provide valuable ongoing support and services. Interestingly, in many distribution models the supplier has no direct contact with the purchaser in terms of the marketing or sale of the product, but may have direct ongoing responsibilities in the area of product support and maintenance. And then there is the Internet, which shows incredible promise for helping suppliers develop one-on-one marketing and distribution strategies.

Numerous commercial law impacts result from the particular marketing structures that have developed around the computer industry. Shrinkwrap licences purport to bind the developer of mass market software to the ultimate user even though these two parties may not deal directly with one another in the initial sales process. The various intermediaries that reside between the developer and the user will be concerned about being treated unfairly vis-à-vis their competitors, and they may be able to look to competition law for redress in certain circumstances. Tax issues come to the fore as a result of the constant shifting in the nature and functions of the various participants in the diverse distribution chains. This was true even before the Internet created yet additional uncertainty as to the place and identity of the tax-payer in an international, digital environment, particularly in respect of the sale and transmission of digital-based products.

B. COMPETITION LAW

Canada's *Competition Act* contains numerous prohibitions on anti-competitive conduct.[6] This statute applies in the context of the computer business because of the multitiered marketing and distribution channels in the high-technology industries and because of the strategic importance of these industries in the wider economy. The purpose of the *Competition Act* is to promote efficiency within the Canadian economy and provide consumers with competitive prices and product choices.[7] The statute provides for a number of criminal offences, contained in Part VI, which typically carry penalties consisting of fines and imprisonment for officers of the company for up to five years.[8] The statute also permits a private right of action for a party that has suffered damages as a result of conduct that constitutes a violation of the statute's criminal provisions. The *Competition Act* also contains in Part VIII a number of reviewable practices, which are civil proceedings brought before the Competition Tribunal, a body better suited than a judge alone to sift through the complex economic evidence to determine if a particular practice has an anti-competitive impact in the marketplace.[9] The Competition Tribunal can make a number of remedial

---

6   R.S.C. 1985, c. C-34, as amended.
7   Section 1.1 of the *Competition Act* provides: "The purpose of this Act is to maintain and encourage competition in Canada in order to promote the efficiency and adaptability of the Canadian economy, in order to expand opportunities for Canadian participation in world markets while at the same time recognizing the role of foreign competition in Canada, in order to ensure that small and medium-sized enterprises have an equitable opportunity to participate in the Canadian economy and in order to provide consumers with competitive prices and product choices."
8   Although it is not common for individuals to be charged under the statute, in a case involving price fixing among driving-school operators a one-year prison term was imposed on one of the individual principals of the companies involved, and another individual was sentenced to 100 hours of community service and a fine of $10,000: see *CompAct: News From the Competition Bureau*, Issue 3, July–September 1996.
9   The Competition Tribunal is a hybrid body composed of judges and lay experts, constituted under the *Competition Tribunal Act*, R.S.C. 1985, c. 19 (2d Supp).

orders where it finds a reviewable practice to lessen competition substantially. Recently, the *Competition Act* was also amended to permit a private right of action in respect of the "refusal to deal" and certain other reviewable practices (though with the remedy in such a case limited to obtaining a prohibition order, and excluding damages).[10] The Competition Bureau, a unit within Industry Canada, plays a central role in investigating alleged infractions under the *Competition Act*; it negotiates consensual settlements if possible and brings cases to the Competition Tribunal, or in the case of criminal offences, to the regular court system through the Department of Justice, if a voluntary solution was unattainable. Through speeches, and more formal (but non-binding *Enforcement Guidelines*), the Competition Bureau attempts to educate Canadians as to the *Competition Act* and the Competition Bureau's approach to enforcing it. For example, the Competition Bureau released *Intellectual Property Enforcement Guidelines* that give a good sense, through the use of eight hypothetical situations, of how the Competition Bureau would approach various issues posed by the intersection of intellectual property rights and competition law.[11] Most companies view the Competition Bureau as a type of government regulator and approach the *Competition Act* in a defensive mode, trying to avoid running afoul of it. Although such an attitude is certainly warranted, organizations should also regard the Competition Bureau in a more offensive light, as a department that can help when they are adversely affected by the anticompetitive behaviour of competitors, suppliers, or others. Laws similar to the *Competition Act* exist in other nations, notably the United States and Europe, but they can differ significantly from Canada's in terms of substance and procedure.[12] A Canadian com-

---

10 These changes were effected by Bill C-23, which came into force on June 21, 2002.

11 Competition Bureau, *Intellectual Property Enforcement Guidelines*, 2000 <competition.ic.ca>. These guidelines are modelled generally after similar initiatives in Japan, Europe, and especially the United States. The guidelines state that the exercise of intellectual property rights, *per se*, is not an anti-competitive activity, and that the Competition Bureau's primary focus is on situations where owners of intellectual property rights engage in conduct that goes beyond their statutory or common law rights, where such behaviour results in an adverse impact on competition. The Competition Bureau has also released very helpful guidelines regarding the application to the Internet of the *Competition Act's* misleading advertising provisions.

12 Both the United States and Europe have very well-developed competition law regimes, with significant government agencies to enforce them. The United States also has a vibrant tradition of "private law enforcement" in the antitrust area (as its competition law is called), courtesy of the ability of the plaintiff to claim treble damages in some cases. The United States has also seen some very high-pro-

pany doing business through non-Canadians accessing its Web site should review what laws apply to such activity in the foreign jurisdiction, such as local competition law that often prohibits misleading advertising (see chapter 7, section B, "Jurisdiction," for a discussion about the Internet from the perspective of jurisdiction and regulation).

1) Criminal Offences

a) Conspiracy and Bid Rigging

The *Competition Act*, in subsection 45(1), makes it a criminal offence for two or more parties to conclude an agreement, or otherwise conspire in any manner, that would lessen competition unduly, as was the case in the early 1990s when a number of companies participated in an illegal conspiracy to fix prices in Canada and the United States for thermal fax paper.[13] Agreements that could also run afoul of the conspiracy offence include dividing up customers or markets in a manner that unduly lessened competition. Competitors in the high-technology industry, however, can collaborate for certain purposes enumerated in subsection 45(3) of the *Competition Act*, in particular to define product standards or to participate in research and development. Subsection 45(4), however, denies this exemption if, in the course of this permitted collaboration, the parties stray into the areas of pricing, production,

---

file antitrust cases brought against leading technology companies, including IBM in the 1970s, and in the past few years Microsoft. For the key decisions in the government's monopolization claim against Microsoft, see *United States* v. *Microsoft Corp.*, 87 F.Supp. 2d 30 (D.D.C. 2000); *United States* v. *Microsoft Corp.*, 253 F.3d 34 (D.C. Cir. 2001); and *State of New York* v. *Microsoft Corporation*, 2002 WL 31439450 (D. D.C. 2002) (in the latter case the court upheld a consent decree agreed to by Microsoft and the U.S. government, but opposed by a number of states, that settled the federal government's litigation). For short pieces on this monumentally important case, see "Microsoft and the Future: Busted," *The Economist*, 13 November 1999; and "Microsoft Trial: A Loss of Trust," *The Economist*, 7 July 2001. For longer treatments, see John Heilemann, "The Truth, the Whole Truth, and Nothing but the Truth: The Untold Story of the Microsoft Antitrust Case," *Wired*, November 2000; chapter 6 of Debora L. Spar, *Ruling the Waves: Cycles of Discovery, Chaos, and Wealth From the Compass to the Internet* (New York: Harcourt, 2001), and Ken Auletta, *World War 3.0* (New York: Random House, 2001). For a short chronology of the case, see David Akin, "Microsoft Penalties Upheld," *The Globe and Mail* (2 November 2002).

13 This case is referred to in "Enforcement: Current Activities," in *CompAct: News From the Competition Bureau*, Issue 3, July–September 1996, which publication also mentions that up to September 1996, $2.6 million in fines had been levied in this case.

customer, or distribution matters. Accordingly, computer and software companies involved in such collaborative research, or participating in high-tech trade shows or industry trade associations or other activities where there is contact between competitors, have to be extremely vigilant not to run afoul — or be even perceived as running afoul — of the *Competition Act*'s conspiracy provisions. Section 46 of the statute also prohibits "bid rigging," the practice of colluding on the submission of bids in response to tender calls by a government or a private sector purchaser, such tenders being a very common practice when procuring high-tech products. Interestingly, the bid-rigging provision creates a *per se* offence, thus requiring there to be no adverse impact on competition.

b) Resale Price Maintenance

Given the plethora of multitiered distribution channels in the computer business, perhaps the single most important provision in the *Competition Act* related to this industry is subsection 61(1), which reads as follows:

> 61(1) No person who is engaged in the business of producing or supplying a product, who extends credit by way of credit cards or is otherwise engaged in a business that relates to credit cards, or who has the exclusive rights and privileges conferred by a patent, trade-mark, copyright, registered industrial design or registered integrated circuit topography shall, directly or indirectly,
>
> (a) by agreement, threat, promise or any like means, attempt to influence upward, or to discourage the reduction of, the price at which any other person engaged in business in Canada supplies or offers to supply or advertises a product within Canada; or
>
> (b) refuse to supply a product to or otherwise discriminate against any other person engaged in business in Canada because of the low pricing policy of that other person.

The prohibition in paragraph 61(1)(a) effectively precludes an entity in the product distribution chain from engaging in resale price maintenance, namely, dictating what an entity lower down in the chain charges for a particular product, with the proviso that maximum prices can be set (so long as they do not become, by virtue of practice or an ancillary agreement, the minimum price as well!). The reference to patent, copyrights, and other intellectual property rights at the end of the lead-in paragraph in subsection 61(1) has the effect of confirming that licensing and distribution arrangements for software and related products are covered by the provision. Activity that is not direct resale price maintenance is also problematic, as illustrated by the *Epson* case, where a manufacturer was held to have violated the predecessor of paragraph 61(1)(a) by requiring dealers, through a clause in the dealer agreement, not to advertise the manufacturer's computer products for sale at a price lower than the manufacturer's suggested retail price.[14] The court concluded that this clause violated this provision of the statute, even though the evidence indicated that no dealer actually honoured the clause, and notwithstanding the expert testimony of an economics professor to the effect that such a clause is not always economically harmful. In refusing to accept this economic evidence, the court stated that resale price maintenance is *per se* criminal conduct, again not requiring any adverse impact on competition, like the bid-rigging offence. It should be noted, however, that under subsection 61(3), a supplier can suggest resale prices, but it must be made clear to the distributor, preferably in writing in the agreement between the parties, that failure to follow the suggestions will in no way adversely affect the relationship between the supplier and the distributor. The upshot of paragraph 61(1)(a) is that distribution channels in the computer industry must be carefully planned and implemented. Indeed, a software developer that considered it very important that its particular product not sell for less than a certain price to end-users would likely have to change its proposed relationship with the distributor as a result of subsection 61(1). For instance, the software developer could appoint a sales representative, where the latter would drum up business for the developer, but the end-user's price would be set by the developer, and the representative would receive only a sales commission from the developer once each sale is concluded.

c) Refusal to Deal

Many companies in the computer business attempt to obtain a copy of a competitor's new software product or a unit of a new hardware item as soon as it is released in order to study it and, if permitted by relevant agreements, take it apart and study its inner workings (a practice sometimes termed *reverse engineering*).[15] Many suppliers comply with such a request as they believe that competition law requires them to sell to anyone who demands to buy. This is an erroneous belief. Generally, anyone can refuse to sell to anyone else, subject to a couple of important exceptions, the first one being paragraph 61(1)(b) of the *Competition Act*, which makes it an offence not to supply someone because of

---

14 *R. v. Epson (Canada) Ltd.*, (1987) 19 C.P.R. (3d) 195 (Ont. Dist. Ct.).

15 As for whether reverse engineering of software is permitted by intellectual property law, see chapter 2, section B.3, "Copyright."

the low pricing policy of that person. In other words, paragraph 61(1)(b) prohibits refusing to supply product to discounters, of which there are a number in the computer business. This prohibition applies even if the supplier had never before conducted business with the discounter. Certain exceptions to this rule are contained in subsection 61(10), as where the distributor would use the supplier's products as "loss leaders," or where the distributor has shown that it is unable to provide adequate service for the relevant product, a not unimportant consideration with a high-technology product. As well, paragraph 61(1)(b) would not be triggered if the reason for refusing to supply was a rational business purpose, such as concern over the creditworthiness of the potential distributor, or simply the fact that the supplier already had a sufficient number of distributors, though in each such case real evidence should bolster the rationale. It would, for example, be difficult for a supplier to rely on the latter argument if, within a short time after refusing the discounter, the supplier appoints another distributor for the same market. In effect, great care must be taken in operationalizing the provisions of the *Competition Act*.

Several other criminal provisions in the *Competition Act* are worth mentioning. Under paragraph 50(1)(a) it is an offence to make a practice of giving a discount, rebate, allowance, or any other advantage to one customer that is not made available to all competitors of that customer with respect to sales of like quantity or quality. This prohibition on price discrimination essentially requires entities in the distribution chain to treat in a consistent manner those of their customers who are competitors with one another. Also, paragraph 50(1)(b) makes it illegal for a supplier to engage in a policy of selling products or services at prices that are unreasonably low if the intent, effect, or tendency of the policy is to lessen competition substantially or to eliminate a competitor. Although it is not entirely clear when a price is "unreasonably low," predatory pricing, as this practice is often called, probably includes a price that is not covering fixed and variable costs of the supplier.[16] The predatory pricing provisions of the *Competition Act* can be relevant to the computer industry where the practice is to give away product at low prices in certain circumstances. The intent behind the activity,

---

16   In the leading case, *R. v. Hoffman-La Roche Ltd.* (*Nos. 1 and 2*) (1981), 33 O.R. (2d) 694 (C.A.), the enterprising defence was put forward that giving away pharmaceuticals to hospitals for free did not constitute a sale, and hence the predatory pricing section should not apply, but this argument was refused by the court, which held that giving away something still implied a price, albeit an extremely low one.

however, is what is critical. If it was merely to meet the competitive pricing of another supplier then paragraph 50(1)(b) should not come into play; a different conclusion, however, may be warranted where the intent of the discounting supplier, which intent is often evidenced by incriminating memos or e-mails, is to eliminate a competitor.

d) Misleading Advertising

Under subsection 52(1) of the *Competition Act*, it is a criminal offence to make, knowingly or recklessly, a false or misleading representation to the public, or to make a claim to the public regarding a product or service, for instance about performance, that is not based on a proper or adequate test, or to make a warranty to the public that is misleading. The civil provisions of the *Competition Act* also create a remedial regime involving orders or fines for the practice of misleading advertising. Misleading advertising provisions apply in the computer industry, where short product cycles, changing technology, and intense competition may tempt suppliers to make unfounded claims about their products. For example, in the United States, a technology company was convicted for advertising a product as available when it was not,[17] and another company settled a prosecution brought against it by the U.S. Federal Trade Commission (the equivalent of the Canadian Competition Bureau) for advertising that a product would increase the memory and performance of personal computers when it did not.[18] In another U.S. case, a manufacturer of computer terminals was found liable for false advertising for describing its products as "compatible" with those of another product when the evidence showed that a manual, intermediate step had to be undertaken by the user to make the two items work together, thereby leading the court to conclude that the items were not compatible as that term is understood in the computer industry.[19] Also in the United States there was a class action lawsuit brought on behalf of millions of buyers of 14-inch computer monitors when the actual measurement of the screens proved to be 7 percent smaller.[20]

---

17   *United States v. Commodore Business Machines, Inc.*, 2 Computer Cases (CCH) ¶46,281 at 62,120 (E.D. Penn. 1990).

18   *Re Syncronys Software Corp. et al.*, Guide to Computer Law, New Developments (CCH) ¶60,544 at 82,183 (F.T.C. 1996).

19   *Princeton Graphics Operating, L.P. v. NEC Home Electronics (U.S.A.), Inc.*, 732 F. Supp. 1258 (S.D.N.Y. 1990). See also *Creative Labs Inc. v. Cyrix Corp.*, 42 U.S.P.Q.2d 1872 (N.D. Cal. 1997).

20   "Read This and Become ($6) Richer," *The Economist*, 21 June 1997.

Another aspect to the misleading advertising provisions relates to the use of the Internet by companies, individuals, and organizations, both in the high-tech industry as well as those in other businesses, to make claims to the public by posting material on their Web sites. In April 1997 the Competition Bureau announced that it had moved against a number of Web sites and usegroups that contained potentially misleading descriptions of business opportunities.[21] Interestingly, given the global nature of the Internet, the Competition Bureau undertook these actions in coordination with its counterpart in the United States, the Federal Trade Commission. Such joint activity is the product of an agreement signed in September 1996 between these two enforcement authorities that established a Canadian–U.S. Task Force on Cross-Border Deceptive Marketing Practices.[22] These actions indicate two important points about the Internet as a business communications medium. First, if the content is problematic in the physical world, it is equally problematic in the online, electronic world. Indeed, the same representations made on Web sites may raise even more concerns than their hard copy paper counterparts, because of the use of various Web-based features such as linking. Thus, in 2001 the Competition Bureau published draft guidelines to assist advertisers and others to stay clear of the *Competition Act*'s misleading advertising provisions.[23] For example, the guidelines recommend that online disclaimers be placed on the same screen as the main message and close to the relevant representation. The guidelines also suggest a "notice and take down" liability regime for Internet service providers when they are hosting a customer's Web site; the ISP would be shielded from liability unless they knowingly or recklessly hosted the misleading representation, but once they are put on notice of it, they have to act to

---

21 Competition Bureau, New Release, *Online Anti-competitive Behaviour Hit by Canadian Competition Bureau and U.S. Federal Trade Commission*, 24 April 1997, available at <strategis.ic.gc.ca/competition>.

22 See "Bureau News," *CompAct: News From the Competition Bureau*, Issue 3, July–September 1996. See also Brian Livingston, "Even Web Not Immune to Pyramid Schemes," *CNET News.com* (23 June 2000) <news.com/Perspectives/Column/0,176,453,00.html>, which describes the efforts of authorities in the United States, Canada, and Australia to shut down a multilevel marketing scheme in which participants, upon payment of $295, were offered fees from subsequent subscribers for Web site creation services: gullible Internet surfers from more than eighty countries ponied up a total of $12.8 million for Web sites that never materialized.

23 Competition Bureau, *Staying "On-Side" When Advertising On-line: A Guide to Compliance with the Competition Act When Advertising on the Internet*, May 2001, available at <strategis.ic.gc.ca/ssg/ct02186e.html>. The final form of the Guidelines was issued on 18 February 2003, and is available at <strategis.ic.gc.ca/ssg/ct02500e.html>.

determine the truthfulness of the impugned statement. And if all this was insufficient for the Canadian entity to worry about, it has to realize that its representations may be even more problematic in the electronic world because authorities in other countries may take jurisdiction over a Web site operated on a computer located in a foreign state if the Web site is aimed at or targeting nationals of that other state, and possibly merely for being accessed by its nationals.[24] Thus, even if the content of the Canadian Web site is acceptable under Canadian law, the operator of the Web site may have to be concerned whether the content is contrary to the laws of another country. This point illustrates well the fourth dynamic of computer law, namely, the blurring of national and international.

2) Reviewable Practices

a) Abuse of Dominant Position
A number of reviewable practices under Part VIII of the *Competition Act* can influence distribution, development, and other activities in the computer, networks, and related sectors of the economy. The abuse of dominant position provision in section 79 of the statute provides that where an entity substantially controls, alone or with others, a class of business throughout or in a region of Canada, and that entity (or entities) engages in anticompetitive acts that are likely to prevent or lessen competition substantially, the Competition Tribunal may order the entity(ies) to prohibit engaging in the anticompetitive behaviour. Section 78 sets out a non-exhaustive list of anticompetitive acts, one of which is particularly germane to the computer business, namely, adopting product specifications that are incompatible with products produced by another person and are designed to prevent that person's entry into, or eliminate them from, a market. It was under section 79 that the Competition Bureau commenced an investigation of Interac, a company owned by Canada's major banks and a few other financial institutions and that operates a network of automated banking machines and debit payment systems. The bureau took the view that several aspects of Interac's bylaws were anticompetitive by restricting, among other things, membership in the electronic network and the manner by which it charged its members for services. After lengthy negotiations and a hearing before the Competition Tribunal, in June 1996 the Competition Tribunal approved a consent order negotiated between the bureau and Interac's members that has the effect of adjust-

---

24   See chapter 7, section B, "Jurisdiction."

ing fees and of opening up the network to other participants on a non-discriminatory basis, provided only duly regulated financial institutions can issue cards to access the network.[25] The case, and the significant resources devoted to it by the bureau, illustrate that the Competition Bureau understands the increasingly important role of computer networks in the Canadian economy.[26]

Companies with patented products can run afoul of the abuse of dominant position provision when, upon the expiry of their patents, they attempt to sustain their monopoly market share by having customers enter into supply contracts that implement a number of exclusionary measures vis-à-vis the competition, such as fidelity rebates.[27] At the same time, however, subsection 79(5) of the *Competition Act* provides that any act engaged in pursuant only to the exercise of any right under the Copyright Act, the Patent Act, and the other intellectual property statutes is not an anticompetitive act. In light of this provision, it is also worth noting that subsection 32(2) of the *Competition Act* gives the Federal Court of Canada the power to make remedial orders in a situation where the exclusive rights conferred by a copyright, patent, or trade-mark have been used in a manner that prevents or lessens competition unduly. This provision, which is neither a criminal offence nor a reviewable practice, is aimed primarily at preventing a number of potentially anticompetitive or restrictive provisions in intellectual property licences, such as the requirement that a patent licensee purchase from the patent holder/licensor all the raw materials required to produce the patented product. Where such an act lessens competition unduly, the Federal Court may order one or more of the following remedies: declare the relevant licence agreement to be void, in whole or in part; prohibit the exercise of the objectionable provision in the licence agreement; order that licences be granted to other licensees on terms the court thinks fit, and other acts to be done or omitted as the court sees fit so as to prevent future anticompetitive use of the patent or trade-mark. While these remedial provisions are very broad, this section of the *Competition Act* has been used very little. Nev-

---

25   For background on the Interac case, see "Enforcement: The Interac Case," in *CompAct: News From the Competition Bureau*, Issue 2, April–June 1996. For a discussion of a U.S.-based automated banking machine network and various technical and business aspects of its operation, see *Plus System, Inc.* v. *New England Network, Inc.*, 804 F.Supp. 111 (D. Colo. 1992), a case referred to in chapter 7, section B, "Jurisdiction."

26   See also the *Air Canada* case, at note 36 below.

27   See *Canada (Director of Investigation and Research)* v. *NutraSweet Co.* (1990), 32 C.P.R. (3d) 1 (Comp. Trib.).

ertheless, section 32 of the Act, together with a number of other sections of the *Competition Act*, such as subsection 61(1), illustrates the tension between the intellectual property regimes that, by their very nature, provide more or less extensive monopoly rights to holders of intellectual properties, and the *Competition Act* that attempts to curb perceived and potential abuses of such intellectual property rights.[28]

In the recent *Tele-Direct* case, the Competition Tribunal had occasion to consider subsection 79(5) of the *Competition Act*.[29] In this proceeding the bureau sought an order requiring the owners of the registered trade-mark "Yellow Pages" to grant licences to this trade-mark to third parties who, the bureau argued, were adversely affected by not being able to use the trade-mark. The bureau argued that refusal to licence the trade-mark to certain parties but not others was an anti-competitive act under the abuse of dominant position provision. The Competition Tribunal disagreed, concluding that while there may be instances where a trade-mark is misused,

> The respondents' refusal to license their trade-marks falls squarely within their prerogative. Inherent in the very nature of the right to license a trade-mark is the right for the owner of the trade-mark to determine whether or not, and to whom, to grant a licence; selectivity in licensing is fundamental to the rationale behind protecting trade-marks. The respondents' trade-marks are valuable assets and represent considerable goodwill in the marketplace. The decision to license a trade-mark — essentially, to share the goodwill vesting in the asset — is a right which rests entirely with the owner of the mark. The refusal to license a trade-mark is distinguishable from a situation where anti-competitive provisions are attached to a trade-mark licence.[30]

---

28 Canada is not the only country to struggle with the resolution of the inherent tension between monopoly-supporting intellectual property laws and monopoly-busting competition laws. In Europe, for example, the competition authorities have ordered a pharmaceutical informatics company to license its market-leading copyrighted database to its competitors, as it has attained the status of an "essential facility": "European Competition Law: Battling Over Bricks," *The Economist*, 25 August 2001.

29 *Canada (Director of Investigation and Research)* v. *Tele-Direct (Publications) Inc.* (1997), 73 C.P.R. (3d) 1 (Comp. Trib.) [*Tele-Direct (Publications)*].

30 *Ibid.*, at 32. For an indication of when U.S. antitrust authorities will consider certain intellectual property licensing practices to be anticompetitive, see U.S. Department of Justice and the Federal Trade Commission, *Antitrust Guidelines for the Licensing of Intellectual Property*, 6 April 1995. For a U.S. case somewhat analogous to the decision in *Tele-Direct (Publications)*, see *Morris Communications Corp.* v. *PGA Tour, Inc.*, 117 F.Supp. 1322 (M.D. Fla. 2000), where the court

The Competition Tribunal also determined that a trade-mark owner's motivation for refusing to license a competitor is irrelevant, given that the *Trade-Marks Act* does not place any limits on the exercise of the right to license a trade-mark.

b) Refusal to Deal

Another reviewable practice is "refusal to deal," contained in section 75 of the *Competition Act*. Under this provision, if a customer can show that it is substantially affected in its business because of its inability to continue to obtain adequate supplies of a product because of insufficient competition among suppliers, and provided the refusal to deal adversely affects competition in a market,[31] the customer may be able to obtain an order from the Competition Tribunal requiring a supplier to provide it with product, provided the product is in ample supply and the customer is willing to meet the usual trade terms of the supplier. This provision can be of particular relevance to companies that provide maintenance and support services for computer products manufactured or supplied by others. For example, in the *Xerox* case, the Competition Tribunal ordered Xerox to supply a third-party service organization with spare parts as without these the third party could not continue its business of servicing Xerox machines.[32] In essence, participants in the computer industry need to keep this provision in mind when establishing their distribution networks and appointing dealers and others who will carry their products.

c) Exclusive Dealing, Market Restriction, and Tied Selling

Three other reviewable practices under subsection 77(1) of the *Competition Act* are

- "exclusive dealing": the practice of requiring or inducing a customer to deal only or primarily in products of the supplier;

---

concluded that the PGA, under the American "essential facilities" antitrust doctrine, did not have to give the plaintiff access to real-time golf scores, as the plaintiff's service would have competed with the PGA's existing golf scores distribution business.

31   This last requirement was added only recently, as part of Bill C-23, that came into effect on 21 June 2002.

32   *Canada (Director of Investigation and Research)* v. *Xerox Canada Inc.* (1990), 33 C.P.R. (3d) 83 (Comp. Trib.). In the U.S., where a different statutory regime exists for competition law, it has been held that Xerox's refusal to sell patented spare parts and copyright materials to independent service organizations is not a violation of American anti-trust law: In *Re Independent Service Organizations Antitrust Litigation, OSU, L.L.C.* v. *Xerox Corporation,* 203 F.3d 1322 (Fed. Cir. 2000).

- "market restriction": the practice of requiring a customer, as a condition of supplying him with the product, to sell a product only in a defined market area;
- "tied selling": the practice of requiring or inducing a customer as a condition of supplying him with one product (the "tying" product) to buy another of the supplier's products (the "tied" product).

These three practices are quite common in the computer industry. A hardware or software supplier will often require a distributor or dealer not to carry any products that compete with the supplier's products. When establishing a distribution system, a supplier may also require that dealers sell only in predetermined geographic areas. A supplier may also insist that in order to be supplied with a preferred product in which the supplier has competitive advantage courtesy, perhaps, of a patent or copyright, the dealer or end-user must also purchase a less attractive product in which the supplier has no particular competitive advantage, such as paper sales being tied to patented computer-based document imaging equipment. These practices, however, are not in and of themselves problematic under the *Competition Act*; they only become so if they are engaged in by suppliers with significant market power and have the effect of excluding others from the marketplace or have some other substantial adverse effect on competition.[33] It should be noted, however, that the Competition Tribunal is directed under subsection 77(4) not to make an order in respect of exclusive dealing or market restriction where they are engaged in only for a reasonable period of time in order to facilitate entry of a new supplier or of a new product into a market. Similarly, the *Competition Act* provides a defence to the tied selling reviewable practice where it is reasonable having regard to the technological relationship between the two products at issue. This defence can be particularly relevant to participants in the computer industry where the two products at issue have a *bona fide* functional rationale for being intertwined.

The defences to exclusive dealing, market restriction, and tied selling noted above illustrate why these practices and the other reviewable practices in Part VIII of the *Competition Act* are not criminal offences but rather are reviewable practices — namely, in certain circumstances these practices can be procompetitive or at least neutral in their effect on competition; that is, the same exclusive dealing behaviour may be

---

33   For a discussion of one of the first (and one of the few) exclusive dealing cases, see George S. Takach, "Exclusive Dealing after Bombardier: The Law Is Not a Great Deal Clearer Than Before" (1983) 8 C.B.L.J. 226.

either beneficial or detrimental to competition, depending largely on the market share of the supplier engaging in the activity. The same observation is valid in respect of the list of anticompetitive acts set out in the abuse of dominant position provision. For example, a requirement by a software or CD-ROM product supplier with a small share of the market that an exclusive dealer not carry competitive products may be procompetitive because it causes the dealer to devote all its energies to the supplier's new product, thereby increasing the prospect for meaningful *inter*-brand competition, namely, between the supplier's new product and the existing products of other suppliers. If, after time, the same product captures 90 percent of the relevant market, the same exclusive arrangement may be anticompetitive if it has the effect of precluding *intra*-brand competition, namely, the ability to purchase a very popular product from more than one source. Similarly, in some cases it might be reasonable, at least for a period of time, to require customers to purchase service contracts only from the supplier of a sophisticated technology-based product, whereas this practice may constitute tied selling in other cases.[34] Thus, the key in these reviewable practices matters is to understand thoroughly the dynamics and parameters of the relevant product market and the roles played by the various participants in it, and then to monitor these factors vigilantly. Some commentators believe that the robust nature of the computer industry precludes the need for intervention by competition law authorities, since the market continually self-corrects as very few participants are able to hold significant market share for very long. In some industries the Internet will permit competition law authorities to consider the relevant geographic market to be much more international, particularly with respect to digital assets that can be distributed electronically; but this also applies where the Internet is still primarily a marketing tool and shipment is overland (but much improved with next day delivery).[35] In effect, the argument can be made that the first and third dynamics of computer law (the rapid pace of technological change and the blurring of private/public) make it more difficult for any one company to achieve monopoly market share, as both of these dynamics promote

---

34   See Drew Fagan, "Digital Access to Change Its Ways: Government Alleges 'Tied Selling,'" *The Globe and Mail* (31 October 1992).

35   See, for example, Patrick Butler *et al.*, "A Revolution in Interaction" (1997) 1 McKinsey Quarterly 4, which argues that networks like the Internet dramatically decrease the transaction costs related to searching for and contracting with partners.

competition. The Competition Bureau, while generally sensitive to these sorts of arguments, nonetheless looks at each case before it on its specific merits, including those involving the high-technology sector.

d) Mergers

This case-by-case approach can be seen in the bureau's handling of the computerized airline reservation case almost a decade ago. Under the merger provisions in section 92 of the *Competition Act*, the Competition Tribunal has the power to dissolve, or to order the disposal of assets related to, a merger of two or more businesses that prevents or lessens competition substantially. Since its addition to the *Competition Act* in 1986, the merger provision has been used by the bureau to block certain business combinations it viewed as anticompetitive, or more commonly, to allow them to proceed provided the parties took certain steps to alleviate the bureau's concerns, typically by divesting certain assets of the combined business that would decrease the level of their postmerger market share. It was under this merger provision that the proposed combination in 1987 of the computerized reservation systems of Air Canada and Canadian Airlines was challenged. A number of parties objected to the merger on the grounds that it would permit Air Canada and Canadian Airlines to benefit from their computer reservation system favouring the two "host airlines" over third parties. The dissolution proceeding was settled by the merged entity agreeing to establish rules relating to the new, combined network information system that would not portray flight booking and other information of any airline in a biased manner, but would give nondiscriminatory treatment to the data of all carriers, as well as give the computerized reservation system of other airlines access to all Air Canada and Canadian Airlines booking information on the same basis.[36] This case recognized the potential for anticompetitive conduct when vital information networks are operated in an exclusionary or discriminatory manner, and in a sense presaged the Interac matter some years later, discussed in section B.2(a), "Abuse of Dominant Position."[37]

---

36 *Canada (Director of Investigation and Research)* v. *Air Canada* (1989), 44 B.L.R. 154 (Comp. Trib.) [*Air Canada*].
37 Airline computer reservation systems have been the subject of litigation, and regulation, in the United States as well. For a sense of the issues, see a short piece by Thomas Hoffman & Mitch Betts, "Scheduling Software Ignites Airline Battle," *Computerworld*, 28 August 1995. See also *United Air Lines, Inc.* v. *Civil Aeronautics Board*, 766 F.2d 1107 (7th Cir. 1985).

e) B2B and B2B2C Exchanges

A number of the concerns raised in the *Air Canada* and *Interac* cases have been expressed in the context of B2B and B2B2C Internet-based exchanges, which are essentially online marketplaces that bring together different businesses to trade with another and/or with consumers.[38] On the positive side, these exchanges can be procompetitive, when they streamline supply management, reduce overhead costs, and facilitate market integration and transparent pricing behaviours; indeed, many suppliers do not want to participate in these exchanges precisely because they result in too much customer benefit as a result of squeezing supplier prices. On the other hand, competition agencies have expressed concerns about the potential for anticompetitive behaviour that can be associated with such exchanges. In particular, commentators and the U.S. Federal Trade Commission[39] have highlighted the following aspects of B2B exchanges that could be problematic from a competition law perspective:

- **Price Fixing:** by facilitating the sharing of sensitive price, production, sales and other data among exchange participants, the exchange might foster collusion among suppliers (from this perspective, the B2B affects competition potentially in the market for goods traded on the B2B exchange);
- **Monopolization:** the exchange itself may begin to wield market power in a manner that violates competition law particularly if the exchange results from a merger of two or more previous operations (from this perspective, the B2B possibly affects competition in the market for marketplaces);
- **Foreclosure:** if the exchange prevents some parties from joining, or discriminates in favour of certain parties, it might result in the type of behaviour that prompted the *Interac* case;
- **Buying Groups:** exchanges might shift too much power to several large purchasers who, courtesy of the exchange, are able to gang up on suppliers in an anti-competitive manner.

---

38   "A Market For Monopoly," *The Economist*, 17 June 2000. But see also Robert McGarvey, "B2B Co-operation Isn't Necessarily the End of Competition," *The Globe and Mail* (30 July 2000).

39   Federal Trade Commission, *Entering the 21st Century: Competition Policy in the World of B2B Electronic Marketplaces: A Report by Federal Trade Commission Staff* (October, 2000) [*Competition Policy*].

As a result of these sorts of concerns, the U.S. government has investigated at least one of them,[40] and the FTC has given some guidance on its thinking about them through the *Competition Policy* report.

C. LICENCES FOR SOFTWARE AND CONTENT

Copies of books are sold; copies of software are typically licensed.[41] There are a number of historic reasons for licensing software, as well as certain contemporary rationales for the practice. A common vehicle for licensing mass market software is the so-called shrinkwrap licence, a form of agreement whose enforceability has been questioned by a number of courts, though recent American cases seem to be more amenable to it. There is also controversy regarding the rights granted to licensees and whether they are broad enough to cover new technical delivery mechanisms and media. The following cases illustrate some of the difficulties inherent in the field of technology licensing given the first dynamic of computer law, namely, the rapid rate of technological change.

1) Why Software and Content Are Licensed

There are three ways in which the owner of the intellectual property rights — the copyright, trade secrets, and patent rights — in a software program or other information-based work could permit another entity to use those rights. First, it could assign those intellectual property rights outright, in which case it would be transferring, for example, the entire and exclusive right to make copies of the work under the *Copyright Act*. Given that after such an assignment the original owner of the

---

40   The FTC has reviewed Covisint, the auto industry's B2B. In a letter dated 11 September 2000 (*Re: Covisint, File No. 001 0127*) available at <ftc.gov/os/2000/09/covisintchrysler.htm>, the FTC indicated that no further action was warranted at that time, but also stated: "Because Covisint is in the early stages of its development and has not yet adopted by-laws, operating rules, or terms for participant access, because it is not yet operational, and in particular because it represents such a large share of the automobile market, we cannot say that implementation of the Covisint venture will not cause competitive concerns."

41   Software is so rarely sold that in *Adobe Systems, Inc.* v. *One Stop Micro, Inc.*, 84 F.Supp 2d 1086 (N.D. Cal. 2000), the court concluded a distributor did not own copies of the software, notwithstanding that the relevant contract included words like "sale," because, among other things, software is invariably licensed and not sold.

work could no longer make copies of it or otherwise exploit it for financial gain, such an assignment is not used where a customer merely wishes to use a copy of the work, and the original owner wishes to continue to exploit it to other users. By contrast, where the owner of the work is selling the business related to the work by virtue of a sale of assets, there typically would be an outright assignment of the intellectual property rights related to the work. Incidentally, as discussed in chapter 2, any such assignment, to be legally effective, must be in writing given subsection 13(3) of the *Copyright Act*.

The second way the owner of the intellectual property rights in a work can exploit the intellectual property is to sell copies of the work, as when the owner of the copyright in a book sells copies of the book. Selling title in a copy of a book or other work is a very different proposition from selling title in the intellectual property of the work.[42] Selling title to a copy of a work merely gives the purchaser the right to use that particular copy of the work; it does not generally afford the right to make further copies of the work because the intellectual property rights granted by the *Copyright Act* are not transferred to the purchaser of the copy of the work. When the holder of the copyright in a book sells title to a copy of the book, however, it cannot control the use, resale, or other exploitation of that copy of the book, subject always to the restriction that the owner of the copy cannot make further copies of it.[43] The various rights provided to the copyright owner under the *Copyright Act* do not include a right that prohibits use or even distribution of copies of the work, and thus once a copy of a work is sold into the stream of commerce with the permission of the copyright owner, that copyright owner cannot further control the resale, distribution, or use of the work, with the exception that the copyright owner can prohibit rental of certain works if such rental is done for a motive of gain.[44] It is sometimes said the copyright owner's rights are "exhausted," subject always to the ongoing right to control further copying. Even in the United States, where that country's copyright law provides copyright owners a right of distribution, there is a "first sale doctrine" that precludes a copyright owner from exercising control over the use or distribution of a copy of a work once it is released into the stream of commerce.

---

42   This distinction is made clear in *Société d'informatique R.D.G. Inc.* v. *Dynabec Ltée* (1984), 6 C.P.R. (3d) 299 (Que. Sup. Ct.), aff'd (*sub nom. Dynabec Ltée.* v. *La Société d'informatique R.D.G. Inc.*) (1985), 6 C.P.R. (3d) 322 (Que. C.A.).

43   *Fetherling* v. *Boughner* (1978), 40 C.P.R. (2d) 253 (Ont. H.C.J.). See also the discussion in the *Théberge* case, at note 100 in chapter 2.

44   See chapter 2, section B.3, "Copyright."

The third way to exploit intellectual property rights in a work is to license copies of the work. In intellectual property terms, a licence is a permission to a user from the owner of the work to do something that the user would not otherwise have the right to do.[45] This method allows the owner of the intellectual property to retain maximum control over it. Thus, in the case of many software-based or other information-based works, the related licence contains the restriction that the work may only be used for the benefit of the licensed user, and that it cannot be used to process the data of third parties. Similarly, the licence agreement would place restrictions on the ability of the licensee to transfer the work to a third party.[46] In this way, the owner of the intellectual property rights is better able to control the exploitation of the work and can reap greater economic returns by prohibiting a resale market for copies of the work. A licence also permits the owner of the intellectual property in software to permit copies of it to be exploited on a temporary or evaluation basis, as is the case with *shareware*, which typically allows use for a short period of time, say thirty days, after which the user must make payment or cease using the software.[47] Shareware should be contrasted with "freeware," which is software in

45 *Electric Chain Company of Canada Limited* v. *Art Metal Works Inc.*, [1933] S.C.R. 581. In this case the court cites a passage from an earlier English decision that states that a licence confers no interest or property in a patent, but that rather a grant is required to convey an interest in property, and that a pure licence is not a grant and does not convey an interest in property. See also *Beckman Instruments, Inc.* v. *Cincom Systems, Inc.*, 2000 U.S. App. Lexis 18166 (9th Cir. 2000), where the court held that a software licence did not permit a licensee to transfer the software to an outsourcing firm that would use the software on the licensee's behalf.

46 *Perry Engineering Ltd.* v. *Farrage* (1989), 28 C.P.R. (3d) 221 (B.C.S.C.). In this case one party argued it should be unenforceable to have a non-transferable software licence as this would make unusable the related hardware that operated only in conjunction with the software upon a subsequent sale of the hardware, but the court did not decide this issue as the case before it involved only the licensee and the subsequent transferee and not the owner of the intellectual property in the software. There is also some authority for the proposition that in the United States some software licences are unenforceable as they conflict with the essence of the transaction, which the court finds to be a sale of a copy of software: see *Softman Products Company, LLC*, v. *Adobe Systems Inc.*, 171 F.Supp. 2d 1075 (C.D. Cal. 2001).

47 For an Australian decision that discusses shareware, see *Trumpet Software Pty. Ltd. & Another* v. *OzEmail Pty. Ltd. & Others*, [1996] ACL Rep. 240 FC 32 (Austl.). For a U.S. discussion of shareware, see *CompuServe, Incorporated* v. *Patterson*, 89 F.3d 1257 (6th Cir. 1996) [*CompuServe*], a case discussed in chapter 7, section B, "Jurisdiction."

which the intellectual property rights are still owned by someone who gives copies of it away, and "public domain software" in which there are no further intellectual property rights either through waiver or expiry. As well, if the work contained trade secrets and confidential information, as is the case with most software, the licence would also require the user to keep confidential the work and not disclose it to third parties. Without such a restriction imposed on the user, the owner of the work would be hard-pressed to preserve trade secret rights in the work. The licence agreement also serves other purposes from the perspective of the developer or supplier of the software product. As discussed in sections D, "Negligence," and E, "Computer Contracts and Sales Law," poorly functioning software can cause users harm, and so software companies attempt to limit their liability contractually (via a licence agreement in the case of software) by shifting to the user certain risks related to the software, as well as limiting the company's liability for certain types of damages.

The phenomenon of the electronic database was described in chapter 1, section A.4, "Data and Databases"; and the current uncertainty surrounding the legal protection afforded databases and the underlying data in them was discussed in chapter 2, section C.4, "Copyright Protection for Electronic Databases." Accordingly, creators of databases and other providers of online services that supply fact-intensive information increasingly resort to having their customers sign licence agreements that restrict the ability of the user, for example, to make the database or the underlying facts or information available to others. These sorts of restrictions were upheld in the line of *Exchange Telegraph* cases that began in England more than one hundred years ago, in which a news wire service company was successful in prohibiting subscribers from conveying news feeds to non-subscriber third parties.[48] In these cases the courts were prepared to restrict further dissemination of financial information and horse racing results by customers of the news wire service on the basis that such use and transfer of them constituted a breach of their subscriber contracts with the news wire service. It may also well be that the increasing use of CD-ROM and other digital technologies will encourage suppliers of these products to use licence agreements to prevent the development of sec-

---

48   *Exchange Telegraph Company Limited v. Giulianotti*, [1959] Scots Law Times 293 (O.H.); *Exchange Telegraph Company v. Gregory & Co.*, [1896] Q.B. 147; *Exchange Telegraph Company Limited v. Central News, Limited*, [1897] 2 c. 48. These cases are discussed in chapter 2, section C.8, "Other Measures of Protection."

ondary markets in their products. One rationale for not licensing paper-based products, such as books or directories, is that these items degrade with use over time, such that secondhand bookstores do not represent a serious threat to mainstream book retailers and publishers. Similarly, the resale market for vinyl records and tape-based music cassettes was fairly limited by the deterioration these products experienced on each subsequent play. By contrast, the digitized signals derived from CD-ROMs retain their initial quality regardless of the amount of use, and therefore a secondary market in CDs presents the music industry with significant economic challenges. It will be interesting to see if the music industry moves to a licensing model at some point (perhaps through secured online distribution over the Internet) in order to stem the resale of their products.[49] Moreover, when content distribution systems become more common on the Internet, they may include mechanisms, such as digital metering systems, that will authorize the use of the digital content on only specific machines, or on a set number of machines, so that again limits are put on the use that the user can make of the particular item. Such systems will be a practical, technologically oriented response to the second dynamic of computer law, namely, the elusive nature of information.[50]

2) Shrinkwrap Licences

Many licences for software are paper-based documents that are signed by representatives of both the software company and the user organization. Such signed software licences usually apply to more expensive, complex software programs where the parties have usually negotiated a number of matters within the licence agreement, such as delivery schedules, customization work and training to be performed by the software developer, and payment milestones. This kind of software, and negotiated software licence, can be contrasted with mass market software that is typically supplied to the public by retailers and requires no customization by the software developer. Given the price of this

---

49   For example, in *Palmer* v. *Braun*, 287 F.3d 1325 (11th Cir. 2002), expensive educational course materials were made available to users only under a non-disclosure agreement that required the eventual return of the materials. Consider, for a low-tech example, that an auto manufacturer is using a contract with the purchasers of a hot model of car to help ensure that the initial purchasers in Canada do not sell them to eager buyers in the U.S.: Greg Keenan, "BMW Wants to Keep Minis Parked in Canada," *The Globe and Mail* (15 February 2002).

50   See also the discussion of "digital rights management technologies," and anticircumvention laws, in chapter 2, section C.6, "Copyright and the Internet."

kind of software, often less than $100 a copy, it would be too expensive in terms of transaction costs for the software supplier to enter into a signed licence agreement in respect of each purchase of a licence. Accordingly, such software typically comes with a licence statement inside the box to which reference is often made on the outside packaging of the box. Alternatively, the diskette containing the software can be in an envelope inside the box, on the cover of which is the licence statement. Or, more recently, the software comes on a CD, and the first screen of the computer program, whenever it is loaded in the computer, displays the relevant licence statement. At one time the actual licence statement was placed on the back of the box containing the software disk, and then the box was tightly cellophane-wrapped so that the prospective user could see the licence statement before purchasing the product. It was this practice that gave rise to the term *shrinkwrap licences*.[51] The licence statement contains various use permissions and restrictions, some of which were discussed in section C.1, "Why Software and Content Are Licensed," together with warranty disclaimers and limitations on liability in favour of the software developer. There is also included, typically in bold, capital letters, the statement that if the user does not accept the various licence terms, then the user can return the software for a full refund, and that commencing to use the software confirms the user's agreement with the licence terms. The chances of enforceability can be improved if the licence is presented by the initial screen of the software and the user has to click on an "I Agree" button at the end of the licence statement before being able to proceed to use the product.[52]

a)   The *Systemshops* Case

In Canada, and elsewhere, there has traditionally been uncertainty as to whether these shrinkwrap licences are enforceable. In Canada, the uncertainty was engendered by the *Systemshops* case, in which a purchaser argued that he could make and use multiple production copies of a single copy of a mass market software program because the licence statement was not brought to his attention at the time he paid for the

---

51   For an overview of the history of the shrinkwrap licence, see Robert W. Gomulkjewicz & Mary L. Williamson, "A Brief Defense of Mass Market Software License Agreements" (1996) 22 Rutgers Computer & Technology Law Journal 335.

52   See the discussion of "express click-consent agreements" in chapter 6, section A.3(c), "Express and Implied Click-Consent Agreements."

product.[53] The court agreed with this position, noting that the licence statement was included in the back of the manual for the product, which was wrapped in cellophane, and thus the licence restrictions were not made known to the defendant at the time of purchase. The court then went on to conclude that as the licence restrictions were without effect, the defendant could do "whatever the purchaser [defendant] wished with the product,"[54] which in this case included making multiple production copies of it. Leaving aside for a moment the question as to the enforceability of the licence statement, the court's conclusion that in the absence of a licence restriction a purchaser of a copyright work can make unlimited copies of it is questionable. Rather, the *Copyright Act* would still apply such that the user would, at most, be able to make such copies as are required to reasonably use the original copy; that is, it would be reasonable to make a copy on the user's hard drive for his own subsequent ease of use of the software, but this is a far cry from the multiple additional hard drives onto which the software was copied in the *Systemshops* case. Of course, in the absence of a licence agreement, a user could resell and transfer (but not rent, as noted earlier) the original copy of the software, but again only so long as additional copies were not made.

As for the question whether shrinkwrap licences are enforceable in Canada, it is too rigid a reading of the *Systemshops* case to conclude that it requires that notice of all the terms be brought to the purchaser's attention at the time of purchase. Obviously this is the ideal scenario, but the outside surfaces of the boxes containing mass market software simply do not provide enough space to contain the whole licence. Hence some software companies indicate on the outside of the box that a full licence agreement is contained within the box. This sort of notice given to the purchaser prior to or at the time of sale should be sufficient to legally bind the purchaser to the terms of the full licence inside the box, but the process can be made extremely certain if the software, when it loads, presents a licence statement on the first screen that must be assented to by clicking an "I Agree" button in order to make further use of the software. This is particularly true given that today these licences have become so standard and ubiquitous that the average user would be hard-pressed to argue that he did not know about them or the various terms contained within them. Indeed, the

53   *North American Systemshops Ltd.* v. *King* (1989), 68 Alta. L.R. (2d) 145 (Q.B.) [*Systemshops*].
54   *Ibid.*, at 155.

court in *Systemshops* acknowledged that in contrast to the practice of the plaintiff in that particular case, it had subsequently become commonplace to insert the disk in a sealed envelope that prominently displays both a warning that the disk is sold subject to licence conditions and a licence agreement. This envelope is then found in the box after the purchaser has left the store, at which point the purchaser has the option of agreeing to the licence terms or returning the software for a refund. Similarly, it should be sufficient if before using the software, and right after loading it into the computer for the first time, one of the first screens to appear on the computer contained the licence agreement, together with a clear statement that further use of the software would be deemed to be consent to the licence terms by the user, though ideally the screen would be designed to require an express manifestation of consent by having the user click an "I Agree" button. If the user did not agree to the terms, the agreement would reiterate the option of returning the software for a full refund.

b)   The *ProCD* Case

In the U.S. case, *ProCD, Incorporated* v. *Zeidenberg*,[55] a shrinkwrap licence contained in a box, only notice of which was included on the outside of the box, was held to be enforceable by an appeals court, overturning a contrary lower court decision that had decided that all the licence terms had to be brought to the purchaser's attention at the time of sale. Distinguishing several previous cases that had essentially stood for the proposition supported by the trial court, the appellate court pointed out that the practice of printing a notice of a licence on

---

55   86 F.3d 1447 (7th Cir. 1996) [*ProCD*]. In *ProCD*, the item being licensed was a directory database contained on a CD-ROM. For U.S. cases upholding a shrinkwrap licence for a software product, see *M.A. Mortenson Company, Inc.* v. *Timberline Software Corp.*, 998 P.2d 305 (Wash. Sup. Ct. 2000) [*Timberline Software*] and *Mudd-Lyman Sales and Service Corporation* v. *United Parcel Service, Inc.*, 2002 WL 31687683 (N.D. Ill. 2002). In this latter case, a computer software sign-in screen was used, as in ProCD, but so was a true shrinkwrap-sealed mechanism; the court found that both vehicles were used to create a binding agreement. But see also *Softman Products Company, LLC* v. *Adobe Systems Inc.*, 2001 U.S. Dist. LEXIS 17723, though this case did not involve an end-user of software, and thus can be distinguished from the facts of *ProCD*. For an early predecessor of the shrinkwrap agreement, see *Primrose* v. *Western Union Telegraph Company*, 154 U.S. 1 (1894), where the limitation of liability terms printed on the back of the form used to submit handwritten messages for telegraphing were held to be operative, given the notice of such terms on the front of the form, including just below the signature line, that indicated the terms on the reverse would apply.

the outside of the box, and including the licence inside the box with a right of refund if the terms are unacceptable, is consistent with numerous other mass market contracting practices, such as buying theatre or airline tickets over the telephone, or buying insurance when the customer pays the premium first and agrees to the general terms (such as amount of coverage, number of years, etc.) and then the detailed policy, with the various exclusions, follows; or indeed numerous examples of the purchase of consumer goods where the customer buys, say, a radio, and then only comes across the product warranty that was inside the box containing the product later, when unpacking the radio at home. Thus, the court concluded that while a final contract can be formed at the point of purchase, a contract can also be formed subsequently when, after the user reads the licence statement accompanying the product, the user can denote acceptance by commencing to use the software or clicking an "I Agree" button to expressly consent to the licence terms.[56]

It remains to be seen whether courts in Canada will adopt reasoning similar to that found in the *ProCD* case.[57] An Ontario case involving the purchase of a truck (rather than computer equipment) held that warranty limitation provisions brought to the attention of the purchaser of the vehicle several months after he purchased it were ineffective because they were not made known at the time of the purchase.[58] The court in this case held that "[t]imely notification of these clauses

---

56   For a recent case that follows *ProCD*, see *I.LAN Systems, Inc. v. Netscout Service Level Corp.*, 183 F.Supp. 2d 328 (D. Mass. 2002) [*Netscout*]. This case supports the "money now, terms later" method of contract formation articulated by *ProCD*, and concludes, at 337, that *ProCD* stands for the proposition "that the absence of a timely rejection was sufficient to show assent." Interestingly, the judge in *Netscout* begins his judgment, at 329, with the following useful passage: "Has this happened to you? You plunk down a pretty penny for the latest and greatest software, speed back to your computer, tear open the box, shove the CD-ROM into the computer, click on 'install' and, after scrolling past a licence agreement which would take at least fifteen minutes to read, find yourself staring at the following dialog box: 'I agree.' Do you click on the box? You probably do not agree in your heart of hearts, but you click anyway, not about to let some pesky legalese delay the moment for which you've been waiting. Is that 'clickwrap' licence agreement enforceable? Yes, at least in the case described below."

57   See *Beta Computers (Europe) Limited v. Adobe Systems (Europe) Limited*, [1996] 23 F.S.R. 367, where a Scottish court, in considering when a contract arose in the context of a shrinkwrap licence, concluded that no contract was concluded until the purchaser accepted the licence terms of the software developer, thereby echoing the holding in the *ProCD* case under Scots law.

58   *Gregorio v. Intrans-Corp.* (1994), 115 D.L.R. (4th) 200 (Ont. C.A.) [*Gregorio*].

is especially important where they purport, as they do in this case, to extinguish or limit common law rights."[59] The court cited another Canadian case in which it was held that a limitation clause is not effective unless the party wishing to rely on it took reasonable steps to bring it to the attention of the other party at or prior to the time of making the contract.[60] Notwithstanding these decisions, a court in Canada faced with a standard shrinkwrap licence should follow the *ProCD* decision where a standard licence statement is at issue, particularly where notice of a fuller licence statement is contained on the outside of the box containing the relevant software, and the first screen of the software, after it is loaded into the computer, displays the licence and requires the user to consent to it by clicking an "I Agree" button at the end of the licence. This would be an important result not just for suppliers selling software in boxes at retail outlets, but also for the increasingly important practice of distributing software to users over the Internet where, as the court in the *ProCD* case points out, there is no box at all but merely a stream of electrons that will include an initial screen containing the licence terms, with a statement that commencing to use the software denotes acceptance of the terms. In Internet situations, however, it is possible to create contracting processes where the user, before being transmitted the digitized content, signifies his or her consent to the relevant licence or other agreement by sending an affirming keystroke or message. Thus, such an "express click-consent agreement" concluded over the Internet should not even raise the issue discussed in the cases above.[61]

3) Licensing in a Digital Environment

In addition to licensing end-users, creators and owners of software and content regularly grant licences to other entities in the distribution

---

59   *Ibid.*, at 205. Presumably in this case the warranty terms were in the owner's manual buried in the glove compartment, where they might never be seen after the truck is driven off the lot. This is distinguishable from the shrinkwrap licence situation where, as soon as the software is first used, the licence is presented on the screen with the option to click "I Agree," and continue use of the software, or to click "I Decline," and to receive a refund of the licence fee.

60   *Trigg v. MI Movers International Transport Services Ltd.* (1991), 84 D.L.R. (4th) 504 (Ont. C.A.).

61   Such an agreement was upheld in *Rudder v. Microsoft Corporation*, [1999] O.J. No. 3778 (Ont. Sup. Court). For a discussion of this case, and other aspects of "express click-consent agreements," and the related "implied click-consent agreement," see chapter 6, section A.3(c), "Express and Implied Click-Consent Agreements."

chain to market and distribute their products. The particular rights licensed in all these circumstances can give rise to disputes, particularly where technological developments occurring after the date of the licence allow the licensed content to be used or distributed in a manner that may not have been contemplated by one or both parties at the time of the original licence agreement. For example, the ability of newspapers to distribute their material in electronic form both over the Internet as part of a database-type service, as well as on CD-ROM-type products, has resulted in lawsuits by freelance journalists who contended that traditionally their articles were licensed for one-time use in the paper-based edition of the newspaper, and that any subsequent online or other electronic use requires the further permission of the journalists.[62] For their part, the newspapers argued that as owners of the copyright in the newspaper, namely, the compilation of the various articles when taken together, they can exploit the newspaper as they please. In the United States initially, and subsequently in Canada, this dispute has been resolved in favour of the freelancers. In *New York Times Co. v. Tasini*,[63] the freelancers argued that they licensed their articles to the *New York Times* for "first publication rights" only, and under the U.S. *Copyright Act*, this meant the newspaper could use it only as part of the paper edition of the newspaper or any revisions of it.[64] The freelancers argued that the online databases in which their articles were placed were not revisions of the paper edition of the paper, and the U.S. Supreme Court agreed, finding the newspaper to have violated the authors' copyrights. A similar conclusion was reached in the initial substantive court decision in *Robertson v. Thomson Corp.*,[65] where freelancers for the *Globe and Mail* brought a similar proceeding to that in *Tasini*. And again, the court found for the freelancers, concluding that InfoGlobe, the electronic database where the articles were available online and in a CD format, is a database and not a newspaper. On the other hand, putting past editions of the *Globe and Mail's* paper edition onto microfilm or microfiche presumably does not violate the freelancers' copyrights, because with these media actual photographic

---

62 For a discussion of class action suits brought by freelance authors against Thomson Corp. and Southam Inc., respectively, see Elizabeth Raymer, "Electronic Copyright Fight Heads to Court," *The Lawyers Weekly* (21 February 1997), and Elizabeth Raymer, "Electronic Copyright Battle Heats Up: Quebec Freelancers Launch $30 Million Class Action," *The Lawyers Weekly* (27 June 1997).

63 121 S. Ct. 2381 (2001) [*Tasini*].

64 Section 201(c), U.S. *Copyright Act*, 17 U.S.C.

65 [2001] O.J. No. 3868 (Sup. Ct.).

images of the newspaper are made and preserved, exactly as the editor of the original newspaper planned them and laid them out. By contrast, InfoGlobe is a database system for retrieving individual, stand-alone articles, the court found, and therefore the *Globe* was held to have infringed the freelancers' copyrights. As more and more content from the paper-based era is scanned or otherwise transformed for use in the electronic era, it can be expected that these sorts of lawsuits will multiply as the parties review their original licence agreements and disagree as to the scope of the rights originally granted, and in particular whether electronic rights are included in the grant clauses.[66]

These sorts of cases (which exemplify the first and second dynamics of computer law, namely, the rapid pace of technological change and the elusive nature of information) are not new in the content industries (such as music, books, and broadcasting), particularly in the motion picture business where, in the United States especially, there have been a number of court decisions dealing with the question whether the language of prior licence grants is broad enough to permit the distributor to exercise distribution rights in new technology platforms or environments. For example, in a number of cases courts have had to decide whether the right to exhibit motion pictures (or to use music) included the ability to exercise these rights in the context of television broadcasts, and subsequently whether television rights included the videocassette market. In one line of cases,[67] these questions are answered in the affirmative, based on a combination of the following factors: the broad, often expansive nature of the licence language; the

---

66   Indeed, on the strength of the *Tasini* decision, above note 63, other organizations representing authors have brought similar proceedings against other database companies. See also M.J. Rose, "Discontent in Contentville.com," *Wired News* (27 July 2000), which chronicles the negotiations Jonathan Tasini, who is president of the National Writers Union, had with the producers of the Contentville.com site that sells online, among other things, articles from 1800 magazines, journals, and newspapers. In this regard, it is interesting to note that the *Globe and Mail* has launched a service where digitized full-image versions of the newspaper are available online: Jack Kapica, "Globe to Offer Pages from Past On-Line," *The Globe and Mail* (4 July 2002).

67   *Bartsch v. Metro-Goldwyn-Mayer, Inc.*, 391 F.2d 150 (2d Cir. 1968) [*Bartsch*]; *Rooney v. Columbia Pictures Industries, Inc.*, 538 F.Supp. 211 (S.D.N.Y. 1982), aff'd without reasons 714 F.2d 117 (2d Cir. 1982); *Brown v. Twentieth Century Fox Film Corporation*; 799 F.Supp. 166 (D.C.D.C. 1992), aff'd without reasons 15 F.3d 1159 (D.C. Cir. 1994); *Bourne v. Walt Disney Company*, 68 F.3d 621 (2d Cir. 1995), cert. denied 116 S. Ct. 1890 (1996); *Boosey & Hawkes Music Publishers, Ltd. v. Walt Disney Company*, 934 F.Supp. 119 (S.D.N.Y. 1996) [*Boosey & Hawkes*].

absence of limiting language in the grant clause; the level of sophistication of the content owner, and the related inference that the new technology was at least recognized by knowledgeable people at the time of the licence grant; and a finding that the two distribution streams are linked technologically; for example, television includes videocassettes because both are still seen through the mechanism of the television. By contrast, in those cases where it has been held that motion picture exhibition rights do not include television, or that television rights do not include videocassettes, courts have focussed on language that is narrower and where sweeping grants of rights are not present; the licensor often being less sophisticated; and an analysis of the mechanics of, for example, television and videocassette distribution that concludes that they are very different market segments and indeed quite distinct media.[68] Frankly, reconciling some of the cases in these two lines of authorities can be difficult; one has the sneaking suspicion that in a few of them the court decided for some reason (not apparent from reading the case) who should be entitled to the unexpected windfall represented by the new technology, and then the court partook of results-oriented reasoning by parsing words and the like.

To the so-called new use cases referred to above can be added the very interesting decision in *Random House, Inc.* v. *Rosetta Books LLC*.[69] In this case, a number of authors had granted to Random House the right to "print, publish and sell the work in book form," but then they granted to Rosetta Books the right to publish these same works in digital versions over the Internet. The Rosetta versions contained the same text as the paper-based editions, but because they were digital the reader could search them electronically by keyword, add text to them, and adjust the layout on the screen (in terms of font size and style, number of words per screen, and the like). Based on these facts, the court concluded that the initial grant to Random House of publication in "book form" (as opposed to some agreements, where the right granted is to "publish the book") did not include the digital, Internet rights granted to Rosetta. One factor that influenced the court was that the electronic, digital signal sent over the Internet was a separate medium from the

---

68   *Cohen* v. *Paramount Pictures Corp.*, 845 F.2d 851 (9th Cir. 1988); *Tele-Pac, Inc.* v. *Grainger*, 570 N.Y.S. 2d 521 (1991), leave to appeal dismissed 588 N.E.2d 99 (N.Y. 1991); *Rey* v. *G.D. Lafferty*, 990 F.2d 1379 (1st Cir. 1993).

69   150 F.Supp. 2d 613 (S.D.N.Y. 2001); affirmed, 2002 U.S. App. LEXIS 3673 (2nd Cir. 2002). See also *Rodgers and Hammerstein Organization* v. *UMG Recordings, Inc.*, 60 U.S.P.Q. 2d 1354 (S.D.N.Y. 2001), where a mechanical licence for a musical composition from the Harry Fox Agency was held not to cover streaming over the Internet.

original paper-based books. Thus, the court was able to distinguish the facts before it from those in the *Bartsch* and *Boosey & Hawkes* cases, where the court held the new uses were within the same medium.

The two lines of licensing referred to in the cases above, together with the *Random House* case, signify the importance of careful drafting of licence grants in these industries. Those desiring broad rights should try to include in licence grant clauses phrases such as "through any and all media, now or hereafter known," or "by present or future methods or means," or "in any medium, manner or form," while of course content owners wishing to keep their options open with respect to new media will likely resist such broad grants of rights. Since business and technological models of content distribution are not worked out in detail for the Internet, content owners will likely be wary for some time before they enter into long-term licence agreements. For example, it is still not clear how consumers will be most willing to pay for content delivered over the Internet.[70] Many paradigms can be envisaged, ranging from subscriber models that allow unlimited access upon payment of a monthly fee to per-byte models where the consumer pays only for what she takes, or broadcast models where the service is free to consumers but paid for by advertisers. And during the current embryonic stage of the Internet, service providers might shift between these and other models until they hit upon the right one. Thus, content owners will likely want to see how these various models with end-users pan out before locking themselves into any particular upstream licensing arrangement with an Internet service provider or content distributor.

D. NEGLIGENCE

Under the law of negligence, someone (referred to here as the defendant) who causes harm to someone else (referred to here as the plaintiff) for failing to comply with a reasonable standard of care will be liable to the plaintiff for the damages caused to the plaintiff provided the law determines that the defendant owed the plaintiff a duty of care. In negligence law, courts determine what the reasonable standard of care is in any given situation and, assuming the standard has not been met, courts then determine who is entitled to be compensated by the defendant's failure to adhere to the standard. The purpose of negligence

---

70   See "A Survey of Electronic Commerce: In Search of the Perfect Market," *The Economist*, 10 May 1997.

law is to compensate certain plaintiffs who are harmed by certain actions of certain defendants, and thereby also to encourage safer behaviour through the adoption of cost-effective measures to avoid situations that cause damage. Under negligence law, these obligations are imposed by the courts, and hence are non-voluntary, in contrast to contract law, which deals with voluntarily assumed obligations.[71]

Given the widespread presence of computers and computer networks in our society, it is not surprising that computers raise a number of issues under the law of negligence, some of them unique. There are questions related to negligence in the creation of computer-based products, particularly in light of ever-shortening product cycles — the alter ego of the first dynamic of computer law — and the fact that bug-free software is, practically speaking, an unattainable goal. As well, computers can be used in ways that are negligent. And ironically, negligence can also arise when computers are not used. In all these scenarios the general law of negligence will apply, but often with particular nuances given the unique characteristics of the computer industry. It should also be noted that in many of these scenarios contract and sales law will also be relevant, particularly in attempts to limit exposure for negligence, and these topics are discussed in the next part of this chapter.

1) Negligence in Creation

There are relatively few reported cases involving negligence claims brought against the developers of computers, software, and related products. This is probably attributable to several factors, including that to date, for the most part, the harm caused by malfunctioning computers has been economic loss rather than injury to persons or damage to physical property. As a result, most claims against suppliers for defective computer resources have been in contract, which is more receptive than negligence to compensating for pure economic loss. Indeed, one way that courts limit the scope of negligence law is to severely curtail the circumstances under which they will award compensation for pure economic loss, thereby reserving negligence, in a practical sense, primarily to the domain of compensation for personal injury or loss to tangible, physical property although, as can be seen in the cases in this section, negligence law can be pressed into action from

---

71   This is a ridiculously short description of negligence law. For a full discussion of this fascinating area of the law, and its development over the years, see Allen M. Linden, *Canadian Tort Law*, 6th ed. (Toronto: Butterworths, 1997).

time to time to compensate for pecuniary losses. As software finds its way into more and more tangible products, however, the likelihood of physical injuries resulting from substandard software will increase.[72] For example, in a pair of U.S. cases, the design and lack of repair, respectively, of computer-based devices led to automobile accidents that caused personal injury and damage to tangible property.[73] The paucity of negligent design and build cases to date should not be taken as an indicator of future expectations.

A negligence case relating to the creation of a computer-based product has the potential to raise some unusual issues. Consider a computer/software system used to help doctors diagnose medical patients by analysing a patient's symptoms relative to a knowledge base contained within the program. These so-called medical expert systems often exhibit artificial intelligence by being able to store previous patient histories and diagnoses in a large database and "to learn" from these previous cases to improve the accuracy and quality of their diagnoses. A threshold issue relative to such a system is who would be liable if a doctor using such a program arrived at an incorrect diagnosis. The candidates for liability include the doctor; the hospital that acquired the system; the supplier of the system; the developer of the system; the medical research team that provided the knowledge base for the system; the developers of the artificial intelligence inference engine that is used in the system; and some combination of all or some of the above. In essence, many computer systems and software products are the result of collaborative efforts among a number of participants, and determining the boundaries of responsibility among them for purposes of a negligence analysis can be a challenge. Nonetheless, courts engage in such delineation all the time, as in the decision in *A.T. Kearney v. International Business Machines Corporation*.[74] This case arose out of a lawsuit brought by a retailer against its consultant, A.T. Kearney, for proposing 100 IBM AS/400 midrange computers that ulti-

---

72   See, for example, Barbara Wade Rose, "Fatal Dose," *Saturday Night*, June 1994, which chronicles the physical harm inflicted on cancer patients by overdoses of radiation attributable to a software glitch in a radiation therapy machine. As for property damage, see the short mention in *The Economist*, 8 June 1996, of the destruction of $500 million worth of uninsured spacecraft and scientific satellite when apparently a software glitch made the launch rocket go off course just after lift-off.

73   *Roberts v. Rich Foods, Inc.*, 654 A.2d 1365 (N.J. 1995); and *Arizona State Highway Department v. Bechtold*, 460 P.2d 179 (Ariz. 1969).

74   *A.T. Kearney, Inc. v. International Business Machines Corporation*, 867 F.Supp. 943 (D. Or. 1994), aff'd 73 F.3d 238 (9th Cir. 1995).

mately proved to be inadequate; instead, the retailer ended up buying an IBM mainframe computer. The retailer sued the consultant for $110 million for negligence, breach of contract, negligent misrepresentation, and breach of fiduciary duty, and they settled for a payment from the consultant to the retailer of $13.25 million. The consultant then sued IBM for negligence, for failure to disclose its doubts about the ability of the proposed system to meet the needs of the retailer. The court dismissed the consultant's claim, finding that IBM was merely a seller of goods and had no special relationship with the consultant and had no consulting or services obligations.

In addition to determining who the proper parties are in a computer-related negligence claim, another difficult challenge lies in determining what standard of care to apply to the development of a computer system or software program, whether it be a medical expert system or any other application. There are, for instance, no general licensing or certification requirements for software developers. One must be a licensed engineer in order to design a bridge that will span a street or highway; no such licence is required by the software programmers designing a key network bridge along the information superhighway. Similarly, although there are many textbooks on software design, programming, and testing, there are no general standards as there are, for example, in the *CICA Handbook* for the accounting profession. Thus, there are no widely accepted standards among software programmers as to how much testing a new product should undergo — as to how many bugs per line of code can remain — before the software is released commercially. On large software development projects the user relies on express contractual provisions to address these concerns; in the mass market environment most users are content to wait for a subsequent release of the product to fix the known bugs.

2) Negligence in Use

a)   Malfunctioning Computers

A wide variety of situations can be contemplated where users of computers are negligent in the manner in which they employ computers. In one type of case, the computer malfunctions with the result that it processes an erroneous result. In such cases, courts have generally been unwilling to let users argue as a defence to liability that the particular computer had malfunctioned. For example, in an early U.S. case, a car leasing company repossessed a customer's car for non-payment even though the customer had promptly paid the required monthly accounts.[75] The problem was that the computer would not register the payments, and therefore it issued the notice to repossess the car. The customer brought a claim for compensatory and punitive damages. The company admitted liability, but tried to explain the whole incident because of a computer error. The court did not accept this excuse, and concluded:

> Men feed data to a computer and men interpret the answer the computer spews forth. In this computerized age, the law must require that men in the use of computerized data regard those with whom they are dealing as more important than a perforation on a card. Trust in the infallibility of a computer is hardly a defense, when the opportunity to avoid the error is as apparent and repeated as was here presented.[76]

In a more recent Nova Scotia case, an insurance company failed to send out a renewal notice on an insurance policy due to a computer error.[77] This caused the policy to lapse, and the previously insured individual

---

75 *Ford Motor Credit Company* v. *Swarens*, 447 S.W.2d 53 (Ky. App. 1969). For a similar result involving lawyers, see *Martinelli* v. *Farm-Rite Inc.*, 785 A.2d 33 (N.J. Sup. Ct. App. Div. 2001), where the court held that glitches in a law firm's computer were insufficient justification for extending a filing deadline; the court noted that computer malfunction, like the human variety, must be expected, and alternatives should be in place to ensure that there is no failure to make timely filings.

76 *Ibid.*, at 57. A similar sentiment was expressed by a court in a later U.S. case, *Poullier* v. *Nacau Motors, Inc.*, 439 N.Y.S.2d 85 at 86 (N.Y. Sup. Ct. 1981) [*Poullier*]: "At first blush, it would appear that this court must determine the guilt or innocence of a computer. But such is not the case. In our modern machine age, it's tempting to shift the ills of society onto the heartless, mechanical world of computers. Yet, responsibility cannot be so easily escaped since a computer, not unlike an infant of tender years, is totally dependent on being spoon-fed by a human world. A computer error must always relate back to a human error, whether it be the human as source of the information fed into it, the human as creator of its programming or the human as mechanic for its proper functioning."
   Equally, in the American case *Re McCormack*, 203 B.R. 521 at 524 (Bankr. D.N.H. 1996) [*McCormack*], the court found that a bank should not be allowed to hide behind its computer: "The testimony by Chase's witness that its software at the time would not accommodate separate accounting and recording of payments coming from the trustee under the plan I find amounts to the 'computer did it' defense. That defense is a nonstarter in this Court's judgment since intelligent beings still control the computer and could have altered the programming appropriately. ... To paraphrase the old quote 'garbage-in' adage a version here pertinent would be 'contempt-of-court in' and 'contempt-of-court out.'"

77 *Judgment Recovery (N.S.) Ltd.* v. *Sun Alliance Insurance Co.* (1986), 74 N.S.R. (2d) 412 (T.D.).

brought a claim for compensation resulting from an automobile accident. The court found the insurance company liable, and again a computer glitch was not permitted to excuse negligent behaviour. In yet another case, the computer of a lottery corporation erroneously indicated to a ticket holder that he had won $835, when in fact he really only won $5.[78] Before the error was pointed out to the ticket holder, he had spent about $400 wining and dining friends to celebrate the lottery win. When the lottery corporation refused to pay the $835, the winner brought a claim and the court agreed with him, concluding that the corporation "in effect, invited him to depend on the computer and he had every reason to believe it was accurate."[79] The court did suggest, however, that if the prize had been greater than $835, then at some point it would have been negligence on the part of the winner not to confirm the win, and actually receive the money, before incurring significant expenses in the expectation of using the lottery winnings to pay for such expenses.

Not all malfunctioning computers, however, will result in liability being visited upon their users. In one case a customer certified a cheque for $7500 on the strength of the amount shown in a bank passbook that had not been updated, and that could not be updated at the time the cheque was drawn because the bank's computers were inoperable.[80] Once the computers came back online, and all the interim postings were made to the account, it turned out the customer was in an overdraft position of roughly $950. The customer refused to pay, ostensibly on the grounds that had he known the true balance in his account he would have reduced the amount of the certified cheque accordingly. The court, ignoring estoppel arguments and the authorities that indicate that the customer's passbook is the only record of the true state of a customer's account, found for the bank and ordered the customer to pay the $950 on the basis of unjust enrichment. In another case, a stockbroker, on the strength of a malfunctioning computer, quoted $7.00 as the price he could get for options held by the customer; in fact, the price the computer should have shown was around $2.50, and the stockbroker unknowingly sold the options for this amount, kicking up a substantial loss for the customer.[81] When the customer sued the broker for the loss, the court, interestingly, held for the broker on the

---

78   *Budai v. Ontario Lottery Corp.* (1983), 142 D.L.R. (3d) 271 (Ont. H.C.J.).

79   *Ibid.*, at 273.

80   *Bank of Nova Scotia v. Butt* (1978), 11 A.R. 616 (Dist. Ct.).

81   *Walwyn Stodgell Cochrane Murray Ltd. v. Ryan* (1981), 36 N.B.R. (2d) 187 (Q.B.T.D.).

basis that the price of the options deteriorated even further after their sale by the broker, such that, ironically, selling at the erroneous price nevertheless saved the customer money by reducing his potential loss. In other words, the misrepresentation by the computer did not cause the investor's damage. Ironically, however, the court did not let the broker collect any commission on the trade as the inaccuracy in the information provided by the broker had so little value to the customer.

b) Negligent Design

In addition to these cases where the particular computer malfunction leads to erroneous processing or computation, there are the intriguing cases where the user's fault lies in the design of the computer being used by it; that is, the computers are working the way they were programmed to work, but the particular way they work (i.e., the design programmed into them) is itself negligent. A good example of this is *Remfor Industries Ltd. v. Bank of Montreal*.[82] In this case, a customer of a bank wished to stop payment on a cheque, and to this end gave the bank the date and number of the cheque, the name of the payee, and the amount of $10,800, which was $53 short of the actual amount of the cheque. The bank's computer was programmed only to register the account number and the precise amount of the cheque, and therefore the bank failed to stop payment because the number given to the bank was incorrect by $53. In the subsequent claim between the customer and the bank, the court held in favour of the customer, concluding that the customer gave a reasonably accurate description to the bank, which was all it had to do, and thereafter it was up to the bank to have an adequate system to properly act on this information:

> I am of the opinion that the learned trial Judge was correct in holding that having regard to the information given to it by the plaintiff, the bank was under a duty to inquire from its customer as to whether the cheque presented for certification was the cheque with respect to which the direction to stop payment had been given. The bank's failure to do so constituted negligence. The information given to the bank was correct in every respect other than the amount. The instructions clearly related to the cheque, the number of which had been given to the bank. The bank's internal procedure in limiting the information supplied to its computer, by reference to account number and the

---

82   (1978), 90 D.L.R. (3d) 316 (Ont. C.A.) [*Remfor*].

amount of the cheque only, cannot relieve the bank of its duty where the customer has supplied such precise additional information.[83]

In other words, a human bank clerk, faced with the same information from the customer, invariably would have called to enquire of the customer to sort out the discrepancies in the amounts at issue, and hence would have effected the stop payment. The computer program used by the bank, because it was poorly designed, required precise information and therefore was not as flexible as the human system it replaced.

Several American cases have come to conclusions similar to that in the *Remfor* case. In one case, *Parr v. Security National Bank*, the court was faced with facts identical to those in *Remfor*, and the court also held in favour of the customer.[84] The court concluded that the customer simply had to identify the cheque on which the customer wished to stop payment with "reasonable accuracy," and therefore the court did not take into account the actual state of the computer program used by the bank or any other matter relating to how the bank handled stop payment orders, notwithstanding that, as the court stated, this result might place a burden on banks. In another U.S. case, however, the bank was able to shift this burden from its back and put it squarely on that of the customer by notifying the customer, in advance, that the bank needs the precise amount of the cheque given that the bank's computer is programmed in a manner to recognize only precise numbers.[85] Thus, even though the customer was out by only one digit (the plaintiff told the bank the amount was $4,287.65, when it was really $4,247.65), the court held in favour of the bank:

> Had plaintiff presented the bank with the correct amount of the check, and thereafter, the computer failed to detect the stop payment order, plaintiff would then be correct in her contention that the computer through its master, the bank, had erred. However, such is not the case. Defendant Bank's request for the exact amount was not unreasonable and is in fact mandated by a stop payment system, necessarily computerized due to the large number of branch offices where such an instrument could be negotiated. Nor is plaintiff's contention that she should not be held responsible for a mere "1 digit

---

83   *Ibid.*, at 320. For a similar result in an online stock trading environment, see *Zhu v. Merrill Lynch HSBC*, [2002] BCPC 0535, where the court found the online broker's computer system confusing, and hence negligently designed when it tripped up a fairly sophisticated user.

84   680 P.2d 648 (Okla. App. 1984).

85   *Poullier*, above note 76.

mistake," a valid one in that one digit can be a world of difference to a computer, who by nature, is quite finicky.[86]

A Canadian court followed a similar rationale involving a dispute regarding Ontario's computerized personal property registration system.[87] In this case, the plaintiff argued the registration system's computer failed to give it adequate information in that it did not display a second variation of a name for a particular debtor. The lower court accepted this argument, but the appellate court did not, noting that the government's computer did not give a wrong answer, rather the plaintiff asked the wrong question. The court noted, in a manner reminiscent of the decision in the *Poullier* case, that the precise rules dictated by the computerized registration system were made available to all users of the system, and therefore the onus was on the plaintiff to comply with its requirement for precision.

A trio of other cases are worth mentioning that echo the result in the *Remfor* case and highlight the requirement for users to ensure that their computers are adequately designed. One decision dealt with a computerized trading system developed and used by a gas pipeline operator.[88] When inputting data into this system, an employee of the company confused two entities with virtually identical names, with the result that delivery of the gas went to the wrong party. The court found both parties to the litigation 50 percent responsible for the error. With respect to the pipeline company, its negligence stemmed from, among other things, failing to design and implement a system that would avoid the kinds of errors encountered in the case. The court cited six specific elements of negligence against the pipeline company, two particularly noteworthy ones being failure to warn the public that its trading system was not free of the types of errors it experienced in the case; and the other a failure to confirm transfers of gas early enough to allow customers to detect any mistakes. In another case, negligence was found when an electric utility disconnected power to a newly built and not yet occupied house in the middle of winter due to non-payment of the utility's bills, causing the pipes to burst and damages to the premises.[89] Again the court castigated the utility for blindly relying on the

---

86   *Ibid.*, at 86.

87   *Federal Business Development Bank* v. *Registrar of Personal Property Security* (1984), 45 O.R. (2d) 780 (H.C.J.).

88   *Shell Pipeline Corporation* v. *Coastal States Trading, Inc.*, 788 S.W.2d 837 (Tex. App. 1990).

89   *Pompeii Estates, Inc.* v. *Consolidated Edison Co. of New York, Inc.*, 397 N.Y.S.2d 577 (N.Y. City Civ. Ct. 1977).

computer when it gave the order to terminate service, and for the failure to verify the situation by a human intervention, which the court concluded would have quickly led the utility to realize the new home had just been built and was unoccupied.

A final case worth noting involved a bank's failure to keep track of appropriate amounts in a bankruptcy administration where the bank was also a secured creditor.[90] The bank pleaded its computers could not handle the particular nuances of the various court awards. The court refused to accept this excuse (see note 83 above), and indeed, went on to award punitive damages against the bank:

> Perhaps a less knowledgeable and less sophisticated business enterprise might not be charged with punitive damages for failing to set up appropriate computer or specialized accounting procedures with appropriate instructions to employees to avoid violations of the automatic stay in this context. Be that as it may, the Court does not believe that that concept or that defense should be available to an enterprise of the nature of Chase. ... Sophisticated commercial enterprises have a clear obligation to adjust their programming and procedures and their instruction to employees to handle complex matters correctly.[91]

The court concluded that if the bank was in fact unable to modify its computer systems appropriately, it should have adopted adequate manual procedures. Instead, much to the chagrin of the court, the bank was content to let its computer spew forth a large volume of printouts that did not meet the requirements of the situation:

> The panoply of computer printouts presented to the debtor in this case bring to mind the phrase "cruelty to dumb animals" in that no borrower in my judgment should have been subjected to that barrage of incomprehensible accounting printouts in response to a simple question of what has happened to the obligations cured under the plan as opposed to post-confirmation transactions. The barrage of totally meaningless and in fact misleading printouts employed by Chase in this instance was truly outrageous and egregious conduct.[92]

In chapter 1 the question arose whether Immanuel Kant, who exalted humans as the only species capable of moral, autonomous judgment, would be pleased by the computer revolution if he were alive today. Clearly, the cases referred to in this section would distress

---

90   *McCormack*, above note 76.
91   *Ibid.*, at 525.
92   *Ibid.*

him, but the responses of the courts would hearten him. In effect, computers are wonderful, indispensable tools, but they are only tools. They do our bidding. Therefore, it is up to people to ensure that their computers and the business or administrative processes of which they are a part are designed in a manner that is appropriate to the task. On occasion this will require that a human intervention step (or two) be factored into the business process design implemented by the computer. Third parties must be given clear and advance notice of the limitations of the computer system. Where a computer user does not do this, and the resulting computer-based business process fails to address the requirements of the particular situation — and not just the exigencies of the computer user — courts will stick the users with liability, rather than permit them to hide behind the computer.

In a similar vein, sometimes it is not the computer that is designed poorly, but the overall workflow process of a company. For example, in *State Farm Mutual Automobile Insurance Company* v. *Bockhorst*,[93] an insured's car insurance had lapsed a number of months previously, but when he was in an accident he quickly sent in his renewal. At the same time, he informed the insurer's agent and adjuster that he had the accident. However, neither of the company's representatives notified the policy services division of the company, which promptly issued the policy renewal. The insurance company tried to rescind the policy, arguing, among other things, that the inexorable process of its computerized policy renewal system should not be held against it and should not lead to the conclusion that it had waived its right to contest the renewal. The trial judge and the appellate court were not moved, and found for the insured, the latter in the following terms:

> Holding a company responsible for the actions of its computer does not exhibit a distaste for modern business practices as State Farm asserts. A computer operates only in accordance with the information and directions supplied by its human programmers. If the computer does not think like a man, it is man's fault. The reinstatement of Bockhorst's policy was the direct result of the errors and oversights of State Farm's human agents and employees. The fact that the actual processing of the policy was carried out by an unimaginative mechanical device can have no effect on the company's responsibilities for those errors and oversights. State Farm's reinstatement of Bockhorst's policy while in full possession of information establishing its right to refuse reinstatement constituted a binding waiver, and the reinstated

---

93   453 F.2d 533 (10th Cir. 1972). See, especially, at 536–37.

policy effectively extended coverage for the period during which Bockhorst's accident occurred.

3) Negligent Non-Use

Although users of computers and technological devices can be negligent when they use computers in a careless manner, they can also be negligent if they fail to use computers, or more up-to-date computers. An important early U.S. case on the question of failing to use readily available and relatively inexpensive technology is the *T.J. Hooper* case, where the distinguished American jurist Learned Hand concluded that a tugboat owner was negligent in not fitting the vessel with a radio receiving set that could have warned the captain of the ship about an impending storm which, in the event, caused the ship to lose one of the barges it was towing.[94] The court found negligence on the basis that an adequate radio set could be purchased at a small cost and was reliable if kept maintained, and would have greatly helped avoid the kind of harm experienced in this case. Importantly, the court also determined that it was no defence to argue that not all ships had yet adopted the radio device; the court rationalized that there are times when a whole industry might lag behind in adopting new and available technology, and the court should not hesitate to set higher standards in such circumstances. In a more recent case, also in the United States, an airline was held to be negligent when its existing computer system failed to detect a forged airline ticket.[95] The court refused to accept the airline's argument that it should not be faulted for its inability to detect the alteration in the tickets due to the nature of its then current computer system. Instead, the court concluded:

> Plaintiff could have prevented the passengers from using altered tickets by maintaining a system capable of confirming which passengers are scheduled for a particular flight. In light of the advanced computer technology available today, this is not an unreasonable burden to place on the plaintiff. ... I do not recognize Swiss Air's reliance on its computer system as a legally cognizable defense. Had Swiss Air been properly equipped with a more sophisticated computer system, it could have promptly discovered the irregularity of the defendant's ticket.[96]

---

94 The *T.J. Hooper*, 60 F.2d 737 (2d Cir. 1932) [*T.J. Hooper*].
95 *Swiss Air Transport Company, Ltd. v. Benn*, 467 N.Y.S.2d 341 (N.Y. City Civ. Ct. 1983).
96 *Ibid.*, at 344.

This reasoning is illustrative of an interesting twist on the first dynamic of computer law, namely, that in certain circumstances the law will require users to stay reasonably current with the pace of technological change. In a somewhat similar vein, a court in Alberta recently concluded that the Crown may make documentary disclosure by delivering to defence counsel electronic copies of material, they do not have to provide "hard copies," and that defence counsel cannot argue that they have no or inadequate computers, or lack of computer training, to handle the electronic material.[97]

A finding of negligence can also be made where a particular technology is installed but then not utilized, as happened in an American case where a bank was held liable when its teller paid on a stopped

---

97   R. v. *Cheung*, [2000] A.J. No. 704 (Alta. Prov. Ct.). After showing no sympathy for the fact that one counsel had no computer, another counsel had a computer too old to support the Crown's software and yet another had an Apple system when the software required a PC, the court concluded, at para. 57: "It is with considerable surprise to me that in the year 2000 with the seemingly pervasive use of personal computers in business, education and even the home, a lawyer practising as a barrister and solicitor, would not already be employing a personal computer in his or her practice. It seems to me that the use of a computer today in a law practice is as much an expectation as a telephone or a photocopy machine. Surely it is today a tool of the trade one reasonably expects a lawyer to possess and employ. It could, I suppose, be argued that a computer is today a necessity to the proper and efficient practice of law. It is however my view that if it is not a necessity, its absence is unnecessarily limiting and restricting to that proper and efficient practice. If a lawyer so wishes to restrict himself or herself that is his or her choice; but that choice ought not to restrict opposing counsel, even if it is counsel for the Crown, particularly in the circumstances of a complex, voluminous piece of litigation, whether criminal or civil." As for the excuse of computer illiteracy, the court dispensed with this purported defence by observing, at para. 62: "I would expect that any active member of the Law Society of Alberta would be able to master, within 60 minutes, the operation of a personal computer had he or she never seen one before, to the degree necessary to adequately access the data provided by the Crown in its electronic or soft copy disclosure, including the search capabilities of the Supertext software. For most members it should take no more than 30 minutes." And finally, the court, at para. 59, found that cost should not be relevant: "In making these comments I am not unmindful of the fact that most of the counsel representing the accused in this case are sole practitioners, and that some of them may have been practising for only a short period of time. I recognize that their financial resources are likely far more limiting to them because of those factors. Still, it is my view that the lack of computers, appropriate computers or incompatible technology, are irrelevant to the determination of the issue, when one considers their cost balanced against their utility and advantages in the practice of law." This is, essentially, the test for negligence vis-à-vis the failure to adopt new technology, as articulated in the *T.J. Hooper* case, above note 94.

cheque without consulting the computer terminal, which, had it been accessed, would have indicated the stop payment order.[98] In this case, the bank argued it did not have sufficient time to act on the customer's stop payment notice as it was given at one branch and the cheque presented the next day at another branch. The court disagreed, and concluded that if the bank employee at the second branch had checked the computer, the stop payment notice would have appeared. Similarly, a pharmacy was held liable in a U.S. case when it advertised its computer system as being able to detect harmful prescription interactions; in fact, the pharmacy failed to spot such an interaction that led a customer to suffer a stroke and subsequently commit suicide.[99] The failure to detect the interaction, however, was not due to a malfunction of the computer but rather was the result of the failure to use the computer system by the person at the pharmacy dispensing drugs. All these cases reaffirm the general sentiment in legal and business circles that technological progress is a positive development, and companies should strive to take advantage of it. Likewise, it is worth noting a line of case law in the United States that stands for the proposition that franchisors may lawfully terminate their relationships with franchisees that refuse to adopt new computer technology proposed by the franchisor.[100]

Once a computer system is installed, however, courts will not generally require an inordinately high standard of redundancy or fail-safe technology, particularly if such back-up systems are quite expensive. Thus, in an American case, a bank was not considered negligent when it failed to have a back-up computer system available when its newly acquired system failed to operate.[101] The court in this case concluded

---

98 *Chute v. Bank One of Akron, N.A.*, 460 N.E.2d 720 (Ohio App. 1983).

99 *Baker v. Arbor Drugs, Inc.*, 544 N.W.2d 727 (Mich. App. 1996), leave to appeal denied 558 N.W.2d 725 (Mich. App. 1997).

100 In *J.I. Case Company v. Early's, Inc.*, 721 F.Supp. 1082 (E.D. Mo. 1989), the court concluded that the new system was necessary for effective communications between franchisor and franchisees; in *Re Groseth International, Inc.*, 442 N.W.2d 229 (S.D. 1989), the court, in addition to noting that the new computer system would save the franchisor money and staff costs, found that it was an essential and reasonable requirement to impose on franchisees in order that the whole franchise system could compete in the marketplace; and in *Crim Truck & Tractor Co. v. Navistar International Transportation Corporation*, 823 S.W.2d 591 (Tex. 1992), the court upheld the franchisor's decision to terminate a franchisee partly on the strength of the franchisee's refusal to participate in mandatory computer-based dealer communication network that would share computerized information between the manufacturer/franchisor and its dealers.

101 *Port City State Bank v. American National Bank*, Lawton, Oklahoma, 486 F.2d 196 (10th Cir. 1973).

that the bank had exercised adequate due care when it promptly called upon the computer maintenance company to correct the problems as quickly as possible. In a similar manner, in *Moss v. Richardson Greenshields of Canada Ltd.*, a cancellation of a sale order could not be communicated to the relevant office as a result of a computer network linking offices in several different cities becoming inoperable.[102] One important issue was whether the company was grossly negligent in not having a back-up system in place to deal with such a contingency. The court concluded it was not grossly negligent to forgo such a system as the main computer network had never failed previously. Just as important, if not more so, the company shifted the risk of such problems to users by means of clauses in their contracts that excluded their liability except in the case of gross negligence or wilful misconduct, thus precluding claims that were based on mere negligence. It is, of course, open to speculation whether similar facts would give rise to similar decisions today if it could be shown that technically sound back-up systems, and so-called disaster recovery services, are available to computer users on relatively reasonable financial terms.

E. COMPUTER CONTRACTS AND SALES LAW

Computers, software, information-based products, and related services are typically provided to users under a wide variety of written contracts. Software is typically licensed, as has been noted previously in this chapter. Hardware can be sold outright pursuant to a purchase agreement under which the user obtains title to the equipment, or leased or rented pursuant to agreements that merely permit the user to use the equipment for a period of time in return for a periodic fee. Ongoing maintenance services are typically provided for both hardware and software. Where there exists no off-the-shelf software that meets a user's requirements, a software development firm may be retained by a user to develop custom software pursuant to a software development agreement, or perhaps the specifications are first developed for the software under a consulting agreement. Instead of acquiring hardware or software, under an outsourcing or service bureau agreement, a user may buy computer services, with the supplier operating the computer system on behalf of the user. All these arrangements present both suppliers and users of computing resources with a

---

102 [1988] 4 W.W.R. 15 (Man. Q.B.), aff'd [1989] 3 W.W.R. 50 (Man. C.A.).

number of risks. As noted in chapter 1, section C.4, "Dependency on Computers," computer system implementation projects can encounter serious technical or financial difficulties. Even if implemented, the system can exhibit tendencies to crash or malfunction on an ongoing basis. In either case, the supplier and user can accumulate significant liability. In the context of two commercial parties undertaking such activities, in the absence of a written agreement to the contrary, the implied warranties and conditions found in sale of goods legislation may apply to the transaction. In many cases, however, suppliers insist on displacing these implied provisions, which in turn results in most users insisting on the computer contract addressing certain issues expressly. In effect, a computer contract is a means of voluntarily assuming certain obligations and avoiding others. Contracts can effectively allow parties to create something of their own law in circumstances where law reform has not kept up with the rapid pace of technological change or has not adequately addressed any of the other dynamics of computer law.[103]

1) Implied Warranties and Conditions

The sale of goods statutes of the common law provinces[104] contain a number of warranties and conditions that are implied into all contracts for the sale of goods, unless they are expressly disclaimed (except, as noted below, in the case of consumer sales, where other statutes generally prohibit disclaiming these implied warranties and conditions). It therefore becomes important in the context of commercial sales, in situations where express disclaimers are not in place, to determine as a preliminary matter whether the sales statute applies to the particular transaction; that is, is there a sale of a good? Where the object of the transaction is a sale of hardware, it is invariably easy to answer this question in the affirmative, for an item of equipment clearly falls within the *chattels personal* definition of goods in the sales statute. Where

---

103 The following discussion only scratches the surface of several important issues related to computer contracts. For an overview of a range of other issues, see George S. Takach, *Contracting for Computers*, 2d ed. (Toronto: McGraw-Hill Ryerson, 1992) [*Contracting*]; for an in-depth treatment of the case law, see chapter 2 of Barry Sookman, *Sookman Computer Law: Acquiring and Protecting Information Technology* (Toronto: Carswell, 1991) (looseleaf, updated) [*Sookman Computer Law*]; and for precedent clauses together with helpful commentary, see Esther C. Roditti, *Computer Contracts: Negotiating, Drafting* (New York: Matthew Bender, 1997) (looseleaf, updated).

104 For example, Ontario's *Sale of Goods Act*, R.S.O. 1990, c. S.1.

the deal involves a bundled system consisting of hardware and soft-ware, courts also generally do not have difficulty concluding the sales statute should apply, particularly where the software component can be characterized as being *incidental* to the hardware.[105] Moreover, there is even American authority for the proposition that the supply of existing software, without any hardware, should come within sales legislation — in the case of the United States, the *Uniform Commercial Code (UCC)*, even when the software was accompanied by customization services.[106] In these cases, courts are wrestling with the second dynam-ic of computer law, specifically the intangible nature of software. By focusing on the fact that software is distributed on a tangible media (for example, a disk or a tape), these courts understood pre-existing soft-ware to be a widely distributed product, and hence they concluded that the "goods aspect" dominates in the case of a software purchase, par-ticularly where services such as training are a small or incidental part of the transaction. The court in the *Advent* case stated that by bringing software sales under the purview of the *UCC*, it would be interpreting the *UCC* in light of commercial and technological developments.

By contrast, agreements solely for the provision of custom software development services have been held not to come within the purview of the *UCC*.[107] In the *Data Processing* case, there was no sale of hard-ware or even a sale of pre-existing software; rather, the supplier was retained to design, develop, and implement a computer system to meet the customer's specific needs.[108] The court, in concluding that the *UCC* did not apply, held that the essential purpose of the contract was to obtain skill, knowledge, and ability, and not a product, not unlike a client seeking legal advice or a patient obtaining medical treatment. The court acknowledged that a computer disk containing software did pass from the supplier to the customer, but this was merely a device utilized to deliver the results of the services. In the *Micro-Managers* case it was also found to be an important factor that the supplier was paid on a time and materials basis, again indicating a strong services

---

105 *Burroughs Business Machines Ltd.* v. *Feed-Rite Mills (1962) Ltd.* (1973), 42 D.L.R. (3d) 303 (Man. C.A.), appeal dismissed without reasons (1976), 64 D.L.R. (3d) 767 (S.C.C.) [*Burroughs*].

106 *Advent Systems Limited* v. *Unisys Corporation*, 925 F.2d 670 (3d Cir. 1991) [*Advent*]. See also *RRX Industries, Inc.* v. *Lab-Con, Inc.*, 772 F.2d 543 (9th Cir. 1985).

107 *Data Processing Services, Inc.* v. *L.H. Smith Oil Corporation*, 492 N.E.2d 314 (9 Ind. App. 1986) [*Data Processing*]; *Micro-Managers, Inc.* v. *Gregory*, 434 N.W.2d 97 (Wis. App. 1988) [*Micro-Managers*].

108 *Data Processing*, above note 107.

rather than product orientation.[109] It should be noted, however, that in the *Data Processing* case, in the absence of the *UCC* substantive rules applying, the court found the supplier liable under common law negligence for having provided substandard services. Similarly, in a controversial United Kingdom case, an appeal court judge concluded that even if the U.K. sales law did not apply to a software development project, an implied warranty that the software is capable of achieving its intended purpose would nevertheless be applicable under a negligence rule governing computer programming services.[110]

If the sales legislation applies, then, in the absence of an agreement to the contrary, several implied warranties and conditions will apply to the particular transaction.[111] One of them provides that if the seller is a merchant, and the goods are bought from a description given by the seller who deals in goods meeting the description, the supplier's products must be of a "merchantable quality," that is, suitable for their intended purposes. The second important implied warranty and condition provides that where a purchaser relies on the skill and knowledge of the seller, the seller has specific knowledge of the purpose to which the goods will be put at the purchaser's premises, and where the purchaser relies on the skill of the seller, then the supplier must deliver goods that are fit for their purpose. To be in effect, this implied warranty and condition requires that the supplier be informed of the specific requirements of the user. Thus, in one case, a supplier of a computer system was held not to be liable for failure of the system to perform a key function as the supplier was not apprised of the need for such a function by the user; the supplier was not told that the inventory management aspect of the business included a manufacturing component, something the supplier's system did not support.[112] In another case, a supplier was not found liable under the fitness for purpose warranty and condition when its optical disk drive device did not work properly with the other computer equipment of the buyer, because the buyer failed to communicate to the supplier what it needed the device for, and

---

109 *Micro-Managers*, above note 107.
110 *St. Albans City and District Council* v. *International Computers Ltd.*, [1997] FSR 251 (C.A.).
111 The *UCC* only has implied warranties, while Canadian sales statutes have implied warranties and conditions: see *Gregorio*, above note 58. For a case that discusses the distinction between implied warranties and implied conditions, see *Michael's Pizzeria Ltd.* v. *LP Computer Solutions Inc. et al.* (1996), 433 A.P.R. 294 (P.E.I. S.C.).
112 *Saskatoon Gold Brokers Inc.* v. *Datatec Computer Systems Ltd.* (1986), 55 Sask. R. 241 (Q.B.).

there was also a question whether the defect was the fault of the supplier's device.[113] By contrast, where the customer makes known to the supplier why the customer needs a particular software product, and the supplier's employee indicates that the software can meet this specific need, then the implied warranty and condition as to fitness for purpose will apply.[114] Indeed, this implied warranty and condition can apply even where the user has employees knowledgeable in computer matters, so long as there is reliance on the expertise of the supplier.[115]

Sales statutes also address the question when a buyer of goods is deemed to have accepted the goods, in the absence of a written agreement. This is important because once an item is accepted, the user is generally limited to money damages for any subsequent malfunctions in the item, where prior to acceptance the remedy of rescinding the sale agreement and receiving a full refund is still available. Sales statutes generally provide that acceptance can occur in one of three ways: the buyer indicates to the seller it has accepted the goods; the buyer does anything in relation to the goods inconsistent with the ownership of the seller; or after a reasonable time, the buyer retains the goods without indicating to the seller that they have been rejected. The application of these provisions to sophisticated computer systems can often be difficult. In one case, a court concluded a computer system was still not accepted after seven months.[116] In another case, a court found that the system was not accepted even fourteen months after its delivery to the

---

113 *Classified Directory Publishers Inc.* v. *Image Management Technologies Inc.*, [1995] O.J. No. 36 (Gen. Div.). In this case, the supplier's device provided secondary online storage, whereas the user needed primary online storage. The supplier, however, was not responsible for this mismatch because the court concluded at para. 31: "The plaintiff chose the defendant's equipment without fully informing the defendant of the purpose to which it would be put and without sufficient expertise on its own part and without relying upon consultants which were available to it for that purpose. It has not been established that the failure of the system can be ascribed to the equipment supplied by the defendant. There is no evidence that it would be impossible to determine the reason for such a failure. The essential elements needed to invoke the warranty protection under section 15 have therefore not been established."

114 *Western Engineering Service Ltd.* v. *Canada Malting Co.*, [1994] O.J. No. 2026 (Gen. Div.). See also *Caul (W.J.) Funeral Home Ltd.* v. *Pearce* (1997), 475 A.P.R. 252 (Nfld. S.C.).

115 *Public Utilities Commission (Waterloo)* v. *Burroughs Businesss Machines Ltd.* (1974), 6 O.R. (2d) 257 (C.A.) [*Waterloo*]. In this case the supplier was liable because the employees of the customer, although generally knowledgeable about computers, did not have specific knowledge concerning the supplier's system.

116 *Burroughs*, above note 105.

buyer because it never worked properly, the computer system consist-ed of very complicated equipment and components, the supplier knew of the problems (and was working to correct them), and the customer needed to keep the supplier's poorly functioning system until it acquired a new one in order to mitigate its damages; hence, the buyer could still reject the system.[117] In a U.S. case, however, a buyer was held to be unable to argue the same position where it used the computer for nineteen months without intimating any problems to the seller.[118]

2) Limitations on Liability

Sales statutes are, for the most part, approximately one hundred years old. The original U.K. *Sale of Goods Act*, on which the Canadian com-mon law provinces sales statutes are modelled, was intended to codify the law of sales related to the products pouring out of England's new industrial era factories of the mid to late 1800s. It is not surprising, therefore, that in many respects the sales statutes are not well suited to the nuances involved in computer systems.[119] In effect, these are statutes covering the sale of tangible goods, and therefore do not expressly address issues related to the licensing of intangible software and infor-mation-based products. As a result, most suppliers of computing resources, in their contracts with customers, expressly disclaim all implied warranties and conditions. Also, because computers and soft-ware can be put to so many uses by purchasers, some entailing a high amount of risk — such as when a personal computer operates a large factory's automated processes — suppliers are also keen to provide a general limitation of their liability in the contract with the user, typical-ly by capping their responsibility for direct damages at a certain dollar

---

117 *Waterloo*, above note 115.

118 *Softa Group, Inc. v. Scarsdale Development*, 5 Computer Cases (CCH) ¶47,055 at 66,304 (Ill. Appl. 1993).

119 It is for this reason that in the United States there has been an effort to codify a "new" sales law in respect of software that addressed such issues as applicability to mass market software; confirming enforceability of shrinkwrap licences; abili-ty to assign and relocate licensed software; and software-related warranties and disclaimers on questions such as infringement, performance, protection against viruses, and disabling routines: see Raymond T. Nimmer, "Article 2B [of the UCC] Meeting the Information Age," in *The Law of Computer Technology: Rights, Licenses, Liabilities* (Boston, MA: Warren, Gorham & Lamont, 1992) (looseleaf, updated), at Appendix SC-3 to 1996 Cumulative Supplement No. 3. One result of this has been the *Uniform Computer Information Transactions Act*, which to date has been adopted as law in several states.

amount and excluding all other damages, especially lost profits or other consequential damages.[120] Even without such contractual-based limitations on liability, courts in a wide variety of situations have expressed an unwillingness to impose unlimited liability on the providers of information-related products and services, particularly for what courts call "pure economic loss."[121] In an early Canadian telegraph case, *Kinghorne* v. *The Montreal Telegraph Company*, the court noted that in some cases telegraph companies limit their liability through contract.[122] In the *Kinghorne* case, the telegraph company did not utilize this device, and still the court was willing to severely curtail its exposure, as the court was reluctant to visit the company with "ruinous damages" that might flow to a customer for a message not being delivered even though the telegraph company stood to gain such little revenue from sending the one message. The court stated that if a particular message is so important, the customer must bring that fact expressly to the attention of the telegraph company. In a more recent American case, a similar sentiment was expressed when the court failed to hold an online information service provider strictly liable for the accuracy of the content of its messages, as this "would open the doors 'to a liability in an indeterminate amount for an indeterminate time to an indeterminate class,'" to cite a phrase used in one of the judgments referred to in this case.[123]

---

120   For a thoughtful discussion of the distinction between direct and consequential damages in a computer contract context, see *Applied Data Processing, Inc.* v. *Burroughs Corporation*, 394 F.Supp. 504 (D. Conn. 1975).

121   In *Ontario (A.G.)* v. *Fatehi* (1984), 15 D.L.R. (4th) 132 (S.C.C.), the Supreme Court of Canada summarized "pure economic loss" as a diminution of worth incurred without any physical injury to any asset of the plaintiff.

122   (1859), 18 U.C.Q.B.R. 60 [*Kinghorne*]. See also the American case *Primrose* v. *Western Union Telegraph Company*, 154 U.S. 1 (1894), where the court confirmed that given the peculiar risks of sending messages by telegraph, it was reasonable for a telegraph operator, in its standard terms and conditions, to limit its liability for ordinary negligence to the amount of fees paid where the customer did not pay for repetition of the message or for insurance. In effect, this contractual construct allowed the customer to send the message (for 1.5 times the regular price) in a manner that would have the successful and accurate delivery at the company's risk (in this case, if negligence occurred with a repeated message, the company's liability was 50 times the sum paid for the service), or the customer could send it at the regular price at the customer's own risk.

123   *Daniel* v. *Dow Jones & Company Inc.*, 520 N.Y.S.2d 334 at 338 (N.Y. City Civ. Ct. 1987). This quote is originally found in *Ultramares Corporation* v. *Touche*, 174 N.E. 441 at 444 (N.Y. 1931). In a similar vein, U.S. courts have held that a rock group is not responsible for a boy's suicide (*McCollum* v. *Columbia Broadcasting Systems Inc.*, 202 Cal. App.3d 989 (2nd Dist. 1988)); a computer game maker is

A recent decision from British Columbia illustrates the judicial reluctance to award economic damages, in this case specifically in the context of a computer system. In *Seaboard Life Insurance Co. v. Babich*, the defendant hit a hydro pole with his truck causing minimal damage to the pole — it cost only $200 to fix — but dislodging some step-down conductors that caused some wires to fall, with the result that power was disrupted for ninety minutes for about 1500 customers of B.C. Hydro.[124] As a result, the plaintiff insurance company's computers were inoperable for about five hours, causing some loss of data. The plaintiff sued the defendant for the downtime of its employees and their loss of productivity. In light of those cases that have awarded damages for economic loss only where there is also some property damage, the plaintiff argued that its data (that was lost) should be characterized as property. The court disagreed and concluded that

> There may be contexts in which computer data will be held, in law, to constitute property. But for the purposes of distinguishing between pure economic loss and damage to property in the law of damages, I consider that it would simply be productive of confusion to treat the loss of the data as anything other than economic loss. In this case, the loss was purely economic. Some employees had to stand by until the computers were operational. Others had to spend some time checking them and "reinputting" data. All, essentially, a matter of increasing the cost of doing business.[125]

This finding is reminiscent of the decision of the Supreme Court of Canada in *R. v. Stewart*, where the court held that confidential information cannot constitute property for purposes of the *Criminal Code's* theft or fraud provisions.[126] The case also illustrates, once again, the second dynamic of computer law — namely, the elusive nature of infor-

---

not responsible for a teenager's suicide (*Watters v. TSR Inc.*, 904 F.2d 378 (6th Cir. 1990)); a video-game maker is not responsible for the Columbine High School shootings (*Sanders v. Acclaim Entertainment, Inc.*, 188 F.Supp. 2d 1264 (D. Colo. 2002)), and the distributor of a movie (and related video game and Web site) is not responsible for "copycat" acts of violence committed by a four-teen-year-old boy (*James v. Meow Media, Inc.*, 90 F.Supp. 2d 798 (W.D. Ky., 2000)). In the latter case the court concluded, among other reasons, that the defendant could not be expected to know the mental state of every potential consumer of its products.

124 [1995] 10 W.W.R. 756 (B.C.S.C.) [*Babich*].

125 *Ibid.*, at 760.

126 (1988), 41 C.C.C. (3d) 481 (S.C.C.). This case is discussed in chapter 3, section B.1, "Theft."

mation — and demonstrates, at a practical level, how important it is for users of computers to have adequate back-up and disaster recovery plans in place, including uninterruptible power supply systems, to help deal with a power outage or some other unforeseeable event that knocks out their computer systems.

That is not to say, however, that courts do not award damages in computer-related cases, because of course they do.[127] And because they do, suppliers try to limit their exposure contractually, as a government corporate name search agency did when its computers failed to perform adequately; the trial judge found the agency liable, but the appeal court reversed on the grounds that the arrangements under which the agency provided the service disclaimed the agency's responsibility.[128] Indeed, courts will generally enforce these provisions in agreements between businesses, provided they are set out in clear and unambiguous language.[129] Moreover, such limit of liability clauses can also be used to deflect negligence claims that might otherwise be brought against the supplier by the user, given that tort and contract claims can be sustained simultaneously by the same facts.[130] These limitation of liability clauses in computer contracts can also be meaningful for users, and thus increasingly they are being made mutual in software development

---

127 For a useful list of the types of damages that courts in Canada and elsewhere have awarded in computer-related litigation, see chapter 2, section 19(c) of Sookman, *Sookman Computer Law*, above note 103. Companies often agree to large settlements as well. See *Shaw v. Toshiba America Information Systems, Inc.*, 91 F.Supp. 2d 942 (E.D. Tex. 2000), wherein Toshiba agreed to settle a class action claim alleging defects in Toshiba's laptop computers, for $2.1 billion, and legal fees of $147.5 million.

128 *R. v. 87118 Canada Ltd.* (1981), 56 C.P.R. (2d) 209 (F.C.A.).

129 *Hunter Engineering Co. v. Syncrude Canada Ltd.* (1989), 57 D.L.R. (4th) 321 (S.C.C.) [*Hunter*]; *Group West Systems Ltd. v. Werner's Refrigeration Co. Ltd.* (1988), 85 A.R. 82 (Q.B.) [*Group West Systems*]; but note that under Article 1474 of Quebec's *Civil Code*, one cannot limit liability with respect to gross default. For a recent American decision that upheld a limitation of liability clause in a software shrinkwrap licence, even though the user likely did not read it, see *Timberline Software*, above note 55.

130 *BG Checo International Ltd. v. British Columbia Hydro & Power Authority*, [1993] 2 W.W.R. 321 (S.C.C.); *Kinghorne*, above note 122; and *Queen v. Cognos Inc.* (1993), 99 D.L.R. (4th) 626 (S.C.C.). Another mechanism for limiting liability is for the contract to provide for an abridged limitations period. For example, in *Wilson Pharmacy, Inc. v. General Computer Corp.*, 2000 Tenn. App. Lexis 648 (Ct. App. Tenn. 2000), the court upheld a provision requiring claims to be brought within one year. Some jurisdictions, however, prohibit such contracting-out of statutory limitation periods.

and other such agreements.[131] If there is any ambiguity in the wording of the limitation or disclaimer, or if the court concludes that the supplier is in fundamental breach of its obligations under the contract, then courts may decline to enforce the exclusionary clauses.[132] As well, suppliers who merely disclaim "implied warranties," typically being affiliates of U.S. entities that only have implied warranties to contend with under the American *UCC*, can be rudely surprised when a court in Canada finds them liable under the implied conditions of Canadian sales statutes, given that, in contrast to the *UCC*, the Canadian sales statutes have both implied warranties and conditions.[133] It should also be noted that the implied warranties and conditions in the sales statutes cannot be disclaimed in the context of consumer sales, such as where personal computers are purchased for home use.[134] Indeed, where computer and information-based products are being sold to "consumers" (i.e., non-businesses), the consumer protection laws of each province

---

131 See *Computrol, Inc.* v. *Newtrend, L.P.*, 203 F.3d 1064 (8th Cir. 2000) [*Computrol*], where such a clause allowed the appellate court to reduce a jury award against the user of $2,663,000 to $469,206, as a result of the user's wrongful termination of a software development project.

132 *Listo Products Ltd.* v. *Phillips Electronics Ltd.*, [1983] B.C.J. No. 432 (S.C.) (QL) [*Listo*]; *Hunter*, above note 129. For similar recent results outside of the computer industry, see *Solway* v. *Davis Moving & Storage Inc.* (2001), 57 O.R. (3d) 205, [2001] O.J. No. 5049 (Sup. Ct.), varied, [2002] O.J. No. 4760 (C.A) (limitation of liability clause in storage agreement not upheld as it would be unreasonable or unconscionable to do so); and *Gore Motors Ltd.* v. *National Leasing Group Inc.*, [2000] O.J. 2351 (Ont. Sup. Ct.) (limitation of liability in equipment lease not upheld where customer pressured to sign acceptance certificate even before the equipment was delivered). In a number of cases, however, courts have upheld limit of liability provisions in contracts even where there has been a fundamental breach: see *Group West Systems*, above note 129, and *Fraser Jewellers (1982) Ltd.* v. *Dominion Electric Protection Co.* (1997), 34 O.R. (3d) 1 (C.A.).

133 See, for example, *Gregorio*, above note 58 at 207, where the court stated: "The express terms of the Peterbilt [truck maker] Warranty do not exclude the statutory conditions of fitness for a purpose and merchantable quality in s. 15. There is a difference between a breach of warranty and a breach of condition. Words that exclude only implied warranties do not also exclude implied conditions. Although a vendor may exclude the implied conditions contained in the *Sale of Goods Act*, he must use explicit language to do so."

134 See, for example, Ontario's *Consumer Protection Act*, R.S.O. 1990, c. C.31, s. 34. As well, under Article 1474 of Quebec's *Civil Code*, one cannot contract out of liability for gross default in a contract with a consumer or a business. Similarly, in many jurisdictions, parties cannot contractually circumscribe their gross negligence. See also chapter 6, section A.3(d), "Unconscionable Terms," in the context of the enforceability of especially onerous terms, particularly in a consumer context.

in which sales are made need to be reviewed as they often contain specific rules regarding consumer warranties and other matters.

3) Express Warranties

Given the practice of suppliers in the computer industry to disclaim implied warranties and conditions, and given the difficulty of applying these warranties and conditions to computer-related transactions even if they were not disclaimed, many users of computing resources provide for express warranties in their contracts with suppliers. These are often coupled with an acceptance test provision, as well as express remedies in favour of the user if these obligations are not met by the supplier. Provisions such as these can be beneficial to both the purchaser and supplier if they are even-handed and the performance benchmarks in them are based on reasonable, objective criteria.[135] The Listo case illustrates well the unfortunate fate that can befall parties that do not provide for express warranties, acceptance tests, and remedies in a contract for the supply of computer equipment.[136] In this case, the supplier and its subcontractor bungled along for five years trying to install a computer system when a court finally put an end to the miserable tale by awarding judgment for fundamental breach against the supplier. Of course, one cannot really talk of a "winner" of such a lawsuit, since the user had by this point suffered excruciatingly, largely because it did not have the contractual means to bring to a speedy end a project that clearly was in dire straits soon after it began. By contrast, in the *Hawaiian Telephones* case the user had a series of express remedies that it brought

---

135 In *USM Corporation v. First State Insurance Company*, 652 N.E.2d 613 (Mass. Sup. Ct. 1995) [*USM Corporation*], for example, a computer consultant warranted that the computer system would be free of defects in design and in substantial accordance with certain functional specifications. For a discussion of reasonable, win-win computer contract clauses generally, see Takach, *Contracting*, above note 103. Also, it is important in these computer contracts to stipulate clearly whether the work to be done by the supplier will be on an "all-in, fixed price" basis, or whether the "time and materials" methodology is intended to apply: based on an ambiguous computer system development contract, the court in *Continental Commercial Systems Corp. v. Minerva Technology Inc.*, [1998] B.C.J. No. 143 (B.C.S.C.), concluded in favour of the supplier, finding a time and materials agreement.

136 *Listo*, above note 132. For more recent examples of the multiple problems that can scuttle a relationship between a software developer/system integrator and a client, see *Lalese Enterprises Inc. v. Arete Technologies Inc.* (1994), 59 C.P.R. (3d) 438 (B.C.S.C.); and *Bridgesoft Systems Corp. v. British Columbia* (2000), 74 B.C.L.R. (3d) 212 (B.C.C.A.).

to bear quickly upon non-performance by the supplier, thereby making the best of a bad situation.[137] Users must be very careful, however, in exercising remedies that purport to terminate contracts. In a number of cases, courts have recognized that computer technology is usually sophisticated, and complicated, and therefore suppliers should be afforded a reasonable period of time to fix bugs within the system. Thus, in the *Gerber Scientific* case, the trial court stated:

> In contracts for computer systems, especially complex ones, it is reasonable to contemplate start-up problems. The defendant's position presumes that the vendors installed a perfectly functioning system. This presumption does not reflect reality. Problems in a newly installed system are inevitable.[138]

Similarly, even when a user has the right to terminate a contract, it must exercise the provision with great care and with a clear, unambiguous notice, or else a court may find in favour of the supplier on the basis that the user terminated the agreement prematurely.[139]

F. TECHNOLOGY LICENCES UPON BANKRUPTCY

Several questions arise when a licensee, or especially a licensor, of technology goes bankrupt. These questions are particularly important because of the nature of software licences. As noted in chapter 1, section C.4, "Dependency on Computers," virtually all businesses, governments, and other organizations have become reliant on licensed software. It could be extremely disruptive if, upon a bankruptcy of the licensors of such software, the users were to lose the right of continued use of the software. Yet such a possibility cannot be dismissed — the question has not yet been decided in Canada. Another view, however, holds that Canadian bankruptcy law should not be interpreted to afford such a result. By contrast, the *Bankruptcy and Insolvency Act* (*BIA*

---

137 *Hawaiian Telephone Co. v. Microform Data Systems, Inc.*, 829 F.2d 919 (9th Cir. 1987).

138 *Gerber Scientific Instrument Co. v. Bell-Northern Research Ltd.* (1991), 5 B.L.R. (2d) 20 at 29 (Ont. Gen. Div.) [*Gerber Scientific*], rev'd (1994), 17 B.L.R. (2d) 21 (Ont. C.A.).

139 *M.L. Baxter Equipment Ltd. v. Geac Canada Ltd.* (1982), 133 D.L.R. (3d) 372 (Ont. H.C.J.). For a more recent American case with the same lesson, see *Computrol*, above note 131.

Act) makes quite clear the rights of technology licensors when their licensees file a proposal under the *BIA Act*.[140]

1) Bankruptcy of Licensor

The uncertainty in Canadian bankruptcy law as to the ability of a licensee of technology to continue to use it upon a bankruptcy of the licensor arises, ironically, because of subsection 365(a) of the U.S. bankruptcy code.[141] This permits a trustee who is vested with the property of the debtor upon a bankruptcy to reject "executory contracts," contracts that contain ongoing obligations of the licensor. This ability on the part of a trustee in the United States to reject executory contracts led a court to conclude in the *Lubrizol* case that the trustee for a bankrupt licensor of metal coating process technology could disclaim all the debtor's non-exclusive licences in order to improve the terms of sale of the technology to another company from the bankrupt licensor.[142] The result in *Lubrizol* was that the licensee lost its rights to work the technology. The harsh result of the *Lubrizol* decision led to the addition of paragraph 365(1)(n) to the U.S. *Bankruptcy Act*, which provides that if a trustee disclaims an intellectual property licence, the user may nevertheless affirm the licence, in which case the user can continue to use it in return for giving up the right to sue for any damages from the bankrupt estate.[143] Some observers in Canada of the Lubrizol case have commented that a trustee in bankruptcy in Canada could come to the same result as in that U.S. case, with an extremely unfortunate result given that no equivalent to paragraph 365(1)(n) of the U.S. statute exists in the Canadian one. Thus, some users insist that in source code escrow agreements (an arrangement whereby a neutral party, such as a trust company, holds the source code version of a supplier's product in order to make it available to a user upon a specified default of the supplier, but until such release keeping the important confidential information out of the hands of users), the supplier sell

---

140   *Bankruptcy and Insolvency Act*, R.S.C. 1985, c. B-3, as amended. Prior to 1992, this statute was the *Bankruptcy Act*.

141   *Bankruptcy Reform Act of 1978*, 11 U.S.C.A. 101.

142   *Lubrizol Enterprises, Inc. v. Richmond Metal Finishers, Inc.*, 756 F.2d 1043 (4th Cir. 1985) [*Lubrizol*].

143   In an early case involving para. 365(1)(n) of the U.S. *Bankruptcy Act* and Ontario Hydro, the software licensee, the court held that the extent of the claims are to be determined by U.S. bankruptcy law and not Ontario law (the law provided for in the relevant software licence agreement): *Re EI International, Debtor*, 123 B.R. 64 (Bankr. D. Idaho 1991).

title in a copy of the source code to the trustee to try to get it out of the estate of the supplier upon any bankruptcy. This is a very dangerous practice for the supplier given that any related restrictions on the trustee may not be enforceable; see section C.1, "Why Software and Content Are Licensed," for an explanation why a software company would not want to sell title to a copy of its software. It is open to question, however, whether the concern generated in Canada over the *Lubrizol* case is entirely warranted, for a number of reasons.

First, most software licences are not all that executory in nature. In *Lubrizol* the main factor that made it executory from the licensor's perspective was that, involving a licence for a metal coating product (and not a software licence), the licensor had undertaken a duty to inform the licensee if it granted a third party better licence terms, and then such more favourable terms had to be granted to the original licensee. These sorts of provisions are quite rare in commercial software arrangements involving off-the-shelf products. Similarly, the licensee's primary ongoing activity in *Lubrizol* was to pay the licensor royalties; again, most software licences involve a single, lump sum payment, so this is yet another factor by which to distinguish *Lubrizol*. Most importantly, the court in *Lubrizol* focused on the specific wording in the U.S. bankruptcy statute to permit the disclaimer by the bankruptcy trustee. As noted below, however, the *BIA Act* does not contain such a general provision. Thus, a court in Canada, if faced with the question whether a trustee in bankruptcy can disclaim the software licences granted prior to the bankruptcy of a Canadian software company, may not follow the *Lubrizol* case and instead might follow the decision in the *Erin Features* case.[144]

In *Erin Features*, a trustee in bankruptcy brought a motion to disclaim an agreement in which the debtor had previously granted exclusive marketing rights in a film to a distributor. The court refused to grant the motion, concluding that the "property rights" conveyed to

---

144 *Re Erin Features #1 Ltd.* (1991), 8 C.B.R. (3d) 205 (B.C.S.C.) [*Erin Features*]. But a court might come to the same result as in *Lubrizol*, particularly after the decision in *T. Eaton Co. (Re)* (1999), 14 C.B.R. (4th) 288, [1999] O.J. No. 4216 (Sup. Ct.) , where the court refused to grant a licensee specific performance in respect of a trade-mark licence that the licensor repudiated in the proceedings. Accordingly, what would be useful in this area is a legislative solution in Canada, perhaps along the lines of the U.S. s. 365(1)(n) of the U.S. bankruptcy as noted above, which seems to working fairly well. Until such law reform comes to pass, licensees of technology might consider the use of various structures and mechanisms, such as trusts and security interests, in an attempt to bolster their licence rights, but these measures usually entail significant transactions costs that effectively limit their use to situations involving material amounts of money or risk.

the distributor cannot subsequently be disturbed by the trustee. Although the court in this case reached the right conclusion, the reasoning in the case may be open to some criticism given that it is not clear that the grant of even exclusive marketing rights conveys a property interest. Nonetheless, there are several other reasons why the same result should occur again if similar facts present themselves. First, as opposed to the U.S. and U.K.[145] bankruptcy statutes, which contain express provisions allowing trustees to disclaim executory contracts, no similar general right exists in the BIA Act.[146] Second, paragraph 30(1)(k) of the BIA Act does address when a trustee can disclaim contracts, namely, allowing a bankrupt lessee to disclaim real property leases or similar contracts. Accordingly, in Canada a correct conceptual analysis of the rights of trustees in respect of technology licences would be that, except as otherwise provided by statute, a trustee receives the same quality of title in the debtor's estate as was enjoyed by the debtor. A trustee in bankruptcy for a software company, for example, should acquire the intellectual property rights in the software subject to the licences granted prior to the bankruptcy. Incidentally, this produces an extremely just result, as the same situation would have come to pass had the assets of the software company been sold while the company was still solvent.

2) Bankruptcy of Licensee

Where a trustee for a bankrupt technology company may be interested in terminating the previous licences granted by the company, the trustee for a bankrupt company that is the licensee of various technologies has just the opposite objective. It wants to ensure that the tenure that the bankrupt estate has in the technology, such as a software licence, continues. In this regard, where the insolvent licensee wishes to make a proposal under the BIA Act, which then allows the company to attempt to restructure its affairs and avoid bankruptcy, section 65.1 of the BIA Act makes it clear that licences for intellectual

---

145 Insolvency Act 1986 (U.K.), 1986, c. 45, s. 315.
146 For example, the Canadian case Stead Lumber Company Limited v. Lewis (1957), 37 C.B.R. 24 (Nfld. S.C.), cites Halsbury's Laws of England for authority that a trustee in bankruptcy can disclaim certain executory contracts. These references to Halsbury's in turn rely on provisions in the United Kingdom's then prevailing bankruptcy statute. Thus, it is open to question how relevant this case is to an analysis of the current Canadian bankruptcy legislation.

property rights — such as software licences — cannot be terminated by the licensor for failure to make past payments. The licensor can, however, insist on being paid currently for future obligations, such as software maintenance services, and if there is a failure to pay these amounts then the licence can be terminated. By contrast, where there is a bankruptcy (and not just a proposal), many software licences will provide that the agreement is terminated by such an event.

A similar issue arises in respect of the ability of the trustee in bankruptcy to deal with the licence in a manner that was not available to the pre-bankrupt debtor. For example, trustees in bankruptcy often purport to sell or assign software or other intellectual properties that are licensed to the bankrupt on a non-assignable basis. In effect, however, a trustee should only acquire such rights as the debtor itself had in the licensed material. Thus, a licensor should be able to stop a trustee from transferring the intellectual property to a third party where the debtor did not have this right in the first place. Indeed, this point is buttressed by the discussion in section C.1, "Why Software and Content Are Licensed," that explained that a software licence generally does not convey to the licensee (and hence does not convey to the trustee in bankruptcy upon the licensee's bankruptcy) a property interest; rather, the licence is merely a contractual-based permission to do something that otherwise would not be permitted. Thus, in the absence of a specific clause in the licence agreement to the contrary, the trustee in bankruptcy for the licensee's estate should not be able to deal with the software for purposes of transferring it.

There may be an exception to this rule if the software licence is silent on assignment, in which case, depending on all the facts of the situation, it may be argued that it is an implied term of the contract that it be able to be assigned, at least to a purchaser of the assets of the original licensee's business. Of course, this raises the point that licensees, when negotiating the terms of their licence agreements, should be careful to ensure that the software can be assigned at least to an entity that purchases all or substantially all of the assets of the licensee, or at least intends to carry on the licensee's business, as discussed.[147] Where a licensee fails to achieve this flexibility, however, the bankruptcy law should not be interpreted to afford such rights to trustees in bankruptcy.

---

147 See section C.1, "Why Software and Content Are Licensed," earlier in this chapter.

G. TAX ISSUES

The marketing, licensing, and sale of computer software and other information-based products present the tax system with numerous challenges. The intangible nature of these items (emblematic of the second dynamic of computer law) and the many ways they can be supplied to the end-user often make the exercise of applying tax laws to them akin to putting the proverbial square peg in the round hole. This is illustrated by the treatment afforded software under provincial retail sales tax legislation, as well as by the manner in which the withholding tax provisions of the *Income Tax Act* (*IT Act*) have been historically applied to software licence payments.[148] Applying tax laws in the Internet environment also raises some novel questions. In each of these areas the four dynamics of computer law are quite evident. There are, of course, other tax issues germane to the computer industry, such as the important research and experimental development tax credit regime in the *IT Act* and various other tax-related measures relevant to the funding of computer-based innovation activity, but these are beyond the purview of this short section.[149] The diversity of tax issues relevant to computers and networks can also be seen from a recent case that determined that a community-based "freenet" in Vancouver could qualify for tax purposes as a charity.[150]

1) Software and Sales Tax

Most provincial sales tax statutes provide for a tax to be levied on the sale of items of tangible personal property.[151] Two immediate issues are raised by such statutory language in the context of software and other information-based assets. First, is software sold? Second, is software tangible personal property? Both questions require negative answers, at least on a liberal reading of the statute. Thus, in the *Telecheque* case, a

---

148 *Income Tax Act*, R.S.C. 1985, c. 1 (5th Supp.), as amended.
149 Eligibility for research tax credits is also an important question in the United States. For example, in *Wicor, Inc.* v. *United States* 116 F.Supp. 2d 1028 (E.D. Wisc. 2000), the court agreed with the disallowance of the tax credit for, among other reasons, the fact that the taxpayer company retained a consultant to help on the project, and this consultant had completed previous projects that were not dissimilar, thereby decreasing the taxpayer's risk.
150 *Vancouver Regional FreeNet Assn.* v. *M.N.R.* (1996), 137 D.L.R. (4th) 206 (F.C.A.).
151 See, for example, Ontario's *Retail Sales Tax Act*, R.S.O. 1990, c. R.31.

court concluded that operating system software and application software licensed under software licences were not tangible personal property under British Columbia's *Social Service Tax Act*.[152] In this case the taxpayer, as part of a sale of its entire business, sold hardware, software, and data pursuant to a sale agreement that listed these items separately and allocated a portion of the total purchase price to each of them. The minister of finance, in a manner reminiscent of the sales legislation cases where installations of hardware and software were treated as a single "good" (see section E.1, "Implied Warranties and Conditions"), argued that the hardware, software, and data made up a single bundle of assets all subject to tax. The court disagreed, concluding that the data/information component represented "experience" and was separate from the computer (i.e., the business could have used this information in a manual mode), and similarly the hardware was separate from the software as the former would have value by having some other software operated on it (i.e., the software was not so intimately linked to the hardware as to constitute one object).

A provincial taxing authority wishing to realize tax revenues from the burgeoning information sector, however, may focus on the fact that most software transactions involve the supply of a physical diskette or CD-ROM on which the intangible software is resident. This would then allow them to tax the physical item, based on the value of the intangible information it contained. This was the result in the *Kia-Ora Video* case where the sale of videotapes was found to be the sale of tangible personal property, much like the sale of a book.[153] In this case the taxpayer, in reliance on the *Telecheque* decision, argued that the movie content portion of the videos was intangible and therefore should not be subject to tax. The court disagreed, holding that the price of the videos was not allocated among different components, as was the case in the *Telecheque* case. As well, the court found that each of the software and hardware in *Telecheque* could be used separately, whereas in the case of a videocassette, the physical tape and the content were one indivisible unit. In a subsequent case, the court struggled with the question whether customized application software provided to operate with telephone switching equipment should be subject to Newfoundland's retail sales tax.[154] In a confusing judgment, the court ultimately

---

152 *Continental Commercial Systems Corporation (Telecheque Canada) v. R.*, [1982] 5 W.W.R. 340 (B.C.C.A.) [*Telecheque*].
153 *Re Kia-Ora Video Ltd.* (1984), 56 B.C.L.R. 242 (Co. Ct.).
154 *Newfoundland Telephone Co. v. Newfoundland (A.G.)* (1992), 43 C.P.R. (3d) 40 (Nfld. S.C.).

found the software to be a taxable product, though the court seemed to concede that some software may be capable of being acquired in a non-taxable form.[155]

In an attempt to avoid questions such as these, Ontario amended its *Retail Sales Tax Act* to expressly cover computer programs under the definition of "tangible personal property."[156] This statutory amendment continues the previous policy of treating off-the-shelf software as a good and subject to provincial sales tax. Under the previous policy, pre-existing software subject to a written licence agreement was also exempt from tax, but this is no longer the case under the new law. As well, there is no exemption from the sales tax on the basis of how the software is delivered; thus, whether it is provided to the user on a CD-ROM, diskette, tape, or by electronic transmission, there is no impact on its tax status. Under the new statutory rules, however, custom software designed and developed to meet the specific requirements of the initial purchaser is non-taxable as it is considered a service rather than a good. Moreover, it is not necessary that the custom software be developed "from scratch." Rather, modifications to existing programs will also qualify for tax-exempt status, provided the price of the modification is greater than the price of the pre-written program.

---

155 In another interesting technology tax case from the Maritimes, in *Halifax (City) v. Canadian Imperial Bank of Commerce*, [1987] N.S.J. No. 104, 37 D.L.R. (4th) 187 (S.C.), the court concluded that computer equipment was not "assessable property" under Nova Scotia's *Assessment Act*, as the definition of this term was intended to capture machinery that made goods but not those that facilitated the provision of services, notwithstanding that the statute defined "assessable property" to include equipment used in "processing" (the court read this phrase together with "manufacturing").

156 *An Act to stimulate job growth, to reduce taxes and to implement other measures contained in the 1997 budget* (Bill 129), S.O. 1997, c. 10, subs. 30(3), received royal assent June 26, 1997. See also O. Reg. 383/99, which amends Regulation 1012 under the *Retail Sales Tax Act*, with respect to the taxation of computer software. The Ontario government has published a helpful guide to their approach to taxing software and related services: Ontario, Retail Sales Tax Branch, *650 RST Guide, Computer Programs and Related Services*, February 2001. The Ontario government proposed yet further clarifications to these rules in a *Consultation Draft of the Retail Sales Tax Amendment Act (Computer Programs)* and related Backgrounder as of July 19, 2002, as part of the government's 2002 Ontario budget, which would introduce new definitions of "taxable services," and would make clear, among other things, that the following would not be taxable: testing of a program (unless done in conjunction with a taxable service); training; advisory services; and data management (these materials are available at <gov.on.ca/FIN>).

The federal government makes a distinction between off-the-shelf software and all other software, for purposes of various collection procedures related to the federal Goods and Services Tax.[157] Under the current policy of the Canada Customs and Revenue Agency (CCRA) (formerly Revenue Canada), pre-packaged off-the-shelf software marketed with a shrinkwrap licence is treated as tangible personal property. If such software is delivered to the Canadian user from outside of Canada, the user acts as the importer for purposes of paying the GST at the time of importation. In contrast, all other software is treated as custom software, is categorized as the supply of intangible personal property, and is considered to be supplied to the user's premises in Canada regardless of how and where it was actually delivered, even if transmitted to the user electronically. Accessing an online computer by means of a modem is considered to be the supply of a service, not of personal property.

2) Software and Withholding Tax

The application to software-related payments of Canada's withholding tax provision in the *IT Act* represents a rich and varied tale driven by a number of seemingly unconnected factors, such as whether software is protected by copyright, whether there is a one-time payment or running royalties, the nature of the particular media on which the software is resident, and how the software is distributed in this country. The core withholding tax provision is set out in paragraph 212(1)(d)(i) of the *IT Act*, which requires persons in Canada to deduct and remit to Ottawa a 25 percent withholding tax on rental or royalty payments for the use or right to use in Canada any property, invention, trade-name, patent, or similar property right. In the *Saint John Shipbuilding* case in the mid-1970s, it was held that one-time, lump sum licence fee payments are not caught by these withholding tax provisions.[158] In this case the court found that a "rental" denoted a payment that was applicable for a limited term, and that "royalties" were payments calculated in reference to use or production from property or from profits; the court held that a lump sum payment for the right to use software for an indefinite term did not fall into either of these categories. It should be noted, however,

---

157 See CCRA, *GST Technical Information Bulletin B-037R*, "Imported Computer Software," 1 November 1994; and *Customs Memorandum D13-11-6*, "Determining Value for Duty of Computer Software," 2 July 1997.

158 R. v. *Saint John Shipbuilding & Dry Dock Co. Ltd.*, 80 D.T.C. 6272 (F.C.A.) [*Saint John Shipbuilding*].

that various bilateral tax treaties between Canada and other countries, which generally reduce the 25 percent withholding tax rate to 10 percent, have been amended over time to include language broader than that in the *IT Act* withholding tax provision; the result is that CCRA now takes the view that lump sum licence fees, of the kind exempted in the *Saint John Shipbuilding* case, are covered by the 10 percent withholding tax obligation. Also, however, several of these bilateral treaties, such as those with the United States and the Netherlands, have been amended to completely exclude from withholding tax payments in respect of software licence fees (but not, for example, in respect of fees paid for software customization services that are performed in Canada by the staff of an American software supplier).

An important exemption from the withholding tax is found in paragraph 212(1)(d)(vi) of the *IT Act*, which provides that the tax is not payable in respect of the reproduction of copyright. Originally intended to cover situations such as the printing and distribution in Canada of foreign-owned books, there have always been several nagging doubts about its applicability to software. First there was the question, in the 1970s and early 1980s, whether copyright covered software. This question was resolved definitively in 1988 with the insertion of computer program into the *Copyright Act* as a protectable work. On the other hand, the CCRA does not allow the exemption to end-users of software, taking the view that an end-user's act of copying is merely incidental to its use of the product. Rather, CCRA is of the view that "right to produce" means, essentially, putting the copies made by the distributor into the stream of commerce. The typical beneficiary of this provision is the distributor that is given a master copy of the product and the associated rights to produce copies in Canada for further distribution.

3) Tax and Internet-Related Activities

The Internet raises several taxation issues, primarily as a result of the second and fourth dynamics of computer law. The elusive nature of information causes the Internet to pose similar tax categorization questions as discussed earlier in this section, but even more tellingly because a number of information-based products — text, sound, music, graphics, all sorts of digital content — can now be transmitted over the Internet, and (from the perspective of CCRA) particularly problematically sourced from a non-Canadian Web site; in effect, the fourth dynamic of computer law (namely, the blurring of private/public) has conspired to make the second dynamic even more troublesome. A key question is whether the particular transaction should be characterized as a sale of a product, a licensing of an intangible, or the provision of a service. Things are simple to define in the physical world. For example, the sale of a copy of a newspaper is a sale of a good. Accessing the same newspaper content online raises the questions whether the essence of the transaction is still the sale of a product, or is it now more reasonable to refer to the essence of the deal being the licensing of intellectual property (particularly if search software accompanies the content), or is it the provision of a service (especially if the newspaper is but one database that can be accessed from the information service supplier's Web site). And these characterizations matter in some jurisdictions, such as in Europe, where value-added tax would apply, for example, to a purchase of a physical disk containing software, but would not if the non-European software company transmitted the software to the European customer over the Internet.[159] Most tax laws have origins in an environment of manufactured physical goods, and the digital ether created by the Internet (again, emblematic of all four dynamics of computer law) does not mesh well with such a tax regime.

In addition to the dephysicalization challenge posed by digitization, the tax laws have to cope with the fourth dynamic of computer law, the blurring of national/international. This issue predates the Internet, since the general increase in mobility and international commerce has seen capital, people, technology, and even production capacity move offshore for a number of years. This issue occurs, too, in distance selling through mail-order and catalogue operations, but is greatly augmented and exacerbated by the ability of the Internet to reach customers globally. In the United States, state tax authorities are quite concerned about tax erosion. The concern arises because of the decision in the *Quill* case, in which the U.S. Supreme Court concluded that a state cannot require an out-of-state mail-order house to collect tax on its sales made to residents of the state where the vendor did not have a physical outlet or sales representatives in the state.[160] Interestingly, the court below took the opposite view, partly on the basis that given the new computer technologies used by such vendors, it would no longer be a significant burden for them to collect and remit taxes for

---

159 Elaine Erickson and Michael Loten, "On-Line Transactions Blur Goods vs. Services Distinction for VAT Purposes," *High-Tech Industry*, November–December 1996.

160 *Quill Corp. v. North Dakota*, 504 U.S. 298 (1992).

multiple states; this was long one of the rationales for not making them subject to various tax regimes (i.e., it was simply too difficult to comply). The U.S. Supreme Court, however, did not agree. In coming to its conclusion, the court noted that the "due process" clause of the U.S. constitution no longer was an impediment to imposing sales tax on non-resident vendors, because clearly they had sufficient contacts with the state; this is consistent with the general trend in the non-tax Internet jurisdiction cases discussed in chapter 7, section B, "Jurisdiction." The court, however, held that the "substantial nexus" required by the U.S. constitution's commerce clause (that bans state actions that impede or place a burden on interstate commerce) required more than the communication and other links found sufficient for the purposes of the due process clause; that is, the court decided to maintain the "physical presence" rule, largely, it seems, because it provides a clear demarcation line that businesses can easily understand and then factor into their operational plans.

The amount of physical presence in a U.S. state required to meet the *Quill* test as articulated in subsequent decisions, however, does not have to be significant. For example, in one recent case, a company that sold computers by mail order to residents of New York State also sent employees into the state on occasion to provide installation, training, and error correction services.[161] These minimal contacts were sufficient for the court to uphold the state government's right to require the company to collect and remit New York State sales tax. What has state and other tax authorities particularly worried, however, is that in an Internet environment even these services can be provided online, thereby obviating the need for any physical presence in the state that wishes to levy sales tax. Similarly, in the context of income tax, many jurisdictions have adopted, in their bilateral tax treaties, the concept that they will not consider income to be sourced in their jurisdiction, and hence will not levy tax, unless the entity has a "permanent establishment" in

---

161 *Orvis Company, Inc.*, v. *Tax Appeals Tribunal of the State of New York*, 654 N.E.2d 954 (N.Y. 1995). See also *America Online, Inc.* v. *Johnson*, No. M2001-00927-COA-R3-CU (Tenn. C.A. 2002), where the court concluded that AOL may well have a sufficient nexus with the taxing jurisdiction; and *In the Matter of the Petition for Redetermination under the Sales and Use Tax Law of Borders Online, Inc.*, SC OHA 97-638364-56270 (Cal. Bd. of Equalization 2001), the presence requirement was satisfied because an affiliate of the online company had physical outlets in the taxing state which accepted returns of the products sold by the Internet retailer. See also *Geoffrey, Inc.* v. *South Carolina Tax Commission*, 437 S.E.2d 13 (Sup. Ct. S.C. 1993), where the mere licensing of intangibles (in this case trade-marks) was sufficient to find jurisdiction for tax purposes.

the jurisdiction. The permanent establishment concept, however, has always had a physical orientation, and its application in an Internet environment is made much more problematic. For instance, does a Canadian company have a permanent establishment in the United States when it contractually agrees to have a U.S. company load the Canadian company's valuable database onto a server at the U.S. company's premises, from which server the U.S. company will provide access to its subscribers around the world and pay the Canadian company a royalty in respect of such exploitation?[162]

These questions are causing a number of tax authorities to assess their legal regimes in light of the Internet.[163] There is even talk of a "bit tax," which would not tax products or services but rather the transmission of data itself. This suggestion has been criticized, but the very fact that it has been advanced indicates the degree to which certain taxing authorities consider the Internet to be a threat to critical tax revenues.[164] Indeed, in the early days of the commercial Internet the U.S. federal government, in a wide-ranging report titled *A Framework for Global Electronic Commerce*, proposed that no new taxes be imposed on

---

162 For a general discussion of these and related Internet tax conundrums, see James D. Cigler, Harry C. Burritt & Susan E. Stinnett, "Cyberspace: The Final Frontier for International Tax Concepts?" (1996) 7 J. of Int. Tax 340.

163 Richard G. Cohen & Paul Terry, "Online Taxation Issues Undergo Federal Scrutiny" (5 May 1997) The National Law Journal.

164 Organization for Economic Co-operation and Development, *Electronic Commerce: Opportunities and Challenges for Government* (The "Sacher Report") (Paris: OECD, 1997). This is a short but useful conspectus of a wide range of issues related to electronic commerce, including questions pertaining to commercial (including tax), security, infrastructure, social, and cultural questions. The OECD has prepared a number of reports and technical papers on international direct tax, consumption tax, and tax administration issues which the OECD believes represent a major step forward toward reaching an international consensus on the taxation treatment of e-commerce: they are available at <oecd.org>. As for concerns about the Internet eroding a government's tax base, see "The Mystery of the Vanishing Taxpayer," *The Economist*, 29 January 2000; and Heather Scoffield, "E-commerce Eluding Tax Net: Ottawa Finding it 'Difficult' to Collect," *The Globe and Mail* (4 April 2002). This latter article reports on concerns expressed in internal government documents (obtained through an access to information request) to the effect that (among other things) e-commerce conducted through encryption allows taxpayers to hide their activities, and no taxes are paid when music is illegally downloaded over the Internet. In the United States, various states are trying to stem the loss of taxes by cracking down on direct shipments of out-of-state wine: see *Swedenburg v. Kelly*, 232 F. Supp. 2d 135 (S.D.N.Y.)

Internet commerce.[165] As for existing taxes, this report noted that the U.S. government wants to ensure that any taxation of commerce over the Internet avoids double taxation, and that any taxation of Internet sales follows these principles:

- It should neither distort nor hinder commerce. No tax system should discriminate among types of commerce, nor should it create incentives that will change the nature or location of transactions.
- The system should be simple and transparent. It should be capable of capturing the overwhelming majority of appropriate revenues, be easy to implement, and minimize burdensome record keeping and costs for all parties.
- The system should be able to accommodate tax systems used by the United States and its international partners today.[166]

These sentiments are echoed in a lengthy Canadian report prepared by an advisory committee comprising industry representatives and tax professionals.[167] This *Advisory Report* emphasizes that neutrality as between offline and online commerce is an important objective for the tax system, and therefore is also critical of a "bit tax." The *Advisory Report* raises more than twenty-five other issues, and made over seventy recommendations.

Three of the most difficult questions, from an Internet perspective, raised by the *Advisory Report* relate to "residency," "carrying on business," and "permanent establishment." Residency is important because most countries tax the worldwide income of a resident. The Internet poses a particular challenge in respect of corporate taxpayers, to the extent that historically courts looked to the physical location of the

---

165 President William J. Clinton & Vice President Albert Gore, Jr., *A Framework for Global Electronic Commerce* (Washington, DC: White House, 1997). This paper, which contained the then U.S. Administration's views on a broad range of topics, such as financial (including customs, taxation, and electronic payment), legal (including a *UCC* for electronic commerce, intellectual property, privacy, and security), and market access (including telecommunications infrastructure and information technology, content, and technical standards) matters, is available at <ljx.com/internet/ecommframe.html>.

166 *Ibid.*, at 4–5.

167 *Electronic Commerce and Canada's Tax Administration: A Report to the Minister of National Revenue from the Minister's Advisory Committee on Electronic Commerce*, 30 April 1998 [*Advisory Report*]. Other countries have also been studying the impact of the Internet on taxation: New Zealand, Inland Revenue Department, *Guidelines to Taxation and the Internet*, 1998 <ird.govt.nz/resource/taxaint/index.htm>; and Australian Taxation Office, *Tax and the Internet: Second Report*, 1999 <ato.gov.on>.

members of the board of directors to determine a corporation's locale of "central management and control."[168] This determination is made more problematic in today's world of video and teleconferencing, where directors routinely participate in such meetings by remote electronic access.[169] As for carrying on business, this concept is important because many jurisdictions impose tax when a foreign corporation is found to be carrying on business in a jurisdiction (or, for example, they have to register in Canada for GST purposes). Thus the question becomes what quality of Internet activity would cause a company to be carrying on business in the relevant jurisdiction. And in a similar vein, as already noted above, the question of permanent establishment creates a similar challenge vis-à-vis the Internet, given that traditionally this concept keyed off a physical "fixed" place of business, such as an office in a building.

The government responded favourably to the *Advisory Report*,[170] and put in motion a further process that resulted in the publication in the summer of 2002 of a very helpful information bulletin that outlines how the CCRA will approach consumption tax questions involving e-commerce.[171] The *GST Information Bulletin*, on the issue of carrying on business (which is important to determine whether a non-resident has to register for GST purposes), replaces the "place of contract" test with a multifactored "place of operations" test that de-emphasizes the relevance of physical location. As for "permanent establishment," the *GST Information Bulletin* states that a Web site alone does not create a permanent establishment, nor would a Web-hosting arrangement (nor would an ISP's fixed, physical place of business constitute a permanent establishment for a user who merely used the ISP for hosting services;

---

168 *De Beers Consolidated Mines, Limited v. Howe*, [1906] 5 Tax. Cas. 198 (H.L.); and *Unit Construction Co., Ltd. v. Bullock*, [1960] AC 251 (H.L.). A CCRA interpretation bulletin cites both of these cases for the proposition that usually management and control exist where the board meets and holds its meetings, but if management and control are actually exercised by some other party (such as the directors of its parent company or its principal shareholder, who are resident in another country, then the company will be resident in that other country: Canada Customs and Revenue Agency, *IT391R Status of Corporations* (14 September 1992).

169 See chapter 4, section E.2, "Corporate Meetings," for a discussion of cases and statutory amendments that facilitate the holding of directors meeting by electronic means.

170 *A Response by the Minister of National Revenue to his Advisory Committee's Report on Electronic Commerce* (29 September 1998).

171 CCRA, *GST/HST And Electronic Commerce*, July 2002 [*GST Information Bulletin*].

of course, this physical facility would be a permanent establishment for the ISP itself). The bulletin also gives guidance as to when an electronic supply of digital material (which the bulletin concludes is not a supply of goods) is either a supply of intangible personal property or a service; the CCRA document helpfully provides twenty-eight examples that apply a "factor" approach. In effect, the *GST Information Bulletin* provides helpful guidance to companies attempting to navigate the previously uncharted waters of e-commerce taxation.

H. OTHER ISSUES

The foregoing discussion in this chapter has covered a broad range of commercial issues. Two more are worth noting — international trade law and labour law. Neither topic is primarily related to computing and network technologies. Nonetheless, the important economic role of computer technology and the large international market for buying and selling these products (about 10 percent of all international trade) make several legal issues relevant. In labour law, the significant impact of computing technologies in the workplace requires a brief survey of legal questions. And in both these areas several of the four dynamics of computer law are busily at work.

1) International Trade

a) Customs Classifications
One international trade issue that illustrates the first dynamic of computer law involves the customs classification process, whereby, new products have to be slotted into existing tariff classifications in order to determine the rate of duty to be paid upon the importation into Canada of the particular product. As with all categorization exercises involving the computer industry, the hazard here is that often the authorities are being asked to fit square pegs into round holes. In one case, computerized branch exchanges (CBX) were imported, which are small digital telephone switches that also contain a computerized call tracking function so that businesses and organizations that install these systems in their offices can keep track of calling patterns by employees.[172] The Tariff Board, the agency that heard appeals from the decisions of the Department of National Revenue, determined that the CBX product

---

172 *IBM Canada Ltd.* v. *Deputy M.N.R., Customs and Excise*, [1992] 1 F.C. 663 (C.A.).

should come under the category of electric telephone apparatus because its primary function was telecommunications, and its data processing capability was only an ancillary feature. The Federal Court of Appeal overturned this decision and concluded instead that the proper tariff category was electronic data processing machines. The court reasoned that the word *telephone* related only to the transmission of sound and voices, whereas the CBX product was used to transmit data as well, and also that there was a distinction between *electronic* and *electric* that, although not apparent from the decision, favoured treating the CBX product as electronic rather than electric.[173] The decision of the court is less than satisfying, but the importer appreciated it because the tariff rate on data processing equipment (about 3.9 percent) at the time was lower than for telephone equipment (17.5 percent). This area of the law has witnessed a number of instances where the language in the government regulations has not kept pace with technological developments, again illustrating the first dynamic of computer law.

As a result of a number of international trade agreements, there is less opportunity for arbitrage among different tariff categories because the tariffs on most computer (and telecommunications) products are being reduced over time. Since the Second World War, most of the industrialized countries, and even the less developed ones, have participated in successive rounds of tariff reduction under the *General Agreement on Tariffs and Trade* (GATT) and, since 1995, the World Trade Organization (WTO). Regional free trade agreements, such as the 1989 *Canada–U.S. Free Trade Agreement* (FTA) and the 1994 *North American Free Trade Agreement* among Canada, the United States, and Mexico (NAFTA), also provided for the elimination of tariffs on a wide range of goods, either immediately or during a phaseout schedule over several years.[174] For example, under the FTA, duties on computers and central office switching telephone equipment were eliminated on January 1, 1989, provided the products qualified under the FTA's complex

---

173 For a similar determination in favour of finding computerized telecommunications equipment to be data processing rather than telephone equipment, see *General Datacomm Ltd. v. Deputy M.N.R. (Customs and Excise)* (1984), 9 T.B.R. 78 (T. Bd.).

174 For an overview of the NAFTA generally, see Jon R. Johnson, *The North American Free Trade Agreement: A Comprehensive Guide* (Aurora, ON: Canada Law Book, 1994), and for a treatment of the NAFTA specifically from the perspective of the computer industry, see Barry B. Sookman, *North American Free Trade Agreement and Computers: A Summary*, presented to the Fourth Annual Significant Developments in Computer Law Conference sponsored by the University of Dayton School of Law, Program in Law and Technology, June 11, 1993.

but useful "rules of origin" as being either Canadian or American in origin. Forty countries under the auspices of the WTO agreed to eliminate customs duties by the year 2000 on many high-technology products, including computers, telecom equipment (which, interestingly in light of the *IBM* decision noted in the previous paragraph, includes switching apparatus and modems), semiconductors, semiconductor manufacturing equipment, software and scientific instruments, but not consumer electronic goods.[175] This benefited Canadian importers of telecommunications products from certain non–North American countries and, more importantly, has been a boon to Canadian exporters of high-tech goods because tariffs are as high as 50 percent on these products in many developing countries.

b) Government Procurement

Although governments have largely given up the tariff as a means of protecting domestic industry, they have discovered other mechanisms — non-tariff barriers to trade — to assist companies within their jurisdictions. One such method, particularly in the high-tech sector, is government procurement, since governments purchase huge volumes of computers, software, and related services. In 1981 a number of GATT members agreed to a set of rules contained in the *Government Procurement Code* that was aimed at reducing discrimination against foreign suppliers. This agreement was augmented and superseded by the WTO's *Government Procurement Agreement*, as well as by government procurement provisions in trade agreements such as the FTA and NAFTA. For contracts above a certain dollar value, governments must put the tender out to competitive bid and cannot devise the tender criteria to favour one supplier over another. This rule is especially important in the computer sector where specifications for a tender can easily be skewed to favour a particular vendor. Sometimes, however, tender requirements that might seem unfair can be found to be reasonable, as in an American case that held that the U.S. government could specify a certain software operating system for handheld computers based on past procurements and the necessity to have interoperability.[176] And, of course, in awarding these contracts, the government cannot favour domestic suppliers, but must base its decision solely on the neutral criteria set out in the tender request. The NAFTA also implemented a bid

---

175 WTO, "Elimination of Tariffs on Computer Products by Year 2000 Agreed," *Focus Newsletter*, No. 17, March 1997.

176 *Integrated Systems Group, Inc.* v. *Department of the Army*, Guide to Computer Law, New Developments (CCH) ¶60,446 at 81,580 (1993).

protest mechanism whereby disgruntled parties can request the Canadian International Trade Tribunal (CITT) to investigate (but not reverse) questionable tender situations. This mechanism has been used with positive results in several high-tech procurements.[177] Bidders wishing to use this vehicle, however, must do so quickly; complaints must be lodged with the CITT within ten days of learning of the bases for the complaints.[178]

c) GATT, GATS, and TRIPs

The WTO oversees a number of agreements among its members intended generally to implement the following three principles in the international trade in goods and services: national treatment (the government of a WTO member state must extend to the nationals of other member states the same treatment it affords to its own nationals); most favoured nation (a government that extends a benefit to the national of another member state must extend the same benefit to the nationals of all member states, even if the benefit is not offered to its own nationals); and transparency (a government's rules relating to trade in goods and services should be clear to all member states).[179] The GATT, which covers trade in tangible, physical goods, is the oldest of the WTO's agreements, and the most detailed in terms of rules. As noted above, particularly in the context of supplemental regional trade agreements such as NAFTA, the GATT has been quite successful in reducing customs duties in WTO member countries on a range of goods, including computers, telecom equipment, and other high-tech products.

By contrast, the GATS (General Agreement on Trade in Services) dates only from 1993, and to date represents a more modest effort to liberalize trade in services, typically by focusing on specific market access initiatives that various members agree to from time to time.

---

177 See, for example, Simon Tuck, "Ottawa to Pay Corel in RFP Dispute," *The Globe and Mail* (26 June 1999), which details the events leading up to the federal government's payment to Corel of $9.9 million arising out of a tender that Corel argued discriminated against it. This settlement came in the wake of a CITT ruling in Corel's favour: Heather Scoffield, "Court Rules that Ottawa Must Compensate Corel," *The Globe and Mail* (27 April 1999). In a more recent U.S. decision, however, Corel was unsuccessful in preventing the U.S. federal Department of Labor from standardizing its software onto the Microsoft platform: *Corel Corp. v. United States*, 165 F.Supp. 2d 12 (D.D.C. 2001).

178 The rules on government procurement bid protests before the CITT are set out in the *North American Free Trade Agreement Procurement Inquiry Regulations*, SOR/93-602, 15 December 1993.

179 For information on the WTO, see <wto.org>.

Conceptually, the GATS contemplates four modalities of international service delivery, namely, cross-border supply (where a service supplier in one country provides the service directly into the territory of another WTO member country); consumption abroad (in the territory of a member country to the consumer in another member's country); commercial presence (where the service supplier establishes a commercial presence in another country); and presence of natural persons (where the service supplier establishes a presence through natural persons in another country). WTO members have agreed to a series of commitments based on these various modes of service delivery. A problem, however, arises when one overlays on this construct the fact that e-commerce delivery systems may not pigeonhole well into these categories.[180] Another difficulty is that certain copyright works, such as music and videos, can be delivered either as goods (when copied onto a CD-ROM, DVD, or videocassette) or a service (as a stream of bits over the Internet), thereby causing a regulatory short circuit as a result of differences in approach between the GATT and the GATS (and once again illustrating the impact of the second dynamic of computer law).[181] The WTO countries also acknowledge that the global trading environment requires adherence by member states to an effective legal regime of intellectual property protection. Thus the WTO's TRIPs Agreement (Agreement on Trade-Related Intellectual Property Rights) requires member countries to abide by most favoured nation and national treatment principles for a wide variety of intellectual property rights.[182] The TRIPs also requires member countries to provide effective remedial mechanisms to ensure that intellectual property rights can be enforced by all rights holders, both domestic and international.

---

180 The WTO defines e-commerce as the "production, distribution, marketing, sale or delivery of goods and services by electronic means": see WTO, *Work Programme on Electronic Commerce* (1998), para. 1.3, online at <wto.org>.

181 For example, in 1998 the WTO declared a moratorium on the collection of customs duties on goods purchased through e-commerce. See WTO, *The Geneva Ministerial Declaration on Electronic Commerce*, available at <wto.org>. This created a distortion that favoured the streaming of bits over the delivery of CDs, DVDs, or videocassettes, to continue with the same example, thereby creating an incentive to conduct business over the Internet.

182 These rights include patents, trade secrets, trade-marks, copyrights, industrial designs; for a discussion of these rights, see chapter 2.

2) Employment Law

The computer revolution has changed the nature of the workplace. Information technology has become a fixture in the factory as well as at the office. Computers have raised a cluster of labour law issues in the contexts of union and non-union employment environments. A critic of computerization lists the labour movement's concerns with the microchip as follows:

- job loss: last century the Industrial Revolution's factories absorbed the displaced agricultural workers; after the Second World War, the service sector absorbed the displaced factory workers; this cycle will not continue with workers displaced by the computer;[183]
- job degradation: the computer takes over the more interesting tasks associated with a job;[184]
- electronic monitoring: terribly stress-inducing as each keystroke is recorded by management;
- loss of job mobility: lower-level employees cannot move into middle management because the role of middle managers to collect and aggregate information is now performed by computers;
- increase in part-time work: as information is stored in computers rather than in brains, fewer fulltime staff are needed to serve as the institutional memory of an organization;
- health hazards from video display terminals: carpal tunnel syndrome, pain in the hand and wrist, and musculoskeletal conditions could be added to this category;[185]
- telecommuting: by keeping workers at home, connected to the office by computers and networks, management can facilitate the break-up of unions or prevent them from organizing;[186]

---

183 See, for example, Marian Stinson, "Assembly-line Robots Taking Workers' Jobs: UN Report," *The Globe and Mail* (8 February 2000).

184 In "George Bush, Union-Basher?" *The Economist*, 12 October 2002, the point is made that a key issue in the labour dispute that shut down twenty-nine ports on the American West Coast in 2002 was the union's determination to achieve control over jobs created by new technology.

185 Though some research suggests that there may not be a link between keyboard use and carpal tunnel syndrome: "Light at the End?" *The Economist*, 16 June 2001. Modern technological devices, however, can cause other, indirect injuries; this is why some U.S. states have banned the use of cellphones while driving: "Yada, Yada, Yada ...," *The Economist*, 30 June 2001.

186 Though e-mail can also be used to help establish unions, or to decertify them: "E-mail's Sacred Unions," *The Economist*, 4 October 2000; and Virginia Galt, "Web Redraws Labour Battle Lines," *The Globe and Mail* (26 December 2000).

- an adverse impact on women: many of the above concerns apply disproportionately to women.[187]

Of course, each microchip has two sides, and there is a counterargument to most of these points. Job loss, for example, is contentious because it is not at all clear that the economy, on a macro level, is unable to generate the necessary number of new jobs; indeed, thousands of high-tech jobs were unfilled over the past decade.[188] Nevertheless, at a micro level workers have been displaced by technology, and for many older workers made redundant by the computer it is little consolation that the firm has hired young computer programmers to maintain the overall employment level. In many unionized environments the method by which new technology is introduced into the workplace is a subject for collective bargaining and results in grievance arbitrations. For example, in a U.S. case, the arbitrator determined that a collective agreement's management rights clause allowed the employer to introduce a computerized receiving system that had the effect of eliminating a clerk's job.[189] Similarly, in Canadian unionized environments joint management–labour committees address the contentious issues presented by the first dynamic of computer law, namely, the rapid pace of technological change.

New technologies in the workplace have also led to problems in non-unionized environments. For example, in one adjudication under the *Canada Labour Code*, an employee had inadvertently obtained access to the company's payroll file that listed all the staff salaries. While printing his own work on a local area network, he wondered why it was taking so long and noticed that another job in the print queue was the payroll run; "out of curiosity" he made a copy of the payroll file to see what his co-workers earned.[190] The employee was fired when senior management learned he had copied the payroll file — extremely confidential information — because as a television station it did not want the salaries of its on-air personalities known by advertisers. The employee sought redress under the *Canada Labour Code*,

---

187 David Bishop Debenham, "Clipping Away at Labour Relations: Legislative Policy in the Age of the Microchip" (1988) 17 Man. L.J. 232.

188 For an even-handed assessment of the job loss issue, see Zavis Zeman & Robert Russell, "The Chip Dole: An Overview of the Debates on Technological Unemployment," *CIPS Review* (January-February 1980): 10.

189 *Teamsters, Local Union No. 878 and Harvest Foods, Inc.*, Guide to Computer Law, New Developments (CCH) ¶60,386 at 81,245 (1992).

190 *Leech v. British Columbia Television Broadcasting System Ltd.* (8 April 1991) [unreported].

and the adjudicator, noting that the employee had not misused the information for any personal gain nor disclosed it to any third party, ordered reinstatement of the employee. One lesson from this case is that it is incumbent upon management to take appropriate steps to keep certain information confidential if they in fact do not want it accessed by staff generally. Thus, rather than running the payroll on the company's local area network where other users can access it, it should have been run off a stand-alone system not accessible to other staff. Management's response to the situation upon learning of the employee's access to the information was arguably also poorly handled; in effect, employers are struggling with new situations presented by computer technology.

Another case showing poor management skills when dealing with computer-related issues involved a financial institution where the computer password of one of its employees was used to steal $1850 from several dormant customer accounts.[191] The employer, assuming that the person who stole the money was the employee to whom this password was assigned, fired her on the day before she was to move from Halifax to Ottawa to take up a promotion with the company; she had already sold her car, shipped her belongings, cancelled her lease in Halifax, and entered into a new one in Ottawa. Moreover, the company gave her no reasons for the firing. The court found that it could not be proved she stole the money, and in fact it was likely not her because on one of the occasions that money was taken the plaintiff was out of the country and could not have accessed the computer remotely. Some other employee had obtained the plaintiff's computer password and used it to steal the funds, and the plaintiff was exonerated. The court found the employer terminated the employee wrongfully and awarded punitive damages against the employer for its callous treatment of the plaintiff.

Another employment case worth noting is *Russell v. Nova Scotia Power Inc.*[192] The plaintiff, a long-time employee in the financial information systems group of a large company, had completed overseeing the implementation of a major new software application when a new controller was appointed to whom the plaintiff reported. The plaintiff and the controller did not get along well, and the company eventually dismissed the plaintiff for incompetence. To make matters worse, the controller sent an e-mail to hundreds of the plaintiff's co-workers indicating not only that he was no longer in the information systems

---

191 *Conrad v. Household Financial Corp.* (1992), 327 A.P.R. 56 (N.S.C.A.).
192 (1996), 436 A.P.R. 271 (N.S.S.C.).

department (which the court found would be a legitimate purpose for such an e-mail), but also that he was terminated for incompetence. The court found that there was no evidence supporting the claim of incompetence (i.e., many of the "problems" the controller attributed to the difficulties with the new software application were not the fault of the plaintiff), and that the plaintiff was wrongfully terminated and entitled to eighteen months' notice or pay in lieu of such notice. Moreover, while not finding the employer deserving of punitive damages, the court did award $40,000 in aggravated damages because the e-mail message was sent in order to embarrass the plaintiff and make an example of him and led to a serious aggravation of a pre-existing anxiety disorder. The court dismissed the plaintiff's claim for defamation, largely because it might result in double compensation in light of the award of aggravated damages for many of the same factors that underpinned the defamation claim. This is another example of an employer behaving badly in light of new computer technology and then using the new technology to make matters even worse.[193]

3) Insurance

Companies purchase insurance contracts in order to spread the risks presented by unforeseeable, harmful events that cause them damage. Accordingly, insurance is extremely relevant to organizations supplying or using various computing resources, including those conducting e-commerce over the Internet. Virtually every section of this book has highlighted activity that presents a meaningful risk to modern enterprises. In general terms, intellectual property infringement,[194] various types of criminal conduct,[195] invasion of privacy,[196] malfunctioning computers,[197]

---

193 For a discussion of employee-related e-mail issues from another perspective, see chapter 4, section A.1(d), "Monitoring Employee E-mails."
194 Intellectual property questions, including infringement issues, are dealt with primarily in chapter 2.
195 Chapter 3 covers comprehensively the various types of computer crime activities for which companies would want insurance coverage, including hacking (including denial of service attacks); viruses; computer-based fraud; and the transmission of obscene material.
196 Threats to personal privacy are enumerated in chapter 4 (see section A, "Privacy and Data Protection").
197 The risks posed by computer errors are covered in chapter 1 (see section C.4, "Dependency on Computers") and chapter 5 (see sections A.2, "Imperfect Software," and D, "Negligence").

inappropriate e-mail,[198] and online libel[199] are all activities for which companies would do well to have insurance coverage, given how simple it is to cause harm to third parties through, or to be adversely impacted by, these events. There are also the more traditional yet equally serious problems of power outages and other similar risks beyond a company's control that can cause material computer problems for which insurance cover would be desirable. In all these circumstances, companies can sustain various first-party losses (i.e., damages suffered by themselves), including loss of data or access to data, data recovery costs, loss of computer functionality, business interruption caused by computer down time, loss of profits due to lost sales when an e-commerce Web site goes down, and costs associated with investigating and recovering from hacker or virus attacks. The list of third-party losses (i.e., damages a policyholder's negligence may cause to third parties) includes damages caused by breach of computer security leading to public disclosure of confidential customer data, transmission of a virus to a third party, misuse of a third party's trade-mark, and posting libellous messages to a third-party Web site. In all these cases, in theory insurance could play a useful role in spreading risk among many insureds. That is not to say insurance is or should be a panacea. It cannot alone constitute an organization's risk management strategy. Rather, insurance should be included as part of an overall plan for minimizing and mitigating the effects of computer-related risks, along with pro-active management, and contractual and other risk reduction measures.

An insurance contract is just that, a contract that sets out the specific risks against which the insurance company has agreed to provide coverage to the insured, in return for the payment of a premium by the insured. There are, however, a number of different types of insurance, including all-risk property,[200] commercial general liability

---

198 The harm that can be done by unfortunate e-mail is explained in chapter 4 (see section A.1(d), "Monitoring Employee E-mails") and chapter 6 (see section B.3(b), "E-mail Policies").

199 Libel and defamation are dealt with in chapter 7 (see section A, "Cyber Libel").

200 As its name suggests, the "all-risk" policy provides the most expensive coverage available, usually including all causes of damage except those specifically excluded: *Santa Advertising Inc. v. Wawanesa Mutual Insurance Co.*, [2001] O.J. No. 2675 (Sup. Ct.) [*Santa Advertising*]. For example, in *Datatab Inc. v. St. Paul Fire and Marine Insurance Co.*, 347 F.Supp. 36 (S.D.N.Y. 1972), a court held that such a policy applied in the case of an interruption of business caused by the shutdown of a computer system, in turn indirectly caused by a water main break, that damaged some pumps, knocked out the air conditioning; and forced the company to turn off its computers.

(CGL),[201] errors and omissions (E&O),[202] directors and officers (D&O),[203] business interruption,[204] and employee dishonesty.[205] What is key, and legally operative, is the wording of the specific policy and, in terms of determining the scope of coverage under it, the interpretation given to such words by the courts.[206] Not surprisingly, the first two dynamics of computer law (namely, the rapid pace of technological change and the elusive nature of information) have prompted a number of judicial decisions, as courts have been asked to interpret traditional insurance contract phrases in light of new computer-based realities. The balance of this section on insurance will explore how courts have been faring in this difficult exercise.

---

201 CGL insurance usually covers amounts that an insured becomes responsible for due to personal injury or property damage.

202 E&O coverage insures professionals (including software designers, system integrators, and computer consultants) for damages resulting from errors, mistakes, omissions, and negligence made by the professional as they performed their services. In *USM Corporation*, above note 135, a computer consultant was entitled to rely on an E&O policy for cover, even where the underlying dispute with the customer did not sound directly in negligence, as it was characterized by the court as a breach of contract.

203 D&O insurance covers the defence and indemnification of directors and officers of a corporation for lawsuits brought against them arising out of their acts (or omissions) on behalf of the corporation.

204 Business interruption insurance indemnifies against loss of income resulting from the insured's inability to operate its business due to events beyond the insured's control. In *Home Indemnity Co.* v. *Hyplains Beef*, 89 F.3d 850 (10th Cir. 1996), the court held that a computer glitch that resulted only in business delays, but not a total suspension of operations, was not covered due to the specific wording of the policy. But see *Maher* v. *Continental Casualty Co.*, 76 F.3d 535 (4th Cir. 1996), a case not involving computers, where coverage was found even though there was not a complete cessation of operations.

205 Employee dishonesty insurance is purchased in the event the rogue employees cause harm by theft, vandalism or some other wrongful act.

206 It is a mistake to assume that a specific insured's policy is like any other policy. While there has been a move to harmonize certain standard form policy templates, there are lots of nuances between the actual phrases used by different insurers, and often there are negotiations between the insured and the carrier that result in various endorsements, extensions, or exclusions becoming part of the insurance contract. There simply is no substitute for reading the precise policy in effect in each instance. Some policies, however, are not easy to read. In *Computer Corner, Inc.* v. *Fireman's Fund Insurance Company*, 46 P.3d 1264 (C.A.N.M. 2002) [*Computer Corner*], the court found an exclusion too vague, to the benefit of the insured, who operated a computer repair shop.

a)   Coverage for Software and Data

A core coverage of the all-risks and CGL insurance policies is "property damage," often qualified by the terms *physical* or *tangible* property. This language poses little difficulty when the harm occasioned is to the actual, physical componentry of the computer.[207] The issue arises, however, as to whether these same phrases can encompass software and data. There is no case law directly on this point in Canada,[208] and interestingly the U.S. cases are divided. For example, in *America Online, Inc. v. St. Paul Mercury Insurance Co.*,[209] the court concluded that "computer data, software and systems" are not "tangible" property for purposes of a Technology Commercial General Liability Protection Policy.[210] In coming to this conclusion, the court noted that *tangible* means property that "can be touched"; data, software, and systems do not qualify, argued the court, as they are incapable of perception by any of the senses and are therefore intangible.[211] Other American cases have come to

---

207 See *State Auto Property and Casualty Insurance Co.* v. *Midwest Computers & More*, 147 F.Supp. 2d 1113 (W.D. Okl. 2001) [*Midwest Computers*]. In this case, the relevant insurance policy provided that "property damage" comprised "physical injury to tangible property," as well as "loss of use of tangible property that is not physically injured." Interestingly, under the second prong, the court held that there could be recovery for loss of data (although in this specific case, there was a further exclusion in the policy that blocked recovery).

208 In one Canadian case, however, the court held that the term "property damage" in an insurance contract did not cover an alleged interference with an inventor's claim to a right to exploit a patent: *Canadian Universities Reciprocal Insurance Exchange* v. *GAN Canada Insurance Co.* (1999), 12 C.C.L.I. (3d) 18 (Ont. Gen. Div.) [*Canadian Universities*]. Interestingly, in this case two insurance policies were at issue, and one did not qualify the word *property* by "physical" or "tangible," as the other one did. Nevertheless, the court concluded that "property damage" contemplated a physical injury. In another Canadian case, *Kogan* v. *Chubb Insurance Co. of Canada*, [2001] O.J. No. 1697 27 C.C.L.I. (3d) 16 (Sup. Ct.), the court held that a residential fire and other perils policy, for coverage in respect of computer data replacement, did not cover software lost in the house fire.

209 207 F.Supp. 2d 459 (E.D.Va. 2002) [*St. Paul Mercury*].

210 Equally, in *Midwest Computers*, above note 207, the court concluded at 1116: "Although the medium that holds the information can be perceived, identified, or valued, the information itself cannot be. Alone, computer data cannot be touched, held, or sensed by the human mind; it has no physical substance. It is not tangible property."

211 The court in *St. Paul Mercury*, above note 209, looked no further than *Black's Law Dictionary*, which defines "tangible" as: "Having or possessing physical form. Capable of being touched and seen; perceptible to the touch; tactile; palpable; capable of being possessed or realized; readily apprehensible by the mind; real; substantial." From a broader perspective, the court in *St. Paul Mercury* was mindful that a finding in favour of the insured would eviscerate the long-stand-

a similar conclusion, including one involving misappropriated trade secrets,[212] and another where electronic serial numbers and mobile telephone identification numbers used to activate cell phones were stolen by a rogue employee.[213]

There are cases, however, going the other way. In an Australian decision,[214] the court was willing to find that software was covered (but not data). With respect to data, a U.S. case found that a computer tape and data on it together were covered.[215] And in a very interesting and potentially important decision, *American Guarantee & Liability Ins. Co.* v. *Ingram Micro, Inc.*,[216] a court was willing to hold that "physical damage"

---

ing damages doctrine of refusing recovery in tort for economic loss. In this regard the court was animated by the same motivation as found in the *Babich* case, above note 124.

212 *St. Paul Fire & Mutual Marine Insurance Co.* v. *National Computer Systems*, 490 N.W.2d 626 (Minn. Ct. App. 1992).

213 *Peoples Telephone Company, Inc.* v. *Hartford Fire Insurance Company*, 36 F.Supp. 2d 1335 (S.D. Florida 1997). Similar results have been seen in non-technology cases: see *Old Republic Insurance Company* v. *West Flagler Associates, Ltd.*, 49 So. 2d 1174 (Dist. C.A. Florida 1982), where a horse-racing betting ticket was held not to be tangible property, or *Schaefer/Karpf Productions* v. *CNA Ins. Companies*, 76 Cal. Rptr. 2d 42 (Cal. Ct. App. 1998), where loss of use of a script for a children's video, because the script could not be touched or felt, was held not to be covered under the relevant CGL policy. In this latter case, through a series of unfortunate events, the plaintiff's kids' production of "The Best Christmas Pageant Ever" was copied onto hundreds of tapes that previously carried a hardcore porn video, with the result that when the Christmas video was over, if the tape was kept running (because, for example, in a school setting, the teacher was busy setting the table for Christmas lunch), young viewers were exposed to their first experience of hard-core pornography. In concluding that no coverage was afforded under the standard CGL policy, the court argued that there was no harm to the physical cassettes comprising the plastic box with the reel of tape inside; the judge noted, colourfully, at 47, "Here, the medium is not the message."

214 *Switzerland Insurance Australia Ltd.* v. *Dundean Distributors Pty. Ltd.*, [1998] Vic. S.C. 25 (Vict. C.A.).

215 *Retail Systems, Inc.* v. *CNA Insurance Companies*, 469 N.W.2d 735 (Minn. C.A. 1991).

216 2000 WL 726789 (D. Ariz. 2000). In coming to this conclusion, the court stated at 2: "At a time when computer technology dominates our professional as well as personal lives, the Court must side with Ingram's broader definition of 'physical damage.' The Court finds that 'physical damage' is not restricted to the physical destruction or harm of computer circuitry but includes loss of access, loss of use, and loss of functionality." The court concluded that reading the policy as proposed by the insurer would be "archaic." See also *Computer Corner*, above note 206, where the appellate court noted, at 266, that "the computer data in question 'was physical, had an actual physical location, occupied space and was capable of being physically damaged and destroyed.' The district court concluded 'computer data is tangible property.' These rulings are not challenged on appeal."

included "loss of use and functionality," thereby giving coverage for the costs of reconstructing data. This decision, however, was expressly considered and not followed in the *St. Paul Mercury* case, thereby setting the stage for a resolution of this jurisprudential dichotomy through the appellate process. In the meantime, companies worried about the coverage afforded them under traditional insurance policies for computer and e-commerce-related risks might wish to consider what new insurance products are available specifically for these activities.[217] For example, in a recent Ontario case, an advertising company was able to recover from an insurance company the former's costs incurred in recreating files lost by a computer outage given that the company had purchased a specific Electronic Data Processing coverage.[218]

b) Coverage for Intellectual Property Infringement

There are numerous cases on the question whether a CGL policy's "advertising liability" clause covers various forms of intellectual property infringement and other actions regarding intellectual property rights.[219] From a copyright perspective, this type of insurance is intended to cover situations such as the use of infringing music in an advertisement. Notwithstanding the efforts of fairly creative counsel for

---

217 See Caroline Alphonso, "Lloyd's to Offer E-biz Insurance: Will Cover Damage by Computer Hackers," *The Globe and Mail* (23 August 2000). As well, some first-party policies can be expanded to include a "corruption of data" clause, that would provide for destruction, distortion, or corruption of any data or software, though often these add-ons include an exclusion for viruses.

218 *Santa Advertising*, above note 200. In this case the court also held that an exclusion in the EDP policy that read "Human errors or omissions in processing, recording or storing information onto electronic media" did not deny coverage as a result of the insured failing to make back-up copies of its data.

219 Again, there is no such thing as a "typical" advertising liability clause. The one that was at issue in *Canadian Universities*, above note 208, covered
   (i) libel, slander or defamation;
   (ii) any infringement of copyright or of title or of slogan;
   (iii) piracy or unfair competition or idea misappropriation under an
       implied contract;
   (iv) any invasion of right of privacy;

   committed or alleged to have been committed in any advertisement, publicity article, broadcast or telecast and arising out of your advertising activities.

   In "insurance-speak," the subcategories (i) to (iv) are known as "offences" (not to be confused, however, with criminal offences under the *Criminal Code*). Thus, one asks, in insurance coverage litigation, whether the insured's conduct in a particular instance comes under, for example, the "offence" of "libel, slander or defamation."

insureds, the advertising injury provision has not been extended by the courts to the copying and distribution of software,[220] nor to the misappropriation of software code;[221] similarly, the injury has to arise from the advertising, and not the activities that were advertised or the steps necessary to conduct the advertising campaign.[222] The provision has been used recently, however, in an Ontario case where a company was alleged to have made unauthorized use of photographs in a commercial product.[223]

Just as the scope for the advertising injury clause in insurance contracts is relatively narrow in respect of software infringement, insureds sued for direct patent infringement have also had great difficulty convincing courts that they should be covered by the advertising injury policy language. Two hurdles are presented to insureds. First, courts typically do not find that patent infringement comes within one of the enumerated offences, be it "infringement of copyright, title or slogan,"[224]

---

220 In *GAF Sales Service, Inc. v. Hastings Mut. Ins. Co.*, 568 N.W.2d 165 (Mich. Ct. App. 1997), copyright infringement related to the copying and distribution of software was not covered under the advertising injury provision as the loss was not related to advertising (rather, it arose directly from the software infringement).

221 In *Microtec Research, Inc. v. Nationwide Mutual Ins. Co.*, 40 F.3d 968 (9th Cir. 1994) [*Microtec Research*], the harm was attributable to misappropriation of the software code, not the indirect ability of the company to advertise that its product was as good as that of a third party.

222 In *Robert Bowden, Inc. v. Aetna Casualty & Surety Co.*, 1997 U.S. Dist. LEXIS 14632 (N.D. Ga. 1997), the court refused the plaintiff's argument that it needed the software that was copied illegally to conduct an advertising campaign; that is, using illegally copied software to create the advertising copy does not result in the software being used in the advertisement, for insurance purposes.

223 *Corel Corp. v. Guardian Insurance Co. of Canada*, [2001] O.J. No. 368 (Ont. S.C.).

224 In *St. Paul Fire & Marine Inc. Co. v. Advanced Interventional Sys.*, 824 F.Supp. 583 (E.D. Va. 1993); affirmed, 21 F.3d 424 (4th Cir. 1994), the trial court concluded, at 586: "And it is nonsense to suppose that if the parties had intended the insurance policy in question to cover patent infringement claims, the policy would explicitly cover infringements of 'copyright, title or slogan,' but then include patent infringement, *sub silento*, in a different provision, by reference to 'unauthorized taking of ... [the] style of doing business.'" Similarly, in *Gencor Industries v. Wausau Underwriters Insurance Company*, 857 F.Supp. 1560 (M.D. Fla. 1994) [*Gencor*], the court stated, at 1564: "It is even more absurd to suggest that the phrase 'infringement of ... title,' as used in the clause 'infringement of copyright, title or slogans,' encompasses patent infringement or inducement to infringe. Basic common sense dictates that if these policies covered any form of patent infringement, the word 'patent' would appear in the quoted 'infringement' clauses."

"piracy,"[225] "unfair competition,"[226] or "idea misappropriation";[227] in a similar vein, in an Ontario case none of these offences was found to fit an unusual fact pattern involving the "wrongful interference with patent rights."[228] Second, even if an offence can be made out, as has been done in some cases where the court finds an ambiguity in the policy language, most courts have denied coverage on the basis that there is no causal connection between the underlying claim (direct patent infringement) and the activity of advertising (which is the object of coverage for this specific insurance coverage).[229] Thus, many courts have held that patent injury (for insurance purposes) is caused by (as set out in the *Patent Act*) the manufacture, use, and sale of an allegedly infringing product, and not by its use, in advertising; put another way, using or displaying an infringing product in an advertisement does not comprise use of infringing material in the course of the insured's advertising.[230] An exception to this line of reasoning might be

225 See *Gencor, ibid.*, and *Atlantic Mutual Insurance Co.* v. *Brotech Corporation* v. *Planet Insurance Company*, 857 F.Supp. 423 (E.D. Pa. 1994); affirmed 60 F.3d 813 (3rd Cir. 1995). In *Iolab Corporation* v. *Seaboard Surety Company*, 15 F.3d 1500 (9th Cir. 1994) [*Iolab*], the court, at 1506, put it as follows: "In the context of policies written to protect against claims of advertising injury, 'piracy' means misappropriation or plagiarism found in the elements *of the advertisement itself* — in its text form, logo, or pictures — rather than in the product being advertised" [emphasis in original]. See also *United States Fidelity & Guaranty Company* v. *Star Technologies, Inc.*, 935 F.Supp. 1110 (D. Ore. 1996) [*Star Technologies*], where the court concluded that the terms "advertising activity" and "piracy" were ambiguous enough to allow patent infringement to come under the former, although the court nevertheless held for the insurer on the basis that there was a lack of causal connection between the infringement and any advertising. This case cites another for a pithy test for the causal connection required: the advertising activity must cause the damage, not merely expose it.
226 See *Gencor*, above note 224, as well as *Aetna Casualty And Surety Company, Inc.* v. *Superior Court (Watercloud Bed Co., Inc.)*, 19 Cal. App. 4th 320 (Cal. Ct. App. 4th). But see also *Rymal* v. *Woodcock*, 896 F.Supp. 637 (W.D. La. 1995), where the court determined that the "gross ambiguity" of the insurance policy at least required the insurance company to defend the claim, whether or not it subsequently would be responsible for indemnification of the actual damages.
227 See *Gencor*, above note 224. See also *Fluoroware, Inc.* v. *Chubb Group of Insurance Companies*, 545 N.W.2d 678 (Minn. Ct. App. 1996).
228 See *Canadian Universities*, above note 208.
229 See *Star Technologies*, above note 225.
230 For example, in *Iolab*, above note 225, the court, at 1506, citing an earlier case, stated: "a patent is infringed by making, using or selling a patented invention, not by advertising it."

available in those jurisdictions, like the U.S. since 1996,[231] where a fourth patent right, namely "offering to sell," has been added to the traditional trio of "make, use and sell."[232] In any event, companies concerned about the scope of coverage afforded them under general, traditional insurance policies for potential patent infringement should explore obtaining insurance specially aimed at this risk.[233]

With respect to trade-marks, the typical CGL advertising injury language (such as that at note 219 above) makes no express mention of trade-marks, and this has led some courts to deny coverage.[234] In many other decisions, however, coverage has been found either by relying on the term "misappropriation of advertising ideas or style of doing

---

231 The *TRIPS Agreement* (Trade Related Aspects of Intellectual Property Rights), concluded under the auspices of the GATT (as discussed in section H.1(c) of this chapter, "*GATT, GATS and TRIPs*") resulted in 35 U.S.C. §271(a), reading [since 1996] as follows: "whoever without authority makes, uses, *offers to sell*, or sells any patented invention, within the United States or imports into the United States any patented invention during the term of patent therefore, infringes the patent" [emphasis added to identify the new phrase].

232 Thus, in *Everett Associates, Inc. v. Transcontinental Insurance Company*, 57 F. Supp. 2d 874 (N.D. Cal. 1999), the court concluded that the pre-1996 case law was inapplicable to new cases involving the amended U.S. *Patent Act*, and on the strength of the new "offer to sell" language, held the insurance company responsible to extend coverage for patent infringement; on appeal (35 Fed. Appx. 450 (9th Cir. 2002)), the appellate court reversed this finding, holding that patent infringement cannot come under the enumerated offence of "misappropriation of a style of doing business," but concluding as well that due to the 1996 Patent Act revision, patent infringement may arise from advertising activity. Similarly, in *Clark Manufacturing Inc. v. Northfield Insurance Company*, 187 F.3d 646 (9th Cir. 1999) [*Northfield Insurance*], the court also denied coverage; notwithstanding that the underlying activity involved an "offer of sale" of a patent infringing product, the plaintiff did not overcome the initial hurdle that patent-infringement was held by the court not to come within the enumerated offence of "misappropriation of advertising ideas."

233 In one case, *Den-Tal-Ez, Inc. v. Reliance Ins. Co.*, No. 92-05352, (Ct. Comm. Pleas, Montgomery County Penn., 10 November 1993), the court was apparently assisted in finding that "piracy" does not include patent infringement by the fact, noted by the court in its judgment, that the insured could have purchased insurance that expressly covered patent infringement.

234 See, for example, *Advance Watch Co., Ltd. v. Kemper National Ins. Co.*, 99 F.3d 795 (6th Cir. 1996, where the court held, at 802, that "misappropriation of advertising ideas or style of doing business" does not refer to a category or grouping of actionable conduct which includes trademark or trade dress infringement." Indeed, in some policies there is an express exclusion of advertising injury arising out of infringement of a trade-mark, as was the case in *Microtec Research*, above note 221.

business" or the phrase "infringement of title."[235] And unlike the situation with patents (noted above), once the determination is made that the trade-mark infringement comes within one of the enumerated offences, it is relatively simple for insureds to make out the causal connection as the relevant trade-mark invariably is used in the insured's advertising.[236] As for trade secrets, again there is a dichotomy in the U.S. jurisprudence. On the one hand, where the trade secret relates to technology, and is not related to advertising, courts have not found in favour of the insureds.[237] On the other hand, a court found coverage where the trade secrets included "customer lists, methods of bidding jobs, methods and procedures for billing, marketing techniques, and other inside and confidential information."[238] In effect, with such vari-

---

235 *J. A. Brundage Plumbing and Roto-Rooter, Inc.* v. *Massachusetts Bay Insurance Company*, 818 F.Supp. 553 (W.D.N.Y. 1993); *B.H. Smith Inc.* v. *Zurich Insurance Company*, 676 N.E.2d 221 (Ill. App., 1st Dist. 1996); and *Energex Systems Corporation* v. *Fireman's Fund Insurance Company*, 1997 WL 358007 (S.D.N.Y. 1997).

236 See, for example, *P.J. Noyes Company* v. *American Motorists Insurance Company*, 855 F.Supp. 492 (D.N.H. 1994), where the court, at 495, concluded: "Although the underlying action is one for trademark infringement, the infringement occurred as a result of Noyes using the term 'Dustfree Precision Pellets' in their advertising. But for the use of the term in the packaging, literature and advertisements, there would have been no trademark infringement. Accordingly, the court finds that the underlying suit comes within the terms of the policy."

237 *Northfield Insurance*, above note 232, and *Winklevoss Consultants, Inc.* v. *Federal Insurance Co.*, 991 F.Supp. 1024 (N.D. Ill. 1998). In the latter case, the court held that a claim for trade secret misappropriation, in the context of the insured's alleged copying of a third-party's software program to create a competing product, did not fall under the advertising injury provisions of a CGL policy. The decision in this case begins, at 1024, with the following observation: "An insurance company's duty to defend intellectual property claims under the rubric of 'advertising injury' is the subject of countless lawsuits — indeed, a recent litigation explosion — throughout the country." Interestingly, in a subsequent decision (111 F.Supp. 2d 995 (N.D. Ill. 1998)), the insured was successful in having the insurance company provide coverage, but only because trademark–related claims were added to the underlying misappropriation lawsuit at a later date.

238 *Sentex Systems, Inc.* v. *Hartford Accident & Indemnity Company*, 93 F.3d 578 (9th Cir. 1996). In this case, the plaintiff in the underlying trade secret case denied having identified its trade secrets in the insured's written sales material, but testified that the proprietary information was used by the insured in other sales-related ways. In coming to its conclusion that insurance coverage should be found, the court stated, at 580: "In this day and age, advertising cannot be limited to written sales materials, and the concept of marketing includes a wide variety of direct and indirect advertising strategies. It is significant that ESSI's claims for misappropriation of trade secrets relate to marketing and sales and not to

ability of results in the intellectual property-related insurance cover decisions, companies who are heavy users of intellectual property, or who develop and market technology-related products, would do well to enquire as to the specific insurance products available for intellectual property-type assets.

---

secrets relating to the manufacture and production of security systems." But see also *Pierce Companies, Inc. v. Wausau Underwriters Insurance Company,* 201 F.3d 444 (9th Cir. 1999), where the misappropriation of marketing techniques and customer lists did not result in a finding for coverage, because the court concluded that the "gravamen" of the complaint was misappropriation of a toner formulation and production process rather than the printing of a marketing brochure or any other advertising.

CHAPTER 6

E-COMMERCE
CONTRACT AND
EVIDENCE LEGAL ISSUES

For the past few hundred years, paper-based documents — in the form of contracts, purchase orders, invoices, and bills of lading — have been the predominant means to record and share commercial information. With the advent of the telegraph 150 years ago, for the first time commercial information was communicated electronically without paper. The telex and fax continued this trend, as did direct computer-to-computer communications, often referred to as electronic data interchange (EDI), an important means for transmitting commercial information in certain industries. Today, the Internet is poised to become a very important means of doing business electronically, both in the context of the one-on-one transactions of early electronic communications, as well as in the online environment of many-on-many.[1] As well, data are

---

1   In this chapter, the term *electronic commerce* will be considered to encompass a broad range of previous and current technologies, though today its primary focus is on business being done by means of fax, telephone, e-mail, and the Internet. See chapter 1, section C.3, "Mass Customization," for a discussion of Internet-based electronic commerce. In one of its reports on the online world, the Canadian government has defined electronic commerce as follows: "Electronic commerce, which is at the heart of the information economy, is the conduct of commercial activities and transactions by means of computer-based information and communications technologies. It generally involves the processing and transmission of digitized information": Government of Canada (Task Force on Electronic Commerce, Industry Canada), *A Cryptography Policy Framework for Electronic Commerce: Building Canada's Information Economy and Society*

515

today stored electronically; even previously paper-based documents are scanned and their contents stored electronically through imaging systems to save money and to improve access through indexing and retrieval systems. This shift from a paper-based to an electronic-based environment raises numerous legal issues related to contract formation,[2] evidence law, records retention, and e-mail. This is not surprising given that the four dynamics of computer law, namely, the rapid rate of technological change, the elusive nature of information, and the blurring of private/public and national/international, are very much in evidence vis-à-vis doing business electronically.[3] The legal system has had several hundred years to craft rules, through statutes as well as judge-made common law, to address the risks and problems presented by paper. By contrast, electronic-based communications systems, from the telegraph to the Internet, have presented the subdisciplines of contract and evidence/records retention law with novel and sometimes difficult hurdles. Nevertheless, through sensible judge-made law, and more recently by means of legislated law reform, the legal rules relating to electronic commerce are becoming more certain, with the ultimate goal of making them as predictable as those applicable to doing business with paper-based information; indeed, in case after case, judges are concluding that electronic communications and record-keeping practices offer greater, not less, certainty and trustworthiness

---

(Ottawa: Industry Canada, 1998), available at <strategis.ic.gc.ca/crypto> [*Cryptography Policy Framework*]. Electronic commerce refers to business arrangements effected through electronic instead of paper-based mechanisms.

2   Contract formation issues are particularly important given that, as John Gregory notes in "Solving Legal Issues in Electronic Commerce" (1999) 32 C.B.L.J. 84 at 86 ["Solving Legal Issues"], "Electronic commerce rests largely on the law of contract." Mr. Gregory, who is with Ontario's Ministry of the Attorney General, is the prime architect of Ontario's recent law reform initiatives in the electronic commerce area. This article by Mr. Gregory provides a wide-ranging survey of the "areas of uncertainty" related to electronic commerce (involving contracts, electronic devices, shrinkwrap licences, webwrap and clickwrap licences, negotiable instruments, electronic payment systems, jurisdiction, and intellectual property); various statutory barriers including evidence law and writing requirement impediments; and the means to promote electronic commerce, including enhanced signatures, licensing information, consumer protection, privacy, and dispute resolution. Usefully, Gregory divides his analysis by those measures intended to remove barriers to doing business electronically, and those that actively promote e-business.

3   These dynamics are important, and are a unifying theme throughout this book. For a discussion of these dynamics, see chapter 8, section A, "Computer Law: Dynamics."

than their paper-based predecessors. The new legal rules related to the electronic business environment, however, are not self-applying; that is, when designing and implementing electronic commerce delivery systems, significant care and attention must be expended in order to achieve online legal relationships that are effective and enforceable.

A. CONTRACT LAW ISSUES

Contracts are agreements that give rise to obligations the law will enforce.[4] Contract law facilitates the efficient operation of markets by establishing rules for concluding contracts and making payment under them. To this end, contract law has developed a number of principles and doctrines intended to promote certainty among business people in their commercial relations.[5] In particular, the law has promulgated several rules related to the formation of contracts, addressing such questions as what formalities need to be observed, and when and where contracts arise. With respect to contracts and other commercial documents that are paper-based, these rules are quite elaborate and well developed, as might be expected from a body of law that has matured over several hundred years. Since the advent of the telegraph, commercial relations effected through electronic means have presented the law with a number of challenges, primarily because of the first and second dynamics of computer law; that is, courts have been confronted by technologies that have obviated the need for paper, and once free of a paper-based medium, judges have had to contend with the truly ephemeral nature of information. Generally, however, by focusing on the policy objectives intended to be achieved by contract law rules related to writing and signature (for example, the core functional purpose of writing

---

4   Joseph Chitty, *Chitty on Contracts*, 28th ed. (London: Sweet & Maxwell, 1999) para. 1-001. Another renowned commentator conceptualizes contracts in terms of private legal obligations that effect economic exchange: P.S. Atiyah, *An Introduction to the Law of Contract*, 5th ed. (Oxford: Clarendon Press, 1995).

5   Professor Lon Fuller, in his classic article "Consideration and Form" (1941) 41 Colum. L. Rev. 799, conceptualizes these as the "channelling function" of contracts, essentially the use of certain rules to ensure transactors know when they have a contract. Fuller's other two important functions are "evidentiary" (in effect, having a record of the transaction so that transactors can recall with precision what they agreed to), and "cautionary" (in essence, the contracting process serves as a warning that legally binding commitments are being made resulting in obligations that will need to be discharged).

is memory, that is, to record for future reference), courts have been receptive to the new technologies, have taken pains to understand them and the risks and opportunities they represent, and have assisted business people in adopting them by recognizing their legal legitimacy; in short, judges in this area have not had much trouble dealing with the first dynamic of computer law. More recently, with the enactment of various electronic commerce statutes and amendments to evidence and other laws, legislators have also signalled their intention to help make more certain the legal environment for electronic commerce.

1) The Writing Requirement

a) The *Statute of Frauds*
Contract formation law has for several hundred years frowned upon the practice, once widespread, of entering into oral contracts for certain types of agreements, in which two or more parties do not reduce their oral agreement to any fixed form of record. Some three hundred years ago, the problems presented by oral contracts and the rules of civil procedure and evidence were so acute — and the number of disputes over oral contracts brought before the local magistrates so numerous — that post-Cromwellian England passed the *Statute of Frauds*.[6] This legislation, which should really be called the Statute Against Frauds, established the requirement that certain contracts, in order to be enforceable, must be in "writing." The statute, whose purpose was to reduce the likelihood of fraud and fabrication and to promote certainty in commercial relations, was repealed in England in 1954, but survives to this day in the common law provinces, such as in Ontario's version of the statute that still requires a number of agreements, such as guarantees and those related to land transactions, to be in writing.[7]

---

6   The original *Statute of Frauds* was passed in 1677, as 29 Charles II C.3, "An Act for the Prevention of Frauds and Perjuries." For a discussion of the historic context for this legislation, see Douglas Stollery, "Statute of Frauds" (1976) 14 Alberta Law Review 222 ["Frauds"]. For a wide-ranging discussion, from an American perspective, of the challenges raised by the *Statute of Frauds* in relation to electronic commerce contract formation, see: Shawn Pompian, "Is the *Statute of Frauds* Ready for Electronic Contracting?" (1999) 85 Va. L. Rev. 1447.

7   *Statute of Frauds*, R.S.O. 1990, c. S.19. For a good example of why oral agreements should be discouraged and written agreements promoted, see *Ben-Israel* v. *Vitacare Medical Products Inc.*, [1997] O.J. No. 4540 (Ont. Gen. Div.); affirmed, *Ben-Israel* v. *Vitacare Medical Products Inc.*, [1999] O.J. No. 2272 (Ont. C.A.). In this case the customer of a contract manufacturer claimed that the latter agreed to a non-competition arrangement when they first entered into business togeth-

Moreover, the concept that particular contracts must be reduced to writing has been imported from the Statute of Frauds into numerous other statutes and regulations.[8] Accordingly, while the following discusses the writing requirement and related issues generally, it is always important to understand what, if any, statutory rules apply in a given situation, and then to approach the particular rule from the context of the purpose of the applicable statute. Nevertheless, the general principles articulated here should assist in any such specific exercise.

b) Telegraph Cases

In all likelihood the English Parliament in 1677 contemplated a "writing" to be words and figures written in ink on paper, given that this was the predominant method of recording commercial information at the time (having superseded stone tablets, clay tablets, metal papers, papyrus, and parchment used by earlier civilizations). With the intro-

---

er. This agreement was never reduced to writing, and of course the manufacturer denied its existence five years later when it went into competition against the customer. The trial judge ultimately ended up believing the customer, because its representative appeared to the judge as "credible, logical and cautious," while the manufacturer's witnesses demonstrated a "condescending, evasive and manipulative mind set." These types of judgment calls, which make the inherent uncertainty of litigation positively lottery-like, can be avoided when agreements are reduced to writing for posterity's sake. See also *James W. Smith* v. *International Paper Company*, 87 F.3d 245 (8th Cir. 1996) for a decision applying strictly a writing requirement in the context of a real estate deal, and refusing to find a contract in a mixture of oral and e-mail exchanges.

8   For example, s.139 of Ontario's *Insurance Act*, c. I.8, which requires contracts for title insurance be in writing; *The Cost of Borrowing (Banks) Regulations* (under the federal *Bank Act*) S.O.R./2001-101 [*Borrowing Regulations*], which require a disclosure statement to be provided to the borrower in writing (as to how this can be done electronically, see below note 77); s. 19 Ontario's *Consumer Protection Act*, R.S.O. 1990, c. C.31, which contains a writing requirement for certain types of consumer agreements, and subs. 36(2) of the same statute, which does not allow a credit card company to bring an action against a cardholder unless the borrower "requested or accepted the credit arrangement and card in writing"; and s. 7 of Alberta's *Sale of Goods Act*, R.S.A. 1980, c. S-2, which provides that certain contracts for the sale of goods must be made in writing. Various writing and other formalities exist in statutes governing intellectual property exchanges. For example, subs. 13(4) of the *Copyright Act*, R.S.C. 1985, c. C-42, as amended, requires any copyright assignment to be in writing. As well, subs. 13(1) of the *Bills of Exchange Act*, R.S.C. 1985, c. B-4, provides that any bill or note related to the purchase money of a patent right must have prominently across its face the words "Given for a patent right."

duction of the telegraph some 160 years ago,[9] the question arose whether telegraphic messages would satisfy the writing requirement in the *Statute of Frauds*. For the most part, this question was answered in the affirmative in Canada,[10] England,[11] and the United States.[12] In some cases, courts simply assumed that a telegram constituted a writing. In other cases, the courts took the view that the "original" writing is the paper-based message provided to the telegraph company by the sender and that the message sent by the telegraph company is merely a transcript confirming the original writing.[13] Courts even were able to overcome a break in the paper trail when they were confronted with the practice of clients of telegraph companies telephoning their messages to the telegraph office, sometimes (but not always) relying on the legal construct that the telegraph clerk, for this narrow purpose, was the agent of the client. Thus, in the *Selma Sav. Bank* case,[14] the court (without relying on the agency construct), concluded that the writing requirement of the applicable statute was met by the telegraph clerk transcribing the signature on behalf of the customer as fully as if the customer's own staff had written out and signed the message, because the "mechanical means of making and signing the writing are not important," in view of the definition of writing in the applicable law "providing that 'written' includes printed, and 'writing' includes print." In coming to this conclusion, the court cited in full the following passage from an earlier American case:

> So when a contract is made by telegraph, which must be in writing by the statute of frauds, if the parties authorize their agents either in writing or by parol, to make a proposition on one side and the other party accepts it through the telegraph, that constitutes a contract in writing under the statute of frauds; because each party authorizes his agents, the company or the company's operator, to write for him; and it makes no difference whether that operator writes the offer or the

---

9   For a fascinating study of the telegraph, see Tom Standage, *The Victorian Internet: The Remarkable Story of the Telegraph and the Nineteenth Century's Online Pioneers* (London: Phoenix, 1999).

10 *Kinghorne v. The Montreal Telegraph Co.* (1859), 18 U.C.Q.B.R. 60 [*Kinghorne*].

11 *McBlain v. Cross* (1871), 25 L.T. 804; and *Coupland v. Arrowsmith* (1868), 18 L.T. 755 [*Coupland*]. See also Evelyn G.M. Carmichael, *The Law Relating to the Telegraph, the Telephone and the Submarine Cable* (London: Knight & Co., 1904).

12 See the various telegraph cases in S. Walter Jones, *A Treatise on the Law of Telegraph and Telephone Companies*, 2d ed. (Kansas City: Vernon Law Book Company, 1916).

13 *Kinghorne*, above note 10; and *Howley v. Whipple*, 48 N.H. 487 (1869) [*Howley*].

14 *Selma Sav. Bank v. Webster County Bank*, 206 S.W. 870 at 872 (Ky. App. 1918).

acceptance in the presence of his principal and by his express direction, with a steel pen an inch long attached to an ordinary penholder, or whether his pen be a copper wire a thousand miles long. In either case the thought is communicated to the paper by the use of the finger resting upon the pen; nor does it make any difference that in one case common record ink is used, while in the other case a more subtle fluid, known as electricity, performs the same office.[15]

This case is indicative of a predilection on the part of judges to sensibly accommodate new developments in technology. In short, in the area of contract formation courts have been able to cope successfully with the first dynamic of computer law — the rapid pace of change in technology and the equally constant advances in business practices engendered thereby.

c) Fax Cases

More recently, courts have had to determine whether fax communications satisfy the writing requirement. In the British Columbia case of

---

15 *Ibid.*, at 872 from *Howley*, above note 13 at 488. It should be noted that even where a traditional handwritten signature is at issue, courts have accepted a lead pencil in addition to ink: *Brown v. The Butchers' & Drovers' Bank*, 1844 N.Y. LEXIS 47 (N.Y. Sup. Ct. 1844). See also *Bradshaw v. Unity Marine Corporation, Inc.*, 2001 WL 739951 (S.D. Tex. 2001), a colourful decision from Texas, where the pleadings were drafted in crayon on the back of gravy-stained paper placemats. But see also *In Re Kaspar*, 125 F.3d 1358 (10th Cir. 1997) [*Kaspar*], where a computer-based form completed by a telemarketing representative from answers given orally over the telephone was held not to constitute a writing. In coming to this conclusion, the court stated, at 1361: "[A] statement of financial condition is a solemn part of significant credit transactions; therefore, it is only natural that solemnity be sanctified by a document which the debtor either prepares or sees and adopts. In a world where important decisions relating to the extensions of credit and service will be made upon the contents of a statement relating to financial condition, too much mischief can be done by either party to the transaction were it otherwise. Somewhere in the commercial risk allocation picture, the writing must stand as a bulwark which tends to protect both sides. A creditor who forsakes that protection, abandoning caution and sound business practices in the name of convenience, may find itself without protection." But for a decision coming to a different conclusion on virtually equivalent facts, see *Chevy Chase Federal Savings Bank v. Graham (In RE Graham)*, 122 B.R. 447 (Bank M.D. Fla. 1990). It is interesting to speculate whether the deficiency observed by the court in Kaspar could have been cured by the creditor sending, either through the regular paper-based mails or by e-mail, a confirmatory copy of the completed form to the debtor at the time the loan was applied for. In any event, the court proposed that Congress might deal with this issue if it felt that the *Bankruptcy Act* needed to be updated in light of new technology.

Beatty v. First Explor. Fund 1987 & Co.,[16] a partner argued that proxies for a special meeting of the partners that were sent by telecopier should be declared invalid, on the basis that the partnership agreement required proxies to be "written" and "signed by the appointer." The court disagreed, stating that

> the law has endeavoured to take cognizance of, and to be receptive to, technological advances in the means of communication. … The conduct of business has for many years been enhanced by technological improvements in communication. Those improvements should not be rejected automatically when attempts are made to apply them to matters involving the law. They should be considered and, unless there are compelling reasons for rejection, they should be encouraged, applied and approved.[17]

The Ontario Court of Appeal, in *Rolling v. Willann Investments Ltd.*, came to a similar conclusion when it held that a fax transmission of an offer was valid:

> Where technological advances have been made which facilitate communications and expedite the transmission of documents we see no reason why they should not be utilized. Indeed, they should be encouraged and approved.[18]

The sentiments in the *Beatty* and *Rolling* cases encapsulate the common-sense, practical approach taken by Canadian judges to new technologies and related business practices in the area of contract formation legal issues. Similarly, in an English case a court held that service of certain legal documents could be effected by fax, with the judge stating that he could see no reason why "advantage should not be taken

---

16   (1988), 25 B.C.L.R. (2d) 377 (S.C.) [*Beatty*].

17   *Ibid.*, at 383 and 385. In coming to this conclusion, the court in Beatty cited the following passages from *Re English, Scottish and Australian Chartered Bank*, [1891-4] All E.R. 775 (Eng. C.A.), at 779 and 783, a telegraph case almost a hundred years before where proxies were, for the first time, allowed to be telegraphed, with the court in that case finding that: "[I]t is ingeniously using the improved methods of communication," and that the telegraph "can be brought into play to carry out what was eminently needed, and indeed was absolutely necessary to carry out, justice in this case." This case is discussed further in chapter 4, section E.2, "Corporate Meetings." See also *Sadgrove v. Bryden*, [1907] 1 Ch. 318 (Ch. Div.), where the court permitted instructions related to proxies to be conveyed by cablegram.

18   (1989), 70 O.R. (2d) 578 at 581 (C.A.) [*Rolling*].

of the progress in technology which fax represents to enable documents to be served by fax."[19] Interestingly, the party arguing against use of fax in this case made the point that the paper quality from the fax was poor, and that if the fax was left on a radiator the writing would come off. The court responded to this concern by stating that in practice this technological shortcoming can be dealt with by making a photocopy of the fax. In the United States there are also fax cases that have adopted reasoning commensurate with that articulated in the *Beatty* and *Rolling* cases. For example, in one decision a court held that a fax of a certified copy of a court judgment is admissible as evidence.[20] In another case, a court concluded that where a statute required that a particular document be under seal, a fax copy of the seal satisfied the statutory condition.[21] But in at least one case a fax did not suffice, because the legislation clearly required paper-based originals.[22]

In the *Beatty* and *Rolling* cases, the respective judges took comfort from the fact that the faxed document was a copy of an original document, and that underlying the faxes were paper-based originals with signatures consisting of human autographs. These cases reflect a particular type of fax technology where original, paper-based documents are reproduced by a system akin to photocopying and then transmitted. More modern fax technology, however, allows a sender of a message to transmit directly from a computer, without first creating a paper document. Similarly, EDI involves direct computer-to-computer transmission of data, without the creation of paper-based records at either the sender's or recipient's end. The older fax cases illustrate an important legal side effect of the first dynamic of computer law; the rapid pace of technological change means that great care and sensitivity must be exhibited when "classifying" a decision for jurisprudential, precedential purposes. One should not, for example, say that the *Beatty* case stands for the proposition that all fax technology has been held to satisfy the writing requirement. Rather, forms of fax technology other than those at issue in the *Beatty* and *Rolling* cases should be approached from the perspective of a functional analysis of the purpose

---

19   *Hastie & Jenkerson v. McMahon*, [1991] 1 All E.R. 255 at 259 (C.A.).

20   *Englund v. State*, 907 S.W.2d 937 (Tex. App. 1995).

21   *State v. Smith*, 832 P.2d 1366 (Wash. App. 1992).

22   *Department of Transportation v. Norris*, 474 S.E.2d 216 (C.A. Ga 1996). See also the dissent in the appeal of this case: *Norris v. Department of Transportation*, 486 S.E.2d 826 (S.C. Ga 1997).

of the writing requirement and the underlying technical and business process aspects of the communication in issue.[23]

d) Electronic Messages

With respect to electronic messages, courts in Canada and the United States have come to the same conclusions as in the telegraph and fax cases noted in sections A.1(b), "Telegraph Cases," and A.1(c), "Fax Cases," respectively.[24] Some commentators, however, did not predict the outcome of these cases. One concern that was raised in Ontario (and jurisdictions with Interpretation Acts similar to Ontario's) regarding electronic messages and the writing requirement is that the definition of writing in the Ontario *Interpretation Act* provides that "'writing,' 'written,' or any term of like import, includes words printed, painted,

---

23   Indeed, even the technology underpinning photocopying is shifting from one based on a process of optical and mechanical "dry photography" to one that involves digital scanning, printing, and transmission all in one: Kevin Marron, "Digital Copiers Save Time and Shoe Leather," *The Globe and Mail*, Technology Quarterly (3 June 1997).

24   See *Newbridge Networks Corp. (Re)* (2000), 48 O.R. (3d) 47 (Ont. Sup. Ct.) [*Newbridge Networks*], and *Re RealNetworks Inc. Privacy Litigation*, 2000 U.S. Dist. LEXIS 6584 (N.D. Ill. 2000) [*RealNetworks*]. And prior to the new millennium, it was reported that a court in the United Kingdom approved a law firm serving a writ by means of the Internet for a libel action: see "Libel Writ Served by E-mail," *Electronic Telegraph*, Issue 374, 1 May 1996, at <telegraph.co.uk/index.html>. More recently, in *Rio Properties, Inc. v. Rio International Interlink*, 284 F.3d 1007 (9th Cir. 2002), the court stated at 1017–18, in a decision that concluded that e-mail was an appropriate mechanism for effecting alternative service: "Although communication via e-mail and over the Internet is comparatively new, such communication has been zealously embraced within the business community. RII particularly has embraced the modern e-business model and profited immensely from it [RII was an Internet gaining site]. In fact, RII structured its business such that it could be contacted only via its e-mail address" [emphasis in original]. It should be noted, however, that the court in this case, at 1019, also expressed reservations about using e-mail to effect service: "Despite our endorsement of service of process by email in this case, we are cognizant of its limitations. In most instances, there is no way to confirm receipt of an email message. Limited use of electronic signatures could present problems in complying with the verification requirements of *Rule 4(a)* and *Rule 11*, and system compatibility problems may lead to controversies over whether an exhibit or attachment was actually received. Imprecise imaging technology may even make appending exhibits and attachments impossible in some circumstances. We note, however, that, except for the provisions recently introduced into *Rule 5(b)*, email service is not available absent a *Rule 4(f)(3)* court decree. Accordingly, we leave it to the discretion of the district court to balance the limitations of email service against its benefits in any particular case."

engraved, lithographed, photographed, or represented or reproduced by any other mode in a visible form."[25] The question was whether this definition requires the writing to be visible to the *unaided eye*, or whether the use of technical intermediaries, such as a computer monitor, would be accommodated under the definition. Without making reference to any case law, a pair of English commentators, considering a similarly worded definition in their *Interpretation Act*, had concerns regarding EDI messages that are passed between computers and that are not normally viewed by humans: one had expressed the view that the "reference to 'visible form' might militate against the characterization of a purely electronic document as a writing,"[26] and the other had taken an even harder line, being of the opinion contracts will not be enforceable using EDI until the writing definition in the Interpretation Act is amended.[27] These assessments, particularly the latter, misconstrue the relevant conclusion to be drawn on this point from the second dynamic of computer law and, in short, are not warranted, having regard to the purpose and wording of the writing definition in the context of modern day computer-based communications, and the *Newbridge Networks* and *RealNetworks* cases comprise two decisions that support this conclusion.

Where the electronic message is displayed on a computer monitor, the *Interpretation Act* definition of writing is satisfied because words are directly represented in a visible form.[28] Even where a monitor is not used in each case, however, the writing definition should be satisfied

---

25   *Interpretation Act* (Ontario), R.S.O. 1990 c. I.11, subs. 29(1). Generally, this type of language is used in the other common law provinces. Slightly different wording is used in the federal *Interpretation Act*, R.S.C. 1985, c. I-21. Other words in Interpretation Acts can also cause some uncertainty from a nomenclature perspective. For example, in British Columbia's statute (R.S.B.C. 1996, c. 238), "mail" is linked inexorably to that which is deposited in the "Canada Post Office," thus raising the question as to the interpretation to be given to any reference to "e-mail" in a B.C. statute.

26   Christopher Millard, "Contractual Issues of EDI," in *EDI and the Law*, ed. Ian Walden (London: Blenheim Online Publications, 1989) [*EDI and the Law*], at 47. In this same book another British author argues that the *Interpretation Act* definition of writing arguably is wide enough to cover EDI messages: Rob Bradgate, "Evidential Issues of EDI," in Walden, *EDI and the Law*. For a concern similar to that raised by Millard, see Mark J. Selick, "E-Contract Issues and Opportunities For the Commercial Lawyer" (2000) 16 B.F.L.R. 1.

27   Chris Reed, "EDI — Contractual and Liability Issues" (1989) 6:2 Computer Law and Practice 36.

28   Three commentators from Quebec agree: D. Johnston, S. Handa, & C. Morgan, *Cyberlaw: What You Need to Know About Doing Business Online* (Toronto: Stoddart, 1997), at 192.

for a couple of reasons. Consider, for example, an EDI system where the computers of both users participate in the creation of the electronic contract and both retain an electronic version of the various EDI messages, all of which can be printed out on paper if desired. Or consider an Internet-based transaction where two parties, through their computers, satisfy the requirements of offer and acceptance by means of transmitting electronic e-mail messages, each of which is retained by both computers and susceptible to being reproduced in a paper-based form if so desired. In these cases, the judicial focus on reliability of records, which at base is the purpose of the Statute of Frauds' writing requirement, should shift from a document-specific enquiry to a systemic analysis of the various technological devices and business processes that gave rise to the contract. In the case of these examples, indicia of trustworthiness include the fact that both parties actively participated in the creation of the contract, and that from the time of creation and thereafter each party can access the contract electronically through computer terminals or by printing out a hard copy. Thus, these examples should satisfy the writing definition in the *Interpretation Act* for two reasons. The definition is not exhaustive, and therefore the definition should not be limited to a paper-based environment when, as in the above-noted examples, reliable forms of writing have been created. As well, these examples should also satisfy the visible form requirement given that at all relevant times a version of the contract was and continues to be available in a visible form, whether displayed on a computer screen or by being printed out. In other words, in an electronic contracting environment the writing requirement should be interpreted as admitting of more than one legally relevant version of the contract, given the second dynamic of computer law. This would be consistent with the decisions in several cases discussed in sections B.2(a), "Computer-Generated Business Records," and B.2(b), "Multiple Originals."

The approach to the writing requirement noted in the previous paragraph is echoed by an American court that had to determine whether a computer disk (or more precisely, the information contained electronically on it) provided to an insurance agent would constitute "written notice."[29] The court noted that no previous case had dealt with this issue in the context of a computer disk, although various cases had held that videotapes and tape recordings constituted a "writing" for various statutory purposes. In coming to its conclusion that the computer disk did satisfy the writing requirement, the court stated the following:

---

29   *Clyburn v. Allstates Insurance Company*, 826 F.Supp. 955 (D.S.C. 1993).

Although, as noted, these cases [related to videotapes and tape recordings] arise in entirely different contexts and stem from different statutes or rules, the cases do suggest that other media forms are recognized as "writings." The storage of information on tape recordings and videotapes is not that much different from that on floppy diskettes for computers, but rather is more a difference in the devices used to read the information. The information can be retrieved and printed as "hardcopy" on paper. In today's "paperless" society of computer generated information, the court is not prepared, in the absence of some legislative provision or otherwise, to find that a computer floppy diskette would not constitute a "writing" within the meaning of [the relevant statute].[30]

Bolstering the court's finding were the facts that (a) there was no evidence to suggest that the insurance agent did not have the necessary equipment to access or read the computerized document, and (b) the sending of such computer disks was a standard method for the insurance company to communicate with its agent. In effect, the court applied a very sensible approach to coming to terms with the challenges posed by the second dynamic of computer law.

In the *Newbridge Networks* and *RealNetworks* cases even more direct authority can be found for the proposition that electronic messages satisfy the writing requirement. In the former case, the court, in the context of discussing various proposed amendments to the corporations law that would facilitate electronic communications to shareholders, made the following comment:

I do not find the distinction in the legislative amendments between "written" or "printed" format to be helpful when contradistincted to the electronic format. When the electronic format is extracted from its envelope sent to me, it is in written form on a screen and may, at my choice, be printed out on a printer for hard copy.[31]

---

30 *Ibid.*, at 956—57.
31 *Newbridge Networks*, above note 24 at 50. Note as well that the court in *Apple v. McIntosh* (1986), 10 C.P.R. (3d) 1 (F.C.T.D.), at 30, held that software residing on a chip is a literary work and satisfies a writing requirement so long as there is "a method" by which the two programs can be visibly compared in order to test whether there has been copying. It can also be added that courts in copyright cases have held information to be reproduced in "material form" when displayed on a screen: *Matrox Electronic Systems Ltd.* v. *Gaudreau*, [1993] R.J.Q. 2449 (C.S.); and *Bookmakers' Afternoon Greyhound Services* v. *Wilf Gilbert (Staffordshire) Ltd.*, [1994] F.S.R. 723 (Ch. D.).

In the *RealNetworks* case the court concluded that a licence pulled down and viewed electronically from a Web site satisfies the relevant statutory writing requirements (that were quite similar in phraseology to the *Interpretation Acts* in Canada), in large part (apparently) because the licence could be printed and stored. In coming to its conclusion the court stated:

> The word "written," used in a statute, may include printing and any other mode of representing words or letters. ... Thus, although the definition of a writing included a traditional paper document, it did not exclude representations of language on other media. Because electronic communications can be letters or characters formed on the screen to record or communicate ... , it would seem that the plain meaning of the word "written" does not exclude all electronic communications.[32]

In approaching the writing issue, particularly in the context of sales transactions, courts should also be wary of the context in which many of these cases arise. Typically, an agreement is struck for the future delivery of a product, and between the time of concluding the contract and making delivery the price of the product fluctuates such that the seller could sell the same product for more to another buyer, or the buyer could obtain the product for less from another source. Thus, one or other party brings a claim under the writing requirement as a pretext for extricating itself from the initial bargain. In one such Ontario case during the telegraph era, where the plaintiff argued that a series of letters and telegrams did not constitute an agreement in writing for the purpose of the Statute of Frauds, the court was not persuaded and upheld the contract, using the following language:

> The fact that the price of leather had increased, and the unwillingness of the defendants to deliver it after such increase at the price they had named for it in their first letter, and at which the plaintiff had offered to take it, suggest that the view of the contract now contended for by the defendants is an attempt to get rid of a bargain by an ingenious interpretation of the correspondence, rather than frankly carrying out what they had really agreed to, and what both parties at the time understood.[33]

---

32 *RealNetworks*, above note 24 at 2.
33 *Thorne v. Barwick* (1866), 16 U.C.C.P. 369 at 377 [*Thorne*].

Such judicial sentiment and conclusions are consistent with and supportive of the rule that the *Statute of Frauds* should not be used to perpetrate a fraud.[34]

e) Contractual Measures

One approach to the writing requirement involves parties to electronic commerce transactions dealing with the issue contractually. For example, more than a decade ago, the EDI Council of Canada published a *Model Form of Electronic Data Interchange Trading Partner Agreement and Commentary (Model TPA)*.[35] The *Model TPA* is intended to be used by organizations engaging in EDI. The *Model TPA*, which has numerous counterparts around the world, addresses a number of the technical, operational, contractual, and legal issues that arise in EDI relationships.[36] With respect to the writing requirement, section 6.04 of the *Model TPA*, titled "Enforceability," provides as follows:

> The parties agree that as between them each Document [being an electronic message] that is received by the Receiver shall be deemed to constitute a memorandum in writing signed and delivered by or on behalf of the Sender thereof for the purposes of any statute or rule of law that requires a Contract to be evidenced by a written memorandum or be in writing, or requires any such written memorandum to be signed and/or delivered. Each party acknowledges that in any legal proceedings between them respecting or in any way related to a Contract it hereby expressly waives any right to raise any defence or waiver of liability based upon the absence of a memorandum in writing or of a signature.

It is open to question, however, as the commentary to the *Model TPA* points out, whether parties can "contract out" of a writing requirement, or whether such a provision would be void as against public policy. Accordingly, if possible, parties should choose to have their EDI

---

34   For cases that discuss the rule that the *Statute of Frauds* should not be used to perpetrate frauds, see Stollery, "Frauds," above note 6.

35   Legal and Audit Issues Committee of the Electronic Data Interchange Council of Canada, *Model Form of Electronic Data Interchange Trading Partner Agreement and Commentary*, 1990 [*Model TPA*].

36   For the version developed by the American Bar Association, see ABA Electronic Messaging Services Task Force, "Model Electronic Data Interchange Trading Partner Agreement and Commentary" (1990) 45 Bus. L. 1717. See also Amelia H. Boss, "Electronic Data Interchange Agreements: Private Contracting Towards a Global Environment" (1992) 3 Nw. J. Int'l L. & Bus. 31.

contract governed by the laws of a jurisdiction that no longer contains a writing requirement; for example, it would be wise to have an EDI agreement between parties in Alberta and British Columbia governed by British Columbia law, given that British Columbia's *Sale of Goods Act* does not contain a writing requirement. It should also be noted that such contractual measures to address the writing requirement and other issues need not be restricted to EDI situations. Organizations doing business over the Internet could implement the same type of provision in agreements with subscribers or other parties.[37]

f) Law Reform Approaches

Even if contracts were able to address all outstanding legal issues adequately, they would still not be a perfect solution. As noted later in this book,[38] contracts are not a panacea because, among other things, they usually entail non-trivial transaction costs. Relying solely on judge-made common law also has its shortcomings. While the previous sections of this chapter note many decisions where judges have had little difficulty with the writing requirement in the context of electronic commerce, every now and then an unfortunate decision mars this record. For example, in one American case the court concluded that a fax transmission did not satisfy the statutory writing requirement because while such a transmission is an audio signal from which a writing may be accurately duplicated, the transmission itself was a series of "beeps and chirps" that do not constitute a writing.[39] Thus, the legal uncertainties resulting from the new electronic trading and communications technologies could usefully be addressed by law reform. Accordingly, this section deals with law reform generally, while the next section deals specifically with the recently enacted electronic commerce statutes.

Legislators could consider several solutions to deal with the writing requirement in the context of electronic messages. One approach is the "functional equivalent" method. This method has been taken by

---

37   See below, at note 293, for a provision that effects a similar purpose in respect of evidence law in a set of Web site terms and conditions.

38   See chapter 8, section C.4, "Law Reform."

39   *Department of Transportation* v. *Norris*, 474 S.E.2d 216 (C.A. Ga 1996). Fortunately, this decision was reversed, but not by expressly repudiating the unfortunate statements about fax transmissions: *Norris* v. *Department of Transportation*, 486 S.E.2d 826 (S.C. Ga 1997). See also *Walgreen Co.* v. *Wisconsin Pharmacy Examining Board,* 577 N.W.(2d) 387 (Wisc. C.A. 1998), where the court, having to jump through statutory hurdles to accommodate physicians submitting prescriptions to pharmacies by e-mail, ends up analogizing e-mail to oral telephone calls for purposes of the relevant legislation.

the United Nations Commission on International Trade Law (UNCI-TRAL) in its Working Group on EDI, which has prepared a set of model provisions for uniform rules on the legal aspects of EDI.[40] Article 6 of the UNCITRAL Model Law, for example, provides that whenever a rule of law requires a writing, that rule is satisfied by an electronic data message having certain characteristics. It is interesting to note, as John Gregory does in *Solving Legal Issues*,[41] that much of the UNCITRAL Model Law was influenced by the content of the various model EDI trading partner agreements referred to in the previous section on Contractual Measures.[42] The UNCITRAL Model Law also had a significant influence on the development of the *Uniform Electronic Commerce Act* prepared by the Uniform Law Conference of Canada, and the resulting federal and provincial electronic commerce legislation referred to in the next section.[43]

Illustrating another approach to law reform is the 1988 version of the United Kingdom's copyright law that contains a broad definition of writing: "any form of notation or code, whether by hand or otherwise and regardless of the method by which, or medium in or on which, it is recorded."[44] More simply, Ontario's Hospital Management Regulation was amended to provide that "writing includes an entry in a computer."[45] A similar methodology is to statutorily deem electronic and related messages to be writings. In the early 1990s, such a solution on a large scale was proposed to the Ontario government, namely, to expand the definition of writing in the *Interpretation Act* to include information recorded by electronic, magnetic, or optical means. The government chose not to implement this approach because at the time the Ontario statutes contained over 2000 references to writing, many of which were to consumer notices where the government believed it inappropriate to permit electronic communications. The government's concern was somewhat misplaced. There should not be a problem deeming electronic messages to satisfy the writing requirement. The real problem is

---

40   See the UNCITRAL Model Law on Electronic Commerce, adopted in 1996, available at <uncitral.org/english/texts/electcom/ml-ec.htm>.

41   "Solving Legal Issues," above note 2.

42   See section A.1(e) of this chapter, "Contractual Measures."

43   See section A.1(g) of this chapter, "Electronic Commerce Statutes." Usefully, the UNCITRAL Model Law has served as the inspiration for law reform in this area in a number of countries around the world, including Slovenia, Bermuda, India, Singapore, Australia, Colombia, and the United States. For a list of such legislation around the world, see <pkilaw.com>.

44   *Copyright, Designs and Patents Act 1988* (U.K.), 1988, c. 48, s. 178.

45   Hospital Management, R.R.O. 1990, Reg. 965, subs. 1(1).

ensuring the delivery of the notice, whether it is in paper-based or electronic form. Thus, someone should be entitled to give a consumer notice electronically so long as the sender can show that it was given (i.e., that the recipient had adequate computer technology, etc.). And, of course, occasionally it may be more difficult to give the notice electronically, as in the situation where a landlord and tenant statute requires the posting of a message in a lobby of an apartment building. However, this would be a snap electronically if a lobby is outfitted with a digital display device that carries all sorts of tenant programming, including official notices. This is not such a far-fetched idea — office elevators are often equipped with compact computer monitors that display news, weather, information, and advertising. For an interesting twist on the writing definition approach to law reform, consider that the court in the *Ellis Canning* case in the United States had to decide whether a tape of a telephone conversation comprised a writing under the *Uniform Commercial Code* (UCC).[46] The court answered this question in the affirmative because in the UCC the definition of writing includes "printing, typewriting *or any other intentional reduction to tangible form*" [italics in original]. The court found that the tape recording of the oral contract was a reduction in tangible form, but that "probably the opposite result would be required under historical statutes of frauds which do not contain the tangible form language of this somewhat unusual definition of the word 'written.'"[47] In order to comfortably accommodate an electronic environment, any reference to tangible form should be avoided in writing definitions, unless it is made clear that the tangible form may be printed out as a second or indirect step.

A third approach to the writing requirement has been simply to delete the particular requirement altogether. For example, a *Statute of Frauds* writing requirement has historically been part of sale of goods legislation in the common law provinces (for example, Ontario's *Sale of Goods Act* prior to December 1994 contained a provision that contracts for the sale of goods to be delivered in the future having a value of over $40 must be in writing).[48] England repealed the equivalent provision in

---

46   *Ellis Canning Company* v. *Bernstein*, 348 F.Supp. 1212 (D. Colo. 1972) [*Ellis Canning*].

47   *Ibid.*, at 1228.

48   *Sale of Goods Act*, R.S.O. 1990, c. S.1. In the United States, the state-based *Uniform Commercial Code* also contains a *Statute of Frauds* provision in respect of the sale of goods, together with a "merchant's exception," whereby a commercial party can be held to an agreement simply by not disputing a confirmatory communication sent by another commercial party: see *Bazak International Corp.* v. *Mast Industries*, 73 N.Y.2d 113 (N.Y.C.A., 1989).

its *Sale of Goods Act* in the 1950s, and, in keeping with the general trend over the past few decades to reduce formal requirements for contracts, British Columbia, Manitoba, and New Brunswick have also repealed the provision in their sales statutes (but not, for example, Alberta). As well, Ontario and most other provinces effectively repealed this provision in May 1992 for international sales contracts given that the *United Nations Convention on Contracts for the International Sale of Goods* provides that a contract of sale need not be evidenced in writing (though a signatory to this convention could derogate from this provision, thus continuing to require certain formal requirements for contracts).[49] This results in the perverse situation where two parties conducting EDI, Web-based purchasing, or some other form of electronic commerce within a province that still has a writing requirement in its *Sale of Goods* statute do so with less certainty than if either of them contracted electronically with an entity in the United States, given that in the latter case the U.N. International Sales Convention, to which the United States is also a signatory, effectively repeals the writing requirement. This ironic state of affairs was rectified in Ontario in December 1994 when that jurisdiction finally repealed section 5 of its *Sale of Goods Act*,[50] but the bizarre situation still exists in those provinces that have not taken this step.[51] Indeed, even in provinces that have repealed the writing provision in their sales statutes applicable to commercial sales, a similar writing provision in respect of consumer sales may continue to exist in another statute.[52]

g) Electronic Commerce Statutes

In an effort to address the legal uncertainties caused by information in electronic form discussed elsewhere in this chapter, governments in Canada have enacted legislation based, generally speaking, on the

---

49   Each province and the federal government implemented this U.N. Convention by passing enabling legislation; for Ontario's see *International Sale of Goods Act*, R.S.O. 1990, c. I.10.

50   The repeal was effected by s. 54 of the *Statute Law Amendment Act (Government Management and Services), 1994*, S.O. 1994, c. 27. For criticism of the state of affairs prior to the repeal, see George S. Takach, "Preventing Ambulance-Chasing On the Info Highway," *The Globe and Mail* (11 February 1994).

51   For example, Alberta still has a writing requirement in its sale of goods legislation: *Sale of Goods Act*, RSA 1980, c. S-2, s.7.

52   For Ontario, for example, see s. 19 of the *Consumer Protection Act*, R.S.O. 1990, c. C.31, which provides that "executory contracts" must be in writing; an executory contract is a sale of goods or services to a consumer worth more than $50 where delivery of the goods or performance of the services is to be made after the agreement is entered into.

UNCITRAL Model Law and the *Uniform Electronic Commerce Act* (UECA) prepared by the Uniform Law Conference of Canada.[53] This flurry of law reform is very welcome, as it resolves a number — but not all — of the outstanding issues surrounding the enforceability of doing business online. What follows is a description of Ontario's *Electronic Commerce Act* (ECA),[54] with specific references to the other provincial enactments,[55] and the federal law[56] (referred to in this book as PIPE-DA), as appropriate. Similar laws, again generally based on the UNCI-TRAL template, have been passed in the United States.[57] Although all these laws have the same general objective of removing statutory bar-

---

53   The Uniform Law Conference of Canada adopted the UECA in September 1999. The UECA is available at <law.ualbertaca/alri/ulc/current/euecafa.htm>.

54   *Electronic Commerce Act, 2000*, S.O. 2000, c. 17, in force as of October 16, 2000 [*ECA*].

55   Saskatchewan — *The Electronic Information and Documents Act*, 2000, S.S. c. E-7.22 (in force November 1, 2000); Nova Scotia — *Electronic Commerce Act*, S.N.S. 2000 c. 26 (in force November 30, 2000); Manitoba — *The Electronic Commerce and Information Act*, S.M. 2000 c. E55 (in force October 23, 2000, except Parts 2 and 6, Part 6 in force March 19, 2001); Alberta — *Electronic Transactions Act* (not yet proclaimed); British Columbia — *Electronic Transaction Acts*, S.B.C. 2001, c. 10 (in force April 19, 2001); Quebec — *An Act to Establish a Legal Framework for Information Technology*, S.Q. 2001, c. 32 (in force November 1, 2001); Prince Edward Island — *Electronic Commerce Act*, s. P.E.I. 2001, c. 31 (in force May 15, 2001); New Brunswick — *Electronic Transactions Act*, S.N.B. 2001, c. E-5.5 (not yet in force); Newfoundland and Labrador — *Electronic Commerce Act*, S.N.L. 2001, c. E-5.2 (in force December 13, 2001); Yukon — *Electronic Commerce Act*, S.Y. 2000, c. 10 (in force March 27, 2001). For a helpful comparative analysis of the Canadian and U.S. model laws, and their similarity "in inspiration," as befits the world's two largest trading partners, see John D. Gregory, "The UETA and UECA: Canadian Reflections" (2001) Idaho L. Rev. 441 ["The UETA and UECA"].

56   *Personal Information Protection and Electronic Documents Act*, S.C. 2000, c. 5, Part 2 [PIPEDA]. Part 1 of PIPEDA contains the privacy law regime that applies to personal information, and is discussed in chapter 4, section A.4(b), "Private Sector Coverage."

57   See the U.S. federal *Electronic Signatures in Global and National Commerce Act*; at the state level, over half the states have enacted legislation based on the U.S. *Uniform Electronic Transactions Act* <law.upenn.edu/library/ulc/fnact99/1990s/ueta.htm>; see also <uetaonline.com> for related materials. Again, it must be emphasized that while all these statutes have a similar genesis, they can differ in important respects. For example, the U.S. federal law does not have a consent requirement for businesses, only for consumers. In the United States, see also the *Uniform Computer Information Transactions Act* <law.upenn.edu/bll/ulc/ucita/citam99.htm>, which as of December 31, 2001, was translated into law in two states, Virginia (the state where America Online is headquartered) and Maryland.

riers to the use of, and helping facilitate the adoption of, information in electronic form, they are not identical to one another: the statutes in the common law provinces are quite similar inasmuch as they are all based on the UECA and are "minimalist" in their approach,[58] but these differ importantly from PIPEDA, and the Quebec law has a number of unique nuances given that province's civil law system; as well, the Quebec law addresses several areas not covered by the UECA.[59]

In terms of the scope of the ECA, the statute expressly provides that it does not require anyone to use information in an electronic form without their consent.[60] It is merely enabling legislation, and voluntary. Thus if parties are nervous about using electronic-based information or documents, or if they are content to continue using paper, they may do so and do not have to use, for example, the Internet.[61] On the other hand, the ECA provides that consent to use electronic information may be "inferred from a person's conduct."[62] This likely means if a person uses the Internet to place an order for some goods, the ECA has been invoked. It will be interesting to see what the outer parameters of such inferred consent might be: for instance, is it enough that a person's paper-based letterhead or business card contains an e-mail address? The other key point about the scope of the ECA is that it does not apply to certain types of documents, including wills, powers of attorney for financial affairs or personal care, negotiable instruments, documents that may be prescribed by regulation, land transfer documents that require registration, and documents of title.[63] There are generally

---

58   But even the provincial common law statutes can differ importantly from one another. For example, the Manitoba law reflects the "opt-in" approach, which, like PIPEDA, makes it apply only to those statutes that are designated in a schedule. The Ontario *ECA*, by contrast, and as noted below, takes the opt-out approach: it applies to all provincial statutes unless expressly excluded.

59   For example, the Quebec law addresses, among other non-UECA subjects, the liability of different service providers involved in transmitting, hosting, and retaining technology-based documents.

60   *ECA*, subs. 3(1). For a form of consent used in the securities industry for effecting notice and delivery electronically, see "National Policy 11-201," and the discussion of this policy in chapter 4, section E.1, "Securities Law."

61   See the testimony of John Gregory, the principal draftsperson behind the *ECA*, before the Standing Committee on Justice and Social Policy of the Ontario Legislature regarding the *ECA* (then Bill 88), on Monday, August 28, 2000, available at <ontla.on.ca> [*Bill 88 Testimony*].

62   *ECA*, subs. 3(2).

63   *ECA*, s. 31. Here is another example of how the different provincial electronic commerce statutes can differ. New Brunswick's law, for instance, does not contain any statutory exceptions to its coverage, and while the law does allow for

two reasons put forward for these exclusions. In the case of a will, a power of attorney or a negotiable instrument, the ECA reflects the view that these are documents for which there should only be a single, unique original.[64] As for land transfer documents, there is another legislative regime dealing with electronic registration of such materials.[65] Similarly, the ECA does not override other reform efforts that have already made it into Ontario law.[66]

An important distinction relating to coverage of the respective statutes exists between the ECA and the federal law. With the former, once the ECA is invoked expressly or by inferred consent, its rules apply to all Ontario statutes in respect of their application to private parties unless the ECA expressly excludes a particular statute. PIPEDA, by contrast to Ontario's "opt-out" approach, takes an "opt-in" approach, and only covers those other federal statutes listed in schedules to the legislation.[67] Thus, PIPEDA is subject to an incremental,

---

exceptions to be made by regulation, it would appear the New Brunswick government is going to be extremely forward-thinking and not exclude any by regulation, for the time being.

64　Of course the solution for transferring value between business parties that do not know each other may not be an electronic negotiable instrument, but rather an electronic title recordation system, operated by a neutral and trusted intermediary, that serves the same purpose, and indeed more conveniently. For wisdom on this subject, see Jane K. Winn, "Couriers without Luggage: Negotiability and Digital Signatures" (1998) 49 S. Carol. L. Rev. 739. As for wills, it is a pity the Ontario *ECA* excludes this genus of document, and kudos to New Brunswick for adopting the view that any person who makes a deliberate attempt to prepare a will electronically should be capable of having it admitted to probate as a testamentary document. Just as there are today services where one can buy a will online (see <canadawills.com>, <yourwill.net>, and <willkit.net>), in the not too distant future one can envisage a service where one completes a will online and has the service provider store it safely for future reference: see the author's testimony before the legislative committee considering the Ontario *ECA* when it was in bill form, in *Bill 88 Testimony*, above note 61. Thankfully, the ULCC is reconsidering the whole area of wills: see its discussion paper on electronic wills and powers of attorney at <ulcc.ca/en/poam2/e-wills-power-attorney.pdf>.

65　*Land Registration Act*, R.S.O. 1990, c. L.4, as amended by S.O. 1994, c. 27, s. 85. See also <teranet.on.ca/>.

66　Thus, the province's electronic filing system for personal property security registrations is not affected by the *ECA*: see, *Electronic Registration Act* (Ministry of Consumer and Commercial Relations Statutes), 1991, S.O. 1991, c. 44.

67　PIPEDA, s. 40. For a discussion of the rationales behind the "opt-out" and "opt-in" approaches to coverage under such legislation, see *Solving Legal Issues*, above note 2. See also the approach taken to electronic documents in the recent amendments to the *Criminal Code* implemented by the *Criminal Law Amendment Act*, 2001, S.C. 2002, c. 13 [*2002 Criminal Law Amendments*]. These amendments enact, in the

statute-by-statute rollout, versus the across-the-board approach under the ECA. Depending on what is ultimately listed in its schedule, PIPEDA could have a much narrower application than the ECA.[68] Also with respect to scope, it is worth noting that, with one exception, the ECA is technology-neutral.[69] The definition of "electronic" is broad, and does not favour one or other particular technology.[70] The exception to this in the ECA relates to biometric information, and a provision that only extends the benefits of the ECA to the use of biometric information if all parties to the transaction expressly consent to its use,[71] thereby denying biometric technologies the benefit of the inferred consent principle applicable to all other technologies.[72] PIPEDA also exhibits a technology bias, specifically in respect of encryption for certain types of signatures, as is discussed in section 2, "Signatures." The core objective of the ECA is to create a media-neutral legal environment for information.[73] This essentially means the removal of the paper bias that exists in many laws. This is done, in the ECA, by a provision that stipulates that "[I]nformation or a document to which this Act applies is

---

new s. 841 of the *Criminal Code*, a definition of "electronic document," which means "data that is recorded or stored on any medium in or by a computer system or other similar device and that can be read or perceived by a person or a computer system or other similar device." The new ss. 844 and 845 provide that any requirements under the *Criminal Code* that documents be in writing or signed may be satisfied by means of a document in electronic form, or a signature in an electronic document, in each case as prescribed by a statute or the rules of court.

68   As of November 26, 2002, no statutes were listed in the schedules to the federal law.

69   Although given that the *ECA* can only be invoked by consent, in a broader sense the whole statute is not technology neutral, and indeed favours paper-based communications over electronic ones, because the former needs no consent of any kind to be effective.

70   The definition of *electronic* in s. 1 of the *ECA* reads as follows: "includes created, recorded, transmitted or stored in digital form or in other intangible form by electronic, magnetic or optical means or by any other means that has capabilities for creation, recording, transmission or storage similar to those means and "electronically" has a corresponding meaning."

71   *ECA*, subs. 29(1). Subsection 29(2) of the *ECA* defines "biometric information" to mean "information derived from an individual's unique personal characteristics, other than a representation of his or her photograph or signature." Thus, it would cover technologies related to fingerprint and retina scans. For a discussion of biometrics, see section A.2(b) of this chapter, "The Authentication Function."

72   This exception for biometric information was requested by Ontario's Information and Privacy Commissioner, and does not appear in the Canadian *Uniform Electronic Commerce Act* or in several of the provincial counterparts to the *ECA*: see *Bill 88 Testimony*, above note 61.

73   The point of the *ECA* is not to make the law better, just neutral: see Gregory, "The UETA and UECA," above note 55, at 459.

not invalid or unenforceable by reason only of being in electronic form."[74] The non-discrimination principle, which effectively provides equal treatment to paper-based and computer-based information, is then operationalized by several "functional equivalency rules." That is, the ECA establishes a handful of rules that must be satisfied for electronic information to have the same legal effect as paper-based information; put another way, the statute provides a useful mechanism for overcoming the second dynamic of computer law — namely, the elusive nature of information — in a commercial setting. For example, a legal requirement that information be in "writing," is satisfied by information or a document in electronic form "if it is accessible so as to be usable for subsequent reference."[75] Therefore, the effectiveness of electronic information will not be denied if the intended user can read it and call it up at a later time by appropriate computer equipment.[76] Similarly, if the law requires that certain information be *provided*, this can be satisfied if the electronic information is both accessible to the user and capable of being retained by the user.[77] Thus the recipient must be

---

74   *ECA*, s. 4. The reason for the seemingly awkward double negative is that the *ECA* is not intended to provide that every contract concluded electronically is valid. There are various reasons why a contract — whether concluded electronically or on paper or otherwise — may be invalid, including duress, capacity to contract, mistake, etc. The point of the *ECA* is simply to provide that a contract will not be invalid because it is in electronic form. With respect to capacity to contract, and given the great numbers of youth that frequent the Internet, it is useful to note that the age of majority is generally 18 or 19 in Canadian provinces: for example, see s. 1, *Age of Majority and Accountability Act*, R.S.O. 1990, c. A-7.

75   *ECA*, s. 5.

76   The *ECA* does not stipulate for how long the electronic information must be kept. This will be determined by, among other things, statute-based record-retention rules, or a company's own record-retention policy based on, among other things, an analysis of relevant limitation periods. In short, a company should apply its paper-based record retention rules to electronic information in terms of period of retention, with the possible exception of certain e-mail communications: see the discussion in section B.3(b), "E-mail Policies," later in this chapter.

77   *ECA*, subs. 6(1). For a similar regime, see the *Internet Sales Contract Regulation*, Alta. Reg. 81/2001 under the *Alberta Fair Trading Act*, which stipulates that the statute's requirement for a written sales contract can be met electronically if (1) the contract is sent to an e-mail address provided by the consumer; (2) the contract is made accessible to the consumer on the Internet in a manner that ensures that the contract is capable of being retained and printed by the consumer; or (3) the contract is sent to a location and in a manner specified by the consumer. Similarly, under the *Borrowing Regulations*, above note 8, if the borrower consents (in writing), then the disclosure statement may be provided by electronic means in an electronic form that the borrower can retrieve and retain.

able to keep, store, and print the electronic information. A further rule stipulates that electronic information is not provided to a person if it is merely made available for access, for example on a Web site.[78] Therefore, simply posting information to a Web site is insufficient.[79] One sensible way to comply is to send the user an e-mail with the relevant information. It will be interesting to see if the jurisprudence under the ECA will allow someone to send a user an e-mail indicating that information has been posted in the Web site, and inviting the user to download it from the Web site. In effect, the ECA is fairly flexible on how its functional equivalence rules should be satisfied, and indeed there are a number of different ways they can be. One suggestion is for persons undertaking online commercial relationships to specify in their contracts precisely how they agree to satisfy these equivalency rules.[80]

The *quid pro quo* for being able to use electronic documents is the need to use particular care in their creation and preservation. For example, with respect to the *retention* of documents, the ECA provides that a legal requirement to retain a document that is originally created, sent or received in written form is satisfied if the electronic document is retained in the same format as the one in which the written document was created or in a format that accurately represents the information in the written document, and the electronic information is accessible so as to be usable for subsequent reference.[81] A similar rule applies for the retention of documents that were originally created, sent, or received electronically, with the additional proviso that where the electronic document was sent or received, information (if any was created) regarding its origin, destination, and date and time when sent or

---

78 *ECA*, s. 10. But provision of information electronically as part of an interactive Web-based e-commerce transaction should suffice.

79 John D. Gregory gives the rationale for this in the following terms: "Just as I cannot deliver a paper document to you by simply showing it to you, I cannot deliver an electronic document by putting it on a web site. The addressee must be able to decide how long to keep the information, without risk that the person providing it will alter or delete it": "The UETA and UECA," above note 55 at 455.

80 For example, in the securities law area, public companies often go to great lengths to stipulate the precise technical criteria surrounding how disclosure documents will be transmitted by the company, with the investor acknowledging that it will be capable of receiving electronic materials in this form; see chapter 4, section E.1, "Securities Law." For a public example of this, see the job recruitment advertisement on page 111 of the October 21, 2000, edition of *The Economist* for the NATO Spokesman position that stipulates that "any application sent via e-mail **must** be sent using **WORD 97, A4 format** with **only one attachment**" [emphasis in original].

81 *ECA*, subs. 12(1).

received should also be retained. Therefore, if electronic time stamp records are created, these should be kept. The ECA also contains a rule that if there is a legal requirement for one or more copies of a document to be provided, this can be satisfied by sending a single version of the electronic information.[82] As for original documents, the ECA provides that electronic documents may serve as originals if the electronic document is accessible so as to be used for subsequent reference and is capable of being retained, and there exists a reliable assurance as to the integrity of the information.[83] For this latter purpose, integrity is a function of whether the information has remained complete and unaltered, and, in turn, whether the assurance is reliable is to be determined in light of all the circumstances, including the purpose for which the document was created.[84] If this sounds vague, it is intentionally so, to permit flexibility as different technologies come and go. It is useful to note, however, that the UNCITRAL Model Law contains a list of factors that could be relevant to this determination.[85] Generally speaking, however, "the electronic system does not have to be better than the paper system it replaces."[86]

The application to public bodies of the foregoing rules in the ECA is conditional upon each Ontario ministry, agency, board, commission, municipality, and other governmental entity agreeing expressly to be bound by these rules (and not simply through inferred consent, which is enough for private sector entities) for purposes of the communica-

---

82   *ECA*, s. 13.

83   *ECA*, subs. 8(1).

84   *ECA*, subs. 8(2).

85   UNCITRAL Model Law, para. 58, states that in determining whether a particular method is appropriate, various legal, technical, and commercial factors could be considered, including the following: "(1) the sophistication of the equipment used by each of the parties; (2) the nature of their trade activity; (3) the frequency at which commercial transactions take place between the parties; (4) the kind and size of the transaction; (5) the function of signature requirements in a given statutory and regulatory environment; (6) the capability of communication systems; (7) compliance with authentication procedures set forth by intermediaries; (8) the range of authentication procedures made available by any intermediary; (9) compliance with trade customs and practice; (10) the existence of insurance coverage mechanisms against unauthorized messages; (11) the importance and the value of the information contained in the data message; (12) the availability of alternative methods of identification and the cost of implementation; (13) the degree of acceptance or non-acceptance of the method of identification in the relevant industry or field both at the time the method was agreed upon and the time when the data message was communicated; and (14) any other relevant factor."

86   Gregory, "The UETA and UECA," above note 55.

tions that persons have with the public sector.[87] Similarly, the government can stipulate the specific technical standards and other rules that will apply to any such communications between it and private sector entities and persons.[88] Thus, while governments have generally indicated their willingness to allow people to interact with them electronically, these provisions recognize that governments need to roll out their electronic access plans carefully and in a structured format, and probably in stages, so as not to be overwhelmed. By the same token, however, the ECA confirms that through the ECA government cannot force anyone to deal with it electronically;[89] of course the government could do this in some other separate statute.

2) Signatures

Many of the statutes that call for certain types of contracts or notices to be in writing also stipulate that the writing be "signed" by the party against whom the writing is being enforced. As with the writing issue discussed above, the question arises whether the signature requirement can be met in an environment of electronic messages. In 1677, when the first *Statute of Frauds* was promulgated, the predominant form of signature would have arguably been the human autograph.[90] In a number of cases, however, courts have taken a purposive approach to the signature requirement and have concluded that various means will suffice in addition to the human autograph. In a Quebec case, a court had to decide whether the then current rule of civil procedure requiring legal documents to be signed by a lawyer would permit the lawyer's name to be stamped on a relevant document.[91] The court noted an early French definition for signature that described an individual writing his name by his hand at the end of a document, but then went on to dis-

---

87   *ECA*, s. 14.
88   For example, in 1998, British Columbia's *Business Paper Reduction Act*, S.B.C. c. 26 was passed to allow electronic filing of government mandated information. See the *Electronic Filing Act*, S.S. 1998, c. E-7.21, for a similar initiative by Saskatchewan.
89   *ECA*, subs. 15(4).
90   In earlier times, the Bible tells how a merchant would authenticate a commercial transaction by giving one of his sandals to another trader; subsequently, the trader could verify the party he was dealing with by comparing the comparative wear on the soles of the pair of sandals: Ruth 4:7. This example leads to the conclusion that what we are striving for in modern times is not the electronic signature, but the "electronic sandal"!
91   *Grondin v. Tisi & Turner* (1912), 4 D.L.R. 819 (Que. Ct. Rev.).

cuss and adopt more liberal interpretations of signature that included stamping and other means of inscription, so long as no prejudice can be shown to the contesting party, and hence the court held that the legal document under consideration with only a stamp of the lawyer's name satisfied the particular writing requirement. More recently, the English Court of Appeal also found that solicitors could sign their accounts by stamping them in addition to signing them by hand.[92] These cases are consistent with a number of others where the rapid pace of technological change (the first dynamic of computer law), and the novel business practices engendered by it, have not distracted courts from understanding that the true function of the signature requirement is to authenticate a document, and from concluding that this purpose can be satisfied in a number of ways in addition to the use of the human autograph.

a) Telegraph and Fax Cases

In an early case, a party argued that a telegram cannot be a document for *Statute of Frauds* purposes because it was not signed.[93] The court disagreed, and held that telegrams, together with previous correspondence, did constitute a binding contract. In an American telegraph case, a court held that a typed signature, effected by the telegraph company on behalf of a customer, satisfied the relevant signature requirement; the court stated that "[i]n view of the way in which business is done nowadays, any other view would be unrealistic and would produce pernicious consequences, impeding the conduct of business transactions."[94] In another American case, the court was confronted by

---

92   *Goodman v. J. Eban, Ltd.,* [1954] 1 All E.R. 763 (C.A.). In this case Lord Denning registered a dissenting view, stating at 769: "This is such common knowledge that a rubber stamp is contemporaneously used to denote the thoughtless impress of an automaton in contrast to the reasoned attention of a sensible person." The point that Lord Denning missed, but that the majority understood, and that courts in virtually all other cases in this area have grasped, is that automated systems and business processes can, in fact, be extremely sensible, reliable, and trustworthy. But see *Milliken & Co. v. Interface Flooring Systems (Canada) Inc.* (1998), 149 F.T.R. 125 (F.C.T.D.), where the court held that an artist's stamp did not constitute a signature for purposes of section 13(4) of the *Copyright Act* (which requires that assignments of copyrights be in writing signed by the copyright owner) because no evidence was led to show that this was a customary manner of identifying artists for purposes of an assignment.

93   *Coupland,* above note 11.

94   *La Mar Hosiery Mills, Inc. v. Credit and Commodity Corporation,* 216 N.Y.S.2d 186 at 190 (City Ct. of N.Y. 1961). See also *Hessenthaler v. Farzin,* 388 Pa. Super. 37 (Sup. Ct. Penn. 1989), where a mailgram's use of the phrase "We, Dr. Mehdi and

the teletype form of telegraphy, where machines took the place of the transmission/receiver clerks.[95] In this case the court "conceded that these teletype messages do not bear the signature in writing of the party to be charged in the sense that they were not literally signed with pen and ink in the ordinary signature of the sender."[96] Nevertheless, the court noted that each party was readily identifiable and known to the other by the symbols and code letters used. In approaching the question what constitutes a signature in order to satisfy the California *Statute of Frauds*, the court stated it must "take a realistic view of modern business practices, and can probably take judicial notice of the extensive use to which the teletype machine is being used today among business firms, particularly brokers, in the expeditious transmission of typewritten messages."[97] The court, not being able to find any other case on point with respect to teletype machines, nevertheless held teletype messages to satisfy its jurisdiction's *Statute of Frauds*, illustrating again how well courts, for the most part, have been able to handle the challenges posed by the first dynamic of computer law when operating in the contract formation arena. In a later U.S. case, a court decided that a taped telephone conversation satisfied the signature requirement, given that the purpose of this requirement is to identify the contracting party, and this was effected through the audio tape, since both parties admitted and did not contest.[98]

Courts are willing to look at the purpose of the signature requirement, which they have determined to be to connect a person to a document in order to denote authenticity and consent; that is, to make it attributable to the author and to signify the author's approval of the document in order to give it legal effect. Put another way, a signature essentially serves three objectives: identify the signer; show the signer's intent to be bound by the document; and link the signer with the document. By focusing on this functional analysis, courts have avoided stumbling over the various technological obstacles thrown up by the first dynamic of computer law. Instead, like Olympic hurdlers, courts jump over these different and successive challenges, apparently without effort, but in fact thankful for the diligent conditioning undergone

---

Marie Farzin," without more by way of signatures or names, was found sufficient to constitute the mailgram a "signed" writing given the context of the entire, lengthy telegram.

95 *Joseph Denunzio Fruit Co. v. Crane*, 79 F.Supp. 117 (S.D. Cal. 1948).
96 *Ibid.*, at 128.
97 *Ibid.*, at 128–29.
98 *Ellis Canning*, above note 46.

by the common law with all previous technologies. In this regard, it is useful to note that Interpretation Acts do not generally contain a definition for signature, thus permitting a very flexible environment in which the term can operate. Of course, for certain documents the human autograph remains a useful signature. And sometimes the legislature will expressly require a signature by hand, as in one U.S. case where a faxed version of a document was held not to conform to the strict signature requirements of the regulations.[99] This case, however, is not in conflict with the others noted above. Indeed, it may be taken to support them indirectly in the sense that it can be said to stand for the proposition that today, with fax technology as ubiquitous as it is, the judicial presumption ought to be for its acceptance in meeting formal writing and signature requirements, and the onus should be on Parliament to expressly exclude it or other similar communications technologies from satisfying such requirements in the rare circumstances where this is thought to be necessary.

Moreover, the human autograph is not foolproof, even for paper-based documents.[100] Indeed, the entire field of handwriting analysis developed from the legal challenges to the authenticity and genuineness of autographs. A similar sentiment was presciently pointed out in the *Debtor* case in the United Kingdom that considered whether a faxed proxy was valid for a meeting of creditors where the relevant rules required the proxy to be "signed."[101] The court, approaching the question from first principles, noted that the purpose of the signing requirement is to provide some measure of authentication to the proxy form. In this regard the court pointed out the following:

---

99 *Gilmore v. Lujan*, 947 F.2d 11409 (9th Cir. 1991). While upholding the ability of the government department to reject the fax based on its regulations, the court commented on how this rule served no sensible purpose, effectively encouraging the agency to revise its finicky, counterproductive, and unfair procedures. Indeed, to illustrate how out of date this agency's policy was, consider that in Ontario a contract, to be under "seal," no longer requires a wax impression or even a paper wafer, but merely a party's signature over the word *seal* in the signature area of the document: see *872899 Ontario Inc. v. Iacovoni* (1997), 33 O.R. (3d) 561 (Gen. Div). The appellate decision in this case also discounts the benefit of using a seal: *872899 Ontario Inc. v. Iacovoni* (1998), 40 O.R. (3d) 715 (Ont. C.A.).

100 See, for example, *Stan-Ka Auto Corp. v. Blinkova*, [1998] O.J. No. 1047 [*Stan-Ka*], where a bank was held not to be negligent for relying on forged faxed payment instructions, a case illustrating the ease with which signatures may be counterfeited for purposes of a fax communication given today's various copying technologies. See also *Bank of Nova Scotia v. Toronto-Dominion Bank* (2001), 200 D.L.R. (4th) 549 (Ont. C.A.), another recent case involving the forging of human signatures.

101 *Re a Debtor (No. 2021 of 1995)*, [1996] 2 All E.R. 345 (Ch. D.) [*Debtor*].

Of course even if the rule were strictly limited to signature by direct manual marking of the form, the authentication is not perfect. Signatures are not difficult to forge. Furthermore, in the overwhelming majority of cases in which the chairman of a creditors' meeting receives a proxy form, the form will bear a signature which he does not recognise and may well be illegible. Authenticity could only be enhanced if the creditor carrying suitable identification signed the form in person in the presence of the chairman. Even there the possibility of deception exists.[102]

This observation is important because it reminds anyone considering the actual or potential shortcomings of electronic messaging systems, from the perspective of security and alterability, that modern technology systems and business practices should not be compared to some nirvanalike method of perfection, but rather to a paper-based environment that also has its weaknesses.[103] When a court is being asked to judge the trustworthiness of some new computer- or network-based technology or business practice, it should not demand that the system be 100 percent accurate or foolproof, because, of course, perfection is a status that no system — whether paper-based or electronic — can hope to achieve. Rather, the standard should be whether organizations in the real economy entrust their daily operations to the particular technology or administrative mechanism.[104] If so, the procedure that meets the everyday needs of thousands of enterprises should meet the requirements of the law, insofar as contract formalities are concerned.

In the *Debtor* case, the court concluded that the faxed proxy did satisfy the signature requirement. In doing so the court noted that the fax method of transmitting the proxy was superior to sending it by post (which the party also did in this case):

---

102 *Ibid.*, at 351.

103 For a recent Ontario decision echoing this point, see the passage in para. 7 of the *Newbridge Networks* case, above note 24, where Farley J. recounts how variable and unconvincing, especially to a U.S. bureaucrat, a human signature can be. Interestingly, in *Brown v. The Butchers' & Drovers' Bank*, 1844 N.Y. LEXIS 47 (Sup. Ct. N.Y., 1844), the court accepted as a good signing within the then New York State *Statute of Frauds* an endorsement on a bill of exchange comprising the figures "1, 2, 8," rather than the endorser's name, as the endorser, concluded the court, intended to be bound by this designation as a substitute for his own name.

104 A good example of where this analysis was followed can be seen in Ontario's *Business Regulation Reform Act*, S.O. 1994, c. 32. Under this statute, a member of the public can register a business style by using a paper form, or by electronic filing (under O. Reg. 442/95, s. 3). As the signatures on the paper form were never verified, the government decided not to require a signature on the electronic version.

When a creditor faxes a proxy form to the chairman of a creditors' meeting he transmits two things at the same time, the contents of the form and the signature applied to it. The receiving fax is in effect instructed by the transmitting creditor to reproduce his signature on the proxy form which is itself being created at the receiving station. It follows that, in my view, the received fax is a proxy form signed by the principal or by someone authorised by him. The view which I have reached appears to me to be consistent with the realities of modern technology. If it is legitimate to send by post a proxy form signed with a rubber stamp, why should it not be at least as authentic to send the form by fax?

The facts of the present case illustrates [sic] the point well. Here the proxy form was sent both by post and by fax. Such being the nature of postal delivery, the creditor could not be certain whether his proxy was received at all or on time. On the other hand, when the fax is transmitted he knows that it has been received because, first, he obtains an answerback code and, secondly, an activity report is normally printed out. From the chairman's point of view, there is nothing about a received fax which puts him in a worse position to detect forgeries than when he receives through the post or by hand delivery a document signed by hand by a person whose signature he has never seen before or one signed by stamping. The reality is that fax transmission is likely to be a more reliable and certainly is a more speedy method of communication than post.[105]

The court in the *Debtor* case made another important point when it stated that the chairman who receives a proxy by fax is entitled to treat it as authentic unless there are surrounding circumstances that indicate otherwise. The presumption ought to be that messages sent by fax are authentic (for contract law purposes) and admissible (for evidence law purposes), but of course this presumption can always be rebutted. This same approach was taken in R. v. *Kapoor*, in which the accused challenged the validity of an information, the official document issued by a justice of the peace that contained the charges against the accused, on the basis that the signature of the justice of the peace was unintelligible.[106] The signature was in fact unintelligible, and there was no printing of the name to indicate who the signature belonged to (illustrating another shortcoming of the human autograph — it is often a very messy and incomprehensible example of penmanship!).[107] Nonetheless, the

---

105 *Debtor*, above note 101 at 351–52.
106 R. v. *Kapoor* (1989), 52 C.C.C. (3d) 41 (Ont. H.C.J.).
107 Again, see Farley J.'s decision in *Newbridge Networks*, above note 24, for confirmation of this point.

court turned down the challenge to the official document on the basis of the legal dictum *omnia praesumuntur rite et solemniter esse acta donec probetur in contrarium*, which, as all Latin scholars know, means "everything is presumed to be rightly and duly performed until the contrary is shown." It is suggested that this is a sensible rule to apply to all formal and evidentiary matters related to computer-generated documents, and not just to those emanating from a public office.

b) The Authentication Function

A final important point worth noting in the Debtor case is that the court, based on its salutary "first principles" approach, went on to consider messages in a form beyond the fax immediately before the court and concluded that

> Once it is accepted that the close physical linkage of hand, pen and paper is not necessary for the form to be signed, it is difficult to see why some forms of non-human agency for impressing the mark on the paper should be acceptable while others are not.
>
> For example, it is possible to instruct a printing machine to print a signature by electronic signal sent over a network or via a modem. Similarly, it is now possible with standard personal computer equipment and readily available popular word processing software to compose, say, a letter on a computer screen, incorporate within it the author's signature which has been scanned into the computer and is stored in electronic form, and to send the whole document including the signature by fax modem to a remote fax. The fax received at the remote station may well be the only hard copy of the document. It seems to me that such a document has been "signed" by the author.[108]

---

108 *Debtor*, above note 101 at 351. See also *Shattuck* v. *Klotzbach*, 2001 WL 1839720 (Mass. Sup. Ct.) [*Shattuck*], where the court accepted the typewritten signature at the end of an e-mail. In this case, dealing with the sale of land and therefore bringing into play the statute of frauds requirement that a contract for the sale of lands be in writing and signed, the court noted that telegrams have satisfied the writing requirements of the statute of frauds; moreover, at 3, the court concluded: "This court believes that the typed name at the end of an e-mail is more indicative of a party's intent to authenticate than that of a telegram as the sender of an e-mail types and sends the message on his own accord and types his own name as he so chooses. In the case at bar, the defendant sent e-mails regarding the sale of the property and intentionally and deliberately typed his name at the end of all such e-mails. A reasonable trier of fact could conclude that the e-mails sent by the defendant regarding the terms of the sale of the property were intended to be authenticated by the defendant's deliberate choice to type his name at the conclusion of all e-mails."

Although this passage relates to a hypothetical example raised by the court, its analysis is unassailable. The fact is the technical and business foundations of these electronic messages make them hugely reliable. This explains why, in contrast to the telegraph technology of the last century that spawned a rash of litigation arising out of garbled messages and the like, courts in Canada, the United States, and elsewhere are witnessing so few contract formation disputes arising out of the new computer and network technologies.

A recent case in Ontario echoes much of the analysis in the *Debtor* decision.[109] In *Newbridge*, a public company in Canada asked the court to approve an option holder's voting procedure whereby option holders would be sent notices electronically, and then transmit their proxies electronically as well. In considering this question Farley J., in a useful and colourful decision, reasoned that the key enquiry is "whether the notice and voting concepts can utilize the present technology and retain the integrity required."[110] The court answered in the affirmative, concluding that in various ways the electronic procedures were more trustworthy than the traditional paper-based processes. For example, expressing a sentiment akin to that found in the *Debtor* case, the court indicated that a password-based electronic signature is more secure than a human autograph that is not confirmed or verified by a third party, notwithstanding that each is susceptible to tampering. Accordingly, the court concluded that

> Overall for most intents and purposes and on balance the electronic procedure is a safer and more reliable system than is that which relies on the mails or other delivery systems. Password integrity has been built in. Notice of non-delivery is rather instantaneous.[111]

To the trenchant and helpful analysis in the *Debtor* and *Newbridge* cases can be added the point that in today's commercial environment there are many ways of authenticating particularly sensitive documents and messages. We see payroll or mass-produced cheques and banknotes

---

109 *Newbridge Networks*, above note 24.

110 *Ibid.*, at para. 4.

111 *Ibid.*, at para. 6. It should be noted, however, that there is authority for the rebuttable presumption that where a company uses its regular procedures for mailing letters, those letters are actually received in the usual time and by the person to whom they are addressed: *Hagner* v. *United States*, 285 U.S. 427 (1932) and *Godfrey* v. *United States*, 997 F.2d 335 (7th Cir. 1993); but note that in this latter case the government department was unable to invoke the presumption of delivery because it merely introduced an ambiguous computer-generated record of the taxpayer's account without anything more.

mechanically stamped or printed with a copy of a human autograph — quite a silly practice if one considers that the whole point of a human autograph is that it be done by a human; there are other much more effective ways to authenticate mass-produced documents, such as the thin film reflective patches used on certain Canadian banknotes. Moreover, even more sophisticated electronic authentication mechanisms can be deployed to meet signature requirements for particularly sensitive documents. Generally, they can be based on something a person knows (such a password or PIN — personal identification number), something a person has (such as a card key, smart card or token), or something a person is (namely, a biometric device). Token-based devices, for example, such as smart cards or credit cards with magnetic strips containing security functionality are used in many electronic environments, such as automated cash dispenser machines.[112] Biometric devices, such as equipment that scans retinas, hand geometries or fingerprints against an existing database to determine authenticity, are also growing in popularity.[113] Biometrics measure a person's physical (fingerprint,[114] hand geometry,

---

112 For example, in *States v. Miller*, 70 F.3d 1353 (D.C. Cir. 1995) a PIN number was effectively equated to a signature, when the court found that unauthorized use of a PIN to withdraw funds from an ATM constituted forgery, such use of the PIN being equated to cashing a cheque with a forged signature. See also *Speavak, Cameron & Boyd v. National Community Bank of New Jersey*, 677 A.2d 1168 (App. Div. 1996) where an account number used as an endorsement on a cheque was held to constitute a signature, the court finding that "... in this age, use of numbers as identification has become pervasive. Indeed, numbers are more readily recognized and handled than signatures."

113 See Ann Davis, "The Body as Password," *Wired*, July 1997, which mentions the "traditional" biometric technologies of retina scans, as well as less-known ones such as hand contours involving the knuckles, voice modulation, and head resonances. One press report quotes developers of biometric devices as predicting a large increase in sales of their wares in the wake of the September 11, 2001, terrorist attacks: Kevin Marron, "Biometric Security Blossoms in Business," *The Globe and Mail* (28 March 2002).

114 Law enforcement agencies have used ink-based fingerprints for more than one hundred years. In this format, they have come under some criticism lately, especially when only partial, or poor quality, prints can be recovered from a crime scene: see "Fingering Fingerprints," *The Economist*, 16 December 2000; "Printing Errors," *The Economist*, 19 January 2002; and the decision in *United States v. Plaza*, 2002 WL 389163 (E.D. Pa. 2002). Fingerprint-scan systems used for identification (i.e., the question "who is this person?" is answered by conducting a one-to-many comparison of the subject's biometric against a database of stored records) or verification (i.e., the question "is this person who they claim to be?" is answered by performing a one-to-one comparison of the subject's biometric against one known to come from the same subject) are presumably more accurate and less prone to error.

retina, iris, or facial contours) or behavioural (signature, voice, or key-stroke pattern) characteristics to confirm identity.[115] With these biometric systems, a central registry logs an authentic version of the biometric, and then subsequent usage of the particular vehicle is compared to the master version kept on file electronically. By one estimate, police, computer firms, and other corporations spent more than $500 million on fingerprint and other biometric devices in 1995, with sales projected to grow 40 percent annually.[116] Another estimate is less gregarious, but nevertheless shows a steady increase in sales, although most players in the biometric industry are still waiting for the "killer biometric application" that causes truly widespread adoption of one or more of its several products.[117] Indeed, with the growing use of electronic pads that can record signatures, the oldest of biometric mechanisms — the signature — will find new applications in the electronic environment.[118] Other types of authentication in the computer and network environment draw

---

115 A recent article on the use of e-mail by physicians mentions how one doctor uses a fingerprint reader to help ensure that only he has access to the sensitive e-mails sent by his patients: Joanne Sommers, "Doctors Bring Back the House Call, Virtually," *The Globe and Mail*, Report on E-Business (28 June 2002).

116 Estimate by the Yankee Group, a U.S. consultancy, reported in Tom Abate, "New Chip Can Verify Fingerprints" *The Globe and Mail*, Technology Quarterly (3 June 1997) ["New Chip"]. As with all projections in the technology business, however, this one was too optimistic: sales of biometric systems did not hit $500 million in the United States until 2001 (Clive Thompson, "User Unfriendly," *The Globe and Mail, Report on Business Magazine* (November 2002)); this article then goes on to predict sales hitting $1.9 billion by 2005. In any event, the point is not to get caught up in the numbers, but to track the legally relevant trends. In this regard, the "New Chip" article refers to a company with a new postage stamp-sized fingerprint pad and related chip and software that can read and verify fingerprints. Another company mentioned in the article uses optical technology to verify fingerprints, apparently with the competitive advantage that it can detect when a live finger is used, to differentiate from one that has been chopped off to gain access to the restricted area. See also David Berman, "Mytec's Secret Identity," *Canadian Business*, September 1997.

117 "Biometrics: The Measure of Man," *The Economist*, 9 September 2000 ["The Measure of Man"].

118 For an analysis of a signature-based biometric system, contrasted with an encryption-based system, see Benjamin Wright, "A Cyberspace Perspective: Eggs in Baskets: Distributing the Risks of Electronic Signatures" (1997) 15 J. Marshall J. Computer & Info. L. 189. In footnote 7 of this article, Wright, one of the pioneers of e-commerce law in the United States, puts the authentication debate in the following useful perspective: "In practice, disputes over the authenticity of commercial documents are rare. Of the many billions of commercial documents created every year, the authenticity of only a tiny fraction of the total is seriously contested in court. Among the reasons for this are that most people are happy

on knowledge-based systems involving passwords and/or personal identification numbers. For particularly sensitive transactions or documents, mathematic encryption systems can be used. As noted in the next section of this chapter, some jurisdictions are supporting the use of encryption systems by enacting digital signature statutes.

None of these authentication mechanisms are foolproof. The knowledge-based ones can be forgotten, or compromised if not enough thought is put into them, token-based devices can be lost, and even biometrics are not perfect.[119] A cut finger or laryngitis can wreak havoc with a fingerprint or voice recognition system. And these are just the problems caused by inadvertence. The more nefarious scenario has the intruder cutting off someone else's finger to gain unauthorized entry (though the latest fingerprint scanners can now also check for temperature, to ensure that the finger is part of a live body). In short, while the technological solution can be useful, it too (like the legal and contractual skill sets proposed in this book) has to be approached thoughtfully, and ministered with care, and constantly updated and refreshed.

As well, persons have to use all such authentication and communications systems in a manner that convinces a court (if challenged) that the person truly intended to be bound by the specific electronic transmission. For example, there are two lines of U.S. authorities on the point whether a company's paper-based letterhead, with the name of the company printed on top of the page, satisfies the signature requirement where no actual autograph or other mark is left by the person sending the document. One line is evident in a leading decision, when Justice Cardozo explained that in such cases the court must

---

with their commercial transactions most of the time, and the facts and circumstances surrounding the documents (including the signatures, but also including the context and content of the documents) tend to show their origin and authenticity."

119 In one recent survey in the United Kingdom, commuters were willing to disclose their passwords in order to receive a free ballpoint pen, while in another nearly half the British respondents admitted to using their own name, or the name of a family member or pet as their password; also, in Japan recently, a security researcher has perfected a simple way to fool the fingerprint scanner by employing a moulded gelatine skin on top of a regular finger: "Securing the Cloud," *The Economist*, 26 October 2002. Also, biometric devices can raise legal concerns, including privacy issues: see Patrick J. Waltz, "On-Site Fingerprinting in the Banking Industry: Inconvenience or Invasion of Privacy" (1998) 16 J. Marshall J. Computer & Infor. L. 597. Privacy advocates argue that systems that routinely identify people will erode privacy and human rights: see their comments in "The Measure of Man," above note 117.

assess all the relevant facts to ascertain whether the party sending the letterhead intended to be bound, or was simply using the letterhead as a non-binding "scratch pad."[120] A similar question was asked in a more recent American case where a document alleged to be a financial guarantee was sent by fax without a human signature but contained the name of the sender company on the top of the page because the sender's fax machine imprinted this corporate name automatically on each page that was faxed by the machine. The lower court concluded there was no question but that the sender intended to be bound by the faxed guarantee, and that the plaintiff acted in reliance upon it, and that the guarantor "should not be permitted to evade its obligation because of the current and extensive use of electronic transmissions in modern business transactions."[121] A second line of reasoning was shown when the appellate court reversed this finding (although for reasons that are not altogether apparent from the judgment), and instead treated the corporate name imprinted by the fax machine as insufficient to denote intent on the part of the defendant to authenticate the document.[122] In effect, this case illustrates that all the fancy computer and communications paraphernalia in the world still do not obviate the need for sensible and sound business processes, which can then be implemented by the newfangled technology. As with the negligence cases reviewed in chapter 5, section D.2, "Negligence in Use," computer technology in these contexts should be viewed as a means to an end, rather than as an end in itself.

Accordingly, out of an abundance of caution, as with the writing requirement, parties to EDI and other agreements that contemplate electronic messages are also stipulating contractually in their EDI TPAs that the various electronic messages constitute signed writings.[123] Even in the absence of such contractual confirmation, the signature requirement in *Statute of Frauds*-type provisions should be satisfied by messages produced by those electronic-based systems that implement a trustworthy system for the exchange and recording of information where the identity of the sender of the message is conveyed by a rea-

---

120 *Mesibov, Glinert & Levy v. Cohen Bros. Mfg. Co.*, 157 N.E. 148 (N.Y. 1927).

121 *Parma Tile Mosaic & Marble Co., Inc. v. Estate of Short*, 590 N.Y.S.2d 1019 at 1021 (N.Y. Sup. Ct. 1992).

122 *Parma Tile Mosaic & Marble Co., Inc. v. Estate of Short*, 663 N.E.2d 633 (N.Y. 1996). It will be interesting to see how courts approach the "From:" line in e-mail, which is generally automatically generated by the e-mail system.

123 See s. 6.04 of the *Model TPA*, above note 35, which covers the signature as well as the writing issue.

sonably secure technical means and the parties, through the applicable electronic commerce delivery system, clearly indicate an intention to become legally bound.[124] The cases show that in such circumstances courts will not block the use by business people of new technologies that are accepted by them to provide the signature requirement where the underlying rationale of the signature requirement can be achieved through one or more technological devices or business processes. Courts should continue this approach when considering documents and messages emanating from new communication networks, always focussing their analysis on the underlying functions of the relevant technological devices and business processes.

c) Law Reform

Earlier this chapter discussed how the recently enacted federal and provincial electronic commerce statutes addressed the writing requirement and, essentially, created a media-neutral legal environment for information.[125] These statutes generally effect the same result in the signature area as well. Thus, Ontario's *Electronic Commerce Act* (ECA) provides that a legal requirement that a document be signed or endorsed is satisfied by an electronic signature.[126] The definition of "electronic signature" in the ECA is very broad and technology-neutral: "electronic information that a person creates or adopts in order to sign a document and that is in, attached to or associated with the document."[127] Therefore, the electronic signature does not have to resemble a human autograph when it is viewed or printed out. It can be any type of symbol, or some mathematical/alphanumeric code, or even a sound. Nor does the electronic signature have to be part of the underlying document, as is usually the case in the paper-based world. So long as the two can be related functionally, the signature and the information to which it relates may be transmitted separately. The ECA, however, permits the government to prescribe by regulation certain documents, or

---

124 As for general Quebec law, the definition of "signature" in the *Civil Code* is broad enough to capture both paper-based and electronic authentication means, the only relevant question being evidentiary in nature: namely, can it be demonstrated that the electronic signature is a "distinctive mark regularly used to signify intention."

125 See section A.1(g) of this chapter, "Electronic Commerce Statutes." Readers should review this earlier section to understand the scope and application of these electronic commerce statutes.

126 *ECA*, above note 54, subss. 11(1) and 11(2).

127 *ECA*, s. 1.

classes of documents, for which the electronic signature must be reliable, and in some cases the government can even dictate the specific signature technologies to be used.[128]

PIPEDA, Canada's federal law in this area,[129] takes this latter concept even further by using the concept of "secure electronic signature," which is one that results from a technology or process that can ensure that in respect of the person using the technology or process the resulting electronic signature is unique to the person; the technology used to create the signature was under the sole control of the person; the signature identifies the person; and the signature is linked with the document to determine whether the document was changed since the time the signature was attached to it.[130] A secure electronic signature, therefore, is one that can ensure identity (the user is who he purports to be); non-repudiation (the user cannot deny sending the message); confidentiality (it does not permit unauthorized access); and integrity of the signed document (it was not tampered with after the user sent it). PIPEDA requires that only secure electronic signatures be used in respect of electronic documents that are to be under seal,[131] originals,[132] made under oath,[133] statutory declarations,[134] or witnessed.[135]

At the time PIPEDA was enacted, the federal government believed that only encryption technology supported by a public key infrastructure (PKI) satisfied the requirements for a secure electronic signature.[136] Greatly simplified, in a PKI a so-called Certification Authority confirms the identity of a person, for example through a face-to-face registration where a person shows two pieces of photographic-based identification, and issues to the person a software program that can encrypt electronic communications (such as e-mail). The typical encryption methodology is based on public and private key pairs, or

---

128 ECA, subss. 11(3) and (4).
129 Personal Information Protection and Electronic Documents Act, S.C. 2000, c. 5. [PIPEDA].
130 PIPEDA, subss. 31(1), 48(1) and (2).
131 PIPEDA, s. 39.
132 PIPEDA, s. 42.
133 PIPEDA, s. 44.
134 PIPEDA, s. 45.
135 PIPEDA, s. 46. Interestingly, the new electronic document provisions in the Criminal Code, being the new s. 846 enacted by the 2002 Criminal Law Amendments, above note 67, seemingly call for a looser standard, by merely requiring that the electronic document has been made in accordance with the laws of the place where it was made.
136 Michael Power, "Bill C-6: Federal Legislation in the Age of the Internet" (1999) 26 Man. L.J. 235, at 244.

unique mathematical algorithms, generated by the software. The user encrypts a message with the private key (the private key is known only to one person), and a recipient can decrypt it with the public key (the public key is known to many people).[137] The recipient confirms the identity of the sender by checking a directory of keys/digital certificates kept by the Certification Authority. Public key cryptography[138] is a relatively recent revolutionary breakthrough.[139] Codemaking — and codebreaking — have gone on for 2500 years,[140] but until the advent of

---

137 The technology uses scrambling, "hashing," and other exotic technologies and processes: for accessible descriptions, see Philip R. Zimmermann, "Crytography for the Internet," *Scientific American*, October 1998 ["Cryptography for the Internet"] (Zimmermann is the developer of the PGP [Pretty Good Privacy] encryption software, which is widely used on the Internet; <pgpi.com>); and Stewart A. Baker, "International Developments Affecting Digital Signatures" (1998) 32 Int'l Lawyer 963. See also the discussion of cryptology in chapter 4, sections B.3, "Regulating the Export of Encryption Technologies," and C, "Regulating the Domestic Use of Encryption Technologies." For an example of a working PKI in Canada, see the description of Teranet, Ontario's electronic land registry system, at <teranet.ca> and in the remarks of Susan Elliot in the *Bill 88 Testimony*, above note 61. For a description of the federal government's PKI, see <cse-cst.gc.ca/cse/english/gov.html> and <cio-dpi.gc.ca/pki/Initiatives/initiatives.e.html>.

138 "Cryptography" is the activity of making secret codes for communication, "cryptanalysis" is the study of attempting to compromise these codes, and "cryptology" is both disciplines: Zimmerman, "Cryptography for the Internet," above note 137 at 112.

139 The new industry was kicked-off by the publication in 1976 of "New Directions in Cryptography," by two Stanford professors, Whitfield Diffie and Martin E. Hellman. An important type of public key cryptography, known as elliptic curve, was invented by a Canadian at the University of Waterloo in the 1980s, and was commercialized by Certicom, a Canadian public company whose shares were initially listed on the Toronto Stock Exchange and more recently the Nasdaq in the United States as well.

140 For an entertaining survey of cryptology through the ages, see Simon Singh, *The Code Book: The Evolution of Secrecy from Mary Queen of Scots to Quantum Cryptography* (New York: Doubleday, 1999), and for a related review of this work: "Cryptography: Tijguz Cvtjoftt," *The Economist*, 28 August 1999 (the title can be decrypted to read "Shifty Business" by applying the "Caesar shift," namely, by inserting for each letter its immediate lower neighbour in the alphabet. Singh chronicles how cryptology is almost as old as writing itself, as kings and other powerful people (including Roman emperors) wanted to keep secret their communications. Singh explains how computer-based public key cryptography has changed radically the crypto business, including by democratising it so that average folk can use what was previously the preserve of governments, in order to send credit card numbers over the Internet. This argument, that encryption technologies have undergone a fascinating democratization, is also made by Debora L. Spar, in *Ruling the Waves: Cycles of Discovery, Chaos, and Wealth From the Compass to the Internet* (New York: Harcourt, 2001).

public key cryptography always depended on the sender and receiver agreeing in advance on their secret code, which then was extremely susceptible to compromise. Based on complex mathematics, and operationalized through sophisticated but relatively inexpensive software, public key cryptography allows computer users to agree on a key even though they do not know one another.[141] Encryption-based authentication systems could become very important over the coming years because of the opportunities for perpetrating fraud by means of electronic communications. For example, faxed signatures could be forged[142] or a telex system could be infiltrated,[143] with the result in each case that the innocent recipient could rely on the communication, hence leaving the entity impersonated holding the bag. Computer-based cryptography systems, however, raise a host of public policy issues, particularly concern from the law enforcement community that data encryption permits criminals, terrorists, and spies to conduct communications in a way that eludes tracking by government agencies.[144]

PKI systems also raise many legal issues for the three parties involved in them — the key holder, the Certification Authority, and the

---

141 Math-based, software-powered digital encryption can be made very secure. As explained in *Cryptography Policy Framework*, above note 1, a cryptographic algorithm is used to encrypt "plaintext" into "ciphertext," and then to decrypt back into plaintext. Security in cryptography comes from the fact that even if the algorithm is known, there are millions or trillions of possible "keys" that could have been used for encryption: a bit-length of 56 bits makes possible roughly 72 quadrillion keys. Of course, encryption is not entirely secure; code-breakers are always just behind the codemakers. In 1997, 78,000 volunteered computers over the Internet took 96 days to crack a single 56-bit key. Cryptographic strength is increased by adding to the length of the key: these same resources would take 67 years to crack a 64-bit key, and over 13 billion times the average age of the universe to crack a 128-bit key. But, with improved technology, the codebreakers will accelerate these times. Therefore, it is important that the new technology of light-based quantum cryptography promises to produce even stronger strength security: "Quantum Cryptography: The End of the Code War?" *The Economist*, 23 June 2001; and D. Stucki, N. Gisin, O. Guinnard, G. Ribordy & H. Zbinden, "Quantum Key Distribution Over 67km With a Plug & Play System" (2002) New Journal of Physics 4 at 41.1–41.8.

142 *Stan-Ka*, above note 100.

143 *Standard Bank London Ltd.* v. *The Bank of Tokyo Ltd.*, [1995] 2 Lloyd's Rep. 169 (Q.B.D.).

144 For a contrary view by one of the pioneers of public key cryptography, arguing that government should not have access to cryptographic keys used in the private sector, see Ronald L. Rivest, "The Case Against Regulating Encryption Technology," *Scientific American*, October 1998. See also chapter 4, section C, "Regulating the Domestic Use of Encryption Technologies."

party relying on the digital certificates issued by the Certification Authority. The technology might be compromised, fraud might seep into the system at the point of registering the key holder, or the Certification Authority might fail to withdraw a certificate from the register after it is compromised, to name but three eventualities. No Canadian jurisdiction has yet adopted general legislation devoted entirely to governing PKI systems to deal with these kinds of issues, though the new Quebec electronic commerce law does have a chapter dealing with the certification of identities, including addressing the accreditation of certification service providers pursuant to government promulgated standards, and defining the parameters of their certification practice statements.[145] Several U.S. states have passed legislation that focuses on certification service providers,[146] and Europe has moved in this direction as well,[147] though some commentators have cautioned against legislation that is overly specific in its technological presumptions.[148] In the absence of a statutory regime dealing with the liability of Certification Authorities, it is difficult to predict how much responsibility a court would have a Certification Authority shoulder if any of the risk scenarios noted above, or others, come to pass.[149] UNCITRAL is in the process

---

145 *An Act to Establish a Legal Framework for Information Technology*, S.Q. 2001, c. 32, c. 111, Div. 111.

146 For example, Utah's *Digital Signature Act*, 46 Utah Code Ann. ch.3, Utah. For a detailed discussion of the various provisions of the Utah legislation, see Barry B. Sookman, *Sookman Computer, Internet and E-Commerce Law*, rev. ed. (Toronto: Carswell, 2001), at §5.7.

147 See the *European Community Directive on Electronic Signatures, European Directive* 1999/93/EC, December 13, 1999. This Directive calls for implementation by national law by July 19, 2001: see, for example, the German *Act on Electronic Signatures* (Signaturgesetzes), which came into force on May 22, 2001.

148 "Laws such as the Utah *Digital Signature Act*, which prescribe a specific implementation of asymmetric cryptography within a public key infrastructure, have been consigned to the margins of electronic commerce when the market place failed to embrace their vision of digital signatures"; Jane K. Winn, "The Emperor's New Clothes: The Shocking Truth About Digital Signatures And Internet Commerce" (2001) 37 Idaho L. Rev. 353 at 379.

149 Interestingly, quality certification might provide a potentially analogous activity with which to compare the service offered by a Certification Authority. Several British cases involving certification of the seaworthiness of ships have found that where such certification or classification proves to be in error, the certifier or classifier is not liable when the ships subsequently prove to be unseaworthy: see *Marc Rich & Co. A.G. v. Bishop Rock Marine Co. Ltd.*, [1996] 1 A.C. 211 (H.L.); and *Reeman v. Dep't of Transport* (1997), 2 Lloyd's Rep. 648 (C.A.). Although these cases may not be directly comparable to the role of a Certification Authority, they suggest a range of potentially analogous situations and case law that

of reviewing this whole area as a follow-on project to its Model Law,[150] with its work focusing on the interpretation and application of the signature and attribution of data message articles of the UNCITRAL Model Law, standards of conduct of certification authorities and related parties, and cross-border recognition of certificates and digitally signed documents.[151] The new Quebec information technology legislation is also noteworthy for setting into motion a technical harmonization exercise that is quite unique. This law creates a multidisciplinary committee that will establish guidelines regarding such matters as signature algorithms and encryption methods (among other technical subjects the committee can investigate). Once each year the committee will report to the government on the voluntary adoption of these guidelines, and if the relevant minister is not satisfied with the progress being made, the government may substitute compulsory provisions for the guidelines.[152]

3) Offer and Acceptance

A contract arises when, in response to an offer made by an offeror, the offeree's acceptance is received by the offeror.[153] Where parties conclude a contract in face-to-face, simultaneous communications, the existence of an offer and an acceptance is usually clear. Where parties negotiate a contract and they are distant from one another, and particularly if they

---

may apply as courts attempt to determine the appropriate duty and level of care owed by Certification Authorities in the absence of statutory guidance. It is worth noting that in the absence of a statutory liability regime, Certification Authorities will probably rely heavily on limiting their liability by means of contract: for a discussion of this approach, see chapter 5, section E.2, "Limitations on Liability."

150 The UNCITRAL Model Law on Electronic Commerce; see above note 40.

151 See UNCITRAL Model Law on Electronic Signatures (2001), and the related Guide to Enactment, A/CN.9/493.

152 *An Act to Establish a Legal Framework for Information Technology*, S.Q. 2001, c. 32, Ch. IV, Div. 1.

153 More precisely, the following elements must be present to conclude a binding contract: the parties intended to create legal relations when they entered into the agreement; one party to the contract made an offer; the other party or parties accepted that offer; the promises contained in the contract were made for valuable consideration; and the terms of the contract are certain: *New Zealand Law Commission, Electronic Commerce, Part One* (1998), para. 50. This useful report is available at <lawcom.govt.nz>. By contrast, under Quebec's *Civil Code*, a contract need not have consideration flowing between parties to be enforceable; what is important is that the contract has a cause and object.

are not communicating in real time[154] but through a telecommunications mechanism that involves delays between respective transmissions, it may not be clear what communications actually constitute an offer or an acceptance. In a number of cases involving telegraphed messages, disputes arose as a result of the differing conclusions that could be drawn from the various words and phrases used in the telegrams that passed to and fro between the parties; each telegram added ambiguity to the core question as to whether the parties had come to a meeting of the minds on quantity and price (in a sale of goods context).[155] Indeed, in an early Canadian telegraph case, the court noted that the fee for telegrams was charged by the word and was expensive, so senders limited the number of words used and this increased the likelihood of misunderstanding and dispute.[156] On the other hand, with modern, inexpensive means of telecommunications, we currently also have a problem of misunder-

---

154 For an example of a brief contract, in this case for taxicab services, concluded by telephone in real-time, see *Fraser* v. *U-Need-A-Cab Ltd.* (1985), 50 O.R. (2d) 281, 17 D.L.R. (4th) 574 (C.A.).

155 For a discussion of some of these cases, see *Thorne*, above note 33.

156 *Kinghorne*, above note 10. As for the high cost of telegrams, see footnote 43 in chapter 1. The high price of telegraphic communication, for example, led to the use of elaborate code systems in an effort to reduce costs. For instance, the court in *Falck* v. *Williams*, [1900] A.C. 176 (H.L.), recounts how the telegraphed message "Shale Copyright Semiramis Begloom Escorte Sultana Brilliant Argentina Bronchil," in fact was intended to mean: "Shale. Your rate is too low, impossible to work business at your figures. Semiramis [the name of a ship]. Have closed in accordance with your order. — Confirm. Two ports Fiji Islands. Sultana. Brilliant. Argentina. Keep a good look-out for business for this vessel, and wire us when anything good offers." The court determined the coded message was ambiguous, and that the dispute could have been avoided by spending "a few more shillings" on the message. Some courts, however, were quite adept at working within the constraints of sparsely worded telegrams. In *George C. Brewer* v. *Hurst and Lachmund Company*, 127 Cal. 643 (Sup. Ct. Cal., 1900), the court deciphered the shortened code used by one of the parties to find an enforceable contract. The court, at 647, justified its reasoning as follows: "Any other conclusion than the one here reached would certainly impair the usefulness of modern appliances to modern business, tend to hamper trade, and increase the expense thereof." See also *Bibb* v. *Allen*, 149 U.S. 481 (U.S. Sup. Ct.), where the court upheld the use of a code system that replaced long corporate names with monikers such as "Albert" or "Alfred" to save space on the telegram. As for the modern-day code used by teenagers to text-message one another over cellphones, see Erin Anderssen, "R U Sure U No Wht Yr Kds R Doin?" *The Globe and Mail* (15 February 2003). This vowel-challenged system of efficient, but often times hard to decipher, messages, will likely produce its own stream of litigation if today's teens carry it forward as they move into the work force.

standings, but now caused by the uncertainty created by too many messages. For example, in one case involving a cascade of telexes, the court concluded, notwithstanding that a formal written agreement had been forwarded by one party to the other but never signed, that a contract did arise from a preceding flurry of telexes.[157] More disturbing are recent cases involving torrents of e-mail messages where courts, after surveying the mass of electronically transmitted messages, concluded that no contracts arose.[158] These cases are troublesome because the high volume of messages makes it very difficult to discern discreet offers and acceptances. These cases likely portend much more litigation to come as e-mail becomes the ubiquitous means of written business communication over the next few years. The problem is that much e-mail virtually approximates oral conversation in terms of frequency and informality; but before we conclude we need a new type of *Statute of Frauds* for this new medium, let us be thankful that e-mail is at least reduced to writing, and thus an accurate evidentiary trail of it is kept.[159]

Conflicts about offer and acceptance also can arise in the context of other recent technology, and one such falling-out involving a computerized telephone ordering system led to the decision in the U.S. case *Corinthian Pharmaceutical Systems, Inc.* v. *Lederle Laboratories.*[160] In this case, a drug wholesaler ordered a large quantity of a particular product the day before a material price increase was to take effect. The wholesaler used the manufacturer's automated telephone order system, and after placing the order message with the computer, was issued a "tracking number" by the manufacturer's computer system. No human representative of the manufacturer participated in taking the order. Subsequently, the manufacturer did not wish to supply the large quan-

---

157 *Sydney Steel Corp.* v. *Mannesmann Pipe & Steel Corp.* (1986), 75 N.S.R. (2d) 211 (S.C.S.C.).

158 See *Bogdanovic* v. *Buchanan*, [1999] B.C.J. No. 3006 (S.C.), and *Boon* v. *Boon* (2000), 585 A.P.R. 143 (N.S.S.C.), where the court was unable to identify a specific offer and acceptance among the avalanche of e-mail, and therefore concluded the series of messages had not crystallized into an agreement. In *John Hansen* v. *Transworld Wireless TV-Spokane, Inc.*, 44 P. 3d 929 (Wash. C.A. 2002), the court held that a series of internal company e-mails did not establish that a contract had been made for purposes of a writing requirement under the *Uniform Commercial Code*. But see also *Shattuck*, above note 108, where the court found that a contract had been formed through the exchange of various e-mails.

159 See section B.3(b), "E-mail Policies," later in this chapter, for a related discussion on e-mail from an evidence law perspective that discusses the literature that argues in favour of an express e-mail retention policy.

160 724 F.Supp. 605 (S.D. Ind. 1989) [*Corinthian*].

tity of product to the wholesaler at the lower price, and therefore argued that the tracking number issued by its computer was not an acceptance of the wholesaler's order, but merely an acknowledgment of receipt of the order (which, the manufacturer argued, was the offer in contract law terms). The court agreed, concluding that no contract had been consummated, with the result that the wholesaler was denied the lower price for the manufacturer's products.[161]

In order to avoid misunderstandings of the kind that arose in the *Bogdanovic, Boon,* and *Corinthian* cases, the EDI Council of Canada's *Model TPA* encourages parties to be extremely precise as to what electronic messages constitute a purchase order, a functional acknowledgment (the equivalent of the non-binding tracking number in the *Corinthian* case), and a purchase order acknowledgment. Indeed, EDI, if properly utilized, can help avoid the problems encountered in the cases referred to in the previous paragraphs because it is a system based on a structured protocol of standard electronic messages, the meaning of each of which is well settled. Again, it is worth asking why there is a lack of case law involving contract formation disputes in an EDI environment. The answer, quite simply, is that the current computer-based technologies are more effective than previous technologies at permitting parties to come to a meeting of the minds in an unambiguous manner.[162] In effect, the pace of technological change, articulated as the first dynamic of computer law, presents the law with numerous challenges, but at the same time technical progress assists the law by devising even more reliable means of communication.

a)   Battle of the Forms

EDI messages, however, only address core contract formation issues, such as quantity, price, and time of shipment, and generally do not cover secondary matters such as warranty terms, interest on overdue

---

161 It is interesting to speculate, in light of the negligence cases referred to in chapter 5, section D.1, "Negligence in Creation," involving the design of computer-based systems, whether the plaintiff in the *Corinthian* case, above note 160, might not have had a reasonable negligence claim arising out of the facts of the case.

162 Another, at least partial, answer might be that the EDI Council of Canada's *Model TPA*, above note 35, provides that disputes be resolved by private arbitration; that is, there may in fact be many more problem situations than we think, we just do not hear about them because the arbitration awards are not publicly available. On the other hand, modern communications technology is not perfect. See *Yamada v. Silver Dollar Cabaret Ltd.*, [2000] B.C.J. No. 2387 (B.C.S.C.), for a case that recounts a "keystone cops"–type account of problems with computers that prevent critical e-mails from being received in a timely manner.

payments, etc. Thus, the *Model TPA* addresses another fertile source of conflict that arises in the traditional paper-based commercial environment, namely the so-called battle of the forms regarding these secondary contract conditions. This is the term given to the phenomenon of the various commercial documents of trading partners containing differing, and often conflicting, terms and conditions regarding warranty, etc. The price list of a manufacturer, generally considered not an offer but an invitation to treat, will contain certain product warranty terms, which may be different from the warranty terms contained in the buyer's purchase order, and which may differ from the warranty terms of the manufacturer's purchase order acknowledgment. In Canada, this battle is usually won by the party taking the last shot,[163] for example, the manufacturer if the goods are shipped after it sent its own form of purchase order acknowledgment.[164] In contrast, the manufacturer can lose the battle if it ships product in a situation where the last paper to cross the trenches is the buyer's purchase order (which is accepted by the shipping of the goods).[165]

Recreating the battle of the paper-based forms in an EDI trading environment is quite difficult because the standard messages used for EDI, or transaction sets as they are called, do not include legal terms and conditions. Therefore, the *Model TPA* stipulates that the parties attach a mutually agreeable set of terms and conditions to the TPA, which will then govern the various sales of product made under the agreement. This is an eminently sensible approach, but it does require trading partners to negotiate terms and conditions they normally

---

163 Ontario Law Reform Commission, *Report on Sale of Goods: The Battle of the Forms* (1979) Vol. 1, at 181. For a U.K. case with a pithy analysis by Lord Denning, see *Butler Machine Tool Co. v. Ex-Cell-O Corpn*, [1979] 1 All E.R. 965 (C.A.) [*Butler Machine Tool*].

164 But not always: see *Tywood Industries Ltd. v. St. Anne-Nackawic Pulp & Paper Co. Ltd.* (1979), 100 D.L.R. (3d) 374 (Ont. H.C.J.). Lord Denning, in the *Butler Machine Tool* case, above note 163, also acknowledges that sometimes the battle of the forms is not decided by the last shot, but by an approach that reconciles what is common amongst the two offers and replacing contradictory terms with what the transactors might reasonably have implied under the circumstances. This latter approach is closer to the mechanism provided under the United States *Uniform Commercial Code*: see the decisions in *Step-Saver Data Systems, Inc. v. Wyse Technology*, 939 F.2d 91 (3rd Cir. 1991) and *Arizona Retail Systems, Inc. v. Software Link, Inc.*, 831 F.Supp. 759 (D. Ariz. 1993); these cases are also referred to in chapter 5, section C.2, "Shrinkwrap Licences."

165 To understand how a wise general counsel at IBM Canada managed the battle of the forms some years ago, see Grant Murray, "A Corporate Counsel's Perspective of the 'Battle of the Forms'" (1979-80) 4 C.B.L.J. 290.

would not in a paper-based environment (where they rely instead on the hope that their particular standard form will win the battle of the forms if a dispute ever crops up). Accordingly, not wishing to spend time negotiating terms and conditions, some EDI trading partners perversely attach their various paper-based forms to the TPA and stipulate that the terms in these forms will apply as if the forms were actually being used (which, of course, they are not). The result may well be that the whole arrangement is void for uncertainty. Of course, parties not wishing to spend the time negotiating items such as warranties could remain silent on the issue and simply let the various implied warranties and conditions of sales legislation, either domestic or international, apply to the transactions. This is a risky approach, however, as the scope, coverage, and meaning of these implied warranties can be extremely uncertain.[166] There is, therefore, really no better course of action vis-à-vis the battle of the forms problem than to take the time to negotiate a mutually acceptable set of warranties and other terms that will govern the relationship between the parties; and of course the time spent on such negotiations will decrease dramatically if both sides take a sensible, middle-ground approach right from the beginning instead of spinning their wheels in interminable discussions of mutually unreasonable positions.

b) Online Offers, Acceptances, and Auctions

One risk that confronts parties selling products in an online environment is that their Web site displays of merchandise, if accompanied by prices and other sales terms, may be construed as offers and hence open to acceptance by purchasers without further consideration by the seller.[167] Although this might not pose a problem generally, it would,

---

166 See chapter 5, section E.1, "Implied Warranties and Conditions."
167 For example, in the United States a retailer's advertisement to sell a particular item at a specific sale price on a "first come, first served" basis created a binding, unilateral offer that the retailer had to honour for a male shopper even though the retailer intended the offer for women only: *Morris Lefkowitz* v. *Great Minneapolis Surplus Store, Inc.*, 86 N.W.2d 689 (S.C. Minn. 1957). See also *Johnson* v. *Capital City Ford Co.*, 85 So (2d) 75 (La. App. 1955), where an offline car dealer was found to have made a binding offer presenting his vehicles in the showroom with prices attached to them. And every graduate of first-year law school will remember fondly *Carlill* v. *Carbolic Smoke Ball Co.*, [1893] 1 Q.B. 256 (C.A.), where the manufacturer of the smoke ball was held by the court to have to pay the amount it advertised it would pay to anyone who caught the flu after using the ball; that is, one can accept a unilateral binding offer even through performance.

for example, if the product were in limited supply. On the other hand, the United Kingdom common law has held that advertisements and catalogues, including the display of goods in a shop with a price tag, constitute "invitations to treat," rather than offers.[168] Until a Canadian court, however, comes to the same conclusion in respect of product listings on a Web site, online merchants would be well advised to state clearly in their online terms and conditions and in their promotional editorial copy that the material on the site constitutes advertisements, and that the merchant reserves the right to accept or reject all offers submitted to it. If merchants don't heed this advice, the result is confusion. In a perceptive article, Professor Mark Budnitz details how he surveyed a number of U.S. shopping Web sites and found that it is not at all clear, given the confusing geography and presentation of these sites, when offers are made and by whom, and what communication or action constitutes acceptance.[169] It is indeed fair to say that a haze of uncertainty accompanies many Web sites, due in equal measure to poor design and failure to provide adequate information regarding offer, acceptance, and other key legal terms.[170]

Online auctioneers must be particularly careful about delineating the rules of invitation to treat offer and acceptance when conducting Internet auctions, a particularly popular form of e-commerce.[171] For example, in a recent case, *Je Ho Lim v. The .TV Corporation International*,[172] the court noted that under general American law an auction is generally with reserve, unless a contrary intention is expressed (as

---

168 *Fisher v. Bell*, [1961] 1 Q.B. 394. Similarly, the display of products on the shelves of a "self-service" retailer is merely an invitation to treat, an offer is made when a customer takes an item to the counter to pay, and this offer is accepted when the retailer accepts the consumer's money (and thus the contract is not concluded when the consumer takes the item off the shelf and puts it into his or her shopping basket): *Pharmaceutical Society of Great Britian v. Boots Cash Chemists (Southern) Ltd.*, [1953] 1 Q.B. 401 (C.A.). Presumably the same analysis would apply to an online shopping experience using the typical electronic shopping cart at an Internet retailer's Web site.

169 Mark E. Budnitz, "Consumers Surfing for Sales in Cyberspace: What Constitutes Acceptance and What Legal Terms and Conditions Bind the Consumer" (2000) 16 Ga. St. U.L. Rev. 741.

170 Thus the initiative for online consumer protection, including Canada's Internet Sales Contract Template referred to in chapter 4, section E.4(c), "Internet Sales Contract Template."

171 The Internet is extremely well suited for the auction model of e-commerce. It is no surprise that eBay, the leading Internet auctioneer, is perhaps the most successful pure-play Internet company to date.

172 2002 Cal. App. LEXIS 4315 (Cal. App.).

when goods are offered "without reserve"), and therefore an auctioneer can withdraw goods if he pleases. In the .*TV* case, however, the domain name registrar offered "golf.tv" in an online auction, the plaintiff offered the highest bid ($1010), and the registrar confirmed the plaintiff as the winner by e-mail. Shortly thereafter, the registrar had second thoughts, and tried to rescind the deal by arguing that the reserve bid had not been met, and the confirmatory e-mail was sent by error.[173] The court sided with the plaintiff, concluding on these facts that either the defendant's advertisement of the "golf.tv" domain name was an offer and accepted by the plaintiff's highest bid, or if the plaintiff's bid was merely an offer, it was accepted by the defendant's e-mail.

c) Express and Implied Click-Consent Agreements

Until fairly recently, there was doubt in Canada whether contracts could be formed online by having a customer denote consent to various terms and conditions posted on a Web site by clicking an icon or button that says "I Agree." This uncertainty exists no longer, courtesy of the *Rudder* decision and the electronic commerce statutes discussed earlier in this chapter.[174] At issue in the *Rudder* case was the enforceability of the Microsoft Network's Member Agreement. The plaintiffs in the case had launched a class action, alleging a breach of certain provisions of the subscriber agreement. They argued, however, that the governing law and place of legal proceedings clauses of the Agreement, which provided for the State of Washington (Microsoft's approach to dealing with the uncertainty caused by the fourth dynamic of computer law was to provide a specific forum for the hearing of disputes), should not be

---

173 The defendant's motivation in trying to rescind the plaintiff's agreement can be understood by the fact that the registrar subsequently offered the domain name "golf.tv" with an opening reserve bid of $1,000,000. Some might ask whether, in substance, the ability of an entity to distribute at differential prices top-level domain names of a country (here, "tv" denotes the island nation of Tuvalu) does not constitute institutionalized cybersquatting, an activity frowned upon by the official Internet naming authorities when conducted by individuals: see chapter 2, section C.7(b), "Cybersquatting."

174 *Rudder v. Microsoft Corporation* (1999), 2 C.P.R. (4th) 474 (Ont. Sup. Ct.) [*Rudder*]. For a similar case in the United States with the identical result, see *Caspi v. The Microsoft Network,* 732 A.2d 528 (N.J. Super. Appellate 1999) [*Caspi*]. For a decision that predates *Rudder* where the court, in a cursory opinion, assumed the validity of a click-consent agreement in granting an *ex parte* motion to enforce an injunction, see *I.D. Internet Direct Ltd.* v. *Altelaar,* [1999] O.J. No. 1804 (Sup. Ct.). As for the e-commerce statutes, see section A.1(g) of this chapter, "Electronic Commerce Statutes."

enforced because they had not been given adequate notice of it. The court disagreed. The judge found that potential members of the Microsoft Network were required to acknowledge their acceptance of the terms of the Members Agreement by clicking on an "I Agree" button at the time the terms of the agreement were displayed. The court noted that while the entire agreement was not displayed at once, all the terms could be read by scrolling through several screens, and that this was no different than having to turn the pages of a multi-page paper-based document. It did not help the plaintiffs' cause that they wished to rely on certain provisions of the Members Agreement but not on others. The court said that such a finding would result in a "commercial absurdity," and "would lead to chaos in the marketplace, render ineffectual electronic commerce and undermine the integrity of any agreement entered into through this medium."[175] Rather, the court concluded, "on the present facts, the Membership Agreement must be afforded the sanctity that must be given to any agreement in writing."[176] This decision is consistent with several previous US decisions that have upheld what may be termed *express click-consent agreements*, namely contracts concluded over the Internet when people either typed "I Agree" or clicked on an "I Agree" icon at the end of the specific agreement they were agreeing to.[177] As such, this Canadian decision will help bolster confidence in the

---

175 *Rudder*, above note 174 at 482. On the same issue, the court in *Caspi*, above note 174, held at 532 that "… and no good purpose, consonant with the dictates of reasonable reliability in commerce, would be served by permitting them to disavow particular provisions or the contract as a whole."

176 *Rudder*, above note 174 at 482.

177 See *Compuserve, Incorporated v. Patterson*, 89 F.3d 1257 (6th Cir. 1996). See also the *Caspi* decision, above note 174, where the court, at 530, pointed out that the consumer could become a subscriber to the Microsoft service only after having an opportunity to review the subscription agreement and clicking on a button labelled "I Agree"; for greater certainty, there was even a button labelled "I Don't Agree." In *Forest v. Verizon Communications*, 2002 D.C. App. LEXIS 509 [*Verizon*], the court upheld a user contract that appeared on the screen in a scroll box, where only a small portion of the contract was visible at any one time, given that the subscriber clicked an "Accept" button below the scroll box. In upholding the forum selection clause in this agreement, the court was of the view that absent fraud or mistake, a person is bound by a contract that he had an opportunity to read whether he actually did or not; at page 7 of the opinion the court concluded: "A contract is no less a contract simply because it is entered into via a computer." See also *Hughes v. McMenamon*, No. 2001-10981-RBC1 (D. Mass. 2002), which followed *Caspi* and upheld the forum selection clause in an AOL user agreement.

enforceability of contracts concluded over the Internet, thereby making the legal environment for e-commerce more certain.[178]

The *Rudder* decision dealt with a Web site design whereby the user was presented with the relevant terms and conditions, and expressly required to agree to them (or decline them) before the user could go on to the next screen in the site. In this sense, the *Rudder* case dealt with an express click-consent agreement. Often, however, the Web designer does not want to present the user with the terms and conditions expressly. This need not be an insurmountable obstacle to creating an enforceable online agreement. In one recent American decision, the court held that assent to terms and conditions may be manifested by conduct, in this case by using the site for its intended purpose.[179] In another case the court seemed to be willing to agree that an online agreement can be created where a customer clicks a box at the bottom of the screen on which the application is provided, a link to the text of the User Agreement is provided at the bottom of the same screen, and the link to the user agreement need not be activated for the application to be processed.[180] In other cases, however, courts have concluded that

---

178 For a G2C (government to consumer) example of an express click-consent agreement, consider the Ontario government's kiosks where a member of the public can renew a driver's licence. After the person's credit card and vehicle registration details are verified, the kiosk screen requires the person to certify that she has insurance, by means of touching an "I Agree" icon. The statutory authority for this is the *Compulsory Automobile Insurance Act*, R.S.O. 1999, c. C.25, while the kiosk system of certification is legally underpinned by O. Reg. 278/95, which permits a certificate of insurance to be in electronic form.

179 *Register.com v. Verio, Inc.*, 126 F.Supp. 2d 238 (S.D.N.Y. 2000) [*Verio*]. The final paragraph of Register.com's Web site terms and conditions provided that "by submitting this query [for the WHO IS domain name database], you agree to abide by these terms." Therefore, the court concluded, by entering the search request, the defendant assented to the terms, notwithstanding that the defendant did not manifest assent by an express click on an "I Agree" icon. For an earlier version of this sort of agreement, see *Primrose v. Western Union Telegraph Company*, 154 U.S. 1 (1894), where the limitation of liability terms printed on the back of the form used by customers to submit handwritten messages for telegraphing were held to be operative, given the notice of such terms on the front of the form, including just below the customer's signature line, that indicated that the terms on the reverse would apply.

180 *Comb v. PayPal, Inc.*, 2002 U.S. Dist. LEXIS 16364 (N. Cal.) [*PayPal*]. However, while the court was willing to assume for purposes of the motion (without deciding) that the user agreement was effective, the court went on to find the agreement unconscionable and therefore its submission to arbitration provisions unenforceable; see the discussion in the next section on unconscionable terms.

the terms and conditions are not binding on the user because insufficient efforts were taken to bring the terms, or even the existence of the
terms, to the user. Thus, in one case the court found the link on the
home page to the contract terms too small to be noticed,[181] and in
another case the link was in a colour that did not stand out.[182] In yet
another case, the language on the screen referencing the terms was
considered merely an invitation to link to the terms, rather than a firm
condition, with the result that the user was able to download the software without having either to view the page containing the terms of the
software licence or to click a button that manifested acceptance of
these terms; in these circumstances the court held the user had not
assented to the licence terms.[183] And in one case the terms were con-

---

181 *Ticketmaster Corp.* v. *Tickets.com Inc.*, 2000 U.S. Dist. LEXIS 4553 (C.D. Cal.). In
this case the court concluded, at 3: "Many websites make you click on 'agree' to
the Terms and Conditions before going on, but Ticketmaster does not. Further,
the Terms and Conditions are set forth so that the customer needs to scroll
down the home page to find and read them. Many customers instead are likely
to proceed to the event page of interest rather than reading the 'small print.' It
cannot be said that merely putting the Terms and Conditions in this fashion
necessarily creates a contract with anyone using the website." The court, however, did leave open the possibility of Ticketmaster amending its claim if in fact it
could show that the defendant had knowledge of the terms and conditions
together with facts showing implied agreement to them.

182 *Pollstar* v. *Gigmania Ltd.*, 2000 WL 33266437 (E.D. Cal).

183 *Specht* v. *Netscape Communications Corp. and America Online, Inc.*, (2001) U.S.
Dist. LEXIS 9073. This decision is particularly useful because it takes a "first
principles" approach to online contracting, as illustrated by the judgment's opening paragraph, which highlights the "timeless issue of assent": "Promises become
binding when there is a meeting of the minds and consideration is exchanged. So
it was at King's Bench in common law England; so it was under the common law
in the American colonies; so it was through more than two centuries of jurisprudence in this country; and so it is today. Assent may be registered by a signature,
a handshake, or a click of a computer mouse transmitted across the invisible
ether of the Internet. Formality is not a requisite; any sign, symbol, or action, or
even wilful inaction, as long as it is unequivocally referable to the promise, may
create a contract." See also *Softman Products Company, LLC* v. *Adobe Systems Inc.*,
171 F.Supp. 2d 1075 (C.D. Cal. 2001), where the court declined to find an
enforceable agreement because the distributor of the software (who was not an
end-user of the software) never had occasion to load the software and hence
interact with the sign-up screen; moreover, the court also held that the one-sen-
tence notice to users on the outside of the box that indicated that the software
was offered subject to licence terms was insufficient to bind the distributor.

sidered unenforceable because the damage caused by the Web site owner occurred before the user could even assent to the terms.[184]

These latter cases are often referred to by commentators as dealing with "click wrap" or "browse wrap" agreements. In so doing, they are trying to draw a parallel to the "shrinkwrap" software licences, discussed in chapter 5, section C.2, "Shrinkwrap Licences." Unfortunately, the intended analogy is not a good one, as most shrinkwrap software licences today do not involve any cellophane packaging, and instead utilize the "pay now, contract later, with full refund if refuse licence" model, as in the *ProCD* case.[185] In the *ProCD* case, the user purchased the product at retail, but when he took it home and loaded the disk into his computer, a screen appeared that presented the licensor's licence terms. The user had to expressly agree to these terms in order to continue into the product. If the user declined to agree with the contract, the user could return the product for a full refund. Thus, the *ProCD* case is akin to the *Rudder*-type situation, and each dealt with express click-consent agreements because in both scenarios the user is given the opportunity to read the contract and then to immediately and expressly agree (or not) to it before commencing to use the relevant service or product.

This does not mean that the only type of online agreement that will be enforceable is the kind where the user is expressly required to scroll

---

184 *Mark Williams* v. *America Online, Inc.*, 2001 Mass. Super. LEXIS 11 (February 8, 2001). But note also the decision in *Verizon*, above note 177, where pre-agreement damages were ultimately limited by contract when an agreement subsequently was entered into by the user of the online service.

185 *ProCD* v. *Ziedenberg*, 86 F.3d 1447 (7th Cir. 1996) [*ProCD*]. For a more recent American case that follows *ProCD*, see *Moore* v. *Microsoft Corporation*, 741 N.Y.S. 2d 91 (N.Y.A.D. 2002), where the court concluded the following: "We agree with the Supreme Court that the End-User License Agreement (hereinafter the EULA) contained in the defendant's software program is a validly binding contract between the parties which bars the plaintiffs claims (see *Brower* v. *Gateway* 246 A.D. 2d 246 (N.Y.A.D., 1998)). The terms of the EULA were prominently displayed on the program user's computer screen before the software could be installed. Moreover, the program's user was required to indicate assent to the EULA by clicking on the 'I agree' icon before proceeding with the download of the software. Thus, the defendant offered a contract that the plaintiff accepted by using the software after having an opportunity to read the licence at leisure. As a result, the plaintiff's claims are barred by the clear disclaimers, waivers of liability, and limitations of remedies contained in the EULA." For another recent click-consent agreement that follows *ProCD*, see *I.LAN Systems, Inc.* v. *Netscout Service Level Corp.*, 183 F.Supp. 2d 328 (D. Mass. 2002) [*Netscout*]. Both the *ProCD* and *Netscout* decisions are discussed in more detail in chapter 5, section C.2(b), "The *ProCD* Case."

through the terms and conditions and then click "I Agree" at the end of these terms. There is no doubt, of course, that such an "express click-consent agreement" is the preferred vehicle for creating binding online contracts. Nevertheless, "implied click-consent agreements" will be recognized by the courts as well, provided they are designed and presented carefully, as they were in the *Verio* case and (arguably) in the *PayPal* decision. Three conditions need to exist. First, the link to the terms must be readily accessible, and ideally should take the user directly to the terms. Second, there should be a prominent notice on the home page, requiring (not merely requesting) users to read and assent to the terms, and stressing the importance of the terms. Finally, the home page (or other screen where the online contract is intended to be created) should have a button that has the user confirm that he or she has read the terms and agrees to be bound by them, thereby manifesting assent to the terms.

The recent decision in *Kanitz v. Rogers Cable Inc.*[186] gives support to the enforceability of implied click-consent agreements. The legal proceedings in this case were prompted by the service difficulties experienced by users of the Rogers Internet-over-cable service several years ago as Rogers was rolling out this high-speed Internet access service. The plaintiffs were customers of this service who signed up either with Rogers or with Shaw (in the latter case, they became Rogers subscribers when Rogers and Shaw swapped certain cable assets subsequently). The plaintiffs estimated that they should each receive a refund of $240 to compensate for service outages. Of course, it hardly makes sense for an individual to sue for such a small amount of money, so the plaintiffs brought their claim as a class action on behalf of some 370,000 Rogers subscribers. Rogers countered that the relevant user agreement provides for arbitration as the exclusive dispute resolution mechanism, and therefore the class action should be dismissed. What prompted this skirmish in the case, however, is that the original user agreement did not provide for arbitration. Rather, in January 2001, Rogers posted to its Web site an amendment to the user agreement that included an arbitration clause.

At the time Rogers posted its new user agreement (that contained the new arbitration clause), it did not give subscribers notice by an e-mail or postal mail. It merely put the new agreement in a subarea of its Web site that was at least five clicks away from its main home-page. The plaintiffs, accordingly, argued that subscribers did not have sufficient notice of the revised terms, including the new arbitration clause, and

---

186 (2002), 58 O.R. (3d) 299 (Ont. Sup. Ct.) [*Kanitz*].

therefore the new terms should not be binding on subscribers. They argued that this process amounted to a unilateral imposition of terms, which the court should not sanction. The court did not agree with the plaintiffs, and instead found in favour of Rogers. The court noted that the original user agreement expressly provided that Rogers could amend the agreement so long as it gave notice either by e-mail or postal mail, or by "notifying any changes to this Agreement by posting notice of such changes on the Rogers@Home web site." Thus, although the court stated that Rogers could have done more to alert subscribers to the new terms, such as by sending an e-mail to this effect, the court concluded that, given this wording in its user agreement, it did not have to do so and instead could give notice by the Web site posting. (It should be noted, however, that a different conclusion may result in another jurisdiction if the relevant arbitration law required that arbitration agreements be in writing (Ontario's law has no such requirement) and the relevant electronic commerce statute did not recognize a mere Web posting to satisfy a writing requirement; in such a situation it would be sensible to communicate the new provision by e-mail).

Rogers, however, did not post this notice on the first page of its Web site. Rather, the notice was contained on a page fairly deep into the site. Not a problem, concluded the court. It is reasonable in this situation, the court found, to place an obligation on the user to check the Web site from time to time to determine if changes have been made to the terms and conditions. Moreover, the court continued, it is equally reasonable to expect Internet-over-cable subscribers to visit that portion of Rogers' site that deals with the Internet access business. In coming to this conclusion, the court noted that locating a specific piece of information on any given Web site can sometimes require a process of "trial and error until one becomes familiar with the web site and where items are located on it." In a passage that undoubtedly will be cited in future cases, the court concluded (at para. 32):

> We are here dealing with people who wish to avail themselves of an electronic environment and the electronic services that are available through it. It does not seem unreasonable for persons, who are seeking electronic access to all manner of goods, services and products along with information, communication, entertainment and other resources, to have the legal attributes of their relationship with the very entity that is providing such electronic access, defined and communicated to them through that electronic format.

A final point worth noting is that the user agreement, after enumerating the three methods by which notice may be given to users of an amendment (as noted above), went on to provide that a subscriber's continued use of the Rogers service following the notice of change means that the subscriber agrees to the change. Based on this language, the court concluded that by virtue of the plaintiffs' continued use of the service, they were deemed to have accepted the amendments to the terms and conditions, including the new arbitration clause.[187]

d) Unconscionable Terms

Whether the Web site utilizes an express click-consent agreement or an implied click-consent agreement, Web site owners need to be mindful of the jurisprudence that stipulates that particularly onerous or unusual terms need to be brought to the express attention of the user for them to be enforceable.[188] Indeed, particularly in a B2C context, it should be remembered that judges in the offline world have jettisoned entire contracts where they believed unfair bargaining power or unconscionability was at work.[189] In a similar vein in one recent case, *Robet* v. *Versus Brokerage Services (c.o.b. E*Trade Canada)*,[190] involving a claim by a user of an Internet stock trading service, the court refused to

---

187 For a similar result where the new consumer contract was provided by regular mail, see *Boomer* v. *AT&T Corporation*, 309 F.3d 404 (7th Cir. 2002). In this case the telecommunications company mailed its new consumer agreement in an envelope that stated: "ATTENTION: Important information concerning your AT&T service enclosed." A cover letter also stated that continued use of the services will deem acceptance of the new terms, and that if the consumer does not agree with the new terms, a 1-800 number may be called to cancel the service. On these facts, the new agreement was held enforceable, including the new arbitration clause that precluded class actions.

188 *Tilden Rent a Car Co.* v. *Clendenning* (1978), 83 D.L.R. (3d) 400 (Ont. C.A.) [*Tilden*]. See also the *Thorsteinson* case, at note 189 below. Though, in other cases it has been held that transactors are deemed to have read and understood all the provisions in the agreement they sign: *Fraser Jewellers (1982) Ltd.* v. *Dominion Electronic Protection Co.* (1997), 34 O.R. 3d (1) (Ont. C.A.) [*Fraser Jewellers*]; and *Rudder*, above note 174. In any event, one way to bring unusual terms to the attention of users is to have additional "I Agree" click icons throughout the agreement immediately following such terms. That is, in *Thornton*, at note 200 below, Lord Denning, at 689, used the famous phrase that to give sufficient notice to particularly onerous terms, "it would need to be printed in red ink with a red hand pointing to it, or something equally startling." In fact the Internet affords an efficient medium in which to effect the equivalent of red ink and the red hand.

189 *W.W. Distributors & Co. Ltd.* v. *Thorsteinson* (1960), 26 D.L.R. (2d) 365 (Man. C.A.) [*Thorsteinson*].

190 [2001] O.J. No. 1341 (Sup. Ct.) [*Robet*]. For an American decision concluding that a user agreement providing for arbitration of disputes was unconscionable both procedurally and substantively, see *PayPal*, above note 180.

enforce the limit of liability clause (contained in an account agreement concluded partly online and partly by hard copies exchanged by regular mail) because, essentially, it felt the agreement was overly one-sided and unfair, and the court concluded that exclusionary clauses should not be enforced where the supplier failed to supply the very thing contracted for.[191] In *Robet*, a client of E-Trade purchased 3000 shares, but due to computer and human error, an extra 9000 shares were shown as having been purchased by the client. Instead of complaining to E-Trade (as many other clients did), the client sold the 9000 shares (as many other clients affected by the same error sold their excess shares), which started a chain of events that eventually required the client to cover a short sale position. When the client refused to do so, E-Trade did. The resulting loss was apportioned by the court: E-Trade was at fault for the original posting of the erroneous account balance showing the extra 9000 shares,[192] but the client was at fault for not mitigating damages as soon as he was able to do so by promptly covering the short-sale position. In effect, a plague on both your houses, said the court. One lesson reinforced by the court in *Robet* was that the whole sorry story could have been avoided had E-Trade promptly notified the client that a computer glitch had occurred, and that therefore there might be anomalous postings in their account balances. A short e-mail to this effect would have done the trick. The court observed that since the computer meltdown that gave rise to this case, E-Trade in fact had added such an e-mail–based warning functionality to its system. Indeed, considered more broadly, e-mail can solve a great number of the online contracting challenges noted in this chapter. It can, for example, serve as a primary vehicle for delivery of electronic information in order to meet the various functional equivalency requirements in the new electronic commerce statutes. E-mail is also very effective for confirming online purchases.[193] E-mail is easy and simple to use,

---

191 See also *Wei Zhu v. Merrill Lynch HSBC*, [2002] BCPC 0535 (B.C. Prov. Ct.), in which the court refused to enforce disclaimers presented on the screen of an online stock trading service. For a different view of the law, see the *Fraser Jewellers* case referred to in chapter 5, section E.2, "Limitations on Liability," where the Ontario Court of Appeal held that a limitation of liability clause would apply even in the case of fundamental breach.

192 This result is reminiscent of the decision in *Budai v. Ontario Lottery Corporation* (1983), 142 D.L.R. (3d) 271 (Ont. H.C.J.), discussed in chapter 5, section D.2(a), "Malfunctioning Computers."

193 For an example of a problem that could have been avoided by a confirmatory e-mail, see Douglas McArthur, "The Perils of 'Electronic' Air Tickets," *The Globe and Mail* (26 November 1997). This piece recounts how a dispute arose when a

and relatively inexpensive. It is an extremely valuable handmaiden to electronic commerce and should be considered as a useful utility to achieve a number of legal objectives in the online world.[194]

It should be noted, however, that in the *Kanitz* case, the court was also unsympathetic to the plaintiffs' secondary and tertiary arguments, namely, that the arbitration clause was "buried" in the agreement so that it could not be seen, and that it was "unconscionable." On the first point, the court concluded that the arbitration clause is simply presented like every other clause of the agreement, and so it is not the same as the fine print on the back of a car rental contract (that led to a finding of unenforceability in *Tilden*). In coming to this conclusion, the court in the *Kanitz* case echoed the sentiment in the *Rudder* decision, where the court found that scrolling through multiple screens is akin to flipping the pages of a paper-based agreement. (Incidentally, the other parallel between the *Kanitz* and *Rudder* cases is that they both had rather sophisticated representative plaintiffs. In *Kanitz*, the court noted that the lead plaintiff had a master's degree in computer science, whereas the plaintiffs in *Rudder* were law school graduates. One gets a sense from these failed class-action suits that persons with less technical and legal sophistication would make better plaintiffs.) Nor was the arbitration clause unconscionable, notwithstanding that it did preclude collective litigation. The court held that if the legislature wishes to prevent arbitration proceedings from thwarting class-action litigation, then it could amend the class action legislation[195] accordingly; but in the meantime, the court would uphold the objective of the *Arbitration Act*,[196] namely, to give effect to arbitration agreements. The court, however, does offer a faint glimmer of hope to the plaintiffs, by noting that under the arbitration statute an arbitrator may be able to consolidate a number of arbitrations

---

person booked a discount airfare over the phone; no record was made of the phone conversation by the airline, the passenger was issued no receipt or ticket, and then to the passenger's surprise (and dismay), the invoice (sent after the flight had been taken) showed not the low-cost fare but the regular price. A quick (and virtually automatic) e-mail sent immediately after the booking (or even a fax) could have avoided this dispute.

194 The other lesson from *Robet*, above note 190, and the other cases noted above in this section, is that great care should be taken in the "legal design" of the Web site. Also, plain language should be used, whenever possible.

195 For example, in Ontario: *Class Proceedings Act*, S.O. 1992, c. 6.

196 *Arbitration Act*, S.O. 1991, c. 17. But see Ontario's new *Consumer Protection Act, 2002*, S.O. 2002, c. 30 (Bill 180, 2002), which makes any contractual term providing for arbitration invalid that purports to prevent a consumer from utilizing the regular court system. This new law also allows a consumer to institute class proceedings even if the relevant consumer agreement says he or she cannot.

that raise the same issue. While this might be of some help to plaintiffs desiring to bring a mass claim, it is a far cry from a class proceeding. In short, in *Kanitz*, Rogers' tactic of inserting an arbitration clause has paid fairly material dividends. By contrast, however, in the American *PayPal* decision, an arbitration clause in a user agreement for an online payment service was held to be unenforceable as being unconscionable.

e) Law Reform

The electronic commerce statutes discussed earlier in this chapter in the context of the writing and signature rules[197] also contain provisions relating to electronic transactions. For example, the Ontario ECA provides that an offer, an acceptance, or any other matter material to the formation or operation of a contract may be expressed by electronic information or by an act intended to result in electronic communication, such as touching or clicking on an appropriate icon or other place on a computer screen, or by speaking.[198] This echoes the result in the *Rudder* decision, and confirms that click-consent agreements will not be unenforceable because they are concluded by electronic means but, as noted in the previous section of this chapter, it is still incumbent on the Web site designer to structure the electronic offer and acceptance in a way that effectively forms a binding agreement. The ECA also provides specific rules, consistent with the other "writing" provisions of the ECA, related to contracts for the carriage of goods.[199] Another section of the ECA confirms that a contract may be formed by the interaction of an individual with a computer, such as the server and software that operates a Web site, or by two computers without any direct human interaction.[200] Although this rule is helpful in confirming

---

197 See sections A.1(g), "Electronic Commerce Statutes," and A.2(c), "Law Reform," in this chapter.

198 Thus, a voice-activated response would be effective: see Gregory, "The UETA and UECA," above note 55 at 461.

199 *ECA*, s. 23.

200 *ECA*, s. 20. The *ECA* uses the unfortunate phrase electronic agent, which seemingly denotes some form of principal–agent legal relationship between the user and the technology, but a close reading of the definition confirms that electronic agent is simply the Web site, for example, that a user interacts with while ordering a book online. For a pre-*ECA* case that enforced a contract concluded with a parking ticket machine, see *Thornton v. Shoe Lane Parking*, [1971] 1 All E.R. 686 (C.A.) [*Thornton*], but note that in this decision additional onerous provisions on the back of the ticket issued by the parking ticket machine were held invalid to the extent they contradicted the terms brought to the customer's attention in the notice placed on or near the machine that the customer first saw when he drove up to the ticket dispensing machine. See also L. Wein, "The Responsibility of Intelligent Artifacts: Towards an Automation Jurisprudence" (1996) 6 Harv. J. Law & Techn. 103.

that a valid agreement can be made even if the electronic contract formation process is automated at one or both ends of the transaction, the provision does not, by itself, solve the problem raised by the *Corinthian* case; that is, it is still important for business people to stipulate, by contract, which electronic transmissions will, when taken together, constitute a binding agreement. Similarly, as noted in the previous section, businesses selling goods online should be careful to ensure that their marketing material on the Web site is not construed to be a formal offer, but merely what is called an "invitation to treat," in response to which potential customers submit offers, which in turn are only accepted by the e-tailer when they confirm such in a subsequent e-mail or an online confirmation given immediately upon receipt of the order. On the other hand, an e-tailer may construct its Web presence such that its detailed online terms and conditions constitute the offer, which a user accepts when he types "I Agree" or clicks on the "I Agree" icon at the end of the online terms.

4) Garbled Messages

Where contracts are not negotiated in a face-to-face environment, but by means of a telecommunications device, there is always the risk that the messages intending to create contractual obligations do not reach their destination or, perhaps more dangerously, are received by the recipient but not in precisely the form sent by the sender. The telegraph was notoriously susceptible to errors, particularly at the various points where human actors were involved in the process of dictating, transcribing, transmitting, receiving, or deciphering a telegraphic message. So many different things could go wrong in the transmission of a telegram. In *Henckel* v. *Pape*, for example, two commercial parties had exchanged several messages regarding the possible purchase of up to fifty rifles, the number that the plaintiff had available for sale.[201] The defendant finally wrote out a telegram ordering three rifles. By mistake, the telegraph clerk telegraphed "the" for "three," with the result that the plaintiff sent all fifty rifles. In the ensuing action by the seller against the purchaser, the court held that the purchaser should not be responsible for the error of the telegraph clerk, that there was no contract between the parties, and thus the defendant was not responsible to pay for the rifles. A similar result was arrived at in an American telegraph case, with the court concluding that no contract came into existence when the telegraph company understated the price actually

---

201 (1870), 23 L.T. 419 [*Henckel*].

quoted by the sender of the telegram.[202] Another American case gives a good example of the dangers inherent in the telegraph system; the seller wired a quotation of a particular commodity at $1.70, but it was delivered to the buyer at $1.07.[203] In addition to the very common problem illustrated in these cases, including the difficulty of differentiating between dots and dashes, numerous other inherent weaknesses in the telegraph system caused a flood of litigation surrounding this technology in the mid-1800s.[204] Often a telegraph message had to be relayed through multiple telegraph companies, compounding the risks all around, as well as introducing the opportunity for the message to fall between the cracks during the stages where typically boys delivered the message on foot between the offices of different telegraph companies in the same city.[205] The telegraph technology effecting the transmission was also extremely prone to malfunction. Poorly insulated telegram wires disrupted many transmissions, and perhaps not surprisingly, given that many early insulators were made of cowhorns or

---

202 *Harper v. Western Union Telegraph Co.*, 130 S.E. 119 (S.C. 1925). See also *Bowen & McNamee v. The Lake Erie Telegraph Company*, 1 American Law Register 685 (Ct. of Common Pleas, 1853), where a telegraph company was held responsible for the damages caused by its transposition of the phrase "one handsome" into "one hundred" in a commercial telegram.

203 *Postal Tel. Cable Co. v. Schaefer*, 62 S.W. 1119 (Ky. App. 1901). In some of the cases, the problem was caused by the fact that in Morse code, the telegraph language in which letters were different combinations of dots and dashes, and most importantly, for liability purposes, spaces between letters, it was difficult except for the most expert telegraph clerk to differentiate between a dot and a dash. Thus, in *John Wann v. Western Union Telegraph Company*, 37 Mo. 472 (Sup. Ct. Miss. 1866), a merchant stipulated "Ship by sail" when ordering some goods, but the "s" (three dots following each other) became an "r" (essentially, a dot with a space followed by two more dots), so that the goods were shipped by "rail." This extra space caused $1000 in damages (a lot of money in 1866), the difference in the cost between rail and ship transport. See also *Primrose v. Western Union Telegraph Company*, 154 U.S. 1 (1894) where the problem arose because of a single dot: in a critical word, a "u" (two dots and a dash) had been changed to an "a" (one dot, one dash). For the outcome in this case, see note 122 in chapter 5.

204 For a review of many of these cases, see William L. Scott & Milton P. Jarnagin, *A Treatise upon the Laws of Telegraphs* (Boston: Little, Brown, 1868), as well as the books in the above notes 11 and 12.

205 In *Kinghorne*, above note 10, the telegraph message was sent from Kingston, Ontario, to Ogdensburg, New York, where the recipient telegraph company was to send the message by hand to another company's office in Ogdensburg for onward transmission to its office in Oswego. The message never did arrive in Oswego, and the lawsuit against the initial telegraph company ensued.

cloth soaked in beeswax. Electrical storms played havoc with early telegraph transmission systems. In short, it is no wonder that in the *Kinghorne* decision the court stated in respect of telegraphic messages:

> We must look, I think, in the case of each communication, at the papers delivered by the party who sent the message, not at the transcript of the message taken through the wire at the other end of the wire, with all the chances of mistakes in apprehending and noting the signals, and in transcribing for delivery.[206]

a)   Contractual Measures

Compared to early telegraph systems that caused numerous misadventures, current telecommunications networks are much more reliable and trustworthy. This is one reason why today, notwithstanding the huge increase in telecommunications traffic over the last thirty years, there is a relative dearth of litigation over garbled messages and the like. Another reason, of course, is that in certain jurisdictions the telephone companies operate under tariffs and limitations of liability that restrict the claims that can be brought against them. Also helping to reduce basic communication mix-ups in today's computerized networked environments are technologies that permit the testing of certain parameters of an electronic message to ensure it accords with past practice and the anticipated relationship between the parties.[207] A contract provision that reflects this is section 5.04 of the EDI Council of Canada's *Model TPA* that requires each party to undertake reasonableness testing on messages received so that a recipient does not act upon erroneous messages, such as where 10,000 units of a product are ordered by a single electronic purchase order when, historically, no more than 1000 were ordered at a time, probably indicating that an extra zero was mistakenly added to the electronic purchase order. Such verification procedures were available to persons using the telegraph, but they were time-consuming and cumbersome. For example, in the *Henckel* case, it was noted that on the back of the pre-printed form that a customer used to write down the contents of the telegram, there was offered for an additional fee a procedure whereby, if the sender desired to adopt an "extra security against risk of error," it could have the telegram, as prepared by the telegraph clerk from the originator's handwritten message, delivered to the sender by a messenger for a confirmation check, only

---

206 *Ibid.*, at 66.
207 Of course, this does not mean electronic systems are infallible: see *Shell Pipeline Corporation v. Coastal States Trading, Inc.*, 788 S.W.2d 837 (Tex. App. 1990), referred to in chapter 5, section D.2, "Negligence in Use."

after which it would be transmitted by the telegraph company.[208] Of course such "repetition," as it was called, took extra time and was charged as an additional service. One doubts if it was used very often. By contrast, in an EDI or other electronic environment, a party agreeing to undertake reasonableness testing in, for example, an EDI trading partner agreement can do so because it has software that carries out this function, thereby illustrating yet another example of how sophisticated technology can assist parties in bringing greater precision to their contract formation activities. This is an important point. All too often the first dynamic of computer law is viewed merely as a challenge to the law, indeed often as an adversary, as in the criminal law area discussed in chapter 3, where the law has a difficult time keeping up with new technological means of causing harm. In other areas, however, the first dynamic of computer law means a rash of new products, such as encryption programs, authentication mechanisms (such as biometric devices), and more stable transmission technologies, to help promote stability and certainty. In essence, contract formation processes can be made very reliable, and the evidence for this is the relative scarcity of lawsuits in this area of the law today.

b) Law Reform

It is interesting to note that the Ontario ECA, discussed throughout this chapter,[209] includes a provision that stipulates that an electronic transaction between an individual and another person's computer (i.e., their Web site) has no legal effect if the individual makes a material error in the transaction; the computer does not give the individual an opportunity to prevent or correct the error; on becoming aware of the error, the individual promptly notifies the other person; and the individual does

---

208 *Henckel*, above note 201 at 420. Another form of defensive measure adopted by the telegraph companies was the "repeated message," whereby a receiving station sent the message back to the originating station for confirmation, after which corrections could be effected. Of course, there was an extra fee for this service, often as high as 50 percent of the cost of the message: see *Camp v. Western Union Telegraph Company*, 58 Ky. 167 (Louisville Ch. Ct. 1858), wherein the court stated at 164: "The system of telegraphing, however perfect it may be, [was] seriously affected by atmospheric causes, which are uncontrollable; and if a man want[ed] to send a message of an important character, prudence and wisdom would seem to dictate that he should have it repeated, in order to be assured of its direct transmission. And as the repetition imposes additional labor, it is surely justice that an enhanced price should be paid."

209 See sections A.1(g), "Electronic Commerce Statutes," A.2(c), "Law Reform," and A.3(e) "Law Reform," in this chapter.

not benefit from any consideration received as a result of the error.[210] This provision raises several issues. What is a "material" error, as opposed to a non-material one? The courts will have to answer this. Also, the "confirmation defence," if it can be called that, will likely lead many businesses to design their Web sites or other electronic ordering mechanisms to permit individuals to unambiguously review and correct errors in their orders before processing them. This will likely put a higher onus on Internet-based merchants than, for example, their paper-based catalogue sales counterparts. Moreover, some Internet e-tailers see material marketing advantage in facilitating a "one-click" check-out system that does not require the use of any confirmatory screen (see the discussion surrounding the Amazon.com one-click patent in chapter 2, section C.2, "Patent Protection for Software and Business Methods"). Nevertheless, the confirmatory screen device is a sensible mechanism for trying to avoid the occurrence of errors in online contracting. It is similar to the "repetition" service offered by telegraph companies 150 years ago.[211] The principle was the same then as now; an ounce of prevention is worth a pound of cure.

5) Time and Place of Contract

a) The *Post Box Rule*
When parties sign a contract simultaneously in a face-to-face setting, there is no doubt as to when and where the contract came into being. When either an offer, or an acceptance, or both, are sent by telegraph,

---

210 *ECA*, s. 21. For an example of the kind of error this provision is aimed at avoiding, consider the following blunder described in "How About Now: A Survey of the Real-Time Economy," *The Economist*, 2 February 2002: "Last November a simple typing error left it [UBS Warburg, a European investment bank] at least $50m out of pocket. The morning that Dentsu, one of the world's biggest advertising companies, went public on the Tokyo stock exchange, a UBS Warburg trader mistakenly entered a 'sell' order of 610,000 Dentsu shares at ¥16 each — instead of 16 Dentsu shares at ¥610,000. Although the trade was cancelled two minutes later, the bank's computers had already sold several thousand shares which it had to buy back at market price."

211 See *John Wann v. The Western Union Telegraph Company*, 37 Mo. 472 (Sup. Ct. Miss. 1866), and *Primrose v. Western Union Telegraph Company*, 154 U.S. 1 (U.S. Sup. Ct. 1894), where the "repetition" service offered by telegraph companies is described. Telegraph companies would typically charge 50 percent more for this service, but as it resulted in vastly more accurate messages, the company also agreed to take on much more liability if the repetition service was purchased by the customer.

telex, fax, EDI, e-mail, or via the Internet, or are communicated by tele-phone, it is often not a trivial legal task to determine when and where the contract arose. The uncertainty began even before the advent of the telegraph, with the mail delivery system. The general contract law rule is that an offer is not considered accepted until the acceptance of the offer is received by the offeror. In the 1800s in England an exception to this rule was developed by judges for offers and acceptances sent by the mail. The so-called *post box rule* holds that where an offer is made by the mail, the contract is made immediately at the time acceptance is posted in the mail (rather than when the acceptance is actually received by the offeror) where use of the mail is reasonable in the cir-cumstances or expressly contemplated by the parties.[212] This rule effec-tively operates to place the burden of uncertainty of the waiting period on the offeror; that is, the offeror does not know that it has earlier con-cluded a binding contract until it receives the offeree's acceptance in the mail, whereas the offeree knew the contract came into existence the moment it posted its reply letter. Shifting this risk to the offeror, and giving the concomitant comfort to the offeree, was reasonable for sev-eral reasons, including because of the increased reliability of the Royal Mail in the 1800s, and because the offeror typically chooses the mode of communication and could require that acceptance be received by it before it is effective. The *post box rule* is a good example of a legal doc-

---

212 *Imperial Life Assurance Co. of Canada v. Colmenares* (1967), 62 D.L.R. (2d) 138 (S.C.C.) [*Colmenares*]. The rule, however, will not apply where the parties did not contemplate the mails to be used: see *Moscovitch's Estate et al. v. South End Development Company Ltd.* (1968), 4 N.S.R. 1965–69, 182 (N.S.C.A.). Similarly, and for a good recent discussion of the *post box rule*, see *Trans-Pacific Trading, a division of Tyrer Enterprises Ltd. v. Rayonier Canada Ltd.*, [1998] 9 W.W.R. 226, [1998] B.C.J. No. 890 (C.A.). In this case the offeror, on August 25, 1995, faxed his offer, a copy of the contract, with the statement "Please sign and fax back ASAP." The offeror also sent the offeree by mail three copies of the contract with a note that the offeree should sign and return these so that the offeror could "complete our files in this matter." For some unknown reason, the offeree did not fax back the agreement on August 25, but rather put the signed copies in the mail on August 30. When the offeror revoked the offer on August 31, the offeree argued it already had a binding contract on August 30, courtesy of the *post box rule*. The trial judge and B.C. Court of Appeal disagreed, concluding that the offeror's fax of August 25 contemplated an acceptance by fax, the copies of the contract mailed by the offeror were for "housekeeping" purposes only, thus the mailing by offeree of the signed contracts on August 30 was not an effective acceptance, and therefore the offeror's revocation by fax on August 31 of its orig-inal offer was effective. A case like this illustrates why, generally speaking, it is no longer sensible to circulate "originals" for ink signatures once the deal is done on the strength of a faxed document; this practice merely leads to confusion.

trine being firmly grounded in the communication environment and business processes of its day.[213]

As the telegraph, telephone, and each other new communications technology came into widespread use, cases developed for each one as to when and where contracts were consummated. Telegraph messages,[214] and telegrams,[215] for example, are treated like the mail, and an acceptance by telegraph or telegram of an offer was considered effective when sent and not when it was received. Thus, as with the post (or courier), where the delay is instrinsic to the technology chosen by the offeror, the courts have sided with the offeree. Thorny inconsistencies, however, in the case law appeared. In *Carow Towing*, an early Canadian telephone case, it was held that a contract entered into by telephone should be treated like a letter and should follow the *post box rule*, with acceptance occurring at the place the acceptance is spoken and not where the offeror hears the acceptance.[216] By contrast, in the *Entores* case, a later British decision, Lord Denning concluded that for simultaneous communications like the telephone, the place where the contract is entered into is where the offeror hears the acceptance, and thus, if the line goes dead during the telephone conversation, the onus is upon the offeree to ring back the offeror to ensure the words of acceptance had gotten through to the offeror.[217] Subsequent cases in Canada have followed the decision in *Entores* rather than the approach in *Carow Towing*,[218] with the exception of Quebec where, up until relatively recently, the preponderance of cases have followed the rule that telephone contracts arise when and where the offeree speaks its acceptance;[219] since

213 The *post box rule* has been extended to couriers: see *Nova Scotia v. Weymouth Sea Products Ltd.* (1983), 4 D.L.R. (4th) 314 (N.S.C.A.); that is, it does not matter whether the paper-based agreement is mailed or carried by a courier. See also John Gregory, "Receiving Electronic Messages," 15 B.F.L.R. 473 (2000), an insightful article that argues for not extending the *post box rule* to newer, electronic-based methods of communication.

214 *Henthorn v. Fraser*, [1892] 2 c. 27.

215 *Malady v. Jenkins Steamship Co.* (1909), 18 O.L.R. 251 (Div. Ct.).

216 *Carow Towing Co. v. The "Ed. McWilliams"* (1919), 46 D.L.R. 506 (Ex. Ct.).

217 *Entores, Ltd. v. Miles Far East Corporation*, [1955] 2 All E.R. 493 (C.A.) [*Entores*].

218 See, for example, *McDonald & Sons Ltd. v. Export Packers Co. Ltd.* (1979), 95 D.L.R. (3d) 174 (B.C.S.C.) [*Export Packers*]. See also *Re Viscount Supply Co. Ltd.* (1963), 40 D.L.R. (2d) 501 (Ont. S.C.); *Senneth v. Tape Estate*, [1986] S.J. No. 223 (Sask. Q.B.) [*Senneth*]; *England v. Surfwood Supply (1964) Ltd.*, [1987] O.J. No. 1412 (Ont. Dist. Ct.); *National Bank of Canada v. Clifford Chance* (1996), 30 O.R. (3d) 746 (Gen. Div.) [*Clifford Chance*]; and *Ungar (c.o.b. "Parkland Mobile Repair Co.") v. Sayisi Dene*, [1999] S.J. No. 402 (Sask. Q.B.).

219 *Rosenthal & Rosenthal Inc. v. Bonavista Fabrics Ltd.*, [1984] C.A. 52 (Que. C.A.).

the enactment of the current *Civil Code* in January 1994, Article 1387 makes it clear that in respect of telephone (and all other) contracts acceptance occurs when and where the acceptance is received. Indeed, the existence of Article 1387 means that in Quebec there is no *post box rule* for any kind of communications, even those effected by mail. Elsewhere, the *Entores* decision was followed in several fax cases, in each of Nova Scotia,[220] New Zealand,[221] and Ontario,[222] all essentially holding that a contract made by fax arises when the offeror receives by fax the acceptance of the offeree.[223]

The *Entores* decision also held that telex technology results in instantaneous communications with the result that acceptance occurs when the message is received by the offeror. This approach was confirmed in a useful and insightful pronouncement by the House of Lords in the *Brinkibon* case.[224] In this case, the court determined that although telex communications should be categorized as simultaneous, in each case the specific constituent elements and factors in the communications system need to be carefully considered, such as the following:

> The senders and recipients may not be the principals to the contemplated contract. They may be servants or agents with limited authority. The message may not reach, or be intended to reach, the designated recipient immediately: messages may be sent out of office hours, or at night, with the intention, or on the assumption, that they will be read at a later time. There may be some error or default at the recipient's end which prevents receipt at the time contemplated and believed in by the sender. The message may have been sent and/or received through machines operated by third persons. And many other variations may occur. No universal rule can cover all such cases; they must be resolved by reference to the intentions of the parties, by sound business practice and in some cases by a judgment where the risks should lie.[225]

---

220 *Balcom (Joan) Sales Inc. v. Poirier* (1991), 288 A.P.R. 377 (N.S. Co. Ct.).
221 *Gunac Hawkes Bay (1986) Ltd. v. Palmer*, [1991] 3 N.Z.L.R. 297 (H. Ct.).
222 *Eastern Power Ltd. v. Azienda Communale Energia and Ambiente* (1999), 178 D.L.R. (4th) 409 (Ont. C.A.) [*Eastern Power*].
223 But see also *Bickmore v. Bickmore*, [1996] O.J. No. 4572, 7 C.P.C. (4th) 294 (Gen. Div.) , where it was held, in a confusing decision that did not refer to previous authorities in the fax area, that faxed acceptance was effective when transmitted by the offeree, though the court in this case noted that with respect to fax transmissions receipt is virtually simultaneous with transmission.
224 *Brinkibon Ltd. v. Stahag Stahl and Stahlwarenhandelsgesellschaft mbH*, [1982] 1 All E.R. 293 (H.L.) [*Brinkibon*].
225 *Ibid.*, at 296.

These factors articulated in the *Brinkibon* case, particularly in view of the first and fourth dynamics of computer law (namely, the rapid pace of technological change and the blurring of national and international) raise a number of questions in respect of EDI, e-mail, and Internet communications. Certain EDI transmissions, for example, will fall into the simultaneous communications category. Equally, many communications over the Internet exhibit features of instantaneous, or near instantaneous, communications. A good deal of EDI is effected not between the trading principals, however, but by the use of intermediaries, so-called value-added networks (VANs), or service providers. An EDI message could likely route through the message sender's VAN, then through the recipient's VAN, and finally to the recipient. Similarly, e-mail messages over the Internet may be sent to electronic mailboxes of a service provider from which an intended recipient has to then download the message. In such circumstances it may be more difficult to conclude that the simultaneous communication rules should apply. Or, it may be challenging to discern when exactly an electronic message has arrived at the recipient's location for purposes of being legally effective. For instance, there is an old British case that held that a paper-based letter sent in a sealed envelope is not considered received until it is opened by the addressee personally.[226] Should such a rule apply in the case of e-mail, or should an e-mail message be deemed received when it is available to be viewed by the intended recipient, regardless of the time at which the recipient actually reads the message?[227] Or when should a telex or fax be deemed to have arrived at a workplace? In one case, the answer was when the message is received by the recipient's machine (on a Friday after business hours and not three days later on a Monday morning when a person actually read the telex).[228]

b) Contractual Measures

Given these uncertainties, prudent users of electronic commerce should try to avoid having to refer these sorts of questions to a judge

---

226 *Arrowsmith v. Ingle* (1810), 3 Taunt. 234.
227 See, for example, *Tenax Steamship Co. v. The Brimnes* (1974), [1975] Q.B. 929 (C.A.), where a fax was held to be effective even though the recipient of the message did not actually read it. In those jurisdictions that have an electronic commerce statute similar to Ontario's *ECA*, this question is now answered: see section A.5(c) of this chapter, "Law Reform."
228 The "*Pendrecht*," [1980] 2 Lloyd's Rep. 56 (Q.B.). But see also *Schelde Delta Shipping B.V. v. Astart Shipping Ltd. (The Pamela)*, [1955] 2 Lloyd's Rep. 249, which held that an acceptance sent by fax after regular business hours was effective the next business day.

by providing, in their EDI trading partner agreement or other similar document, precisely what electronic message must be received by which computer (i.e., the recipient's or the recipient's VAN or service provider) in order for a contract to arise, thereby bringing certainty to the dual questions of when and where the electronic contract arose. Indeed, as to the "where" question, the parties to the TPA or other agreement would do well to select a governing law in advance, and to make sure the VAN or other service provider agreements contain the same jurisdiction, so that there is no question which law would apply if resort to the courts were ever required. This is particularly true for EDI and Internet transactions where each trading party's VAN, or Internet service provider, may be in a jurisdiction separate from the customer, with the result that possibly the laws of four different jurisdictions may come into play if the parties remain silent on the governing law question. In such circumstances, as Lord Denning noted in the *Entores* case dealing with simply two parties in different jurisdictions, the problems arise because the laws of the respective jurisdictions are different. Therefore, predicting a court's probable response is difficult, given that the court will invariably try to do the just thing under the circumstances, but in some cases this is truly a difficult task. Consider, for example, the court's commentary in the *Export Packers* case where the judge advocated that the various rules developed by the law over the years, such as the simultaneous communication rule in the *Entores* case, should not be applied in a dogmatic fashion:

> When the common law rules relating to offer and acceptance were under development the telephone did not exist. At that time agreements were made by two or more persons getting together and reaching a common understanding. As the postal system came into being elaborate rules were made by the Courts covering the mechanics of reaching a bargain by mail. Today a person ordinarily resident in British Columbia may telephone from Japan where he is on a business trip to a person ordinarily resident in Ontario but who is also then visiting Italy. They may agree to the same kind of contract which is the subject matter of this writ. It does not necessarily follow the place where the contract was made was Japan and that Japanese law governs its interpretation. Alternatively, it would be hard to argue the place where the contract was made was Italy and the law of that country ought to apply to its interpretation.[229]

---

229 *Export Packers*, above note 218 at 178.

A passage such as this (which resonates with the fourth dynamic of computer law) clearly confirms the benefit in users of electronic commerce crafting their own rules for dealing with contract formation issues, including stipulating, in their written contract, which jurisdiction's law will govern the contract. Where this is not done, as in the *Eastern Power* case, the agreement or relationship will be subject to the jurisdiction having the most substantial connection to it.[230] This determination, however, is not self-defining, and often not at all predictable.[231] Thus, dealing with the governing law question in advance in the contract between the parties can save a lot of angst subsequently.[232]

c) Law Reform

Making commercial relationships more secure and predictable through contract, however, can be a costly and time-consuming exercise. Therefore, usefully, the ECA contains several rules relating to the time of sending of electronic information. One provision sets out a firm rule that electronic information is sent when it enters an information system outside of the sender's control, or if the sender and addressee use the same system, when the information becomes capable of being retrieved and processed by the addressee.[233] As for receipt, another provision establishes a presumption (not a firm rule) that electronic information is presumed to be received by the addressee when it enters the addressee's information system and becomes capable of being retrieved and processed, provided that if the addressee has not designated or does not use the information system for the purpose of receiving such information, then receipt only occurs once the addressee becomes aware of the information in the addressee's information system.[234] As well, to deal with the challenge posed by the peripatetic business person raised

---

230 See also *Colmenares*, above note 212. The factors considered in this exercise include the nature and location of the subject matter of the contract, the residence of the parties, and where the contract will be performed.

231 For example, in the *Senneth* decision, above note 218, while the court held that the telephone-originated contract was concluded in Saskatchewan, the court went on to find that the governing law should be that of Ontario given the other factors in this case.

232 Canadian courts have generally upheld the right of the parties to a commercial arrangement to choose the governing law of the contract, unless the choice is not *bona fide*, is illegal, is against public policy or where the choice of law has little or no connection with the transaction: see J.-G. Castel, *Canadian Conflicts of Laws*, 4th ed. (Toronto: Butterworths, 1997), ¶449.

233 *ECA*, subs. 22(1).

234 *ECA*, subs. 22(3). Once aware of it, however, the addressee is deemed to be in receipt of it, even he or she fails (or refuses) to retrieve it.

by the passage from the *Export Packers* case noted in the previous paragraph, the ECA provides that electronic information is deemed to be sent from a sender's place of business and received at the addressee's place of business, thereby making it irrelevant, for contract formation purposes, where the actual computers/servers facilitating, or individuals participating in, the communication might be located.[235] These rules can be changed, or supplemented, by the agreement of the relevant parties. Thus, as noted in the previous paragraph, the terms and conditions of an Internet Web site used for e-commerce should also address expressly when and where the contract arises. With respect to the latter, for example, it might provide that the online agreement will be deemed to have been made in the jurisdiction where the office of the Web site operator is located, and that the customer cannot bring any legal proceeding against the supplier except in such jurisdiction.[236]

B. EVIDENCE LAW

Evidence law strives to ensure that only reliable evidence is permitted to be provided to judicial and other decision makers in legal, administrative, and related proceedings. To this end, a number of evidence law rules have been developed, initially in the context of oral testimony and, more recently, for documents and records. Statutory records retention rules also attempt to ensure that companies and other organizations maintain trustworthy information in order to permit the relevant government agency to carry out its regulatory and other functions properly. In the jurisdictions that have evidence laws that do not address computer-generated records directly, questions from time to time can be raised as to whether the traditional rules of evidence are adequate to deal with the economy's shift from paper-based to electronic record keeping. The first two dynamics of computer law — the rapid pace of technological change and the elusive nature of information — have presented a number of challenges to the laws of evidence. Nonetheless, as in the contract law area, the judiciary's approach to computer-generated

---

235 *ECA*, subs. 22(4). Note that the *ECA* did not address whether or not the *post box rule* should apply to communications because, as noted earlier, the *ECA* is focused on making the law media-neutral, not substantively changing any particular area of the law.

236 Such a provision was upheld in the *Rudder* decision, above note 174, and such forum selection clauses, as they are known, are generally upheld by Canadian courts: see *Sarabia v. "Oceanic Mindaro" (The)* (1996), 4 C.P.C. (4th) 11 (B.C.C.A.).

records has generally been adequate to deal with these challenges. Courts have endeavoured to understand the technology underpinning the computer-generated record, and then have sensibly applied the common law or traditional statutory evidence law rule, almost invariably with the result that a copy of the computer-generated record has been admitted into evidence. More recently, jurisdictions in Canada have enacted changes to their evidence statutes that expressly address computer-generated records, in one fashion or another. These law reform efforts make more certain the legal environment for electronic commerce and the other means of doing business electronically. The result is that today virtually all e-mails, for example, are allowed to be admitted as evidence.[237] Indeed, some commentators are advocating carefully structured e-mail retention policies for organizations to try to prevent them from drowning in the flood of unsolicited e-mail filling up users' computers.

1) Admissibility of Business Records

Traditionally, the form of evidence preferred by judges was oral testimony given by live witnesses, in order that the veracity of the witnesses, and their credibility, might be tested by rigorous, and sometimes withering, cross-examination. Moreover, a live witness would only be allowed to testify as to matters of which he or she had personal knowledge; information that the witness heard someone else say — referred to as "hearsay" — would be excluded, given that such other person should be compelled to testify firsthand so that, again, the reliability testing mechanism of cross-examination could be brought to bear.[238] Under such a hearsay rule, documents were also frowned upon as evidence because, strictly speaking, they constituted hearsay; again, the theory was that the actual author of the document should also have to appear personally in court. By the early 1800s, however, business records were becoming such a prevalent means of storing information it was no longer practical to bring to court the author of every single document in the company. As important, judges took comfort in the trustworthiness of these business records because they were the very same documents that were used to organize and operate in some cases vast and impressive corporate or financial empires; in effect, if they were good enough for the business, they were good enough for the

---

237 *Sabourin & Sun Group of Cos. v. Laiken*, [2000] O.J. No. 1445 (Sup. Ct.), is a good example; most of the evidence in the case is e-mail–based, but no questions are raised as to its admissibility.

238 See *R. v. O'Brien*, [1978] 1 S.C.R. 591, for an articulation of the hearsay rule.

legal system. Thus developed an important exception to the common law hearsay rule: business records created in the ordinary course of business could be admitted into evidence.[239] Accompanying the common law business records exception to the hearsay rule was the "best evidence" rule, which required that the best evidence possible be provided to the court. In the context of documents, this meant, for example, that original documents were to be preferred to copies.[240] This best evidence rule can be seen operating, for example, in some of the old telegraph cases referred to in the previous part of this chapter, where courts preferred to see before them the actual paper-based message written out by the customer rather than the transcript of this message produced by the telegraph company.[241] More recently, however, there has been a loosening of the application of the best evidence rule.[242]

Over time, the business records common law exception to the hearsay rule became enshrined in many of Canada's evidence law statutes. For example, in respect of bank records, the *Canada Evidence Act* provides in section 29 that[243]

29 (1) Subject to this section, a copy of any entry in any book or record kept in any financial institution shall in all legal proceedings be admitted in evidence as proof, in the absence of evidence to the

---

239 *Ares v. Venner* (1970), 73 W.W.R. 347 (S.C.C.) [*Ares*]. In *R. v. Monkhouse*, [1988] 1 W.W.R. 725 (Alta. C.A.) [*Monkhouse*], the Alberta Court of Appeal put the common law rule thusly: "Where an established system in a business or other organization produces records which are regarded as reliable and customarily accepted by those affected by them, they should be admitted as *prima facie* evidence." The Supreme Court of Canada's current general "principled" approach to hearsay is that "hearsay evidence will be substantively admissible when it is necessary and sufficiently reliable": Lamer C.J. in *R. v. U (F.J.)*, [1995] 3 S.C.R. 764, at 787. See also *R. v. Hawkins*, [1996] 3 S.C.R. 1043, and the cases cited at footnote 249 below.

240 *R. v. Cotroni* (1979), 45 C.C.C. (2d) 1 (S.C.C.).

241 See *Kinghorne*, above note 10, and *Howley*, above note 13.

242 See *R. v. Papalia*, [1979] 2 S.C.R. 256, where re-recordings of certain key conversations from the original tape recordings were admitted where no question was raised as to the authenticity of the re-recordings. See also *R. v. Hall*, [1998] B.C.J. No. 2515 (B.C.S.C.) [*Hall*], where the court, in overriding the defendant's objection that computer printouts did not pass muster under the best evidence rule, stated at para. 52: "The law must be applied in accordance with the rapidly changing reality of today notwithstanding that it was drafted in the past. For this Court to hold in the context of this application that the printouts were not admissible would be to ignore the realities of the computer age, wherein technological change has rendered the former distinctions between originals and copies a moot distraction in many areas."

243 *Canada Evidence Act*, R.S.C. 1985, c. C-5.

contrary, of the entry and of the matters, transactions and accounts therein recorded.

(2) A copy of an entry in the book or record described in subsection (1) shall not be admitted in evidence under this section unless it is first proved that the book or record was, at the time of the making of the entry, one of the ordinary books or records of the financial institution, that the entry was made in the usual and ordinary course of business, that the book or record is in the custody or control of the financial institution and that the copy is a true copy of it, and such proof may be given by any person employed by the financial institution who has knowledge of the book or record or the manager or accountant of the financial institution, and may be given orally or by affidavit sworn before any commissioner or other person authorized to take affidavits.

The first predecessor of section 29 was added to the *Canada Evidence Act* in 1927, illustrating that quite early on Parliament was comfortable with the circumstantial trustworthiness that resulted from the well-kept records of Canada's banks, this confidence being fostered no doubt in part by the close government regulation of these financial institutions and the fact that customers relied on these records as well. Forty years later, a general business records provision was added, now section 30 of the *Canada Evidence Act*:

30 (1) Where oral evidence in respect of a matter would be admissible in a legal proceeding, a record made in the usual and ordinary course of business that contains information in respect of that matter is admissible in evidence under this section in the legal proceeding on production of the record.

... (6) For the purpose of determining whether any provision of this section applies, or for the purpose of determining the probative value, if any, to be given to information contained in any record admitted in evidence under this section, the court may, on production of any record, examine the record, admit any evidence in respect thereof given orally or by affidavit including evidence as to the circumstances in which the information contained in the record was written, recorded, stored or reproduced, and draw any reasonable inference from the form or content of the record.

The essential scheme created by sections 29 and 30 is to admit the bank or business record subject to the court's ability to probe the so-called foundation evidence relating to the process that created the record to ensure its trustworthiness.

Section 31 of the *Canada Evidence Act* also contains provisions providing for the admissibility of microfilm copies:

(2) A print, whether enlarged or not, from any photographic film of

(a) an entry in any book or record kept by any government or corporation and destroyed, lost or delivered to a customer after the film was taken,

(b) any bill of exchange, promissory note, cheque, receipt, instrument or document held by any government or corporation and destroyed, lost or delivered to a customer after the film was taken, or

(c) any record, document, plan, book or paper belonging to or deposited with any government or corporation,

is admissible in evidence in all cases in which and for all purposes for which the object photographed would have been admitted on proof that

(d) while the book, record, bill of exchange, promissory note, cheque, receipt, instrument or document, plan, book or paper was in the custody or control of the government or corporation, the photographic film was taken thereof in order to keep a permanent record thereof, and

(e) the object photographed was subsequently destroyed by or in the presence of one or more of the employees of the government or corporation, or was lost or was delivered to a customer.[244]

To complete the picture, it should be noted that section 26 of the *Canada Evidence Act* provides for the admission of certain government documents, including material in government books in subsection 26(1):

26(1) A copy of any entry in any book kept in any office or department of the Government of Canada, or in any commission, board or other branch of the public service of Canada, shall be admitted as evidence of that entry, and of the matters, transactions and accounts therein recorded, if it is proved by the oath or affidavit of an officer of the office or department, commission, board or other branch of the public service of Canada that the book was, at the time of the making of the entry, one of the ordinary books kept in the office, department, commission, board or other branch of the public service of

---

244 Subsection 31(1) defines "photographic film" to include "any photographic plate, microphotographic film and photostatic negative." For a case applying the microfilm provisions of the *Canada Evidence Act*, see *R. v. Sanghi* (1971), 6 C.C.C. (2d) 123 (N.S.C.A.) [*Sanghi*].

Canada, that the entry was made in the usual and ordinary course of business of the office, department, commission, board or other branch of the public service of Canada and that the copy is a true copy thereof.

A number of the provincial evidence statutes, but not all of them, contain provisions similar to these and those in the previous paragraph. Moreover, although animated by the same general principles, the specific bank, general business records, microfilm, and government document provisions in the various provincial and federal evidence statutes are by no means uniform, and important differences exist between them.

2) Admissibility of Computer-Based Evidence

a) Computer-Generated Business Records
In those jurisdictions that have to date not implemented or in the future do not implement evidence law provisions similar to those noted later in this chapter that expressly address computer-generated records, parties arguing for the admissibility of those records tend to rely on either the statutory business records rules in the various evidence acts or on the common law business records exception to the hearsay rule, both of which are outlined in the previous section of this chapter. Generally, courts have expressed very little reluctance to admit computer-generated records under these approaches. In an early case, the British Columbia Court of Appeal concluded, without any discussion, that printouts from a computerized accounting system were clearly admissible under section 30 of the *Canada Evidence Act*.[245] A dozen years later the same court confirmed this position, again without any substantive discussion.[246] And where an evidence statute is found to be unavailable because one of its conditions is not met, the common law principle has been used to admit the computer-based record.[247] Thus, in *Kinsella* v. *Logan*,[248] a 1995 New Brunswick case that predates the amendments to the New Brunswick evidence statute referred to in the next section of this chapter, the court determined that the business

---

245 *R.* v. *Vanlerberghe* (1976), 6 C.R. (3d) 222 (B.C.C.A.). See also *Sanghi*, above note 244, where computer-related evidence was admitted without a discussion of reliability issues.

246 *R.* v. *Bicknell* (1988), 41 C.C.C. (3d) 545 (B.C.C.A.).

247 See, for example, *R.* v. *Sunila and Solayman* (1986), 26 C.C.C. (3d) 331 (N.S.S.C.) [*Sunila*].

248 (1995), 163 N.B.R. 1 (N.B.Q.B.) [*Kinsella*].

records provision of this statute did not apply to computer-generated credit reports because of the statutory requirement (not found in the *Canada Evidence Act*) that the business record be made at or near the time of the acts or events recorded. The credit report, which is produced by the computers of the credit-reporting agency by sorting and processing data provided by the computers from many merchants and financial institutions, is constantly being updated, and hence did not fit the contemporaneity requirement in the statute. Undaunted, the court reviewed the recent Supreme Court of Canada decisions on the common law hearsay rule,[249] which essentially permit the admission of any document that is reliable, and admitted the credit report on the strength of the fact that such credit reports are extensively used in banking and business, and hence the court ought to consider them to be reliable as well.

The *Kinsella* case exhibited an eminently sensible approach to computer-generated evidence. The computer-based record at issue in this case was the lifeblood of the company that generated it. In almost all organizations today, computer-based records and the printouts derived from them serve as the informational bricks and mortar that support the whole infrastructure and operations of the entity. Indeed, as noted in chapter 1, section C.4, "Dependency on Computers," this phenomenon has led to a large number of business and other organizations becoming entirely dependent on the computer. In some respects this can be a risky situation, and even an unfavourable state of affairs, as when a new project to upgrade all or some of the computer system fails to come to fruition, as discussed in chapter 5, section E.3, "Express Warranties." From an evidentiary perspective, however, this inordinate reliance on computers is a reassuring fact. It means that judges should defer to the computer-generated document, given its tremendous degree of circumstantial trustworthiness.

From time to time, however, the traditional business records provisions in the evidence law statutes have raised questions in the context of computer-generated material since their wording pre-dated computer concepts. Thus, in *R. v. McMullen* the trial judge excluded a computer printout related to an accused's account at a bank branch on the basis that the branch itself had no written record other than the printouts, and the printouts were generated from information obtained from other locations through computer connections.[250] Thus, given

---

249 *R. v. Khan*, [1990] 2 S.C.R. 531; and *R. v. Seaboyer*, [1991] 2 S.C.R. 577.
250 (1978), 42 C.C.C. (2d) 67 (Ont. H.C.J.) [*McMullen*].

that no person in the particular branch could be said to be in charge of the operation of the computer system in terms of overall input, processing, and output, the trial judge concluded that section 29 of the *Canada Evidence Act* does not apply to computer-type evidence, and specifically the word "record" in section 29 does not include computer-generated evidence. On appeal, Linden J. disagreed with the trial judge and held that a computer printout is a copy of a record kept by a financial institution. In reaching this conclusion he stated in a passage reproduced in the Court of Appeal decision:

> The types of records that have been kept have varied through the ages. Human beings have used stone tablets, papyrus, quill pen entries in dusty old books, typewritten material on paper, primitive mechanical devices and now sophisticated electronic computer systems. All, however, serve the same function of recording and this had been recognized by the American authorities that were cited to me. Parliament has indicated its faith in the reliability of the records of financial institutions in whatever form they may have been kept through the years. I conclude, therefore, that the language used by Parliament in the *Canada Evidence Act* includes records kept in computers.
>
> Methods of copying have also changed much over the years. At one time, copies were done by scribes by hand. Then printing was invented. Eventually, primitive copying machines were designed. Now the sophisticated xeroxing equipment can produce copies that can hardly be distinguished from the original. In my view, a computer printout is a copy of what is contained within that computer, whether it be on tape or disc, though it is in a different form than the original record. It is merely a new type of copy made from a new type of record. Though the technology changes, the underlying principles are the same.[251]

On a further appeal, the Ontario Court of Appeal upheld Linden J.'s decision, and then went on to discuss the type of foundation evidence regarding the relevant computer system the court believed necessary in the case of computer-generated evidence:

> I accept that the demonstration of reliability of computer evidence is a more complex process than proving the reliability of written records. I further accept that as a matter of principle a Court should carefully scrutinize the foundation put before it to support a finding of reliability, as a condition of admissibility. ... The nature and quali-

---

251 *Ibid.*, at 69.

ty of the evidence put before the Court has to reflect the facts of the complete record keeping process — in the case of computer records, the procedures and processes relating to the input of entries, storage of information, and its retrieval and presentation. ... If such evidence be beyond the ken of the manager, accountant or the officer responsible for the records ... then a failure to comply with s. 29(2) must result and the printout evidence would be inadmissible.[252]

With respect to the question of foundation evidence, it is worth noting that in a case that predates the decision in *McMullen*, the court refused to admit a computer printout because the human witness of the party wishing to introduce it did not know where the documents came from, how they were created, the origin of the data, and the processes used to produce them.[253] In the later *R. v. Bell and Bruce* case noted in the next paragraph, however, a much more sensible approach to foundation evidence was exhibited — it was simply not an issue.[254] Similarly, in *R. v. Hall*,[255] the court did not require foundation evidence, given that trustworthiness of reliability was concluded from the fact that the company relied on the computer-generated records for its day-to-day operations.[256] Moreover, the court in this case went on to find that evidence of computer glitches would not deny admissibility, but would merely go to the weight of the evidence.[257] In effect, given that data

---

252 *R. v. McMullen* (1979), 100 D.L.R. (3d) 671 at 678-79 (Ont. C.A.).

253 *R. v. Rowbotham* (1977), 33 C.C.C. 411 (Ont. Gen. Sess.).

254 *R. v. Bell and Bruce* (1982), 35 O.R. (2d) 164 (C.A.) [*Bell and Bruce*].

255 *Hall*, above note 242. See also *Sunila*, above note 247, where the court concluded that "[T]he required circumstantial guarantee of trustworthiness flows from the presumption that businesses will create 'systems' which ensure the reliability of their records."

256 The court in *Hall*, above note 242, stated, at para. 56: "In contrast to the dusty shelves of account books in a Victorian bank, most large institutions these days have huge amounts of information, much of it retained as mere data with no tangible form." Indeed, in this case, the court concluded, at para. 58, that the fact that the data was billing information automatically recorded by the computer lent even more trustworthiness to the electronic evidence: "The recorder of the information, a passionless mechanical computer with no subjectivity, surpasses the [common law rule against hearsay] requirement of 'a person having personal knowledge' [who makes the entry in the computer]. This computer was under a duty of sorts, being programmed to make the entry or record."

257 The court in *Hall*, above note 242, stated, at para. 64: "As common experience and the evidence above show, even computers are subject to error. These problems, however, go to weight rather than admissibility. No evidence is perfect, and hearsay evidence need not be perfectly reliable for admissibility. ... This Court can seek further solace in the fact that the usual fears of hearsay ... namely perception, memory and credibility — are irrelevant to a computer-generated record."

itself is subject to the second dynamic of computer law — namely, the elusive nature of information — these statutory and common law evidence rules lead courts to consider the trustworthiness of the computer system itself, and most importantly the organization's reliance on the reports generated by the computer, in order to have comfort in the admissibility of evidence generated by such computer.

b) Multiple Originals

A few years after the *McMullen* decision, a further peculiarity of computer-based records came under scrutiny in the *Bell and Bruce* case.[258] In this latter case, the Crown wished to introduce copies of the paper-based monthly records of a bank account that were generated by the bank's computer. This particular computer stored electronically all the deposits and withdrawals that occurred in a month, but at the end of the month printed out a paper-based cumulative record, and then the electronic memory was wiped clean, leaving the monthly paper-based account statement as the sole record. The defence argued that the *Canada Evidence Act* only permits the admission of a copy of the original record, that the electronically stored data was the original record in this case, and therefore a copy of the paper-based record was inadmissible as it was not a copy of the original record. The trial judge accepted this argument and acquitted the accused. The Ontario Court of Appeal, however, disagreed with the argument. In a manner reminiscent of the decisions in the *Beatty* and *Brinkibon*[259] cases, the appellate court in *Bell and Bruce* indicated that "[b]ecause of the rapidly changing nature of the technology, it would be impossible to lay down general rules to govern every case"[260] involving computer-generated evidence. Nonetheless, the court went on to stipulate several general propositions, including the following: a record may be in any form, even an illegible one; and the form in which information is recorded may change from time to time, and the new form is equally a record of that kind of information. Based on these principles, the court held that the information in the bank's computer changed its form when it was printed out as a paper-based monthly statement, and that this hard copy thereupon became the record that was kept by the financial institution, and hence a copy of it was admissible. In effect, *Bell and Bruce* raises the important point that in the Information Age, and particularly in light of the second dynamic of computer law, it is not helpful to

---

258 *Bell and Bruce*, above note 254.
259 *Beatty*, above note 16; and *Brinkibon*, above note 224.
260 *Bell and Bruce*, above note 254 at 166.

speak in terms of the "original" when attempting to decide whether it is reasonable to admit into evidence certain material. The concept of original, and its handmaiden the "best evidence rule," made a lot more sense in an age that predated the computer and the Internet. These concepts have very little to commend themselves to us today, when our focus instead should be on the trustworthiness of the system that produced the information being proposed to be admitted into evidence.

In this regard, interestingly, there is in the *Bell and Bruce* case no extended discussion of foundation evidence the way there was in the *McMullen* decision. This is indicative of the attitude of most judges when considering computer-generated evidence emanating from financial institutions in particular. For example, in a U.S. case an appellate court stated that

> In this case, there was no error in admitting the evidence without requiring that technical information be supplied. Certainly when the computer-generated evidence is provided by a well-established national banking institution, maintaining numerous branches in the state, it is reasonable for a court to assume that the "electronic-computer" equipment is reliable.[261]

The court in this case noted that perhaps a stronger foundation could have been laid if the prosecutor had provided information regarding the type of data in the computer and other matters, but even without this foundation evidence the court was comfortable admitting the computer-generated evidence from the bank. And this comfort was not misplaced. It is not clear what foundation evidence regarding the computer is really intended to achieve. Suppose, for a moment, that the foundation evidence shows that the computer did experience some downtime, as all computers are wont to do on occasion. So what? In order for the business to run, and survive, the reason for the downtime was fixed. If information was lost, it was recovered. If files were corrupted, they were redone. In short, probably the only meaningful foundation evidence would be the admission that the company went bankrupt as a result of its computer system not working. Short of this, the only foundation question that really needs to be asked is, quite simply, "Does the organization rely on this computerized information on a daily basis either directly or indirectly as data for other reports and records that the organization relies on directly?" If the answer to this question is affirmative (as it invariably will be, unless the organization

---

261 *State v. Kane*, 594 P.2d 1357 at 1361 (Wash. App. 1979).

has superfluous computer systems on its premises), then the document containing such data should be viewed as being sufficiently reliable to permit its introduction as evidence.

The cases above illustrate that courts have had little difficulty applying the existing rules of evidence to computer-generated records. By focusing on the purpose of these rules, and understanding the technologies and business processes involved in the fact situations before them, courts have arrived at sensible decisions when confronted with computer-generated evidence, invariably by admitting the computer-generated record where they have direct or circumstantial confidence in the reliability of the computer system that generated them. At the risk of stating the obvious, this process is only called into play on those rare occasions when one party challenges the admissibility of computer-generated evidence; that is, for the most part litigators do not feel the need to fight this battle. Where, however, courts are asked to pass on this matter, the process noted above has been assisted by the fact that many of the cases involved computer-generated records held by a person unconnected with the particular matter being litigated, that is, a disinterested third party, and this added to the sense of trustworthiness of the records at issue. Nevertheless, in other cases the computer-based records of a party to the litigation were at issue, and a similar positive approach to admissibility was displayed by the court.[262] In a case not involving computer-generated evidence, it was held that any records of a business, and not just those related to its routine business activities, could be admitted under the business records rule of Ontario's evidence statute.[263] This decision is particularly useful in the context of imaging technologies where a company may be scanning and storing records that do not relate to its core business functions. This is not to say, however, that electronic-based material cannot present problems from time to time. There is no doubt that, in one sense, electronically stored material is more volatile, changeable, and at the very least prone to updating and, more ominously, alteration and even deterioration.[264] For example, academic

---

262 *Tecoglas, Inc. v. Domglas, Inc.* (1985), 51 O.R. (2d) 196 (H.C.J.). In this case the court permitted a construction company's own computer printouts, containing expenditure data, to be admitted.

263 *Setak Computer Services Corporation Ltd.* v. *Burroughs Business Machines Ltd.* (1977), 76 D.L.R. (3d) 641 (Ont. H.C.J.).

264 Marcia Stepanek, "From Digits to Dust: Surprise — Computerized Data Can Decay before You Know It," *Business Week*, 20 April 1998. Or consider the decision in *Monotype Corporation PLC v. International Typeface Corporation*, 43 F.3d 443 (9th Cir. 1994), where the e-mail of an employee of a company not included in the litigation was held inadmissible as not coming within the business

journals that are available only online on the Internet in an electronic format without any paper-based version being published raise concerns if, say, the journal's Web site is discontinued; that is, how does one prove what the official version of the article was? There are, of course, several ways of dealing with these exigencies, such as lodging electronic copies (or at least one hard copy that is a faithful reproduction of what was on the Web site) with deposit libraries or other trusted third parties.

Another factor arguing in favour of trustworthiness of electronic documents is that although they may be more volatile (as a result of the second dynamic of computer law), they are also more numerous from the perspective of the number of copies made and maintained of all the different versions of the material, because storage capacity is no longer an issue for electronic documents. Indeed, it is difficult to destroy electronic documents. Thus, in one U.S. case a felon thought he had deleted the copy of the ransom note used in the crime, but electronic retrieval measures allowed the note to be recovered from the computer's hard drive.[265] Simply pressing the delete keystroke on a computer does not destroy the relevant information; rather, it is posted to an area of the hard drive waiting to be overwritten, but can be recovered with certain software utilities if it has not yet been overwritten. The defendants in the *Prism* software copyright case learned this lesson when their denial of accessing the plaintiff's source code was disproved by such a "smoking gun" electronic retrieval.[266] In this regard it should also be noted that

---

record rule in contrast, the court concluded, to an earlier decision where computer printouts were held admissible. In coming to this conclusion, the court stated that "The difference between *Catabran* [the earlier decision] and the present case is that E-mail is far less of a systematic business activity than a monthly inventory printout. E-mail is an ongoing electronic message and retrieval system whereas an electronic inventory recording system is a regular, systematic function of a bookkeeper prepared in the course of business." See also *United States v. Ferber*, 966 F.Supp. 90 (D. Mass. 1997), where an employee's e-mail also did not come within the business records rule as his employer did not require him to generate that specific kind of e-mail message. Interestingly, however, the e-mail was admitted under another U.S. rule of evidence, namely as a "present sense impression," given, in this case, the virtual contemporaneity of the perception with the e-mail declaration. Given the spontaneity of much e-mail (as discussed in section B.3(b), "E-mail Policies," later in this chapter) this could prove to be an important basis for arguing admissibility.

265 *Commonwealth v. Copenhefer*, 587 A.2d 1353 (Pa. 1991).

266 *Prism Hospital Software Inc. v. Hospital Medical Records Institute* (1994), 57 C.P.R. (3d) 129 (B.C.S.C.). See also Linda Himelstein, "The Snitch in the System: Old Data Are Showing Up in Court — and Winning Cases," *Business Week*, 17 April 1995 [*Snitch*].

in Ontario a case has held that a computer disk must be produced for discovery in litigation, and not just the information contained on it (i.e., printouts), given that the old authorities defining "document" spoke in terms of "any matter expressed or described upon any substance by means of letters, figures, or marks."[267] Similarly, tape recordings[268] have been held to be "documents" under the applicable rule of civil procedure. There has even been a case in the United States where e-mail messages, never before printed out until the trial, were admitted even though they arose in a completely paperless environment.[269] The court in this case acknowledged that messages in the e-mail system could be erased or altered, but the court was satisfied that the various password and other controls in place for the system reduced the likelihood that the message was modified. In effect, the ability of courts to handle the peculiar dynamics of computer-generated evidence under the general business records rules and the common law — that is, their facility in

---

267 *Reichmann v. Toronto Life Publishing Co.* (1988), 66 O.R. (2d) 65 at 67 (H.C.J.). The ambit of "electronic discovery" is very broad indeed. For example, Rule 30.02 of Ontario's *Rules of Civil Procedure* defines the scope of discovery in civil cases; para. 30.02(1) requires disclosure of every "document"; and para. 30.1(1)(a) defines "document" to include … "and information recorded or stored by means of any device." This would allow access to metadata, residual data, "file-properties" data, and other information beyond the core document at issue: this additional information would reveal who created the document, when, how many versions it went through, etc.

268 *Tide Shore Logging Ltd. v. Commonwealth Insurance Company* (1979), 100 D.L.R. (3d) 112 (B.C.S.C.). In this case, at 115–16, the court included the following passage from an earlier U.K. decision, *Grant v. Southwestern and County Properties Ltd.*, [1974] 2 All E.R. 465: "A litigant who keeps all his documents in microdot form could not avoid discovery because in order to read the information extremely powerful microscopes or other sophisticated instruments would be required. Nor again, if he kept them by means of microfilm which could not be read without the aid of a projector." In this case the court took a very broad view of the meaning of document, stating it was derived from the Latin *documentum*, meaning to "instruct" or "provide information." The judge concluded that there should be no difference between the treatment of information recorded on paper and that captured on an audio tape, stating at 475: "It appears to me that written or printed words are, after all, only encapsulated sound — and in a sense badly encapsulated sound, in that they often do not, when they purport to be a record of direct speech, embody the tone of voice, the inflexions, the subtleties of phrasing and pauses, which form the warp and woof of real-life conversation. If two parties to litigation have a record of a vital conversation, one in the form of a shorthand note, and the other in the form of a tape recording, I think that both would be justified, under normal English usage, in saying that they held 'documentary proof' of the conversation."

269 *United States v. Poindexter*, 951 F.2d 369 (D.C. Cir. 1991).

handling the first two dynamics of computer law when it comes to evidence law issues — have led some commentators to question the need for special computer-related statutory provisions.[270]

c) Computer-Generated Evidence

Where the records in the computer are generated by the computer itself, rather than through human-related input or manipulation, yet another approach has been taken to admissibility, as illustrated in the decision in R. v. McCulloch.[271] In these sorts of cases, the computer is not recording data inputted by a human. Rather, the computer is generating, or gathering, information without human intervention.[272] For example, in McCulloch, the Crown wanted to admit data from the telephone company's computers that recorded when and for how long a phone call is made. As there was no human involvement in generating this data, the defence argued that subsection 30(1) of the Canada Evidence Act was inapplicable, as its lead-in phrase requires that an individual be able to give oral evidence as to the facts that are recorded. The judge agreed, finding that this business records exemption contemplated the traditional situation where a clerk originally entered the data, but later could not speak to each item of data stored in the computer; in other words, section 30 did not apply where the record is mechanically created without human input. On the other hand, to the relief of the Crown, the court held that the proper characterization of this type of computer-generated evidence is not that it is hearsay (and therefore does not require either the statutory or the common law exception to the hearsay rule), but rather that it is admissible as real evidence.[273]

---

270 J. Douglas Ewart, Documentary Evidence in Canada (Toronto: Carswell, 1984).

271 R. v. McCulloch, [1992] B.C.J. No. 2282 (B.C. Prov. Ct.) [McCulloch]. See also the last part of the decision in the Hall case, note 242 above.

272 For example, an automated bank teller machine records withdrawals of cash, and posts this information to a bank's central account tracking computer. No human facilitates the collection or posting of this data.

273 The court in McCulloch, above note 271, encapsulated its rule as follows: "Where evidence is automatically recorded by any means, other than by human labour, and the evidence so recorded can be reproduced in any form, intelligible to the human mind, the reproduction is admissible as real evidence. The recording may be mechanical, chemical, electronic, photographic, or auditory, to name a few examples, and the reproduction may be by computer printout, audiovisual playback, photographs, or other means. The weight to be attached to such evidence will depend on the accuracy and integrity of the process employed." For a decision involving the same sort of technology as in the McCulloch case, but with a less satisfying result, see R. v. Sheppard (1992), 97 Nfld. P.E.I.R. 144 (Nfld. Sup. Ct.).

d) Text Residing on a Web Site

The type of electronic evidence referred to above, namely, business records generated by a computer, is to be contrasted with text-based information that resides on a Web site, which has been viewed by at least a couple of courts with serious reservations as to its authenticity and trustworthiness. For example, the court in *Teddy St. Clair v. Johnny's Oyster & Shrimp, Inc.*,[274] refused to admit data from an online database in these terms at 774:

> While some look to the Internet as an innovative vehicle for communication, the Court continues to warily and wearily view it largely as one large catalyst for rumor, innuendo, and misinformation. So as to not mince words, the Court reiterates that this so-called Web provides no way of verifying the authenticity of the alleged contentions that Plaintiff wishes to rely upon in his Response to Defendant's Motion. There is no way Plaintiff can overcome the presumption that the information he discovered on the Internet is inherently untrustworthy. Anyone can put anything on the Internet. No web-site is monitored for accuracy and nothing contained therein is under oath or even subject to independent verification absent underlying documentation. Moreover, the Court holds no illusions that hackers can adulterate the content on any web-site from any location at any time. For these reasons, any evidence procured off the Internet is adequate for almost nothing ...
>
> Instead of relying on the voodoo information taken from the Internet, Plaintiff must hunt for hard copy back-up documentation in admissible form from the United States Coast Guard or discover alternative information verifying what Plaintiff alleges.[275]

The court in this case touches on various negative aspects of the Internet, discussed in other chapters of this book, dealing with criminal law, consumer protection, and libel matters (and each exacerbated by the four dynamics of computer law), including that it is very difficult to ensure that only truthful content is conveyed over the Internet, and indeed unscrupulous people can very easily perpetrate hoaxes and

---

274 76 F.Supp. 2d 773 (S.D. Tex. 1999).

275 See also *United States of America v. Angela L. Jackson*, 208 F.3d 633 (7th Cir. 2000) for a similar result, where the court refused to conclude that Web postings were business records of Internet service providers, and hence found the material to be untrustworthy.

frauds over the Internet.[276] This "Wild-West" dimension of the Internet (which public authorities are attempting to tame, as noted elsewhere in this book), however, should not be confused with the business records generated by computers which, for the reasons noted in the previous sections, are a far more trustworthy category of evidence.

e) Law Reform

Although, as noted above, some commentators have asked whether special computer-related evidence rules are required, the business records and other traditional provisions of the *Canada Evidence Act* do contain some shortcomings in the context of computer-generated evidence. For example, in one case the term book in subsection 26(1) was held not to include a computer.[277] It probably would make sense, therefore, to at least add the concept of "record" to subsection 26(1) so as to capture electronic-based materials, given the broad definition of "record" in subsection 29(12). As well, while cases such as *McMullen*, *Bell and Bruce*, and *Kinsella* are indeed helpful and demonstrate the flexibility inherent in the business records provisions, they also illustrate some of the limitations of these traditional statutory rules. First, the inconsistency in the coverage of these statutory business records provisions across the country can be a problem, particularly for organizations with operations in more than one province. Then there is the simple fact that the words in the business records provisions, given the first dynamic of computer law, simply do not reflect computer-related reality that well. Of course appellate courts in *McMullen* and *Bell and Bruce* have managed to overcome this language problem, but it should

---

276 Marian Stinson, "April Fool's Joke Helps Sink Loonie: Fake Report Said Finance Minister to Quit," *The Globe and Mail* (2 April 2002). E-mail can also be fabricated in an attempt to gain an advantage illegally: Walter Olson, "Shut Up, They Explained," *Reason Magazine*, June 1997, online at reason.com; in this case the girlfriend of the CEO of Oracle created false e-mail in support of her wrongful termination lawsuit against Oracle. Interestingly, the fabrication was rebutted by cellular phone records that indicated that the CEO was driving his car at the time the allegedly incriminating e-mail was sent, thus proving he could not have sent the message.

277 *Sunila*, above note 247. In this decision, the court, after noting that in an earlier case the term book was held to apply to files loosely fastened together, concluded at 336 that "[W]hile it is one thing to stretch the meaning of a well-known word used in a statute within a certain context, to equate book with computer would be to ignore completely the common and accepted meaning of the word 'book.' It would be tantamount to legislating a new word into the statute. That is the sole responsibility of our legislators, not of judges."

not be forgotten that in both cases the judges at first instance went in the other direction. Indeed, two cases that came after *Bell and Bruce* illustrate that some courts are still having difficulty dealing with computer-generated materials as business records.[278] Accordingly, most jurisdictions in Canada have concluded it would be useful to address some of the traditional statutory shortcomings and uncertainties of the legal regime related to computer-generated evidence.

As a result, the Uniform Law Conference of Canada (ULCC), which comprises representatives of all the offices of attorneys general in the Canadian provinces, the federal government, and the two territories, adopted a *Uniform Electronic Evidence Act* in the summer of 1998.[279] Even before this ULCC initiative, however, Quebec and New Brunswick took express cognizance of computer-generated evidence in their evidence law statutes. The previous Article 2837 of the Quebec *Civil Code* recognized data stored in a computer, so long as the document reproducing the data is intelligible and its reliability is sufficiently guaranteed; and the previous Article 2838 provided that reliability is presumed in respect of computers when the data entry is carried out systematically and without gaps and the computerized data is protected against alterations. These provisions, as well as Article 2839 of the *Civil Code*, have been superseded by the evidence law provisions of Quebec's recently enacted electronic commerce law.[280] In 1996, the *Evidence Act* of New Brunswick was amended by adding thereto the following provision:[281]

> 47.2(1) Where, in the normal course of business or affairs, a document that was created in electronic form by a person is recorded or stored electronically in order to keep a permanent record of the document, a printout of the document generated by or produced from a computer record or other electronic medium is admissible in evidence in all cases and for all purposes for which the document would have been admissible had it been created in a tangible form.

> 47.2(2) A printout described in subsection (1) is not admissible in evidence unless

---

278 See *R. v. Hanlon* (1985), 69 N.S.R. 266 (N.S. Co. Ct.); and *R. v. Cordell* (1982), 39 A.R. 281 (C.A.), where ultimately the computer printout was admitted by the appellate court, but only after being excluded by the trial judge.

279 Uniform Law Conference of Canada, *Uniform Electronic Evidence Act,* August 1997, available at <law.ualberta.ca/alri/ulc/acts/eeeact.htm>.

280 *An Act to Establish a Legal Framework for Information Technology,* S.Q. 2001, c. 32.

281 R.S.N.B., 1973, c. E-11. The amendments are found in *An Act to Amend the Evidence Act,* S.N.B. 1996, c. 52.

(a) the document was recorded or stored electronically in the normal course of business or affairs, and

(b) the contents of the document being tendered are as originally recorded and stored and have not been altered.

A further provision was also added to this statute that recognizes the practice of electronic imaging, a process whereby paper-based documents are scanned and stored electronically:

47.1(2) Where a document kept or held by a person is copied by a process of electronic imaging or similar process and is recorded or stored electronically in the course of an established practice in order to keep a permanent record of the document, a printout of the document generated by or produced from a computer record or other electronic medium is admissible in evidence in all cases and for all purposes for which the original document would have been admissible.

47.1(3) A printout described in subsection (2) is not admissible in evidence unless

(a) the original document was copied by a process of electronic imaging or similar process and was recorded or stored electronically in the course of an established practice in order to keep a permanent record of it,

(b) the original document was destroyed after being copied and recorded or stored in accordance with paragraph (a), and

(c) the printout is a true copy of the original document.

Interestingly, this provision does not reference the national standard for imaging that has been published by the Canada General Standards Board (CGSB).[282] This standard sets out a number of practices and procedures recommended for imaging systems. Usefully, the lack of a reference to this standard in subsection 47.1(2) of the New Brunswick statute ostensibly will permit imaging systems to comply with it that fall below the rather rigorous processes set out in the CGSB standard. On the other hand, it is unfortunate that paragraph 47.1(3)(b) requires the original of the document to be destroyed; while many users of imaging systems may well do this, it really should not be a statutory requirement. As well, it would have been useful if the New Brunswick statute had made it clear that with respect to paragraph 47.1(3)(c), one could prove that a printout is a copy of the original by relying on the reliability of the system that produced the printout.

---

282 Canadian General Standards Board, *Microfilm and Electronic Images as Documentary Evidence*, CAN/CGSB-72.11-93 [*Microfilm*].

With respect to the ULCC *Uniform Electronic Evidence Act*, a key objective of the uniform act is to provide that the best evidence rule is satisfied in respect of electronic records by proof of the integrity of the electronic records system by which the data was recorded or preserved. Moreover, the draft statute allows the integrity of the record-keeping system to be implied from the operation of the underlying computer. This proposal for a uniform electronic evidence statute usefully achieves a number of objectives. It supports the admissibility of electronic evidence, while still permitting a party to challenge it if the reliability of the computer system or network that produced it can be put into question. Perhaps most importantly, the uniform act effectively resolves the issue of what constitutes the "original" record in the context of the creation, storage, and communication of electronic information by effectively abandoning the concept of original in an electronic environment. This would serve as a useful recognition of a trend articulated by decisions such as *Bell and Bruce*. The concept of original is paper-based — it applies where a person types or writes directly onto a piece of paper, thereby clearly creating an original of the letter. Where computers send messages electronically, the second dynamic of computer law kicks in and it is no longer meaningful to talk in terms of which is the original — the copy of the message in the sender's or recipient's computer — and which is a reproduction. The thrust of the ULCC proposals is to shift the analysis from an assessment of a particular electronic document to the computer-based system that produced it, and then to take comfort about this system based on its operational track record. The ephemeral nature of information should lead to an enquiry at the systemic level of the processes that produced the information, rather than focusing on any particular manifestation of that information. The ULCC proposal requires, sensibly, that the party seeking to introduce an electronic record also proves its authenticity; that is, that the record is indeed what the party claims it to be. Equally, it would always be possible for a party to object to the admission of any particular item based on evidence of tampering or alteration, but it would be the rare situation indeed where this would occur. The general rule ought to be along the lines of a variation on the adage "I think, therefore I am" transcribed as "the document is produced in the normal course of business (whether electronically or in any other mode) and relied upon by the business, and therefore it should be admitted."[283]

---

283 This is similar to the following articulation of the common law document exception to the hearsay rule in *Monkhouse*, above note 239: "... where an established system in a business or other organization produces records which are regarded

The ULCC proposals regarding authentication, the best evidence rule, and the presumption of integrity have been adopted by the Canadian government,[284] Ontario,[285] Saskatchewan,[286] and Manitoba.[287] For example, sections 31.2 and 31.3 of the *Canada Evidence Act* now read as follows:

> 31.2(1) The best evidence rule in respect of an electronic document is satisfied
>
> (a) on proof of the integrity of the electronic documents system by or in which the electronic document was recorded or stored; or
>
> (b) if an evidentiary presumption established under section 31.4 applies [section 31.4 allows the government to make evidentiary presumptions through regulations].
>
> (2) Despite subsection (1), in the absence of evidence to the contrary, an electronic document in the form of a printout satisfies the best evidence rule if the printout has been manifestly or consistently acted on, relied on or used as a record of the information recorded or stored in the printout.
>
> 31.3 For the purposes of subsection 31.2(1), in the absence of evidence to the contrary, the integrity of an electronic documents system by or in which an electronic document is recorded or stored is proven
>
> (a) by evidence capable of supporting a finding that at all material times the computer system or other similar device used by the electronic documents system was operating properly or, if it was not, the fact of its not operating properly did not affect the integrity of the electronic document and there are no other reasonable grounds to doubt the integrity of the electronic documents system;
>
> (b) if it is established that the electronic document was recorded or stored by a party who is adverse in interest to the party seeking to introduce it; or
>
> (c) if it is established that the electronic document was recorded or stored in the usual and ordinary course of business by a person who is not a party and who did not record or store it under the control of the party seeking to introduce it.

---

as reliable and customarily accepted by those affected by them, they should be admitted as prima facie evidence."

284 *Personal Information Protection and Electronic Documents Act*, S.C. 2000, c. 5, Part 3.

285 *Red Tape Reduction Act*, S.O. 1999, c. 12, s. 7.

286 *The Saskatchewan Evidence Amendment Act*, 2000, R.S.S. 1978, c. S-16, amended.

287 *The Electronic Commerce and Information Act*, S.M. c. 32, c. C.S.M. c. E55.

Law reform through statutory amendment is no panacea. Even new legislative provisions have to be monitored to ensure they remain up to date, given the relentless effect of the first dynamic of computer law. This need for legislators to stay vigilant can be seen in the amendment in 1968 of the U.K. civil evidence statute to provide that any "document produced by a computer" is admissible.[288] A commentator writing about this section has suggested that the U.K. government, indirectly, has put into question whether this provision is broad enough to cover EDI or other electronic messages where, in effect, the record in one computer has been created by and sent by another computer.[289] Thus, the ULCC, and others, should always be careful to use language that encompasses a wide spectrum of technologies and potential business practices, such as where documents arise out of the interconnected collaboration of different parties over the Internet or other networks. And the ULCC should not consider its task complete upon the adoption of its *Uniform Electronic Evidence Act*.[290]

f)   Contractual Measures

In those provinces that do not have modern evidence laws that either expressly address computer-generated evidence (as Quebec and New Brunswick have done, as noted above) or implement the ULCC proposals, private parties may wish to bolster the admissibility of electronically generated evidence through contract. It is, for instance, quite common for EDI trading partners to stipulate contractually how records of their electronic messages are to be kept. Moreover, just as EDI trading partners will often deem these electronic messages to be writings for contract law purposes (as noted above), so too does the EDI Council of Canada's *Model TPA*, in section 7.04, contain a similar provision addressing evidence law issues:

> Each party hereby acknowledges that a copy of the permanent record of the Transaction Log certified in the manner contemplated by this Agreement shall be admissible in any legal, administrative or other proceedings between them as *prima facie* evidence of the accuracy and completeness of its contents in the same manner as an original document in writing, and each party hereby expressly waives any

---

288   *Civil Evidence Act 1968* (U.K.), 1968, c. 64, subs. 5(1).

289   Rob Bradgate, "Evidence Issues of EDI," in *EDI and the Law*, above note 26.

290   See the author's testimony before the Ontario legislative committee considering Bill 88 on the need for continual law reform in this area, in *Bill 88 Testimony*, note 61 above.

right to object to the introduction of a duly certified permanent copy of the Transaction Log in evidence.[291]

The transaction log referred to in this provision refers to the electronically stored summary or index of messages sent between the EDI trading partners.[292] As with the equivalent provision dealing with the "writing" issue, it is open to question whether such a provision is enforceable; nonetheless, it is still a useful provision to include in TPAs today. And organizations transacting business over the Internet could use a similar provision in a set of Web site terms and conditions.[293]

3) Records Retention Rules and Policies

a) Statutory Requirements
A similar issue to the one of evidence law arises in connection with the records retention requirements stipulated by numerous statutes in many jurisdictions. A large number of laws require companies, organizations, and individuals to maintain certain books and records in order that a particular government department be able to have access to the information contained therein for regulatory and other purposes. Traditionally, the records retention provisions of various statutes either expressly, or impliedly, contemplated paper-based documents as the manner in which information must be retained. Over time, some of these provisions have been amended to include the recording and storage of information in electronic form. As with the writing requirement caveat given above, however, it must be understood that there are a multitude of these record retention provisions, and the specific ones relevant to any entity's situation must be reviewed in detail. Nevertheless, in order to illustrate the phenomenon by way of an example, consider the records retention rules under the *Income Tax Act*, contained in

---

291 *Model TPA*, above note 35.

292 In *Roberts* v. *United States*, 508 A.2d 110 (D.C. 1986), a similar electronic-based log was admitted into evidence, in that case being summaries of the transactions of automated teller machines, which were compiled from the bank's computerized transaction records.

293 For example, consider the following term from the online contract found at ING's online bank Web site at <ingdirect.ca>: "A copy of any electronic communication will be admissible in any legal, administrative or other proceedings as conclusive evidence as to the contents of such communication in the same manner as an original document in writing, and you hereby waive any right to object to the introduction of any such copy of electronic communication in evidence."

an *Information Circular*,[294] which provide that Canada Customs and Revenue (CCRA, formerly Revenue Canada) recognizes two types of books and records: the traditional books of account with supporting source documents and records produced and retained in an electronically readable format that can be related back to the supporting source documents, and which is supported by a system capable of producing accessible and readable copy.[295]

With respect to records kept electronically, the CCRA policy contains a number of rules and requirements. The taxpayer must keep documentation describing the system controls that existed to prevent unauthorized alteration or loss of records.[296] Similarly, the electronic records must show an audit trail from the source documents, and where there are no paper source documents, as in EDI transactions, the electronic records have to be kept; specifically, the policy stipulates that it is the record keeper's responsibility to ensure the trustworthiness and readability of the EDI transaction records.[297] The policy also makes it clear that the taxpayer is responsible for storing electronic records in appropriate media[298] and for dealing with any deficiencies in the software used to process the data.[299] Equally, the taxpayer is responsible for ensuring that upon a system conversion, the converted records are "trustworthy and readable."[300] If the taxpayer retains a third-party computer services company to maintain its computers, for example, on a time-share, service-bureau, or outsourcing basis, the policy makes it

294 *Income Tax Act* (Canada), R.S.C. 1985, c. 1 (5th Supp.). The *Income Tax Act's* record retention rules are contained in *Income Tax Information Circular No. IC78-10R3, Books and Records Retention/Destruction*, October 5, 1998, which cancelled and replaced Information Circular No 78-10R (SR), February 1, 1995, and Information Circular 78-10R2, July 14, 1989 [*Information Circular*].
295 Ontario's tax laws also permit the keeping of electronic records: *Corporations Tax Act*, R.S.O. 1990, c. C.40, ss. 93 (6.1) to (6.3), added by S.O. 1994, c. 14, s. 42(2).
296 *Information Circular*, s. 19, above note 294.
297 *Ibid.*, s. 20.
298 *Ibid.*, s. 21.
299 *Ibid.*, s. 23.
300 *Ibid.*, s. 24. Although microfilm is a relatively low-tech solution, and not nearly as useful for purposes of indexing and retrieval as digital-based archival systems, at least with microfilm there is the high level of confidence that for those documents that are intended to be stored for tens of years, microfilm will survive and keep the integrity of the images. Unfortunately, the same cannot be said for data in a digital format, given that there are significant issues involving long-term storage (CD's, for instance, have a tendency to degrade after a period of time), migration (i.e., how to shift digital information from one medium to another), and obsolescence (i.e., what is to be done when a storage or retrieval technology is no longer supported by its previous manufacturer).

clear that the taxpayer remains responsible for compliance with the policy's obligations.[301] This latter responsibility would typically lead to a provision in the contract between the taxpayer and the service provider that requires the service provider to make any changes to the computer system, or the related services, that may be required for the taxpayer to comply with applicable law.

The CCRA policy also permits imaging and microfilm (including microfiche) reproduction of some documents, provided the imaging methodology employed complies with the imaging standard of the Canadian General Standards Board.[302] The CCRA policy provides that each imaging program should include the following:

(a) someone in the organization has confirmed in writing that the program will be part of the usual and ordinary activity of the organization's business;

(b) systems and procedures are established and documented;

(c) a log book is kept showing:
   (i)   the date of imaging;
   (ii) the signatures of the persons authorizing and performing the imaging;
   (iii) a description of the records imaged; and
   (iv) whether source documents are destroyed or disposed of after imaging, and the date a source document was destroyed or disposed of;

(d) the imaging software maintains an index to permit the immediate location of any record, and the software inscribes the imaging date and the name of the person who does the imaging;

(e) the images are of commercial quality, and are legible and readable when displayed on a computer screen or reproduced on paper;

(f) a system of inspection and quality control is established to ensure that c), d) and e) above are maintained; and

(g) after reasonable notification, equipment in good working order is available to view, or where feasible, to reproduce a hard copy of the image.[303]

---

301 *Ibid.*, s. 22.

302 Canadian General Standards Board, *Microfilm and Electronic Images as Documentary Evidence*, CAN/CGSB-72.11-93. Note also that source documents or records that are in an electronic format must be kept in addition to the microfilm and/or electronic image: *Information Circular*, s. 15, above note 294.

303 For another example of a legal regime that permits imaging, see s. 10.2 of the *Public Guardian and Trustee Act*, R.S.O. 1990, c. P.51 [as inserted by S.O. 1997, c. 23, s. 11(5)], which allows this government agency to image documents and discard the paper-based originals.

Several other examples exist of how computer and network technologies might be addressed from a records retention perspective.
Ontario's *Vital Statistics Act*, the statute under which the government
registers and stores documents relating to births, marriages, deaths,
and other similar events, has been amended to permit it to accommodate new data storage technologies.[304] Thus, subsection 4(1) of this
statute now provides that the registrar may cause registrations and
other documents to be accurately recorded by any technology, so long
as an accurate and easily readable paper copy of the registration or
other document can be made from the record. Moreover, the statute
provides in subsection 46(1) that a certified copy of a registration
signed by the registrar general or deputy registrar general or on which
the signature of either of them is reproduced by any method is admissible as evidence in any Ontario court as proof of the facts so certified,
in the absence of evidence to the contrary. Similarly, the statute also
provides in subsection 46(3) that a paper copy made from the record
of a document, other than a registration, that is made under section 4
is admissible in evidence to the same extent as an original document.
The result is a statutory regime of certification and document storage
that is malleable enough to accommodate a wide range of new technologies. Equally, the provision in the *Canada Business Corporations
Act* specifying how certain records are to be maintained contains a flexible computer-related option at the end of it:

> All registers and other records required by this Act to be prepared and
> maintained may be in a bound or loose-leaf form or in a photograph-
> ic film form, or may be entered or recorded by any system of mechan-
> ical or electronic data processing or any other information storage
> device that is capable of reproducing any required information in
> intelligible written form within a reasonable time.[305]

b) E-mail Policies

E-mail is the "killer application" of the Internet. It is estimated that 9.7
billion e-mails were sent daily in 2000, up from 5.9 billion in 1999.[306]

---

304 R.S.O. 1990, c. V.4.
305 Canada *Business Corporations Act*, R.S.C. 1985, c. C-44, subs. 22(1). Section
139 of Ontario's *Business Corporations Act*, R.S.O. 1990, c. B.16, provides a similar regime, though somewhat more onerous from the perspective of the record
keeper, but still sensibly flexible and electronically friendly.
306 IDC (International Data Corporation), cited in Stacy Lawrence, "The Agony and
the Ecstasy," *The Industry Standard*, 25 December 2000. The amount of intracompany e-mail is even higher, in the United States alone perhaps as high as
25.2 billion messages daily: David S. Bennahum, "Daemon Seed: Old Email

In a few short years it has become, at least in the workplace, an indispensable means of communication. It is inexpensive and easy to use. It travels well and cheaply across time zones. Today, one cannot imagine functioning without it, nor could any corporation or government department. And other text-based messaging systems are becoming equally ubiquitous, including instant messaging systems and wireless service equivalents. The phenomenon of e-mail, however, presents challenges for the law, and particularly for practising lawyers, for several reasons. The first problem posed by e-mail is that people say the darndest things via this new medium. Through e-mail people have a propensity to say things they otherwise would likely never record.[307] In short, e-mail is a dream come true for plaintiff's counsel, and a defendant's counsel's worst nightmare. For example, incriminatory or otherwise important e-mails have been relevant in reported cases involving anti-trust,[308] sexual harassment,[309] age discrimination,[310] a trade secret misappropriation dispute,[311] a former employee non-competition

---

Never Dies," *Wired*, May 1999 ["Daemon Seed"]. If this number at first seems high, consider the math at a company of, say, 20,000 employees. If each employee receives 100 e-mails a day, the result is 730,000,000 million e-mails a year.

307 Of course, some pretty surprising admissions can be made in paper-based mail as well: see *Apotex Fermentation Inc.* v. *Novopharm Ltd.* (1998), 80 C.P.R. (3d) 449 (Man. C.A.), at para. 145. See, for example, Lina Saigol, "Merrill Lynch Sends Brokers to E-mail School: Think Before You Write," *Financial Post* (28 December 2002). Technology solutions are also being considered, such as e-mail that deletes itself after a period of time: Guy Dixon, "E-mail Hits the Shredder," *The Globe and Mail* (4 April 2002).

308 The role of e-mails in the United States government's antitrust trial against Microsoft is by now the stuff of legends: *United States of America* v. *Microsoft Corporation*, 253 F.3d 34 (U.S.C.A., Dist. Col. 2001). The government's use of e-mails written by senior Microsoft executives against Microsoft at trial is chronicled by Ken Auletta in *World War 3.0* (New York: Random House, 2001). This is not the first time Microsoft has been stung by its own e-mails; see also *Karen Strauss* v. *Microsoft Corporation*, 1995 U.S. Dist. LEXIS 7433 (S.D.N.Y.) [*Strauss*], where several inappropriate and offensive sexually-related e-mail messages were discovered on Microsoft's back-up tapes.

309 *Knox* v. *State of Indiana*, 93 F.3d 1327 (7th Cir. 1996). See also *Strauss*, above note 308. There are many other cases in the United States where inappropriate e-mail forms part of a sexual harassment claim, including *Yamaguchi* v. *United States Department of the Air Force*, 109 F.3d 1475 (9th Cir. 1997); and *Hickey-McAllister* v. *British Airways*, 978 F.Supp. 133 (E.D. N.Y. 1997).

310 *Kelley* v. *Airborne Freight*, 140 F.3d 335 (1st Cir. 1998). In this case the court found one of the e-mails "vitriolic," a phrase that indicates the displeasure of the court.

311 *Vermont Microsystems, Inc.* v. *Autodesk, Inc.*, 5 Computer Cases (CCH) ¶47,210 at 67,224 (D. Vt. 1994); 88 F.3d 142 (2d Cir. Vt. 1996); 132 F.3d 449 (2d Cir. Vt. 1998). See also *Snitch*, above note 266, where the lawyer for Vermont Microsys-

case,[312] sale of a business dispute,[313] and insider trading investigations.[314] And the problem is not just e-mail, but voicemail as well. In a case involving insider trading of stock, the court reproduced the portion of the voicemail that the court labelled "an ill-advised admission":

> Anyway, finally I sold all my stock off on Friday and I'm going to short the stock because I know it's going to go down a couple of points here in the next week, as soon as Lou releases the information about next year's earnings.[315]

Several years ago, an article in *Wired* chronicled the kind of embarrassing truths that are fairly regularly communicated by e-mail.[316] While it is hard to believe that the following e-mails were ever sent, the article's author confirms they were collected by a firm specializing in forensic e-mail discovery. Here is an example:

---

tems is quoted as follows: "There's no question in my mind that the E-mail and evidence that files had been wiped convinced the judge that there had been hanky-panky."

312 In *EarthWeb Inc.* v. *Mark Schlack*, 71 F.Supp. 2d 299 (S.D.N.Y. 1999) the plaintiff's argument that the defendant had access to trade secrets and proprietary information of the plaintiff prompted the production of over 1100 documents, a large percentage of which were intracompany e-mails. On the other hand, in this case, in finding for the former employee, the court ignored a potentially devastating e-mail as merely being a "glib remark." This case is also discussed in chapter 2, section B.1, "Trade Secrets/Breach of Confidence."

313 *Siemens Solar Industries* v. *Atlantic Richfield Co.* (1994), Fed. Sec. Rep. ¶98,167: 1994 WL 86368 (S.D.N.Y.) (March 16, 1994). In this case the purchaser of a technology business sued the vendor for, among other things, misrepresenting that the business's technology was further developed than it actually was. Apparently, one of the e-mails of the vendor said, "As it appears that [the technology] is a pipedream, let Siemens have the pipe": reported in *Snitch*, at note 266 above.

314 Steven Edwards, "'ImClone Is Going to Start Trading Downward'," *National Post* (10 August 2002) (this case involves the allegations against Martha Stewart, the home-decorating celebrity). Indeed, it would appear that virtually all the corporate upheavals that rocked America in 2002 were fuelled by revelatory e-mails: Charles Gasparino, "N.Y. Expanding Merrill Probe to Most Major Wall Street Firms," *The Globe and Mail* (11 April 2002); Mark Wigfield, "WorldCom E-mails Build Case," *The Globe and Mail* (27 August 2002); "E-mail Reveals Vivendi Tension," *The Globe and Mail* (14 December 2002); "The Value of Trust," *The Economist*, 8 June 2002; Laurie P. Cohen & Mark Maremont, "E-mails Reveal Tyco Lawyers Knew of Funds," *The Globe and Mail* (27 December 2002); and John Saunders, "Remarks Misunderstood: Ex-Banker: CSFB Point Man Still Won't Explain E-mail," *The Globe and Mail* (19 October 2002).

315 *Smith* v. *SEC*, 129 F.3d 356 (6th Cir. 1997) at 359.

316 Bennahum, "Daemon Seed," above note 306.

> Yes I know we shipped 100 barrels of [deleted], but on our end, steps have been taken to ensure that no record exists. Therefore it doesn't exist. If you know what I mean. Remember, you owe me a golf game next time I'm in town.

Or, how about this for a career-limiting message:

> [National retail chain] would like 2,500 free units of [our product] in order to conduct a test marketing study. If the study goes well, they will place an order for 100,000 units. I recommend we provide the free units for the following reasons:
> 1.   2,500 free units is cheap compared with the profit from an order for 100,000 units.
> 2.   They will provide the names and addresses of the stores involved in the study so that we can drop-ship the product.
> 3.   Since we will know where the product will be, I will send someone around to buy all of it, thereby ensuring a successful test.

The author of "Daemon Seed" calls e-mail "truth serum." No kidding — if these samples are any indication of what is being composed by e-mailers around the world. It is as though the normal adult speech filter is not activated when using e-mail. It likely has something to do with the immediacy of e-mail. Particularly with technologies like ICQ, e-mail now feels like a virtual extension of oral speech. Inhibition melts, candour takes over, and in a split second the most senior executive has composed and sent what subsequently will become the opposition's smoking-gun e-mail if litigation ensues. It would almost be humorous – a modern-day version of *Candid Camera*, the television show in the 1960s that secretly filmed people in laugh-inducing situations — if the legal ramifications were not so serious.

The legal conundrum posed by e-mail derives from the fact that although it feels like conversation, and people say the sorts of things they might while talking casually, unlike speech it is recorded and is permanent. It is as if all conversations in a company were held in the hallways, and all hallways had powerful recording devices that captured every word of every conversation. This is a frightening thought but quite an appropriate image for understanding the legal implications of our computer networks — huge repositories of all our reservoirs of raw indiscretion. "Daemon Seed," at 104, characterizes it this way:

> The technology of electronic communications is moving so quickly that it has outpaced both the law and our own sense of propriety. In a weird and still unclear turn, our vast pools of saved email have mutated into personal surveillance mechanisms. Big Brother isn't some dark

figure of distant, central control. He's us: the decentralized record of all our thoughts and feelings, preserved in the electronic platters of hard disks on desktops and in archives across the country.

Put another way, with e-mail we are witnessing the ultimate extension of the third dynamic of computer law, namely, that an individual's "private world" has so perfectly fused with his public one that the hapless individual does not realize (until it is too late) that his seemingly private statements on e-mail have become public. Accordingly, organizations that utilize e-mail (and it is the rare one today that does not) would be well advised to consider policies that address various aspects of the e-mail phenomenon.[317] First and foremost, employees need to be reminded that e-mail is truth serum, and that it is virtually permanent, with the result that discretion is invariably the better avenue to follow when sending or replying to e-mail, given that what one says can and will be used subsequently, either in court, or in more routine fora, such as an annual performance review. The test should be, therefore, "would I be embarrassed to see this e-mail message on the front page of the *Globe and Mail*," because that is indeed where it might one day appear.[318]

On the other hand, it is no answer to simply dictate to staff that no e-mail be sent, even if such an unrealistic command could be contemplated. The fact is there is also good e-mail, that tells a court a good

---

317 For a discussion of company policies that contemplate the monitoring of employee e-mails, see chapter 4, section A.1(d), "Monitoring Employee E-mails." But the real problem with e-mail, and particularly with instant text messaging, is that these "written" forms of communication approximate very closely the oral conversation. Abbreviations such as "LOL" (laughed out loud) and the smiley symbols — ;-) the "winking" smiley, :-(the "unhappy" smiley, and :-) the "happy" smiley — help online participants interact with one another through a seemingly steady information flow that blends the oral with the literal, as if it were the visualization of conversation.

318 The "Daemon Seed" article, above note 306, recounts how a headline in the *New York Times* about the Salt Lake City Olympics scandal read: "E-Mail Trail Adds Details to U.S.O.C.'s Role." The piece reprinted e-mails circulated among members of the U.S. Olympic Committee who were granting favours to foreign delegates to secure votes. It was all quite unsavoury, and all captured for posterity by e-mail. As early as AD 604, the regret attributable to an unfortunate written passage was well captured in quatrain 51 of the *Rubáiyát of Omar Khayyám* (Collins: London, 1947):

> The Moving Finger writes; and, having writ,
> Moves on: nor all thy Piety nor Wit
> Shall lure it back to cancel half a Line,
> Nor all thy Tears wash out a Word of it.

This wisdom imparted by a Persian poet almost 1500 years ago resonates for the world of e-mail today just as well.

story — provided the e-mails are sensible. Indeed, if, for example, a company is having difficulty with a business partner, any failure to chronicle, by means of e-mail, the dissatisfaction at the time it arose, may well preclude the company complaining at a later date. This is precisely what happened in a recent Ontario case, when a court refused to believe the principal of a company that retained a consultant, when the principal argued it had always been dissatisfied with the consultant's performance.[319] The court had found a steady flow of e-mail between the parties at all times, and therefore the lack of e-mails critical of the consultant at the time of performance led the court to conclude that the principal was then satisfied with the consultant's performance. Care must also be taken with the "copy" function of e-mail. Again, the problem arises because the utility is so powerful and easy to use. When used indiscriminately, however, it can raise several concerns. For example, when a business person sends a sensitive e-mail to the company's in-house lawyer, there may be a knee-jerk tendency to copy this message to a raft of business people within the organization. Doing so, however, may cause the sender to lose the right to argue solicitor-client privilege in these messages at a later date, if a court were to conclude that the widespread e-mail distribution to non-lawyers took the document out of the realm of seeking legal advice, and placed it squarely in the purview of management communication.[320]

Another e-mail legal issue arises today because such a huge volume of spam and intracorporate personal and generally unimportant e-mail is inundating the computer systems of organizations. This e-mail avalanche is itself a problem.[321] As a result, some commentators argue that it can be extremely expensive to comply with the request for documentary evidence as part of the civil litigation process when reams of junk e-mail must be ferreted through electronically.[322] Thus, some companies are organizing their e-mail to permit easier recovery in the event

---

319 *Nad Business Solutions Inc.* v. *Inasec Inc.*, [2000] O.J. No. 1585 (Sup. Ct.).

320 See, for example, *NRS Block Bros. Realty Ltd.* v. *Co-Operators Development Corp.* (1994), 24 C.P.C. (3d) 132 (Sask. Q.B.), for a decision holding that an internal company electronic memo is not privileged.

321 See chapter 4, section E.5(a), "Spam," for a discussion of the various steps that might be taken to address the spam problem.

322 See *In Re Brand Name Prescription Drugs Antitrust Litigation,* 1995 U.S. Dist. LEXIS 8281 (S.D. Ill.). In this procedural motion, a pharmaceutical company wanted to avoid having to organize 30 million pages of e-mail for purposes of discovery by the plaintiff, at a cost of $50,000 to $70,000. The court disagreed, essentially finding that a company that decides to store records electronically must then pay the price of having them discovered electronically.

of litigation, or otherwise. Governments, for example, have for some time instituted e-mail retention policies, even before spam was a problem.[323] Today, a number of entities are instituting e-mail retention/destruction policies along the lines suggested by Ian C. Ballon, an American lawyer.[324] Spam, for example, is the equivalent of paper-based junk mail. In the physical office world, one simply discards junk mail in the trash, thereby never permitting it to enter the corporate filing system. Electronic spam, however, penetrates into a user's personal e-mail box automatically (illustrating yet another intrusive aspect of the third dynamic of computer law, namely, the blurring of private/public), and has to be actively deleted, which most people do not have the time to do. Therefore, Ballon proposes that people keep "official" e-mail messages by either printing them out and then storing them in traditional paper-based files, or storing them in an appropriate electronic folder.[325] As for the unimportant e-mail that is left, Ballon argues that these electronic messages can be destroyed at regular intervals. He concludes, on the strength of several evidence spoliation[326] cases that

---

323 For an example of a comprehensive records retention policy that includes e-mail, emanating from The White House, see *Scott Armstrong* v. *Executive Office of the President*, 877 F.Supp. 690 (D.C.D.C. 1995).

324 Ian C. Ballon, "Spoliation of E-Mail Evidence: Proposed Intranet Policies and a Framework for Analysis," in *Cyberspace Lawyer*, March 1999, Glasser Legal-Works, available at FindLaw for Legal Professionals <library.lp.findlaw.com>. Other commentators have advised of the merits of a document retention policy for electronic messages that, among other things, provides for the regular purging of electronic materials that are no longer relevant: for example, see Patrick R. Grady, "Discovery of Computer Stored Documents and Computer Based Litigation Support Systems: Why Give Up More Than Necessary" (Spring 1996) 14 J. Marshall J. Computer Info. & L. 523.

325 A recent article on the use of e-mail by physicians mentions how one doctor prints out all e-mail that relates to a patient's care and stores these printed e-mails with the hard copy patient chart: Joanne Sommers, "Doctors Bring Back the House Call, Virtually," *The Globe and Mail, Report on E-Business* (28 June 2002).

326 Although Ballon is an American, and is addressing American cases, his analysis arguably is of some interest in Canada given that the tort of spoliation of evidence seems to have arrived in this country. For example, in *Spasic Estate* v. *Imperial Tobacco Ltd.* (2000), 49 O.R. (3d) 699 (Ont. C.A.), the Ontario Court of Appeal concluded that it could see no reason why a trial court would be unable to rely on a separate tort of spoliation where pertinent evidence had been destroyed; in the case the plaintiff is alleging that tobacco companies shredded research documents about the addictive qualities of nicotine and the link between smoking and cancer: Jane Gadd, "Tobacco Firms Ordered to Stop Stalling Case," *The Globe and Mail* (3 March 2003). In *Enterprise Excellence Corp.* v. *Royal Bank of Canada*, [2002] O.J. No. 3086 (Ont. Sup. Ct.), the court con-

predated e-mail,[327] that such a policy, if administered properly, including not destroying any messages pertaining to a matter once a claim is likely,[328] is reasonable in today's e-mail environment.

---

cluded, at para. 75, "it is clear that the spoliation inference, evidently an American term, can apply in Canada." For a trade secrets case involving extremely lengthy and involved sanctions proceedings arising out of alleged spoliation, and in which the plaintiff is castigated for performing its review of the defendant's computer evidence in a manner that destroyed some of it, see *Gates Rubber Company v. Bando Chemical Industries, Limited*, 167 F.R.D. 90 (D. Colo. 1996).

327 In *Carlucci v. Piper Aircraft Corporation*, 102 F.R.D. 472 (S.D. Fl. 1984) the court, while acknowledging that good faith disposal of documents pursuant to a *bona fide*, consistent, and reasonable document retention policy might be a justification for failure to produce documents in discovery, found that the defendant utterly failed to implement such a policy. Indeed, this case is a striking example of how not to implement a document destruction policy. The recent case brought against Enron's auditors for obstruction of justice based on, among other things, the destruction of documents, also shows just how carefully any e-mail retention policy must be constructed and then administered (and indeed why some companies will decide not to institute such a policy): see Alexei Barrionuevo & Jonathan Weil, "Andersen's Duncan Admits: 'I Obstructed Justice,'" *The Globe and Mail* (14 May 2002); and Anne Marie Stolley, "Judge Denies Andersen Bid for Acquittal," *The Globe and Mail* (28 May 2002). See also *Lewy v. Remington Arms Co. Inc.*, 836 F.2d 1104 (8th Cir. 1988). It should also be noted that recently several American banks were subject to significant financial penalties for failing to maintain certain records, including e-mails: Tom Cahill, "Brokerages Fined for Lost E-mails," *The Globe and Mail* (4 December 2002); and "Address Unknown," *The Economist*, 7 December 2002 (this latter piece argues the confidential settlement is extremely unsatisfactory as no guidance is given as to what the transgressions were, and thus how they should be addressed in the future.

328 See, for example, *Computer Associates International, Inc. v. American Fundware, Inc.*, 133 F.R.D. 166 (D. Colo. 1990), where, in a case alleging software copyright infringement, the court entered default judgment against the defendant upon learning that it destroyed all but the current version of the program's source code. The court found that although deleting prior versions of the source code was in keeping with standard industry practice, the defendant should have modified this policy, and preserved all electronic data, once the litigation commenced. In coming to this conclusion, the court asserted, "In this post Iran-gate era of widely publicized evidence destruction by document shredding, it is well to remind litigants that such conduct will not be tolerated in judicial proceedings. Destruction of evidence cannot be countenanced in a justice system whose goal is to find the truth through honest and orderly production of evidence under established discovery rules. I hold that nothing less than default judgment on the issue of liability will suffice to both punish this defendant and deter others similarly tempted."

INTERNET LIBEL AND JURISDICTION ISSUES

There has already been much discussion in this book of the Internet and the legal issues engendered by this network of computer networks.[1] This book, however, has consciously not devoted a separate chapter to the Internet, nor has it opted to treat the Internet as an altogether novel or unique phenomenon. Rather, approaching the Internet as another step along the steady path of the evolution of computers and networks, this book has attempted to integrate the analysis of Internet issues into the technologies and business processes that were its predecessors, such as telegraphy, telephony, and broadcasting. Indeed, the four dynamics of computer law that have driven these industries are currently driving the Internet as well; moreover, the Internet may well be the phenomenon that best exemplifies the active and sustained

---

1   A brief description of the Internet was offered in chapter 1, section A.6, "The Internet"; intellectual property issues related to it were canvassed in chapter 2, particularly in sections C.6, "Copyright and the Internet" and C.7, "Trademarks, Domain Names, and the Internet"; the impact of it on criminal law was discussed in chapter 3; the issues related to regulation of it were discussed in chapter 4, including its possible regulation by the CRTC in section D.3, "Regulating Broadcasting over the Internet," and various regulatory aspects of e-commerce in section E, "Regulating E-Commerce"; licensing and tax issues germane to it were discussed in chapter 5, sections C.3, "Licensing in a Digital Environment" and G.3, "Tax and Internet-Related Activities," respectively; and contract and evidence law legal questions related to doing business on it electronically were discussed in chapter 6.

operation of the rapid pace of technological change, the elusive nature of information, and the blurring of private/public and national/international.[2] Nonetheless, while there are some truly revolutionary characteristics of the Internet, the legal issues presented by it are best understood in their historic context, drawing on existing and prior analogies and metaphors; that is, in approaching the Internet it is sensible not to overreact (and, for example, to be "overwhelmed" by its novelty), but neither to underreact (and, for example, to be lulled into a sense of *déjà vu* by its sameness with what has come before). Thus, the following discussions of Internet libel and jurisdiction issues are firmly rooted in the principles and analyses developed by the law in response to a series of pre-Internet technologies and business practices.

A. CYBER LIBEL

1) Libel Law and the Internet

The Internet provides unprecedented opportunities for local, regional, national, and global communications of text and other content. Chapter 1 described the technology that makes the e-mail, Web site, usegroups, and other features of the Internet an important advance in the history of message passing among humans.[3] Included in such messages, of course, will be defamatory ones. Defamation is a published false or derogatory statement that discredits a person, or impugns that person's honesty or integrity, or brings into doubt the person's financial solvency, provided the statement is made known to a third party and is not excused because it is the truth or fair comment or protected by privilege.[4] In the recent Hill case, the Supreme Court of Canada spoke eloquently about the danger of defamation, and the laudatory objective

---

2   These dynamics are important, and are a unifying theme throughout this book. For a discussion of them, see chapter 8, section A, "Computer Law: Dynamics."

3   As mentioned in chapter 1, section A.6, "The Internet," *American Civil Liberties Union v. Reno*, 929 F.Supp. 824 (E.D. Pa. 1996) [*ACLU*] provides a solid analysis of how the Internet works and also how it differs from other electronic communication media. Although the *ACLU* case dealt with the constitutionality of U.S. legislation aimed at certain pornography, its observations about the Internet are also relevant to formulating sensible and practical libel rules for the Internet.

4   For a good discussion of the intricacies of defamation law, see Raymond E. Brown, *The Law of Defamation in Canada*, 2d ed. (Toronto: Carswell, 1994) (looseleaf, updated) [*Defamation*].

of protecting a person's reputation being the essential purpose of the law of libel:

> Although much has very properly been said and written about the importance of freedom of expression, little has been written of the importance of reputation. Yet, to most people, their good reputation is to be cherished above all. A good reputation is closely related to the innate worthiness and dignity of the individual. It is an attribute that must, just as much as freedom of expression, be protected by society's laws. ...
>
> Democracy has always recognized and cherished the fundamental importance of an individual. That importance must, in turn, be based upon the good repute of a person. It is that good repute which enhances an individual's sense of worth and value. False allegations can so very quickly and completely destroy a good reputation. A reputation tarnished by libel can seldom regain its former lustre. A democratic society, therefore, has an interest in ensuring that its members can enjoy and protect their good reputation so long as it is merited.[5]

The court in the *Hill* case also gives a brief historic overview of the libel law to the present day, including its important role in the age of the Star Chamber in seventeenth-century England to replace duelling and blood feuds. The civil law of Quebec also provides for the protection of reputation by enshrining the principle in both the Quebec *Civil Code* and the Quebec *Charter of Human Rights and Freedoms*.[6] Defamation may also be criminal in its nature; see the discussion of criminal libel in chapter 3, section B.7, "Criminal Libel."

The law of defamation is extremely relevant to the Internet because just as the Internet is the ultimate vehicle developed to date to effect copyright infringement, a subject discussed in chapter 2, section C.6, "Copyright and the Internet," so too does the Internet promise to be the supreme mechanism for perpetrating libellous statements. Indeed, it is truly unique in that it is the only means of mass communication where the author of the disseminated material is generally not subject to an editorial filter prior to publication, at least at the point of initial

---

5   *Hill v. Church of Scientology of Toronto*, [1995] 2 S.C.R. 1130 at 1175 [*Hill*].
6   Article 3 of the Civil Code of Quebec provides: "Every person is the holder of personality rights, such as the right to life, the right to the inviolability and integrity of his person, and the right to the respect of his name, reputation and privacy. These rights are inalienable." Section 4 of the Quebec *Charter of Human Rights and Freedoms*, R.S.Q. c. C-12, states: "Every person has a right to the safeguard of his dignity, honour and reputation."

publication. Contrast this with broadcasting, newspapers, or book publishing, where a producer, editor, or publisher vets an author's content before it hits the airwaves, newsstands, or the bookstore. The Internet makes each user — all 500 million and counting — a publisher in his or her own right, at least from the perspective of launching the libellous statement into cyberspace.[7] This aspect of the Internet highlights the third dynamic of computer law, namely, the blurring of private and public. Interestingly, in other areas of this book where the impact of this dynamic is chronicled, the focus is on the public world intruding on the private sphere courtesy of the Internet and other technologies. With Internet libel, it is somewhat in reverse, whereby the private individual can make him- or herself felt around the world in a unique and revolutionary manner. Of course, the Internet does not represent a fundamental departure from certain communications technologies and practices with respect to all activities on it. As emphasized in the other analyses of the Internet provided earlier in the context of copyright and criminal law, it must always be remembered that the Internet comprises a myriad of communication and related activities, undertaken by a broad range of actors. Thus, the multifarious nature of the Internet must be kept in mind as the various scenarios for liability for libel on it are discussed below.

a) Slander or Defamation
An intriguing threshold question about defamatory statements on the Internet is whether they are libel or slander, the two subcategories of defamation. The distinction matters, at least in those provinces where the two have not been combined in defamation statutes.[8] Slander, which is an oral defamation, generally attracts smaller monetary damage awards and requires the proof of financial loss on the part of the plaintiff. Libel, which is a written defamation, requires no actual damages, and is generally considered the more serious of the two, given the assumption that a written statement is more deliberate and premeditated, and is also more permanent in its longevity. Most messages on the Internet are text-based and are characterized as libel. Many spon-

---

7   This was also seen, for example, in R. v. Pecciarich (1995), 22 O.R. (3d) 748 (Prov. Ct.), discussed in chapter 3, section B.5(b), "Intermediary Liability," where the accused single-handedly created and disseminated child pornography over the Internet.

8   Such as Ontario's Libel and Slander Act, R.S.O. 1990, c. L.12. In some libel statutes, the distinction between libel and slander is almost completely eliminated: see, for example, Manitoba's The Defamation Act, R.S.M. 1987, c. D20.

taneous messages, however, also contain libellous sentiments. As well, many areas of the Internet are not permanent. Messages on bulletin boards and usegroups are regularly purged and content is deleted as Web sites are updated. But telephony and radio broadcasting over the Internet raise the possibility of slander, and the fluidity of instant messaging systems such as ICQ resembles more oral conversation than it does formal, paper-based letters. And voice recognition systems where data is entered into a computer orally and then transmitted in a text-based format truly blur the distinction between libel and slander. In provinces like Ontario that have a *Libel and Slander Act*, these distinctions may well be moot since the legislation provides that defamatory words in a "broadcast" are deemed to be a libel[9] and *broadcasting* is broadly defined and would capture most Internet-based messages.

While the definition of broadcasting in Ontario's *Libel and Slander Act* is quite technology-neutral,[10] the definition of *newspaper*, the other key concept in the statute, is quite closely aligned to the traditional paper-based journal.[11] This raises the question whether a journal published in an online environment would be a broadcast or a newspaper, an important distinction. For example, subsection 8(1) of the statute provides that certain other provisions of the statute that are of benefit to newspapers by providing for short limitation periods are only available to the newspaper if the name of the proprietor and publisher and address of the publication are stated either at the head of the editorials or on the front page of the newspaper. In a recent case an appellate court construed this provision very strictly, holding that placing of the editorial information at the bottom of the editorial page did not comply with subsection 8(1).[12] In the context of a newspaper put up on a Web site, for example, what constitutes "the head of the editorials" or the "front page of the newspaper"? In the case of the latter, is it the absolutely first screen of the Web site? Or what if an icon on this screen, once clicked, brings up the editorial information; is this sufficient? Or what if another screen from another service of the publisher hotlinks the viewer directly into the editorials, bypassing the first

---

9 See, for example, *Libel and Slander Act*, R.S.O. 1990, c. L.12, s. 2.
10 *Ibid.*, s. 1.
11 *Ibid.*, s. 1.
12 *Hermiston* v. *Robert Axford Holdings Inc.* (1994), 120 D.L.R. (4th) 283 (Ont. Div. Ct.); but see also *Elliott* v. *Freisen* (1984), 6 D.L.R. (4th) 338 at 343 (Ont. C.A.), where "some attempted compliance at the head of the editorial page" was found to be sufficient by the court.

page? This practice may also raise copyright and trademark issues.[13] In the non-linear environment of the Web, and the Internet generally, how does one apply concepts like "the head of" and the "front page"? Somewhat more broadly, what if the electronic forum in which the libel appeared offers a particularly effective and timely method for a rejoinder by the subject of the libel?

Questions not unlike these were addressed in a recent U.S. decision, *It's In the Cards, Inc.* v. *Fuschetto*.[14] In this case the court concluded that messages by subscribers to an electronic bulletin board on the Internet were not "periodicals" for purposes of a Wisconsin statute similar to Ontario's *Libel and Slander Act*.[15] The court held that posting a message to the bulletin board was a random communication of a computerized message analogous to posting a written notice on a public bulletin board, and not a publication that appears at regular intervals. Moreover, the court offered the view that the Wisconsin statute, by using the words *magazines, newspapers, and periodicals* contemplated paper-based writings involving the print media; the court stated the electronic bulletin board postings could not be classified as print. In coming to this conclusion the court referred to an earlier case, *Hucko* v. *Jos. Schlitz Brewing Co.*, where it had held that the particular Wisconsin provision did not apply to broadcast media; ostensibly the court in the *Fuschetto* case was unwilling to accept a third type of media between

---

13   See chapter 2, section C.9, "Internet Linking and Framing."

14   535 N.W.2d 11 (Wis. App. 1995) [*Fuschetto*]. See also *George Firth* v. *State of New York*, 747 N.Y.S.2d 69, 98 N.Y.2d 365 (N.Y. Ct. Apps. 2002), where the court adopted the single publication rule for defamation on a Web site; this means that the relevant date for libel posted on a Web site is the first day it was posted (if it was available, or even updated regularly thereafter), and therefore limitation periods can be determined for cyber libel with precision. See also *Weiss* v. *Sawyer* (2002), 217 D.L.R. (4th) 129 (Ont. C.A.), where it was held that the *Libel and Slander Act's* "newspaper" provisions applied equally when the material was posted on a Web site. The Court of Appeal endorsed the lower court's view that "a newspaper is no less a newspaper because it appears in an online version."

15   The Wisconsin statute provided that any party claiming to be defamed in a "newspaper, magazine or periodical" must provide the other party an opportunity to retract the alleged libel: see *Fuschetto* at 12, footnote 1. Although the Ontario statute refers only to "newspaper," the definition of *newspaper* in s. 297 in the *Criminal Code*, with respect to the criminal libel provisions, refers to "paper, magazine or periodical" that are "printed." The reference to "printed" is in the Ontario statute as well, but interestingly, given the court's view on the matter referred to below, not in the Wisconsin statute.

paper-based and broadcast, that is, the Internet.[16] The court in the *Fuschetto* case justified its conservative approach on the following basis:

> Additionally, subsec. (2) of [the Wisconsin statute] was repealed in 1951 and reenacted in its present form, years before cyberspace was envisioned. The magnitude of computer networks and the consequent communications possibilities were non-existent at the time this statute was enacted. Applying the present libel laws to cyberspace or computer networks entails rewriting statutes that were written to manage physical, printed objects, not computer networks or services. Consequently, it is for the legislature to address the increasingly common phenomenon of libel and defamation on the information superhighway.
>
> The rate at which technological developments are growing coupled with the complexity of technology is beyond many laypersons' ken. A uniform system of managing information technology and computer networks is needed to cope with the impact of the information age. It is the responsibility of the legislature to manage this technology and to change or amend the statutes as needed. Therefore, we conclude that extending the definition of "periodical" under [the Wisconsin statute] to include network bulletin board communications on the SportsNet computer service is judicial legislation in which we will not indulge.[17]

In this regard, however, it should be noted that in the *Chuckleberry* case discussed in section B.2(a), "Regulatory/Criminal Jurisdiction," the court concluded that the words *magazine* and *periodical* in a 1981 injunction order could include a Web site containing text and pictures of the defendant.[18] The court found that the word *magazine* meant a *"storehouse of information,"* and that the word *periodical* was appropriate because the material on the Web site was updated from time to time. Readers are also directed to the discussion of criminal libel in

---

16   In *Hucko v. Jos. Schlitz Brewing Company*, 302 N.W.2d 68 at 72 (Wis. App. 1981), the court concluded that it was obvious from the unambiguous language of the Wisconsin statute that by referring only to magazines, newspapers, and periodicals, the statute did not cover radio or television because it did not refer to these means of communication expressly. Although this may be a reasonable conclusion, for the *Fuschetto* court to draw the inference from this that magazines, newspapers, and periodicals might not find some form of existence on the Internet in other than the traditional paper-based format is less convincing.

17   *Fuschetto*, above note 14 at 14–15.

18   *Playboy Enterprises, Inc. v. Chuckleberry Publishing, Inc.*, 939 F.Supp. 1032 (S.D.N.Y. 1996) [*Chuckleberry*].

chapter 3, section B.7, "Criminal Libel," which discusses a case that was willing to view "printed" as including photocopied, thereby supporting as well the position that the court in *Fuschetto* took too narrow an approach.[19] Nonetheless, as suggested by the court in *Fuschetto* in respect of its own libel law, and in light of the first dynamic of computer law — namely, the rapid pace of technological change — governments with statutes such as Ontario's *Libel and Slander Act* should consider updating them to capture issues germane to the Internet. In short, libel statutes were enacted to implement desirable policy objectives with respect to certain important channels of communication, some of which apply in an Internet environment. Accordingly, this statutory regime needs to be brought current with today's online technologies and business practices.

A recent British Columbia case worth noting in light of the foregoing is *Reform Party of Canada* v. *Western Union Insurance Co.*[20] In this case a political party had posted allegedly defamatory material on its Web site aimed at several Senators. When the Senators brought suit against the party, the party looked to its insurance company to defend the claim. The insurance company denied coverage, on the basis that the act of "publishing" was expressly excluded from the policy. The key question, therefore, was whether the posting of material to a Web site constituted "publishing." The political party argued in the negative, relying on the fact that a user must take positive steps to visit the site and browse it. The court disagreed, and concluded that posting the material on the Web site was the equivalent of publishing, which is defined, the court noted, as "to make public; to circulate; to make known to people in general," given that the Web site made the material available to a vast audience (regardless of the actual number of users of the site) and that the number of potential users was not limited or restricted.

2) Intermediary Liability

There is little doubt that the author of a libellous statement can commit the act of defamation by transmitting it to third parties over the

---

19   *Xerox of Canada Ltd.* v. *IBM Canada Ltd.* (1977), 33 C.P.R. (2d) 24 (F.C.T.D.).

20   (1999), 3 C.P.R. (4th) 289 (B.C.S.C.). The British Columbia Court of Appeal upheld the trial judge on this point regarding "publishing" including posting material to a Web site (although only 173 hits were registered on the relevant pages), but also found another means of having the insurer defend the insured: *Canadian Reform Conservative Alliance* v. *Western Union Insurance Co.* (2001), 12 C.P.R. (4th) 475 (B.C.C.A.).

Internet or other electronic networks. In the *Finucan* case, a court in Ontario found that a professor's defamation claim was a separate and distinct cause of action from his wrongful termination claim when his superior's highly critical performance evaluation and termination letter were distributed to all professors in the college via an internal e-mail network.[21] In an Australian case, a professor was awarded A$40,000 in damages when a libel was communicated over a bulletin board available to thousands of students and academics.[22] In many cases, however, it is not worth proceeding against the author of the libellous message because they are either judgment-proof by virtue of having no meaningful assets, or they are out of the defendant's jurisdiction and hence difficult or expensive to pursue (for a discussion of jurisdiction in the context of the Internet, which is the quintessential problem caused by the fourth dynamic of computer law, see the next part of this chapter). In other cases, the author's identity is simply not known, given the ability of a person to communicate on the Internet in an anonymous manner by using a name, or handle, other than his real name.[23] In such circumstances plaintiffs may well want to pursue other persons who, although not involved in the actual writing of the defamatory message, participated in its transmission in some way. Are the various intermediaries who provide Internet services liable for the part they play in the transmission of libellous messages? These issues are similar to those discussed elsewhere in this book regarding the liability of Internet intermediaries for copyright infringement or criminal law offences (see section C.6, "Copyright and the Internet," in chapter 2 and section B.5, "Obscenity and Child Pornography," in chapter 3).

Defamation law has long recognized that in addition to the author of the libellous statement, third parties involved in its publication are also to be held responsible. The publisher of a book is liable for any libel contained in it, given that through the exercise of the editorial function the publisher has thorough knowledge of the contents of the book and the ability to excise the offending libel. Newspapers are sim-

---

21 *Egerton v. Finucan*, [1995] O.J. No. 1653 (Gen. Div.). See also *Russell v. Nova Scotia Power Inc.* (1996), 436 A.P.R. 271 (N.S.S.C.), discussed in chapter 5, section H.2, "Employment Law." For a brief description of other civil libel actions brought in Canada, see Michael Geist, *Internet Law* (North York, ON: Captus Press, 2000), at 187. See also *Reichman v. Berlin*, [2002] O.J. No. 2732 (Ont. Sup. Ct.), where the plaintiff was awarded $200,000 in general damages, $100,000 in aggravated damages, and a further $100,000 in punitive damages for an Internet libel.

22 *Rindos v. Hardwick*, [1994] ACL Rep. 145 WA 4 (Sup. Ct.).

23 See section A.3 of this chapter, "Anonymity and the Internet."

ilarly liable for defamatory statements contained in them, and indeed they are responsible for any republications that are a "natural and probable consequence of the original publication," as in the *Holt* case, when a Toronto newspaper was held liable for defamatory remarks republished by another newspaper in British Columbia.[24] This rule, coupled with the principle that each republication is a separate libel, may hold serious adverse ramifications for persons who transmit libellous e-mail over the Internet. Given its electronic makeup, and the ease with which e-mail can be retransmitted by its recipient, it would not be surprising for a court, in the appropriate circumstances, to find that the original sender of an e-mail message is responsible for its subsequent transmission, as this was a natural and probable consequence of the original e-mail transmission.[25] E-mail raises several other issues in respect of libel. A libellous message sent in a sealed envelope through the mail will not be deemed published until it is opened after being delivered by the postal service. By contrast, a postcard is deemed to be published to the post office as well, given the ease with which it can be read.[26] As noted in chapter 3, section B.10, "Interception of Communications," with respect to the application to e-mail of the *Criminal Code*'s interception of communications provisions, this question will be determined by the characteristics of the type of e-mail message in question, such as whether it is encrypted or not. Another important factor will be whether the ultimate destination of the message was to be posted to a public message board, such as one belonging to a usegroup.

In this regard, another line of non-electronic libel cases that may be relevant to crafting statutory or judge-made rules for third-party liability are those that have addressed liability for failure to remove derogatory statements from physical premises. For example, in *Byrne* v. *Deane*, a golf club was held to be liable for participating in the publication of a defamatory statement when it did not remove from its interior walls such a statement about the plaintiff after the club acquired knowledge of the statement.[27] Similarly, in *Hellar* v. *Bianco*, a court in a preliminary proceeding held that an owner of a bar could be held to participate in a republication of an offending message about the plain-

24   *Chinese Cultural Centre of Vancouver* v. *Holt* (1978), 7 B.C.L.R. 81 (S.C.).
25   By contrast, several courts have held that publication of a libellous statement posted continually on a Web site occurs only once, namely, the first day it was available from the site: *Firth* v. *State of New York*, 2000 WL 306865 (Ct. Cl. N.Y. 2000).
26   See s. 7.12(1) of Brown, *Defamation*, above note 4.
27   [1937] 1 K.B. 818 (C.A.).

tiff in the men's room if it failed to remove it promptly enough after being notified of it; the court decided to leave up to the jury whether the plaintiff gave sufficient time to the defendant (in this case, about thirty minutes), given all the surrounding circumstances (i.e., the bartender was busy when the plaintiff initially called to complain).[28]

In an earlier U.S. case, the proprietor of an office was held to have ratified the libel in a newspaper article when he posted the article on a bulletin board in his office for a period of forty days and declined to remove it even after notified of its libellous nature.[29] In *Scott v. Hull* a proprietor of a building was not found responsible for offensive graffiti on an exterior wall, based on the rationale (and the distinguishing fact from the preceding cases) that the defendant did not invite the public onto the premises where the offending material was situated;[30] that is, in the other cases, the libellous material was posted by invitees (or the proprietor in the *Fogg* case) and viewed by invitees. If these cases are cited as analogous in an Internet case, it will be necessary to understand, for example, whether the forum where the libel took place online was a "public place," such as an open-to-all-the-public usegroup, or whether it was a "private" gathering of selected e-mailers. In determining such questions involving the third dynamic of computer law, see the discussion of the cases regarding "distribution to the public," "public place," and "exposure to the public" in chapter 3, sections B.5(c), "Internet Distribution," and B.6, "Illegal Speech."

a) Pre-Internet Innocent Dissemination

With respect to the various intermediaries that operate on the Internet, it is important that in contrast to the book and magazine publisher, defamation law does not hold liable the so-called innocent disseminator, such as bookstores, newsvendors, and libraries, provided that (a) they do not know of the libel contained in the work disseminated by them; (b) there are no circumstances that ought to have led them to

---

28   244 P.2d 757 (Cal. App. 1952). The "shocking" matter complained of, and that led the court to conclude at 759 that a "[r]epublication occurs when the proprietor has knowledge of the defamatory matter and allows it to remain after a reasonable opportunity to remove it," indicated to the court at 758 that the "appellant was an unchaste woman who indulged in illicit amatory ventures." See also *Tacket v. General Motors Corporation*, 836 F.2d 1042 (7th Cir. 1987), where an employer was held liable for failing to remove a defamatory sign on its wall painted by an unknown third party.

29   *Fogg v. Boston & L.R. Co.*, 20 N.E. 109 (Mass. 1889) [*Fogg*].

30   259 N.E.2d 160 (Ohio App. 1970).

suppose it contained a libel; *and* (c) it was not negligence on their part that they did not know it contained a libel.[31] Interestingly, something akin to this test has been codified in the U.K. *Defamation Act 1996*, one of the purposes of which was to modernize the defences in the law of defamation having regard to the current and future technologies of communications.[32] Key provisions in this statute relevant to the present analysis read as follows:

s.1(1) In defamation proceedings a person has a defence if he shows that
(a) he was not the author, editor or publisher of the statement complained of,
(b) he took reasonable care in relation to its publication, and
(c) he did not know, and had no reason to believe, that what he did caused or contributed to the publication of a defamatory statement.

...

(3) A person shall not be considered the author, editor or publisher of a statement if he is only involved
(a) in printing, producing, distributing or selling printed material containing the statement;
(b) in processing, making copies of, distributing, exhibiting or selling a film or sound recording (as defined in Part I of the *Copyright, Designs and Patents Act* 1988) containing the statement;
(c) in processing, making copies of, distributing or selling any electronic medium in or on which the statement is recorded, or in operating or providing any equipment, system or service by means of which the statement is retrieved, copied, distributed or made available in electronic form;
(d) as the broadcaster of a live programme containing the statement in circumstances in which he has no effective control over the maker of the statement;
(e) as the operator of or provider of access to a communications system by means of which the statement is transmitted, or made available, by a person over whom he has no effective control.

---

31 *Menear v. Miguna* (1996), 30 O.R. (3d) 602 (Gen. Div.), reversed for other reasons (1997), 33 O.R. 223 (C.A.) [*Menear*]. See also *Newton v. Vancouver* (1932), 46 B.C.R. 67 (S.C.); in this case a municipality and a hospital were denied the innocent disseminator defence, and became liable as publishers, when they supervised the printing and circulation of a report containing defamatory statements.
32 *Defamation Act 1996* (U.K.), 1996, c. 31.

In a case not within paragraphs (a) to (e) the court may have regard
to those provisions by way of analogy in deciding whether a person
is to be considered the author, editor or publisher of a statement.

...

(5) In determining for the purposes of this section whether a person
took reasonable care, or had reason to believe that what he did caused
or contributed to the publication of a defamatory statement, regard
shall be had to
(a) the extent of his responsibility for the content of the statement or
the decision to publish it,
(b) the nature or circumstances of the publication, and
(c) the previous conduct or character of the author, editor or publisher.

Stating the test for innocent dissemination is relatively simple —
the intermediary will only be liable if it knew or ought to have known
of the libel — but its application can be a challenge, particularly as new
technologies and business practices present novel fact patterns. In
crafting sensible rules for Internet-based libel, it is worth having regard
to the pre-Internet case law. In *Emmens* v. *Pottle*, the modern concept
of innocent disseminator was first propounded, and in that case a
newsvendor was held not to be liable because he did not have knowledge of the libel among the materials he sold.[33] By contrast, the innocent disseminator defence was denied a book retailer where it was
given clear notice of the libel and the retailer continued to sell the
offending work.[34] In two British cases, however, the duty to act reasonably (effectively the requirement of the second two prongs of the test
articulated at the beginning of the previous paragraph) was held not to
require a bookseller to review each title in its shop. Thus, in one case
the bookseller was able to rely on the fact that the libel was in scholarly publications by authors of high character,[35] and in the other case a
large chain of stores that distributed 400 to 500 different magazine
titles, for a total of 50,000 copies a week, was exonerated because there
was nothing in the nature of the particular magazine that contained the
libel that should have led them to suppose it contained a libel.[36] However, in two other British cases intermediaries were found liable. In one
case, the operator of a circulating library claimed the defence should

---

33   (1885), 16 Q.B. 354 (C.A.).
34   *Lambert* v. *Roberts Drug Stores Ltd.*, [1933] 4 D.L.R. 193 (Man. C.A.).
35   *Weldon* v. *"The Times" Book Company (Limited)* (1911), 28 T.L.R. 143.
36   *Bottomly* v. *F.W. Woolworth and Co. Limited* (1932), 48 T.L.R. 521 (C.A.).

apply given the large number of books it handled, but then went on to admit that it made a conscious decision not to hire anyone to screen books because this was too expensive, and that it preferred to run the risk of having to defend the odd claim in court, an admission found to be particularly damning by the court.[37] In the other case, a large book retailer argued that its throughput of books and other materials at head office was so great that it did not have the ability to screen materials, thereby not catching a libellous advertising poster from one of its suppliers that went out to its bookstall locations.[38] The court found, however, that the managers of the bookstalls did read the posters as they were being put up or soon thereafter, and that they should have been instructed to screen for libel, or the company should have had someone at head office do so. In short, the court found the company liable because the company's "system" was faulty and negligent in this regard. These cases, and the ones referred to in the next few paragraphs, emanate from circumstances that present several useful analogies to a number of situations found on the Internet.

A number of libel cases have examined whether printers should be entitled to the innocent disseminator defence. Traditionally, the answer has been negative, given the knowledge that the printer gained of the libellous work through the activity of typesetting. Indeed, in one case the officers of a printing company were found liable for allowing their employees to use the company's presses to put into circulation defamatory statements.[39] In a recent case, however, a printer was entitled to the innocent disseminator defence because the particular technology used by the printer did not require the printer to compose type nor in any other way read or learn of the contents of the work being printed.[40] In this decision the court was cognizant of the impact of new technology and its ability to relieve the printer from liability. It is interesting to note that subsection 1(3) of the U.K. *Defamation Act* now excludes from liability someone involved only in printing printed material containing the defamatory statement.

---

37 *Vizetelly v. Mudie's Select Library, Limited*, [1900] 2 Q.B. 170 (C.A.).

38 *Sun Life Assurance Co. of Canada v. W.H. Smith & Son Ltd.*, [1993] All E.R. 432 (C.A.).

39 *Lobay v. Workers and Farmers Publishing Association Limited*, [1939] 1 W.W.R. 220 (Man. K.B.).

40 *Menear*, above note 31. It should be noted, however, that the lower court decision in this case was set aside, not for substantive reasons, but because the Ontario Court of Appeal concluded that matters in dispute in the case were not properly the subject of a summary judgment proceeding, which is how the lower court dealt with the matter.

b) Telegraphy and Broadcasting

Several pre-Internet communication technologies have presented vexing dilemmas in the application of the innocent disseminator rule. For example, courts in Canada and elsewhere have had to wrestle with whether telegraph companies should come within the defence. In one decision the court permitted an action to proceed against the telegraph company, but at the same time was mindful of the difficult position this puts the company in because of, among other things, the large volume of messages transmitted by it:

> The question raised by the motion is of extreme importance. It is manifestly not desirable that any person may, by going to a telegraph office and filing a message with libellous matter in it, make the company liable to an action for libel and put it to the expense of defending an action. On the other hand, it is not desirable that irresponsible persons should make the telegraph company the instrument for libelling innocent persons. One cannot easily conceive how the law could intend that every telegraph operator should be a judge of whether any particular message is or is not a libel.[41]

In an earlier telegraph case, the Supreme Court of Canada wrestled with the same Gordian knot.[42] In the *Dominion Telegraph* case, a telegraph company was sued for its role in transmitting a libellous story from Halifax to a newspaper in Saint John, which subsequently reprinted it. Of the six Supreme Court judges who heard the case, two expressed no views on the liability issue. Another pair held that a common carrier such as the telegraph company should not be immunized from defamation actions. Chief Justice Ritchie, expressing this position, believed that exempting telegraph companies from liability for defamation would give them the power to perpetrate injustices and wrongs of all manner. Nevertheless, the Chief Justice recognized the difficult upshot of holding telegraph companies liable for all messages:

> In the transmission of messages for publication, especially letters and news for the public newspapers, it would seem that telegraph companies assume a responsibility similar to that of the publishers. By this agency libellous matter would be necessarily brought to the knowledge of operators who otherwise would not have cognizance of it. By their immediate and indispensable agency, "press despatches"

---

41   *Kahn v. Great Northwestern Telegraph Co. of Canada* (1930), 39 O.W.N. 11 at 11-12, aff'd (1930), 39 O.W.N. 143 (First Div. Ct.).
42   *Dominion Telegraph Co. v. Silver* (1881), 10 S.C.R. 238 [*Dominion Telegraph*].

and the like are brought before the public. In communications specially designed for the press, we see no reason why they should not stand on the same footing with publishers. But in strictly private messages the reason for so stringent a rule does not obtain, perhaps should not be applied at all.[43]

It should be noted that a factor that seemed to colour Chief Justice Ritchie's finding of liability for the news despatch was the fact that it appeared that the telegraph company not only transmitted the libellous news from Halifax to Saint John, but collected the news in Halifax as well. Thus, in an Internet context, the telegraph company may have been more than a passive conduit, but an information provider as well.

In the *Dominion Telegraph* case, two judges took a view contrary to that of Chief Justice Ritchie and expressed the following view:

I do not see how this verdict can be sustained, nor how the defendants can be held responsible for the publication in the *St. [sic] John Daily Telegraph*, which is the publication complained of, unless they are responsible in all cases for the use which the receivers of telegraphic messages transmitted over the defendants' line may make of such messages when received, and so to hold would, as it appears to me, be subversive of the telegraphic system and destructive of the benefits conferred upon the public by an invention without which it would be impossible that the affairs of the world could in the present age be conducted. The company by their charter are bound to transmit all despatches received by them for transmission in the order in which they are received, (subject to certain specific exceptions,) under heavy pecuniary penalties. It would be impossible for them to comply with this provision of the statute if they should be compelled, or it was a duty imposed upon them by law in order to their own protection [sic], to enquire into the truth of matter stated in the despatches delivered to them for transmission at the peril, in case of neglect to do so, of being responsible in damages if such matter should be libellous.[44]

American courts wrestled with the same conundrum presented by the telegraph business process; given that human telegraph operators read each message in the course of sending it, it was tempting to place an onus on them to be responsible for transmitting libellous ones; on the other hand, to hold them to such a duty would slow down the service

---

43   *Ibid.*, at 261–62.
44   *Ibid.*, at 265–66.

immeasurably. Thus, in the United States, the compromise was articulated that the telegraph company should not be responsible for messages where, knowing nothing of the parties or their circumstances, a person of ordinary intelligence and acting in good faith would conclude that defamation was not the object of the message.[45] In other words, the telegraph company would only be responsible if the message was libellous on its face.

This test was applied in an early Canadian telegraph libel case where a telegraph company transmitted to the office of a news service a message that impugned the character of a federal politician.[46] All five judges agreed with the chief justice that the message was "libellous on its face,"[47] and therefore, although they recognized they were dealing with a novel action without much precedent, they had no trouble finding the telegraph company liable, citing by analogy the newsvendor who sells a newspaper knowing it to contain a libel. While unanimous on the issue of liability, the justices disagreed on the appropriate quantum of damages. Two of them thought the trial judge's award of $50 was sufficient since there was no malice, the telegraph company's employees erroneously believed they were under an obligation to send every message, and as the two judges put it, the plaintiff did not suffer "one cent of damage"[48] and "there is very little in the terms of the telegram itself that is injurious."[49] The three judges in the majority disagreed. Finding the telegram to constitute a libellous defamation, and noting that the telegraph company did not reveal to the plaintiff the identity of its sender, they increased the libel award from $50 to $500, a substantial sum in 1886. This case illustrates that standards such as "libellous on its face," even if they can be operationalized for purposes of liability determination, still present a challenge in calculating dam-

---

45   *Nye v. Western Union Tel. Co.*, 104 F.R. 628 (D. Minn 1900). In articulating this "libellous on its face test," the court in this case concluded at 631: "Any rule imposing a stricter responsibility upon telegraph companies in respect to the character of messages transmitted than is above indicated would be productive of such embarrassment and delays, and make necessary such annoying inquiries, as to greatly diminish the efficiency of the service, and subject telegraph companies on the one hand to danger of prosecutions and suits for refusal to transmit messages or to transmit them promptly, and on the other to vexatious actions for fancied injuries, and even to conspiracies between senders and addressees to mulct these supposedly wealthy corporations."

46   *Archambault v. The Great North Western Telegraph Co.* (1886), M.L.R. 4 Q.B. 122.

47   *Ibid.*, at 131.

48   *Ibid.*, at 133.

49   *Ibid.*

ages, an issue extremely relevant in the Internet environment. Nevertheless, these telegraphy cases, and the broadcasting ones referred to in the next paragraph, address a number of the central issues that are germane to the Internet libel analysis.

Another pre-Internet communications technology worth noting is broadcasting. Broadcasters traditionally have been responsible for libellous statements emanating from the shows they produce, for much the same reason as book publishers or newspaper editors. In an Australian case, a television company was even held liable when it was merely retransmitting a program that it relayed from another broadcaster.[50] In this case, the broadcast was a current affairs program where the broadcaster producing the show knew what the guest was going to say and that it would be controversial. Nevertheless, the rebroadcaster did not know any of this, and thus it is not surprising that a strong dissent was lodged in this case in favour of finding that the innocent disseminator defence should apply on the basis that the rebroadcaster was just the conduit in the channel of distribution. Consistent with this minority decision is a U.S. case that held that a local broadcaster that serves as a "mere conduit" does not republish a libel contained in an unedited feed.[51] Interestingly, the court in this case cited as authority for this proposition the *Cubby, Inc. v. CompuServe Inc.*[52] Internet case discussed in section A.2(c), "Internet Intermediaries." A type of broadcasting that has several similarities in the Internet world is the radio talk show. In one case, a radio station was held liable for adopting the defamatory statements of a call-in guest when the host of the show agreed with the guest's statements.[53] In another case, however, the station was not liable because it did not have knowledge of the defamatory nature of the statement.[54] In the United States several states have addressed the issue of the "outside speaker" by legislating that radio stations are not liable for such statements so long as they took due care to prevent the statement and were not guilty of negligence or malice.

c) Internet Intermediaries

The Internet raises a host of issues related to libel. For example, one intriguing question is whether a party can be liable merely for having

---

50 *Thompson v. Australian Capital Television Pty. Ltd.* (1994), 127 A.L.R. 317 (Austl. Fed. Ct.).

51 *Auvil v. CBS "60 Minutes,"* 800 F.Supp. 928 (E.D. Wash. 1992).

52 776 F.Supp. 135 (S.D.N.Y. 1991) [*Cubby*].

53 *Lawson v. Burns*, [1976] 6 W.W.R. 362 (B.C.S.C.).

54 *Smith v. Matsqui (Dist.)* (1986), 4 B.C.L.R. (2d) 342 (S.C.).

links from her Web site to another Web site that contains libellous material. Pre-Internet cases have held that a publication of a libel occurs where the defendant, in addition to showing the libellous letter herself, requested third parties visit a place where the defamatory material was available to be read;[55] or where a defendant's letter to a newspaper simply made reference to a speech that included the defamation which was reported in another publication;[56] or where the defendant, without saying anything, sat by a placard containing libel and directed attention to it.[57] In another U.S. case, however, no responsibility was visited upon a radio commentator who made an on-air reference to a libellous article that appeared in a magazine because, the court concluded, the commentator did not repeat the libel verbatim or in substance, and the words actually broadcast were not themselves libellous.[58] In light of these cases, it will be interesting to see the result in a recently launched California case where apparently liability is being claimed against a college student association merely for linking to a third-party Web site containing allegedly defamatory material regarding a professor of the college.[59]

In Canada, no cases have yet considered the liability of Internet-related disseminators of defamatory statements, but a couple have been brought in the United States. In the Cubby case, an online services company, CompuServe, made available some 150 special interest fora and newsletters, one of which was the "Journalism Forum," which in turn contained a daily newsletter entitled "Rumourville USA."[60] CompuServe contracted with a third party, Cameron Communications, Inc. (CCI) to create and run this forum, and the newsletter was contracted for by CCI from the newsletter's publisher, Don Fitzpatrick Associates (DFA). The contract between CCI and DFA provided that all editorial responsibility for the contents of the newsletter resided with DFA, and CompuServe had no opportunity to view the newsletter's contents before DFA made it available to CompuServe subscribers by means of the "Journalism Forum." When an issue of the newsletter contained defamatory statements, the plaintiff brought an action against DFA and CompuServe. CompuServe argued it should not be visited with liability because it was only a distributor and not a publisher, and the court agreed:

---

55   *Lindley v. Delman*, 26 P.2d 751 (Okla. 1933).
56   *Lawrence v. Newberry* (1891), 64 L.T. 797 (Q.B.).
57   *Hird v. Wood* (1894), 38 S.J. 234 (C.A.).
58   *MacFadden v. Anthony*, 117 N.Y.S.2d 520 (Sup. Ct. N.Y. 1952).
59   *Curzon-Brown v. San Francisco Community College District et al.*, No. 307335 (Cal. Super. Ct., San Francisco County, January 21, 2000), reported in *Computer & Online Industry Reporter*, May 16, 2000.
60   *Cubby*, above note 52.

> CompuServe has no more editorial control over such a publication than does a public library, book store, or newsstand, and it would be no more feasible for CompuServe to examine every publication it carries for potential defamatory statements than it would be for any other distributor to do so. ... Technology is rapidly transforming the information industry. A computerized database is the functional equivalent of a more traditional news vendor, and the inconsistent application of a lower standard of liability to an electronic news distributor such as CompuServe than that which is applied to a public library, book store, or newsstand would impose an undue burden on the free flow of information.[61]

The court also found that CompuServe did not know, nor had reason to know, of the defamatory statements in the newsletter, and so the court, influenced to an important degree by the U.S. First Amendment (which provides constitutional protection for free speech) protection of distributors considerations, found in favour of CompuServe's motion for summary judgment. This finding is similar to the decision in *Daniel* v. *Dow Jones & Company, Inc.*, where a non-interactive online service was held not to be liable for erroneous data if it simply distributed it and did not have knowledge of the inaccuracy in it.[62] The important fact that CompuServe shifted editorial control to a third party over the particular forum also is somewhat analogous to the situation contemplated in subsection 303(2) of the *Criminal Code*, in the criminal libel provisions, where a proprietor of a newspaper gives to another person the authority for the editorial affairs of the paper.

The other important American Internet libel case, *Stratton Oakmount, Inc.* v. *Prodigy Services Company*,[63] declined to follow the *Cubby* case as a result of the very different facts found by the court in the *Prodigy* case. Prodigy, an online service provider like CompuServe, distinguished itself from other service providers by presenting itself as a family-oriented service that screened its public message areas for offensive messages. One such area was "Money Talk," where subscribers could post messages regarding financial matters, investment views, and the like. One such message was a defamatory one, and the plaintiff, after being unable to find the message's originator, sued Prodigy. The court reviewed whether Prodigy was a publisher or a distributor, and found it to be the former on the strength of Prodigy's own statements that it exercised content guidelines, had employed board leaders to

61 *Ibid.*, at 140.
62 520 N.Y. S.2d 334 (N.Y. City Civ. Ct. 1987) [*Daniel*].
63 5 Computer Cases (CCH) ¶47,291 at 67,772 (N.Y. Sup. Ct. 1995) [*Prodigy*].

moderate the online discussions, and implemented a software-based screening program. On appeal, Prodigy argued that while it did exercise screening techniques, these were only to exclude certain key offensive words and could not possibly screen for libellous statements. The case was never heard on appeal as the parties settled in the meantime.

In another case involving Prodigy,[64] the plaintiff sued the ISP for allowing an imposter to open an account with the ISP in the plaintiff's name; the case arose, and the imposter's actions came to light, when the imposter sent extremely vulgar e-mail messages to a scoutmaster that lived in the plaintiff's community. The court rejected the plaintiff's claim that Prodigy was a publisher of these e-mails, concluding that in respect of these communications the ISP played a passive role, was merely a conduit, and hence not a publisher.[65] With respect to messages posted by the imposter on Prodigy's electronic bulletin board, the plaintiff argued that inasmuch as Prodigy reserves the right in its membership agreements to screen these messages, it should be liable as a publisher. The court disagreed, holding that an ISP's decision to screen some messages does not alter its passive character in respect of the millions of other messages it does not screen, and hence it is not the guarantor of those other messages.[66] Finally, the plaintiff argued that Prodigy was negligent for failing to employ a verification process of applicants so as to weed out imposters. The court declined this invitation, concluding that to do so would open up ISPs to liability for the wrongful acts of its subscribers, and that there is "no justification for such limitless field of liability."[67] It should also be noted that the court held in favour of the ISP in this case without resorting to the statutory immunity provided by U.S. law for ISPs and referred to in the next section of this chapter; the court did not want to determine whether the new law applied to this case on a retroactive basis.

---

64   *Lunney v. Prodigy Services Company*, 94 N.Y.2d 242 (N.Y. App 1998) [*Lunney*].

65   The court in *Lunney*, above note 64, at 249, concluded: "The public would not be well served by compelling an ISP to examine and screen millions of e-mail communications, on pain of liability for defamation."

66   The court recognized the fact-specific nature of the investigation that gave rise to its particular conclusion, stating at 250: "In some instances, an electronic bulletin board could be made to resemble a newspaper's editorial page; in others it may function more like a 'chat' room. In many respects, an ISP bulletin board may serve much the same purpose as its ancestral version, but uses electronics in place of plywood and thumbtacks. ... We see no occasion to hypothesize whether there may be other instances in which the role of an electronic bulletin board operator would qualify it as a publisher."

67   *Lunney*, above note 64, at 251.

Facts somewhat similar to those in *Lunney* gave rise to a recent U.K. interlocutory decision, *Godfrey* v. *Demon Internet Ltd.*[68] The plaintiff, Godfrey, was a professor who asked Demon, then the U.K.'s largest ISP, to remove a "squalid, obscene and defamatory" posting in a newsgroup made by an unknown person masquerading as the plaintiff. The defendant refused, and so the posting remained on the ISP's news server for another ten days, when it was deleted in the ordinary course of the ISP's two-week removal schedule. The ISP argued that it did not publish this posting, or if it was found to do so, it was entitled to the defence in section 1 of the U.K. *Defamation Act*,[69] as it was merely the owner of an electronic device through which the postings were transmitted. The defendant relied heavily on U.S. cases for bolstering its position, especially the *Anderson*, *Cubby*, *Prodigy*, and *Lunney* decisions. The court disagreed strongly with the defendant, crucially finding as a fact that the ISP chose to store the defamatory posting in its computers and that the ISP did have the ability to delete it, as it eventually did. Thus, the court concluded that the ISP could not take advantage of the innocent disseminator defence once it had been put on notice about the defamatory posting by the plaintiff.[70] In the course of its judgment, the court observed that the defence in the U.K. *Defamation Act* is markedly different from the U.S. statutory defence for ISPs (discussed in the next session).[71] Ultimately, this case settled just

---

68 [1999] 4 All E.R. 346 [*Demon Internet*].

69 See above note 32.

70 The court in *Demon Internet*, above note 68, cited various background material to the U.K. Defamation Act that essentially made clear the legislative intention that the statutory innocent dissemination defence not protect those who knew that the material they were handling was defamatory, or ought to have known; that is, it is available to those who unwittingly provide a conduit for the publication of defamatory material, but someone is disqualified from using the defence if he has knowledge or cause for suspicion.

71 The court in *Demon Internet*, above note 68, at the outset of its decision, stated at 343–44: "According to counsel this is the first defamation action involving the Internet to come up for judicial decision within this jurisdiction. However I had a number of American cases cited before me. The United States was in the forefront of the early development of the Internet. Care has to be taken before American cases are applied in English defamation cases. The impact of the First Amendment has resulted in a substantial divergence of approach between American and English defamation law. For example in innocent dissemination cases in English law the defendant publisher has to establish his innocence, whereas in American law the plaintiff who has been libelled has to prove that the publisher was not innocent. Nevertheless the American decisions are educative and instructive as to the workings of the Internet and the problems which arise when defamatory material finds its way onto the Internet."

before going to trial, with the ISP paying the plaintiff £15,000 and his legal costs of £230,000 (and having to bear its own legal costs).

d) U.S. Law Reform

Partly to counteract the decision in the first *Prodigy* case, section 230(c) was added to the U.S. *Telecommunications Act of 1996*, which provides as follows:

> (1) No provider or user of an interactive computer service shall be treated as the publisher or speaker of any information provided by another information content provider.
>
> (2) No provider or user of an interactive computer service shall be held liable on account of —
> (A) Any action voluntarily taken in good faith to restrict access to or availability of material that the provider or user considers to be obscene, lewd, lascivious, filthy, excessively violent, harassing, or otherwise objectionable, whether or not such material is constitutionally protected; or
> (B) any action taken to enable or make available to information content providers or others the technical means to restrict access to material described in paragraph (1).[72]

In a number of cases this provision has been used by an ISP to shield itself from liability.[73]

To understand how far-reaching the section 230 defence is, consider the decision involving Matt Drudge, the self-proclaimed "Thomas Paine of the Internet," who through his notorious Drudge Report served up extensive Washington D.C. gossip and rumour. AOL, then the world's largest interactive computer service, licensed the Drudge Report for distribution over the AOL network, retaining the right to

---

72   *Telecommunications Act of 1996*, 47 U.S.C.A. §230. This statute is also discussed in chapter 3, section B.5(e), "Legislative Responses."

73   *Zeran* v. *America Online, Inc.*, 958 F.Supp. 1124 (E.D. Va. 1997) [*Zeran*]; and *Doe* v. *America Online Inc.*, 1997 WL 374223 (Fla. Cir. Ct.). The section, however, can be used by entities other than ISPs. It has been held to apply to Web site operators as well: see *Stoner* v. *EBay Inc.*, 56 U.S.P.Q 2d 1852 (Cal. Super. 2000) (in this case eBay was held not to be responsible for bootleg copies of music sold over its auction service); and *Schneider* v. *Amazon.Com Inc.*, 29 Media L. Rep. 2421 (Wash. Ct. App. 2001) (in this case Amazon was held not to be liable for negative book reviews posted on its site), but not if they actually provide content, such as developing online questionnaires (*Carafano* v. *Metrosplash Inc.*, 207 F.Supp. 2d 1055 (C.D. Cal. 2002)) (though in this latter case the plaintiff's claim was dismissed on other, substantive grounds).

remove content that AOL determined was objectionable. AOL herald-ed its delivery of the report by stating, in a press release, "AOL Hires Runaway Gossip Success Matt Drudge." So there was no question that AOL knew generally the kind of material that Drudge was going to write, and equally AOL had the right to exert editorial control over it before its dissemination. Nevertheless, because of section 230, the court was unwilling to find AOL liable when Drudge wrote a particu-larly problematic piece insinuating that a senior White House staffer had a spousal abuse past:

> If it were writing on a clean slate, this Court would agree with plain-tiffs. AOL has certain editorial rights with respect to the content pro-vided by Drudge and disseminated by AOL, including the right to require changes in content and to remove it; and it has affirmatively promoted Drudge as a new source of unverified instant gossip on AOL. Yet it takes no responsibility for any damage he may cause ... it would seem only fair to hold AOL to the liability standards applied to a publisher or, at least, like a book store owner or library, to the lia-bility standards applied to a distributor. But Congress has made a dif-ferent policy choice by providing immunity even where the interactive service provider has an active, even aggressive role in making available content prepared by others. In some sort of tacit *quid pro quo* arrangement with the service provider community, Con-gress has conferred immunity from tort liability as an incentive to Internet service providers to self-police the Internet for obscenity and other offensive material, even where the self-policing is unsuccessful or not even attempted.[74]

e) Intermediary Liability in Canada

It is too early to tell what influence the *Cubby* and *Prodigy* cases will have in Canada. In the United States a number of commentators view these two cases as standing for the proposition that an online service provider improves its chances of avoiding liability by not screening content or otherwise exercising any editorial control over the public message space on its network. Whatever the merits of this position in the United States, it would appear to be a dangerous approach in Cana-da given that if a network operator does nothing in this country it

---

74 *Blumenthal v. Drudge*, 992 F.Supp. 44 (U.S. Dist. Col. 1998) at 51. See also *Ben Ezra, Weinstein & Co., Inc. v. America Online, Inc.*, 206 F.3d 980 (10th Cir. 2000), where Section 230 of CDA served to deflect liability from AOL in respect of alleged inaccurate stock quotations about the plaintiff's company.

could still be found liable, even if it did not have actual knowledge of the libel. In order for a participant on the Internet in Canada to argue successfully the innocent disseminator defence it must show it did not have knowledge of the libel and that there are no conditions that would lead it to suspect libel, and the entity was not negligent in failing to know about the libel. Therefore, the first step in analysing an intermediary's liability for libel publication over the Internet should begin with a detailed assessment of the defendant's role and activities on the Internet as they specifically and actually pertain to the alleged libel. This requires going beyond labelling the defendant an Internet service provider, or an online content supplier, or a bulletin board service operator, or a common carrier, or a discussion forum or usegroup moderator, or one of any number of other labels. Similarly, the urge to label the defendant by analogy to a newsvendor, library, newspaper, broadcaster, or one of any number of other pre-Internet categories should be avoided. Rather, a functional assessment of the defendant's specific activities related to the alleged libel should be undertaken, focusing on the degree of knowledge and control (if any of either) that the defendant had of the libel.

Similarly, to the extent that pre-Internet cases are drawn upon for jurisprudential support, such cases must also be analysed from the perspective not of "labels," but rather the degree of knowledge and control exercised by the relevant defendant. Armed with this information, the court must then approach the defendant by being cognizant of the competing policy positions at issue in Internet libel cases. On the one hand, the law must be mindful of the admonition of the Supreme Court of Canada in the *Hill* case as to the great importance and value of a person's unsullied reputation, and how it would be unfortunate indeed if the Internet became a medium where libellous statements went unchecked.[75] On the other hand, it would be equally extreme to take the position that disseminators of other people's messages over the Internet were absolutely liable for their content, regardless of the actual measures taken by the defendant. Clearly, justice and practicality lie somewhere in between. Thus, where the defendant has knowledge of the libel, and the ability to control its further dissemination or storage, liability should follow if, within a reasonable period of time after being notified of it, the defendant does not take measures to delete the libellous material or block access to it. In this regard, where the defendant is involved in some form of forum moderation and has the opportuni-

---

75   *Hill*, above note 5.

ty to review messages prior to their posting on a public message board or soon after, the test of "libellous on its face" might usefully be employed to determine, in the context of a time-sensitive service, whether the defendant was negligent in letting libellous material through its screen.

Where the facts present themselves in as straightforward a manner as the *Godfrey* case, the action to be taken by the ISP, or the operator of any other Web presence, is also straightforward: if you are notified of an allegedly libellous posting, and on its face it is arguably libellous, remove it. There are, of course, many other situations where the facts, and the sensible course of action, are not so clear. For example, what if you are merely linking to material that contains the allegedly defamatory material? Or, what if you are linking to the home page of a site that in material several clicks away from the home page contains the problematic material? What if the complainant is someone other than the person allegedly being defamed? What if you are hosting a discussion group, and the first posting of a thread contains the allegedly defamatory material, do you have to remove subsequent entries merely because they refer to the first posting (but do not reproduce it)? How quick should you be to suspend the privileges of a subscriber who is posting problematic material who then tells you the material is forged (as in the *Lunney* and *Godfrey* cases)? In essence, there are many nuances to the day-to-day application of the knowledge-based version of the defamation test, and judicial guidance in these issues would be welcome.

Actual knowledge, however, should not be the sole test for libel liability in respect of Internet intermediaries; rather, the second and third prongs of the innocent disseminator defence should apply equally in cyberspace. Thus, where actual knowledge of the libel is absent, the court should also ask whether there are circumstances that ought to have led the defendant to suppose that, for example, the online discussion forum would contain a libel, or whether the defendant was negligent in letting it happen. This should not mean, however, that the defendant must screen every message of every type. In most cases this simply will not be practical. A large online service provider like America Online currently delivers some 11,000,000 messages a day. At some point in the future software may well be intelligent enough to screen all this traffic for libel, but it certainly cannot be done today. Nor should the defendant be made to do so, as this would bring the fast-flow, low-cost, ease-of-use aspects of the Internet communications model into serious question. A defendant should be expected, however, to monitor a bulletin board that is notorious for its ability to attract defamatory statements. Or a defendant should be expected to monitor

closely the messages sent by persons known to participate in abusive
or offensive behaviour. In effect, the Internet is a fabulous information
resource of immense help. The Internet will not, however, be able to
maintain or develop this role if it becomes a cesspool of defamation. All
intermediaries on the Internet have to take reasonable measures to
deter, or neutralize the effects of, persons who would make defamatory statements on the Internet. The standards and approaches noted
above will ensure that the various participants on the Internet do their
fair share in preserving and enhancing the value of the Internet.

3) Anonymity and the Internet

One of the fairly novel aspects of the Internet is the ability to communicate over it anonymously. Many people use pseudonyms or aliases to
mask their real identity. There is a saying among Netizens, that on the
Internet no one knows you're a dog, which prompted the wonderful cartoon with the same caption, with the picture of a dog sitting in front of
the computer typing away on a keyboard. As well, various technologies
have been developed to enable Internet users to operate online anonymously.[76] Anonymity makes the Internet environment ripe for fraud,
forgery, and similar objectionable behaviour that leads to many legal
challenges. Chapter 6 discusses legal and technological measures aimed
at verifying authentication online.[77] At least one U.S. state has passed a
law prohibiting users of the Internet from operating anonymously.[78]

From the perspective of libel, the *Lunney* and *Godfrey* cases illustrate the perniciousness and ease of posting counterfeit messages over
the Internet. In Ontario, courts will assist plaintiffs who bring defamation actions against such persons to ascertain their identity. This can
usually be done because even though the imposter attempts to hide
under a fake name for purposes of her communications, her computer
still generates a unique IP address that is known to the ISP. Thus, in
most cases an ISP can track down the address of a sender of defamatory e-mail. In Ontario, courts have facilitated this in a couple of recent
orders. In the summer of 1998, Philip Services Corporation (PSC), a
Canadian public company, believed that a number of messages posted
to a Yahoo! discussion group by anonymous participants were defam-

76   See, for example, the products of Montreal-based Zero Knowledge Systems,
     <zeroknowledge.com>.
77   See chapter 6, section A.2(b), "The Authentication Function."
78   See the discussion on the 1996 amendment to the Georgia *Computer Systems
     Protection Act* in chapter 4, section E.4(b), "False Claims."

atory. PSC obtained an order, on an *ex parte* basis, against a number of ISPs, requiring them to provide PSC with the names of these participants, as well as their addresses (both physical, as well as the IP address where PSC had no name for the subscriber).[79] In a similar recent decision,[80] a company claimed that an individual had committed defamation as well as breach of confidence and conversion by attaching the company's internal files to allegedly defamatory e-mails sent to seventy-five recipients. The company did not know the identity of the sender of these messages, and therefore brought a legal proceeding to compel the ISP to disclose the relevant coordinates of the potential perpetrator. The court concluded that the ISP did not have to voluntarily disclose such information, and that ISPs may indeed be under contractual duties of confidence not to do so without being ordered to do so by a court. Similarly, it would not be enough that the plaintiff merely started a lawsuit and then demanded disclosure by the ISP. At the same time, however, the court held that where the plaintiff, before a judge, can make out a *prima facie* case against the poster of the messages (as it did in this case), the ISP would be required to turn over the identification information to the plaintiff. This is a sensible compromise on this difficult issue, and finds a good balance between protecting freedom of speech and freedom from libel.[81]

---

79   *Philip Services Corp.* v. *John Doe*, (No. 4592/98) (Ont. Gen. Div., June 24, 1998); and *Financial Post*, July 10, 1998. It is interesting to note that the user agreements of various ISPs contain a range of different confidentiality obligations vis-à-vis their customers' data: see Ian R. Kerr, "*The Legal Relationship Between Online Service Providers and Users*," 35 C.B.L.J. 419. Professor Kerr finds that these provisions can be said to come within one of five types: (a) confidential; (b) confidential within the limits of the law; (c) disclosure when illegality is suspected; (d) disclosure to protect the service provider or in extraordinary circumstances; and (e) voluntary disclosure and active monitoring.

80   *Irwin Toy Limited* v. *Joe Doe*, [2000] O.J. No. 3318 (Sup. Ct.). For a similar U.S. case, see *America Online, Inc.* v. *Anonymous Publicly Traded Company*, 542 S.E.2d 377 (Sup. Ct. Va. 2001). This case is interesting because the plaintiff did not reveal its identity.

81   An American case, *Dendrite International, Inc.* v. *John Doe No. 3 et al*, A-2774-00T3 (N.J. Sup. Ct. App. DIV. 2001), arguably animated by strong First Amendment freedom of speech traditions, provides the anonymous poster with greater protection by requiring, in addition to the showing of a *prima facie* case, that the ISP first attempt to inform the poster that a claim has been brought against them; the ISP indicate the exact statements complained of; the ISP produce its specific evidence supporting the *prima facie* case; and the court balance First Amendment freedom of (anonymous) speech rights against the strength of the *prima facie* case and the necessity for this particular disclosure in order for the case to proceed.

B. JURISDICTION

1) Pre-Internet Law

As a general proposition, the jurisdiction of a government to pass and enforce laws is limited, in terms of physical proximity, to the land mass comprising the particular country, province, state, municipality, or other substate entity under the control of such government. This principle is based on the fundamental tenet of international law, namely, that all countries are independent and sovereign, and that for reasons of international comity, no state will exceed its inherent jurisdiction.[82] Thus, the general rule is that law is based on geographic communities, and that courts should take jurisdiction over an entity and its actions when they are both in the court's physical jurisdiction. The Internet presents a fundamental challenge to such a physically based legal system. In terms of function, the Internet has no physical boundaries, and its communities are virtual rather than physical in nature. Cyberspace appears to have no geographic borders. On reflection, however, it is clear that the Internet has not wiped away borders, but that it allows borders to be crossed with great ease. The fourth dynamic of computer law postulates a blurring of domestic and international frontiers, rather than the elimination of national ones.

a) Canadian Civil Matters

The ability of communications technologies and business practices to breach national boundaries predates the Internet. As transnational activities increased through the acceleration of international trade and travel and the transmission of information across national frontiers by means of the mail, telegraph, telex, phone, and fax, a number of exceptions to the strict territorial principle of legal jurisdiction began to develop. Courts in Canada today are prepared to assume jurisdiction in a number of situations where domestic actors have an impact on persons outside of Canada, and conversely where foreign actors affect persons within Canada. Numerous hybrid situations, involving both domestic and foreign parties, can also be envisaged. For example, the rules of some Canadian courts will permit jurisdiction to be exercised when the parties themselves have agreed contractually to be bound by the laws of a province of Canada.[83] In the context of tort law, Canadi-

---

82 Ruth Sullivan, ed., *Driedger on the Construction of Statutes*, 3d ed. (Toronto: Butterworths, 1994).

83 See, for example, *Ontario Rules of Civil Procedure*, Rule 17.02.

an courts, following well-established conflicts of laws principles, will assert jurisdiction if there is a real and substantial connection between the wrongdoing and the Canadian jurisdiction.[84] In a libel case, for example, the plaintiff brought a claim in Ontario against a U.S. broadcaster for a radio broadcast by the defendant's station in the United States and heard across the border in Canada.[85] The defendant brought a motion to dismiss the action, arguing that the Ontario court had no jurisdiction to entertain the matter. The Ontario court disagreed, holding that the U.S. broadcasts were so transmitted as to be published in Ontario, and in its reasons stated the following:

> A person may utter all the defamatory words he wishes without incurring any civil liability unless they are heard and understood by a third person. I think it a "startling proposition" to say that one may, while standing south of the border or cruising in an aeroplane south of the border, through the medium of modern sound amplification, utter defamatory matter which is heard in a Province in Canada north of the border, and not be said to have published a slander in the Province in which it is heard and understood. I cannot see what difference it makes whether the person is made to understand by means of the written word, soundwaves or etherwaves in so far as the matter of proof of publication is concerned. The tort consists in making a third person understand actionable defamatory matter.[86]

A similar conclusion was reached in a later Ontario libel case with respect to a television broadcast that originated in the United States and was received in Canada either directly via U.S. television stations or indirectly after being retransmitted by Canadian-based cable companies.[87]

---

84 See, for example, *Hunt* v. *T&N plc* (1993), 109 D.L.R. (4th) 16 (S.C.C.) [*Hunt*], where the court concluded that some of the traditional rules on enforcement of foreign judgments that emphasized sovereignty are no longer reasonable in the new international environment of the constant flow of products, wealth, and people across the globe. For earlier cases that articulate the "real and substantial connection" test for finding jurisdiction, see *Morguard Investments Ltd.* v. *De Savoye*, [1990] 3 S.C.R. 1077 and *Amchem Products Incorporated* v. *British Columbia (Workers' Compensation Board)*, [1993] 1 S.C.R. 897.

85 *Jenner* v. *Sun Oil Co. Ltd.* (1952), 16 C.P.R. 87 (Ont. H.C.J.).

86 *Ibid.*, at 98–99. See also *United States Satellite Broadcasting Company* v. *WIC Premium Television*, (2000 ABCA 233), where the Alberta Court of Appeal took jurisdiction over American direct-to-home satellite signal distributors when their programming spilled over into Alberta.

87 *Pindling* v. *National Broadcasting Corp.* (1984), 49 O.R. (2d) 58 (H.C.J.). For a similar result in a more recent case involving dissemination by newspaper across a provincial boundary, see *Direct Energy Marketing Ltd.* v. *Hilson*, [1999] A.J. No. 695 (Alta. Q.B.).

This latter case may also be said to illustrate "forum shopping" in the modern world of transnational communications and business, given that the plaintiff, the prime minister of the Bahamas, decided to bring his suit in Canada instead of the United States, which he was clearly entitled to do.

Where, however, a court believes it would be unreasonable for a plaintiff to bring a claim in a certain case, it could steer the plaintiff away on grounds of *forum non conveniens*, the rule that some other jurisdiction is better placed to entertain the matter because of, for instance, the location of witnesses. For example, in one case involving allegations of negligence by a U.K.-based law firm, the court decided that the contract by a Toronto-based party to retain the U.K. firm was concluded in Toronto because the offer emanated from Toronto over the telephone and hence the contract arose in Toronto when the offer-or received the U.K. firm's acceptance over the phone.[88] Nevertheless, because the opinion was rendered by U.K. lawyers in the United Kingdom, on matters of U.K. law, involving a U.K.-based project, and for other similar reasons involving the U.K., the court held that the litiga-tion should be moved to the United Kingdom under the doctrine of *forum non conveniens*. The fundamental determination in these cases is whether it is inherently reasonable for a court to take jurisdiction over a person not resident within the court's physical territorial boundary.[89] In making this determination courts should not consider a mechanical counting of contacts and connections, but instead should focus on what promotes order and fairness in the given situation.[90]

b) Canadian Criminal Matters

With respect to criminal matters, the Supreme Court of Canada in the *Libman* case provided a thorough review of the U.K. and Canadian law as to when a court should take jurisdiction where a foreign actor or action is relevant.[91] The court concluded that "all that is necessary to

---

88   *National Bank of Canada* v. *Clifford Chance* (1996), 30 O.R. (3d) 746 (Gen. Div.). This decision is consistent with the current trend in determining the place of contracts effected by telephone as noted in chapter 6, section A.5, "Time and Place of Contract."

89   *Moran* v. *Pyle National (Canada) Ltd.* (1973), 43 D.L.R. (3d) 239 (S.C.C.) [*Moran*].

90   *Hunt*, above note 84. In a case involving the charge of criminal libel arising out of postings on the Internet, the venue for prosecution was moved from Guelph, Ontario (where the complainant lived) to Ottawa (where the accused live), part-ly because the server initially used to host the offending Web site was in Ottawa: *R.* v. *Barrett*, [2000] O.J. No. 2055 (Ont. Sup. Ct.).

91   *Libman* v. *R.* (1985), 21 D.L.R. (4th) 174 (S.C.C.) [*Libman*].

make an offence subject to the jurisdiction of our courts is that a significant portion of the activities constituting that offence took place in Canada … it is sufficient that there be a 'real and substantial link' between an offence and this country."[92] The court found that even in the late nineteenth century, with the invention and development of modern communications, courts in England exercised criminal jurisdiction over transnational transactions so long as a significant part of the chain of action occurred in the United Kingdom. Since that time, the court noted the "means of communications have proliferated at an accelerating pace,"[93] and therefore the interests of states in continuing this judicial trend, as well as being "our brothers' keepers" in a shrinking world, have only increased, even if this means that many countries may be able to take jurisdiction (a development the court stated can be handled by the doctrines of *autrefois acquit* and *convict*). Similarly, in the area of securities regulation, in the pre-Internet era courts did not have difficulty finding that accused can commit infractions via the telephone and traditional mail, without ever setting a physical foot in the court's province.[94] The *Criminal Code* addresses a number of circumstances where it might not otherwise be clear which territorial division within Canada (which province or smaller judicial division) is to have control over a particular offence.[95] For example, paragraph 476(d) of the *Criminal Code* provides that where an offence is committed in an aircraft in the course of a flight, the offence can be said to have been committed where the flight commenced or ended or in any jurisdiction over which it passed. Similarly, paragraph 476(e) provides that where an offence is committed in respect of the mail in the course of its door-to-door delivery, the offence shall be deemed to have been committed in any jurisdiction through which the mail was carried on that delivery. With respect to the offence of defamatory libel, subsection 478(2) of the *Criminal Code* provides that anyone charged with this offence in respect of a newspaper be tried where he resides or where the newspaper is published.

c) U.S. Law
It is useful to consider the American experience with the question of jurisdiction for a number of reasons, including the sheer number of

---

92   *Ibid.*, at 200.
93   *Ibid.*, at 201.
94   See, for example, *R. v. Mckenzie Securities Ltd.* (1966), 56 D.L.R. (2d) 56 (Man. C.A.) [*Mckenzie*]. This case is discussed in chapter 4, section E.1., "Securities Law."
95   R.S.C. 1985, c. C-46.

pre-Internet cases, and now the virtual avalanche of Internet jurisdiction cases emanating from the United States, as well as the fact that Canadian courts increasingly find U.S. analysis of technology law issues influential.[96] Each U.S. state has a statute (a "long-arm statute") that extends the jurisdiction of the courts of that state beyond its own physical boundaries. These statutes typically permit "general jurisdiction" to be exercised over a person (or other entity) if it is resident in the state or has some permanence or continuity of presence in the state. The statutes also allow for "specific jurisdiction" (sometimes called "personal jurisdiction") to be exercised where the non-resident makes some "purposeful availment" of doing business or conducting transactions in the state or commits some tortious act in the state or outside the state that has an effect in the state, provided the taking of jurisdiction does not offend notions of fair play or substantial justice and there are no *forum non conveniens* reasons for declining jurisdiction.[97] In effect, the U.S. rules are similar to the Canadian rules, with courts essentially asking whether there is sufficient connection between the non-resident defendant and the forum state for the court to reasonably take jurisdiction.

In pre-Internet cases in the United States, as has been the situation in Canada, the trend has been for courts to more readily allow an out-of-jurisdiction resident to be brought into the courts of the forum state. In a case some forty years ago, a Texas-based insurance company was held to be subject to California's jurisdiction on the basis of issuing a single insurance contract through the mails.[98] In a leading U.S. Supreme Court decision, which (like the Supreme Court of Canada in the *Hunt* and *Moran* cases) rejected any "talismanic jurisdictional formula" (i.e., there is no mechanical system of approaching the "contacts with the jurisdiction" issue), the court, echoing the fourth dynamic of

---

96   See footnote 4 of the Updated Preface to the First Edition of this book for a sampling of computer law cases where Canadian judges have found useful the opinions of their American counterparts.

97   *Burger King Corp. v. Rudzewicz*, 471 U.S. 462 (1985) [*Burger King*].

98   *McGee v. International Life Insurance Co.*, 355 U.S. 220 (1957) [*McGee*]. In this case, the court observed at 222–23: "Looking back over this long history of litigation a trend is clearly discernible toward expanding the permissible scope of state jurisdiction over foreign corporations and other non-residents. In part this is attributable to the fundamental transformation of our national economy over the years. Today many commercial transactions touch two or more States and may involve parties separated by the full continent. With this increasing nationalization of commerce has come a great increase in the amount of business conducted by mail across state lines."

computer law, made it clear that physical presence in the jurisdiction is not necessary to a finding of jurisdiction:

> Jurisdiction in these circumstances may not be avoided merely because the defendant did not *physically* enter the forum State. Although territorial presence frequently will enhance a potential defendant's affiliation with a State and reinforce the reasonable foreseeability of suit there, it is an inescapable fact of modern commercial life that a substantial amount of business is transacted solely by mail and wire communications across state lines, thus obviating the need for physical presence within a State in which business is conducted. So long as a commercial actor's efforts are "purposefully directed" toward residents of another State, we have consistently rejected the notion that an absence of physical contacts can defeat personal jurisdiction there.[99]

Pre-Internet, Canadians have been subject to U.S. jurisdiction based on, for example, trade-marked products and mail-order sales effected in the United States[100] and in one libel case on a single telephone call.[101] In several of the U.S. pre-Internet cases, listings and advertisements in telephone directories in the forum state did not result in a finding of jurisdiction,[102] but something more such as posting a message to a pre-Internet computer-based bulletin board did.[103] In coming to this conclusion, the court in this latter case stated that

> Through the use of computers, corporations can now transact business and communicate with individuals in several states simultaneously. Unlike communication by mail or telephone, messages sent through computers are available to the recipient and anyone else who

---

99 *Burger King*, above note 97 at 476.

100 *Vanity Fair Mills, Inc.* v. *T. Eaton Co. Limited*, 234 F.2d 633 (2nd Cir. 1956).

101 *Brainerd* v. *Governors of the University of Alberta*, 873 F.2d 1257 (9th Cir. 1989). Typically, in these cases the Canadian company is resisting being hauled into the U.S. court. On occasion, however, the shoe is on the other foot and the Canadian company is vying to achieve jurisdiction in the United States because the relevant U.S. law is more favourable than its Canadian counterpart: see *Nowsco Well Service, Ltd.* v. *Home Insurance Company*, 799 F.Supp. 602 (S.D. W. Va. 1991), where the Canadian company tried to achieve jurisdiction in the United States but was sent back to Alberta for reasons of *forum non conveniens*.

102 See, for example, *Baird* v. *Day & Zimmerman, Inc.*, 390 F.Supp. 883 (S.D.N.Y. 1974); and *Ziperman* v. *Frontier Hotel of Las Vegas*, 374 N.Y.S.2d 697 (Sup. Ct. App. N.Y. 1975).

103 *California Software Incorporated* v. *Reliability Research, Inc.*, 631 F.Supp. 1356 (C.D. Cal. 1986).

may be watching. Thus, while modern technology has made nation-wide commercial transactions simpler and more feasible, even for small businesses, it must broaden correspondingly the permissible scope of jurisdiction exercisable by the courts.[104]

2) Internet Cases

The pre-Internet cases in Canada and the United States, such as *Hunt, Moran, Libman, Burger King*, and *McGee*, raise the question what connections or effects, in an Internet context, are sufficient to make the initiator of a particular activity subject to the jurisdiction of a forum court. In Canada this query has been answered in a half dozen or so cases, while in the United States, the land of litigation, a veritable flood of Internet jurisdiction cases have been decided. Rather than cite all of (or even the majority of) the latter, it is more efficient to note the trends in analysis that have been brought to bear on these multifarious fact patterns. It is also worth noting that different considerations can apply depending on the type of matter at hand. For example, courts and regulators have been extremely reluctant to deny themselves jurisdiction in criminal, quasi-criminal, and regulatory matters. On the other hand, in civil matters, different results can flow depending on whether the gravaman of the claim involves intellectual property infringement, breach of contract, defamation, or some other substantive area of the law.

a) Regulatory/Criminal Jurisdiction

In the criminal, quasi-criminal, and regulatory arenas, courts and regulators seem to have little hesitation assuming jurisdiction over foreign-originated Internet-related conduct they view as harmful to the public good so long as there is a real and substantial connection to the court's or regulator's own jurisdiction. Thus, the Alberta Securities Commission exercised jurisdiction over the World Stock Exchange (WSE), a fledgling Internet-based stock market that was incorporated in the Cayman Islands and whose Web site was operated from a server located in Antigua.[105] Importantly, the principals behind the WSE were resident in Edmonton, promoted the exchange to residents of Alberta, and initially operated their site using a hosting service in Edmonton. Following the reasoning in *Libman*, the Commission seized jurisdic-

---

104 *Ibid.*, at 1363.
105 *Re World Stock Exchange*, Alberta Securities Commission Decision, 15 February 2000 [*World Stock Exchange*]: available at <albertasecurities.com/DATA/items/EOL/orders/494580.pdf>.

tion largely because there was no real regulatory oversight otherwise being brought to bear on the WSE, and the Commission felt it had to fill the regulatory lacunae.[106] In a similar vein, the Canadian Human Rights Commission has concluded that it has jurisdiction over the Internet hate dissemination activities of Ernst Zündel; although Zündel's Web site was operated on a server in California, Zündel was still resident in Canada, he posted materials to the Web site, and the site was accessed by Canadians in Canada.[107] In effect, in the regulatory/criminal arena, the challenge posed by the fourth dynamic of computer law (namely, the blurring of national/international) is being resolved by Canadian courts and regulators taking jurisdiction over alleged wrongdoers physically located in foreign venues where their Internet activity allows them to have a meaningful connection with Canada. Indeed, the extent to which the criminal oversight/regulatory urge will be exercised in the Internet space can be seen from the decision in *Alteen* v. *Informix*,[108] where the court held that local plaintiffs in St. John's should be entitled to bring a claim involving misleading consumer information in part because the defendant's securities disclosure documents disseminated over the Internet were often picked up in news stories by the Canadian financial or business press.

In the United States, the criminal and quasi-criminal cases also illustrate a dogged determination of courts, governments, and law enforcement authorities to overcome the challenges posed by the fourth dynamic of computer law and to retain control over harmful activities they perceive to be occurring in their jurisdiction. For example, in the *Chan* case, the court was confronted with evidence of a complicated, multinational fraud and money-laundering scheme with funds flowing from a bank in Macau to Nigeria through a New York–based bank.[109] There were extensive wire transfers of funds effected through the

---

106 The Commission bristled at the "flag-of-convenience" behaviour of the WSE, departing Edmonton for the Cayman Islands, and then being chased from there to Antigua by the Cayman authorities. The Commission summed up its position as follows at 38 of *World Stock Exchange*, *ibid.*: "There would be no purpose in having an elaborate framework of securities regulation to protect the public interest if the law permitted entities like the WSE to circumvent it all by using modern technology and communications to step beyond our jurisdiction."

107 *Sabrina Citron, Toronto Mayor's Committee on Community and Race Relations, and Canadian Human Rights Commission* v. *Ernst Zündel*, Canadian Human Rights Tribunal, 18 January 2002. See the discussion of this case in chapter 3, section B.6(a), "The *Canadian Human Rights Act*."

108 [1998] N.J. No. 122 (Nfld. T.D.).

109 *Banco Nacional Ultramarino, S.A.* v. *Chan*, 641 N.Y.S.2d 1006 (Sup. 1996).

accused's bank account in the New York bank, but the accused was never physically in New York. When the victim sued in New York to recover its monies, the defendant argued the courts of New York should not take jurisdiction over the matter as he was never present in New York. The court declined to hold that physical presence was required for purposes of New York's long arm statute and concluded:

> [T]o allow a defendant to conspire and direct tortious activities in New York, in furtherance of that conspiracy, and then avoid jurisdiction because it directs those activities from outside the state or country, is to ignore the reality of modern banking and computer technology in the end of the twentieth century! A defendant with access to computers, fax machines, etc., no longer has to physically enter New York to perform a financial transaction which may be criminal or tortious, i.e., conversion. He may secrete himself and/or direct activities from locations where jurisdiction may be impossible to acquire, including a boat beyond the three mile limit. Thus, the emphasis should be on the locus of the tort, not whether defendant was physically here when the tortious act occurred. Once the court finds that the tort occurred within the state, it should look at the totality of the circumstances, to determine if jurisdiction should be exercised. ... Having found that the tort occurred within New York the court concludes that defendant's bodily presence is not an indispensable requirement for long-arm jurisdiction. It would be a travesty to permit the use of our institutions to channel stolen funds and/or the proceeds from heroin sales by those who impudently claim they are beyond our borders! It would be a gross violation of common sense and reality to shelter such activities.[110]

In the United States, the federal and state governments are generally anti-Internet gaming, as noted in chapter 3, section B.8, "Gaming and Betting." Thus, in the *Granite Gate* case, the attorney general of Minnesota brought a consumer protection action against the operator of a sports betting Web site on the Internet.[111] The attorney general's claim of consumer fraud, deceptive trade practices, and false advertising was based on U.S. federal law that prohibits betting by telephone, wire, or facsimile, as well as on Minnesota state law that prohibits sports betting. The defendant was not resident in Minnesota, being

---

110 *Ibid.*, at 1009–10.
111 *State of Minnesota v. Granite Gate Resorts, Inc.*, 1996 WL 767431 (D. Minn.) (Westlaw) [*Granite Gate*]. See also the Minnesota Attorney General's "*Warning to All Internet Users and Providers*," at <state.mn.us/ebranch/ag/memo.txt>.

based in Nevada with the computer for the Web site being in Belize, and argued that the Minnesota courts lacked jurisdiction over him and his operation. The court disagreed, finding that the Web site's ability to be accessed by Minnesota residents was sufficient to find jurisdiction. The court analysed the quantity and quality of contacts, the connection between these contacts and the cause of action, the interest of the state in providing a forum, and the convenience of the parties. The court concluded that the Web site operator was conducting a direct marketing campaign in Minnesota, and that by advertising in Minnesota he was purposefully availing himself of the privilege of conducting business in the state. Interestingly, the judge noted that Internet advertising through a Web site is more sustained than traditional paper-based advertising that is often discarded and reaches fewer people. The court also noted the defendant's tracking technology that could tell him in which state a user of the Web site was resident; indeed, the defendant knew that a specific number of its customers were Minnesota residents. A final factor relevant to the court was the defendant's own statement on the Web site that customers who were delinquent in payment would be sued either in Belize or in the customer's home state. The court concluded it was impossible for the defendant to argue inconvenience once it had itself made the offer of using the Minnesota jurisdiction for this particular purpose. In a more recent online gaming case, *People* v. *World Interactive Gaming*,[112] the accused argued that when a New York

---

112 714 N.Y.S.2d 844 (N.Y. Supp. 1999); affirmed 1999 N.Y. Misc. LEXIS 425
(S.C.N.Y.) [*World Interactive Gaming*]. In this case the court concluded that it is
irrelevant that Internet gaming is legal in Antigua, where the online bets were
received, given that the act of entering and transmitting the information from
New York was illegal in New York. In effect, the court concluded that the
respondents could not use the computer server as a shield against liability. Interestingly, the court also noted that the Web site's mechanism for supposedly permitting only users from states that allowed gaming, namely requiring the user to
type in his or her state, could easily be circumvented by merely typing in another state. Similarly, in *United States of America* v. *$734,578.82 in U.S. Currency*,
No. 00-2500 (3rd Cir. 2002), a British-based sports betting company was found
violating U.S. law by taking bets from the United States; the court ignored the
principle that a gaming transaction takes place where the wager is accepted, and
instead focused on the broad language of the relevant New Jersey statute that
makes illegal any conduct that materially aids any form of gaming activity. For a
decision in Canada that similarly ignores the technical determination of where a
lottery ticket is purchased through an analysis of offer and acceptance, and opts
instead for a broader view of regulating gaming, see *Earth Future Lottery, Re*
(2002), 633 A.P.R. 311 (PEI C.A.), discussed in chapter 3, section B.8, "Gaming
and Betting."

State resident accessed a Web site hosted by a server operated in Antigua, it was as though the American citizen hopped on an airplane, flew to Antigua, and physically entered the casino there, which Americans are allowed to do. The court disagreed, and concluded that the better analysis was that the accused was making its casino available in New York State, which it was not licensed to do.

Another case worth considering in some detail arises out of a 1981 injunction that was granted in favour of *Playboy* magazine prohibiting the importation into the United States by an Italian publisher of a publication titled *Playmen* on the grounds of trade-mark infringement (the *Chuckleberry* case).[113] Fifteen years later, the Italian publisher established a Web site in Italy on the Internet that carried the *Playmen* trademark. Users visiting the site could become subscribers to the electronic magazine by paying the requisite fee, after which a password would be issued. The court in the 1996 contempt proceeding found that this activity, in respect of U.S. subscribers, violated the 1981 injunction order. The court was not swayed by the defendant's argument that as the Internet did not exist in 1981, the injunction could not possibly have contemplated, nor should it apply to, the defendant's Internet-based activities. The court disagreed, stating:

> The Injunction's failure to refer to the Internet by name does not limit its applicability to this new medium. Injunctions entered before the recent explosion of computer technology must continue to have meaning.[114]

The court also did not accept the defendant's argument, reminiscent of the accused's defence in the *World Interactive Gaming* case, that when someone in the United States accessed the Italian Web site, it was essentially the same as that person getting on a plane and flying to Italy. Rather, the court found that merely uploading the material onto the Web site in contemplation of Internet users downloading the material in the United States constituted distribution of the material in the United States. Accordingly, the court concluded that sufficient contacts were made with the United States when would-be subscribers faxed completed application forms to Italy and were issued passwords in return. The court found the Italian publisher advertising and distributing material in the United States through this Internet site, and it was not important to the analysis whether the actual activity was charac-

---

113 *Chuckleberry*, above note 18.
114 *Ibid.*, at 1037.

terized as a subscriber pulling down the infringing material or the publisher sending it down to the subscriber. With respect to the resulting remedial order, the court required the Italian publisher to either shut down the Internet site or cease to accept new subscribers from the United States, indicate on the site that no new subscriptions will be offered to U.S. residents, invalidate existing U.S. users and refund them the remaining portions of their subscriptions, and pay damages to the U.S. plaintiff in respect of past sales to U.S. customers.

A final U.S. criminal case worth noting is *United States v. Thomas*.[115] In this case, the accused operated a subscription bulletin board system from a computer in California that permitted subscribers to download sexually explicit material. Instead of bringing an obscenity case in the San Francisco area where the accused lived and operated the system, law enforcement authorities deliberately brought it in Tennessee where a postal inspector had downloaded some materials from the service. The accused was convicted of transmitting obscenity and appealed on several grounds, including that the venue of Tennessee was improper. The appellate court dismissed the appeal, concluding that the prosecution can be brought where the material originates or where it is received. Indeed, the court felt that the community standard for obscenity in Memphis (which would be more conservative than in San Francisco) was preferred because it was the community affected by the distribution. Not surprisingly, the court denied the accused's argument that a cyberspace community standard for judging obscenity among like-minded users was more important than a physical place's standards.

b) Pre-*Zippo* Case Law

While the trend in criminal and regulatory matters has been to discern a real and substantial connection in virtually all cases sufficient to find in favour of jurisdiction, on the civil side the law has approached the fourth dynamic of computer law by exhibiting more complexity and nuance. Even before the *Zippo* case discussed below, in the United States two lines of authorities emerged. In one, courts refused to find access to a Web site or the creation of a Web site sufficient to bring the out-of-state person into the jurisdiction of the forum court. For example, in the *Pres-Kap* case, the court refused to take jurisdiction in Florida over a New York user of a Florida-based online information network service when the non-resident used the service simply to gain access to

---

115 74 F.3d 701 (6th Cir. 1996).

a database.[116] The relevant contract between the parties was negotiated and signed in New York, and the customer was serviced by the Florida company in New York; these findings make the court's conclusion more understandable, in light of the following cases. In another case, the Blue Note jazz club in Missouri established a Web site where it advertised.[117] Persons wishing to frequent this club, however, had to call to order tickets and had to pick them up at the club. The Web site contained a disclaimer that this club was not associated with the well-known New York jazz club of the same name. When the New York club brought a trade-mark infringement proceeding against its Missouri namesake, the court refused to find infringement, concluding that the Web site was intended to give information and was not the equivalent of advertising, promoting, or selling in New York City; a clubgoer could not order tickets over the Internet, but had to go to Missouri for them. The court also found it important that 99 percent of the patrons of the Missouri club were local residents; the club serviced the local university and the Web site took the place of putting posters up on the walls of university buildings. Similarly, the court in the *SunAmerica* case refused to find jurisdiction in a trade-mark case solely on the basis of the defendant's operation of a general access Web site, and concluded:

> Plaintiffs ask this court to hold that any defendant who advertises nationally or on the Internet is subject to its jurisdiction. It cannot plausibly be argued that any defendant who advertises nationally could expect to be haled into court in any state, for a cause of action that does not relate to the advertisements. Such general advertising is not the type of "purposeful activity related to the forum that would make the exercise of jurisdiction fair, just or reasonable."[118]

Similar decisions were given in the *Goldberger*[119] and *McDonough*[120] cases, with equivalent sentiments expressed by the respective courts,

---

116 *Pres-Kap, Inc.* v. *System One, Direct Access, Inc.*, 636 So.2d 1351 (Fla. App. 1994). For a similar holding, see *Cook* v. *Holzberger*, 3 Computer Cases (CCH) ¶46,736 at 64,613 (S.D. Ohio 1992).

117 *Bensusan Restaurant Corporation* v. *King*, 937 F.Supp. 295 (S.D.N.Y. 1996), aff'd 126 F.3d 25 (2nd Cir. 1997) [*Bensusan*]. For a similar decision involving the respective "Leopard Lounges" in Chicago and Atlanta, see *Donmar, Inc.* v. *Swanky Partners, Inc.*, 2002 WL 1917258 (N.D. Ill. 2002).

118 *IDS Life Insurance Co.* v. *SunAmerica, Inc.*, 958 F.Supp. 1258 at 1268 (N.D. Ill.1997), aff'd in part, vacated in part, 1998 WL 51350 (7th Cir.).

119 *Hearst Corporation* v. *Goldberger*, 1997 WL 97097 (S.D.N.Y.). In this case the court stated at para. 1: "Where, as here, defendant has not contracted to sell or actually sold any goods or services to New Yorkers, a finding of personal juris-

the sole activity in each case being the operation of a "passive" general access Web site. At issue in the McDonough case was the question of general jurisdiction, and U.S. courts to date have declined to find general Web site access sufficient for the purposes of finding general jurisdiction, even in those cases that find it sufficient for personal jurisdiction;[121] though in *McDonough* the court also found it did not have personal jurisdiction. The *Goldberger* decision, however, was based on only personal or specific jurisdiction, and the court in that case considered, but refused to follow, the *Inset* and *Maritz* decisions.[122]

In contrast to these cases, a second line of U.S. jurisdiction jurisprudence arose in civil matters where courts did take jurisdiction over non-resident defendants on the basis that their Internet-related activities progressed beyond low intensity interactivity or mere advertising. Thus, in *CompuServe, Incorporated* v. *Patterson*, the court held a Texas-based computer programmer subject to Ohio law given the nature of this person's dealings with CompuServe, the Ohio-based online service that had contracted to distribute and sell copies of the programmer's software.[123] The Texas-based individual had never visited Ohio during their dealings, yet Ohio jurisdiction was established given that an electronic contract was concluded (that was governed by Ohio law) and CompuServe was distributing the product from Ohio. Similarly, in other cases courts have taken jurisdiction on the basis of sales

---

diction in New York based on an Internet web site would mean that there would be nationwide (indeed, worldwide) personal jurisdiction over anyone and everyone who establishes an Internet Web site. Such nationwide jurisdiction is not consistent with traditional personal jurisdiction case law nor acceptable to the Court as a matter of policy." For a similar result, see *Cybersell, Inc.* v. *Cybersell, Inc.*, 44 U.S.P.Q.2d 1928 (9th Cir. 1997) [*Cybersell*]; and *Blackburn* v. *Walker Oriental Rug Galleries*, No. 97-5704 (E.D. Pa., 7 April 1998), reported in *Computer & Online Industry Litigation Reporter*, 21 April 1998 at 4.

120 *McDonough* v. *Fallon McElligott Inc.*, 40 U.S.P.Q. 2d 1826 (S.D. Cal. 1996). In this case the court stated at 1828: "Because the Web enables easy world-wide access, allowing computer interaction via the Web to supply sufficient contacts to establish jurisdiction would eviscerate the personal jurisdiction requirement as it currently exists; the Court is not willing to take this step. Thus, the fact that Fallon has a Web site used by Californians cannot establish jurisdiction by itself."

121 See, for example, *Panavision International, L.P.* v. *Toeppen*, 938 F.Supp. 616 (C.D. Cal. 1996) [*Panavision*], where general jurisdiction was declined, but personal jurisdiction was found in an Internet-related trade-mark/domain name dispute.

122 See below note 128.

123 89 F.3d 1257 (6th Cir. 1996).

made to customers through the defendant's Web site,[124] or based on soliciting donations,[125] or based on subscribers signed up by the defendant for services delivered over the Internet,[126] or for having follow-on contacts, negotiations, and other dealings in addition to, and often as a result of, the initial Internet-based communication.[127] The common sentiment expressed by courts in these cases is that parties who avail themselves of technology in order to do business in a distant place should not then be able to escape that place's legal jurisdiction. These cases run the gamut from contract breach claims to tort, including trade libel; in several cases, courts have even found jurisdiction in trade-mark infringement matters merely on the basis of a defendant's general access Web site,[128] or linking to a national ATM network

---

124 *Digital Equipment Corporation v. AltaVista Technology, Inc.*, 960 F.Supp. 456 (D. Mass. 1997). See also *Cody v. Ward*, 954 F.Supp. 43 (D. Conn. 1997), where a court took jurisdiction based on telephone and e-mail communications that consummated a business relationship begun over *Prodigy's* "Money Talk" discussion forum for financial matters. In partially justifying this decision, the court noted that the use of fax technology, and even live telephone conferences, can greatly reduce the burden of litigating out-of-state.

125 *Heroes, Inc. v. Heroes Foundation*, 958 F.Supp. 1 (D.D.C. 1996).

126 *Zippo Manufacturing Company v. Zippo Dot Com, Inc.*, 952 F Supp. 1119 (W.D. Pa. 1997) [*Zippo*].

127 *Resuscitation Technologies, Inc. v. Continental Health Care Corp.*, 1997 WL 148567 (S.D. Ind.). The court in this case was not concerned that the defendants had never visited the forum state in person and concluded at para. 5: "Neither is the matter disposed of by the fact that no defendant ever set foot in Indiana. The 'footfalls' were not physical, they were electronic. They were, nonetheless, footfalls. The level of Internet activity in this case was significant." See also *EDIAS Software International, L.L.C. v. BASIS International Ltd.*, 947 F.Supp. 413 (D. Ariz. 1996). In this case the court summed up the essence of many of the Internet jurisdiction cases by stating at 420: "BASIS [the defendant] should not be permitted to take advantage of modern technology through an Internet Web page and forum and simultaneously escape traditional notions of jurisdiction." See also *Gary Scott International, Inc. v. Baroudi*, 981 F.Supp. 714 (D. Mass. 1997).

128 *Panavision*, above note 121; *Maritz, Inc. v. CyberGold, Inc.*, 947 F.Supp. 1328 (E.D. Mo. 1996) [*Maritz*]; *Inset Systems, Inc. v. Instruction Set, Inc.*, 937 F.Supp. 161 (D. Conn. 1996) [*Inset*]. In the latter case the court observed at 165: "In the present case, Instruction has directed its advertising activities via the Internet and its toll-free number toward not only the state of Connecticut, but to all states. The Internet as well as toll-free numbers are designed to communicate with people and their businesses in every state. Advertisement on the Internet can reach as many as 10,000 Internet users within Connecticut alone. Further, once posted on the Internet, unlike television and radio advertising, the advertisement is available continuously to any Internet user. ISI has therefore, purposefully availed itself of the privilege of doing business within Connecticut."

through a telephone line indirectly through an independent data processor in a third state.[129]

c) *Zippo* and Beyond

In the *Zippo* case, the court articulated a sliding scale test for determining the degree of interactivity necessary for a determination of jurisdiction. At one end of the continuum, offered the court, was the passive Web site that simply posts information that, by virtue of the nature of the Internet, is available to all users in all jurisdictions; such a site, concluded the court, without more should not lead to a finding of jurisdiction. By contrast, where the operator of the Web site does business over the Internet, by entering into contracts that involve, among other things, the knowing and repeated transmission of files over the Internet to and from the site, that should lead to a finding of jurisdiction. And in the middle would be the difficult, fact-dependent analyses where the court would have to determine with precision the exact nature and quality of interactivity and the commercial nature of the exchange of information. Thus can be articulated the sliding scale test for jurisdiction formulated in *Zippo*, which has been followed in numerous cases in the late 1990s and early in the new millennium, including in an important Canadian case, *Braintech, Inc. v. Kostiuk*.[130] This decision of the B.C. Court of Appeal applied *Zippo* and the general Canadian principles enumerated in various pre-Internet cases, and held that the mere posting of libellous material on a Web site was insufficient for a finding of jurisdiction in the absence of proof that someone in the relevant jurisdiction actually accessed the material.

As Web site technology and design evolved to the point where, currently, most commercial sites include some amount of interactivity (illustrating the inevitable confluence of the first and fourth dynamics of computer law), some courts and commentators[131] took the view that the *Zippo* analysis would lead inexorably to a finding of jurisdiction in the case of most Web sites, and that this would be too far reaching a result. Thus, various courts have articulated different, more difficult tests for Web sites and Internet activity in order to find jurisdiction,

---

129 *Plus System, Inc. v. New England Network, Inc.*, 804 F.Supp. 111 (D. Colo. 1992). In the United States, yet a third test for jurisdiction is taking shape, that focuses not on the degree of interactivity of the Web site, but on the "effect" it has on the actor in the other jurisdiction: *Millennium Enterprises, Inc. v. Millennium Music L.P.*, 33 F.Supp. 2d 907 (D. Or. 1999).

130 (1999), 171 D.L.R. (4th) 46 (B.C.C.A.).

131 See, for example, the criticism of *Zippo*, above note 126, in Michael Geist, *Internet Law in Canada*, 2d ed. (North York, ON: Captus Press, 2001), at 64–78.

including "something more" than interactivity,[132] the "effects" test,[133] "purposeful availment,"[134] "targeting,"[135] and "deliberate action."[136] To some degree or other all these articulations drive off the core concept that jurisdiction should only be exercised in those circumstances where the Web site operator expressly aimed its activity at the forum state.

Keeping in mind these various tests for finding jurisdiction in the Internet context, it is worth noting that in the following circumstances (and cases), courts refused to take jurisdiction where there was no online ordering of products;[137] there was a sale through eBay;[138] there was merely registration of a domain name;[139] there was merely use of a

---

132 *Panavision International, L.P.* v. *Toeppan*, 141 F.3d 1316 (9th Cir. 1998); and *Cybersell*, above note 119.

133 See *Calder* v. *Jones*, 465 U.S. 783 (1984), for the original articulation of the "effects test"; to witness its application in an online situation, see *Nissan Motor Co. Ltd.* v. *Nissan Computer Corporation*, 89 F.Supp. 2d 1154 (C.D. Cal. 2000).

134 *People Solutions, Inc.* v. *People Solutions, Inc.*, 2000 WL 1030619 (N.D. Tex. 2000).

135 *American Information Corporation* v. *American Infometrics, Inc.*, 139 F.Supp. 2d 696 (D. Md. 2001).

136 *Millennium Enterprises, Inc.* v. *Millennium Music L.P.*, 33 F.Supp. 2d 907 (D. Or. 1999).

137 *Ty Inc.* v. *Clark*, 2000 WL 51816 (N.D. Ill. 2000). In this case the consumer had to print out an order form, and fax it or mail it to the merchant. Interestingly, in *S. Morantz, Inc.* v. *Hang & Shine Ultrasonics, Inc.*, 79 F.Supp. 2d 537 (E.D. Pa. 1999), a handful of sales were not even sufficient when the site was fairly passive. In *Barret* v. *Catacombs Press*, 44 F.Supp. 2d 717 (E.D. Pa. 1999), several e-mails were considered insufficient connectivity to establish jurisdiction. Interestingly, this case also held that for jurisdictional purposes, postings to list-serves and USENETs should be treated as similar to a passive Web site because they were not targeted at a particular place; that is, once such a posting is submitted, the sender cannot determine in which regions it is or is not available.

138 In *Winfield Collection Ltd.* v. *McCauley*, 105 F.Supp. 2d 746 (E.D. Mich. 2000), the court recognized that by first principles, a seller using eBay cannot choose his or her preferred bidder, as it goes to the highest bidder, and therefore there was no purposeful availment. Similarly, in *Machulsky* v. *Hall*, 210 F.Supp. 2d 531 (D.N.J. 2002), negative comments on eBay about a seller in New Jersey were insufficient to cause a New Jersey court to take jurisdiction, as the comments were not targeted at New Jersey, but rather were posted to a "global audience."

139 *America Online, Inc.* v. *Huang*, 2000 WL 991587 (E.D. Va. 2000). Similarly, in *Nexgen Solutions Inc.* v. *Nexgen Solutions Corp.*, No. AW-02-736 (D. Md. 2002), the court held that use by the defendant in its domain solution of a registered trade-mark of the plaintiff was not capable of supporting a finding of jurisdiction where the defendant's Web site was relatively passive: it allowed users to enter contact information and send feedback e-mails. For a similar result involving a Canadian defendant who had registered in its dot-com domain name its own Canadian registered trade-mark, but also the U.S. registered trade-mark of the U.S.-based plain-

trade-mark;[140] the defamatory materials were on a passive Web site;[141] and where the Web site was merely passive.[142] By contrast, courts in the

---

tiff, see *Desktop Technologies, Inc.* v. *Colorworks Reproduction & Design, Inc.*, 1999 WL 98572 (E.D. Pa. 1999), where the court concluded, at 6: "Defendant's Internet presence and e-mail link are its only contacts with Pennsylvania. As established earlier, Defendant maintains the web site to advertise and post information about its services and employment opportunities. The web site does not exist for the purpose of entering into contracts with customers outside of Canada or for the purpose of attracting customers from Pennsylvania. Instead, its web site specifically states that it is servicing clients in British Columbia, Alberta, and Yukon. Defendant has never entered into any contracts in Pennsylvania, made sales or earned income in Pennsylvania, or sent messages over the Internet to users in Pennsylvania. While visitors to the web site are able to exchange information over the web site via Internet FTP and e-mail, receiving a file through Internet FTP or an e-mail does not constitute placing an order. Thus, while Defendant is exchanging information over the Internet, it is not doing business over the Internet with residents of Pennsylvania. Accordingly, this Court finds that Defendant's registration of 'ColorWorks' as a domain name and posting a web site on the Internet are insufficient to subject Defendant to specific personal jurisdiction in Pennsylvania." This case will be of particular interest to Canadians who operate a Web site but wish, and take appropriate measures, to reach customers only in Canada.

140 In *Citigroup* v. *City Holding*, 97 F.Supp. 2d 549 (S.D.N.Y. 2000) the court reasoned that the tort of trade-mark infringement occurs where the Web site is created and operated; otherwise, a "where viewed" approach would result in jurisdiction everywhere in the world; at the same time, however, the court also concluded that use of marks in an online chat transmission would constitute infringement. See also *Accuweather Inc.* v. *Total Weather Inc.*, 223 F.Supp. 2d 612 (M.D. Pa. 2002).

141 *Lofton* v. *Turbine Design, Inc.*, 100 F.Supp. 2d 404 (N.D. Miss. 2000); and in *Bailey* v. *Turbine Design, Inc.*, 86 F.Supp. 2d 790 (W.D. Tenn. 2000), the court applied the "effects doctrine," concluding that there would be no finding of jurisdiction unless the plaintiff's state was deliberately targeted. But see *Dow Jones & Company Inc.* v. *Gutnick*, [2002] HCA 56 (H.C.A.) [*Gutnick*], where the court held that a claimant residing in Australia could bring a defamation action in Australia against an American company that had the offending material on its Web site that was hosted on a computer server in the United States (but accessible worldwide); this important case is discussed further below.

142 In *Mid City Bowling Lanes* v. *Sports Palace, Inc.* v. *Ivercrest, Inc.*, 35 F.Supp. 2d 507 (E.D. La. 1999), aff'd 208 F.3d 1006 (5th Cir. 2000), in a finding reminiscent of *Bensusan*, above note 117, the court held that it was unlikely patrons would travel from Louisiana to Chicago to bowl after viewing the Chicago bowling alley's Web site. See also *Perry* v. *Righton.com*, 90 F.Supp. 2d 1138 (D. Or. 2000), where the court found that no activities were targeted at persons in the plaintiff's state; and *Miller* v. *Asensio*, 101 F.Supp. 2d 395 (D.S.C. 2000), where the court held that merely posting a fraudulent report on a Web site in New York was not deemed to cause a transaction or act in South Carolina for purposes of the *Securities Exchange Act*, even if it was read in South Carolina.

U.S. have taken jurisdiction in circumstances where there have been a large number of visitors to the site from the state,[143] online hacking;[144] solicitation of membership;[145] the conduct of contracting activities;[146] the making of offers to sell domain names by e-mail;[147] and online order taking.[148]

---

143 *National Football League* v. *Miller d/b/a NFL Today,* 2000 WL 335566 (S.D.N.Y. 2000).

144 *Peridyne Technology Solutions, LLC* v. *Matheson Fast Freight, Inc.,* 117 F.Supp. 2d 1366 (N.D. Ga. 2000).

145 In *Online Partners.com Inc.* v. *Atlantic Media Corp.,* 2000 Dist. Lexis 783 (N.D. Cal. 2000) the Web site actively solicited membership by having people fill out forms and provide payment by credit card.

146 In *Peyman* v. *Johns Hopkins University,* 2000 U.S. Dist. Lexis 9987 (E.D. La. 2000), the university's office of technology licensing Web site included interactive pages, where it solicited and concluded patent licence agreements. In finding jurisdiction, the court noted that the "nationalization of commerce" no longer made it inconvenient to conduct litigation from another state.

147 In *Nutrisystem.com, Inc.* v. *Easthaven, Ltd.,* 58 U.S. P.Q. (2d) 1160 (E.D. Pa. 2000) and *Cello Holdings, LLC* v. *Lawrence-Dahl Companies,* 89 F.Supp. 2d 464 (S.D.N.Y. 2000), there were e-mail offers and follow-up telephone calls. See also *McRae's Inc.* v. *Hussain,* 105 F.Supp. 2d 594 (S.D. Miss. 2000).

148 In *Carrot Bunch Co. Inc.* v. *Computer Friends, Inc.,* 218 F.Supp. 2d 820 (N.D. Texas 2002), jurisdiction was found where a user could buy products online by browsing interactively, completing an online order form, and receiving an e-mail confirming purchases; there was also evidence of the defendant having made actual sales through this process to residents in the forum state. In *Ty, Inc.* v. *Sullivan,* 2002 WL 500663 (N.D. Ill. 2002), the selling of Beanie Babies over a Web site that took orders and effected payment online invoked jurisdiction; again, there was evidence of actual online sales to residents in the forum state. In *Euromarket Designs, Inc.* v. *Crate & Barrell Limited,* 96 F.Supp. 2d 284 (N.D. Ill. 2000), consumers in Illinois visited a virtual store operated by an Irish Web site. In *American Eyewear, Inc.* v. *Peeper's Sunglasses and Accessories, Inc.,* 106 F.Supp. 2d 895 (N.D. Tex. 2000), users submitted orders containing credit card information. The Web site in *Student Advantage, Inc.* v. *International Student Exchange Cards, Inc.,* 2000 U.S. Dist. Lexis 13138 (S.D.N.Y. 2000) allowed users to buy products by providing payment and shipping instructions. In *Hsin Ten Enterprises United States* v. *Clark Enterprises,* 2000 U.S. Dist. Lexis 18717 (S.D.N.Y. 2000) users could purchase, and ask questions, online. In *Citigroup Inc.* v. *City Holding Co.,* 97 F.Supp. 2d 549 (S.D.N.Y. 2000), although there was no finding of jurisdiction based on trade-mark principles (see above note 140), jurisdiction was found on the basis of online loan applications, e-mail exchanges with online representatives, and online chats. In *Sports Authority Michigan Inc.* v. *Justballs, Inc.,* 97 F.Supp. 2d 806 (E.D. Mich. 2000), the Web site enabled purchases of products online through a virtual store, and use of a virtual shopping cart and check-out counter.

Australia's highest court has also delivered a very important decision dealing with Internet-based jurisdiction.[149] In this case Dow Jones argued that in Internet libel cases the appropriate law should be that of the jurisdiction where the server is located, except where it is clear the server has been housed in a country of convenience (such as a "libel haven"). Dow Jones urged the court to view the Internet as a revolutionary new medium where it simply could not control dissemination of material, as broadcasters, for example, can do by limiting the strength of their signals. This approach, Dow Jones argued, would bring certainty to Internet jurisdiction issues, at least so far as libel is concerned. These arguments were all rebutted by the court. As for the argument that a publisher could not realistically screen all 190 countries for their libel laws on any given publication, the court noted that generally it merely had to determine where the subject of the story lived, and enquire as to that country; an elegant, yet simple response to the good question.[150] The court also mentioned that given that most

149 *Gutnick*, above note 141. For a similar decision within the U.S. see *Northwest Healthcare Alliance Inc. v. Healthgrades.com Inc.*, 50 Fed. Appx. 339 (9th Cir. 2002), where jurisdiction in Washington State was found in respect of a Web site operated in Colorado, because the site rated health care facilities in (among other places) Washington State; thus the operator knew that these ratings would be of particular interest to residents of Washington State, thereby producing the bulk of the harm of any defamation in that state. Thus, the court concluded, at 341: "Specifically, we find that defendant Healthgrades.com has purposefully interjected itself into the Washington state home health care market through its intentional act of offering ratings of Washington medical service providers. This act was expressly aimed at plaintiff's forum state, since defendant was well aware that its ratings of Washington home health care providers would be of value primarily to Washington consumers. Though defendant gleaned its information from various public sources, including the federal government, the information was obtained originally from Washington sources, and the allegedly defamatory rating received by plaintiff on defendant's web site concerned the Washington activities of a Washington resident. Finally, the brunt of the harm allegedly suffered by plaintiff occurred in Washington — where plaintiff is incorporated, where plaintiff has its principal place of business, and where plaintiff's reputation is likely to suffer if in fact it has been injured by defendant's actions. The effects, therefore, of defendant's out-of-state conduct were felt in Washington, plaintiff's claims arise from that out-of-state conduct, and defendant could reasonably expect to be called to account for its conduct in the forum where it understood the effects of its actions would be felt." For a similar result in a preliminary procedural decision in Ontario, see *Kitakufe v. Oloya*, [1998] O.J. No. 2537 (Gen. Div.).

150 In a similar, pre-Internet vein, the U.S. Supreme Court held, in *Calder v. Jones*, 465 U.S. 783 (1984) [*Calder*], that the *National Enquirer*, which was published outside of California, could be sued by a well-known Hollywood actress in California as she lived and worked in California, and the *National Enquirer* knew

publishers will only have substantial assets in one jurisdiction, the practical reality of enforcing foreign judgments may lead claimants to bring claims in the publisher's home jurisdiction in any event. In this regard, see the discussion of the *Bachchan* case at note 151 below.

d) Enforcement

The foregoing American cases do not, of course, answer all the questions posed by Internet jurisdiction issues. There is, for example, also the enforcement issue. In the civil context, a decision like *Bachchan* v. *India Abroad Publications Incorporated* should be noted.[151] In this case the plaintiff, a national of India, brought a libel claim in the United Kingdom against a New York publisher because England's libel laws were more plaintiff-friendly than those in the United States. The plaintiff was successful in England, but when it came time to execute on his judgment in New York (the defendant had no assets in the United Kingdom), the New York court declined to enforce the judgment in New York on the basis that the lack of a U.S. First Amendment free speech law in the United Kingdom made it contrary to public policy to enforce the judgment in the United States. Also with respect to enforcement, it can reasonably be asked how a court would take effective steps to enforce a judgment against a foreign Web site operator. How would, for example, the court in the *Chuckleberry* case enforce its order against the Italian Web site operator if the latter refused to comply with it? Does it commence extradition proceedings against the principals behind it? Can it require Internet service providers to block their subscribers from accessing the site?

These questions were at issue in the case brought against Yahoo! U.S. in France arising out of the display of Nazi symbols on the Yahoo! U.S. site, contrary to French law (no action was brought against Yahoo! France as it was compliant with this French law). The French court ordered Yahoo! U.S. to re-engineer its servers in the U.S. to permit them

---

that the bulk of the injury to her reputation would occur among her acquaintances in California. Similarly, in *Hustler* v. *Keeton*, 465 U.S. 770 (1984), the U.S. Supreme Court permitted a defamation action be brought in New Hampshire against an out-of-state publisher solely on the strength of its mailing the magazine to subscribers in that state. Although Dow Jones did not "mail" material to its online subscribers in the same, physical manner, presumably it knew that a subscriber from Australia would download material from its service. But see *Revell* v. *G.W. Lidov*, 317 F.3d 467 (5th Cir. 2002), and the other Internet defamation cases mentioned therein, where jurisdiction was not found due to a lack of "targetting," in contrast to the facts in the *Calder* case.

151 585 N.Y.S.2d 661 (Sup. 1992) [*Bachchan*].

to recognize French Internet protocol (IP) addresses, and to block access to the illegal material to such IP addresses.[152] The court also ordered these measures to be implemented in three months; failure would result in a daily fine of 100,000 francs. Interestingly, the court also ordered that such a fine could not be collected from Yahoo! France (the affiliate of the defendant), but rather was exigeable only against Yahoo! U.S. This meant that the plaintiffs who brought the case in France would have to enforce their French judgment in the United States. This prompted Yahoo! U.S. to seek a pre-emptive, declaratory judgment in California, where the court refused to enforce the French court's ruling as it would be inconsistent with the First Amendment freedom of speech protections of the U.S. Constitution.[153] The fourth dynamic of computer law produced a classic standoff along the Internet frontier.

Some regulators are taking a more practical approach to their regulatory purview. For example, Quebec's *Charter of the French Language* applies generally to all commercial advertising, regardless of the medium used to convey the advertising.[154] Accordingly, the Office de la langue française, the agency that enforces this law, has stipulated that advertising posted on a Web site must be in French.[155] Nonetheless, the Office has stated that it will apply this rule only in respect of companies physically located in Quebec for their products or services made available in Quebec; thus, it will not bother companies located outside of Quebec, even though their Web sites are accessible to residents of Quebec. The office has prosecuted companies located within Quebec, however, for maintaining English-only Web sites.[156]

---

152 *La Ligue Contre Le Racisme et l'Antisemitisme* v. *Yahoo! Inc.*, No. RG: 00/05308 (County Court of Paris, 20 November 2000).

153 *Yahoo! Inc.* v. *La Ligue Contre Le Racisme et l'Antisemitisme*, 169 F.Supp. 2d 1181 (N.D. Cal. 2001).

154 *Charter of Human Rights and Freedoms*, R.S.Q., c. C-12. Title I, ch. VII, s. 52. The same law requires software to be made available in Quebec at the same time the English version is made available if in fact a French language equivalent is in existence; that is, a software supplier does not have to produce a French version, but if it has one it must make it available simultaneously with the English one.

155 The office's Web site is at <olf.gouv.qc.ca>.

156 In *R. c. Frances Muriel Waldie-Reid*, [2002] J.Q. No. 1167, the court found that the requirement, in section 52 of the *Charter of the French Language*, R.S.Q., e. C-11, that "catalogues, brochures, folders, commercial directories and any similar publications must be drawn up in French" applied equally to commercial advertising on an Internet site operated by an entity physically doing business at a location in Quebec. In *R. c. Hyperinfo Canada Inc.*, [2001] J.Q. No. 7210, 19 C.P.R. (4th) 386 (C.Q.) [*Hyperinfo*] a similar conclusion was arrived at, and the court did not accept as a defence that the Quebec-based Web site operator posted a written notice on his site that it was intended for non-Quebec residents only.

e)   Disclaimers and Express Governing Law

Based on the cases to date, operators of Web sites would be well advised to consider the following measures if they wish to decrease the likelihood of their being haled into a particular jurisdiction's court. Through express contracts with subscribers, Web site operators should try to choose a governing law for the relationship, together with the forum in which any disputes would be settled.[157] Written disclaimers should also be used if the Web site operator wishes to control with whom it does business. So, if a Web site operator puts a promotional contest online that is accessible by residents in all provinces, and the operator does not find it cost effective to comply with the contest rules of one or another province (or of the United States or other jurisdictions), then the site should clearly state that the contest is open only to persons from a particular province(s).[158] The Web site operator should employ technology and business procedures to ensure that contestants for the contest, or subscribers for other purposes, do not come from prohibited jurisdictions. In a similar vein, the following is a guideline from Canada's Competition Bureau as to the steps a company outside of Canada should take to ensure that its foreign representations do not put the company offside the Canadian misleading advertising rules:

(g) Clearly indicating for whom the representations are intended or, alternatively, indicating those for whom the representations are not intended;

(h) Requiring visitors to supply their country of origin, and then linking them to a web site intended for their use;

---

157 As discussed in chapter 6, section A.3(c), "Express and Implied Click-Consent Agreements," these agreements, for the most part, are being enforced by courts in Canada and the United States. For example, choice of law and forum clauses were upheld in *Rudder v. Microsoft Corporation* (1999), 2 C.P.R. (4th) 474 (Ont. Sup. Ct.) and *Caspi v. The Microsoft Network*, 732 A.2d 528 (N.J. Super. Appellate 1999).

158 The previous discussion of jurisdiction has focused on Canada and its largest trading partner, the United States. The Internet, of course, is supremely global, and so Canadians must also consider the ramifications of their Web and other Internet activities in the context of non-North American jurisdictions. For example, an American university learned this lesson recently when it was hauled into a Paris courtroom because its website (accessible around the world, including in France), which offered information about the university's courses conducted in France, was not in the French language, thereby violating a French law that information offering goods and services in France must be in French: see Wendy R. Leibowitz, "National Laws Entangle the Net: It's a Small, Small, Litigious Web" (30 June 1997) *The National Law Journal,* also available at <www.ljx.com/internet/0630natlaw.html>.

(i) Using screening technologies to ensure that only consumers from the countries that the advertiser is trying to reach have access to the web site;

(j) Only entering into contracts with consumers in countries that the advertiser is trying to reach where their country of origin can be identified by such factors as delivery address, credit card holder address information, etc.; and

(k) Ensuring that the representations are not directed at Canadians. For example, pictorial representations such as a Canadian flag, maple leaf or a map of Canada would likely create the general impression that the site is intended for the Canadian public. Similarly, displaying a Canadian address or telephone number for contact information, or indicating that Canadian laws will govern in the event of a dispute, will increase the likelihood that a site will be treated as having been directed at Canadian consumers. E-mail sent to Canadians will also likely be treated as having been directed at Canadian consumers.[159]

It will be interesting to see how these targeting mechanisms, if applied in a *bona fide* manner, stand up to judicial scrutiny in future cases. Based on the *Granite Gate, Chuckleberry*, and *Bensusan* cases (in the first case the attorney general of Minnesota asked that the Web site clearly state that its services were void in Minnesota; in the second case the Italian Web site was permitted to operate so long as it precluded access by Americans; and in the third case the Columbia, Missouri, defendant's Web site stated it was for Columbia residents only), such measures to "localize" the reach of a particular Web site should be met with a positive judicial reception; but note that in the *Hyperinfo* case, a Web site operator was not able to "contract out" of a "public order" law by means of a written disclaimer. Nonetheless, given the fourth dynamic of computer law — namely, the blurring of national and international — people who use the Internet to do business in foreign countries should be prepared to become subject to the laws of those countries, and therefore should review related issues pertaining to tax, insurance, legal compliance, trade-marks, misleading advertising, etc., just as if they were establishing offices in the foreign jurisdictions. The huge benefits of the Internet must be cultivated prudently.

---

159 Competition Bureau, *Staying 'On-Side' When Advertising On-line: A Guide to Compliance with the Competition Act When Advertising on the Internet*, May 2001, available at <www.strategis.ic.gc.ca/ct02186e.html>.

CHAPTER 8

COMPUTER LAW: DYNAMICS, THEMES, AND SKILL SETS

This book presents a wide-ranging analysis of intellectual property law, criminal law, regulatory legal regimes, commercial law, and electronic commerce and Internet legal issues in terms of four principal dynamics. First, there is the impact on the law of rapid technological change and the law's response to this. A second dynamic is the elusive nature of information, particularly in its digital form, and how the law is coping with the challenges posed by this. A third dynamic is the increasing fusion of the public and private spheres in many computer law matters. Finally, there is a blurring in computer law of the dividing line that has traditionally separated that which is national and that which is international. Each of these dynamics presents computer law and its practitioners with several fundamental challenges.

In meeting these challenges, the legal system can consider four themes, the elements of which weave through this book. First, there is the need for consistency in computer laws. Then one needs to understand something about regulatory control points and the law. A third theme recurs around the liability of intermediaries; and finally, the law must consider the dangers of mischievous metaphors. Armed with an appreciation of the aforementioned dynamics and themes, the legal practitioner can approach virtually any present or future legal problem by employing one or more skill sets: the common law, by which reliance is placed on judge-made interpretations of the current law; contract, by which persons, companies, and organizations craft their own rules, particularly in the absence of meaningful judicial precedent (or in the face of conflicting jurisprudence); technology, which involves using technical measures to overcome perceived weaknesses in the law; and law reform, which entails changes in statute-based law (or the adoption of new statutes) to solve a problem in the previous state of statute or judge-made law and, in certain cases, to reduce the need for contractual and technological solutions.

A. COMPUTER LAW: DYNAMICS

1) The Rapid Pace of Technological Change

The first and most important dynamic in the computer law field is the relentless pace of technological change. As discussed in chapter 1, the computer industry rides a roller coaster that appears — and in fact is — out of control. No other industry produces new products and services at such a dizzying pace. Each new product that is launched engenders other products, some competitive, some complementary. There are also continual developments in the formats, methodologies, and technologies for delivering traditional content — such as music, images, and text. Relatively recent developments include multimedia products on CD-ROM, and most recently, of course, there is the use of the Internet for commercial purposes. And wireless delivery capabilities now make information, software, and content available to everyone, everywhere, at all times. In a word, developments in the computer field are breathtaking, especially when considered in light of the fact that the microchip is only thirty years old. It is an exhilarating time for this industry. While the cadence of technological change has perhaps never been as peripatetic as it is today, the phenomenon of one technology-driven device leapfrogging the other to produce a competitive and dynamic environment is not new. The thrust and parry between the telegraph and the telephone created an analogous situation, and later devices such as the radio, teletype, telex, television, cable transmission, and other technologies all added to the mix, each leaving new legal challenges in its wake. With the microchip and the computer revolution, coupled with the latest networks (including the Internet), however, this process has been accelerated, with enormous implications for the law.

The dynamic of rapid technological change is evident in the area of intellectual property law, as articulated in chapter 2. Developers of new technologies and information-based products are constantly agitating for intellectual property protection for the fruits of their labour. The

Copyright Act, for example, has been amended on numerous occasions to recognize new works resulting from new technologies. In 1988, computer programs were included as protected literary works. Today, defining the contours of protection for software under copyright and patent, determining the scope of protection for electronic databases, and wrestling with the impact of the Internet (courtesy of online technologies that have resulted in file sharing, framing, and linking) are difficult technologically induced challenges to intellectual property laws. The problems are not entirely new (though the challenges posed by the technologies underpinning Napster and iCraveTV[1] do present a number of unique legal nuances), but the current breakneck pace with which the issues are arising is unprecedented.

Chapter 3 of this book makes clear that technological changes have also been a constant driver of the amendments over the years to the *Criminal Code*. Courts in Canada have been reluctant to interpret the provisions in the *Criminal Code* in a technologically expansive manner, thereby resulting in numerous acquittals when the law was challenged by the rapid pace of technological change. Indeed, it seems that the *Criminal Code* has been one or two technologies behind the latest mischief-causing development. The *Criminal Code* was brought somewhat up to date in the mid-1980s with the addition of the computer abuse and data abuse provisions. Nevertheless, the first dynamic of computer law continues to present a fundamental challenge to the criminal law, as illustrated by recent developments in the electronic dissemination of child pornography.

As discussed in chapter 4, in the regulatory arena, the law and policy surrounding data protection and the privacy of personal information is being affected by the first dynamic of computer law. Given the development of technologies that collect huge volumes of data (such as point-of-sale systems in retail stores and most B2C Web sites), and gargantuan databases that aggregate, sort, and profile the data and then transmit them instantaneously to the four corners of the globe, how should the data protection laws covering the government sectors be extended to the private sector, as has already been done in Quebec and is being done under the federal private sector privacy law? It remains to be seen, for example, if this can be done in a manner that produces consistent regimes across the country, assuming the common law provinces follow the lead of Quebec and the federal government. There is also the possibility that these new laws will harness technological

---

1   These cases are discussed in chapter 2, section C.6, "Copyright and the Internet."

progress to assist in the preservation of privacy; that is, in addition to presenting the law with questions, the first dynamic of computer law may also hold within itself certain solutions.

The need to keep pace with technology is particularly telling in the area of export control. There is, of course, the requirement to stay current with new technological developments so as to know when to add a new item to the Export Control List. Just as important, however, is to be able to remove an item from the ECL promptly after it is widely available on the world market. Not doing so will adversely affect Canadians who, because of anachronistic export controls, will be disadvantaged in pursuing sales or other commercial opportunities abroad. In effect, there is a danger in underregulating when some new technology appears that provides Canada and its allies with some strategic military benefits. On the other hand, with the rapid pace of technology diffusion around the world even without a breach of export control rules, the ECL should be pruned regularly.

The CRTC also faces fundamental regulatory challenges from the onslaught of technology. Of course the CRTC, and its predecessors, have been confronted with new technologies and services before, such as the introduction of cable distribution in the 1960s. On the telecommunications front, since the early 1980s the CRTC's work has become more complicated as technological advances permitted telephone sets and other terminal equipment supplied by businesses other than the phone company to be connected to the main telephone network. Regulatory complexity increased as the technical means developed to permit competition in long distance telephone services. Similarly, a complex regulatory environment arises when competition in local telephone service appears, again a regulatory option made possible by new technologies. From a regulatory perspective, however, all these technologically driven new developments have been manageable because they all involve relatively substantial companies, each with a physical presence in Canada, and therefore the CRTC can effectively assert jurisdiction over them pursuant to the *Telecommunications Act* and the *Broadcasting Act*. In contrast, several newer technologies do not fit comfortably within the traditional regulatory models, and they will prove to be far more difficult to regulate. Direct to home satellite transmissions from foreign-service providers is one such technology. Already an estimated 250,000 Canadian homes have satellite dishes that receive these unauthorized signals. Similarly, an Internet with broadband capacity allows computer users in Canada to access literally thousands of sites around the world in order to obtain a wide variety of programming. Indeed, the Internet poses squarely the question whether there are certain technologies that the CRTC should simply not even attempt to regulate. The recent *Bell ExpressVu*[2] and *New Media*[3] decisions address these issues, but likely they will not be the last words on these subjects.

New technologies that have given us spam, Web-crawling capabilities and advertising systems such as pop-up ads and page-jacking (where a consumer is not let out of a labyrinth of interconnected Web pages), are taxing the ingenuity of government agencies charged with protecting consumers. And the relentless, driving cadence of change does not help: just as the agency gets its head around one new technology, it is confronted by yet another. Riding the Internet tiger is not for the faint of heart.

As discussed in chapter 5, the relentless march of technology is keenly felt in the commercial law area. New technology-oriented products and technology-based distribution structures for old and new products and services often have implications, both positive and negative, under the *Competition Act*. Technology also drives the evolution of the various licensing models used in the computer industry and with information-based products. Successive new technologies produce the familiar dilemma whether the licence grant language for a particular deal includes the subsequent new medium on which the product is now available (for example, does the book publishing agreement give to the publisher the e-book rights to the work, or just the traditional paper-based rights?). Rapid technological developments also raise a host of negligence questions, including the perennial conundrum of when it is negligent not to adopt new technology. It is also a challenge to determine appropriate standards of care for the creation and use of new technology-based products, such as software, precisely because they are new and ever-changing.

Developments in technology can also wreak havoc on established tax rules, particularly where the rule is intended to cover a specific activity; then a new technology appears that reflects the previous activity but in a new manner. In the context of electronic commerce/Internet issues, the analysis in chapter 6 makes it clear that new technologies are also constantly challenging the core principles of contract and evidence law. Much of the law of contract contemplates a

---

2   The *Bell ExpressVu* case is discussed in chapter 2, section C.8, "Other Measures of Protection."

3   The *New Media* decision is discussed in chapter 4, section D.3(c), "The *New Media* Decision."

paper-based written agreement, signed by the parties simultaneously in a face-to-face setting. Since the advent of the telegraph, however, more and more contracts have been effected at a distance using means other than paper. Thus, each new technological trend, from the telegraph to the Internet (including ubiquitous e-mail), has prompted the law of contract to reassess when and where offer and acceptance occurred and the time and place of the contract. Computers and related technologies, such as imaging, optical disks, and even direct output from computer to microfilm, have also raised questions as to the admissibility of evidence that is collected, stored, or altered by a computer. Thankfully, as noted in section C.1, "Common Law," courts have consistently risen to meet these challenges in the contract and evidence law arenas, thereby facilitating the use of electronic means to communicate and store business data. In the libel area, a completely new cluster of legal issues in the law of defamation has been created in a few short years as a result of the Internet connection of millions of personal computers to the vast global computer network. Today, untold numbers of "publishers" can access communication vehicles without editorial filters to monitor or control them. The first dynamic of computer law continues to churn up a host of legal issues in its wake.

2) The Elusive Nature of Information

The second dynamic of computer law is the elusive nature of information. Information is intangible. Unlike land and goods, which both have tangible, physical properties, information is ephemeral, and only begins to take on a physical presentation when it is reproduced on a medium such as paper. Intangible information, however, should not be confused with the physical vessels it tends to be carried in. Indeed, now that information in its electronic state has been freed from the constraints of paper, it can fully reveal its fluid, plastic nature. The dephysicalization of information has set it free. It is not only its intangibility, however, that makes information elusive. Another unusual aspect of this malleable asset is that it takes its value from its context. Traditional assets sometimes exhibit this, for example, when agricultural land is rezoned for residential or industrial use, but usually the purpose to which a particular plot of real estate is put is unchanging for a lengthy period of time. Similarly, tangible, moveable goods, like chairs, retain their single purpose throughout their existence. Information, in contrast, can gain or lose value and regain it again, for reasons completely extraneous to itself. Yet another aspect of elusiveness is that much information is incomplete, and therefore is continually in a state of becoming. Fact-intensive information (imagine a stock market feed) and scientific knowledge, even software, is constantly being improved and updated, like a service rather than a commodity. To define the parameters of information-based assets from a legal perspective or to regulate the use, reproduction, and movement of information-based assets is fiendishly difficult.

Intellectual property regimes face difficult challenges when confronted by the elusive nature of software and information-based products. While a court can easily delimit the contours of a parcel of land or the physical outlines of a chair, it cannot easily formulate sensible ownership regimes for information-based assets. It is no simple task to determine where the line between the protected and unprotected should be drawn, for example, with respect to facts contained in electronic databases. And even if the data were to be protected in some manner, would higher levels of aggregation based on the underlying data also be protected? Practices as diverse as the "digital sampling" of music, and the "reverse engineering" of software, raise similar issues fuelled by the second dynamic of computer law. Dissemination of ephemeral information over the Internet also raises a number of challenges for intellectual property law, again as is evident in the *Napster* and *iCraveTV* cases. The Supreme Court's decision in the *Stewart*[4] case not to protect confidential information under the *Criminal Code*'s theft provision illustrates a similar difficulty caused by the second dynamic of computer law, and this lacuna in the criminal law has not been rectified with a statutory amendment. As well, the wire-tap cases in the criminal law area that recognize only the contents of conversations as deserving of protection and deny protection to seemingly peripheral information, such as the number of calls and their duration, again show the difficulty the legal system has with the ephemeral nature of data, though the recent decisions in *Kyello* and *Tessling*[5] indicate a more sophisticated approach to this important question. The proponents of data protection legislation note that the intangible nature of personal information makes it so easy to disseminate it that it should be protected before the data begin their travels around the vast computer and telecommunications networks of the world. In certain commercial law contexts, such as the sale of goods and tax statutes, the challenge is to determine whether software is a good or a service. The

---

4   The *Stewart* case is discussed in chapter 3, section B.1, "Theft."
5   These cases are discussed in chapter 3, section B.10(a), "What Information Is Protected."

dephysicalization of information — primarily through the substitution of electronic networks for stand-alone paper-based communications — also has important ramifications for contract and evidence law. In all these areas the second dynamic of computer law is clearly at work.

3) The Blurring of Private/Public

A third dynamic in the computer law area is the blurring of the dividing line between the public and private spheres. There are many elements to this dynamic. In terms of our lifestyles, the new electronic gadgetry (including cellphones, faxes, and e-mail through broadband access, and especially "always-on" email devices such as the Blackberry) suppresses the distinction between the home and the office. We dress casually at the office (so that it feels more like home), and we have lots of gadgetry at home (so it feels more like the office). We use a "personal computer" in the office. In essence, information technology has shredded the traditional barrier between our private and most important public space, our workplace. And as we sit at our computers at home and surf the Internet, we are quickly removing yet another dividing line between private and public.

The third dynamic of computer law is being driven in part by technological developments that permit individuals to assume greater powers of creation, storage, and dissemination of information-based works. In the past, the function of creating content-based works was restricted to businesses or organizations that could amass the financial and technical resources required to publish a book or produce a music record. Although these major content developers and distributors continue to exist, a multitude of smaller players now participate in the content creation business, aided by inexpensive personal computers, image scanners, and related technology. And the Internet will permit these players to bypass the traditional distribution infrastructures in order to market and transmit their content products directly to end-users. Similarly, the Internet and CD-ROMs, for example, permit individuals to receive content in their homes or offices (which are increasingly partly or wholly at home). The same dynamic applies to data, especially personal information, which is now being recorded in many ways, as people sit in the privacy of their homes but transmit data about themselves to the whole world on the Internet. All these developments fuse the public and private realms of human activity into one seamless, interconnected medium.

This third dynamic of computer law confronts intellectual property laws in several ways. Traditionally, infringers were businesses that sold their illegal wares to the public. This was dictated largely by technological constraints; a large printing press was required in order to make unauthorized copies of a book, and sophisticated technology was required to make bootleg copies of films and vinyl long-playing records. Recently, since high-quality photocopiers are still beyond the means of individuals, most legal cases of unauthorized photocopying still involve larger defendants, such as companies, governments, or educational institutions. Current technologies, however, bring to the fore a whole new category of infringer, the private individual. Cheap handheld scanners, inexpensive computers, small and affordable photocopiers, and a raft of similar devices have permitted individuals to get into the reproduction business. And not just for their personal use. Machines that can produce copies of CD-ROMs are now within easy reach of an individual's budget. Most importantly, the Internet represents an extremely low-cost distribution mechanism for information-based products. Whether these trends are viewed as the extension of the public sphere into the private, or vice versa, the upshot for intellectual property owners is that the battlefield on which they will defend their assets will increasingly be private homes and offices. This is an uncomfortable venue for intellectual property law. It also raises very relevant questions about the practicalities of dealing with a multitude of infringers. Thus a number of years ago the *Copyright Act* was amended to permit the home copying of music, in return for a tax on blank media. Is this increasingly the intellectual property law model for digital-centred challenges?

As noted in chapter 3, the third dynamic of computer law also has important ramifications for criminal law. The home and other private places like a person's automobile were considered by the law to be important sanctuaries, zealously protected from outside interference. Then homes began to be wired and otherwise connected to the outside world. In came the mail, radio, and television, each more forceful but still passive in nature. The telephone was the first interactive device, and now, of course, there is the Internet that brings the world to the desktop in an immediate and sustained manner. The physical membrane separating the private home from the public world is in tatters, and its penetration is having a profound impact on the law. The criminal law protections against search and seizure have been expanded to extend beyond the home, to cover the person, and in some cases to apply to information as well. This may be the ironic result of the public intruding into the private; the private person in the comfort of her private study can perpetrate crime in the public sphere by connecting to the multitude of networks and computers accessible to her personal computer.

The proponents of a legal regime for data protection argue that a prime rationale for such a law is to prevent the fusion of public and private in the realm of personal information. Similarly, in the traditional world of export control the border was a relevant place at which to stop the export from Canada of items that cannot legally be shipped out of the country. However, software and technical data that are controlled items under the ECL can now be transmitted from an office or private home; indeed, even taking them out of the country by more traditional means is facilitated by putting the information on a small tape or CD-ROM or loading them into a laptop computer, which would be far more difficult to detect than a sheaf of blueprints. Satellite signals and electrical impulses sent over the Internet are extremely difficult to control, let alone block completely. Moreover, since they are received by private individuals, there are precious few intermediaries that the regulatory apparatus could use to help implement its goals. The "push" model of public broadcasting is far more amenable to CRTC regulatory oversight than the "pull" model of narrowcasting over the Internet; the blurring of private/public will present significant challenges to the CRTC over the coming years.

As pointed out in chapter 7, libel on the Internet provides a compelling example of the fusion of private and public. There are no editorial filters or controlling intermediaries in the Internet environment, with the result that the border between private and public is erased and in its place is seamless cyberspace. E-mail is a trenchant example of the third dynamic of computer law; the same electronic message that can be sent seemingly privately to one recipient can, with the push of a few keystrokes, be distributed to millions. Courts and legislatures will have to respond creatively in order to deal with the challenges posed by the third dynamic of computer law.

4) The Blurring of National/International

A final dynamic involves another blurring, this time between the national and the international boundaries. The computer business is probably the most global industry in the world. Computers, software, and other information-based products are traded around the world at a frenzied pace. Since the invention of the telegraph, information has been flowing between countries at an increasing rate, to the point where today, with the Internet and other international private and public networks, enormous volumes of data, information, and content are transmitted over geographic frontiers every minute.[6] These networks ignore geography in an increasing number of areas of human endeavour.

This dynamic is being felt keenly by the owner of intellectual property, as noted in chapter 2. There was a time when the business responsible for the infringement was located in the same jurisdiction as the content creator, when the authority of the intellectual property law clearly applied, and when the assistance of the local police could be called upon for large-scale infringement. Intellectual property was a national affair, since production centres were close to their markets. As international trade in books and other content-based product increased, Canadian content owners could still rely on customs officers to help keep out infringing products. These options began to erode once paper, vinyl, and celluloid were no longer the primary media for the carriage and presentation of content. Today, computer disks and CD-ROMs are much more difficult to control, and the Internet and other networks, which allow the digital bits and bytes themselves to be sent across the border, make it extremely difficult for national border guards to assist the domestic content creators. It's a very small world after all the technological advances of the last decade. At a conceptual level, international intellectual property treaties are making progress. Achieving redress for piracy in the real world, however, is an expensive, time-consuming, and imperfect exercise. It would also seem, at first blush, that the fusion of the national with the international would not cause too many conceptual concerns for the criminal law, given that extraditing criminals from abroad and gathering evidence in foreign lands has been a traditional activity in the criminal law realm. Nevertheless, the volume and sophistication of harmful computer-based conduct effected in one state adversely affecting persons, businesses, and organizations in another is unprecedented. For example, child pornography flows into Canada over the Internet, all but ignoring the electronically porous border. Most police forces are slowly beginning to grapple with the consequences of Internet crime. The evidentiary and enforcement issues will tax to the limit the current structures in place for international cooperation in crime prevention.

---

6   Or, as the Federal Court of Appeal put it in the first sentence of their recent decision in *Society of Composers, Authors and Music Publishers of Canada v. Canadian Association of Internet Providers*, [2001] F.C.J. No. 166 (C.A.), at para. 1, "In a remarkably short time, the Internet has become a global medium of communication that operates sans frontières."

The supporters of data protection legislation for the private sector are well aware of the international dimensions of the issue, as is chronicled in chapter 4. With huge amounts of personal data being transmitted around the world, there is the need for some mechanism to ensure consistent data protection globally. Otherwise, countries or sub-state jurisdictions will appear that are willing to ignore data protection laws in order to become "data havens." And just as data protection laws fight valiantly to keep alive the distinction between private and public, so too the export control laws endeavour to enforce the separateness of the national and the international. Nevertheless, the technological developments noted above, culminating in an Internet that ignores borders with impunity, make it more and more difficult to stand on guard at the border. The sources of many of the transmissions that the CRTC will find problematic lie outside of Canada. Regulation works best when there are intermediate control points, or choke points, within Canada where the regulator, by exercising control over a larger entity relatively high up in the distribution chain, can efficiently dictate the options available to the millions of individuals lower down in the chain. Radio and television stations, cable companies and telephone companies, each with significant operations and physical plants in Canada, have served admirably as control points in the past and will continue to do so for the foreseeable future as their product offerings continue to find a market in this country. Foreign satellite and Internet transmissions effectively bypass these control points and, for the most part, are requested and received directly by the end-user in the privacy of his or her home. Although Internet transmissions are carried by Internet service providers, they generally act simply as conduits, and attempting to regulate content through them would be an enormous task for the CRTC. Such an effort, however, pales in comparison with regulating individual Internet users who access Web sites around the world in order to receive the new broadcasting programming. In short, the new technologies pose fundamental challenges to the manner in which the CRTC carries out its mandate.

The theme of national/international fusion also permeates electronic commerce/Internet issues. Initially, in the contractual setting, the focus was on determining which jurisdiction's law applies given that the electronic contractors were in different countries. More recently, the Internet has challenged the very concept of the nation state by eliminating geography as a factor in its use. Courts, governments, and regulators, sensing a profound threat, are responding in a manner that they hope will maintain national sovereignty in a networked world. Thus, foreign actors are being made subject to the jurisdiction of a country when their conduct over the Internet has an impact on that country. It is a small world, courtesy of the new technology, but one still consisting of separate and distinct countries. Therefore, users of the new technologies should not forget that the fourth dynamic of computer law speaks not in terms of the elimination of the national, but of its fusion with the international. Travellers on the Internet should not forget that when they extend their presence through the Internet into other countries, the laws of those countries may well come into play to regulate their activities.

B. COMPUTER LAW: THEMES

In addition to approaching computer law issues from the perspective of the four dynamics, four themes run throughout the legal subtopics that have been discussed in this book. The first is consistency. This theme emphasizes that legal rules for the computer industries should be consistent with the best jurisprudence applied to earlier technologies. As well, they should be consistent in different jurisdictions and in different subdisciplines of the law. A second theme relates to what may be termed *regulatory control points*, to order and enforce behaviour. The upshot of this theme is that in an electronic world the traditional control points are under pressure and new ones may have to be devised. A third theme relates to the rules of liability applicable to intermediaries. Entities that indirectly facilitate infringing, criminal, or libellous activities in a computer and networked environment, but who do not initiate the offending activity themselves, pose some difficult questions for the law, particularly in the Internet setting. A final theme concerns what may be termed mischievous metaphors. The legal system tends to analyse current activities, and persons or entities associated with them, in terms of categories developed in the past. This is a useful approach, but one fraught with dangers as it risks trapping its participant in outdated and ill-fitting legal paradigms.

1) Consistency in Computer Laws

Consistency should play a role in computer law in at least three distinct but interrelated ways. First there is the objective of striving for historic consistency in the jurisprudence. This means, for example, that the preferred analytical approach to the Internet is an even-handed, measured one. The Internet should not be viewed as a completely revolutionary and "never-seen-before" communication vehicle that "breaks all the rules." Nor should it be seen as representing "business as usual." The ideal approach is to see the Internet as another stage in the evolution of communications technologies that consist of mail, the telegraph, the telephone, radio, telex, fax, television, and the like. The new statutes and case law should be consistent with that of the past. Of course, this will not always be possible or even desirable, but in a surprising number of cases it will be, much to the delight of today's legal and business communities who are searching for sensible and predictable rules to order relations in the Information Age.

Consistency should also be an objective in national (i.e., among the Canadian provinces) and international contexts. In an industry as global as the computer business, countries can benefit from similar legal solutions in other countries. Thus, Canadian courts should regularly read the decisions of courts in the United States, Europe, Asia, and elsewhere, particularly where a point appears to be new in Canada. Where the foreign decision displays sound judgment and a sensible resolution of a thorny problem, the Canadian court should not hesitate to draw heavily on it. Lawmakers should also not be averse to drawing generously on another jurisdiction's law, if it is well done and the jurisprudence under it appears sound. The tendency in some jurisdictions to insert unusual provisions solely to differentiate a law from its predecessors in other countries ought to be discouraged; indeed, uniform law exercises within a country (i.e., among the various provinces and the federal government) and between countries should be the norm for moving ahead with new legislative initiatives. Legislators should realize that the nation state cannot resolve some of the world's more intractable problems alone.

There is also a need for achieving consistency among the different subdisciplines of computer law. It is common for two or more areas of computer law to consider the same issue, albeit from a different perspective (which should never be forgotten). Both the civil law of intellectual property and the criminal law have had to cope with the contours of what constitutes confidential information. Sales statutes and tax statutes have had to wrestle with the intangible properties of software. The concepts of public and private are germane to copyright, criminal law, and privacy laws. Originality is a concept native both to intellectual property law and evidence law. On these and other points there has been some cross-fertilization among different areas of the law, but not nearly enough. Obviously, this should not be done unthinkingly, but there is no reason why, for example, the concepts of public and private should not be the same (or at least broadly similar) across all the laws that utilize these words, particularly where use on the Internet is concerned.

This book hopes to promote these three levels of consistency. By drawing on case law from a variety of countries, and highlighting the common threads in the various subareas of computer law, the foregoing illustrates those situations where harmonization is present and working, and where it is not. And while some progress is being made, much work remains to be done.

2) Control Points and the Law

The law has traditionally relied heavily on several regulatory control points to help enforce its rules. One important control point used to be geography and its various physical derivatives and associated principles. Historically, most intellectual property enforcement focused on the businesses that made or distributed infringing copies of protected works. The retail establishment on the street sold the illegal music records produced by the infringing pressing plant in the industrial park. Illegal goods crossing the border could be intercepted by customs authorities.[7] These geographic control points continue to exist, but they are handling fewer and fewer information-based products because they are being bypassed altogether by consumers who can obtain digital content directly, on disk, by mail order, or over the Internet. And regulating the individual in the comfort of his or her own home is onerous and not politically popular, hence the change in the copyright law to permit private copying of music in exchange for a levy on blank tapes.

Another important control point has been the physical identity of an individual. In a number of contexts, such as pornography, gaming, and even with some contract/evidence law issues, the ability of a gate-

---

7   One author describes the difficulty of patrolling borders in the Information Age in the following terms: "Because digital technologies allow information to flow seamlessly and invisibly across national borders, they make it very difficult for governments to do many of the things to which they have grown accustomed. Governments can't patrol their physical territories in cyberspace; they can't easily enforce property rights over ephemeral ideas and rapidly moving bits; they can't control information flows; they even may not be able to collect taxes. Such is the nature of politics along the technological frontier": Debora L. Spar, *Ruling the Waves: Cycles of Discovery, Chaos, and Wealth From the Compass to the Internet* (New York: Harcourt, 2001) [*Ruling the Waves*], at 3.

keeper or ticket-taker to look at a person and to judge his age or other physical characteristics was a key part of the legal regime regulating that activity. With the move to electronic environments that no longer require physical presence, the law is confronted with either banning non-physical access to the computer-based environment or striving to recreate the same security of identity but in an online context. While this will be a challenging task, there are new biometric and other authentication technologies being developed that may assist. At the same time, however, other technologies have been developed that permit people to participate in Internet activities anonymously, thereby decreasing the efficacy of implementing a "personal control point" mechanic on the Internet. The widespread availability and use by individuals of high-strength encryption products has the same effect of allowing people to "hide out" in cyberspace.

Paper has traditionally been an important control point for information. In many areas the existence of paper, and the process leading up to the creation of the particular paper-based document, served as an important legal ordering function. Putting "pen to paper" usually meant a single author, or a small subset of authors, could clearly identify their discrete contributions to the work. In contract and evidence law, a signed paper document gives comfort, not just because the signatory put her autograph on it, but because the very process of signing most documents usually entails being present, physically, with the document, and therefore probably reading it (or at least discussing it with someone else). These factors cannot be taken for granted in a non–paper-based environment. That is not to say new control points cannot be created in a digital environment. Their focus, however, may not be on a particular letter or document, but on whether the system creating them is working properly, in which case the authenticity and veracity of the information will simply be assumed.

3) Intermediary Liability

A recurring theme in computer law is that often the direct protagonist of a particular mischief is unavailable to the person harmed. Thus, the infringer of a copyright work, or the creator of the obscene material, or the author of the libellous statement, cannot be found, or is impecunious, or is otherwise not worth pursuing. In each case, however, one or more parties providing one or more services is associated with some technology or business practice that in some way assists the perpetrator of the blameworthy conduct. The question in such a context is straightforward: Should the intermediary be liable for the harm?

While the question may be put simply, the answer, as discussed throughout the previous chapters of this book, is complicated. The first step in responding to it is to understand the intermediary's precise role in the allegedly harmful activity. Then the analysis should focus on what knowledge and control the intermediary had on either the creation or dissemination of the problematic message. And by knowledge, more is meant than actual knowledge. In a libel case, for example, negligence might also suffice if the entity had reason to know that the perpetrator was a "regular" on the network, and the entity took no steps to minimize the harm. Or, in a criminal context, a similar standard is referred to by the term *wilful blindness*; that is, the operator of the service suspected a problem but consciously decided not to look further. In these and related sorts of situations, visiting the intermediary with liability may be appropriate. And again, the law ought to strive for consistency in the various subareas that deal with intermediary liability.

4) Mischievous Metaphors

There are many situations in computer law where the lawyer, judge, academic, or legislator is confronted with what seems to be a novel situation and, in order to make sense of it, a similar example — a metaphor — for the new activity is found in past experience. When determining an Internet participant's liability for libel, for example, there is a strong urge to categorize the participant as "publisher," "news vendor," "bookstore," "library," "broadcaster," etc., because then the entire legal schema associated with the category can be utilized without having to expend too much time and effort. This tendency to use metaphor, incidentally, is not unique to lawyers. The etymology of the Internet is full of it. One "surfs the Web," or uses a "bookmark" to save the location of a site. Metaphors are used elsewhere in computing: one "cuts and pastes" text in a word processing program. And, of course, outside the computer industry, car engines are still measured in "horsepower," a holdover from the days when cars and buggies shared the same road.

Metaphors can help the novice quickly grasp something new by putting it in the context of something old. They can also, however, become substitutes for vigorous, independent thought and analysis. Lawyers often have problems explaining what something is; rather, they describe what it is like. After a point, metaphors can do as much harm as good. Similarly, legal classification systems can also be counterproductive if not approached with great care. Consider one author's assessment of the predilection of scientists to slot phenomena into pigeonholes:

Early zoologists classified as mammals those that suckle their young and as reptiles those that lay eggs. Then a duck-billed platypus was discovered in Australia laying eggs like a perfect reptile and then, when they hatched, suckling the infant platypi like a perfect mammal.

The discovery created quite a sensation. What an enigma! it was exclaimed. What a mystery! What a marvel of nature! When the first stuffed specimens reached England from Australia around the end of the eighteenth century they were thought to be fakes made by sticking together bits of different animals. Even today you still see occasional articles in nature magazines asking, "Why does this paradox of nature exist?"

The answer is: it doesn't. The platypus isn't doing anything paradoxical at all. It isn't having any problems. Platypi have been laying their eggs and suckling their young for millions of years before there were any zoologists to come along and declare it illegal. The real mystery, the real enigma, is how mature, objective, trained scientific observers can blame their own goof on a poor innocent platypus.

Zoologists, to cover up their problem, had to invent a patch. They created a new order, monotremata, that includes the platypus, the spiny anteater, and that's it. This is like a nation consisting of two people.[8]

Like good scientists, lawyers must not allow their classification systems to become confining straightjackets. So, in assessing the liability of an Internet participant, the focus should be on function rather than status. Then a very careful assessment of the participant and technology involved in the cases being compared should be undertaken. Again, function should be the hallmark. For example, it is not enough to say that a particular case stands for the proposition that a fax can be used to deliver a message in writing, or that a cellular phone message comes under the wire-tap prohibition of the *Criminal Code*; in both cases a detailed understanding of the particular kind of fax and cellular technology is required as this will have enormous impact on their jurisprudential value. And where there is a dearth of applicable metaphors — where we are confronted by a legal platypus — courts and legislators should not hesitate to carve out new categories, essentially the monotremata of computer law.

---

8   Robert M. Pirsig, *Lila: An Inquiry into Morals* (New York: Bantam, 1991) at 101–2.

C. COMPUTER LAW: SKILL SETS

The dynamics inherent in computer law, and in the technological trends driving it, present lawyers and other participants in the legal system with a number of daunting challenges. In tackling these challenges, four primary skill sets, or approaches, can be contemplated. Recourse can be had to the common law by relying on judge-made decisions to address the various novel and pressing legal issues presented by the computer and information-based assets. A second skill set centres on contract law, and the ability of entities, when confronted with new or uncertain situations, to craft their own laws, as it were, for use between the private parties. Technology can also be employed to fill gaps and fissures in the law by channelling behaviour through the use of specific technological devices contained within computers, networks, and software programs. The fourth skill set relates to law reform, which involves shepherding through the parliamentary process legislation that will address the specific needs of participants in the computer, networking, and information-based industries. These skill sets should not be viewed as mutually exclusive. This book concludes with a discussion of the parameters of these four skill sets.

1) Common Law

The genius of the common law lies in its tremendously flexible nature. It would appear, therefore, that the common law would be extremely well suited to coping with the four dynamics of the computer industry. Through the good offices of a presiding judge (or arbitrator), the common law can quickly accommodate existing rules to apply to a new technology or product. Judges should also be able to assess the economic differences between tangible assets, on the one hand, and information, on the other hand. As for the public/private dimension, judges act as guardians of the private sphere of human existence, just as they can delineate national boundaries to ensure that the international nature of the computer business does not defeat the protective objectives of various national laws, though the common law regularly falls short in achieving this goal.

As discussed in chapter 2, in the intellectual property area, several decisions, such as in the American *Altai* and Canadian *Delrina* and *Prism* cases,[9] craft tests for infringement that, while not satisfying everyone

---

9   These cases are covered in chapter 2, section C.3, "Copyright Protection for Software."

with their precise contours, nevertheless indicate an effective understanding of the relevant technology. Moreover, the reduction in the scope of protection between the *Whelan* and *Altai* cases illustrates the common law's ability to recalibrate itself where a consensus begins to emerge that the previous standard is either incorrect, dysfunctional, or merely dated. In the area of electronic commerce, again judges have shown their willingness to adapt the law of contract and evidence to new technological conditions. In doing so, judges have striven to distill the policy rationale of a particular contract formation or evidence law rule, and have concluded that the new electronic process (whether it involved the telegraph, telephone, fax, EDI, or Internet-based e-mail), if designed and executed properly, satisfied the underlying purpose of the law. In short, in a host of situations judges have shown a receptiveness to new technology, and an ability to tackle the four dynamics of computer law. Accordingly, a participant in the computer industry, when confronted with a new legal problem, should be willing to consider making use of the common law skill set, at least in certain circumstances.

Not in all circumstances, however. For all the court decisions that are made with a sensitivity to the new technologies and with a willingness to wade into new fact situations armed only with analogies from a low-tech past, there are other decisions that show the court's aversion to tackling technological subject matter. In some cases, there is an admitted lack of understanding of the technical material presented by the parties. There is also the problem that in most civil law disputes between two parties, courts rarely venture beyond the specific issues presented by the particular case before them. One court recently articulated this approach in the following manner, highlighting its particular appropriateness for Internet-related legal issues:

> We recognize of course that parties to a lawsuit, and surely others interested in the field, will look to decisions for points of guidance. For every new rule that a court sets down doubts are minimized, and practitioners are able to give counsel based on settled doctrine, rather than on open questions. While many decisions serve to establish rules that advance predictability, courts cannot go beyond the issues necessary to decide the case at hand. An ambition of that sort would entail something very much like drafting advisory opinions. Misdirected or misapplied, they can create the very kind of uncertainty, or confusion, that purposeful decisional law seeks to eliminate. These general observations apply even more compellingly when dealing with Internet law. Given the extraordinarily rapid growth of this technology and its developments, it is plainly unwise to lurch pre-

maturely into emerging issues, given a record that does not at all lend itself to their determination.[10]

In the criminal law area, there is the added unwillingness on the part of judges to perform a role they believe rightfully rests with Parliament, namely, keeping the *Criminal Code* abreast of new technological developments. In other areas, such as data protection until recently, there is not a relevant statutory regime, and judges are reluctant to create a new branch of the law when the jurisprudential underpinnings are so weak. In yet other areas, the Internet-related legal issue is not just old wine in a new bottle, but rather it is a fairly different beverage. Consider online libel. What makes it different is (in no particular order) the incredibly higher volume of messages involved; the fact that most messages emanate from individuals under circumstances where no third-party editorial filter has been applied to the communication; and the fact that a Web site operator screening a busy discussion forum might be able to use filtering software to catch certain egregious messages. It is fair to conclude that the libel jurisprudence of the last few hundred years will have to be very carefully drawn upon in order to apply it to many kinds of Internet-related libel questions.

Moreover, even where a particular judge decides to venture forth boldly and tackle a new technological conundrum confronting the law, there is always the problem that the decision will stand alone for some time, while participants in the computer industry wait anxiously to see if it will be adopted in their own jurisdiction. This was the situation Canadians faced in the trial judgment in the *Tele-Direct* case that considered the scope of protection for material in a Yellow Pages telephone directory. The U.S. *Feist* case was briefed before the trial judge in this case, but the court declined to decide whether the principles animating *Feist* were directly applicable, or not, in Canada. Unfortunately, the result was that Canadian database developers did not know precisely what degree of protection they had for their products on the two sides of the Canada–U.S. border. Put another way, the common law, because of its very nature as a vehicle that is national in scope, is often poorly equipped to deal with the fourth dynamic of computer law, namely, its international dimension. Fortunately, the Federal Court of Appeal cleared up this uncertainty in the *Tele-Direct* case by indicating that Canadian and U.S. copyright laws provided a similar degree of protection for fact-based compilations. By the same token, however, uncer-

---

10   *Lunney v. Prodigy Services Company*, 94 N.Y.2d 242 (N.Y. App. 1998) at 251.

tainty has once again been injected into the mix by the appellate decision in *CCH* v. *LSUC*.[11] So the roller coaster ride continues.

2) Contract

Contracts are another skill set, or approach, that addresses the four dynamics of computer law. In the intellectual property area, contracts can be harnessed in many ways. For example, where electronic databases are not protected, the particular property can be exploited pursuant to a licence agreement that requires the user to agree to a certain set of rules, including, most importantly, not sharing the information with third parties. In effect, a result not afforded by intellectual property law is achieved through contract. Even with information-based assets that are clearly protected by intellectual property law, such as software, contracts are still used to regulate the use and distribution of the asset. Software licence agreements restrict the use that can be made of the software, such as to process only the data of the user and not of third parties, and also to prohibit a user from transferring the software to a third party. A contract requiring the user to maintain the confidentiality of the information is central to the very preservation of the trade secrecy status of software.

Contracts are also used to clarify the relationship between two parties. In the commercial context, for example, contracts between the users and suppliers of computers and services might specify such matters as when the particular computer system is to be considered accepted by the user. In a similar vein, commercial parties can override the generic implied warranties and conditions provided in sale of goods statutes so that the reasonable expectations of the parties can be managed, and met, with a greater likelihood of success. Achieving greater certainty than the general law is also a prime rationale for the use of contracts in the field of electronic commerce. Parties desiring their electronic messages to constitute binding agreements can provide, in a master written agreement, precisely which messages, when transmitted to specific computers, will give rise to irrevocable contracts. Similarly, they can stipulate what records of these messages will be admissible as evidence. In short, parties endeavour to make their own law by means of contracts. The result has been the development of a wide variety of contracts for the computer industry, including so-called shrinkwrap

---

11   The *Tele-Direct*, *Feist*, and *CCH* cases are discussed in chapter 2, section C.4, "Copyright Protection for Electronic Databases."

licences for software, trading partner agreements for electronic data interchange and express and implied click-consent agreements in a multitude of Internet situations. Indeed, by opting for arbitration over the court system as a means of dispute resolution, in agreements between businesses the parties can also, again through contract, deal privately and precisely with the rules they wish to have applied if they have a falling-out with one another.

If the number and variety of contracts were not proof enough of their important role in the computer industry, consider how well the contract vehicle responds to the four dynamics of computer law. Private parties can agree to stay current with technological change, as when the parties to an EDI trading partner agreement determine, in the contract, how they will keep their system updated. Another example is the detailed consent that public companies obtain from shareholders wishing to receive disclosure material electronically; these agreements list the precise type of computer-based communications, how e-mails will be utilized, and the like. Contracts can also handle the unique indicia of information-based, intangible assets, such as when a software licence, or database exploitation agreement, defines with precision what does, and what does not, constitute the protected material of each party. Similarly, contracting parties can undertake to keep certain information confidential, thus attempting to keep from becoming public that which is private. Finally, contracts travel well across borders, thereby allowing a seamless welding of the domestic with the international, fusing two different domestic legal systems (each party's "international" is invariably the other party's "national"). Indeed, the contract vehicle is so useful in bridging the gap between different nations that international arbitration conducted in a third country is often used to move the legal venue of any dispute out of either party's jurisdiction. In short, contracts have proven themselves, time and again, to be an essential skill set for the legal practitioner seeking to implement secure, lasting solutions in the computer law field.

Contracts, however, are not panaceas. They involve a number of specific costs and disadvantages that should be weighed at the outset.[12]

---

12 For a discussion of the use of various contract vehicles, and their attendant cost structures, see Oliver E. Williamson, "Contract Analysis: The Transaction Cost Approach," in Paul Burrows & Cento Veljanovski, eds., *The Economic Approach to Law* (London: Butterworths, 1981). See also the seminal article by Ronald Coase as to how transaction costs related to contracts might help explain whether a company expands, or outsources various functions to third-party suppliers: R.H. Coase, "The Nature of the Firm" (1937) 4 Economica N.S. 386. See

Transaction costs for negotiating and drafting contracts for high-tech goods can be quite high, when calculated as a percentage of the total value of the deal. There is much risk for both buyer and seller, and much time and effort can be expended on larger deals. For simpler transactions, however, the computer industry has developed the shrinkwrap licence that is enclosed with the mass marketed product; in one variation, it is read but not signed by the user who consents by commencing to use the software, while in another (more recent) form, the user of the software clicks on an "I Agree" button at the end of the agreement that appears in the sign on screen when first loading the software. On the other hand, although this type of contract is increasingly being used across the computer industry, in a number of cases the purported contract was held to be unenforceable because the flawed method of procuring offer and acceptance online did not result in the parties' ultimately agreeing with one another on the relevant terms, or so the court found. And even where the contract is found to be in force, certain clauses can be excised by judges if there are concerns about unfair bargaining power on the side of the supplier and even unconscionability. In short, online agreements have to be designed with great care.

Contracts also raise another concern, which might be called the privatization of the legal system. Consider the use of arbitration as a dispute resolution mechanism. The parties, in their contract, provide for private, speedy arbitration if ever a claim arises between them. One day the arbitration provision is invoked, and the privately appointed arbitrator quietly settles a thorny point of fact and law, perhaps in the area of electronic commerce. From a private perspective (that is, as far as the two businesses are concerned) this has been an efficient episode of dispute resolution. From a public perspective, however, the jurisprudence of computer law has been denied a reported case that could serve to educate others. Contrary to popular wisdom, the objective is not to learn from your own mistakes, but to learn from the mistakes of others. The private arbitration model does not have a pedagogical result, which is provided by the common law in the publicly available decisions of trial and appeal courts that canvass the facts of the cases they decide. At a micro level the parties are better off, but at a macro level the legal system is disadvantaged. The same problem is encountered

---

also R.H. Coase, "The Problem of Social Cost" (1960) 3 J.L. & Econ. 1. Don Tapscott, one of Canada's leading thinkers about the Internet, argues that Coase's theorem will find full realization in the Internet's ability to facilitate efficient transactions among third parties: see Don Tapscott, David Ticoll & Alex Lowy, "The Business Web: Internet Nirvana," *ecompany*, December 2000.

wherever the general statutory rules are abandoned in favour of private ordering through contract.

3) Technical Solutions

The privatization of computer law through the use of contracts stands to be assisted by another skill set, namely, the use of technical devices to control the dissemination and use of software and other information-based products. Put another way, content creators and owners who perceive there to be serious shortcomings in the common law, or in the current statute-based law, as they apply to the protection and exploitation of high-tech goods and services, often gravitate toward technologically oriented solutions to make up for shortcomings in the law. Some software is already distributed in a copy-protected format; this software is activated in a manner that will make it operate only on a specific computer of the user, thereby preventing the making of unauthorized copies of the program. Although not in widespread use because users find it too cumbersome, and most suppliers of mass market software do not want to put obstacles in the way of the use of their products, the full potential of such copy protection devices will be achieved in the context of protecting the dissemination of content over the Internet. Several forms of digital metering are also being deployed that track authorized transmissions of content over networks and restrict unauthorized distribution of the content. Coupled with sophisticated but inexpensive and user-friendly encryption technologies, such digital metering devices permit content owners to capture 100 percent of the potential returns derived from the use of their products.

Such digital metering technologies and other devices that permit the content owner to control the distribution and use of his or her material have implications for the various intellectual property law regimes. Most pressing, perhaps, is the possibility that such technologies could lead to a displacement of certain important aspects of the *Copyright Act*. The *Copyright Act* represents a carefully measured set of compromises between content creator and user. For example, when a book is purchased from an authorized dealer, the purchaser can resell it or lend it, but cannot make copies of it except in the context of fair dealing for the personal research or study of the user. Moreover, the *Copyright Act* permits potential book buyers to browse through the work at the bookseller before deciding whether to buy it. Libraries can do even more by lending books to patrons on a temporary basis. Important questions arise from proposed widespread digital metering that will restrict all forms of use of the work except those specifically authorized by the content owner. Will practices such as the resale of content, or the lending of content by libraries, or the browsing of content in a retail environment be permitted and at what cost? If these activities are completely curtailed, or made too expensive for the average person, then what would have been achieved is an end run around the *Copyright Act* — a finessing of the public policy tradeoffs inherent in the statute.

Various other technologies are already in (or are increasingly coming into) widespread use to achieve certain solutions to finicky challenges encountered along the information highway. Biometric devices, for example, are used to help parties authenticate themselves in online transactions or other interactions. To combat spam, users can purchase filtering software that is generally somewhat effective against the nuisance of mass, junk e-mail. And yet a third example would be antivirus software that users can install on their computers to help fight, prophylactically, the insidious bits of dangerous software code that are released fairly regularly over the Internet.

It would appear, then, that the technical skill set responds favourably to the four dynamics of computer law noted above. It positively glows from the perspective of the rapid rate of technological change, because this skill set is of technology itself. For example, by being integrated into the content, digital metering and related devices can adapt as the product or delivery mechanism changes. In this regard, the technology skill set is superior to even the contract one. Similarly, the ephemeral nature of software and information-based assets can also be easily accommodated because technology, particularly in the form of encryption devices, is used to respond to the very fact that makes intangible information so elusive. Encryption and other security measures can also be used to keep private information from leaking into the public realm, and so one can anticipate that technological solutions will play an important role in addressing privacy and data protection legal issues. And, of course, the technology can be made to operate globally, so that the technical skill set can be made effective around the world.

Yet the technical skill set carries with it nagging concerns. The fact that it operates outside of established legal regimes raises the problems of uniformity of treatment, cost of access, lack of transparency, and transaction costs. Coupled with the contract skill set, technology pressed into service on behalf of content providers, for example, could have the effect of sidestepping various important dimensions of the current legal system. Those who do not relish such a result can respond in one of two ways. First, they can focus on the contract/technical skill sets and attempt to ameliorate their most objectionable aspects by promoting, for example, access to certain groups such as libraries and schools. The other approach is to focus on the fourth skill set, law reform, in order to convince content owners and other participants in the computer industry not to abandon entirely the public legal systems in favour of private solutions.

4) Law Reform

Law reform is the fourth skill set available to participants in the computer industry. The law has adapted often to the Information Age, such as with the repeal of the writing requirement in Ontario's sales statute to remove doubt as to the enforceability of contracts concluded electronically for the sale of goods. More recently, we have witnessed in Canada a number of important law reform efforts addressing computer law issues; in particular, the electronic commerce acts federally and provincially; various electronic evidence statutes; and the federal private sector privacy law. A number of other areas, however, need a review from the perspective of possible law reform, including intellectual property (such as the protection of databases and the implementation of intellectual property principles on the Internet), and Internet issues such as the liability of service providers for libel and copyright infringement initiated by others. It would also be very useful to pass an amendment to Canadian bankruptcy and other creditor protection laws that make it clear that a trustee in bankruptcy or any similar official cannot interfere with previously granted technology or intellectual property licences. Law reform can play a vital role in alleviating shortcomings in the common law and can obviate the need to rely on contractual and technical mechanisms. Law reform is sometimes required because certain judges, when confronted with a new technology, are unwilling to create a new category of rights, calling instead upon the legislature to do so if they think it appropriate. To achieve such lofty ambitions, however, the particular law reform initiative must respond to the four dynamics of computer law.

First, and perhaps foremost, the process of law reform must stay current with technological developments. To this end, an Institute for the Study of Computer Law could be established, either as a standalone entity or as part of an existing organization. The institute's mandate would be to conduct, on an ongoing basis, studies of existing and new technologies and their impact on the legal system and on the information society more broadly. Such an institute would be multidisciplinary, drawing on expertise in all the legal subdisciplines. There are a few law schools now in Canada with computer law programs that, individually or ideally collectively and collaboratively, have the capability to serve as just such an institute.

The second element in the effort to keep current with the raging pace of technology would be a Parliamentary standing committee (or a subcommittee of one of the current standing committees) that would have as its entire or partial mandate the monitoring of developments in the information society and an assessment, on a continuous and sustained basis, of whether Canadian law is adequate to deal with the new issues and conundrums. Again, as with the institute, one objective would be to build up expertise and develop a rigorous approach to enquiry, as opposed to the *ad hoc* manner in which current efforts are undertaken. For example, in the mid-1990s there was a flurry of research activity surrounding the information highway (as the Internet was then called), and several reports were released. Although this was valuable work and there has been some follow-up, an ongoing commitment to review issues — some identified, some not — is missing

The process of introducing proposed legislation is also *ad hoc*. The history of legislative amendments to the *Copyright Act* is a telling case in point. The amendments in 1988 and the Bill C-32 amendments in April 1997 each proceeded on the basis of trying to make a large number of changes to the law because copyright law reform was seen as an extremely rare occurrence. Consequently, huge lobbying efforts were mobilized in both cases, leading to a number of unsatisfactory provisions in the 1988 amendments. In effect, law reform in the areas discussed by this book all too often become gut-wrenching, pitched battles between vehemently opposed interests, with the result that even relatively uncontroversial proposals are held up, and often get mauled in the crossfire of the larger understandably divisive issues. Arguably better and more effective law reform would result from a cadence of proposed amendments that were less ambitious but more frequent.

These proposals should not be taken to favour a particularly active law reform agenda. The study of issues and new technologies should be ongoing and vigorous; proposing legislative solutions should be a more circumspect exercise. In most cases, Parliament should allow the common law a reasonable period of time to see if it can adequately handle the new challenge. Often it will, possibly assisted by scholarship emanating from the institute or the Parliamentary committee. Where the judicial decisions are inconsistent or in conflict, or where the issues are too numerous and the interests too diverse, or where the common law is too inefficient, or where the courts specifically seek Parliament's assistance — in these cases the law reform process will be prepared to craft more timely and more sensible solutions.

In terms of the actual law reforms, care should be taken to regulate function or behaviour, and not form. Artificial categories with seemingly handy, but ultimately counterproductive, labels should be avoided. Thus, in the age of convergence in the broadcasting and telecommunications areas, references to telephone companies and cable companies need to be increasingly replaced by reference to what a particular entity does, not what it generally calls itself. In the tax area a similar heed should be paid to the underlying business activity, rather than to the formal categories established by the *Income Tax Act*, when dealing with topics such as withholding tax. As well, drafters of new laws should usually strive for technologically neutral legislative provisions so that the resulting law stands a better chance of withstanding the onslaught of the first dynamic of computer law, namely, the rapid pace of technological change.

Equally, we should always be probing the proper degree of specificity in the rules promulgated as a result of the law reform. On the one hand, if the rules are too detailed, they will suffer the same fate as legislation that is too technology-specific; it will soon be overtaken by events, in this case changes in the underlying business model. Nevertheless, the new legislation cannot be too general, or we will forget why we passed it. A law could be as general as the following one-liner: "Everyone will behave with every one else so that justice is served." But this standard, alone, is too amorphous; we need more direction so people and organizations can understand the law in advance. At the same time, a legislative amendment each month to fill a particular gap in the law is too cumbersome. As usual, the truth (and the optimum solution) lies somewhere in between.

Finally, law reform needs to be global or at least to involve Canada's primary trading partners. Thus, the institute and the Parliamentary committee should endeavour to monitor international developments so that Canada's initiatives line up with those similar moves abroad that are reasonable in approach and compelling in rationale. If there are no such international counterparts, then an important role in Canadian law reform will be to help stimulate them, particularly through international bodies such as the World Intellectual Property Organization (WIPO). And, of course, law reform in Canada should be consistent across the provinces; therefore, the Uniform Law Conference of Canada exercises are important. A law reform skill set that is animated by such considerations will serve an extremely useful purpose. It will help fill gaps left by the common law, and may relieve some of the intense pressure to rely overly on contract and technical solutions. Of course, in all likelihood resort to all four skill sets will be required over time, depending on the particular issue confronting computer law.

5) Applying the Skill Sets

The four skill sets of common law, contract, technology, and law reform are not mutually exclusive. In some cases, the computer law practitioner will identify one of them as the most appropriate vehicle given the particular circumstances. In other scenarios, one can envisage applying them in serial order, starting perhaps with the common law, moving on to contract and then technological solutions, and ultimately ending up with law reform as the most permanent solution.[13] In still other circumstances, however, two or more skill sets might usefully be pursued simultaneously. Contract and technology, for example, might complement each other for a "total solution." Or one might be pursuing a test case up the appellate court ladder, all the while lobbying Parliament for new legislation. The sophisticated computer law practitioner will know what mixing and matching of skill sets is best suited to the commercial and legal challenge at hand.

---

13   For a somewhat similar, linear approach to "taming the technological frontier," see Debora L. Spar, *Ruling the Waves*, above note 7. Spar gives a masterful, historical comparative analysis of how different technological breakthroughs (including the telegraph, radio, encryption, and music over the Internet) move through the same three phases driven by first "pirates," then "pioneers" and then "prophets," with each stage relying increasingly heavily on laws and regulation for commercial certainty (though it is startling how important patent protection has been for all stages of each technological development).

GLOSSARY

ACPA	*Anticybersquatting Consumer Protection Act*
actus reus	the physical component of a crime; contrasted with *mens rea*, the mental element
bona fide	in good faith
B2B	business to business
B2C	business to consumer
CAAST	Canadian Alliance Against Software Theft
CBX	computerized branch exchange
CCRA	Canada Customs and Revenue Agency (formerly Revenue Canada)
chip	short hand term for semiconductor integrated circuit
CITT	Canadian International Trade Tribunal
CMI	copyright management information
C2C	consumer to consumer
CDRP	CIRA's Domain Name Dispute Resolution Policy
CIRA	Canadian Internet Registration Authority
DNR	dial number recorder
DRM	digital rights management
DTH	direct-to-home

EDI	electronic data interchange
ex ante	before the fact
ex parte	unilaterally
forum non conveniens	the venue is not appropriate for the bringing of the legal action
GATT	*General Agreement on Tariffs and Trade*
G2C	government to consumer
HTML	hyptertext mark-up language
ICANN	Internet Corporation for Assigned Names and Numbers
ICQ	an instant text messaging service
in personam	relating to a specific person
in rem	relating to the thing; contrasted to *"in personam"*
IP	Internet Protocol
ISP	Internet service provider
mens rea	the mental element of a crime; contrasted with the *actus reus*, the physical element
MIPS	millions of instructions per second
NAFTA	*North American Free Trade Agreement*
per se	in and of itself
PGP	Pretty Good Privacy
PIN	personal identification number
prima facie	on its face
sui genesis	unto itself
UCC	*Uniform Commercial Code*
UCITA	*Uniform Computer Information Transactions Act*
UDRP	Uniform Dispute Resolution Policy
UECA	*Uniform Electronic Commerce Act*
UETA	*Uniform Electronic Transactions Act*
UI	user interface
ULCC	Uniform Law Conference of Canada
VOD	video on demand
WTO	World Trade Organization

TABLE OF CASES

INDEX

hacking, 218n
Information
    contrasted with land and tangible
        personal property, 73, 230
    economics of, 73, 74, 75
    stock market, 62n
    takes value from context, 66n
Information Age
contrasted with Agrarian and Industrial
    eras, 48, 57, 58, 74
court declares "Information Age", 57n
described, 48–58
dot-com shake out, 53n
economics of, 51
mass production v. mass customization,
    60
Information Highway, *see* Internet
Injunctions
    arbitration, 132–36
    difficulty in obtaining for prior
        restraint of publication, 85n
    domain names, 183n
    interim injunctions, 119
    interlocutory injunctions, 119
    permanent injunctions, 121
    springboard doctrine, 121
    the Internet, 658
Innis, Harold
    contrasted with Marshall McLuhan,
        36n
INS Doctrine of Misappropriation
    discussed, 111, 198
    unfair competition, 84
Insolvency, *see* Bankruptcy
Insolvency Act 1986 (U.K.), *see* Bank-
    ruptcy
Insurance
    all-risk property insurance, 506n
    commercial general liability insur-
        ance, 505
    coverage for patent infringement, 510
    coverage for software infringement,
        509
    coverage for trade secret misappro-
        priation, 513
    coverage for trade-mark infringe-
        ment, 513
    errors and omissions insurance, 505n
    for online defamation, 627
    insurance coverage for software and
        data, 507
    technology-related risks, 505
Integrated Circuit Topography Act, *see*
    Chip Protection Law

Intellectual Property Laws, *see* Copy-
    right, Patents, Trade-Marks, Trade
    secrets, Domain names, Passing
    off chip protection laws, INS
    Doctrine of Misappropriation
ability of civil procedure system to
    cope with intellectual property
    cases, 118
alternatives to, 84
contrasted with tangible property, 74
described, 77
international aspects, 124
ownership, 114n, 182
    joint owners, 117
    Crown ownership, 115n
    assignment, 115
    non-human author, 114
    employees, 115
    security interests, 117
    domain names, 182n
protection through technology, 195
quasi-property, 195
rationale for intellectual property
    ownership legal regimes, 76, 78
rationale for private property legal
    regimes, 79n
remedies for infringement, 118
    Anton Piller orders, 118n
    injunctions, 119
    damages, 122
    personal liability, 123
Intermediary Liability
    aiding and abetting, 279
    analysing function rather than sta-
        tus, 267
    Canadian consultation process, 165
    DMCA defences, 168
    for copyright infringement, 168,
        170, 171
    for criminal hate speech, 264
    for criminal law online distribution
        of obscene material, 249
    for human rights law, 264
    for misleading advertising, 433
    for online civil libel, 627, 637
    for online criminal libel, 268
    for possession of child pornography,
        250
    innocent disseminator, 630
International Trade
    customs classification, 496
    GATT, 497
    government procurement, 498
    NAFTA, 497

ABOUT THE AUTHOR

George S. Takach is a Toronto-based partner of McCarthy Tétrault, where he is National Practice Group Leader of the Technology, Communications and Intellectual Property Group. George's practice emphasizes software, computers, technology, tech financing/tech M&A, and related matters. A recent nationwide survey conducted by Lexpert, a peer review-based law directory publisher, ranked George among a handful of leading lawyers in Canada in the computer law field. This survey also found McCarthy Tétrault to have the strongest computer law practice in Canada.

Since 1990 George has been an Adjunct Professor at Osgoode Hall Law School, York University, teaching a course titled "Computers, Information, and the Law." George has a BA (Hons.) in political economy from the University of Toronto; the third year of this degree was completed at the Institut d'Études Politique, Université d'Aix-Marseilles, France. He also has an MA in international relations from the Norman Paterson School of International Affairs, Carleton University in Ottawa. He earned his JD from the Faculty of Law, University of Toronto, where he graduated on the Dean's List.

What spare time George has he spends with the two women in his life: his wife, Janis, and their daughter, Natalie. They especially enjoy skiing and travelling together.

McCarthy Tétrault is Canada's premier law firm with more than eight hundred lawyers in offices in Vancouver, Calgary, London, Toronto, Ottawa, Montreal, Quebec, and London, England. The firm provides Canadian and international clients with a wide range of legal services, including business law, litigation, and numerous specialty areas. The firm's Technology, Communications and Intellectual Property Group has extensive experience serving a wide variety of Canadian and international technology companies and organizations marketing or acquiring various computing and other technology resources and financing tech enterprises.

George S. Takach
Phone: (416) 601-7662
Fax: (416) 601-8249
gtakach@mccarthy.ca
www.mccarthy.ca